2001

2001

WOMEN IN WORLD HISTORY

A Biographical Encyclopedia

WOMEN IN WORLD HISTORY

A Biographical Encyclopedia

VOLUME
1
Aak-Azz

Anne Commire, Editor
Deborah Klezmer, Associate Editor

YORKIN PUBLICATIONS

GALE GROUP

Detroit
San Francisco
London
Boston
Woodbridge, CT

Yorkin Publications

Anne Commire, *Editor*
Deborah Klezmer, *Associate Editor*
Barbara Morgan, *Assistant Editor*

Eileen O'Pasek, Gail Schermer, Patricia Coombs, James Fox,
Catherine Cappelli, Karen Rikkers, *Editorial Assistants*
Karen Walker, *Assistant for Genealogical Charts*

Special acknowledgment is due to Peg Yorkin who made this project possible.

Thanks also to Karin and John Haag, Bob Schermer, and to
the Gale Group staff, in particular Dedria Bryfonski, Linda Hubbard, John Schmittroth, Cynthia Baldwin,
Tracey Rowens, Randy Bassett, Christine O'Bryan, Rebecca Parks, and especially Sharon Malinowski.

The Gale Group

Sharon Malinowski, *Senior Editor*
Rebecca Parks, *Editor*
Linda S. Hubbard, *Managing Editor, Multicultural Team*

Margaret A. Chamberlain, *Permissions Specialist*
Mary K. Grimes, *Image Cataloger*

Mary Beth Trimper, *Production Director*
Evi Seoud, *Assistant Production Manager*

Cynthia Baldwin, *Product Design Manager*
Tracey Rowens, *Cover and Page Designer*

Barbara Yarrow, *Graphic Services Manager*
Randy Bassett, *Image Database Supervisor*
Robert Duncan and Michael Logusz, *Imaging Specialists*
Christine O'Bryan, *Graphics Desktop Publisher*

Library of Congress Catalog Card Number 99-24692
A CIP record is available from the British Library

ISBN 0-7876-4080-8
Printed in the United States of America.

Library of Congress Cataloging-in-Publication Data

Women in world history : a biographical encyclopedia / Anne Commire, editor, Deborah Klezmer, associate editor.
    p. cm.
    Includes bibliographical references and index.
    ISBN 0-7876-3736-X (set). — ISBN 0-7876-4080-8 (v. 1). —
    ISBN 0-7876-4061-1 (v. 2) — ISBN 0-7876-4062-X (v. 3) — ISBN 0-7876-4063-8 (v. 4)
    1. Women—History Encyclopedias.2. Women—Biography Encyclopedias.
    I. Commire, Anne. II. Klezmer, Deborah.
        HQ1115.W6 1999
        920.72'03—DC21   99-24692

10 9 8 7 6 5 4 3 2 1

CONTENTS

CONTENTS

The final volume of *Women in World History* contains a set
of the genealogical charts, the bibliography and sources,
and the indices.

*I*NTRODUCTION

"All history is biography," wrote Thomas Carlyle. But in 1914, Vera Brittain won a scholarship to Oxford challenging Carlyle's qualifier that "all history is the biography of great men." The exclusion of women, as well as minorities, from standard texts has created a history that bears little resemblance to reality. Yet there are those who continue to claim that to supplement traditional history with women's history is a radical or political notion, one that threatens to distort the historical record. We suggest that what is radical is the notion of teaching the history of a few to all.

The idea for *Women in World History* began while we were editing a five-volume set of reference books for Gale Research entitled *Historic World Leaders*. One goal for *Leaders* had been to include biographies of as many women as possible, but as the volumes filled quickly with the requisite men—the Napoleons, the Gandhis, the Churchills—we had too little space for the important women we were uncovering. It soon became clear that as long as women's biographies had to compete for the small percentage of pages set aside for them in traditional collections, history would remain incomplete. The same few women—Florence Nightingale, Joan of Arc, Pocahontas—would continue to represent the thousands of remarkable women who have affected the course of world history. We determined that in order for a general reference series to devote space to women commensurate with their significance, the volumes would have to be devoted to women—100%.

Denied their history, women have been denied the momentum of their own accomplishments; the result has been a loss to history and to the world. Debate about the suitability of women in combat, for example, that remains ignorant of the role Russian women played in World Wars I and II consigns women to the task of proving themselves over and over again (e.g. Soviet fighter pilot Lidiya Litvak shot down 15 enemy planes in 1943.) *Women in World History* represents an attempt on the part of historians from around the world to bring to light the individual achievements made by women of every age and to bolster the cumulative effect that these achievements, once revealed, can have on future generations.

"Except when writing about queens," notes Carolyn Heilbrun, "biographers of women have not . . . been at ease with their subjects—and even with queens, like Elizabeth I of England, there has been a tendency to see them as somewhat abnormal, monstrous." Others tend to see women as shadows of men. Corizon Aquino, for example, who governed the Philippines during a difficult six years and prevented her country from lapsing into chaos, is occasionally perceived as simply the widow of an exceptional man. For 19 centuries, Ban Zhao who, upon the death of her brother, completed the *Han Shu* (*History of the Han*), the second most noted of the many dynastic histories of China, was rarely mentioned as its co-editor, though some modern-day scholars give her credit as its primary author. For 11 years, from 1872 to its completion in 1883, during her husband's illness, Emily Roebling supervised the construction of the Brooklyn Bridge, then the longest span in the world; her work is generally encapsulated in a two-line footnote, if it is mentioned at all.

Many women have been simply forgotten. Poet Lucille Clifton tells of a visit she made to Walnut Grove plantation. During a tour, not a single mention was made of slaves. When she asked the tour guide how many slaves had worked the plantation, the guide responded that there were ten slaves recorded, but there might have been more—only male slaves were listed as property. Because women play a prominent role in literature—often in literature written by men— "a very queer, composite being thus emerges," writes Virginia Woolf. "Imaginatively she is of the highest importance; practically she is completely insignificant. She pervades poetry from cover to cover; she is all but absent from history."

The process of uncovering the stories of the approximately 10,000 women in this series has been fascinating, enlightening, and frequently frustrating. Throughout the ages, fathers and sons have been scrupulously documented in historical records; for mothers and daughters, birth and death dates are often unknown and approximated. Many cultures do not even count daughters as children. The king's daughter was often treated with the same indifference as the daughter of a tavern owner. But, like certain Soviet leaders who made an art form of airbrushing discredited colleagues from the photographic record, history has occasionally left in a hand or an elbow by mistake. We encountered one historic tome that solemnly noted: "Ariadne was a 5th-century Byzantine empress and daughter of the childless Leo I." Leo had no sons. Records of Eliza Lynch, a major figure in the cultural and political development of Paraguay, scrupulously list her children with dictator Francisco Solano López: "Jan (b. 1855); Enrique (b. 1858); Federico (b. 1860); Carlos (b. 1861); Leopoldo (b. 1862); Miguel (b. 1866); and three daughters, names unknown."

For expediency, historians have eliminated what they perceive to be the secondary storyline. When a woman *is* known to exist historically, she has often been the casualty of streamlining. The secret to good writing is brevity. "The Holy Roman emperor Otto I arranged a marriage for his son Otto II to a Byzantine empress" is much more readable than "Empress Adelaide of Burgundy and Holy Roman emperor Otto I arranged a marriage for their son Otto II to Theophano, a Byzantine empress."

In the world's text, women have been relegated to common nouns—the queen, the princess, the sister of Charles IV, the duchess of Carlisle—and possessive pronouns—"and his daughter," "and his mother," "and his wife." In many accounts that chronicle the early years of the 20th century, this phrase appears: "The 1914 assassination of Archduke Franz Ferdinand and his wife led directly to World War I." (Worse, in most reports Archduchess Sophie Chotek's death goes unmentioned; Franz Ferdinand dies alone.) Michael Collins storms the barricade during the Easter Rising, and Michael Collins is named; Constance Markievicz and Winifred Carney storm the same barricade, and they are referred to as "two women activists." The often-used phrase "Einstein and his wife" (he had two) evokes an image of a disheveled genius and a drab, faceless woman when, in fact, Mileva Einstein-Marić did the computations for his theory of relativity.

"Let women do all the sports they wish—but not in public," wrote Pierre de Coubertin, founder of the modern Olympics, in 1937. De Coubertin's dictum, echoing his predecessors, did not stop women from venturing forth; it only cloaked their achievements. For example, many women were already attempting to climb the Matterhorn in the middle of the 19th century. (Lucy Walker ascended in a white print skirt.) In 1867, along with three men and her father, Felicite Carrel came within 350 feet of the Matterhorn's summit. In the appendix to *Scrambles Amongst the Alps* by Edward Whymper, all the men who made that ascent—Caesar Carrel, J.J. and J.P. Maquignaz, and J.A. Carrel—are carefully listed, except the neglected Felicite who is cited as "and a daughter of the last named." Despite Whymper, the point she reached is known as Col Felicite.

We spent months tracking antecedents. Sometimes we found them, sometimes not. If information is sought on a fairly prominent man, one need only start with an encyclopedia. For a woman, an encyclopedia is rarely the place to start. Instead, one starts with the most prominent man with whom she is identified. To find Heloise, look for Abelard. To find Ariel Durant, look for Will Durant. In *Webster's Biographical Dictionary* (1972 ed.), Mary Cassatt is listed as "his sister Mary" at the end of the entry on American railroad executive **Cassatt, Alexander Johnston (1839–1906)**. He has five lines; she has four.

We were determined not to leave a mother, wife, duchess or daughter unturned. Take Ingeborg. Our morning would start simply enough; then we would read: "After his marriage at Amiens, on August 14, 1193, Philip II Augustus, king of France, took a sudden aversion to his 18-year-old Danish bride and sought a divorce." Well, there it was. Obviously, by her marriage to Philip II Augustus, the Danish bride was a queen of France, but who was she? From one source, we learned that she was on good terms with the ensuing French kings; from another, that she lived peacefully, gaining a reputation for kindness. From a third, that she died highly esteemed but, as in the previous sources, nameless, either in 1237 or 1238. Within an hour, we had her name: Ingeborg. By mid-morning, we learned that Ingeborg was the daughter of Waldemar I the Great, king of Denmark. No mother mentioned. Now we had a nameless Danish queen, and a barely named French one.

To give complete and accurate information on Ingeborg, we needed her mother, but while pouring through Palle Lauring's *A History of*

Denmark, we read in passing that Philip Augustus "had threatened to cast off his first wife." Another ball in the air. Now we had a nameless Danish queen, one barely named daughter, and an unnamed first wife. By noon, we had uncovered Isabella, first wife of Philip and daughter of Baldwin V, count of Hainault. No mother mentioned. Unfortunately, we had also uncovered a third wife, known only as the mother of Philip Hurepel. Now we had the aforementioned twosome, a newly named first wife, and an unknown third. By mid-afternoon, we gleaned that the mother of Philip Hurepel was named Agnes; she was also the mother of the nonessential Marie. By late afternoon, we had a headache. The results of our day's exploration can be found under the names Agnes of Meran (d. 1201), Ingeborg (c. 1176–1237/38), Isabella of Hainault (1170–1190), and Marie of France (1198–c. 1223). As far as we were able to ascertain, Ingeborg's mother was either Sophie of Russia or Richezza of Poland. No one knows for sure.

These were not idle chases. Often the woman off-handedly referred to as the "queen-regent" or "queen mother" turned out to be someone of import, like Catherine de Medici or Eleanor of Aquitaine. A towering stack of books would eventually straighten out these problems, but the quantity needed will not be found in a small library collection.

The majority of the time, when we did find the woman for whom we were looking, she didn't have one name; she had five or six. Unlike most men whose various names have been sifted down over time to one or two, Holy Roman Empress Agnes of Poitou strolls through the history books as Agnes of Aquitaine, Agnes of Guienne, Agnes of Bavaria, or Agnes of Germany. The dowager empress of China, in her various transliterations, is known as Cixi or Tz'u-hsi, Tse-Hi, Tsu-Hsi, Tze Hsi, Tzu Hsi, Tsze Hsi An, Yehonala, Xiaoqin Xian Huanghou, Xi Taihou, Nala Taihou, Lao Fuoye, or Imperial Concubine Yi. Running down these names easily added over two years to the project, but we had no choice. Otherwise, the same woman would be scattered throughout our index as Yolande of Brienne on page 29, Jolanta on page 403, and Isabella II of Jerusalem on page 1602.

Name changes that accompany marriage added to the difficulty. Women from outside Russia took on Russian names when they married tsars; one minute they're Sophia Augusta Frederika, princess of Anhalt-Zerbst, the next minute they're Catherine II the Great. East Germany's Christa Rothenburger won the gold medal in speedskating in 1984. In 1992, she won the silver medal as Christa Luding. In some books, Alice Guy Blache can be found under B; in others, Alice Guy-Blache is found under G. Then there's the longtime bugbear: Mrs. Vincent Astor, Mrs. John D. Rockefeller. Which one? Mrs. John D. the 1st, the 3rd, or junior? So often, the dreaded, "the philanthropist, Mrs. Reid," stopped us cold. Is that Mrs. Ogden Mills Reid or Mrs. Whitelaw Reid? (See Helen Rogers Reid and Elizabeth Mills Reid.)

We were not alone in our exasperation. "How are you listing Etta Palm?," queried one of our French historians about an assignment: "As *Palm, Etta Aelders? Palm Aelders, Etta?* or *Palm d'Aelders, Etta?* My best sources call her *Etta Palm d'Aelders,* but I'll put her under *Palm* because she's more widely known to English audiences as *Etta Palm.* Whew! You'd think there would be more uniformity in these matters."

Researching the lives of Roman women in Republican times was also daunting. Free Roman men had three or four names: the *praenomen* or given name, the *nomen* or family name, and sometimes the *cognomen* or distinguishing name: thus, Gaius Julius Caesar. The women, however, were given only one name, the feminine form of the family name. That is why the *daughters* of Julius Caesar and *his sister* are all named Julia. Only Julia. Historians have taken to qualifiers like Julia Minor and Julia Major, but it has not solved the problem. Five of the Julias can be found in *Women in World History,* as well as all eight Cleopatras (Cleopatra VII is the famous one), five Arsinoes, seven sisters Bonaparte, seven Beatrice d'Estes, numerous Euphrosynes, Eurydices, Eudocias, Theopanos, Theodoras, Zoes, Faustinas, and Flavias, many Sforzas and Viscontis, and all 35 women named Medici.

Eventually, we picked up speed. With the material we had accumulated, we could begin to answer our own questions more readily and find the women more quickly. Out of necessity, we were using *Women in World History* as a primary reference source, long before it was completed.

We were also using our charts. Women are rarely included on existing genealogies. A Chinese journalist recalled being handed a copy of her family tree which stretched back 3,000 years. "Not one woman was included on the tree," she noted, "not a mother, a sister, a daughter, a wife." For expediency, women have been left off charts which, while following the male line, are difficult enough to read without adding a cadre of women. When women do appear because of their regal status, usually only their sons are noted on the ancestral line below. In one case, a son was included who had died at age six, while his surviving sister, who had become queen of a neighboring country, was missing.

Determined to come up with an easy-to-use cast list, we set about giving one name to each woman on the world stage as she made her entrances and exits throughout the series. In order to do this, we needed to make our own charts, settle on a name for the subject, and add dates if known. Without identifying dates, five Margarets of Austria all look alike. Thought was given to imposing a rational system on the names, but problems outweighed the advantages. One commonly used data base made a stab at it by changing all Catherines to Katherine. Thus, they had Katherine the Great. Whenever possible, we have tried to use the name by which the subject has been most clearly identified in historical contexts. In so doing, the inconsistencies arise. A Spanish historian might call a queen Isabella; an English historian might call the same queen Elizabeth; a French and German historian, Elisabeth; a Russian historian, Elizaveta.

If the women were difficult for us to locate without knowing the exact name used, we knew the task would be even more difficult for our readers. For this reason, we offer many avenues to find the women sought: by the charts, by indexing, by cross-referencing of collective name variants (*Rejcka. Variant of Ryksa.*), by cross-referencing of name variations within the series (*Gonzaga, Eleanor [1534–1594]. See Eleanora of Austria.*), and by cross-referencing of titles (*Pembroke, countess of. See Clifford Anne [1590–1676].*). Also, each entry includes a section of name variations, shedding light on most of the name incarnations by which a woman has been known.

We began to rely so heavily on our genealogical charts—all 90 of them—that we decided to put them in the front of Volume I, alphabetized by country (see *Contents*). If a woman is bolded on the chart, she appears in both her own entry and throughout the series under the name given. Sometimes her sketch will just be personal data, sometimes a few paragraphs, sometimes many pages, but as Rutger's Kay Vandergrift notes: "The first step for those who are the 'others' in traditional history is to prove their very existence."

In addition to the charts, collective and joint entries (such as Astronauts: Women in Space, Egyptian Feminism, Siege Warfare and Women, Anita Augspurg and Lida Heymann, The Song

Sisters) provide a unique forum for viewing the lives of, and relationships among, the women they feature. Sidebar entries about women related in some manner to the main biographical subject also appear throughout the series. Ranging from one sentence to several paragraphs in length, sidebars feature mothers, daughters, sisters, peers, and partners who are of historical interest in their own right. For instance, a sidebar on Miep Gies can be found in the entry on Anne Frank; Irene Gibson, the original "Gibson girl," can be found in the entry on her sister Nancy Astor; well-known French bookseller Adrienne Monnier appears in the entry on her life-partner Sylvia Beach.

Early in the production of *Women in World History,* we received a note from Tillie Olsen: "You're involved in a daunting task. Selections must be so difficult—who to leave out. Yet the joy in having so *many* from whom to select." This series takes us from around 3100 BCE to the modern age. Our intention was to include only women who are deceased, born before 1926, or currently inactive or retired. However, we felt we could not omit the women of the 1960s' women's movement, nor women whose place in history we believe to be secure, such as Jane Goodall, Aung San Suu Kyi, Helen Caldicott, Toni Morrison, Geraldine Ferraro, and Jocelyn Bell Burnell.

We wanted to include women of historical interest from every walk of life—artists, pirates, scientists, athletes, philanthropists, adventurers, politicians, pacifists, saints, and courtesans, even those famous for just being famous. We also wanted to include women of courage, many of whom challenged us to see new dimensions of the very term *courage,* like Alice of Battenberg who risked her life to save a score of Jews, and the many other valiant women who are featured. This is, however, an encyclopedia, not a book of merit. Women of historical interest, like Ma Barker and Eva Braun, are also included.

We envisioned a series heavily focused on international women, many of whom were enormously important, even revered in their own countries, though seldom known in the United States. Most books in the U.S. cover only American women; by so doing, they isolate women's accomplishments to the last 200 years and neglect about 3,000 years of women's history. An international emphasis, however, did not prove easy. Since much of the information and many of the primary sources we needed for our research were not available in English, we asked professors to undertake translations. More than 300 contributors, from over 20 nations, have participated in this project. (For a complete list, see the *Contributors* section in this volume.)

Readers will inevitably find omissions and inequities in length. Due to the sheer number of women writers, we were not able to include as many of them as we had hoped. Their work is often well-documented, and libraries already contain biographical information for students. Instead, we chose to concentrate on women in areas less documented. We hope that supplements to the series will follow, with emphasis on adding women writers and expanding some of the shorter entries. We invite suggestions for inclusion in every area from our readers. We have also spent years checking our facts. Nonetheless, because women have been ignored historically, the record is replete with inaccuracies that have been given widespread circulation. Thus, there will be errors in this series. We welcome suggestions and corrections.

When we started this project, we expected to find that women of achievement did not, because of their limitations in society, achieve in proportion to the men of their day. It would be our task to document the exceptions. We set out to produce a multivolume series in four years' time that would contain around 5,000 women. Four years turned into five; five turned into six; six turned into nine. *Women in World History* contains more than 10,000 exceptions.

We have just begun.

Finally, our sincerest thanks to Peg Yorkin, a woman legendary for her commitment to women. She gave us her belief, risked over one million dollars, left editorial control to the editors, and, with phenomenal patience, kept this project alive for those nine years. Without her, there would be no *Women in World History*.

Anne Commire

Deborah Klezmer

*U*SER'S GUIDE

The following is the boxed example entry:

1 **Fuller, Margaret** (1810-1850)

2 *Early feminist writer, central figure with the Transcendentalists, and one of the most intellectually gifted American women of the 19th century. Name variations: Sarah Margaret Fuller as a child; Margaret Fuller Ossoli, d'Ossoli, or Marchioness Ossoli after her marriage.* **3** *Born Sarah Margaret Fuller in Cambridgeport, Massachusetts, on May 23, 1810; died in a shipwreck off New York harbor, on July 19, 1850; eldest child of Timothy Fuller (1778-1835, a lawyer, member of the state assembly and U.S. Congress) and Margaret (Crane) Fuller; may have been married to her lover Marquis Giovanni Angelo Ossoli in 1849 or 1850; children: one son, Angelo.*

4 *Taught school in Providence (1837-39); began "conversations" for educated women (1839); was editor of the Dial (1840-42); book reviewer for Greeley's New York Tribune (1844-46); voyaged to Europe (1846); as a journalist, covered the Italian republicans and the revolution (1846-49).*

5 *Selected writings: Günderode (translation of the correspondence between *Karoline von Günderode and *Bettina von Arnim, 1842); Summer on the Lakes in 1843 (Boston: Little Brown, 1844); Women in the Nineteenth Century (New York: Tribune Press, 1845); Papers on Literature and Art (2 vols. New York: Wiley and Putnam, 1846); Collected Works (1855); Life Without and Life Within (collection of essays and poems, Boston, 1860).*

6 Margaret Fuller was one of the most intellectually gifted American women of the 19th century. Thwarted by her family's poverty and by the restrictions of her gender in early life, she matured into a superb speaker and writer in her 30s. Her work as a literary critic and historian of the Italian revolution was cut tragically short by her death in a shipwreck when she was only 40.

*L*et Ulysses drive the beeves [cows] home, while Penelope there piles up the fragrant loaves; they are both well employed. . . . But Penelope is no more meant for a baker or weaver solely, than Ulysses for a cattle-herd.
—Margaret Fuller

7 Fuller was the oldest of nine children, and her ambitious father decided to bring her up as though she were a son. He made her work hard at a difficult educational program while pursuing his own career, first as a lawyer, later as a U.S. Congressional representative, and then as speaker of the Massachusetts Assembly. At age six, she began to learn Latin and soon showed prodigious intellectual gifts, devouring Shakespeare and Cervantes while still very young and reading all of Virgil, Horace, and Ovid by the time she was eight. The price of this forced learning and a harsh streak in her father's manner was a long series of gruesome nightmares, in which she dreamed of being trampled by horses, and of being lost in a blood-soaked forest. She spent two teenage years in Groton, Massachusetts, at Miss Prescott's boarding school, where her intellectual brilliance amazed the teachers and unnerved fellow students. Fuller had violent temper tantrums when other students mocked her eccentricities, followed by paroxysms of remorse when her petty vengeance was discovered. She returned to the family's home in Cambridgeport, near Harvard University, when she was 15. There, she befriended Oliver Wendell Holmes, Sr., William Ellery Channing, and Richard Henry Dana, soon to be famous men, who were then studying at Harvard, and advanced her education by discussions with such professors as the logician Henry Hedge.

The pleasures of Harvard life ended abruptly when her father decided to retire from law and politics to a country farm in 1833. The life did not suit Margaret Fuller, then aged 23; she was bored teaching her young siblings and looking after the family when her mother became an invalid. Her father's death from cholera two years later made matters worse. Responsible for the entire family, Fuller decided to work in Boston as a teacher and send them money rather than remain immured in the countryside. She worked at Bronson Alcott's Temple School as a Latin and French teacher, amazing **8** the father of *Louisa May Alcott, with her brilliance and energy, and taking on extra teaching and translating work to earn money for the family. After a year, Bronson's eccentric methods of religious education scandalized the children's parents, most of whom abandoned his school and drove it into bankruptcy. Fuller's reputation was spreading, however, and the Greene Street School in Providence, Rhode Island, now offered her $1,000 per year to teach just four hours a day, which was the highest teaching salary offered to a woman up to that time. She accepted and spent her leisure time reading Goethe and translating works of German philosophy. Aware that she was not a beauty, Fuller worked hard to make striking

266   *W*OMEN IN *W*ORLD *H*ISTORY

---

1 ENTRY HEADING

Entries in this series are arranged in one strict A–Z alphabet. ENTRY HEADINGS include the subject's name followed by her birth and death dates (in parentheses). When birth and/or death dates are unavailable, the best available date that indicates the subject's era is cited. The following abbreviations are used for dating:

b. = born	fl. = flourished
d. = died	c. = circa
r. = reigned	

2 IDENTIFIER

IDENTIFIERS are located below the ENTRY HEADING. One-sentence in length, these are used to indicate the subject's nationality and to provide a brief summation of the subject's life and achievements. IDENTIFIERS may include information regarding any of the following: the subject's field; discoveries, advancements, or pioneering efforts made by the subject; the historical landscape in which the subject was of import; controversy that surrounded the subject; major awards won by the subject or the legacy left by the subject for future generations.

3 PERSONAL PROFILE

The PERSONAL PROFILE follows the IDENTIFIER. PERSONAL PROFILES vary greatly in length and are dependent on information availability. This section is designed to be a catchall for the subject's "vital statistics." Its components are as follows:

Name variations

Includes spelling and form variations, pseudonyms, married names, nicknames, and titles. These are included to assist a researcher in making a more thorough search of the library for further information about the subject.

Pronunciation

Date and place of birth

Date, place, and manner of death

Parents' names and occupations

Spouse's name, date of marriage, and dates of widowhood or divorce

Children's names and birth dates

Because periods in a woman's life may have gone unchronicled, in some cases children's birth dates provide the best available information on the subject's activities during these years.

10

dresses for herself and to cut a distinctive figure even if not a conventionally attractive one.

In 1841, the family sold its farm in Groton and moved back to the Jamaica Plain section of Boston. There Fuller became a central figure in the Transcendentalist Club, befriending Ralph Waldo Emerson, Henry David Thoreau, the ❧ Sturgis sisters, George and ❧ Sophia Ripley, and *Elizabeth Palmer Peabody. The Transcendentalists rebelled against the conventional, theologically dry religion of Unitarian Boston in favor of their own blend of German philosophical idealism and nature mysticism. A group of talented writers, they were also great conversationalists (Bronson Alcott tried to make a living as a traveling conversationalist) and many of them described Fuller as the greatest talker among them. Her friend James Freeman Clark wrote: "All her friends will unite in the testimony that whatever they may have known of wit and eloquence in others, they have never seen one who, like her, by the conversation of an hour or two, could not merely entertain and inform, but make an epoch in one's life."

From late 1839, Fuller led a series of women's "conversations," which were in effect seminars on contemporary issues. Developing an early feminist insight into the condition of her sex, she urged her "assistants," as the participants were known, to study with the same rigor showed by their men folk and to look on their intellectual lives as vocational rather than merely decorative. The conversations, two hours a week, lasted 13 weeks for each of four consecutive years, gaining steadily in repute and drawing larger audiences each time. Fuller profited from them (at $10 per "assistant") and became an intellectual celebrity in New England but found when she once tried a course of mixed "conversations" that the men dominated the talk and patronized the women. Never subject to false modesty, she told Emerson, who also admired her, "I now know all the people worth knowing in America and I find no intellect comparable to my own."

Relinquishing teaching, she became first editor of The Dial, the Transcendentalists' magazine. Widely renowned, with a large group of clever and influential friends and acquaintances, she had the intellectual, literary, and business skills to make the project succeed. Emerson and George Ripley helped her get the magazine going, but she wrote eight of the articles in the first edition and was The Dial's most prolific contributor throughout its five-year life. When

❧ **Ripley, Sophia** (1803–1861)
American educator and Transcendentalist. Born on July 6, 1803; died in 1861; married George Ripley (1802–1880, a leading Transcendentalist); children.

A close friend of Margaret Fuller, Sophia Ripley also contributed to the Dial. She was the first in that periodical to touch on the "women's question," in her 1841 article "Woman," complaining that women lose themselves in marriage, becoming "an appendage . . . the upper nurse." Even so, Ripley carried on a traditional existence in her marriage to George Ripley, but she was a leading spirit in developing with her husband their utopian Brook Farm, a model community based on the ideals of Christianity and Transcendentalism. Its members included Nathaniel Hawthorne, John Sullivan Dwight, Christopher Cranch, Almira Barlow, and Margaret Fuller's brother Lloyd. Wrote Ralph Waldo Emerson: "Sarah R is wonderfully free from egotism of place and time and blood."

Ripley started the Brook Farm commune in the spring of 1841, he and his wife urged Fuller to join them as the farm's "presiding genius." Fuller was willing to visit for weekends and hold impromptu conversations but, recalling her earlier experiences, felt no attraction to farming and the countryside and refused to live there. She suffered from severe and disabling headaches nearly every afternoon and cherished the privacy she could not have enjoyed in the commune. Nathaniel Hawthorne, who did settle down at Brook Farm for a while, disliked Fuller and modeled his odious character Zenobia, in The Blithedale Romance (1852), on her. He also wrote later that she was "a great humbug with a strong, heavy, unpliable, and, in many respects, defective and evil nature."

Fuller always had her share of opponents, knew she was unattractive to many men, and never expected to marry. "From an early age" she wrote:

I have felt that I was not born to the common womanly lot. I knew that I should never find a being who could keep the key to my character, that there would be none on whom I could always lean; that I should be a pilgrim and sojourner on the earth, and that the birds and foxes would be surer of a place to lay their heads than I.

In the late 1830s, she had fallen in love with Samuel Gray Ward, a man seven years her junior who had studied art and literature in Germany and shared many of her philosophical enthusiasms. She was dismayed when Ward

❧ **Sturgis sisters.** See Adams, Clover for sidebars on Ellen Sturgis Hooper and Caroline Sturgis Tappan.

9

---

4 TIMELINE

This section follows the PERSONAL PROFILE. It lists events of major importance in the subject's life with dates of occurrences, in chronological order. Events listed in the TIMELINE may include those that took place in the subject's own life and those that occurred during the historical landscape of her day thus either impacting her life or providing a portrait of the times in which she lived.

5 VITAE

This section follows the TIMELINE or the PERSONAL PROFILE (when no TIMELINE appears). It is a listing of selected career achievements and applies primarily to sports figures and women in the arts. For sports figures, the VITAE is a listing of selected records; for novelists, selected writings; for filmmakers, selected films; for visual artists, selected works; for musicians, selected discography; etc.

6 CORE BIOGRAPHY

The CORE BIOGRAPHY tells the subject's life story with an emphasis on narration rather than critique. In-depth discussions of events in the subject's life unfold primarily in chronological order and are designed to illumine the sub-

ject's character as much as her activities. As available, comprehensive information regarding the subject's family, childhood, adolescence, and adult and senior years are presented alongside a portrayal of the major issues and events of the given era.

7 QUOTATION

A QUOTATION, either by or about the subject, which exemplifies her.

8 ASTERISKS

In the CORE BIOGRAPHY, an ASTERISK is used to indicate the names of women who have their own entries in the series. The ASTERISK appears in front of the woman's name.

9 CROSS REFERENCE: IN MARGIN

Occasionally a woman is mentioned in the CORE BIOGRAPHY whose entry appears as a SIDEBAR in another location. In these cases, a ❧ appears before her name pointing toward (*i.e.,* ❧ or ❧) a corresponding cross reference in margin. This cross reference is always designed to send the reader to the location of an entry or SIDEBAR about the woman in question.

10 SIDEBAR

SIDEBARS are entries about another woman, or women, who were related in some manner to the main biographical subject. Many women have been included as SIDEBARS rather than as separate entries to help illustrate the interrelatedness of women's activities and to indicate the cumulative effects of their efforts. SIDEBARS include entries about women who were related by family, occupation, time period, or ideology to the main biographical subject. SIDEBARS approximate the format of main entries, most often including ENTRY HEADING, PERSONAL PROFILE, CORE BIOGRAPHY, SOURCES, SUGGESTED READING, RELATED MEDIA, COLLECTIONS, and BYLINE.

A ❧ before a woman's name in the CORE BIOGRAPHY indicates that there is a SIDEBAR about her included within the entry; the direction of the ❧ (*i.e.,* ❧ or ❧) indicates the direction on the page to which to look for the SIDEBAR. (The same symbol, facing in the opposite direction, also appears before the ENTRY HEADING in the SIDEBAR.)

11 REFERENCES SHELF

This section includes reference materials, both those used in constructing the entry and those to which a researcher can turn for additional information about the biographical subject.

Sources
     A list of sources used in the preparation of the entry.

Suggested Reading
     A list of sources, not directly used to construct the entry, which contains further information about the subject.

Related Media
     A list of related media—including feature films, audio tapes, television and radio programs, and plays—that

were not used in constructing the entry but which contain information by or about the subject.

Collections

A list of collections where materials by or about the subject is located.

12 BYLINE

Most entries in the series have been contributed by historians, women's studies professors, or freelance authors (for complete list, see *Contributors* page). Where applicable, the contributor's title, university affiliation, and location are included in the BYLINE. When contributors have also authored larger works on the biographical subject or a related subject, these titles are also indicated.

13 CROSS REFERENCE: BY VARIANT

Cross references by variant apply only to given names (e.g., Marie). The need for these arose from the prevalent variations in given names around the world. Variants here refer to equivalent forms of like names, such as Louise, Louisa, Luise, Lowyse. Cross references by variant for each applicable given name appear in the alphabetical listing. Under "Louise," for example, a researcher will find a cross reference by variant to Luise and Lowyse. Cross references by variant are also used to point out less similar, regional variations in given names; for example, the Spanish name Isabella is cross-referenced by variant to the English equivalent of Elizabeth. Researchers who are initially unable to find the woman whom they are seeking are encouraged to see the cross reference by variant for different forms of the given name and to pursue their subject accordingly.

14 CROSS REFERENCE: BY TITLE

Because oftentimes a reader may know a royal only by her title and approximate dates (*e.g.*, Duchess of Burgundy), cross references by title are designed to send the reader from the royal's title to her primary name, under which her entry can be found. A reader looking up the Duchess of Burgundy, for example, will find several cross references listed, each pointing to a different Duchess of Burgundy. When more than one woman share the same title as in such cases, the women's life and death dates (or best available dates) are included in the cross references, so that readers may identify the particular Duchess of Burgundy whom they are seeking. In these cases, like titles are listed in ascending order by best available date.

15 CROSS REFERENCE: BY NAME

Due to the large number of name variations for women, cross references are used liberally within the alphabetical listing. The name by which a woman is most commonly known (here called her primary name) is the name under which her entry appears. To make this entry easier to find, many name variations are cross-referenced in the al-

phabetical listing, sending the reader to a primary name under which an entry will be found.

Cross references for women who share the same name contain the subject's birth and death dates (or the best available dates for the subject), so that the reader may identify the particular woman they are seeking. These cross references are listed in ascending order by best available date.

16 FURTHER NOTES ON CROSS REFERENCING

Cross references by name and by title are designed to send the reader to the location of a particular entry. When the entry in question is contained as a SIDEBAR within another main entry, the cross reference indicates the name of the main entry in which the SIDEBAR is contained and, when applicable, the primary name of the SIDEBAR subject. In the first example, the woman in question is the Duchess of Burgundy whose primary name is Michelle Valois, and she can be found as a SIDEBAR within the entry about Isabeau of Bavaria.

FULLER

of our country as the land of the future. It is so, but that spirit which made it all it is of value in my eyes, which gave all hope with which I can sympathize for that future, is more alive here [in Italy] at present than in America. My country is at present spoiled by prosperity, stupid with the lust of gain, soiled by crime in its willing perpetuation of slavery.

She was depressed to discover that the American republic refused to give diplomatic recognition to the Roman republic but instead stood by and watched it fall. The Romans, in the face of overpowering odds, surrendered unconditionally on July 4, 1849, after a prolonged French bombardment had shattered many familiar Roman landmarks. Fuller and Ossoli had survived but now feared reprisals and had to leave the city rapidly. Going to collect Angelo, their son, they found him sick and half starved because of recent privations brought on by the war.

Angelo recovered, and Fuller realized that she must now break the fact of his existence to her relatives and friends back in States. The news at once started rumors and gossip going in America; Greeley terminated her contract at the Tribune, and she found she was unable to get a contract for the book she was writing about the Roman revolution. With her son and Ossoli, whom she now introduced as her husband, she went to Florence where she found a temporary job as a governess and was befriended by Robert and *Elizabeth Barrett Browning, the English poets. Aware that the authorities were seeking former republican soldiers, however, they were not safe anywhere in Italy, and Fuller decided they must return to America and face the risk of scandal and ostracism.

After borrowing the money for passage on the cheapest ship they could find, the family set sail for New York on the American merchant ship Elizabeth in May 1850. En route the captain died and an inexperienced mate was forced to take over. Approaching New York harbor in high wind on the early morning of July 19, 1850, the ship ran aground on a reef off Fire Island. The storm worsened and the ship began to break up. The shore was in sight, but the lifeboats had been smashed, and one of the men who tried to swim ashore for help was swept away and drowned. Fuller and Ossoli, with their son Angelo, apparently resolved that they would stay together at all costs, and when the captain cried "Abandon ship" they stayed behind and were drowned.

Mourned by relatives and friends who had been waiting with eager anticipation to see her

as a wife and mother and to meet her exotic husband, Fuller's death seemed tragic and, to many, unnecessary. Three of her Transcendentalist friends, Emerson, Clark, and Channing, published a eulogistic memoir of her life and work in 1852 and paid tribute to her lasting influence on their lives. Fuller was largely forgotten by the end of the 19th century, however, and only with the more recent feminist movement have her history and her work been thoroughly revived.

SOURCES: **11**

Allen, Margaret V. The Achievement of Margaret Fuller. University Park, PA: Pennsylvania State University Press, 1979.

Capper, Charles. Margaret Fuller: An American Romantic Life. NY: Oxford University Press, 1992.

Slater, Abby. In Search of Margaret Fuller. NY: Delacorte Press, 1978.

Stern, Madeleine. The Life of Margaret Fuller. Westport, CT: Greenwood Press, 1991.

Wade, Mason, ed. The Writings of Margaret Fuller. NY: Viking, 1941.

SUGGESTED READING:

Blanchard, Paula. Margaret Fuller: From Transcendentalism to Revolution. NY: Delacorte Press, 1978.

Emerson, Ralph Waldo, W.H. Channing, and J.F. Clarke. Memoirs of Margaret Fuller Ossoli. Boston, MA: Phillips, Sampson, 1852.

Miller, Perry, ed. Margaret Fuller: American Romantic. Gloucester, MA: Peter Smith, 1969. Von Mehren, Joan. Minerva and the Muse: A Life of Margaret Fuller. Boston, MA: University of Massachusetts, 1994.

COLLECTIONS:

Fuller Manuscripts and Works, Houghton Library, Harvard University; Margaret Fuller Papers, Massachusetts Historical Society.

Patrick Allitt, Assistant Professor of History, Emory University, Atlanta, Georgia **12**

Abigal **13**
 Variant of Abigal.

Angouleme, countess of
 See Isabella of Valois (1389-1410).
 See Louise of Savoy (1476-1531). **14**
 See Margaret de Rohan (fl. 1449).
 See Margaret of Turenne.

Angouleme, Marguerite d' **15**
 See Margaret of Angouleme ((1492-1549).

Anne, Princess of Orange (1709–1759)
 See Caroline of Ansbach for sidebar. **16**

Duchess of Burgundy
 See Isabella of Bavaria for sidebar on Michelle Valois (d.1942).

270   *WOMEN IN WORLD HISTORY*

ACKNOWLEDGMENTS

Photographs and illustrations appearing in *Women in World History, Volume 1,* were received from the following sources:

Alexander Turnbull Library, Sylvia Ashton-Warner Collection (Wellington, New Zealand): **p. 542** (Reference No. C15948); Courtesy of Dede Allen: **p. 226**; Courtesy of American Museum of Natural History, Department of Library Services: **p. 151,** (Neg. 46353); AP/Wide World Photos: **p. 536**; Archive Photos, Inc.: **p. 262**; Painting by Jean Bourdichon, *Jean Marot Presents His Work to Queen Anne of Brittany*: **p. 381**; Compliments of the British Embassy: **p. 371**; Bruno of Hollywood (New York City): **p. 1**; Painting by Caravaque: **p. 354**; Courtesy of Columbia Pictures Industries: **p. 188**; Commerce Graphics Ltd. (East Rutherford, New Jersey): **pp. 11, 14**; Corbis Corporation: **p. 202**; Photograph by Lars Hansen, courtesy of Curbstone Press: **p. 194**; Courtesy of

Sophie Dickson: **p. 421**; Compliments of Elizabeth Arden Co.: **p. 443**; Courtesy of R.C. Elwood, from the book *Inessa Armand: Revolutionary and Feminist* (Cambridge University Press, 1992): **p. 472**; Courtesy of Embassy of Finland: **p. 411**; Courtesy of Stephen Frank, photographer: **p. 437**; Pencil drawing by Marchioness Granby, Duchess of Rutland: **p. 554**; Painting by J.-B. Greuze: **p. 493**; Courtesy of Harcourt Brace: **p. 453**; Portrait by E.O. Hoppe, reproduced from the original in the Henry E. Huntington Library and Art Gallery by permission: **p. 645**; Courtesy of International Museum of Photography at George Eastman House: **p. 557**; Courtesy of Laura Ashley, Inc.: **p. 538**; Courtesy of Library of Congress: **pp. 25,** Sculpture by Saint-Gauden **46, 129, 172, 241, 248, 279, 299, 303,** Photograph by Susan Mullally Weil **334, 403, 417, 427, 628**; Courtesy of Lodge Portraits: **p. 519**; Photograph by P.N. Luknitsky, 1925: **p. 156**; Courtesy of Marlborough Gallery (New York City), ©Jen Fong **p. 5, p. 6**; Courtesy of Massachusetts Historical Society, Adams Manuscript Trust: **p. 52**; Photograph by Clarence Bull, courtesy of Metro-Goldwn-Mayer: **p. 243**; Courtesy of Museo Nazionale (Florence): **p. 461**; Photograph by Nadar: **p. 36**; Courtesy of National Aeronautics and Space Administration: **pp. 588–594**; Courtesy of National Historic Institute (Manila, the Philippines): **p. 433**; Courtesy of National Park Service, Adams Historical Site: **p. 38**; Courtesy of the National Portrait Gallery (London): **p. 210**, Photograph by Olive Edis **p. 576**; Photograph by Roger-Viollet: **p. 631**; Painting by Peter Paul Rubens (Rijksmuseum, Amsterdam): **p. 373**; Courtesy of University of Illinois at Chicago, Wallace Kirkland Papers, Jane Addams Memorial Collection, Special Collections, The University Library: **p. 69**; Photograph by Jack Vartoogian: **p. 162**; Courtesy of Warner Bros.: **p. 573**; Painting by Francis Xavier Winterhalter: **p. 79**; Courtesy of Madame Yevonde (London): **p. 63**; Courtesy of 20th Century-Fox: **p. 662**.

CONTRIBUTORS

Christina Accomando is Assistant Professor of English at California State University, Humboldt, who teaches multi-ethnic literature; she served as WREI Fellow in the House Judiciary Subcommittee on Civil Rights, and has written on Sojourner Truth, slave resistance in Robert Hayden's and Phillis Wheatley's poetry, race in contemporary legal discourse, and other topics in African-American studies, including "'The laws were laid down to me anew': Harriet Jacobs and the Reframing of Legal Fictions" in *African American Review* (Summer 1998).

Claire Hsu Accomando is a graduate of New York University and author of *Love and Rutabaga: A Remembrance of the War Years* (St. Martin's Press, 1993), "Exploring the Past with Memoir Writing," in *Promising Practices* (The Greater San Diego Council of Teachers of English, 1996) and articles in *American History Magazine* and *The Christian Science Monitor;* she created and presented the series *History through Art* (Sweetwater Union High School District, San Diego, California).

Vanessa H. Agnew received her Ph.D. from the University of Wales at Cardiff in 1998; she is a freelance writer who teaches and lives in Ann Arbor, Michigan.

Tangren Alexander received her Ph.D. in Philosophy from the University of Oregon; she teaches philosophy and has published in the journals *Hypatia, The Journal of Feminist Philosophy, Teaching Philosophy, Sage-Woman, WomanSpirit Magazine,* and *Sinister Wisdom,* and her short stories can be found in the anthologies *Our Lives, Lesbian Personal Writing* (ed. Francis Rooney, Toronto: Second Story Press, 1991), *Riding Desire* and *Intricate Passions* (ed. Tee Corinne, Edwin-William Press, 1991 & 1989 respectively) and *A Woman's Touch* (eds. Nelly and Cedar, Womanshare Books, 1978).

Catherine Allgor is Assistant Professor of History at Simmons College, Boston, Massachusetts, and author of "'A Lady Will Have More Influence': Women and Patronage in Early Washington City," in *Political Identities: American Women and the Emergence of a Secular State* (eds. Alison Parker *et al.,* Texas A&M University Press) and "'A Republican in a Monarchy': Louisa Catherine Adams in Russia," in *Diplomatic History* (Winter 1997); she won the George Egleston Prize for best American history dissertation, Yale University, 1998, for "Political Parties: Society and Politics in Washington City, 1800–1832."

Patrick Allitt is Professor of History at Emory University, Atlanta, Georgia, and author of *Catholic Converts* and *Catholic Intellectuals and Conservative Politics in America, 1950–1985* (both Cornell University Press, 1997 and 1993 respectively); he is writing a book on the intellectual opponents of environmentalism to be published by the same press.

Thomas L. Altherr is Professor of History and American Studies at the Metropolitan State College of Denver, Denver, Colorado, and is the author of *Sports in North America: A Documentary History,* Vol. I: *Early American Sports to 1820* (1997); he has written numerous articles on subjects including baseball, environmental and agricultural history, and Native Americans and the American West.

Abel A. Alves is Associate Professor of History at Ball State University, Muncie, Indiana, and author of *Brutality and Benevolence: Human Ethology, Culture, and the Birth of Mexico* (Greenwood Press, 1996) and "Of Peanuts and Bread: Images of the Raw and the Refined in the Sixteenth-Century Conquest of New Spain," in *Coded Encounters: Writing, Gender, and Ethnicity in Colonial Latin America* (eds. F. Javier Cerallos-Candau *et al.,* University of Massachusetts Press, 1994); he has contributed articles and reviews to *The Sixteenth Century Journal* since 1989.

Don Amerman is a freelance writer and editor in Saylorsburg, Pennsylvania, and managing editor of *The Journal of Commerce* (New York: 1978–1996); he is a frequent contributor to special editions of *The Journal of Commerce*.

Eleanor Amico is a freelance writer, editor of *Readers Guide to Women's Studies* (Fitzroy Dearborn Publishers, 1998), and the author of "Life Path Sexism," in *On the Market: Surviving the Academic Jobs Search* (ed. Christina Boufis and Victoria C. Olsen, Riverhead Books, 1997), a chapter on Biblical Understandings in *Living the Sacred Trust: Clergy Sexual Ethics* (General Board of Higher Education and Ministry, the United Methodist Church), and other articles; she has taught Women's Studies and Biblical Studies.

Fred M.B. Amram is an award-winning professor of Speech Communication and Creativity at the University of Minnesota and has written books and articles about creativity, invention, robotics, and communication; he is the author of *From Indian Corn to Outer Space: Women Invent in America* which was noted by The Women's National Book Association, and he has been an international consultant to industry, government agencies and educational institutions.

Denise H. Amschler is Professor of Health Science at Ball State University, Muncie, Indiana, and the author of "What Do We Really Know about Women and Heart Disease?" in *The Health Educator* (1996) and "The Rising Incidence of HPV Infection and Its Implications for Reproductive Health," in *Journal of Sex Education and Therapy* (1991); she was editor of *The Eta Sigma Gamman* (1977–92), has lectured widely, and has served as a media advocate for women's health issues.

William Anderson is the author of biographies and books on American literature and history such as *The World of the Trapp Family* (Midpoint, 1998), *Laura Ingalls Wilder: A Biography* (Harper Collins, 1992), *A Little House Reader* (Harper Collins, 1998), and *The World of Louisa May Alcott* (Harper Collins, 1995); he contributes to a variety of magazines and has lectured widely at schools, libraries and universities.

Harriet Ann Horne Arrington is a freelance biographer in Salt Lake City, Utah, who has published on Utah pioneers Alice Merrill Horne, Joseph Horne, and Bathsheba Bigler Smith in such works as *Worth Their Salt: Notable but Often Unnoted Women of Utah* (Utah State

University, 1997), *Encyclopedia of Mormonism* (Macmillan, 1992), and *Nearly Everything Imaginable: Everyday Life in Pioneer Utah* (BYU Studies, 1998); she has lectured extensively on pioneer women in Utah.

Patricia A. Ashman is Professor of History at Central Missouri State University, Warrensburg, and associate editor of the *Historical Dictionary of the British Empire* (Greenwood Press, 1996); she is the author of "Carry A. Nation," "Leonore K. Sullivan," "Nettie Tayloe Ross," and "Luella St. Clair Moss," in *Dictionary of Missouri Biography* (University of Missouri Press, 1999).

Dianne Ashton is Professor of Religion at Rowan University, Glassboro, New Jersey, and author of *Rebecca Gratz: Women and Judaism in Antebellum America* (Wayne State University Press, 1998) and *Jewish Life in Pennsylvania* (Pennsylvania History Association, Ethnic History Series, 1998); she compiled *The Philadelphia Group: A Guide to Archival and Manuscript Collections* (Center for American Jewish History at Temple University, 1993), and served as co-editor of *Four Centuries of Jewish Women's Spirituality* (Beacon Press, 1992).

Mary Welek Atwell, Ph.D., is Chair and Associate Professor in the Criminal Justice Department at Radford University, Radford, Virginia; she is the author of "Elsie Dinsmore . . . Haunting the Minds of Millions of Women," in *Women's Studies and the Curriculum* (ed. Marienne Triplette, Salem College, 1983) and has published in *Journal of Negro History, Virginia Social Science Journal, Capitol Studies, Diplomatic History, Dictionary of Internationalists, American National Biography* and *Children's Literature Association Quarterly*.

Patricia Backhaus is a band-music historian who has published and lectured widely on women in band music; an adjunct instructor of trumpet and brass techniques at Wisconsin Lutheran College, Milwaukee, she is also the portrayer of "The Female Sousa: Helen May Butler," and has performed nationwide, telling the story of Butler and her American Ladies Concert Band.

Francesca Baines is a freelance writer in London, England, who worked as a civil servant in a policy division of the Department of the Environment, taught English to students at the University of Madrid, and served as editor of the children's publication *Classic Adventures*.

Amanda Carson Banks is Senior Information Officer at Vanderbilt University, Nashville, Tennessee, and a lecturer in the Department of Religious Studies and the Divinity School; she received her Ph.D. in Folklore from the University of Pennsylvania and has published and lectured widely on women and religion, and on alternative belief systems, including the Cult of Elvis, Holy Wells, and Angel Worship.

Jeffrey G. Barlow is a professor in the Department of Social Studies at Pacific University, Forest Grove, Oregon.

Sharon L. Barnes is a Ph.D. candidate at the University of Toledo, Ohio, whose dissertation discusses the poetry and feminist theory of Audre Lorde; she specializes in 20th-century American women poets and is co-author of a book of poetry, *Missing Pieces.*

Tracy Barrett is Senior Lecturer in Italian, Vanderbilt University, Nashville, Tennessee, and author of *Cecco, As I Am and Was: The Poems of Cecco Angiolieri* (Branden, 1994), *Anna of Byzantium* (Bantam Double Dell for Young Readers, 1999); she teaches courses on medieval women authors and was awarded a 1994 grant from the National Endowment for the Humanities for a project entitled "Medieval Women in Their Own Words."

Melissa Barth is Coordinator of the Office of Women's Concerns and Women's Studies and Professor of English at Appalachian State University, Boone, North Carolina.

Paula Bartley is Senior Lecturer in History at the University of Wolverhampton, Dudley, United Kingdom, and author and joint editor of the "Women in History" series (Cambridge University Press); among other works, she is author of *Life in the Industrial Revolution* (Edward Arnold, 1987, published in Braille 1992), co-author and co-editor of *Plains Women* (Cambridge University Press, 1991), co-editor of *Women in India and Pakistan* (Cambridge University Press, 1992), and co-author of *Medieval Islam* (Hodder and Stoughton, 1993).

Ellen T. Bastio is a freelance writer in Maryland.

Karin Bauer is Assistant Professor of German Studies at McGill University, Montreal, Canada; she has written a critical study of Nietzsche, Adorno, and Wagner as well as articles on contemporary German writers.

Dave Baxter is a freelance writer in Waterloo, Ontario, Canada.

Donna Beaudin of Guelph, Ontario, Canada, is a freelance writer in history.

Evelyn Bender, Ed.D., Librarian, Edison/Fareira High School, Philadelphia, Pennsylvania, is author of *Brazil* (Chelsea House, 1990) and "Youssef Chahine," in *Censorship: An International Encyclopedia* (London: Fitzroy Dearborn Publishers); she has written curricula on women's history and Latina writers and has served as an American Memory Fellow at the Library of Congress and as consultant and writer at the Rosenback Museum and Library in Philadelphia.

Edith J. Benkov is Professor of French at San Diego State University, San Diego, California.

June Melby Benowitz, Ph.D., is Instructor of American History at Keiser College, Sarasota, Florida; she is the author of *The Encyclopedia of American Women and Religion* (ABC-CLIO, 1998), a contributor to the *New Handbook of Texas* (Texas State Historical Society, 1997), and author of *From Log Cabin to High Rise: The Washington County Courthouse, 1849–1988* (Hillsboro, Oregon: Washington County, 1988).

Jill Benton received her Ph.D. in English and American Literature from the University of California at San Diego; she is Professor of English and World Literature at Pitzer College, Claremont, California, and author of *Naomi Mitchison: A Biography.*

Kari Bethel is a freelance writer and editor in Columbia, Missouri, who works in several subject areas, including literature, history, psychology, and education; she earned a master's degree in English in 1985 and served as editor and senior editor at the University of Missouri (1987–1997).

Laurie Twist Binder is School Library Media Specialist, City of Buffalo Public Schools, New York, and a freelance graphic artist; she is the illustrator of *Buffals—Streets Tell Our Story* by Carolyn Giambra and Doreen Dell (Chalk It Up Press, 1983).

Allida Black, Ph.D., is a professor of American Studies and History; her publications include *Eleanor Roosevelt and the Shaping of Postwar Liberalism* (Columbia University Press, 1997), "Anna Eleanor Roosevelt," in *America's First Ladies: A Biographical Encyclopedia* (ed. Lewis L. Gould, Garland Publishing, 1994), and "Faith and Politics: Hillary Rodham Clinton and 'the Politics of Meaning,'" in *Current World Leaders* (April 1994).

Elizabeth L. Bland is a reporter at *Time* magazine.

Judy Blankenship is a photographer and writer who lived in Latin America from 1985–93.

Robert Bolt is Professor of History, Emeritus, at Calvin College, Grand Rapids, Michigan, and author of *Donald Dickinson* (Eerdmans, 1970); he has written articles on the religions of several 20th-century American presidents.

Stephane E. Booth is Assistant Professor of History at Kent State University, Salem Campus, Salem, Ohio, and has written articles for many publications including *Historical Methods, Talkin' Union, Illinois Historical Journal,* and the *Encyclopedia of the American Left* (eds. Buhle, Buhle, and Georgakas, 1990).

Sara Steinert Borella is Assistant Professor of French at Pacific University, Forest Grove, Oregon; among her publications are "Is Illness Metaphor? The Case of Contemporary Swiss Women Writers," in *The Translation Review* (December 1992) and "From the Swiss Alps to the Elburz Mountains: Traveling with Ella Maillart and Annemarie Schwarzenback," in *La voie creuelle* and *Das glückliche Tal* (International Swiss Literature Conference).

Wes Borucki is a doctoral candidate in the Department of History of the University of Alabama, Tuscaloosa, and editor (1998–1999) of *Southern Historian,* the University of Alabama's annual journal; he lectures on "Yankees in King Cotton's Court: Northerners in Antebellum and Wartime Alabama" and has contributed biographical sketches to *Civil Rights in the United States* (Macmillan Press).

Kathleen Brady is author of *Lucille: The Life of Lucille Ball,* an essay on Hazel Brannon Smith in *Lost Heroes of American History,* and a short story in the anthology *The Confidential Casebook of Sherlock Holmes;* she was named a Fellow of the Society of American Historians after the publication of her biography *Ida Tarbell: Portrait of a Muckraker.*

Daniel E. Brannen, Jr., is an attorney who left the practice of law to work as a freelance writer; he frequently writes legal, historical, governmental, and biographical entries for reference textbooks published by the Gale Group.

Peter Harrison Branum is a freelance writer in Auburn, Alabama.

Susan Brazier is a freelance writer in Ottawa, Ontario, Canada.

Carol Brennan is a freelance writer in Grosse Pointe, Michigan.

Catherine Briggs is a freelance writer and a Ph.D. candidate at University of Waterloo, Ontario, Canada.

Jeff Broadwater, Ph.D., J.D., is Assistant Professor of History at Barton College, Wilson, North Carolina, whose publications include *Dwight Eisenhower and the Anti-Communist Crusade, 1952–1961* (University of North Carolina Press).

Kendall W. Brown is Professor of History at Brigham Young University, Provo, Utah, and author of *Bourbons and Brandy: Imperial Reform in Eighteenth-Century Arequipa* (Duke University Press, 1986), "The Spanish Imperial Mercury Trade and the American Mining Expansion under the Bourbon Monarchy," in *The Political Economy of Spanish America in the Age of Revolution 1750–1850* (eds. Andrien and Johnson, University of New Mexico Press, 1994), and "Jesuit Wealth and Economic Activity within the Peruvian Economy: The Case of Colonial Southern Peru," in *The Americas* (July 1987); he served as area editor of *The Americas* and has published and lectured widely on Iberian and Latin American history.

David L. Bullock, Ph.D., directs a history office for the government and is an adjunct associate professor at Colorado Technical University; he has published one book and 50 articles, the majority in European and British history. Bullock is a former military officer and has traveled in 41 countries.

June K. Burton is Associate Professor Emeritus at the University of Akron, Ohio, and author of *Napoleon and Clio* (Carolina Academic Press, 1979); she served as associate editor of *Historical Dictionary of Napoleonic France* (Greenwood Press, 1985), has authored articles and papers on Napoleonic women's medicine, legal medicine, and education and historiography. Burton received an honorary doctor of laws degree from Stetson University in 1992, and has served since 1997 as contributing editor of *Napoleon* magazine and as editor of its series "Featured Scholars."

Kimberly A. Burton, B.A., M.I.S. (University of Michigan).

Linnea Goodwin Burwood's publications include "The Island of Crimea," in *Masterplots II: World Fiction* (ed. Frank N. Magill, Salem Press, 1988) and "Nikon" in *Great Lives from History: Renaissance to 1900* (ed. Frank N. Magill, Salem Press, 1989).

Robert W. Cape, Jr. is Associate Professor of Classics and Director of Gender Studies at Austin College, Sherman, Texas; he has written and lectured on Women in Antiquity, Roman Rhetoric, and Gender Studies.

Tanya Carelli is a freelance writer in science fiction and women's history in San Diego, California.

Juliet Carey is Curatorial Assistant at the National Museums and Galleries of Wales, Cardiff, Wales, United Kingdom.

Toni Caribillo was a feminist leader and historian who served as president of the Los Angeles chapter of NOW and as NOW's national vice president and board member, a major fund raiser and organizer for the Equal Rights Amendment ratification, and vice president of the Fund for the Feminist Majority, the organization she helped create; she was co-author of *The Feminization of Power* (1988) and *Feminist Chronicles, 1953–1993* (1993), which was published four years before her death in 1997.

Stanley D.M. Carpenter is Associate Professor of Strategy at the United States Naval War College, Newport, Rhode Island.

Michael D. Cary is a professor in the Department of History and Political Science at Seton Hill College, Greensburg, Pennsylvania; his publications include "Political Dimensions of the Blues," in *Popular Music and Society* (14, Summer 1990).

Maria Casalini is Researcher of Contemporary History, Florence, at Florence University, Italy, and author of *La Signora del Socialismo italiano: Vita di Anna Kuliscioff* (Roma: Editori Riuniti, 1978) and *Servitú, nobili e borghesi nella Firenze dell'Ottocento* (Firenza: Olschki, 1997); she has published essays about domestic servants in 19th-century Florence and about gender construction in Italian Socialist Party politics, most recently "'Sebben che siamo donne': Il movimonto oparaio e la questione delle lavoratrioi," in *Passato e presente* (no. 43, 1998).

Susan E. Cayleff is Professor and Chair of the Department of Women's Studies at San Diego State University, California, and the author of *Babe: The Life and Legend of Babe Didrikson Zaharias* (University of Illinois Press, 1995/96), *"Wings of Gauze": Women of Color and the Experience of Health and Illness* (Wayne State University), and *Wash and Be Healed: The Water Cure Movement and Women's Health* (Temple University Press, 1987).

Lamar Cecil is William R. Kenan, Jr., Professor of History at Washington and Lee University, Lexington, Virginia.

Beth Champagne is a freelance writer who lives in East Ryegate, Vermont.

Henry Y.S. Chan is Associate Professor of History at Moorhead State University, Moorhead, Minnesota, co-editor of *World History: A Reader,* 2 vols. (American Heritage, 1996), author of "Chen Shou," "Fang Xuanling," "John King Fairbank," "Huang Zongxi," "Wei Yuan," in *Making History: A Global Encyclopedia of Historical Writing* (Greenwood Press, 1998), and "Anti-Russia Volunteer Army," "Assassinationism," "Baohuanghui," "Guangfuhui," and "Zou Rong/Revolutionary Army," in *Modern China: An Encyclopedia of History, Culture and Nationalism* (Garland Publishing, 1998); he has published and lectured widely on China in the modern world.

William L. Chew III is Professor of History at Vesalius College, Vrije Universiteit, Brussels, Belgium, and author of *A Bostonian Merchant Witnesses the Second French Revolution* (Brussels: Center for American Studies, 1992), editor of *Images of America: Through the European Looking-Glass* (Brussels: VUBPress, 1997) and contributor to *The Historical Encyclopedia of World Slavery* (ed. Junius P. Rodriquez); he has published widely on Franco-American national stereotypes in travel literature.

Gloria Ifeoma Chuku, Ph.D., is Lecturer in History at the School of Humanities of Imo State University, Owerri, Imo State, Nigeria, author of a number of articles published in Nigeria and Pakistan, a member of the Editorial Board of the Historical Society of Nigeria Occasion Publications, and has been a visiting scholar in Women's Studies at the University of Arizona and a research scholar at the CODESRIA Institute in Senegal; she has published and lectured widely on women in Africa (Nigeria) and on history and cultural development of the African world community.

Geoffrey Clark is Assistant Professor of History at Emory University, Atlanta, Georgia.

Ann Mauger Colbert is Journalism Coordinator at Indiana University—Purdue University at Fort Wayne, Indiana, and author of "Philanthropy in the Newsroom—Women's Editions of Newspapers," in *Journalism History 22* and "Susan B. Anthony," in *Feminist Writers;* she is a former reporter for the *Indianapolis Star and News* and the recipient of two reporting awards.

Deborah Conn is a freelance writer and editor, based in Falls Church, Virginia.

Steven Conn is Assistant Professor of History at Ohio State University, Columbus, Ohio; his publications include "The Politics of Corporate Architecture: Skyscrapers in Penn's Greene Country Towne," and (with Max Page) "Shop Till You Drop: The Development of the Shopping Mall," in *American Landscapes* (ed. Neil Silberman), "Henry Chapman Mercer and the Search for American History," in *Pennsylvania Magazine of History and Biography* (Vol. CXVI, no. 3), and "Thoughts on National Service: An Open Letter to William Buckley," in *Change Magazine*.

Stacy A. Cordery is Associate Professor of History and Coordinator of Women's Studies at Monmouth College in Monmouth, Illinois; she received her Ph.D. from the University of Texas and is the author of an article on Alice Roosevelt as a celebrity first daughter, studies of United States first ladies and an analysis of women in the Gilded Age; Cordery is completing a biography of Alice Roosevelt Longworth and serves as an editor for *H-Women*.

Marilyn Costanzo, of Grove City, Pennsylvania, is a freelance writer in history.

John M. Craig, Ph.D., is Professor of History at Slippery Rock University, Slippery Rock, Pennsylvania, and author of *Lucia Ames Mead and the American Peace Movement* as well as numerous articles on American activist women.

Carlos Ulises Decena is a Ph.D. candidate in American Studies at New York University.

Jacqueline DeLaat is McCoy Professor of Political Science and Leadership at Marietta College, Ohio, where she is a teacher of American politics and public policy, as well as of women and politics; she is the author of *Gender Issues in the Workplace: A Case Study Approach* (Sage Publications, 1999) and has consulted on gender issues in the contemporary workplace.

Frenzella Elaine De Lancey, Ph.D., is an assistant professor in the Department of Humanities and Communications at Drexel University in Philadelphia, Pennsylvania; her publications include "Afrocentricity, Science, and Technology: Implications for Curriculum & Pedagogy," in *Afrocentric Scholar* and "Mandombian Scientists: Assaying an Afrocentric Analysis," in *Journal of Black Studies*.

Justus D. Doenecke is Professor of History at the New College of the University of South Florida, Sarasota, Florida; he has written books and articles centering on American history in the late 19th and the 20th centuries, including *Not to the Swift: The Old Isolationists in the Cold War Era* (Bucknell University Press, 1979), *The Presidencies of James A. Garfield and Chester A. Arthur* (University of Kansas Press, 1981), and *The Battle Against Intervention, 1939–1941* (Krieger, 1997).

Shirley Dunkley, Ph.D., is Tutor in History at the Department of Adult Continuing Education, University of Sheffield, England, and author of works on local women's history such as "Women in Public," in *The History of the City of Sheffield 1843–1993* (Sheffield Academic Press, 1993); her research interests include women in local government in the 19th and 20th centuries, and she leads a research group that examines the history of domestic service in Sheffield.

Anita DuPratt received her Ph.D. from the University of Washington and is Professor of Theatre at California State University Bakersfield, Bakersfield, California; her publications include "A Quest for Legitimacy: A Study of the New City Theatre, London, 1831–1835," in *From Pen to Performance* (Vol. III, 1983), "Popular Appeal in English Drama to 1850," in *Theatre Journal* (May 1983), "The Relationship Between Theatre Repertoire and Theatre Location: A Study of the Pavilion Theatre," in *All the World, Drama, Past and Present* (Vol. II, 1982), and "Shipwrecks and Spectacles," in *Theatre News* (May 1982).

Natania T. East is a historian and freelance writer in British Columbia, Canada.

Maria Sheler Edwards is a freelance writer in Ypsilanti, Michigan. She holds a B.A. in English from the University of Michigan and a M.A. in written communications from Eastern Michigan University.

Uche Egemonye, former Attorney for the United Nations Compensation Commission, is a graduate student in the Department of History at Emory University, Atlanta, Georgia; she is the author of "Judicial Paternalism and the Justification for Assaults Against Black Women, 1865–1910," in *Lethal Imagination: Violence and Brutality in American History* (ed, Michael Bellesiles, New York University Press, 1999) and is writing a dissertation on the legal strategies that blacks employed in

Savannah, Georgia, from 1865 to 1910, to secure their rights.

Grant Eldrige is a freelance writer living in Pontiac, Michigan.

R.C. Elwood is Professor of History at Carleton University, Ottawa, Canada, and served as general editor of the *Proceedings of the III World Congress for Soviet and East European Studies* (15 vols., 1985–90); he has published seven books, serving as author or editor, including *Inessa Armand: Revolutionary and Feminist* (Cambridge: Cambridge University Press, 1993), which won the 1992 Heldt Prize for the Best Book in Slavic Women's Studies.

M.C. English is a freelance writer in Boston, Massachusetts.

Barbara Evans is Research Associate in Women's Studies at Nene College, Northampton, England.

Elizabeth Evans is a retired school teacher who lives in Bowen, North Queensland, Australia, and the mother of fellow contributor Lekkie Hopkins.

Mark L. Evans is Assistant Keeper (Fine Art) at the Department of Art, National Museum and Gallery of Cardiff, Cathays Park, Cardiff, Wales, and author of "Die Miniaturen des Münchner Medici-Gebetbuchs," in *Das Gebetbuch Lorenzos de Medici* (Stuttgart, 1991), *The Sforza Hours* (Luzern, 1995), and numerous exhibition and permanent-collection catalogues and essays, largely on Renaissance art.

Rocío Evans is a Chicana feminist writer who resides in Cambridge, Massachusetts; her publications include "Athena" (April 1993), "Hermes, Guide of Souls" (May 1992), and "Demeter and Persephone" (May 1990) in *New Moon Rising, Journal of Wicca,* and "Women in the Military" (March 1991) for *Peace and Freedom Partisan.*

Margery Evernden is Professor Emerita at the English Department of the University of Pittsburgh, Pennsylvania, and a freelance writer.

Maura Jane Farrelly is a freelance writer and a graduate student in history at Emory University, Atlanta, Georgia, working on a dissertation entitled "Papist Patriots: Catholic Identity and Revolutionary Ideology in Maryland, 1689–1783."

Mara Faulkner, O.S.B., is Assistant Professor of English at the College of St. Benedict, St. Joseph, Minnesota, and the author of *Protest and Possibility in the Writing of Tillie Olsen* (University Press of Virginia).

Anita Clair Fellman is an associate professor of History and Director of Women's Studies at Old Dominion University, Norfolk, Virginia, and co-editor of *Rethinking Canada: The Promise of Women's History,* 3rd ed. (Toronto: Oxford University Press, 1997); she is a member of the Broad Minds Collective which edited *Ourselves as Students: Multicultural Voices in the Classroom* (Southern Illinois University Press, 1996), and is working on a book about Laura Ingalls Wilder's Little House books in American culture.

Suzanne Ferriss is an assistant professor in the Liberal Arts Department of Nova University, Fort Lauderdale, Florida.

Gayle Veronica Fischer is a historian and author of several articles on dress reform movements in the United States.

Sibelan Forrester is Assistant Professor of Russian at Swarthmore College, Swarthmore, Pennsylvania, whose publications include "Marina Tsvetaeva as Literary Critic and Critic of Literary Critics," in *Russian Writers on Russian Writers* (ed. Faith Wigzell, Berg Publishers), "Bells and Cupolas: The Structuring Role of the Female Body in Marina Tsvetaeva's Poetry," in *Slavic Review* (Vol. 51, no. 2, Summer 1992), and numerous entries for the *Dictionary of Russian and Soviet Women Writers* (ed. M. Astman, *et al.,* Greenwood Press, 1993)

Julia L. Foulkes recently completed a year as a Rockefeller Foundation Postdoctoral Fellow at the Center for Black Music Research, Columbia College, Chicago, Illinois; she is at work on the manuscript "Dancing America: Modern Dance and Cultural Nationalism 1925–1960," and is the author of a number of articles including "Dance Is for American Men: Ted Shawn and the Intersection of Gender, Sexuality, and Nationalism in the 1930s," in *Queer Theory and the Dancing Body* (Wesleyan University Press, 1998).

Joan Francis is Professor of History and Women's Studies at Atlantic Union College, South Lancaster, Massachusetts, and lectures on Women and African American Studies; she is currently researching women in New England, has taught in the Caribbean, and is published in *Dialogue: Journal of Adventist Education.*

Ernest Freeberg received his Ph.D. in American History from Emory University, Atlanta, Georgia, and is a freelance writer.

Ellen Dennis French is a freelance writer and editor who has contributed to many Gale Research reference publications; she serves as an adjunct instructor in Interpersonal and Public Communication and resides in Murrieta, California.

Lorely French is Professor of German and Chair of the Humanities Division at Pacific University, Forest Grove, Oregon, and author of *German Women as Letter Writers 1750–1850* (Madison, London: Fairleigh Dickinson University Press/ Associated University Presses, 1996) and numerous articles on 19th-century German women writers; she was the recipient of the first John Meyer Faculty Award at Pacific University, received grants from the German Academic Exchange Service, American Council of Learned Societies, and Pro Helvetia, and served as vice-president and president of the Oregon Association of Teachers of German.

Janet Owens Frost is Professor of Anthropology at Eastern New Mexico University, Portales, New Mexico; she participates in local and regional women's studies activities and is the author of "Making Connections: Teaching Anthropology of Third World in New Mexico," in *Women's Studies International Forum* (Pergamon Press, 1991) and "H. Marie Wormington," in *Women Anthropologists: A Biographical Dictionary* (eds. Gacs, Khan, McIntyre and Weinbery, Greenwood Press, 1988).

Kathleen E. Garay, Ph.D., is Acting Director of the Women's Studies Programme at McMaster University, Hamilton, Canada, and a contributor to *Florilegium, Historical Journal* and *Mystics Quarterly*; she produced a CD-ROM on medieval women *Sybils!2* (McMaster University, 1997), serves as coordinator of a forthcoming television series on medieval female spirituality (Vision T.V., 1999), and has written primarily about women and crime and female spirituality, with emphasis on the later medieval period.

Lydia M. Garner is Associate Professor of History at Southwest Texas State University, San Marcos, and author of articles and reviews in the United States and Brazil; she specializes in the research of institutions in new nations, lectures on Brazilian and Latin American history, serves on the board of editors of *The Journal of Third World Studies*, and has

served as president of the World History Association of Texas.

Karen Gernant is Professor of History at Southern Oregon University, Ashland, Oregon, and the author of *Imagining Women: Fujian Folk Tales* (Interlink, 1995) for which she translated 37 stories; she has written and lectured widely on China and Chinese women's history, has translated a contemporary novella for Chinese Literature Press (Beijing), and serves on the board of the Oregon Council for the Humanities. An anonymous donor has endowed a scholarship in her name.

Christopher Gibb is author of *Food and Famine* (Wayland, 1987), which was runner-up for the T.E.S. non-fiction award, *The Dalai Lama* (London: Exley, 1990), *Church and State in England: 1500–1750* (Wayland, 1997), and nine other books; he is a scholar of Oxford University, a freelance writer of children's educational books, and a historical consultant for Heinemann Books, who has worked as an editor for Wayland Publishers, served as a volunteer in N. India starting a publishing project for Tibetan refugees, and acted as Youth and Schools Manager for the Save the Children Fund (London).

Virginia Gibbs is Assistant Professor of Spanish Language and Literature at Luther College, Decorah, Iowa; her publications include "Roman Spain: Conquest and Assimilation," in *Religious Studies Review, Las Sonatas de Valle-Inclán* (Madrid: Editorial Pliegos, 1992), "Latin American Film," in *Latin American Research Review* (Vol. 27, no. 3, Fall 1992), and "Valle-Inclán's Bradomín and Montenegro and the Problem of Hispanic Caciquismo" in *Bridging the Atlantic: Iberian and Latin American Thought in Historical Perspective* (eds. Marina Pérez de Mendiola and Panivong Norindr).

Kathryn E.I. Gibson is Assistant Professor of English/Speech at City University of New York, New York, and recipient of a W.K. Kellogg Foundation Fellowship (1997); her research project, "African-American Grandparents Raising Grandchildren," was profiled on CBS News, and she is the founder and Director of the Grandparents Advocacy Project, as well as curator of the "A Tribute to Black Women" art exhibit.

Cheryl Gillard is a musicologist and freelance writer of Ottawa, Canada, who has served as music consultant for the National Library of Canada's "Celebrating Women's Achievements" digital project, has published and lectured widely on women and music, and has provided archival research for several publications on the work of Canadian pianist Glen Gould.

Emily Gilbert Gleason is a freelance writer in history, who presents impersonations and monologues of Catharine Macaulay.

Sabine Gless, Ph.D., is a freelance writer in Basel, Switzerland.

Howard Gofstein, M.A., Wayne State University, Detroit, Michigan, is a freelance writer and contributor to reference works, including *Encyclopedia of World Biography* (Gale Research), and ghost writer of *ISO 14000 Road Map to Registration* (McGraw-Hill).

Vibha Bakshi Gokhale, Ph.D., is the author of *Walking the Tightrope: A Feminist Reading of Therese Huber's Prose Narratives* (Camden House, 1995) and several entries for *The Feminist Encyclopedia of German Literature* (eds. Friederike Eigler and Susanne Kord, Greenwood Press, 1996) and for *Masterplots: Twentieth Anniversary Revised Second Edition* (ed. Eric Howard, Salem Press, 1995).

Susan Gonda is Instructor of History at Grossmont College, San Diego, California; she is the author of *Strumpets and Angels: Rape, Seduction, and the Criminal Boundaries of Sexuality, 1786–1860* and serves as co-president of San Diego's Women's History Reclamation Project.

Alice Goode-Elman is Professor of English and Women's Studies at Suffolk County Community College, Selden, New York; under the pen name Alice Neufeld, she is author of "One Step Away from Mother: A Stepmother's Story," in *Women and Stepfamilies: Voices of Anger and Love* (Temple University Press, 1989), and is working on a memoir, "Women's Studies."

Paul B. Goodwin is Professor of History at University of Connecticut, Storrs, Connecticut, author of *Global Studies: Latin America*, 8th edition (Dushkin/McGraw-Hill, 1998), 15 articles for *The Encyclopedia of Latin American History*, 5 vols. (Scribners, 1996), and "United States-Argentine Relations, 1824–1849," in *The Early Relations of the United States with Latin America* (ed. T. Ray Shurbutt, University of Alabama, 1991); he has lectured for the Smithsonian Institution throughout southern South America.

Bertram M. Gordon is Professor of History at Mills College, Oakland, California, author of *Collaborationism in Europe during the Second World War* (Cornell University Press, 1980), and editor of *Historical Dictionary of World War II France* (Greenwood Press, 1998); he serves on the editorial board of *French Historical Studies*, the International Editorial Advisory Board of *Modern Contemporary France*, and has published and lectured widely on the history of food and of tourism.

Karen Gould of Austin, Texas, is an independent scholar and expert on medieval art history; she has written extensively about women and art in the Middle Ages and is author of *The Psalter and Hours of Yolande of Soissons* (The Medieval Academy, 1978) as well as articles and catalogues on medieval manuscripts.

Lewis L. Gould is Eugene C. Barker Centennial Professor in American History, Emeritus, at University of Texas at Austin, and a nationally recognized expert on first ladies; he is the author of a number of books and the editor of *American First Ladies: Their Lives and Their Legacy* (1996).

Patricia Greene is an assistant professor in the Department of Romance and Classical Languages, and in Women's Studies, at Michigan State University, East Lansing, Michigan; she is co-editor of *Spain Today: Essays on Literature, Culture and Society* (Dartmouth College, 1995) and author of *Federica Montseny: La mujer y el ideal* (Madrid, Spain: Editorial Orto, 1999).

William S. Greenwalt is Associate Professor of Classical History at Santa Clara University, Santa Clara, California.

Brahmjyot K. Grewal is Assistant Professor of History at Luther College, Decorah, Iowa; her publications include "Eugene Genovese's *Roll, Jordan, Roll* As a Seminal Text in the Marxist Interpretation of Southern Planter Class," in *Agora* (Spring 1993) and "The United States and Japan in Siberia, 1918–1920: Co-Operation or Co-Optation?" in *Pakistan Journal of American Studies* (Spring 1993).

Susan Grogan is Senior Lecturer in History at Victoria University of Wellington, New Zealand; she is the author of *French Socialism and Sexual Difference: Women and the New Society, 1803–1844* (London: Macmillan; New York: St. Martin's Press, 1992), *Flora Tristan: Life Stories* (London & New York: Routledge, 1998) and several articles on Flora Tristan.

John Haag, Associate Professor of History at the University of Georgia, Athens, Georgia, is the author of chapters in books including *Who Were the Fascists?, Austria in the Age of the French Revolution 1789–1815,* and *Austria 1938–1988: Anschluss and Fifty Years;* in addition to publishing in journals including *The Journal of Contemporary History* and *Central European History,* he has participated in several research projects including the University of Vienna Pernkopf Anatomy Atlas investigation and the University of Hamburg Musical Exiles survey.

Karin Loewen Haag of Athens, Georgia, is a writer and editorial consultant who has published articles in professional journals and newsletters; she writes for Millennium III, an educational publishing firm, and is working on a book "From Slavery to Subdivision," an account based on local history about the black women and men whose skills and energy helped build the South.

Cara Hall, a New Zealand concert pianist now retired and living in Perth, Western Australia, has contributed articles to *Music Maker, Skywest, Artswest* and other magazines.

Susan A. Hallgarth was Coordinator of Women's Studies at Empire State College, State University of New York; her publications include "Across the Great Divide" (9, July 1992), "Golden Opportunities" (8, September 1991) and "Cather Custody Battles" (8, October 1990) in *Women's Review of Books,* "Willa Cather: The Woman Who Would Be Artist in *Song of the Lark* and "Lucy Gayheart," in *Willa Cather: Family, Community, and History* (ed. John J. Murphy, Brigham Young University, 1990), and "Women Settlers on the Frontier: Unwed, Unreluctant, Unrepentant," in *Women's Studies Quarterly* (27, Fall/Winter 1989).

Richard Clay Hanes, Ph.D., is a freelance writer in Eugene, Oregon, who was Adjunct Professor in Historic Preservation at the University of Nevada, Reno, Nevada, and served as advisor to the state and communities of Oregon promoting historical interpretation; he is an author and lecturer on various topics related to early settlement of the American West and its legacy, including "Cultural Persistence in Nevada: Current Native American Issues," in *Journal of California and Great Basin Anthropology* (1982), and "The Barlow Road," in *Overland Journal* (1995).

Blake Harper is a freelance writer in Amherst, Massachusetts.

Taylor Harper of Amherst, Massachusetts, is a freelance writer in travel and history who has contributed articles for local, national, and international periodicals including *The Christian Science Monitor, Winds* (The Inflight Magazine of Japan Airlines), *Maryland, International Living,* and the *Sunday Republican.*

Judith Harris is Assistant Professor of English at George Washington University, Washington, D.C., and has written articles on poetry and psychoanalysis including "Women's Confessionalist Poetry and Ideology," in *AWP Chronicle* (Dec. 1994), "Giotto's Invisible Sheep: Lacanian Mirroring and Modeling in Walcott's Another Life," in *South Atlantic Quarterly* (Spring 1997), and "Using the Psychoanalytic Process in Creative Writing Classes," in *Journal for the Psychoanalysis of Culture and Society* (Winter 1998); her creative work has appeared in *Tikkun, Prairie Schooner, Storming Heaven's Gate* (eds. Vecchione and Sumrall, Penguin Books), *The American Scholar, Antioch Review, The Daily Forward, The Women's Review of Books, Her Face in the Mirror* (Beacon Press) and *13th Moon.*

Katherine G. Haskell of Jeffersonville, Pennsylvania, is a freelance writer and medical editor.

Steven C. Hause is Professor of History and Fellow in International Studies at the University of Missouri-St. Louis, co-author of *Women's Suffrage and Social Politics in Third Republic France* (Princeton, 1984), and author of *Hubertine Auclert: The French Suffragette* (Yale, 1987); he is also co-editor of *Feminisms of the Belle Epoque* (Nebraska, 1994) and co-author of *Western Civilization* (Wadsworth, 1998).

Patricia B. Heaman is Professor of English at Wilkes University, Wilkes-Barre, Pennsylvania; she teaches courses in Victorian literature and the modern novel, and has lectured on British and American writers of the 19th and 20th centuries.

Leslie Heaphy is Assistant Professor of History at Kent State University, Stark Campus, Kent, Ohio, and the author of numerous book reviews and a number of encyclopedia entries on sports figures.

Dagmar Herzog is Assistant Professor of History at Michigan State University, East Lansing, Michigan, and author of "The Feminist Conundrum," in *Intimacy and Exclusion: Religious Politics in Pre-Revolutionary Baden*

(Princeton University Press, 1996) and "Liberalism, Religious Dissent and Women's Rights: Louise Dittmar's Writings from the 1840s," in *In Search of a Liberal Germany: Studies in the History of German Liberalism from 1789 to the Present* (eds. Konrad Jarausch and Larry Eugene Jones, Oxford: Berg, 1990).

Carol Lakey Hess, Ph.D., is the author of "Education as the Art of Getting Dirty with Dignity," in *The Arts of Ministry: Feminist and Womanist Approaches* (ed. Christie Cozad, Westminster/John Knox Press, 1996), "Becoming Midwives to Justice: A Feminist Approach to Practical Theology," in *Liberating Faith Practices: Feminist Practical Theologies in Context* (eds. Denise Ackermann and Riet Bons-Storm, Peeters, 1998), and *Caretakers of Our Common House: Women's Development in Communities of Faith* (Abingdon Press, 1997).

Robert H. Hewsen is Professor of History at Rowan University of New Jersey, and author of *The Geography of Ananias of Shirak* (University of Tübingen, Wiesbaden, 1992) and *Armenia: A Historical Atlas* (University of Chicago); he co-founded and was the first President of the Society for the Study of Caucasia, University of Chicago.

Neil M. Heyman is Professor of History at San Diego State University, San Diego, California, and the author, with H. Herwig, of *Biography of World War I* (Greenwood Press, 1982), *Russian History* (McGraw-Hill), and other works on modern European history.

Alison Duncan Hirsch, Ph.D., is Assistant Professor of American Studies and History at Penn State Harrisburg and a freelance writer.

Roberta A. Hobson teaches history at Herbert Hoover High School in San Diego and received her master's degree in history from San Diego State University; her publications include a biography and critique of Judith McDaniel in *Contemporary Lesbian Writers of the United States* (Greenwood Press, 1993).

Wilson J. Hoffman is Thorn and Frances Pendleton Professor of History at Hiram College, Hiram, Ohio, whose publications include numerous contributions to *Victorian Britain: An Encyclopedia* and *The Encyclopedia of Stuart History.*

Jan Holden is a freelance writer in Los Angeles, California.

Catherine Dybiec Holm is a freelance writer in Cook, Minnesota, author of "The Green Cadillac" in *End of the Road Reader* (Ely, MN: Northwoods Writers Guild), "Trash Can Tom" in *North Coast Review* (Duluth, MN: Poetry Harbor), and articles in numerous periodicals and reference publications. Recipient of Blandin Foundation/COMPAS (St. Paul, Minnesota) grant to facilitate art dialog in rural communities.

Niles R. Holt is Professor of History at Illinois State University, Normal, Illinois, and co-author of *The Best Test Preparation for the Graduate Record Examination* (Research and Education Association, 1996) and *The Best Test Preparation for the Advanced Placement Examination in European History* (Research and Education Association, 1992); he was the recipient of grants from the National Endowment for the Humanities and the American Philosophical Society, has spoken by invitation in Germany on German religious history, and has published and lectured widely in the United States on the history of science and European intellectual history.

Lekkie Hopkins is Coordinator of Women's Studies at Edith Cowan University, Perth, Western Australia; she is a former high school teacher, archivist, oral historian and radio broadcaster who has written journal articles on Australian women's fiction and the history of Australian women peace activists.

Catherine Hundleby received her M.A. in Philosophy from the University of Guelph, Canada, and is a Ph.D. candidate in Philosophy at the University of Western Ontario, Canada, working on feminist theories of knowledge; she is the author of "Where Standpoint Stands Now," in both *Women in Politics,* (Vol. 18, no. 3, 1997) and *Politics and Feminist Standpoint Theories* (eds. Sally J. Kenney and Helen Kinsella, The Haworth Press).

Sarah Hunt is a freelance writer and historian in Las Cruces, New Mexico.

Ann Hollinshead Hurley is Assistant Professor of English at Wagner College, Staten Island, New York, and co-editor of *So Rich a Tapestry: The Sister Arts and Cultural Studies* (Bucknell University Press, 1995); she has written numerous essays on women writers of the 17th century and on the poetry of John Donne.

Janet Hyer is a Ph.D. candidate in the Department of Political Science at the University of Toronto, Ontario, and Program Assistant at the Centre for Russian and East European Studies at the University of Toronto; her publications include "Managing the Female Organism: Doctors and the Medicalization of Women's Paid Work in Soviet Russia during the 1920s" in *Women in Russia and the Former USSR* (ed., Rosalind J. Marsh, Cambridge University Press, 1996) and "Soviet Women Tell Their Story: Letters to the Editor from *Rabotnitsa* and *Krest'ianka*" in *Canadian Woman Studies/les cahiers de la femme* (Vol. 10, no. 4, Winter 1989).

Nancy Hynes, O.S.B., is Professor of English, College of Saint Benedict, St. Joseph, Minnesota.

Alexander Ingle is a lecturer in the Department of Classical Studies at the University of Michigan.

Cathy Jorgensen Itnyre is Professor of History at Copper Mountain College in Joshua Tree, California; she edited *Medieval Family Roles* (Garland Publishing, 1996) and contributed biographies to *Historic World Leaders* (Gale Research, 1994).

Douglas C. Jansen is a freelance writer in history in Austin, Texas.

Jennifer W. Jay is Professor of History and Classics at the University of Alberta, Canada, author of *A Change in Dynasties: Loyalism in Thirteenth-Century China* (Western Washington University, 1991) and co-editor of *East Asian Cultural and Historical Perspectives* (Edmonton: Research Institute for Comparative Literature and Cross-Cultural Studies, 1997); she teaches and publishes on women in East Asian history.

Janice Lee Jayes, of American University, Washington, D.C., is a cultural historian who specializes in U.S.-Mexican relations.

Madeleine Jeay is Professor of Medieval Literature at McMaster University, Hamilton, Canada, author of an analysis (Montreal, CERES, 1983) and a critical edition (Montreal-Paris, Presses University of Montreal-Urin, 1985) of the *Evangiles des Quenouilles* (Fifteenth Century Popular Beliefs) and of *Donner la parole: L'histoire-cadre dans les recueils de nouvelles des xve–xvie siécles* (Montreal, CERES, 1992); she has published articles and lectured on medieval French literature, folklore and popular religion.

Richard Bach Jensen, Assistant Professor of History at Louisiana Scholars' College, Northwestern State University, Natchitoches, Louisiana, is author of *Liberty and Order: The Theory and Practice of Italian Public Security Policy, 1848 to the Crisis of the 1890s* (Garland Publishing, 1991), "The Euturists and the Fascist Conquest of Power," in *History Today* (November 1995), "The International Anti-Anarchist Conference of 1898 and the Origins of Interpol," in *Journal of Contemporary History* (April 1981), and other articles and dictionary entries on Italian and Spanish history.

Angela V. John is Professor of History at the University of Greenwich, London, England, and author of *By the Sweat of Their Brow* (London: Croom Helm, 1980, and Routledge, 1984), (with Revel Guest) *Lady Charlotte: A Biography of the Nineteenth Century* (London: Weidenfeld and Nicolson, 1989); and *Elizabeth Robins: Staging a Life* (London and New York: Routledge, 1995); she is editor of *Unequal Opportunities: Women's Employment in England 1800–1918* (Oxford: Basil Blacknell, 1986) and *Our Mother's Land: Chapters in Welsh Women's History 1830–1939* (Cardiff: University of Wales Press, 1991 and 1997), and co-editor (with Claire Eustance) of *The Men's Share* (London: Routledge, 1997).

Mara M. Johns is translator of Moa Martinson's *Kyrkbröllop* (Church Wedding) and a freelance writer in San Diego, California.

Linda L. Johnson is Professor of History at Concordia College, Moorhead, Minnesota, and author of "The Feminist Politics of Takako Doi and the Social Democratic Party of Japan," in *Women's Studies International Forum* (1992) and "Women's History in Cross-Cultural Perspective," in *Women's Studies Quarterly* (1989); she is the recipient of the Asiatic Society of Japan Award (1989).

Yvonne Johnson is Associate Professor of History at Central Missouri State University, Warrensburg, Missouri, and has published and lectured widely on African-American women; she is author of *The Voices of African American Women* (Peter Lang, 1998), (with Michael Meacham) "African Traditional Religions and African American Liberation Theology," in *African Philosophy in the Twenty-First Century* (Harcourt Brace), "Alice Walker" and "Harriet Tubman," in *Great Lives from History* (Salem Press, 1995), and the "Toni Morrison," "bell hooks," "John Hope," and "Emanuel Cleaver" entries in *The African American Encyclopedia Supplement* (Salem Press, 1996).

Deborah Jones is a screenwriter in Los Angeles, California, who wrote, produced, and directed *The Last Laugh* (PBS, 1992); she has written movies for Lifetime, USA, CBS, NBC, ABC, and Paramount Pictures.

Martha Jones, M.L.S., is head of the technical services department at the Morse Institute Library, Natick, Massachusetts, and is an Internet trainer, electronic resources specialist, researcher, and freelance writer.

Kathleen M. Joyce is an assistant professor in the Department of Religion at Duke University, Durham, North Carolina; she writes on the interplay of gender, medicine, and religion in American history.

Cynthia Jurisson is Associate Professor of American Church History at the Lutheran School of Theology at Chicago, Illinois; she is a member of the Council of Editorial Advisors for *The Lutheran Quarterly* and lectures widely on women in the history of Christianity.

Ackson M. Kanduza is Professor of History at the University of Swaziland, Kwaluseni, Swaziland.

Sylvia Gray Kaplan, M.A., is Instructor of History at Portland Community College, Oregon, and Adjunct History Faculty of Marylhurst University, Marylhurst, Oregon; she writes a monthly column, "Ask the Ancients," for *The Omen* (Mensa) and has contributed entries on Caligula, Claudius, and Seneca to *Historic World Leaders* (Gale Research, 1994).

Juanita Karpf is Assistant Professor of Music and Women's Studies at the University of Georgia, Athens, Georgia; her research has appeared in numerous publications including *African American Women, Alabama Review, American National Biography, International Review of the Aesthetics and Sociology of Music, Music Review, Notable Black American Women, Popular Music and Society, Powerful Black Women, Signs: Journal of Women in Culture and Society,* and *Transformations.*

Galina Kashirina is a teacher of the English language at the State Gymnasium #11 in St. Petersburg, Russia.

Bette J. Kauffman is Associate Professor of Mass Communication at Northeast Louisiana University, Monroe, Louisiana, and author of "Feminist Facts: Interview Strategies and Political Subjects in Ethnography," in *Communication Theory* (Vol. 2, no. 3), "Woman Artist: Between Myth and Stereotype," in *On the Margins of Art Worlds* (Westview Press, 1995), "Missing Persons: Working Class Women and Movies, 1940–1990," in *Feminism, Multiculturalism and the Media: Global Diversities* (Sage Publications, 1995), and "Media Realities: Visual Competence in Social Context," in *Journal of Visual Literacy* (Vol. 17, no. 2); she is currently writing *Woman Artist: Communicating Social Identity.*

Marjorie Dearworth Keeley is a Latin teacher for Adams-Cheshire Regional School District, Adams, Massachusetts; she is the author of "The Vigiles" and "The Commissatio," in *The Romans Speak for Themselves: Book II* (Longman, 1989) and of "A Classical Magnet Program," in *New England Classical Newsletter and Journal* (Vol. XVIII, no. 3, February 1991).

Brigid Kelly is a ballet instructor at Desert Ballet Centre, Yucca Valley, California.

Andrea Moore Kerr, Ph.D., is a women's historian and independent scholar living in Washington, D.C.; her publications include *Lucy Stone: Speaking Out for Equality* (Rutgers, 1992) as well as numerous articles for *Woman's Journal and Women's History in the United States: A Handbook* (Garland Publishing, 1992 and 1995 revision); a consultant to television series "One Woman, One Vote" (PBS, 1995); biographer-in-residence, Boston Public Schools; lectures widely on 19th century American women.

Muhonjia Khaminwa is a freelance writer in Cambridge, Massachusetts; she has been a Fellow, MacDowell Colony for Artists, Peterborough, New Hampshire (December 1996); the recipient of a Massachusetts Cultural Council Professional Development Grant (February 1997); and a contributor to *Encarta Africana* (Afropaedia L.L.C., 1998).

Penelope Ann Kines is a freelance writer and a drama instructor in New York City.

Carolyn Kitch, Ph.D., is Assistant Professor of Magazine Journalism at The Medill School of Journalism, Northwestern University, Evanston, Illinois, and the author of articles on women's media history in *Journalism & Mass Communication Quarterly* and *American Journalism* as well as chapters in *Mass Media and Society* (eds. Alan Wells and Ernest Hakanen, Ablex, 1997) and *Significant Contemporary Feminists: A Biocritical Sourcebook* (ed. Jennifer Scanlon, Greenwood Press); she is former senior editor of *Good Housekeeping* and associate editor of *McCall's.*

Barbara Koch, freelance writer and researcher based in Farmington Hills, Michigan, is a

M.L.I.S. candidate at Wayne State University, Detroit, Michigan.

Phillip E. Koerper is Professor of History at Jacksonville State University, Jacksonville, Alabama, and editor of *Classics in Western Civilization*, 2 vols. (Ginn Press, 1986–87); he has contributed to such works as *Great Lives from History*, *Modern Encyclopedia of Russian and Soviet History*, *Historic World Leaders*, *Harper Encyclopedia of Military History*, *International Military Encyclopedia*, *Biographical Dictionary of British Radicals*, *Historical Dictionary of the British Empire*, *Hawaiian Journal of History*, *Alabama Review*, *Encyclopedia USA* and *Encyclopedia of the War of 1812*.

Claudia Marie Kovach is Professor of English and French at Neumann College, Aston, Pennsylvania, and author of "Floating Tristan: Distortions, Indeterminacy and Difference Within the Integrated Corpus," *Tristania* (Vol. IV, Edwin Mellon Press) and several other articles on Isabel Allende and Amy Tan; she has published and lectured widely on medieval literature and literature by women.

Joanna H. Kraus is Professor Emeritus, Theater, at the State University of New York College at Brockport and an award-winning playwright; her works include *Sunday Gold* (1998), *Angel in the Night* (1996), *Remember My Name* (Samuel French, 1989), *Ms. Courageous: Women of Science* (New Plays, 1997) and *Tall Boy's Journey* (Carolrhoda Books, 1992).

Noeline J. Kyle is Professor of History at Queensland University of Technology, Australia, and author of *Her Natural Destiny: The Education of Women in New South Wales* (Kensington: NSW University Press, 1986), *We Should've Listened to Grandma: Women and Family History* (Sydney: Allen & Unwin, 1988), (with Catherine Manathunga and Joanne Scott) *A Class of Its Own: A History of QUT* (Sydney: Hale & Iremonger, 1999); she is co-editor of *History of Education Review* and is writing a critical biography of Mother Vincent "Ellen" Whitty, a leading educator in 19th-century Queensland.

Robert S. La Forte is Professor of History at the University of North Texas, Denton, and author of *Leaders of Reform* (University of Kansas Press, 1974), *Down the Corridor of Years* (University of North Texas Press, 1989), *Remembering Pearl Harbor* (SR Books, 1991), *Building the Death Railway* (SR Books, 1993), and *With Only the Will to Live* (SR Books, 1994); he has edited several readings in American history books and published entries in *American National Biography* (Oxford Press, 1998) and articles in *Kansas History, A Journal of the Plains*.

Mary M. Lacey is Assistant Professor of English and Humanities at Earlham College, Richmond, Indiana; she teaches courses in 19th- and 20th-century literature, poetry, creative writing, and humanities.

Anil Lal is a freelance writer in Chicago who is at work on a book entitled "A Cultural Poetics for Economics: Of Imaginative and Commercial Economies."

Christine Lambert is a Ph.D. candidate in history at Emory University, Atlanta, Georgia, working on a dissertation "Citizenship and Identity in New Orleans and the New Nation, 1803–1836."

Kathleen A. Waites Lamm is Professor of English and Women's Studies at Nova University, Fort Lauderdale, Florida.

Kate Lang received her Ph.D. in Near Eastern Languages from the University of Chicago; she is Assistant Professor of History at the University of Wisconsin-Eau Claire.

Gaynol Langs is an independent scholar in Redmond, Washington.

Denise M. Larrabee is a writer, historian, and former Curator of Women's History Collection at the Library Company of Philadelphia; she publishes and lectures on women's history and is the author of *Anne Hampton Brewster: 19th-Century Author and "Social Outlaw"* (Library Company of Philadelphia, 1992), as well as numerous short stories and essays; Larrabee is a co-founder of the Meridian Writers Collective, an assistant editor for *American Writing: A Magazine,* and has served as scholar and speaker for the Pennsylvania Humanities Council.

Kristine Larsen is Associate Professor of Astronomy and Physics at Central Connecticut State University, New Britain, Connecticut.

Leslie Larson is Copywriting and Catalog Manager at the University of California Press; she has written two novels and her criticism has appeared in *FM: Five, The Lesbian Review of Books,* and *The Women's Review of Books.*

Shirley A. Leckie is Professor of History at the University of Central Florida, Orlando; she is author of *Elizabeth Bacon Custer and the*

Making of a Myth (University of Oklahoma Press, 1993), editor of *The Colonel's Lady on the Western Frontier: The Correspondence of Alice Kirk Grierson* (University of Nebraska Press, 1989), and co-author of *Unlikely Warriors: General Benjamin Grierson and His Family* (University of Oklahoma Press, 1984).

Matthew Lee is a freelance writer in Colorado Springs, Colorado.

Barbara S. Lesko is Research Assistant in the Department of Egyptology at Brown University, Providence, Rhode Island, and author of *The Remarkable Women of Ancient Egypt,* 3rd ed. (B.C. Scribe Publications, 1996) and *Great Goddesses of Egypt* (University of Oklahoma Press); she edited Women's *Earliest Records* (Scholars Press of Atlanta, 1989) and has contributed to two editions of the textbook *Becoming Visible: Women in European History* (Houghton Mifflin, 1987, 1997).

Lucy A. Liggett is Professor of Telecommunications and Film, Eastern Michigan University, Ypsilanti, Michigan; she is the author of *Ida Lupino as Film Director, 1949–1953* (Arno Press) and contributor to *The Encyclopedia of Television* (ed. Horace Newcomb, Museum of Broadcast Communication, 1997) and has produced documentaries and lectured on women in film and public life.

Elisa A. Litvin is a secondary educator and independent historian who lives in Farmington Hills, Michigan.

Nancy L. Locklin is a Ph.D. candidate in history at Emory University, Atlanta, Georgia, and a Fulbright scholar; she specializes in the economic role of women in early modern Europe.

Meghan K. Lowney, M.S.W., is Executive Director of Operation Hope of Fairfield, Fairfield, Connecticut.

Margaret E. Lynch, M.A., is a Teaching Fellow in the Department of History at Lancaster University, Lancaster, United Kingdom, and an independent scholar.

Barbara J. MacHaffie is Molly C. Putnam and Israel Ward Andrews Associate Professor of History and Religion at Marietta College, Marietta, Ohio, and author of *Her Story: Women in Christian Tradition* (Fortress Press, 1986) and *Readings in Her Story: Women in Christian Tradition* (Fortress Press, 1992).

Anna Macías is Professor Emerita of History at Ohio Wesleyan University, Delaware, Ohio, and author of *Genesis del Gobierno Constituciala en Mexico: 1808–1820* (Mexico: SEP/SETENTAS 94, 1973) and *Against All Odds: The Feminist Movement in Mexico to 1940* (Greenwood Press, 1982); she has written numerous articles on feminism in Mexico and the United States in scholarly journals in both countries.

William MacKenzie is a graduate student at the Department of History, University of Guelph, Ontario, Canada, and a freelance writer.

Cheryl Knott Malone has worked as a lecturer, reference librarian, and bibliographer; her publications include *Gender, Unpaid Labor, and the Promotion of Literacy: A Selected, Annotated Bibliography* (Garland Publishing, 1987) and "Women's Unpaid Work in Libraries: Change and Continuity," in *Reclaiming the American Library Past: Writing the Women In* (ed. Suzanne Hildenbrand, Ablex).

James M. Manheim, freelance writer and editor in Ann Arbor, Michigan, has written widely about music; he has contributed numerous articles to the Gale encyclopedias *Contemporary Black Biography* and *Contemporary Musicians.*

Michael Tomasek Manson is Assistant Professor of Literature at The American University in Washington, D.C.

Crista Martin is a freelance writer in Boston, Massachusetts.

D.E. Martin lectures in the Department of History at the University of Sheffield, United Kingdom, and is author of *John Stuart Mill and the Land Question* (Hull: Hull University Press, 1981) and contributor of articles on British women to *Dictionary of Labour Biography,* 9 vols. (London: Macmillan, 1972–93) and *Dictionary of National Biography* (Oxford: Oxford University Press); he is co-editor of the *Labour History Review* (1987–97) and of *The History of the City of Sheffield, 1843–1993* (Sheffield: Sheffield Academic Press, 1993).

Ingrid Martínez-Rico received her Ph.D. in Comparative Literature from Pennsylvania State University and is an adjunct professor at the University of Georgia, Athens, Georgia; she has taught at universities in Spain, Kenya, Lithuania and the U.S., is collaborating with Ray Fleming on a work on Romanticism, and will soon publish a book on Rosalia de Castro.

Fraidie Martz is a freelance writer in Vancouver, British Columbia, Canada, and author of *"Open*

Your Hearts": The Story of the Jewish War Orphans in Canada (Montreal, Quebec: Véhicule Press, 1997); she is co-curator of the traveling exhibit "Open Hearts—Closed Doors" (Vancouver Holocaust Education Centre, 1997).

Susan J. Matt is a freelance writer in history.

Jacqueline Maurice is an American freelance writer living in Calgary, Alberta, Canada; she worked in the information technology field at Xerox Corporation for 12 years, studies Native American and First Nations' history and current events, and is a contributor to the Gale Research publications *Native American Tribes* and *Exploring Law and Society.*

Malinda Mayer, B.F.A. in theater direction (Boston University), M.Sc.Ed. in multiple handicapped education (Lesley College), is a manual therapist and a freelance writer and editor based in Falmouth, Massachusetts; she has also served as senior technical writer for a computer software company.

Jane McAvoy is Associate Professor of Theology at Lexington Theological Seminary, Kentucky; she is the editor of *Table Talk: Resources for the Communion Meal* and is completing a book on women mystics and understandings of salvation.

Susan W. McCarter received her master's degree in education from the University of South Carolina; she is a freelance writer in Wayne, Pennsylvania, with a dual background in education and corporate communications.

Helga P. McCue, a freelance writer in Waterford, Connecticut, has edited *Something About the Author* and *Authors and Artists for Young Adults,* and has contributed to *Yesterday's Authors of Books for Children* (all Gale Research). She is also managing editor for Garland Publishing's academic and reference divisions.

Marcia Phillips McGowan is Professor of English and Director of Women's Studies at Eastern Connecticut State University, Willimantic, Connecticut, co-editor (with Sandra M. Boschetto-Sandoval) of *Claribel Alegría and Central American Literature* (Ohio University Press, 1994), and author of articles on Edith Wharton's fiction in *Connecticut Review;* she has published and lectured widely on women writers and women's studies pedagogy.

Margaret McIntyre is Instructor of Women's History at Trent University, Peterborough, Ontario, Canada; she has presented several conference papers on women and power in early modern Scotland and is currently completing a master's degree in Archival Studies at the University of Toronto.

Elsie Anne McKee is Archibald Alexander Professor of Reformation Studies and the History of Worship at Princeton Theological Seminary, Princeton, New Jersey, and specializes in the history and theology of the Protestant Reformation; she is the author of *John Calvin on the Diaconate and Liturgical Almsgiving* (Geneva: Droz, 1984), *Elders and the Plural Ministry: The Role of the Exegetical History in Illuminating Calvin's Theology* (Geneva: Droz, 1988), *Diakonia in the Classical Reformed Tradition and Today* (Wm. B. Eerdmans, 1989), *Reforming Popular Piety in Sixteenth-Century Strasbourg: Katharina Schütz Zell and Her Hymnbook* (Princeton Theological Seminary, 1994), *Katharina Schütz Zell: The Life and Thought of a Sixteenth Century Reformer* (Leiden: E.J. Brill, 1998), *The Writings of Katharina Schütz Zell: A Critical Edition* (Leiden: E.J. Brill, 1998).

Deirdre McMahon is Lecturer in History at Mary Immaculate College, University of Limerick, Limerick, Ireland, and author of *Republicans and Imperialists* (Yale University Press, 1984); she has contributed articles and reviews to *Bullán, Irish Archives, Irish Historical Studies, Irish Jurist,* and *Irish Studies in International Affairs.*

Kathryn M. McMahon, Ph.D., is the author of *Heroes and Enemies: War, Gender and Popular Culture* for the series "Gender and Political Theory: New Contexts" (Lynne Rienner Publishers).

Linda A. McMillin is Associate Professor, Head of the History Department, and Director of University Honors Program at Susquehanna University, Selinsgrove, Pennsylvania, whose research and publications focus on religious women in the Middle Ages.

Francesca Medioli is Lecturer in Italian Studies at the University of Reading, Reading, United Kingdom, and author of *L'"Inferno monacale" di Arcangela Tarabotti* (Torino: Rosenberg e Sellier, 1990) and several articles including "The Dimensions of the Cloister: Enclosure, Constraint and Protection in XVIIth C. Italy" in *Time and Space in Early Modern Women's Life* (eds. A. Jacobson Schutte, T. Kuhn, Thomas Jefferson University Press, 1999); she has published and lectured widely on cloistered women in Early Modern Italy.

Bonnie Hurren Meech is a freelance actor, director and tutor at The Bristol Old Vic Theater School, and co-founder and Artistic Director of Show of Strength Pub Theater Company, Bristol, England (1989–96).

Margaret L. Meggs is an independent scholar on women's and disability issues and on feminism and religion; her articles and essays have appeared in *Women's VU, Citizenne*, "Womanspirit" newsletter, *The Montana Professor, The (Nashville) Tennessean*, and the *Havre (Montana) Daily News*, and she presents lectures and workshops on feminist earth-based spirituality.

Jo Anne Meginnes, of Brookfield, Vermont, is a freelance writer whose experience includes 13 years in the journalistic field, nine of which were spent as the copyeditor for an award-winning, small town, weekly newspaper; she has written many feature stories and is working on two children's books.

Linda E. Merians is Associate Professor of English at La Salle University, Philadelphia, Pennsylvania, and editor of *The Secret Malady: Venereal Disease in Eighteenth-Century Britain and France* (University Press of Kentucky, 1996); she has published widely on topics related to 18th-century British literature and culture.

Denise D. Meringolo is Curator at the Jewish Historical Society of Greater Washington, Washington, D.C., and a freelance writer and researcher; her exhibits at the Jewish Historical Society have included *Tzedakah: Jewish Women Creating a Capital Community, 1895–1948* and *Don't Whisper a Prayer, Sing Aloud a Song of Peace: Yitzhak Rabin in Washington*.

Kim L. Messeri is a freelance writer and researcher based in Austin, Texas, and has contributed to reference works, including the *International Directory of Company Histories* (St. James Press, Farmington Hills, Michigan).

Barbara H. Milech, Ph.D., is Senior Lecturer in the School of Communication and Cultural Studies at Curtin University of Technology, Perth, Western Australia, and teaches in the areas of narrative, gender, and cultural studies; recent publications include "Feminist Figures, Ethical Narratives," in *When Plot Meets Knot: Narrative and Metaphor across the Disciplines* (Ohio State University Press), "Counter-memories, Counter-identifications: Aboriginal Women's Life Writings," in *Aus-*

tralian Feminist Law Journal, and "'Sophisticated Spaces': Fiction, Autobiography, and Reading Elizabeth Jolley," in *a/b: Auto/Biography Studies*, and she is editor of *Fellow Passengers: Elizabeth Jolley's Collected Stories* (Penguin, 1987).

Kristie Miller is an independent historian, correspondent for the La Salle (Illinois) *News Tribune*, and author of *Ruth Hanna McCormick: A Life in Politics 1880–1944* (University of New Mexico Press, 1992), "Grace Coolidge," in *American First Ladies* (ed. Lewis L. Gould, Garland Publishing, 1996), and other essays on women in American politics in journals and encyclopedias; she co-edited *American Women in Political Parties 1880–1960* (University of New Mexico Press, 1999).

Sally M. Miller is Professor of History at the University of the Pacific, Stockton, California, and author of *From Prairie to Prison: The Life of Social Activist Kate Richards O'Hare* (University of Missouri Press, 1993), *Race, Ethnicity and Gender in Early 20th Century American Socialism* (Garland Publishing, 1996) and "A Path Approaching Full Circle: Kate Richards O'Hare," in *Socialism and Christianity* (ed. Jacob Dorn, Greenwood Press, 1998).

Elizabeth Milliken received her Ph.D. in American History from Cornell University, Ithaca, New York, and is a freelance writer.

Christine Miner Minderovic, B.S., is a freelance writer from Ann Arbor, Michigan, who has worked in the medical field for 30 years; she has contributed to many reference publications on topics including science, biography, art and modern dance.

Lois A. Monteiro, Ph.D., R.N., is Professor of Medical Science at Brown University School of Medicine, Providence, Rhode Island; she is the author of numerous publications including *Monitoring Health Status and Medical Care* (Ballinger/Lippincott, 1976), "Florence Nightingale on Public Health Nursing," in *American Journal of Public Health* (February 1985), "Funding, Training and Human Resources for Contraceptive Development," in *Developing New Contraceptives: Obstacles and Opportunities* (Institute of Medicine, National Academy Press, February 1990), and "Nightingale and Her Correspondents," in *Nightingale and Her Era: New Scholarship about Women and Nursing* (eds. V. Bullough, et al., Garland Publishing, 1990)

Diane Moody is a freelance writer in London, England, with a B.A. in Art History, from Princeton University, Princeton, New Jersey.

Annabelle Mooney is a freelance writer in Canberra, Australia.

Heather Moore, of Northampton, Massachusetts, is a freelance writer in the history of photography and women's studies.

Patrick Moore, Associate Professor of English, University of Arkansas at Little Rock, has contributed many articles in reference works about leaders in science, technology, and history; he is also the author of many journal articles about technical communication, technical disasters, literature, and discourse analysis.

Susan Morehouse is Associate Professor of English at Alfred University, Alfred, New York; her publications include "Imagining Flight When I Am Still" (Fall 1989) and "My Mothers Who Wrote" (Fall 1987) in *The Southern Review,* "Somebody's Lover," in *The Madison Review* (Fall 1988), and "If You Lived Here You'd Be Home Now," in *The Laurel Review* (Summer 1987).

Paula Morris, B.A. (Auckland, New Zealand), is a freelance writer in Brooklyn, New York, currently working on "The Real Things: On the Trail of Laura Ingalls Wilder."

Joseph C. Morton is Professor of History at Northeastern Illinois University, Chicago, Illinois, and author of "Stephen Bordley of Colonial Annapolis," in *Winterthur Portfolio 5* (University Press of Virginia, 1969) and "Bordley Family" and "Regulators," in *Encyclopedia of Southern History* (Louisiana State University Press, 1979); he has written biographical sketches of John Quincy Adams, Daniel Boone, Benjamin Franklin, Alexander Hamilton, Patrick Henry, Lyndon Baines Johnson and John Paul Jones for *Historic World Leaders* (Gale Research, 1994) and has lectured in the People's Republic of China.

Karen E. Mura, Ph.D., is Associate Professor of English at Susquehanna University, Selinsgrove, Pennsylvania.

Cliona Murphy is Professor of History at California State University, Bakersfield, and author of *The Women's Suffrage Movement and Irish Society in the Early Twentieth Century* (Temple University Press, 1989).

Sally A. Myers, Ph.D. in American Studies, Bowling Green State University in Ohio, is a freelance writer and editor in Defiance, Ohio. She is former assistant professor of English, Defiance College and Ohio Northern University. She has written widely on American women's history and 19th-century American literature for scholarly journals, and is working on a book about northwest Ohio women's literary clubs at the turn of the 20th century.

Doan Thi Nam-Hau is a freelance writer in Los Angeles, California.

Jenny Newell is a research and editing assistant at the Centre for Cross-Cultural Research, Australian National University, Canberra; her publications as a freelance writer include articles in the *Australian Dictionary of Biography* (Melbourne University Press, 1996, 1999).

David S. Newhall, Ph.D., Harvard University, is Pottinger Distinguished Professor of History, Emeritus, Centre College, Danville, Kentucky, and author of *Clemenceau: A Life at War* (Edwin Mellen Press, 1991); he has contributed many entries to *Historical Dictionary of the Third French Republic* (Greenwood Press, 1986) and *Historic World Leaders* (Gale Research, 1994).

Kate Newmann is a full-time writer who lives in County Donegal, Ireland; she served as editor at the Institute of Irish Studies, Queen's University, Belfast, N. Ireland, and compiled *The Dictionary of Ulster Biography* (Belfast: The Institute of Irish Studies, Queen's University, 1994).

Laurie Norris is an intercultural relations consultant who works with immigrants and refugees encountering U.S. culture and making work transitions; she is the author of a study of Russians working in the U.S., a nongovernmental organization (NGO) delegate to the United Nations for International Union for Health Promotion and Education, and served as oral historian for the Henry Street Settlement Urban Life Center Centennial Oral History Project (1993).

Kathleen Banks Nutter is Manuscripts Processor at the Sophia Smith Collection, Smith College, Northampton, Massachusetts, and author of "Organizing Women During the Progressive Era: Mary Kenney O'Sullivan and the Labor Movement," in *Labor's Heritage* (1997) and "Women Reformers and the Limitations of Labor Politics in Progressive Era Massachusetts," in *Massachusetts Politics: Selected Historical Essays* (Westfield State College, 1998); she has taught U.S. history at the University of Massachusetts, Westfield State College, and Greenfield Community College.

Gerard O'Brien is Senior Lecturer in History at the University of Ulster, Northern Ireland.

Peter Hart O'Brien teaches English and Classics at Boston University Academy, Boston, Massachusetts.

Jeanne A. Ojala is Professor of History at the University of Utah, Salt Lake City, Utah, and author of *Auguste de Colbert: Aristocratic Survival in an Age of Upheaval, 1793–1809* (University of Utah Press, 1979), *Madame de Sévigné: A Seventeenth Century Life* (Oxford: Berg Publishers, 1990), and "The Peninsular Marshal—Suchet," in *Napoleon's Marshals* (ed. David G. Chandler, Macmillan, 1987); she has contributed articles and dictionary entries on prostitution in Paris, the French Revolution, and Napoleon, and contributed entries on European women writers for *Continental Women Writers* (ed. K.M. Wilson, Garland Publishing, 1991).

Kenneth J. Orosz is a Ph.D. candidate in European History at Binghamton University, Binghamton, New York, working on the dissertation "Language, Race and Nationhood: German and French Language Policy in Colonial Cameroon, 1885–1939."

Joseph F. Patrouch is Assistant Professor of History at Florida International University in Miami, Florida, and a historian of early modern Central Europe.

Elena Pavlova is a graduate of the Leningrad State University, Russia, and a Ph.D. candidate in Russian history at the University of Chicago, Chicago, Illinois; her publications include "The Coinless Period in the History of Northeastern Russia," in *Russian History* and "From Turf to Icon: the Ritual of Legal Confirmation (OTVOD) in Private Legal Documents of Northeastern Russian Principalities of the 1380–1460s," in *Chicago Anthropology Exchange* 21 (1995).

Reina Pennington is a Ph.D. candidate in the Department of History of the University of South Carolina, Columbia, South Carolina, and author of "Offensive Women: Women in Combat in the Red Army," in *Time to Kill: The Soldier's Experience of War in the West* (London: Pimlico Press, 1997); she is at work on *Military Women Worldwide: A Biographical Dictionary* for Greenwood Press and *Wings, Women and War: Soviet Women's Military Aviation Regiments in the Second World War* for University Press of Kansas, Modern War Studies Series.

Barbara Bennett Peterson, Ph.D., is Professor of History at the University of Hawaii, Honolulu, editor of *Notable Women of Hawaii* (University of Hawaii Press, 1984), and author of *Britons View America* (Fulbright Association, 1988); she is an associate editor for the *American National Biography* (Oxford University Press), and editor of *The Pacific Region* with Wilhelm G. Solheim II (Fulbright Association, 1991), *American History, 17th, 18th, and 19th Centuries* (American Heritage, 1993), *America, 19th and 20th Centuries* (American Heritage, 1993), and *Notable Women of China.*

Christopher Phelps is Editorial Director at Monthly Review Press in New York City; he has taught American history at the University of Oregon and Simon Fraser University, is author of *Young Sidney Hook: Marxist and Pragmatist* (Ithaca: Cornell University Press, 1997), and has contributed to *American Quarterly, The Nation,* and other publications.

Margaret Dorsey Phelps, Ph.D., is an adjunct assistant professor at the University of Iowa, Iowa City, Iowa, and a freelance writer.

Donald K. Pickens is Professor of History at the University of North Texas, Denton, and author of *Eugenics and the Progressives* (Vanderbilt University Press, 1969), many articles on American history, and numerous reference-book entries; he has lectured on American national character on the History Channel, established the "Women in America" History course at UNT in 1968, and is writing a study of Leon H. Keyserling and the rise and fall of integrative liberalism.

Steven Plank is Professor of Musicology at Oberlin College, Oberlin, Ohio, and author of *The Way to Heavens Doore: An Introduction to Liturgical Process and Musical Style* (Scarecrow Press, 1994); he has written many studies of early music, which have appeared in *Musical Times, Music & Letters* and *Early Music.*

Jeannie G. Pool of Los Angeles, California, is a freelance writer on music history.

Kimberly A. Powell, Ph.D., is Assistant Professor of Communication at Luther College, Decorah, Iowa, and co-author of "Jessie Daniel Ames, Suffragette and Anti-lynching Crusader: Militant Reform through Local Action," in *Women Public Speakers in the U.S., 1925–1993* (Greenwood Press, 1993) and several articles on Daniel-Ames published in communications journals; she publishes and lectures on argumentation and debate, public speaking and feminist issues.

Norman Powers is a writer and producer at Chelsea Lane Productions, New York, New York, whose works include *The Greengage Summer* (adaptation; screenplay), *Foreign Land* (adaptation; screenplay), *Maybe* (screenplay), *Wild Horse Annie* (teleplay) and *The House of Seven Gables* (adaptation; teleplay).

Mansah Prah, Ph.D., is Lecturer in Sociology at the University of Cape Coast, Cape Coast, Ghana, West Africa, and has published and lectured widely on women in Africa with specific reference to Ghana; her publications include *Introduction to Women's Studies with a Focus on Ghana* (Schriescheim, Germany: Books on African Studies, 1995) and "The Development of Women's Studies in Ghana," in *Women's Studies Quarterly* (Vol. XXIV, June 1996).

Heather Munro Prescott is Associate Professor of History and Co-coordinator of Women's Studies at Central Connecticut State University, New Britain, Connecticut, and the author of *"A Doctor of Their Own": The History of Adolescent Medicine* (Harvard University Press, 1998); she has published and lectured widely on the history of gender and medicine, and is working on a project entitled "Student Bodies: The History of College and University Health."

Jenifer Presto is Assistant Professor of Slavic Languages and Literatures at the University of Southern California, Los Angeles, California, and the author of articles on Zinaida Gippius and women writers in Russian Modernism.

Mary A. Procida is Visiting Assistant Professor of History, Temple University, Philadelphia, Pennsylvania.

Maria Sophia Quine is a lecturer at Queen Mary and Westfield College, University of London, England, and the author of *Population Politics in Twentieth-Century Europe: Fascist Dictatorships and Liberal Democracies* (London, England: Routledge, 1996); her research interests lie in the social history of Modern Italy and Italian Fascism.

Jesse T. Raiford is President of Raiford Communications, Inc., New York, New York.

Martha Rampton is Assistant Professor of History at Pacific University, Forest Grove, Oregon, and author of "The Peasants' Revolt of 1381 and the Written Word," in *Comitatus* 24 (1993), "The Significance of the Banquet Scene in the Bayeux Tapestry," in *Medievalia*

et Humanistica 21 (1994), and "Up From the Dead: Magic and Miracle" in *Death in the Middle Ages;* she is currently working on a book entitled "The Gender of Magic in the Early Middle Ages."

Rosemary Raughter is a lecturer at the Women's Education, Research and Resource Centre, at University College, Dublin, Ireland, and the author of a number of articles on women in 18th-century Ireland, including "A Natural Tenderness: the Reality and the Ideal of Eighteenth-Century Female Philanthropy," in *Women and Irish History* (eds. Maryann Valiulis and Mary O'Dowd, Dublin: Wolfhound Press, 1997) and "A Discreet Benevolence: Female Philanthropy and the Catholic Resurgence," in *Women's History Review* (Vol. 6, no. 4, 1997).

Boris Raymond, Ph.D., is an adjunct professor in the Department of Sociology and Anthropology at Dalhousie University, Halifax, Nova Scotia, Canada, author of *Krupskaia and Soviet Russian Librarianship, 1917–1939* (Scarecrow Press, 1979), and contributor to *Canadian Journal of Information Science, Canadian Library Journal, Library Quarterly,* and *Journal of Library History.*

Michaela Crawford Reaves, Ph.D., is Professor of History at California Lutheran University, Thousand Oaks, California, and has published on American culture and women in history, most recently "Wilma Pearl Mankiller," in *Significant Contemporary Feminists* (Greenwood, 1998), and has served as commentator in *Women: First and Foremost* (Monterey Movie Co., 1996) and as secondary curriculum designer for "Shiloh," the play based on Shelby Foote's novel *Shiloh;* her current research topics include "The Farmer's Revolt: Arms and Fraternity in California."

Rhoda E. Reddock is a Senior Lecturer and Head of the Centre for Gender and Development Studies at The University of the West Indies, St. Augustine Campus, Trinidad and Tobago, a founding member and past Chair of The Caribbean Association of Feminist Research and Action (CAFRA), and the past Chair of Research Committee 32 (Women and Society) of the International Sociological Association (ISA); she is the author of numerous publications including *Women, Labour and Politics in Trinidad and Tobago* (ZED Books, 1994) and *Ethnic Minorities in Caribbean Society* (ISER, 1996), and is co-editor of the collection *Women Plantation Workers: International Experiences* (Berg, 1998).

Lyn Reese is Director of Women in World History Curriculum, Berkeley, California, and author of *Spindle Stories, I Will Not Bow My Head: Documenting Women's Political Resistance, Muslim Women in World History,* and *Personalities from the Past* (Women in World History Curriculum, 1990–1998); she consults for textbook publishers, creates user's guides for television series, and presents teacher workshops on women's history.

Judith C. Reveal, former president of the Maryland Writers' Association (1997–98), is a freelance writer in Greensboro, Maryland.

C. David Rice, Ph.D., is Chair and Professor at the Department of History of Central Missouri State University, Warrensburg, Missouri.

Doris L. Rich has been a newspaper reporter, a Red Cross field assistant in World War II, a photographer, and teacher of English and civics in Bangladesh, Ghana, and Hong Kong, and has lived in, traveled through, and written extensively about Asia; she is author of *Amelia Earhart: A Biography* (Smithsonian Institution Press, 1989)—which was the basis of *Amelia Earhart: The Last Flight* (Turner Network Television)—as well as *Queen Bess: Daredevil Aviator* (Smithsonian Institution Press, 1993) and *The Magnificent Moisants* (Smithsonian, 1998).

Pamela Riney-Kehrberg is Associate Professor of History at Illinois State University, Normal, Illinois; she is the author of *Rooted in Dust: Surviving Drought and Depression in Southwestern Kansas* (University Press of Kansas, 1994) and is conducting research on the history of women and children in rural America.

Elizabeth Rokkan is a retired associate professor in the Department of English at the University of Bergen, Norway, and a recipient of St. Olav's Medal (Norway); she is translator of such novelists as Johan Borgen, Jostein Gaarder, Cora Sandel, and Tarjei Vesaas, and the author of articles on British and American studies and Norwegian literature.

Kathy Rubino is a freelance writer in Boston, Massachusetts.

Nancy Ellen Rupprecht is Associate Professor of History and Director of Women's Studies at Middle Tennessee State University, Murfreesboro, Tennessee.

Reinhilde Ruprecht is a freelance writer in the Federal Republic of Germany whose publications include "The Feminist and Womanist Critique of Reinhold Niebuhr's Understanding of Sin: Ethical Considerations" (Arbeitsgemeinschaft ökumenische Forschung, Villigst, Federal Republic of Germany).

Anne J. Russ received her Ph.D. from Cornell University and is Professor of Sociology and Education at Wells College, Aurora, New York, and the author of several articles on the history of higher education.

Constance B. Rynder is Professor of History at the University of Tampa, Florida, and author of numerous articles on women in history, including "All Men and Women Are Created Equal (the 1848 Seneca Falls Women's Rights Convention)," in *American History* (August 1998); she has lectured on women in American and Irish history and politics.

Meredith Sabini, M.A., Ph.D., is a licensed psychologist and Mandatory Continuing Education Provider in Berkeley, California, whose career combines teaching, writing, dream research, and public speaking; she is associate editor at *Psychological Perspectives* and has contributions in *The Sacred Heritage*.

Santosh C. Saha is a history professor at Mount Union College, Alliance, Ohio, and author of articles in *Canadian Journal of African Studies, Journal of Negro History,* and *International Journal of African Historical Studies,* and of biographical essays in *Historic World Leaders* and *Dictionary of Human Rights Advocacy Organizations in Africa;* he served as editor of the *Cuttington Faculty Research Journal* and is on the editorial board of *Indian Journal of Asian Affairs.*

John Sainsbury is Associate Professor of History at Brock University, St. Catharines, Ontario, Canada, and the author of *Disaffected Patriots: London Supporters of Revolutionary America, 1769–1782* (Kingston and Montreal, McGill-Queen's University Press, 1987).

Christopher Saunders is Associate Professor of History at the University of Cape Town, South Africa, and author of *The Making of the South African Past* (Cape Town and New York, 1988), *A Dictionary of South African History* (Cape Town, 1998) and a number of other books and articles on the history of South Africa.

Pamela G. Sayre is Instructor in History at Henry Ford Community College, Dearborn, Michigan; her publications include "The Mistress of Robes—Who Was She?" in *Byzantine Studies/Etudes Byzantines* (Vol. 13, fasc. 2, 1986).

Kristina R. Sazaki is Assistant Professor of German at the College of the Holy Cross in Worcester, Massachusetts, and author of "The Crippled Text/Woman: Annette von Droste-Hülshoff's *Ledwina*," in *Monatshefte* (Vol. 89. no. 2, 1997) and "Mimicking Theater: Charlotte Birch-Pfeiffer's *Dorf und Stadt* in Relation to Berthold Auerbach's *Die Frau Professorin*," in *Thalia's Daughters: German Women Dramatists from the Eighteenth Century to the Present* (Tübingen: Günther Narr, 1996); she teaches German language and German literature and culture of the 18th and 19th centuries.

Elizabeth D. Schafer of Loachapoka, Alabama, is an independent scholar who received her Ph.D. in the history of science and technology from Auburn University; she is co-author of *Women Who Made a Difference in Alabama* (1995) and a contributor to many encyclopedias, journals and magazines.

Mark Schneider is the author of *Boston Confronts Jim Crow, 1890–1920* (Northeastern University Press, 1997).

Ann Schwalboski, English teacher and writing specialist, University of Wisconsin-Baraboo/Sauk County, is a freelance biography writer who is working on a forthcoming book of fiction.

Scout is a freelance writer in Washington, D.C.

Pamela Scully is Assistant Professor of History at Kenyon College, Gambier, Ohio, and author of *Liberating the Family? Gender and British Slave Emancipation in the Rural Western Cape, South Africa, 1823–1853* (Heinemann, 1997) and "Rape, Race and Colonial Culture: The Sexual Politics of Identity in the Nineteenth-Century, Cape Colony, South Africa," in *American Historical Review* (100, 2, April 1995); she is currently conducting research on race and women's suffrage in South Africa.

Kirsten A. Seaver is a historian, novelist and translator, in Palo Alto, California, and author of *The Frozen Echo: Greenland and the Exploration of North America ca. 1000–1500* (Stanford University Press, 1996), articles on early exploration and cartography, three historical novels (Gyldendal, Oslo, 1994, 1996, 1998), and translations including Camilla Collett's *The District Governor's Daughters* (Norvik Press, 1992); in addition to reviews, lectures and television work, she has translated Norwegian poetry, winning the American Scandinavian Foundation Translation Prize in 1994 for Henrik Ibsen, *Love's Comedy*.

Willa Seidenberg has worked as a television-news writer and producer, a freelance reporter, and a teacher of courses on radio journalism; she is co-author of *A Matter of Conscience: GI Resistance during the Vietnam War* (Addison Gallery of American Art, 1992) and of "A Matter of Conscience: Resistance within the US Military during the Vietnam War," in *Vietnam Generation* (Vol. 2, no. 1, 1990), and is co-director of two Oral History/Photographic Projects: *A Matter of Conscience,* a national traveling exhibition, and *Memories of the American War.*

Karen A. Shaffer is a Maud Powell biographer and president of the Maud Powell Foundation in Arlington, Virginia.

John Shean received his Ph.D. from the University of Wisconsin-Madison and is Visiting Assistant Professor of History at Clarion University of Pennsylvania; he has published articles and lectured on various aspects of Greek, Roman, Byzantine, and religious history and is converting his dissertation on the Christianization of the Roman army into a book.

Carole Shelton is Adjunct Professor of History at Middle Tennessee State University, Murfreesboro, Tennessee; her publications include "War, Heroism, and Shellshock—Siegfried Sassoon: A Case Study," in *Focus on Robert Graves and His Contemporaries* (Winter 1992).

Kenneth R. Shepherd is Adjunct Instructor in History at Henry Ford Community College, Dearborn, Michigan, and Washtenaw Community College, Ann Arbor, Michigan; he is a contributor to *Contemporary Authors* and *Something About the Author* (both Gale Research).

Mona Siegel is Assistant Professor of History at the University of Cincinnati, Cincinnati, Ohio; she is author of "'To the Unknown Mother of the Unknown Soldier': Pacifism, Feminism, and the Politics of Sexual Difference in France between the Wars" and is finishing a book-length study of patriotism and pacifism in post-World War I French education.

Chris Sitka is a freelance writer and researcher in Sydney, Australia.

Susie Slosberg is Adjunct Professor of Public Relations at Baruch College, The City University of New York, and a lyricist whose work has been recorded on Signature Sounds Recording; she is a member of ASCAP

(American Society of Composers, Authors and Publishers), NSAI (Nashville Songwriters International), NARAS (National Academy of Recording Arts & Sciences), and SGA (Songwriters Guild of America).

Suzanne Smith is a freelance writer and editor in Decatur, Georgia; her publications include "Howl about Wolves: The Controversial Plan to Bring Wolves Back to Yellowstone Park" and "The Science of Forensic Anthropology," in *Science World Magazine* and "New Discoveries for Managing Sleep Problems in the Elderly," in *New Choices Magazine*.

Robert Sobel is retired Professor Emeritus of business history at Hofstra University, Hempstead, New York, and the author of *Coolidge: An American Enigma* (Regnery 1998).

Kimberly Estep Spangler is Associate Professor of History and Chair of the Division of Religion and Humanities at Friends University, Wichita, Kansas, and has published biographical sketches in *Historic World Leaders* (Gale Research, 1994) and *Great Lives from History II: American Women* (Salem Press, 1995).

Terry E. Sparkes received her Ph.D. from the University of Chicago and is Assistant Professor of Religion at Luther College, Decorah, Iowa, and author of "Religion and Utopia," in *Utopian Visions of Work and Community* (Iowa Humanities Board, 1996) and "The 'Pernicious Effects' of Religion in America: A Dissenting View of the 'Good Society' from the 1820s," in *Agora* (Fall 1995); she has lectured and written on the history of freethinkers in the U.S., on American civil religion, and on contemporary American religious pluralism and diversity issues.

Jane E. Spear is a freelance writer and editor based in Canton, Ohio.

John C. Spurlock is Associate Professor of History at Seton Hill College, Greensburg, Pennsylvania; his publications include *Free Love: Marriage and Middle-Class Radicalism in America, 1825–1860* (New York University Press, 1988), "Utopian Communities," in *Encyclopedia of Social History* (Garland Publishing), "Marr Fenn Davis" and "Marian Olden," in *Past and Promise: The Lives of New Jersey Women* (Scarecrow Press, 1990), and "Anarchy and Community at Modern Times, 1851–1863," in *Communal Societies* (1983).

N.J. Stanley is Visiting Assistant Professor of Theater at Bucknell University, Lewisburg, Pennsylvania; she is the author of "Nina Vance," in *The Handbook of Texas,* 3rd ed. (Texas State Historical Association, 1996) and "Ford Foundation Begins a Program to Fund Nonprofit Theaters," in *Great Events in History II: Arts and Culture,* 2nd ed. (Salem Press, 1993), and has published numerous theater reviews.

Monique Stavenuiter received her Ph.D. from the University of Groningen and is a researcher at the University of Nijenrode, the Netherlands; she is the author of *Ouderen En De Leuensloop* (Zwolle: Waanders, 1993), co-author of *Lange Levens, Stille Getuigen* (Zutphen: Walburg Pers, 1994), and co-editor of the *Dutch Yearbook of Women's History (Jaarboek voor Vrouwengeschiedenis).*

Paula A. Steib worked as a freelance writer in Kaneohe, Hawaii, and London, England, where she also served as an editor for the U.S. Navy.

David R. Stevenson was Associate Professor of History at the University of Nebraska at Kearney; he was author of "David Hume, Historicist," in *The Historian* 52 (Feb. 1990), "Vico's Sciencza Nuova: An Alternative to the Enlightenment Mainstream," in *The Quest for the New Science: Language and Thought in Eighteenth Century Science* (eds. Karl J. Fink and James W. Marchand, Southern Illinois University Press, 1979), and numerous other works on modern intellectual history. He died in 1997.

Hugh A. Stewart, M.A., Guelph, Ontario, Canada, has worked as an Associate Corporate Freelance Writer.

Kearsley A. Stewart, a lecturer in the Women's Studies Program and Department of Anthropology at the University of Georgia, Athens, Georgia, is author of "Challenging Stereotypes: Teaching about HIV/AIDS in Africa," in *Teaching Africa: African Studies in a New Millennium* (Lynne Rienner Publishers, 1998) and other publications on women's health in Africa; she is also a Medical Anthropologist with the Faculty of Medicine at Emory University on a clinical research project to improve patient adherence to the new drug therapies for HIV/AIDS.

Christine Stolba is a Ph.D. candidate in history at Emory University, Atlanta, Georgia, and the co-author, with Diana Furchtgott-Roth, of *Women's Figures: The Economic Progress of Women in America* (American Enterprise Institute and The Independent Women's Forum, 1996).

Carla Stoner is a freelance writer in American literature.

Margaret M. Storey is Assistant Professor of History at DePaul University, Chicago, Illinois, and works on the history of Southern unionists during the American Civil War.

Ginger Strand, Ph.D. (Princeton University), has taught English and Humanities at Princeton and Columbia Universities and is a freelance writer and consultant in New York City.

Darlene M. Suarez is a freelance writer whose publications include "Oral History Interview with Jane Dumas, Kumeyaay Indian Elder/Herbalist," in *Women's Times* (November 1993) and "Cigarette and Alcohol Use among Migrant Hispanic Adolescents," in *Journal of Family and Cummunity Health* (January 1994).

Joan E. Supplee is Associate Professor of History and Director of Latin American Studies at Baylor University, Waco, Texas, and author of "Women and the Counterrevolution in Chile," in *Women and Revolution in Africa, Asia, and the New World* (University of South Carolina Press, 1994) and "'Agua a Vino': "Recusos publicos y ganacias privadas en Mendoza, Argentina," in *Siglo XIX* II:5 (febrero 1993) and "Wine and Wine-making in Argentina," in *Encyclopedia of Latin American History* (Scribners, 1996); she has written other articles on Argentine economic history and women in Chile.

Denise Sutherland is a freelance writer in Canberra, Australia, who has worked with the Australian Science Archives Project.

Andrew Swenson is a freelance writer in Michigan whose publications include "Vampirism in Gogol's Short Fiction," in *Slavic and East European Journal* (37.4, Winter 1993) and "Demons, Dualities, and Other Developments: Lermontov's Metaphysical Statement in 'The Demon,'" in *Graduate Essays on Slavic Languages and Literatures* (1989).

Emily Taitz is Adjunct Professor of Women's Studies at Adelphi University, Garden City, New York, and author of *The Jews of Medieval France: The Community of Champagne* (Greenwood, 1994) and "Kol Ishah: The Voice of Women in Medieval Europe," in *Daughter of the King* (JPS, 1992); she is also co-author of *Remarkable Jewish Women* (JPS, 1996) and *Written Out of History: Jewish Foremothers* (Biblio Press, 1980; reprints

1985, 1990, 1996), as well as several young-adult biographies.

Sarolta A. Takács is Associate Professor of the Classics at Harvard University, Cambridge, Massachusetts.

C. Anita Tarr is Assistant Professor of English at Illinois State University in Normal, Illinois; her teachings and publications focus primarily on children's and young-adult literature like *Peter Pan, Johnny Tremain,* and *The Yearling,* but also include Virginia Woolf and Ernest Hemingway.

B. Kim Taylor, author of *The Great New York City Trivia and Fact Book* (Cumberland House, 1998), is a freelance writer and CD-ROM scriptwriter based in New York City.

JoAnne Thomas is Instructor of History and Women's Studies and a Ph.D. candidate at Western Michigan University; she is author of "Cosmetics and Beauty Industry" and "Dress Reform," in *Ready Reference: Women's Issues* (ed. Margaret McFadden, Salem Press, 1997), and researches popular music of the Civil War.

Ileana Tozzi, D. Litt., is a secondary school teacher in Rieti, Italy, and member of Società Italiana delle Storiche and Deputazione di Storia Patria; she is the author of *Bellezza Orsini: Cronaca di un processo per stregoneria* (1990), *Petronilla Paolini Massimi: Una donna in Arcadia* (1991), *Foemina in fabula: Gli stereotipi del femminile nella cultura popolare* (1991), *Colomba da Rieti: Una scelta di vita religiosa nella prima età moderna* (1996), and *Colomba da Rieti: Itinerari di religiosità femminile in Umbria* (1998).

Jean Truax, Ph.D., Medieval History, University of Houston, is an independent scholar.

Sherrie Tucker is a freelance writer and jazz disc jockey in the San Francisco Bay Area, California; her publications include "The Politics of Impermanence: Effects of World War Two on All-Woman Bands," in *Hot Wire: The Journal of Women's Music and Culture* and "Where the Blues and the Truth Lay Hiding: Rememory of Jazz in Black Women's Fiction," in *Frontiers, A Journal of Women's Studies* (Vol. XIII, no. 2, 1993).

Mark Vajcner is Assistant Archivist at the University of Alberta, Edmonton, Canada, and the author of "Stuart Garson and the Manitoba Progressive Coalition," in *Manitoba History* (Vol. 26, Autumn 1993).

Laga Van Beek is a Ph.D. candidate at Brigham Young University, Provo, Utah, co-author of "The Mormon Practice of Plural Marriage: The Social Construction of Religious Identity and Commitment," in *Sex, Lies and Sanctity: Religion and Deviance in Contemporary North America* (JAI Press, 1995) and "How Common the Principle?: Women as Plural Wives in 1860," in *Dialogue: A Journal of Mormon Thought* (Vol. 26, 1993), and was a consultant for the video "Utah Women Reconsidered, 1896–1996."

Jaime B. Veneracion is Chair of the Department of History at the University of the Philippines, Diliman, Quezon City, Philippines, whose works include *Kasaysayan ng Bulakan* (1986), *Merit and/or Patronage: A History of the Philippine Civil Service* (1983), and *Malolos: The Legacy of Its Past* (1981).

Wanda Wakefield has served as an adjunct lecturer at SUNY College at Brockport and Millard Fillmore College, SUNY University at Buffalo; she served as associate editor and reviewer for *Southern Historian,* and is co-author of "After the Riots of 1964: Community Response to the Housing Situation," in *Afro-Americans in New York Life and History* (Summer 1994).

Sherry Nanninga Walker received her M.A. in Biblical Studies from the Iliff School of Theology and is Adjunct Instructor in the Education and Developmental Studies Division of Pikes Peak Community College, Colorado Springs, Colorado; she is also a freelance writer in the fields of religion and women's religious history.

Linda Walton is an attorney and freelance writer based in Grosse Pointe Shores, Michigan.

Harry M. Ward is William Binford Vest Professor of History at the University of Richmond, Richmond, Virginia, and the author of a dozen books including *Colonial America: 1607–1763* (Prentice Hall, 1991), *American Revolution: Nationhood Achieved, 1763–1788* (St. Martin's Press, 1995), and *General William Maxwell and the New Jersey Continentals* (Greenwood Press, 1997); his next book is a social history of the American Revolution (London, England: University of London Press).

Stephen Webre is Professor of History at Louisiana Tech University, Ruston, Louisiana, and specializes in colonial and modern Spanish American history; he is the author of publications including *José Napoleón Duarte and the Christian Democratic Party in Salvadoran Politics, 1960–1972* (Louisiana State University Press, 1979) and *La sociedad colonial en Guatemala: Estudios locales y regionales* (Antigua, Guatemala: CIRMA, 1989), and numerous scholarly articles.

Gregory Weeks is a freelance writer living in Austria whose publications include "Der Traum von einem Deutsch-Mittelafrikanischen Reich, 1933–1943," in *Geschichte und Gegenwart* (3/95), and "Nazis Ban Emil Nolde" and "Group 47 Formed in Germany," in *Great Events from History II: Arts and Culture* (Salem Press, 1993).

Lisa S. Weitzman, a graduate of Yale University and the Johns Hopkins University School of Advanced International Studies, is a Russian trade specialist. She serves as a trustee for a large public library system outside Cleveland, Ohio. A freelance writer, she has contributed to Gale's *Contemporary Black Biography* and to a variety of local publications.

Thomas Whigham is Professor of Latin American History at the University of Georgia, Athens, Georgia, and has twice served as Fulbright Scholar in South America; he is a proponent of Argentine, Paraguayan, and Brazilian studies in the United States, and author of works including *The Politics of River Trade: Tradition and Development in the Upper Plata, 1780–1870* (University of New Mexico Press, 1991). Whigham is currently writing a study of the 1864–1870 Paraguayan War, and has served as an advisor to the U.S. State Department.

Inga Wiehl is a native of Denmark who teaches English at Yakima Valley Community College, Yakima, Washington; she has published articles on Scandinavian writers in a variety of journals and lectured on Scandinavian literature throughout the state on behalf of the Washington Commission for the Humanities.

John Hoyt Williams is Distinguished Professor of Arts and Sciences at Indiana State University, Terre Haute, Indiana, and author of *Sam Houston: A Biography of the Father of Texas* (Simon and Shuster, 1993).

Laura Wimberley is an independent scholar best known for her work on the history of the Edwards Aquifer and articles about historical water problems; she earned her Ph.D. at Texas A&M University with specializations in American environmental history, the social history of the American West, and Texas water history.

Kelly Winters is a freelance writer and author of *A Guide to Nature and Outdoor Adventures on Long Island* (Side Roads Press, 1999). Having hiked the Appalachian Trail from Georgia to Maine and having written about the trek in *Walking Home,* she is currently at work on a book about people who have gone on endurance treks that changed their lives.

Lisa Wolffe, Ph.D., is Assistant Professor at Louisiana Scholar's College, Natchitoches, Louisiana, and a freelance history writer.

Marivic Wyndham, Ph.D., is the author of *Eleanor Dark: A World-Proof Life* (Australian National University, 1995).

Laura York received her B.A. in history from the University of California, San Diego (1992), and her M.A. in history from the University of California, Riverside (1998); her research interests include Early Modern Europe and the history of women and gender in the West.

Hoda M. Zaki is Associate Professor of Political Science at Hood College, Frederick, Maryland.

GENEAOLOGICAL CHARTS

Designed to show the relation of ancestors to descendants, the following genealogical charts are family trees that begin with the original rulers on the highest branch. From this extends a lower branch that shows their children and those whom their children married (when known). The next branch shows their children's children and corresponding spouses (when known), and so on.

Charts are grouped alphabetically by country, and headings for each country are located at the top of every chart. Each chart displays a House Title, which identifies the name of the ruling house.

The following symbols and abbreviations are used:

| indicates the descent of children

= indicates marriage, liaison, or other intimate relationship

⋮ indicates illegitimate descent of children

m. indicates marriage

(1) indicates first wife or husband

(2) indicates second wife or husband

(3) indicates third wife or husband (etc.)

(illeg.) illegitimate

Women whose names appear in bold on the charts have entries in the Women in World History series.

The House of Saxe-Coburg
(1831–)

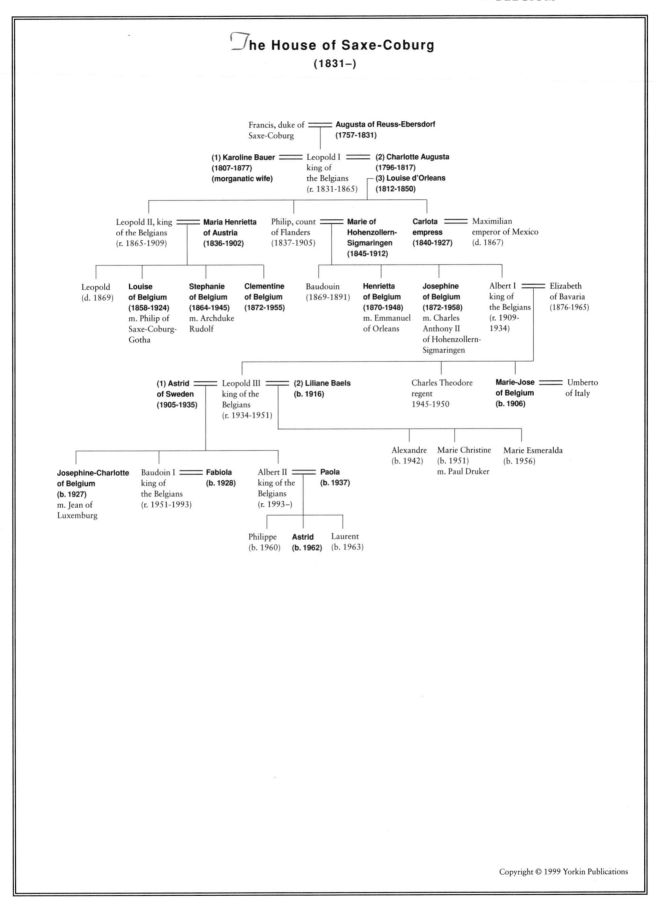

Francis, duke of ══ **Augusta of Reuss-Ebersdorf**
Saxe-Coburg   **(1757-1831)**

(1) Karoline Bauer ══ Leopold I ══ **(2) Charlotte Augusta**
(1807-1877)   king of   **(1796-1817)**
(morganatic wife)   the Belgians ── **(3) Louise d'Orleans**
                         (r. 1831-1865) **(1812-1850)**

Leopold II, king ══ **Maria Henrietta**   Philip, count ══ **Marie of**   **Carlota** ══ Maximilian
of the Belgians   **of Austria**   of Flanders   **Hohenzollern-** **empress**   emperor of Mexico
(r. 1865-1909)   **(1836-1902)**   (1837-1905)   **Sigmaringen**   **(1840-1927)** (d. 1867)
                                                            (1845-1912)

Leopold   **Louise**   **Stephanie**   **Clementine**   Baudouin   **Henrietta**   **Josephine**   Albert I ══ Elizabeth
(d. 1869)   **of Belgium**   **of Belgium**   **of Belgium**   (1869-1891)   **of Belgium**   **of Belgium**   king of   of Bavaria
             (1858-1924)   **(1864-1945)**   **(1872-1955)**   **(1870-1948)**   **(1872-1958)**   the Belgians (1876-1965)
             m. Philip of   m. Archduke   m. Emmanuel   m. Charles   (r. 1909-
             Saxe-Coburg-   Rudolf   of Orleans   Anthony II   1934)
             Gotha   of Hohenzollern-
                                                                                                        Sigmaringen

(1) Astrid ══ Leopold III ══ **(2) Liliane Baels**   Charles Theodore   **Marie-Jose** ══ Umberto
of Sweden   king of the   **(b. 1916)**   regent   **of Belgium**   of Italy
(1905-1935)   Belgians   1945-1950   **(b. 1906)**
                   (r. 1934-1951)

                                                           Alexandre   Marie Christine   Marie Esmeralda
                                                           (b. 1942)   (b. 1951)   (b. 1956)
                                                                        m. Paul Druker

Josephine-Charlotte   Baudoin I ══ **Fabiola**   Albert II ══ **Paola**
of Belgium   king of   **(b. 1928)** king of the   **(b. 1937)**
(b. 1927)   the Belgians   Belgians
m. Jean of   (r. 1951-1993)   (r. 1993–)
Luxemburg

                                                      Philippe   **Astrid**   Laurent
                                                      (b. 1960)   **(b. 1962)**   (b. 1963)

The House of Saxe-Coburg-Gotha
(1887–1946)

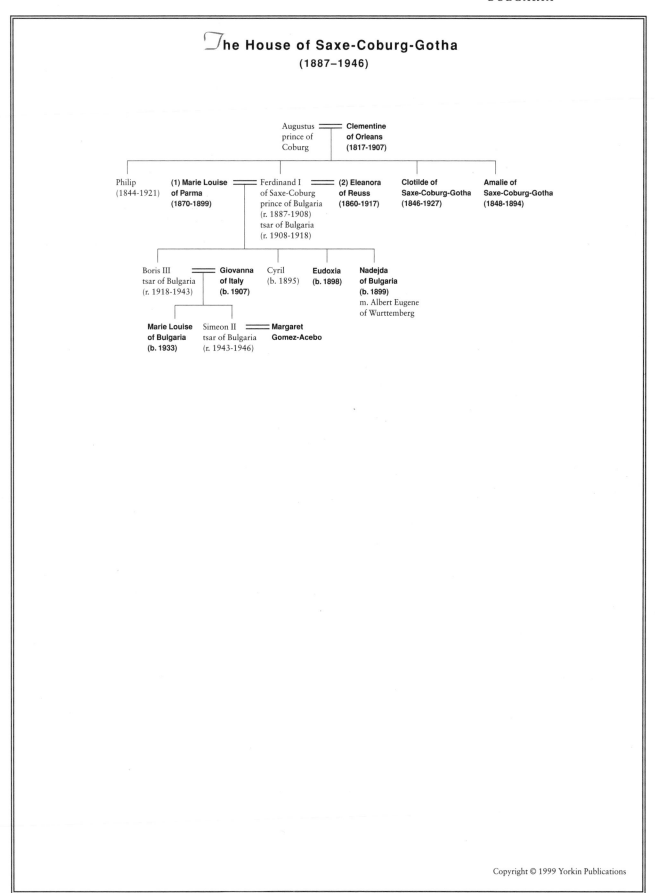

Augustus prince of Coburg ═══ **Clementine of Orleans (1817-1907)**

Philip (1844-1921)

(1) Marie Louise of Parma (1870-1899) ═══ Ferdinand I of Saxe-Coburg prince of Bulgaria (r. 1887-1908) tsar of Bulgaria (r. 1908-1918) ═══ **(2) Eleanora of Reuss (1860-1917)**

Clotilde of Saxe-Coburg-Gotha (1846-1927)

Amalie of Saxe-Coburg-Gotha (1848-1894)

Boris III tsar of Bulgaria (r. 1918-1943) ═══ **Giovanna of Italy (b. 1907)**

Cyril (b. 1895)

Eudoxia (b. 1898)

Nadejda of Bulgaria (b. 1899) m. Albert Eugene of Wurttemberg

Marie Louise of Bulgaria (b. 1933)

Simeon II tsar of Bulgaria (r. 1943-1946) ═══ **Margaret Gomez-Acebo**

ℰmpresses & Emperors of Byzantium

REIGN	EMPRESS OR EMPEROR	SPOUSE
306-337	Constantine I the Great	Fausta (d. 324)
337-361	Constantius II	Galla (fl. 320)
		Eusebia of Macedonia (fl. 300 CE)
		Faustina of Antioch
361-363	Julian	Helena (c. 320-?)
363-364	Jovian	Charito
364-378	Valens	Albia Domnica
379-395	Theodosius I the Spaniard	Flaccilla (c. 355–386) and Galla (c. 365–394)
395-408	Arcadius	Eudocia of Byzantium (r. 400-404)
408-450	Theodosius II the Calligrapher	Eudocia (c. 400-460)
	Pulcheria (c. 398-453) sister of and joint ruler with emperor Theodosius II	
450-457	Marcian	Pulcheria (c. 398-453)
457-474	Leo I	Verina (fl. 437-483)
474	Leo II	
474-491	Zeno the Isaurian	Ariadne (fl. 457-515)
491-518	Anastasius I [Anastasios I]	Ariadne (fl. 457-515)
518-527	Justin I [Flavius Justinus]	Lupicinia-Euphemia (d. 523)
527-565	Justinian I, the Great	Theodora (c. 500-548)
565-578	Justin II [Flavius Justinus]	Sophia (c. 525-after 600)
	administered affairs of empire jointly with Tiberius II Constantine	
578-582	Tiberius II Constantine	Ino-Anastasia
582-602	Maurice Tiberius [Mauritius]	Constantina (fl. 582-602)
602-610	Phocas I [Phokas I]	Leontia (fl. 602-610)
610-641	Heraclius I [Herakleios I] of Carthage	Fabia-Eudocia (fl. 600s)
		Martina
641	Heraclonas-Constantine	Gregoria-Anastasia
641	Heraclonas II [Heracleon; Heraklonas]	unmarried
641-668	Constantine III [Constans II]	Fausta (fl. 600s)
668-685	Constantine IV [Pogonatus]	Anastasia (fl. 600s)
685-695 and		
705-711	Justinian II Rhinotmetos	Eudocia (fl. 700s)
		Theodora of the Khazars (fl. 700s)
695-698	Leontius II [Leontios]	unknown
698-705	Tiberius III Apsimar	unknown
711-713	Philippikos Vardan [Philippicus]	unknown
713-715	Anastasius II Artemius	Irene (fl. 700s)
715-717	Theodosius III	unknown
717-741	Leo III the Iconoclast	Maria (fl. 700s)
741-775	Constantine V [Kopronymus]	Irene of the Khazars (d. 750?)
		Maria (fl. 700s)
		Eudocia (fl. 700s)
775-780	Leo IV the Khazar	Irene of Athens (c. 752-803)
780-797	Constantine VI [Porphyrogenitus]	Maria of Amnia (fl. 782)
		Theodote (fl. 795)
780-790	**Irene of Athens (c. 752-803)** regent and co-emperor	
792-797	**Irene of Athens (c. 752-803)** co-emperor	
797-802	**Irene of Athens (c. 752-803)**	
802-811	Nicephorus I	unknown
811	Stauracius [Stavrakios]	Theophano of Athens
811-813	Michael I Rhangabé	Prokopia (fl. 800s)
813-820	Leo V Gnuni the Armenian	Barca-Theodosia
820-829	Michael II of Amorion	Thecla (fl. 800s)
		Euphrosyne (fl. 800s)
829-842	Theophilos I [Theophilus]	Theodora the Blessed (fl. 842-856)
842-867	Michael III the Drunkard	Eudocia Decapolita (fl. 800s)
842-866	Bardas	
867	Theophilus II	
867-886	Basil I the Macedonian	Maria of Macedonia
		Eudocia Ingerina (fl. 800s)
886-912	Leo VI the Wise	St. Theophano (866-893)
		Zoe Zautzina (c. 870-c. 899)
		Eudocia Baiane (d. 902)
		Zoe Carbopsina (c. 890-920)
912-913	Alexander [III]	unknown
913-959	Constantine VII Porphyrogenetos	Helena Lekapena (c. 920-961)
919-944	Romanus I Lecapenus	Theodora (early 900s)
959-963	Romanus II	Bertha-Eudocia the Frank
		Theophano (c. 940-?)
963-969	Nicephoros II Phocas	Theophano (c. 940-?)
969-976	John I Tzimisces	Theodora (late 900s)
976-1025	Basil II the Bulgar Slayer	unmarried
1025-1028	Constantine VIII	Helena of Alypia

REIGN	EMPRESS OR EMPEROR	SPOUSE
1028-1050	**Zöe Porphyrogenita (980-1050)**	Romanus III Argyrus
1028-1034	**Zöe Porphyrogenita (980-1050)**	(co-emperor) Romanus III Argyrus
1034-1041	**Zöe Porphyrogenita (980-1050)**	Michael IV Paphlagonian
1041-1042	Michael V Kalaphates	unknown (probably unmarried)
1042-1050	**Zöe Porphyrogenita (980-1050)**	(co-emperor) Constantine IX Monomachus
1050-1056	**Theodora Porphyrogenita (c. 989-1056)**	unmarried
1056-1057	Michael VI Bringas	unknown
1057-1059	Isaac I Comnenus	**Catherine of Bulgaria (fl. 1050)**
1059-1067	Constantine X Ducas	**Eudocia Macrembolitissa (1021-1096)**
1067	**Eudocia Macrembolitissa (1021-1096)**	
1068-1071	Romanus IV Diogenes	**Eudocia Macrembolitissa (1021-1096)**
1071-1078	Michael VII Ducas	**Maria of Alania (fl. 1070-1081)**
1078-1081	Nicephorus III Botaneiates	**Verdenia**
		Maria of Alania (fl. 1070-1081)
1081-1118	Alexius I Comnenus [Alexios I Komnenos]	**Irene Ducas (c. 1066-1133)**
1118-1143	John II Comnenus	**Priska-Irene of Hungary (c. 1085-1133)**
1143-1180	Manuel I Comnenus	**Bertha-Irene of Sulzbach (d. 1161)**
		Marie of Antioch (fl. 1180-1183)
1180-1183	Alexius II Comnenus	**Agnes-Anne of France (b. 1171)**
1183-1185	Andronicus I Comnenus	**Agnes-Anne of France (b. 1171)**
1185-1195	Isaac II Angelus [Angelos-Comnenus]	**Margaret-Mary of Hungary (c. 1177-?)**
1195-1203	Alexius III Angelus	**Euphrosyne (d. 1203)**
1203-1204	Isaac II Angelus [restored]	
1203-1204	Alexius IV Angelus	unmarried
1204	Alexius V Ducas Mourtzouphlos	**Eudocia Angelina (fl. 1204)**

In April 1204, when Crusaders and Venetians attacked the imperial palace in Constantinople, thousands were killed and the emperor, Alexius V, fled. The conquerors crowned a Latin emperor, Baldwin of Flanders. Shortly after, a young Byzantine noble, Theodore Lascaris, organized a government-in-exile 40 miles away across the Straits of Nicaea. These Nicaean emperors—Theodore and his successors—are considered by some to have continued the Byzantine line.

Nicaean emperors

1204-1222	Theodore I Lascaris	**Anna Angelina (d. 1210?)**
		Philippa of Lesser Armenia
		Marie de Courtenay (fl. 1215)
1222-1254	John III Ducas Vatatzes	**Irene Lascaris (fl. 1222-1235)**
		Constance-Anna of Hohenstaufen
1254-1258	Theodore II Lascaris	**Helen Asen of Bulgaria (d. 1255?)**
1258-1261	John IV Lascaris	unmarried
1261-1282	Michael VIII Paleologus [Palaiologos]	**Theodora Ducas (c. 1200s)**
1282-1328	Andronicus II Paleologus	**Anna of Hungary (d. around 1284)**
		Irene of Montferrat (fl. 1300)
1328-1341	Andronicus III Paleologus	**Irene of Brunswick (fl. 1300s)**
		Anne of Savoy (c. 1320-1353)
1341-1347	John V Paleologus	**Helena Cantacuzene (fl. 1340s)**
1347-1354	John VI Cantacuzene [Kantakouzenos]	**Irene Asen**
1355-1391	John V Paleologus (restored)	**Helena Cantacuzene (fl. 1340s)**
1376-1379	Andronicus IV Paleologus	**Maria-Kyratza Asen**
1390	John VII Paleologus	**Eugenia Gattilusi**
1391-1425	Manuel II Paleologus	**Helena Dragas (fl. 1400)**
1425-1448	John VIII Paleologus	**Anna of Moscow (1393-1417)**
		Sophie of Montferrat
		Maria of Trebizond (d. 1439)
1448-1453	Constantine XI Paleologus	**Magdalena-Theodora Tocco**
		Caterina Gattilusi

The Byzantine empire—an empire that had endured for over 1,000 years—ceased to exist on May 29, 1453, when the Turks "scaled the walls."

Latin emperors (in Constantinople)

1204-1205	Baldwin I of Constantinople	**Marie of Champagne (c. 1180-1203)**
	(also known as Baldwin IX; count of Flanders & Hainault)	
1205-1216	Henry	
1216-1217	Peter de Courtenay	**Yolande of Courtenay (d. 1219)**
1218-1228	Robert de Courtenay	
1228-1261	Baldwin II of Constantinople	

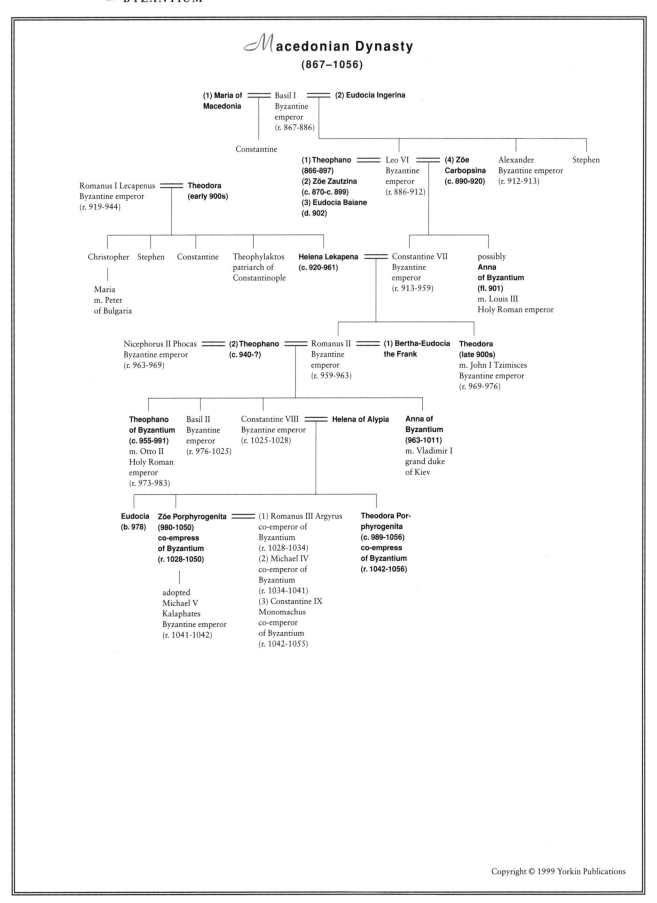

Macedonian Dynasty
(867–1056)

(1) Maria of Macedonia ══ Basil I Byzantine emperor (r. 867-886) ══ **(2) Eudocia Ingerina**

Constantine

(1) Theophano (866-897) ══ Leo VI Byzantine emperor (r. 886-912) ══ **(4) Zöe Carbopsina (c. 890-920)**   Alexander Byzantine emperor (r. 912-913)   Stephen
(2) Zöe Zautzina (c. 870-c. 899)
(3) Eudocia Baiane (d. 902)

Romanus I Lecapenus Byzantine emperor (r. 919-944) ══ **Theodora (early 900s)**

Christopher   Stephen   Constantine   Theophylaktos patriarch of Constantinople   **Helena Lekapena (c. 920-961)** ══ Constantine VII Byzantine emperor (r. 913-959)   possibly **Anna of Byzantium (fl. 901)** m. Louis III Holy Roman emperor

Maria m. Peter of Bulgaria

Nicephorus II Phocas Byzantine emperor (r. 963-969) ══ **(2) Theophano (c. 940-?)** ══ Romanus II Byzantine emperor (r. 959-963) ══ **(1) Bertha-Eudocia the Frank**   **Theodora (late 900s)** m. John I Tzimisces Byzantine emperor (r. 969-976)

Theophano of Byzantium (c. 955-991) m. Otto II Holy Roman emperor (r. 973-983)   Basil II Byzantine emperor (r. 976-1025)   Constantine VIII Byzantine emperor (r. 1025-1028) ══ **Helena of Alypia**   **Anna of Byzantium (963-1011)** m. Vladimir I grand duke of Kiev

Eudocia (b. 978)   **Zöe Porphyrogenita (980-1050) co-empress of Byzantium (r. 1028-1050)** ══ (1) Romanus III Argyrus co-emperor of Byzantium (r. 1028-1034) (2) Michael IV co-emperor of Byzantium (r. 1034-1041) (3) Constantine IX Monomachus co-emperor of Byzantium (r. 1042-1055)   **Theodora Por-phyrogenita (c. 989-1056) co-empress of Byzantium (r. 1042-1056)**

adopted Michael V Kalaphates Byzantine emperor (r. 1041-1042)

The Comneni & Angeli
(1057–1204)

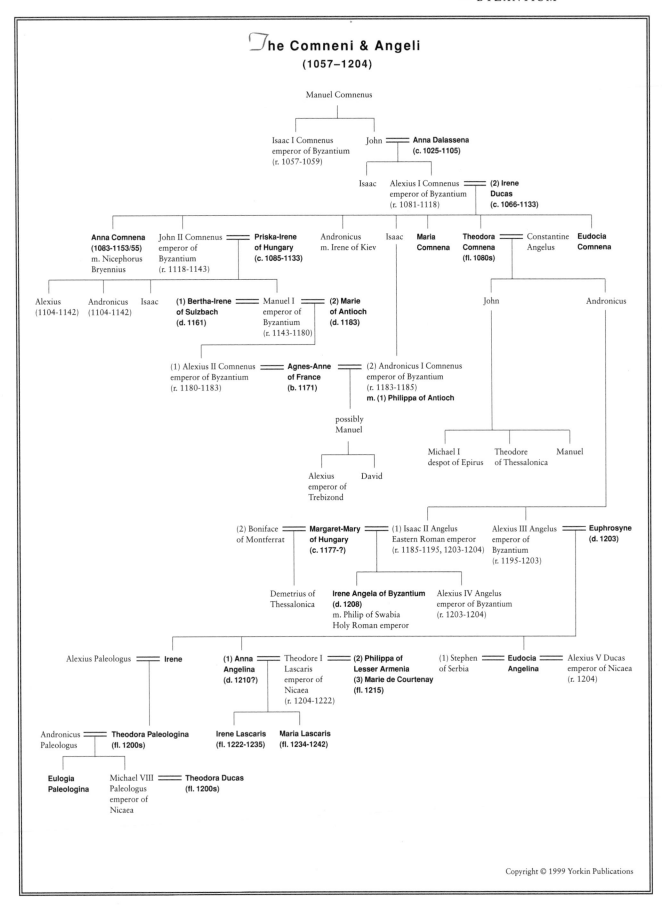

Manuel Comnenus

Isaac I Comnenus
emperor of Byzantium
(r. 1057-1059)

John === **Anna Dalassena**
(c. 1025-1105)

Isaac

Alexius I Comnenus === **(2) Irene**
emperor of Byzantium **Ducas**
(r. 1081-1118) **(c. 1066-1133)**

Anna Comnena
(1083-1153/55)
m. Nicephorus
Bryennius

John II Comnenus === **Priska-Irene**
emperor of **of Hungary**
Byzantium **(c. 1085-1133)**
(r. 1118-1143)

Andronicus
m. Irene of Kiev

Isaac

Maria
Comnena

Theodora === Constantine **Eudocia**
Comnena Angelus **Comnena**
(fl. 1080s)

Alexius
(1104-1142)

Andronicus
(1104-1142)

Isaac

(1) Bertha-Irene === Manuel I === **(2) Marie**
of Sulzbach emperor of **of Antioch**
(d. 1161) Byzantium **(d. 1183)**
(r. 1143-1180)

John

Andronicus

(1) Alexius II Comnenus === **Agnes-Anne** === (2) Andronicus I Comnenus
emperor of Byzantium **of France** emperor of Byzantium
(r. 1180-1183) **(b. 1171)** (r. 1183-1185)
m. (1) Philippa of Antioch

possibly
Manuel

Alexius
emperor of
Trebizond

David

Michael I
despot of Epirus

Theodore
of Thessalonica

Manuel

(2) Boniface === **Margaret-Mary** === (1) Isaac II Angelus
of Montferrat **of Hungary** Eastern Roman emperor
(c. 1177-?) (r. 1185-1195, 1203-1204)

Alexius III Angelus === **Euphrosyne**
emperor of **(d. 1203)**
Byzantium
(r. 1195-1203)

Demetrius of
Thessalonica

Irene Angela of Byzantium
(d. 1208)
m. Philip of Swabia
Holy Roman emperor

Alexius IV Angelus
emperor of Byzantium
(r. 1203-1204)

Alexius Paleologus === **Irene**

(1) Anna === Theodore I === **(2) Philippa of**
Angelina Lascaris **Lesser Armenia**
(d. 1210?) emperor of **(3) Marie de Courtenay**
Nicaea **(fl. 1215)**
(r. 1204-1222)

(1) Stephen === **Eudocia** === Alexius V Ducas
of Serbia **Angelina** emperor of Nicaea
(r. 1204)

Andronicus === **Theodora Paleologina**
Paleologus **(fl. 1200s)**

Irene Lascaris
(fl. 1222-1235)

Maria Lascaris
(fl. 1234-1242)

Eulogia
Paleologina

Michael VIII === **Theodora Ducas**
Paleologus **(fl. 1200s)**
emperor of
Nicaea

The Dynasty of the Ducas
(1059–1078)

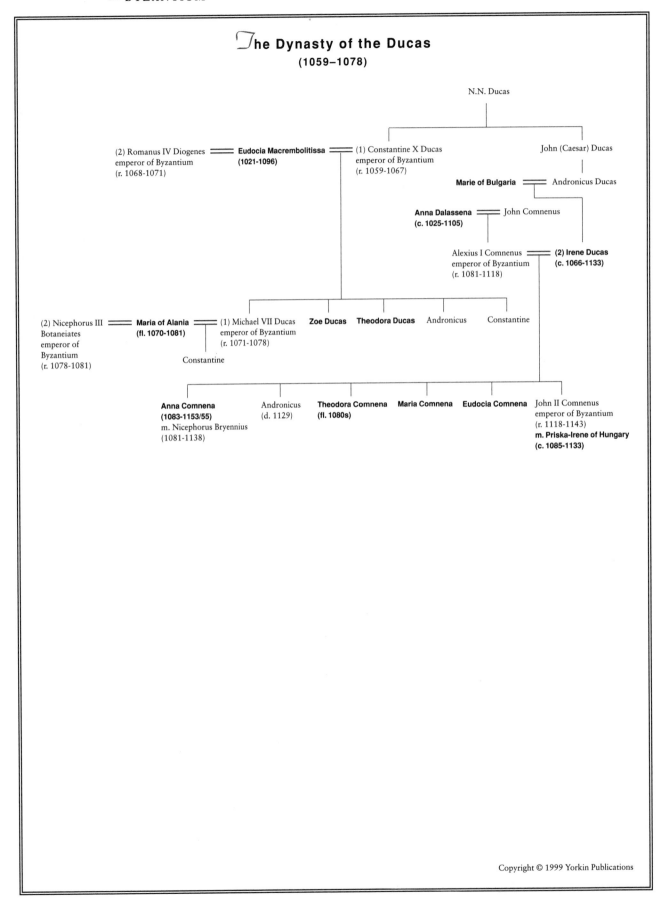

N.N. Ducas

(2) Romanus IV Diogenes
emperor of Byzantium
(r. 1068-1071)

Eudocia Macrembolitissa
(1021-1096)

(1) Constantine X Ducas
emperor of Byzantium
(r. 1059-1067)

John (Caesar) Ducas

Marie of Bulgaria

Andronicus Ducas

Anna Dalassena
(c. 1025-1105)

John Comnenus

Alexius I Comnenus
emperor of Byzantium
(r. 1081-1118)

(2) Irene Ducas
(c. 1066-1133)

(2) Nicephorus III
Botaneiates
emperor of
Byzantium
(r. 1078-1081)

Maria of Alania
(fl. 1070-1081)

(1) Michael VII Ducas
emperor of Byzantium
(r. 1071-1078)

Zoe Ducas   **Theodora Ducas**   Andronicus   Constantine

Constantine

Anna Comnena
(1083-1153/55)
m. Nicephorus Bryennius
(1081-1138)

Andronicus
(d. 1129)

Theodora Comnena
(fl. 1080s)

Maria Comnena

Eudocia Comnena

John II Comnenus
emperor of Byzantium
(r. 1118-1143)
m. Priska-Irene of Hungary
(c. 1085-1133)

The Dynasty of the Lascarids
(1204–1261)

```
(1) Anna Angelina ═══ Theodore I Lascaris ═══ (2) Philippa
(d. 1210?)            Nicaean emperor            of Lesser Armenia
                      (r. 1204-1222)             (3) Marie de Courtenay
                                                 (fl. 1215)

   Marie Lascaris      (1) Irene Lascaris ═══ John III Ducas Vatatzes ═══ (2) Constance-Anna
   (fl. 1234-1242)     (fl. 1222-1225)        Nicaean emperor                of Hohenstaufen
   m. Bela IV                                 (r. 1222-1254)
   of Hungary
              Helen Asen ═══ Theodore II Lascaris              Basil Vatatzes
              of Bulgaria     Nicaean emperor                        |
                             (r. 1254-1258)                    Isaac Ducas
                                                                     |
   Irene Lascaris      Maria ═══ Nicephorus I   John IV Lascaris    John
   (d. around 1270)              of Epirus       Nicaean emperor          |
   m. Constantine Tich                           (r. 1258-1261)    Theodora Ducas
                                                                   m. Michael VIII
                                                                   Paleologus
```

The Paleologi Family
(1260–1453)

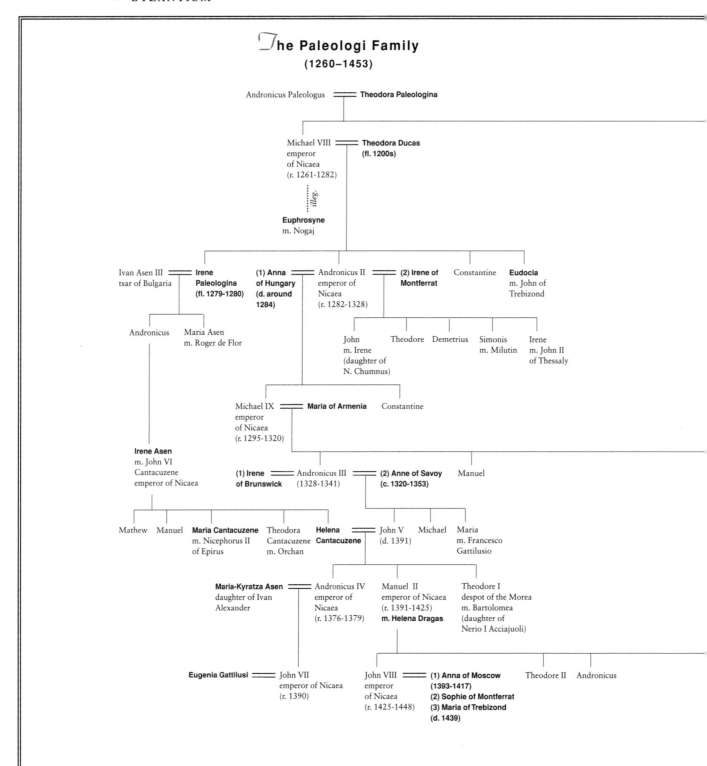

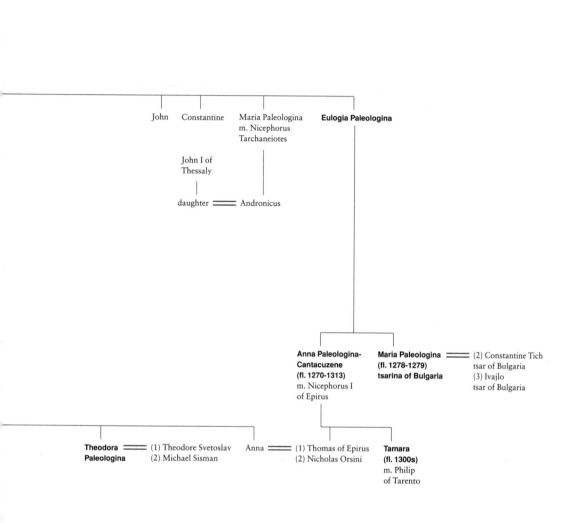

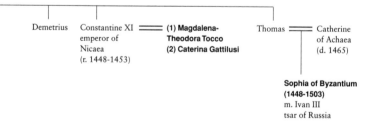

Bohemia: The House of Premyslid
(900–1000?)

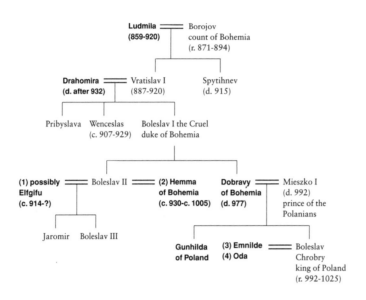

Ludmila
(859-920)
═══ Borojov
count of Bohemia
(r. 871-894)

Drahomira ═══ Vratislav I
(d. after 932)   (887-920)

Spytihnev
(d. 915)

Pribyslava   Wenceslas   Boleslav I the Cruel
(c. 907-929)   duke of Bohemia

(1) possibly ═══ Boleslav II ═══ (2) Hemma
Elfgifu   of Bohemia
(c. 914-?)   (c. 930-c. 1005)

Dobravy ═══ Mieszko I
of Bohemia   (d. 992)
(d. 977)   prince of the
              Polanians

Jaromir   Boleslav III

Gunhilda   (3) Emnilde ═══ Boleslav
of Poland   (4) Oda   Chrobry
                             king of Poland
                             (r. 992-1025)

Bohemia: The House of Premyslid
(1198–1378)

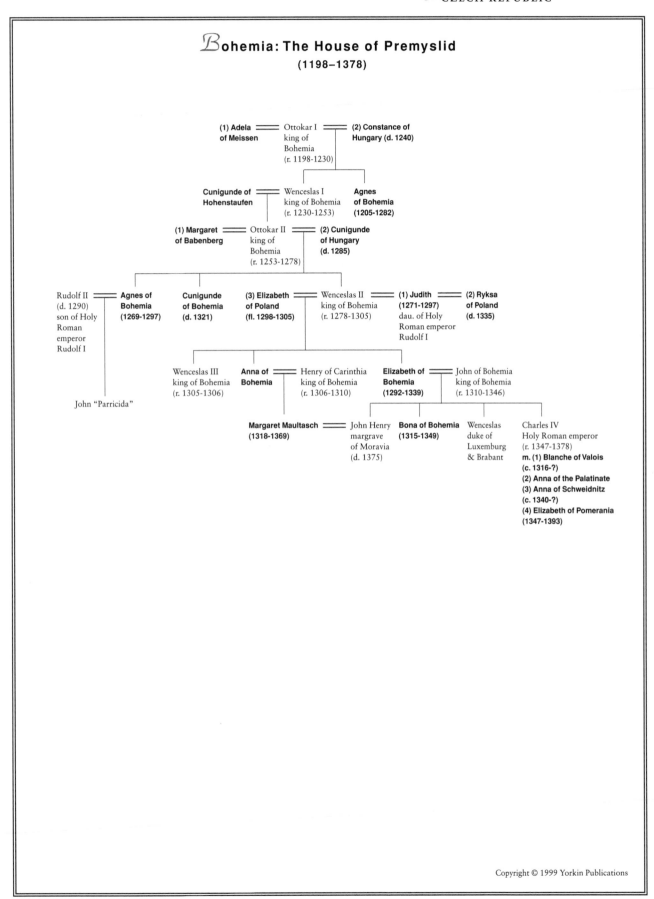

The Descendants of Waldemar the Great

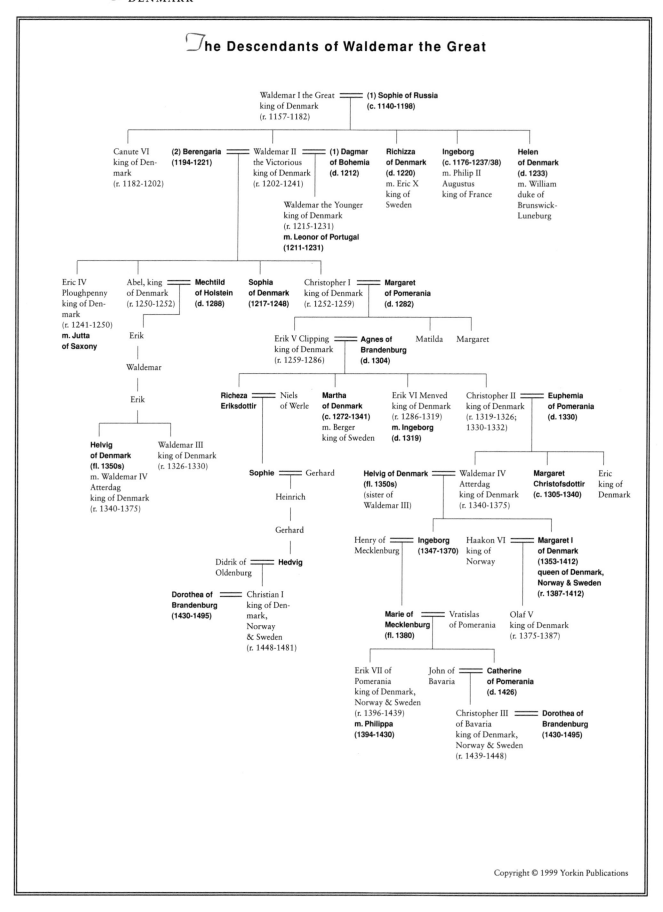

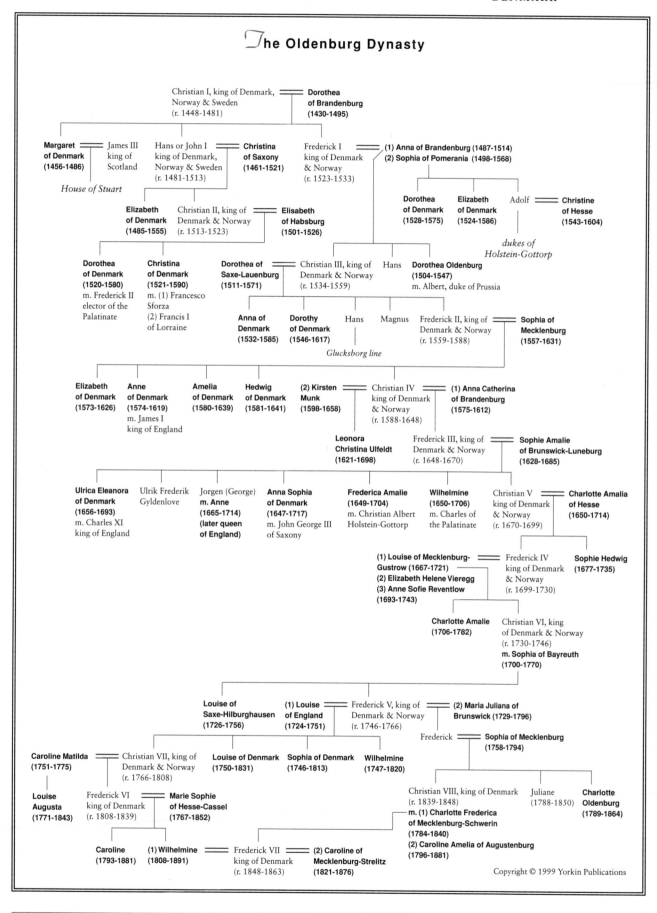

The Oldenburg Dynasty

Christian I, king of Denmark, Norway & Sweden (r. 1448-1481) === **Dorothea of Brandenburg (1430-1495)**

Margaret of Denmark (1456-1486) === James III king of Scotland

House of Stuart

Hans or John I king of Denmark, Norway & Sweden (r. 1481-1513) === **Christina of Saxony (1461-1521)**

Frederick I king of Denmark & Norway (r. 1523-1533) === **(1) Anna of Brandenburg (1487-1514)** / **(2) Sophia of Pomerania (1498-1568)**

Dorothea of Denmark (1528-1575)   **Elizabeth of Denmark (1524-1586)**   Adolf === **Christine of Hesse (1543-1604)**

dukes of Holstein-Gottorp

Elizabeth of Denmark (1485-1555)   Christian II, king of Denmark & Norway (r. 1513-1523) === **Elisabeth of Habsburg (1501-1526)**

Dorothea of Denmark (1520-1580) m. Frederick II elector of the Palatinate

Christina of Denmark (1521-1590) m. (1) Francesco Sforza (2) Francis I of Lorraine

Dorothea of Saxe-Lauenburg (1511-1571) === Christian III, king of Denmark & Norway (r. 1534-1559)   Hans   **Dorothea Oldenburg (1504-1547)** m. Albert, duke of Prussia

Anna of Denmark (1532-1585)   **Dorothy of Denmark (1546-1617)**   Hans   Magnus   Frederick II, king of Denmark & Norway (r. 1559-1588) === **Sophia of Mecklenburg (1557-1631)**

Glucksborg line

Elizabeth of Denmark (1573-1626)   **Anne of Denmark (1574-1619)** m. James I king of England   **Amelia of Denmark (1580-1639)**   **Hedwig of Denmark (1581-1641)**   **(2) Kirsten Munk (1598-1658)** === Christian IV king of Denmark & Norway (r. 1588-1648) === **(1) Anna Catherina of Brandenburg (1575-1612)**

Leonora Christina Ulfeldt (1621-1698)   Frederick III, king of Denmark & Norway (r. 1648-1670) === **Sophie Amalie of Brunswick-Luneburg (1628-1685)**

Ulrica Eleanora of Denmark (1656-1693) m. Charles XI king of England   Ulrik Frederik Gyldenlove   Jorgen (George) **m. Anne (1665-1714) (later queen of England)**   **Anna Sophia of Denmark (1647-1717)** m. John George III of Saxony   **Frederica Amalie (1649-1704)** m. Christian Albert Holstein-Gottorp   **Wilhelmine (1650-1706)** m. Charles of the Palatinate   Christian V king of Denmark & Norway (r. 1670-1699) === **Charlotte Amalia of Hesse (1650-1714)**

(1) Louise of Mecklenburg-Gustrow (1667-1721) / **(2) Elizabeth Helene Vieregg** / **(3) Anne Sofie Reventlow (1693-1743)** === Frederick IV king of Denmark & Norway (r. 1699-1730)   **Sophie Hedwig (1677-1735)**

Charlotte Amalie (1706-1782)   Christian VI, king of Denmark & Norway (r. 1730-1746) **m. Sophia of Bayreuth (1700-1770)**

Louise of Saxe-Hilburghausen (1726-1756)   **(1) Louise of England (1724-1751)** === Frederick V, king of Denmark & Norway (r. 1746-1766) === **(2) Maria Juliana of Brunswick (1729-1796)**

Frederick === **Sophia of Mecklenburg (1758-1794)**

Caroline Matilda (1751-1775) === Christian VII, king of Denmark & Norway (r. 1766-1808)   **Louise of Denmark (1750-1831)**   **Sophia of Denmark (1746-1813)**   **Wilhelmine (1747-1820)**

Louise Augusta (1771-1843)   Frederick VI king of Denmark (r. 1808-1839) === **Marie Sophie of Hesse-Cassel (1767-1852)**

Christian VIII, king of Denmark (r. 1839-1848) **m. (1) Charlotte Frederica of Mecklenburg-Schwerin (1784-1840)** / **(2) Caroline Amelia of Augustenburg (1796-1881)**   **Juliane (1788-1850)**   **Charlotte Oldenburg (1789-1864)**

Caroline (1793-1881)   **(1) Wilhelmine (1808-1891)** === Frederick VII king of Denmark (r. 1848-1863) === **(2) Caroline of Mecklenburg-Strelitz (1821-1876)**

The Danish Royal House
(1699–)

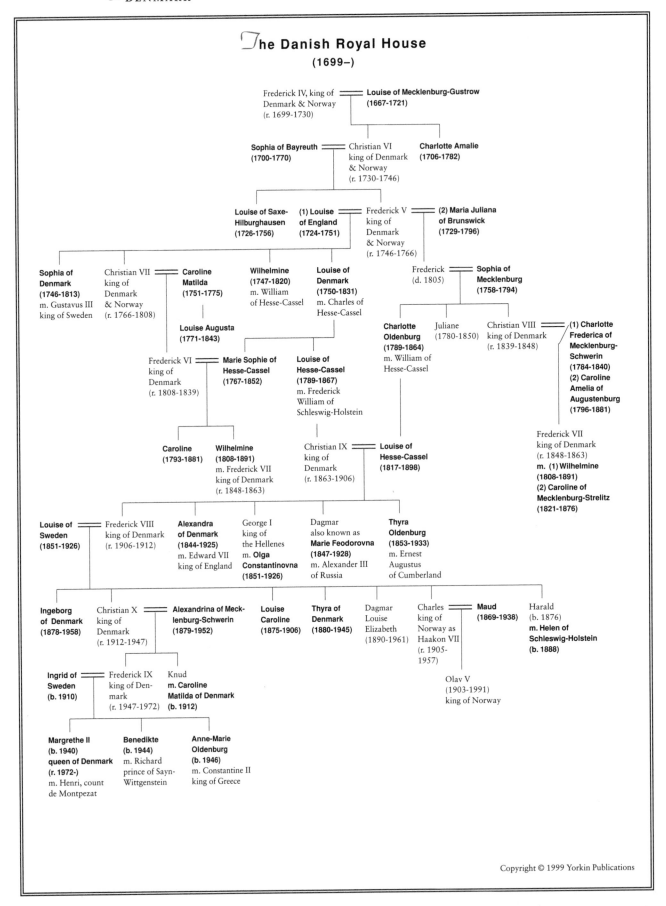

Frederick IV, king of Denmark & Norway (r. 1699-1730) ══ **Louise of Mecklenburg-Gustrow (1667-1721)**

Sophia of Bayreuth (1700-1770) ══ Christian VI king of Denmark & Norway (r. 1730-1746) **Charlotte Amalie (1706-1782)**

Louise of Saxe-Hilburghausen (1726-1756) **(1) Louise of England (1724-1751)** ══ Frederick V king of Denmark & Norway (r. 1746-1766) ══ **(2) Maria Juliana of Brunswick (1729-1796)**

Sophia of Denmark (1746-1813) m. Gustavus III king of Sweden

Christian VII king of Denmark & Norway (r. 1766-1808) ══ **Caroline Matilda (1751-1775)**

Wilhelmine (1747-1820) m. William of Hesse-Cassel

Louise of Denmark (1750-1831) m. Charles of Hesse-Cassel

Frederick (d. 1805) ══ **Sophia of Mecklenburg (1758-1794)**

Louise Augusta (1771-1843)

Frederick VI king of Denmark (r. 1808-1839) ══ **Marie Sophie of Hesse-Cassel (1767-1852)**

Louise of Hesse-Cassel (1789-1867) m. Frederick William of Schleswig-Holstein

Charlotte Oldenburg (1789-1864) m. William of Hesse-Cassel

Juliane (1780-1850)

Christian VIII king of Denmark (r. 1839-1848) ══ **(1) Charlotte Frederica of Mecklenburg-Schwerin (1784-1840) (2) Caroline Amelia of Augustenburg (1796-1881)**

Caroline (1793-1881)

Wilhelmine (1808-1891) m. Frederick VII king of Denmark (r. 1848-1863)

Christian IX king of Denmark (r. 1863-1906) ══ **Louise of Hesse-Cassel (1817-1898)**

Frederick VII king of Denmark (r. 1848-1863) m. (1) Wilhelmine (1808-1891) (2) Caroline of Mecklenburg-Strelitz (1821-1876)

Louise of Sweden (1851-1926) ══ Frederick VIII king of Denmark (r. 1906-1912)

Alexandra of Denmark (1844-1925) m. Edward VII king of England

George I king of the Hellenes m. **Olga Constantinovna (1851-1926)**

Dagmar also known as **Marie Feodorovna (1847-1928)** m. Alexander III of Russia

Thyra Oldenburg (1853-1933) m. Ernest Augustus of Cumberland

Ingeborg of Denmark (1878-1958)

Christian X king of Denmark (r. 1912-1947) ══ **Alexandrina of Mecklenburg-Schwerin (1879-1952)**

Louise Caroline (1875-1906)

Thyra of Denmark (1880-1945)

Dagmar Louise Elizabeth (1890-1961)

Charles king of Norway as Haakon VII (r. 1905-1957) ══ **Maud (1869-1938)**

Harald (b. 1876) **m. Helen of Schleswig-Holstein (b. 1888)**

Ingrid of Sweden (b. 1910) ══ Frederick IX king of Denmark (r. 1947-1972)

Knud **m. Caroline Matilda of Denmark (b. 1912)**

Olav V (1903-1991) king of Norway

Margrethe II (b. 1940) queen of Denmark (r. 1972-) m. Henri, count de Montpezat

Benedikte (b. 1944) m. Richard prince of Sayn-Wittgenstein

Anne-Marie Oldenburg (b. 1946) m. Constantine II king of Greece

Copyright © 1999 Yorkin Publications

𝒫tolemaic Dynasty
(Greek Epoch)

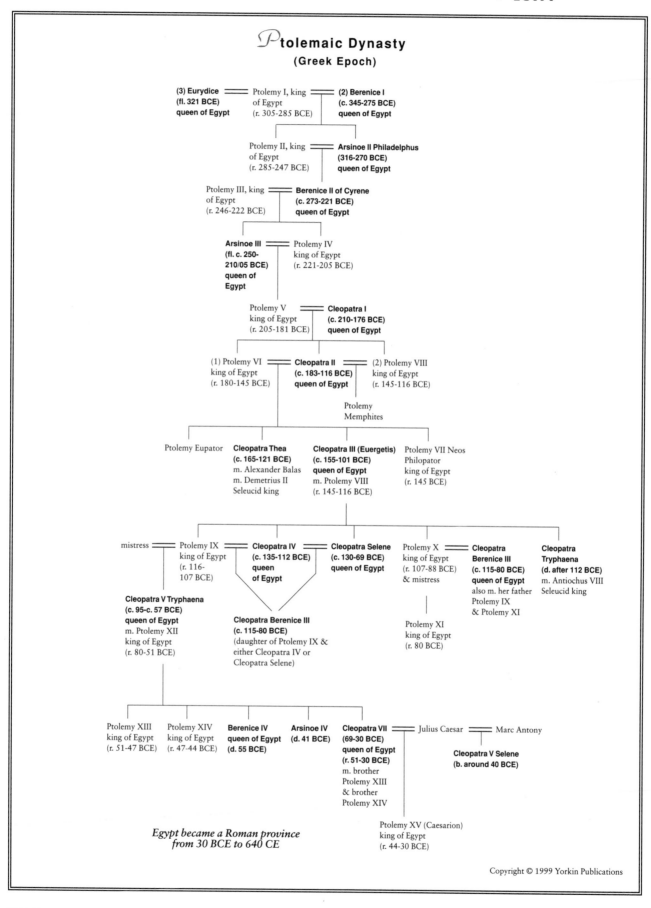

(3) Eurydice ══ Ptolemy I, king ══ **(2) Berenice I**
(fl. 321 BCE) of Egypt **(c. 345-275 BCE)**
queen of Egypt (r. 305-285 BCE) **queen of Egypt**

Ptolemy II, king ══ **Arsinoe II Philadelphus**
of Egypt **(316-270 BCE)**
(r. 285-247 BCE) **queen of Egypt**

Ptolemy III, king ══ **Berenice II of Cyrene**
of Egypt **(c. 273-221 BCE)**
(r. 246-222 BCE) **queen of Egypt**

Arsinoe III ══ Ptolemy IV
(fl. c. 250- king of Egypt
210/05 BCE) (r. 221-205 BCE)
queen of
Egypt

Ptolemy V ══ **Cleopatra I**
king of Egypt **(c. 210-176 BCE)**
(r. 205-181 BCE) **queen of Egypt**

(1) Ptolemy VI ══ **Cleopatra II** ══ **(2) Ptolemy VIII**
king of Egypt **(c. 183-116 BCE)** king of Egypt
(r. 180-145 BCE) **queen of Egypt** (r. 145-116 BCE)

Ptolemy
Memphites

Ptolemy Eupator | **Cleopatra Thea** | **Cleopatra III (Euergetis)** | Ptolemy VII Neos
| **(c. 165-121 BCE)** | **(c. 155-101 BCE)** | Philopator
| m. Alexander Balas | **queen of Egypt** | king of Egypt
| m. Demetrius II | m. Ptolemy VIII | (r. 145 BCE)
| Seleucid king | (r. 145-116 BCE) |

mistress ══ Ptolemy IX ══ **Cleopatra IV** ══ **Cleopatra Selene** | Ptolemy X ══ **Cleopatra** | **Cleopatra**
king of Egypt **(c. 135-112 BCE)** **(c. 130-69 BCE)** | king of Egypt **Berenice III** | **Tryphaena**
(r. 116- **queen** **queen of Egypt** | (r. 107-88 BCE) **(c. 115-80 BCE)** | **(d. after 112 BCE)**
107 BCE) **of Egypt** | & mistress **queen of Egypt** | m. Antiochus VIII
| also m. her father | Seleucid king
Cleopatra V Tryphaena Ptolemy IX
(c. 95-c. 57 BCE) **Cleopatra Berenice III** & Ptolemy XI
queen of Egypt **(c. 115-80 BCE)**
m. Ptolemy XII (daughter of Ptolemy IX & Ptolemy XI
king of Egypt either Cleopatra IV or king of Egypt
(r. 80-51 BCE) Cleopatra Selene) (r. 80 BCE)

Ptolemy XIII Ptolemy XIV **Berenice IV** **Arsinoe IV** **Cleopatra VII** ══ Julius Caesar ══ Marc Antony
king of Egypt king of Egypt **queen of Egypt** **(d. 41 BCE)** **(69-30 BCE)**
(r. 51-47 BCE) (r. 47-44 BCE) **(d. 55 BCE)** **queen of Egypt** **Cleopatra V Selene**
(r. 51-30 BCE) **(b. around 40 BCE)**
m. brother
Ptolemy XIII
& brother
Ptolemy XIV

Egypt became a Roman province
from 30 BCE to 640 CE

Ptolemy XV (Caesarion)
king of Egypt
(r. 44-30 BCE)

Copyright © 1999 Yorkin Publications

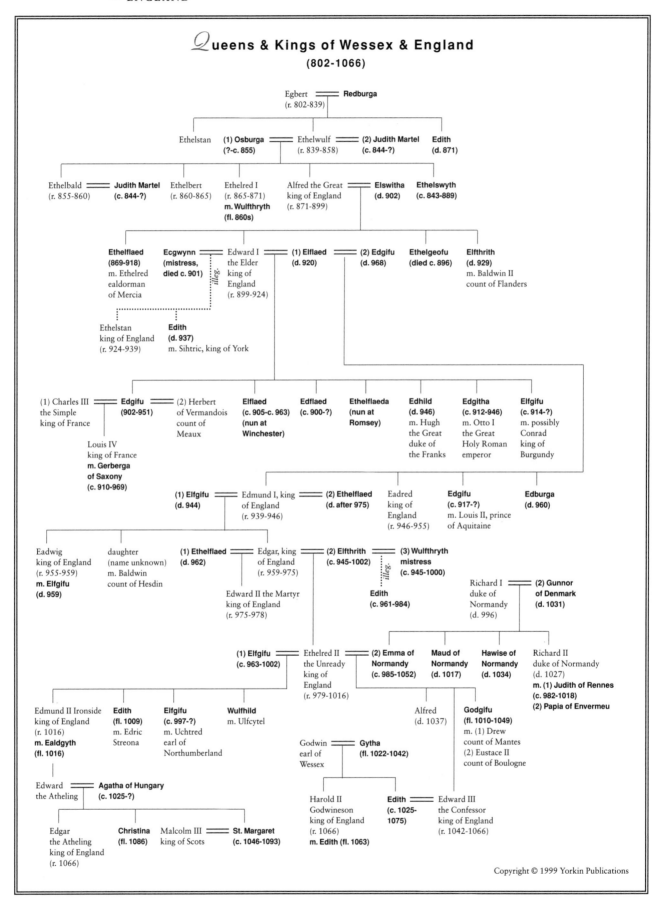

Queens & Kings of Wessex & England
(802-1066)

Egbert
(r. 802-839) ═══ Redburga

Ethelstan | (1) Osburga (?-c. 855) ═══ Ethelwulf (r. 839-858) ═══ (2) Judith Martel (c. 844-?) | Edith (d. 871)

Ethelbald (r. 855-860) ═══ Judith Martel (c. 844-?) | Ethelbert (r. 860-865) | Ethelred I (r. 865-871) m. Wulfthryth (fl. 860s) | Alfred the Great king of England (r. 871-899) ═══ Elswitha (d. 902) | Ethelswyth (c. 843-889)

Ethelflaed (869-918) m. Ethelred ealdorman of Mercia | Ecgwynn (mistress, died c. 901) ═══ Edward I the Elder king of England (r. 899-924) ═══ (1) Elflaed (d. 920) ═══ (2) Edgifu (d. 968) | Ethelgeofu (died c. 896) | Elfthrith (d. 929) m. Baldwin II count of Flanders

illeg.

Ethelstan king of England (r. 924-939) | Edith (d. 937) m. Sihtric, king of York

(1) Charles III the Simple king of France ═══ Edgifu (902-951) ═══ (2) Herbert of Vermandois count of Meaux | Elflaed (c. 905-c. 963) (nun at Winchester) | Edflaed (c. 900-?) | Ethelflaeda (nun at Romsey) | Edhild (d. 946) m. Hugh the Great duke of the Franks | Edgitha (c. 912-946) m. Otto I the Great Holy Roman emperor | Elfgifu (c. 914-?) m. possibly Conrad king of Burgundy

Louis IV king of France m. Gerberga of Saxony (c. 910-969)

(1) Elfgifu (d. 944) ═══ Edmund I, king of England (r. 939-946) ═══ (2) Ethelflaed (d. after 975) | Eadred king of England (r. 946-955) | Edgifu (c. 917-?) m. Louis II, prince of Aquitaine | Edburga (d. 960)

Eadwig king of England (r. 955-959) m. Elfgifu (d. 959) | daughter (name unknown) m. Baldwin count of Hesdin | (1) Ethelflaed (d. 962) ═══ Edgar, king of England (r. 959-975) ═══ (2) Elfthrith (c. 945-1002) ═══ (3) Wulfthryth mistress (c. 945-1000)

Edward II the Martyr king of England (r. 975-978) | Edith (c. 961-984)

illeg.

Richard I duke of Normandy (d. 996) ═══ (2) Gunnor of Denmark (d. 1031)

(1) Elfgifu (c. 963-1002) ═══ Ethelred II the Unready king of England (r. 979-1016) ═══ (2) Emma of Normandy (c. 985-1052) | Maud of Normandy (d. 1017) | Hawise of Normandy (d. 1034) | Richard II duke of Normandy (d. 1027) m. (1) Judith of Rennes (c. 982-1018) (2) Papia of Envermeu

Edmund II Ironside king of England (r. 1016) m. Ealdgyth (fl. 1016) | Edith (fl. 1009) m. Edric Streona | Elfgifu (c. 997-?) m. Uchtred earl of Northumberland | Wulfhild m. Ulfcytel | Alfred (d. 1037) | Godgifu (fl. 1010-1049) m. (1) Drew count of Mantes (2) Eustace II count of Boulogne

Edward the Atheling ═══ Agatha of Hungary (c. 1025-?)

Godwin earl of Wessex ═══ Gytha (fl. 1022-1042)

Edgar the Atheling king of England (r. 1066) | Christina (fl. 1086) | Malcolm III king of Scots ═══ St. Margaret (c. 1046-1093)

Harold II Godwineson king of England (r. 1066) m. Edith (fl. 1063) | Edith (c. 1025-1075) ═══ Edward III the Confessor king of England (r. 1042-1066)

Copyright © 1999 Yorkin Publications

Danish Queens & Kings of England
(1013–1066)

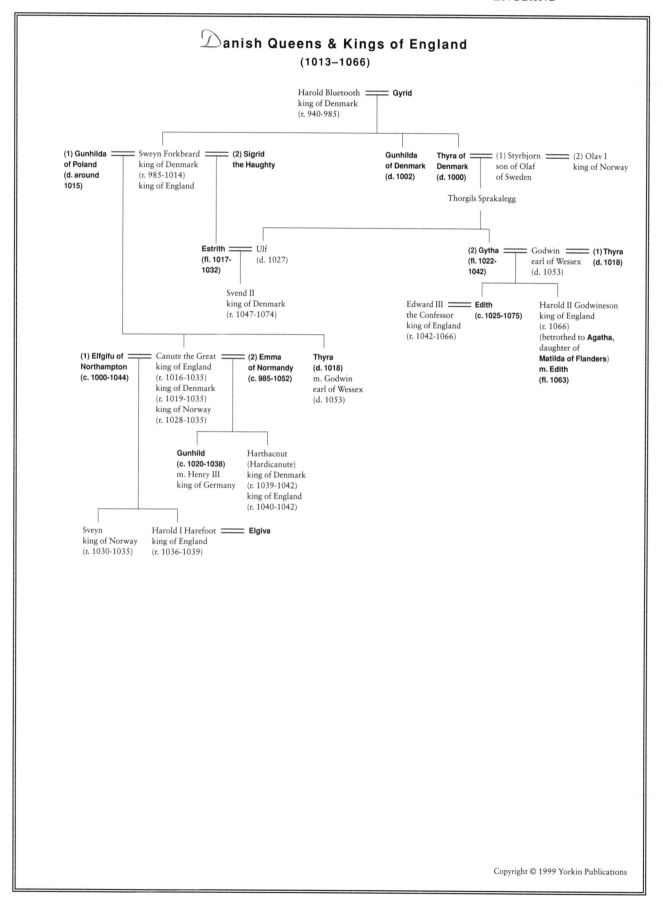

Harold Bluetooth
king of Denmark
(r. 940-985) ═══ **Gyrid**

**(1) Gunhilda
of Poland
(d. around
1015)** ═══ Sweyn Forkbeard
king of Denmark
(r. 985-1014)
king of England ═══ **(2) Sigrid
the Haughty**

**Gunhilda
of Denmark
(d. 1002)**

**Thyra of
Denmark
(d. 1000)** ═══ (1) Styrbjorn
son of Olaf
of Sweden ═══ (2) Olav I
king of Norway

Thorgils Sprakalegg

**Estrith
(fl. 1017-
1032)** ═══ Ulf
(d. 1027)

**(2) Gytha
(fl. 1022-
1042)** ═══ Godwin
earl of Wessex
(d. 1053) ═══ **(1) Thyra
(d. 1018)**

Svend II
king of Denmark
(r. 1047-1074)

Edward III
the Confessor
king of England
(r. 1042-1066) ═══ **Edith
(c. 1025-1075)**

Harold II Godwineson
king of England
(r. 1066)
(betrothed to **Agatha**,
daughter of
Matilda of Flanders)
**m. Edith
(fl. 1063)**

**(1) Elfgifu of
Northampton
(c. 1000-1044)** ═══ Canute the Great
king of England
(r. 1016-1035)
king of Denmark
(r. 1019-1035)
king of Norway
(r. 1028-1035) ═══ **(2) Emma
of Normandy
(c. 985-1052)**

**Thyra
(d. 1018)**
m. Godwin
earl of Wessex
(d. 1053)

**Gunhild
(c. 1020-1038)**
m. Henry III
king of Germany

Harthacnut
(Hardicanute)
king of Denmark
(r. 1039-1042)
king of England
(r. 1040-1042)

Sveyn
king of Norway
(r. 1030-1035)

Harold I Harefoot
king of England
(r. 1036-1039) ═══ **Elgiva**

The Normans & Angevins

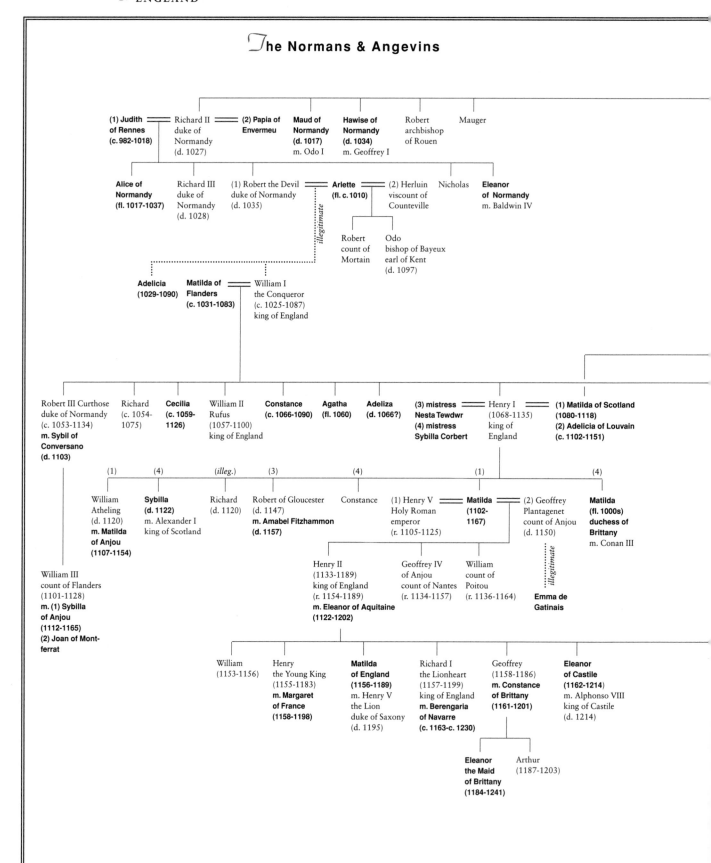

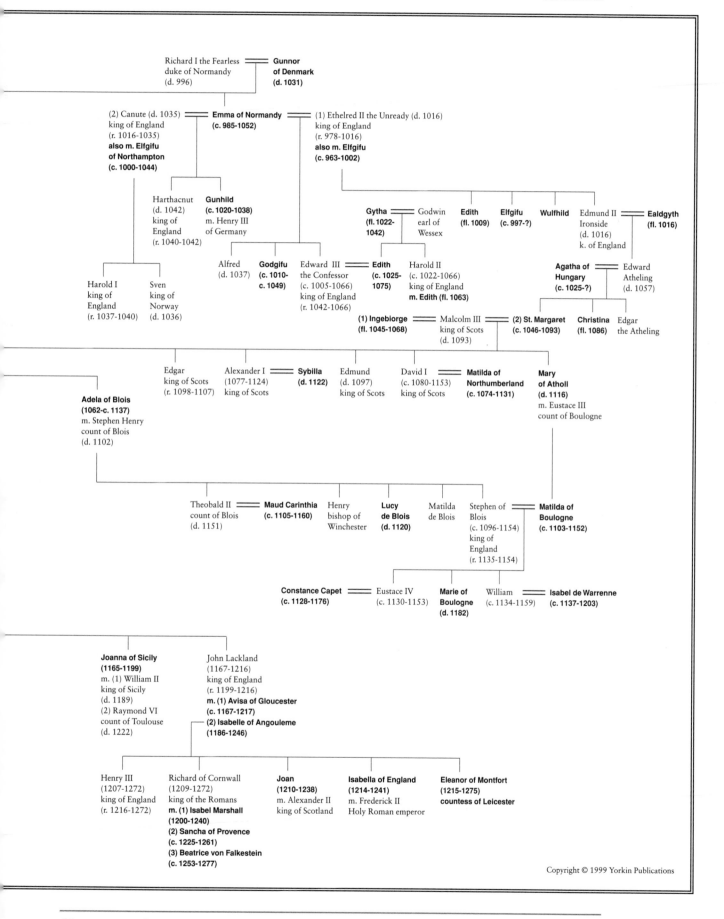

Richard I the Fearless
duke of Normandy
(d. 996)
═══ **Gunnor
of Denmark
(d. 1031)**

(2) Canute (d. 1035)
king of England
(r. 1016-1035)
**also m. Elfgifu
of Northampton
(c. 1000-1044)** ═══ **Emma of Normandy
(c. 985-1052)** ═══ (1) Ethelred II the Unready (d. 1016)
king of England
(r. 978-1016)
**also m. Elfgifu
(c. 963-1002)**

Harthacnut
(d. 1042)
king of
England
(r. 1040-1042)

**Gunhild
(c. 1020-1038)**
m. Henry III
of Germany

**Gytha
(fl. 1022-
1042)** ═══ Godwin
earl of
Wessex

**Edith
(fl. 1009)**

**Elfgifu
(c. 997-?)**

Wulfhild

Edmund II
Ironside
(d. 1016)
k. of England ═══ **Ealdgyth
(fl. 1016)**

Alfred
(d. 1037)

**Godgifu
(c. 1010-
c. 1049)**

Edward III
the Confessor
(c. 1005-1066)
king of England
(r. 1042-1066) ═══ **Edith
(c. 1025-
1075)**

Harold II
(c. 1022-1066)
king of England
m. Edith (fl. 1063)

**Agatha of
Hungary
(c. 1025-?)** ═══ Edward
Atheling
(d. 1057)

Harold I
king of
England
(r. 1037-1040)

Sven
king of
Norway
(d. 1036)

**(1) Ingeborge
(fl. 1045-1068)** ═══ Malcolm III
king of Scots
(d. 1093) ═══ **(2) St. Margaret
(c. 1046-1093)**

**Christina
(fl. 1086)**

Edgar
the Atheling

Edgar
king of Scots
(r. 1098-1107)

Alexander I
(1077-1124)
king of Scots ═══ **Sybilla
(d. 1122)**

Edmund
(d. 1097)
king of Scots

David I
(c. 1080-1153)
king of Scots ═══ **Matilda of
Northumberland
(c. 1074-1131)**

**Mary
of Atholl
(d. 1116)**
m. Eustace III
count of Boulogne

**Adela of Blois
(1062-c. 1137)**
m. Stephen Henry
count of Blois
(d. 1102)

Theobald II
count of Blois
(d. 1151) ═══ **Maud Carinthia
(c. 1105-1160)**

Henry
bishop of
Winchester

**Lucy
de Blois
(d. 1120)**

Matilda
de Blois

Stephen of
Blois
(c. 1096-1154)
king of
England
(r. 1135-1154) ═══ **Matilda of
Boulogne
(c. 1103-1152)**

Constance Capet
(c. 1128-1176) ═══ Eustace IV
(c. 1130-1153)

**Marie of
Boulogne
(d. 1182)**

William
(c. 1134-1159) ═══ **Isabel de Warrenne
(c. 1137-1203)**

**Joanna of Sicily
(1165-1199)**
m. (1) William II
king of Sicily
(d. 1189)
(2) Raymond VI
count of Toulouse
(d. 1222)

John Lackland
(1167-1216)
king of England
(r. 1199-1216)
**m. (1) Avisa of Gloucester
(c. 1167-1217)**
**(2) Isabelle of Angouleme
(1186-1246)**

Henry III
(1207-1272)
king of England
(r. 1216-1272)

Richard of Cornwall
(1209-1272)
king of the Romans
**m. (1) Isabel Marshall
(1200-1240)
(2) Sancha of Provence
(c. 1225-1261)
(3) Beatrice von Falkestein
(c. 1253-1277)**

**Joan
(1210-1238)**
m. Alexander II
king of Scotland

**Isabella of England
(1214-1241)**
m. Frederick II
Holy Roman emperor

**Eleanor of Montfort
(1215-1275)
countess of Leicester**

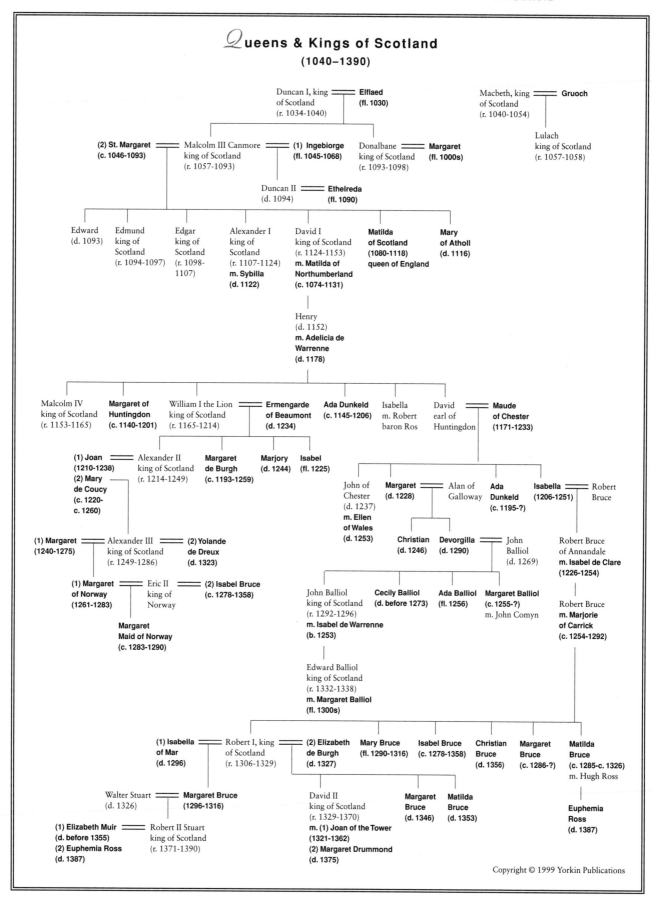

𝒬ueens & Kings of Scotland
(1040–1390)

Copyright © 1999 Yorkin Publications

The Plantagenets

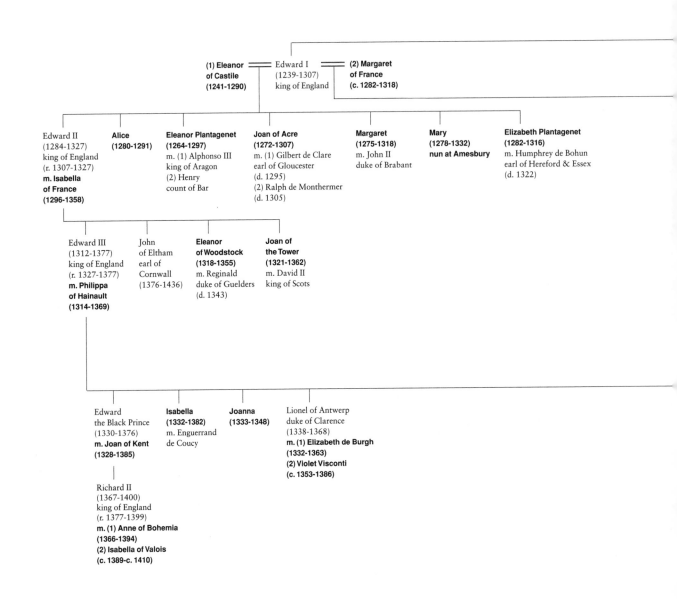

(1) Eleanor of Castile (1241-1290) ═══ Edward I (1239-1307) king of England ═══ **(2) Margaret of France (c. 1282-1318)**

Edward II (1284-1327) king of England (r. 1307-1327) **m. Isabella of France (1296-1358)**

Alice (1280-1291)

Eleanor Plantagenet (1264-1297) m. (1) Alphonso III king of Aragon (2) Henry count of Bar

Joan of Acre (1272-1307) m. (1) Gilbert de Clare earl of Gloucester (d. 1295) (2) Ralph de Monthermer (d. 1305)

Margaret (1275-1318) m. John II duke of Brabant

Mary (1278-1332) nun at Amesbury

Elizabeth Plantagenet (1282-1316) m. Humphrey de Bohun earl of Hereford & Essex (d. 1322)

Edward III (1312-1377) king of England (r. 1327-1377) **m. Philippa of Hainault (1314-1369)**

John of Eltham earl of Cornwall (1376-1436)

Eleanor of Woodstock (1318-1355) m. Reginald duke of Guelders (d. 1343)

Joan of the Tower (1321-1362) m. David II king of Scots

Edward the Black Prince (1330-1376) **m. Joan of Kent (1328-1385)**

Isabella (1332-1382) m. Enguerrand de Coucy

Joanna (1333-1348)

Lionel of Antwerp duke of Clarence (1338-1368) **m. (1) Elizabeth de Burgh (1332-1363) (2) Violet Visconti (c. 1353-1386)**

Richard II (1367-1400) king of England (r. 1377-1399) **m. (1) Anne of Bohemia (1366-1394) (2) Isabella of Valois (c. 1389-c. 1410)**

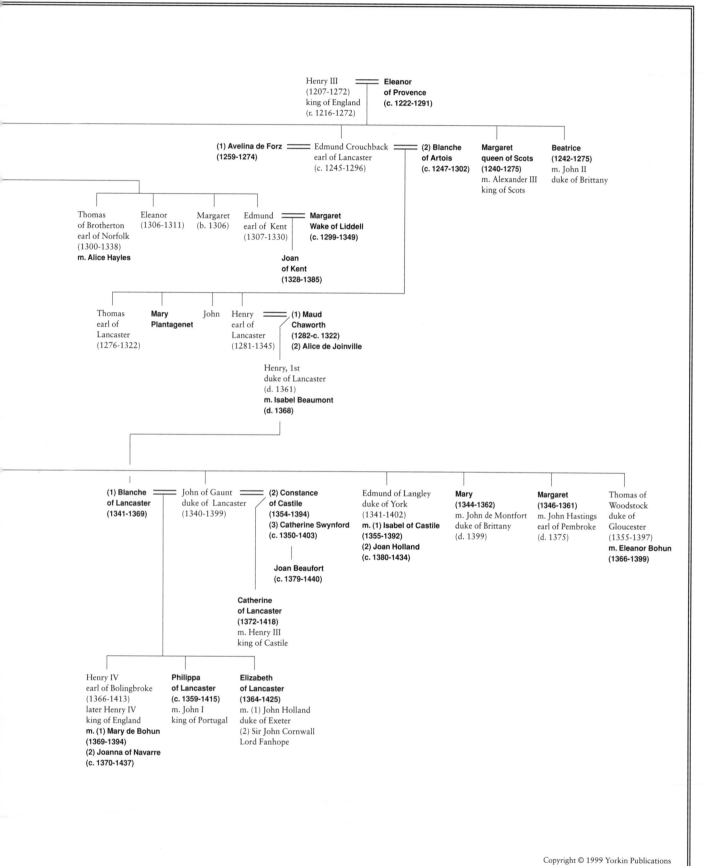

Henry III
(1207-1272)
king of England
(r. 1216-1272)

Eleanor
of Provence
(c. 1222-1291)

(1) Avelina de Forz
(1259-1274)

Edmund Crouchback
earl of Lancaster
(c. 1245-1296)

(2) Blanche
of Artois
(c. 1247-1302)

Margaret
queen of Scots
(1240-1275)
m. Alexander III
king of Scots

Beatrice
(1242-1275)
m. John II
duke of Brittany

Thomas
of Brotherton
earl of Norfolk
(1300-1338)
m. Alice Hayles

Eleanor
(1306-1311)

Margaret
(b. 1306)

Edmund
earl of Kent
(1307-1330)

Margaret
Wake of Liddell
(c. 1299-1349)

Joan
of Kent
(1328-1385)

Thomas
earl of
Lancaster
(1276-1322)

Mary
Plantagenet

John

Henry
earl of
Lancaster
(1281-1345)

(1) Maud
Chaworth
(1282-c. 1322)
(2) Alice de Joinville

Henry, 1st
duke of Lancaster
(d. 1361)
m. Isabel Beaumont
(d. 1368)

(1) Blanche
of Lancaster
(1341-1369)

John of Gaunt
duke of Lancaster
(1340-1399)

(2) Constance
of Castile
(1354-1394)
(3) Catherine Swynford
(c. 1350-1403)

Joan Beaufort
(c. 1379-1440)

Edmund of Langley
duke of York
(1341-1402)
m. (1) Isabel of Castile
(1355-1392)
(2) Joan Holland
(c. 1380-1434)

Mary
(1344-1362)
m. John de Montfort
duke of Brittany
(d. 1399)

Margaret
(1346-1361)
m. John Hastings
earl of Pembroke
(d. 1375)

Thomas of
Woodstock
duke of
Gloucester
(1355-1397)
m. Eleanor Bohun
(1366-1399)

Catherine
of Lancaster
(1372-1418)
m. Henry III
king of Castile

Henry IV
earl of Bolingbroke
(1366-1413)
later Henry IV
king of England
m. (1) Mary de Bohun
(1369-1394)
(2) Joanna of Navarre
(c. 1370-1437)

Philippa
of Lancaster
(c. 1359-1415)
m. John I
king of Portugal

Elizabeth
of Lancaster
(1364-1425)
m. (1) John Holland
duke of Exeter
(2) Sir John Cornwall
Lord Fanhope

The House of Tudor
(1485–1603)

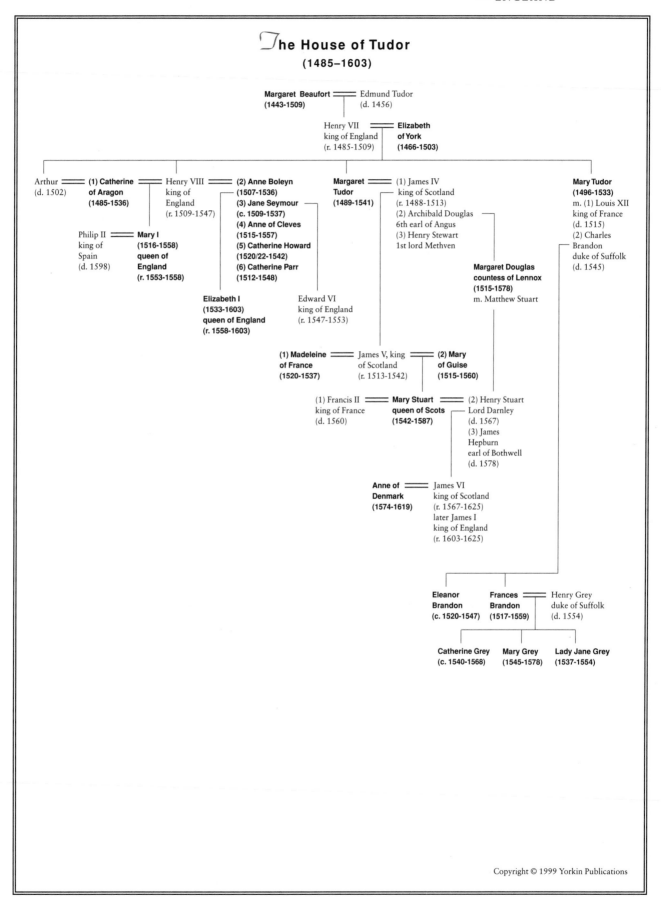

Margaret Beaufort (1443-1509) ══ Edmund Tudor (d. 1456)

Henry VII king of England (r. 1485-1509) ══ **Elizabeth of York (1466-1503)**

Arthur (d. 1502) ══ **(1) Catherine of Aragon (1485-1536)** ── Henry VIII king of England (r. 1509-1547) ══ **(2) Anne Boleyn (1507-1536)**
(3) Jane Seymour (c. 1509-1537)
(4) Anne of Cleves (1515-1557)
(5) Catherine Howard (1520/22-1542)
(6) Catherine Parr (1512-1548)

Margaret Tudor (1489-1541) ══ (1) James IV king of Scotland (r. 1488-1513)
(2) Archibald Douglas 6th earl of Angus
(3) Henry Stewart 1st lord Methven

Mary Tudor (1496-1533) m. (1) Louis XII king of France (d. 1515) (2) Charles Brandon duke of Suffolk (d. 1545)

Philip II king of Spain (d. 1598) ══ **Mary I (1516-1558) queen of England (r. 1553-1558)**

Margaret Douglas countess of Lennox (1515-1578) m. Matthew Stuart

Elizabeth I (1533-1603) queen of England (r. 1558-1603)

Edward VI king of England (r. 1547-1553)

(1) Madeleine of France (1520-1537) ══ James V, king of Scotland (r. 1513-1542) ══ **(2) Mary of Guise (1515-1560)**

(1) Francis II king of France (d. 1560) ══ **Mary Stuart queen of Scots (1542-1587)** ══ (2) Henry Stuart Lord Darnley (d. 1567)
(3) James Hepburn earl of Bothwell (d. 1578)

Anne of Denmark (1574-1619) ══ James VI king of Scotland (r. 1567-1625) later James I king of England (r. 1603-1625)

Eleanor Brandon (c. 1520-1547)

Frances Brandon (1517-1559) ══ Henry Grey duke of Suffolk (d. 1554)

Catherine Grey (c. 1540-1568)

Mary Grey (1545-1578)

Lady Jane Grey (1537-1554)

The Stuarts
(1603–1714)

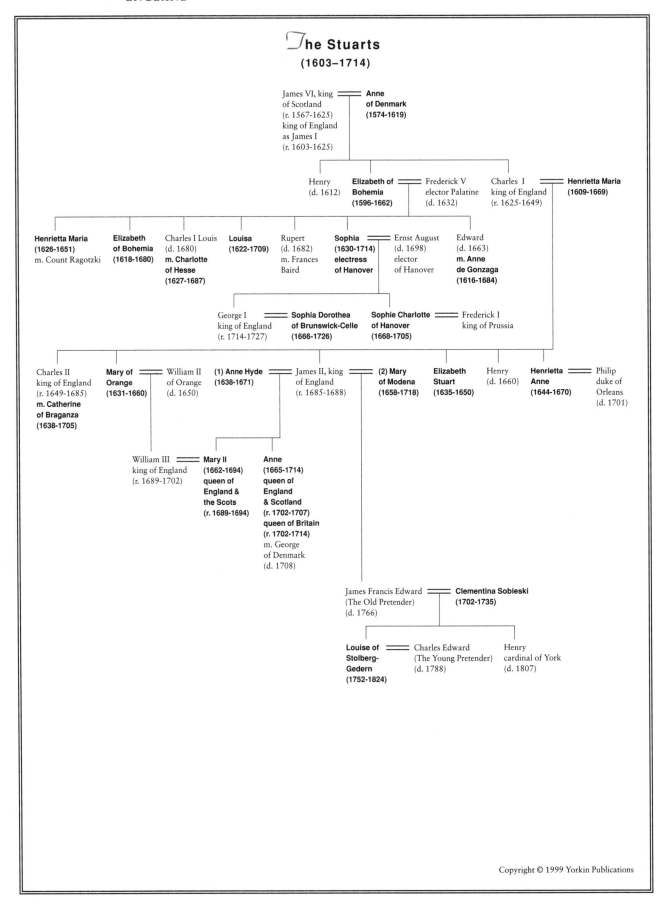

James VI, king
of Scotland
(r. 1567-1625)
king of England
as James I
(r. 1603-1625)
**═══ Anne
of Denmark
(1574-1619)**

Henry
(d. 1612)

**Elizabeth of
Bohemia
(1596-1662)** ═══ Frederick V
elector Palatine
(d. 1632)

Charles I
king of England
(r. 1625-1649) ═══ **Henrietta Maria
(1609-1669)**

**Henrietta Maria
(1626-1651)**
m. Count Ragotzki

**Elizabeth
of Bohemia
(1618-1680)**

Charles I Louis
(d. 1680)
**m. Charlotte
of Hesse
(1627-1687)**

**Louisa
(1622-1709)**

Rupert
(d. 1682)
m. Frances
Baird

**Sophia
(1630-1714)
electress
of Hanover** ═══ Ernst August
(d. 1698)
elector
of Hanover

Edward
(d. 1663)
**m. Anne
de Gonzaga
(1616-1684)**

George I
king of England
(r. 1714-1727) ═══ **Sophia Dorothea
of Brunswick-Celle
(1666-1726)**

**Sophie Charlotte
of Hanover
(1668-1705)** ═══ Frederick I
king of Prussia

Charles II
king of England
(r. 1649-1685)
**m. Catherine
of Braganza
(1638-1705)**

**Mary of
Orange
(1631-1660)** ═══ William II
of Orange
(d. 1650)

**(1) Anne Hyde
(1638-1671)** ═══ James II, king
of England
(r. 1685-1688) ═══ **(2) Mary
of Modena
(1658-1718)**

**Elizabeth
Stuart
(1635-1650)**

Henry
(d. 1660)

**Henrietta
Anne
(1644-1670)** ═══ Philip
duke of
Orleans
(d. 1701)

William III
king of England
(r. 1689-1702) ═══ **Mary II
(1662-1694)
queen of
England &
the Scots
(r. 1689-1694)**

**Anne
(1665-1714)
queen of
England
& Scotland
(r. 1702-1707)
queen of Britain
(r. 1702-1714)
m. George
of Denmark
(d. 1708)**

James Francis Edward
(The Old Pretender)
(d. 1766) ═══ **Clementina Sobieski
(1702-1735)**

**Louise of
Stolberg-
Gedern
(1752-1824)** ═══ Charles Edward
(The Young Pretender)
(d. 1788)

Henry
cardinal of York
(d. 1807)

Copyright © 1999 Yorkin Publications

Women in World History

𝒯he House of Hanover
(1714–1837)

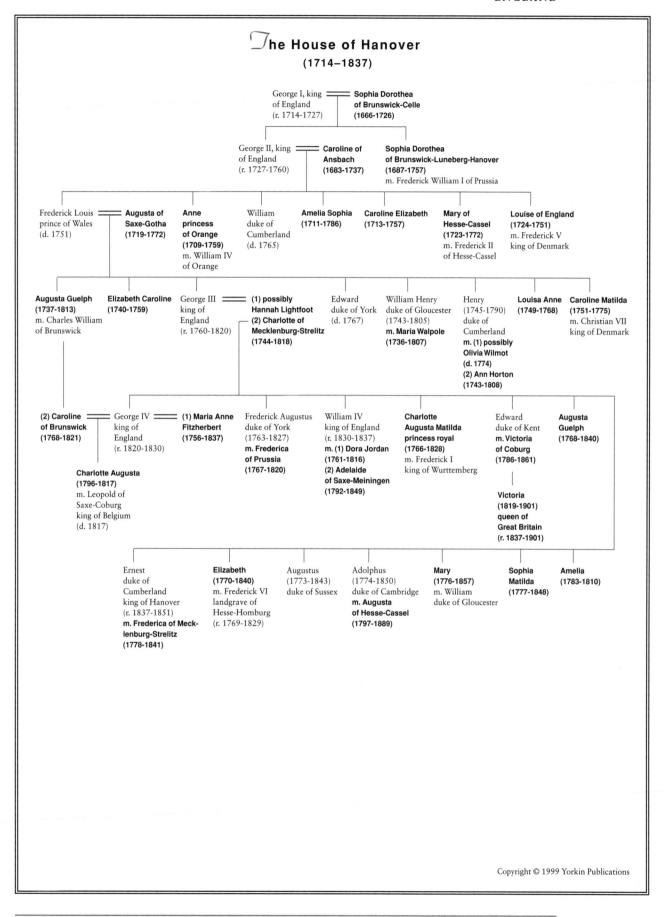

George I, king of England (r. 1714-1727) ══ **Sophia Dorothea of Brunswick-Celle (1666-1726)**

George II, king of England (r. 1727-1760) ══ **Caroline of Ansbach (1683-1737)**

Sophia Dorothea of Brunswick-Luneberg-Hanover (1687-1757) m. Frederick William I of Prussia

Frederick Louis prince of Wales (d. 1751) ══ **Augusta of Saxe-Gotha (1719-1772)**

Anne princess of Orange (1709-1759) m. William IV of Orange

William duke of Cumberland (d. 1765)

Amelia Sophia (1711-1786)

Caroline Elizabeth (1713-1757)

Mary of Hesse-Cassel (1723-1772) m. Frederick II of Hesse-Cassel

Louise of England (1724-1751) m. Frederick V king of Denmark

Augusta Guelph (1737-1813) m. Charles William of Brunswick

Elizabeth Caroline (1740-1759)

George III king of England (r. 1760-1820) ══ **(1) possibly Hannah Lightfoot (2) Charlotte of Mecklenburg-Strelitz (1744-1818)**

Edward duke of York (d. 1767)

William Henry duke of Gloucester (1743-1805) **m. Maria Walpole (1736-1807)**

Henry (1745-1790) duke of Cumberland **m. (1) possibly Olivia Wilmot (d. 1774) (2) Ann Horton (1743-1808)**

Louisa Anne (1749-1768)

Caroline Matilda (1751-1775) m. Christian VII king of Denmark

(2) Caroline of Brunswick (1768-1821) ══ George IV king of England (r. 1820-1830) ══ **(1) Maria Anne Fitzherbert (1756-1837)**

Frederick Augustus duke of York (1763-1827) **m. Frederica of Prussia (1767-1820)**

William IV king of England (r. 1830-1837) **m. (1) Dora Jordan (1761-1816) (2) Adelaide of Saxe-Meiningen (1792-1849)**

Charlotte Augusta Matilda princess royal (1766-1828) m. Frederick I king of Wurttemberg

Edward duke of Kent **m. Victoria of Coburg (1786-1861)**

Augusta Guelph (1768-1840)

Charlotte Augusta (1796-1817) m. Leopold of Saxe-Coburg king of Belgium (d. 1817)

Victoria (1819-1901) queen of Great Britain (r. 1837-1901)

Ernest duke of Cumberland king of Hanover (r. 1837-1851) **m. Frederica of Mecklenburg-Strelitz (1778-1841)**

Elizabeth (1770-1840) m. Frederick VI landgrave of Hesse-Homburg (r. 1769-1829)

Augustus (1773-1843) duke of Sussex

Adolphus (1774-1850) duke of Cambridge **m. Augusta of Hesse-Cassel (1797-1889)**

Mary (1776-1857) m. William duke of Gloucester

Sophia Matilda (1777-1848)

Amelia (1783-1810)

The Houses of Saxe-Coburg-Gotha

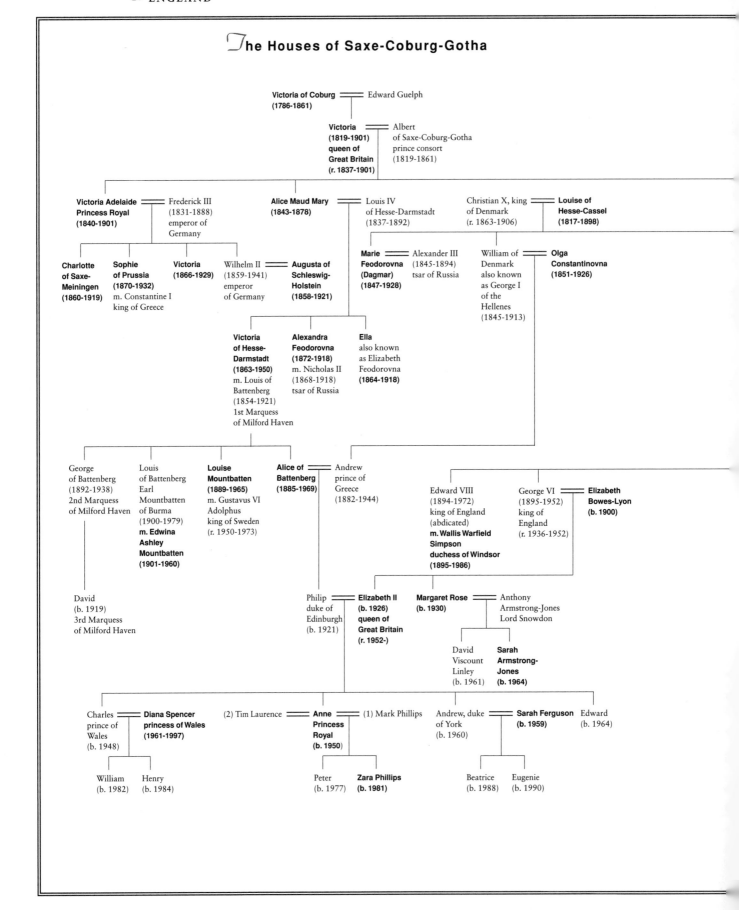

Victoria of Coburg (1786-1861) ═══ Edward Guelph

Victoria (1819-1901) queen of Great Britain (r. 1837-1901) ═══ Albert of Saxe-Coburg-Gotha prince consort (1819-1861)

Victoria Adelaide Princess Royal (1840-1901) ═══ Frederick III (1831-1888) emperor of Germany

Alice Maud Mary (1843-1878) ═══ Louis IV of Hesse-Darmstadt (1837-1892)

Christian X, king of Denmark (r. 1863-1906) ═══ Louise of Hesse-Cassel (1817-1898)

Charlotte of Saxe-Meiningen (1860-1919)

Sophie of Prussia (1870-1932) m. Constantine I king of Greece

Victoria (1866-1929)

Wilhelm II (1859-1941) emperor of Germany ═══ Augusta of Schleswig-Holstein (1858-1921)

Marie Feodorovna (Dagmar) (1847-1928) ═══ Alexander III (1845-1894) tsar of Russia

William of Denmark also known as George I of the Hellenes (1845-1913) ═══ Olga Constantinovna (1851-1926)

Victoria of Hesse-Darmstadt (1863-1950) m. Louis of Battenberg (1854-1921) 1st Marquess of Milford Haven

Alexandra Feodorovna (1872-1918) m. Nicholas II (1868-1918) tsar of Russia

Ella also known as Elizabeth Feodorovna (1864-1918)

George of Battenberg (1892-1938) 2nd Marquess of Milford Haven

Louis of Battenberg Earl Mountbatten of Burma (1900-1979) m. Edwina Ashley Mountbatten (1901-1960)

Louise Mountbatten (1889-1965) m. Gustavus VI Adolphus king of Sweden (r. 1950-1973)

Alice of Battenberg (1885-1969) ═══ Andrew prince of Greece (1882-1944)

Edward VIII (1894-1972) king of England (abdicated) m. Wallis Warfield Simpson duchess of Windsor (1895-1986)

George VI (1895-1952) king of England (r. 1936-1952) ═══ Elizabeth Bowes-Lyon (b. 1900)

David (b. 1919) 3rd Marquess of Milford Haven

Philip duke of Edinburgh (b. 1921) ═══ Elizabeth II (b. 1926) queen of Great Britain (r. 1952-)

Margaret Rose (b. 1930) ═══ Anthony Armstrong-Jones Lord Snowdon

David Viscount Linley (b. 1961)

Sarah Armstrong-Jones (b. 1964)

Charles prince of Wales (b. 1948) ═══ Diana Spencer princess of Wales (1961-1997)

(2) Tim Laurence ═══ Anne Princess Royal (b. 1950) ═══ (1) Mark Phillips

Andrew, duke of York (b. 1960) ═══ Sarah Ferguson (b. 1959)

Edward (b. 1964)

William (b. 1982)

Henry (b. 1984)

Peter (b. 1977)

Zara Phillips (b. 1981)

Beatrice (b. 1988)

Eugenie (b. 1990)

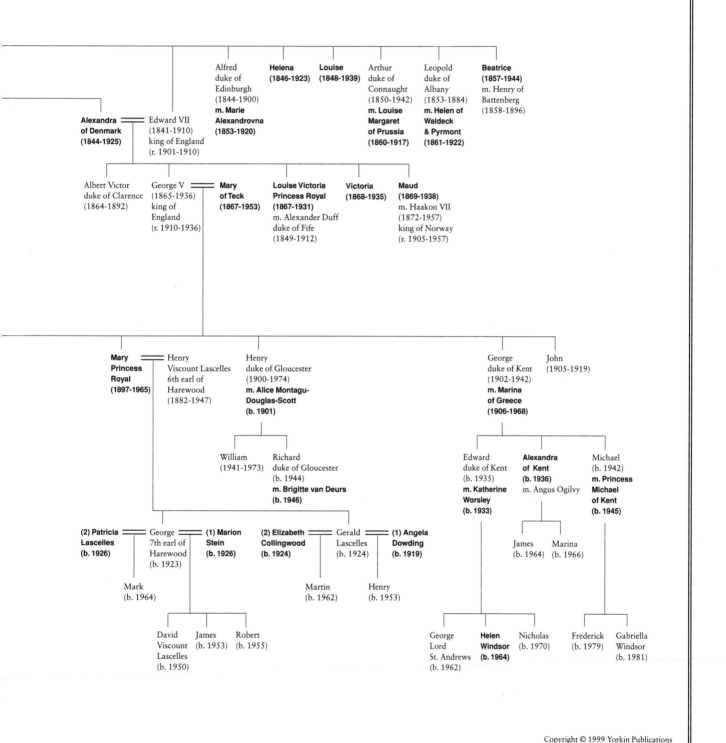

Alfred
duke of
Edinburgh
(1844-1900)
**m. Marie
Alexandrovna
(1853-1920)**

**Helena
(1846-1923)**

**Louise
(1848-1939)**

Arthur
duke of
Connaught
(1850-1942)
**m. Louise
Margaret
of Prussia
(1860-1917)**

Leopold
duke of
Albany
(1853-1884)
**m. Helen of
Waldeck
& Pyrmont
(1861-1922)**

**Beatrice
(1857-1944)**
m. Henry of
Battenberg
(1858-1896)

**Alexandra
of Denmark
(1844-1925)**

Edward VII
(1841-1910)
king of England
(r. 1901-1910)

Albert Victor
duke of Clarence
(1864-1892)

George V
(1865-1936)
king of
England
(r. 1910-1936)

**Mary
of Teck
(1867-1953)**

**Louise Victoria
Princess Royal
(1867-1931)**
m. Alexander Duff
duke of Fife
(1849-1912)

**Victoria
(1868-1935)**

**Maud
(1869-1938)**
m. Haakon VII
(1872-1957)
king of Norway
(r. 1905-1957)

**Mary
Princess
Royal
(1897-1965)**

Henry
Viscount Lascelles
6th earl of
Harewood
(1882-1947)

Henry
duke of Gloucester
(1900-1974)
**m. Alice Montagu-
Douglas-Scott
(b. 1901)**

George
duke of Kent
(1902-1942)
**m. Marina
of Greece
(1906-1968)**

John
(1905-1919)

William
(1941-1973)

Richard
duke of Gloucester
(b. 1944)
**m. Brigitte van Deurs
(b. 1946)**

Edward
duke of Kent
(b. 1935)
**m. Katherine
Worsley
(b. 1933)**

**Alexandra
of Kent
(b. 1936)**
m. Angus Ogilvy

Michael
(b. 1942)
**m. Princess
Michael
of Kent
(b. 1945)**

**(2) Patricia
Lascelles
(b. 1926)**

George
7th earl of
Harewood
(b. 1923)

**(1) Marion
Stein
(b. 1926)**

**(2) Elizabeth
Collingwood
(b. 1924)**

Gerald
Lascelles
(b. 1924)

**(1) Angela
Dowding
(b. 1919)**

James
(b. 1964)

Marina
(b. 1966)

Mark
(b. 1964)

Martin
(b. 1962)

Henry
(b. 1953)

David
Viscount
Lascelles
(b. 1950)

James
(b. 1953)

Robert
(b. 1955)

George
Lord
St. Andrews
(b. 1962)

**Helen
Windsor
(b. 1964)**

Nicholas
(b. 1970)

Frederick
(b. 1979)

Gabriella
Windsor
(b. 1981)

ℳerovingian Queens and Kings

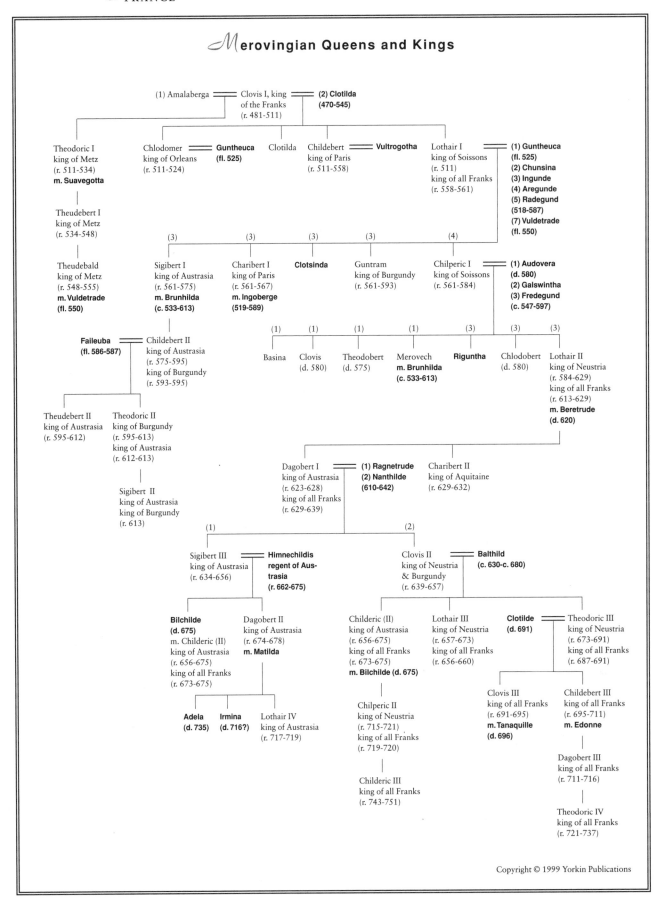

The House of Pepin
(640–814)

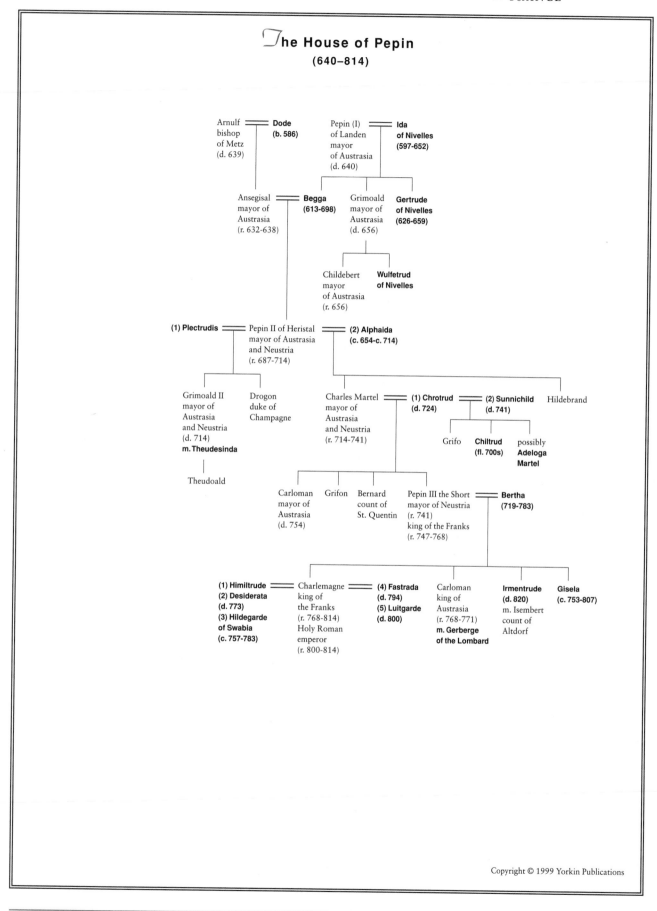

Arnulf bishop of Metz (d. 639) ══ **Dode (b. 586)**

Pepin (I) of Landen mayor of Austrasia (d. 640) ══ **Ida of Nivelles (597-652)**

Ansegisal mayor of Austrasia (r. 632-638) ══ **Begga (613-698)**

Grimoald mayor of Austrasia (d. 656) — **Gertrude of Nivelles (626-659)**

Childebert mayor of Austrasia (r. 656) — **Wulfetrud of Nivelles**

(1) Plectrudis ══ Pepin II of Heristal mayor of Austrasia and Neustria (r. 687-714) ══ **(2) Alphaida (c. 654-c. 714)**

Grimoald II mayor of Austrasia and Neustria (d. 714) **m. Theudesinda**

Theudoald

Drogon duke of Champagne

Charles Martel mayor of Austrasia and Neustria (r. 714-741) ══ **(1) Chrotrud (d. 724)** ══ **(2) Sunnichild (d. 741)**   Hildebrand

Grifo   **Chiltrud (fl. 700s)**   possibly **Adeloga Martel**

Carloman mayor of Austrasia (d. 754)   Grifon   Bernard count of St. Quentin   Pepin III the Short mayor of Neustria (r. 741) king of the Franks (r. 747-768) ══ **Bertha (719-783)**

(1) Himiltrude
(2) Desiderata (d. 773)
(3) Hildegarde of Swabia (c. 757-783) ══ Charlemagne king of the Franks (r. 768-814) Holy Roman emperor (r. 800-814) ══ **(4) Fastrada (d. 794)** **(5) Luitgarde (d. 800)**

Carloman king of Austrasia (r. 768-771) **m. Gerberge of the Lombard**

Irmentrude (d. 820) m. Isembert count of Altdorf

Gisela (c. 753-807)

𝒯he Carolingian Dynasty
(768–987)

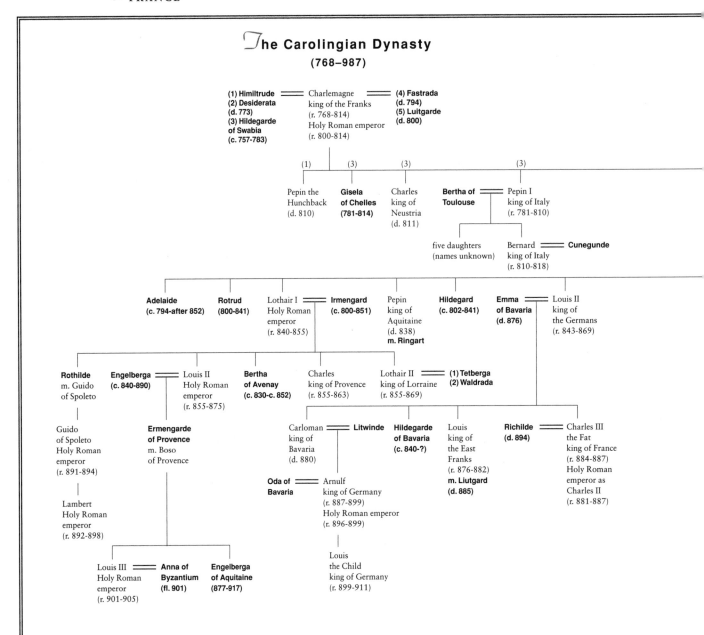

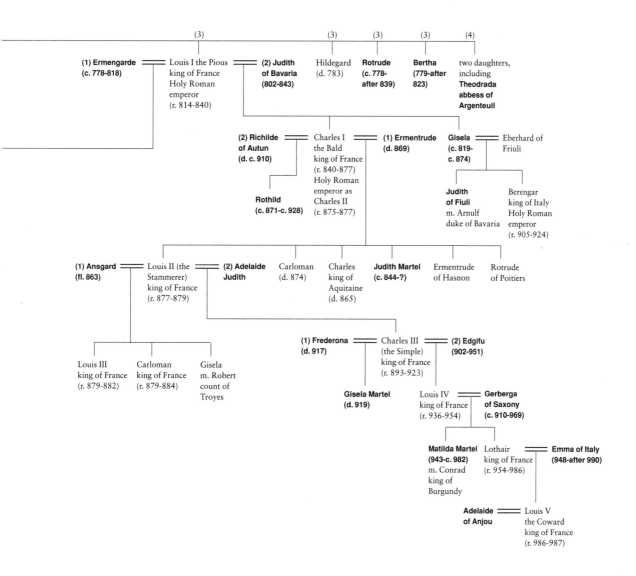

The House of Capet
(987–1328)

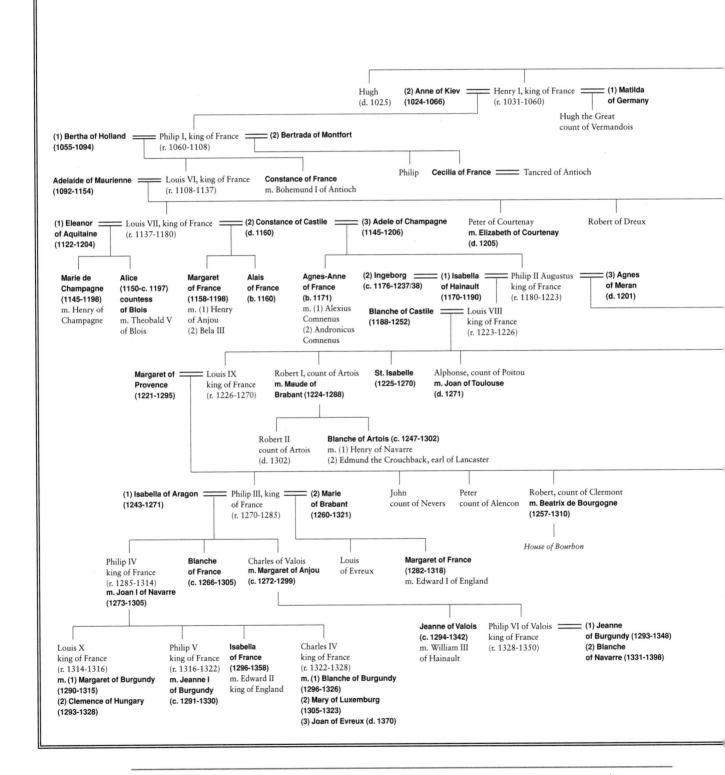

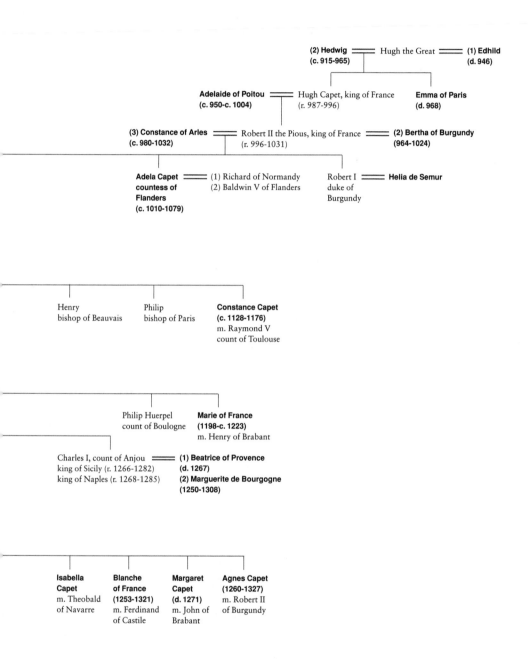

The House of Anjou
(1266–1435)

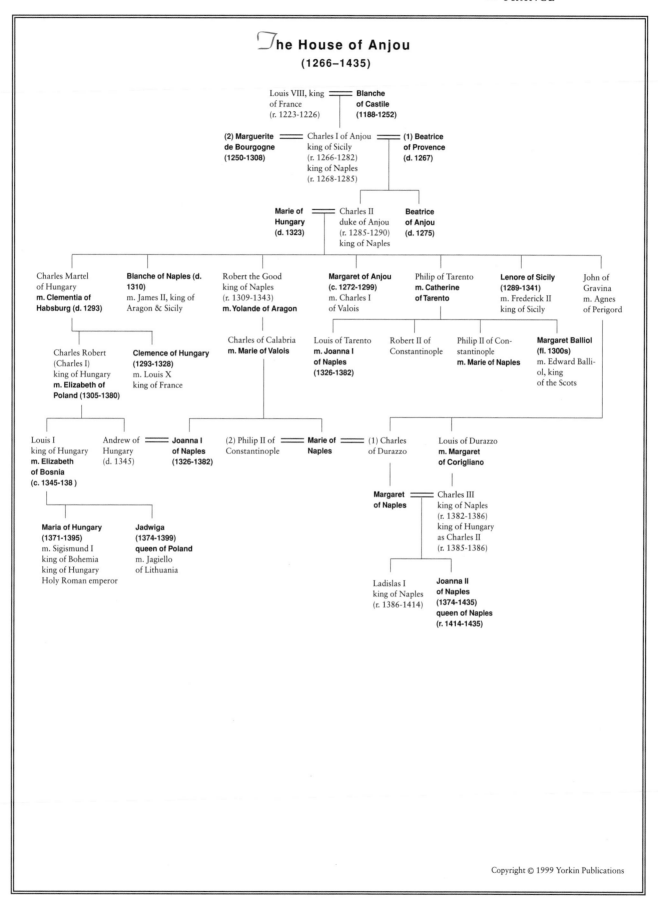

Louis VIII, king of France (r. 1223-1226) ══ **Blanche of Castile (1188-1252)**

(2) Marguerite de Bourgogne (1250-1308) ══ Charles I of Anjou king of Sicily (r. 1266-1282) king of Naples (r. 1268-1285) ══ **(1) Beatrice of Provence (d. 1267)**

Marie of Hungary (d. 1323) ══ Charles II duke of Anjou (r. 1285-1290) king of Naples — **Beatrice of Anjou (d. 1275)**

Charles Martel of Hungary **m. Clementia of Habsburg (d. 1293)**

Blanche of Naples (d. 1310) m. James II, king of Aragon & Sicily

Robert the Good king of Naples (r. 1309-1343) **m. Yolande of Aragon**

Margaret of Anjou (c. 1272-1299) m. Charles I of Valois

Philip of Tarento **m. Catherine of Tarento**

Lenore of Sicily (1289-1341) m. Frederick II king of Sicily

John of Gravina m. Agnes of Perigord

Charles Robert (Charles I) king of Hungary **m. Elizabeth of Poland (1305-1380)**

Clemence of Hungary (1293-1328) m. Louis X king of France

Charles of Calabria **m. Marie of Valois**

Louis of Tarento **m. Joanna I of Naples (1326-1382)**

Robert II of Constantinople

Philip II of Constantinople **m. Marie of Naples**

Margaret Balliol (fl. 1300s) m. Edward Balliol, king of the Scots

Louis I king of Hungary **m. Elizabeth of Bosnia (c. 1345-138)**

Andrew of Hungary (d. 1345) ══ **Joanna I of Naples (1326-1382)**

(2) Philip II of Constantinople ══ **Marie of Naples** ══ (1) Charles of Durazzo

Louis of Durazzo **m. Margaret of Corigliano**

Maria of Hungary (1371-1395) m. Sigismund I king of Bohemia king of Hungary Holy Roman emperor

Jadwiga (1374-1399) queen of Poland m. Jagiello of Lithuania

Margaret of Naples ══ Charles III king of Naples (r. 1382-1386) king of Hungary as Charles II (r. 1385-1386)

Ladislas I king of Naples (r. 1386-1414)

Joanna II of Naples (1374-1435) queen of Naples (r. 1414-1435)

The House of Burgundy
(1312–1477)

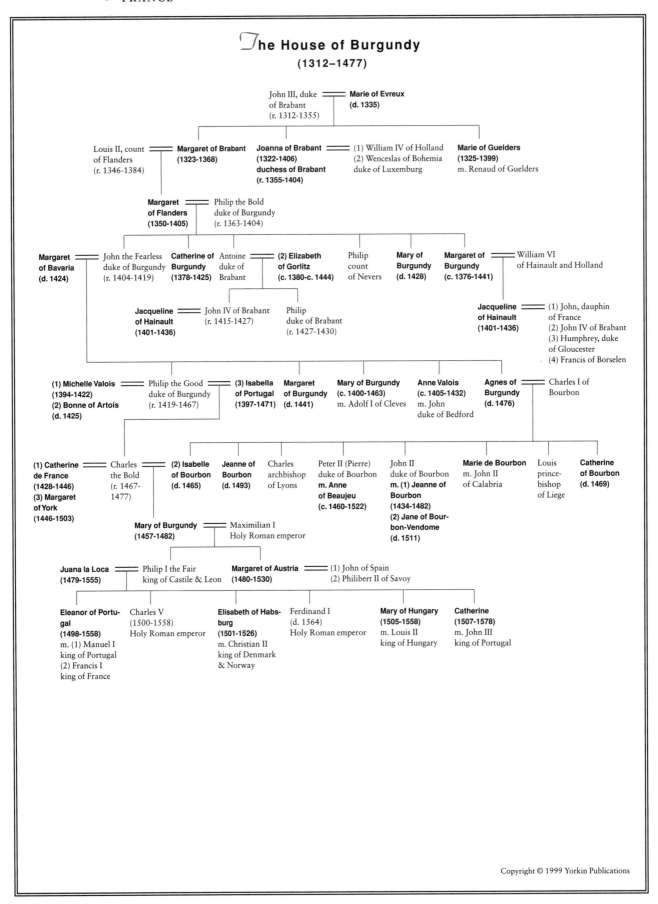

John III, duke of Brabant (r. 1312-1355) ═══ **Marie of Evreux (d. 1335)**

Louis II, count of Flanders (r. 1346-1384) ═══ **Margaret of Brabant (1323-1368)**

Joanna of Brabant (1322-1406) duchess of Brabant (r. 1355-1404) ═══ (1) William IV of Holland (2) Wenceslas of Bohemia duke of Luxembourg

Marie of Guelders (1325-1399) m. Renaud of Guelders

Margaret of Flanders (1350-1405) ═══ Philip the Bold duke of Burgundy (r. 1363-1404)

Margaret of Bavaria (d. 1424) ═══ John the Fearless duke of Burgundy (r. 1404-1419)

Catherine of Burgundy (1378-1425)

Antoine duke of Brabant ═══ **(2) Elizabeth of Gorlitz (c. 1380-c. 1444)**

Philip count of Nevers

Mary of Burgundy (d. 1428)

Margaret of Burgundy (c. 1376-1441) ═══ William VI of Hainault and Holland

Jacqueline of Hainault (1401-1436) ═══ John IV of Brabant (r. 1415-1427)

Philip duke of Brabant (r. 1427-1430)

Jacqueline of Hainault (1401-1436) ═══ (1) John, dauphin of France (2) John IV of Brabant (3) Humphrey, duke of Gloucester (4) Francis of Borselen

(1) Michelle Valois (1394-1422) (2) Bonne of Artois (d. 1425) ═══ Philip the Good duke of Burgundy (r. 1419-1467) ═══ **(3) Isabella of Portugal (1397-1471)**

Margaret of Burgundy (d. 1441)

Mary of Burgundy (c. 1400-1463) m. Adolf I of Cleves

Anne Valois (c. 1405-1432) m. John duke of Bedford

Agnes of Burgundy (d. 1476) ═══ Charles I of Bourbon

(1) Catherine de France (1428-1446) (3) Margaret of York (1446-1503) ═══ Charles the Bold (r. 1467-1477) ═══ **(2) Isabelle of Bourbon (d. 1465)**

Jeanne of Bourbon (d. 1493)

Charles archbishop of Lyons

Peter II (Pierre) duke of Bourbon **m. Anne of Beaujeu (c. 1460-1522)**

John II duke of Bourbon **m. (1) Jeanne of Bourbon (1434-1482) (2) Jane of Bourbon-Vendome (d. 1511)**

Marie de Bourbon m. John II of Calabria

Louis prince-bishop of Liege

Catherine of Bourbon (d. 1469)

Mary of Burgundy (1457-1482) ═══ Maximilian I Holy Roman emperor

Juana la Loca (1479-1555) ═══ Philip I the Fair king of Castile & Leon

Margaret of Austria (1480-1530) ═══ (1) John of Spain (2) Philibert II of Savoy

Eleanor of Portugal (1498-1558) m. (1) Manuel I king of Portugal (2) Francis I king of France

Charles V (1500-1558) Holy Roman emperor

Elisabeth of Habsburg (1501-1526) m. Christian II king of Denmark & Norway

Ferdinand I (d. 1564) Holy Roman emperor

Mary of Hungary (1505-1558) m. Louis II king of Hungary

Catherine (1507-1578) m. John III king of Portugal

The House of Valois
(1328–1515)

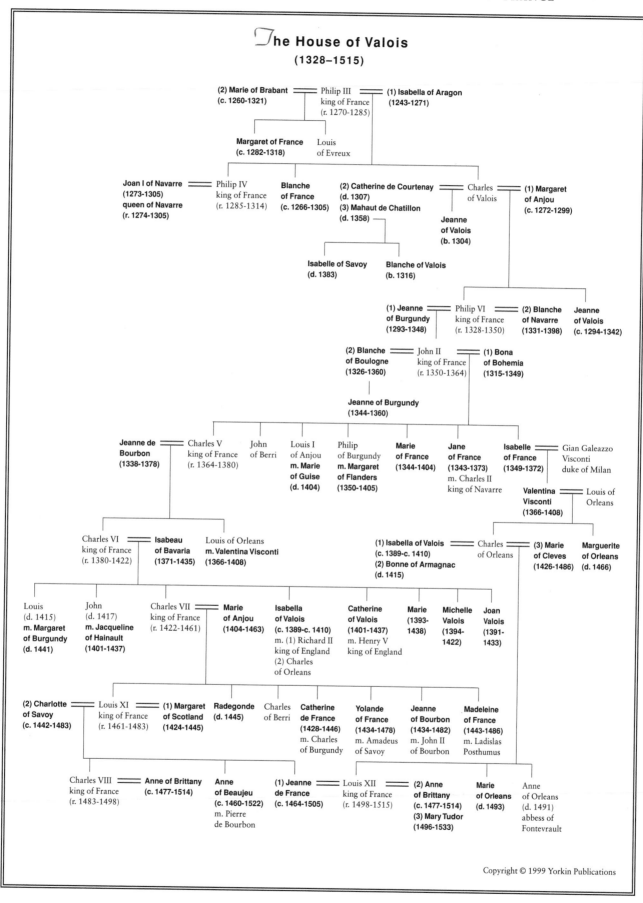

(2) Marie of Brabant ═══ Philip III ═══ **(1) Isabella of Aragon**
(c. 1260-1321) — king of France — **(1243-1271)**
— (r. 1270-1285) —

Margaret of France — Louis
(c. 1282-1318) — of Evreux

Joan I of Navarre ═══ Philip IV — **Blanche** — **(2) Catherine de Courtenay** ═══ Charles ═══ **(1) Margaret**
(1273-1305) — king of France — **of France** — **(d. 1307)** — of Valois — **of Anjou**
queen of Navarre — (r. 1285-1314) — **(c. 1266-1305)** — **(3) Mahaut de Chatillon** — — **(c. 1272-1299)**
(r. 1274-1305) — **(d. 1358)** — Jeanne
— of Valois
— **(b. 1304)**

Isabelle of Savoy — **Blanche of Valois**
(d. 1383) — **(b. 1316)**

(1) Jeanne ═══ Philip VI ═══ **(2) Blanche** — **Jeanne**
of Burgundy — king of France — **of Navarre** — **of Valois**
(1293-1348) — (r. 1328-1350) — **(1331-1398)** — **(c. 1294-1342)**

(2) Blanche ═══ John II ═══ **(1) Bona**
of Boulogne — king of France — **of Bohemia**
(1326-1360) — (r. 1350-1364) — **(1315-1349)**

Jeanne of Burgundy
(1344-1360)

Jeanne de ═══ Charles V — John — Louis I — Philip — **Marie** — **Jane** — **Isabelle** ═══ Gian Galeazzo
Bourbon — king of France — of Berri — of Anjou — of Burgundy — **of France** — **of France** — **of France** — Visconti
(1338-1378) — (r. 1364-1380) — **m. Marie** — **m. Margaret** — **(1344-1404)** — **(1343-1373)** — **(1349-1372)** — duke of Milan
— **of Guise** — **of Flanders** — m. Charles II
— **(d. 1404)** — **(1350-1405)** — king of Navarre

Valentina ═══ Louis of
Visconti — Orleans
(1366-1408)

Charles VI ═══ **Isabeau** — Louis of Orleans — **(1) Isabella of Valois** ═══ Charles ═══ **(3) Marie** — **Marguerite**
king of France — **of Bavaria** — m. Valentina Visconti — **(c. 1389-c. 1410)** — of Orleans — **of Cleves** — **of Orleans**
(r. 1380-1422) — **(1371-1435)** — **(1366-1408)** — **(2) Bonne of Armagnac** — — **(1426-1486)** — **(d. 1466)**
— **(d. 1415)**

Louis — John — Charles VII ═══ **Marie** — **Isabella** — **Catherine** — **Marie** — **Michelle** — **Joan**
(d. 1415) — (d. 1417) — king of France — **of Anjou** — **of Valois** — **of Valois** — **(1393-** — **Valois** — **Valois**
m. Margaret — **m. Jacqueline** — (r. 1422-1461) — **(1404-1463)** — **(c. 1389-c. 1410)** — **(1401-1437)** — **1438)** — **(1394-** — **(1391-**
of Burgundy — **of Hainault** — m. (1) Richard II — m. Henry V — **1422)** — **1433)**
(d. 1441) — **(1401-1437)** — king of England — king of England
— (2) Charles
— of Orleans

(2) Charlotte ═══ Louis XI ═══ **(1) Margaret** — **Radegonde** — Charles — **Catherine** — **Yolande** — **Jeanne** — **Madeleine**
of Savoy — king of France — **of Scotland** — **(d. 1445)** — of Berri — **de France** — **of France** — **of Bourbon** — **of France**
(c. 1442-1483) — (r. 1461-1483) — **(1424-1445)** — **(1428-1446)** — **(1434-1478)** — **(1434-1482)** — **(1443-1486)**
— m. Charles — m. Amadeus — m. John II — m. Ladislas
— of Burgundy — of Savoy — of Bourbon — Posthumus

Charles VIII ═══ **Anne of Brittany** — **Anne** — **(1) Jeanne** ═══ Louis XII ═══ **(2) Anne** — **Marie** — Anne
king of France — **(c. 1477-1514)** — **of Beaujeu** — **de France** — king of France — **of Brittany** — **of Orleans** — of Orleans
(r. 1483-1498) — **(c. 1460-1522)** — **(c. 1464-1505)** — (r. 1498-1515) — **(c. 1477-1514)** — **(d. 1493)** — (d. 1491)
— m. Pierre — **(3) Mary Tudor** — abbess of
— de Bourbon — **(1496-1533)** — Fontevrault

ℐhe House of Lorraine & Guise
(1480–1625)

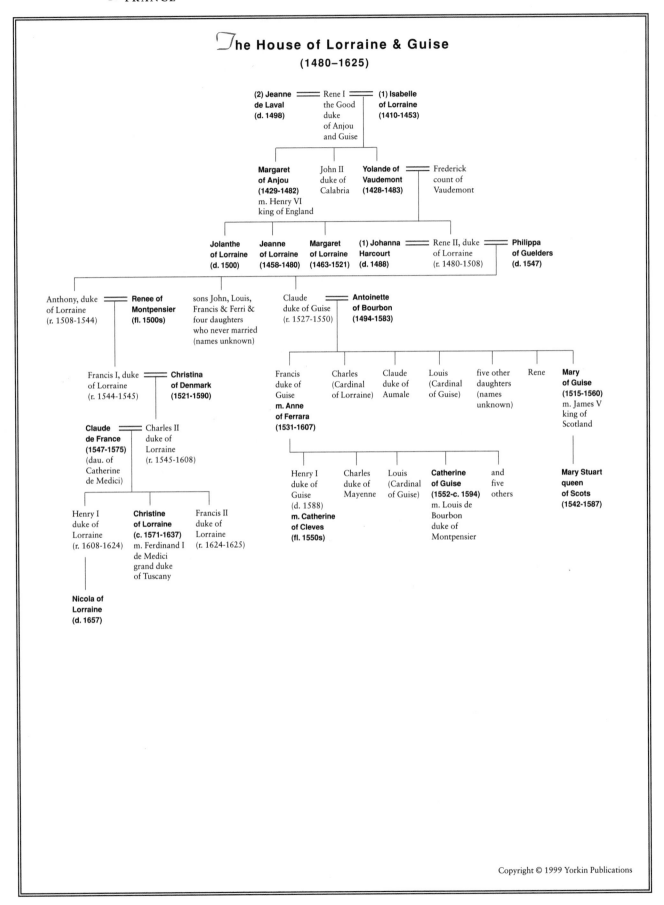

The Last of the Valois Queens & Kings
(1498–1589)

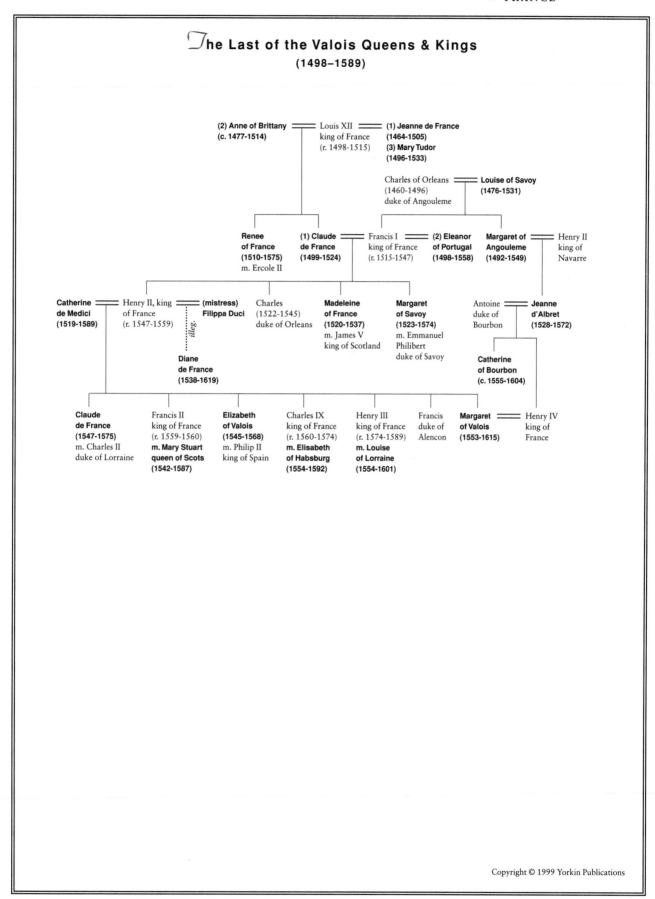

(2) Anne of Brittany ═══ Louis XII ═══ **(1) Jeanne de France**
(c. 1477-1514)   king of France   **(1464-1505)**
   (r. 1498-1515)   **(3) Mary Tudor**
   (1496-1533)

Charles of Orleans ═══ **Louise of Savoy**
(1460-1496)   **(1476-1531)**
duke of Angouleme

Renee   **(1) Claude** ═══ Francis I ═══ **(2) Eleanor**   **Margaret of** ═══ Henry II
of France   **de France**   king of France   **of Portugal**   **Angouleme**   king of
(1510-1575)   **(1499-1524)**   (r. 1515-1547)   **(1498-1558)**   **(1492-1549)**   Navarre
m. Ercole II

Catherine ═══ Henry II, king ═══ **(mistress)**   Charles   **Madeleine**   **Margaret**   Antoine ═══ **Jeanne**
de Medici   of France   **Filippa Duci**   (1522-1545)   **of France**   **of Savoy**   duke of   **d'Albret**
(1519-1589)   (r. 1547-1559)   duke of Orleans   **(1520-1537)**   **(1523-1574)**   Bourbon   **(1528-1572)**
   illeg.   m. James V   m. Emmanuel
   king of Scotland   Philibert
Diane   duke of Savoy   **Catherine**
de France   **of Bourbon**
(1538-1619)   **(c. 1555-1604)**

Claude   Francis II   **Elizabeth**   Charles IX   Henry III   Francis   **Margaret** ═══ Henry IV
de France   king of France   **of Valois**   king of France   king of France   duke of   **of Valois**   king of
(1547-1575)   (r. 1559-1560)   **(1545-1568)**   (r. 1560-1574)   (r. 1574-1589)   Alencon   **(1553-1615)**   France
m. Charles II   **m. Mary Stuart**   m. Philip II   **m. Elisabeth**   **m. Louise**
duke of Lorraine   **queen of Scots**   king of Spain   **of Habsburg**   **of Lorraine**
   (1542-1587)   **(1554-1592)**   **(1554-1601)**

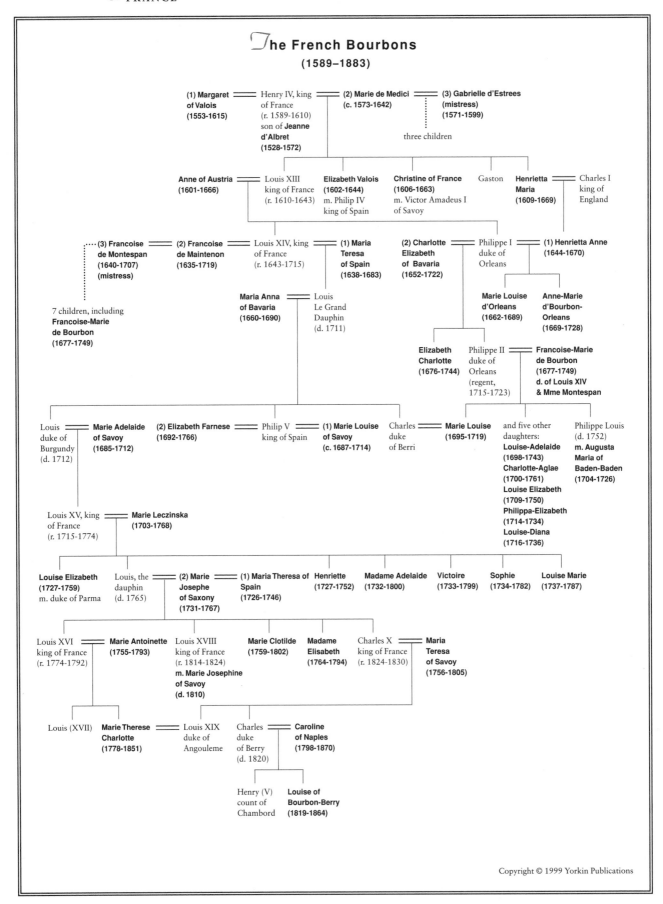

𝒯he French Bourbons
(1589–1883)

(1) Margaret of Valois (1553-1615) ═ Henry IV, king of France (r. 1589-1610) son of **Jeanne d'Albret (1528-1572)** ═ **(2) Marie de Medici (c. 1573-1642)** ═ **(3) Gabrielle d'Estrees (mistress) (1571-1599)**

three children

Anne of Austria (1601-1666) ═ Louis XIII king of France (r. 1610-1643)   **Elizabeth Valois (1602-1644)** m. Philip IV king of Spain   **Christine of France (1606-1663)** m. Victor Amadeus I of Savoy   Gaston   **Henrietta Maria (1609-1669)** ═ Charles I king of England

(3) Francoise de Montespan (1640-1707) (mistress) ═ **(2) Francoise de Maintenon (1635-1719)** ═ Louis XIV, king of France (r. 1643-1715) ═ **(1) Maria Teresa of Spain (1638-1683)**   **(2) Charlotte Elizabeth of Bavaria (1652-1722)** ═ Philippe I duke of Orleans ═ **(1) Henrietta Anne (1644-1670)**

7 children, including **Francoise-Marie de Bourbon (1677-1749)**

Maria Anna of Bavaria (1660-1690) ═ Louis Le Grand Dauphin (d. 1711)

Marie Louise d'Orleans (1662-1689)   **Anne-Marie d'Bourbon-Orleans (1669-1728)**

Elizabeth Charlotte (1676-1744)   Philippe II duke of Orleans (regent, 1715-1723) ═ **Francoise-Marie de Bourbon (1677-1749) d. of Louis XIV & Mme Montespan**

Louis duke of Burgundy (d. 1712) ═ **Marie Adelaide of Savoy (1685-1712)**   **(2) Elizabeth Farnese (1692-1766)** ═ Philip V king of Spain ═ **(1) Marie Louise of Savoy (c. 1687-1714)**   Charles duke of Berri ═ **Marie Louise (1695-1719)**   and five other daughters: **Louise-Adelaide (1698-1743) Charlotte-Aglae (1700-1761) Louise Elizabeth (1709-1750) Philippa-Elizabeth (1714-1734) Louise-Diana (1716-1736)**   **Philippe Louis (d. 1752)** m. Augusta Maria of Baden-Baden **(1704-1726)**

Louis XV, king of France (r. 1715-1774) ═ **Marie Leczinska (1703-1768)**

Louise Elizabeth (1727-1759) m. duke of Parma   Louis, the dauphin (d. 1765) ═ **(2) Marie Josephe of Saxony (1731-1767)** ═ **(1) Maria Theresa of Spain (1726-1746)**   **Henriette (1727-1752)**   **Madame Adelaide (1732-1800)**   **Victoire (1733-1799)**   **Sophie (1734-1782)**   **Louise Marie (1737-1787)**

Louis XVI king of France (r. 1774-1792) ═ **Marie Antoinette (1755-1793)**   Louis XVIII king of France (r. 1814-1824) **m. Marie Josephine of Savoy (d. 1810)**   **Marie Clotilde (1759-1802)**   **Madame Elisabeth (1764-1794)**   Charles X king of France (r. 1824-1830) ═ **Maria Teresa of Savoy (1756-1805)**

Louis (XVII)   **Marie Therese Charlotte (1778-1851)** ═ Louis XIX duke of Angouleme   Charles duke of Berry (d. 1820) ═ **Caroline of Naples (1798-1870)**

Henry (V) count of Chambord   **Louise of Bourbon-Berry (1819-1864)**

Copyright © 1999 Yorkin Publications

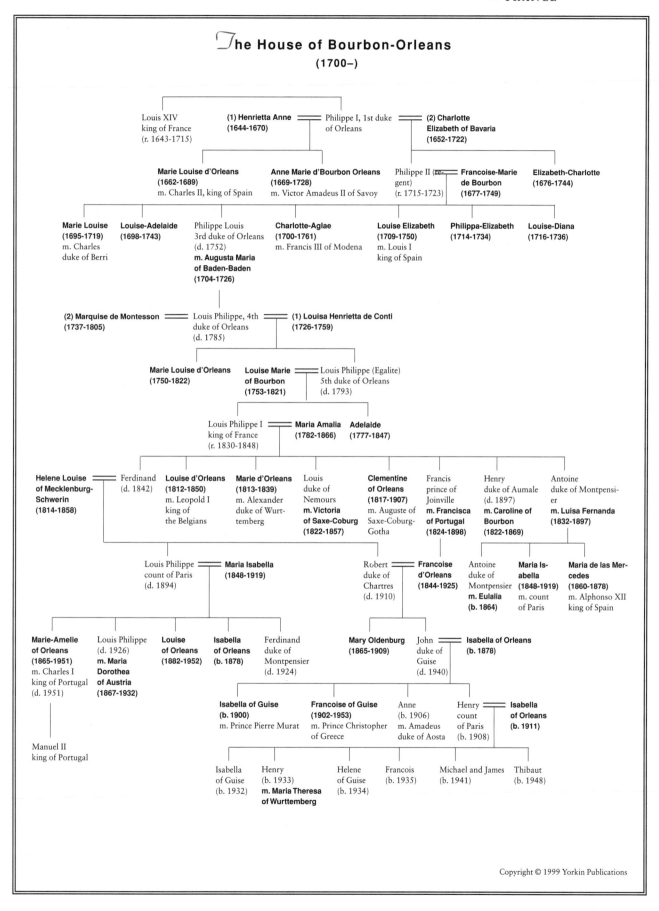

The House of Bourbon-Orleans
(1700–)

Louis XIV
king of France
(r. 1643-1715)

**(1) Henrietta Anne
(1644-1670)** ═══ Philippe I, 1st duke
of Orleans ═══ **(2) Charlotte
Elizabeth of Bavaria
(1652-1722)**

**Marie Louise d'Orleans
(1662-1689)
m. Charles II, king of Spain**

**Anne Marie d'Bourbon Orleans
(1669-1728)
m. Victor Amadeus II of Savoy**

Philippe II (re-gent)
(r. 1715-1723) ═══ **Francoise-Marie
de Bourbon
(1677-1749)**

**Elizabeth-Charlotte
(1676-1744)**

**Marie Louise
(1695-1719)**
m. Charles
duke of Berri

**Louise-Adelaide
(1698-1743)**

Philippe Louis
3rd duke of Orleans
(d. 1752)
**m. Augusta Maria
of Baden-Baden
(1704-1726)**

**Charlotte-Aglae
(1700-1761)**
m. Francis III of Modena

**Louise Elizabeth
(1709-1750)**
m. Louis I
king of Spain

**Philippa-Elizabeth
(1714-1734)**

**Louise-Diana
(1716-1736)**

**(2) Marquise de Montesson
(1737-1805)** ═══ Louis Philippe, 4th
duke of Orleans
(d. 1785) ═══ **(1) Louisa Henrietta de Conti
(1726-1759)**

**Marie Louise d'Orleans
(1750-1822)**

**Louise Marie
of Bourbon
(1753-1821)** ═══ Louis Philippe (Egalite)
5th duke of Orleans
(d. 1793)

Louis Philippe I
king of France
(r. 1830-1848) ═══ **Maria Amalia
(1782-1866)**   **Adelaide
(1777-1847)**

**Helene Louise
of Mecklenburg-
Schwerin
(1814-1858)** ═══ Ferdinand
(d. 1842)

**Louise d'Orleans
(1812-1850)**
m. Leopold I
king of
the Belgians

**Marie d'Orleans
(1813-1839)**
m. Alexander
duke of Wurt-
temberg

Louis
duke of
Nemours

**Clementine
of Orleans
(1817-1907)**
m. Auguste of
Saxe-Coburg-
Gotha
**m. Victoria
of Saxe-Coburg
(1822-1857)**

Francis
prince of
Joinville
**m. Francisca
of Portugal
(1824-1898)**

Henry
duke of Aumale
(d. 1897)
**m. Caroline of
Bourbon
(1822-1869)**

Antoine
duke of Montpensi-
er
**m. Luisa Fernanda
(1832-1897)**

Louis Philippe
count of Paris
(d. 1894) ═══ **Maria Isabella
(1848-1919)**

Robert
duke of
Chartres
(d. 1910) ═══ **Francoise
d'Orleans
(1844-1925)**

Antoine
duke of
Montpensier
**m. Eulalia
(b. 1864)**

**Maria Is-
abella
(1848-1919)**
m. count
of Paris

**Maria de las Mer-
cedes
(1860-1878)**
m. Alphonso XII
king of Spain

**Marie-Amelie
of Orleans
(1865-1951)**
m. Charles I
king of Portugal
(d. 1951)

Louis Philippe
(d. 1926)
**m. Maria
Dorothea
of Austria
(1867-1932)**

**Louise
of Orleans
(1882-1952)**

**Isabella
of Orleans
(b. 1878)**

Ferdinand
duke of
Montpensier
(d. 1924)

**Mary Oldenburg
(1865-1909)**

John
duke of
Guise
(d. 1940) ═══ **Isabella of Orleans
(b. 1878)**

Manuel II
king of Portugal

**Isabella of Guise
(b. 1900)**
m. Prince Pierre Murat

**Francoise of Guise
(1902-1953)**
m. Prince Christopher
of Greece

Anne
(b. 1906)
m. Amadeus
duke of Aosta

Henry
count
of Paris
(b. 1908) ═══ **Isabella
of Orleans
(b. 1911)**

Isabella
of Guise
(b. 1932)

Henry
(b. 1933)
**m. Maria Theresa
of Wurttemberg**

Helene
of Guise
(b. 1934)

Francois
(b. 1935)

Michael and James
(b. 1941)

Thibaut
(b. 1948)

The House of Bonaparte

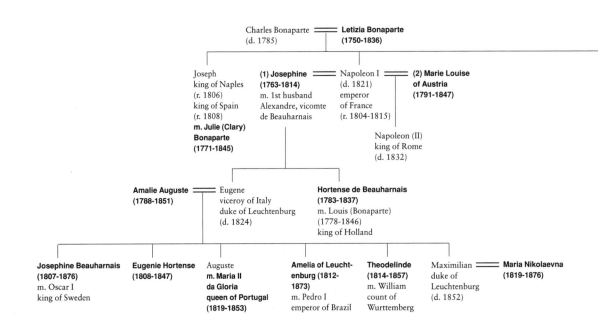

Charles Bonaparte
(d. 1785)
═══ **Letizia Bonaparte**
(1750-1836)

Joseph
king of Naples
(r. 1806)
king of Spain
(r. 1808)
m. Julie (Clary)
Bonaparte
(1771-1845)

(1) Josephine
(1763-1814)
m. 1st husband
Alexandre, vicomte
de Beauharnais
═══ Napoleon I
(d. 1821)
emperor
of France
(r. 1804-1815)
═══ **(2) Marie Louise**
of Austria
(1791-1847)

Napoleon (II)
king of Rome
(d. 1832)

Amalie Auguste
(1788-1851)
═══ Eugene
viceroy of Italy
duke of Leuchtenburg
(d. 1824)

Hortense de Beauharnais
(1783-1837)
m. Louis (Bonaparte)
(1778-1846)
king of Holland

Josephine Beauharnais
(1807-1876)
m. Oscar I
king of Sweden

Eugenie Hortense
(1808-1847)

Auguste
m. Maria II
da Gloria
queen of Portugal
(1819-1853)

Amelia of Leucht-
enburg (1812-
1873)
m. Pedro I
emperor of Brazil

Theodelinde
(1814-1857)
m. William
count of
Wurttemberg

Maximilian
duke of
Leuchtenburg
(d. 1852)
═══ **Maria Nikolaevna**
(1819-1876)

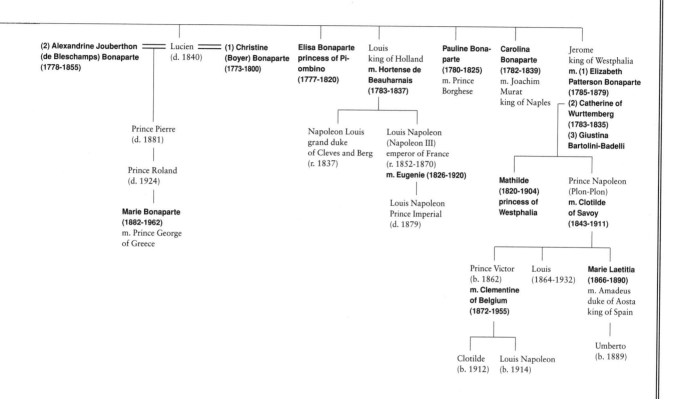

𝒮axon & Salian Empresses & Emperors

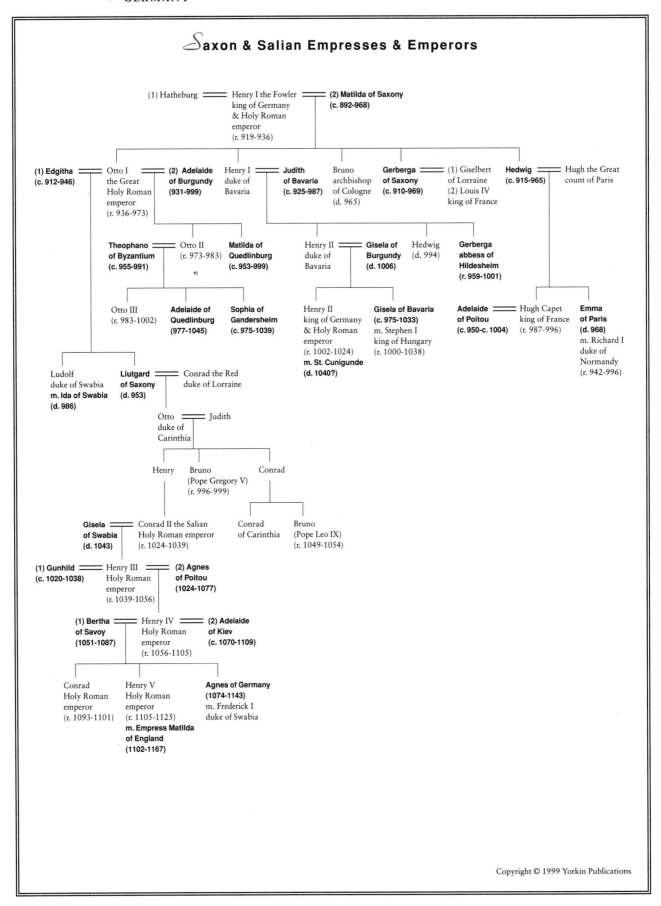

(1) Hatheburg ═══ Henry I the Fowler ═══ **(2) Matilda of Saxony**
king of Germany **(c. 892-968)**
& Holy Roman
emperor
(r. 919-936)

(1) Edgitha ═══ Otto I ═══ **(2) Adelaide** │ Henry I ═══ **Judith** │ Bruno │ **Gerberga** ═══ (1) Giselbert │ **Hedwig** ═══ Hugh the Great
(c. 912-946) the Great **of Burgundy** duke of **of Bavaria** archbishop **of Saxony** of Lorraine **(c. 915-965)** count of Paris
Holy Roman **(931-999)** Bavaria **(c. 925-987)** of Cologne **(c. 910-969)** (2) Louis IV
emperor (d. 965) king of France
(r. 936-973)

Theophano ═══ Otto II │ **Matilda of** │ Henry II ═══ **Gisela of** │ Hedwig │ **Gerberga**
of Byzantium (r. 973-983) **Quedlinburg** duke of **Burgundy** (d. 994) **abbess of**
(c. 955-991) **(c. 953-999)** Bavaria **(d. 1006)** **Hildesheim**
(r. 959-1001)

Otto III │ **Adelaide of** │ **Sophia of** │ Henry II │ **Gisela of Bavaria** │ **Adelaide** ═══ Hugh Capet │ **Emma**
(r. 983-1002) **Quedlinburg** **Gandersheim** king of Germany **(c. 975-1033)** **of Poitou** king of France **of Paris**
(977-1045) **(c. 975-1039)** & Holy Roman m. Stephen I **(c. 950-c. 1004)** (r. 987-996) **(d. 968)**
emperor king of Hungary m. Richard I
(r. 1002-1024) (r. 1000-1038) duke of
m. St. Cunigunde Normandy
(d. 1040?) (r. 942-996)

Ludolf │ **Liutgard** ═══ Conrad the Red
duke of Swabia **of Saxony** duke of Lorraine
m. Ida of Swabia **(d. 953)**
(d. 986)

Otto ═══ Judith
duke of
Carinthia

Henry │ Bruno │ Conrad
(Pope Gregory V)
(r. 996-999)

Conrad │ Bruno
of Carinthia (Pope Leo IX)
(r. 1049-1054)

Gisela ═══ Conrad II the Salian
of Swabia Holy Roman emperor
(d. 1043) (r. 1024-1039)

(1) Gunhild ═══ Henry III ═══ **(2) Agnes**
(c. 1020-1038) Holy Roman **of Poitou**
emperor **(1024-1077)**
(r. 1039-1056)

(1) Bertha ═══ Henry IV ═══ **(2) Adelaide**
of Savoy Holy Roman **of Kiev**
(1051-1087) emperor **(c. 1070-1109)**
(r. 1056-1105)

Conrad │ Henry V │ **Agnes of Germany**
Holy Roman Holy Roman **(1074-1143)**
emperor emperor m. Frederick I
(r. 1093-1101) (r. 1105-1125) duke of Swabia
m. Empress Matilda
of England
(1102-1167)

Welf & Hohenstaufen Families

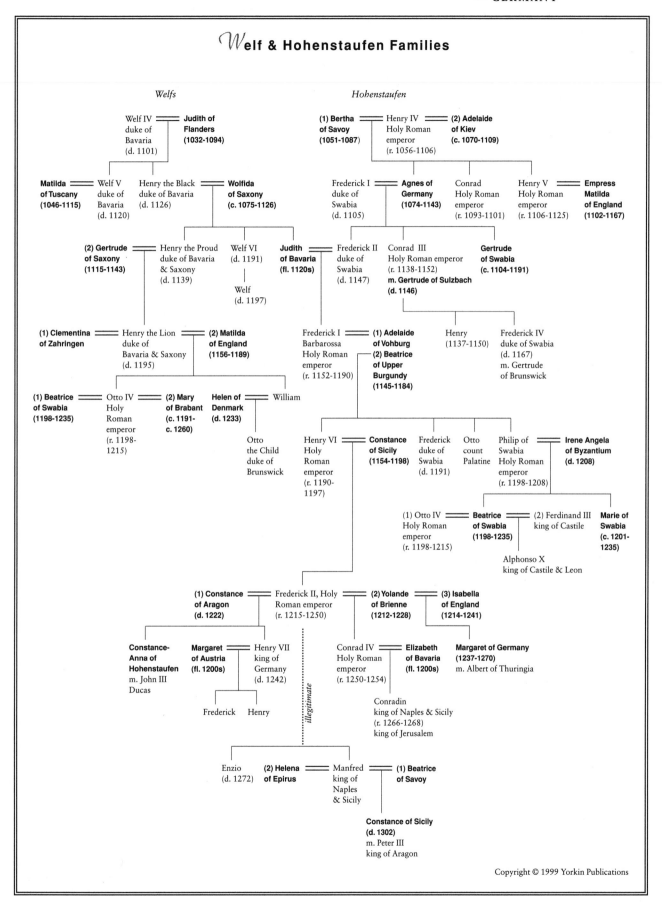

The House of Wittelsbach
Main Line (1180–1508)

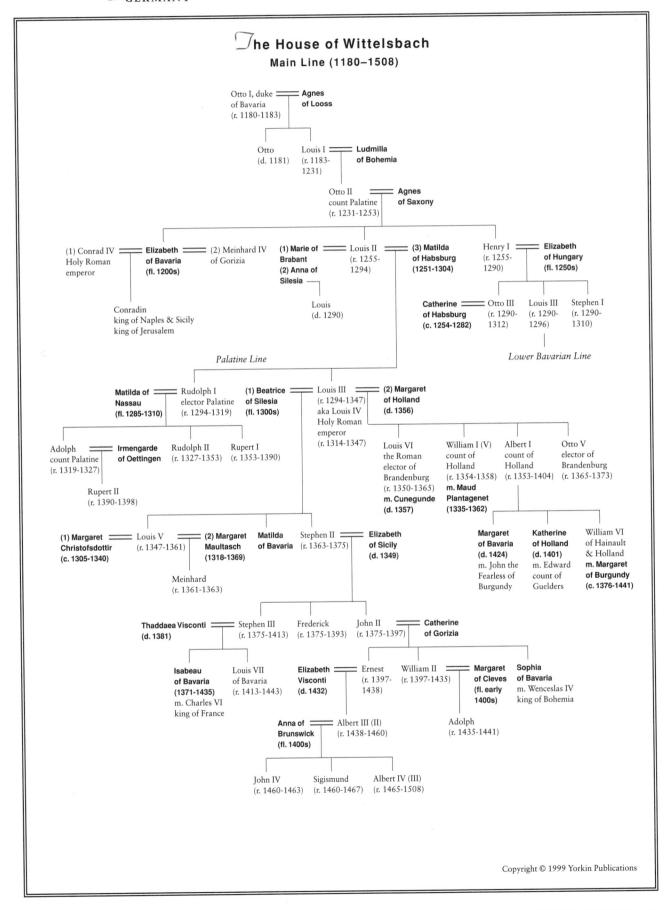

Otto I, duke of Bavaria (r. 1180-1183) ═══ **Agnes of Looss**

Otto (d. 1181)

Louis I (r. 1183-1231) ═══ **Ludmilla of Bohemia**

Otto II count Palatine (r. 1231-1253) ═══ **Agnes of Saxony**

(1) Conrad IV Holy Roman emperor ═══ **Elizabeth of Bavaria (fl. 1200s)** ═══ (2) Meinhard IV of Gorizia

(1) Marie of Brabant (2) Anna of Silesia ═══ Louis II (r. 1255-1294) ═══ **(3) Matilda of Habsburg (1251-1304)**

Henry I (r. 1255-1290) ═══ **Elizabeth of Hungary (fl. 1250s)**

Conradin king of Naples & Sicily king of Jerusalem

Louis (d. 1290)

Catherine of Habsburg (c. 1254-1282) ═══ Otto III (r. 1290-1312)

Louis III (r. 1290-1296)

Stephen I (r. 1290-1310)

Palatine Line

Lower Bavarian Line

Matilda of Nassau (fl. 1285-1310) ═══ Rudolph I elector Palatine (r. 1294-1319)

(1) Beatrice of Silesia (fl. 1300s) ═══ Louis III (r. 1294-1347) aka Louis IV Holy Roman emperor (r. 1314-1347) ═══ **(2) Margaret of Holland (d. 1356)**

Adolph count Palatine (r. 1319-1327) ═══ **Irmengarde of Oettingen**

Rudolph II (r. 1327-1353)

Rupert I (r. 1353-1390)

Louis VI the Roman elector of Brandenburg (r. 1350-1365) **m. Cunegunde (d. 1357)**

William I (V) count of Holland (r. 1354-1358) **m. Maud Plantagenet (1335-1362)**

Albert I count of Holland (r. 1353-1404)

Otto V elector of Brandenburg (r. 1365-1373)

Rupert II (r. 1390-1398)

(1) Margaret Christofsdottir (c. 1305-1340) ═══ Louis V (r. 1347-1361) ═══ **(2) Margaret Maultasch (1318-1369)**

Matilda of Bavaria

Stephen II (r. 1363-1375) ═══ **Elizabeth of Sicily (d. 1349)**

Margaret of Bavaria (d. 1424) m. John the Fearless of Burgundy

Katherine of Holland (d. 1401) m. Edward count of Guelders

William VI of Hainault & Holland **m. Margaret of Burgundy (c. 1376-1441)**

Meinhard (r. 1361-1363)

Thaddaea Visconti (d. 1381) ═══ Stephen III (r. 1375-1413)

Frederick (r. 1375-1393)

John II (r. 1375-1397) ═══ **Catherine of Gorizia**

Isabeau of Bavaria (1371-1435) m. Charles VI king of France

Louis VII of Bavaria (r. 1413-1443)

Elizabeth Visconti (d. 1432) ═══ Ernest (r. 1397-1438)

William II (r. 1397-1435) ═══ **Margaret of Cleves (fl. early 1400s)**

Sophia of Bavaria m. Wenceslas IV king of Bohemia

Anna of Brunswick (fl. 1400s) ═══ Albert III (II) (r. 1438-1460)

Adolph (r. 1435-1441)

John IV (r. 1460-1463)

Sigismund (r. 1460-1467)

Albert IV (III) (r. 1465-1508)

The House of Habsburg
(1273–1519)

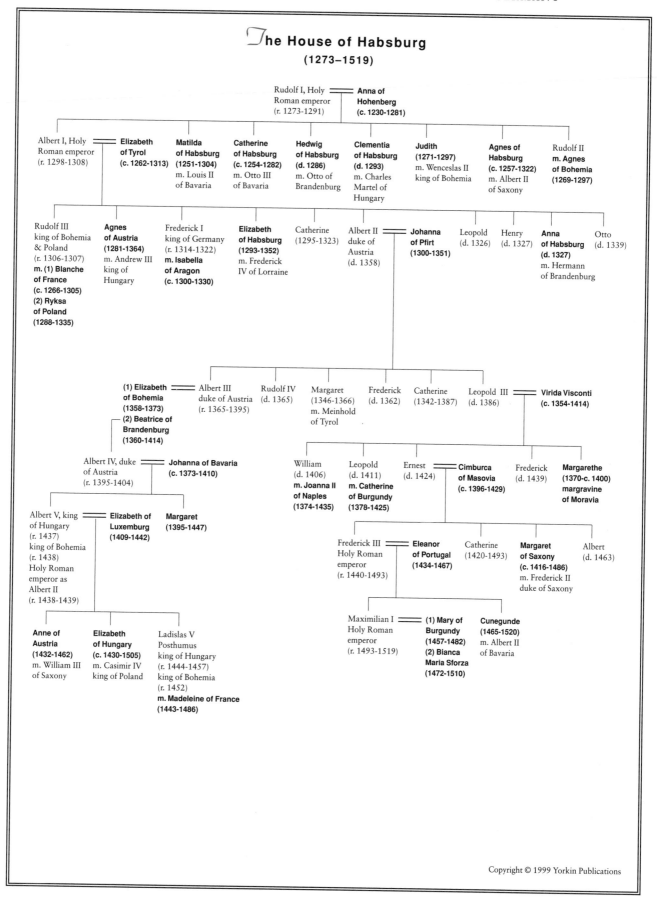

The House of Habsburg
(1493–1780)

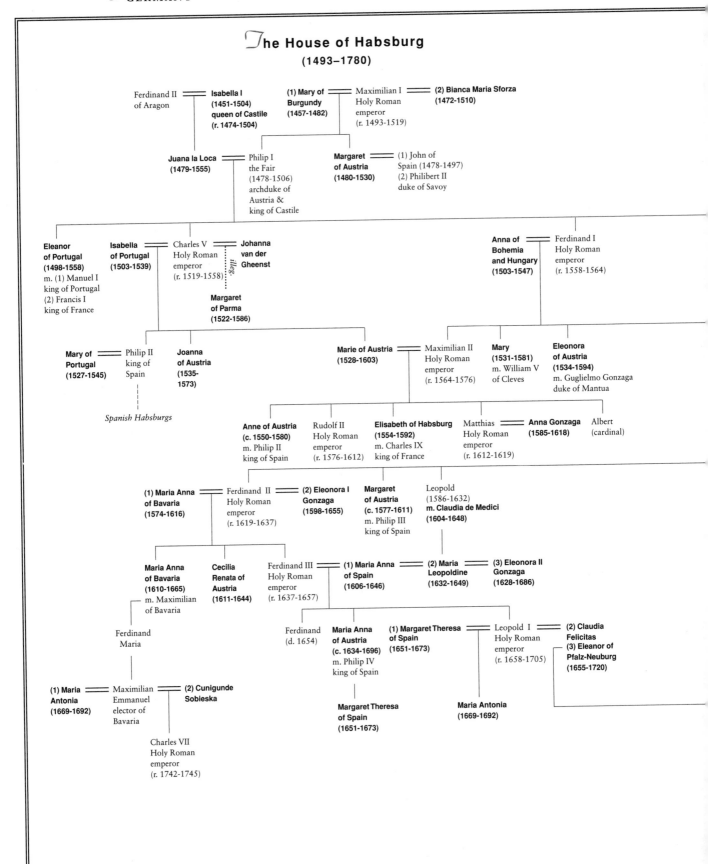

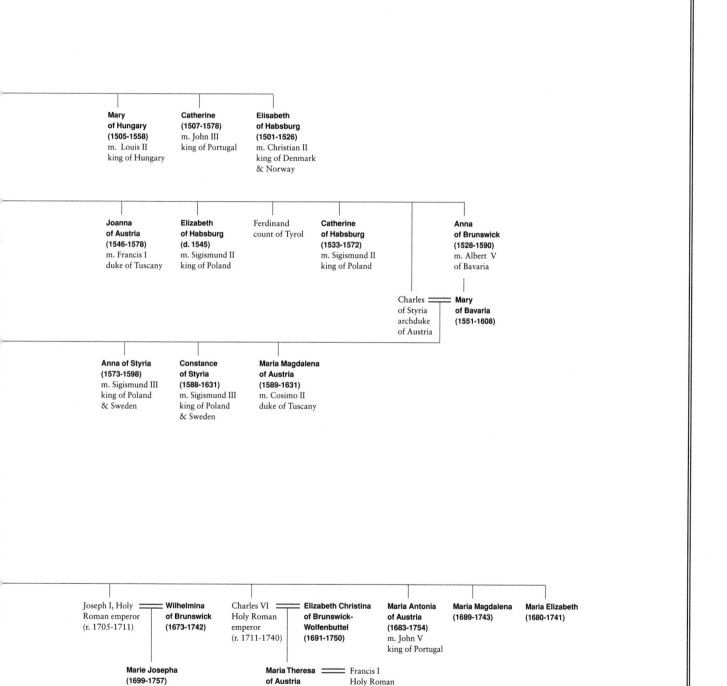

**Mary
of Hungary
(1505-1558)**
m. Louis II
king of Hungary

**Catherine
(1507-1578)**
m. John III
king of Portugal

**Elisabeth
of Habsburg
(1501-1526)**
m. Christian II
king of Denmark
& Norway

**Joanna
of Austria
(1546-1578)**
m. Francis I
duke of Tuscany

**Elizabeth
of Habsburg
(d. 1545)**
m. Sigismund II
king of Poland

Ferdinand
count of Tyrol

**Catherine
of Habsburg
(1533-1572)**
m. Sigismund II
king of Poland

**Anna
of Brunswick
(1528-1590)**
m. Albert V
of Bavaria

Charles ════ **Mary
of Styria   of Bavaria
archduke   (1551-1608)**
of Austria

**Anna of Styria
(1573-1598)**
m. Sigismund III
king of Poland
& Sweden

**Constance
of Styria
(1588-1631)**
m. Sigismund III
king of Poland
& Sweden

**Maria Magdalena
of Austria
(1589-1631)**
m. Cosimo II
duke of Tuscany

Joseph I, Holy ════ **Wilhelmina
Roman emperor   of Brunswick
(r. 1705-1711)   (1673-1742)**

Charles VI ════ **Elizabeth Christina
Holy Roman   of Brunswick-
emperor   Wolfenbuttel
(r. 1711-1740) (1691-1750)**

**Maria Antonia
of Austria
(1683-1754)**
m. John V
king of Portugal

**Maria Magdalena
(1689-1743)**

**Maria Elizabeth
(1680-1741)**

**Marie Josepha
(1699-1757)**
m. Frederick
Augustus III
king of Poland

**Maria Theresa ════ Francis I
of Austria   Holy Roman
(1717-1780)   emperor
                      (r. 1745-1765)**

The House of Hohenzollern
(1417–1713)

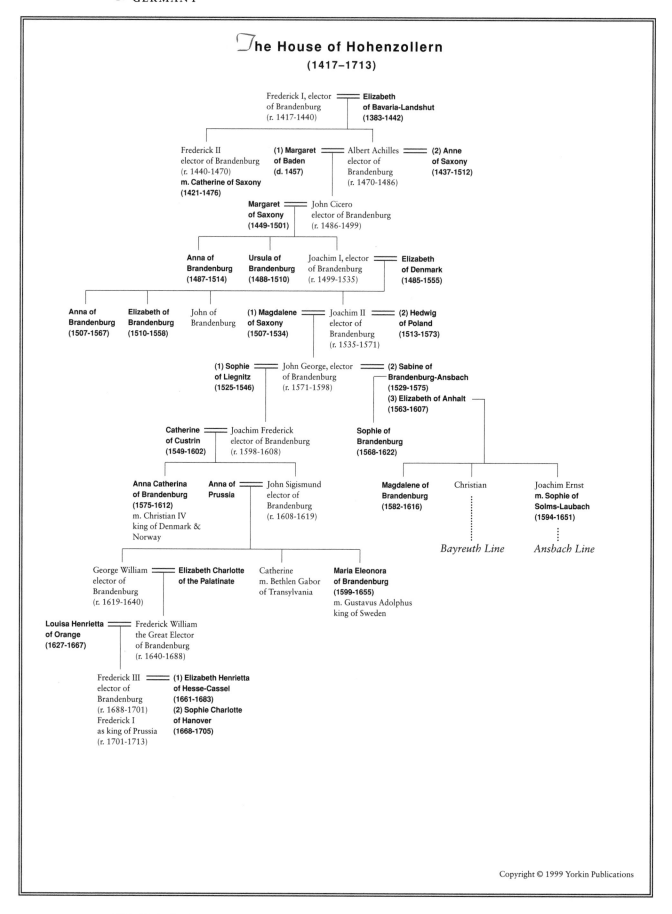

Frederick I, elector
of Brandenburg
(r. 1417-1440)

**Elizabeth
of Bavaria-Landshut
(1383-1442)**

Frederick II
elector of Brandenburg
(r. 1440-1470)
**m. Catherine of Saxony
(1421-1476)**

**(1) Margaret
of Baden
(d. 1457)**

Albert Achilles
elector of
Brandenburg
(r. 1470-1486)

**(2) Anne
of Saxony
(1437-1512)**

**Margaret
of Saxony
(1449-1501)**

John Cicero
elector of Brandenburg
(r. 1486-1499)

**Anna of
Brandenburg
(1487-1514)**

**Ursula of
Brandenburg
(1488-1510)**

Joachim I, elector
of Brandenburg
(r. 1499-1535)

**Elizabeth
of Denmark
(1485-1555)**

**Anna of
Brandenburg
(1507-1567)**

**Elizabeth of
Brandenburg
(1510-1558)**

John of
Brandenburg

**(1) Magdalene
of Saxony
(1507-1534)**

Joachim II
elector of
Brandenburg
(r. 1535-1571)

**(2) Hedwig
of Poland
(1513-1573)**

**(1) Sophie
of Liegnitz
(1525-1546)**

John George, elector
of Brandenburg
(r. 1571-1598)

**(2) Sabine of
Brandenburg-Ansbach
(1529-1575)
(3) Elizabeth of Anhalt
(1563-1607)**

**Catherine
of Custrin
(1549-1602)**

Joachim Frederick
elector of Brandenburg
(r. 1598-1608)

**Sophie of
Brandenburg
(1568-1622)**

**Anna Catherina
of Brandenburg
(1575-1612)
m. Christian IV
king of Denmark &
Norway**

**Anna of
Prussia**

John Sigismund
elector of
Brandenburg
(r. 1608-1619)

**Magdalene of
Brandenburg
(1582-1616)**

Christian

⋮

Bayreuth Line

Joachim Ernst
**m. Sophie of
Solms-Laubach
(1594-1651)**

⋮

Ansbach Line

George William
elector of
Brandenburg
(r. 1619-1640)

**Elizabeth Charlotte
of the Palatinate**

Catherine
m. Bethlen Gabor
of Transylvania

**Maria Eleonora
of Brandenburg
(1599-1655)
m. Gustavus Adolphus
king of Sweden**

**Louisa Henrietta
of Orange
(1627-1667)**

Frederick William
the Great Elector
of Brandenburg
(r. 1640-1688)

Frederick III
elector of
Brandenburg
(r. 1688-1701)
Frederick I
as king of Prussia
(r. 1701-1713)

**(1) Elizabeth Henrietta
of Hesse-Cassel
(1661-1683)
(2) Sophie Charlotte
of Hanover
(1668-1705)**

𝒯he House of Hohenzollern
(1701–1918)

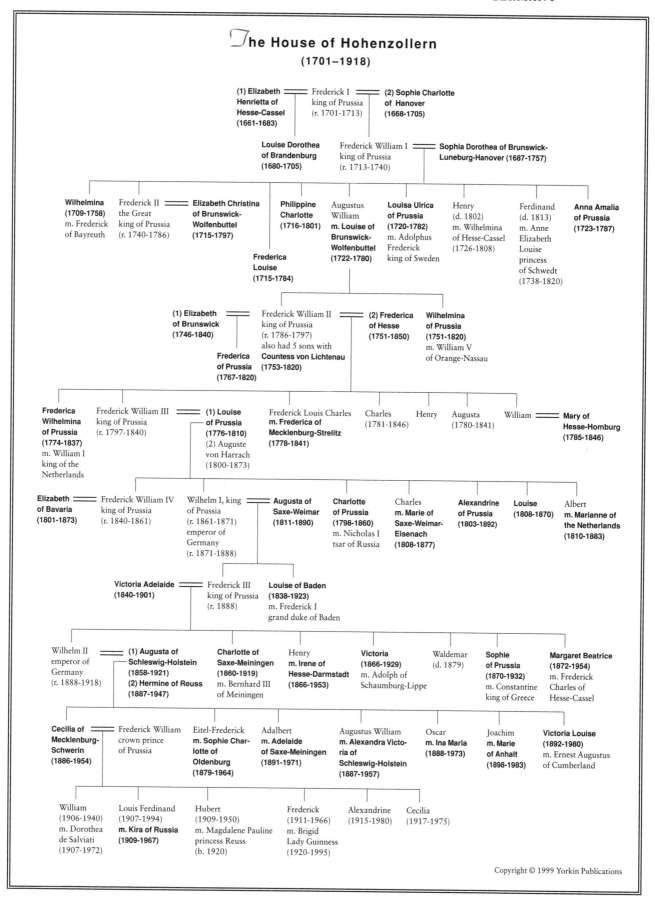

*C*leves-Julich Succession
(1609)

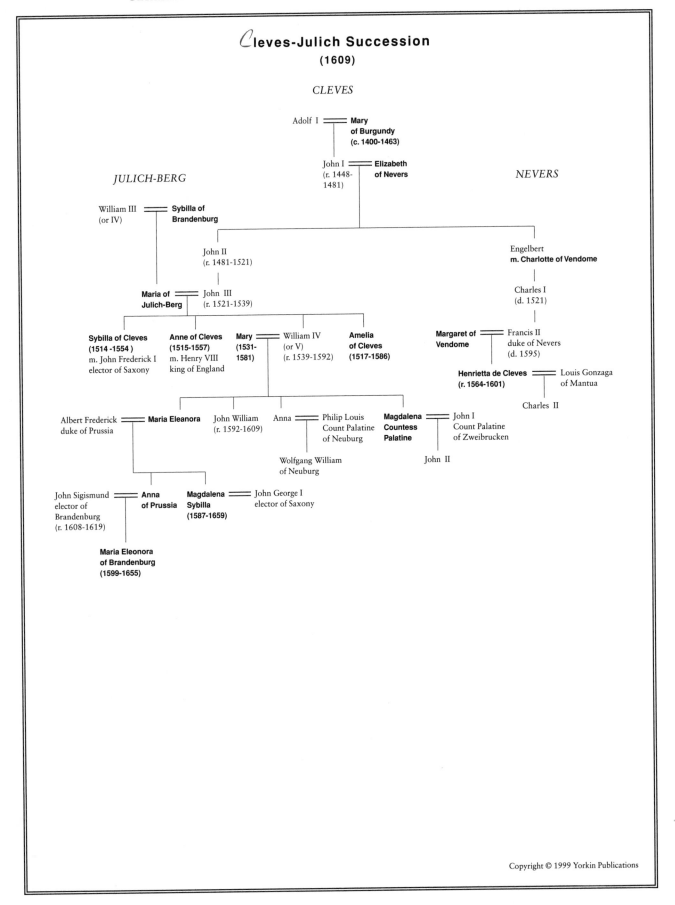

CLEVES

Adolf I ══ **Mary of Burgundy (c. 1400-1463)**

John I (r. 1448-1481) ══ **Elizabeth of Nevers**

JULICH-BERG

NEVERS

William III (or IV) ══ **Sybilla of Brandenburg**

John II (r. 1481-1521)

Engelbert **m. Charlotte of Vendome**

Charles I (d. 1521)

Maria of Julich-Berg ══ John III (r. 1521-1539)

Sybilla of Cleves (1514-1554) m. John Frederick I elector of Saxony

Anne of Cleves (1515-1557) m. Henry VIII king of England

Mary (1531-1581) ══ William IV (or V) (r. 1539-1592)

Amelia of Cleves (1517-1586)

Margaret of Vendome ══ Francis II duke of Nevers (d. 1595)

Henrietta de Cleves (r. 1564-1601) ══ Louis Gonzaga of Mantua

Charles II

Albert Frederick duke of Prussia ══ **Maria Eleanora**

John William (r. 1592-1609)

Anna ══ Philip Louis Count Palatine of Neuburg

Magdalena Countess Palatine ══ John I Count Palatine of Zweibrucken

Wolfgang William of Neuburg

John II

John Sigismund elector of Brandenburg (r. 1608-1619) ══ **Anna of Prussia**

Magdalena Sybilla (1587-1659) ══ John George I elector of Saxony

Maria Eleonora of Brandenburg (1599-1655)

Copyright © 1999 Yorkin Publications

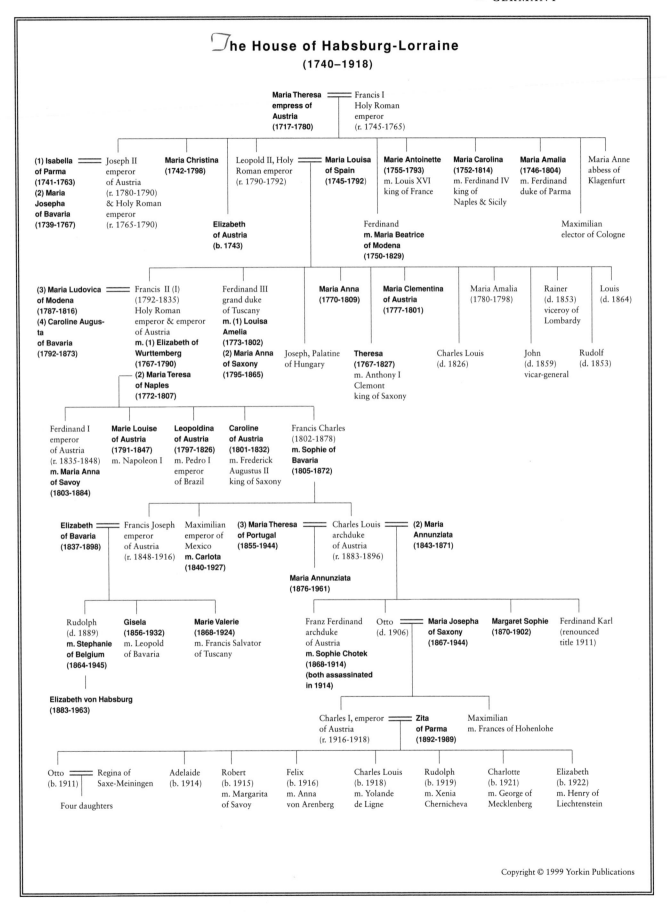

𝒯he House of Habsburg-Lorraine
(1740–1918)

Maria Theresa empress of Austria (1717-1780) ═══ Francis I Holy Roman emperor (r. 1745-1765)

(1) Isabella of Parma (1741-1763) (2) Maria Josepha of Bavaria (1739-1767) ═══ Joseph II emperor of Austria (r. 1780-1790) & Holy Roman emperor (r. 1765-1790)

Maria Christina (1742-1798)

Leopold II, Holy Roman emperor (r. 1790-1792) ═══ **Maria Louisa of Spain (1745-1792)**

Marie Antoinette (1755-1793) m. Louis XVI king of France

Maria Carolina (1752-1814) m. Ferdinand IV king of Naples & Sicily

Maria Amalia (1746-1804) m. Ferdinand duke of Parma

Maria Anne abbess of Klagenfurt

Elizabeth of Austria (b. 1743)

Ferdinand m. Maria Beatrice of Modena (1750-1829)

Maximilian elector of Cologne

(3) Maria Ludovica of Modena (1787-1816) (4) Caroline Augusta of Bavaria (1792-1873) ═══ Francis II (I) (1792-1835) Holy Roman emperor & emperor of Austria **m. (1) Elizabeth of Wurttemberg (1767-1790) (2) Maria Teresa of Naples (1772-1807)**

Ferdinand III grand duke of Tuscany m. (1) Louisa Amelia (1773-1802) (2) Maria Anna of Saxony (1795-1865)

Maria Anna (1770-1809)

Maria Clementina of Austria (1777-1801)

Maria Amalia (1780-1798)

Rainer (d. 1853) viceroy of Lombardy

Louis (d. 1864)

Joseph, Palatine of Hungary

Theresa (1767-1827) m. Anthony I Clemont king of Saxony

Charles Louis (d. 1826)

John (d. 1859) vicar-general

Rudolf (d. 1853)

Ferdinand I emperor of Austria (r. 1835-1848) **m. Maria Anna of Savoy (1803-1884)**

Marie Louise of Austria (1791-1847) m. Napoleon I

Leopoldina of Austria (1797-1826) m. Pedro I emperor of Brazil

Caroline of Austria (1801-1832) m. Frederick Augustus II king of Saxony

Francis Charles (1802-1878) **m. Sophie of Bavaria (1805-1872)**

Elizabeth of Bavaria (1837-1898) ═══ Francis Joseph emperor of Austria (r. 1848-1916)

Maximilian emperor of Mexico **m. Carlota (1840-1927)**

(3) Maria Theresa of Portugal (1855-1944) ═══ Charles Louis archduke of Austria (r. 1883-1896) ═══ **(2) Maria Annunziata (1843-1871)**

Maria Annunziata (1876-1961)

Rudolph (d. 1889) **m. Stephanie of Belgium (1864-1945)**

Gisela (1856-1932) m. Leopold of Bavaria

Marie Valerie (1868-1924) m. Francis Salvator of Tuscany

Franz Ferdinand archduke of Austria **m. Sophie Chotek (1868-1914) (both assassinated in 1914)**

Otto (d. 1906) ═══ **Maria Josepha of Saxony (1867-1944)**

Margaret Sophie (1870-1902)

Ferdinand Karl (renounced title 1911)

Elizabeth von Habsburg (1883-1963)

Charles I, emperor of Austria (r. 1916-1918) ═══ **Zita of Parma (1892-1989)**

Maximilian m. Frances of Hohenlohe

Otto (b. 1911) ═══ Regina of Saxe-Meiningen

Adelaide (b. 1914)

Robert (b. 1915) m. Margarita of Savoy

Felix (b. 1916) m. Anna von Arenberg

Charles Louis (b. 1918) m. Yolande de Ligne

Rudolph (b. 1919) m. Xenia Chernicheva

Charlotte (b. 1921) m. George of Mecklenberg

Elizabeth (b. 1922) m. Henry of Liechtenstein

Four daughters

𝒬ueens and Kings of Bavaria
(1805–1918)

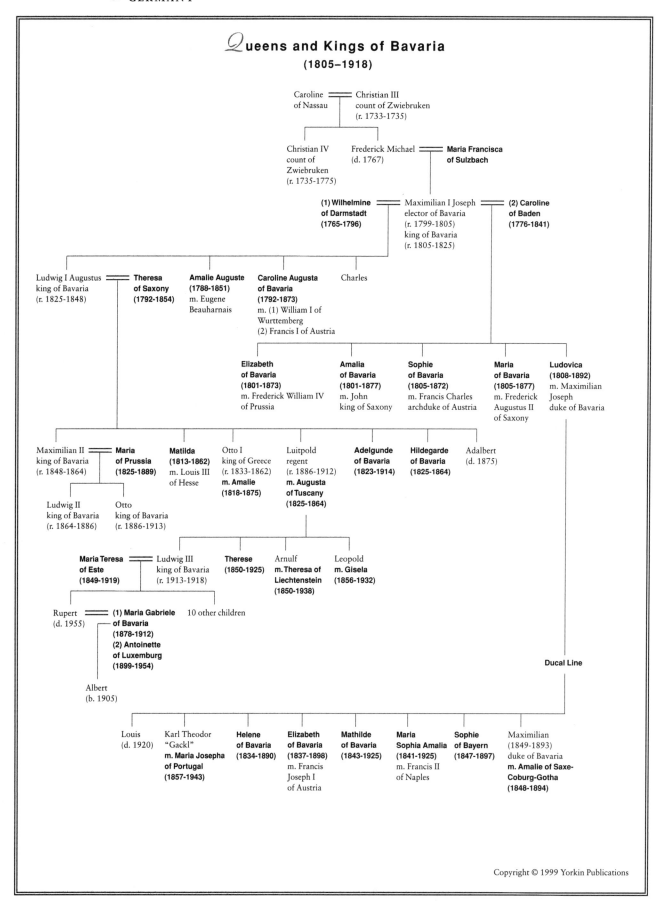

Caroline of Nassau ═══ Christian III count of Zwiebruken (r. 1733-1735)

Christian IV count of Zwiebruken (r. 1735-1775)

Frederick Michael (d. 1767) ═══ **Maria Francisca of Sulzbach**

(1) Wilhelmine of Darmstadt (1765-1796) ═══ Maximilian I Joseph elector of Bavaria (r. 1799-1805) king of Bavaria (r. 1805-1825) ═══ **(2) Caroline of Baden (1776-1841)**

Ludwig I Augustus king of Bavaria (r. 1825-1848) ═══ **Theresa of Saxony (1792-1854)**

Amalie Auguste (1788-1851) m. Eugene Beauharnais

Caroline Augusta of Bavaria (1792-1873) m. (1) William I of Wurttemberg (2) Francis I of Austria

Charles

Elizabeth of Bavaria (1801-1873) m. Frederick William IV of Prussia

Amalia of Bavaria (1801-1877) m. John king of Saxony

Sophie of Bavaria (1805-1872) m. Francis Charles archduke of Austria

Maria of Bavaria (1805-1877) m. Frederick Augustus II of Saxony

Ludovica (1808-1892) m. Maximilian Joseph duke of Bavaria

Maximilian II king of Bavaria (r. 1848-1864) ═══ **Maria of Prussia (1825-1889)**

Matilda (1813-1862) m. Louis III of Hesse

Otto I king of Greece (r. 1833-1862) **m. Amalie (1818-1875)**

Luitpold regent (r. 1886-1912) **m. Augusta of Tuscany (1825-1864)**

Adelgunde of Bavaria (1823-1914)

Hildegarde of Bavaria (1825-1864)

Adalbert (d. 1875)

Ludwig II king of Bavaria (r. 1864-1886)

Otto king of Bavaria (r. 1886-1913)

Maria Teresa of Este (1849-1919) ═══ Ludwig III king of Bavaria (r. 1913-1918)

Therese (1850-1925)

Arnulf **m. Theresa of Liechtenstein (1850-1938)**

Leopold **m. Gisela (1856-1932)**

Rupert (d. 1955) ═══ **(1) Maria Gabriele of Bavaria (1878-1912) (2) Antoinette of Luxemburg (1899-1954)**

10 other children

Albert (b. 1905)

Ducal Line

Louis (d. 1920)

Karl Theodor "Gackl" **m. Maria Josepha of Portugal (1857-1943)**

Helene of Bavaria (1834-1890)

Elizabeth of Bavaria (1837-1898) m. Francis Joseph I of Austria

Mathilde of Bavaria (1843-1925)

Maria Sophia Amalia (1841-1925) m. Francis II of Naples

Sophie of Bayern (1847-1897)

Maximilian (1849-1893) duke of Bavaria **m. Amalie of Saxe-Coburg-Gotha (1848-1894)**

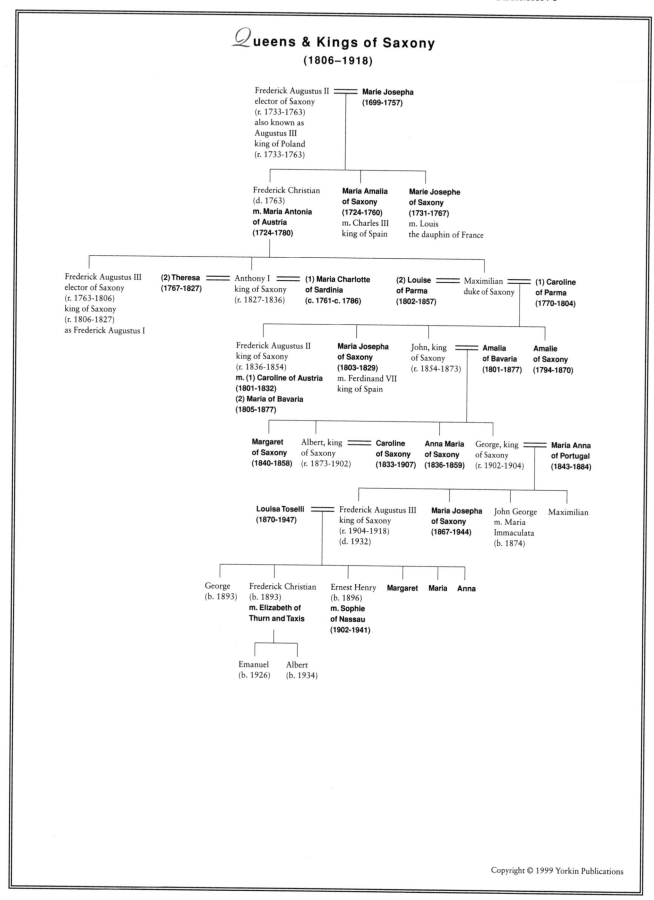

Queens & Kings of Saxony
(1806–1918)

Frederick Augustus II
elector of Saxony
(r. 1733-1763)
also known as
Augustus III
king of Poland
(r. 1733-1763)
═══ **Marie Josepha
(1699-1757)**

Frederick Christian
(d. 1763)
**m. Maria Antonia
of Austria
(1724-1780)**

**Maria Amalia
of Saxony
(1724-1760)**
m. Charles III
king of Spain

**Marie Josephe
of Saxony
(1731-1767)**
m. Louis
the dauphin of France

Frederick Augustus III
elector of Saxony
(r. 1763-1806)
king of Saxony
(r. 1806-1827)
as Frederick Augustus I

**(2) Theresa
(1767-1827)** ═══ Anthony I
king of Saxony
(r. 1827-1836) ═══ **(1) Maria Charlotte
of Sardinia
(c. 1761-c. 1786)**

**(2) Louise
of Parma
(1802-1857)** ═══ Maximilian
duke of Saxony ═══ **(1) Caroline
of Parma
(1770-1804)**

Frederick Augustus II
king of Saxony
(r. 1836-1854)
**m. (1) Caroline of Austria
(1801-1832)
(2) Maria of Bavaria
(1805-1877)**

**Maria Josepha
of Saxony
(1803-1829)**
m. Ferdinand VII
king of Spain

John, king
of Saxony
(r. 1854-1873) ═══ **Amalia
of Bavaria
(1801-1877)**

**Amalie
of Saxony
(1794-1870)**

**Margaret
of Saxony
(1840-1858)**

Albert, king
of Saxony
(r. 1873-1902) ═══ **Caroline
of Saxony
(1833-1907)**

**Anna Maria
of Saxony
(1836-1859)**

George, king
of Saxony
(r. 1902-1904) ═══ **Maria Anna
of Portugal
(1843-1884)**

**Louisa Toselli
(1870-1947)** ═══ Frederick Augustus III
king of Saxony
(r. 1904-1918)
(d. 1932)

**Maria Josepha
of Saxony
(1867-1944)**

John George
m. Maria
Immaculata
(b. 1874)

Maximilian

George
(b. 1893)

Frederick Christian
(b. 1893)
**m. Elizabeth of
Thurn and Taxis**

Ernest Henry
(b. 1896)
**m. Sophie
of Nassau
(1902-1941)**

Margaret   **Maria**   **Anna**

Emanuel
(b. 1926)

Albert
(b. 1934)

Queens & Kings of Wurttemberg

(1806-1918)

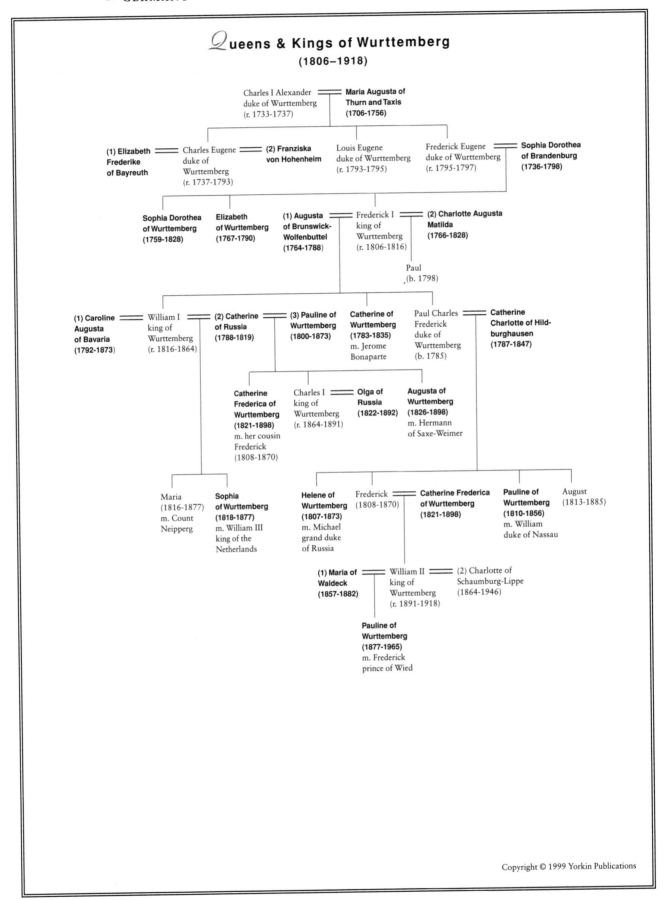

Charles I Alexander
duke of Wurttemberg
(r. 1733-1737)
=== **Maria Augusta of
Thurn and Taxis
(1706-1756)**

**(1) Elizabeth
Frederike
of Bayreuth** === Charles Eugene
duke of
Wurttemberg
(r. 1737-1793) === **(2) Franziska
von Hohenheim**   Louis Eugene
duke of Wurttemberg
(r. 1793-1795)   Frederick Eugene
duke of Wurttemberg
(r. 1795-1797) === **Sophia Dorothea
of Brandenburg
(1736-1798)**

**Sophia Dorothea
of Wurttemberg
(1759-1828)**   **Elizabeth
of Wurttemberg
(1767-1790)**   **(1) Augusta
of Brunswick-
Wolfenbuttel
(1764-1788)** === Frederick I
king of
Wurttemberg
(r. 1806-1816) === **(2) Charlotte Augusta
Matilda
(1766-1828)**

Paul
(b. 1798)

**(1) Caroline
Augusta
of Bavaria
(1792-1873)** === William I
king of
Wurttemberg
(r. 1816-1864) === **(2) Catherine
of Russia
(1788-1819)** === **(3) Pauline of
Wurttemberg
(1800-1873)**   **Catherine of
Wurttemberg
(1783-1835)
m. Jerome
Bonaparte**   Paul Charles
Frederick
duke of
Wurttemberg
(b. 1785) === **Catherine
Charlotte of Hild-
burghausen
(1787-1847)**

**Catherine
Frederica of
Wurttemberg
(1821-1898)
m. her cousin
Frederick
(1808-1870)**   Charles I
king of
Wurttemberg
(r. 1864-1891) === **Olga of
Russia
(1822-1892)**   **Augusta of
Wurttemberg
(1826-1898)
m. Hermann
of Saxe-Weimer**

Maria
(1816-1877)
m. Count
Neipperg   **Sophia
of Wurttemberg
(1818-1877)
m. William III
king of the
Netherlands**   **Helene of
Wurttemberg
(1807-1873)
m. Michael
grand duke
of Russia**   Frederick
(1808-1870) === **Catherine Frederica
of Wurttemberg
(1821-1898)**   **Pauline of
Wurttemberg
(1810-1856)
m. William
duke of Nassau**   August
(1813-1885)

**(1) Maria of
Waldeck
(1857-1882)** === William II
king of
Wurttemberg
(r. 1891-1918) === **(2) Charlotte of
Schaumburg-Lippe
(1864-1946)**

**Pauline of
Wurttemberg
(1877-1965)
m. Frederick
prince of Wied**

Copyright © 1999 Yorkin Publications

𝒬ueens & Kings of Greece: Danish Line
(1863–1974)

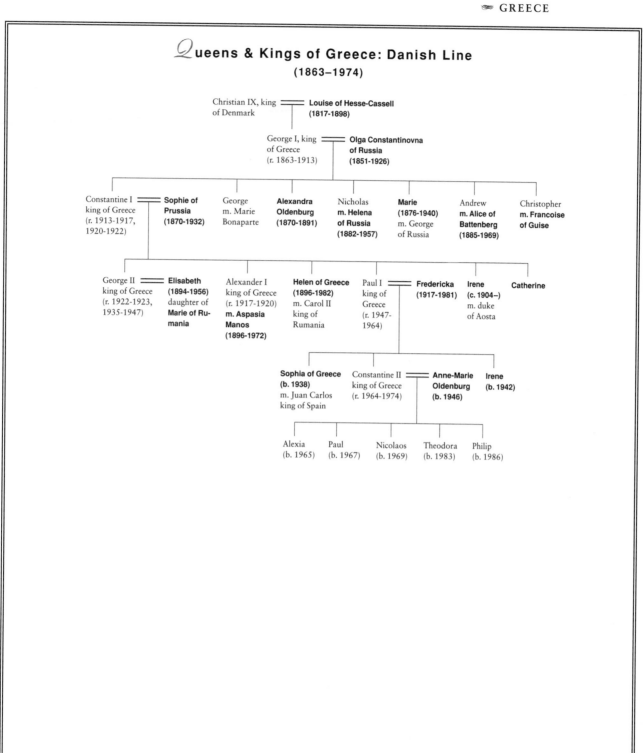

Christian IX, king of Denmark ═══ **Louise of Hesse-Cassell (1817-1898)**

George I, king of Greece (r. 1863-1913) ═══ **Olga Constantinovna of Russia (1851-1926)**

Constantine I king of Greece (r. 1913-1917, 1920-1922) ═══ **Sophie of Prussia (1870-1932)**

George m. Marie Bonaparte

Alexandra Oldenburg (1870-1891)

Nicholas **m. Helena of Russia (1882-1957)**

Marie (1876-1940) m. George of Russia

Andrew **m. Alice of Battenberg (1885-1969)**

Christopher **m. Francoise of Guise**

George II king of Greece (r. 1922-1923, 1935-1947) ═══ **Elisabeth (1894-1956) daughter of Marie of Ru-mania**

Alexander I king of Greece (r. 1917-1920) **m. Aspasia Manos (1896-1972)**

Helen of Greece (1896-1982) m. Carol II king of Rumania

Paul I king of Greece (r. 1947-1964) ═══ **Fredericka (1917-1981)**

Irene (c. 1904–) m. duke of Aosta

Catherine

Sophia of Greece (b. 1938) m. Juan Carlos king of Spain

Constantine II king of Greece (r. 1964-1974) ═══ **Anne-Marie Oldenburg (b. 1946)**

Irene (b. 1942)

Alexia (b. 1965)

Paul (b. 1967)

Nicolaos (b. 1969)

Theodora (b. 1983)

Philip (b. 1986)

The Arpad Dynasty
(907–1301)

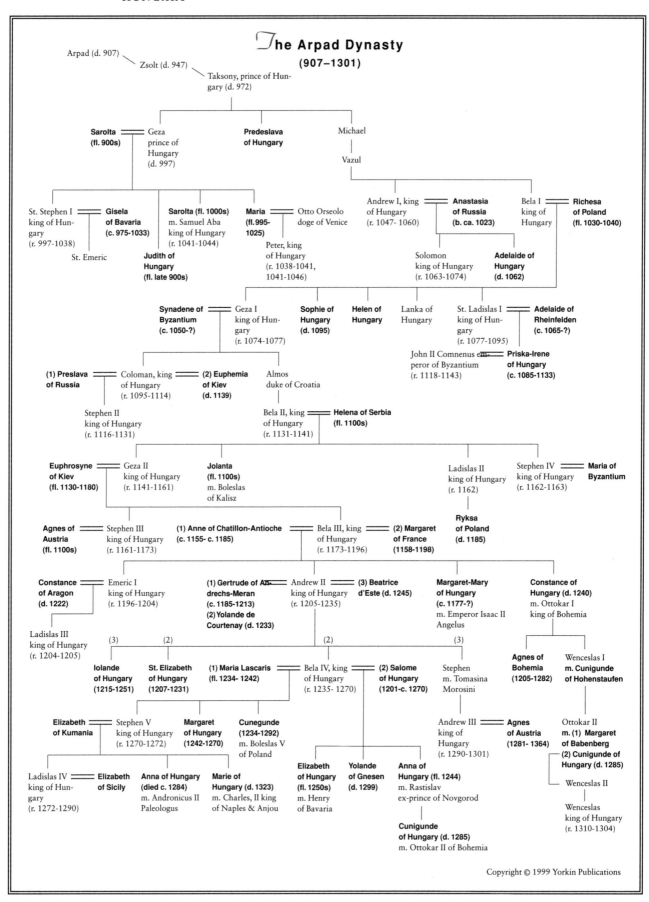

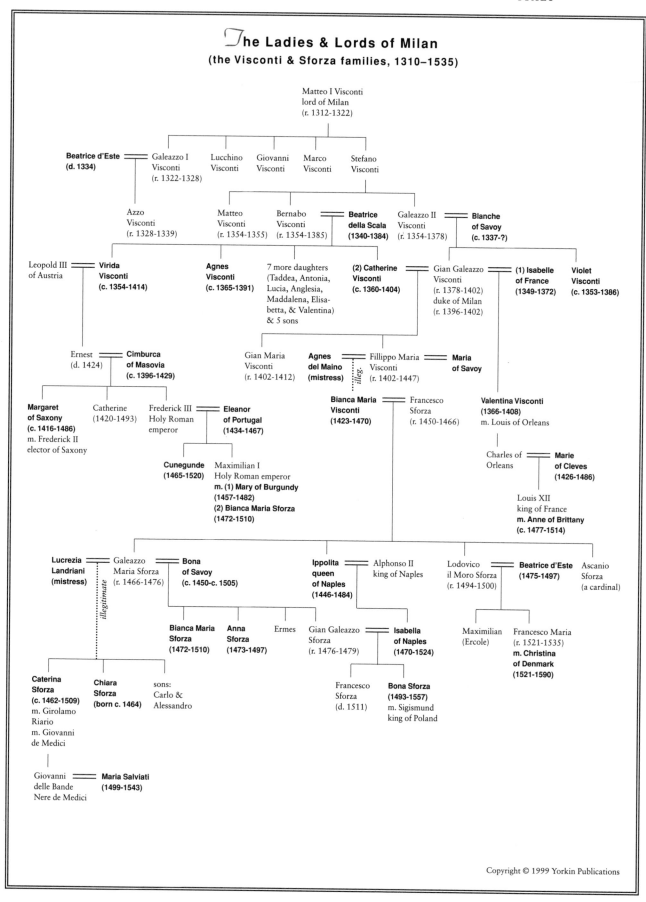

The Ladies & Lords of Milan
(the Visconti & Sforza families, 1310–1535)

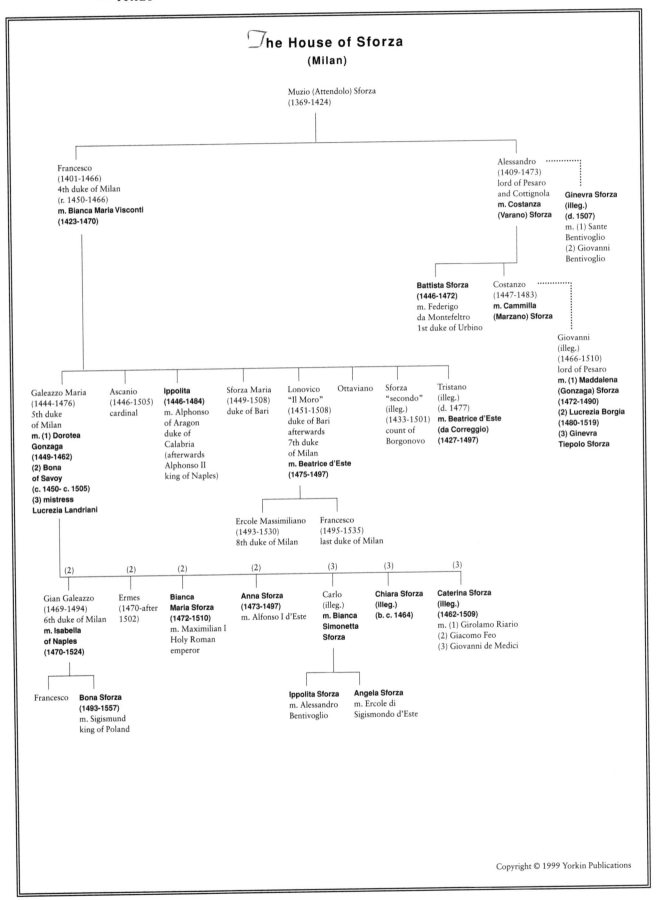

The House of Sforza
(Milan)

Muzio (Attendolo) Sforza
(1369-1424)

Francesco
(1401-1466)
4th duke of Milan
(r. 1450-1466)
m. Bianca Maria Visconti
(1423-1470)

Alessandro
(1409-1473)
lord of Pesaro
and Cottignola
m. Costanza
(Varano) Sforza

Ginevra Sforza
(illeg.)
(d. 1507)
m. (1) Sante
Bentivoglio
(2) Giovanni
Bentivoglio

Battista Sforza
(1446-1472)
m. Federigo
da Montefeltro
1st duke of Urbino

Costanzo
(1447-1483)
m. Cammilla
(Marzano) Sforza

Giovanni
(illeg.)
(1466-1510)
lord of Pesaro
m. (1) Maddalena
(Gonzaga) Sforza
(1472-1490)
(2) Lucrezia Borgia
(1480-1519)
(3) Ginevra
Tiepolo Sforza

Galeazzo Maria
(1444-1476)
5th duke
of Milan
m. (1) Dorotea
Gonzaga
(1449-1462)
(2) Bona
of Savoy
(c. 1450- c. 1505)
(3) mistress
Lucrezia Landriani

Ascanio
(1446-1505)
cardinal

Ippolita
(1446-1484)
m. Alphonso
of Aragon
duke of
Calabria
(afterwards
Alphonso II
king of Naples)

Sforza Maria
(1449-1508)
duke of Bari

Lonovico
"Il Moro"
(1451-1508)
duke of Bari
afterwards
7th duke
of Milan
m. Beatrice d'Este
(1475-1497)

Ottaviano

Sforza
"secondo"
(illeg.)
(1433-1501)
count of
Borgonovo

Tristano
(illeg.)
(d. 1477)
m. Beatrice d'Este
(da Correggio)
(1427-1497)

Ercole Massimiliano
(1493-1530)
8th duke of Milan

Francesco
(1495-1535)
last duke of Milan

(2)

Gian Galeazzo
(1469-1494)
6th duke of Milan
m. Isabella
of Naples
(1470-1524)

(2)

Ermes
(1470-after
1502)

(2)

Bianca
Maria Sforza
(1472-1510)
m. Maximilian
I Holy Roman
emperor

(2)

Anna Sforza
(1473-1497)
m. Alfonso I d'Este

(3)

Carlo
(illeg.)
m. Bianca
Simonetta
Sforza

(3)

Chiara Sforza
(illeg.)
(b. c. 1464)

(3)

Caterina Sforza
(illeg.)
(1462-1509)
m. (1) Girolamo Riario
(2) Giacomo Feo
(3) Giovanni de Medici

Francesco

Bona Sforza
(1493-1557)
m. Sigismund
king of Poland

Ippolita Sforza
m. Alessandro
Bentivoglio

Angela Sforza
m. Ercole di
Sigismondo d'Este

Copyright © 1999 Yorkin Publications

The House of Savoy
(1553–1946)

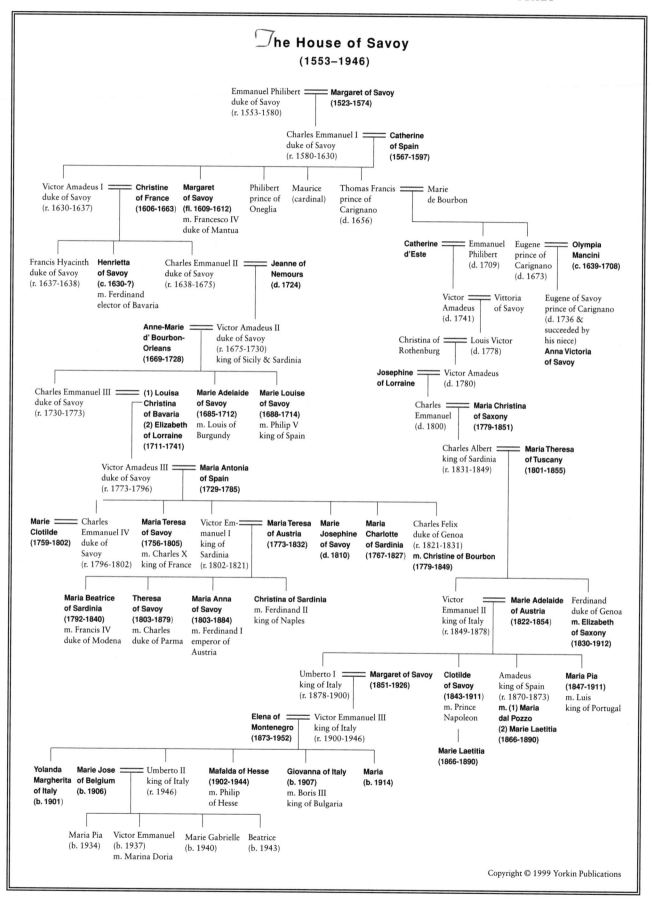

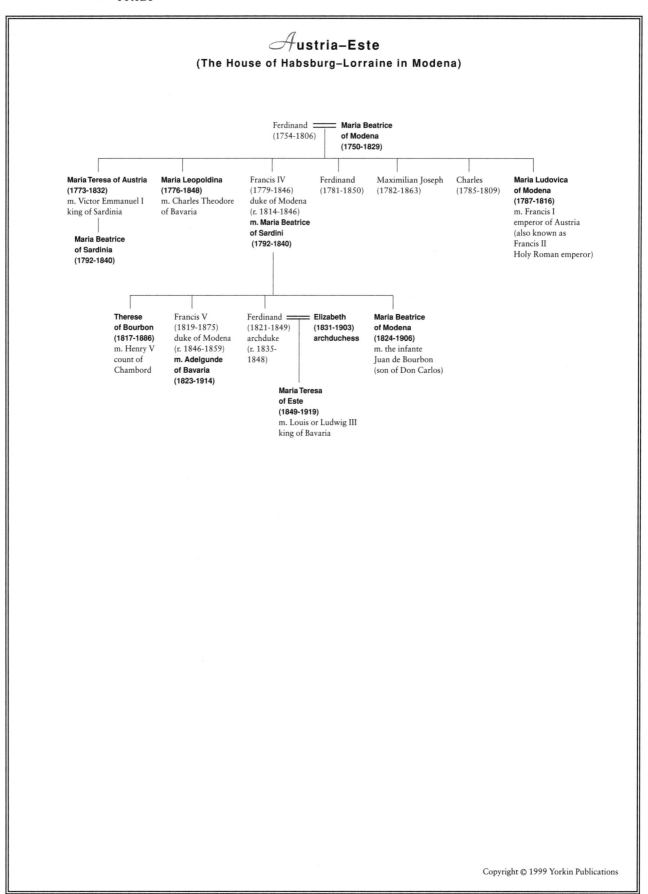

Austria–Este
(The House of Habsburg–Lorraine in Modena)

Ferdinand (1754-1806) ══ **Maria Beatrice of Modena (1750-1829)**

Maria Teresa of Austria (1773-1832)
m. Victor Emmanuel I
king of Sardinia

Maria Beatrice of Sardinia (1792-1840)

Maria Leopoldina (1776-1848)
m. Charles Theodore
of Bavaria

Francis IV
(1779-1846)
duke of Modena
(r. 1814-1846)
m. Maria Beatrice of Sardini (1792-1840)

Ferdinand
(1781-1850)

Maximilian Joseph
(1782-1863)

Charles
(1785-1809)

Maria Ludovica of Modena (1787-1816)
m. Francis I
emperor of Austria
(also known as
Francis II
Holy Roman emperor)

Therese of Bourbon (1817-1886)
m. Henry V
count of
Chambord

Francis V
(1819-1875)
duke of Modena
(r. 1846-1859)
m. Adelgunde of Bavaria (1823-1914)

Ferdinand
(1821-1849)
archduke
(r. 1835-
1848) ══ **Elizabeth (1831-1903) archduchess**

Maria Teresa of Este (1849-1919)
m. Louis or Ludwig III
king of Bavaria

Maria Beatrice of Modena (1824-1906)
m. the infante
Juan de Bourbon
(son of Don Carlos)

The House of Este I

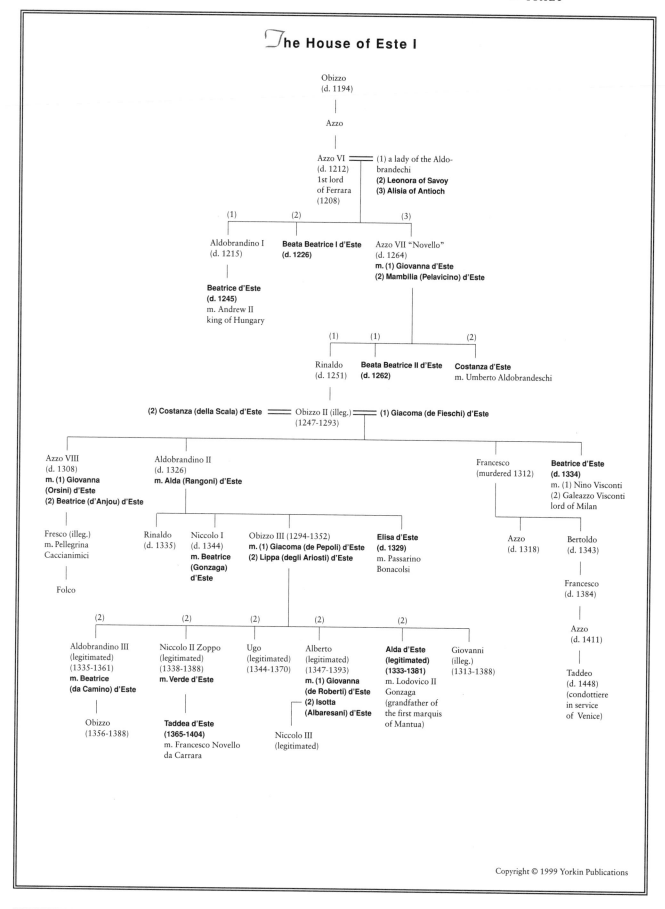

Obizzo
(d. 1194)

Azzo

Azzo VI
(d. 1212)
1st lord
of Ferrara
(1208)
(1) a lady of the Aldo-
brandechi
(2) Leonora of Savoy
(3) Alisia of Antioch

(1)
Aldobrandino I
(d. 1215)

(2)
Beata Beatrice I d'Este
(d. 1226)

(3)
Azzo VII "Novello"
(d. 1264)
m. (1) Giovanna d'Este
(2) Mambilia (Pelavicino) d'Este

Beatrice d'Este
(d. 1245)
m. Andrew II
king of Hungary

(1)
Rinaldo
(d. 1251)

(1)
Beata Beatrice II d'Este
(d. 1262)

(2)
Costanza d'Este
m. Umberto Aldobrandeschi

(2) Costanza (della Scala) d'Este ═══ Obizzo II (illeg.) ═══ (1) Giacoma (de Fieschi) d'Este
(1247-1293)

Azzo VIII
(d. 1308)
m. (1) Giovanna
(Orsini) d'Este
(2) Beatrice (d'Anjou) d'Este

Aldobrandino II
(d. 1326)
m. Alda (Rangoni) d'Este

Francesco
(murdered 1312)

Beatrice d'Este
(d. 1334)
m. (1) Nino Visconti
(2) Galeazzo Visconti
lord of Milan

Fresco (illeg.)
m. Pellegrina
Caccianimici

Rinaldo
(d. 1335)

Niccolo I
(d. 1344)
m. Beatrice
(Gonzaga)
d'Este

Obizzo III (1294-1352)
m. (1) Giacoma (de Pepoli) d'Este
(2) Lippa (degli Ariosti) d'Este

Elisa d'Este
(d. 1329)
m. Passarino
Bonacolsi

Azzo
(d. 1318)

Bertoldo
(d. 1343)

Folco

Francesco
(d. 1384)

Azzo
(d. 1411)

(2)
Aldobrandino III
(legitimated)
(1335-1361)
m. Beatrice
(da Camino) d'Este

(2)
Niccolo II Zoppo
(legitimated)
(1338-1388)
m. Verde d'Este

(2)
Ugo
(legitimated)
(1344-1370)

(2)
Alberto
(legitimated)
(1347-1393)
m. (1) Giovanna
(de Roberti) d'Este
(2) Isotta
(Albaresani) d'Este

(2)
Alda d'Este
(legitimated)
(1333-1381)
m. Lodovico II
Gonzaga
(grandfather of
the first marquis
of Mantua)

Giovanni
(illeg.)
(1313-1388)

Taddeo
(d. 1448)
(condottiere
in service
of Venice)

Obizzo
(1356-1388)

Taddea d'Este
(1365-1404)
m. Francesco Novello
da Carrara

Niccolo III
(legitimated)

The House of Este II

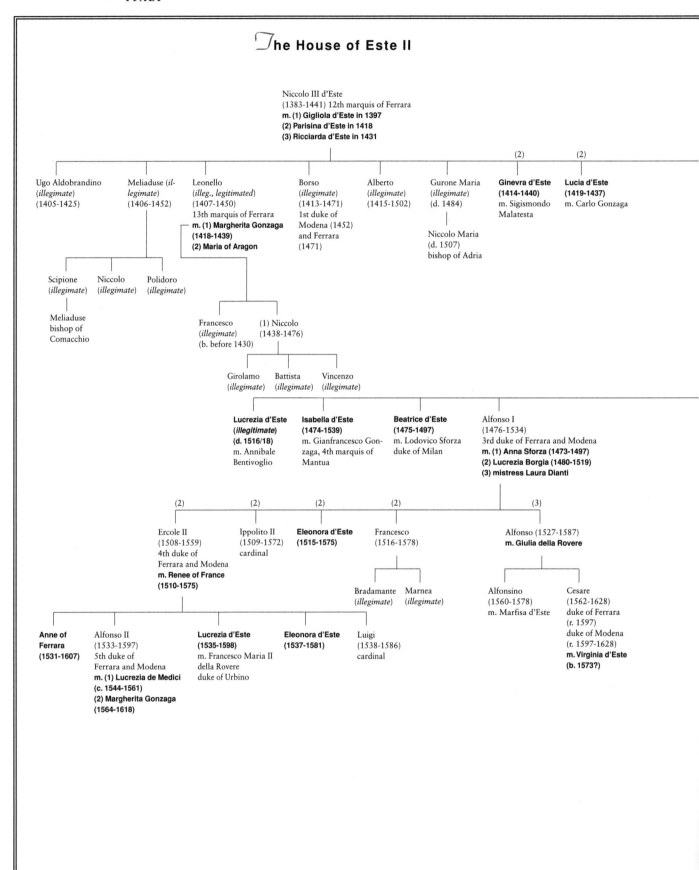

Niccolo III d'Este
(1383-1441) 12th marquis of Ferrara
m. (1) Gigliola d'Este in 1397
(2) Parisina d'Este in 1418
(3) Ricciarda d'Este in 1431

Ugo Aldobrandino
(*illegimate*)
(1405-1425)

Meliaduse (*il-
legimate*)
(1406-1452)

Leonello
(*illeg., legitimated*)
(1407-1450)
13th marquis of Ferrara
m. (1) Margherita Gonzaga
(1418-1439)
(2) Maria of Aragon

Borso
(*illegimate*)
(1413-1471)
1st duke of
Modena (1452)
and Ferrara
(1471)

Alberto
(*illegimate*)
(1415-1502)

Gurone Maria
(*illegimate*)
(d. 1484)

Niccolo Maria
(d. 1507)
bishop of Adria

(2)
Ginevra d'Este
(1414-1440)
m. Sigismondo
Malatesta

(2)
Lucia d'Este
(1419-1437)
m. Carlo Gonzaga

Scipione
(*illegimate*)

Niccolo
(*illegimate*)

Polidoro
(*illegimate*)

Meliaduse
bishop of
Comacchio

Francesco
(*illegimate*)
(b. before 1430)

(1) Niccolo
(1438-1476)

Girolamo
(*illegimate*)

Battista
(*illegimate*)

Vincenzo
(*illegimate*)

Lucrezia d'Este
(***illegitimate***)
(d. 1516/18)
m. Annibale
Bentivoglio

Isabella d'Este
(1474-1539)
m. Gianfrancesco Gon-
zaga, 4th marquis of
Mantua

Beatrice d'Este
(1475-1497)
m. Lodovico Sforza
duke of Milan

Alfonso I
(1476-1534)
3rd duke of Ferrara and Modena
m. (1) Anna Sforza (1473-1497)
(2) Lucrezia Borgia (1480-1519)
(3) mistress Laura Dianti

(2)
Ercole II
(1508-1559)
4th duke of
Ferrara and
Modena
m. Renee of France
(1510-1575)

(2)
Ippolito II
(1509-1572)
cardinal

(2)
Eleonora d'Este
(1515-1575)

(2)
Francesco
(1516-1578)

(3)
Alfonso (1527-1587)
m. Giulia della Rovere

Bradamante
(*illegimate*)

Marnea
(*illegimate*)

Alfonsino
(1560-1578)
m. Marfisa d'Este

Cesare
(1562-1628)
duke of Ferrara
(r. 1597)
duke of Modena
(r. 1597-1628)
m. Virginia d'Este
(b. 1573?)

**Anne of
Ferrara
(1531-1607)**

Alfonso II
(1533-1597)
5th duke of
Ferrara and Modena
m. (1) Lucrezia de Medici
(c. 1544-1561)
(2) Margherita Gonzaga
(1564-1618)

**Lucrezia d'Este
(1535-1598)**
m. Francesco Maria II
della Rovere
duke of Urbino

**Eleonora d'Este
(1537-1581)**

Luigi
(1538-1586)
cardinal

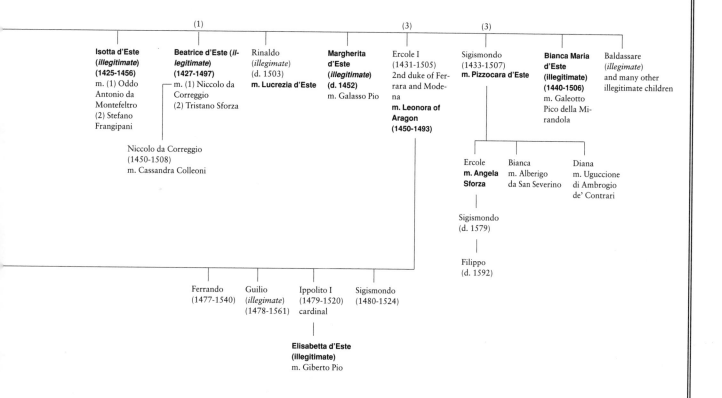

Isotta d'Este
(***illegitimate***)
(1425-1456)
m. (1) Oddo
Antonio da
Montefeltro
(2) Stefano
Frangipani

Beatrice d'Este (***il-legitimate***)
(1427-1497)
— m. (1) Niccolo da
Correggio
(2) Tristano Sforza

Niccolo da Correggio
(1450-1508)
m. Cassandra Colleoni

Rinaldo
(*illegimate*)
(d. 1503)
m. Lucrezia d'Este

**Margherita
d'Este**
(***illegimate***)
(d. 1452)
m. Galasso Pio

Ercole I
(1431-1505)
2nd duke of Fer-
rara and Mode-
na
**m. Leonora of
Aragon
(1450-1493)**

Sigismondo
(1433-1507)
m. Pizzocara d'Este

**Bianca Maria
d'Este**
(***illegimate***)
(1440-1506)
m. Galeotto
Pico della Mi-
randola

Baldassare
(*illegimate*)
and many other
illegitimate children

Ercole
**m. Angela
Sforza**

Sigismondo
(d. 1579)

Filippo
(d. 1592)

Bianca
m. Alberigo
da San Severino

Diana
m. Uguccione
di Ambrogio
de' Contrari

Ferrando
(1477-1540)

Guilio
(*illegimate*)
(1478-1561)

Ippolito I
(1479-1520)
cardinal

Sigismondo
(1480-1524)

**Elisabetta d'Este
(illegitimate)**
m. Giberto Pio

The Gonzagas, Rulers of Mantua
(marquisate 1432, dukedom 1530)

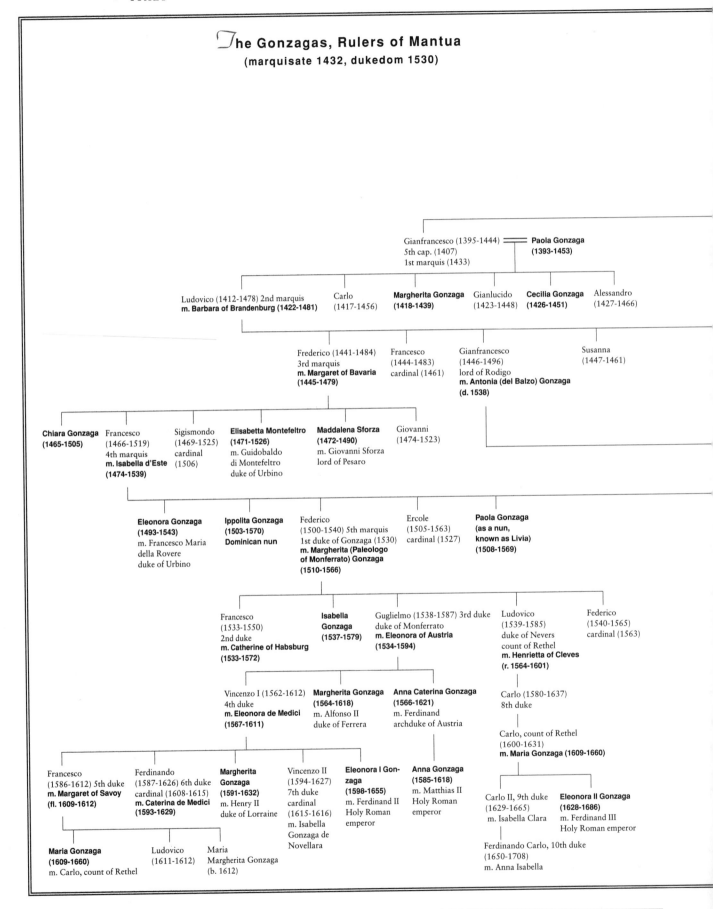

Gianfrancesco (1395-1444)
5th cap. (1407)
1st marquis (1433)
Paola Gonzaga (1393-1453)

Ludovico (1412-1478) 2nd marquis
m. Barbara of Brandenburg (1422-1481)

Carlo (1417-1456)

Margherita Gonzaga (1418-1439)

Gianlucido (1423-1448)

Cecilia Gonzaga (1426-1451)

Alessandro (1427-1466)

Frederico (1441-1484)
3rd marquis
m. Margaret of Bavaria (1445-1479)

Francesco (1444-1483) cardinal (1461)

Gianfrancesco (1446-1496) lord of Rodigo
m. Antonia (del Balzo) Gonzaga (d. 1538)

Susanna (1447-1461)

Chiara Gonzaga (1465-1505)

Francesco (1466-1519) 4th marquis
m. Isabella d'Este (1474-1539)

Sigismondo (1469-1525) cardinal (1506)

Elisabetta Montefeltro (1471-1526) m. Guidobaldo di Montefeltro duke of Urbino

Maddalena Sforza (1472-1490) m. Giovanni Sforza lord of Pesaro

Giovanni (1474-1523)

Eleonora Gonzaga (1493-1543) m. Francesco Maria della Rovere duke of Urbino

Ippolita Gonzaga (1503-1570) Dominican nun

Federico (1500-1540) 5th marquis 1st duke of Gonzaga (1530)
m. Margherita (Paleologo of Monferrato) Gonzaga (1510-1566)

Ercole (1505-1563) cardinal (1527)

Paola Gonzaga (as a nun, known as Livia) (1508-1569)

Francesco (1533-1550) 2nd duke
m. Catherine of Habsburg (1533-1572)

Isabella Gonzaga (1537-1579)

Guglielmo (1538-1587) 3rd duke duke of Monferrato
m. Eleonora of Austria (1534-1594)

Ludovico (1539-1585) duke of Nevers count of Rethel
m. Henrietta of Cleves (r. 1564-1601)

Federico (1540-1565) cardinal (1563)

Vincenzo I (1562-1612) 4th duke
m. Eleonora de Medici (1567-1611)

Margherita Gonzaga (1564-1618) m. Alfonso II duke of Ferrera

Anna Caterina Gonzaga (1566-1621) m. Ferdinand archduke of Austria

Carlo (1580-1637) 8th duke

Carlo, count of Rethel (1600-1631)
m. Maria Gonzaga (1609-1660)

Francesco (1586-1612) 5th duke
m. Margaret of Savoy (fl. 1609-1612)

Ferdinando (1587-1626) 6th duke cardinal (1608-1615)
m. Caterina de Medici (1593-1629)

Margherita Gonzaga (1591-1632) m. Henry II duke of Lorraine

Vincenzo II (1594-1627) 7th duke cardinal (1615-1616) m. Isabella Gonzaga de Novellara

Eleonora I Gonzaga (1598-1655) m. Ferdinand II Holy Roman emperor

Anna Gonzaga (1585-1618) m. Matthias II Holy Roman emperor

Carlo II, 9th duke (1629-1665) m. Isabella Clara

Eleonora II Gonzaga (1628-1686) m. Ferdinand III Holy Roman emperor

Maria Gonzaga (1609-1660) m. Carlo, count of Rethel

Ludovico (1611-1612)

Maria Margherita Gonzaga (b. 1612)

Ferdinando Carlo, 10th duke (1650-1708) m. Anna Isabella

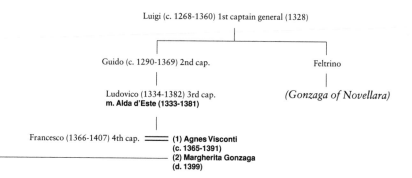

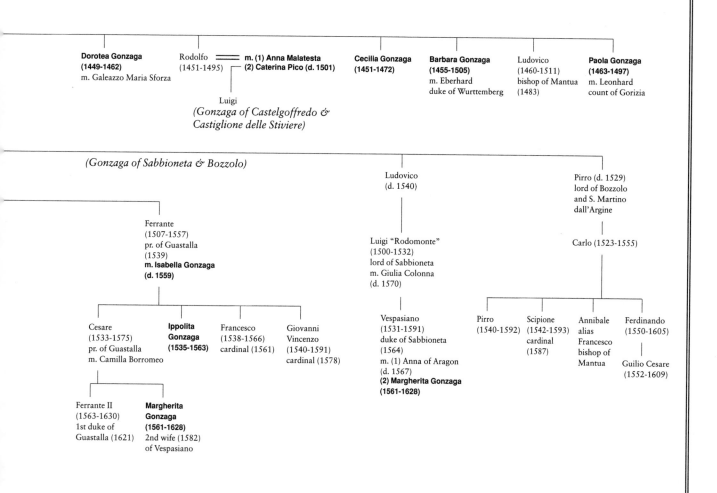

Luigi (c. 1268-1360) 1st captain general (1328)

Guido (c. 1290-1369) 2nd cap.

Feltrino

Ludovico (1334-1382) 3rd cap.
m. Alda d'Este (1333-1381)

(Gonzaga of Novellara)

Francesco (1366-1407) 4th cap. === (1) Agnes Visconti
(c. 1365-1391)
(2) Margherita Gonzaga
(d. 1399)

Dorotea Gonzaga (1449-1462)
m. Galeazzo Maria Sforza

Rodolfo (1451-1495) === m. (1) Anna Malatesta (2) Caterina Pico (d. 1501)

Cecilia Gonzaga (1451-1472)

Barbara Gonzaga (1455-1505) m. Eberhard duke of Wurttemberg

Ludovico (1460-1511) bishop of Mantua (1483)

Paola Gonzaga (1463-1497) m. Leonhard count of Gorizia

Luigi
(Gonzaga of Castelgoffredo & Castiglione delle Stiviere)

(Gonzaga of Sabbioneta & Bozzolo)

Ludovico (d. 1540)

Pirro (d. 1529) lord of Bozzolo and S. Martino dall'Argine

Ferrante (1507-1557) pr. of Guastalla (1539) m. Isabella Gonzaga (d. 1559)

Luigi "Rodomonte" (1500-1532) lord of Sabbioneta m. Giulia Colonna (d. 1570)

Carlo (1523-1555)

Cesare (1533-1575) pr. of Guastalla m. Camilla Borromeo

Ippolita Gonzaga (1535-1563)

Francesco (1538-1566) cardinal (1561)

Giovanni Vincenzo (1540-1591) cardinal (1578)

Vespasiano (1531-1591) duke of Sabbioneta (1564) m. (1) Anna of Aragon (d. 1567) (2) Margherita Gonzaga (1561-1628)

Pirro (1540-1592)

Scipione (1542-1593) cardinal (1587)

Annibale alias Francesco bishop of Mantua

Ferdinando (1550-1605)

Guilio Cesare (1552-1609)

Ferrante II (1563-1630) 1st duke of Guastalla (1621)

Margherita Gonzaga (1561-1628) 2nd wife (1582) of Vespasiano

The Medici

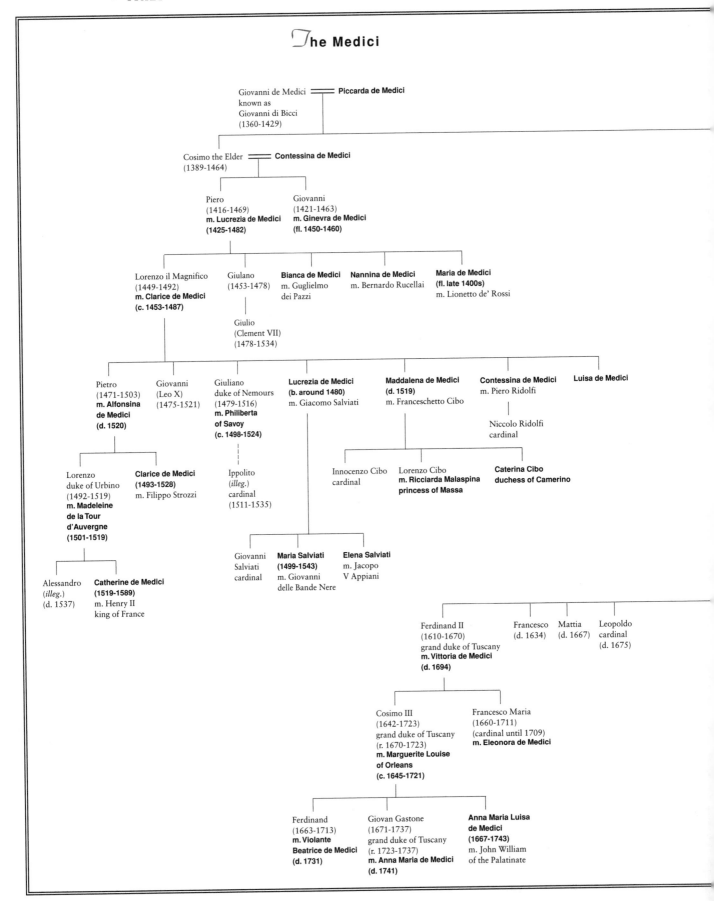

Giovanni de Medici known as Giovanni di Bicci (1360-1429) ═══ **Piccarda de Medici**

Cosimo the Elder (1389-1464) ═══ **Contessina de Medici**

Piero (1416-1469) **m. Lucrezia de Medici (1425-1482)**

Giovanni (1421-1463) **m. Ginevra de Medici (fl. 1450-1460)**

Lorenzo il Magnifico (1449-1492) **m. Clarice de Medici (c. 1453-1487)**

Giuliano (1453-1478)

Bianca de Medici m. Guglielmo dei Pazzi

Nannina de Medici m. Bernardo Rucellai

Maria de Medici (fl. late 1400s) m. Lionetto de' Rossi

Giulio (Clement VII) (1478-1534)

Pietro (1471-1503) **m. Alfonsina de Medici (d. 1520)**

Giovanni (Leo X) (1475-1521)

Giuliano duke of Nemours (1479-1516) **m. Philiberta of Savoy (c. 1498-1524)**

Lucrezia de Medici (b. around 1480) m. Giacomo Salviati

Maddalena de Medici (d. 1519) m. Franceschetto Cibo

Contessina de Medici m. Piero Ridolfi

Luisa de Medici

Niccolo Ridolfi cardinal

Lorenzo duke of Urbino (1492-1519) **m. Madeleine de la Tour d'Auvergne (1501-1519)**

Clarice de Medici (1493-1528) m. Filippo Strozzi

Ippolito (illeg.) cardinal (1511-1535)

Innocenzo Cibo cardinal

Lorenzo Cibo **m. Ricciarda Malaspina princess of Massa**

Caterina Cibo duchess of Camerino

Alessandro (illeg.) (d. 1537)

Catherine de Medici (1519-1589) m. Henry II king of France

Giovanni Salviati cardinal

Maria Salviati (1499-1543) m. Giovanni delle Bande Nere

Elena Salviati m. Jacopo V Appiani

Ferdinand II (1610-1670) grand duke of Tuscany **m. Vittoria de Medici (d. 1694)**

Francesco (d. 1634)

Mattia (d. 1667)

Leopoldo cardinal (d. 1675)

Cosimo III (1642-1723) grand duke of Tuscany (r. 1670-1723) **m. Marguerite Louise of Orleans (c. 1645-1721)**

Francesco Maria (1660-1711) (cardinal until 1709) **m. Eleonora de Medici**

Ferdinand (1663-1713) **m. Violante Beatrice de Medici (d. 1731)**

Giovan Gastone (1671-1737) grand duke of Tuscany (r. 1723-1737) **m. Anna Maria de Medici (d. 1741)**

Anna Maria Luisa de Medici (1667-1743) m. John William of the Palatinate

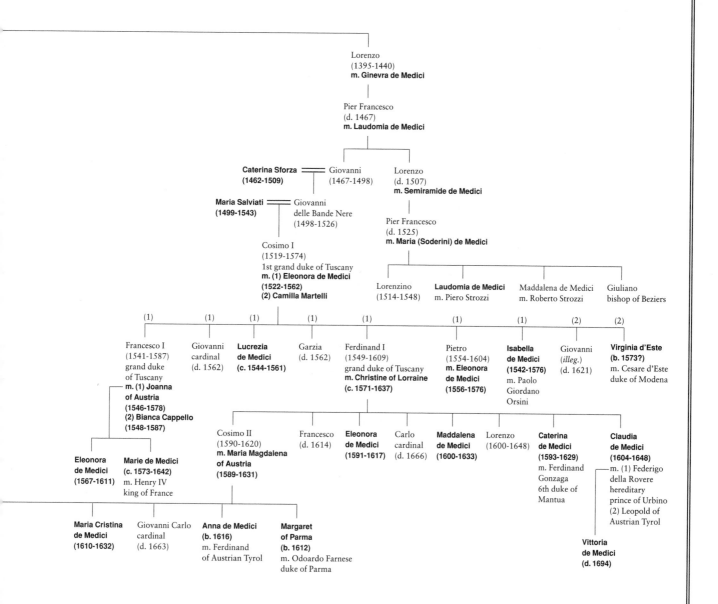

Lorenzo
(1395-1440)
m. Ginevra de Medici

Pier Francesco
(d. 1467)
m. Laudomia de Medici

Caterina Sforza ═══ Giovanni
(1462-1509) (1467-1498)

Lorenzo
(d. 1507)
m. Semiramide de Medici

Maria Salviati ═══ Giovanni
(1499-1543) delle Bande Nere
(1498-1526)

Pier Francesco
(d. 1525)
m. Maria (Soderini) de Medici

Cosimo I
(1519-1574)
1st grand duke of Tuscany
m. (1) Eleonora de Medici
(1522-1562)
(2) Camilla Martelli

Lorenzino
(1514-1548)

Laudomia de Medici
m. Piero Strozzi

Maddalena de Medici
m. Roberto Strozzi

Giuliano
bishop of Beziers

(1) Francesco I
(1541-1587)
grand duke
of Tuscany
m. (1) Joanna
of Austria
(1546-1578)
(2) Bianca Cappello
(1548-1587)

(1) Giovanni
cardinal
(d. 1562)

(1) **Lucrezia**
de Medici
(c. 1544-1561)

(1) Garzia
(d. 1562)

(1) Ferdinand I
(1549-1609)
grand duke of Tuscany
m. Christine of Lorraine
(c. 1571-1637)

(1) Pietro
(1554-1604)
m. Eleonora
de Medici
(1556-1576)

(1) **Isabella**
de Medici
(1542-1576)
m. Paolo
Giordano
Orsini

(2) Giovanni
(*illeg.*)
(d. 1621)

(2) **Virginia d'Este**
(b. 1573?)
m. Cesare d'Este
duke of Modena

Eleonora
de Medici
(1567-1611)

Marie de Medici
(c. 1573-1642)
m. Henry IV
king of France

Cosimo II
(1590-1620)
m. Maria Magdalena
of Austria
(1589-1631)

Francesco
(d. 1614)

Eleonora
de Medici
(1591-1617)

Carlo
cardinal
(d. 1666)

Maddalena
de Medici
(1600-1633)

Lorenzo
(1600-1648)

Caterina
de Medici
(1593-1629)
m. Ferdinand
Gonzaga
6th duke of
Mantua

Claudia
de Medici
(1604-1648)
m. (1) Federigo
della Rovere
hereditary
prince of Urbino
(2) Leopold of
Austrian Tyrol

Maria Cristina
de Medici
(1610-1632)

Giovanni Carlo
cardinal
(d. 1663)

Anna de Medici
(b. 1616)
m. Ferdinand
of Austrian Tyrol

Margaret
of Parma
(b. 1612)
m. Odoardo Farnese
duke of Parma

Vittoria
de Medici
(d. 1694)

The Neapolitan Bourbons
(1735–1860)

The Kingdom of Naples was united with Sicily in
1130-1282, 1435-1458, 1503-1713, 1720-1806, 1815-1860

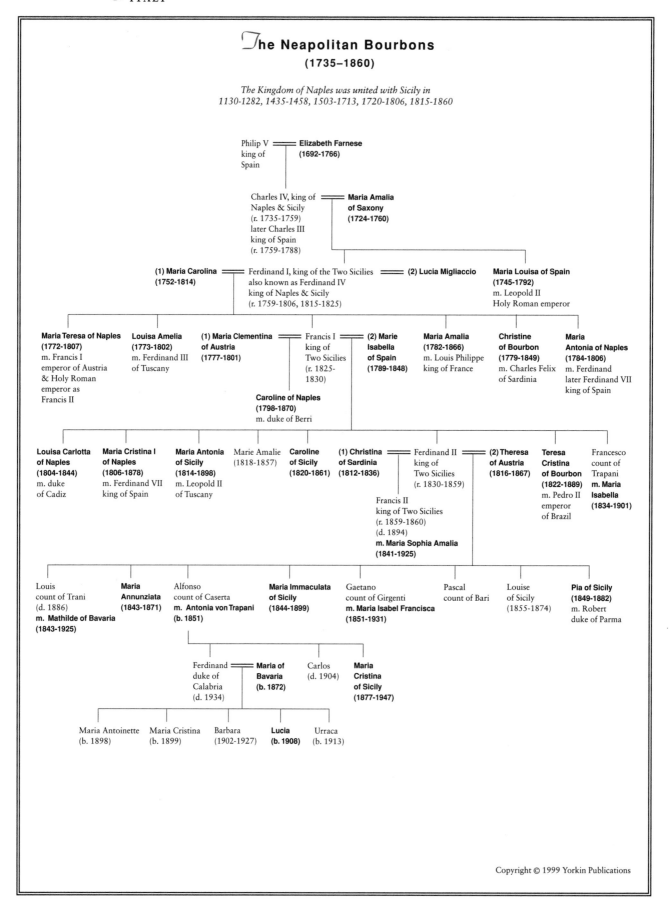

Philip V
king of
Spain
===
**Elizabeth Farnese
(1692-1766)**

Charles IV, king of
Naples & Sicily
(r. 1735-1759)
later Charles III
king of Spain
(r. 1759-1788)
===
**Maria Amalia
of Saxony
(1724-1760)**

**(1) Maria Carolina
(1752-1814)**
===
Ferdinand I, king of the Two Sicilies
also known as Ferdinand IV
king of Naples & Sicily
(r. 1759-1806, 1815-1825)
===
(2) Lucia Migliaccio

**Maria Louisa of Spain
(1745-1792)**
m. Leopold II
Holy Roman emperor

**Maria Teresa of Naples
(1772-1807)**
m. Francis I
emperor of Austria
& Holy Roman
emperor as
Francis II

**Louisa Amelia
(1773-1802)**
m. Ferdinand III
of Tuscany

**(1) Maria Clementina
of Austria
(1777-1801)**
===
Francis I
king of
Two Sicilies
(r. 1825-
1830)
===
**(2) Marie
Isabella
of Spain
(1789-1848)**

**Maria Amalia
(1782-1866)**
m. Louis Philippe
king of France

**Christine
of Bourbon
(1779-1849)**
m. Charles Felix
of Sardinia

**Maria
Antonia of Naples
(1784-1806)**
m. Ferdinand
later Ferdinand VII
king of Spain

**Caroline of Naples
(1798-1870)**
m. duke of Berri

**Louisa Carlotta
of Naples
(1804-1844)**
m. duke
of Cadiz

**Maria Cristina I
of Naples
(1806-1878)**
m. Ferdinand VII
king of Spain

**Maria Antonia
of Sicily
(1814-1898)**
m. Leopold II
of Tuscany

Marie Amalie
(1818-1857)

**Caroline
of Sicily
(1820-1861)**

**(1) Christina
of Sardinia
(1812-1836)**
===
Ferdinand II
king of
Two Sicilies
(r. 1830-1859)
===
**(2) Theresa
of Austria
(1816-1867)**

**Teresa
Cristina
of Bourbon
(1822-1889)**
m. Pedro II
emperor
of Brazil

Francesco
count of
Trapani
**m. Maria
Isabella
(1834-1901)**

Francis II
king of Two Sicilies
(r. 1859-1860)
(d. 1894)
**m. Maria Sophia Amalia
(1841-1925)**

Louis
count of Trani
(d. 1886)
**m. Mathilde of Bavaria
(1843-1925)**

**Maria
Annunziata
(1843-1871)**

Alfonso
count of Caserta
**m. Antonia von Trapani
(b. 1851)**

**Maria Immaculata
of Sicily
(1844-1899)**

Gaetano
count of Girgenti
**m. Maria Isabel Francisca
(1851-1931)**

Pascal
count of Bari

Louise
of Sicily
(1855-1874)

**Pia of Sicily
(1849-1882)**
m. Robert
duke of Parma

Ferdinand
duke of
Calabria
(d. 1934)
===
**Maria of
Bavaria
(b. 1872)**

Carlos
(d. 1904)

**Maria
Cristina
of Sicily
(1877-1947)**

Maria Antoinette
(b. 1898)

Maria Cristina
(b. 1899)

Barbara
(1902-1927)

**Lucia
(b. 1908)**

Urraca
(b. 1913)

The Tuscan Branch of Habsburg-Lorraine

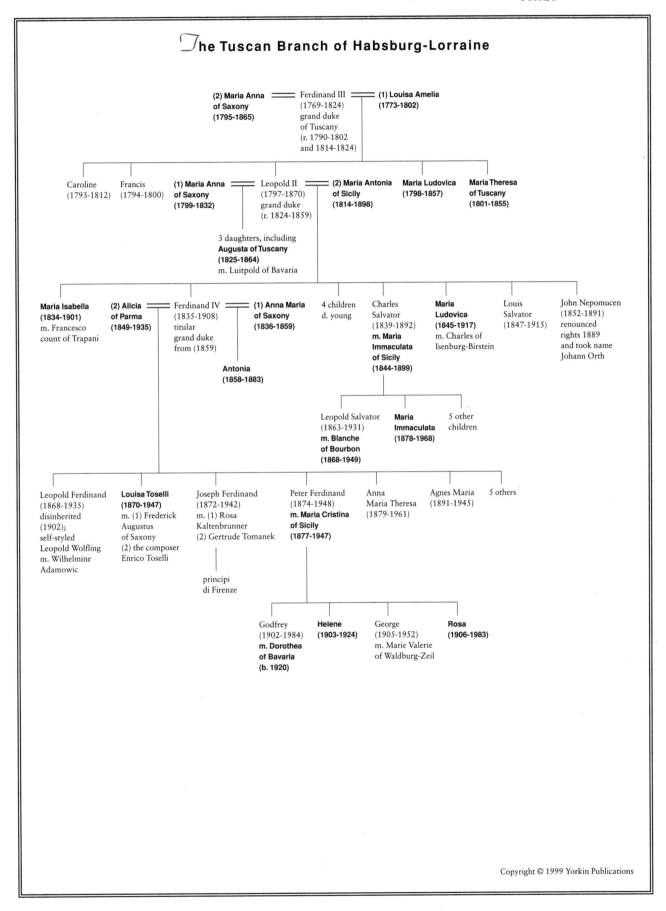

(2) Maria Anna of Saxony (1795-1865) ══ Ferdinand III (1769-1824) grand duke of Tuscany (r. 1790-1802 and 1814-1824) ══ **(1) Louisa Amelia (1773-1802)**

Caroline (1793-1812) — Francis (1794-1800) — **(1) Maria Anna of Saxony (1799-1832)** ══ Leopold II (1797-1870) grand duke (r. 1824-1859) ══ **(2) Maria Antonia of Sicily (1814-1898)** — Maria Ludovica (1798-1857) — Maria Theresa of Tuscany (1801-1855)

3 daughters, including **Augusta of Tuscany (1825-1864)** m. Luitpold of Bavaria

Maria Isabella (1834-1901) m. Francesco count of Trapani — **(2) Alicia of Parma (1849-1935)** ══ Ferdinand IV (1835-1908) titular grand duke from (1859) ══ **(1) Anna Maria of Saxony (1836-1859)** — 4 children d. young — Charles Salvator (1839-1892) **m. Maria Immaculata of Sicily (1844-1899)** — **Maria Ludovica (1845-1917)** m. Charles of Isenburg-Birstein — Louis Salvator (1847-1915) — John Nepomucen (1852-1891) renounced rights 1889 and took name Johann Orth

Antonia (1858-1883)

Leopold Salvator (1863-1931) **m. Blanche of Bourbon (1868-1949)** — **Maria Immaculata (1878-1968)** — 5 other children

Leopold Ferdinand (1868-1935) disinherited (1902); self-styled Leopold Wolfling m. Wilhelmine Adamowic — **Louisa Toselli (1870-1947)** m. (1) Frederick Augustus of Saxony (2) the composer Enrico Toselli — Joseph Ferdinand (1872-1942) m. (1) Rosa Kaltenbrunner (2) Gertrude Tomanek — Peter Ferdinand (1874-1948) **m. Maria Cristina of Sicily (1877-1947)** — Anna Maria Theresa (1879-1961) — Agnes Maria (1891-1945) — 5 others

principi di Firenze

Godfrey (1902-1984) **m. Dorothea of Bavaria (b. 1920)** — **Helene (1903-1924)** — George (1905-1952) m. Marie Valerie of Waldburg-Zeil — **Rosa (1906-1983)**

Copyright © 1999 Yorkin Publications

ℰmpresses & Emperors of the Imperial House of Japan

According to Japanese tradition, the imperial house of Japan has ruled without interruption from Jimmu to Akihito. Legend depicts Jimmu as a descendant of the sun goddess Amaterasu, and each succeeding empress or emperor has been given the title of tenno *(heavenly ruler). Modern historians generally agree that the forced abdication of Empress Kogyoku in 645 is a trustworthy starting point for more reliable sources of Japanese history.*

		BIRTH AND DEATH DATES	REIGN DATES
1	Jimmu		
2	Suizei		
3	Annei		
4	Itoku		
5	Kosho		
6	Koan		
7	Korei	*legendary emperors*	
8	Kogen		
9	Kaika		
10	Sujin		
11	Suinin		
12	Keiko		
13	Seimu		
14	Chuai		
15	Ojin	*late 4th to early 5th century*	
16	Nintoku		
17	Richu	*first half of the 5th century*	
18	Hanzei		
19	Ingyo		
20	Anko	*mid-5th century*	
21	Yuryaku		
22	Seinei		
23	Kenzo	*latter half of the 5th century*	
24	Ninken		
25	Buretsu		
26	Keitai		
27	Ankan	*first half of the 6th century*	
28	Senka		
29	Kimmei	509-571	531 or 539-571
30	Bidatsu	538-585	572-585
31	Yomei	?-587	585-587
32	Sushun	?-592	587-592
33	**Suiko**	**554-628**	**593-628**
34	Jomei	593-641	629-641
35	**Kogyoku**[1]	**594-661**	**642-645**

Taika Reforms

36	Kotoku	597-654	645-654
37	**Saimei**	**594-661**	**655-661**
38	Tenji	626-672	661-672
39	Kobun	648-672	672
40	Temmu	?-686	672-686
41	**Jito**	**645-703**	**686-697**
42	Mommu	683-707	697-707

Nara Period

43	**Gemmei**	**661-721**	**707-715**
44	**Gensho**	**680-748**	**715-724**
45	Shomu	701-756	724-749
46	**Koken**[2]	**718-770**	**749-758**
47	Junnin	733-765	758-764
48	**Shotoku**	**718-770**	**764-770**
49	Konin	709-782	770-781

Heian Period

50	Kammu	737-806	781-806
51	Heizei	774-824	806-809
52	Saga	786-842	809-823
53	Junna	786-840	823-833
54	Nimmyo	810-850	833-850
55	Montoku	827-858	850-858
56	Seiwa	850-881	858-876
57	Yozei	869-949	876-884
58	Koko	830-887	884-887
59	Uda	867-931	887-897
60	Daigo	885-930	897-930
61	Suzaku	923-952	930-946
62	Murakami	926-967	946-967
63	Reizei	950-1011	967-969
64	En'yu	959-991	969-984
65	Kazan	968-1008	984-986
66	Ichijo	980-1011	986-1011
67	Sanjo	976-1017	1011-1016

		BIRTH AND DEATH DATES	REIGN DATES
68	Go-Ichijo	1008-1036	1016-1036
69	Go-Suzaku	1009-1045	1036-1045
70	Go-Reizei	1025-1068	1045-1068
71	Go-Sanjo	1034-1073	1068-1073
72	Shirakawa	1053-1129	1073-1087
73	Horikawa	1079-1107	1087-1107
74	Toba	1103-1156	1107-1123
75	Sutoku	1119-1164	1123-1142
76	Konoe	1139-1155	1142-1155
77	Go-Shirakawa	1127-1192	1155-1158
78	Nijo	1143-1165	1158-1165
79	Rokujo	1164-1176	1165-1168
80	Takakura	1161-1181	1168-1180
81	Antoku	1178-1185	1180-1185

Kamakura Period

82	Go-Toba	1180-1239	1183-1198
83	Tsuchimikado	1195-1231	1198-1210
84	Juntoku	1197-1242	1210-1221
85	Chukyo	1218-1234	1221
86	Go-Horikawa	1212-1234	1221-1232
87	Shijo	1231-1242	1232-1242
88	Go-Saga	1220-1272	1242-1246
89	Go-Fukakusa	1243-1304	1246-1260
90	Kameyama	1249-1305	1260-1274
91	Go-Uda	1267-1324	1274-1287
92	Fushimi	1265-1317	1287-1298
93	Go-Fushimi	1288-1336	1298-1301
94	Go-Nijo	1285-1308	1301-1308
95	Hanazono	1297-1348	1308-1318

Ashikaga Period

96	Go-Daigo	1288-1339	1318-1339
97	Go-Murakami	1328-1368	1339-1368
98	Chokei	1343-1394	1368-1383
99	Go-Kameyama	?-1424	1383-1392
N1	Kogon	1313-1364	1331-1333
N2	Komyo	1322-1380	1336-1348
N3	Suko	1334-1398	1348-1351
N4	Go-Kogon	1338-1374	1351-1371
N5	Go-En'yu	1359-1393	1371-1382
100	Go-Komatsu	1377-1433	1382-1412
101	Shoko	1401-1428	1412-1428
102	Go-Hanazono	1419-1471	1428-1464
103	Go-Tsuchimikado	1442-1500	1464-1500
104	Go-Kashiwabara	1464-1526	1500-1526
105	Go-Nara	1497-1557	1526-1557

Period of Military Dictatorships

106	Ogimachi	1517-1593	1557-1586
107	Go-Yozei	1572-1617	1586-1611

Tokugawa Period

108	Go-Mizunoo	1596-1680	1611-1629
109	**Meisho**	**1624-1696**	**1629-1643**
110	Go-Komyo	1633-1654	1643-1654
111	Gosai	1637-1685	1655-1663
112	Reigen	1654-1732	1663-1687
113	Higashiyama	1675-1709	1687-1709
114	Nakamikado	1702-1737	1709-1735
115	Sakuramachi	1720-1750	1735-1747
116	Momozono	1741-1762	1747-1762
117	**Go-Sakuramachi**	**1740-1813**	**1762-1771**
118	Go-Momozono	1758-1779	1771-1779
119	Kokaku	1771-1840	1780-1817
120	Ninko	1800-1846	1817-1846
121	Komei	1831-1867	1846-1867

Modern Period

122	Meiji	1852-1912	1867-1912
	Meiji empress (Haruko)	1850-1914	
123	Taisho	1879-1926	1912-1926
	Taisho empress (Sadako)		
124	Hirohito	1901-1989	1926-1989
	& Empress Nagako	**b. 1903**	
125	Akihito	**b. 1989**	1989-
	& Empress Michiko	**b. 1934**	

Note: The numbers on the left designate the place of rulers in the order of succession. The names of all the empresses and emperors, except for Hirohito and Akihito, were given posthumously.

[1]Kogyoku (35) later reigned as Saimei (37).
[2]Koken (46) later reigned as Shotoku (48).

Queens & Kings of Jerusalem
(1099-1489)

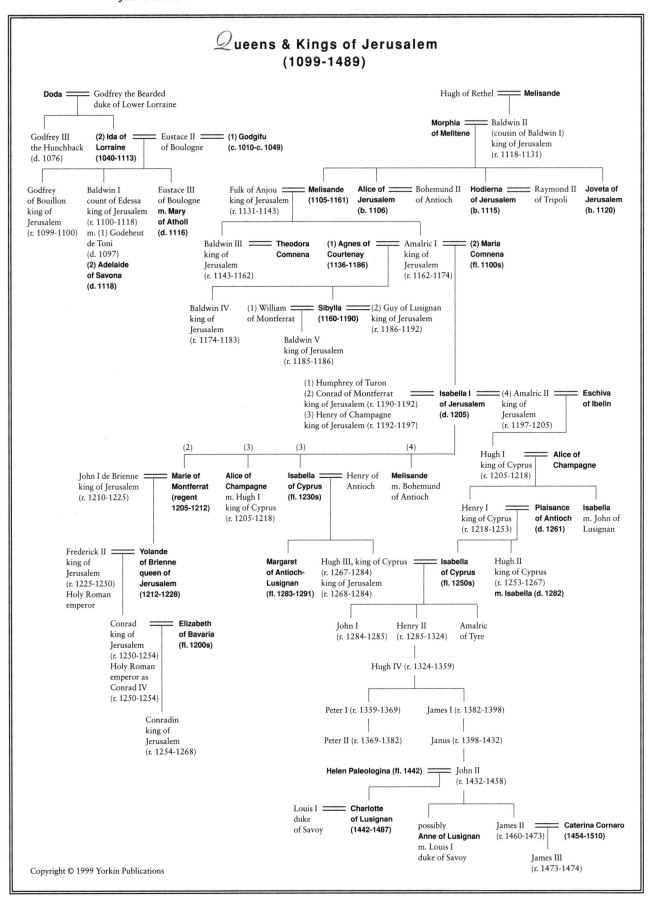

Copyright © 1999 Yorkin Publications

*L*uxemburg Rulers
(1308–1437)

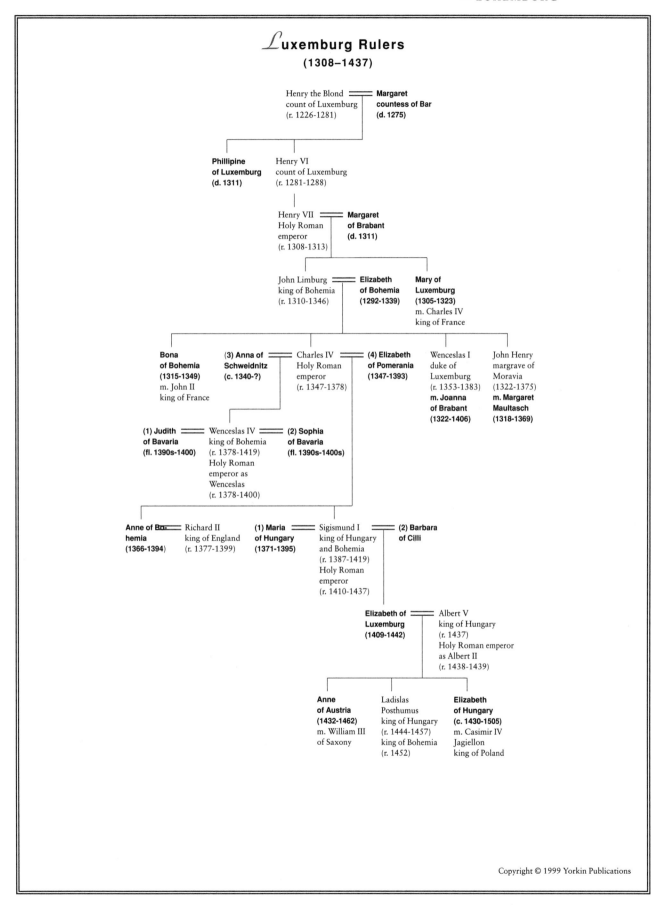

Henry the Blond
count of Luxemburg
(r. 1226-1281)
══ **Margaret
countess of Bar
(d. 1275)**

**Phillipine
of Luxemburg
(d. 1311)**

Henry VI
count of Luxemburg
(r. 1281-1288)

Henry VII
Holy Roman
emperor
(r. 1308-1313)
══ **Margaret
of Brabant
(d. 1311)**

John Limburg
king of Bohemia
(r. 1310-1346)
══ **Elizabeth
of Bohemia
(1292-1339)**

**Mary of
Luxemburg
(1305-1323)
m. Charles IV
king of France**

**Bona
of Bohemia
(1315-1349)
m. John II
king of France**

**(3) Anna of
Schweidnitz
(c. 1340-?)**
══ Charles IV
Holy Roman
emperor
(r. 1347-1378)
══ **(4) Elizabeth
of Pomerania
(1347-1393)**

Wenceslas I
duke of
Luxemburg
(r. 1353-1383)
**m. Joanna
of Brabant
(1322-1406)**

John Henry
margrave of
Moravia
(1322-1375)
**m. Margaret
Maultasch
(1318-1369)**

**(1) Judith
of Bavaria
(fl. 1390s-1400)**
══ Wenceslas IV
king of Bohemia
(r. 1378-1419)
Holy Roman
emperor as
Wenceslas
(r. 1378-1400)
══ **(2) Sophia
of Bavaria
(fl. 1390s-1400s)**

**Anne of Bo-
hemia
(1366-1394)**
══ Richard II
king of England
(r. 1377-1399)

**(1) Maria
of Hungary
(1371-1395)**
══ Sigismund I
king of Hungary
and Bohemia
(r. 1387-1419)
Holy Roman
emperor
(r. 1410-1437)
══ **(2) Barbara
of Cilli**

**Elizabeth of
Luxemburg
(1409-1442)**
══ Albert V
king of Hungary
(r. 1437)
Holy Roman emperor
as Albert II
(r. 1438-1439)

**Anne
of Austria
(1432-1462)
m. William III
of Saxony**

Ladislas
Posthumus
king of Hungary
(r. 1444-1457)
king of Bohemia
(r. 1452)

**Elizabeth
of Hungary
(c. 1430-1505)
m. Casimir IV
Jagiellon
king of Poland**

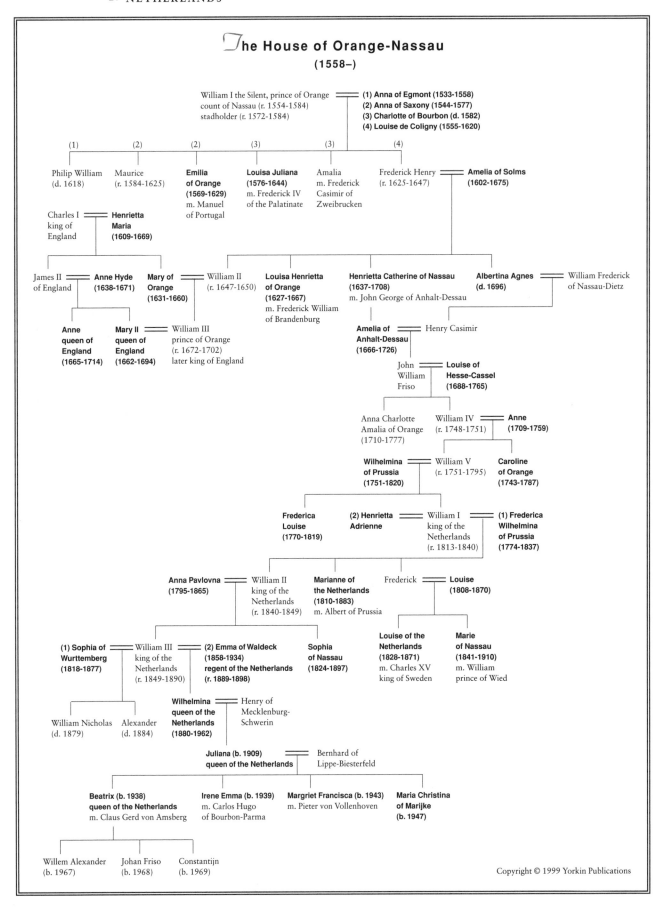

The House of Orange-Nassau
(1558–)

William I the Silent, prince of Orange == **(1) Anna of Egmont (1533-1558)**
count of Nassau (r. 1554-1584) — **(2) Anna of Saxony (1544-1577)**
stadholder (r. 1572-1584) — **(3) Charlotte of Bourbon (d. 1582)**
— **(4) Louise de Coligny (1555-1620)**

(1) — (2) — (2) — (3) — (3) — (4)

Philip William (d. 1618) — **Maurice** (r. 1584-1625) — **Emilia of Orange (1569-1629)** m. Manuel of Portugal — **Louisa Juliana (1576-1644)** m. Frederick IV of the Palatinate — **Amalia** m. Frederick Casimir of Zweibrucken — **Frederick Henry** (r. 1625-1647) == **Amelia of Solms (1602-1675)**

Charles I king of England == **Henrietta Maria (1609-1669)**

James II of England == **Anne Hyde (1638-1671)** — **Mary of Orange (1631-1660)** == **William II** (r. 1647-1650) — **Louisa Henrietta of Orange (1627-1667)** m. Frederick William of Brandenburg — **Henrietta Catherine of Nassau (1637-1708)** m. John George of Anhalt-Dessau — **Albertina Agnes (d. 1696)** == **William Frederick** of Nassau-Dietz

Anne queen of England **(1665-1714)** — **Mary II** queen of England **(1662-1694)** == **William III** prince of Orange (r. 1672-1702) later king of England — **Amelia of Anhalt-Dessau (1666-1726)** == **Henry Casimir**

John William Friso == **Louise of Hesse-Cassel (1688-1765)**

Anna Charlotte Amalia of Orange (1710-1777) — **William IV** (r. 1748-1751) == **Anne (1709-1759)**

Wilhelmina of Prussia (1751-1820) == **William V** (r. 1751-1795) — **Caroline of Orange (1743-1787)**

Frederica Louise (1770-1819) — **(2) Henrietta Adrienne** == **William I** king of the Netherlands (r. 1813-1840) == **(1) Frederica Wilhelmina of Prussia (1774-1837)**

Anna Pavlovna (1795-1865) == **William II** king of the Netherlands (r. 1840-1849) — **Marianne of the Netherlands (1810-1883)** m. Albert of Prussia — **Frederick** == **Louise (1808-1870)**

(1) Sophia of Wurttemberg (1818-1877) == **William III** king of the Netherlands (r. 1849-1890) == **(2) Emma of Waldeck (1858-1934)** regent of the Netherlands (r. 1889-1898) — **Sophia of Nassau (1824-1897)** — **Louise of the Netherlands (1828-1871)** m. Charles XV king of Sweden — **Marie of Nassau (1841-1910)** m. William prince of Wied

William Nicholas (d. 1879) — **Alexander** (d. 1884) — **Wilhelmina** queen of the Netherlands **(1880-1962)** == **Henry of Mecklenburg-Schwerin**

Juliana (b. 1909) queen of the Netherlands == **Bernhard of Lippe-Biesterfeld**

Beatrix (b. 1938) queen of the Netherlands m. Claus Gerd von Amsberg — **Irene Emma (b. 1939)** m. Carlos Hugo of Bourbon-Parma — **Margriet Francisca (b. 1943)** m. Pieter von Vollenhoven — **Maria Christina of Marijke (b. 1947)**

Willem Alexander (b. 1967) — **Johan Friso** (b. 1968) — **Constantijn** (b. 1969)

Copyright © 1999 Yorkin Publications

Queens & Kings of Norway
(1905–)

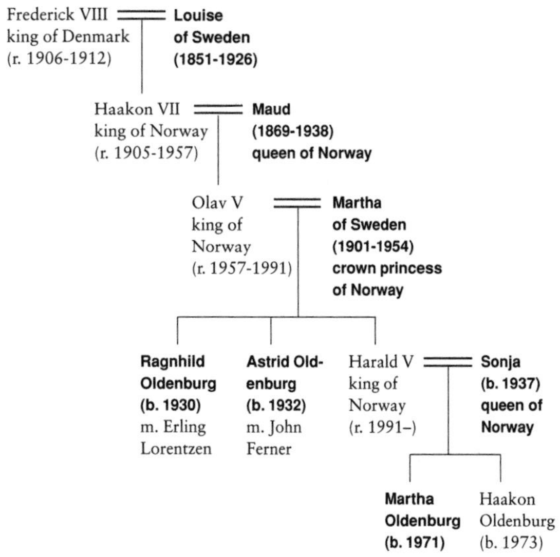

Frederick VIII ══════ **Louise**
king of Denmark   **of Sweden**
(r. 1906-1912)   **(1851-1926)**

Haakon VII ══════ **Maud**
king of Norway   **(1869-1938)**
(r. 1905-1957)   **queen of Norway**

Olav V ══════ **Martha**
king of   **of Sweden**
Norway   **(1901-1954)**
(r. 1957-1991) **crown princess**
of Norway

Ragnhild   **Astrid Old-**   Harald V ══════ **Sonja**
Oldenburg   **enburg**   king of   **(b. 1937)**
(b. 1930)   **(b. 1932)**   Norway   **queen of**
m. Erling   m. John   (r. 1991–)   **Norway**
Lorentzen   Ferner

Martha   Haakon
Oldenburg   Oldenburg
(b. 1971)   (b. 1973)

Rulers of Poland, Hungary, & Lithuania
(1205–1492)

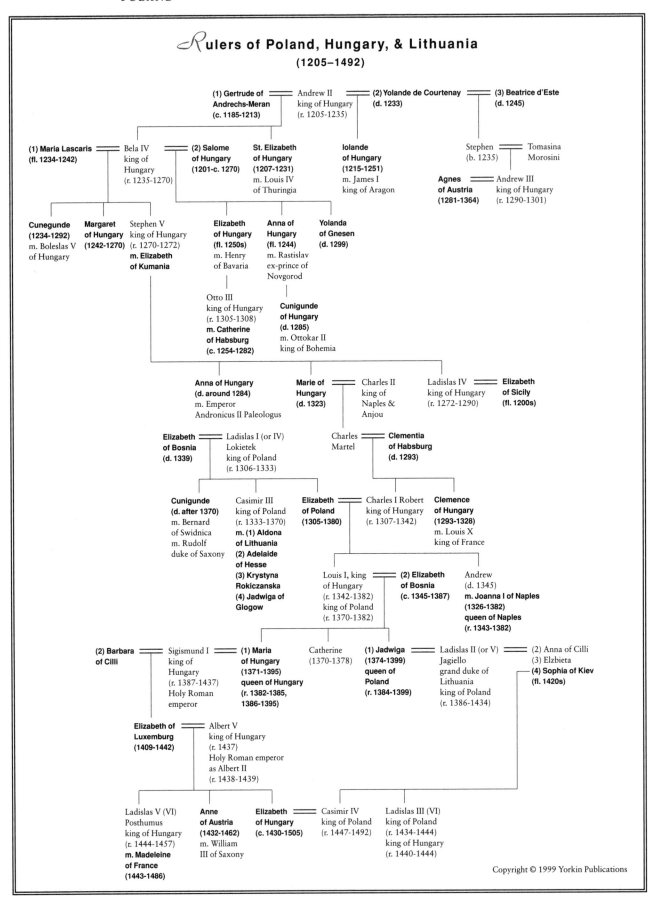

(1) Gertrude of Andrechs-Meran (c. 1185-1213) ═ Andrew II king of Hungary (r. 1205-1235) ═ **(2) Yolande de Courtenay (d. 1233)** ═ **(3) Beatrice d'Este (d. 1245)**

Stephen (b. 1235) ═ Tomasina Morosini

Agnes of Austria (1281-1364) ═ Andrew III king of Hungary (r. 1290-1301)

(1) Maria Lascaris (fl. 1234-1242) ═ Bela IV king of Hungary (r. 1235-1270) ═ **(2) Salome of Hungary (1201-c. 1270)** 　 **St. Elizabeth of Hungary (1207-1231)** m. Louis IV of Thuringia 　 **Iolande of Hungary (1215-1251)** m. James I king of Aragon

Cunegunde (1234-1292) m. Boleslas V of Hungary 　 **Margaret of Hungary (1242-1270)** 　 Stephen V king of Hungary (r. 1270-1272) **m. Elizabeth of Kumania** 　 **Elizabeth of Hungary (fl. 1250s)** m. Henry of Bavaria 　 **Anna of Hungary (fl. 1244)** m. Rastislav ex-prince of Novgorod 　 **Yolanda of Gnesen (d. 1299)**

Otto III king of Hungary (r. 1305-1308) **m. Catherine of Habsburg (c. 1254-1282)** 　 **Cunigunde of Hungary (d. 1285)** m. Ottokar II king of Bohemia

Anna of Hungary (d. around 1284) m. Emperor Andronicus II Paleologus 　 **Marie of Hungary (d. 1323)** ═ Charles II king of Naples & Anjou 　 Ladislas IV king of Hungary (r. 1272-1290) ═ **Elizabeth of Sicily (fl. 1200s)**

Elizabeth of Bosnia (d. 1339) ═ Ladislas I (or IV) Lokietek king of Poland (r. 1306-1333) 　 Charles Martel ═ **Clementia of Habsburg (d. 1293)**

Cunigunde (d. after 1370) m. Bernard of Swidnica m. Rudolf duke of Saxony 　 Casimir III king of Poland (r. 1333-1370) **m. (1) Aldona of Lithuania (2) Adelaide of Hesse (3) Krystyna Rokiczanska (4) Jadwiga of Glogow** 　 **Elizabeth of Poland (1305-1380)** ═ Charles I Robert king of Hungary (r. 1307-1342) 　 **Clemence of Hungary (1293-1328)** m. Louis X king of France

Louis I, king of Hungary (r. 1342-1382) king of Poland (r. 1370-1382) ═ **(2) Elizabeth of Bosnia (c. 1345-1387)** 　 Andrew (d. 1345) m. Joanna I of Naples (1326-1382) queen of Naples (r. 1343-1382)

(2) Barbara of Cilli ═ Sigismund I king of Hungary (r. 1387-1437) Holy Roman emperor ═ **(1) Maria of Hungary (1371-1395) queen of Hungary (r. 1382-1385, 1386-1395)** 　 Catherine (1370-1378) 　 **(1) Jadwiga (1374-1399) queen of Poland (r. 1384-1399)** ═ Ladislas II (or V) Jagiello grand duke of Lithuania king of Poland (r. 1386-1434) ═ **(2) Anna of Cilli (3) Elzbieta (4) Sophia of Kiev (fl. 1420s)**

Elizabeth of Luxemburg (1409-1442) ═ Albert V king of Hungary (r. 1437) Holy Roman emperor as Albert II (r. 1438-1439)

Ladislas V (VI) Posthumus king of Hungary (r. 1444-1457) **m. Madeleine of France (1443-1486)** 　 **Anne of Austria (1432-1462)** m. William III of Saxony 　 **Elizabeth of Hungary (c. 1430-1505)** ═ Casimir IV king of Poland (r. 1447-1492) 　 Ladislas III (VI) king of Poland (r. 1434-1444) king of Hungary (r. 1440-1444)

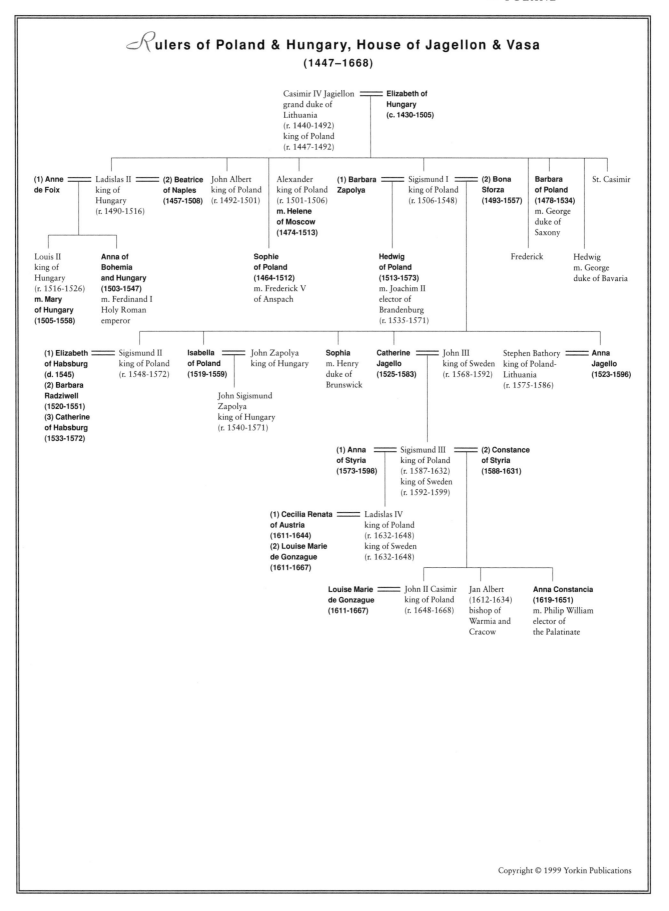

Rulers of Poland & Hungary, House of Jagellon & Vasa
(1447–1668)

Casimir IV Jagiellon
grand duke of
Lithuania
(r. 1440-1492)
king of Poland
(r. 1447-1492)
═══ **Elizabeth of
Hungary
(c. 1430-1505)**

**(1) Anne
de Foix** ═══ Ladislas II
king of
Hungary
(r. 1490-1516) ═══ **(2) Beatrice
of Naples
(1457-1508)**　　John Albert
king of Poland
(r. 1492-1501)　　Alexander
king of Poland
(r. 1501-1506)
**m. Helene
of Moscow
(1474-1513)**　　**(1) Barbara
Zapolya** ═══ Sigismund I
king of Poland
(r. 1506-1548) ═══ **(2) Bona
Sforza
(1493-1557)**　　**Barbara
of Poland
(1478-1534)**
m. George
duke of
Saxony　　St. Casimir

Louis II
king of
Hungary
(r. 1516-1526)
**m. Mary
of Hungary
(1505-1558)**　　**Anna of
Bohemia
and Hungary
(1503-1547)**
m. Ferdinand I
Holy Roman
emperor　　**Sophie
of Poland
(1464-1512)**
m. Frederick V
of Anspach　　**Hedwig
of Poland
(1513-1573)**
m. Joachim II
elector of
Brandenburg
(r. 1535-1571)　　Frederick　　Hedwig
m. George
duke of
Bavaria

**(1) Elizabeth
of Habsburg
(d. 1545)
(2) Barbara
Radziwell
(1520-1551)
(3) Catherine
of Habsburg
(1533-1572)** ═══ Sigismund II
king of Poland
(r. 1548-1572)　　**Isabella
of Poland
(1519-1559)** ═══ John Zapolya
king of Hungary　　**Sophia**
m. Henry
duke of
Brunswick　　**Catherine
Jagello
(1525-1583)** ═══ John III
king of Sweden
(r. 1568-1592)　　Stephen Bathory
king of Poland-
Lithuania
(r. 1575-1586) ═══ **Anna
Jagello
(1523-1596)**

John Sigismund
Zapolya
king of Hungary
(r. 1540-1571)

**(1) Anna
of Styria
(1573-1598)** ═══ Sigismund III
king of Poland
(r. 1587-1632)
king of Sweden
(r. 1592-1599) ═══ **(2) Constance
of Styria
(1588-1631)**

**(1) Cecilia Renata
of Austria
(1611-1644)
(2) Louise Marie
de Gonzague
(1611-1667)** ═══ Ladislas IV
king of Poland
(r. 1632-1648)
king of Sweden
(r. 1632-1648)

**Louise Marie
de Gonzague
(1611-1667)** ═══ John II Casimir
king of Poland
(r. 1648-1668)　　Jan Albert
(1612-1634)
bishop of
Warmia and
Cracow　　**Anna Constancia
(1619-1651)**
m. Philip William
elector of
the Palatinate

The Burgundian House
(1112–1325)

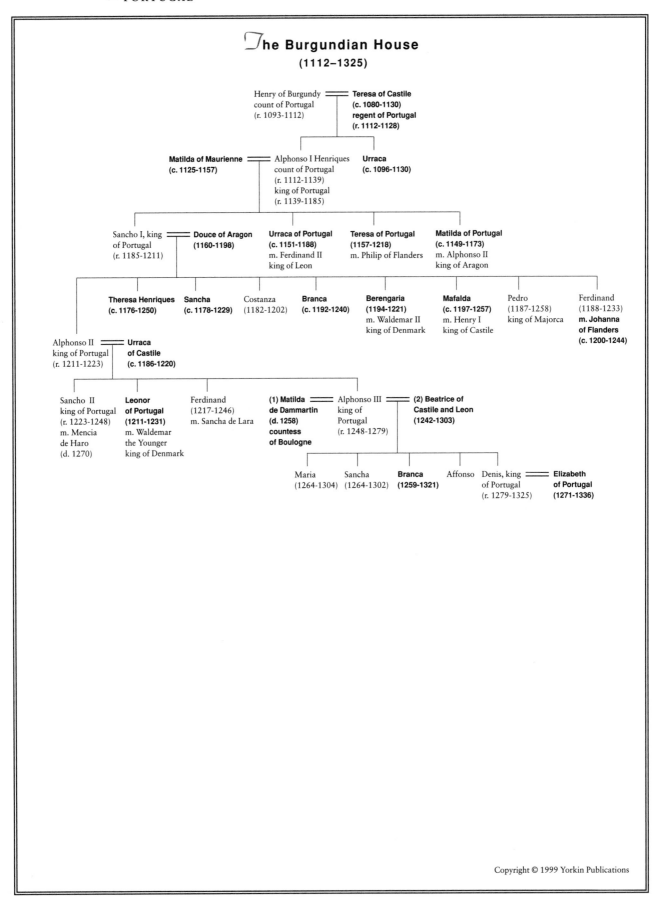

Henry of Burgundy ══ **Teresa of Castile**
count of Portugal   **(c. 1080-1130)**
(r. 1093-1112)   **regent of Portugal**
                         (r. 1112-1128)

Matilda of Maurienne ══ Alphonso I Henriques   Urraca
(c. 1125-1157)   count of Portugal   **(c. 1096-1130)**
                             (r. 1112-1139)
                             king of Portugal
                             (r. 1139-1185)

Sancho I, king ══ **Douce of Aragon**   **Urraca of Portugal**   **Teresa of Portugal**   **Matilda of Portugal**
of Portugal   **(1160-1198)**   **(c. 1151-1188)**   **(1157-1218)**   **(c. 1149-1173)**
(r. 1185-1211)   m. Ferdinand II   m. Philip of Flanders   m. Alphonso II
                                           king of Leon   king of Aragon

Theresa Henriques   **Sancha**   Costanza   **Branca**   **Berengaria**   **Mafalda**   Pedro   Ferdinand
(c. 1176-1250)   **(c. 1178-1229)** (1182-1202)   **(c. 1192-1240)** **(1194-1221)**   **(c. 1197-1257)** (1187-1258)   (1188-1233)
                                                                           m. Waldemar II   m. Henry I   king of Majorca   **m. Johanna**
                                                                           king of Denmark   king of Castile   **of Flanders**
                                                                                                                                      (c. 1200-1244)

Alphonso II ══ **Urraca**
king of Portugal **of Castile**
(r. 1211-1223)   **(c. 1186-1220)**

Sancho II   **Leonor**   Ferdinand   **(1) Matilda** ══ Alphonso III ══ **(2) Beatrice of**
king of Portugal   **of Portugal**   (1217-1246)   **de Dammartin**   king of   **Castile and Leon**
(r. 1223-1248)   **(1211-1231)**   m. Sancha de Lara   **(d. 1258)**   Portugal   **(1242-1303)**
m. Mencia   m. Waldemar   **countess**   (r. 1248-1279)
de Haro   the Younger   **of Boulogne**
(d. 1270)   king of Denmark

Maria   Sancha   **Branca**   Affonso   Denis, king ══ **Elizabeth**
(1264-1304)   (1264-1302)   **(1259-1321)**   of Portugal   **of Portugal**
                                                            (r. 1279-1325) **(1271-1336)**

*Q*ueens & Kings of Portugal
(1248–1521)

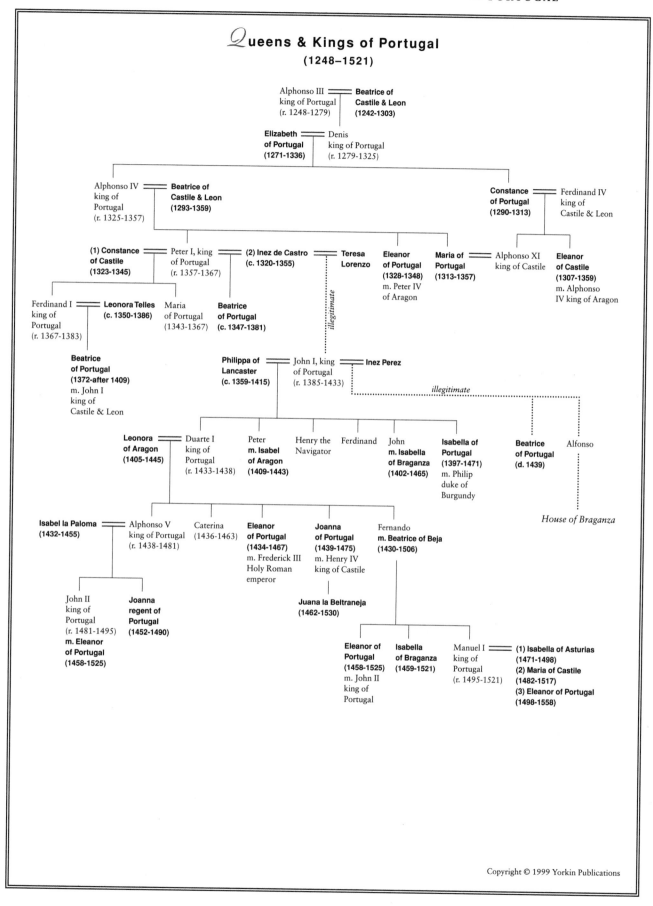

Alphonso III
king of Portugal
(r. 1248-1279)
**Beatrice of
Castile & Leon
(1242-1303)**

**Elizabeth
of Portugal
(1271-1336)**
Denis
king of Portugal
(r. 1279-1325)

Alphonso IV
king of
Portugal
(r. 1325-1357)
**Beatrice of
Castile & Leon
(1293-1359)**

**Constance
of Portugal
(1290-1313)**
Ferdinand IV
king of
Castile & Leon

**(1) Constance
of Castile
(1323-1345)**
Peter I, king
of Portugal
(r. 1357-1367)
**(2) Inez de Castro
(c. 1320-1355)**
**Teresa
Lorenzo**
**Eleanor
of Portugal
(1328-1348)**
m. Peter IV
of Aragon
**Maria of
Portugal
(1313-1357)**
Alphonso XI
king of Castile
**Eleanor
of Castile
(1307-1359)**
m. Alphonso
IV king of Aragon

illegitimate

Ferdinand I
king of
Portugal
(r. 1367-1383)
**Leonora Telles
(c. 1350-1386)**
Maria
of Portugal
(1343-1367)
**Beatrice
of Portugal
(c. 1347-1381)**

**Beatrice
of Portugal
(1372-after 1409)
m. John I
king of
Castile & Leon**

**Philippa of
Lancaster
(c. 1359-1415)**
John I, king
of Portugal
(r. 1385-1433)
Inez Perez

illegitimate

**Leonora
of Aragon
(1405-1445)**
Duarte I
king of
Portugal
(r. 1433-1438)
Peter
**m. Isabel
of Aragon
(1409-1443)**
Henry the
Navigator
Ferdinand
John
**m. Isabella
of Braganza
(1402-1465)**
**Isabella of
Portugal
(1397-1471)**
m. Philip
duke of
Burgundy
**Beatrice
of Portugal
(d. 1439)**
Alfonso

House of Braganza

**Isabel la Paloma
(1432-1455)**
Alphonso V
king of Portugal
(r. 1438-1481)
Caterina
(1436-1463)
**Eleanor
of Portugal
(1434-1467)**
m. Frederick III
Holy Roman
emperor
**Joanna
of Portugal
(1439-1475)**
m. Henry IV
king of Castile
Fernando
**m. Beatrice of Beja
(1430-1506)**

John II
king of
Portugal
(r. 1481-1495)
**m. Eleanor
of Portugal
(1458-1525)**
**Joanna
regent of
Portugal
(1452-1490)**

**Juana la Beltraneja
(1462-1530)**

**Eleanor of
Portugal
(1458-1525)**
m. John II
king of
Portugal
**Isabella
of Braganza
(1459-1521)**
Manuel I
king of
Portugal
(r. 1495-1521)
**(1) Isabella of Asturias
(1471-1498)
(2) Maria of Castile
(1482-1517)
(3) Eleanor of Portugal
(1498-1558)**

Queens & Kings of Portugal
(1495–1640)

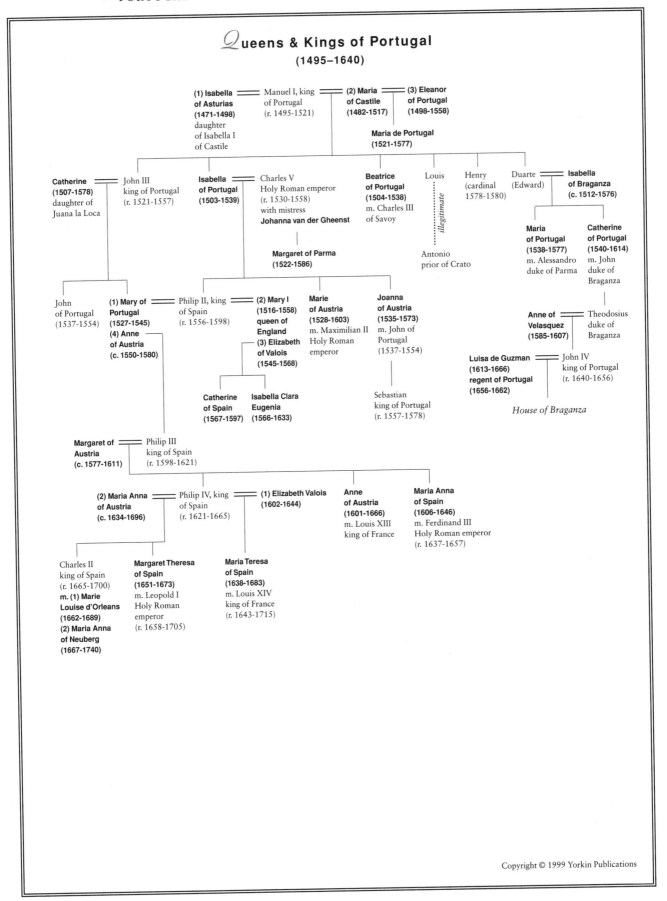

(1) Isabella of Asturias (1471-1498) daughter of Isabella I of Castile ═══ Manuel I, king of Portugal (r. 1495-1521) ═══ **(2) Maria of Castile (1482-1517)** ═══ **(3) Eleanor of Portugal (1498-1558)**

Maria de Portugal (1521-1577)

Catherine (1507-1578) daughter of Juana la Loca ═══ John III king of Portugal (r. 1521-1557)

Isabella of Portugal (1503-1539) ═══ Charles V Holy Roman emperor (r. 1530-1558) with mistress **Johanna van der Gheenst**

Beatrice of Portugal (1504-1538) m. Charles III of Savoy

Louis — *illegitimate* — Antonio prior of Crato

Henry (cardinal 1578-1580)

Duarte (Edward) ═══ **Isabella of Braganza (c. 1512-1576)**

Maria of Portugal (1538-1577) m. Alessandro duke of Parma

Catherine of Portugal (1540-1614) m. John duke of Braganza

Margaret of Parma (1522-1586)

John of Portugal (1537-1554)

(1) Mary of Portugal (1527-1545) ═══ Philip II, king of Spain (r. 1556-1598) ═══ **(2) Mary I (1516-1558) queen of England**

(4) Anne of Austria (c. 1550-1580)

(3) Elizabeth of Valois (1545-1568)

Marie of Austria (1528-1603) m. Maximilian II Holy Roman emperor

Joanna of Austria (1535-1573) m. John of Portugal (1537-1554)

Anne of Velasquez (1585-1607) ═══ Theodosius duke of Braganza

Catherine of Spain (1567-1597)

Isabella Clara Eugenia (1566-1633)

Sebastian king of Portugal (r. 1557-1578)

Luisa de Guzman (1613-1666) regent of Portugal (1656-1662) ═══ John IV king of Portugal (r. 1640-1656)

House of Braganza

Margaret of Austria (c. 1577-1611) ═══ Philip III king of Spain (r. 1598-1621)

(2) Maria Anna of Austria (c. 1634-1696) ═══ Philip IV, king of Spain (r. 1621-1665) ═══ **(1) Elizabeth Valois (1602-1644)**

Anne of Austria (1601-1666) m. Louis XIII king of France

Maria Anna of Spain (1606-1646) m. Ferdinand III Holy Roman emperor (r. 1637-1657)

Charles II king of Spain (r. 1665-1700) **m. (1) Marie Louise d'Orleans (1662-1689) (2) Maria Anna of Neuberg (1667-1740)**

Margaret Theresa of Spain (1651-1673) m. Leopold I Holy Roman emperor (r. 1658-1705)

Maria Teresa of Spain (1638-1683) m. Louis XIV king of France (r. 1643-1715)

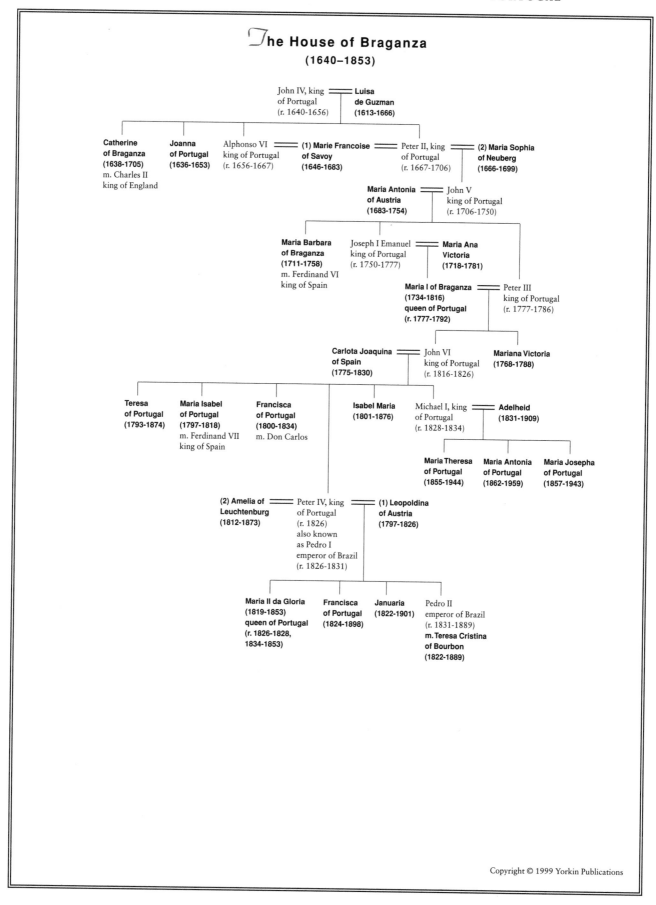

The House of Braganza
(1640–1853)

John IV, king of Portugal (r. 1640-1656) ══ Luisa de Guzman (1613-1666)

Catherine of Braganza (1638-1705) m. Charles II king of England

Joanna of Portugal (1636-1653)

Alphonso VI king of Portugal (r. 1656-1667) ══ (1) Marie Francoise of Savoy (1646-1683) ══ Peter II, king of Portugal (r. 1667-1706) ══ (2) Maria Sophia of Neuberg (1666-1699)

Maria Antonia of Austria (1683-1754) ══ John V king of Portugal (r. 1706-1750)

Maria Barbara of Braganza (1711-1758) m. Ferdinand VI king of Spain

Joseph I Emanuel king of Portugal (r. 1750-1777) ══ Maria Ana Victoria (1718-1781)

Maria I of Braganza (1734-1816) queen of Portugal (r. 1777-1792) ══ Peter III king of Portugal (r. 1777-1786)

Carlota Joaquina of Spain (1775-1830) ══ John VI king of Portugal (r. 1816-1826)

Mariana Victoria (1768-1788)

Teresa of Portugal (1793-1874)

Maria Isabel of Portugal (1797-1818) m. Ferdinand VII king of Spain

Francisca of Portugal (1800-1834) m. Don Carlos

Isabel Maria (1801-1876)

Michael I, king of Portugal (r. 1828-1834) ══ Adelheid (1831-1909)

Maria Theresa of Portugal (1855-1944)

Maria Antonia of Portugal (1862-1959)

Maria Josepha of Portugal (1857-1943)

(2) Amelia of Leuchtenburg (1812-1873) ══ Peter IV, king of Portugal (r. 1826) also known as Pedro I emperor of Brazil (r. 1826-1831) ══ (1) Leopoldina of Austria (1797-1826)

Maria II da Gloria (1819-1853) queen of Portugal (r. 1826-1828, 1834-1853)

Francisca of Portugal (1824-1898)

Januaria (1822-1901)

Pedro II emperor of Brazil (r. 1831-1889) m. Teresa Cristina of Bourbon (1822-1889)

The House of Coburg-Braganza
(1826–1910)

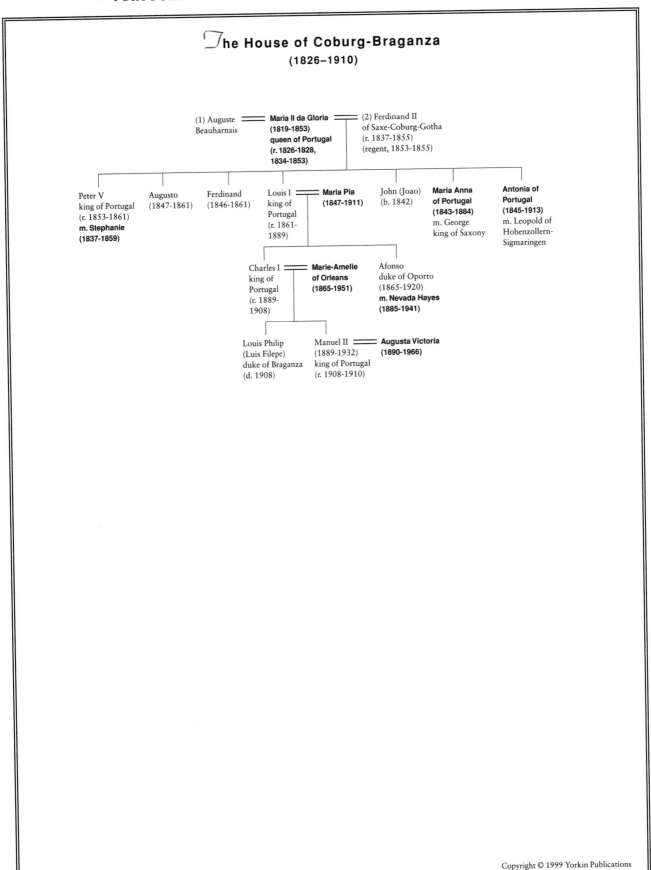

(1) Auguste Beauharnais ══ **Maria II da Gloria (1819-1853) queen of Portugal (r. 1826-1828, 1834-1853)** ══ (2) Ferdinand II of Saxe-Coburg-Gotha (r. 1837-1855) (regent, 1853-1855)

Peter V king of Portugal (r. 1853-1861) **m. Stephanie (1837-1859)**

Augusto (1847-1861)

Ferdinand (1846-1861)

Louis I king of Portugal (r. 1861-1889) ══ **Maria Pia (1847-1911)**

John (Joao) (b. 1842)

Maria Anna of Portugal (1843-1884) m. George king of Saxony

Antonia of Portugal (1845-1913) m. Leopold of Hohenzollern-Sigmaringen

Charles I king of Portugal (r. 1889-1908) ══ **Marie-Amelie of Orleans (1865-1951)**

Afonso duke of Oporto (1865-1920) **m. Nevada Hayes (1885-1941)**

Louis Philip (Luis Filepe) duke of Braganza (d. 1908)

Manuel II (1889-1932) king of Portugal (r. 1908-1910) ══ **Augusta Victoria (1890-1966)**

The Julian Line

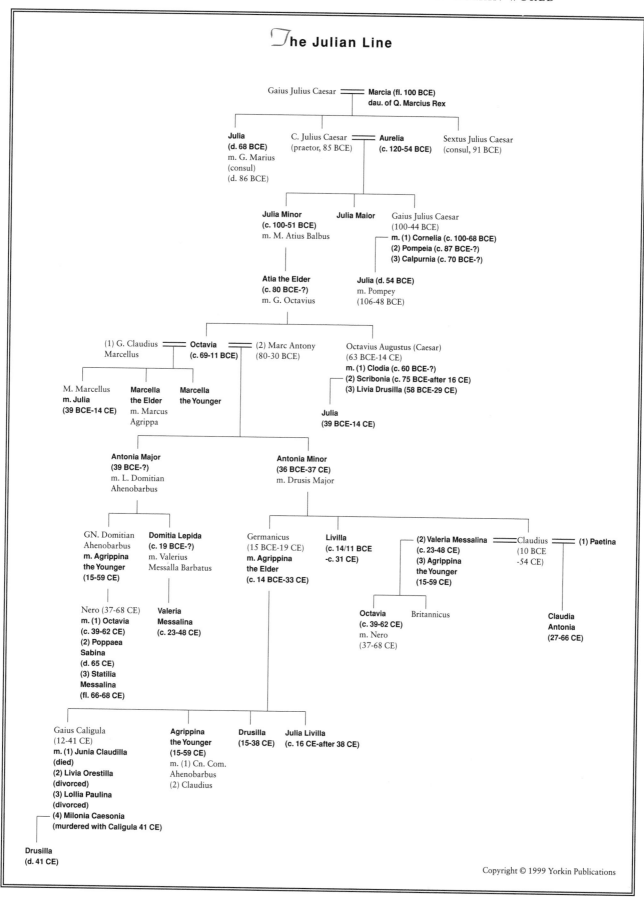

Gaius Julius Caesar ══════ **Marcia (fl. 100 BCE)**
dau. of Q. Marcius Rex

Julia
(d. 68 BCE)
m. G. Marius
(consul)
(d. 86 BCE)

C. Julius Caesar
(praetor, 85 BCE) ═══ **Aurelia**
(c. 120-54 BCE)

Sextus Julius Caesar
(consul, 91 BCE)

Julia Minor
(c. 100-51 BCE)
m. M. Atius Balbus

Julia Maior

Gaius Julius Caesar
(100-44 BCE)
m. (1) Cornelia (c. 100-68 BCE)
(2) Pompeia (c. 87 BCE-?)
(3) Calpurnia (c. 70 BCE-?)

Atia the Elder
(c. 80 BCE-?)
m. G. Octavius

Julia (d. 54 BCE)
m. Pompey
(106-48 BCE)

(1) G. Claudius
Marcellus ═══ **Octavia**
(c. 69-11 BCE) ═══ (2) Marc Antony
(80-30 BCE)

Octavius Augustus (Caesar)
(63 BCE-14 CE)
m. (1) Clodia (c. 60 BCE-?)
(2) Scribonia (c. 75 BCE-after 16 CE)
(3) Livia Drusilla (58 BCE-29 CE)

M. Marcellus
m. Julia
(39 BCE-14 CE)

Marcella
the Elder
m. Marcus
Agrippa

Marcella
the Younger

Julia
(39 BCE-14 CE)

Antonia Major
(39 BCE-?)
m. L. Domitian
Ahenobarbus

Antonia Minor
(36 BCE-37 CE)
m. Drusis Major

GN. Domitian
Ahenobarbus
m. Agrippina
the Younger
(15-59 CE)

Domitia Lepida
(c. 19 BCE-?)
m. Valerius
Messalla Barbatus

Germanicus
(15 BCE-19 CE)
m. Agrippina
the Elder
(c. 14 BCE-33 CE)

Livilla
(c. 14/11 BCE
-c. 31 CE)

(2) Valeria Messalina
(c. 23-48 CE)
(3) Agrippina
the Younger
(15-59 CE)

Claudius
(10 BCE
-54 CE) ═══ **(1) Paetina**

Nero (37-68 CE)
m. (1) Octavia
(c. 39-62 CE)
(2) Poppaea
Sabina
(d. 65 CE)
(3) Statilia
Messalina
(fl. 66-68 CE)

Valeria
Messalina
(c. 23-48 CE)

Octavia
(c. 39-62 CE)
m. Nero
(37-68 CE)

Britannicus

Claudia
Antonia
(27-66 CE)

Gaius Caligula
(12-41 CE)
m. (1) Junia Claudilla
(died)
(2) Livia Orestilla
(divorced)
(3) Lollia Paulina
(divorced)
(4) Milonia Caesonia
(murdered with Caligula 41 CE)

Agrippina
the Younger
(15-59 CE)
m. (1) Cn. Com.
Ahenobarbus
(2) Claudius

Drusilla
(15-38 CE)

Julia Livilla
(c. 16 CE-after 38 CE)

Drusilla
(d. 41 CE)

Flavian Dynasty
(69–96 CE)

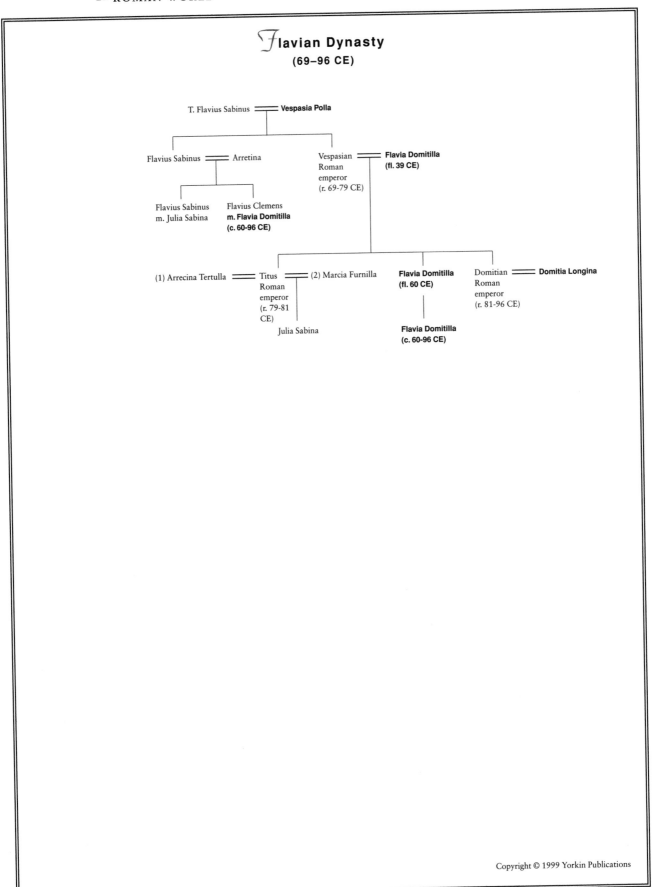

T. Flavius Sabinus ══════ **Vespasia Polla**

Flavius Sabinus ═════ Arretina

Vespasian
Roman
emperor
(r. 69-79 CE) ═════ **Flavia Domitilla (fl. 39 CE)**

Flavius Sabinus
m. Julia Sabina

Flavius Clemens
m. Flavia Domitilla (c. 60-96 CE)

(1) Arrecina Tertulla ═════ Titus
Roman
emperor
(r. 79-81
CE) ═════ (2) Marcia Furnilla

Julia Sabina

Flavia Domitilla (fl. 60 CE)

Flavia Domitilla (c. 60-96 CE)

Domitian
Roman
emperor
(r. 81-96 CE) ═════ **Domitia Longina**

𝓕amily Connections of Plotina-Trajan & Sabina-Hadrian
(97–138 CE)

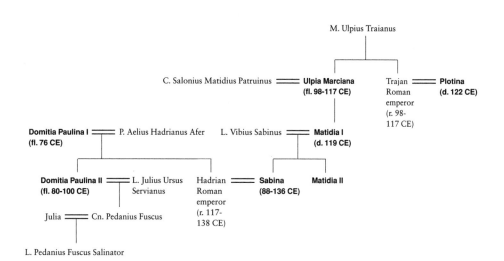

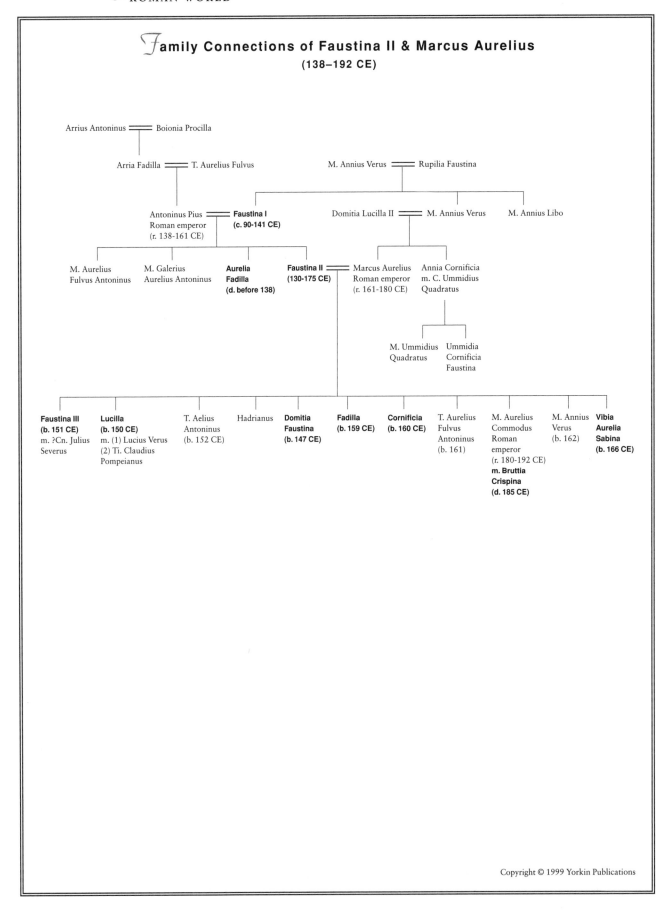

ℱamily Connections of Faustina II & Marcus Aurelius
(138–192 CE)

Arrius Antoninus ═══ Boionia Procilla

Arria Fadilla ═══ T. Aurelius Fulvus

M. Annius Verus ═══ Rupilia Faustina

Antoninus Pius
Roman emperor
(r. 138-161 CE) ═══ **Faustina I
(c. 90-141 CE)**

Domitia Lucilla II ═══ M. Annius Verus

M. Annius Libo

M. Aurelius
Fulvus Antoninus

M. Galerius
Aurelius Antoninus

**Aurelia
Fadilla
(d. before 138)**

**Faustina II
(130-175 CE)** ═══ Marcus Aurelius
Roman emperor
(r. 161-180 CE)

Annia Cornificia
m. C. Ummidius
Quadratus

M. Ummidius
Quadratus

Ummidia
Cornificia
Faustina

**Faustina III
(b. 151 CE)**
m. ?Cn. Julius
Severus

**Lucilla
(b. 150 CE)**
m. (1) Lucius Verus
(2) Ti. Claudius
Pompeianus

T. Aelius
Antoninus
(b. 152 CE)

Hadrianus

**Domitia
Faustina
(b. 147 CE)**

**Fadilla
(b. 159 CE)**

**Cornificia
(b. 160 CE)**

T. Aurelius
Fulvus
Antoninus
(b. 161)

M. Aurelius
Commodus
Roman
emperor
(r. 180-192 CE)
**m. Bruttia
Crispina
(d. 185 CE)**

M. Annius
Verus
(b. 162)

**Vibia
Aurelia
Sabina
(b. 166 CE)**

The House of Constantine
(293–363 CE)

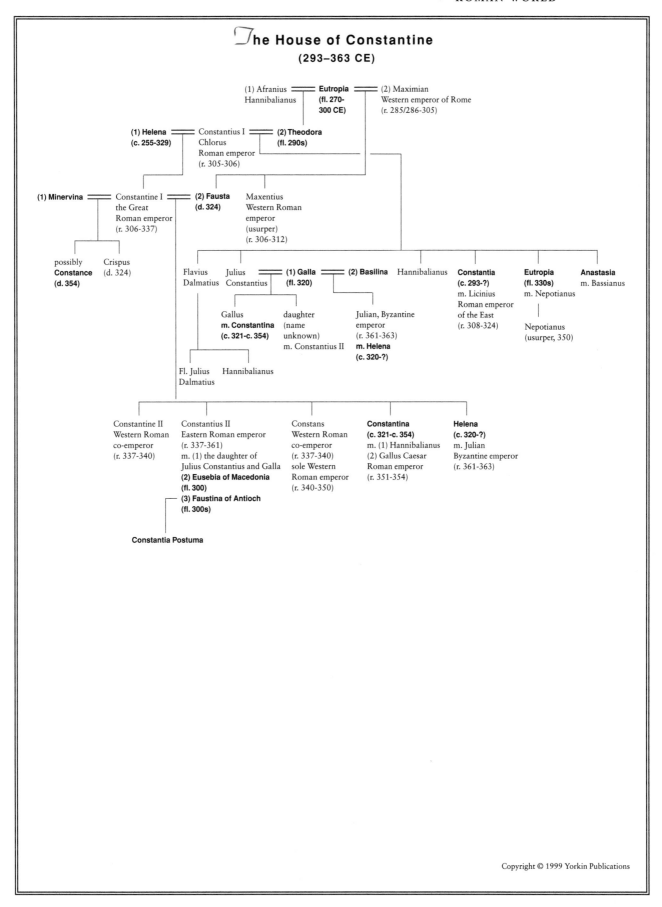

(1) Afranius Hannibalianus ══ **Eutropia (fl. 270-300 CE)** ══ (2) Maximian Western emperor of Rome (r. 285/286-305)

(1) Helena (c. 255-329) ══ Constantius I Chlorus Roman emperor (r. 305-306) ══ **(2) Theodora (fl. 290s)**

(1) Minervina ══ Constantine I the Great Roman emperor (r. 306-337) ══ **(2) Fausta (d. 324)**   Maxentius Western Roman emperor (usurper) (r. 306-312)

possibly **Constance (d. 354)**   Crispus (d. 324)

Flavius Dalmatius   Julius Constantius ══ **(1) Galla (fl. 320)** ══ **(2) Basilina**   Hannibalianus   **Constantia (c. 293-?)** m. Licinius Roman emperor of the East (r. 308-324)   **Eutropia (fl. 330s)** m. Nepotianus   **Anastasia** m. Bassianus

Gallus **m. Constantina (c. 321-c. 354)**   daughter (name unknown) m. Constantius II   Julian, Byzantine emperor (r. 361-363) **m. Helena (c. 320-?)**

Nepotianus (usurper, 350)

Fl. Julius Dalmatius   Hannibalianus

Constantine II Western Roman co-emperor (r. 337-340)   Constantius II Eastern Roman emperor (r. 337-361) m. (1) the daughter of Julius Constantius and Galla **(2) Eusebia of Macedonia (fl. 300)** **(3) Faustina of Antioch (fl. 300s)**   Constans Western Roman co-emperor (r. 337-340) sole Western Roman emperor (r. 340-350)   **Constantina (c. 321-c. 354)** m. (1) Hannibalianus (2) Gallus Caesar Roman emperor (r. 351-354)   **Helena (c. 320-?)** m. Julian Byzantine emperor (r. 361-363)

Constantia Postuma

The House of Hohenzollern-Sigmaringen
(1866–1947)

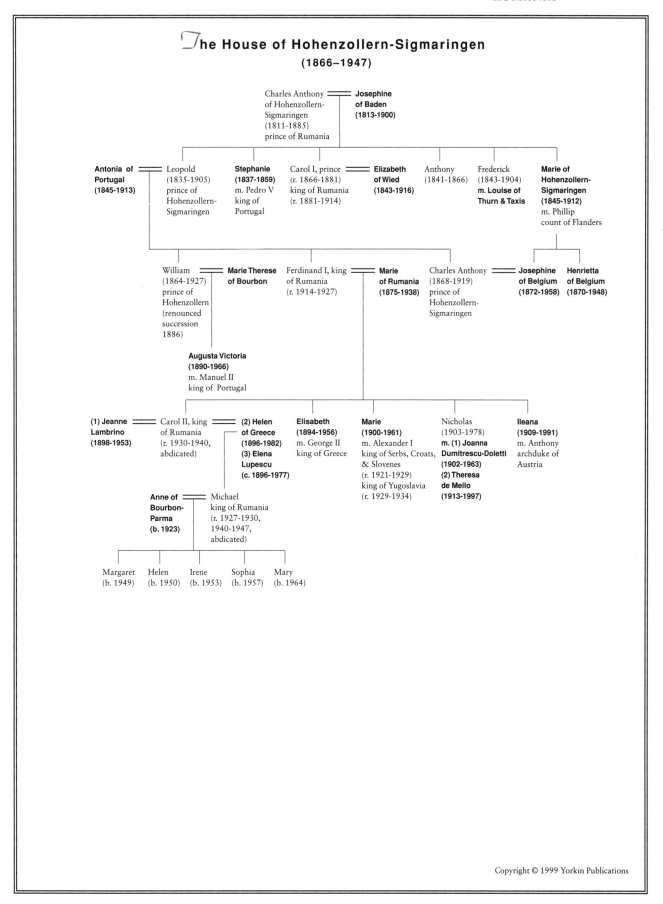

Charles Anthony of Hohenzollern-Sigmaringen (1811-1885) prince of Rumania ═══ **Josephine of Baden (1813-1900)**

Antonia of Portugal (1845-1913) ═══ Leopold (1835-1905) prince of Hohenzollern-Sigmaringen

Stephanie (1837-1859) m. Pedro V king of Portugal

Carol I, prince (r. 1866-1881) king of Rumania (r. 1881-1914) ═══ **Elizabeth of Wied (1843-1916)**

Anthony (1841-1866)

Frederick (1843-1904) **m. Louise of Thurn & Taxis**

Marie of Hohenzollern-Sigmaringen (1845-1912) m. Phillip count of Flanders

William (1864-1927) prince of Hohenzollern (renounced succession 1886) ═══ **Marie Therese of Bourbon**

Ferdinand I, king of Rumania (r. 1914-1927) ═══ **Marie of Rumania (1875-1938)**

Charles Anthony (1868-1919) prince of Hohenzollern-Sigmaringen ═══ **Josephine of Belgium (1872-1958)**

Henrietta of Belgium (1870-1948)

Augusta Victoria (1890-1966) m. Manuel II king of Portugal

(1) Jeanne Lambrino (1898-1953) ═══ Carol II, king of Rumania (r. 1930-1940, abdicated) ═══ **(2) Helen of Greece (1896-1982) (3) Elena Lupescu (c. 1896-1977)**

Elisabeth (1894-1956) m. George II king of Greece

Marie (1900-1961) m. Alexander I king of Serbs, Croats, & Slovenes (r. 1921-1929) king of Yugoslavia (r. 1929-1934)

Nicholas (1903-1978) **m. (1) Joanna Dumitrescu-Doletti (1902-1963) (2) Theresa de Mello (1913-1997)**

Ileana (1909-1991) m. Anthony archduke of Austria

Anne of Bourbon-Parma (b. 1923) ═══ Michael king of Rumania (r. 1927-1930, 1940-1947, abdicated)

Margaret (b. 1949)

Helen (b. 1950)

Irene (b. 1953)

Sophia (b. 1957)

Mary (b. 1964)

ℛussian Empresses & Emperors
(1462–1762)

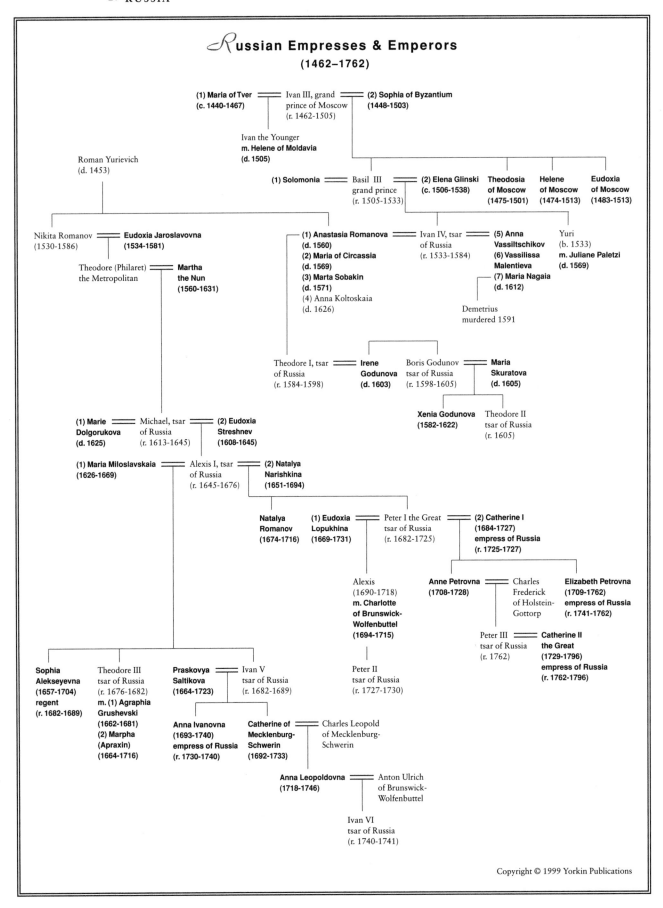

(1) Maria of Tver (c. 1440-1467) ═ Ivan III, grand prince of Moscow (r. 1462-1505) ═ **(2) Sophia of Byzantium (1448-1503)**

Ivan the Younger **m. Helene of Moldavia (d. 1505)**

(1) Solomonia ═ Basil III grand prince (r. 1505-1533) ═ **(2) Elena Glinski (c. 1506-1538)** | **Theodosia of Moscow (1475-1501)** | **Helene of Moscow (1474-1513)** | **Eudoxia of Moscow (1483-1513)**

Roman Yurievich (d. 1453)

Nikita Romanov (1530-1586) ═ **Eudoxia Jaroslavovna (1534-1581)**

(1) Anastasia Romanova (d. 1560) (2) Maria of Circassia (d. 1569) (3) Marta Sobakin (d. 1571) (4) Anna Koltoskaia (d. 1626) ═ Ivan IV, tsar of Russia (r. 1533-1584) ═ **(5) Anna Vassiltschikov (6) Vassilissa Malentieva (7) Maria Nagaia (d. 1612)** | Yuri (b. 1533) **m. Juliane Paletzi (d. 1569)**

Theodore (Philaret) the Metropolitan ═ **Martha the Nun (1560-1631)**

Demetrius murdered 1591

Theodore I, tsar of Russia (r. 1584-1598) ═ **Irene Godunova (d. 1603)** | Boris Godunov tsar of Russia (r. 1598-1605) ═ **Maria Skuratova (d. 1605)**

Xenia Godunova (1582-1622) | Theodore II tsar of Russia (r. 1605)

(1) Marie Dolgorukova (d. 1625) ═ Michael, tsar of Russia (r. 1613-1645) ═ **(2) Eudoxia Streshnev (1608-1645)**

(1) Maria Miloslavskaia (1626-1669) ═ Alexis I, tsar of Russia (r. 1645-1676) ═ **(2) Natalya Narishkina (1651-1694)**

Natalya Romanov (1674-1716)

(1) Eudoxia Lopukhina (1669-1731) ═ Peter I the Great tsar of Russia (r. 1682-1725) ═ **(2) Catherine I (1684-1727) empress of Russia (r. 1725-1727)**

Alexis (1690-1718) **m. Charlotte of Brunswick-Wolfenbuttel (1694-1715)**

Anne Petrovna (1708-1728) ═ Charles Frederick of Holstein-Gottorp | **Elizabeth Petrovna (1709-1762) empress of Russia (r. 1741-1762)**

Peter III tsar of Russia (r. 1762) ═ **Catherine II the Great (1729-1796) empress of Russia (r. 1762-1796)**

Peter II tsar of Russia (r. 1727-1730)

Sophia Alekseyevna (1657-1704) regent (r. 1682-1689)

Theodore III tsar of Russia (r. 1676-1682) **m. (1) Agraphia Grushevski (1662-1681) (2) Marpha (Apraxin) (1664-1716)**

Praskovya Saltikova (1664-1723) ═ Ivan V tsar of Russia (r. 1682-1689)

Anna Ivanovna (1693-1740) empress of Russia (r. 1730-1740) | **Catherine of Mecklenburg-Schwerin (1692-1733)** ═ Charles Leopold of Mecklenburg-Schwerin

Anna Leopoldovna (1718-1746) ═ Anton Ulrich of Brunswick-Wolfenbuttel

Ivan VI tsar of Russia (r. 1740-1741)

ℛussian Empresses & Emperors
(1762–1917)

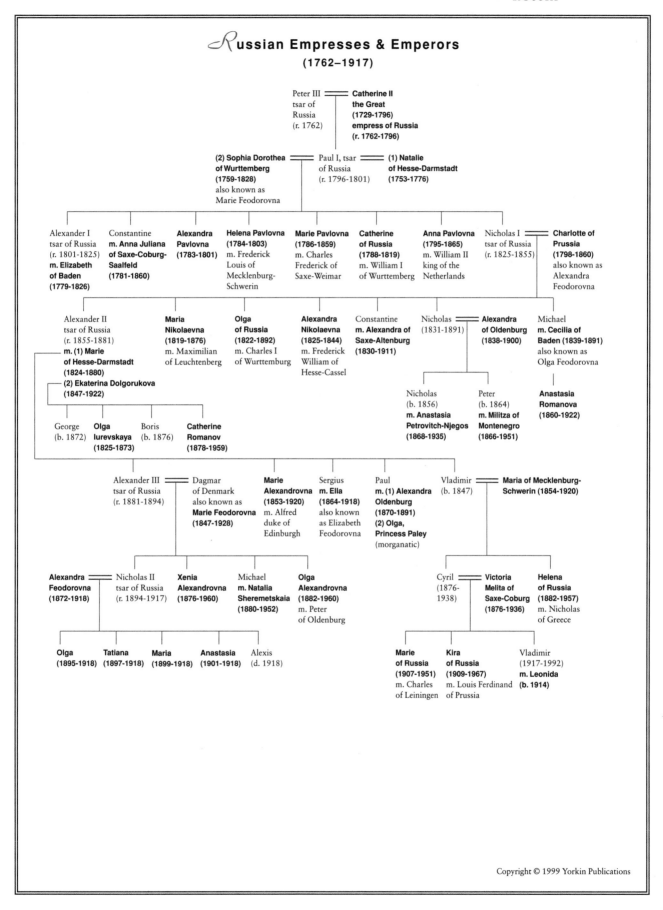

Peter III
tsar of
Russia
(r. 1762)
═══ **Catherine II
the Great
(1729-1796)
empress of Russia
(r. 1762-1796)**

**(2) Sophia Dorothea
of Wurttemberg
(1759-1828)**
also known as
Marie Feodorovna
═══ Paul I, tsar
of Russia
(r. 1796-1801)
═══ **(1) Natalie
of Hesse-Darmstadt
(1753-1776)**

Alexander I
tsar of Russia
(r. 1801-1825)
**m. Elizabeth
of Baden
(1779-1826)**

Constantine
**m. Anna Juliana
of Saxe-Coburg-
Saalfeld
(1781-1860)**

**Alexandra
Pavlovna
(1783-1801)**

**Helena Pavlovna
(1784-1803)**
m. Frederick
Louis of
Mecklenburg-
Schwerin

**Marie Pavlovna
(1786-1859)**
m. Charles
Frederick of
Saxe-Weimar

**Catherine
of Russia
(1788-1819)**
m. William I
of Wurttemberg

**Anna Pavlovna
(1795-1865)**
m. William II
king of the
Netherlands

Nicholas I
tsar of Russia
(r. 1825-1855)
═══ **Charlotte of
Prussia
(1798-1860)**
also known as
Alexandra
Feodorovna

Alexander II
tsar of Russia
(r. 1855-1881)
**m. (1) Marie
of Hesse-Darmstadt
(1824-1880)
(2) Ekaterina Dolgorukova
(1847-1922)**

**Maria
Nikolaevna
(1819-1876)**
m. Maximilian
of Leuchtenberg

**Olga
of Russia
(1822-1892)**
m. Charles I
of Wurttemburg

**Alexandra
Nikolaevna
(1825-1844)**
m. Frederick
William of
Hesse-Cassel

Constantine
**m. Alexandra of
Saxe-Altenburg
(1830-1911)**

Nicholas
(1831-1891)
═══ **Alexandra
of Oldenburg
(1838-1900)**

Michael
**m. Cecilia of
Baden (1839-1891)**
also known as
Olga Feodorovna

Nicholas
(b. 1856)
**m. Anastasia
Petrovitch-Njegos
(1868-1935)**

Peter
(b. 1864)
**m. Militza of
Montenegro
(1866-1951)**

**Anastasia
Romanova
(1860-1922)**

George
(b. 1872)

**Olga
Iurevskaya
(1825-1873)**

Boris
(b. 1876)

**Catherine
Romanov
(1878-1959)**

Alexander III
tsar of Russia
(r. 1881-1894)
═══ Dagmar
of Denmark
also known as
**Marie Feodorovna
(1847-1928)**

**Marie
Alexandrovna
(1853-1920)**
m. Alfred
duke of
Edinburgh

Sergius
**m. Ella
(1864-1918)**
also known
as Elizabeth
Feodorovna

Paul
**m. (1) Alexandra
Oldenburg
(1870-1891)
(2) Olga,
Princess Paley**
(morganatic)

Vladimir
(b. 1847)
═══ **Maria of Mecklenburg-
Schwerin (1854-1920)**

**Alexandra
Feodorovna
(1872-1918)**
═══ Nicholas II
tsar of Russia
(r. 1894-1917)

**Xenia
Alexandrovna
(1876-1960)**

Michael
**m. Natalia
Sheremetskaia
(1880-1952)**

**Olga
Alexandrovna
(1882-1960)**
m. Peter
of Oldenburg

Cyril
(1876-
1938)
═══ **Victoria
Melita of
Saxe-Coburg
(1876-1936)**

**Helena
of Russia
(1882-1957)**
m. Nicholas
of Greece

Olga
(1895-1918)

Tatiana
(1897-1918)

**Maria
(1899-1918)**

**Anastasia
(1901-1918)**

Alexis
(d. 1918)

**Marie
of Russia
(1907-1951)**
m. Charles
of Leiningen

**Kira
of Russia
(1909-1967)**
m. Louis Ferdinand
of Prussia

Vladimir
(1917-1992)
**m. Leonida
(b. 1914)**

Scandinavian Rulers
(1263–1533)

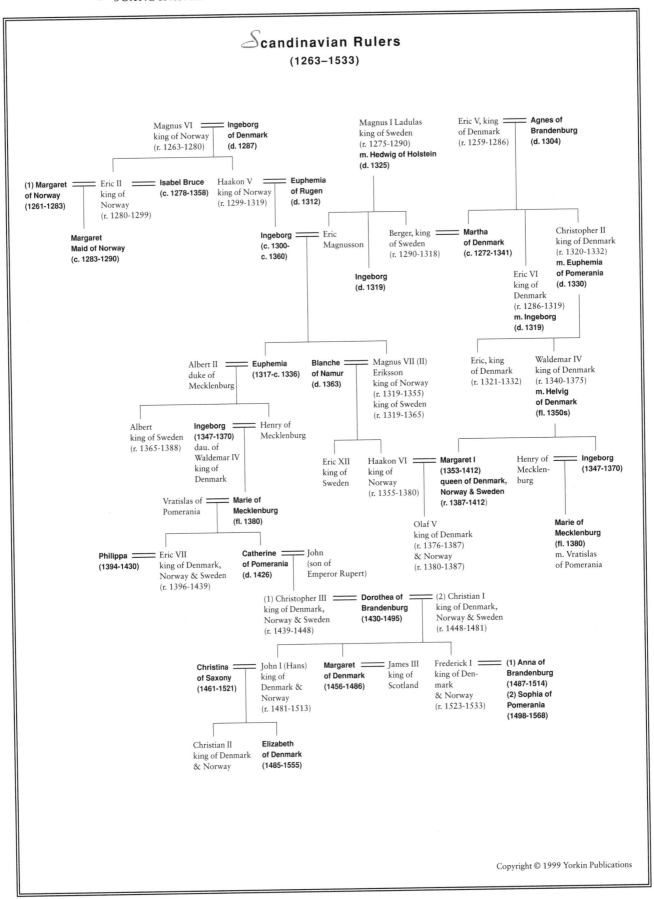

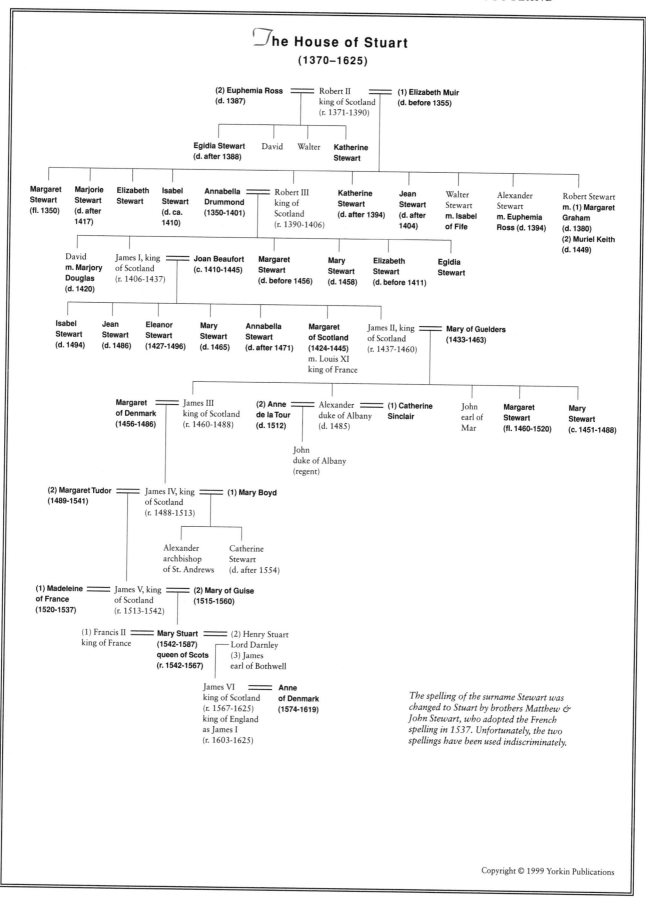

The House of Stuart
(1370–1625)

(2) Euphemia Ross (d. 1387) ═══ Robert II king of Scotland (r. 1371-1390) ═══ **(1) Elizabeth Muir (d. before 1355)**

Egidia Stewart (d. after 1388) — David — Walter — **Katherine Stewart**

Margaret Stewart (fl. 1350) — Marjorie Stewart (d. after 1417) — Elizabeth Stewart — Isabel Stewart (d. ca. 1410) — **Annabella Drummond (1350-1401)** ═══ Robert III king of Scotland (r. 1390-1406) — Katherine Stewart (d. after 1394) — Jean Stewart (d. after 1404) — Walter Stewart m. Isabel of Fife — Alexander Stewart m. Euphemia Ross (d. 1394) — Robert Stewart m. (1) Margaret Graham (d. 1380) (2) Muriel Keith (d. 1449)

David m. Marjory Douglas (d. 1420) — James I, king of Scotland (r. 1406-1437) ═══ **Joan Beaufort (c. 1410-1445)** — Margaret Stewart (d. before 1456) — Mary Stewart (d. 1458) — Elizabeth Stewart (d. before 1411) — Egidia Stewart

Isabel Stewart (d. 1494) — Jean Stewart (d. 1486) — Eleanor Stewart (1427-1496) — Mary Stewart (d. 1465) — Annabella Stewart (d. after 1471) — Margaret of Scotland (1424-1445) m. Louis XI king of France — James II, king of Scotland (r. 1437-1460) ═══ **Mary of Guelders (1433-1463)**

Margaret of Denmark (1456-1486) ═══ James III king of Scotland (r. 1460-1488) — **(2) Anne de la Tour (d. 1512)** ═══ Alexander duke of Albany (d. 1485) ═══ **(1) Catherine Sinclair** — John earl of Mar — **Margaret Stewart (fl. 1460-1520)** — **Mary Stewart (c. 1451-1488)**

John duke of Albany (regent)

(2) Margaret Tudor (1489-1541) ═══ James IV, king of Scotland (r. 1488-1513) ═══ **(1) Mary Boyd**

Alexander archbishop of St. Andrews — Catherine Stewart (d. after 1554)

(1) Madeleine of France (1520-1537) ═══ James V, king of Scotland (r. 1513-1542) ═══ **(2) Mary of Guise (1515-1560)**

(1) Francis II king of France ═══ **Mary Stuart (1542-1587) queen of Scots (r. 1542-1567)** ═══ (2) Henry Stuart Lord Darnley (3) James earl of Bothwell

James VI king of Scotland (r. 1567-1625) king of England as James I (r. 1603-1625) ═══ **Anne of Denmark (1574-1619)**

The spelling of the surname Stewart was changed to Stuart by brothers Matthew & John Stewart, who adopted the French spelling in 1537. Unfortunately, the two spellings have been used indiscriminately.

Spanish Rulers
(970–1285)

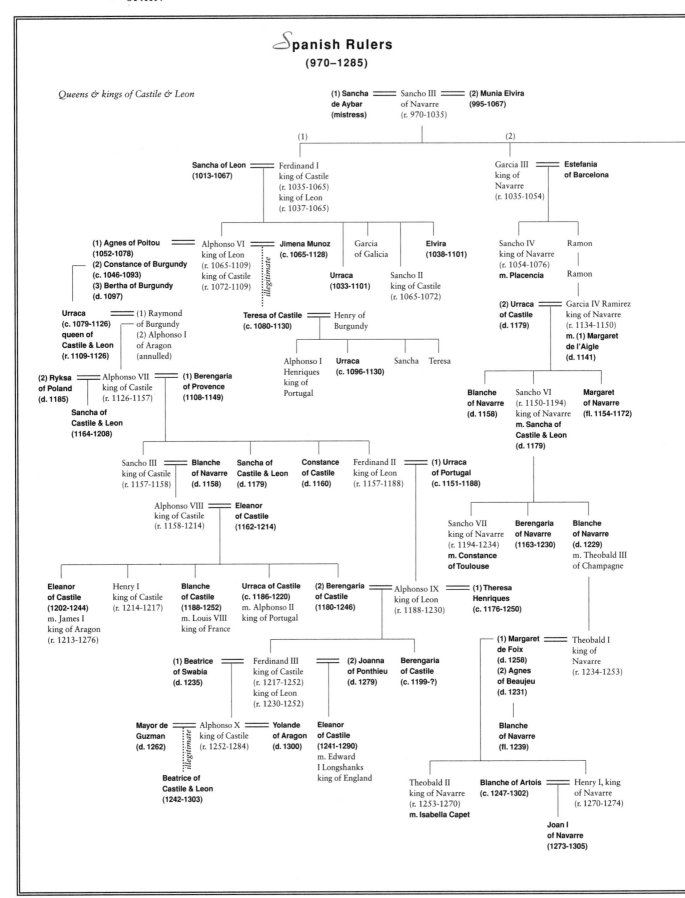

Queens & kings of Castile & Leon

(1) Sancha de Aybar (mistress) ══ Sancho III of Navarre (r. 970-1035) ══ **(2) Munia Elvira (995-1067)**

(1)

(2)

Sancha of Leon (1013-1067) ══ Ferdinand I king of Castile (r. 1035-1065) king of Leon (r. 1037-1065)

Garcia III king of Navarre (r. 1035-1054) ══ **Estefania of Barcelona**

(1) Agnes of Poitou (1052-1078)
(2) Constance of Burgundy (c. 1046-1093)
(3) Bertha of Burgundy (d. 1097) ══ Alphonso VI king of Leon (r. 1065-1109) king of Castile (r. 1072-1109) ══ **Jimena Munoz (c. 1065-1128)** *illegitimate*

Garcia of Galicia

Elvira (1038-1101)

Sancho IV king of Navarre (r. 1054-1076) **m. Placencia**

Ramon

Urraca (1033-1101)

Sancho II king of Castile (r. 1065-1072)

Ramon

Urraca (c. 1079-1126) queen of Castile & Leon (r. 1109-1126) ══ (1) Raymond of Burgundy (2) Alphonso I of Aragon (annulled)

Teresa of Castile (c. 1080-1130) ══ Henry of Burgundy

(2) Urraca of Castile (d. 1179) ══ Garcia IV Ramirez king of Navarre (r. 1134-1150) **m. (1) Margaret de l'Aigle (d. 1141)**

(2) Ryksa of Poland (d. 1185) ══ Alphonso VII king of Castile (r. 1126-1157) ══ **(1) Berengaria of Provence (1108-1149)**

Alphonso I Henriques king of Portugal

Urraca (c. 1096-1130)

Sancha Teresa

Blanche of Navarre (d. 1158)

Sancho VI (r. 1150-1194) king of Navarre **m. Sancha of Castile & Leon (d. 1179)**

Margaret of Navarre (fl. 1154-1172)

Sancha of Castile & Leon (1164-1208)

Sancho III king of Castile (r. 1157-1158) ══ **Blanche of Navarre (d. 1158)**

Sancha of Castile & Leon (d. 1179)

Constance of Castile (d. 1160)

Ferdinand II king of Leon (r. 1157-1188) ══ **(1) Urraca of Portugal (c. 1151-1188)**

Alphonso VIII king of Castile (r. 1158-1214) ══ **Eleanor of Castile (1162-1214)**

Sancho VII king of Navarre (r. 1194-1234) **m. Constance of Toulouse**

Berengaria of Navarre (1163-1230)

Blanche of Navarre (d. 1229) m. Theobald III of Champagne

Eleanor of Castile (1202-1244) m. James I king of Aragon (r. 1213-1276)

Henry I king of Castile (r. 1214-1217)

Blanche of Castile (1188-1252) m. Louis VIII king of France

Urraca of Castile (c. 1186-1220) m. Alphonso II king of Portugal

(2) Berengaria of Castile (1180-1246) ══ Alphonso IX king of Leon (r. 1188-1230) ══ **(1) Theresa Henriques (c. 1176-1250)**

(1) Margaret de Foix (d. 1258)
(2) Agnes of Beaujeu (d. 1231) ══ Theobald I king of Navarre (r. 1234-1253)

(1) Beatrice of Swabia (d. 1235) ══ Ferdinand III king of Castile (r. 1217-1252) king of Leon (r. 1230-1252) ══ **(2) Joanna of Ponthieu (d. 1279)**

Berengaria of Castile (c. 1199-?)

Blanche of Navarre (fl. 1239)

Mayor de Guzman (d. 1262) ══ Alphonso X king of Castile (r. 1252-1284) ══ **Yolande of Aragon (d. 1300)** *illegitimate*

Eleanor of Castile (1241-1290) m. Edward I Longshanks king of England

Beatrice of Castile & Leon (1242-1303)

Theobald II king of Navarre (r. 1253-1270) **m. Isabella Capet**

Blanche of Artois (c. 1247-1302) ══ Henry I, king of Navarre (r. 1270-1274)

Joan I of Navarre (1273-1305)

Queens & kings of Aragon

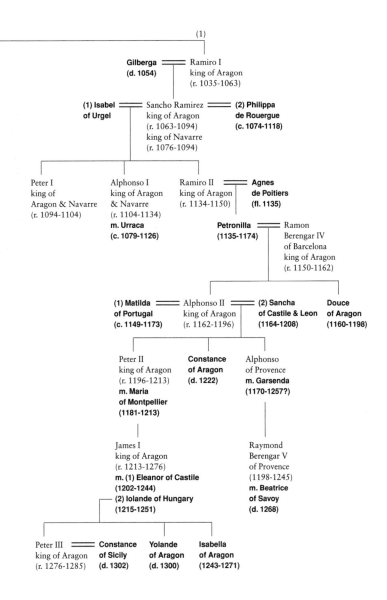

(1)

Gilberga ═══ Ramiro I
(d. 1054)   king of Aragon
              (r. 1035-1063)

(1) Isabel ═══ Sancho Ramirez ═══ (2) Philippa
of Urgel   king of Aragon   de Rouergue
                (r. 1063-1094)   (c. 1074-1118)
                king of Navarre
                (r. 1076-1094)

Peter I   Alphonso I   Ramiro II ═══ Agnes
king of   king of Aragon   king of Aragon   de Poitiers
Aragon & Navarre & Navarre   (r. 1134-1150)   (fl. 1135)
(r. 1094-1104)   (r. 1104-1134)
                 m. Urraca   Petronilla ═══ Ramon
                 (c. 1079-1126)   (1135-1174)   Berengar IV
                                                    of Barcelona
                                                    king of Aragon
                                                    (r. 1150-1162)

(1) Matilda ═══ Alphonso II ═══ (2) Sancha   Douce
of Portugal   king of Aragon   of Castile & Leon of Aragon
(c. 1149-1173)   (r. 1162-1196)   (1164-1208)   (1160-1198)

Peter II   Constance   Alphonso
king of Aragon   of Aragon   of Provence
(r. 1196-1213)   (d. 1222)   m. Garsenda
m. Maria   (1170-1257?)
of Montpellier
(1181-1213)

James I   Raymond
king of Aragon   Berengar V
(r. 1213-1276)   of Provence
m. (1) Eleanor of Castile   (1198-1245)
(1202-1244)   m. Beatrice
(2) Iolande of Hungary   of Savoy
(1215-1251)   (d. 1268)

Peter III ═══ Constance   Yolande   Isabella
king of Aragon   of Sicily   of Aragon   of Aragon
(r. 1276-1285)   (d. 1302)   (d. 1300)   (1243-1271)

The House of Castile & Leon
(1252–1504)

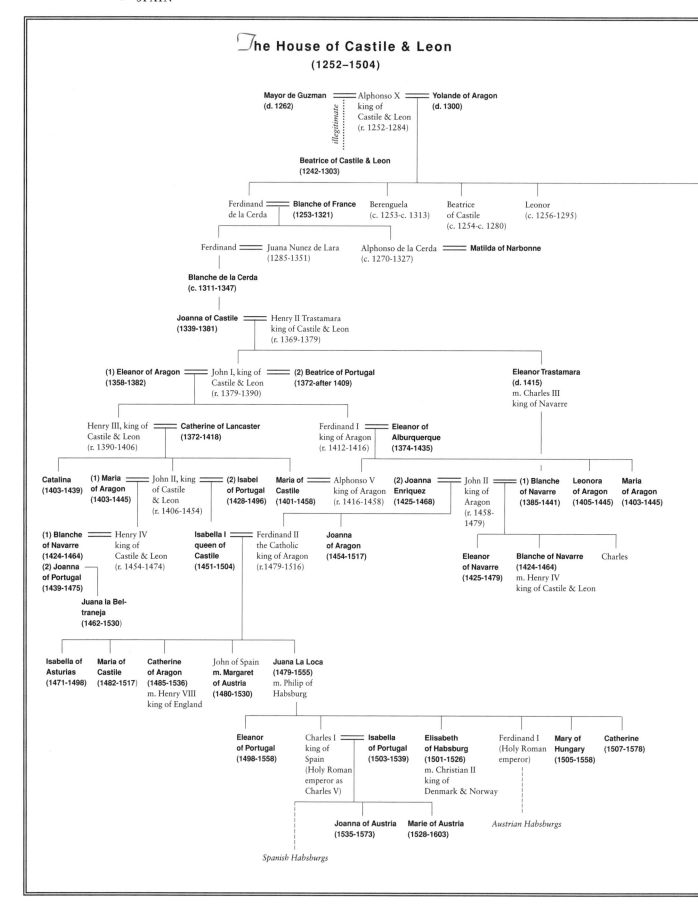

Mayor de Guzman (d. 1262) ═══ *illegitimate* ═══ Alphonso X king of Castile & Leon (r. 1252-1284) ═══ **Yolande of Aragon (d. 1300)**

Beatrice of Castile & Leon (1242-1303)

Ferdinand de la Cerda ═══ **Blanche of France (1253-1321)** | Berenguela (c. 1253-c. 1313) | Beatrice of Castile (c. 1254-c. 1280) | Leonor (c. 1256-1295)

Ferdinand ═══ Juana Nunez de Lara (1285-1351) | Alphonso de la Cerda (c. 1270-1327) ═══ **Matilda of Narbonne**

Blanche de la Cerda (c. 1311-1347)

Joanna of Castile (1339-1381) ═══ Henry II Trastamara king of Castile & Leon (r. 1369-1379)

(1) Eleanor of Aragon (1358-1382) ═══ John I, king of Castile & Leon (r. 1379-1390) ═══ **(2) Beatrice of Portugal (1372-after 1409)** | **Eleanor Trastamara (d. 1415)** m. Charles III king of Navarre

Henry III, king of Castile & Leon (r. 1390-1406) ═══ **Catherine of Lancaster (1372-1418)** | Ferdinand I king of Aragon (r. 1412-1416) ═══ **Eleanor of Alburquerque (1374-1435)**

Catalina (1403-1439) | **(1) Maria of Aragon (1403-1445)** ═══ John II, king of Castile & Leon (r. 1406-1454) ═══ **(2) Isabel of Portugal (1428-1496)** | **Maria of Castile (1401-1458)** ═══ Alphonso V king of Aragon (r. 1416-1458) | **(2) Joanna Enriquez (1425-1468)** ═══ John II king of Aragon (r. 1458-1479) ═══ **(1) Blanche of Navarre (1385-1441)** | **Leonora of Aragon (1405-1445)** | **Maria of Aragon (1403-1445)**

(1) Blanche of Navarre (1424-1464) **(2) Joanna of Portugal (1439-1475)** ═══ Henry IV king of Castile & Leon (r. 1454-1474) | **Isabella I queen of Castile (1451-1504)** ═══ Ferdinand II the Catholic king of Aragon (r.1479-1516) | **Joanna of Aragon (1454-1517)** | **Eleanor of Navarre (1425-1479)** | **Blanche of Navarre (1424-1464)** m. Henry IV king of Castile & Leon | Charles

Juana la Bel-traneja (1462-1530)

Isabella of Asturias (1471-1498) | **Maria of Castile (1482-1517)** | **Catherine of Aragon (1485-1536)** m. Henry VIII king of England | John of Spain m. Margaret of Austria (1480-1530) | Juana La Loca (1479-1555) m. Philip of Habsburg

Eleanor of Portugal (1498-1558) | Charles I king of Spain (Holy Roman emperor as Charles V) ═══ **Isabella of Portugal (1503-1539)** | **Elisabeth of Habsburg (1501-1526)** m. Christian II king of Denmark & Norway | Ferdinand I (Holy Roman emperor) | **Mary of Hungary (1505-1558)** | **Catherine (1507-1578)**

Joanna of Austria (1535-1573) | **Marie of Austria (1528-1603)** | *Austrian Habsburgs*

Spanish Habsburgs

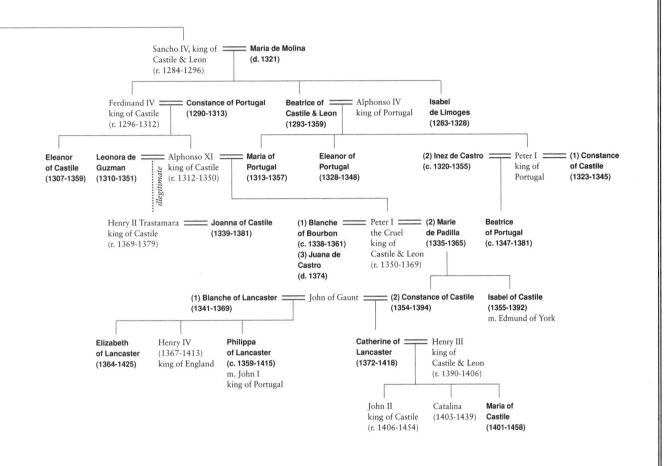

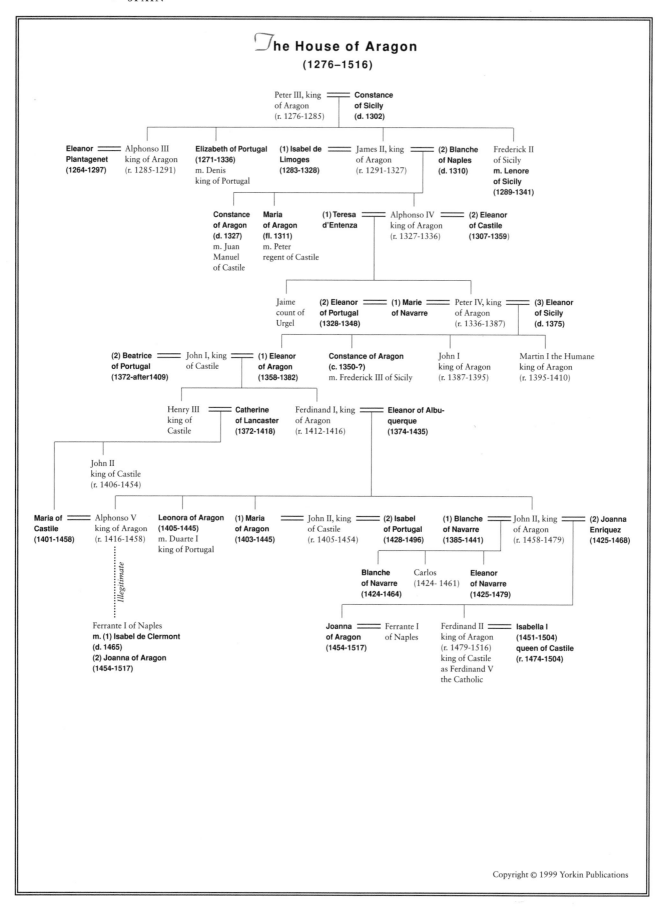

The House of Aragon
(1276–1516)

Peter III, king of Aragon (r. 1276-1285) ═══ **Constance of Sicily (d. 1302)**

Eleanor Plantagenet (1264-1297) ═══ Alphonso III king of Aragon (r. 1285-1291)

Elizabeth of Portugal (1271-1336) m. Denis king of Portugal

(1) Isabel de Limoges (1283-1328) ═══ James II, king of Aragon (r. 1291-1327) ═══ **(2) Blanche of Naples (d. 1310)**

Frederick II of Sicily **m. Lenore of Sicily (1289-1341)**

Constance of Aragon (d. 1327) m. Juan Manuel of Castile

Maria of Aragon (fl. 1311) m. Peter regent of Castile

(1) Teresa d'Entenza ═══ Alphonso IV king of Aragon (r. 1327-1336) ═══ **(2) Eleanor of Castile (1307-1359)**

Jaime count of Urgel

(2) Eleanor of Portugal (1328-1348) ═══ **(1) Marie of Navarre** ═══ Peter IV, king of Aragon (r. 1336-1387) ═══ **(3) Eleanor of Sicily (d. 1375)**

(2) Beatrice of Portugal (1372-after1409) ═══ John I, king of Castile ═══ **(1) Eleanor of Aragon (1358-1382)**

Constance of Aragon (c. 1350-?) m. Frederick III of Sicily

John I king of Aragon (r. 1387-1395)

Martin I the Humane king of Aragon (r. 1395-1410)

Henry III king of Castile ═══ **Catherine of Lancaster (1372-1418)**

Ferdinand I, king of Aragon (r. 1412-1416) ═══ **Eleanor of Albuquerque (1374-1435)**

John II king of Castile (r. 1406-1454)

Maria of Castile (1401-1458) ═══ Alphonso V king of Aragon (r. 1416-1458)

Leonora of Aragon (1405-1445) m. Duarte I king of Portugal

(1) Maria of Aragon (1403-1445) ═══ John II, king of Castile (r. 1405-1454) ═══ **(2) Isabel of Portugal (1428-1496)**

(1) Blanche of Navarre (1385-1441) ═══ John II, king of Aragon (r. 1458-1479) ═══ **(2) Joanna Enriquez (1425-1468)**

Illegitimate

Ferrante I of Naples **m. (1) Isabel de Clermont (d. 1465) (2) Joanna of Aragon (1454-1517)**

Blanche of Navarre (1424-1464) — Carlos (1424-1461) — **Eleanor of Navarre (1425-1479)**

Joanna of Aragon (1454-1517) ═══ Ferrante I of Naples

Ferdinand II king of Aragon (r. 1479-1516) king of Castile as Ferdinand V the Catholic ═══ **Isabella I (1451-1504) queen of Castile (r. 1474-1504)**

Copyright © 1999 Yorkin Publications

The Spanish Succession
(1700)

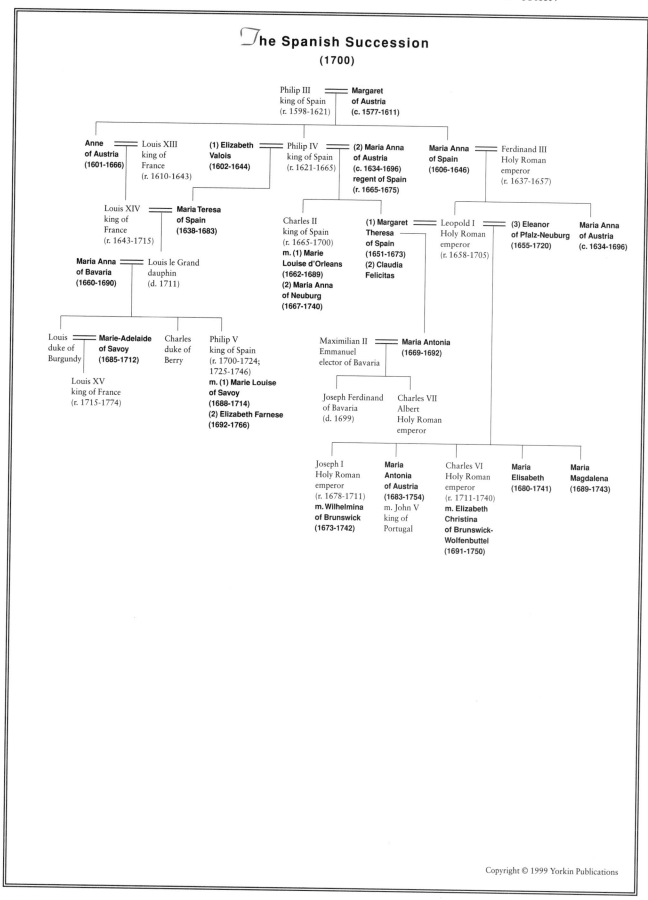

Philip III
king of Spain
(r. 1598-1621) ═══ **Margaret
of Austria
(c. 1577-1611)**

**Anne
of Austria
(1601-1666)** ═══ Louis XIII
king of
France
(r. 1610-1643)

**(1) Elizabeth
Valois
(1602-1644)** ═══ Philip IV
king of Spain
(r. 1621-1665) ═══ **(2) Maria Anna
of Austria
(c. 1634-1696)
regent of Spain
(r. 1665-1675)**

**Maria Anna
of Spain
(1606-1646)** ═══ Ferdinand III
Holy Roman
emperor
(r. 1637-1657)

Louis XIV
king of
France
(r. 1643-1715) ═══ **Maria Teresa
of Spain
(1638-1683)**

Charles II
king of Spain
(r. 1665-1700)
**m. (1) Marie
Louise d'Orleans
(1662-1689)
(2) Maria Anna
of Neuburg
(1667-1740)**

**(1) Margaret
Theresa
of Spain
(1651-1673)
(2) Claudia
Felicitas** ═══ Leopold I
Holy Roman
emperor
(r. 1658-1705) ═══ **(3) Eleanor
of Pfalz-Neuburg
(1655-1720)**

**Maria Anna
of Austria
(c. 1634-1696)**

**Maria Anna
of Bavaria
(1660-1690)** ═══ Louis le Grand
dauphin
(d. 1711)

Louis
duke of
Burgundy ═══ **Marie-Adelaide
of Savoy
(1685-1712)**

Charles
duke of
Berry

Philip V
king of Spain
(r. 1700-1724;
1725-1746)
**m. (1) Marie Louise
of Savoy
(1688-1714)
(2) Elizabeth Farnese
(1692-1766)**

Maximilian II
Emmanuel
elector of Bavaria ═══ **Maria Antonia
(1669-1692)**

Louis XV
king of France
(r. 1715-1774)

Joseph Ferdinand
of Bavaria
(d. 1699)

Charles VII
Albert
Holy Roman
emperor

Joseph I
Holy Roman
emperor
(r. 1678-1711)
**m. Wilhelmina
of Brunswick
(1673-1742)**

**Maria
Antonia
of Austria
(1683-1754)**
m. John V
king of
Portugal

Charles VI
Holy Roman
emperor
(r. 1711-1740)
**m. Elizabeth
Christina
of Brunswick-
Wolfenbuttel
(1691-1750)**

**Maria
Elisabeth
(1680-1741)**

**Maria
Magdalena
(1689-1743)**

৵panish Bourbons
(1700–1833)

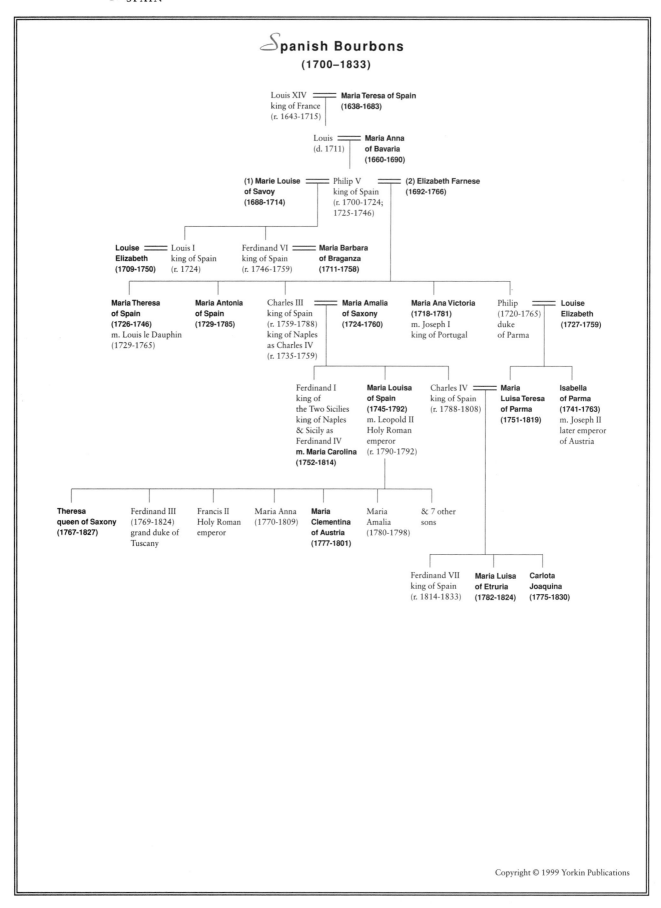

Louis XIV
king of France
(r. 1643-1715)
═══ **Maria Teresa of Spain**
(1638-1683)

Louis
(d. 1711)
═══ **Maria Anna**
of Bavaria
(1660-1690)

(1) Marie Louise
of Savoy
(1688-1714)
═══ Philip V
king of Spain
(r. 1700-1724;
1725-1746)
═══ **(2) Elizabeth Farnese**
(1692-1766)

Louise
Elizabeth
(1709-1750)
═══ Louis I
king of Spain
(r. 1724)

Ferdinand VI
king of Spain
(r. 1746-1759)
═══ **Maria Barbara**
of Braganza
(1711-1758)

Maria Theresa
of Spain
(1726-1746)
m. Louis le Dauphin
(1729-1765)

Maria Antonia
of Spain
(1729-1785)

Charles III
king of Spain
(r. 1759-1788)
king of Naples
as Charles IV
(r. 1735-1759)
═══ **Maria Amalia**
of Saxony
(1724-1760)

Maria Ana Victoria
(1718-1781)
m. Joseph I
king of Portugal

Philip
(1720-1765)
duke
of Parma
═══ **Louise**
Elizabeth
(1727-1759)

Ferdinand I
king of
the Two Sicilies
king of Naples
& Sicily as
Ferdinand IV
m. Maria Carolina
(1752-1814)

Maria Louisa
of Spain
(1745-1792)
m. Leopold II
Holy Roman
emperor
(r. 1790-1792)

Charles IV
king of Spain
(r. 1788-1808)
═══ **Maria**
Luisa Teresa
of Parma
(1751-1819)

Isabella
of Parma
(1741-1763)
m. Joseph II
later emperor
of Austria

Theresa
queen of Saxony
(1767-1827)

Ferdinand III
(1769-1824)
grand duke of
Tuscany

Francis II
Holy Roman
emperor

Maria Anna
(1770-1809)

Maria
Clementina
of Austria
(1777-1801)

Maria
Amalia
(1780-1798)

& 7 other
sons

Ferdinand VII
king of Spain
(r. 1814-1833)

Maria Luisa
of Etruria
(1782-1824)

Carlota
Joaquina
(1775-1830)

𝒯he Spanish Bourbons
(1814–)

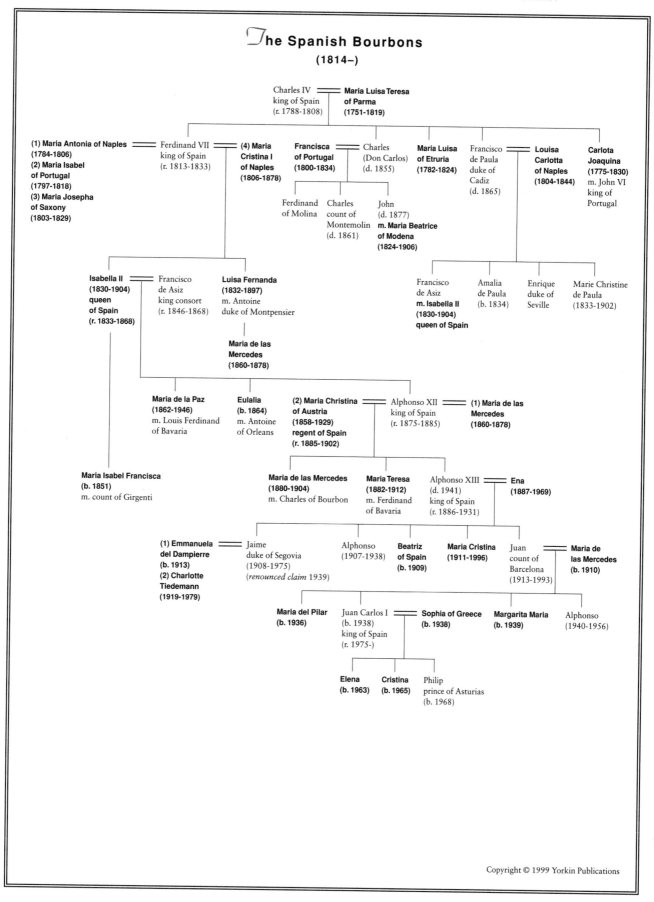

Charles IV
king of Spain
(r. 1788-1808) ═══ **Maria Luisa Teresa
of Parma
(1751-1819)**

**(1) Maria Antonia of Naples
(1784-1806)
(2) Maria Isabel
of Portugal
(1797-1818)
(3) Maria Josepha
of Saxony
(1803-1829)** ═══ Ferdinand VII
king of Spain
(r. 1813-1833) ═══ **(4) Maria
Cristina I
of Naples
(1806-1878)**

**Francisca
of Portugal
(1800-1834)** ═══ Charles
(Don Carlos)
(d. 1855)

**Maria Luisa
of Etruria
(1782-1824)**

Francisco
de Paula
duke of
Cadiz
(d. 1865) ═══ **Louisa
Carlotta
of Naples
(1804-1844)**

**Carlota
Joaquina
(1775-1830)**
m. John VI
king of
Portugal

Ferdinand
of Molina

Charles
count of
Montemolin
(d. 1861)

John
(d. 1877)
**m. Maria Beatrice
of Modena
(1824-1906)**

Francisco
de Asiz
**m. Isabella II
(1830-1904)
queen of Spain**

Amalia
de Paula
(b. 1834)

Enrique
duke of
Seville

Marie Christine
de Paula
(1833-1902)

**Isabella II
(1830-1904)
queen
of Spain
(r. 1833-1868)** ═══ Francisco
de Asiz
king consort
(r. 1846-1868) ═══ **Luisa Fernanda
(1832-1897)**
m. Antoine
duke of Montpensier

**Maria de las
Mercedes
(1860-1878)**

**Maria de la Paz
(1862-1946)**
m. Louis Ferdinand
of Bavaria

**Eulalia
(b. 1864)**
m. Antoine
of Orleans

**(2) Maria Christina
of Austria
(1858-1929)
regent of Spain
(r. 1885-1902)** ═══ Alphonso XII
king of Spain
(r. 1875-1885) ═══ **(1) Maria de las
Mercedes
(1860-1878)**

**Maria Isabel Francisca
(b. 1851)**
m. count of Girgenti

**Maria de las Mercedes
(1880-1904)**
m. Charles of Bourbon

**Maria Teresa
(1882-1912)**
m. Ferdinand
of Bavaria

Alphonso XIII
(d. 1941)
king of Spain
(r. 1886-1931) ═══ **Ena
(1887-1969)**

**(1) Emmanuela
del Dampierre
(b. 1913)
(2) Charlotte
Tiedemann
(1919-1979)** ═══ Jaime
duke of Segovia
(1908-1975)
(*renounced claim* 1939)

Alphonso
(1907-1938)

**Beatriz
of Spain
(b. 1909)**

**Maria Cristina
(1911-1996)**

Juan
count of
Barcelona
(1913-1993) ═══ **Maria de
las Mercedes
(b. 1910)**

**Maria del Pilar
(b. 1936)**

Juan Carlos I
(b. 1938)
king of Spain
(r. 1975-) ═══ **Sophia of Greece
(b. 1938)**

**Margarita Maria
(b. 1939)**

Alphonso
(1940-1956)

Elena
(b. 1963)

Cristina
(b. 1965)

Philip
prince of Asturias
(b. 1968)

Copyright © 1999 Yorkin Publications

The House of Vasa
(1523–1818)

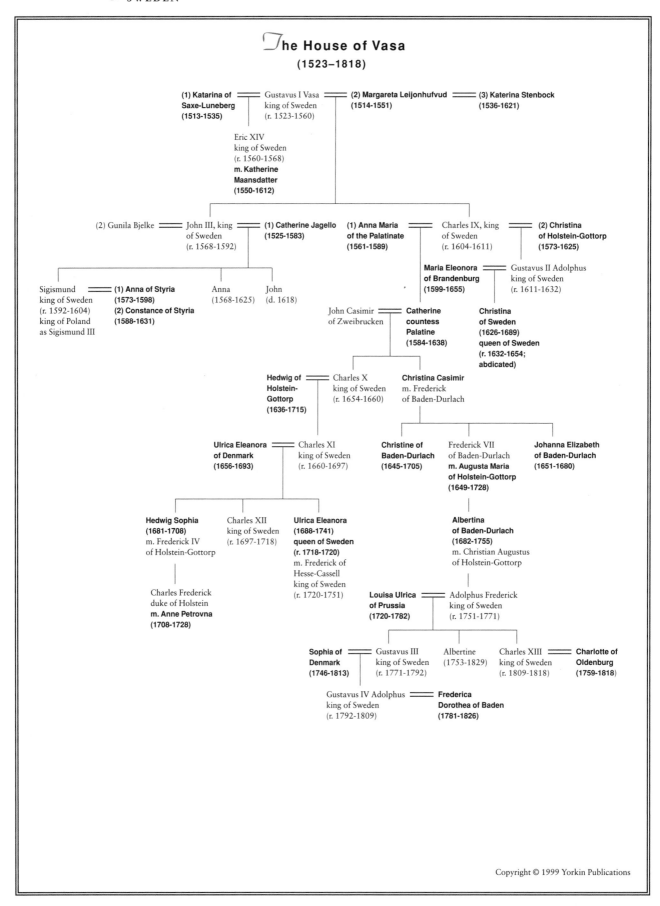

(1) Katarina of Saxe-Luneberg (1513-1535) ═══ Gustavus I Vasa king of Sweden (r. 1523-1560) ═══ **(2) Margareta Leijonhufvud (1514-1551)** ═══ **(3) Katerina Stenbock (1536-1621)**

Eric XIV king of Sweden (r. 1560-1568) **m. Katherine Maansdatter (1550-1612)**

(2) Gunila Bjelke ═══ John III, king of Sweden (r. 1568-1592) ═══ **(1) Catherine Jagello (1525-1583)**   **(1) Anna Maria of the Palatinate (1561-1589)** ═══ Charles IX, king of Sweden (r. 1604-1611) ═══ **(2) Christina of Holstein-Gottorp (1573-1625)**

Maria Eleonora of Brandenburg (1599-1655) ═══ Gustavus II Adolphus king of Sweden (r. 1611-1632)

Sigismund king of Sweden (r. 1592-1604) king of Poland as Sigismund III ═══ **(1) Anna of Styria (1573-1598)** **(2) Constance of Styria (1588-1631)**   Anna (1568-1625)   John (d. 1618)

John Casimir of Zweibrucken ═══ **Catherine countess Palatine (1584-1638)**   **Christina of Sweden (1626-1689) queen of Sweden (r. 1632-1654; abdicated)**

Hedwig of Holstein-Gottorp (1636-1715) ═══ Charles X king of Sweden (r. 1654-1660)   **Christina Casimir m. Frederick of Baden-Durlach**

Ulrica Eleanora of Denmark (1656-1693) ═══ Charles XI king of Sweden (r. 1660-1697)   **Christine of Baden-Durlach (1645-1705)**   Frederick VII of Baden-Durlach **m. Augusta Maria of Holstein-Gottorp (1649-1728)**   **Johanna Elizabeth of Baden-Durlach (1651-1680)**

Hedwig Sophia (1681-1708) m. Frederick IV of Holstein-Gottorp   Charles XII king of Sweden (r. 1697-1718)   **Ulrica Eleanora (1688-1741) queen of Sweden (r. 1718-1720) m. Frederick of Hesse-Cassell king of Sweden (r. 1720-1751)**   **Albertina of Baden-Durlach (1682-1755) m. Christian Augustus of Holstein-Gottorp**

Charles Frederick duke of Holstein **m. Anne Petrovna (1708-1728)**

Louisa Ulrica of Prussia (1720-1782) ═══ Adolphus Frederick king of Sweden (r. 1751-1771)

Sophia of Denmark (1746-1813) ═══ Gustavus III king of Sweden (r. 1771-1792)   Albertine (1753-1829)   Charles XIII king of Sweden (r. 1809-1818) ═══ **Charlotte of Oldenburg (1759-1818)**

Gustavus IV Adolphus king of Sweden (r. 1792-1809) ═══ **Frederica Dorothea of Baden (1781-1826)**

The House of Bernadotte
(1818–)

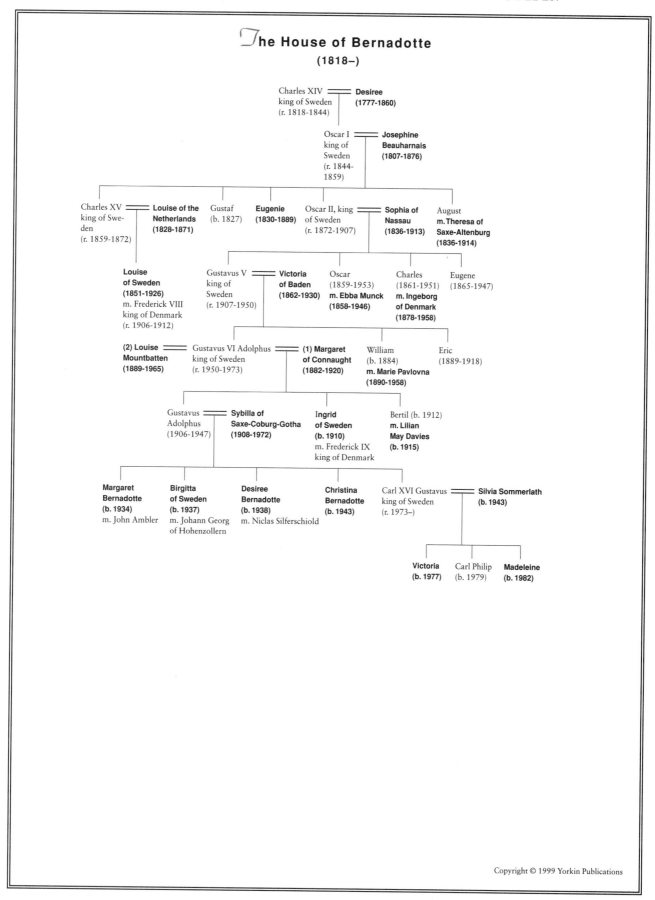

ℛulers of Serbia
(1804–1945)

Obrenovich Family

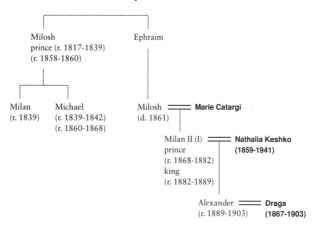

```
                    ┌──────────────────┴──────────────────┐
                Milosh                              Ephraim
              prince (r. 1817-1839)
              (r. 1858-1860)
         ┌──────────┴──────────┐            ┌──────────┴──────────┐
     Milan              Michael         Milosh ═══ Marie Catargi
     (r. 1839)          (r. 1839-1842)  (d. 1861)
                        (r. 1860-1868)
                                            Milan II (I) ═══ Nathalia Keshko
                                            prince              (1859-1941)
                                            (r. 1868-1882)
                                            king
                                            (r. 1882-1889)
                                            Alexander ═══ Draga
                                            (r. 1889-1903)  (1867-1903)
```

Karadjordjevic (or Karageorgevich) Family

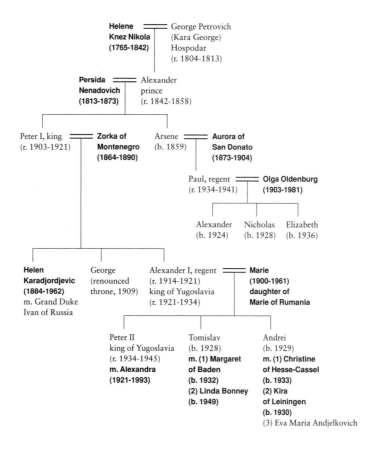

```
Helene ═══ George Petrovich
Knez Nikola    (Kara George)
(1765-1842)    Hospodar
               (r. 1804-1813)

Persida ═══ Alexander
Nenadovich    prince
(1813-1873)   (r. 1842-1858)

Peter I, king ═══ Zorka of      Arsene ═══ Aurora of
(r. 1903-1921)    Montenegro    (b. 1859)   San Donato
                  (1864-1890)               (1873-1904)

                              Paul, regent ═══ Olga Oldenburg
                              (r. 1934-1941)    (1903-1981)

                      Alexander    Nicholas    Elizabeth
                      (b. 1924)    (b. 1928)   (b. 1936)

Helen          George          Alexander I, regent ═══ Marie
Karadjordjevic (renounced      (r. 1914-1921)           (1900-1961)
(1884-1962)    throne, 1909)   king of Yugoslavia       daughter of
m. Grand Duke                  (r. 1921-1934)           Marie of Rumania
Ivan of Russia

        Peter II              Tomislav          Andrei
        king of Yugoslavia    (b. 1928)         (b. 1929)
        (r. 1934-1945)        m. (1) Margaret   m. (1) Christine
        m. Alexandra          of Baden          of Hesse-Cassel
        (1921-1993)           (b. 1932)         (b. 1933)
                              (2) Linda Bonney  (2) Kira
                              (b. 1949)         of Leiningen
                                                (b. 1930)
                                                (3) Eva Maria Andjelkovich
```

A

Aakesson, Birgit.

See Wigman, Mary for sidebar.

Aarons, Ruth Hughes (1918–1980)

World champion table tennis player and only world singles champion to ever represent the United States. Born Ruth Hughes Aarons in June 1918; died in 1980; daughter and one of three children of Alfred E. (a theatrical producer) and Leila (Hughes) Aarons (a singer and actress).

For ten weeks in the summer of 1936, New York's renowned Rainbow Room headlined Ruth Aarons and her European opponent Sandor Glancz in one of the most unlikely acts to play the posh supper club: an exhibition of table tennis. After the show, the management offered a bottle of their best champagne to anyone wishing to challenge the winner—usually the newly crowned world champion, Aarons. Reputedly, the champagne is still on ice.

Ruth Hughes Aarons, one of the few high-class American players before World War II, rose to the top of a game that was just finding its niche in the United States. When she won the world title in Prague, Czechoslovakia, in 1936, she became the first American to reach the final rounds in a sport hitherto dominated by Europeans, especially the Hungarians. At the close of the 20th century, Aarons remained the only world singles champion—man or woman—the United States ever produced.

Daughter of Broadway producer Alfred Aarons and actress **Leila Hughes**, the petite Aarons grew up in homes in New York City and Connecticut and dreamed of becoming a fashion designer. But at 13, while passing time during a rain shower at a New York tennis club, she was introduced to table tennis. Fascinated, she began to study the game and practiced daily. The following year, she won her first title at the national women's championships in Cleveland. Before long, she drove the ball over the net at bullet speed and mastered an unreturnable serve. At 18, Aarons was world champion, a title she held in 1936 and 1937. (The final match of the 1937 singles championship was halted when it exceeded a new time-limit ruling, thereby leaving the title vacant. Since she had not been officially beaten, Aarons retained the championship.)

Ruth Aarons

In April of 1937, Aarons' forays into show business created a furor when she was suspended for three months by the English Table Tennis Association because of a paid exhibition tour in British nightclubs. With backing from the U.S. Table Tennis Association, which threatened to break with the international organization, Aarons claimed her exhibition provided promotion for the sport and refused to curtail her appearances. Since Aarons had no upcoming matches of importance, her suspension was of little consequence and, within a year, the incident was largely forgotten. Show business eventually prevailed over championship play. Though Aarons continued her exhibition tours into the 1940s, she went on to become a theatrical agent of some note. Both her half-brother Alex and her brother Lisle also pursued careers in the theater.

SOURCES:
New York Evening Sun (Entertainment Section). August 1, 1936.
New York World Telegram. April 10, 1937.
The Washington Post. July 25, 1937.
Interview with Tim Boggan, historian for U.S. Table Tennis Association.

Sarah
Aaronsohn

Aaronsohn, Sarah (1890–1917)

Zionist pioneer, spy, and patriot, known as "the Joan of Arc of the New Palestine," who is one of the few women in the pantheon of Jewish Palestine's national martyrs and heroes. Name variations: Aaronson. Born in the agricultural settlement of Zikhron Ya'akov, Turkish Palestine, in 1890; killed herself to avoid divulging information during extended torture by Turks in October 1917; daughter of Efrayim Fishel Aaronsohn (1849–1939) and Malkah Aaronsohn (Jewish pioneer settlers); sister of Aaron (1876–1919) and Alexander (1888–1948) Aaronsohn; married Bulgarian-born Hayyim Abraham, in 1914.

Born in 1890 in an agricultural settlement in the Palestinian province of the Ottoman Empire, Sarah Aaronsohn grew up as part of a remarkable family of Zionist pioneers. When Jews were persecuted and massacred in bloody pogroms in Eastern Europe, her father Efrayim Fishel Aaronsohn and her mother Malkah left their native Rumania and settled in Turkish-controlled Palestine. Here they helped found the agricultural settlement of Zikhron Ya'akov. Enterprising and hardworking, the Aaronsohns became prosperous farmers, making the desert bloom and raising a family of three, Aaron, Alexander, and last-born Sarah, who came of age in the heady atmosphere of hard labor and high hopes for a future independent Zionist state, a refuge for persecuted Jews the world over.

Sarah's brothers recognized Palestine's precarious status in the declining but still powerful Ottoman Empire. In 1913, her brother Alexander founded a short-lived self-defense organization, Gidonim, to defend Zikhron Ya'akov and other Jewish agricultural settlements against Turkish aggression. In 1906, her other brother Aaron discovered wild Emmer wheat in Galilee—the precursor of all strains of modern wheat. As an agricultural expert, he established important links with government officials in Europe and the United States.

Unlike her brothers, Sarah seemed destined for a quiet domestic life. In 1914, the year World War I began, she married Bulgarian-born Hayyim Abraham and moved to Constantinople with her new husband. The marriage quickly failed, however, and the next year she returned to Zikhron Ya'akov. On her arrival, Sarah Aaronsohn witnessed the first of the 20th century's many holocausts as the Turks systematically exterminated the Armenian minority—men, women, and children—living in the Ottoman Empire. Shocked by the massacre, Aaronsohn interpreted the genocide as Ottoman state policy; it was clear to her that under the appropriate circumstances the Jews, too, would find themselves systematically destroyed.

When Aaron started an organization dedicated to the eventual overthrow of Turkish rule in Palestine, she readily joined. Although some like Avshalom Feinberg called for an armed uprising of Jewish settlers against the Turkish forces, Sarah and her brothers felt a spy ring—that would provide important military intelligence for the British—would be more useful. They believed their assistance could lead to the creation of a British-protected Zionist republic. Consisting of a handful of members, the secret group was called Nili. The name—which also served as a password—was taken from a Biblical quotation, "*Netzah yisrael lo yishaker*" (I Samuel 15:29), "The Strength of Israel will not die."

Sarah Aaronsohn, her brothers, and members of Nili quickly began gathering information to assist British military strategists in the Middle

East. In 1916, Aaron used his prewar scientific contacts as a pretext for a trip to Germany. From there, he went to neutral Denmark where he relayed valuable information to British agents. In August, he went to London and created a permanent arrangement between the Nili organization and British intelligence. The British were grateful for Nili's collaboration, as they knew the information would help plan a successful campaign against the Turks. Agents from British ships began landing off the coast of Athlit to stay in close contact with members of his group.

Sarah Aaronsohn was in charge of dispersing the money sent by the British, especially to aid the Jews who were expelled from the cities of Jaffa and Tel Aviv by Ottoman authorities during Passover. She also used the money to bribe Turkish officials who would look the other way. In April 1917, Aaronsohn secretly went to British-occupied Egypt with her brother Aaron for consultations with British intelligence officials. During this visit, she very likely came in contact with T.E. Lawrence, the legendary Lawrence of Arabia. Impressed by Aaronsohn's courage, intelligence, and idealism, many in Egypt feared for her safety and pleaded with her not to return to Palestine. In June, however, she returned to Zikhron Ya'akov.

Aided by information provided by Nili, British forces were moving in on Palestine. On a regular basis, the British supply ship *Monegan* sailed to a point off the coast near Athlit and put an agent ashore who collected the intelligence reports. Aaronsohn, upon seeing the ship's smoke on the horizon, would hang out a sheet to indicate it was safe to land. On those nights, she rode her horse down to the ruins of Crusader Castle carrying a satchel of reports that were otherwise kept hidden in a secret panel in her home. After handing over the reports, she received more money for Nili's operations. Aaronsohn's clandestine activities were controversial. Some Jewish leaders in Palestine feared savage Turkish retaliation, while others were not certain that British rule would ever replace the Ottoman government in Palestine.

Her work was always dangerous. By September 1917, the presence of German submarines on the coast near Athlit made the customary dropping of a British agent too risky. In order to transmit intelligence to Nili, carrier pigeons were used to send coded messages to the British forces in Egypt. Soon a pigeon landed in a Turkish army camp. Within a week, the Turks broke the complicated Nili code, which used not only Hebrew but also Aramaic, French, and English. The message confirmed the Turks' long-held suspicion that valuable information was being passed to their enemies by treasonous Jews in Palestine. Turkish troops rounded up a number of Jewish suspects whom they imprisoned and tortured. Learning of the crackdown, Aaronsohn ordered the Nili members to disperse while she remained at home to preserve the appearance of normal life. Her cool-headed courage allowed many of the Nili members to escape.

On October 1, 1917, Turkish troops surrounded her settlement, arresting Aaronsohn and her father. For four days, they were tortured. Using the infamous *bastinado* method—beating on the soles of the victim's feet—her Turkish interrogators subjected Aaronsohn to indescribable suffering, but she refused to reveal information. Lashed to the gatepost of her home, she was whipped relentlessly but refused to talk. After four days, her Turkish captors decided to take her to Nazareth, where "expert" interrogators could force her to reveal the information they were certain she possessed. Aaronsohn persuaded her captors that her bloodstained dress might create a bad impression on the trip and obtained permission to change her clothes. In the bathroom, she took out a pistol concealed there and killed herself.

By the end of the year, the British had achieved major military victories in Palestine. Though some have debated the importance of Nili intelligence to the war, General MacDonough, chief of British military intelligence in the Near East, countered that "General Allenby knew with certainty from his intelligence in Palestine all the movements of the enemy. All the cards of the enemy were revealed to him, and so he could play his hand with complete confidence. Under these circumstances, victory was certain before he began."

Sarah Aaronsohn's idealism and courage were not forgotten. Some think that the unidentified "S.A." to whom Lawrence of Arabia dedicated *The Seven Pillars of Wisdom*, his epic account of the Arab revolt against the Turks, is in fact Sarah Aaronsohn. The dedication reads:

> To S.A.
> I loved you, so I drew these tides of men into my
>   hand and wrote my will across the sky in stars
> To earn you, Freedom, the seven pillared worthy
>   house that your eyes might be shining for me
> When we came.

The end of war in 1918 opened a new chapter for Jews throughout the world. For the first time in almost 2,000 years, they could envision a homeland, a place where all Jews could return. Today many call Aaronsohn "the Joan of Arc of the New Palestine." Every October, hushed pilgrimages are made to her grave in Zikhron Ya'akov. In February 1991, she was honored by an Israeli commemorative postage stamp. Sarah Aaronsohn gave her life to further the Zionist ideal more than 30 years before the birth of Israel in May 1948.

SOURCES:

Cowen, Ida, and Irene Gunther. *A Spy for Freedom: The Story of Sarah Aaronson*. NY: Lodestar Books, 1984.

Engle, Anita. *The Nili Spies*. London: Hogarth Press, 1959.

Frost, Murray. "Judaica Philately," in *Global Stamp News*. No. 55. February 1995, p. 58.

Tsur, Jacob. *Zionism: The Saga of a National Liberation Movement*. New Brunswick, NJ: Transaction Books, 1977.

John Haag, Associate Professor of History, University of Georgia, Athens, Georgia

Abaijah, Josephine (1942—)

Papua New Guinea health educator, political leader, and entrepreneur. Name variations: Josephine Abayah; Dame Josephine Abaijah. Born in Wamira Village, Milne Bay, Papua New Guinea, in 1942; one of the first women to be educated in New Guinea.

Became a health-education administrator and the first female member of the House of Parliament (1972–82); an entrepreneur with several retail businesses, returned to politics to serve as chair of the Interim Commission (governing body) of the National Capital District; created Dame of the British Empire (1991); published novel A Thousand Coloured Dreams; *leader of the Papua Besena Party.*

Some 100 miles north of Australia, Papua New Guinea is one of the last "unknown" areas of the globe. With fewer than four million people, the country is underpopulated. Many tribes—cut off from one another by precipitous mountain ranges, tropical rain forests, and fast-flowing rivers—speak over 700 languages. One-third of the population lives in the mist-shrouded Highlands. Though born in 1942, Josephine Abaijah grew up in the ways of her ancestors because her people had not been discovered by Europeans until the 1930s. Until then, they knew nothing of metal tools or the wheel. Sorcery and tribal wars were a part of everyday existence, though during Abaijah's youth it became increasingly common to halt warlike contests to permit tourists to cross the battlefield. In her lifetime, Papua New Guinea would make the remarkable transition from the age of stone to that of the microchip. During these decades of change, Josephine Abaijah, born in Wamira Village, Milne Bay, was one of the country's most successful denizens.

Education first separated Abaijah from the members of her tribe. Educated in the late 1940s and early 1950s, she was the first girl to attend the Misima government school, where she remained the only girl in her class throughout her schooling. She then attended an Anglican boarding school in Queensland, Australia. An excellent student, she earned certificates in health education, public health, teacher training, and rural reconstruction. She also finished courses in nursing, serving as secretary at Papuan Medical College. Her skills as a health educator brought her into a number of positions of responsibility, including regional health educator at Lae, the second largest city of Papua New Guinea. As an administrator in the health-education field, she served in a senior capacity in the Department of Public Health and as principal of the Institute of Health Education.

In 1972, Abaijah and her Australian advisor Dr. Eric Wright founded the Papua Besena ("Hands off Papua") movement to push for independence from Australian governance. She initially appeared on the national political stage in April 1972 when she became the first woman delegate to the national parliament, the 100-seat House of Assembly of Papua New Guinea. As Papua's leading feminist and a passionate political activist, she raised a number of bitterly controversial issues in her campaign speeches, including what she characterized as the "suppression, isolation and the brutal treatment of the people by patrol officers." Abaijah's political career in the House of Assembly ended in 1982 with her defeat at the polls. She used her new freedom to prosper in the private sector, successfully managing several retail businesses. In 1989, she returned to center stage of public life as the first woman to serve as chair of the Interim Commission (governing body) of the National Capital District. In 1991, she was named a Dame of the British Empire. That same year, Abaijah published her novel *A Thousand Coloured Dreams*, which was based on her life story; it was the first novel ever published by a Papua New Guinea woman. In 1992, she ran unsuccessfully for a seat in the House of Assembly. She remained, however, the leader of the Papua Besena Party.

SOURCES:

Abaijah, Josephine, with Eric Wright. *A Thousand Coloured Dreams*. Mount Waverly, Victoria, Australia: Dellasta Pacific, 1991.

"New Guinea Leader Sets Self-government Date," in *The Times* [London]. April 21, 1972, p. 8.

"Papua New Guinea," in *1975 Britannica Book of the Year*. Chicago, IL: Encyclopaedia Britannica, 1975, pp. 543–544.

Turner, Ann. *Historical Dictionary of Papua New Guinea*. Metuchen, NJ: Scarecrow Press, 1994.

"Unknown Past to Famous Future," in *The Economist*. Vol. 313, no. 7633, December 16, 1989, pp. 70–72.

John Haag, Associate Professor of History, University of Georgia, Athens, Georgia

Abakanowicz, Magdalena

(1930—)

Polish sculptor. Name variations. Marta Abakanowicz-Kosmowska. Born in Falenty, Poland, on June 20, 1930; daughter of a Polish mother who descended from landed knights and a Russian father who escaped the Bolshevik revolution; studied at Academy of Fine Arts, Warsaw, 1950–55, granted M.A., 1955; married Jan Kosmowski (a civil engineer), in 1956.

Instructor, State College of Arts in Poznan, 1965–74, associate professor, 1974—. Awards: first prize from the Polish Ministry of Culture (1965); gold medal from the Polish Artists' Union (1965); gold medal from the VIII Sao Paulo Bienal, Brazil (1965); grand prize of the Polish Minister for Foreign Affairs (1970); state prize of the Polish Folk Republic (1972); honorary doctorate, Royal College of Art, London (1974); golden cross of merit from the Polish Folk Republic (1974).

Selected works: Abakans; Black Garment (1969); a series called Alterations, *which includes* Heads *(1975),* Seated Figures *(1974–79),* Backs, *and* Embryology *(1978–81);* Katharsis *(1985);* War Games; Trunks; Arboreal Architecture; Wheel and Rope; Marrow Bone *(1987);* Zyk *(1989);* Winged Trunk *(1989);* Anasta *(1989);* Great Ursa; Infantes *(1992);* Circus *(1992).*

Magdalena Abakanowicz was born in a 32-room mansion on the outskirts of Warsaw into the aristocratic world of 1930 Poland, nine years before Hitler's troops marched in and laid claim to the country. In her prose poem "Portrait X 20," she describes her stern father and aloof mother, and the solace she found in the woods and fields of Falenty. "For hours I looked at the grass and the water," she said. "I wanted to subordinate myself to them, so that I might understand the mysteries that separated me from them."

When the Germans invaded in 1939, her father joined the Polish Resistance; their house became a refuge for partisans and Jews; and Mag-

dalena learned to shoot. In 1943, when drunken Wehrmacht soldiers entered the house, firing at random, her mother's right arm was severed by a bullet. The following year, with the Soviet Army advancing into Poland, the family moved into Warsaw for safety just before the Warsaw Uprising of August–September. During the two months of bloody fighting, when the Polish Home Army was defeated by Germans in all-out warfare, 14-year-old Magdalena Abakanowicz served as a nurse's aide in an improvised hospital. Memories of pain, death, and disfigurement would accompany her throughout life. At war's end, her parents sold what was left of their household on the black market and opened a newspaper stand.

One repressive regime followed another, and at the close of the war and the ouster of the Nazis, Poland was occupied by the Soviet army. By 1947, Polish Communists had taken full control, and deputy prime minister Wladyslaw Gomulka helped crush non-Communist political parties. As minister of the recovered territories, he established Polish control over regions an-

Magdalena Abakanowicz

nexed from Germany. This involved deporting large portions of the population: under Gomulka's direction, 5,000 people a day were sent westward to Germany at the start of 1946.

Abakanowicz longed to take up art but first had to overcome parental objection as well as Stalin's ban of prewar bourgeoisie from attending universities. Concealing her family history, she entered an art school in Sopot, on the Baltic coast, in 1949. A year later, she attended Warsaw's Academy of Fine Arts. While living with families who took her in, she supported herself by giving blood. She also worked nights, holding a lantern for men who repaired streetcar lines. Communism's restrictions infiltrated everything, including the academic atmosphere. "Socialist realism," a kind of propaganda-art with paintings of peasants smiling into the sun, dominated Soviet academies. But completion of her courses was a prerequisite for joining the Polish Artists' Union and working as a sculptor.

Despite the oppressive atmosphere, Abakanowicz graduated in 1954. Two years later,

with the help and encouragement of weaver and tapestry artist **Maria Laszkiewicz**, Abakanowicz's work was entered into the First International Biennial of Tapestry in Lausanne, Switzerland. The works from Poland "started a movement," recalled Abakanowicz. Lausanne gallery owner Pierre Pauli "understood immediately the search for freedom that we Polish artists represented in our work, a search for a new expression, for the participation of fiber in contemporary conceptualist sculpture and painting." When Pauli died in 1971, his wife **Alice Pauli** became the main commercial agent for Magdalena's work.

In the early 1960s, Abakanowicz turned to organic materials like burlap, rope, and thread, developing an individualistic, rebellious vision of human freedom. "My intention was to extend the possibilities of man's contact with a work of art through touch and by being surrounded by it," she told *Contemporary Artists.* "I have looked to those slowly growing irregular forms for an antidote against the brilliance and speed of contemporary technology. I wanted to impose a slower rhythm on the environment as a contrast to the immediacy and speed of our urban surroundings."

"While many of Abakanowicz's works are purely abstract," writes **Nancy Heller**, "her most haunting sculptures represent fragmented human figures. Such works as *Heads* (1975), a group of ovoid burlap shapes, each four feet high, placed on end on a gallery floor, or *Seated Figures* (1974–79), a row of eighteen headless burlap bodies, reflect a curious combination of savagery and calm. Their crudely sown seams and escaping stuffing underscore the impression of violence." Her 1985 work *Katharsis* comprising 33 bronze figures, standing alone though herded together, is said to be suggestive of endless mourning. John Dornberg called the piece "haunting, anguished, personal art charged with energy and emotions that jar the senses."

"We find out about ourselves only when we take risks, when we challenge and question," Abakanowicz told Dornberg. "I was searching for the greatest risk; to make art of something that is not considered art." Each figure in a group is sculpted by hand. "I select [the material] with my hands," she notes. "I shape it with my hands. My hands transmit my energy to it. In translating idea into form, they always pass on to it something that eludes conceptualization. They reveal the unconscious." Her pieces require years of work. *Embryology* was completed in four years, *Seated Figures* in five.

Abakanowicz maintains that there are as many ways to view her work as there are viewers. To some, *Backs* may evoke Auschwitz, to others a ritual in Bali or Poland's Solidarity movement. While acknowledging that all of her work is concerned with human problems, she wants the precise meaning to vary with each person. "When I leave them to the imagination of people, I am never disappointed by the reception. Only, people today are afraid to judge or understand such objects in their own way. We have got accustomed to having everything explained, explained and explained away."

The works of Magdalena Abakanowicz can be seen in over 40 museums, including the Muzeum Narodowe (Warsaw); Stedelijk Museum (Amsterdam); Nationalmuseum (Stockholm); Kustindustrimuseet (Oslo); Musee des Beaux-Arts (La Chaux-de-Fonds, Switzerland); Malmo Museum (Sweden); Kunsthalle (Mannheim, Germany); Museum of Modern Art (New York); Museum of Contemporary Crafts (New York); Museu de Arte Moderna (Sao Paulo, Brazil); Bank of America (San Francisco); Australian National Gallery (Canberra); Kyoto National Museum of Modern Art (Japan); Centre Georges Pompidou (Paris); and Museum of Contemporary Art (Chicago).

If you think it needs explaining, you wouldn't understand it anyway. At the bottom of all art there is mystery.

—Magdalena Abakanowicz

SOURCES:

Dornberg, John. "One Way to Create Fine Art Is to Take the Greatest Risks," in *Smithsonian*. April 1985, pp. 110–114.

Heller, Nancy G. *Women Artists*. NY: Abbeville Press, 1987.

Hughes, Robert. "Dark Visions of Primal Myth," in *Time*. June 7, 1993, p. 64.

Naylor, Colin, and Genesis P-Orridge, eds. *Contemporary Artists*. NY: St. Martin's Press, 1977.

Plagens, Peter. "Sculpture to the Point," in *Newsweek*. May 31, 1993.

Rose, Barbara. *Magdalena Abakanowicz*. NY: Abrams, 1994.

SUGGESTED READING:

Jacob, Mary Jane, Magdalena Abakanowicz, and Jasia Reichardt. *Magdalena Abakanowicz*. NY: Abbeville Press, 1982.

Abassa (fl. 8th c.)

Arabian noblewoman. Name variations: Abbasa. Born around 765; died in 803 or later; daughter of a Persian maiden and al-Mahdi, 3rd Abbasid caliph (or ruler) of Baghdad (present-day Iraq); half-sister of Musa al-Hadi (4th Abbasid caliph, r. 785–786), Harun al-Rashid (Haroun al-Raschid; 5th Abbasid caliph, r. 786–809), *Ulayya (an Arabian singer), and Ibrahim ibn al-Mahdi; stepdaughter of *al-Khaizaran; married Jafar (or Jaffar) ibn Yahya al-Barmeki, member of the powerful Barmak (Barmek, Barmakis, Barmakids or Barmecide) family; children: twin boys.

Abassa was the half-sister of Harun al-Rashid, whose 8th-century court, depicted by the mythical storyteller Scheherazade in the *Arabian Nights*, was known for its opulence and learning. Harun was a dynamic ruler during the golden age of the Abbasid Empire, which stretched from India to North Africa and was celebrated by poets, musicians, and writers of the time. As the fifth and most famous Abbasid caliph of Baghdad, he encouraged the arts and foreign influence. He could also, however, be treacherous.

Harun's loyal friend and grand vizier (high officer or minister) was Yahya, a member of the powerful, wealthy Persian family originally founded by Barmak. The Barmakis had considerable influence over the Abbasid caliphs. Yahya, who had tutored Harun, had a daughter, the songstress *Dananir al Barmakiyya, and two sons, Fazl (Fadl) and Jafar. Because the sons grew up with Harun and were loyal during a struggle for succession, they earned a reputation as the "little viziers" and continued their influence over him.

Thanks to his eloquence, intelligence, and charm, Jafar (named Giafar in the *Arabian Nights*) was a close companion to caliph Harun. Suffering from insomnia, Harun liked to have someone knowledgeable to talk with through the long nights and to join him on after-hour carousals. In some sections of the *Nights*, Jafar is one of Harun's late-night companions in sorties through Baghdad.

Harun al-Rashid's half-sister Abassa was another who drew his affection. Abassa was said to be so beautiful and accomplished that Harun lamented their status as brother and sister; he believed no other husband to be worthy of her. Longing to have Abassa join him on his evening excursions (which would have gone against Islamic convention), Harun decided to marry Abassa to his friend Jafar. This enabled him to indulge in the camaraderie of his two boon companions during his nocturnal roaming. The marriage, arranged for appearances and convenience, was conditional. Jafar was never to treat Abassa as his wife. But legend tells us that Abassa fell in love with Jafar and arranged to take the place of a slave girl who was sent to his rooms on Friday nights. Jafar, initially horrified and fearful of the consequences, went along with the subterfuge nonetheless. When twin sons were born in secret, they were sent away to Mecca to be reared. Their deceit was discovered in 803, and Harun had nearly the entire Barmakis family destroyed: Yahya was killed, Jafar was put to death while praying, and Fazl was paralyzed from shock.

One story contends that Harun also had Abassa and her two sons killed, while another reports that, dismissed from his court, Abassa wandered about, desolate, reciting her own story in song. Some Arabic verses composed by her, which commemorate her misfortune, are still extant. In the divan (a collection of poems) entitled *Juba*, Abassa's genius for poetry is mentioned, and a specimen of her composition addressed to her husband Jafar, in six Arabic lines, appears in a book written by Ben Abu Haydah.

Abayah, Josephine (b. 1942).

See Abaijah, Josephine.

Abayomi, Oyinkansola
(1897–1990)

Nigerian feminist and nationalist. Name variations: (nickname) Oyinkan; Lady Oyinkansola Abayomi. Born Oyinkansola Ajasa in Lagos, Nigeria, on March 6, 1897; died in Lagos on March 19, 1990; daughter of Sir Kitoyi and Lady Cornelia Olayinka (Moore) Ajasa; studied at the Young Ladies Academy at Ryford Hall, Gloucestershire; studied music at the Royal Academy, London, 1917; married Moronfolu Abayomi (a lawyer), on May 10, 1923 (died 1923); married Kofoworola Abayomi, in 1930 (died 1979).

Into the cultured and educated Nigerian family Ajasa, a girl was born and given six names, of which the first was Oyinkansola (she also answered to Olaosebikan, Ajibike, Morenike, Ajibati, and Moronkeji). Oyinkan, as her mother and father called her, was the oldest of two children, though her brother Akuisola died when he was two years old. The Ajasa home was busy with the political and journalistic business of her father Sir Kitoyi Ajasa, a lawyer and later inaugural member of the Nigerian Legislative Council and publisher of the newspaper *The Standard*. Abayomi was schooled at the Anglican Girls' Seminary in Lagos from the fall of 1903 until 1909. Then, as her mother had done, she traveled to England and studied at the Young Ladies Academy at Ryford Hall, Gloucestershire. World war broke out during her time in England, so she continued on to the Royal Academy in London in 1917, where she studied music. In 1920, after 11 years away from Nigeria, Abayomi returned home to Lagos. She took work as a music teacher at her old school, which had been renamed the Anglican Girls' School.

In England, she had been a member of the Girl Guides. After discovering that the first Nigerian chapter of the Guides had been established in Lagos by a native Englander who was teaching there, Abayomi joined and became the first aboriginal supervisor of the group. In August of 1923, she married Moronfolu Abayomi, a lawyer. Following a brief honeymoon, they returned to Lagos and their respective jobs. Two months later, Moronfolu was shot and killed while in court. In despair, Abayomi returned home to live with her parents.

Shortly after studying in England, Oyinkan Abayomi had joined those who demanded that Nigerian women's education be equal to that of their male peers. In particular, activists sought a secondary school for girls, an institution parallel to the boys' King's College. As a member of the Lagos Women's Organization, Abayomi campaigned and raised funds for Queen's College, which was established in Lagos in 1927. She was invited to be a member of the two-person teaching staff, and was the only Nigerian working for the school. In 1930, she married Dr. Kofoworola (Kofo) Abayomi.

Work for the Girl Guides escalated as they sought government support and recognition equal to that of the local Boy Scouts. In 1931, support was granted. Abayomi rose in administration of the Girl Guides, until she received the top posting of chief commissioner. Meanwhile, her husband Kofo cofounded the Lagos Youth Movement, later the Nigerian Youth Movement, intent upon bringing Nigerian government into native, rather than British, hands. Abayomi joined the cause and in 1944 founded the Nigerian Women's Party, which helped unite several diffuse women's organizations. They rallied for nationalism and continued recognition of equal opportunities for women.

On January 1, 1979, Kofo died. Three years later, in 1982, Abayomi retired from the Girl Guides and was given the honorary title Life President. This was not, however, her only title. In 1954, Kofo had been knighted by the king, and she was thus known as Lady Oyinkan. In recognition for her work on behalf of Nigeria and women, Abayomi was also honored with several traditional chieftaincies, receiving five chief titles in all, the last of which was Iya Abiye of Egbaland. Lady Oyinkan Abayomi died in 1990 at the age of 93.

SOURCES:
Awe, Bolanle. *Nigerian Women in Historical Perspective.* Victoria Island: Sankore-Bookcraft, 1992.
Coker, Folarin. *A Lady.* Nigeria: Evans Brothers, 1987.

Crista Martin, Boston, Massachusetts

ABBA (1974–1982)
Swedish singing group.

Agnetha Fältskog (1950—). Name variations: Agnetha Ulvaeus; Agnetha Faltskog; in the group's early days, known in Great Britain as Anna. Pronunciation: Ann-yetta. Born Agnetha Ase Faltskog on April 15, 1950, in Jonkoping in the south of Sweden; married Björn Ulvaeus (separated in 1978, then divorced).

*Agnetha Fältskog, who idolized *Connie Frances, began singing with bands at age 15. Within three years, she had topped the Swedish chart with her single "I Was So In Love" and would enjoy other solo hits before and during her period with ABBA. By*

1970, Fältskog was living with Björn Ulvaeus, then a songwriter for Stig Anderson, a music-business entrepreneur, and appearing in Jesus Christ Superstar *as *Mary Magdalene. She scored a massive hit with her Swedish cover recording of "I Don't Know How to Love Him." Following her stint with ABBA, Agnetha released the solo albums,* Wrap Your Arms Around Me *(1983),* Eyes of a Woman *(1985), and* I Stand Alone *(1988).*

Frida Lyngstad (1945—). Name variations: Anni-Frid Lyngstad-Fredriksson. Born Anni-Frid Synni Lyngstad in Norway, near the large town of Narvik, on November 15, 1945; married Ragnar Frederiksson (a bass player); married Benny Andersson, in 1978 (divorced 1981); children: (first marriage) Hans and Liselotte.

*Frida Lyngstad had a tragic start in life. She was conceived during the occupation of Norway in World War II, the product of a relationship between *Synni Lyngstad *and a German soldier. Her birth brought only scorn to her mother Synni who would be dead within two years at age 21. Two-year-old Frida was sent to Sweden to live with her grandmother and grew up in Eskilstuna, about 100 miles from Stockholm. While in her teens, Frida sang with Bengt Sandlund's jazz group, then formed her own band, the Anni-Frid Four, around 1964. She married fellow band member Ragnar Frederiksson and had two children. Soon, she was awarded a solo recording contract. Following ABBA, Frida recorded her first solo album* Something's Going On *(1982); her second was* Shine *(1984).*

The singing group ABBA had more than a dozen Top 40 hits in the United States, including their easy-listening "Dancing Queen," "Knowing Me, Knowing You," and "Fernando." Composed of Frida Lyngstad, her keyboard player husband Benny Andersson, Agnetha Fältskog, and Fältskog's guitarist husband Björn Ulvaeus (ABBA is an acronym of their collective first initials), the group first gained international recognition when their single "Waterloo" won the 1974 Eurovision Song Contest. They then went on to become one of the 1970s' most successful acts, particularly outside America. After the reign of the Beatles, no group has sold more singles.

With their marriages on the rocks, the group split up in 1982, and Lyngstad and Fältskog went off on solo careers. Despite their unwillingness to reunite, ABBA enjoyed an enormous resurgence in the 1990s. Popular with gays, grunge rockers, and the most hardened critics, their greatest hits collection, *Gold*, sold over five million copies in Europe and was No. 1 on Billboard charts. Notes

ABBA

Richard Locayo in *Time*: "Embracing Abba is a way for Generation X to repudiate the baby boomers and their wrinkled artifacts. No less a figure than Kurt Cobain of Nirvana had declared himself a fan. To a generation apt to think of McCartney, Jagger and Dylan as millionaires who once posed as rebels, Abba has the virtue of forthright artificiality. . . . As music, they'll do. But as ironic heroes to a different kind of counterculture, they'll do perfectly."

SOURCES:

Locayo, Richard. "What's that Chirping," in *Time*. October 11, 1993.

RELATED MEDIA:

ABBA—The Movie, produced in Australia by Stig Anderson and Reg Grundy.

Abbasa (fl. 8th c.).

See Abassa.

Abbe, Kathryn (1919—)

American photographer. Born in New York City in 1919; grew up in Wallingford, Connecticut; twin sister of Frances McLaughlin-Gill; studied photography with Walter Civardi and graduated with a B.F.A., Pratt Institute, 1941; studied painting with Yasuo Kuniyoshi at the New School for Social Research, 1939–41; married James Abbe, Jr. (a photographer and art historian); children: Tom (b. 1948), Lucinda (b. 1950), Eli (b. 1952).

In 1941, photographer Kathryn Abbe won *Vogue*'s "Prix de Paris" contest; the following year, she began working with the magazine's fashion photographer *Toni Frissell. As a freelancer from 1944 on, Abbe contributed photographs to *Good Housekeeping*, *Better Homes and Gardens*, and *Parents*. Her subjects included actors, actresses, musicians, and especially children. She and her twin sister **Frances McLaughlin-Gill** spent three years working on a book about twins, which was published in 1980.

Abbéma, Louise (1858–1927)

French painter. Name variations: Abbema.

Like her contemporary *Rosa Bonheur, Louise Abbéma donned the clothes of a man. Unlike Bonheur, who used the guise to escape notice, Abbéma dressed as a captain of the dragoons to draw attention. Notes **Germaine Greer** in *Obstacle Race*, Abbéma was "not without talent, as her early *Lunch in the Hothouse* in the Museum at Pau shows, but she did not develop any further as an artist. Instead she settled for the fashionable limelight that her flamboyant behavior attracted." In 1876, as an 18-year-old painter, Abbéma undertook a portrait of *Sarah Bernhardt who was then performing at the Comédie Française. It was the beginning of an intense relationship. Joining Bernhardt's coterie, Abbéma continued executing portraits of the actress until 1922. For her work, Louise Abbéma was awarded the Chevalier de la Légion d'Honneur by the French government.

SOURCES:
Greer, Germaine. *The Obstacle Race.* NY: Farrar, Straus, 1979.

Abbott, Berenice (1898–1991)

American photographer, outspoken proponent of photographic realism, and archivist of the work of Eugéne Atget. Name variations: changed the spelling of her first name from Bernice to Berenice. Born Bernice Abbott on July 17, 1898, in Springfield, Ohio; died at her home in Monson, Maine, on December 10, 1991; daughter of Charles E. and Alice (Bunn) Abbott; attended Ohio State University for a year and a half; never married; no children.

Traveled to New York City to study sculpture (1918); continued studies in Europe, under Bourdelle in Paris and at the Kunstschule in Berlin (1921); worked as assistant to American photographer Man Ray in Paris (1923–25); established her own reputation in portraiture (1925–29); returned to New York and began her masterwork: a photographic documentation of the city (1929); also taught photography at the New School for Social Research in New York (1934–58); purchased home in Maine (1956) and moved there permanently (1968).

Selected works: Changing New York *(NY: E.P. Dutton, 1939; reprinted as* New York in the Thirties, *NY: Dover, 1973);* A Guide to Better Photography *(NY: Crown, 1941);* The View Camera Made Simple *(Chicago: Ziff-Davis, 1948);* Greenwich Village Today and Yesterday *(NY: Harper, 1949);* New Guide to Better Photography *(NY: Crown, 1953);* Eugéne Atget Portfolio: Twenty Photographic Prints from his Original Glass Negatives *(1956);* The World of Atget *(NY: Horizon Press, 1964);* Magnet *(Cleveland, Ohio:*

World, *1964);* Motion *(Cleveland: World, 1965);* A Portrait of Maine *(NY: Macmillan, 1968);* The Attractive Universe *(Cleveland: World, 1969);* Berenice Abbott Photographs *(NY: Horizon Press, 1970);* Berenice Abbott: The Red River Photographs *(NY: McGraw-Hill, 1979);* Berenice Abbott Photographs *(Washington, D.C.: Smithsonian Institution Press, 1990).*

Selected exhibitions: "Portraits Photographiques" *(Au Sacre du Printemps, Paris, 1926);* "Photographs for Henry-Russell Hitchcock's Urban Vernacular of the Forties, Fifties and Sixties" *(Yale University, New Haven, Connecticut, 1934);* "Changing New York: 125 Photographs" *(Museum of the City of New York, 1937);* "Pageant of Photography" *(Golden Gate Exposition, San Francisco, 1940);* "Science Photographs" *(Smithsonian Institution, Washington, D.C., 1960, and widely circulated);* "Women, Cameras and Images III" *(Hall of Photography, Smithsonian Institution, Washington, D.C.); and many more.*

Berenice Abbott's theory on photography— "It has to walk alone; it has to be itself"—has

Berenice Abbott

come to summarize her photographic legacy. But as **Erla Zwingle** first pointed out, the fiercely independent Abbott could have been speaking of her personal life as well.

*P*hotography can never grow up if it imitates some other medium. It has to walk alone; it has to be itself.

—Berenice Abbott

The pattern of standing alone and remaining true to herself was established early. Abbott left home at the age of 19 to attend Ohio State University; little is known about what came before. Her biographer Hank O'Neal reports only that Abbott's childhood was unhappy, for her parents divorced when she was an infant and she was raised alone by her mother, rarely seeing her father and separated from her sister and two brothers. Though O'Neal suggests that Abbott and her siblings were reunited when Abbott was six, Zwingle's feature article for *American Photographer,* published several years later, mentions only brothers and reports that Abbott never saw them again. Whichever the case, Abbott discouraged discussion of her early life. She allowed only occasional tantalizing glimpses, such as the fact that she had changed her own first name. The pronunciation of "Bernice," she explained to Zwingle, was unpleasant: "*Burrnees.*" Adding a letter "made it sound better."

Ohio State failed to provide the escape Abbott sought. She stayed for just one semester, finding the structured lifestyle oppressive, the faculty uninspiring, and compulsory courses irrelevant. On borrowed train fare, she headed for New York to join **Susan Jenkins**, a friend and former classmate who, along with her fiancé Jimmy Light, kept a spacious Greenwich Village apartment by taking roomers. Undaunted by the flu epidemic and blizzard that greeted her, Abbott set out to pursue her interest in journalism by enrolling in Columbia University. Again the factory conditions of higher education failed to provide the intellectual challenge she sought; she withdrew after one week and began casting about for a new direction.

That new direction, which would become such a singular focus of her life, did not emerge for some time, though the seeds of it were planted during her three years in Greenwich Village. It was a period of adjustment for the shy young Midwesterner. She was considered by acquaintances of the time as somehow out of her ele-

ment. Writer ***Agnes Boulton** remembers "a thin, interesting, pallid, and dazed young girl . . . who seemed indeed to belong to another world." Wrote Boulton:

> Abbott supported herself with odd jobs in the restaurants and garment factories of New York City. More importantly, her roommates introduced her to bohemian society. She helped out at the Village's famous Provincetown Playhouse where Jimmy Light was a director, and even played a minor role in Eugene O'Neill's *The Moon of the Caribbees.* The large apartments she and the Lights shared, first on MacDougal Street and later on Greenwich Avenue where they were joined by the writer ***Djuna Barnes** and critics Malcolm Cowley and Kenneth Burke, were favorite gathering places of Village literati. Among the influential friends she gained was **Hippolyte Havel**, who claimed her as a "daughter" and 20 years later was able to get her into the all-male McSorley's saloon to photograph.

During this period, Abbott became interested in sculpture, and her work in the theater pushed her more firmly in that direction. While in rehearsal for a now-forgotten play, the entire cast was stricken with Spanish influenza. Some did not survive. Already in a weakened condition due to work and diet, Abbott spent six weeks gravely ill in St. Vincent's Hospital and, upon her release, could scarcely walk. After a long convalescence at the Dobbs Ferry, New York, home of wealthy cousin Guy Morgan, she returned to the city with new priorities: a place of her own and sculpting.

Taking two rooms on "Clothesline Alley," she focused on developing as a sculptor. Among her new artist friends and early supporters was the surrealist Marcel Duchamp, who commissioned a set of chesspieces. More important, Duchamp introduced Abbott to the photographer Man Ray. The three became a threesome, frequenting Village restaurants and dance clubs together, but the greater consequence of these relationships would be realized some years later in Paris when Man Ray put a camera in Berenice Abbott's hands.

It was another influential artist friend, the Baroness ✦ **Elsa von Freytag-Loringhoven,** who inspired Abbott to go to Europe to study sculpture with the likes of Bourdelle and Brancusi. Abbott had concluded that she could not live off her work in New York, and she was no longer willing to take mundane employment. In a spirit reminiscent of her earlier escape to the city, Abbott set sail for France on a one-way ticket, with a handful of dollars in her pocket, in March of

1921. She would return to New York eight years later a successful photographic portraitist.

When she arrived in Paris, there were few photographers, and photography was the prodigal child of the arts. It might have remained thus except for the arrival of Man Ray later in 1921. However, it was not until 1924, after Abbott had pursued sculpting with marginal success in Paris and even less in Berlin, that she had a life-changing conversation with Ray. He was among the first she encountered upon her return from Berlin, where she—symbolically, as it turned out—abandoned a large sculpture on the station platform when she had to run to catch her train to Paris. Ray was unhappy with his darkroom assistant, a young man who knew too much about photography to be sufficiently malleable in the artist's hands. Fortunately, Abbott knew nothing about photography, and when she asked, "How about me?" Ray hired her on the spot.

It took another year before Ray literally put a camera into her hands. Abbott had become by then a highly skilled technician. Having taken to the work, she learned quickly and invested long hours in the mastery of developing and printing. Ray loaned her a small Brownie-type camera that she took on holiday to Amsterdam and there made her earliest photographs. Some, in fact, "turned out"; her work in photography from the beginning showed an exceptional sensibility with the medium. In his biography, *Berenice Abbott: American Photographer*, O'Neal quotes her remembrance of the influence of Man Ray:

> Man Ray did not teach me photographing techniques. He took the portraits on the balcony in his studio while I was in the darkroom. One day he did, however, suggest that I ought to take some myself; he showed me how the camera worked and I soon began taking some on my lunch break. I would ask friends to come by and I'd take pictures of them. The first I took came out well, which surprised me. I had no idea of becoming a photographer, but the pictures kept coming out and most of them were good. Some were very good and I decided perhaps I could charge something for my work. Soon I started to build up a little business.

Abbott always sought to minimize the competition between herself and Ray, but her success as a portraitist eventually led to their parting company. When *Peggy Guggenheim requested a sitting from Abbott rather than Ray, he would not allow it, contending that those who could afford his prices ought to sit for him. Though Abbott had been paying Ray for the materials she used and had continued to do all the darkroom work for his prodigious output, squeezing in her own after hours, she now felt the need to work alone. With loans and help from Guggenheim and others, she set up a studio and began building a remarkable clientele; the portraitist phase of her photographic career was off and running.

Finding historical phases in the works of many artists involves tracking the development of technical skill or a distinctive creative voice. Berenice Abbott's photography exhibited both from the beginning. In her case, historical phases have to do largely with subject matter that inspired her in changing social contexts. The three phases that comprise her photographic contribution as artist are the Paris portraits; the documentation of New York City and later documentary projects; and the photographs of scientific phenomena. As Man Ray had discovered, there was a healthy market for portraiture in Paris, but virtually none for other forms of photographic expression. Abbott's life as a portraitist clearly grew out of her association with Ray and thrived in this context, for there was no shortage of writers, poets, artists, philosophers, philanthropists, and other cultural luminaries, including expatriate Americans, in Paris in the 1920s. There are many whose portraits by Abbott remain to this day their definitive representations, including James Joyce, Jean Cocteau, André Gide, *Janet Flanner, Princess Eugéne Murat, Peggy Guggenheim, *Djuna Barnes, *Marie Laurencin, *Edna St. Vincent Millay, ✍▶ A'Lelia Walker, and Eugéne Atget.

It must be conceded that certain of Abbott's portraits of men are among her most known and reproduced. For example, James Joyce *is* his Ab-

◀✍
Walker, A'Lelia.
See Women of
the Harlem
Renaissance.

✍▶ **Freytag-Loringhoven, Elsa von** (1875–1927)
Danish-French poet. Name variations: Baroness von Freytag-Loringhoven. Born in Denmark in 1875; died of asphyxiation in 1927 at age 52.

As reported by *Janet Flanner in *Paris Was Yesterday,* the Baroness Elsa von Freytag-Loringhoven was by birth a "great Danish lady" and "by marriage various nationalities." An advocate of modern art and a published poet in the *Little Review,* she also posed for many artists, including William Glackens, Robert Henri, and George Bellows. After the Bolshevik Revolution effectively wiped out her fortune, Elsa was found selling newspapers in Germany. When sympathetic Parisian friends paid for a room and put her up, "she and her little dog were asphyxiated by gas in the night," writes Flanner, "both victims of a luxury they had gone too long without."

"Theoline, Pier 11, East River, New York City," by Berenice Abbott, 1936; courtesy of Commerce Graphics, Ltd.

bott portrait. But that is surely because some of the men she photographed were more famous than many of the women. In fact, critics tend to agree that she had a particular sensibility for photographing women, and, by her own analysis, it was one of the aspects of her work that

separated her from her teacher. As she reported to Zwingle, "Ray's portraits were good, but he always made the women look like pretty objects. He never let them be strong characters in themselves." Abbott declined to flatter anyone, or to instruct them in ways to pose themselves to good advantage. One reviewer's description of an unidentified Abbott portrait of a woman displayed in the First Salon of Independent Photographers (May 24–June 7, 1928, Paris) conveys the result, albeit with perhaps a touch more sentiment than Abbott herself would approve: "[W]ith the most naked, the most modest, the least pretentious truth, this human representation evokes a spiritual emotion. It is a bare countenance, bathed by the morning light, which stands out, which presents itself. In simplicity here is her soul to gaze at, given as simply as a handshake." Abbott's women sitters present themselves to her camera in many ways—assertive, hesitant, direct, distracted—but always on their own terms and never as decorative mannequins. (Interestingly, it was the critical acclaim Abbott's entries into this exhibition received and the critical panning Man Ray's received that drove the final wedge between them.)

While Man Ray was Abbott's teacher of technique, Eugéne Atget was her inspiration. She first encountered Atget's work through Ray, who owned several Atget prints, and she describes her response in *The World of Atget*: "There was a sudden flash of recognition—the shock of realism unadorned." After establishing her own studio, Abbott sought out Atget, bought a few of his prints, and encouraged friends to do the same. The following year, she asked to take his photograph. He agreed, and the three photographs she made are the only ones of him except for a snapshot from his youth. By the time she took prints to his home for him to see, he had died.

Abbott had been virtually alone in supporting Atget. Even Ray advised her against helping the reclusive, dedicated, maverick photographer who had made recording everyday life in and about Paris his life's work. Moreover, he photographed in a particular way: with a minimalist, realist eye, eschewing all technical tricks and experimentations, all artistic affectations. This was Abbott's own philosophy, which she theorized and definitively expressed in the article "It Has To Walk Alone," first published in *Infinity* in 1951. Indeed, she became a leading proponent of the view that because photography's *forté* was the direct, sharply focused, unblinking, documenting eye, therefore photography's greatest expressive achievement was the unflinching record of life as it is. Attempts by many of her contemporaries to secure the status of photography as art by such manipulations as soft focusing, scratching negatives, and treating prints with chemicals for special effects were

viewed by Abbott as insults to the medium and its audience.

Abbott not only fulfilled the aesthetic vision she shared with Atget but, in a sense, she completed his career as well, for she purchased his entire accumulation of prints and negatives, and worked tirelessly for decades, sometimes at the expense of her own career, to fix his place in history. That the Atget archive was purchased by the Museum of Modern Art in 1968, after 50 years in Abbott's care, is testimony to her success. As Zwingle notes, it is ironic that this woman, who never married and never regretted it, for she viewed marriage as "the finish for women who want to do their work," should have given so much to a single man. That the subject of her commitment should be another "loner" dedicated to his work and a vision, having no regard for trend and popularity, is entirely in keeping with her character.

The clearest, fullest expression of the Abbott ideology remains her powerful and unique documentation of New York during a period of explosive growth. She returned to the city in 1929 in order to photograph it, having visited earlier the same year and been swept away by its exhilarating pace and rapidly changing appearance. Back in Paris, she closed a highly successful studio, sold most of her things, carefully packed the Atget collection, her studio equipment and art objects, bought a small camera for street use, and set sail.

The difficulties she encountered would have quickly deterred a less driven person. Abbott was not prepared for the cost of living in New York City. She set up a portrait studio, which was to fund the documentary project, but she was much less successful than she had been in Paris; her reputation in the United States was modest, her fees high, and she proudly refused to advertise. Moreover, when the stock market crashed, the portrait business suffered. But she persisted, spending one day a week on the street with her camera (the small one was soon exchanged for a large view camera), supplementing her income by selling some of the early results to magazines.

For six years, Abbott sought funding for the project that she began to call "Changing New York." Among those who turned her down were the Guggenheim Foundation, the Museum of the City of New York, the New York Historical Society, and 30-some privately solicited patrons of the Museum of Modern Art. Nevertheless, she continued to photograph with urgency, except when financial circumstances forced her to engage in more lucrative ventures. One of these interruptions was a two-part project with the architectural historian Henry-Russell Hitchcock. Together, they documented the buildings of Henry Hobson Richardson and recorded American cities from Boston to Savannah as they had been before the Civil War. This latter work clarified for Abbott the distinctiveness of New York City and gave her a new sense of urgency to capture its metamorphosis on film.

Finally in September 1935, just after she had begun teaching photography part-time at the New School for Social Research in New York City, the Federal Art Project (FAP) of the Works Progress Administration (WPA) approved Abbott's "Changing New York" proposal. For the next four years, Abbott would receive funding for supplies and a staff, and a salary for herself ($145 per month) to carry out her ambition. As O'Neal notes, her extraordinary portrait of a city's transformation is testimony to what government funds can do when put into the hands of an artist who is then left alone. Tardily recognizing the worth of the project, the Museum of the City of New York mounted a huge exhibition—110 of the best photographs—in December 1937, to wide enthusiasm and recognition for Abbott.

The project culminated in a book, *Changing New York* (1939), also well received, but whose proceeds went to the FAP. Thereafter, the FAP's support declined rapidly; in the fall of 1939, Abbott resigned and essentially closed a chapter of her life and career. That she had embodied her philosophy of photography in the work is evident. Upon seeing the Museum of New York exhibition, writer-photographer Carl Van Vechten wrote to her: "[T]hey were all completely magnificent. They all compose. They have clarity and sympathy. Technically they are flawless. Most of all they definitely are lacking in any strain after novelty or angle. I must say I find you are pretty much the master (or mistress) of all living photographers."

There were other documentary projects: a tour through the poor, rural South with writer-critic and supporter **Elizabeth McCausland**, which foreshadowed the extensive depression-era work produced by Roy Stryker's Resettlement and Farm Security Administrations, and a summer of traveling U.S. Route 1 from Maine to Florida. This latter tour produced an enormous document that remains Abbott's most unrecognized work, for she never found a publisher for the book proposed. But the next major commitment Abbott made was to a marriage between art and science. Again she faced difficulties. Again she persisted and ultimately produced the body of work which, along with the early human portraits and the New York City portrait, comprises Berenice Abbott's threefold contribution as an artist.

"Like a flea attacking a giant" is how Abbott later characterized her turn to science as the subject with enough substance to inspire and engage her mind and camera for the next several decades. Lacking any formal training in science, she acquired physics and chemistry texts, and immediately realized that the illustrations in them were poor. She resolved to interpret science for the layperson, to photograph scientific phenomena with both "popular appeal and scientific correctness," as she wrote in an early statement of purpose.

Unfortunately, in an age in which science was full of hope and promise, no one else was interested. It was not until 1944—after four years of countless overtures and appeals, several publication projects that failed for lack of support, and ongoing experimentation supported by her commercial work and teaching—that Abbott gained a toehold in the scientific community: she was hired to be photography editor for *Science Illustrated,* then a small, struggling magazine. Indeed, the position lasted for only a year; the magazine was sold to a new publisher who dismissed Abbott as part of a major reorganization. Nevertheless, the scientific work continued. Abbott became an inventor: photographic technology of the day was not adequate to the task she had set herself. She needed, for example, lighting that moved in order to capture a wrench spinning through velvet-black space. She needed a camera that would tilt at heretofore unimagined angles in order to capture an enlarged eye refracted many times over in a parabolic mirror, without including the stand that held the mirror.

Finally in October 1957, persistence and dedication paid off. Inspired by a newspaper account of the Soviet launch of Sputnik, which criticized the United States for falling behind in science, Abbott renewed her appeals. The first call, to Robert C. Cook of the Bureau of Population Reports in Washington, D.C., produced a referral to Doubleday, publishers of a new textbook planned by the Physical Science Study Committee of Educational Services, Inc. (PSSC), which was to revamp the study of high-school physics. When she was hired to illustrate it, her life changed dramatically once again. With the finest equipment available, under the direction of a professional scientist who respected her ability, and with a salary that freed her from worry and distraction, Abbott began producing a body of work that gained a wider audience. In his biographical statement that accompanied an illustrated article written by Abbott for *Art in America,* photography editor and historian Beaumont Newhall wrote of the pictures: "In her approach to photography as an ally of physics, all the drama, beauty and arresting suspense of the physical laws and the natural phenomena are excitingly presented."

The work with the PSSC brought Berenice Abbott wide recognition and, for the first time, financial security. She was now in her 50s and her health was deteriorating. Abbott had never been robust, and several bouts with pneumonia, years of smoking, and New York City smog had taken their toll. On a mid-1950s' trip to Maine, which she had discovered while documenting U.S. Route 1, Abbott had purchased a dilapidated stagecoach inn and had been gradually restoring it. After surgery to remove part of a lung and doctor's orders to stop smoking and leave the city, the pace of work on the house picked up. In the early 1960s, she began spending more and more time there, first commuting to the city to do studio and darkroom work, then completing the move of all her equipment to Maine in 1966.

But her work was not yet finished. Abbott documented Maine, not just the postcard pretty coastal parts so popular with other photographers, but the inland industries and people as well. These photographs were published as the book *A Portrait of Maine.* She produced additional works from the Atget collection, and assisted with various retrospectives and publications of her own life and work. She ventured back to Paris for an exhibition of her portraits, astonishing the young photographers who had assumed the artist had died but who gathered to listen in delight to her tales of Paris life early in the century. She played ping pong and softball with her friends and neighbors, and in her 90th year visited New York City to be made an Officer in the Order of Arts and Letters by the French government.

As O'Neal concludes, the range and variety of her accomplishments are surely unique. She recognized and rescued the seminal work of a French street photographer from certain oblivion, and, with hard work that she might well have devoted to her own career, ensured his place in history. She began teaching out of necessity, continued for 25 years, and, in the process,

established one of the first and best photography programs in higher education. She produced several photography textbooks and dozens of inventions. As a photographer, she moved from portraiture to documentary to science's artist, producing in each some of the most memorable images of her—and our—time.

SOURCES:

Abbott, Berenice. *Berenice Abbott/Photographs.* Foreword by *Muriel Rukeyser. Introduction by David Vestal. Washington and London: Smithsonian Institution Press, 1990.

———. "It Has to Walk Alone," in *Photographers on Photography.* Edited by Nathan Lyons. Englewood Cliffs, NJ: Prentice Hall, 1966 (first published in *Infinity,* Vol. 7, no. 11, 1951).

O'Neal, Hank. *Berenice Abbott: American Photographer.* Introduction by John Canaday. Commentary by Berenice Abbott. NY: McGraw-Hill, 1982.

Stretch, Bonnie Barrett. "No More Softball," in *ARTnews.* Vol. 87. October 1988, p. 20.

Zwingle, Erla. "A Life of Her Own," in *American Photographer.* Vol. 16. April 1986, pp. 54–67.

SUGGESTED READING:

Berenice Abbott: Documentary Photographs of the 1930s. Exhibition catalog. Essay by Michael G. Sundell, Guest Curator. Cleveland, OH: The New Gallery of Contemporary Art, 1980.

Hagen, Charles. "Berenice Abbott," in *Artforum.* Vol. 23. March 1985, p. 95.

Hambourg, Maria Morris. "Photography Between the Wars: Selections from the Ford Motor Company Collection," in *The Metropolitan Museum of Art Bulletin.* Vol. 45. Spring 1988, pp. 1–56.

Kramer, Hilton. "Berenice Abbott," in *Art & Antiques.* Vol. 9. February 1992, pp. 75–77.

Starenko, Michael. "I to eye—Self portrait: The photographer's persona, 1840–1985," in *Afterimage.* Vol. 13. January 1986, p. 17.

Woodward, Richard B. "Berenice Abbott's Many Lives," in *ARTnews.* Vol. 91, February 1992, p. 29.

COLLECTIONS:

The Museum of Modern Art; The Brooklyn Museum; National Collection of Fine Arts, Smithsonian Institution; Lunn Gallery-Graphics International, Washington, D.C.; New Gallery for Contemporary Art, Cleveland, Ohio; and many more public and private collections. Before her death, Abbott turned over her cameras, prints, and negatives to collector Ronald Kurtz, East Rutherford, New Jersey.

RELATED MEDIA:

Berenice Abbott: A View of the 20th Century (56 min.), a film by **Kay Weaver** and **Martha Wheelock,** Ishtar Films, 1992.

Bette J. Kauffman, Assistant Professor of Communications, Pennsylvania State University, University Park, Pennsylvania

Abbott, Edith (1876–1957)

American social worker and educator. Born on September 26, 1876, in Grand Island, Nebraska; died on July 28, 1957; daughter of Othman A. and Elizabeth (Griffin) Abbott (a noted pioneer in educational work

in the West); sister of social worker *Grace Abbott; graduated from the University of Nebraska, 1901.

During her nearly 50-year career, Edith Abbott advocated the use of social research to advance social reform. After a brief stint teaching economics at Wellesley College (1907–08), she became a resident of Hull House (1908–20) and a member of the faculty of the University of Chicago (1911–23), before becoming dean of the School of Social Service Administration (1924–42) and dean emeritus (1942–53). Abbott was the author of several books on crime, immigration, and labor, including *Women in Industry* (1910), *The Tenements of Chicago* (1936), and *Public Assistance* (1939). A critic of politics in welfare programs, she fought against injustices in the treatment of the poor.

Abbott, Emma (1850–1891)

American soprano. Born in Chicago, Illinois, on December 9, 1850 (some sources cite 1849); died in Salt Lake City, Utah, on January 5, 1891; studied in New York with Achille Errani and in Europe with Wartel, Sangiovanni, and Delle Sedie; married Eugene Wetherell, in 1875.

Debuted at Covent Garden in London as Marie in La fille du régiment *(1876); debuted in New York in the same role (1877).*

Emma Abbott began her musical education in the choir of Plymouth Church, Brooklyn, and afterward studied in Milan and Paris. She made her debut at Covent Garden, London, before she and her husband Eugene Wetherell came to the United States, where she appeared successfully in the operas of Verdi, Gounod, and Bellini. One of the most popular sopranos of her time, she became the first woman to establish an opera company. The Emma Abbott English Grand Opera Company, formed in 1878, presented shortened versions of contemporary operas, sometimes interspersed with current ballads. The ensemble toured throughout the United States, including the

West, until one month before Abbott's death in January 1891.

Abbott, Evelyn (1843–1901)

British classical scholar. Born in 1843; died in 1901; educated at Lincoln Grammar School, Somerset College, Bath, and Balliol College, Oxford.

Evelyn Abbott, who endured a spinal cord injury at age 23 that paralyzed her lower limbs for life, was the author of *History of Greece* (3 vols., 1888–1900) and the editor of *Hellenica* (1880).

Abbott, Gertrude (1846–1934).

See Abbott, Mother.

Abbott, Grace (1878–1939)

American social worker. Born on Grand Island, Nebraska, on November 17, 1878; died in Chicago, Illinois, on June 19, 1939; daughter of Othman A. and Elizabeth (Griffin) Abbott (a noted pioneer in educational work in the West); younger sister of Edith Abbott (dean of School of Social Service Administration, University of Chicago); graduated Grand Island College, Ph.B., 1898; attended University of Nebraska, 1902; awarded M.A. in political science from University of Chicago, 1909; never married; no children.

Grace Abbott's social work began with a residency at *Jane Addams' Hull House in 1907. Following that, she helped organize the Immigrants' Protective League with *Sophonisba Breckinridge. Abbott's involvement with the League eventually led to her studying conditions on Ellis Island, testifying before Congress, and publishing numerous articles along with her book *The Immigrant and the Community* (1917).

Abbott devoted most of her life to child welfare. In 1917, at the invitation of *Julia Lathrop, she joined the staff of the U.S. Children's Bureau. From 1921 to 1934, Abbott succeeded Lathrop as chief of its Child Labor Division and turned her attention to the Sheppard-Towner Act, which extended federal aid for maternal and infant health care; the bureau opened 3,000 child-health and prenatal-care clinics throughout the United States. During her involvement with the bureau, Abbott was also president of the National Conference of Social Workers (1924). After 1934, she served as professor of public welfare at the University of Chicago, where her sister *Edith Abbott was dean. In 1934–35, Grace was editor of *Social Service Review* and a member of President Franklin Delano Roosevelt's Council on Economic Security, which helped devise the social security system. She also authored works on social welfare, including the two-volume *Child and the State* (1931).

Abbott, Margaret (1878–1955)

American golfer and first American woman to win an Olympic gold medal. Name variations: Margaret Abbott Dunne. Born on June 15, 1878; died on June 10, 1955; grew up in Chicago; began playing golf at a private club in 1897; married Finley Peter Dunne (1867–1936), in 1902; children: three sons and one daughter.

The sport of golf was represented in the Olympics only once: in 1900 in Paris, France. That year also marked the first Olympic games in which women were allowed as contestants. The winner of the nine-hole event was the unlikely Margaret Abbott, who was then an art student living in Paris; she was described as a "fierce competitor" with a "classy backswing." Beating out Switzerland's **Polly Whittier** by two strokes, Abbott became the first American woman to win an Olympic gold medal. The first female gold medalist from any country was *Charlotte Cooper of Great Britain who won the lawn tennis singles and mixed doubles. Margaret Abbott accompanied her husband Finley Peter Dunne, the humorist and popular creator of Mr. Dooley, when he cut short his career in mid-course and retired to Long Island in 1911.

Abbott, Maude (1869–1940)

Canadian cardiologist and promoter of medical education for women. Born in 1869 in Montreal, Canada; died of a cerebral hemorrhage on September 2, 1940; graduated from McGill University, Montreal; graduated from Bishop's College, Montreal, 1894.

The following remark from a contemporary male doctor was indicative of the late 19th-century attitude Maude Abbott faced when she attempted to gain admission to the medical school of McGill University: "Women may be useful in some departments of medicine, but in difficult work—surgery, for instance—they would not have the nerve. Can you think of a patient in a critical case waiting while the medical lady fixes her bonnet, or adjusts her bustle?" Undaunted, Abbott pioneered in the area of congenital heart disease, and hundreds of "blue babies" indirectly owe their lives to her. She became an interna-

tional authority on medical museums and worked tirelessly to break down barriers against women in medicine.

Born in 1869, Maude Abbott was orphaned early when her father deserted the family, and she and her sister Alice were adopted by their grandparents. Alice later contracted an illness that left her with a mental disorder. In coming years, Maude would spend a fortune unsuccessfully looking for a cure.

Abbott was awarded an undergraduate degree at McGill University but was subsequently denied admission to its medical school. Bishop's College, which would merge with McGill in 1905, was the first institution in Quebec to admit women as medical students. Though Bishop accepted her, the road was not easy. Abbott was denied a "ticket" for clinics at Montreal General Hospital until widespread publicity induced some of the hospital's wealthier patrons to threaten to withhold their donations unless she was granted admittance. Her case reports were stolen from the wards by male students in hopes that she would fail. Despite such acts of sabotage, she graduated in 1894, winning both the chancellor's prize and the senior anatomy medal.

After three years in Europe, Abbott was appointed assistant curator of the medical museum at McGill. In 1900, she became curator and would manage the museum for over 30 years. It was here that she developed the *Osler Catalogue of the Circulatory System*, named for Dr. William Osler. In 1907, the same year a fire nearly destroyed the museum and its contents, Abbott organized and edited the *Bulletin of the International Association of Medical Museums*. By 1910, she had also been appointed a research fellow in pathology and was formally recognized by McGill with the honorary degree of M.D., the degree for which she had unsuccessfully petitioned to study 20 years before.

In 1923, Abbott served a two-year appointment as visiting professor of pathology and bacteriology at the Woman's Medical College of Pennsylvania. Returning to McGill, she continued her work in the museum along with writing and teaching. She established her medical reputation with a section she contributed on congenital heart defects for Osler's *System of Medicine*. Her major work was a massive volume, *Atlas of Congenital Cardiac Disease*, a classified bibliography of Osler's writings, which identified 1,000 cases.

Abbott received many awards for her work, including a gold medal—McGill's highest honor—for her presentation on congenital heart disease. The exhibit, a culmination of years of research, was featured at the centenary meeting of the British Medical Association in London, and was displayed at the Graduate Fortnightly in Cardiology at the New York Academy of Medicine in 1931. Following her retirement in 1936, the Carnegie Foundation granted her $2,500 to complete a book on heart disease. Unfortunately, the book was never completed. While sitting for a portrait, which was to be the first likeness of a woman to hang in the medical building of McGill, Abbott was stricken and taken to the hospital. She died of a cerebral hemorrhage on September 2, 1940.

SUGGESTED READING:

Macdermot, H.E. *Maude Abbott*, 1941.

Abbott, Mother (1846–1934)

Australian founder of St. Margaret's hospital. Name variations: Gertrude Abbott, Mary Jane O'Brien. Born Mary Jane O'Brien in Sydney, Australia, on July 11, 1846; died in Sydney on May 12, 1934; daughter of Thomas (a schoolmaster) and Rebecca (Matthews) O'Brien.

When Mary Jane O'Brien entered the order of St. Joseph of the Sacred Heart (founded two years before by ***Mary MacKillop** and **Julian Tenison Woods**), the 22-year-old assumed the name Sister Ignatius. "Influenced by Julian Woods," writes Chris Cunneen, "she and another nun claimed to witness visions." A scandal followed when the other nun was found to have fabricated the apparitions. Though blameless, O'Brien left the convent in July 1872 and returned to Sydney. There, she became known as Mrs. Gertrude Abbott, or Mother Abbott, and eventually founded St. Margaret's Maternity Home, which she managed for the next 40 years. By the time of Mother Abbott's death in 1934, St. Margaret's had become the third largest obstetric hospital in Sydney.

Abegg, Elisabeth (1882–1974)

Early critic of Hitler's Third Reich who rescued countless Jews in Berlin and has been honored for her work during the Holocaust. Born on March 3, 1882; died in 1974; grew up in Alsace; earned a doctorate.

Elisabeth Abegg was born on March 3, 1882, in more tolerant times than those on her horizon. She grew up in Alsace (now a part of France) when it was a province of the German Reich, but moved to Berlin after France reclaimed the disputed border territory in 1918. In Berlin, she became involved with the relief work of the Quakers, who, true to their Christian beliefs, were among the first to provide food and medical assistance to the German populace after the November armistice of 1918 was signed. These experiences strengthened Abegg's commitment to the Quaker faith and instilled beliefs that would mark her life.

Abegg earned a doctorate and became a history teacher at the prestigious *Luisenschule*, an all-girls' school. Her career suffered with Hitler's rise to power after 1933 when she became increasingly disparaging of the Nazi regime. Transferred to another school because of her outspoken criticisms, by 1940 she was denied the right to teach because of her continued refusal to either accept or advance the Nazi party line.

Throughout the 1930s, Germany's Jews suffered the systematic loss of fundamental human rights. By 1939, as persecution and degradation became the norm, they had no shred of legal or moral protection. In September 1941, all Jews in the German Reich were ordered to wear a Star of David on their clothing when appearing in public. Germany's Jews were either working as slave laborers or being deported to the Eastern territories to be annihilated as part of Hitler's "Final Solution" of the "Jewish Question."

Refusing to remain uninvolved, the 60-year-old Elisabeth Abegg began to actively rescue Jews. Though responsible for her ailing older sister Julie and her 86-year-old bedridden mother, both of whom lived with her in her home in Berlin's Tempelhof district, she used her apartment at Berliner Strasse 24A (now Tempelhofer Damm 56) on countless occasions to provide temporary shelter for Jews hiding from the Nazi dragnet. Creating an extensive rescue network consisting of her Quaker friends as well as former students, she saved the lives of dozens of Jews who were sheltered either in her own apartment, which consisted of three and one-half rooms, or in temporarily empty adjoining apartments. She continued these activities at serious risk, especially considering that several of her neighbors at Berliner Strasse 24A were fanatical Nazis who suspected her of disloyalty because she refused their requests to fly the Nazi flag.

Abegg found safe and permanent hideaways in Berlin, East Prussia, and her beloved Alsace for Jewish refugees. Selling off her jewelry, she used her remaining wealth to raise enough funds to finance the successful escape into Switzerland of several of her most endangered charges. Concerned that the Jewish children were missing an education, she tutored them at her home. Almost daily, she spent long hours traveling by streetcar and subway to visit her wards at their secret locations, bringing food, money, and forged identification papers. **Charlotte Herzfeld**, a girl whose parents had committed suicide on the eve of their "resettlement," was saved by Abegg. She wrote Abegg many years later: "You were there—calm, serene, courageous. . . . I regained trust, I sensed warmth, I felt safe. You reminded me of my mother's calmness, warmth and equanimity."

On Abegg's 75th birthday in 1957, a group of individuals whose lives she had saved published a commemorative booklet to honor her. *And a Light Shined in the Darkness* contained a number of moving testimonials, including that of **Hertha Blumenthal**: "With Fräulein Dr. Abegg was revealed the truth that a life of love for one's fellow human beings, together with respect for others, is the most elevated and eternal value. . . . Her rectitude, straightforwardness, and endless love will always be the model . . . upon which I pattern my life and will come into play whenever anyone needs my help."

SOURCES:

Dick, Lutz van, ed. *Lehreropposition im NS-Staat: Biographische Berichte über den 'aufrechten Gang.'* Frankfurt am Main: Fischer Taschenbuch Verlag, 1990.

Grossman, Kurt R. *Die unbesungenen Helden: Menschen in Deutschlands dunkelsten Tagen.* 2nd edition, Berlin-Grünewald: Arani Verlag, 1961.

Keim, Anton M., ed. *Yad Vashem: Die Judenretter aus Deutschland.* Mainz: Matthias Grünewald Verlag, 1983.

Leuner, H.D. *When Compassion was a Crime: Germany's Silent Heroes, 1933–1945.* London: Oswald Wolf, 1966.

Schilde, Kurt. *Vom Columbia-Haus zum Schulenburgring: Dokumentation mit Lebensgeschichten von Opfern des Widerstandes und der Verfolgung von 1933 bis 1945 aus dem Bezirk Tempelhof.* Berlin: Edition Hentrich, 1987.

Schwersenz, Jizchak, and Edith Wolff. *Jüdische Jugend im Untergrund. Eine zionistische Gruppe in Deutschland während des 2. Weltkrieges.* Tel Aviv: Bulletin 45 des Leo-Baeck-Instituts, 1969.

Und ein Licht leuchtet in der Finsternis. Festschrift für Elisabeth Abegg, die in ihrer Wohnung Tempelhofer Damm 56 eine Vielzahl jüdischer Mitbürger versteckte. Berlin: Freundeskreis, 1957.

John Haag, Associate Professor of History, University of Georgia, Athens, Georgia

Abel, Annie Heloise (1873–1947)

English-American historian. Name variations: Abel-Henderson. Born Annie Heloise Abel on February 18, 1873, in Fernhurst, Sussex, England; died in Aberdeen, Washington, on March 14, 1947; graduated from the University of Kansas, 1898, M.A., 1900; attended Cornell; awarded Ph.D., Yale, 1905; married George C. Henderson (an Australian scholar), in 1922 (separated 1924).

In 1885, 12-year-old Annie Abel boarded an English ship to join her parents in Salina, Kansas, to which they had immigrated the previous year. Noted for her work with relations between Native Americans and whites, Abel taught at Wells College before teaching at the Woman's College of Baltimore (Goucher College), where she became full professor and head of the department in 1914. She also taught English at Johns Hopkins (1910–15) and joined the faculty of Smith College (1916–22). Her most important work was the three-volume *The Slaveholding Indians* published between 1915 and 1925. After a brief stay in Australia and an unhappy marriage (1922–24), Abel returned to the States and moved to Aberdeen, Washington, though still using her married name, Abel-Henderson. From 1924 to 1925, she taught at Sweet Briar College, then, in 1928, became professor of history at University of Kansas where she researched British colonial and Indian policy while continuing to publish her findings.

Abiertas, Josepha (1894–1929)

Filipino lawyer and feminist who was the first woman to graduate from the Philippine Law School. Born in Capiz, Philippines, in 1894; died of tuberculosis in 1929.

Born in 1894 and orphaned along with her brother at an early age, Josepha Abiertas attended school in Capiz before enrolling at the Philippine Law School. Because she devoted her short life to bettering the position of women and poor farmers, the Josepha Abiertas House of Friendship was dedicated to her after her death at age 33.

Abigail (fl. 1010 BCE)

Biblical woman. Name variations: Abigal. Flourished around 1010 BCE (chronology of the Old Testament is based on textual and archaeological evidence and cannot be exactly pinpointed); daughter of Jesse of Bethlehem; sister of David (r. 1010–970 BCE); married Jether (an Ishmaelite); children: Amasa.

Abigail was the sister of King David who ruled Judah and Israel from about 1010 to about 970 BCE, capturing Jerusalem in about the year

1000. She was the mother of Amasa who commanded the army of Absalom.

Abigail (fl. 1000 BCE)

Biblical woman. Name variations: *The Beautiful Peacemaker. Born in Carmel, a town in the hill country of Judah (the ruins of which still remain under the name Kurmul, about ten miles south-southeast of Hebron); flourished around 1000 BCE; married Nabal (died); married King David (David appears to have ruled Judah and Israel from approximately 1010 BCE to approximately 970 BCE, capturing Jerusalem in about 1000 BCE); children: Chileab (in Bible called also Daniel).*

After the future king David fled from the jealous and insane King Saul, he became an outlaw chieftain, gathering about him a band of debtors and malcontents numbering about 600. Once a year, Abigail's husband Nabal, a wealthy sheepmaster who pastured his 4,000 animals on the southern slopes of Carmel, held a great banquet for his men at the time of sheep shearing. David's men, at one of their encampments, had protected Nabal's shepherds and flocks, then at sheep shearing time, partly requested, partly demanded, a gift of food for themselves. Nabal imperiously refused and, in so doing, placed himself at the mercy of David and his men. Nabal's men perceived the danger but did not dare approach him; so they told Abigail his wife, a woman, it is said, of "good understanding, and of a beautiful countenance."

Bringing offerings of bread, wine, grain, raisins, figs, and dressed sheep, Abigail hastened down to David's encampment with her attendants. There, 400 men, fully armed, were on their way to kill Nabal and his men. But Abigail's diplomacy and bearing softened David's heart, and his small army turned back. When Abigail reached home, her husband Nabal was in the midst of revelry, too drunk to comprehend his proximity to danger. Told the next day how near he had come to death, Nabal suffered a shock so great that he died.

Summoned to David's camp, Abigail became his second wife. David was crowned king after the death of Saul, and Abigail shared the honors of royalty. One son, Chileab, was born to them. Though Abigail was David's companion in all future fortunes, she was also obliged to submit to a division of his affections with other wives: *Michal (who was Saul's daughter and David's first wife), *Ahinoam of Jezreel, *Abishag of Shunem, *Bathsheba (widow of Uriah and mother of Solomon), *Haggith (mother of Absalom and Adonijah), and several others, unnamed.

Abigal.

Variant of Abigail.

Abihail (fl. 970 BCE)

Biblical woman. Flourished around 970 BCE; second wife of King Rehoboam (r. 975–958 BCE), a descendant of Eliab, David's oldest brother.

Abington, Frances (1737–1815)

English actress. Name variations: *Frances or Fanny Barton. Born Frances Barton in London, England, in 1737; died in London on March 4, 1815; daughter of a private soldier in the King's Guards; married her music-master, one of the royal trumpeters (soon separated).*

From the position of domestic servant, flowergirl, and streetsinger in St. James's Park who went by the name of "Nosegay Fan," Fanny Abington rose to prominence on the English stage and enjoyed a successful career for 43 years. Her first appearance was as Miranda in *The Busybody* in 1755. She originated over 30 characters, including Lady Bab in *High Life Below Stairs,* Betty in the *Clandestine Marriage,* Charlotte in the *Hypocrite,* Charlotte Rusport in the *West Indian,* Roxalana in the *Sultan,* Miss Hoyden in the *Trip to Scarborough,* and, her crowning triumph, Lady Teazle in *The School for Scandal.* Abington starred at the Drury Lane from 1764–82 and at Covent Garden from 1782–90. Her last appearance was in 1799.

Abishag of Shunem (fl. 1000 BCE)

Biblical woman. Flourished around 1000 BCE; Shunammite woman taken by David to comfort him in his old age.

The First Book of Kings tells of King David's last days, when the young beauty Abishag of Shunem was brought to serve him and keep him warm in bed, though they had no sexual relations. She became one of his wives (1 Kings 1:3, 4, 15). After David's death, his son Solomon ascended to the throne. His half-brother Adonijah persuaded *Bathsheba, Solomon's mother, to entreat the king to permit him to marry Abishag. Solomon, who suspected in this request a craving for the throne, had Adonijah put to death.

Abital (fl. 1000 BCE)

Biblical woman. Fifth wife of King David.

Abla Pokou (c. 1700–c. 1760).

See Pokou.

Abrabanel, Benvenida (d. 1560)

Jewish noblewoman of Italy. Born in Naples, Italy; birth date unknown; died in 1560 in Ferrara, Italy; daughter of Joseph Abrabanel; married first cousin Samuel Abrabanel (d. 1547), before 1541 in Naples.

Benvenida Abrabanel, a wealthy Jewish entrepreneur and benefactor, came from a family that had enjoyed great prosperity and royal favor in Spain until 1492, the year the Spanish monarchs *Isabella I and Ferdinand expelled all practicing Jews from the Iberian peninsula. Although the king and queen offered the Abrabanels the opportunity to remain in their native land, the family left Spain and made Naples, Italy, their new home. In Naples, young Benvenida received an excellent education. Her intelligence and learning led the Spanish viceroy to request that she tutor his daughter *Eleonora de Medici (1522–1562), later duchess of Tuscany.

Benvenida eventually married her first cousin, the merchant Samuel Abrabanel, with whom she moved to Ferrara in 1541, when the government of Naples expelled the Jews from that city. Samuel's business thrived in Ferrara, allowing the highly educated Benvenida the opportunity to create a sort of salon, opening her home to scholars and artists from across Italy. After Samuel died in 1547, Benvenida took over his commercial enterprises, which prospered under her management, partly due to important trading rights she earned from her former student, Eleonora de Medici. Abrabanel gained renown for her learning, business acumen, and charity, for she gave freely of her wealth to aid the less fortunate Jews of Ferrara.

Laura York, Anza, California

Abrahams, Ottilie Grete (1937—)

Namibian political leader and physician whose efforts were crucial in the establishment of an independent Namibia. Born Ottilie Grete Schimming in 1937 in Windhoek, South West Africa (now Namibia); educated in Windhoek and Cape Town, South Africa; graduated University of Cape Town, 1961; married Kenneth Godfrey Abrahams, in 1961.

Founding member of the South West Africa Student Body (SWASB), a predecessor of the major nationalist parties; deeply involved with the newly formed South West Africa People's Organisation (SWAPO); served as secretary-general of the Namibian Independence Party (NIP).

In 1937, Ottilie Grete Schimming was born into a family of mixed race (designated by the derogatory terms "Rehoboth Baster" or "Coloured" in South Africa) and was educated in Windhoek and Cape Town, South Africa. An activist while still in secondary school, Ottilie was a founding member of the South West Africa Student Body (SWASB), a predecessor of the major nationalist parties that were to emerge several decades later. This organization was founded by Namibian students enrolled in South African secondary and post-secondary schools, and was inspired by South Africa's Defiance Campaign of 1952 led by the African National Congress (ANC). When Ottilie and many of her contemporaries returned to South West Africa, she and the other militants among them wished to create a permanent entity that reflected their growing sense of national identity. Consequently, in late 1955, she founded the South West Africa Progressive Association.

After graduating from the University of Cape Town in 1961, where she was granted a medical degree, she married Kenneth Godfrey Abrahams (1936—), a South African medical student of mixed race who also received his degree from the University of Cape Town. The couple returned to South West Africa where Ottilie set up a medical practice in Rehoboth, and both began to engage in dangerous political activities. In the early 1960s, they became deeply involved with the newly formed South West Africa People's Organization (SWAPO). Soon they were also active in a small guerrilla group, Yo Chi Chan, which attracted the attention of the South African intelligence services. By 1963, Kenneth was forced to flee to Botswana where he was captured by South African police and taken to Cape Town. Ottilie led the movement to free her husband, which took place when the British pressured the South African government. The reunited couple went to Tanzania where they worked in the SWAPO office with Sam Nujoma (1929—), then went on to create a dissident organization, SWAPO-Democrats (SWAPO-D) in June 1978.

After returning to Namibia, Ottilie Abrahams and her husband split from SWAPO-D and joined another dissident group, the Namibian Independence Party (NIP). Ottilie served as secretary-general. Their leadership during the 1989 elections paved the way for Namibia's independence. One year later, Sam Nujoma was elected president of a new, independent Namibia. In time, Ottilie and Kenneth would become estranged from Nujoma, claiming that he had used party funds for an extravagant lifestyle. With the achievement of independence, the Abrahams moved away from the center stage of political life, concentrating instead on activities that were considerably less dramatic but greatly constructive for their nascent nation. Drawing on their joint experiences of several decades of revolutionary journalism, they worked together to edit and publish a highly regarded journal, *The Namibian Review*. While Kenneth concentrated on his medical practice, Ottilie Abrahams devoted much effort and time to essential self-improvement projects, including supervising an adult-education center in the shantytowns around the national capital of Windhoek in the 1990s.

SOURCES:

Grotpeter, John J. *Historical Dictionary of Namibia.* Metuchen, NJ: Scarecrow Press, 1994.

John Haag, Associate Professor of History,
University of Georgia, Athens, Georgia

Abramova, Anastasia (b. 1902)

Russian ballerina with the Bolshoi Theater. Born in Russia in 1902; studied with Yekaterina Geltzer and Yekaterina Vazem; entered the Bolshoi School, 1910, graduated, 1917; trained together with Liubov Bank, Valentina Kudriavtseva, and Nina Podgoretskaya under the direction of Alexander Gorsky and Vassily Tikhomirov at the Bolshoi Theater.

Anastasia Abramova made her debut as Lise in *La Fille Mal Gardée* (1922) and was known for her Swanilda in *Coppélia* and Aurora in *The Sleeping Beauty.* Her Soviet ballets included Jeanne in *Flames of Paris,* Tao-Hoa in *The Red Flower,* and Stepmother and Fairy in *Cinderella.* She retired from the Bolshoi in 1948.

Abrams, Harriett (c. 1758–c. 1822)

English composer and soprano, well known in London for her beautiful compositions and voice. Born of Jewish descent around 1758; died around 1822; sister of singers Theodosia Abrams (c. 1765–c. 1834) and Eliza Abrams (c. 1772–c. 1830).

Hard facts are scarce concerning Jewish composer and singer Harriett Abrams. Her sister Theodosia had a beautiful contralto voice and sang with Harriett as did another sister Eliza. Harriett studied with the composer Thomas Arne and, in 1775, she made her debut in *May Day.* By 1780, she left Drury Lane to become a singer in fashionable concerts. In 1784, she appeared in the Handel Commemoration concerts and in some of the Antient Music concerts. By the 1790s, Abrams had limited her appearances to exclusive programs in the homes of the nobility like the Ladies' Concerts she organized at Lord Vernon's. She also staged annual benefits where Haydn played the piano in 1792, 1794, and 1795. A composer as well as a singer, Harriett Abrams published two sets of Italian and English canzonets, a collection of Scottish songs, and a number of ballads. One of these ballads, "Crazy Jane," was quite the rage in 1799–1800. Though musical programs and newspapers of the period document her popularity, she all but faded from the view of modern history.

John Haag, Associate Professor of History,
University of Georgia, Athens, Georgia

Abrantès, Laure d' (1784–1838)

French novelist. Name variations: Laurette de St. Martine-Permon, Laure Permon, Duchesse d'Abrantès or Abrantes; (pseudonym) Madame Junot. Born at Montpellier, France, in 1784 (some sources cite 1785); died in Paris, on June 6(?), 1838; daughter of a Corsican mother who was a friend of Letizia Bonaparte; married General Junot (one of Napoleon's generals), later the duke of Abrantès or duc d'Abrantès; children: *Constance Aubert (b. 1803).

Following her marriage, the society leader Laure d'Abrantès became lady-in-waiting to *Letizia Bonaparte, mother of Napoleon. When Abrantès' alcoholic husband committed suicide, leaving her in financial straits, she began to write. Though her novels are mostly forgotten, her 18-volume *Mémoires de Mme la duchesse d'Abrantès ou Souvenirs historiques sur Napoléon, la Révolution, le Directoire, le Consulat, l'Empire et la Restauration* (Paris: Ladvocat, 1831–35) include the first years of the reign of Louis-Philippe. Along with her *Histoire des salons de Paris* (1836–38), they have been said to give an excellent, ribald, though sometimes inaccurate portrait of the 19th-century French court. Although the sales of her memoirs earned her 70,000 francs, it was not enough to sustain her, and Abrantès died in poverty.

SUGGESTED READING:

Cosland, M. *Women of Iron and Velvet.*

Abzug, Bella (1920–1998)

U.S. Representative, attorney, and peace activist who worked to advance the role of women in U.S. politics and win representation for women's issues. Born Bella Savitsky in New York, New York, on July 24, 1920; died of complications from heart surgery in New York City on March 31, 1998; daughter of Emmanuel (a Russian immigrant and meat-market owner) and Esther Savitsky; attended local Bronx elementary schools; graduated from Walton High School; attended and graduated from Hunter College; enrolled in Columbia Law school, 1942, but subsequently left due to World War II; returned to law school and was awarded the LL.B. degree and admitted to the bar, 1947; married Martin Abzug (a stockbroker), in June 1945; children: two daughters, **Eve Gail (Egee) Abzug; Liz Abzug**.

Helped found the Women's Strike for Peace (1961) and was active in the peace movement (1960s and 1970s); was an early supporter and founder of the National Organization for Women (NOW) and remained active in feminist issues (late 1960–98); was active in reform politics in New York City and elected to Congress, serving in the U.S. House of Representa-

Bella Abzug

tives (1970–76); gained fame for her outspoken support of the women's liberation movement and supported legislation that promoted federal job programs, public transportation, and individual right to privacy; ran unsuccessfully for the U.S. Senate from New York (1976); served as chair of the National Advisory Council on Women (1977–78); remained active in women's issues and co-founded the National Women's Political Caucus (1971), one of the largest financial contributors to women seeking political office.

Selected publications: Bella! Ms. Abzug Goes to Washington *(edited by Mel Ziegler, Saturday Review Press, 1972);* Gender Gap: Bella Abzug's Guide to Political Power for American Women *(with Mim Kelber, 1984).*

Bella Abzug was a teenager when her father died. After his death, she broke tradition in her synagogue, where segregation of the sexes disturbed her, by reciting the Kaddish, a ritual then reserved for male relatives. She would later write about the day in *Gender Gap:* "No one tried to stop me, and as I stood in a corner reciting my mourner's prayers, I came to understand that one way to change outmoded traditions was to challenge them."

Abzug ranks as one of the most flamboyant and politically effective women activists of the mid-20th century. As an outspoken supporter of the women's liberation movement in the United States and an early, active participant in the peace movement, she directed her career toward civil-rights and civil-liberties issues, legislation promoting job equality, the founding of the modern women's liberation movement, the attempt to pass the Equal Rights Amendment to the U.S. Constitution, and the advancement of U.S. women in electoral politics. Wrote one biographer at the outset of her years in Congress: "The Ninety-second Congress has a number of new Representatives who are impatient with archaic House rules and anxious to make the national legislative body more responsive to the needs of the people, but none is more vocal than flamboyant, fearless Bella Abzug." Indeed, this straightforward, assertive political style set her apart from other politically active women of her era.

Born in the Bronx section of New York City in 1920, Abzug was one of two daughters of Emmanuel and **Esther Savitsky**. Her father, a Russian immigrant, owned and operated Manhattan's Live and Let Live Meat Market. Bella attended local elementary schools in the Bronx and graduated from the all-girl Walton High School. While a student at Hunter College in Manhattan, she was elected student-body president and also became active in the Zionist movement prior to World War II. Encouraged by many to go to "the best" law school, she applied to Harvard but received a letter informing her that it did not admit women. Outraged, Abzug turned to her mother, who replied: "Why do you want to go to Harvard anyway? It's far away, and you can't afford the carfare. Go to Columbia." After graduation from New York's Hunter College in 1942, she did enroll in the Columbia Law School but dropped out after a short time to work toward the war effort in a shipbuilding factory.

Returning to Columbia Law School after World War II, Abzug became an editor of the prestigious *Columbia Law Review*. While there, she met her future husband Martin Abzug. Before marrying in June of 1945, the two had long discussions about "who would do what," and it was agreed that she would work at her legal career even after having children (they would soon raise two daughters). In the meantime, she completed law school in 1947 and was admitted to the bar. Abzug later referred to her husband as a "role-model feminist husband" and frequently praised him for the equality of their career and family concerns throughout their long, successful relationship. She expressed her views about career and family to a reporter for *New Woman* (June 1971):

> You try to adjust the family situation to the realities of your life. You don't put one ahead of the other. There is a balance, and you strive to keep that balance. The family grows with it. And the kids also know that the mother is a woman, wife, and lawyer. A total person. It makes them better people.

After admission to the bar, Abzug developed two primary legal interests. First, she was a labor-law specialist who represented, among others, unions for restaurant workers, fur workers, auto workers, and the first longshoremen strikers. Outside her labor-law practice, however, she also served (often for minimal or no fee) a variety of civil-rights and civil-liberties litigants. She was chief counsel in the appeal of Willie McGee, a young Mississippi black man convicted of raping a white woman and sentenced to death. In her defense arguments, Abzug challenged the practice of excluding blacks from Southern juries and of applying the death sentence for rape convictions only in the case of black defendants. While she lost this case and McGee was executed in 1951, it drew worldwide attention and helped establish Abzug as a noted civil-liberties attorney.

Similarly, Abzug's defense of several persons accused of subversive activities by the late Senator Joseph McCarthy, in the period of his investigations of alleged communists in the 1950s, further contributed to her notoriety as an activist attorney on behalf of unpopular or controversial defendants. During the same period, she was also defense lawyer for New York State teachers accused of leftist activities. In these cases, Abzug was among the first attorneys to appeal to the First Amendment's guarantee of the rights to free speech, press, and association. In the 1950s, she also served as counsel to various tenant and minority groups, and helped write model legislation that was later incorporated into the Civil Rights Act of 1964 and the Voting Rights Act of 1965.

In addition to her reputation as an active participant in the civil-rights movement, Abzug is also well known for her early and sustained involvement in the peace movement of the mid-20th century, prompting Jimmy Breslin's remark: "Some came early, others came late. Bella has been there forever." In 1961, she helped found the Women's Strike for Peace, one of the largest and most active peace organizations of this period. She led many demonstrations and lobbying efforts on behalf of this group throughout the 1960s, in favor of a nuclear test ban, disarmament, and an immediate end to the war in Vietnam. She also worked within the Democratic Party in New York to back the campaigns of a number of peace candidates, and, in 1967, she helped rally unhappy Democrats and various peace groups into a combined effort to "Dump Lyndon Johnson." She was also an active supporter of Senator Eugene McCarthy, who ran as the Democratic "peace candidate," challenging President Johnson in the 1968 presidential primaries. This candidacy is often credited with forcing Johnson's withdrawal from the presidential campaign.

In this same period, Abzug was engaged in a number of Democratic Party activities, which would later lead to her own candidacy for Congress. After the Democratic loss in 1968, she was a founder of the New Democratic Coalition, a reform movement within the party. In the New York City mayoral campaign of 1969, she contributed to the successful reelection campaign of Mayor John V. Lindsay by organizing and serving as chair of the Taxpayers' Campaign for Urban Priorities. She also served as an advisor to Lindsay.

When she announced her candidacy for the Democratic nomination to Congress from the 19th Congressional District of New York in March of 1970, Abzug was endorsed as the official candidate of the reform Democrats. Her campaign stressed three issues: peace and ending the war in Vietnam; reordering national spending priorities; and women's equality. Abzug believed hers was the first winning campaign in her era that stressed women's equality. When she ran, there were only nine women serving in the House of Representatives, and one in the U.S. Senate.

The victory, however, was a hard-fought one. For 14 years, the district in which Abzug was running had been represented by Leonard Farbstein, a Democrat who sat quietly in the House, attending to district issues and maintaining a moderately liberal voting record. The reform Democrats had tried unsuccessfully to unseat him in the past, and, in 1970, the incumbent was confident of again winning his predominantly Jewish but ethnically diverse district, which included both rich and poor constituents.

But the forces behind Farbstein underestimated the energies of the galvanized Bella. With "This woman belongs in the House" as her slogan, Abzug offered her constituents a new, stronger voice in Washington. She committed to working for better housing, cuts in defense spending, equal rights for women, and an immediate end to the Vietnam War. Defeating Farbstein in the May primary in her race against Republican Barry Farber, Abzug gained the support of a wide range of prominent New Yorkers, including Mayor Lindsay, peace groups, and several Broadway entertainers who campaigned on her behalf. Many young women were attracted to and worked in the campaign. As one of the most colorful political personalities in New York, Abzug drew much attention, even nationally. She was loud, good natured, and a tireless campaigner. Wrote Abzug:

> I've been described as a tough and noisy woman, a prizefighter, a man-hater, you name it. They call me Battling Bella, Mother Courage and a Jewish mother with more complaints than Portnoy. There are those who say I'm impatient, impetuous, uppity, rude, profane, brash and overbearing. Whether I'm any of these things, or all of them, you can decide for yourself. But whatever I am—and this ought to be made very clear at the outset—I am a very serious woman.

The 19th Congressional District had four times as many Democrats as Republicans in 1970, so Abzug was expected to win. A number of regular Democrats, alienated by the primary battle, defected to her opponent. Others cited her manner and strong views on such controversial issues as women's liberation. The battle grew acrimonious as election day neared, but, on November 3, 1970, Abzug won easily.

As a representative, Bella Abzug made her presence known on Capitol Hill immediately. Her first day in the House, refusing to wait the rookie's traditional time before addressing that body, she introduced a resolution calling for withdrawal of all troops from Indochina by July 4, 1971, and later that afternoon fellow New York Representative *Shirley Chisholm administered a special peace oath to Representative Abzug, while hundreds of supporters looked on. Abzug also campaigned early and vigorously for a seat on the Armed Service Committee—an assignment seldom granted to a new representative—on the grounds that the committee needed a woman and a critic of the military. This attempt proved unsuccessful, and she was assigned to the Government Operations and Public Works committees; she later chaired a subcommittee on Government Information and Individual Rights.

*W*e women must get used to thinking of ourselves as a mighty multitude. . . . We can learn to become political leaders and activists, or we can sit back and let a minority of men in government, backed by powerful money and military interests, run our country and try to run the whole world. It's up to us.

—Bella Abzug

During her first year, Abzug introduced several antiwar amendments, none of which passed. She also opposed the draft, describing compulsory military service as "slavery." She met repeatedly, and very publicly, with antiwar demonstrators in Washington. After some were arrested in May 1971, she questioned the constitutionality of the mass arrests, a position the courts later upheld.

Abzug also worked from the first for the enactment of the Equal Rights Amendment (ERA) and other legislation of importance to women, including the Equal Credit Act of 1972 and various increases in entitlement programs benefitting women and families. She was active in the attempt to pass national childcare legislation in the early 1970s, and in oversight of the Equal Opportunity Commission's handling of gender discrimination issues, after the Equal Pay Act was extended to include professionals. Abzug also introduced an Abortion Rights Act,

just prior to the Supreme Court's landmark decision extending abortion rights in *Roe* v. *Wade* (1973). She also supported Title IX of the Education Amendments of 1972, which made it illegal to discriminate on the basis of sex in any federally funded educational institutions. Those measures that were successful created dramatic changes in the lives of American women. (Thousands of women active in college sports today have Title IX to thank.) Indeed, even those causes that were unsuccessful would lay important groundwork for campaigns on similar issues that would be launched during the 1980s.

Other milestones of Abzug's House service included authoring a provision that allowed transfer of interstate highway funds to public mass transportation, and the coauthoring of the amended Freedom of Information Act and the Privacy and Sunshine laws. She also brought major programs into New York State for transportation, public works, economic development, and water and sewage. Home often, conferring regularly with constituents, Abzug was ranked by a *U.S. News and World Report* survey of House delegates as the third most influential member of that body.

Successful in the House and widely known as a lecturer and advocate of issues important to women, minorities, and peace activists, Abzug felt it was a "worthwhile risk" to run for the Senate in 1976. *Margaret Chase Smith had been defeated, there were no women in the upper house, and no woman had ever been the nominee of a major New York party for Senate. Abzug was popular, well known, with important New York supporters; nonetheless, the chair of the state Democratic Party recruited Daniel Patrick Moynihan to oppose her in the Democratic primary. Two other well-known liberals, Ramsey Clark and Paul O'Dwyer, also entered the primary along with a millionaire builder, Abe Hirschfield. Bella Abzug lost the primary by less than one percent of the vote, and Moynihan went on to become the New York senator. Abzug credited her loss to division in the liberal ranks within New York City.

While she did not return to legislative office, Abzug remained vigorously involved in politics throughout the 1970s and 1980s, primarily through her work with the National Women's Political Caucus (NWPC), which she helped found in 1971. Having experienced firsthand the difficulties faced by women running for elected office, she became convinced of the need to increase political activity on behalf of women candidates. Reminding women that they are an electoral majority in the United States, the NWPC raises and contributes funds to women candidates of either party who work to advance women's issues and legislation, and promotes interest in party and election reforms favorable to women candidates. The organization grew tremendously during the 1970s and 1980s, and many women elected to office in this period credit the NWPC with contributing to their success.

From this organizational base, Abzug worked to reform the political parties, so that by 1980 women delegates became equal in numbers to male delegates in both party conventions. She served as political action director of the NWPC and worked tirelessly for many women candidates. She also served for a time as chair of the National Advisory Council on Women, resigning in a policy dispute with President Jimmy Carter over his efforts for the passage of the ERA after the Houston Conference on Women (1978). As a leader in both the NWPC and the National Organization for Women, she continued activity in support of the ERA, childcare, and other legislation favorable for women. As a lawyer, author, noted lecturer, and experienced political analyst, Abzug remained at the forefront of women's political action during the "gender gap" years of the 1980s. At this time, women increased their political activity and began voting in patterns clearly differentiated from those of male voters.

Bella Abzug once observed: "I have been and still am often described as 'aggressive,' 'abrasive,' and 'strident.' Friends and coworkers have observed, and I concur, that had I been a male politician with my record of accomplishment in Congress and the movements for social change, the adjectives would have been transformed into 'strong,' 'courageous,' and 'dynamic.'"

SOURCES:
Abzug, Bella S., with Mim Kelber. *Gender Gap: Bella Abzug's Guide to Political Power for American Women.* Boston: Houghton Mifflin, 1984.
————. *Bella! Ms. Abzug Goes to Washington.* Edited by Mel Ziegler. NY: Saturday Review Press, 1972.

SUGGESTED READING:
LeVeness, Frank P., and Jane P. Sweeney, eds. *Women Leaders in Contemporary U.S. Politics.* Boulder, CO: Lynne Rienner, 1987.

Jacqueline DeLaat, Associate Professor of Political Science,
Marietta College, Marietta, Ohio

Acarie, Barbe (1566–1618)

French nun and mystic. Name variations: Jeanne Avrillot; Marie de l'Incarnation. Born Jeanne Avrillot in 1566; died in 1618; daughter of Nicolas Avrillot (a wealthy aristocrat) and a mother who belonged to one of the oldest Parisian families; educated at the convent of Longchamps; married Pierre Acarie (d. 1613), viscount of Villemare, in 1584; children: six.

Though known for her piety and dreams of becoming a nun, Barbe Acarie was married in 1584 at the urgings of her parents to Pierre Acarie, viscount of Villemare. She was 16. From then on, Barbe successfully served both Parisian high society and the poor. Throughout her life, she suffered from chronic pain and relied on the use of crutches. While her husband squandered the family fortune, she turned her Paris home into a spiritual salon, which was frequented by many, including Vincent de Paul and Francis de Sâles. When Pierre was exiled and their property confiscated, Barbe Acarie determined to restore the family fortune and educate her six children.

In 1603, stirred by the work of *Teresa of Avila, she influenced the court of King Henry IV to introduce the reformed order of the Carmelites to France. She was also instrumental in helping **Madame de Sainte-Beuve** in establishing the French Ursulines. Following the death of her husband, Acarie entered the Carmelite convent at Amiens where her eldest daughter was sub-prioress. Two other daughters joined them. Acarie, who became a lay sister and assumed the religious name of Marie de l'Incarnation, was later transferred to Pontoise where she died in 1618, age 52. She was beatified in 1794.

SUGGESTED READING:
Menzies, Lucy. *Mirrors of the Holy.*
Sheppard, L.C. *Barbe Acarie, Wife and Mystic,* 1953.

Accaiuoli, Laudomia.
See Medici, Laudomia de.

Acca Larentia.
See Larentia, Acca.

Accoramboni, Vittoria
(c. 1557–1585)

Duchess of Bracciano. Name variations: Virginia; Vittoria Corombona. Pronunciation: Ah-KHO-rum-BOH-nee. Born around 1557; murdered in Padua on December 22, 1585; married Francesco Peretti, in 1573 (murdered in 1581); married Paolo or Paulo Giordano Orsini (d. 1585), duke of Bracciano (or Brachiano).

Vittoria Accoramboni's name reaches down through history because of passion, revenge, treachery, and a series of intrigues culminating in multiple murders, including her own and those of her two husbands. In 16th-century Italy, Accoramboni's first husband Francesco Peretti was murdered at the instigation of Paolo Orsini, who was already married, so that he might wed Accoramboni, a woman known for her great beauty and wit. (The death of Paolo Orsini's wife *Isabella de Medici, daughter of *Eleonora de Medici, is also open to questions of foul play.) Eventually, Orsini married Accoramboni. Upon his death, on November 13, 1585, she became involved in litigation with Ludovic Orsini, concerning her inheritance, and was murdered by him. These events were altered and adapted by John Webster for his play *The White Devil or Vittoria Corombona*, first presented around 1612. In the revenge tragedy, Isabella de Medici dies while kissing a poisoned portrait of her husband, and Francesco meets his end when pushed off a gymnasium horse vault. Accoramboni's history has also been written by Gnoli (1870), and was made the subject of a novel by L. Tieck, *Vittoria Accoramboni* (1840).

Achmatowa, Anna (1889–1966).

See Akhmatova, Anna.

Achsah

Biblical woman. Only daughter of Caleb (1 Chr. 2:49).

Achsah was offered in marriage to Othniel, as a reward for his conquest of the city of Debir, or Kirjath-sepher. As a wedding gift, Achsah requested the springs of Upper and Lower Gullath.

Achurch, Janet (1864–1916)

English actress. Born in Lancashire, England, on January 17, 1864; died on September 11, 1916; descended from an old acting family; great granddaughter of Achurch Ward, who managed the Theatre Royal in Manchester; married Charles Charrington (an actor).

"She was a feminist before her time," wrote Sheridan Morley of Janet Achurch in *The Great Stage Stars*. The first English actress to play Ibsen, Achurch won acclaim as Nora in *A Doll's House* in 1899. *Elizabeth Robins recalled the shock of seeing Achurch, decked out in the shabby but pretty "clothes of Ibsen's Nora," breaking the then unspoken theatrical rule that "an actress invariably comes on in new clothes, unless she is playing a beggar." The unstagey effect of the entire production, writes Robins, made the play "less like a play than like a personal meeting—with people and issues that seized us and held us, and wouldn't let go." Soon after, Achurch formed her own company and toured with the play in Australia, India, and America. Considered a genius by George Bernard Shaw, Achurch was cast in the title role of his *Candida* as well as in the role of Cecily Waynflete in his *Captain Brassbound's Conversion*. Her promise, however, gave way to morphine, cocaine, a rocky marriage, and a financially incompetent husband. Departing from the stage at 49, Janet Achurch died at age 52.

SOURCES:

Morley, Sheridan. *The Great Stage Stars*. London: Angus & Robertson, 1986.

Ackermann, Louise Victorine (1813–1890)

French poet. Born Victorine Choquet in Paris, France, on November 30, 1813; died in Nice, on August 3, 1890; grew up in the Oise; educated by her Voltaire-an-atheist father; married Paul Ackermann (d. 1846, a German poet and philologist), in 1843.

Widowed after three years of marriage, Louise Ackermann wrote poems that resonate with pessimism, passion, and despair. An admirer of German philosophy and of Victor Hugo, she retired near Nice where she wrote *Contes* (1855), *Poésies, Premières poésies* (1863), *Poésies philosophiques* (1871), and *Pensées d'une solitaire* (*Thoughts of a Lonely Woman*, 1882). Her autobiography *Ma Vie* appeared in *Oeuvres* in 1885, while her journal, spanning the years 1848–69, was published in the *Mercure de France* on May 1, 1927.

Ackermann, Rosemarie (1952—)

East German high jumper. Name variations: Rosi. Born on April 4, 1952.

Broke the world record with 1.94 meters in 1974; won the gold medal in women's high jump in Montreal Olympics at 1.93 meters (6'4", 1976); cleared the bar at 2.0 meters in West Berlin (1977).

Between 1974 and 1977, Rosemarie Ackermann was nearly unbeatable in the women's high jump. Until she endured an Achilles tendon operation, her only rival was the Italian champion *Sara Simeoni. In the 1976 Olympic games in Montreal, Rosi Ackermann won the gold medal and was the first woman to jump two meters over her own height, while Simeoni took the silver. In a memorable encounter at the European games in Prague in 1978, Simeoni defeated Ackermann with a jump of 2.01 meters (6'7") to Ackermann's 1.99. The following year, 1979, Ackermann, using her "old fashioned" straddle-style jump, defeated Simeoni at the European Cup in Turin with 1.99 meters, but stress fractures took their toll and Ackermann never again regained her dominance. She took 4th in Moscow at the 1980 Olympic games while Simeoni took the gold with an Olympic record-breaking jump of 6'5.5".

Ackland, Valentine (1906–1968).

See Warner, Sylvia Townsend for sidebar.

Ackté, Aino (1876–1944)

Finnish soprano. Name variations: Aïno Ackté or Ackte. Born in Helsinki, Finland, on April 23, 1876; died in Nummela on August 8, 1944; daughter of Lorenz Nikolai Ackté (a baritone and conductor) and **Emmy Strömer** *Ackté (a soprano); sister of* **Irma Tervani** *(1887–1936, a leading mezzo-soprano); studied with her mother before entering the Paris Conservatoire, 1894; studied with Duvernoy.*

Aino Ackté made her 1897 debut at the Grand Opera in Paris as Marguerite in Gounod's *Faust.* Subsequently, she interpreted many parts with great success, including Elsa in *Lohengrin,* Elizabeth in *Tannhäuser,* Benjamin in Méhul's *Joseph,* and other leading roles. Under the baton of Sir Thomas Beecham, she was triumphant as the first British Salome in Strauss' opera. Ackté helped found the Finnish National Opera and was its director from 1938–39. Two volumes of her autobiography were published: the first in 1925, the second in 1935.

Acland, Lady Harriet (1750–1815)

English memoirist. Born Christian Henrietta Caroline on January 3, 1750; died at Tetton, near Taunton, England, on July 21, 1815; daughter of Stephen, 1st earl of Ilchester; married Major John Dyke Acland.

Following her marriage, Lady Harriet Acland accompanied her husband, who was under the command of General John Burgoyne when the British army invaded New York in 1777. She was there when Burgoyne was defeated at Stillwater on September 19 and October 7, and when he surrendered all 5,791 of his troops to Major General Horatio Gates at Saratoga on October 17, 1777. Lady Acland recorded her adventures in her memoirs, which helped chronicle this facet of the Revolutionary War.

Acosta, Mercedes de.

See Garbo, Greta for sidebar.

Acosta de Samper, Soledad
(1833–1913)

Colombian journalist and novelist who wrote more than 45 historical romances, including **Los Piratas en Cartagena.** *Name variations: Soledad Samper; (pseudonyms) Bertilda Aldebarán, Olga Aldebarán. Born Soledad Acosta on May 5, 1833, in Bogotá, Colombia; died on March 17, 1913, in Colombia; daughter of Joaquín Acosta (a Colombian scholar and politician) and Caroline Kemble Acosta; married José Maria Samper, in 1855; children: four daughters.*

Born in Bogotá, Colombia, Soledad Acosta was the only child of Joaquín Acosta, a South American with political aspirations, and **Caroline Kemble Acosta**, who was born in England. At the Acosta home in Guaduas, prominent figures from governmental, scientific, and cultural Colombian circles came to spend time with Joaquín, a popular and influential scholar. During these visits, Joaquin's daughter sat close by, soaking up the conversations. Though she was not close with her English-teacher mother, Soledad let her father influence her education and interests; his political stature accounts heavily for her superior education, an uncommon accomplishment for a Colombian woman of the early 19th century. At 12, she traveled to Nova Scotia with her father and was schooled in Halifax for a year. Then, beginning in 1846, she went to Paris for three more years of formal education.

Back in Colombia, she met José Maria Samper, who edited the journal *El Neo-Granadino* (*The New Granadan*). They were married in 1855. Within two years, the Sampers welcomed two daughters. A productive writer and liberal politician, José was of the opinion that women were inferior and best suited for homemaking. Though he recognized exceptions, including his wife and his sister, he remained convinced that females largely had little to offer outside the home. Soledad, however, thought the sexes to be equal, particularly if women were allowed the same educational opportunities as men. Nevertheless, she consciously avoided publicly disagreeing with her husband. This avoidance strongly influenced her writing; she chose subjects that presented no opportunity for comparison with her husband's writing.

Her literary career began in José's journal, with translations from the French of *George

Sand and Alexander Dumas. In 1858, the family left Colombia because the country had grown hostile to their liberal views. First they traveled to Europe, where Soledad began writing fashion, drama, and literary reviews, as well as travel columns, for journals back in Bogotá. They then left Europe for Peru, where José and Soledad coedited *Revista Americana* (American Review). By the time they returned to Colombia in 1863, the family had grown to four daughters, and Soledad had turned her literary sights away from journalism. Drawing on her homeland, but never on her own life, she began to write historical romances. Intensely private, she did not incorporate her personal experiences into her books, but rather the history of the country which she had learned, in part, from her father. Over the next four decades, she produced more than 45 books—in excess of one a year. She also helped found and edit *La Mujer* (*Woman*), the first periodical sustained exclusively by women, which ran from 1878 to 1881. In 1888, José Samper died. Soledad spent the following years writing and traveling to Europe. She died in 1913, two months before her 80th birthday.

Crista Martin, Boston, Massachusetts

Acte (fl. 55–69 CE)

Imperial freedwoman and mistress of the Roman emperor Nero. Pronunciation: ACT-ay. Name variations: Claudia Acte or Akte. Born in Asia Minor and brought to Rome as a slave in the imperial house of Nero or Claudius; flourished between 55 and 69 CE.

Became the mistress of Nero (55); helped to avert the incest of Nero and Agrippina (59); assisted at Nero's funeral (69).

*A*cte repaid his very genuine love with a fidelity which survived his faithlessness.

—Bernard W. Henderson

Among the group of four or five women who loved and influenced the Emperor Nero, the freedwoman Acte stands out as the one whose motives are least suspect and whose faith in a notoriously promiscuous man lasted to his death. The figure of Nero's mother ***Agrippina the Younger** looms large in the first five years of the young emperor's reign, and Acte's entrance into his life coincides portentously with two signal events in Agrippina's career.

Acte was apparently a lowborn native of Greek Asia Minor; she was bought as a slave by the imperial household of Nero or of his great uncle and adoptive father Claudius. Though slavery in Rome certainly meant membership in a class of subservient non-citizens, slaves (especially Greek-speaking slaves) were not necessarily uneducated or unsophisticated by the standards of high society. Indeed, the fact that Acte was procured for the emperor's staff may be an indication of her particular aptitude in noble circles. At some point, she (or her father) was legally manumitted or "freed"; this means that theoretically she could have attained a fairly high social standing in Neronian Rome. However, the 17-year-old Nero fell in love with her in 55, and this precipitated a power struggle in the imperial court.

It was clear to the young ruler's elder advisors, Seneca (the Stoic philosopher) and Burrus, that the affair must be handled delicately: Nero's attraction to his wife ***Octavia** (39–62 CE) was waning, and the force of his potentially destructive libido was already known. As Tacitus, the best ancient commentator on the situation, observed, "It was feared that prohibition of his affair with Acte might result in seductions of noblewomen instead." Added to Seneca's fear, perhaps, was the carefully considered possibility that as a rival to Agrippina for Nero's attention, Acte might help to break that redoubtable woman's influence on policy.

To this end, Seneca had the liaison carefully shielded at its inception, and persuaded one of his friends to put his own name to Nero's gifts to Acte. According to Tacitus, by the time Agrippina found out about the affair, her opposition was fruitless. Deep in the throes of love, Nero had even begun to make noises about marrying Acte, smoothing over the gross social disparity between them by claiming her descent from the royal family of Hellenistic Pergamum (the Attalids), a patent fiction. Agrippina's reaction to this development was violent—she displayed a rage at "having an ex-slave as her rival and a servant girl as her daughter-in-law," says Tacitus. Not surprisingly, this sort of opposition produced only an intensification of Nero's desire for his new love. When Agrippina realized she had lost the battle for her son's obedience, she changed her tactics and went so far as to offer her own bedroom for the couple's "secret, surreptitious, sensual meetings." But the about-face was too obvious, and the disaffection of mother and son became permanent. Nero sealed the change in situation by the murder of Agrippina's son and his own stepbrother Brittanicus, a perceived rival to the throne.

The next report we have of Acte is in 59, in connection with one of Agrippina's most notorious misdeeds. Tacitus relates that she was so desperate to maintain the power she had held at court that she one day appeared before her drunken son "all decked out and ready for incest." Seneca had Acte called in to help avert disaster, and she helped willingly: "She feared for Nero's reputation—and for her own safety." Tacitus tells us that Acte's efforts were a success insofar as she was able to convince Nero that his mother had been boasting about her intimacy with him, and by warning him that the army (a very conservative body) would never tolerate the sacrilege of incest. Soon after, Nero had his mother Agrippina killed.

After a few years, it seems that the emperor's single-minded devotion to Acte faded. The assassination of Agrippina occurred amidst the machinations of the aristocratic and ambitious matron ❧ **Poppaea Sabina** to marry Nero, a goal that would necessitate his divorce of his wife Octavia, and which his mother had opposed. His eventual marriage with Poppaea in 62 CE is indication that if Nero was ever really serious about marrying Acte, he finally decided, or was persuaded, that such a union was not expedient. During Nero's principate, his love life and politics were often inextricably entwined. Yet we have some evidence of Acte's continued love for, and proximity to, Nero through these years: an inscription records her consecration of a temple to the goddess Ceres in Pisa with a prayer that Nero's love for her not be lost and his marriage with Poppaea be prevented. There is also reason to believe that Nero's move away from Acte as an object of marriage had more to do with political and social considerations than any loss of love. Tacitus informs us that M. Salvius Otho—senator, close confidant of Nero, husband of Poppaea Sabina, and himself future emperor—was banished by Nero after Poppaea Sabina cast aspersions on Acte's character.

The last we hear of Acte is her administration of Nero's funeral rites with a few others after his deposal and suicide in 69 CE. The fact that she alone of all Nero's women (his third wife *Messalina deserted him and lived on with high social standing) deigned to honor a cruel, unjust, and probably insane man after his death is testimony not only of the fearlessness of her devotion, but also of the authenticity of their love.

Besides her consecration of the temple to Ceres (which is preserved in a wall of the present-day Cathedral in Pisa), inscriptions found on waterpipes, bricks, and pottery have given us some information about Acte's life away from court. She was apparently very well off, having a good number of slaves and estates in Italy and Sardinia. A late antique rumor that Acte became a Christian is a romantic one with little basis in fact.

SOURCES:

Cassius Dio. *Dio's Roman History.* Translated by Ernest Cary. Vol. 8. MA: Harvard University Press, 1992.

Gaius Suetonius Tranquillus. *The Twelve Caesars.* Translated by Robert Graves; revised with an introduction by Michael Grant. Hammondsworth: Penguin Books, 1957.

Henderson, Bernard W. *The Life and Principate of the Emperor Nero.* London: Methuen, 1903.

Stein, A. *Paulys Real-Encyclopädie der Klassischen Alterumswissenschaft.* Edited by Georg Wissowa. Stuttgart: J.B. Metzlersche Buchhandlung, 1897.

Tacitus. *The Annals of Imperial Rome.* Translated with an introduction by Michael Grant. Hammondsworth: Penguin Books, 1956.

SUGGESTED READING:

Balsdon, J.P.V.D. *Roman Women: Their History and Habits.* London: Bodley Head, 1962 (reprint by Westport, CT: Greenwood Press, 1975).

Bauman, Richard A. *Women and Politics in Ancient Rome.* London and NY: Routledge, 1992.

The Oxford Classical Dictionary. Edited By N.G.L. Hammond and H.H. Scullard. Oxford: The Clarendon Press, 1970.

Peter H. O'Brien, Boston University

❧
*Poppaea Sabina
(d. 65). See
Agrippina the
Younger for
sidebar.*

Acton, Eliza (1799–1859)

English writer. Born in Battle, England, on April 17, 1799; died in Hampstead, on February 13, 1859.

During her early years, Eliza Acton wrote poetry, but she is best remembered as one of the first women to prepare a cookbook. Her popular work, *Modern Cookery for Private Families* (published in 1845), went through numerous editions. In 1857, she brought out her last work, *The English Bread Book.* Acton's cookery books influenced domestic-science expert *Isabella Beeton** (1836–1865).

Ada (c. 380–c. 323 BCE)

Ruler of Caria. Born around 380 BCE in Caria (Southwestern Turkey); died around 323 BCE; daughter of Hecatomnus, satrap of Caria (r. 392–377); sister of Mausolus (r. 377–353), Artemisia (r. 353–351), Idrieus (r. 351–344), and Pixodarus (r. 341–336); married her brother Idrieus; children: none; adopted Alexander the Great and made him her royal heir (334).

Ruled Caria jointly with her brother-husband, Idrieus (351–344), before assuming the throne on his death; her rule contested by her younger brother, Pixodarus, who seems to have seized most of Caria by 341; refusing to surrender her claim to the throne, regained control of Caria with the help of Alexander the

Great, whom she (being childless) adopted and made her royal heir (334); after her death (c. 323), her family died out and Caria, already absorbed into the Macedonian sphere of influence, came to be ruled by the Macedonian, Philoxenus.

Ada's father Hecatomnus was a product of the Carian aristocracy and probably of the family that traditionally laid claim to that region's throne. However, during the 4th century, Caria was a part of the Persian Empire and Hecatomnus' official status was that of a Persian satrap (governor). Hecatomnus had five children (three sons and two daughters), all of whom eventually assumed power in Caria: Mausolus (r. 377–353), *Artemisia II (r. 353–351), Idrieus (r. 351–344), Ada (r. 344–341 and 334–c. 323), and Pixodarus (r. 341–336). (Between 336 and 334, Caria was ruled by an Orontobates—the Persian husband of Pixodarus' daughter, **Ada II**. Pixodarus alone of his siblings fathered a child who survived into adulthood.) Perhaps the most famous member of this dynasty was Mausolus, whose tomb was so spectacular that his name has ever after been associated with funeral monuments (mausoleums).

The regnal dates here noted disguise the fact that for much of Mausolus' reign, Artemisia ruled beside her brother as his wife and queen. Similarly, Idrieus married Ada and the two jointly ruled after both Mausolus and Artemisia had died. In each case, the sister-wife of the established king succeeded her brother-husband and ruled (at least for a time) as Caria's sole ruler. In the case of Artemisia, uncontested legitimacy lasted until her death, after which her brother and sister (Idrieus and Ada respectively) assumed authority in lieu of any surviving children. Ada, however, was not so fortunate, for not long after the death of Idrieus, Caria was beset by a civil war that saw Pixodarus challenge his sister. The specific issues and events behind Pixodarus' insurrection are unknown, but he was not completely successful in unseating Ada. Although he seems to have seized her satrapal authority, she continued to hold an inland citadel (Alinda) and its region until Pixodarus' death in 336. Despite an inability to dispossess his sister, Pixodarus was ambitious to assert some autonomy from the Persians, for—in perhaps his most famous diplomatic gambit—he offered a daughter in marriage to Arrhidaeus (337), the son of Philip II and half-brother of Alexander the Great of Macedonia. Philip (in the process of laying the foundation for an invasion of Asia) was intrigued by Pixodarus' proposal, but negotiations fell through when Alexander intervened in the negotiations by offering himself to Pixodarus for marriage to his daughter in Arrhidaeus' stead.

Exactly what prompted Pixodarus to seek powerful European friends is unknown, but, when one considers the Hecatomnid dynasty's history, it is quite likely that Pixodarus acted more out of a fear of Ada than out of a desire to free himself from Persia. Full brother-sister marriages such as those between Mausolus-Artemisia and Idrieus-Ada are frequently indicative of matriarchal societies, and it is most likely that this was the case in Caria. In such societies, a king almost always exercises effective sovereignty, yet his claim to legitimacy comes not directly from a royal father, but from his sister-spouse, who is in fact the conduit of sovereignty from her father to her husband. As a result, for the sons of kings to aspire to their fathers' powers, they must marry their sisters—and this appears to have been the primary reason why Mausolus married Artemisia, and Idrieus married Ada. Although power seems to have been the primary motive behind the Hecatomnid endogamy (marriage with near relatives), affection almost certainly played a role in the unfolding of the dynasty's history. Artemisia was famous for her love of Mausolus—a love which in part was manifested in the construction of the Mausoleum. Ada, too, might have been so fond of Idrieus that she refused the overtures of Pixodarus upon the death of her husband.

Whether or not Pixodarus attempted to marry the eligible Ada before trying to overthrow her, it is clear that he alone of his brothers married a woman who was not of his family, and, it is also clear that he alone of these three Carian dynasts had difficulty in winning the uncontested loyalty of his people. In addition, when Orontobates was appointed to rule Caria after his father-in-law's demise, he was secured as the region's satrap not by the good will of his Carian subjects, but by the reality of superior Persian strength. Ada's claims to Caria after 336 were thus buoyed by the expectations of a population used to seeing one of its own ruling locally, albeit one willing to rule as a client of the Persians. If Caria was in fact a matriarchy, then Orontobates could not have expected to have replaced Ada in local hearts, for Pixodarus' wife—the mother of Orontobates' spouse—was not a Hecatomnid, and thus would not have been in line to inherit that dynasty's public legacy.

Having outlived Pixodarus, Ada continued to dispute Orontobates' position within Caria. In this, she was helped enormously by Alexander the Great's invasion of Asia. By the summer of 334, Alexander had advanced into Caria, where Orontobates, working in conjunction with other Persian officials, attempted a vigorous defense of Halicarnassus, Caria's most important port. When that defense fell, Orontobates fled his satrapy, allowing it to fall under the Macedonian sphere of influence. Alexander, wishing to be accepted by the Carians as their overlord, yet not wanting to get bogged down in local politics when the vast majority of the Persian Empire still lay beyond his grasp, shrewdly took stock of the existing situation and approached Ada. Detouring to Alinda, Alexander met with her and hailed her as his "Mother," after which he displayed notable filial piety toward her. Even more important, Alexander confirmed Ada as the ruler of Caria on his behalf. In return for having her rights thus ratified, the childless Ada adopted Alexander as her "son."

Thereafter, Ada appears to have ruled her native land as a loyal dependent of Alexander. Though little evidence exists about her reign, it seems clear that Ada continued the Hellenization of Caria, which had begun in earnest earlier in the 4th century. Greek artists and intellectuals seem to have been welcomed at her court where they helped to redirect Carian culture generally to the west. The process of Hellenization was thorough, and Caria, along with the rest of Anatolia, became completely Greek, to remain so for the better part of 1,500 years. Ada died about the time of her "son" Alexander, and with her passed the Hecatomnid house. After Ada, Caria initially passed under the authority of the Macedonian satrap, Philoxenus. Nevertheless, the turmoil that beset the Macedonian world in the wake of Alexander's death swamped Caria as well. Before becoming a peaceful part of the Roman Empire some 300 years after Ada's death, Caria would pass from political hand to hand, as the great Hellenistic dynasties of the eastern Mediterranean fought for the advantage offered by the control of southwestern Anatolia.

William S. Greenwalt, Associate Professor of Classical History, Santa Clara University, Santa Clara, California

Adah

Biblical woman. First wife of Lamech; children: Jabal and Jubal.

Adah

Biblical woman. Name variations: Bashemath. Daughter of Elon the Hittite; first of Esau's three wives.

Adam, Juliette la Messine

(1836–1936)

French feminist, journalist, and political activist, who was the only woman present at the ceremonial signing of the Treaty of Versailles. Name variations: Juliette Lamber Adam, Juliette Lamber, Juliette Lambert; (pseudonyms) La Messine or de la Messine, Paul Vasili, La Grande Française. Born Juliette Lambert in Verberie, Picardy, on October 4, 1836; died in Callian, on August 25, 1936; daughter of a physician and advocate of women's rights; educated at home; married to Alexis de la Messine (a government official) until 1867; married to Edmond Adam (journalist and political activist), from 1868 to 1877; children: (first marriage) one daughter.

Ran a Parisian salon; founded the journal La Nouvelle Review *(1879); known particularly for fighting for women's suffrage and for her work against the German threat to France.*

Selected works: many contributions to journals, beginning with a letter to the editor of Le Siècle *(1856); essays, including* Idées anti-proudhoniennes sur l'amour, la femme et le mariage *(1858);* Blanches de Coucy *(1858); the biography* Garibaldi, sa vie d'après des documents inédits *(1859); novels, including* Grecque *(1879),* Païenne *(1883),* Chrétienne *(1913); plays for her salon; her memoirs.*

Juliette Adam, educated only at home by her father and maternal grandmother, became well known as an intellectual, a writer, and a political activist. Her first marriage was to Alexis de la Messine, when she was in her late teens. They had one daughter and moved to Paris, but the marriage was unhappy.

Adam began spending time with a literary group, including former members of the Order of Saint-Simon Charles Renouvier and Charles Fauverty who founded and edited *La Revue Philosophique.* Her own views were anticlerical and egalitarian, particularly concerned with achieving the vote for women.

Her treatise *Idées anti-proudhoniennes sur l'amour, la femme et le mariage* ("Anti-Proudonist Ideas on Love, Women and Marriage") was a response to the socialist Pierre-Joseph Proudhon's assessment of the social worth of women in *De La Justice Dans la Révolution et dans l'Église* ("On Justice in the Revolution and in the Church," published in 1858). Proudhon had argued that it would be a great mistake to grant women, the inferior helpmates of men, the vote. Adam believed that the differences between men and women were appropriate and complementary, but she ar-

Juliette
Adam

gued for their equality, calling masculine and feminine qualities different but equal. She also argued that masculine and feminine characteristics are not necessarily attached to biological sex. There is variation within the genders, she wrote, so that some women may have masculine characteristics and some men have feminine characteristics. On this basis, and because of the need for moral autonomy, she argued that women should be given the vote, and that contracts between equals should replace traditional marriage. (Adam also convinced the better-known *Jenny d'Hericourt, despite her initial reluctance, to publish her own response to Proudhon.)

Though Adam had begun to publish under the name "Lamber," a variation of her maiden name Lambert, in the hopes of keeping royalties for her work, French law stated that a wife's income belonged to her husband. Alexis succeeded in obtaining the initial royalties for this, his wife's first book, which had been published at her own expense in 1858. Under his own name, he republished her biography of Garibaldi, *Garibaldi, as vie d'après des documents inédits* (originally printed in 1859). Seven years later, in 1866, they separated (divorce was not legal in France), and Alexis would die a year later.

For the last four decades of the 19th century, Adam ran a successful Parisian salon, which included women and attracted many intellectuals and Republicans, those concerned with supporting sovereign democracy in France. Adam's own concerns became more nationalistic in her later life, and she was particularly known for her opposition to German political presence in France. In 1868, she married Edmond Adam, a journalist and political activist. They were both deeply involved in the Republican movement, with Juliette Adam being particularly prominent in efforts to retrieve the region of Alsace-Lorraine from Germany, earning her the name "La Grande Française" (The Great Frenchwoman). She was the only woman present at the ceremonial signing of the Treaty of Versailles.

In 1879, two years after the death of Edmond, her second husband, Adam founded a journal, *La Nouvelle Review* (The New Review), as a forum for Republicanism and continued to edit it until 1899. The journal published papers by Guy de Maupassant, Pierre Loti, Gustave Flaubert, *George Sand, and Frédéric Mistral, as well as a body of work by Adam, who provided the international coverage, with a particular emphasis on the relations between France and Germany.

She also often published elsewhere and wrote in many forms: essays, biography, drama for her salon, and novels. Some of her work was released under the pseudonym "Paul Vasili," which was shared by several authors. Antiquity was a favorite interest of Adam's, and her novel *Grecque* (1879) chronicles the life of an ancient Greek woman. *Païenne* (The Pagan Woman, 1883) is a fictional exchange of passionate letters. The novel *Chrétienne* (The Christian Woman), published in 1913, marks her return to Catholicism. Before her death in 1936, less than

two months shy of her 100th birthday, Juliette Adam also published her memoirs.

Catherine Hundleby, M.A. Philosophy,
University of Guelph, Guelph, Ontario, Canada

Adams, Abigail (1744–1818)

American first lady and early advocate of gender equality in the American revolutionary and early national eras. Born Abigail Smith on November 11, 1744, in the Congregational church parsonage in Weymouth, Massachusetts; died on October 28, 1818, at home in Quincy, Massachusetts; daughter of the Reverend William Smith (1706–1783, pastor) and Elizabeth (Quincy) Smith (1721–1775); no formal schooling, largely self-taught; married John Adams (1735–1826), on October 25, 1764; children: Abigail (Nabby, 1765–1813); John Quincy (b. July 11, 1767–1848); Susanna (Suky, b. December 28, 1768–1770); Charles (b. May 29, 1770–1800); Thomas Boylston (b. September 15, 1772–1832).

Admitted to church membership (1759); married John Adams and took up residence in Braintree (October 25, 1764); suffered through a severe case of whooping cough (1766); managed family and farm during husband's absences to the Continental congresses (1774–77) and during his stay in Europe (1778–84); witnessed Battle of Bunker Hill (June 17, 1775); inoculated against smallpox (July 1776); gave birth to a still-born daughter (July 11, 1777); resided in Europe (1784–88); served as wife of the first vice president (1789–97); served as first lady (1797–1801); reigned as matriarch of the Adams family (1801–18).

In a letter dated March 31, 1776, Abigail Adams admonished her husband, away attending to affairs of the Continental Congress, to "Remember the Ladies, and be more generous and favourable to them than your ancestors." Born into a male-dominated society, this stout-hearted woman spent a lifetime working to overcome the disadvantages suffered by women of her day. Primarily by example, but also through hundreds of letters, she advocated a philosophy that refused to accept female inferiority. Instead, she viewed women and men as partners, each having separate but equal spheres. A woman's sphere was in the home. Adams firmly believed that the wife or mother had a sacred duty to raise the children to a godly and useful life and to be a true and ever-present partner and helpmate to the husband or father whose sphere was outside the home. As she put it, "Nature has assigned to each sex their particular duties and sphere of action." But, given opportunities denied most of her female contemporaries, Abigail

Adams also demonstrated convincingly that an intelligent, widely read, widely traveled, high-spirited woman could live a productive, influential, and rewarding life.

Second child of William Smith and ❦▶ **Elizabeth Quincy Smith,** Abigail's ancestral roots went deep into the rocky soil of colonial Massachusetts. As pastor of the Congregational church in Weymouth, her father occupied a position of influence and respectability among his Puritan neighbors. Upon graduation in 1725 from Harvard, where he developed a love of books, William sought and obtained a pastorate and a wife. On the slender salary afforded ministers and on the proceeds of two small farms, Pastor Smith was able to provide a comfortable but not luxurious living for his growing family. There were always servants to do the menial labor and money enough to purchase books, furniture, and fine china. The Weymouth parsonage provided a comfortable and secure home for Abigail and her siblings.

It was, however, from her mother, Elizabeth Quincy, that Abigail inherited what would pass

Abigail Adams, *by Jane Stuart, copied from the original by Gilbert Stuart.*

as near-aristocratic status in 18th-century New England. For five generations, the Quincys had occupied positions of influence, wealth, and respectability. In 1633, the first Quincy had emigrated from Northamptonshire, England, and would serve as an elected representative of the town of Boston in the first General Court held in Massachusetts. Carrying on this tradition of public service, his grandson, Abigail's maternal grandfather Colonel John Quincy, served for many years as speaker of the House of Representatives.

The Colonel and his wife, **Elizabeth Norton Quincy**, lived in a spacious mansion some four miles from the Smith parsonage. Frequent and often lengthy stays in Mount Wollaston brought the impressionable young Abigail into contact with the Bay Colony elite. The Puritan values of learning, hard work, and public service exhibited at the Quincy family mansion greatly influenced Abigail during her adolescent years. As she would write repeatedly in later years to children and grandchildren, you should "daily grow in virtue and useful Learning, and be a bright Orniment in Church or State."

Pastor Smith and wife Elizabeth were to have four children: ❧▶ **Mary Smith Cranch** (1741–1811), Abigail, William "Billy" (1746–1787), and ❧▶ **Elizabeth "Betsy" Smith** (1750–1815). The three Smith sisters not only grew up together, but remained lifelong friends. Except for the many letters Adams wrote to her husband during periods of separation, the epistles to Mary and Betsy were the most revealing and informative. As for the only son, Billy was a constant disappointment to his family. Unable to gain church membership, denied entrance to Harvard, and unable to stay out of the clutches of the law, Billy would lead a life of dissipation that would be a source of continual comment by his straightlaced sisters. It was rumored that Pastor William Smith's dying breath in 1783 was a plea for Billy's reformation and salvation. William, Jr.'s premature death in the winter of 1787, during Abigail's four-year stay in Europe, was viewed by many, including his sisters, as perhaps the inevitable consequence of a life ill-spent.

Growing up in a family that provided both comfort and security, Adams learned early about the proper role of a woman in 18th-century Massachusetts. The Smith sisters were taught "patient submission" to their duty as wives and mothers. Denied opportunities for formal schooling and relegated to second-class status legally and politically, proper New England women were to provide a secure, loving environ-

❧▶ **Smith, Elizabeth Quincy** (1721–1775)
Mother of Abigail Adams. Name variations: Elizabeth Quincy. Born in 1721; died in 1775; daughter of Colonel John Quincy (speaker of the House of Representatives) and Elizabeth Norton; married Reverend William Smith (1706–1783, a pastor); children: *Mary Smith Cranch (1741–1811); *Abigail Adams (1744–1818); William "Billy" (1746–1787); *Elizabeth "Betsy" Smith (1750–1815).

❧▶ **Cranch, Mary Smith** (1741–1811)
Sister of Abigail Adams. Name variations: Mary Smith. Born Mary Smith in 1741; died in 1811; daughter of the Reverend William Smith (pastor, 1706–1783) and Elizabeth (Quincy) Smith (1721–1775); sister of Abigail Smith Adams (1744–1818); married Richard Cranch, in 1762; children: three.

❧▶ **Smith, Elizabeth "Betsy"** (1750–1815)
Sister of Abigail Adams. Name variations: Betsy Shaw, Betsy Peabody, Betsy Smith. Born in 1750; died in 1815; daughter of the Reverend William Smith (pastor, 1706–1783) and Elizabeth (Quincy) Smith (1721–1775); sister of *Abigail Adams (1744–1818); married Reverend John Shaw (died 1794); married Reverend Stephen Peabody.

ment for their husbands and children. Mothers were to set the example of lives spent to further the careers of husbands. They were to be the family educators. Sons were to be taught the rudiments of an education so as to prepare them for formal schooling. Daughters, on the other hand, were to be taught only enough, and usually not formally, to enable them to assume their proper roles as future wives and mothers. Although Abigail Adams generally accepted the subordinate role assigned to females outside the home, she would become an articulate advocate for equality of the sexes within the home. Thus, she expanded significantly on the female role preached by her grandmother and mother.

Adams had no formal education. Instead, she and her sisters were allowed, and even encouraged, to peruse the several scores of books in Pastor Smith's library. Up to the age of 11, Abigail was largely self-taught, though numerous conversations with her learned father undoubtedly aided in her education. In 1755, Richard Cranch came to live with the Smith family. This 30-year-old Harvard graduate became a home tutor to the Smith sisters. He instilled a love of learning that remained with them throughout their eventful and, in the case of Betsy, somewhat tragic lives. Especially after he married Abigail's sister Mary in 1762, Richard Cranch was to open up for the sisters the world of literature and broad-minded religion. As Abigail was to write in old age: "To our dear and venerable Brother Cranch do I attribute my early taste for letters; and for the nurture and cultivation of those qualities which have since afforded me much pleasure, and satisfaction. He it was who put proper Bookes into my hands, who taught me to love the Poets and to distinguish their Merrits." Her writings (there are over 2,000 extant letters) demonstrate the lack of formal training, for her grammar and spelling leave much to be desired. These same writings, however, show that their author possessed a keen mind capable of insightful comment on political, social, economic, and religious topics.

Adams would adopt the mildly liberal but still orthodox religious views of her parson father. Pastor Smith was one of a growing number of New England Congregational clergy who espoused a mild form of Puritanism. Although distrusting the fervent religious enthusiasm of the Great Awakening, these liberal divines rejected the rigid Doctrines of Election and Original Sin. Instead, they preached a rejection of Calvinism by promoting a limited doctrine of free will. It would be this revised and up-dated Puritanism that 14-year-old Abigail Smith embraced as she was admitted to church membership in 1759. Over the years, her religious views would change very little from those learned at her father's knee and at the Weymouth meeting house. These rational utilitarian views were those adopted and practiced by a large number of America's founding fathers, including John Adams. To her dying day, Abigail Smith Adams believed in and practiced a mild form of Puritanism with its emphasis on virtuous living and total submission to an omnipotent deity.

Since marriage and child-bearing were considered the proper roles for young women, Abigail no doubt thought long and hard about the selection of a lifemate. Her husband must be a partner who did not exploit his legal rights to dominance. Abigail apparently met John Adams when she was 15. Though nine years his junior, she undoubtedly saw much of him through his close friendship with Richard Cranch. By 1761, John Adams was making frequent visits to the Weymouth Parsonage. Though friends with all three sisters, the young attorney was paying particular attention to the middle daughter. By 1762, their friendship had blossomed into a romance, which resulted in Abigail's marriage to the ambitious barrister on October 25, 1764—less than a month before her 20th birthday. John brought middle-class respectability to this union, whereas Abigail brought a socially superior family name, a handsome dowry, and prospects for a considerable inheritance.

Ever after 1764, Abigail's name would be inextricably linked with that of John Adams. Their marriage would be one of "hills" and "valleys." The "hills" were those times of togetherness, raising the children and enjoying each other's company intellectually and physically and later in old age the almost 18 years of a comfortable, secure, leisurely retirement at what John was wont to call his "Peacefield," the Adams mansion in what is today Quincy, Massachusetts. The "valleys" were the frequent separations, the first when John attended both the first and second Continental Congresses in faraway Philadelphia. By 1774, when John first traveled with his cousin Samuel Adams to America's largest city, Abigail had become the household manager of the modest but growing Adams estate. Left with the care of four small children and the Adams farm, Abigail handled domestic duties with such efficiency as to allow her ambitious, and often absent, husband to pursue unimpeded both his legal and political careers. The second major "valley" was the agonizing four-year period (1784–88) when her husband and their oldest son were in Europe. In a fit of despair in 1775 during the first long separation, Adams described herself as a "nun in a cloister." For the most part, however, she endured these periods with stoicism.

It was barely nine months after her wedding that Adams gave birth to a daughter. Named ❧ **Abigail** but always called Nabby, she was not only the oldest of the children, but became one of Abigail's closest and dearest friends. Following Nabby were the births of John Quincy in July 1767, Susanna (Suky) in 1768 (she died in early 1770), Charles in 1770, Thomas Boylston in 1772, and a still-born daughter in July 1777.

During the first decade of marriage, Adams was kept busy caring for her young children and supervising the farm work. Despite a hectic schedule, she kept up a lively correspondence, especially with her husband, but also with her sisters and a growing list of letter writers. Her letters to and from *Mercy Otis Warren** are particularly revealing as to the views they shared on the need for formal female education and on the proper role of women in the newly created

American republic. It was in these missives, written in what she called her "untutored Stile," that Abigail revealed her innermost aspirations. Unlike most of her contemporaries, both male and female, she was well-informed, well-read, and quite willing to express her thoughts forcefully and persuasively.

The epistles to and from John Adams are of special interest. They reveal a marriage that was a true partnership. Abigail had indeed found, within her own home, an equality of the sexes. John readily admitted that his talented wife was superior to him in the many facets of "domestic duties." Out of necessity rather than inclination, Abigail balanced the family budget, oversaw the running of the farm, paid the taxes, invested the surplus funds, and purchased land. Often all of this and more was done without benefit of the counsel of her preoccupied or absent husband. In praising his "Farmeress" wife, John wrote that "our Neighbours will think Affairs more discreetly conducted in my Absence than at any other Time."

Determined, however, to be more than a "domestick," she snatched spare moments to read voraciously. Among her favorites were the poems of Alexander Pope, James Thomson, and John Milton. Also read and relished were the works of William Shakespeare and the novels of Samuel Richardson. Richardson seemed to have had a noticeable and profound influence on Adams' thinking about the role of women. With sensitivity and refinement, this English author wrote numerous novels that depicted the struggles and sufferings of women in the 18th-century. In his seven-volumed, *Sir Charles Grandison,* he created a model husband who allowed his wife equality. Abigail's ideas on marriage seemed to have been gleaned in part from a girlhood reading of this series.

As a young wife and mother, Adams moved frequently during the first years of marriage. Immediately after the wedding, the young couple had moved into the small salt-box home in Braintree that John had inherited from his father. Living as she did just a few feet from John's mother ❧ **Susan Boylston Adams** and a few miles from her parents in Weymouth, Abigail was surrounded and supported by her family. Even after the family moved to Boston in April of 1768, she was still surrounded by family and familiar sights. In her rented home on Brattle Square, she lived near her Uncle Isaac Smith's mansion. In 1771, the growing family moved back to the Adams homestead in Braintree. Soon, however, they returned to Boston, this

time acquiring a large brick house in November of 1772. Finally in the summer of 1773, having purchased his father's homestead from his mother (Susan Adams had remarried in 1766 five years after his father's death), John moved back to Braintree. This rustic village (to be renamed Quincy after Abigail's grandfather) was to be Abigail's permanent home for the rest of her life.

> *I* desire you would Remember the Ladies, and be more generous and favourable to them than your ancestors. . . . If perticuliar care and attention is not paid to the Laidies we are determined to foment a Rebelion, and will not hold ourselves bound by any Laws in which we have no voice, or Representation.
>
> —**Abigail Adams to John Adams, March 31, 1776**

By 1776, John had become "Mr. Congress," serving on some 90 congressional committees and chairing some 25. "Mrs. Delegate," as Adams was sometimes called, was proud of her husband. She found quiet satisfaction in knowing that most of his views on public policy and political theory were her views as well. Intellectually, Abigail and John were true partners. Even when she twitted her husband to "Remember the Ladies" just prior to the writing of the Declaration of Independence, John did not totally disagree. Instead, he wrote her of the impracticality of her "radical" idea. He also agreed with his wife when she mildly admonished him to "Regard us then as Beings placed by providence

❧▶ **Adams, Abigail** (1765–1813)
Daughter of Abigail Adams. Name variations: (nickname) Nabby; Abigail Adams Smith. Born July 14, 1765; died of cancer in 1813; daughter of Abigail Adams (1744–1818) and John Adams (U.S. president); sister of John Quincy Adams (U.S. president); married Colonel William Stephens Smith; children: four.

❧▶ **Adams, Susan Boylston** (d. 1797)
Mother of John Adams. Born Suzanne or Susan Boylston; died on April 21, 1797; came from a family of some small distinction; married Deacon John Adams (a farmer and cordwainer, who died in 1761); remarried, 1766; children: John Adams (1735–1826, second president of the United States); Peter (b. 1737); Elihu (b. 1741).

under your protection and in immitation of the Supreem Being make use of that power only for our happiness."

In 1784, Abigail finally gave in to John's pleas to join him in Europe. She bade farewell to friends and family—two of her sons were to continue their education at Haverhill—and departed in June from Boston in the company of Nabby and two servants. Up to this time, Adams had never traveled more than 50 miles from Braintree. She was now fulfilling a girlhood dream to see the mother country. As she wrote to John a few weeks before departure, her sex and station had not afforded "the least prospect of gratifying that inclination" to see England. In typical fashion, Abigail, after suffering from a ten-day siege of seasickness, took charge of the cleaning of the vessel and of instructing the ship's cook on how to prepare more appetizing meals. These domestic tasks and reading enabled the frequently seasick Abigail to survive what was described as a hard crossing.

After a brief reunion with her oldest son John Quincy in London (Abigail had not seen him since 1779), Abigail, Nabby, and John Quincy set out for Paris. Following a tearful reunion with her husband, Abigail and family moved into a villa in Auteuil, a village near Versailles. Although she described Paris as the "very dirtiest place" she had ever seen and was seemingly shocked by the moral "looseness" everywhere apparent, she came to enjoy her brief stay in the French capital. However, in 1785, John Adams was appointed the first United States minister to the Court of St. James and the family moved to London, which was to be home for almost four years.

Abigail's managerial skills were sorely tested as "Mrs. Ambassador." She found a suitable house on Grosvenor Square and soon was overseeing a household that included eight servants. The Adamses did not entertain lavishly. Instead, Abigail preferred to give small informal dinner parties. As one visitor related after dining with the American minister and his accomplished wife, the "dinner was plain, neat, and good." On the meager allowance and salary afforded American diplomats, Adams was surprisingly able to balance her household budget.

While in England, she took full advantage of the many cultural and historical attractions in and around London. Despite her Puritan upbringing, she found that she enjoyed going to the theater. Her favorite actress was the celebrated Mrs. *Sarah Siddons. She particularly admired

Siddons because she was a woman who happily combined a professional career with that of a home. There were also trips to the famous Roman resort town of Bath and to nearby castles and formal English gardens. With the frequent entertaining, periodic visits to Queen *Charlotte of Mecklenburg-Strelitz's "circle," and serving as John's soundingboard, the London years went by quickly for the increasingly homesick wife. In 1787, as the family prepared to return to America, Abigail and John learned that her uncle, Cotton Tufts, had been successful in purchasing for them the Vassall-Borland House in Braintree. As one of the finest houses in the village, this would become the "Peacefield" of their retirement years.

Arriving home, the Adamses were greeted with adoration and acclaim. There was speculation that John Adams would take a leading role in the establishment of the new government created by the recently ratified Constitution of 1787. As it turned out, he received the second highest number of electoral votes (George Washington was the unanimous choice of every elector and thus was elected president) and thereby became the first vice president. As the first second lady, Adams performed her official duties with the same efficiency shown earlier in managing the Massachusetts farm. She shared her husband's admiration for the president and for *Martha Washington, the first lady. John, in a public way, and Abigail, privately, supported the Washington policy of neutrality in foreign affairs and the Washington-Hamilton financial program. With the impending retirement of George Washington in 1796, John Adams became the heir-apparent. Running against his former good friend and colleague Thomas Jefferson, John was narrowly elected the second president of the United States.

As first lady, Abigail patterned her public demeanor after that of the mild-mannered, amiable, non-controversial Martha. In private, however, she was more outspoken and caustic. In sharing her husband's political conservatism, Abigail became particularly critical of Jefferson, the man she had once characterized as "one of the most estimable characters on earth." Along with his Virginia neighbor and good friend James Madison, Jefferson, although vice president under Adams, had founded the opposition Republican Party. In an earlier time, Abigail had carried on an extensive correspondence with the multitalented Virginian. She appeared to be one of the few women Jefferson related to on an intellectual level. Their correspondence, carried on primarily in the 1780s when Jefferson was in France and the Adamses were in England, showed Abigail to be a keen observer. As vice president, Jefferson became the leader of the party that opposed John's reelection in 1800. To Abigail, as to her husband, Thomas Jefferson had indeed fallen from grace. The controversial election of 1800 resulted in Jefferson becoming president and John Adams being returned to private life. The two founding fathers, formerly close friends and colleagues, remained estranged until 1812, when a mutual friend convinced them to resume a correspondence that would last almost to the day of their death. They both died on July 4, 1826.

Returning at last to her Quincy homestead, Abigail once again took up management of the farm, this time with the active help of her husband. She described John as the "farmer" and herself as the "dairy-woman." Through diligence and frugality, Abigail was able to make ends meet. Indeed, the Adamses were one of the few founding fathers' families to remain debt-free during the years of public service and retirement.

The "Peacefield" years after 1801 were generally happy ones. Always of delicate health, Abigail had survived whooping cough in the spring of 1766, at least one epidemic of dysentery in 1775, a smallpox inoculation in 1776, numerous bouts of "melancholy," and frequent malarial fever attacks. Now in retirement, she was increasingly "sickly," rarely missing a year in which she did not have to spend weeks and even months in bed. Most of these "medical adventures" were probably malaria attacks or arthritis and rheumatism. She endured these disabilities with accustomed fortitude.

In retirement, Adams kept in close touch with her growing family. Nabby had married the personable Colonel William Stephens Smith. There were four children born to this union. However, the Colonel had a hard time providing for his family. Nabby spent years alone with the children as her husband tried to live up to the high expectations of his in-laws. Tragically, Nabby died of cancer in 1813, leaving her three surviving children to the care of Abigail and John.

Adams was extremely proud of her oldest son. Under his mother's care and instruction, John Quincy had displayed a precociousness that augured well for future preferment. Both Abigail and John observed with obvious pride as their oldest son served as minister to Prussia, as U.S. senator from Massachusetts, as chief negotiator drawing up the Treaty of Ghent ending the War of 1812, as U.S. minister to England, and finally as secretary of state under President James Monroe. Thus, Abigail lived long enough to see her son assume the position that had become the traditional stepping-stone to the presidency.

Her second son was to cause great grief. Charles drank himself into an early grave in 1800. His untimely death left his daughter ✤▶ **Susanna Boylston Adams** to be raised by Abigail and John. The third son Thomas Boylston, against the advice of both parents, became a lawyer. With seven children to raise, his life was one of constant struggle and deprivation.

Throughout her adult life, Adams had maintained a close relationship with both of her sisters. Mary's three children were frequent visitors to the Adams home. The almost simultaneous deaths of Mary and Richard Cranch in 1811 would devastate Abigail. Although not destitute, the Cranch family had lived a life of "genteel sufficiency." However, the young sister Betsy lived a life of "genteel poverty." Her first marriage to the amiable but nearly impoverished Reverend John Shaw was followed, after his death in 1794, with her marriage to the equally amiable and equally nearly impoverished Reverend Stephen Peabody.

By October 1818, after years of frequent illnesses and confinements, the increasingly feeble Abigail contracted typhus fever. After a two-week siege, she died on October 28th, just a few weeks before her 74th birthday. Her legacies were determination, achievement, and example. As John Quincy wrote soon after his mother's death, "Her life gave the lie to every libel on her sex that was ever written."

SOURCES:

Akers, Charles W. *Abigail Adams: An American Woman.* Boston: Little, Brown, 1980.

Levin, Phyllis Lee. *Abigail Adams: A Biography.* New York; St. Martin's Press, 1987.

Whitney, Janet. *Abigail Adams.* Boston: Little, Brown, 1947.

Withey, Lynne. *Dearest Friend: A Life of Abigail Adams.* NY: The Free Press, 1981.

SUGGESTED READING:

Adam, James Truslow. *The Adams Family.* Boston: Little, Brown, 1930.

✤▶ Adams, Susanna Boylston

Eldest daughter of Charles Adams and Sarah Smith Adams (1769–1828).

Nagel, Paul C. *The Adams Women: Abigail and Louisa Adams, Their Sisters and Daughters.* NY: University Press, 1987.

———. *Descent from Glory: Four Generations of the John Adams Family.* Oxford: Oxford University Press, 1983.

COLLECTIONS:
Adam Papers, Microfilms, 1639–1889, the Massachusetts Historical Society, Boston, 1954–1959, 609 reels.

Joseph C. Morton, Professor of History, Northeastern Illinois University, Chicago, Illinois

Adams, Abigail (1765–1813).

See Adams, Abigail (1744–1818) for sidebar.

Adams, Abigail Brooks (1808–1889).

See Adams, Clover for sidebar.

Adams, Annette (1877–1956)

American lawyer and jurist. Born on March 12, 1877; died in Sacramento, California, in 1956; graduated from the State Normal School, Chico, California, 1897; graduated from the University of California-Berkeley, 1904, earned J.D., 1912; taught at Alturas High School in California from 1907–10.

When Annette Adams earned her J.D. degree in 1912 from the University of California at Berkeley, she was the only woman in her class. Two years later, after becoming active in the Democratic Party, she was named federal prosecutor for the Northern District of California, the first woman to hold the post. In 1918, she was named special U.S. attorney in San Francisco and was then promoted to assistant attorney general in Washington, D.C. (June 1920), where her position involved overseeing prosecution of violators of prohibition's Volstead Act under A. Mitchell Palmer. Adams returned to private practice in 1921, until Franklin Roosevelt asked her to serve as assistant special counsel under California Supreme Court Judge John Preston to handle prosecution in *U.S.* v. *Standard Oil.* In November 1944, she was elected to a 12-year term as jurist on the California Third District Court of Appeals. Annette Adams was the first woman in that Western state to hold such a high-ranking judicial position.

Adams, Clover (1843–1885)

American Brahmin and spirited wife of Henry Adams. Name variations: Marian Hooper Adams, Marian "Clover" Hooper. Born Marian Hooper in 1843; committed suicide on December 6, 1885, age 42; daughter of Robert William Hooper and Ellen (Sturgis); sister of Ellen "Nella" Hooper Gurney (1838–1887); married

Henry Adams (1838–1918, noted historian and author), in June 27, 1872; no children.

In Rock Creek Cemetery in Washington D.C., there stands a six-foot statue, a memorial to Clover Adams by Augustus Saint-Gaudens, commissioned by her husband. It presents a seated, enigmatic woman in bronze, with one foot resting on a cushion of rock. As her face recedes mysteriously beneath a shroud that blankets her entire body, one arm breaks through the folds, the hand poised beneath her chin. It is not a replica of Clover Adams; rather, it is said to resemble a Buddhistic goddess of compassion.

Clover Adams, the only wife of Henry Adams, killed herself on December 6, 1885, age 42. She is a missing chapter in her husband's famous autobiography, *The Education of Henry Adams.* The autobiography's 20th chapter is dated 1871, the year before he married his wife. The subsequent chapter is entitled "Twenty Years After." Throughout the telling, Clover Adams does not exist.

She was born Marian Hooper in 1843, into two of Boston's oldest families, the Hoopers and the Sturgises. Her mother ✥➤ **Ellen Sturgis Hooper** was an intellectual, a feminist, and a friend of *Margaret Fuller. Wrote Ellen to her younger sister **Susie:** "I read books of women's rights until I feel like the down-trodden women." When Susie suggested that women limit themselves to "women's sphere," Ellen impatiently replied, "I am thankful one woman is in her sphere (as you seem to believe you are) and only wish a visiting committee for the nations may be appointed to ascertain its exact circumference. A woman's sphere seems to me just what she can fill and I don't see why *Charlotte Corday had not as good a right to the dagger as Brutus, although I have no doubt she may have been missed in the kitchen."

Clover's aunt, another of her mother's four sisters, was *Caroline "Carrie" Sturgis Tappan, a Transcendentalist, friend and correspondent of Ralph Waldo Emerson, and builder of Tanglewood. Much of Tappan's unpublished poetry reflects shared feelings with sister Ellen Hooper: "Standing like statues, ever in one place,/ When every man a citizen shall be,/ But I and all my sisters long must wait,/ Enforced obedience our childish fate."

When Clover was five, Ellen Hooper died of tuberculosis. Clover, her brother Ned, and her sister ✥➤ **Nella** were raised by their doctor father. By 1857, 14-year-old Clover was attending

*Elizabeth Agassiz's new school for young ladies on Quincy Street in Cambridge, the forerunner of the college known as Radcliffe. As she grew older, Clover took a keen interest in events. She performed volunteer work for Boston's Sanitary Commission during the Civil War, and at war's end journeyed to Washington to watch Grant and his Army of the Potomac pass in review. She also attended the trial of the conspirators of the assassinated Lincoln. "*Mrs. Surratt only shows her eyes," she wrote, "keeping her fan to her face. All the men except Paine have weak, low faces. Paine is handsome but utterly brutal . . . his great gray eyes rolling about restlessly."

At 28, still unmarried and no suitor in sight, Clover Hooper seemed to be enjoying life. One Sunday morning in March 1871, she wrote to a friend: "I'm so happy sitting on the floor, with my back against the window and hot sun going through me bringing a prophecy of spring and summer and great things. . . . It seems a fitting time for a friendly chat when the gay church bells have rung the good white sheep into their respective fields and left the naughty black ones to enter sunshine and quiet."

One year later, on June 27, 1872, she married historian and teacher Henry Adams, a great grandson of John and *Abigail Adams and grandson of John Quincy and *Louisa Catherine Adams. Soon after Henry met Clover, he had written to a friend: "She knows her own mind uncommon well. Her manners are quiet. She reads German—also Latin—also, I fear, a little Greek." Many were drawn to her. Henry James called the couple the "Clover Adamses," and wrote his brother that she was "a perfect Voltaire in petticoats," with "intellectual grace."

Following their marriage, the couple sailed to London on the S.S. *Siberia*. On board, half of the Brahmins of Boston were either strolling the decks or lying below, suffering from seasickness, as were the Adamses. Clover wrote in her journal: "H. and I lie and gaze at each other. Wonder if life has anything in store for us. Swallow beef tea. Think it may have. Struggle on deck at two. . . . Mr. Parkman confesses he has been happier; Mr. Lowell quotes Shelley." Their recovery brought on another curse, endless days of barbed chats. Historian Francis Parkman's "ideal woman is found in perfection, behind the purdah of Morocco," she wrote. "If I talked much with him, I should take the stump for female suffrage in short time."

The journey was the beginning of a one-year tour of Europe and parts exotic. Clover's faithful

Hooper, Ellen Sturgis (1812–1848)

*American poet. Born on February 17, 1812; died of tuberculosis on November 3 or 4, 1848; daughter of William Sturgis (1782–1863, a sea captain and merchant) and Elizabeth M. Davis (daughter of Judge John Davis); sister of *Caroline Sturgis Tappan; married Robert William Hooper (1810–1885, a doctor); children: *Nella Hooper Gurney (1838–1887); Edward William Hooper (who married Fanny Hudson Chapin, 1844–1881); Marian *Clover Adams (1843–1885). Author of hymns and lyrical verse, including Beauty and Duty.*

Gurney, Nella Hooper (1838–1887)

*American Brahmin. Name variations: Ellen Gurney. Born Ellen Hooper in 1838; died in 1887; daughter of Robert William Hooper and *Ellen Sturgis Hooper (1812–1848); sister of *Clover Adams (1843–1885); married Ephraim Whitman Gurney (1829–1886, a Harvard professor); no children.*

Sunday letters to her father, which document her 13-year marriage, give inklings of the mental fatigue that was taking place. In Egypt, at the beginning of a three-month boat excursion up the Nile, she wrote that Henry was "utterly devoted and tender," and the weather was beautiful, with "the roses and jasmine in bloom." But bad weather came and the confines of their cabin on the small river boat took their toll. "I must confess," she wrote her father, "I hate the process of seeing things which I am hopelessly ignorant of, and am disgusted at my want of curiosity. I like to watch pyramids, etc., from the boat, but excursions for hours in dust and heat have drawbacks to people so painfully wanting in enthusiasm as I am." Harold Dean Cater, in his *Henry Adams and His Friends* (1947), suggests that it was on this trip that her husband witnessed her first "nervous collapse," abetted by extreme depression. On their return to England and London society, Clover's old spirit appeared to revive.

Returning to America in 1873, after another rugged crossing, they bought a four-story house at the corner of Marlborough and Clarendon streets in Boston's Back Bay. The marriage seemed to thrive. Henry taught his own brand of history at Harvard; Clover resumed her classical studies. "My wife flourishes like the nasturtiums," wrote Henry. "She studies Greek. All our young women study Greek. It has become the correct thing to do. As I am innocent of Greek and would have to go back twenty years to pick it up, I have to keep her in check with Mediaeval Latin."

Saint-Gauden's sculpture at grave of Clover Adams.

In 1877, they moved to Washington, D.C., to a home one block from the White House. Immediately, they were welcomed into Washington's upper strata. Clover delighted in reporting to her father that Rutherford B. Hayes and *Lucy Webb Hayes "suffer much from rats in the White House, who run over their bed and nibble the president's toes. 'Uneasy lies the toes that wear a crown.'"

Clover Adams was a woman of strong opinions who was especially irritated by the Washington assumption that wives should remain behind the veil. Intelligent and deeply political, she abhorred the institution of "ladies lunches." "To sit and see 25 women between fifty and seventy years of age eat for two hours is a discipline worthy of the Spanish Inquisition. I said to myself, 'This too shall pass away.'" She soon found that her caustic remarks were being quoted by her father and getting back to her in-laws, Charles Francis Adams and ❧▶ Abigail Brooks Adams, who were not fond of Clover; Abigail called her "a queer woman."

Clover accompanied her husband on his trips for historical research, often helping him. For Henry's continued research into the Jefferson era, they returned to London in May 1879. That autumn, they went to Paris where Clover spent her 36th birthday in the company of Jack and *Isabelle Gardner. The next stop was Spain and the galleries, where they stuffed themselves with "Titian, Tintoretto, Veronese and Velasquez."

But Clover began to tire of helping her husband search for diplomatic documents, and she longed for home. Instead, they returned to London where she studied the social world and the peculiarities of the English political system. She took it upon herself to visit Parliament with a friend and found herself "as if in a harem. We looked down from a lattice screen from the ladies' gallery." She watched Sir Charles Dilke, "who cremated his wife as a sign of wide views, chewing a sheaf of papers and scratching his bald head while the royal family were prayed for," then she went to have tea "in a little room set apart for ladies." She visited Whitehall when the dean of Windsor handed out used shoes and stockings to the poor: "The amount of anthems and prayers and self-glorifications which accompanied the giving away seems to a dissenting mind unnecessary." She listened to the gossip concerning the marriage of George Eliot (*Mary Anne Evans) and American stockbroker John Cross. "She is about 55—J. Cross 38, they say—the comments are likely to be many and hard." It was her opinion, she wrote her father, that "a woman of genius is above criticism." Adams continued to aid her husband in his research: "Before breakfast we get time for writing notes, reading papers, etc., and after that we both go to the British Museum and work till it closes."

Finally stateside once more, they leased a large old house at 1607 H Street in Washington in October of 1880, just across the park from the White House. That same year, Henry anonymously published his notorious political satire *Democracy*. When the city was rife with rumors

❧▶ **Adams, Abigail Brooks** (1808–1889)

American Brahmin. Name variations: Abby. Born in 1808; died in 1889; daughter of Peter Chardon Brooks (a merchant); married Charles Francis Adams (1807–1886, a lawyer, diplomat, and congressional delegate); children: **Louisa** *(1831–1870, who married Charles Kuhn);* John Quincy II *(1833–1894, who married* **Fanny Crowninshield***); Charles Francis, Jr. (1835–1915, who married* **Mary Ogden***); Henry Brooks Adams (1838–1918, a historian, who married* ***Clover Adams***); Arthur (1841–1846);* **Mary** *(1845–1918, who married R.H.P. Quincy); Brooks (1848–1917, a historian, who married* **Evelyn Davis***).*

that the author of the novel was Clover Adams, Henry was delighted. So was Clover Adams, who would sometimes mischievously acknowledge authorship. But when her father heard the rumors, she emphatically denied them. Wrote her biographer Otto Friedrich:

> There is no reason to doubt Clover's denials on the authorship of *Democracy*, but that does not mean that she had no part in it whatsoever. On the contrary, there are numerous descriptions of the Washington landscape that sound remarkably like Clover's letters. . . . "I make it a rule," [Henry] once wrote to [John] Hay, "to strike out ruthlessly in my writings whatever my wife criticises, on the theory that she is the average reader, and that her decisions are, in fact if not in reason, absolute."

The portrait of Madeleine Lee contained in the novel bore a strong resemblance, physically as well as mentally, to Henry's wife. "She read philosophy in the original German," he wrote of his character, "and the more she read, the more she was disheartened that so much culture should lead to nothing." The character of Madeleine Lee is also self-destructive and suicidal. In the novel, Madeleine tells a friend: "We shall grow to be wax images, and our talk will be like the squeaking of toy dolls. We shall all wander round and round the earth and shake hands. No one will have any object in this world, and there will be no other."

Friendship between the Adamses and Henry James thrived. After years as an expatriate, James determined to visit them in Washington when he arrived in America. "That young emigrant has much to learn here," Adams wrote her father.

> He is surprised to find that he can go to the Capitol and listen to debates without taking out a license, as in London. He may in time

get into the "swim" here, but I doubt it. I think the real, live, vulgar, quick-paced world in America will fret him and that he prefers a quiet corner with a pen where he can create men and women who say neat things and have refined tastes and are not nasal or eccentric.

Henry James portrayed Clover as Mrs. Bonnycastle in *Pandora*, while using her also as a model for Marcellus Cockerel in *The Point of View.* It was Cockerel who, in comparing England to America, said that in America there is no "wife-beating class, and there are none of the stultified peasants of whom it takes so many to make a European noble."

The social atmosphere of Washington was beginning to pall. "Her salon was too famous," noted Friedrich, "and too many ambitious people besieged it." Wrote Clover, "No one is admitted now by my majestic Cerberus if they ask if I 'receive' and so only those who walk in without asking come at all."

In 1882, Clover secured a camera and persuaded friends to pose for her: historians George Bancroft and Francis Parkman, six-year-old Jerome Bonaparte, architect Henry Hobson Richardson, Charles Francis Adams, as well as her husband. At a time when photography was difficult, she was good at it. In the last two years of her life, she spent hours in her darkroom. She also went for long walks along the Potomac and reveled in horseback riding in the wilds of Rock Creek Park.

Just before Christmas 1883, the couple decided to build their first house at the corner of H and 16th. They hired H.H. Richardson as the architect and proposed a four-story brick in what she called his "neo-Agnostic style." That same year, *Esther* was published, a novel about a woman's failure to attain religious faith that Henry wrote under the pseudonym Frances Snow Compton. He later acknowledged that his wife served as a model for the character.

Clover Adams suffered from what were then considered mysterious ailments. Even a sore throat, wrote her husband, could bring her to a state where she "could neither speak, nor sleep, nor swallow, nor breathe, nor stand, nor sit, nor lie." In mid-March 1884, when Clover's father was stricken with angina, she hurried to his bedside and nursed him until he died on April 13th. After his death, Clover plunged into depression and enormous guilt. She was, "sorry for every reckless word or act, wholly forgotten by all save her," wrote her sister Nella. Clover said repeatedly to her visiting sister, "I'm not

real. Oh, make me real." When friends came to visit, she would "lapse into silence," wrote Friedrich, "then rub her hand back and forth across her forehead as though trying to remember, or to forget, or to understand, something beyond her control."

While the slow process of building their house continued, she seemed no longer interested. Henry's brother Charles visited and later reported, "She was engaged the whole time in introspection and self-accusation." Clover wrote to her sister, "If I had one single point of character or goodness I would stand on that and grow back to life." In the same letter, she praised Henry as "more patient and loving than words can express."

When Henry Adams ascended the stairs on a bleak December day in 1885 to ask his wife if she was willing to receive visitors, he found her lying on a rug before the fire; she had fallen out of her chair. Lying next to her was a bottle of potassium cyanide, one of the chemicals used in her darkroom. Later scholars would find a notation, handwritten, inside the back cover of her Bible:

I slept and dreamed that life was Beauty, — I woke, and found that life was Duty. . . .

This poem, written by her mother, had been printed in the inaugural issue of *The Dial*.

SOURCES:
Friedrich, Otto. *Clover.* NY: Simon and Schuster, 1979.
Shepherd, Jack. *The Adams Chronicles.* Boston, MA: Little, Brown, 1975.

SUGGESTED READING:
Chalfant, Edward. *Better in Darkness: A Biography of Henry Adams, His Second Life, 1862–1891.* Archon, 1993.

COLLECTIONS:
The Adams Papers in the Massachusetts Historical Society, at 1154 Boylston Street in Boston.

RELATED MEDIA:
"The Adams Chronicles" (13 hour-long dramatizations), produced by PBS, directed by Fred Coe, 1976.

Adams, Diana (1927–1993)

*American ballerina. Born in Staunton, Virginia, in 1927; died in San Andreas, California, in January 1993; studied with her stepmother, **Emily Hadley Adams**, in Memphis, Tennessee; studied at the Ballet Arts School in New York City with Agnes de Mille and Edward Caton; lived in Arnold, California.*

A leading ballerina with both the New York City Ballet and the American Ballet Theater (ABT), Diana Adams was one of George Balanchine's favorite dancers. She performed in many of his major ballets in the 1950s and is especially remembered for the difficult *pas de deux* danced with Arthur Mitchell in the Balanchine-Stravinsky *Agon* in 1957. "Diana's nervous intensity made the whole *pas de deux* work," said Mitchell, "because it's not so much the difficulty of the steps or how flexible you are, it's the precariousness."

A year after making her 1943 debut in the Rodgers and Hammerstein musical *Oklahoma!*, which was choreographed by her former teacher *Agnes de Mille, Adams joined the ABT. She was seen in the title role of David Lichine's *Helen of Troy* and as the Queen of the Wilis in *Giselle*. In 1948, she created the role of the mother in de Mille's *Fall River Legend*. Two years later, Adams joined the New York City Ballet, where she performed until her retirement in 1963. She also appeared in the Danny Kaye film *Knock on Wood* (1954) and Gene Kelly's *Invitation to the Dance* (1956). Following her retirement, Adams taught at the School of American Ballet in New York.

Adams, Evangeline Smith
(1873–1932)

American astrologer who originated "Adams' Philosophy." Born in Jersey City, New Jersey, in 1873; died in 1932; educated at a private school in Andover, Massachusetts.

Evangeline Adams originated "Adams' Philosophy," a synthesis of the occult theories of the Orient and the West. After building a reputation as a successful astrologer in the United States, she attempted to see astrology legalized in Great Britain. There, she was well known as a radio broadcaster and newspaper columnist on the subject of astrology, credited with having correctly forecast the death date of King Edward VII.

Adams, Hannah (1755–1831)

First professional female writer in America. Born in Medfield, Massachusetts, on October 2, 1755; died in Brookline, Massachusetts, on November 15, 1831 (some sources cite 1832); daughter of Eleanor (Clark) Adams and Thomas Adams (a bibliophile); never married; no children.

Hannah Adams was the first American woman to make writing a profession. Interested in political and religious history, she was determined to present the history of the world's various religions. Consequently, she compiled *Views of Reli-*

gious Opinions* (1784; title changed to *Dictionary of Religions* in 4th ed.), which was broken down into the following three parts: (1) An Alphabetical Compendium of the Denominations among the Christians; (2) A Brief Account of Paganism, Mohammedanism, Judaism, and Deism; and (3) An Account of the Religion of the Different Nations of the World. Adams also wrote *History of New England* (1799), *Evidences of Christianity* (1801), and *History of the Jews* (1812). Her *Memoir* was published a year after her death.

Hannah Adams

Adams, Harriet Chalmers (1875–1937)

American explorer and lecturer. Born in Stockton, California, on October 22, 1875; died in Nice, France, on July 17, 1937.

While traveling through Mexico, Harriet Chalmers Adams became a student of Latin American affairs in 1900, after which she made a three-year journey through Central and South America. She traveled 40,000 miles, visiting every country, and reaching many points previously unknown to any white woman. After lecturing in the United States from 1906 to 1908, she crossed Haiti on horseback in 1910. Adams then traveled through the Philippines, and from Siberia to Sumatra, studying ancient races.

In 1916, Adams was a war correspondent at the French front, and she returned to the United States in 1917 to continue her lectures. In 1925, she organized, and became the first president of, the Society of Women Geographers. Adams wrote regularly for *National Geographic* and was a fellow and member of various geographical and scientific associations throughout the world.

Adams, Harriet Stratemeyer
(c. 1893–1982)

American writer and 50-year manager of the Stratemeyer Syndicate, which was responsible for many book series, including Nancy Drew, Hardy Boys, *and*

Harriet Stratemeyer Adams

the Bobbsey Twins. *Name variations: (pseudonyms) Victor Appleton II, May Hollis Barton, Franklin W. Dixon, Laura Lee Hope, Carolyn Keene. Born on October 22, around 1893, in Newark, New Jersey; died on March 27, 1982, in Pottersville, New Jersey; daughter of Edward L. (an author) and Magdalene Stratemeyer; graduate of Wellesley College, 1914; married Russell Vroom Adams, in 1915; children: Russell Jr. (died in World War II), Patricia Adams Harr, Camilla Adams McClave, Edward Stratemeyer Adams.*

Harriet Stratemeyer Adams described her father Edward as a man who could tell an original story at a moment's notice. Indeed, he took this talent to the limit, changing the history of popular children's literature in America. At the time of his death, the Stratemeyer Syndicate, which he founded in 1906, had produced over 700 books for children and young adults, including the popular Tom Swift and Bobbsey Twins series. His talent and business acumen passed to his daughter Harriet, who, with her sister **Edna**, took over

the reigns of the Syndicate after her father's death. For 52 years, like her father before her, Harriet created hundreds of chapter-by-chapter book outlines for various series books, which were completed by a stable of writers, most anonymous, many former journalists. She also authored an estimated 200 books under various pseudonyms: Carolyn Keene for the Nancy Drew series; Franklin W. Dixon for the Hardy Boys; Victor W. Appleton II for Tom Swift, Jr.; and Laura Lee Hope for The Bobbsey Twins.

In 1910, Adams left her girlhood home in Newark, New Jersey, to attend Wellesley College, where she majored in English and also took courses in religion, music, science, and archaeology. Interested in a writing career, she submitted articles to *The Boston Globe* while in college. After graduation, she set her sights on a job in the Syndicate, but her father was against women working outside the home. Edward compromised, however, by allowing her to edit manuscripts and galley proofs as long as she worked at home and did not set foot in the office.

In 1915, Harriet married Russell Vroom Adams, an investment banker. Following her marriage, she could no longer work even at home because her father decided she should focus all her attention on her marriage. For the next 15 years, Adams raised her four children, while contenting herself with writing pieces for Sunday school and women's clubs. This routine changed greatly when her father died in 1930, and she decided to take over management of the Syndicate with the help of her sister Edna. After moving the business closer to her residence in New Jersey, she continued the incredible pace her father had established. With Edna handling day-to-day operations, Adams dealt with publishers and plotted new titles, while doing considerable writing herself, including many of the Nancy Drew and Dana Girls books. (Twenty-three of the first thirty Nancy Drew books, considered classics in the genre, were written by *Mildred Wirt Benson.) In 1935, 14 series—in addition to Nancy Drew and the Dana Girls—were ongoing, including the Bobbsey Twins, Don Sturdy, Bomba the Jungle Boy, Tom Swift, and Honey Bunch. During the early years of her tenure, Adams introduced the Dana Girls and Kay Tracey as two major new series.

In 1942, Edna married and became an inactive partner, leaving Adams to supervise alone until 1961, when Andrew Svenson (who had been hired as an editor and writer in 1948), became a partner. The Syndicate flourished; only the Depression and paper shortages during World War II caused a cutback on the number of books published. The year 1947 ushered in the beginning of a new growth period, and in the '60s the Syndicate began to revise three of its most popular series: The Bobbsey Twins, Nancy Drew, and the Hardy Boys.

In much the same manner as her father, Adams created her books by first composing an outline, linking plot and subplot. The story was then dictated into a recording machine and transcribed by secretaries. Adams typically completed a mystery in two months, maintaining a nine-to-five writing schedule, with a daily goal of dictating three chapters or 7,500 words. Though she and her staff edited the final manuscripts, most of her stories contain exaggerated versions of incidents from her own childhood and teenage years, as well as her later adventures traveling for pleasure and research. Adams made extensive trips through the United States, Canada, Mexico, South America, Europe, Hawaii, the Orient, and Africa, and set many of her stories in the foreign locales she had visited.

The "Stratemeyer formula"—mystery and action, complemented by a smattering of educational material—has not been without its critics. Objections to stories have focused on the "assembly line method of mass production," and their "escapist, wooden, and regressive" nature. The immense popularity of the books through the years has had a mellowing effect on critics, however, and more recently the books have been seen as a way to interest young people in reading fiction, with the hope that this will lead them to higher literary pursuits.

At the time of Adams' death from a heart attack in 1982, four series were still in progress: the Bobbsey Twins, the Hardy Boys, Nancy Drew, and Tom Swift, Jr., all with the most recent titles published in paperback. In the 1980s, two other series were reissued; Kay Tracey and Linda Craig. The appeal of Stratemeyer titles is undeniable, evidenced by the ongoing publication of many of the series books.

SOURCES:

Billman, Carol. *The Secret of the Stratemeyer Syndicate.* NY: Ungar, 1986.

Johnson, Deidre, ed. *Stratemeyer Pseudonyms and Series Books: An Annotated Checklist of Stratemeyer and Stratemeyer Syndicate Publication.* Westport, CT: Greenwood Press, 1982.

Barbara Morgan, Melrose, Massachusetts

Adams, Léonie Fuller (1899–1988)

American poet and educator. Name variations: Leonie. Born in Brooklyn, New York, on December 9, 1899; *died of heart disease in New Milford, Connecticut, on June 27, 1988; married William Troy, in 1933.*

Best known for her lyric poetry, Léonie Adams has penned collections that include *Those Not Elect* (1925), *High Falcon* (1929), and *This Measure* (1933). She won several awards, including the *Harriet Monroe Poetry Award, the Shelley Memorial Award, and the Bollingen Prize. Adams taught and lectured at various colleges, including Sarah Lawrence, Bennington, and Columbia University, and was poetry consultant to the Library of Congress (1948–49).

Adams, Louisa Catherine

(1775–1852)

Wife and political partner of John Quincy Adams who wrote about crucial national and diplomatic events of early republican America, everyday life in the late 18th and early 19th centuries, and her 50-year alliance with America's preeminent ruling family. Name variations: Louisa or Catherine. Born Louisa Catherine Johnson on February 12, 1775, in London, England; died in Washington, D.C., on May 15, 1852; daughter of Joshua Johnson (an American merchant) and Catherine (Nuth or Young; an Englishwoman) Johnson; had private tutors or attended various private schools in France and England; married John Quincy Adams, on July 26, 1797; children: George Washington (1801–1828), John II (1803–1833); Charles Francis (b. 1807); Louisa Catherine Adams II (1811–1812).

Family moved to France (1778); moved back to England (1782); Louisa met John Quincy Adams (1795); joined him on diplomatic mission in Prussia (1797–1801); family sailed to America (1801); became a senator's wife (1803–08); joined husband in diplomatic mission to Russia (1808–15); journeyed alone from St. Petersburg to Paris (1815); went on diplomatic mission to England (1815–17); returned to America as wife to secretary of state and to campaign for husband's presidency (1817–24); organized the Jackson Ball (1824); served as first lady (1824–28), then retired to Quincy, Massachusetts; returned to Washington as U.S. representative's wife (1830); death of John Quincy Adams (1848).

On November 12, 1808, Louisa Catherine Johnson Adams, wife of the newly arrived American plenipotentiary to Russia, was presented in a formal ceremony to Alexander I and *Elizabeth of Baden, the emperor and empress of All Russias. Though beset with a "fluttering pulse," Louisa Adams performed the ritual well and enjoyed "fifteen minutes of affable chat" with the royal couple. After they withdrew, Adams, in all her heavy and elaborate court dress, was conducted to a more informal meeting with the empress mother, *Sophia Dorothea of Wurttemberg. Thinking that the lady before her was an American provincial, Sophia asked Louisa what she thought of St. Petersburg. Diplomatically, Adams extolled the charms of the city, but mentioned that she had also seen London, Paris, Berlin, and Dresden. "*A mon Dieu!*" exclaimed the royal lady, "*Vous avez tout vue!* (You saw everything!)" "She appeared to regret it very much," wrote Adams later, "the Savage had been expected!"

Louisa Catherine Adams was one of the most well traveled and, in the opinion of some, most sophisticated American women of her time. Born in London, England, on February 12, 1775, to Maryland merchant Joshua Johnson and English-woman **Catherine Nuth Johnson**, Louisa was the second daughter in a family that would consist of eight girls and one boy. Though her mother's origins remain uncertain, Louisa's paternal uncle was the governor of Maryland and her father a patriotic American. With the Revolution only a few months away, American politics shaped Louisa Catherine Johnson's life from its start.

Louisa Catherine Adams, *oil by Charles Bird King.*

Joshua Johnson moved his family to Nantes, France, in 1778, when London proved a difficult place for an American businessman. Louisa began school there, mastering the French language, a skill that would stand her in excellent stead in her future career as a diplomat's wife. The Johnsons moved back to England in 1783 and set up a fashionable London household. As befitted the daughters of a wealthy merchant, Louisa and her sisters received extensive training in languages, fancy work, and music, the latter accomplishment of special interest to the young Louisa, whose early talent blossomed into a virtuosity commented upon by observers throughout her life.

The Johnson home also became a meeting place for Americans in England and diplomats from all countries. John and *Abigail Adams dined there when John served as minister from America, and in 1795, their son, 29-year-old John Quincy, on a diplomatic mission from The Hague, also came to dinner at the Johnsons'. He was quickly drawn into their lively household, attracted by the delightful Johnson girls, who sang and played upon the pianoforte. The family assumed his interest lay in the eldest daughter, Nancy Johnson, but three months after his arrival, John Quincy bestowed "decidedly Publick" attentions on 20-year-old Louisa Catherine.

Their courtship—romantic, stormy, diffident—lasted two years, including a long separation when John Quincy returned to The Hague. He took this opportunity to prepare Louisa to be his wife by instructing her on the "republican" way of thinking, with its stress on duty and sacrifice: "every interest and feeling inconsistent with it must disappear." For the most part, Louisa accepted these dictates; when she resisted, John Quincy reproved her for such a show of "spirit."

On July 26, 1797, the pair married at Tower Hill in London, and then prepared to embark for Berlin to begin John Quincy's assignment as plenipotentiary to the Prussian Court. In the meantime, having seen at least one of their daughters safely married, the Johnson family sailed for America. Within days of their departure, Joshua Johnson's business collapsed, an event precipitated by his mismanagement and extravagance. While still on their honeymoon, the young couple fended off creditors, John Quincy remaining "rigourous, inflexible"; he paid "not a shilling." Louisa Catherine never got over the shame of her father's bankruptcy and the appearance of having "palmed herself off" on an unsuspecting John Quincy. As she viewed it, this tragedy blighted her marriage and turned "every sweet thing into gall." Beginning a pattern of emotional distress followed by physical collapse that would continue throughout her life, she became depressed and then ill.

Shortly after this calamity, Louisa and John Quincy, along with his brother, Thomas Boylston Adams, sailed for Prussia. Suffering from the effects of her first pregnancy, Louisa miscarried the child on shore, thus beginning a death-defying reproductive history that would include 15 pregnancies—ten miscarriages, four live births, and one stillbirth. Once recovered, however, Louisa proved an ideal diplomatic companion. Fluent in French, charming, with a zest for "occasions," she became a great favorite in the highly cultivated court, compensating for her quiet, bookish husband.

When the Adamses finally sailed for America in 1801, they had a solid treaty with Prussia in hand and had established a firm and favorable diplomatic position for the United States at the court. In addition, after four miscarriages, Louisa had given birth to her first child, George Washington Adams. But even in possession of the heir to the Adams' dynasty, Louisa felt uncertain and unwelcome when she met her husband's family in Quincy, Massachusetts. To her, the rural life of 18th-century America was completely alien: "Had I stepped into Noah's Ark I do not think I could have been more utterly astonished. . . . Even the church, its forms, the snuffling through the nose, the Singers, the dressing and the dinner hour were all novelties to me." In the face of her mother-in-law Abigail, a woman Louisa called "the equal of every occasion in life," Louisa felt herself deemed "a *fine* Lady" who would "not suit." Only old John Adams made her feel wanted: he "took a fancy to *me* and he was the only one." Their relationship developed over the years, and their correspondence after Abigail's death is one of the liveliest and most affectionate in the Adams' family papers.

The young Adams family moved to Boston, so that John Quincy could begin his law practice. Louisa became a Boston hostess and enjoyed being the mistress of her own house. Another son, John Adams II, was born in 1803, adding to her contentment. Law bored John Quincy, however, and seizing the only respectable outlet open to an Adams he ran for and was elected senator in 1803. For five years, Louisa shuttled between her husband in Washington and her children in Quincy. She suffered a stillbirth alone in Washington and, with John Quincy present, the birth of another son,

Charles Francis, in Boston in 1807. The physical and social crudeness of Washington and its politics alternately disgusted, amused, and intrigued Louisa. She immediately disliked President Thomas Jefferson, granting him only "a kind of sneaking greatness," and disapproved of the increasing democratization of the young republic.

The summer of 1809 proved, in both Louisa's and John Quincy's hindsight, to be a crucial turning point in their lives and careers. President James Madison appointed John Quincy Adams plenipotentiary to Russia. John Quincy considered it "the most important work of any I have ever . . . been engaged in." For Louisa, it marked a disaster in her life and the lives of her children. Apparently without consulting her, John Quincy decided that only little Charles Francis should go to Russia with them and that his two older sons should remain in America for the duration of his appointment, which he expected would be about three years. Recalling the event in her autobiography *Adventures of a Nobody*, Louisa claimed that she fought both John Quincy and Abigail for her sons, but "not a soul entered into my feelings and all laughed to scorn my suffering, crying out that it was affectation." They even prevented Louisa from pleading her case before John Adams, fearing the family patriarch would side with her. So Louisa Catherine set sail for St. Petersburg accompanied by her sister **Kitty** and her youngest son, whom she later described as "the only one of my children I never deserted." The eventual six-year separation of young George Washington and John from their parents, insisted Louisa, caused their troublesome adolescences and early deaths.

Heartbreak aside, Louisa Catherine once again shone at court, winning special regard from the emperor and empress and obtaining crucial access to the inner circles of power. As John Quincy became more absorbed with his books, Louisa Catherine assumed increasing responsibility for attending the social functions that were the lifeblood of an aristocratic court. The two were overjoyed when Louisa Catherine gave birth to a daughter, Louisa Catherine II, in 1811. However, the child lived only a year and her death drove her parents into deep and separate depressions. John Quincy retreated into his study and Louisa wrote.

In 1815, John Quincy was called to Ghent to negotiate the peace treaty that ended the war of 1812. While there, he received word of his new post in London, the "plum" assignment of the corps, and sent Louisa instructions to join him in Paris. Galvanized by quitting the place that had brought her so much unhappiness, on her 40th birthday Louisa packed up the house, sold the furniture and, accompanied only by her maid, seven-year-old Charles Francis, and a couple of rascally servants, she set out to cross the frozen Russian battlefields in an historic 40-day carriage ride. Along the way, she dealt with thieves, retreating armies, and angry mobs with a strength and bravado that amazed her family.

Reunited with all their children in England, Louisa Catherine and John Quincy spent two idyllic years before returning to America so that John Quincy could take up the post as secretary of state under President Monroe. Louisa and John knew this post to be the stepping-stone to the nation's highest office, but, acknowledging her husband's reluctance and awkwardness in campaign and social situations, Louisa assumed almost the entire burden of "smiling for the Presidency." Using her hard-won political savvy, she turned social calls—"The torments of my life"—into a science, in one morning delivering eleven such calls, covering six square miles. John Quincy took her job as seriously as his own. An amused Louisa wrote his father that he made out her calling cards every morning with all the intensity with which he pored over his state papers. Louisa became famous for her Tuesday evening soirees, and her crowning achievement was the ball she gave to celebrate Andrew Jackson's victory at the Battle of New Orleans, an event unparalleled in Washington's social annals for many years.

However, no single candidate received a majority vote in the electoral college. The election of 1824 was therefore thrown to the House of Representatives, which would select a president from the top three candidates: Jackson, Adams, and William H. Crawford of Georgia. Although the celebrated Jackson had received the most popular votes and the most electoral votes, the lower house elected the second highest electoral vote getter as president. John Quincy Adams was, therefore, constitutionally and legally elected the sixth president of the republic, but under a cloud.

After the election, Louisa's job as "campaign manager" ended, leaving her gloomy and depressed. Her White House years were anticlimactic, and she increasingly grew tired of the "Bull bait" of politics. After John Quincy's ignominious defeat in 1828 to Andrew Jackson, she eagerly prepared to quit Washington for the peace of Quincy. But she was not to have a quiet retirement. The Adams' eldest son George Washington died (a possible suicide) on his way to escort his parents from the White House. Five years later, John Adams II also died, after a long, wrenching battle with alcoholism. Fortunately, Charles Francis, while not exhibiting the Adams scintillation, was turning out to be a solid, if stolid, citizen.

On top of these two losses, John Quincy decided to return to Washington as a congressional delegate to serve in the House of Representatives in 1830. Outraged by his "grasping ambition" and "insatiable passion for fame," Louisa reminded John Quincy of the price they had both paid for his political involvement. She stood by his side, however, as he became the only ex-president ever to return to elected office. She lauded his stand against the Gag Rule in Congress and saw him achieve personal popularity. Though sorrows marred her later years, her intellectual life flourished. Throughout her life, she had written poems, plays, and journals. In 1825 and 1840, she wrote two memoirs, *Record of My Life* and *The Adventures of a Nobody,* that provide fascinating portraits of European diplomatic life and the Washington political scene, as well as insight into the thoughts of an intelligent, sensitive woman of the late 18th and early 19th centuries. She sustained a wide correspondence on a variety of subjects, from musings on women's place in the polity with her daughter-in-law ❧ Abigail Brooks Adams (1808–1889) to discussions of abolition with *Angelina E. Grimke (1805–1879).

In 1848, John Quincy had a stroke while at his desk in the House chamber and died several days later. The following year, Louisa also suffered a stroke but survived three more years, honored and respected by the Washington community. Apparently her last days were tranquil ones, and she died peacefully in her Washington, D.C., home. On the day of her funeral in 1852, both houses of Congress adjourned in her memory, making her the first woman ever to receive that honor.

SOURCES:
The Adams Papers. Published by the Adams Manuscript Trust through the Massachusetts Historical Society, Boston, MA, Reels 264, 265.

Butterfield, Lyman H. "Tending A Dragon-Killer: Notes for the Biographer of Mrs. John Quincy Adams," in *Proceedings of the Massachusetts Historical Society.* Vol. 118, April 1974, pp. 165–178.

Challinor, Joan Ridder. "Louisa Catherine Johnson Adams and the Price of Ambition." Ph.D. diss., American University, 1982.

Corbett, Katharine T. "Louisa Catherine Adams: The Anguished 'Adventures of a Nobody,'" in *Women's Being, Women's Place: Female Identity and Voca-*

tion in American History. Edited by Mary Kelley. Boston: G.K. Hall, 1979.

Nagel, Paul C. *The Adams Women: Abigail and Louisa Adams, their Sisters and Daughters.* NY: Oxford University Press, 1987.

Shepherd, Jack. *Cannibals of the Heart: A Personal Biography of Louisa Catherine and John Quincy Adams.* NY: McGraw-Hill, 1980.

SUGGESTED READING:
Bobbe, Dorothie. *Mr. and Mrs. John Quincy Adams: An Adventure in Patriotism.* NY: Minton, Balch, 1930.

Challinor, Joan Ridder. "'A Quarter-Taint of Maryland Blood': An Inquiry into the Anglo-Maryland Background of Mrs. John Quincy Adams," in *Maryland Historical Magazine.* Winter 1985, 409–419.

———. "The Mis-Education of Louisa Catherine Johnson Adams," in *Proceedings of the Massachusetts Historical Society.* Vol. 98, 1987, pp. 21–48.

Nagel, Paul C. *Descent From Glory: Four Generations of the John Adams Family.* NY: Oxford University Press, 1983.

Shepherd, Jack. *The Adams Chronicles: Four Generations of Greatness.* Boston: Little, Brown, 1975.

COLLECTIONS:
The Adams Papers. Published by the Adams Manuscript Trust through the Massachusetts Historical Society, Boston, MA.

Catherine A. Allgor, Assistant Professor of History, Simmons College, Boston, Massachusetts

Adams, Marion Hooper (1843–1885).

See Adams, Clover.

Adams, Mary Grace (1898–1984)

English broadcasting pioneer. Born Mary Grace Campin in England in 1898; died in 1984; daughter of Edward Bloxham Campin; educated at Godolphin School, Salisbury, and University College, Cardiff, first class, botany, 1921; married Samuel Vyvyan Adams, in 1925.

Mary Grace Adams was the first woman television producer for the BBC (1936–39). From 1939 to 1941, she was employed as director of Home Intelligence at the Ministry of Information. Adams worked for the North American Service Broadcasting (1942–45); was head of television talk shows, BBC (1948–54); and wrote for *Punch.* In 1953, she was awarded an Order of the British Empire (O.B.E.).

Adams, Maude (1872–1953)

American actress, lighting designer, and professor of drama, best known for her contributions to her most famous role, as Peter Pan. Born Maude Ewing Adams Kiskadden on November 11, 1872, in Salt Lake City, Utah; died on July 17, 1953, in Tannersville, New York;

Adams, Abigail Brooks (1808–1889). See Adams, Clover for sidebar.

Maude
Adams

daughter of Asenath Ann Adams Kiskadden (Annie Adams, an actress) and James Henry Kiskadden (a businessman); never married; lived with Louise Boynton.

Carried onstage by her mother as a young child; appeared frequently with her as a child and eventually took her mother's maiden name; left school after her father's death (September 22, 1883); after appearing in many roles in San Francisco and other theaters in the Southwest, eventually appeared as the maid in The Paymaster *in New York (1888); played Nell in* Last Paradise, *staged by Charles Frohman's stock company (1891); Frohman made her John Drew's leading lady (October 1892); British playwright James Barrie wrote* Little Minister *for her (1897); as head of her own company, continued to star in Barrie's plays created for her, including* Quality Street, *(1901),* Peter Pan *(1905),* What Every Woman Knows *(1908),* The Legend of Leonora *(1914), and* A Kiss for Cinderella *(1916); performed* Peter Pan *more than 1,500 times, the pinnacle of her career; fell dangerously ill during the 1918 flu epidemic while playing* A Kiss for Cinderella *and retired from the stage for 13 years; at age 49, began another career as a lighting designer and went to work with General Electric, developing an incandescent bulb widely used in color film (1921); returned to theater playing Portia to Otis Skinner's Shylock in a national tour of* The Merchant of Venice *(1934); for the next few years, participated in a series of six radio plays; became a professor of drama at Stephens College in Columbia, Missouri (1937–46).*

Maude Adams was nine months old when she first appeared on stage with her mother in a play entitled *The Lost Child.* Born Maude Kiskadden in Salt Lake City, Utah, on November 11, 1872, she was the daughter of James Henry Kiskadden, a businessman of Scottish descent. Her mother, Asenath Ann Adams Kiskadden, had been raised a Mormon, the child of parents who joined Brigham Young on his way to Utah in 1847. Under the name **Annie Adams**, she became an actor in Young's theatrical company. Before Maude, Annie gave birth to twin boys who lived only briefly. Maude was her only child to survive.

Because her husband was a poor provider, Annie Adams resumed acting shortly after Maude was born. When Maude was two, the family moved to Virginia City, Nevada, and then on to San Francisco in 1875, where the name of "Little Maude" appeared on programs and handbills. On October 17, 1877, Maude was just shy of her fifth birthday when she became a salaried actress for her role in *Fritz,* a popular

melodrama of the time. According to impresario David Belasco, "She could act and grasp the meaning of a part long before she could read," though her frequent appearances did not leave much time for an ordinary childhood. She eventually adopted her mother's maiden name of Adams, as her stage name.

For four years, Maude lived with her grandmother in Salt Lake City and studied at the Collegiate Institute. After the sudden death of her father, on September 22, 1883, when she was 11, she decided to quit school to join her mother in a traveling road company. In an arduous apprenticeship lasting for the next few years, the young girl appeared in theaters large and small throughout the Southwest, drilled in the skills of acting by her mother. Melodramas were a staple on the road, and Adams became a seasoned professional in plays like *Uncle Tom's Cabin* and *The Octoroon,* performed over and over.

In the late 19th and early 20th centuries, before the era of movies, radio, or television, theater was a chief form of entertainment in towns small and large. On the traveling circuit, her life an endless routine of packing and unpacking costumes and scenery, Maude Adams gradually played increasingly important theaters. By 1888, she and her mother had worked their way East in a touring version of *The Paymaster;* in 1890, Maude was cast in a minor role in *All the Comforts of Home* by Charles Frohman, the well-known New York producer. In 1892, Frohman cast Adams as the leading lady opposite the famous actor John Drew, in Clyde Fitch's *Masked Ball.* "Her piquant beauty, slight figure, and rippling laughter captivated audiences," wrote reviewer William W. Appleton, "and she played a tipsy scene in so attractive a fashion that even the staunchest prohibitionists capitulated to her charm."

Always seeking to unite actors and playwrights, Frohman invited the Scottish-born novelist and playwright James Barrie to see Adams in her starring role in *Rosemary,* in 1895. Stage historian Lewis Strang describes the actress at this point in her career:

> In figure almost painfully slight and girlish; her face elfishly bewitching in its very plainness; her eyes large, blue and roguish; her hair ashen brown and delicately rippling; unusually gifted intellectually and with a personality of the most persuasive magnetism, Maude Adams . . . [was] the most popular woman on the American stage.

Until his first play, *Walker, London,* had been produced in 1893, Barrie had been known chiefly as a novelist. Blessed with a creative imagination, he described his business in life as "playing hide and seek with angels." In *Barrie: The Story of a Genius*, J.A. Hammerton wrote: "Like Hans Andersen, he mixed the everyday world with fairyland and like Dickens he entices us to that borderland of laughter where we suddenly find ourselves in tears." Barrie's successful mix of comedy and pathos in light-hearted dramas quickly found an adoring public. When he discovered Adams, Barrie was searching for an actress who could bring his characters to life, and he was immediately taken by the young actress.

In 1897, Barrie decided to adapt his romantic love story, *The Little Minister*, written in 1891, as a play for Adams. The story involves Lady Barbara, who is sympathetic to the plight of the discontented weavers in the town of Thrums. Disguising herself as a gypsy to help the workers, "Lady Babbie" also engages the assistance of an austere minister, the Rev. Gavin Dishart, and, when troops are called in to quell the workers' rebellion, the two are questioned. When Lady Babbie leads a soldier to believe she is the minister's wife, the cleric does not contest, a sign that he has been captivated; by the play's

Maude Adams as Peter Pan.

end, the two are pronounced man and wife according to the old Scottish law by which any couple who declared themselves wed in public were considered married in fact.

The role of Dishart was played by Robert Edeson. Strang writes glowingly of Adams' portrayal, "She was dashing, careless, and free as the tantalizing gypsy girl; as the daughter of Lord Rintoul, graceful and spirited, serious and sympathetic." The play ran for 300 performances and began a collaboration between playwright and actress that was to propel Maude Adams to national prominence. In 1901, she starred in Barrie's *Quality Street* as Phoebe and was enthusiastically acclaimed by audiences and critics alike.

In Shakespearean roles, she was not as well received. Playing the title role in *Romeo and Juliet* in 1899, Viola in *Twelfth Night* in 1908, and Rosalind in *As You Like It* in 1910, Adams was deplored for her lack of passion and depth. Some criticized her avoidance of mature roles and her narrow theatrical range. What she excelled at was playing children, androgynous heroes, and graceful young women, and these were the roles she preferred. The noted Chicago drama critic **Amy Leslie**, wrote of her abilities within her range:

> She is direct and graceful and alive with the finer, more soulful emotions, so that she sighs and melts and droops with supine pleasantness. She is brightly intelligent and reads . . . with much charming intuition and feeling.

In 1905, this ability to be "true to the fairy idea, true to the child nature, lovely, sweet, and wholesome" made Adams a natural for the American production of Barrie's *Peter Pan*. By now a close friend of the playwright, she had great insight into his work. "So much of Barrie's life is second nature to me," she said, "that I have to remind myself that other people do not know it so well."

Withdrawing to the Catskills for a month that summer, Adams prepared for the play, not simply by learning her lines, but shaping many facets of the upcoming production. Rejecting the costumes used in the London production, she designed her own, in what was quickly to become a fashion trend. After they were worn on stage by Adams, the Peter Pan collar and peaked hat were soon seen everywhere. **Nina Boucicault** had originated the play's leading role in London in 1904, but it was Adams who defined the role for posterity, appearing as Peter Pan more than 1,500 times. Said Barrie of Adams, "Charm is a sort of bloom upon a woman. If you have it, you don't need to have anything

else." The "elfin charm, her pathos, and her elusive quality" made her perfectly suited to play his most famous character.

In 1908, Adams starred in *What Every Woman Knows*, her fourth Barrie hit. She next chose two plays by Edmond Rostand, which were excellent vehicles for displaying her talents. In *L'Aiglon* ("The Eaglet," 1910), she portrayed the dreamy and ineffectual son of Napoleon Bonaparte. In Rostand's *Chantecler* (1911), she assumed the identity of a rooster who thinks his crowing makes the sun rise. Captivated by both productions, audiences sometimes demanded as many as 22 curtain calls, and Adams was idolized from coast to coast; "children, corsets, and cigars" were named after her.

In 1914, a year after Barrie was knighted, becoming a baronet, Adams appeared in another of his plays, *The Legend of Leonora*. In May 1915, Charles Frohman was among those who died in the sinking of the *Lusitania*, and Adams' relations with his firm began to deteriorate. Eventually, she formed her own company.

The British playwright and his favorite American star continued their amazingly suc-

Boucicault, Nina (1867–1950)

English actress. Born in Marylebone, England, on February 27, 1867; died on August 2, 1950; daughter of Dion Boucicault the Elder (1822–1890, an actor and dramatist) and *Agnes Robertson (an actress); sister of Dion Boucicault the Younger (1859-1929) and Aubrey Boucicault; married E.H. Kelly; married Donald Innes Smith.

Nina Boucicault starred in the original production of *Peter Pan* at the Duke of York Theatre, London, England, in 1904. Her father Dion Boucicault the Elder was the producer. Twenty years earlier, she had made her stage debut as Eily O'Connor in *The Colleen Bawn* with her father's company in Kentucky. She then accompanied him on a three-year Australian tour. Returning to America in 1888, Nina appeared at Madison Square Theatre in *A Legal Wreck*. In 1892, she made her London debut as Flossie Trivett in *The New Wing* at the Strand and then played Kitty Verdun in *Charley's Aunt* for two years. Boucicault worked continuously on the London stage; her best known roles included that of Suzanne de Villiers in *Le Monde ou L'On S'Ennuie* (she repeated her performance in an English adaptation) and Susan Throssel in *Quality Street* (1914). She also had great success as Bessie Broke in *The Light that Failed* at the Lyric and as Moira Loiney in *Little Mary* at Wyndham's, both in 1903. Nina Boucicault retired around 1936.

cessful partnership when Adams returned to another Barrie production, *A Kiss for Cinderella*, in 1916. Barrie revisited the fairy tale venue in this fantasy comedy, where, according to Hammerton, the scene shifts "from reality into dreamland or into ghostland, and the comedy more than ever seems to be tinged with a deep sense of human tragedy." *Cinderella* was an enormous hit and ran for two years until Adams became dangerously ill, struck down during the deadly flu epidemic of 1918. Forced to leave the production, she withdrew from public life to recover, then remained in virtual retirement for the next 13 years.

Offstage, Maude Adams always avoided the limelight, rarely granting interviews or attending highly publicized events. She never married and from 1905 until her death in 1953, she lived with her devoted companion, **Louise Boynton**, who functioned as her personal secretary. Adams, a nominal Protestant, was intensely religious, and though she never converted to Roman Catholicism, she withdrew a number of times to spend periods in meditation and reflection in Catholic convents. At the height of her fame, the Cenacle Convent in New York City maintained a room always available for Adams. Those who worked with her knew her as generous and high-principled as well as a practitioner of her deep Christian faith. On more than one occasion, she raised the pay of actors and stagehands in her current production, paying them out of her own salary. She also refused to cash in on her fame. Once, when a theater owner doubled the price of tickets of the play in which she was appearing, she refused to go onstage until the difference had been refunded to the playgoers.

"As all my life had been in the theater, it was natural to turn to something akin, not too remote from my former profession," Adams said, explaining her decision in 1921, at age 49, to take up studies as a lighting designer. After receiving an honorary M.A. from Union College, she moved to Schenectady, New York, to conduct lighting experiments at General Electric, where co-workers were amazed by her technical proficiency. During her tenure from 1921–23, she designed a lighting bridge and developed an incandescent bulb that became widely used with color film. Adams did not patent the bulb and refused to sue when others copied her idea, not wishing to attract any negative publicity.

At the time she left General Electric, Adams was fascinated by the emerging film industry and its technology. She wrote a scenario for a screen adaptation of Rudyard Kipling's *Kim* and made trips to Europe and India to scout locations, but despite offers from production companies the movie was never produced. Her autobiography, "The One I Knew Least of All," was serialized in seven installments in the *Ladies' Home Journal* between 1926–27. In the early 1930s, she returned to the stage in the role of Portia, with Otis Skinner as Shylock, in *The Merchant of Venice*. In 1934, she played Maria in a summer stock production of *Twelfth Night*, and she starred on radio that same year in eight productions of her earlier stage triumphs.

At age 65, when many people retire, Maude Adams began a third career, as professor of drama at Stephens College in Columbia, Missouri. In 1937, she plunged into her teaching duties with the same enthusiasm that marked all her ventures. At Stephens, she wrote manuscripts for three textbooks—*The First Steps in Speaking Verse, The Spoken Verse*, and *A Pamphlet on English Speech and English Verse*, now in the Maude Adams Collection in the Library of Congress. She directed many plays, including *Everyman* and *Chantecler*, and continued to live a quiet private life. She regularly withdrew for meditation in convents and spent time on her two estates purchased in 1900, Ronkonkoma on Long Island and Caddam Hill at Onteora in the Catskills.

Maude Adams was 74 when she retired from teaching; she lived another six years before dying of a heart attack at age 80, in Tannersville, New York. In 1922, she had donated her large estate at Ronkonkoma to the Cenacle Convent, where she continued to spend time in retreat until her death, and she was buried in the convent's private cemetery.

Although few by then remembered the actress who had enchanted a large portion of the American public in the early years of the 20th century and had been a dominant presence on the American stage for two decades, the legacy of Maude Adams was to live on. When ***Mary Martin** was chosen to play Peter Pan in a musical revival of Barrie's play, her portrayal was based on Adams' characterization; and when Walt Disney created its cartoon version, it was not by chance that Peter Pan wore the peaked cap Adams had created. Her elfin influence later resurfaced in the movie *Hook*.

SOURCES:

Appleton, William W. "Adams, Maude," in *Dictionary of American Biography. Supplement Five. 1951–1955*. Edited by John A. Garraty. NY: Scribner, pp. 7–8.

Archer, Stephen M. *American Actors and Actresses: A Guide to Information Sources*. Detroit, MI: Gale Research, 1983.

Bordman, Gerald, ed. "Adams, Maude," in *The Oxford Companion to the American Theatre*. NY: Oxford University Press, 1992.

———. *American Theatre: A Chronicle of Comedy and Drama, 1869–1914*. NY: Oxford University Press, 1994.

Brock, H.I. "Her Light Still Glows in the Theatre," in *New York Times Magazine*. November 8, 1942.

Drew, John. *My Years on the Stage*. NY: E.P. Dutton, 1922.

Hart, Columbia. "Adams, Maude," in *Notable American Women: The Modern Period*. Edited by Barbara Sicherman and Carol Hurd Green. Cambridge, MA: The Belknap Press, 1980, pp. 5–7.

Kuehn, Eileen K. *Maude Adams, An American Idol: True Womanhood Triumphant in the Late 19th and Early 20th Century Theater*. Ph.D. Dissertation, Madison, WI: University of Wisconsin, 1984.

Wilmeth, Don B., and Tice L. Miller. *A Cambridge Guide to American Theatre*. NY: Cambridge University Press, 1993.

Woods, Alan. "Adams, Maude," in *Notable Women in the America Theater: A Biographical Dictionary*. Edited by Alice M. Robinson, Vera Mowry Roberts, and Milly S. Barranger. NY: Greenwood Press, 1989.

SUGGESTED READING:

Davies, Acton. *Maude Adams*. NY: Frederick A. Stopes, 1901.

Patterson, Ada. *Maude Adams: A Biography*. NY: B. Blom, 1971, reprint edition.

Robbins, Phyllis. *Maude Adams: An Intimate Portrait*. NY: Putnam, 1956

———. *The Young Maude Adams*. Francestown, NJ: Marshall Jones, 1959.

Karin Loewen Haag, freelance writer, Athens, Georgia

Adams, Sarah Flower (1805–1848)

English poet and hymn writer whose "Nearer, my God, to Thee" was played to comfort passengers on the sinking Titanic. *Name variations: Sally; signed her articles S.Y. Born Sarah Flower at Great Harlow, Essex, England, on February 22, 1805; died in August 1848; one of two daughters of Benjamin and Eliza (Gould) Flower; sister of Eliza Flower (1803–1846); married William Bridges Adams (a noted inventor), in 1834.*

Selected writings: Vivia Perpetua *(a lyrical drama, 1841); "Nearer, my God, to Thee" (hymn, 1840).*

Sarah Flower Adams, who wrote religious poetry and a number of hymns, is probably best remembered for "Nearer, my God, to Thee," heard over the icy deep as the ill-fated *Titanic* took some 1,500 passengers to a watery grave on April 14, 1912. Pastor John Harper, who had volunteered to remain on board the sinking ship because of an insufficient number of lifeboats, requested that the orchestra play the hymn to lift the spirits of those left topside. The words that provided comfort and strength to those awaiting certain death that night were, ironically, the product of the spiritual uncertainty that plagued Sarah Adams throughout her own short life.

Adams was strongly influenced by her father, Benjamin Flower, the controversial publisher of a radical magazine, the *Cambridge Intelligencer*. She and her sister ❧▶ **Eliza Flower** were educated at home, in an atmosphere of strict religious observance. When their mother died in childbirth, their father continued to look after the educational needs of his daughters, often taking them with him on his travels around the country. As strict as Benjamin Flower was about Bible study and prayer, he held extremely tolerant religious views, often contributing articles to the Unitarian magazine *Monthly Repository* and assisting clergy with Sunday services, regardless of the denomination. He loved to engage in long religious dialogues with his friends and encouraged his daughters to accept nothing and question everything.

Perhaps as a result of her father's liberal views, Sarah found herself facing a spiritual crisis at the age of 20. In a letter to the minister of her Unitarian church, W.J. Fox, she expressed her increasing ambivalence. "I would give worlds to be a sincere believer, to go to my Bible as I used to, but I cannot." When her father died in 1829, Adams suffered a complete breakdown, which curtailed her writing for four years.

After her recovery, she wrote articles, stories, and essays for the *Monthly Repository,* as her father had done. An article, written from Luxembourg where she was visiting the galleries and gardens of the city, revealed something of her own renewal of faith. "It is in the divine spirit of love, swelling in our own hearts, that we must seek and find our God," she wrote. "He is a God of hand, and not a God afar off."

In 1834, Sarah married a fellow contributor to the *Repository,* William Adams, and took a

❧▶ **Flower, Eliza** (1803–1846)

*English composer. Born in Essex, England, in 1803; died in 1846; eldest daughter of Benjamin Flower and Eliza (Gould) Flower; sister of *Sarah Flower Adams (1805–1848).*

Eliza Flower published political songs and music to *Hymns and Anthems* (1841–46) for South Place Chapel; these included compositions for words by her sister, poet Sarah Flower Adams.

brief detour into the theater. Through a friend of her minister, she auditioned and was selected for the role of Lady Macbeth, performed at the Little Richmond Theater to the delight of critics. She planned another performance for the touring company at Bath, but was stricken by ill health again. Her disappointment set off another period of depression that lasted for three years.

Returning to her writing in 1840, Sarah produced her longest work *Vivia Perpetua*, a dramatic poem about the early life of the Christians, in which there are further signs of her lingering spiritual struggle. At the first public reading of the work, it is believed that Adams was so overcome that she broke down and sobbed. She later contributed to a hymnal her sister Eliza was compiling for the South Place Chapel. One of her 13 paeans for the book, dated November 1840, was "Nearer, my God, to Thee."

Devastated by the death of Eliza from consumption in 1846, Sarah Adams died from the same disease two years later, in August 1848. She was buried with her father and sister in the nonconformist cemetery in Harlow. One of her own hymns, "He sendeth sun, He sendeth shower," was sung at her funeral.

The hymn "Nearer, my God, to Thee" went on to achieve international recognition. It was a favorite of Queen *Victoria, King Edward VII, and American president William McKinley. It was also played at the funeral of Baptist minister John Harper, who had asked the band to play it aboard the *Titanic*. He too lost his life that night. After seeing his daughter safely into a lifeboat, he gave up his own place to a woman struggling in the water.

SOURCES:

Smith, Susan V. "The 'Titanic' Hymn," in *This England*. Vol. 18, no. 3. Autumn 1985, pp. 20–22.

Adamson, Joy (1910–1980)

Austrian-born writer and naturalist in Kenya whose bestselling book Born Free *was pivotal in changing attitudes worldwide toward the value of preserving wildlife and habitat. Born Friederike Victoria Gessner in Troppau, Silesia, in the Austro-Hungarian monarchy, on January 20, 1910; murdered near her compound "Shabba," 230 miles north of Nairobi, Kenya, perhaps by poachers who resented her conservation efforts, on January 3, 1980; ashes scattered over the plains; daughter of Victor (an architect and town planner) and Trauta Gessner; married Victor von Klarwill (an Austrian), in 1935; married Peter Bally (a Swiss),* in 1938; married George Adamson (senior warden in the Kenya game department), in 1944.

After growing up on an estate near Vienna, educated in Vienna earning a music degree before studying sculpting and medicine; went to Kenya on vacation (1937); painted flowers in Kenya for botanical books for 15 years, spending time camped out in the wild; became interested in African customs, ornaments, and costumes, which she began painting as well; adopted three lion cubs; kept Elsa, the smallest, and wrote Born Free, *followed by* Living Free *and* Forever Free, *which told of experiences living with the lion and returning her to the wild; proved that captive wild animals could be reeducated to live in their natural habitat, a practice widely used today; alerted the world to the loss of species and habitat, a topic on which she became an early crusader.*

Selected writings: Born Free: A Lioness of Two Worlds *(NY: Pantheon, 1960);* Elsa: The True Story of a Lioness *(NY: Pantheon, 1961);* Forever Free *(NY: Harcourt, 1963);* Joy Adamson's Africa *(NY: Harcourt, 1972); (introduction by Sir Julian Huxley)* Living Free: The Story of Elsa and her Cubs *(NY: Harcourt, 1971);* The Peoples of Kenya *(3rd ed., London: Collins & Harvill, 1973);* The Searching Spirit: Joy Adamson's Autobiography *(Harcourt, 1979).*

At the time Joy Adamson wrote *Born Free*, it was commonly assumed that wild animals lived in huge numbers on vast tracts of land. In telling the story of a lion cub that she raised and then successfully returned to life in the wild, Adamson put an end to this conventional wisdom, publicizing the alarming loss of wildlife and habitat in Africa and around the world. Today, growing numbers of eagles, condors, wolves, bears, lions, and countless other creatures are released into surviving segments of their native habitats as a means of guaranteeing the survival of their species, a movement that owes considerable thanks to the public support first inspired by the story of a cub named Elsa.

Adamson, who was to call international attention to one kind of vanishing world, was born into another, that of the late European aristocracy of the Austro-Hungarian Empire. Named Friederike Victoria Gessner, she was the child of Victor Gessner, an architect and town planner, and **Trauta Gessner**, who gave birth to her on January 20, 1910, on a large estate outside Vienna. Under the rule of Kaiser Francis Joseph I, the Austro-Hungarian Empire stretched across Central Europe, including what is now the Czech Republic, Slovakia, Slovenia, Austria, Hungary, Dalmatia, Bosnia, Herzegovina, and parts of Italy. At its heart lay elegant and sophisticated Vienna, with its unending rounds of fashionable dinner parties, operas, and balls attended in horse-drawn carriages. As a woman of her class, Adamson learned to ride and shoot at an early age, and took part in hunts, but preferred from the beginning to watch game animals rather than kill them. A good shot, she killed her first buck at age 16, a feat she then refused to repeat.

In Vienna, Adamson earned a degree in music, which was only one of her talents. Afterward, she studied sculpting for a time before deciding to enter medical school, but the medical studies ended when she married Victor von Klarwill, an Austrian, in 1935. The marriage was over by 1937, when Adamson, at age 27, went to Kenya to visit friends and fell in love with Africa. Fascinated especially by the plant life, she showed a gift for painting the native flowers and plants, which gained her a place on an expedition to the Chyullu mountain range sponsored by the American Museum of Natural History in New York. Adamson's second husband, Peter Bally, was one of the eight scientists on the trip, which became a three-month honeymoon for the couple. Her illustrations for the next edition of a garden book on East Africa flora led to contracts to illustrate seven more books published by the Royal Horticultural Society of East Africa. The artist documented her botanical findings with plant specimens she forwarded to Kew Gardens in England.

This second marriage also proved to be short lived. In 1944, she married George Adamson, senior warden for the Kenya game department, and found a compatible life, as she described it, spent on what "amounted to 360 days a year on safari." According to Gregory Jaynes:

> In the early years of their marriage the Adamsons spent most of their time wandering across the flat East African plain and living in tent camps. They had spent their honeymoon walking around the shores of Lake Rudolph, thick with crocodiles.

"Both of us were nearly killed by rhinos," George told an interviewer. "But Joy discovered some lovely rock engravings. I captured several poachers and learned to call crocodiles. All in all, it was a good trip."

Contact with the many tribes of East Africa led Joy Adamson to begin recording their patterns of dress and ornamentation, which provided clues to their tribal origins, through designs linked to cultures that originated in Asia, Egypt, and Persia. This ethnological work attracted

government interest and financial support, leading the artist to produce more than 750 illustrations, many life-size, of the peoples in tribal dress. She also made book illustrations of the brilliant coral fish found off the Kenyan coast.

In the 1950s, a tragedy typical of wildlife management led to the immense change in Adamson's life. When George Adamson was called out to hunt and kill a lion that had earned a reputation as a man-eater, he was charged by a lioness he assumed to be the culprit. Forced to shoot her in self-defense, he shortly discovered that she had attacked to shield her three cubs, hidden nearby, so young that they were still blind. Knowing his wife's love of animals, George brought the cubs home for her to nurture, and as their eyes began to focus, Adamson became the first face they recognized. Raising three lion cubs was an impossible human task, however. Adamson arranged for the two larger cubs to be sent to zoos, handpicked for their humane treatment of animals, and kept the smallest, named Elsa.

Joy Adamson

From the movie
Born Free
(Columbia,
1966).

Because her infant charge had been born free, Adamson was determined from the outset that the lioness would not be tamed or domesticated; her resolution, however, was to prove difficult to keep. A history of mostly unfortunate experiences had led to the conventional wisdom that captive animals could never successfully return to the wild, and the Adamsons were the only parents the young Elsa knew; they were her protection and her lion tribe. Certainly her early experiences were not those of a lion in the wild. She was nursed from a bottle, slept on a cot, and rode on the roof of a Landrover—that is, until she grew large enough for the roof to cave in. When Elsa was a year old, she accompanied the Adamsons on vacation to a coastal village on the Indian Ocean, where she proved to be a natural swimmer. Weighing almost 200 pounds at this stage, she wrestled and played with Joy in the shallow surf, photographed in a number of pictures George had begun to take to document their daily life together.

But as Elsa approached age two and the onset of sexual maturity, the Adamsons were forced to think increasingly about what it would take for her to return to the wild. The main barrier to Elsa's survival was that she had never learned to hunt for food. Growing up outside a lion pride, she also did not know lion etiquette; once, because she failed to follow the conventions of lion behavior, she was nearly attacked by an angry lioness, before George fired warning shots into the air to save her. Until she learned to fend for herself, she would never be able to live on her own and mate.

The first attempt to wean Elsa from civilized life was made in a sparsely settled region 350 miles from Isiolo. But Elsa's accustomed climate was different, and she became deathly ill. While she was recovering, the Adamsons traveled 400 miles to the area of Elsa's birthplace, where game abounded, to set up camp and teach her to hunt and kill prey. George would fire at an animal to wound it, then encourage Elsa to finish it off.

After the young lioness began to disappear at night, the Adamsons learned that she was spending the time with a young male lion, but she continued to return to the camp during the day to nap on the cot next to George. Finally, the Adamsons broke camp, leaving her on her own for a week. Upon their return, Elsa greeted them joyously and soon showed signs that she had been able during their absence to hunt on her own. One day, in a curious reversal of earlier hunting forays, she grabbed a full-grown water buffalo in mid-stream, but held it by the throat, as if waiting for George to finish it off. More remarkably, Nuru, the Muslim Somali who was Elsa's keeper, rushed to the kill while Elsa still had the warm, bloody body in her clutches. Nuru's religion required that the throat of any animal that was to be eaten be cut before it died, and visions of buffalo steak for dinner caused him to move in and finish the animal off, in preparation for carving off a nice piece of meat. In what Adamson identified as "an astonishing tribute no less to her intelligence than to her self-control," Elsa growled but did not attack Nuru.

After three years with the Adamsons, Elsa made her final transition to life in the wild in a release that Joy found wrenching. Elsa had become "almost like my child," Adamson recorded in the book about their unique relationship. "Because I had no children, I have spent all my emotion on her and my other animals." After a trip to England of several months to arrange for the book's publication, she returned in July. Then she was delayed several more months in paying a visit with George to the area of Elsa's lair, where the two were greeted with an affectionate 300-pound lion hug. Despite this obvious show of affection for her human family, however, Elsa's life was irreversibly changed. She had a mate and had given birth to cubs, and although the cubs showed up in camp, her mate remained shy, never allowing himself to be touched. Elsa also showed signs of how well her lessons had been learned. If the Adamsons became too familiar with the cubs, she would grip the humans by the knee to pull them away; she also discouraged the cubs from too much familiarity. As Adamson writes:

> Elsa tactfully combined this double life—I should say triple life because she had her own wild life, the wild life of her cubs, and life with us. This, in itself, was an important contribution to the knowledge of the psychology of animals. You see, I am convinced that all of these animals can teach us a great deal, far more than we even now suspect.

With the publication of *Born Free: A Lioness of Two Worlds* in 1960, Adamson found her own reclusive life on safari overtaken by the bright lights of intense publicity. The book was a huge success. Selling more than three million copies and translated into many languages, it was also the inspiration for television shows and movies. Drawn into the circuit of talk-show appearances, interviews and lectures, Adamson took this opportunity in the international limelight to publicize the plight of wild animals around the world. "We had no idea when George first brought in Elsa, an adorable cub, that it would lead to anything," she wrote:

> But obviously Elsa started us on the road to something important. I made up my mind, long before *Born Free* was ever published, much less filmed, that every penny of royalties Elsa earned would go toward the survival of wild animals. Watch out. I'll sell you anything for my cause—books, drawings, a life-time membership in the Elsa Wild Animal Appeal. . . . I'm shameless. I'll do anything to help animals.

At a time when the urgency of the problems surrounding wildlife and the reduction of their habitats was barely beginning to be understood, Adamson linked the nature of the problem to the nature of human beings:

> Our brain is wonderful but also frightening because it has so thoroughly separated us from the entire range of other mammals that we are no longer a part of the balance of nature. We must remember what happened to the dinosaur. When his physical bulk became too big to fit into the landscape, he had to go. I'm not joking when I say that the same thing could happen to us because of our mental bulk. Every form of life, from an ant to an elephant, an eagle to a fish, has its function in the balance of nature—except man. We, the highest form of mammal ever recorded in biological history, have overspecialized our brain. We could, like the dinosaur, overstep our limits and become intellectual rather than physical monsters.

Marshalling worldwide enthusiasm for Elsa and the wildlife she represented, Adamson began to raise funds to save a disappearing Africa. After *Born Free*, she wrote three sequels, *Elsa: The True Story of a Lioness* (1961), *Forever Free* (1963), and *Living Free: The Story of Elsa and Her Cubs* (1961). In 1972, she also published *Joy Adamson's Africa*, followed by *The Peoples of Kenya* (1973), a collection of her paintings and photographs. Her autobiography, *The Searching Spirit: Joy Adamson's Autobiography*, appeared in 1979. By the mid-60s, however, celebrity had taken its toll on the Adamson marriage, and the couple began to live separately. The parting was amicable, and the Adamsons kept in constant touch with weekly chats over short-wave radio, still drawn together by a mutual love of Africa and its wildlife. In 1969, when she was 59, Adamson was in an auto accident that left her with a severely injured right hand, causing her great difficulties as a writer and artist, but her hectic schedule continued unabated. Though still traveling frequently overseas for her cause, she spent as much time as she could manage at Shabba, her Kenyan compound, 230 miles north of Nairobi.

Elsa's . . . impact upon the entire world . . . proves the hunger of people to return, in whatever way they can, to a world of genuine proportion, a world in which our balance and basic values have not been destroyed.

—Joy Adamson

On January 3, 1980, a few weeks short of her 70th birthday, Adamson was in robust health and set out for her daily walkabout in the bush. When she did not return at her customary time to listen to the BBC news before supper, her cook dispatched a guard to look for her. Her body was found a short distance away. At first her death was attributed to lions, but subsequent investigations proved human rather than animal intervention; she had been stabbed in the chest and arm, perhaps by local hunters or poachers who saw their way of life threatened.

Toward the end of her life, however, Joy Adamson had begun to feel that her efforts were helping to bring about changes in human behavior. Since the appearance of *Born Free*, the number of books and magazine articles for the popular audience and the wildlife television programs and movies enhancing the value of preserving wildlife had certainly proliferated, and would continue to do so. Increased public enthusiasm was helping to revolutionize the treatment of animals in zoos, popularizing zoo living space in the form of large outdoor habitat areas, and drawing financial support that now allows important discoveries about the preservation of wildlife through zoo institutions. Public interest was stimulating the growth of "ecotourism," which would shift attitudes in many countries in favor of wildlife as an important economic resource. While such circumstances existed before Adamson's accounts of Elsa, her books' tremendous popularity unquestionably accelerated the pace of change. Wrote Adamson:

> Sometimes when I drive along the road and see a giraffe standing tall and beautiful against the sky or an elephant herd drinking unafraid at a water hole, I think to myself, "Elsa helped give that animal to the world."

SOURCES:
Adamson, Joy. "The Lady and the Lion," in *Saturday Evening Post*. Vol. 232, no. 37, March 12, 1960, pp. 24–27.

———. "What Animals Can Tell Us about Ourselves," in *McCall's*. Vol. 94, no. 4, January 1967, pp. 60–61; 104–105.
"Adamson, Joy (Friederike Victoria)," in *Current Biography Yearbook*. NY: H.W. Wilson, 1972.
Dowty, Leonhard. "The Lady Who Listens to Lions," in *Good Housekeeping*. Vol. 174, no. 2, February 1972, p. 14+.
Jaynes, Gregory. "Joy Adamson. Author of 'Born Free' Is Killed in Africa," in *The New York Times Biographical Service*. January 1980, pp. 1–2.
"Kenya: Don't Blame the Lions," in *Newsweek*. Vol. 95, no. 3, January 21, 1980, p. 56.
Marnham, Patrick. "Orphans All," in *Spectator*. Vol. 224, no. 7906, January 19, 1980, pp. 27–28.
Newquist, Roy. *Counterpoint*. NY: Rand McNally, 1964.

SUGGESTED READING:
Cass, Caroline. *Joy Adamson: Behind the Mask*. Weidenfeld and Nicolson, 1993.

Karin Loewen Haag, freelance writer, Athens, Georgia

Adasse (fl. 1348)

German moneylender. Jewish resident of Gorlitz, Germany; granted citizen's rights around 1348.

Adasse, whose name is found in the town citizenship records of Gorlitz, became wealthy lending money to the Christian residents of the town and attained a high social standing in her community. Eventually, the town leaders bestowed upon her the privileges of citizenship, a rare event for a medieval townswoman and extremely rare for a Jew.

Laura York, Anza, California

Adato, Perry Miller.
See O'Keeffe, Georgia for sidebar.

Adawiyya or Adawiyyah, Rabi'a al-
(c. 714–801).
See Rabi'a.

Addams, Jane (1860–1935)

American founder of Hull House, a Chicago settlement house, who advocated progressive reforms, pacifism, and cultural diversity. Born on September 6, 1860, in Cedarville, Illinois; died in Chicago on May 21, 1935; daughter of John (an Illinois entrepreneur and legislator) and Sarah (Weber) Addams (who died when Jane Addams was two); graduated valedictorian Rockford Female Seminary, 1881 (granted a degree when it became Rockford College, 1882); attended Woman's Medical College of Pennsylvania for one year; never married; no children.

Enrolled at Rockford Seminary (1877); made first visit to Europe (1883) and second visit with Ellen

Jane
Addams

Gates Starr (1887); founded Hull House with Starr (1889); elected chair of Women's Peace Party and the Women's International League for Peace and Freedom (1916); awarded the Nobel Peace Prize (1931).

Selected writings: Democracy and Social Ethics *(1902);* Newer Ideals of Peace *(1907);* Twenty Years at Hull House *(1910);* The Spirit of Youth and the City Streets *(1912);* Peace and Bread in Time of War *(1922);* The Second Twenty Years at Hull House *(1930);* The Excellent Becomes the Permanent *(1932);* My Friend, Julia Lathrop *(1935).*

Jane Addams is one of the heroes and legends of American liberalism. In an age dominated by *laissez-faire* conservatism, she worked to restore a fractured sense of American community and to bring the full benefits of national life to the poorest and most recent immigrants. Hull House, her slum settlement in Chicago, became the influential center of a national movement aimed at bringing education, sanitation, recreation, and political representation to the most disadvantaged citizens of the new urban civilization. Disliked by some contemporaries (and subsequent historians) for her middle-class Puritan pieties and her unshakable self-assurance, she was also widely loved and admired, both for her settlement work and for her leadership in the women's peace movement.

Jane Addams' father John was revered for his business acumen and political probity in downstate Illinois and had a large influence on his daughter's moral education. Jane was one of four among his children to survive into adulthood, and she grew up in frail health, suffering from curvature of the spine. Serious, bookish, and delicate, she did not enter easily into her stepmother's outgoing social plans. When she was 17, Jane attended Rockford Female Seminary, a college of which her father was a trustee, though she had hoped to go to Smith College (which, unlike the seminary, already granted degrees). At Rockford, she met *Ellen Gates Starr, who was to be her lifelong friend and collaborator. During vacations, they wrote long earnest letters to one another expressing their half-formed religious longings and doubts, Jane writing that although she could appreciate Jesus as a great man she could not find in him a link with God. Reacting to pressure from her teachers, she categorically refused to devote her life to overseas missionary work.

Graduating at the top of her class in 1881, Addams then moved to Philadelphia to begin studying at the Woman's Medical College, at a time when few women were doctors and when they faced severe opposition from the male medical professionals. After six months, suffering from health problems, depression, and the shock of her father's sudden death earlier that year, she was forced to give up. In 1883, her stepmother took Jane on a European grand tour in the hope that it would speed her recovery. This was the era when many American heiresses were courting the impoverished aristocracy of Europe, exchanging money for titles in a mutually gratifying marriage trade. Meanwhile, the American women used Europe as a cultural finishing-ground, visiting its art galleries, cathedrals, museums, and concerts to gain a little of the social polish that was still unavailable in middle America. Jane Addams found herself unable to focus exclusively on the artistic heritage of Europe. Instead, she was acutely conscious of the suffering of the poor in London and other cities and believed that the job of alleviating their afflictions was more important than that of finding a husband.

Back in America but still unwell and depressed at the apparent lack of direction in her life, Addams submitted to a medical operation performed by her brother Harry, a doctor, in the hope of curing the curvature of her spine. According to Addams' family lore, the operation revealed that she was incapable of bearing children. Believing herself physically unable to follow the normal course of middle-class women, even had she wanted to, Addams felt more than ever cut off from the mainstream of life. Like many of the educated of her generation, she had absorbed the powerfully persuasive idea of evolution, which intellectuals applied to many fields beyond its original biological provenance. She became convinced that the human race as a whole was evolving but that she, and middle-class women like her, had been shunted aside into an evolutionary backwater, where they were denied all chance to compete and strive. In her impatience with inactivity or pointless work, she felt that the "race life" was passing her by, and her decision in 1889 to begin a settlement house was her way of trying to re-enter the invigorating stream. It certainly had a positive effect on her health. After years of suffering, she suddenly found herself endowed with boundless energy and the ability to work hard and creatively for the next 40 or more years.

The original decision to create a settlement came during her second visit to Europe, in 1887, this time with Ellen Starr. They visited Toynbee House in the East End of London, a settlement where privileged Oxford undergraduates went to study and ameliorate the lives of the working

The children of Hull House.

poor. Back in Chicago, they chose a house in the worst of the slums, at 335 South Halsted Street, to set up a similar settlement and spent some of their savings (both had plentiful private incomes) in preparing to move in. Unsure of what to expect, they were soon the center of attention from their curious neighbors and were rapidly drawn into the teeming life of the district. Twenty years later, Addams published *Twenty Years at Hull House,* a memoir of the settlement's first years of work. It became a minor classic, and the Bible of a generation of social settlement workers.

Addams was convinced that many of her era's social problems sprang from the fact that the huge new cities had broken up the older American tradition of community in which every citizen knew all the others on a face-to-face basis. The problem of scale and the growing ethnic and linguistic diversity made the old ways impractical, but she reasoned that bringing the social classes and different ethnic groups into each others' actual physical presence was the best way to respond—hence the importance of actually living in Halsted Street. One of the ob-

stacles she and Starr worked on from the outset was in overcoming the difficulty that peasant immigrants had adjusting to city life. The women tried to teach basic sanitation to farm families, which were now living cheek-by-jowl in crowded tenements, tried to discourage the mothers from feeding infants on bread soaked in wine, and offered to provide day-care for children whose mothers had to work in factories or in domestic service. They soon found that many of the women worked long hours in nearby sweatshops or on gruelling home-based piece work, and so became advocates for the working women against predatory employers and landlords. Hull House offered meeting rooms to the growing trade unions and stood by many Chicago workers during recurrent bitter strikes. Addams early befriended Samuel Gompers, head of the American Federation of Labor.

The size of the Hull House community fluctuated as new volunteers came and went, but the size of the settlement and the scope of its work increased steadily. Addams was a talented fundraiser and asked the wealthy of Chicago to at least contribute if they were not willing to live at Hull House. Many paid up more or less willingly. In the early 1890s, one volunteer and donor, **Mary Rozet Smith**, began to live there and became Addams' closest lifelong friend, confidante, and admirer. As educated, articulate middle-class women, the Hull House staff tackled Chicago's civic leaders, persuading them to install street lights, to arrange regular garbage collection (Addams became the area's garbage commissioner), to provide police patrols for the sake of local safety, and to offer fair legal representation when local people were in trouble with the law. Addams believed strongly in negotiation and discussion and was always willing to think the best of employers and city politicians—that if only they knew what was happening, they would be sure to act reasonably.

Experience soon made her politically astute, however, and she learned how to blend persuasion with gently coercive threats. Moreover, she decided not to accept voluntary contributions to her work if they came from tainted sources, such as the profits of businessmen who had a reputation for underpaying their workers. Her outlook remained for the most part optimistic: she was convinced that villains were more the exception than the rule. Strongly influenced by Christianity without being in any way orthodox, she was a sort of Christian socialist who believed that moral reform, education, and social improvements would eventually usher in a just and harmonious society. One reform she favored strongly, and for which she spoke frequently, was women's suffrage, not least because it would facilitate the re-entry of more American women into the social mainstream and out of the limbo she felt she had inhabited through her 20s.

Some reformers of her era believed that immigrants living in areas like the Hull House district should be "assimilated" as quickly as possible, that they should learn English, adapt to American habits and customs, and surrender the cultural baggage of their earlier lives. Addams saw that the psychic cost of Americanization on these terms was painfully high to many of the immigrants, especially the older ones; she tried to preserve and honor aspects of Old World life that she found among her neighbors rather than hurry them to oblivion. She set up a museum of ethnic labor, arts, and crafts at Hull House, encouraged story tellers and musicians to preserve their folk ways, and made sure that residents who had not yet mastered English were put in touch with city officials or local professors who spoke their own tongues.

Addams also had a more sympathetic view of "troublesome" children than many of her contemporary reformers. In one of her ten published books, *The Spirit of Youth and the City Streets* (1909), she argued that slum neighborhoods such as hers offered children few outlets for the kind of exciting and healthy play they would have been able to enjoy in the countryside or if (again invoking evolution) they lived as primitive hunters and gatherers. She explained juvenile delinquency and prostitution (which she also treated with more lenity and understanding than was then common) as problems created by the stultifying physical and economic environment, and aimed to provide settings at the Hull House complex in which young peoples' energies could be directed along more profitable lines. Women who had turned to prostitution from economic necessity were usually shunned by the neighborhood's married women, and on one occasion Addams and her friend *Julia Lathrop went to the rescue of a young "fallen woman" who was going through a difficult birth unassisted, though neither of them had any training as midwives. (Lathrop went on from Hull House to run the Illinois State Board of Charities and in 1912 became the first head of the U.S. Children's Bureau.)

Hull House soon attracted favorable notice from the press and from other idealistic men and women, many of whom came along to volunteer for occasional or full-time work. As thousands of Chicagoans began visiting the house, it built annexes nearby for a boys' club and a public kitchen (the "Coffee House"). Later a coal-buying cooperative enabled the area's residents to get vital winter fuel at reduced cost, while a residential coop enabled a growing number of families to have a good and philanthropic landlord taking care of their interests. *Florence Kelley (later National Consumers' League president) and *Frances Perkins (later U.S. secretary of labor) were among the better known volunteers from the early years at Hull House who helped with these enlarged projects and gained vital first-hand experience from their years with Jane Addams. Another assistant, *Mary Eliza McDowell, became first director of the University of Chicago Settlement House founded a decade after Hull House. Addams also encouraged visiting literary, academic, and political dignitaries to speak at the settlement, and a great range of European liberals, socialists, and anarchists passed through, each spreading his or her special brand of social transformation, among them the Russian anarchist Prince Kropotkin, the celebrated philosopher John Dewey, and the British Labour Party founder Keir Hardie.

Most reformers of that era favored the prohibition of alcohol. They could see that slum-district saloons, superficially appealing because of their jovial atmosphere and warmth, were really deadly temptations to low-paid workers, leading them to spend badly needed money on beer and spirits instead of on good nutrition and warm clothes for themselves and their families. Addams was no friend of the saloons but neither did she believe in Prohibition. She wanted to avoid condescending to her neighbors (she never called them "cases" or "clients") and honored their widespread acceptance of the saloon. During the prohibition era of the 1920s, she witnessed the hopeless failure of this high-minded reform, and lived long enough to see it abandoned in the early years of the New Deal. On occasion, she would help alcoholics. In the early years of Hull House, a Mrs. Dennis said she was addicted but agreed to take the following pledge: "I hereby solemnly pledge in the presence of Jane Addams that from this day forth, hence forevermore, that I will abstain from all intoxicating liquor. I also promise that in the case of overwhelming temptation I will come and see Jane Addams."

In 1911, Addams helped found the National Federation of Settlements and Neighborhood Centers, and became the organization's first president. She witnessed the continued growth of the movement over the next two decades, so that by her death in 1935 there were settlement houses in every large American city.

Addams was an active member of the pre-First World War peace movement, and her book *Newer Ideals of Peace* (1907), based on a course of lectures given in Wisconsin the previous year, showed evidence of her extensive thinking on the issue. Like most of her published work, it too was cast in evolutionary terms, making the argument that in the early days of mankind fighting had been the only way to resolve disputes, but that now humanity had evolved to a higher point, enabling it to replace physical force with moral suasion. As she said, any community unable to settle its domestic differences without resort to arms ought to regard itself with shame. The same was all the more true with international communities. She regarded the multiethnic community around Hull House as a microcosm of the world, a miniature form of "united nations" which, she argued, lived at peace by the exercise of reason and good will. Her voice of sane reasonableness saturated the book. She spoke the same theme on a hundred public platforms and often quoted Leo Tolstoy's *My Religion*, treating it as an inspirational text for her Hull House work as well as her pacifism.

Despite its confident rhetoric and influential patrons, the peace movement was powerless to prevent the European descent into war in 1914, and Addams found, three years later, that it was equally ineffective in trying to keep America out of the conflict. By then, she had accepted the post of chair for the Women's Peace Party and the Women's International League for Peace and Freedom, and on their behalf had voyaged to a conference in the Netherlands and to visit the British and German prime ministers, begging them unsuccessfully to submit the war to arbitration. Though, to her, the ghastly massacres of the war in France seemed shocking evidence of an evolutionary malfunction, she stayed active in the International League throughout the 1920s (the basis for her 1931 Nobel Peace Prize). In the Red Scare that followed the First World War, some superpatriots denounced Addams for her reluctance to oppose national enemies by force and dismissed all her reform plans as evidence of "Bolshevism." She faced up to these attacks and even intensified them by protesting against breaches of due process when the attorney general A. Michell Palmer ordered the arbitrary arrest and deportation of many suspected radicals.

In newspaper features year after year [Jane Addams] was voted the greatest woman in the United States, the greatest in the world, and, on one occasion, the greatest in history.

—Daniel Levine

By the 1920s, Hull House had become a vast complex of buildings, second in size only to the University of Chicago, involved in a wide variety of reform projects but still with children's welfare near the center of them all. Addams, a national and international celebrity, traveled widely, usually with her best friend Mary Smith, to give talks about her work throughout America and Europe, sometimes facing hostile crowds because of her peace work, but gradually gaining a more benevolent reception as the postwar mood dissipated. In 1923 with *Alice Hamilton, another longtime friend and volunteer, Addams and Smith traveled around the world, giving speeches everywhere and advocating international cooperation. Addams had been dismayed by the American decision not to join the League of Nations: in her view, foreign entanglement was now the best way to *prevent* wars, whatever wisdom to the contrary George Washington had suggested in his Farewell Address.

Addams suffered from a heart condition in the latter part of her life but remained an active writer, working on the biography of her old friend Julia Lathrop. She stayed loyal to the Republican Party of her youth and voted for Herbert Hoover in 1928 and 1932, but still took great pleasure in finding that her former protégé Frances Perkins was appointed secretary of labor by President Franklin Roosevelt at the beginning of the New Deal. Jane Addams died of cancer on May 21, 1935, and was laid to rest at a ceremonious Chicago funeral. Summing up her influence, historian Daniel Levine argued: "Jane Addams was not an original thinker of major importance. One can find predecessors for almost every one of her ideas in the writings of the English Fabians, German political economists, American pragmatists. Her importance was not as a manufacturer of ideas, but as their retailer. . . . In no one area did she possess enormous expertise; yet probably no reformer was so deeply involved in so many facets of reform."

SOURCES:
Addams, Jane. *Twenty Years at Hull House.* NY: Macmillan, 1910.
———. *Newer Ideals of Peace.* NY: Macmillan, 1907.
———. *The Spirit of Youth and the City Streets.* NY: Macmillan, 1912.
Davis, Allen Freeman. *American Heroine: The Life and Legend of Jane Addams.* NY: Oxford University Press, 1973.
Farrell, John C. *Beloved Lady.* Baltimore: Johns Hopkins University Press, 1967.
Lasch, Christopher. *The New Radicalism in America: The Intellectual as a Social Type.* NY: Knopf, 1965.
Levine, Daniel. *Jane Addams and the Liberal Tradition.* Madison, WI: State Historical Society of Wisconsin, 1971.

Patrick Allitt, Assistant Professor of History, Emory University, Atlanta, Georgia

Addie, Pauline Betz (b. 1919).
See Betz, Pauline.

Adea Eurydice (c. 337–317 BCE).
See Eurydice.

Adeheid (931–999).
See Adelaide of Burgundy.

Adela.
Variant of Adele.

Adela (d. 735) and Irmina (d. 716?)
Frankish saints. Birth dates unknown; Adela died on December 24, 735; Irmina died around 716; daugh-

ters of St. Dagobert II, Merovingian king of Austrasia (r. 674–678), and Matilda (an Anglo-Saxon princess); Adela married Alberic (a noble); children of Adela: one son.*

Upon the 656 death of his father St. Sigibert III, king of Austrasia, Dagobert succeeded him. Since Dagobert was a boy of seven, it was easy for the mayor of the palace, Grimoald, to replace him with his own son. Dagobert was then spirited out of the country by defenders and taken to Ireland for refuge. Seventeen years later, in 673, Dagobert returned to Metz, capital of Austrasia in northeast France, and took possession of his throne.

While in exile, he had married and fathered one son (Lothair IV, r. 717–719) and four daughters, including Adela and Irmina. When Irmina's betrothed, Count Herman, died before setting their wedding date, she became a nun and subsequently founded a convent under Benedictine rule in an old castle in Horren, at Trier. Irmina's religious community was threatened when an epidemic broke out, and she asked for help from St. Willibrord, whose prayers, it was thought, ended the danger. In gratitude, Irmina offered Willibrord the land of Echternach, where he established his abbey.

Adela, meanwhile, had married, borne a son, and been widowed. Though she had many suitors, she followed her sister into the religious life. In about 690, Adela founded the convent of Palatiolum, not far from Trier (on the site of the town of Pfalzel), and became its first abbess. Adela died in 735, 20 years after the death of her sister Irmina. Both sisters were canonized as saints.

Adela Capet (c. 1010–1079).
See Matilda of Flanders for sidebar.

Adela of Blois (1062–c. 1137)
Countess of Blois and Chartres, known by historians as "the heroine of the First Crusade." Name variations: Adele; Adela of Normandy; Adela of England. Born in 1062 in Normandy, France; died on March 8 around 1137 or 1138 at the convent of Marcigny, France; fourth daughter of Matilda of Flanders (1031–1083) and William the Conqueror, duke of Normandy (r. 1035–1087), king of England (r. 1066–1087); sister of Henry I, king of England; married Stephen Henry also known as Etienne (d. 1102), count of Blois, Tours, Chartres, and Champagne; children: seven, though some authorities claim nine, including William de Blois;

Stephen, king of England (r. 1135–1154); Thibaut also known as Theobald II, count of Champagne (whose daughter was *Adele of Champagne, 1145–1206); Henry (bishop of Winchester); Philip (held the See of Chalone); *Matilda de Blois (drowned in 1120); *Lucy de Blois (drowned in 1120).

Born and raised in her father's provinces of Normandy, in northwestern France, Adela of Blois was deeply religious, extremely well-educated, and could read and write in several languages, including Latin. She married Stephen Henry of Blois, one of her father's supporters, and became a trusted companion to her husband. At Adela's encouragement, Stephen left their provinces to participate in the First Crusade. He named Adela as regent of their lands.

Setting aside her needlework on the famous Bayeux tapestry, which her mother *Matilda of Flanders had left for her to complete, the countess ruled ably from 1096 to 1109. Called by historians "the heroine of the First Crusade," Adela also became known as a generous patron of poets and writers, inviting them to her court and rewarding them amply for their works. When Stephen died in the battle of Ramula while on crusade in 1102, Adela continued to rule. She was of such importance that Pope Paschal II spent the Easter of 1107 as her guest, and many of the letters written to her by Hildebert, bishop of Le Mans, on ecclesiastical matters are still extant.

On the death of Adela's brother King Henry I in 1135, her son Stephen claimed the throne of England and was crowned, but, with his mother's financial and political support, he had to fight a civil war against Henry's daughter Empress *Matilda, (1102–1167), Adela's own niece and another claimant of the throne. Adela retired to the convent of Marcigny in the diocese of Autun sometime in the 1130s, and she died there at age 75. She is buried, along with her mother and her sister ❧ Cecilia (c. 1059–1126), in the Abbey of the Holy Trinity at Caen, France.

Laura York, Anza, California

Adela of England (1062–c. 1137).
See Adela of Blois.

Adela of Louvain (c. 1102–1151).
See Adelicia of Louvain.

Adela of Meissen (fl. 1100s)
German royal. Born in Meissen, a city in Germany, northwest of Dresden; flourished in the 1100s; daugh-

ter of Otto II, margrave of Meissen; first wife of Ottokar I (d. 1230), king of Bohemia (r. 1198–1230); children: *Dagmar of Bohemia (d. 1212). Ottokar's second wife was *Constance of Hungary.

Adela of Normandy (1062–c. 1137).
See Adela of Blois.

Adelaide.
Variant of Adelicia.

Adelaide (c. 794–after 852)
French princess. Name variations: Alpaid. Born around 794; died after 852; daughter of *Ermengarde (d. 818) and Louis I the Pious (778–840), king of Aquitaine (r. 781–814), king of France (r. 814–840), and Holy Roman emperor (r. 814–840); sister of Lothair I, Holy Roman emperor (r. 840–855); married Count Bego; children: Susannah (b. around 805).

Adelaide (fl. 860s)
Countess of Anjou and Blois. Flourished around 860; daughter of Eberhard III, count of Alsace; married Robert the Strong (c. 825–866), count of Anjou and Blois, marquis of Neustria; children: Eudes or Odo (c. 860–898), count of Paris and king of France (r. 888–898); Robert I (c. 865–923), king of France (r. 922–923).

Adelaide (1777–1847)
Princess of Orléans. Name variations: Adélaïde; Adelaide d'Orleans; Adelaide of Orleans; Mademoiselle d'Orléans or Orleans. Born Adelaide Eugenie Louise in Paris, France, on August 23 or 25, 1777; died on December 31, 1847; daughter of Louis Philippe Joseph (Philippe-Égalité), duke of Orléans (1785–1793), Montpensier (1747–1752), and Chartres (1752–1785), and Louise Marie of Bourbon (1753–1821); sister of Louis Philippe, king of France (r. 1830–1848); married Baron Athelin.

Adelaide's father Louis Philippe Joseph, duke of Orléans, was a liberal reformer, a thorn in the side of Louis XVI, who aided French Revolutionists. He was guillotined, however, not by royalists but by another revolutionary faction in 1793. Her mother *Louise Marie of Bourbon was noted for her charities. Her father's reputation preceded her when Princess Adelaide was returning to France in 1792 from a visit to England, and she found herself listed among the émigrés. She succeeded, however, in making her

❧◀
*Cecilia
(c. 1059– 1126).*
See Matilda of Flanders for sidebar.

escape and remained in exile until 1814. In 1830, Adelaide was influential in persuading her brother Louis Philippe, the Citizen King, to accept the crown of France.

Adelaide, Madame (1732–1800)

French princess. Name variations: Adélaïde; Marie Adelaide de France. Born Marie Adelaide at Versailles, France, on May 3, 1732; died at Trieste, on February 18, 1800; daughter of Louis XV (1710–1774), king of France (r. 1715–1774) and *Marie Leczinska (1703–1768); sister of *Louise Elizabeth (1727–1759), Victoire (1733–1799), and Louise Marie (1737–1787) as well as Louis le dauphin (father of Louis XVI).

The best-loved daughter of Louis XV, Madame Adelaide grew into a haughty royal who loathed her niece-in-law *Marie Antoinette; indeed, it was at Adelaide's home that Queen Marie Antoinette was first labeled "The Austrian." Adelaide and her sister *Victoire were known as King Louis XVI's "aunts" and given the castle of Bellevue to live out their years. Ironically, it was Marie Antoinette's prodding that freed them from their confining rooms at Versailles.

On February 19, 1791, with the Revolution brewing, Adelaide and Victoire sought permission to leave France to "spend Easter in Rome," but their request met with suspicion by the Assembly. In defiance and fear, they made a hasty and discreet departure to seek refuge abroad. After a ten-day delay by the militia, the royal aunts migrated to Rome. Followed by an audience with the pope, they settled in Caserta in 1796; they then moved to Trieste in 1799, where Adelaide died a few months later.

Adelaide, Queen of Lombardy (931–999).
See Adelaide of Burgundy.

Adelaide, Saint (931–999).
See Adelaide of Burgundy.

Adelaide de Condet (fl. 12th c.)

British patron who commanded the translation of the Proverbs of Solomon (c. 1150). Name variations: Alice de Condet. Lived outside Lincoln, England; married Robert de Condet; children: one son, Roger.

Adelaide de Condet, the lady of Thorngate Castle in England, lived just outside Lincoln, where her husband Robert was a landowner. In the early 12th century, she commissioned a translation of the *Proverbs of Solomon*, a moral treatise, into Anglo-Saxon. Sanson de Nanteuil produced the translation for his patron. It is believed that the work was used in the education of Roger de Condet, Adelaide's son.

Adelaide Judith (fl. 879)

Queen of France. Flourished around 879; daughter of Adelard, count of the Palace; second wife of Louis II the Stammerer (846–879), king of France (r. 877–879), children: Charles III the Simple (879–929), king of France (r. 898–923). Louis II's first wife was *Ansgard (fl. 863).

Adelaide of Anjou

Queen of France. Married Stephen, count of Gevaudun; married Louis V the Coward (c. 967–987), king of France (r. 986–987). Louis V's second wife was Blanca, daughter of William II, count of Auvergne, and Gerletta.

Adelaide of Austria (d. 1854).
See Marie Adelaide of Austria.

Adelaide of Burgundy (931–999)

Empress of the Holy Roman Empire at the time of its reorganization under husband Otto I, who was not only active in imperial governments, but also endowed many churches and monasteries so as to earn the title saint. Name variations: Adeheid, Adelheid, Adelheide, Adelaide, Queen of Lombardy; Saint Adelaide. Born Adelaide in 931 in Burgundy; died at Seltz in Alsace on December 16, 999; daughter of Rudolf or Rudolph II of Burgundy and Bertha of Swabia; married Lothar also known as Lothair (d. 950), king of Italy, in 947; became second wife of Otto I the Great (912–973), king of Germany (r. 936–973), Holy Roman emperor (r. 962–973), in 951; children: (first marriage) *Emma of Italy (b. 948); (second marriage) Matilda of Quedlinburg (c. 953–999) and Otto II (955–983), Holy Roman emperor (r. 973–983); grandmother of *Adelaide of Quedlinburg (977–1045), German abbess and founder.

Married Lothair, king of Italy (947), who was poisoned three years later by Berengar II (Berenguer), a rival for the Italian throne; imprisoned for refusing to marry Adalbert, Berengar II's son (951); escaped and married Otto I later the same year; crowned empress by Pope John XII (962); served as regent to her grandson, Otto III (991–95).

On an April day in 951, Adelaide of Burgundy stood hidden behind tall stalks of wheat listening to the crunch of soldiers' boots nearby. She was on the run and being hunted. Several nights before, she and a trusted servant had tunneled for hours to escape the prison of King Berengar of Italy. Now in the disguise of a serving maid, this widowed queen was headed north to seek refuge at Reggio and appeal for protection to Otto, the king of Germany. As the soldiers grew closer, the grass was parted by a sword—first on one side of the hidden queen, then the other. But Adelaide escaped detection. Her perilous journey continued through hills and marshes, with the aid of clerics and fishermen, to a successful rendezvous with her future husband, Otto, in northern Italy.

The dramatic escape of Adelaide from the prison of King Berengar is recorded by two contemporary biographers. These accounts show Adelaide to be a strong, resourceful, and independent woman. Such a woman of character may not coincide with a modern image of the demure medieval lady, but women's access to power in the Middle Ages was greater than most 20th-century observers might suspect. In a society based on feudalism, the control of land was the control of power. Women inherited and controlled property in equal measure to their brothers. And, while eldest sons usually enjoyed some favor in royal succession, daughters without siblings were known to rule as well. Finally, while land could be won through military might, legitimate heirs were needed to achieve a measure of stability from one generation to the next. Therefore, as daughters and wives, women could advance the economic and dynastic ambitions of their families. In particular as widows, they could enjoy independent rule over their own land holdings and serve as regents and guardians for their children and grandchildren. So, while all early medieval queens did not tunnel out of dungeons or hide in grain fields as Adelaide did, her life serves as a good example of the power and limitations of royal women in the 10th century.

Adelaide was born in 931 in Burgundy in what is now southwestern France. Her father Rudolf II was king of Burgundy and her mother **Bertha of Swabia** came from the German province of Swabia. As part of a peace agreement between her father and King Hugh of Italy, Adelaide was betrothed to Hugh's son, Lothair, at the age of two. Rudolf died in 937 and Adelaide's widowed mother married King Hugh placing Adelaide in the odd position of being betrothed to her stepbrother.

In 947, at the age of 14, Adelaide of Burgundy married Lothair who had become king of Italy two years earlier. A year later, she gave birth to a daughter, *Emma of Italy, a future queen of France. Adelaide's marriage to Lothair lasted only three years. On November 22, 950, Lothair died, and Adelaide's life was then thrown into turmoil. Berengar, the Marquis of Ivrea, claimed the Italian throne for himself. Although he had served as an advisor to Lothair, it was rumored that the marquis had poisoned the king in order to carry out this coup. Berengar then proposed that Adelaide marry his son, Adalbert; this union would legitimize Berengar's claim to power in Italy. Adelaide's consent was required for the marriage, however. This she refused to give and so found herself imprisoned in Berengar's Garda Castle.

Locked away in Berengar's dungeon, 19-year-old Adelaide became the classic example of "a lady in distress." After four months of captivity, she used her own wealth, connections, and resourcefulness to execute a daring escape. Liberation, however, was only the first step in countering Berengar's usurpation of her political rights in Italy. Adelaide needed military aid to defeat Berengar. She appealed to Otto I, king of Germany.

A logical choice, Otto was a strong military and political leader whose lands bordered Italy to the north. Years earlier, when Adelaide's father died, Otto had served as a tutor to her brother, Conrad, and had helped Conrad protect his rights as heir to the throne of Burgundy. Adelaide had much to offer Otto in return, for his chief ambition was to revive the Holy Roman Empire, a political entity that united Germany and Italy. Coming to Adelaide's aid gave Otto an excuse to advance his political ambitions in Italy. Therefore, an alliance between Otto and Adelaide brought advantages to both.

In December of 951, only a few months after escaping Berengar's prison, Adelaide of Burgundy married Otto, and he immediately began to advance their claims in Italy. As one of

Bertha of Swabia (fl. 900s)
*Queen of Burgundy. Born in the German province of Swabia; married Rudolf II of Burgundy also known as Rudolf of Lorraine (died 937); married Hugh of Provence, king of Italy; children: (first marriage) *Adelaide of Burgundy (931-999); Conrad of Burgundy.*

Otto's closest advisors throughout their marriage, Adelaide's influence and popularity was key to the Italian campaign. It took over 11 years, but the dream of empire became a reality. In 962, Otto and Adelaide were crowned emperor and empress of the Holy Roman Empire by Pope John II.

The couple had two children: a son, Otto II, and a daughter ◀❧ Matilda of Quedlinburg. (Otto I also had three other children by his first marriage to *Edgitha, sister of the English king Athelstan). Otto II became coemperor with his father in 967 at the age of 12. Five years later, Adelaide and Otto I arranged a marriage for their son with *Theophano (c. 955–991), a Byzantine princess. This union further established the empire's authority over Greek holdings in southern Italy. Adelaide's daughter Matilda chose a career in the church, entering Quedlinburg monastery. She rose to the rank of abbess, an office with responsibility over a wide variety of spiritual and secular matters.

After the death of Otto I in 973, Adelaide of Burgundy devoted much of her energy and

---

❧➤ Matilda of Quedlinburg (c. 953–999)

*Abbess of Quedlinburg and regent of Germany. Name variations: Mathilda. Born around 953; died in 999 at Quedlinburg monastery, Germany; daughter of Emperor Otto I (912–973), king of Germany, and refounder of the Holy Roman empire (r. 936–973), and *Adelaide of Burgundy (931–999); sister of Otto II (955–983), Holy Roman emperor (r. 973–983); never married; no children.*

Born into the imperial family of Germany, Matilda was the daughter of *Adelaide of Burgundy and Otto I. As a girl, she was allowed to enter a convent rather than marry. Highly educated by the nuns of Quedlinburg, especially in the areas of medicine and history, she also showed a talent for artistic work, and became well known for her exquisite embroidery. Matilda was eventually elected abbess; under her rule, Quedlinburg became famous for its production of richly embroidered clothing for clerics and altar cloths, some of which still exist.

Around 980, Abbess Matilda was pulled out of the convent to act as regent, along with her mother Adelaide and her sister-in-law Theophano (c. 955–991), for her nephew, the young Otto III. The peaceful, introverted nun became an excellent leader, even sending an army to defeat an enemy invasion in 983. When Otto came of age, Matilda returned to Quedlinburg, where she died several years later.

Laura York, Northampton, Massachusetts

---

wealth to the church. She was an active benefactor of many religious foundations, and was particularly supportive of the monastic reform movement centered at Cluny. Two abbots of this house, Majouis and Odilo, were close friends and advisors, and the latter wrote her biography. Adelaide's devotion to religious works went beyond the simple donation of money. She was personally active in the care of the poor, especially at her daughter's monastery at Quedlinburg. She often took off her royal garb and dressed as a serving woman in order to distribute food and clothing to the destitute who gathered at the monastery gate.

Adelaide's religious fervor, however, was not appreciated by her son, Otto II, who considered that her wealth might be more appropriately spent on secular-political pursuits. This tension between mother and son caused Adelaide to leave the imperial court of Germany and live with her brother, Conrad, in Burgundy in 978. Two years later, Adelaide and 25-year-old Otto II were reconciled when he appealed to his mother for aid in calming political unrest in Italy. Adelaide used her personal influence to calm the crisis. She then agreed to return to a more active political life in Italy.

The untimely demise of Otto II in December 983 left the empire in an unstable state. His own son and heir, Otto III, was only three years old. Several political rivals saw these circumstances as a perfect opportunity to usurp the Ottonian claim to the imperial crown. Acting in concert with her daughter Matilda and her daughter-in-law, Theophano, Adelaide of Burgundy was able to counter these political challenges and firmly establish Theophano as regent for her grandson. However, when Theophano died in 991, Adelaide assumed responsibility for the administration of the empire. Under her leadership the kingdom remained stable and peaceful until Otto III was old enough to take up the imperial crown in 995.

In her final years, Adelaide returned to a life devoted to religious causes. It was a time of great literary activity in the monasteries, including *Hrotsvitha who was writing at Gandersheim. In her last months, Adelaide undertook a pilgrimage to the various religious shrines of Northern Italy, Burgundy, and Germany. Many of these holy places had benefitted directly from her patronage. Her biographer, Odilo, recorded the journey in great detail. At every site, friends and family greeted Adelaide along with crowds of poor looking for alms. Adelaide continued the practice of ministering to the poor herself. She also spent much time in prayer. Her piety and devotion greatly impressed Odilo and shaped his claim of her saintliness. Adelaide's pilgrimage ended at Selz where she had ordered her tomb built at the convent of Saint Peter and Saint Paul, a religious house she had founded. On December 16, 999, Adelaide of Burgundy died peacefully in her sleep.

SOURCES:

Hroswitha of Gandersheim. *Gesta Ottonis.* Edited by P. Winterfeld. *Monumenta Germania historica, Scriptores rerum germanicarum in usum scholarum.* Hannover: Hahnsche Buchhandlung, 1965.

Odilo of Cluny. *[Epitaph of Adelaide] Die Lebensbeschreibung der Kaiserin Adelheid von Abt Odilo von Cluny.* Edited by H. Paulhart. *Mitteilungen des Instituts für Österreichische Geschichtsforschung,* supplementary vol. 20, part 2. *Festschrift zur Jahrtausendfeier der Kaiserkronung Ottos des Grossen,* part 2. Cologne: H. Boohlaus Nachf, 1962.

SUGGESTED READING:

Baumer, Gertrude. *Adelheid, Mutter der Königreiche.* Stuttgart: R. Wunderlich, 1949.

Stafford, Pauline. *Queens, Concubines, and Dowagers: The King's Wife in the Early Middle Ages.* Athens, GA: University of Georgia Press, 1983.

Linda A. McMillin, Assistant Professor of History, Susquehanna University, Selinsgrove, Pennsylvania

Adelaide of Burgundy (d. 1273)

Duchess of Brabant. Name variations: Adelaide de Bourgogne; Alix of Burgundy. Died on October 23, 1273; daughter of *Yolande de Dreux (1212–1248) and Hugh IV (1213–1272), duke of Burgundy (r. 1218–1272); married Henry III (d. 1261), duke of Brabant (r. 1248–1261), in 1251; children: Henry IV (c. 1251–1272), duke of Brabant; John I (c. 1252–1294), duke of Brabant; *Marie of Brabant (c. 1260–1321), queen of France.

Adelaide of France (1092–1154).

See Adelaide of Maurienne.

Adelaide of Hohenlohe-Langenburg (1835–1900)

Duchess of Schleswig-Holstein-Sonderburg-Augustenberg. Name variations: Adelaide von Hohenlohe-Langenburg. Born on July 20, 1835; died on January 25, 1900; daughter of Ernest, 4th prince of Hohenlohe-Langenburg, and *Feodore of Leiningen (half-sister of Queen *Victoria); married Frederick, duke of Schleswig-Holstein-Sonderburg-Augustenberg, on September 11, 1856; children: five, including *Augusta of Schleswig-Holstein (1858–1921, first wife of Kaiser Wilhelm II); *Caroline Matilda of

Schleswig-Holstein-Sonderburg-Augustenberg (1860–1932).

Adelaide of Hungary (d. 1062)

Queen of Bohemia. Died on January 27, 1062; daughter of *Anastasia of Russia (c. 1023–after 1074) and Andrew I (c. 1001–1060), king of Hungary (r. 1047–1060); became second wife of Vratislav II (c. 1035–1092), king of Bohemia (r. 1061–1092), around 1058.

Adelaide of Kiev (c. 1070–1109)

Holy Roman empress. Name variations: Eupraxia of Kiev. Born around 1070; died on July 10, 1109; daughter of Vsevolod I, prince of Kiev, and *Anna of Cumin (d. 1111); married Henry, count of Stade; became second wife of Henry IV (1050–1106), king of Germany and Holy Roman emperor (r. 1056–1106), on August 17, 1089 (divorced 1093).

Adelaide of Louvain (c. 1102–1151).

See Adelicia of Louvain.

Adelaide of Maurienne (1092–1154)

Queen of France and religious founder who was one of the most dominant queens in French history. Name variations: Adelaide of France; Adelaide of Savoy; Agnes of Maurienne; Alix. Born in 1092 (some sources cite 1110); died on November 18, 1154 at Montmartre, France; daughter of Humbert II of Maurienne also known as Umberto II, count of Savoy, and *Gisela of Burgundy (daughter of William I, count of Burgundy); married Louis VI the Fat (1081–1137), king of France (r. 1108–1137), in 1115; children: Philip (d. 1131); Louis VII (c. 1121–1180) king of France (r. 1137–1180); Robert, count of Dreux; Peter of Courtenay; Henry, bishop of Beauvais and Rouen; Philip, bishop of Paris; ❧ Constance Capet (c. 1128–1176, who married Raymond V, count of Toulouse).

Adelaide of Maurienne was one of the most powerful queens in French history. A French noblewoman, she married King Louis VI in 1115 while in her teens. Clever and insightful, Adelaide revealed a nature well-suited to politics and state affairs, and she quickly became a trusted advisor to her husband as well as an important ruler in her own right as queen. Twelfth-century France differed from later eras in that queen-consorts were allowed to exercise royal authority under their own names. Adelaide performed

See sidebar on the following page

❦▶ **Constance Capet** (c. 1128–1176)

Countess of Toulouse. Name variations: Countess of Boulogne. Born around 1128; died on August 16, 1176, at Rheims, Champagne, France; daughter of Louis VI, king of France (r. 1108–1137), and *Adelaide of Maurienne (1092–1154); married Eustace IV, count of Boulogne, in 1151; married Raymond V, count of Toulouse, in 1154; children: (second marriage) Raymond VI, count of Toulouse; William; Baldwin; Alesia of Toulouse (who married Roger, viscount of Beziers); Laura of Toulouse (who married Odo, count of Comminger).

---

many royal functions, including signing charters, making judicial decisions, and appointing church and lay officials. Royal correspondence and other documents were dated by the reigning year of both King Louis and Queen Adelaide, attesting to her importance as a co-ruler. Adelaide was also a deeply religious woman; she founded the Abbey of Montmartre with her own money.

After Louis died in 1137, Adelaide refused to retire from handling state matters; instead, she remained at the center of government in Paris with the new king, her 15-year-old son Louis (now Louis VII). Though technically her right to exercise power had died with her husband, she counseled her son and continued to exert royal authority. In her later years, however, she was virtually forced to retire due to her advancing age and the growing influence wielded by her daughter-in-law, the young queen ***Eleanor of Aquitaine**. Adelaide lived out her last years at Montmartre.

Adelaide of Montserrat (fl. 1100)

Regent of Normandy. Mother of Count Roger II of Normandy.

Adelaide was one of many medieval noblewomen who, though not in theory allowed to rule, actually governed large domains in practice. When her son Roger left Normandy to participate in the First Crusade (around 1096), he named Adelaide to act as his regent during his years of absence.

Adelaide of Poitou (c. 950–c. 1004)

Queen of France. Name variations: Adelaide of Guyenne; Adelaide of Aquitaine. Born around 950 (some sources cite 945); died around 1004; daughter

of Guillaume also known as William I (or III) Towhead, count of Poitou, duke of Aquitaine, and **Adele of Normandy (c. 917–c. 962); married Hugh Capet, duke of France (r. 956–996), king of France (r. 987–996), first of the Capetian kings, in 970; children: Robert II (b. 972), king of France (r. 996–1031).*

Adelaide of Quedlinburg
(977–1045)

German abbess of Quedlinburg, a convent famous for the erudition of its nuns. Name variations: Adelheid of Germany; Adelheid of Quedlinburg. Born in 977 in the Holy Roman Empire; died at the abbey of Quedlinburg, Germany, in 1045; daughter of Holy Roman emperor Otto II (r. 973–983) and Empress *Theophano of Byzantium (c. 955–991); sister of Otto III, Holy Roman emperor (r. 983–1002); granddaughter of *Adelaide of Burgundy (931–999), Italian queen and empress; never married; no children.

Born into the ruling family of Germany, Adelaide received an excellent education as a child. Her parents planned a cloistered life for her, instead of a politically motivated marriage to a foreign ruler or noble, the more common fate of royal daughters. However, Otto and Theophano's plans were threatened in 984 when the seven-year-old girl was kidnapped to be used as a political pawn by the supporters of her parents' rebellious enemy, Henry the Quarrelsome of Bavaria. Adelaide was eventually returned safely to her family, and a defeated Henry was required to give her the abbey of Vreden as compensation for his treatment of her.

Adelaide entered the religious life as a young woman, taking nun's vows and continuing her studies. She eventually served as the abbess of several convents, including the wealthy establishment of Quedlinburg, famous for the great learning of its nuns. Adelaide executed her many duties as abbess well and became known for both her excellent learning and her true piety. The abbess was about 68 years old when she died at Quedlinburg.

Laura York, Anza, California

Adelaide of Rheinfelden (c. 1065–?)

Queen of Hungary. Born around 1065; married St. Ladislas I (1040–1095), king of Hungary (r. 1077–1095); children: *Priska-Irene of Hungary (c. 1085–1133, who married Emperor John II Comnenus).

Adelaide of Savona (d. 1118)

Countess and regent of Sicily who later became queen of Jerusalem. Name variations: Adelaide of Salona; Adelaide of Sicily. Reigned 1101–1112; died in 1118 in Sicily; daughter of Marquis Manfred of Savona; niece of Boniface of Savona; married Count Roger I of Sicily (1031–1101, brother of Robert Guiscard), in 1089; married Baldwin I of Boulogne, king of Jerusalem (r. 1100–1118), in 1113; children: Simon of Sicily (r. 1101–1103); Roger II of Sicily (1095–1154). Baldwin I was also married to **Godeheut de Toni** *(d. 1097), daughter of Ralf III, seigneur de Conches.*

Adelaide of Savona, an Italian noblewoman, was the daughter of the reigning marquis of Savona. As a young woman, she became the third wife of Roger I, count of Sicily, and moved to Sicily in 1089 as marquessa. Six years later, she gave birth to one child who survived, Roger II. In 1101, her husband died, leaving Adelaide to act as regent of Sicily in the name of their small son. Adelaide was an able ruler and, when her son came of age in 1113, she left him with a fairly prosperous and peaceful island-state.

Soon after Roger II took over the reins of government, Adelaide married again. Her new husband was Baldwin I of Boulogne, king of Jerusalem (again, she was the third wife). Moving to Jerusalem, she began a new life as Baldwin's queen-consort, but when Baldwin fell ill in 1117, he repented his sins and had his third marriage annulled. Stripped of her wealth, Adelaide returned to Sicily. Her marriage contract would give Roger II the motivation to claim the lands of Jerusalem. Adelaide is remembered as a religious founder, for providing the seed money for the monastery of S. Marie del Patirion.

Laura York, Anza, California

Adelaide of Savoy (1092–1154).

See Adelaide of Maurienne.

Adelaide of Saxe-Meiningen
(1792–1849)

Queen of England. Name variations: Adelaide Louisa Theresa. Born in Meiningen, Thuringia, Germany, on August 13, 1792; died on December 2, 1849, in Stanmore, London, England; buried at St. George's Chapel, Windsor, Berkshire, England; daughter of George I, duke of Saxe-Coburg-Meiningen, and ***Louise of Hohenlohe-Langenburg** *(1763–1837); married William, duke of Clarence, on July 18, 1818; became queen of England in 1830 on his accession as William IV until his death in 1837; children: Charlotte Guelph (1819–1819, died day of birth); Elizabeth Guelph (1820–1821, died age three months), and four other unnamed babies who died in childbirth, including twins.*

With worries of English succession in the air, the 53-year-old William, duke of Clarence (later William IV), married the 26-year-old Adelaide of Saxe-Meiningen, considered plain and religious by contemporaries, specifically to bear children—legitimate children. He had already fathered ten children with his mistress, the actress ***Dora Jordan**. Though Adelaide gave birth to six children who did not survive infancy, she proved to be an extremely tolerant wife, accepting without quibble William's other children, who lounged around the castle. She even accepted the arrival of another mistress, ***Mrs. Fitzherbert**.

The reserved and highly moral Adelaide remained in the background. She took interest in the model cottages under construction at Windsor and the children who lived in them, and she

Adelaide of Saxe-Meiningen

showed kindness to her young niece (and future queen) *Victoria whose mother, *Victoria of Coburg, was on bad terms with the court. Despite her virtues, Adelaide's reputation was tarnished by her husband's success. Because William was an extremely popular king, the public found it easier to vindicate him and blame the influence of his wife when he did something to offend. Though William died in 1837, the new queen Victoria returned her aunt's kindness and continued to address Adelaide as queen of England. When Adelaide died in 1849, while living at Bentley Priory in Middlesex, she was buried at Windsor by the side of her husband and their baby Elizabeth. The city of Adelaide in Australia bears her name.

Adelaide of Saxe-Meiningen
(1891–1971)

Duchess of Saxony. Name variations: Adelheid; Countess Lingen. Born Adelaide Erna Caroline on September 16, 1891, in Cassel; died on April 25, 1971, in La Tour de Peilz, Switzerland; daughter of Frederick Johann (b. 1861), duke of Saxony, and Adelaide Caroline Matilde, Princess Lippe (1870–1889); married Adalbert Ferdinand Berengar, count Lingen, on August 3, 1914; children: Victoria Marina (1917–1981), countess Lingen (who married Kirby Patterson); William Victor (b. 1919), count Lingen.

Adelaide of Schaerbeck (d. 1250)

Flemish saint. Name variations: Alix of Schärbeck. Birth date unknown; died on June 11, 1250.

Adelaide of Schaerbeck was a nun at the Cistercian abbey of Cambre, in Brussels, who became a leper and went blind.

Adelaide of Sicily (d. 1118).
See Adelaide of Savona.

Adelaide of Vohburg (fl. 1140s)

*Duchess of Swabia. Name variations: Adelheid von Vohburg. Flourished around 1140s; daughter of Diepold III, margrave of Vohburg, and Adelaide (daughter of Ladislas I Herman, king of Poland); became first wife of Frederick I Barbarossa (1123–1190), duke of Swabia (r. 1147), Holy Roman emperor (r. 1152–1190), in 1147 (divorced 1153). Frederick Barbarossa's second wife was *Beatrice of Upper Burgundy (1145–1184).*

Adele.
Variant of Adela.

Adele (r. 1017–1031)

Co-ruler of Vendôme. Birth and death dates unknown; married Bouchard I, count of Vendôme, Paril, and Corbeil (ruler of Vendôme from 958–1012); children: three sons, Renaud (bishop of Paril); Bouchard II; Foulques d'Oison.

After her husband died in 1012, Adele's eldest son Renaud ruled Vendôme for four years, until his death in 1016. Then a young nephew, though he was not of age, ruled briefly. Sometime after 1016, Adele co-ruled with her second son Bouchard II, but he too died soon after. She then co-ruled with her third son Foulques d'Oison until 1031 when she sold the duchy to Foulques' uncle Geoffrey Martel, count of Anjou.

Adele of Blois (1062–c. 1137).
See Adela of Blois.

Adele of Blois (1145–1206).
See Adele of Champagne.

Adele of Champagne (1145–1206)

*Queen of France whose son Philip II Augustus was one of the most important kings in the development of the French monarchy. Name variations: Adela or Adele of Blois; Alix or Alice of Champagne. Born in 1145 in Champagne; died in Paris in 1206; daughter of Count Theobald II of Champagne also known as Thibaut of Blois (who was the son of *Adela of Blois) and ✿➔ Maud Carinthia (c. 1105–1160); became third wife of Louis VII (1120–1180), king of France (r. 1137–1180), in 1160; children: Philip "Dieudonne" (b. August 21, 1165–1223), later Philip II Augustus, king of France (r. 1180–1123); *Agnes-Anne of France (b. 1171).*

In 1160, at age 15, Adele of Champagne was betrothed to King Louis VII of France. The marriage was Louis' third. His first wife was *Eleanor of Aquitaine; his second, *Constance of Castile, had died giving birth to *Alais of France in 1160. Since his first two wives had borne only girls, Louis needed a new queen to provide him with an heir. Adele's father, Theobald II of Champagne, a powerful feudal lord of France, was one of Louis' most rebellious vassals, and so Adele's marriage to Louis represented a sort of peace treaty between Theobald and the crown.

Five years later, to the joy of the French people and especially Louis, Adele gave birth to the long-awaited male heir, Philip II Augustus. For six generations, from the accession of Hugh Capet in 987, the Capetian dynasty had asserted royal power in France largely because of the unbroken and undisputed succession of male heirs. The great rejoicing and celebration that accompanied Philip's birth by Louis VII's third wife, Adela of Champagne, in 1165, expressed the promise that the Capetian monarchs would continue to rule France.

Though named Philip Augustus, the child was always called Philip "Dieu-Donne" ("God-given"). Adele did not share in the administration of government during Louis' reign, but after Louis died in 1180 she retained her title as queen and acted as ruler during Philip's minority. She proved to be a capable and energetic regent, handling the myriad royal responsibilities with political shrewdness, developed over her years as a member of two eminent feudal houses.

Adele remained at court after Philip came of age, although her direct participation in government lessened. However, in 1190–91, Philip left France to join Richard I of England on the Third Crusade, and Philip appointed Adele to act as regent of the kingdom in his name, a tribute to his respect for her ability as a ruler. After Philip's return, Adele retired from politics. She died at the age of 61. Although it could not have been anticipated in 1165, her son not only continued the Capetian dynasty but also became one of the most important kings in the development of the French monarchy.

SOURCES:
Kelly, Amy. *Eleanor of Aquitaine and the Four Kings.* Cambridge, MA: Harvard University Press, 1950.

Laura York, Anza, California

Adele of Normandy (c. 917–c. 962)

Countess of Poitou. Born around 917 in Normandy, France; died after October 14, 962, in France; daughter of Rollo also known as Robert (b. 870), duke of Normandy, and *Gisela Martel (d. 919); married William I (III) Towhead (c. 915–963), count of Poitou (r. 934–963), duke of Aquitaine, in 935; children: *Adelaide of Poitou (c. 950–c. 1004); William II (IV) Ironarm (b. around 937), count of Poitou.

Adelgunde of Bavaria (1823–1914)

Duchess of Modena. Name variations: Adelgund. Born on March 19, 1823, in Wurzburg; daughter of *Theresa of Saxony (1792–1854) and Ludwig I (b. 1786), king

⚜▶ **Maud Carinthia** (c. 1105–1160)

Countess of Champagne and Blois. Name variations: Maud of Carinthia. Born around 1105; died in 1160; daughter of Inglebert II, duke of Carinthia, and Uta of Passau; married Theobald II, count of Champagne and Blois, in 1123; children: Henry I (d. 1181), count of Champagne (who married *Marie de Champagne); Theobald V, count of Blois (who married *Alice, Countess of Blois); Stephen, count of Sancerre; William of Rheims, cardinal; *Adele of Champagne (1145–1206).

of Bavaria (r. 1825–1848); died on October 28, 1914, in Wurzburg; married Franz or Francis V (1819–1875), duke of Modena (r. 1846–1859), on March 30, 1842; children: Anna Beatrice (1848–1849).

Adelheid.

Variant of Adelaide.

Adelheid (1831–1909)

Queen of Portugal. Name variations: Adelheid Rosenberg. Born Adelheid Rosenberg on April 3, 1831, in Kleinheubach; died on December 16, 1909, at St. Cecilia's Convent, Ryde, Isle of Wight; daughter of Prince Constantine Rosenberg and Marie Agnes, princess of Hohenlohe-Langenburg; married Miguel also known as Michael I (1802–1866), king of Portugal (r. 1828–1834), on September 24, 1851; children: Maria da Neves (1852–1941, who married Aphonse Carlos, duke of San Jaime); Miguel (b. 1853); Maria Theresa of Portugal (1855–1944); *Maria Josepha of Portugal (1857–1943); Adelgunde of Portugal (1858–1946), duchess of Guimaraes (who married Henry, count of Bardi); *Marie-Anne of Braganza (1861–1942); *Maria Antonia of Portugal (1862–1959, who married Robert, duke of Bourbon-Parma).

Adelheide.

Variant of Adelaide.

Adelicia (1029–1090)

Countess of Ponthieu, Lenz, and Champagne. Name variations: Adelaide; Adeliza of Normandy. Born in 1029; daughter of Robert I, duke of Normandy (r. 1027–1035) and *Arlette (fl. 1010); sister of William I the Conqueror, king of England (r. 1066–1087); married Enguerrand III, count of Ponthieu; married Lambert, count of Lenz; married Odo III, count of Cham-

pagne; children: (second marriage) *Judith of Normandy (c. 1054–after 1086).

Adelicia de Warrenne (d. 1178)

*Countess of Huntingdon. Birth date unknown; died in 1178; daughter of William de Warrenne, 2nd earl of Warrenne and Surrey, and *Isabel of Vermandois; married Henry Dunkeld, 1st earl of Huntingdon, in 1139; children: *Margaret of Huntingdon (c. 1140–1201); Malcolm IV (1142–1165), king of Scots (r. 1153–1165); William I the Lion, king of Scots (r. 1165–1214); David Dunkeld (c. 1144–1219), 1st earl of Huntingdon; *Ada Dunkeld (c. 1145–1206); Matilda (c. 1152–1152); Isabella (who married Robert, baron Ros of Wark).*

Adelicia of Louvain (c. 1102–1151)

Queen of England and patron of literature. Name variations: Adeliza; Adelaide; Adela, Fair Maid of Brabant. Born in 1102 or 1103 in Louvain, France; died on March 23, 1151, in Afflighem, Flanders, Belgium; daughter of Count Godfrey (Barbatus) of Louvain, duke of Brabant or Lower Lotharingia; became second wife of Henry I (c. 1068 or 1069–1135), king of England (r. 1100–1135), on January 24, 1121; married William d'Aubigny also known as William de Albini, later named earl of Arundel, in 1138; children: (first marriage) none; (second marriage) seven who survived, including Reyner d'Aubigny, Henry d'Aubigny, Godfrey d'Aubigny, Alice d'Aubigny, Olivia d'Aubigny, and ❧❦ Agatha d'Aubigny.

Adelicia of Louvain was born into a ruling noble family of the Low Countries (modern Belgium and Flanders) and received an excellent education, showing a great interest in language and literature. After the death of Queen ❦❧ **Matilda of Scotland**, the 18-year-old Adelicia married the bereaved ruling monarch of England, Henry I, as part of a political and economic agreement between her father and the king. In her position as queen, Adelicia was able to pursue her literary interests more fully, for she now had the money and authority to commission works and reward their writers amply. She became known as a generous patron, especially of the French troubadours.

❦❧▶
Matilda of Scotland (1080–1118). See Matilda, Empress for sidebar.

❦❧ ▶ **Aubigny, Agatha d'**
*Daughter of William d'Aubigny, earl of Arundel, and *Adelicia of Louvain (second wife of King Henry I of England); sister of Alice and Olivia d'Aubigny.*

In 1135 on Henry's death, Adelicia lost her position and authority when Stephen, son of her sister-in-law *Adela of Blois, claimed the throne of England, though Stephen would have to fight a civil war for many years against Adelicia's stepdaughter Empress *Matilda of England (1102–1167). Three years later, Adelicia married England's William d'Aubigny, who was later was named earl of Arundel. After 11 years of a reputedly happy marriage, Adelicia withdrew to a convent in Flanders. In *Queens of England*, Norah Lofts suggests that the conflict between her stepdaughter and nephew was the probable cause. Adelicia died in 1151 about age 48.

Laura York, Anza, California

Adeliza.
Variant of Adelicia.

Adeliza (d. 1066?).
See Matilda of Flanders for sidebar.

Adelwip (fl. 13th c.).
See Hadewijch.

Adivar, Halide Edib (c. 1884–1964)

Turkish author, warrior, and political activist. Name variations: Halide Salih, Halidé Edip or Edib; Mrs. H.E. Adivar. Born in 1883 or 1884 in Istanbul (then Constantinople); died in Istanbul, Turkey, on January 9, 1964; daughter of Mehmet Edib or Edip; first Muslim Turkish girl to graduate from the American Girls' College; married Salih Zeki (a noted mathematician; divorced); married Dr. Abdülhak Adnan Adivar (1881–1955), in 1917; children: two sons.

Her many novels attacked the traditional concept of a woman's role; an ardent nationalist, Adivar was outspoken in her attacks against the Allied forces occupying Istanbul and risked her life to defy them; joined the nationalist movement of national rebirth led by Mustafa Kemal Pasha (later Kemal Atatürk); commissioned a sergeant major by Atatürk himself; served on the General Staff and then participated directly at the front lines when the Greeks made their ill-fated attack on the infant Turkish Republic (1922); banished from Turkey because of their outspoken notions of individual liberty, Adivar and her husband moved abroad (1920s); returned to Turkey (1938) and continued to write novels and plays; many motion pictures and novels are based on her life.

Selected writings: Doktor Abdulhak Adnan Adivar *(Istanbul: A. Halit Yasaroglu, 1956)*; Memoirs of Halidé Edib *(NY: Arno Press, 1972)*; Shirt of Flame *(NY: Duffield, 1924)*; The Turkish Ordeal: Being the

Further Memoirs of Halide Edib *(New York and London: Century, 1928)*; The Clown and His Daughter *(London: George Allen and Unwin, 1935)*; The Daughter of Smyrna: A Story of the Rise of Modern Turkey *(Lahore: Dar-ül Kutup Islamica, 1940)*; Masks or Souls? *(London: Allen and Unwin, 1953)*; Turkey Faces West *(NY: Arno Press, 1973)*; The Conflict of East and West in Turkey *(Lahore: Sh. M. Ashraf, 1963).*

Halide Adivar was born into a family of minor government officials in Istanbul in 1884. Her father Mehmet Edib was employed by the French-administered Ottoman Tobacco Monopoly *(Régie des Tabacs)* in the Turkish-controlled Greek town of Joannina. Mehmet Edib was an unusually progressive Turkish parent for his day and age, and he believed that his daughter deserved as fine an education as her obvious intellectual gifts would allow. An excellent student, she was admitted to the American Girls' College at Uskudar (Scutari), graduating in 1901 as the first Muslim Turkish girl to complete that institution's course requirements. A perfect command of English allowed her to keep in touch with the most advanced ideas of the time, and in later years she wrote the first version of several of her most important books in that language.

In Adivar's day, the Ottoman Empire was undergoing a difficult process of reform, which included rethinking the role of women, and a small but growing number of females from the elite strata of society were exposed to Western ideas and ideals of emancipation. Determined to continue her education, Halide took courses privately with a number of tutors. She married one of them, the noted mathematician **Salih Zeki**, and gave birth to two sons. This marriage was not a success, and she eventually left her husband. Later she fell in love with a physician, Dr. Abdülhak Adnan Adivar (1881–1955), who was not only interested in medicine but in literature and politics as well. They married in 1917 when the Ottoman Empire was in its final crisis of dissolution. The Adivars led a full life raising children, writing books and essays, and engaging in nationalist politics.

In her first novels, particularly *Seviyye Talib* (1909), *Handan* (1912) and *Son eseri (Her Last Act,* 1912), Adivar successfully created female characters whose strong, positive personalities forever changed the landscape of modern Turkish literature. These were heroines and role models for the new women in the society proclaimed by the revolutionary Young Turks. Her 1910 novel *Raik'in annesi (Raik's Mother)* was a pioneering attack on traditional patriarchal Ottoman society, listing the sufferings endured by women. Adivar's thinking was mixed with nationalism and sometimes gave the impression of being illiberal. A number of fiercely nationalistic Pan-Turanian ideals made their appearance in her novel *The New Turan* (1912). During these formative years, Adivar was profoundly influenced by the ideas of the Turkish nationalist social philosopher and poet Mehmet Zia Gökalp (c. 1875–1924), who argued that the Ottoman Empire had to undergo a profound transformation in order to survive in a highly competitive world of national states. Adivar subscribed to Gökalp's notion that only drastic changes could enable Turkish civilization to survive and retain the core of its unique history. With its argument that strong cultural and historical ties between peoples of common Turkic ancestry justified the creation of an imperial state even larger than the already existing Ottoman Empire, Gökalp's concept of Pan-Turanianism also influenced Adivar.

When Turkey entered World War I as a German and Austro-Hungarian ally in the fall of 1914, Halide Adivar was a well-known writer. During the war years, she founded orphanages and taught in girls' schools in the Lebanese and Syrian provinces of the Ottoman Empire. When Turkey was defeated, she and her husband were determined to help their nation rise from the ashes of humiliation in 1918. The Allied forces occupied Istanbul in early 1919, and both the Adivars were listed on an arrest warrant issued by General Sir Charles Harington, the British commandant, because of "subversive" nationalist activities.

With superb oratorical talents, Adivar spread the nationalistic gospel at countless mass rallies in and around the capital city, infuriating the occupying powers. Utterly indifferent to the death sentence decreed against her, she became the life and soul of massive anti-Allied street demonstrations before the mosques of Sultan Ahmet and Fatih. Such outpourings of anger frightened and frustrated the Allied forces. When her activities threatened her life, she fled the city disguised as an Armenian servant to join her husband in the new Nationalist capital city of Ankara in Anatolia. Here, the Adivars joined the movement of national rebirth led by Mustafa Kemal Pasha (later Kemal Atatürk). While her husband served as the new regime's first minister of Health and Social Assistance, Halide chose to defend the newborn Turkish state in the most direct manner possible. A physically fearless woman, a keen equestrian, and a fine shot, she was commissioned a sergeant major by Atatürk himself, serving for a time on the General Staff and on the front lines when the Greeks made their ill-fated attack on the infant Turkish Republic in 1922.

The victory of the Turkish Nationalists and the proclamation of a republic in 1923 quickly revealed deep divisions within the revolutionary camp. Principled intellectuals like Adivar and her husband discovered they were frozen out of power and seriously threatened both politically and personally. Atatürk and his power-oriented lieutenants scoffed at the Adivars' notion that the new state should be based on multi-party government and freedom of expression. When their own faction, the Republican Progressive Party, was driven out of the public arena, the Adivars decided to move abroad to join a rapidly growing circle of banished intellectuals in 1924.

Adivar and her husband found refuge in France, where both taught for almost a decade at the School of Oriental Languages in Paris. Throughout these years, she wrote with great determination, hoping to bring the essence of Turkish civilization to a growing number of non-Oriental readers. The Adivars also gave lectures in the British Isles and the United States, where they taught in 1931–32 at Columbia University. Halide Adivar's international reputation was well established by the 1930s, and she took advantage of her fame in 1935 by traveling to India, where she gave lectures at the major universities. The years of banishment were busy ones, and she wrote a significant number of novels, historical works and autobiographical statements, many of which appeared in translation. By the time her best-known novel, *The Clown and His Daughter,* was written in English and published in London in 1935, she had become a writer of international stature (the author's own translation of this work into Turkish did not appear in print until 1938 under the title *Sinekli bakkal* [The Fly-Ridden Grocery Store]). Her strongly evocative novel became a bestseller in Turkey and was immediately recognized as a major literary achievement. Few were surprised in 1942 when its author was awarded the first State Prize for the Turkish Novel. *The Clown and His Daughter* was planned as the first section of an epic trilogy surveying life in Turkey in the final decades of the Ottoman Empire. The volume scrutinized the human drama of everyday life and individual personalities in an Istanbul neighborhood during the reign of Sultan Abdul-Hamid II (1842–1918). Critics universally praised the work for its rich evocation of swirling life and cultural clashes in the terminal, decadent phase of the Ottoman state.

After Kemal Atatürk died in November 1938, his successor, Ismet Inönu, was less dogmatic on matters of literary and intellectual freedom, so a number of exiled intellectuals, including the Adivars, returned home in 1939 to find that the political atmosphere, while by no means ideal, had moderated considerably. Halide was appointed professor of English language and literature at the University of Istanbul, while her husband accepted the post of editor-in-chief of the *Islamic Encyclopedia.* Her teaching duties left Adivar sufficient leisure to continue to write, and she published books and articles to the end of her life. Deeply interested in all aspects of English literature since her earliest days as a writer, Adivar spent the 1940s writing a three-volume history of English literature. She also was responsible for translations into Turkish of Shakespeare's *As You Like It* and *Coriolanus.* Throughout her long writing career, she showed remarkable versatility, for example producing in 1918 an opera libretto *Kenan çobanlari (The Shepherds of Canaan).* Her only play *Maske ve ruh,* published in Turkey in 1945, appeared in her own English adaptation in 1953 under the title *Masks or Souls;* this highly imaginative philosophical allegory presented on stage such diverse personalities as Shakespeare, Tamerlane, and Ibn Khaldun.

In the last years of her life, Halide Adivar continued to write and teach, but she was also involved in political life, serving in parliament from 1950 to 1954 as the delegate of the Republican People's Party from Izmir. She retired after the death of her husband in 1955 and concentrated on her writing. Adivar lived long enough to witness the first stages of a strong revival of interest in her writings, which had for a period been neglected by the Turkish reading public because of what some felt were their overly intricate plots and stylistic infelicities. By the 1990s, almost a dozen films based on her novels and stories had been released in Turkey. Halide Edib Adivar died in Istanbul on January 9, 1964. Among the many tributes, the words of *The Times* of London perhaps best summed up the essence of a remarkable public life and artistic career: "She was a woman in whom passion and intellect were remarkably blended."

SOURCES:

Barlas, H. Ugurol. *Halide Edip Adivar: Biyografya—bibliografya.* Istanbul: Yurttas yayinlari, 1963.

Blakemore, Grace. "Turkish Women Step Forward," in *Social Science.* Vol. 6, no. 3. July 1931, pp. 299–303.

Edip, Halide. "Women's Part in Turkey's Progress," in *Open Court.* Vol. 46, 1932, pp. 343–360.

Harris, George Sellers. *The Origins of Communism in Turkey.* Stanford, CA: Hoover Institution on War, Revolution and Peace, 1967.

"Mrs. H.E. Adivar, Turkish Writer and Woman of Action," in *The Times* [London]. January 15, 1964, p. 15.

Tatarli, Ibrahim. "Les grandes étapes dans l'évolution créative de Halide Edip Adivar," in *Études Balkaniques*. Vol. 20, no. 2, 1984, pp. 15–40.

John Haag, Associate Professor of History, University of Georgia, Athens, Georgia

Adler, Celia (1890–1979)

*American actress and first lady of the Yiddish theater. Born in 1890; died in New York City after suffering a stroke on January 31, 1979; daughter of Jacob Adler (an actor) and his first wife Dinah Feinman (an actress); half-sister of actors Luther and *Stella Adler (1902–1993); married three times; children: one son.*

Celia Adler, who began her acting career in the arms of her mother at the age of six months, would eventually become known as the "first lady of the Yiddish Theater." She was a product of the first marriage of the great Yiddish actor Jacob Adler, who had an eye for many women, and actress **Dinah Feinman**. When Celia asked her mother if she was bitter about her father's skirtchasing ways, Dinah replied: "Anger toward him? Never, my daughter. He was not to blame: women just would not leave him alone."

In 1918, Celia—along with Jacob Ben Ami, Ludwig Satz, and **Bertha Gersten**—helped launch the Yiddish company of Maurice Schwartz at the Irving Place Theater. Historians regard their work as the beginning of serious or "art" in the Yiddish theater. An accomplished actress, Celia starred in many productions, including Sholom Aleichem's *Stempenya,* with Lazar Freed and Maurice Schwartz, produced by the Yiddish Art Theater in 1929. She also appeared with Paul Muni and Marlon Brando in *A Flag is Born* in 1946.

Adler, Emma (1858–1935)

Austrian socialist leader of the women's movement in the Habsburg Empire. Born Emma Braun in Debrecen, Hungary, on May 20, 1858; died in exile in Zurich, Switzerland, on February 23, 1935; married Victor Adler, in 1878; children: three, including Friedrich (Fritz) Adler, who assassinated the Austrian Prime Minister, Count Carl Stürgkh.

Editor of anthologies aimed at youth, particularly the influential Buch der Jugend; *forced to flee Vienna with the advent of fascism; died in exile at the home of her son Fritz Adler in Zurich.*

Selected writings: Jane Welsh Carlyle *(Vienna: Akademischer Verlag, 1907);* Die berühmten Frauen der französischen Revolution, 1789–1795 *(Vienna: C.W. Stern, 1906);* Goethe und Frau von Stein *(Leipzig: Toeplitz & Deuticke, 1887); (editor)* Feierabend: Ein Buch für die Jugend *(Vienna: Verlag der Wiener Volksbuchhandlung, 1902); (editor)* Buch der Jugend: Für die Kinder des Proletariats *(Berlin: "Vorwärts," 1895).*

Emma Braun was born in Debrecen, Hungary, on May 20, 1858, where she grew up in an assimilated middle-class Jewish milieu. Her father was an official of the Hungarian National Railroad. In 1878, she married Victor Adler (1852–1918), a Jewish intellectual from a wealthy Prague family. Deeply moved by the suffering of the working classes in an era of unchecked capitalism, her husband studied medicine in order to minister to the material needs of the urban proletariat of Vienna. Determined to bring medical care to the city's slum dwellers, Emma supported her husband in his political and social aims. The Adlers were so convinced that they should practice what they preached that they chose to live with their three children in extremely modest quarters in one of Vienna's working-class districts while Victor used up his family inheritance to bring medical assistance to the poor.

Sharing the same socialist ideals, they traveled to London in the 1880s to observe a conventional parliamentary system in practice as well as to debate the finer points of Marxist theory with the recently deceased Karl Marx's closest collaborator, Friedrich Engels. The couple also shared a love of adventure. In the early years of their marriage, the Adlers regularly swam across the Attersee—an unusual accomplishment in the late Victorian era for a "delicate" middle-class bride.

The socially progressive Emma Adler was a Marxist agnostic, like her husband. Fellow socialist *Rosa Jochmann related an anecdote from the last decades of the 19th century when the Adlers customarily spent their holidays in the charming village of Nussdorf on the Attersee. Taken by Emma's delicate beauty, an artist working on the decoration of the local church asked her to pose as model for the Virgin Mary. She agreed, and the painting has remained in the church for over a century. Few, if any, of the Catholic worshipers have ever realized that the Mother of God was posed for by a young woman who was both Jewish and a Marxist agnostic.

In the late 1880s, Victor Adler was the undisputed leader of the Austrian socialist movement, tirelessly supported by Emma. Despite the responsibilities of childrearing—she was mother to two sons and a daughter—much of her time and energy was spent teaching and writing. She was a foreign-language instructor in the *Arbeiterbildungsverein,* the ambitious system of adult education courses created under Socialist Party auspices. A strong believer in the popularization of knowledge, Emma published a number of clearly written works, including a history of the role of women in the French Revolution and a biography of *Jane Welsh Carlyle, wife of the famous Romantic historian. Emma's abiding interest in the problems of young people motivated decades of work as an editor of juvenile anthologies, particularly the influential *Buch der Jugend.* Her best friend was the remarkable *Adelheid Popp whose journalistic career lasted over 30 years in the *Arbeiterinnen-Zeitung,* the Social Democratic newspaper aimed at the female working class.

The last two decades of Emma Adler's life were marked by crisis and tragedy. By the time World War I began in August 1914, Victor Adler had worn himself out in the cause of Socialism. He, Emma, and the socialists had expected working-class solidarity, instead of a flocking to national colors. The war showed that the ideal of proletarian internationalism was an empty slogan, further undermining Victor's fragile health. In October 1916, their son Friedrich assassinated the Austrian prime minister, Count Carl Stürgkh, while he was dining in one of Vienna's exclusive hotels. The trial of Fritz Adler in 1917 was a terrible ordeal for his parents, and he barely escaped the death sentence.

In November 1918, the Adlers were filled with joy when the collapse of the Habsburg monarchy and the end of World War I brought about their son's release from prison. That same month, Victor was appointed foreign minister, but he died on the very day Austria was proclaimed a Republic. Although she was greatly respected for decades of work in the socialist cause, tragedy continued to dog Emma Adler. Her only daughter died during the Great Depression and the specter of Fascism and war loomed over Central Europe. Fritz now lived in Switzerland, where he worked as a theoretical physicist and attempted to create a militant international force that would be able to combat both Fascism and Stalinism. Democratic Socialism was suppressed in a bloodbath in the Austrian Republic in February 1934, forcing the elderly Emma Adler to flee to Switzerland to live with her son. She died on February 23, 1935, in Zurich. With the passage of time, many of the ideals Emma

Adler fought for became institutionalized social programs. A visionary and idealist like her husband, she was a woman before her time. Many of the ideals Emma Adler fought for as a leader of the socialist movement are taken for granted in the industrialized world.

SOURCES:
"Adler, Emma" file, Arbeitsgemeinschaft "Biografisches Lexikon der österreichischen Frau," Vienna.
Ellenbogen, Wilhelm. *Menschen und Prinzipien.* Edited by Friedrich Weissensteiner. Vienna: Hermann Böhlaus Nachfolger, 1981.
"Emma Adler," in *Volksrecht* [Zurich]. March 9, 1935.
Florence, Ronald. *Fritz: The Story of a Political Assassin.* NY: Dial Press, 1971.
Hahnl, Hans Heinz. *Vergessene Literaten.* Vienna: Österreichischer Bundesverlag, 1984.
Leser, Norbert, ed. *Werk und Widerhall.* Vienna: Verlag der Wiener Volksbuchhandlung, 1964.
Sporrer, Maria, and Herbert Steiner, eds. *Rosa Jochmann: Zeitzeugin.* Vienna: Europaverlag, 1983.
Tausk, Martha. "Emma Adler," in *Arbeiter-Zeitung* [Vienna]. May 16, 1948.

John Haag, Associate Professor of History, University of Georgia, Athens, Georgia

Adler, Julia (1897–1995).

See Adler, Sara for sidebar.

Adler, Lola (1902–1993).

See Adler, Stella.

Adler, Polly (1899–1962)

Successful American madam who ran an opulent bordello in the heart of Manhattan from 1920 to 1945. Name variations: (aliases) Ann Bean, Pearl Davis, Joan Martin. Born Pearl Adler in Yanow, a White Russian village near the Polish border, on April 16, 1899; died on June 10, 1962; eldest of nine children of Isidore (a Jewish tailor) and Sarah Adler; became a naturalized citizen, May 20, 1929; never married; no children.

Polly Adler was born in Yanow, a White Russian village near the Polish border, on April 16, 1899, the daughter of a Jewish tailor who was by nature temperamental. In her autobiography *A House Is Not a Home,* Adler recalled him as a man "with big ideas and a correspondingly large sense of his own importance. In his eyes . . . a wife's place was either in the kitchen or in childbed, and Sarah, my subdued self-effacing little mother, alternated uncomplainingly between them."

In 1913, with the family planning to follow, Adler was packed off to America, accompanied by an older cousin. But after reaching Bremen, her cousin had second thoughts about embarking, and the 14-year-old Adler (the youngest in steerage) sailed on the *Naftar* alone. With her belongings in a potato sack, Adler arrived at Ellis Island knowing no English. She was put on a train to Mt. Holyoke, Massachusetts, where she was to stay with acquaintances of acquaintances until her family could arrive to claim her. Though her foster family was civil, the warm and affectionate Adler had to deal with their indifference. World War I effectively scuttled the family's dreams of joining her, and Adler's brief stayover turned into four years.

As World War I in Europe took its toll, Adler's father could no longer mail her school money out of Russia. Thus, at 16, the "A" student had to quit school and get a job. For the next two years, she worked in a paper factory for $3 a week. Restless and discontented, she decided to seek out a cousin in Brooklyn. To her surprise, she was greeted warmly, offered the couch, and was soon settled in a job at a corset factory at $5 a week, out of which she paid $3 for room and board and $1.20 for carfare and lunches. Up at 6 AM, home for supper, she then walked a mile each way to night school.

In April 1917, with the United States entering the war, Adler found employment manufacturing soldiers' shirts. The 18-year-old, who had now reached her full height—4'11"—went on her first date and was soon caught up in the dance-hall craze. Though reformers were convinced dance halls were the "gilded hell of the *palais de danse*," Adler noted that the Nonpareil Dance Hall was "more like a gymnasium, and, as in a gymnasium, the goings on though strenuous were disciplined." Becoming a regular, she entered dance contests, competing for candy, Kewpie dolls, cups, and cash. But by the time she was 19, she was still sleeping on the leather couch, "still grindingly poor, still minus an education, still without a place in the sun."

Then a new supervisor came on the job. On their first date, he managed to get her alone. When he made an advance, she rose to leave. Recalled Adler in her autobiography: "Instead of answering, he went over to the door and locked it. When I resisted him, he knocked me cold."

A month after the rape, she realized she was pregnant, but the supervisor would have nothing to do with her. Adler chose to have an abortion. "I tried to put all this nightmare behind me," she wrote. "But though I went through the motions of living, I was changed—I had lost heart. I no longer had hope." Moving to Manhattan, she found a room on Second Avenue and 9th Street

and for the next year worked at the Trio Corset Co. It was a time, she wrote, of "unrelieved drabness, of hurry and worry and clawing uncertainty."

The year 1921 brought prohibition. While attending a party, Adler was befriended by an actress. Open and warm, the actress shared her showbusiness friends with Adler and invited her to share a nine-room apartment on Riverside Drive. At first, Adler was thrilled. Soon, however, she learned that the actress was hooked on opium and the *joie de vivre* of the revolving guests turned into "hop" parties. Throughout her life, Adler steered clear of drugs, and she was uncomfortable with the problems of her self-destructive roommate. When Tony, a known gangster, offered to pay the rent on a new apartment if he could use it once in awhile for trysts with a prominent married woman, Adler jumped at the chance. She now had a room of one's own—sort of.

> Now that I can look back over the whole story, it seems obvious that this was my first big step down the so-called primrose path. But then it never even occurred to me to think of Tony's plan and my part in it as being moral or immoral. It did not touch me personally. It simply paid the rent. . . . I am aware that in the judgment of the stratum of society which decides these things I should have drawn myself up and said, "No thank you, keep your dirty money! I'd rather sew shirts for five dollars a week." . . . My feeling is that by the time there are such choices to be made, your life already has made the decision for you.

Before long, Tony's prominent married woman had moved on and he was casting about for a new girlfriend; he proposed to Adler payment of $100 for a "girl" and $50 for a finder's fee. By now, Adler knew many women who were openly available for a price and gladly deposited the $50 into her bank account. Tony, who was making good money bootlegging, began to spend two nights a week at her apartment. Supplying him with two women a week, Adler was now taking in $100 weekly and finding the eco-

Polly Adler

nomic freedom heady. She began to give her address to those she thought discreet, and before long three women were coming in several nights a week to entertain acquaintances. Adler was soon arrested for running a disorderly house and listed in the police files as a procuress, but a trial was dismissed for lack of evidence.

Her reputation already ruined, the 22-year-old began to run a full-time house, while worrying that her family would find out in Russia's little town of Yanow. By the spring of 1922, having saved $6,000, Adler decided to go legit and launched Polly's Lingerie Shop with a friend who was not in the procuring business. "Among our best customers were *Rosa Ponselle and her sister," boasted Adler. But the shop failed in 1923, and Adler took an apartment in the West 70s and reopened her house for business.

She was fussy about clientele. Businessmen were tightwads, gamblers too rough, so she decided to target the upper brackets of society: theater people, artists, and writers. Her house became a gathering place for intellectuals, tycoons, playboys, those in high positions in government, and the exceedingly wealthy—in short: café society. Polly Adler's was a place to "meet friends, play cards, arrange a dinner party, kill time—a sort of combination club and speakeasy with a harem." She recalled:

> I had begun to receive women as my guests. But at first it was only those who were so rich or so famous or so intellectual or so uninhibited that they could go anywhere. Now, however, dropping in at my place had become the thing, and from this time on I was running what amounted to a coeducational bordello.

She was learning her trade. Savvy about raids, she could slip a quick C-note [$100 bill] where it counted. Prospering, she moved to the 50s near Seventh Ave, employed a domestic staff of three—cook, housecleaner and personal maid—and engaged an interior decorator. The place was done up in period French. "Louis Quinze and Louis Seize," noted Adler, "which is sort of traditional for a house." Showgirls would arrive each night from Ziegfeld's or Earl Carroll's Vanities to pick up loose change. Adler, who knew the benefits of fame, now worked at getting her name in the columns, at becoming the "notorious Polly Adler." Her business card contained the logo of a parrot on a perch and the words: LExington 2-1099, New York City.

After a summer season at Saratoga in 1926, Adler moved her house to 59th and Madison. She had a reputation for running an honest, clean, nomadic house; her women were attractive, experienced, and underwent weekly examinations. The rule of the house: "Be a lady in the parlor and a whore in the bedroom." Her main complaint: invasive questions by the slumming demi-monde.

> Many of my customers never seemed to realize that a prostitute is just as much a product of our so-called culture as is a college professor or a boot-black, and, as with them, her choice of occupation has been dictated by environmental and personality factors. No woman is born a whore and any woman may become one.

Though Adler noted that it would lessen a man's pleasure to think that a woman was submitting to him from necessity, she confessed that "despite all the feigned transports of ecstasy (for purposes of increasing the tip), to ninety-nine out of a hundred girls going to bed with a customer is a joyless, even distasteful, experience."

After a major raid on July 22, 1927, Adler's entrance into the courtroom caused quite a stir among the court officials, "for there were my girls," she wrote, "tall and beautiful, gliding down the aisle like swans on a mirrored lake, with me bustling along after them like Donald Duck."

On May 20, 1929, Adler became a naturalized citizen of the United States. A few months later, she was in hiding in Miami, one step in front of a subpoena, trying to avoid an appearance in front of the Seabury Commission (1931). Though she was not in jeopardy, Adler had no intention of "singing" in front of Samuel Seabury who was engaged in weeding out the malefactors of the New York judicial system. By fleeing a subpoena, she became even more infamous, making every front page in town. In the 1931 edition of the Ziegfeld Follies, Mark Hellinger offered a satire on *Grand Hotel*, with *Helen Morgan playing the moody Russian ballerina "Mademoiselle Polly Adlervitch." But Polly Adler was lying low. She eventually returned to face the music, but would not name names.

Though she was soon released, Adler was flat broke and out of luck. By living outside the law, she had no recourse to the law when she was reluctantly introduced to gangster Dutch Schultz at a party and he asked for her phone number. "There were two things I could do. I could give it to him or I could give it to him." Adler hated gangsters, calling them bully boys, but when Schultz told her to find an apartment under his auspices, she felt she had no options. To her horror, the apartment became gang headquarters. She never lost her fear of Schultz.

By now, Adler had been arrested 11 times, but there had been no convictions. In order to meet their monthly quota, on March 5, 1935, the police carried out another raid. Adler was bound over to be tried at Special Sessions and her "girls" were slated for the Lower Courts. The social climate was curiously sympathetic. "The police tap this woman's wires, set spies on her, and in other ways keep her under surveillance as if they suspected her of being the Lindbergh kidnapper," wrote an indignant columnist for the New York *Daily News*. Even Judge Jonah J. Goldstein showed compassion while sentencing:

> I don't think it's fair to spotlight the women and whisper about the men. It takes two to commit the offense, although under the law only one is brought in. Even though the men are in places of that sort by choice, the procedure in these cases, as in prohibition, makes only the seller and not the buyer liable to prosecution. There is no logic in this distinction, but I am compelled to administer the law as it is written.

Adler received her first prison term: 30 days and $500 fine. While in jail, the town's reigning celebrity was interviewed repeatedly. Forever flip, she was quoted by *Dorothy Kilgallen as saying of her cell, "It's not bad. Of course it ain't big, but it's home." Adler enjoyed the interview; she admired Kilgallen, but forever resented the misattributed "ain't."

Once released, Adler was under constant surveillance. She longed to get out of the business, knowing that if the town were raided, she'd be the leading scapegoat. With the help of her friends of the cognoscenti, in her late 40s, she returned to college in Los Angeles, around 1948, and began to write her autobiography, *A House Is Not a Home*. In it, she quotes everyone from Shakespeare to *Clare Boothe Luce. Writes Adler:

> The literature of all countries teems with novels and stories and plays about prostitution, and the prostitute as a character has fascinated the men with the noblest minds, the giants of letters, no less than the hacks and the pornographers. But the great to-the-life portraits in the gallery of "fallen women"—the Nanas and Sonyas and Sadie Thompsons are as few and far between as the Zolas and Doestoievskis and Maughams who created them. The overwhelming proportion of writing on this subject—both fiction, and what purports to be factual—is cheaply sensational, or distorted by prejudice, or uninformed, often all three. In this kind of writing, the prostitute comes in two standard models. Either she is presented as a

brazen hussy who arrived in the world equipped with marabou-trimmed garters, black silk stockings and a sexy leer (heart of gold optional), or as an innocent victim, a babe in the woods, seduced and abandoned by a city slicker, or maybe shanghaied by a white slaver while on her way from choir practice. And, depending in which category she belongs, her life, when there's no company in the parlor, appears to consist entirely of (a) sitting around in a dirty kimono drinking gin, or (b) weeping and wailing and hammering her fists against the door until someone shuts her up with a smack on the chops.

Polly Adler, however, was not the only one to profit from prostitution. She writes of "the pimp, the grocer, the butcher, the baker, the merchant, the landlord, the druggist, the liquor dealer, the policeman, the doctor, the city father and the politician—these are the people who make money out of prostitution, these are the real reapers of the wages of sin." A huge bestseller, the book's profits kept Adler in the style in which she had grown accustomed until she died in 1962.

SOURCES:

Adler, Polly. *A House Is Not a Home*. NY: Rinehart, 1953.

Adler, Sara (1858–1953)

*Russian-American actress and foremost tragedian of the Yiddish stage. Born Sara Levitzky (changed to Lewis) in 1858 in Odessa, Russia; died April 28, 1953, in New York, New York; married Maurice Heine (divorced 1890); married Jacob Adler (1885–1926, the Yiddish actor), in 1890; children: (first marriage) Frances Adler; *Stella Adler (1902–1993, actress, director, teacher of acting);* *Julia Adler (1897–1995, an actress); Luther; Jay.*

See sidebar on the following page

Sara Adler's place in American theater history is often overshadowed by her second husband Jacob Adler's enormous popularity as the leading tragic actor on the American Yiddish stage. However, not only did she play a major part in establishing the Yiddish theater in New York City, she was an impressive actor in her own right, with over 300 leading roles to her credit. She also introduced "realism" in acting before it became a leading theater movement in the United States.

Born in Odessa, Russia, in 1858, Adler grew up in a wealthy Russian-Jewish family and studied singing at the Odessa Conservatory before joining a Yiddish theater troupe managed by Maurice Heine, whom she later married. After the assassination of Russian Tsar Alexander II in 1881,

❧▶ Adler, Julia (1897–1995)

*American actress. Name variations: Julia Adler Foshko. Born July 4, 1897, in Philadelphia, Pennsylvania; died on June 3, 1995, in Englewood, New Jersey; daughter of Jacob P. and Sara (Lewis) Adler (distinguished actors and producing managers in the Yiddish theater); sister of Frances Adler, *Stella Adler, Luther, and Jay; half-sister of Abe, Charles, and *Celia Adler (offspring of her father's two previous marriages and an intervening liaison in Russia); married Joseph Foshko (an artist); children: daughter, Judy.*

All five children born to actors Jacob and *Sara Adler found their way onto the stage early in life, but Julia, the middle child, just missed being born on stage during an afternoon matinee in Philadelphia. Family legend has recorded her arrival, on July 4, 1897, moments after her famous mother, Sara, left the stage.

Julia Adler's theatrical career was overshadowed by her more famous younger siblings, Stella and Luther. On Broadway in the 1920s, Julia portrayed Jessica in the David Warfield production of *The Merchant of Venice,* as well as the title role in David Belasco's *Rosa Machree.* In 1939, she appeared in a revival of the Clifford Odets play *Awake and Sing,* a role originated by her sister Stella in 1935. Of her performance, *The New York Times* critic Brooks Atkinson could not resist the inevitable comparison: "Julia Adler improves a little upon Stella Adler's playing." In 1952, Julia toured with her brother Luther in *Tovarich.* Her marriage to artist Joseph Foshko produced a daughter, Judy, and several grandchildren and great grandchildren. She died at the age of 97, at the Englewood Hospital in Englewood, New Jersey, the last surviving member of a legendary theatrical family.

SOURCES:

Thomas, Robert McG., Jr. The New York Times News Service. June 4, 1995.

when Jewish repression eventually led to a ban on Yiddish theater, Heine brought his troupe to the United States, where Sara soon gained recognition on the Yiddish stage in New York City.

She divorced Heine in 1890, but it is unclear whether it was before, or because of, Jacob Adler. By her own account, when she first saw Jacob on stage, she thought he was ridiculous. "He dressed badly," she said, "wore yellow shoes!" She married him, regardless, and, together with playwright Jacob Gordin, joined in her husband's efforts to revitalize the Yiddish theater, determined to reflect the life of the new urban American Jew.

According to director and critic Harold Clurman, who saw Adler perform and was mar-

ried to her daughter Stella, Sara taught Jacob a few more things about acting. Despite his popularity, he lacked self-confidence and lived in constant fear of public rejection. Once when he was having difficulty with a part for which he later became famous, he broke down in tears, despairing that he would never get it right. Sara slapped his face. "Of course you can play the part; get up and begin. I shall help you with it."

Sara and Jacob Adler's productions, most of which were mounted at their theater on the Bowery, became the center of serious Yiddish theater, and established Adler as "the dowager duchess" of the Yiddish stage. Her greatest role was that of Katusha Maslova in Gordin's dramatization of Tolstoy's *Resurrection.* Sara also won acclaim for her starkly realistic portrayal of the abandoned and unbalanced wife in Gordin's *Homeless.* She enthralled audiences by "acting the way people do in real life." Clurman elaborated: "I observed that her realism—meticulous, subdued, though still intense—never failed to convey a largeness of feeling, the kind of grandeur that comes through only when a sense of life's high drama is present."

Adler gave birth to six children in the course of her marriage, most of them taking their place on the stage as soon as they were steady on their feet. Five went on to establish careers in the theater; Luther and Stella became stars. Marriage to Jacob demanded resourcefulness and tenacity; he was a notorious womanizer, had been married twice previously, and fathered a number of children by other women. Once, when he temporarily left Sara to live with his mistress-servant, she and actor Rudolf Schildkraut formed their own company. She did everything from directing and acting in the plays, designing and sewing the costumes, even polishing the fruit that was sold during intermission.

After Jacob's death in 1926, Sara performed infrequently, although in 1939 she recreated her role in *Resurrection* as part of a tribute to her at the New Yorker Theater. Though age began to undermine her health, Sara was determined to live the remainder of her life to the fullest. She took tango lessons when she was in her 70s. Once, exhausted after a dangerous attack of acute indigestion, her daughter suggested she take a sleeping pill. "No," she yelled, "if I fall asleep, I'll die."

Adler unabashedly lied about her age, sometimes out of vanity, sometimes out of necessity. When she went into the hospital to have a cataract removed, she told the surgeon she was

70, because she didn't think he would operate if he knew she was 80. She was always immaculately turned out and, up until her last illness, stayed out every night past midnight, congregating with her actor friends at the Cafe Royal on Second Avenue. Sara Adler spent her last years living with her daughter Stella and Harold Clurman. She died on April 28, 1953, at the age of 95.

SOURCES:

Clurman, Harold. *All People are Famous (instead of an autobiography).* NY: Harcourt, Brace, Jovanovich, 1974.

Barbara Morgan, Melrose, Massachusetts

Adler, Stella (1902–1993)

American actress, director, acting teacher, and founder of the Stella Adler Theater Studio in New York City. Name variations: Lola Adler (stage name), Stella Ardler (film name). Born Stella Adler on February 10, 1902, in New York, New York; died on December 21, 1992, in Los Angeles, California; daughter of Jacob P. and Sara (Lewis) Adler (distinguished actors and producing managers in the Yiddish theater); sister of Frances, ❦▸ *Julia Adler (1897–1995), Luther, and Jay; half-sister of Abe, Charles, and *Celia Adler (1890–1979), offspring of her father's two previous marriages and an intervening liaison in Russia; attended New York University; studied acting with her father and Maria Ouspenskaya; married Horace Eleascheff (divorced); married Harold Clurman, in 1943 (divorced 1960); married Mitchell Wilson; children: (first marriage) daughter,* **Ellen Oppenheim**.

Theater: made first appearance on stage at her father's theater, The Grand, New York, in Broken Hearts *(1906); played continuously in her father's company throughout the United States; first appeared in London at the Pavilion Theater as Naomi in* Elisha Ben Avia *(1919); returned to New York and appeared in* Martinique, The Man of the Mountains, *and* The World We Live In *(1920); for one season of vaudeville, appeared coast to coast on the Orpheum Circuit; appeared with the American Laboratory Theater in the role of the Baroness Creme de la Creme in* The Straw Hat *(October 1926), as Elly in* Big Lake *(April 1927), and as Beatrice in* Much Ado About Nothing *(November 1927); played a season at the Living Place Theater with* **Bertha Kalich** *(1927), and with Jacob Ben Ami (1928); starred in a repertory of plays in United States, South America, as well as Paris, Antwerp, and Brussels (1929); played a series of leading parts with Maurice Schwartz and Samuel Goldenberg in plays at the Yiddish Art Theater, Second Avenue, including:* Kiddish Hashem, The God of Vengeance, The Witch of Castile, The Lower Depths, The Living Corpse, He

Who Gets Slapped, Liliom, *and* Jew Süss *(1930); played over 100 parts (1927–31); joined the Group Theater (1931), and played Geraldine at the Martin Beck Theater in* The House of Connelly *(September 1931); played Dona Josefa at the Mansfield Theater in* Night over Taos *(December 1931); played Sarah Glassman in* Success Story *at the Maxine Elliott Theater (September 1932), and Myra Bonney in* Big Night *(January 1933); played title role in* Hilda Cassidy *at the Martin Beck Theater (May 1933); played Gwyn Ballantyne in* Gentlewoman *at the Cort Theater (for the Group Theater, March 1934); played* *Adah Isaacs Menken *in* Gold-Eagle Guy *at the Morosco Theater (November 1934); played Bessie Berger in* Awake and Sing! *at the Belasco Theater (February 1935); played Clara in* Paradise Lost *at the Longacre Theater (December 1935); played Catherine Carnick in* Sons and Soldiers *at the Morosco Theater (May 1943); staged* Manhattan Nocturne *at the Forrest Theater (October 1943); played Clotilde in* Pretty Little Parlor *at the National Theater (April 1944); directed* Polonaise *at the Alvin Theater, (October 1945); played Zinaida in* He Who Gets Slapped *for the Theater Guild at the Booth Theater (March 1946); directed* Sunday Breakfast *at the Coronet Theater (May 1952); directed a revival of* Johnny Johnson *at Carnegie Hall Playhouse (October 1956); played Madame Rosepettle in* Oh Dad, Poor Dad, Mama's Hung You in the Closet, and I'm Feelin' So Sad *at the Lyric, Hammersmith Theater, London (July 1961).*

Film: under the name of Stella Ardler, made her film debut in Love on Toast *(Paramount, 1938); subsequently was associate producer of* Du Barry Was a Lady *(MGM, 1943); appeared in* The Thin Man *(MGM, 1944); and* My Girl Tisa *(UA, 1948).*

To chronicle the life and career of Stella Adler is to journey through almost a century of American theater. She was born in 1902, into the rich acting tradition of the Yiddish-American theater in New York, where acting was a noble profession and the truly great were royalty. She studied with the master, Russian actor-director Constantin Stanislavski (1863–1938). She performed in over 200 productions, in comedies and tragedies that ranged from the classics to the new realism and beyond. In the 1930s, she was part of the Group Theater, which gave rise to some of the most talented playwrights, actors, and designers of the day, and was committed to producing the great social and political plays of that era. She directed for the stage and worked in films. Lastly, she was a teacher, a passionate disciple of Stanislavski, and a founder of The Stella Adler Studio, whose graduates include act-

❦▸
Adler, Julia (1897–1995). *See Adler, Sara for sidebar.*

ing giants Marlon Brando, Robert De Niro, and Warren Beatty. In a loving tribute to Adler written shortly after her death in 1992, Robert Brustein, director of the American Repertory Theater at Harvard University, praised her for the profound respect and admiration she had for acting and actors and for her attempt to instill a nobility of purpose in her students. "In her deepest being," he wrote, "Stella embodied the art of our profession and what it could become. Her loss impoverishes us in more ways than I want to think about."

Stella Adler was born in the proverbial trunk, as were her five brothers and sisters. Her parents, Jacob P. ("the Jewish Henry Irving") and *Sara Adler, were the foremost tragedians of the Yiddish stage in America. Her father, described as "large in frame, talent, and appetites," possessed incredible magnetism both on and off stage. Harold Clurman (Stella Adler's second husband) knew the man and saw him perform. "He 'seduced' not only his audiences, but his servants, his colleagues, his community, and most of all his family." Sara Adler, Jacob's third wife, also possessed a daunting talent, playing over 300 leading roles during her career. Clurman recalls her as one of the Jewish Theater's "first realistic actors."

It was no surprise to Stella Adler that her entire clan became actors. "In my family," she said, "immediately, when you could barely walk, you were put on the stage." Adler made her theatrical debut at the age of four in her father's production of *Broken Hearts* at the Grand Street Theater in New York. She trained and performed the classics in repertory with her parents for the next 12 years, including roles in the plays of Shakespeare, George Hauptmann, and Henrik Ibsen. She made her London debut in 1919 at the Pavilion Theater, and first appeared on Broadway in the 1922 smash hit, *The World We Live In* ("The Insect Comedy"), by Karel Capek.

Stella Adler attended New York University and later, in 1925, studied at the American Laboratory Theater with *Maria Ouspenskaya and Richard Boleslavsky, both of whom had come to the United Stages after distinguished careers in Europe. It was Adler's first introduction to the acting techniques of Constantin Stanislavski, who, with Vladimir Nemirovish-Danchenko, had founded the Moscow Art Theater in 1898. Stanislavski's system for training actors—which would eventually become known simply as "the method"—was created out of practical necessity. The old-fashioned acting techniques simply would not accommodate the new schools of

playwriting, described as "realistic" or "naturalistic," depicting the world and society as it was, instead of creating an idealization. Today, every modern approach to realistic acting has its roots in Stanislavski, although his system is rarely taught in its purist form and has, on occasion, been interpreted beyond recognition.

Prior to the 20th century, what there was of actor's training focused on a mechanical response to imaginary stimulus. Responses became fairly standard and therefore were easily taught or just handed down. For Stanislavski, the goal was psychological realism. His system emphasized teaching the actor to be sensitive to the stimulus (the imaginary situations within the play), from which the reactions would more naturally develop.

In its simplest forr , the method comprises six components: (1) formulation of a flexible body and voice, which can respond to all demands; (2) observation of reality, from which the actor can build a character by selecting lifelike action, stage business, and speech; (3) perfection of stage technique by which the character is projected to the audience, without any appearance of artificiality; (4) formation of "emotion memory," which is the ability to recall from one's own experience how it feels to be in the emotional situations of the play; (5) thorough knowledge of the script, including intense analysis focusing on the character's background, environment, and relationships; and (6) concentration upon imagining, feeling, and projecting the truth of the stage situation to the audience.

Interpreters often forget that Stanislavski was a well-trained and skillful actor before he felt a need to create the exercises and disciplines that make up the Stanislavski method. Through years of experience on the stage, he had learned the technique of acting and then had found that technique was not enough. He never, however, claimed that technique was not essential.

In 1931, Adler and her brother Luther joined the Group Theater, which began as a workshop of The Theater Guild and became independent in 1931. (The Theater Guild, part of the little theater movement, was a subscription-based professional organization that in the 1920s introduced many of the leading experimental European and American playwrights and production techniques.) Founded by Harold Clurman, Lee Strasberg, and *Cheryl Crawford, the Group was a repertory company modeled after the Moscow Art Theater, and dedicated to introducing the Stanislavski method of acting and stage production to America. Providing a depression-era alternative to the commercial theater, it developed into one of the most exciting theater companies of the 1930s. Adler described the ensemble nature of the group: "This theater demanded a basic understanding of a complex artistic principle: that all people connected with this theater, the actor, designer, playwright, director, etc., had of necessity to arrive at a single point of view which the theme of the play also expressed."

In the summer of 1931, the two Adlers, along with a 28-member acting ensemble, which included Franchot Tone, Morris Carnovsky, John Garfield, Lee J. Cobb, and Sanford Meisner, retreated to a farmhouse in Connecticut to prepare for their first season under the direction of Lee Strasberg. There, Strasberg unleashed his interpretation of Stanislavski, putting his actors through rigorous rehearsal sessions that stressed improvisational work and exercises in what he called "affective memory." The Group's premier production of Paul Green's Chekovian drama, *The House of Connelly*, featuring Stella Adler in the role of Geraldine Connelly, won critical acclaim. Brooks Atkinson of *The New York Times* wrote: "Their group performance is too beautifully imagined and modulated to concentrate on personal achievements. There is not a gaudy, brittle or facile stroke in their acting. . . . It is not too much to hope that something fine and true has been started in the American theater."

Adler's performances with the Group theater included roles in plays by Maxwell Anderson, Robert Lewis, Sidney Kingsley, and the Group's resident playwright, Clifford Odets. Her role as Bessie Berger in Odets' *Awake and Sing* is considered by some to be her finest work. Robert Lewis recalled that her portrayal "set a standard for Jewish-mother parts that has not been approached since; omitting the usual self-pity and leavening the dominating nature of the woman with lofty humor."

Adler's relationship with the Group was sometimes fragile. There were skirmishes with Clurman, who directed many of the productions, and to whom she was romantically linked at the time. Believing that "actresses were spiritually affected by their roles," she fretted that he was aging her prematurely by forcing her into the more mature roles, particularly those in Odets' plays. Adler also had a penchant for a somewhat high-toned lifestyle, including an apartment on Fifth Avenue and frequent jaunts to Europe, which did not always sit well with her peers, many of whom were young actors

struggling through the dark days of the Depression. She loved fine clothes and was always beautifully turned out. Clurman remembers her hats, something of a trademark, which were "like the hats of stage stars prior to World War I." Brustein recalled that she dressed "like an elegant courtesan," and held court in her lavish digs. "Her roomy Fifth Avenue apartment, where she entertained so many notables, was furnished like a Venetian Bordello, with low-hanging chandeliers, burnished mirrors and overstuffed furniture."

Adler's greatest problem with the Group, however, was a growing resentment of Strasberg's idiosyncratic interpretation of Stanislavski's system, with his emphasis on "truth" and "reality," and his obsession with "affective memory." In 1934, dissatisfied with her performance in *Gentlewoman*, Adler took a leave of absence from the Group and went off to Europe with Clurman. They were on a stopover in Paris when Clurman received word that Stanislavski was in the city and that he should arrange a meeting. Clurman sent a note and received an invitation by return mail. Shy about accompanying Clurman, Adler hesitantly agreed. The details of the actual meeting differ slightly between accounts. Clurman recalls that Stanislavski was alone with his doctor; Adler remembers the presence of two others. Clurman describes the master as tall—6'4" at least—very much like Adler's father, but, unlike Jacob Adler, quite shy about having a woman in his presence. She remembers being the shy one, quite overcome with stage-fright. "I stood completely unable to move, forward or backward. I was paralyzed by the whole moment." Stanislavski suggested an outing on the Champs-Élysees. Adler remembers the laughter and camaraderie of a small group in the park, and watching Stanislavski interact with the others; Clurman only mentions the doctor in attendance because the master had suffered a heart attack the previous year and was under constant care. On the matter of Stanislavski's first words to her, Adler's account is more dramatic. She knew he sensed her reticence, because he "had the 'eye' and nothing got past him." She remembers it was he who finally approached her. "Young Lady, everybody has spoken to me but you." She blurted back, "Mr. Stanislavski, I loved the theater until you came along, and now I hate it." He simply answered, "Well, then you must come to see me tomorrow."

The next day, Adler went to see him—alone. Sensing her awe, Stanislavski broke the ice by telling her he knew of her family and their impact on the theater, especially her father. The relationship finally relaxed, and they became two actors solving problems. For five weeks, they worked together daily, beginning with her difficulties in *Gentlewoman* and working on improvisational exercises in imagination and isolating the circumstances (truth) of each scene. She took copious notes. He shared intimacies of his work as an actor: how it had taken him ten years to understand Ibsen and his part in *An Enemy of the People;* that he worked on his speech for two hours each morning because he was inclined to lisp. After the last session, Adler described wandering the streets of Paris in a daze, savoring the city and her moments with Stanislavski. "I had worked with the master teacher of the world, the man whose words were going to flood the world with truth. That sense he had, of how truthful you had to be; this was his heritage, this is what he gave away." Stella Adler's new passion was to spread the word.

At a big New York party once, Stella arrived late. A little girl watched her entrance with fascination, turned to her mother in awe and said, "Mommy, is that God?" For those of us who've been privileged to be taught by her . . . the answer would be a resounding, "Yes!"

—Peter Bogdanovich

She returned to the Group Theater with a formal report—complete with charts that Stanislavski had made for her—outlining the system as she had experienced it, and openly admonishing Strasberg for concentrating almost exclusively on the element of emotional recall, while de-emphasizing the study of text and character. In 1935, Adler made her final stage appearance with the Group as Clara in *Paradise Lost,* although she returned to stage in the touring production of *Golden Boy* in 1938. In 1940, Strasberg left the Group to found the Actor's Studio. A year later, the Group Theater came to its official end, though Clurman maintained that it never really ceased existing because of the familial ties that it fostered.

Adler married Harold Clurman in 1943; they divorced in 1960. Facts about the union are sketchy, as are those about her first marriage to Horace Eleascheff, and a third to Mitchell Wilson. In her book, Adler refers to Clurman, but only within the context of the Group Theater. "Harold was the man who did the most to open up my talent and my mind, who helped me educate myself about plays. He had significance in my life, in my theatrical life." In his somewhat loose autobiography, *All People Are Famous,* Clurman refers to Adler often—usually by her full name, Stella Adler—but his more intimate portrait is of her mother Sara, who lived with the couple during the later years of her life. He does, however, make much of Stella's "grandness." One story concerns the lean days during their courtship, in 1941, between the dissolution of the Group and the start of his career as a director. Adler evidently complained that he had not come up with a gift for her—jewelry, for example—in some time. He reminded her that he had debts amounting to $20,000. She snapped back, "A man of your stature should be in debt for a hundred thousand."

Brustein illuminates the relationship a bit more. "By his own account, Clurman 'rushed' this 'spiritually vibrant' woman into marriage, and their tumultuous union had the internal strains of any relationship that mixes love with work." Clurman may also have had a roving eye. Once, when Sara Adler was singing his praises, Stella confided that he liked women. Her mother shot back, "If he didn't like women, he wouldn't like you." There is only an aside recorded about Adler's third marriage, noting that she finally found "romantic fulfillment in marriage to the novelist Mitchell Wilson."

Adler did a stint in Hollywood, debuting in *Love on Toast* with a new, more "*goyishe,*" name—Stella Ardler—and, apparently, a newly bobbed nose to match. She appeared in *Shadow of the Thin Man* in 1941, and much later, in 1948, made *My Girl Tisa.* She also worked as an associate producer with Arthur Freed at MGM on *Du Barry Was a Lady* and *Madame Curie,* and was involved with several *Judy Garland films, including *For Me and My Gal.* Adler was instrumental in encouraging studio heads to nurture Garland's formidable talent.

Between the years 1940 to 1961, Adler, who continued to act and direct, taught as well. In 1941, she developed the Dramatic Workshop at the New School for Social Research and taught for two years there. In 1949, she opened the Stella Adler Acting Studio. Following her own interpretation of Stanislavski's method, Adler designed a comprehensive two-year program with emphasis on play analysis and characterization. Hers was a no-nonsense approach that demanded dedication. According to Brustein, her script analysis course was unparalleled, with a syllabus of scene study that displayed the enormous depth of her knowledge of dramatic literature. She would not tolerate tardiness, gum-chewing, or smoking in class.

She was also somewhat deferential to her male students. "She was famously tough on female students, some of whom she bullied and cowed into near paralysis. . . . This is not to say that women didn't adore her, but they usually felt intimidated by her powerful theatricalism."

Adler continued to perform in the United States and abroad until 1961, when a scathing review of her performance in a London production of Arthur Kopit's *Oh Dad, Poor Dad, Mama's Hung You in the Closet and I'm Feelin' So Sad* abruptly ended her stage career. Brustein attempted an acting comeback for her in 1966 at Yale. He envisioned her in the role of the grand actress Arkadina in Anton Chekhov's *The Sea Gull*, but she agreed only if she could be directed by the great Russian, George Tovstonogov. Russian-American relations being what they were at the time made that impossible, so the production was canceled.

By 1960, Adler's studio had been renamed the Stella Adler Conservatory of Acting, and included a staff of more than a dozen faculty members, although she personally continued to teach master classes in acting and script interpretation. Adler also served as adjunct professor of acting at Yale University's School of Drama and was associated with New York University for many years. She opened a second conservatory in Los Angeles in 1986. Her work and contributions were honored with a Doctor of Humane Letters degree from the New School of Social Research, and a Doctor of Fine Arts degree from Smith College.

Late in life, Stella Adler spent more and more time in Los Angeles, remaining active in teaching and managing her conservatory. She died of heart failure in her sleep on December 21, 1992. To the end, she was larger than life, ever the grand dame of the stage, even as she witnessed the American theater begin to lose some of its luster. She remained committed and hopeful, and ever dedicated to what her beloved Stanislavski had taught her: "The source of acting is imagination and the key to its problems is truth, truth in the circumstances of the play. . . . Creating and interpreting means total involvement, the totality of heart, mind, and spirit."

SOURCES:

Adler, Stella. *The Technique of Acting.* NY: Bantam Books, 1988.

Brockett, Oscar G. *The Theater: An Introduction.* NY: Holt, Rinehart and Winston, 1964.

Brustein, Robert. "Stella for Star," in *The New Republic.* Vol. 208, no. 5, February 1, 1993, pp. 52–53.

Clurman, Harold. *All People Are Famous (instead of an autobiography).* NY: Harcourt Brace Jovanovich, 1974.

Strickland, F. Cowles. *The Technique of Acting.* NY: McGraw-Hill, 1956.

Wilson, Edwin, and Alvin Goldfarb. *Living Theater: An Introduction to Theater History.* NY: McGraw-Hill, 1983.

SUGGESTED READING:

Clurman, Harold. *The Fervent Years: The Story of the Group Theater in the Thirties.* NY: Hill and Wang, 1957.

Stanislavski, Constantin. *An Actor Prepares.* Translated by Elizabeth Reynolds Hapgood. NY: Theater Arts Books, 1936.

Strasberg, Lee. "Acting and the Training of the Actor," in *Producing the Play.* Rev. ed. Edited by John Gassner. NY: Holt, Rinehart and Winston, 1953.

Barbara Morgan, Melrose, Massachusetts

Stella Adler in My Girl Tisa.

Adler, Valentine (1898–1942)

Austrian anti-Nazi and editor. Name variations: Vali, Valentine Sas-Adler. Born in Vienna, Austria, on May 5, 1898; died in a labor camp on July 6, 1942; daughter of Alfred Adler (1870–1937, the psychologist who would later gain fame for breaking with the teachings of his mentor Sigmund Freud) and **Raissa Timofejewna**; *sis-*

*ter of **Alexandra Adler** (a research fellow in neurology at Harvard); married Gyula Sas ("Giulio Aquila").*

Radicalized by the events of World War I, joined the Austrian Communist Party (1919); soon after arriving in Berlin, transferred to the German Communist Party (1921); worked in Berlin until 1933 as an editor and translator; moved to Moscow (1933) to be with her husband; arrested during the Great Purge (January 1937); found guilty of "Trotskyite activities" and sentenced to ten years imprisonment; died in a labor camp (1942) and posthumously rehabilitated by a decree of the Military Collegium of the Supreme Court of the USSR (1956).

A Marxist idealist, Vali Adler became one of the many refugees from Nazi terror who succumbed to the bloody purges unleashed by Soviet dictator Joseph Stalin. A "true believer" in a socialist society, Adler came to her revolutionary ideals not out of economic need but because she was convinced that a Utopian world was achievable in the 20th century. She was born in Vienna on May 5, 1898, the daughter of the distinguished psychologist Alfred Adler. A member of the Austrian Communist Party from 1919 through 1921 and of the German Communist Party starting in 1921, she was convinced that a brave new world was in the offing, and that the Soviet Union would lead the way to a new level of human decency and justice. The rise of Nazism in Germany only strengthened this belief, and she doubtless arrived in the Soviet Union in 1933 with high hopes. Her husband Gyula Sas ("Giulio Aquila") had preceded her to Moscow, and for several years they worked together believing that, led by Stalin and the Communist Party, the USSR would be able to create a stable and prosperous state sufficiently strong to lead the world in meeting the growing menace of fascism.

Adler's beliefs proved to be illusory, as an ever-growing reign of terror destroyed the lives of millions of people in the Soviet Union, including many of the Communists and Socialists who had sought refuge there from Hitler since 1933. The constantly shifting party line and the arbitrary nature of Communist power meant that one could never be certain of the "correct" ideological stance. Working at the publishing house of foreign workers in the USSR, Adler voiced her growing concerns about the risks of even a slight ideological misstep to fellow exile and writer, **Susanne Leonhard:** "Keep your hands off; it is like dancing on eggs."

Arrested on January 22, 1937, she was first interrogated at Moscow's infamous Lubianka prison, then held at the Butyrki prison until sentence was passed on September 19 of that year. The Military Tribunal of the USSR Supreme Court found her guilty of illegal Trotskyite activities and having established contacts with foreign Trotskyite groups. One of the charges against her was that her parents had met with Leon Trotsky and that it was through them that she had established her Trotskyite connections. Sentenced to ten years' imprisonment, she did not survive the privations of Soviet labor camps, dying in one on July 6, 1942. It was not until 1952, after Albert Einstein personally petitioned Soviet authorities for information on Adler's case, that the date of her death was released. On August 11, 1956, during the first phase of Nikita Khrushchev's de-Stalinization campaign, the Military Collegium of the USSR Supreme Court declared Valentine Adler to be posthumously rehabilitated.

SOURCES:

In den Fängen des NKWD. Berlin: Dietz Verlag, 1991.

Leonhard, Susanne. *Gestohlenes Leben.* New ed. Frankfurt am Main: Athenäum Verlag, 1988.

McLoughlin, Barry, and Walter Szevera. *Posthum Rehabilitiert.* Vienna: Zentralkomitee der KPÖ, 1991.

John Haag, Associate Professor of History, University of Georgia, Athens, Georgia

Adnan, Etel (1925—)

Lebanese author and painter. Born in 1925 in Beirut, Lebanon; moved to United States in 1955.

Selected works: Moonshots *(1966);* Five Senses for One Death *(1971);* Jebu et l'Express Beyrouth-Enfer *(1973);* Sitt Marie Rose *(1978);* L'Apocolypse Arabe *(1980);* Pablo Neruda is a Banana Tree *(1982);* From A to Z *(1982);* The Indian Never Had a Horse *(1985);* Journey to Mount Tamalpais *(1986);* The Spring Flowers Own and the Manifestations of the Voyage *(1990).*

Though Etel Adnan was born in Beirut, Lebanon, French colonialism in the region most heavily influenced her upbringing and writing. When she was five, Adnan's Syrian father and Greek mother enrolled her at a convent school run by French nuns, where children learned, spoke, and studied in French, a language unknown to Adnan's parents. Etel was not an avid reader since books were rare—in her home there was a Greek religious text, her father's Koran, and a dictionary—but she quickly showed a proficiency for writing. The nuns accused Adnan of plagiarism. Her essays, they claimed, were too good to have been written by a child. They soon learned that she was a genuine talent.

By her early adolescence, the language difference between child and parents caused stress in the family. Adnan's father, 20 years her mother's senior, was the weaker partner; old, ill, and unable to work, he was largely absent from matters involving his daughter. It was Adnan's mother who held the reins. When Etel was 16, her mother demanded she quit school and work to support the family, which included a young boy, the illegitimate child of a cousin. Adnan took a position in the newly assembled French War Office, which had been established in response to the threat of war (WWII); there, Adnan handled secretarial duties and, for the first year, enjoyed being one of Lebanon's first generation of working women. By the following fall, she began to miss school. Her boss Jean Gaulmier, who found her crying one morning, arranged for Adnan to take morning classes in preparation for the French baccalauréat and then work from eleven in the morning until eight at night. At the end of the day, the office chauffeur drove Adnan home, since the streets were unsafe for a woman to travel alone.

Adnan completed her baccalauréat and hoped to move on to college studies in engineering or architecture, but her mother forbade it. Fearing Adnan would lose her femininity, her marriage prospects and her ability to work, her mother instead enrolled her at the École Supérieure des Lettres. When the war bureau closed, Adnan took a new office position that left her afternoons and nights to study literature, art, and philosophy. She worked with Gabriel Bounoure, who encouraged Adnan's writing and recommended her for a scholarship at the Sorbonne in Paris. Adnan won the prize, but that same year, 1947, her father died. Her mother refused to let her go to Paris.

Instead, for three years Adnan taught French literature at the Ahliga School for Girls. Then in 1950, she no longer postponed her scholarship. Disowned, Adnan moved to Paris to study philosophy. By 1955, she had earned invitations to the United States, where she attended both Harvard and Berkeley, before taking a position in 1959 as a philosophy professor at Dominican College in California. Adnan had written her first poem, "The Book of the Sea," in 1947, but it was in America, protesting the Vietnam War, that she began to write political poetry in both French and English. She sent some of her work back to Europe, and her reputation as a literary activist and critic of life in Arabian society began to grow. In 1972, Adnan returned to Beirut for a brief editorial stint at the French Lebanese paper *L'Orient-le Jour*. At the outbreak of civil war there, she left.

Etel Adnan has since made homes in France and America; she continues to write in either French or English and translate her work between the two languages. She also assists in translations to Arabic but does not write in that language. Adnan does, however, paint "in Arabic" she says, and her art, as well as her designs for carpets, continues to grow in renown. She has published ten books, including the novel *Sitt Marie Rose*.

SOURCES:

Badran, Margot, and Miriam Cooke. *Opening the Gates.* Bloomington: Indiana University Press, 1990.

Orfalea, Gregory, and Sharif Elmusa, eds. *Grape Leaves: A Century of Arab American Poetry.* Salt Lake City: University of Utah Press, 1988.

Schipper, Mineke, ed. *Unheard Words.* London: Alisson and Busby, 1985.

Crista Martin, fiction and freelance writer, Boston, Massachusetts

Adolf, Helen (b. 1895)

Austrian-born American professor of German language and literature who made major contributions to several areas of scholarship. Born December 31, 1895, in Vienna, Austria; death date unknown; daughter of Jakob Adolf (an attorney) and Hedwig (Spitzer) Adolf (an artist); sister of Anna Adolf Spiegel (b. 1893, a medical doctor).

After earning a Ph.D. in literature, went to Leipzig, Germany to work in a publishing house; fled from Austria to United States (1939); learned Spanish to obtain a teaching job; finally received an academic post teaching Spanish, French, and Latin; after receiving a job at Pennsylvania State University (1943), worked her way up the ladder becoming a full professor (1953); a wide knowledge of linguistics, religious psychology, aesthetics, poetry and various strands of history and culture influenced Adolf's academic contributions; awarded the Republic of Austria's Cross of Honor, First Class, in Arts and Letters (1972); her 1960 book Visio Pacis *exemplifies Adolf's unique approach to scholarship.*

Selected writings: (editor) Dem neuen Reich entgegen, 1850–1871 (Leipzig: P. Reclam Verlag, 1930); (editor) Im neuen Reich, 1871–1914 (Leipzig: P. Reclam Verlag, 1932); Visio Pacis: Holy City and Grail: An Attempt at an Inner History of the Grail Legend (University Park, PA: Pennsylvania State University Press, 1960); Werden und Sein: Gedichte aus fünf Jahrzehnten (Horn-Niederösterreich, Austria: Verlag Ferdinand Berger, 1964).

When Helen Adolf was born in Vienna, Austria, on December 31, 1895, into an assimilated Jewish middle-class family that was both financially comfortable and culturally active, she did not know she would cross new frontiers. Her father, Jakob Adolf (1850–1926), was a Galician-born attorney, while her mother, **Hedwig Spitzer Adolf** (1864–1936), was a native Viennese with many artistic interests. From the outset, educational accomplishments were stressed in the Adolf family. Helen's older sister, **Anna Adolf Spiegel**, received a medical degree from the University of Vienna, an unusual accomplishment for a woman of the period, and immigrated to the United States in 1930, where she established a successful academic career at Temple University Medical School in Philadelphia.

Helen Adolf earned her doctorate in literature from the University of Vienna in 1923, but no teaching positions were open to women in Austria. She went to Leipzig, Germany, where she worked at the famous Reclam publishing firm, compiling several highly acclaimed collections of documents relating to the period of German history from 1850–1914. These volumes were innovative in that they brought together long-forgotten political poetry, ballads and songs from a crucial phase of German cultural development. Her interests were varied. She wrote poetry as well as studying psychology and religion during this time. From 1923 to 1938, she served as secretary of the International Society for the Psychology of Religion. Gifted at foreign languages, Adolf sharpened her language skills by translating a number of works from French into German including **Jeanne Galzy's** novel on St. *Teresa of Avila.

Renée Adorée

The 1930s were a dangerous period for Jews like Helen Adolf in Europe. When Nazi Germany annexed Austria in 1938, it was clear that her life was in danger. Deciding to start a new life in the United States, she left in April 1939 to join her sister in Philadelphia. Fortunate to have support from friends and family, Adolf was also assisted by the American Friends Service Committee. The lack of good jobs in the closing years of the Depression meant that Adolf had to begin her career all over again. She attended the University of Penn-

sylvania summer school to improve her knowledge of Spanish, the most popular foreign language taught in the United States at that time. Then she took a number of secondary-school positions in Virginia and Colorado, teaching not only Spanish but Latin and French as well. By 1943, however, Adolf returned to Philadelphia to Pennsylvania State University where she began her ascent up the academic ladder, achieving the rank of full professor in 1953.

Although she made major contributions to several areas of scholarship, Helen Adolf was not merely a specialist. She maintained an intense personal as well as professional interest in many areas that cut across the spectrum of human experience. She spent many years cultivating a knowledge of linguistics, religious psychology, aesthetics, and poetry; her interests encompassed wide areas of history and culture. Her wide knowledge was reflected in her work, *Visio Pacis: Holy City and Grail: An Attempt at an Inner History of the Grail Legend,* which is an example of her eclectic approach to scholarship. There were very few women in the ranks of American academia during Adolf's long career, and almost none at all at the rank of full professor.

Despite the traumatic circumstances, which caused Adolf to come to America, she was glad to become a citizen of her new country in 1944. When asked whether she might return to live in Austria at the end of World War II, she stated that she had encountered individuals who exhibited traits of integrity and altruism in both countries, but only in the United States had she seen "courage and optimism" widely practiced. Postwar Austria, she stated, still retained traces of "resignation." Nonetheless, Adolf retained her loyalty to German culture and the German language. She continued to write most of her poetry in German, and in 1964 published an anthology of selected verse with an Austrian publisher. In 1968, a group of devoted students and colleagues published a *Festschrift* about her lifetime achievements. In 1972, Helen Adolf received the Republic of Austria's coveted Cross of Honor, First Class, in Arts and Letters.

John Haag, Associate Professor of History,
University of Georgia, Athens, Georgia

Adorée, Renée (1898–1933)

French actress. Name variations: Renee Adoree. Born Jeanne de la Fonte in Lille, France, on September 30, 1898; died of tuberculosis in 1933; married Tom Moore (an actor), in 1921 (divorced 1924).

Selected filmography: 1500 Reward *(1918);* The Bandelero *(1924);* Man and Maid *(1925);* The Big Parade *(1925);* Parisian Nights *(1925);* La Bohème *(1926);* The Exquisite Sinner *(1926);* The Flaming Forest *(1926);* Mr. Wu *(1927);* On Ze Boulevard *(1927);* Back to God's Country *(1927);* The Cossacks *(1928);* The Michigan Kid *(1928);* Forbidden Hours *(1928);* The Mating Call *(1928);* The Spieler *(1928);* The Pagan *(1929);* Tide of Empire *(1929);* Redemption *(1930);* Call of the Flesh *(1930).*

At age five, Renée Adorée began her career as a circus performer. After a stint as a dancer with the Folies-Bergère and a role in an Australian movie (*1500 Reward,* 1918), she arrived in Hollywood in 1920. Adorée soon found stardom with her 1925 appearance as Melisande, the French peasant, in King Vidor's *The Big Parade.* In a memorable scene, she pushes her way through the massed army ranks to bid farewell to her American soldier (played by John Gilbert), who is about to go into battle. Adorée died in 1933, at age 35, following a losing battle with tuberculosis.

Adorno, Catherine (1447–1510).

See Catherine of Genoa.

AE.

See also, E for names beginning AE. (Originally the Teutonic [Germanic] Æ was used, such as Aethelflaed or Aethelfleda, before the 11th century, but in some citations was later dropped from common usage, becoming Ethelflaed or Ethelfleda).

Aedelers or Aelders, Etta Palm d'
(1743–1799).

See Palm, Etta.

Aelfflaed.

See Elflaed.

Aelfgifu (c. 985–1052).

See Emma of Normandy.

Aelfgifu (d. 1002).

See Emma of Normandy for sidebar on Elfgifu.

Aelfled.

See Elflaed.

Aelfthryth (c. 945–c. 1000).

See Elfthrith.

Aelfwyn.

See Ethelflaed for sidebar on Elfwyn.

Aelgifu (c. 1000–c. 1040).

See Elfgifu.

Aelia Ariadne (fl. 457–515).

See Ariadne.

Aelia Flavia Flaccilla (c. 355–386).

See Flaccilla.

Aelia Galla Placidia (c. 390–450).

See Placidia, Galla.

Aelia Pulcheria (c. 398–453).

See Pulcheria.

Aelith de Poitiers (c. 1123–?).

See Eleanor of Aquitaine for sidebar.

Aemilia (fl. 195 BCE).

See Cornelia for sidebar.

Aemilia Hilaria (fl. 350 CE)

Gallo-Roman doctor. Name variations: Aemilia; Aemilia Hilaria (Aemilia the Jolly); (nickname) Hilarus. Pronunciation: Aye-MEEL-ee-uh Hee-LAH-ree-uh. Born around 300 CE in Roman Gaul (modern France); died at age 63 at an unspecified date; daughter of Caecilius Agricius Arborius and Aemilia Corinthia Maura, apparently both impoverished nobles from Gaul.

Aemilia Hilaria may be one of the few female doctors in the Roman Empire of whom a record has come down to us from antiquity. This assumption rests on a single line of a long Latin poem, the *Parentalia,* written by her nephew, Decimus Magnus Ausonius, the Gallo-Roman senator and tutor to the emperor Gratian: *more virum medicis artibus experiens* ("You were skilled in the medical arts in the fashion of men"). There is ample evidence for midwives in the Roman Empire at this period, and medical writings were available to women, but, as noted by Gillian Clark, the phrase "according to the fashion of men" "may suggest a full-time commitment." The *Parentalia* tells us that Aemilia's brother-in-law, Ausonius' father, was a doctor, and some professional medical association between the two is possible.

Everything we know about Aemilia Hilaria and her family derives from the *Parentalia.* It appears that she was born in the small city of Aquae Tarbellicae (modern Dax) early in the 4th century, a time when the provinces in Gaul were recovering from barbarian invasions and local revolts against imperial authority. Her father's family, partly descended from the native Celtic Aeduan aristocracy, had emigrated there from central Gaul perhaps around 260. Her mother came from the local municipal aristocracy, although Ausonius points out that they were poor. Aemilia had one brother,

Aemilius Magnus Arborius, who became a tutor to an unnamed son of the emperor Constantius, and two sisters: Aemilia Dryadia, who died in infancy, and **Aemilia Aeonia**, the mother of Ausonius. **Hagith Sivan** in her *Ausonius of Bordeaux: Genesis of a Gallic Aristocracy* points out that Aemilia Hilaria and her siblings all took the nomen, or family name, of their mother, contrary to the usual practice of the times.

According to *Parentalia 5*, Aemilia Hilaria was given the male nickname Hilarus while she was still an infant because she was "affable like a boy" (*comis pueri ad effigiem*). In her youth, she "openly imitated a proper young man" (*reddebas verum non dissimulanter ephebum*), and later in life she showed a disdain for her femininity (*feminei sexus odium*), as a result of which she did not marry but remained a virgin for life. One should be cautious in taking these statements literally, however. As Clark, among others, notes, Christian women of this period were encouraged by the male clergy to hide their feminine appearance. While it is difficult to guess if Aemilia was a Christian—the phrase "love of consecrated virginity" (*devotae virginitatis amor*) seems to indicate this—the language and spirit of her nephew may speak more to poetic license than fact. Nevertheless, as he is our only source for Aemilia we have little choice but to accept Ausonius at his word, and so Aemilia Hilaria comes down to us as a woman who rejected a traditional Roman female image and role.

SOURCES:
Ausonius, *Parentalia 5*.

SUGGESTED READING:
Sivan, Hagith. *Ausonius of Bordeaux: Genesis of a Gallic Aristocracy*. London: Routledge, 1993.

> **Alexander Ingle**, Research Assistant, Institute for the Classical Tradition, Boston University, Boston, Massachusetts

Aenor Aimery or Aénor of Châtellerault (d. 1130).

See Eleanor of Aquitaine for sidebar on Aénor of Châtellerault.

Aesara of Lucania (fl. 400s–300s BCE)

Pythagorean philosopher who wrote the Book on Human Nature. *Born in Lucania, Italy.*

Aesara is counted among the Pythagoreans who were scattered after their expulsion from Crotona in the 5th century BCE. From 425 BCE to 100 CE, Pythagoreans no longer acted as a political society but carried on the philosophical tradition, pursuing the intellectual and spiritual endeavors that were started by Pythagoras and his followers. Aesara's writings describe the foundations of honorable personal and social rules based on an analysis of the parts of the soul. Her work earned her such esteem that, although she was from Lucania in southern Italy, her intellectual accomplishments were praised in Roman poetry and Greek lectures.

Aesara maintained that the soul had three parts: the mind, the spirit, and desire. According to Aesara these forces of the soul work in harmony, interacting in different ways for the achievement of different tasks. The forces of the soul, and the appropriate relation between them, are reflected in the laws that Aesara believed should govern individual morality, the family (considered to be the province of women), and the state (considered to be the province of men). She saw introspection as revealing the natural laws on which all conduct should be based; the need for the appropriate interaction of the different parts of the soul overrides other rules, and the cooperation of the three will vary in different situations.

> **Catherine Hundleby**, M.A. Philosophy, University of Guelph, Guelph, Ontario

Aethel-.

See Ethel-.

Aethelburg.

See Ethelberga.

Aethelfleda.

See Ethelflaed.

Aethelfryth (c. 945–c. 1000).

See Elfthrith.

Aethelthrith.

See Elthelthrith.

Afifi, Hidaya (1898–1969).

See entry on Egyptian Feminists.

Aflatun, Inge.

See Inji Efflatoun in entry on Egyptian Feminists.

Afra (fl. c. 304)

German saint. Possibly daughter of St. *Hilaria who was martyred at the tomb of Afra in the 4th century.

Afra is the local saint of Augsburg, who, according to tradition, suffered martyrdom under Diocletian. Said to have originally been a prostitute, Afra is commemorated on August 5.

Afua Koba (fl. 1834–1884).

See Yaa Asantewaa for sidebar.

Aganoor Pompilj, Vittoria (1855–1910).

See Pompilj, Vittoria Aganoor.

Agape of Thessalonica (d. 304).

See Irene, Chionia, and Agape of Thessalonica.

Agar, Eileen (1899–1991)

Argentine-born British surrealist sculptor, whose works were enormously popular in the 1930s. Born Eileen Agar in Buenos Aires, Argentina, on December 1, 1899; died in London on November 17, 1991; daughter of James and Mamie Agar; educated at Heathfield, Ascot; studied art under sculptor Leon Underwood (1924), at the Slade School of Art under Henry Tonks (1925–26), and in Paris (1928–30); married Robin Bartlett (a painter), in 1925 (separated 1926); married Joseph Bard (a Hungarian-born writer), in 1940.

Her artistic works such as Quadriga *were enormously popular (1930s); known as a surrealist sculptor, first exhibited her work* Angel of Anarchy *in the London Gallery as part of the Exhibition of Surrealist Poems and Objects (1937); became a major celebrity in the London gallery scene (1930s); published autobiography* A Look at My Life *(1988); continued artistic work well into old age, remaining influential in London art circles.*

Selected paintings: Self-Portrait *(1927);* Movement in Space *(1931);* The Modern Muse *(1931);* Autobiography of an Embryo *(1933–34);* Quadriga *(1936);* Ceremonial Hat for Eating Bouillabaisse *(1936);* Angel of Anarchy *(1938);* Marine Object *(1939);* Battle Cry/Bullet Proof Painting *(1938). Work in the permanent collections of Tate Gallery, Arts Council, Contemporary Art Society, National Gallery of New Zealand.*

Eileen Agar, born in Buenos Aires on December 1, 1899, was one of three daughters. Her Scottish father was a businessman whose sales of agricultural machinery in Argentina made the family immensely wealthy. Although she was born in Argentina, the family returned to England for extended stays every other year. In 1911, the Agars settled permanently in London, moving into a luxurious house in Belgrave Square, close to Knightsbridge and virtually next to Buckingham Palace. A second opulent home was purchased in Scotland for the autumn holidays after the close of the social season.

Agar's life was typical of an upper-class woman. She was prepared for her introduction to society and a good marriage. Educated at the prestigious Heathfield School, Eileen discovered her artistic talents. Her early interest in art was not only tolerated by her parents but encouraged as an acceptable pastime for a woman of the upper strata. In her late teens, when she decided to break with social convention and make art her life, her mother **Mamie Agar** hired a watercolor teacher. Eileen attended classes at the Byam Shaw School of Art in Kensington, spending long hours mastering oil painting techniques. In 1921, she began studying at the Slade School of Art under Henry Tonks, who was known for his vehement dismissal of the European Modernists and his emphasis on representational art. In keeping with Slade's teaching practice, Agar copied classical busts and painted from male and female models. Her progress is said to have been "respectable but unremarkable." Classmates included Henry Moore, *Gertrude Hermes, Rodney Thomas, and painter Robin Bartlett.

Defying her family in 1925, Agar married Bartlett, partly to elude parental constraints. Both parents refused to attend the wedding, which took place in London's artistic section of Chelsea. Eileen's American-born mother, one of London's best-known hostesses, felt her daughter was marrying far beneath her station. Her father, however, who died a few months later, must have partially forgiven his errant daughter, as he left her an annual income of £1,000, a substantial sum at the time. The couple traveled to Paris and Spain, where Agar first came under the spell of Goya and El Greco. She soon found, however, that marriage had its own constraints. In 1926, she separated from Bartlett and began her lifelong relationship with a married man, Hungarian-born author Joseph Bard. By 1927, she and Bard were living together in London's bohemian district of Bloomsbury.

After Agar began her relationship with Bard, she broke away from conventional art and began developing her own style. *Self-Portrait,* painted in 1927, ushered in a new era for her work; she felt she had "thrown off the shackles and started a new life." Her fortune allowed the couple to travel extensively, and they spent time in Paris and explored picturesque small towns and villages throughout France and Italy. They met and exchanged ideas with many of the leading avant-garde writers of the period, including William Butler Yeats, Ezra Pound, Osbert Sitwell, and Evelyn Waugh. Waugh, who unsuccessfully attempted to seduce Agar, went on to base a character on her in one of his novels. In 1929, Agar set up a studio in the Rue Schoelcher in Paris. There, she met the sculptor Brancusi, Surrealists André Breton and Paul Eluard, and came under the influence of the Czech painter Foltyn, an abstract Cubist.

A frequent visitor to the Jardin des Plantes, Agar became attracted to the formations in natural history, especially fossils. Grimes, Collins, and Baddeley wrote in *Five Women Painters:* "The enigmatic subtlety of nature's transformational powers became the basis of a new aesthetic for Agar." In a December 1931 edition of the *Island* (a literary journal started with Bard), Agar wrote of "womb-magic, the dominance of female creativity and imagination," linking physical and artistic birth. These concepts culminated into her large, 1934 work, *Autobiography of an Embryo.*

By 1930, she and Bard had tired of travel, and, since his books were increasingly successful in England, they had decided to settle in London. At that time it was not socially acceptable for an unmarried couple to live together, so they leased two apartments in the same building in the unfashionable Earl's Court section of London.

Eileen Agar continued to develop her own artistic style, which was turning toward surrealism by the mid-1930s. She spent the summer of 1935 at Swanage, in England, where she met and became friends with Paul Nash, one of the few British painters committed to the Surrealist ideas of representation. The two proved a positive influence on each other. Continuing her fascination with nature, Agar began gathering odd shapes from the Dorset beaches, such as cork, wood, shells, and stone. She also discovered a shell-encrusted anchor chain, which Nash called a bird snake and used in his photomontage entitled *Swanage.* Attentive to the dynamics between the sexes, Agar wrote: "The sea and the land sometimes play together like man and wife, and achieve astonishing results."

Through Nash, Agar met influential critics Herbert Read and Roland Penrose, two of the British organizers of the landmark International Surrealist Exhibition at the New Burlington Gallery in London. Impressed with her work, they chose three oil paintings, including *Quadriga,* and five objects for the 1936 show. "One day I was an artist exploring highly personal combinations of form and content," wrote Agar, "and the next I was calmly informed I was a Surrealist."

In the 1930s, Eileen Agar's studio was centered around an unconventional clock designed by her friend Rodney Thomas. Driftwood and strange rock formations enhanced the room's dreamlike quality. "Normal" objects such as rope and fish netting added to the atmosphere because of their strange placement. Although Agar did not regard herself as a surrealist, her abstract works became increasingly overlaid with figurative images. Perceptive and open-minded critics like Penrose and Read were impressed by the energy and originality of Agar's vision. Two of her works in particular became extraordinarily popular in the late 1930s. *Quadriga,* inspired by a photograph of a horse's head from the Parthenon, was striking. Describing the work, Agar said, "One horse's head became four ghost heads, agitated, beating rhythmic cabalistic convoluted signs expressing movement and anxiety, each square a different mood. Were they the four horses of the Apocalypse?" This powerful painting, which was seen by many as a fitting symbol of the anxieties and ambiguities of life in the 20th century was acquired by the Tate Gallery for its permanent collection.

A second work, the sculpture *Angel of Anarchy,* was an even more biting commentary on modern life. It was first exhibited in 1937 in the London Gallery as part of their Exhibition of Surrealist Poems and Objects. A powerful work, it offended some viewers while it delighted others. Few were indifferent to its form and implied messages. When the original work was lost, a new and even bolder version of the *Angel of Anarchy* was created in 1940. In its new form *Angel of Anarchy* presented a head greatly enriched with feathers, beads, fur, embroidery and even shells. A brilliant final touch was a blindfold, no doubt symbolizing Britain's future in 1940 because of the country's stubborn refusal to accept Adolf Hitler's domination of the European continent. *Angel of Anarchy* also became part of the Tate Gallery's permanent collection.

Agar was one of the few women, and the main British woman, who came to be recognized as part of the predominantly male movement (other noted female Surrealists include *Frida Kahlo, *Meret Oppenheim, and ✥➤ Ithell Colquhoun). "As a movement it may not question the nature of patriarchy but it at least recognizes its existence," note Grimes, Collins, and Baddeley. "The fact that desire and sexuality play a pre-eminent role in much surrealist work, forces an understanding of the presupposed gender of both artist and audience, a recognition frequently subsumed in less overtly masculine art. . . . Tradi-

tional denials of female rationality, of the ability of women to think on an abstract level, combined with equally long-standing associations with nature and the natural, freed ['Women's Art'] from the civilized values so detested by the surrealists." *Angel of Anarchy* was spoken of as "an almost perfect encapsulation of the Surrealist aesthetic while remaining a very female work."

In the summer of 1937, Agar was invited to join a coterie of the avantgarde in the South of France. There, she mingled with Paul and ✥➤ **Nusch Eluard,** Roland Penrose, and photographer *Lee Miller, becoming part of a group

---

✥➤ **Colquhoun, Ithell** (1906–1988)
English painter and poet. Born on October 9, 1906, in Shillong, Assam, India; died on April 11, 1988, in Cornwall, England; educated at Cheltenham College; studied art at the Slade School of Art and in Paris. Work in permanent collections: Tate Gallery, V&A Bradford, Cheltenham and Southampton Galleries, Glasgow and London Universities. Signs work: in early years, Ithell Colquhoun on back; since 1962, by a monogram.

Ithell Colquhoun joined the English Surrealist group in 1939, but she left the group the following year when pressured to abandon her work on occultism. The result of her experiments in automatism, *decalcomania, sfumage, frottage,* and collage were published in an article titled "The Mantic Stain" in the October 1949 issue of *Enquiry.* Colquhoun also authored *The Crying Wind* (1955), *The Living Stones* (1957), the Surrealist occult novel, *Goose of Hermogenes* (Peter Owen, 1961), *Grimoire of the Entangled Thicket* (1973), *Sword of Wisdom* (1975), and travel books on Cornwall and Ireland.

✥➤ **Eluard, Nusch** (1906–1946)
German artist, model, and author. Born Maria Benz in 1906 in Alsace, Mulhouse, France (then annexed by Germany as Mülhausen); died in 1946 in Paris; married Paul Eluard (a Surrealist painter), in 1934.

Born in Alsace, France, Maria Benz began her career as an actress, choosing Nusch as a stage name. Moving to Paris in 1920, she met her husband, painter Paul Eluard, in 1930, while working as a model for postcards and serving as a walk-on at the Théâtre Grand Guignol. They were married in 1934. For the next two years, she modelled for Man Ray and Pablo Picasso and created a series of Surrealist photomontages, essentially using the female nude. (Her collages were published by Editions Nadada in 1978.) During World War II, the Eluards remained in Paris, joining the Resistance. Weakened by the harshness of the German Occupation, Nusch Eluard died suddenly in 1946.

centered around Pablo Picasso. The war years saw the completion of her work *Battle Cry/ Bullet Proof Painting*, her marriage to Bard in 1940, and a reconciliation with her ailing and alcoholic mother. After the war, and frequent visits to Tenerife, Agar's work began to take on the characteristics of Abstract Expressionism, or the "New York School." Her belief in the "power of female imagery," write Grimes, Collins, and Baddeley, "her interest in sexual archetypes and subversion of traditional materials of fine art all serve to deny the inviolability of the male artist. Her work may not be self-consciously feminist but it is certainly an assertion of women's art."

After many years of recognition, Agar's reputation began to fade. The reasons for this are complex, but several conclusions are obvious. Sexism played a role. Gifted women artists were often confronted by hostility and indifference in the art world. Geopolitical and economic forces also played a part. By 1945, the New York School dominated the art world, whose geopolitical center moved from Europe to the United States. A female artist working in a physically impoverished and intellectually threadbare Britain in the postwar world could count on little critical support. Eileen Agar was not discouraged by these shifts in the public mood and continued to produce powerful, visually rich and witty works of art into her final years. In 1971, she was given a much-deserved retrospective exhibition at the Commonwealth Art Gallery. To the end of her long life, she continued to exhibit at the major London galleries, and her final years she was able to delight a growing number of admirers. Her autobiography, *A Look at My Life*, was published in 1988. Eileen Agar died in London on November 17, 1991. Her accomplishments will not be sufficiently appreciated until women's contribution to art is fully assessed.

SOURCES:

Agar, Eileen, with Andrew Lambirth. *A Look at My Life.* London: Methuen, 1988.

Caws, Mary Ann, Rudolf E. Kuenzli, and Gwen Raaberg, eds. *Surrealism and Women.* Cambridge, MA: MIT Press, 1991.

Chadwick, Whitney. *Women Artists and the Surrealist Movement.* Boston: Little Brown, 1985.

"Eileen Agar," in *The Times* [London]. November 18, 1991, p. 9.

Grimes, Teresa, Judith Collins, and Oriana Baddeley. *Five Women Painters.* London: Lennard Publishing, 1989.

Trevelyan, Julian. *Indigo Days.* London: MacGibbon & Kee, 1957.

RELATED MEDIA:

"Five Women Painters," television film, 1989.

John Haag, Associate Professor of History, University of Georgia, Athens, Georgia

Agariste (fl. 515 BCE–490 BCE)

Greek noblewoman. Flourished around 515 BCE–490 BCE; born into the aristocratic Alcemeonid family; married Xanthippus; children: Pericles (c. 495 BCE–429 BCE), Greek general, politician, and diplomat.

Agariste, mother of Pericles, was an Alcemeonid, an old and influential aristocratic family. The Alcemeonids had been among the elite when Athens was a true aristocracy and had intermarried with the houses of autocratic tyrants. Nevertheless, they were also responsible for the overthrow of Athenian tyranny when Agariste's uncle, Clisthenes, inaugurated his democratic reforms in 507 BCE. Agariste's husband was Xanthippus, one of the most important public figures of his generation, whose greatest claim to fame came in 479 when he led Athens to victory over the Persians at Mycale, a battle that virtually assured that Persia would never again invade European Greece.

Agassiz, Elizabeth Cary (1822–1907)

American naturalist who was co-founder and first president of Radcliffe College. Name variations: Elizabeth Cabot Agassiz. Born Elizabeth Cabot Cary in Boston, Massachusetts, on December 5, 1822; died in Arlington Heights, Massachusetts, following a stroke, on June 27, 1907, at age 84; buried beside her husband in Mount Auburn Cemetery in Cambridge; educated at home; daughter of Thomas Graves Cary (a lawyer and businessman) and Mary Ann Cushing Perkins (a homemaker); married Jean Louis Agassiz, in 1850; stepchildren: Alexander Agassiz (an eminent marine zoologist), *Pauline Agassiz Shaw (1841–1917); Ida Agassiz, who married historian Francis Parkman. Louis Agassiz's first wife was Cécile Braun.

Operated a select school for girls out of her home (1856–64); published A First Lesson in Natural History *(1859); published* Seaside Studies in Natural History, *co-written with her stepson Alexander Agassiz (1865); member of a scientific expedition to Brazil (1865); published* A Journey in Brazil, *co-written with her husband Louis Agassiz (1867); embarked on a deep-sea dredging expedition through the straits of Magellan and the Galapagos (1871); co-founded and operated the Anderson School of Natural History (1872); published the two-volume biography,* Louis Agassiz: His Life and Correspondence *(1885); helped found the Society for the Collegiate Instruction of Women, known as the "Harvard Annex" (1879); elected president of the Society (1882); continued in her capacity as president of the newly incorporated Radcliffe College (1894); resigned from active duty and became honorary president of Radcliffe College (1899); a student's hall, the Elizabeth Cary Agassiz House, established at Radcliffe College (1902); resigned as honorary president (1903).*

A self-taught naturalist and educator, Elizabeth Cary Agassiz remains an important figure in the history of women's higher education in America. She began her noteworthy career as an amateur naturalist, wife and intellectual companion to the brilliant Swiss scientist Louis Agassiz and ended it as one of the founders and the first president of Radcliffe College. Intelligent and tenacious, she was responsible for guiding the women's college from its uncertain inception as an independent foundation with no financial endowment and no degree-granting power to an established, well-funded institute of higher learning officially affiliated with Harvard University.

Elizabeth Cary Agassiz was born on December 5, 1822, at the Boston home of her wealthy maternal grandfather, Colonel Thomas Handasyd Perkins, founder of the Perkins Institute for the Blind. She was the second of seven children born to Thomas Cary and **Mary Ann Perkins**, each descended from prominent and established New England families.

Agassiz spent the earliest years of her childhood on the move. At the time of her birth, her parents were splitting their time between her grandfather's home in Boston and Brattleboro, Vermont, where her father practiced law. Shortly after, her father abandoned his unsuccessful legal career and moved the family to New York City where he joined his brothers in business. In 1832, Thomas Cary moved his family back to Boston and entered his father-in-law's mercantile company. After the company's dissolution six years later, Cary became treasurer of the Hamilton & Appleton Mills in Lowell, a position he held until his death in 1859.

Elizabeth Agassiz's maternal grandfather built a house for the family next door to his own. His two other daughters and their families lived on the same street, and Elizabeth and her siblings grew up as part of a large circle of relatives linked by marriages to other prominent Boston families. Though her youth was happy and relatively carefree, she suffered from delicate health; thus, she received no formal schooling. As her siblings entered school upon adolescence, she remained at home and was tutored in languages, drawing, and music.

"Lizzie," as she was known to her family and friends, was popular in upper-class Boston society. Her sister **Mary**'s 1846 marriage to Harvard professor Cornelius C. Felton gained her entree into a circle of Cambridge intellectuals. It was in her sister's home that Elizabeth met the Swiss scientist Louis Agassiz, who had recently arrived at Harvard University as the new chair of the Lawrence Scientific School. On April 25, 1850, the two married. Her new husband was 15 years her senior and a widower with three adolescent children. Moving into his house on Oxford Street in Cambridge, Elizabeth Agassiz took up her new role as wife to a famous scientist with a dedication and single-minded devotedness that remained constant throughout the 23 years of their marriage. She was a domestic and professional partner to her husband, supervising the household affairs and working closely with him on his work, accompanying him on expeditions and transcribing his field notes. She even helped manage his elaborate menagerie of animals—turtles, rabbits, eagles, a tame bear, a

Elizabeth Cary Agassiz

few snakes, and an alligator—which he kept for observation and breeding experiments. In addition, she assumed with equal vigor the role of mother to her three new stepchildren, forging relationships with them that were, by all accounts, uncommonly close and loving. Her stepson, the scientist Alexander Agassiz, later recalled his stepmother as "my mother, my sister, my companion, my friend, all in one." Adorned by Elizabeth Agassiz's hospitable nature and easy-going temperament, the Oxford Street house soon became one of the intellectual and social centers of Cambridge.

Her long experience as a teacher of girls, her almost unerring practical wisdom, and the unfailing common sense which she always brought to the difficult problems . . . have done more . . . to make Radcliffe College what it is now, than all other causes combined.

—William Watson Goodwin

In 1854, the family moved to a larger house on Quincy Street built for them by the college, where Elizabeth Agassiz resided for the rest of her life. During this time, the family was burdened by financial problems, and Agassiz, with the help of her two older stepchildren, decided to bring in extra income by operating a school for girls out of the Quincy house. The school proposed to offer the daughters of Cambridge families the opportunity for advanced study with the brilliant and talented instructors at Harvard—an opportunity denied them by the university itself. The school opened in 1855 with her husband lending his support by teaching geography, natural history, and botany. Louis Agassiz was a brilliant speaker and his Quincy house lectures became enormously popular. Many students attended, as well as friends and neighbors, including *Clover Adams. Soon other Harvard professors agreed to participate in this experiment in women's higher education. The Quincy Street school was the forerunner of the "Harvard Annex," which would later become Radcliffe College. Over the next eight years, while Elizabeth Agassiz operated the school, her husband's career flourished. In 1858, the Museum of Comparative Zoology (known as the "Agassiz Museum") opened; by 1863, the family's finances had improved sufficiently that Agassiz closed her school. She spent the next decade working as a naturalist, joining her husband on scientific expeditions, and authoring several natural history books and articles.

Her first book, *A First Lesson in Natural History*, published in 1859, was an attempt to make the science of natural history accessible to novice scientists and younger readers. Written in the form of letters to her niece and nephew, Agassiz focused on the marine life of the Nahant shore, north of Boston, where she had spent her summers since girlhood and where she had collected marine specimens to study in her aquarium at home. In clear, poetic language, she explored the undersea world of sea-anemones, corals, jellyfish, starfish, and sea urchins, and expressed the joys of scientific discovery. Though her husband's career eclipsed her own, the book revealed her to be an intelligent, thoughtful naturalist in her own right.

When Louis Agassiz's deteriorating health precipitated a change in climate, Elizabeth accompanied her husband on a 14-month research trip to study the flora and fauna of Brazil. The couple and a retinue of assistants and volunteers set sail for Rio de Janeiro on April 1, 1865. The trip, which included extended visits to Rio and the Amazon and excursions into the coastal mountains, was not an easy one; the transportation and lodgings were often primitive. Agassiz kept a daily journal of their work, took detailed notes of her husband's natural history lectures, and transcribed his voluminous observational notes. She later edited the scientific material and added her own personal experiences and notes culled from her diary, which she and her husband published in 1867 as *A Journey to Brazil*. The book was well received, and though Agassiz characteristically underplayed her own role and described the goal of the book as depicting "the comprehensiveness of [Louis'] aims and the way in which he carried them out," much of the book's appeal arose from her intelligent prose and innovative narrative structure. She received many admiring notes, including one from Henry Wadsworth Longfellow, a colleague and friend of her husband. His read: "The idea of mingling the two diaries is most felicitous. It is like the intermingling of masculine and feminine rhymes in a French poem. In fact the whole expedition is highly poetical and honorable to all concerned."

In 1869, Agassiz accompanied her husband on a dredging trip off the coasts of Cuba and Florida. Her account, "A Dredging Excursion in the Gulf Stream," appeared in *The Atlantic Monthly* in October and November 1869. During this and the following year, she spent much of her time caring for her husband, who had suffered a cerebral hemorrhage and was temporarily incapacitated. Though he recovered, his health remained fragile.

Despite this personal setback, in December 1871 Elizabeth Agassiz accompanied her husband, two other naturalists, and Dr. Thomas Hill (a former Harvard president) on a nine-month, deep-sea dredging expedition aboard the vessel *Hassler* that took them from the West Indies to Rio de Janeiro and the Gulf of Mathias, through the straits of Magellan and up the Chilean coast to the Galapagos Islands. Again Agassiz kept a diary of the voyage and although the account was never published in book form, it did appear as three separate articles in *The Atlantic Monthly*: "The Hassler Glacier," "In the Straits of Magellan," and "A Cruise Through the Galapagos."

In 1872, after a wealthy New Yorker, John Anderson, bequeathed her husband an endowment of $50,000 and Penikese Island in Buzzard's Bay off the coast of Massachusetts, Elizabeth Agassiz co-founded a summer school devoted to the study of natural history. In April 1873, the coeducational Anderson School of Natural History was created. The school opened on July 8 with Louis Agassiz and two other naturalists instructing students and Elizabeth Agassiz handling many of the administrative duties. The couple returned to Cambridge in October after which Louis' already fragile health quickly deteriorated. He died on December 14, 1873.

Elizabeth Agassiz's devotion to her husband remained unabated even after his death. She began preparing his biography, which she labored over intermittently during the next ten years. The book *Louis Agassiz: His Life and Correspondence* (1885) was published in two volumes to great acclaim. Despite her continued efforts to perpetuate her husband's memory, however, Louis' death marked a watershed in Elizabeth's life and work. World travel and scientific expeditions no longer absorbed her time. And although she undertook new domestic duties (eight days after her husband's death, her daughter-in-law died and her stepson Alexander moved into her home accompanied by his three young children), she soon became deeply involved in a new passion that would consume her energies over the next 20 years.

On February 11, 1879, Agassiz accepted an invitation from Arthur Gilman, a well-known Cambridge literary figure, to attend an informal meeting to consider the possibility of creating a college for women that would offer a course of instruction similar to the one provided at Harvard. Agassiz did not favor coeducation, but she was greatly interested in augmenting educational opportunities for women. Following the meeting, the group requested permission from Harvard University president Charles William Eliot to employ Harvard professors as private instructors to qualified young women. Eliot agreed, though he stressed that his cooperation did not betoken any official connection with Harvard nor an endorsement of coeducation. Having secured the support of Eliot and the Harvard faculty in general, an official committee on women's education, which included Agassiz and six other Cambridge women, was formed. On February 22, 1879, the committee issued a circular, "Private Collegiate Instruction for Women," which outlined the admission standards, costs, and goals of the new school. The plan was to create a four-year course of study, modeled on Harvard. Although the school would not be empowered to hand out diplomas, it would offer instead certificates signed by instructors upon completion of final examinations.

On September 24, 1879, the first entrance exams were held and 27 young women were admitted to the school. Rooms for classes were rented out in various homes, and lodgings for the students were secured throughout Cambridge. More than two years later, on May 22, 1882, the school committee incorporated itself under its now official name, the Society for the Collegiate Instruction of Women (though it was better known by its nickname, the "Harvard Annex"). Its stated purpose was the advanced education of women with the assistance of the instructors of Harvard University.

On July 6, 1882, Elizabeth Cary Agassiz was elected president of the Society. Though enrollment of the school continued to grow and the support of the Harvard faculty remained constant, the Harvard Annex remained woefully underfunded and the threat of closure always loomed. In personal letters that date back to this time, Agassiz expressed her desire to ensure the future of the school by raising an endowment. To this end, she directed most of her efforts over the next several years. It was also around this time that Agassiz began to contemplate the creation of a more formal relationship with Harvard University in order to solve her school's chronic financial problems and ensure its future.

Agassiz began to preside over parlor meetings in Boston in which she appealed to her society friends and associates to contribute money for an endowment fund. She turned out to be a first-rate fundraiser; by June 1884, she had raised some $70,000—not enough to secure the future of the Annex, but enough to keep it going.

By 1889, after ten years of operation under Elizabeth Agassiz's stewardship, the Harvard Annex had become one of the nation's preeminent educational institutions for women. More than 150 women a year were now entering the school, and the number continued to grow. Yet problems remained. Though the students received first-rate instruction, they were still denied official academic degrees and the endowment remained inadequate. Accordingly, the Society began to lobby Harvard for an official connection with the university. Though Agassiz remained opposed to coeducation, she hoped that the university would formally recognize the Annex as a separate department of Harvard College. Her commitment to the Annex and her concern over its future was apparent in her 1892 commencement address:

> Whatever be its attitude in the future,— whatever its relation to the University,— whatever name it may bear,—I hope it will always be respected for the genuineness of its work, for the quiet dignity of its bearing, for its adherence to the noblest end of scholarship.

On March 24, 1893, Agassiz sent a letter to President Eliot that contained the proposal that the Annex would turn over its endowment and real estate (estimated worth about $150,000) to the university if the Annex could become a department of Harvard College and thus eligible to grant degrees. On May 29, 1893, Eliot replied by letter that the president and fellows at Harvard were willing to consider a more official relationship. Further negotiations between Agassiz and the president and fellows continued through the year until it was finally agreed that the Annex would officially change its name to Radcliffe College (in honor of Lady **Anne Radcliffe**, Harvard's first woman benefactor); that the Harvard Corporation, acting as "Visitors," would approve all faculty appointments; and that Radcliffe diplomas would bear the Harvard seal. All organization and business matters would be left to the college to handle. The governor signed the act for the incorporation of Radcliffe on March 23, 1894.

Elizabeth Cary Agassiz continued in her capacity as president of Radcliffe College for the next five years. In 1899, she resigned from her official position as president, though she retained the title of honorary president until 1903. During that time, a scholarship (1895) and a student hall (1902) were endowed in her honor.

In addition to her work on behalf of Radcliffe, Agassiz remained a devoted naturalist, assisting her stepson Alexander in his research. A lifelong philanthropist, she was a member of the Ladies' Visiting Committee for the Kindergarten for the Blind (established under the direction of the Perkins Institute for the Blind) and served as treasurer of the Cambridge branch of the committee from 1887–1904. In her later years, she remained close to family and friends, read voraciously, and continued to spend summers at Nahant.

In the summer of 1904, Elizabeth Agassiz suffered a cerebral hemorrhage. Three years of invalidism followed, which culminated in a stroke. She died on June 27, 1907, at the age of 84 and was buried beside her husband in Mount Auburn Cemetery in Cambridge.

SOURCES:

Agassiz, Elizabeth Cabot. *A First Lesson in Natural History.* Boston, MA: Little, Brown, 1859.

———. *A Journey in Brazil.* Boston, MA: Ticknor and Fields, 1868.

Agassiz, G.R., ed. *Letters and Recollections of Alexander Agassiz.* Boston, MA: Houghton Mifflin, 1913.

Norwood, Vera. *Made from this Earth: American Women and Nature.* Chapel Hill: The University of North Carolina Press, 1993.

Paton, Lucy Allen. *Elizabeth Cary Agassiz: A Biography.* Boston, MA: Houghton Mifflin, 1919.

COLLECTIONS:

Personal papers of Elizabeth Cary Agassiz are located in the Schlesinger Library, Radcliffe College.

> **Suzanne Smith**, freelance writer, Decatur, Georgia

Agatha (fl. 1060).

See Matilda of Flanders (c. 1031–1083) for sidebar.

Agatha, Saint (d. 251)

Patron saint of Malta and of the cities Catania and Palermo in Sicily. Born at Palermo, though date of birth is unknown; died on February 5, 251.

According to legend, Agatha was a 3rd-century Sicilian noblewoman of great beauty, who repeatedly rejected the illicit advances of the Roman prefect Quintianus, the governor of Sicily. For this, she suffered a cruel martyrdom during the persecutions of the Christians by the emperor Decius in 251 CE. It is said that she was whipped, burnt with hot irons, torn with hooks, and then placed on a bed of live coals and glass. The Roman and Anglican churches celebrate her feast day on February 5.

Agatha of Hungary (c. 1025–?).

See Margaret, Saint (c. 1046–1093) for sidebar.

Agatha of Lorraine

Countess of Burgundy. Name variations: Agathe de Lorraine. Daughter of Simon I, duke of Lorraine; married Rainald also known as Renaud III, count of Burgundy and (1145–1184).

Agnelli, Susanna (1922—)

*Politician and writer who was the first Italian woman to hold the post of foreign minister. Name variations: Susanna Rattazzi, Countess Rattazzi. Born in Turin, Italy, on April 24, 1922; daughter of Edoardo Agnelli and Princess **Virginia Bourbon del Monte Agnelli**; sister of industrialists Giovanni and Umberto Agnelli; married Count Urbano Rattazzi, a lawyer (divorced 1971); children: six.*

Grew up in a family of immense wealth and influence (her paternal grandfather was the industrialist Giovanni Agnelli, founder of the FIAT automobile company); entered the public arena relatively late in life, serving as town councillor and mayor of Monte Argentario (1974–84); elected for two terms to Italian Parliament on the Republican Party ticket (1976 and 1979); member of the European Parliament (1979–81); elected to Italian Senate (1983); appointed to post of undersecretary of state for foreign affairs with responsibility for South and North American Affairs (1983); member of the World Commission on Environment and Development, Geneva (1984–87); became Italy's first woman minister of foreign affairs (January 1995).

Appointed in January 1995 as the first woman foreign minister in the history of Italy, Susanna Agnelli was the only member of her illustrious family to enter government service. The Agnelli family has wielded immense power and influence in Italy for nearly a century, starting when Susanna Agnelli's paternal grandfather Giovanni Agnelli (1866–1945) copied the production techniques of Henry Ford to build the FIAT automobile company of Turin into a major vertical monopoly. When Susanna was born in Turin on April 24, 1922, her grandfather's company controlled everything necessary to manufacture the finished product. Growing up in a world of great wealth and privilege, young Susanna and her entire family struggled to maintain their independence against her paternal grandfather's enormous ego. When Susanna's father died, her grandfather unsuccessfully attempted to gain custody of her and her sibling. Susanna's mother, born Princess Bourbon del Monte, was a woman with strong intellectual and artistic interests who loved her children

dearly. One of her closest friends was the famous writer Curzio Malaparte. When Susanna Agnelli married Count Urbano Rattazzi and gave birth to six children, she had her mother's intellectual independence as a model for her own future career in literature and politics.

As depicted in her prize-winning autobiography *We Always Wore Sailor Suits,* Susanna Agnelli lived the carefree life of a member of the upper elite in prewar Fascist Italy. This complacent world began to crumble when Benito Mussolini joined his Axis partner Adolf Hitler in June 1940. By 1942, Fascist Italy was a corrupt, ramshackle society ready to collapse of its own dead weight without German assistance. Agnelli spent the war years as a volunteer nurse with the Italian Red Cross; even family wealth could not completely shield her from the horrors that war brought to Italy. The restoration of peace in 1945 quickly revived her family's fortunes, despite the fact that her grandfather had been a major supporter of the Fascist regime (he was cleared of charges of political complicity with Fascism shortly before his death in December 1945).

For almost three decades after 1945, Susanna Agnelli concentrated on her personal life, raising six children. But her life was to change. She divorced her husband in 1971, and by the early 1970s her children were grown, leaving Agnelli the time to concern herself with public affairs. Perennial complaints about inefficient and corrupt government extended to her hometown of Monte Argentario. Deciding that she could offer her fellow citizens something better, Agnelli ran for the post of mayor of Monte Argentario, to which she was elected in 1974. She acknowledged that her family's powerful position had been a factor in her victory telling a reporter for *The New York Times* that many believed she "might be able to get more things done." Her family's influence did not always work in her favor, however. Some of her constituents felt her privileged background kept her from understanding the problems of ordinary people. Many also believed that she could never pull free of the influence of her powerful brother, the industrialist Giovanni Agnelli, the "uncrowned King of Italy," but these misgivings were soon dispelled. Most observers looked upon her entrance into public life as a very positive development encouraging Italian women to achieve equality and become more active in the nation's political life.

Agnelli's tenure as mayor was regarded as a success by most observers, and the experience whetted her appetite for greater responsibility on the national level. While still serving as mayor (her last term ended in 1984), she took on increasingly responsible jobs in the national government in Rome. As a member of the small but often influential Italian Republican Party (*Partito Repubblicano Italiano,* PRI), Agnelli was first elected a deputy to Parliament in 1976 and re-elected in 1979. Now a well-known national figure, Agnelli was elected a senator in 1983. Her sophistication, knowledge of foreign languages, and numerous personal contacts abroad made her a natural choice for the job of undersecretary of state for foreign affairs with responsibility for South and North American affairs in 1983. From 1986 through 1991, she held four positions as a junior minister in the Ministry of Foreign Affairs, gaining invaluable experience. Other jobs handled with skill during this period were her service with the independent Commission on International Humanitarian Issues, which met regularly at Geneva from 1984 through 1987, and the World Commission on Environment and Development, which also met at Geneva during the same years.

While her political career flourished, Agnelli's reputation as a writer also thrived. Her autobiography, published in English as *We Always Wore Sailor Suits,* became a bestseller. She was awarded three prestigious literary prizes for this book, the Scanno and Bancarella awards in 1975 and the Premio Speciale Casentino in 1984. Clearly enjoying the art of communicating, she began writing a weekly "Dear Abby" column in the magazine *Oggi* in 1983. Even when she was serving as foreign minister in 1995, Agnelli took time to provide answers to such pressing problems as how to end a husband's affair with the babysitter. In her letter to the troubled wife who had written her, Agnelli's solution was as follows: "Certainly, to change the father is problematical, while changing the baby sitter should present no difficulty. Hire an ugly one."

In January 1995, Susanna Agnelli was appointed foreign minister of Italy, replacing Antonio Martino. She was not only the first Italian woman to hold this important post, but the only woman among the 22 ministers of a "nonpolitical" and "technical" government. Displaying a cool head and a pragmatic approach, Agnelli did her best to keep Italy out of the conflict raging in the former Yugoslavia. After eight months on the job, one assessor of her performance noted that she had managed to renew Italy's commitment to a European monetary union. Of all the foreign ministers of Europe in 1995, Susanna Agnelli's style was without doubt the most colorful, one of

"patrician manners, straight posture and a haughty demeanor that can have a scolding edge." Responding to critics of her dual role as foreign minister and author of a lonely-hearts column in a popular magazine, Agnelli rhetorically asked her interviewer: "But why not? They are not asking me because I am Foreign Minister. They are asking me because I am an old lady, and they think I am full of experience."

SOURCES:

Agnelli, Susanna. *Addio, addio mio ultimo amore.* Milan: Arnaldo Mondadori, 1985.

———. *We Always Wore Sailor Suits.* NY: Viking Press, 1975.

Bohlen, Celestine. "Italian Foreign Minister Also Advises Lovelorn," in *The New York Times.* August 15, 1995, p. A4.

Klemesrud, Judy. "Susanna Agnelli: Firm Voice in Italian Politics," in *The New York Times Biographical Service.* October 1983, pp. 1158–1159.

Phillips, John. "Versatile Agnelli adds touch of class to Italian Cabinet," in *The Times* [London]. January 20, 1995, p. 11.

Sarti, Roland. "Agnelli, Giovanni," in Frank J. Coppa, ed., *Dictionary of Modern Italian History.* Westport, CT: Greenwood Press, 1985.

John Haag, Associate Professor of History, University of Georgia, Athens, Georgia

Agnes, Lore (1876–1953)

German political activist, anti-Nazi, and deputy to the German Reichstag. Born Lore Benning in Bochum, Germany, on June 4, 1876; died in Cologne on June 9, 1953; married Peter Agnes.

Lifelong Social Democrat who represented the Düsseldorf electoral district as a deputy to the German Reichstag (1919–33); after the Nazi takeover (1933), continued to work in the underground Social Democratic movement and was consequently persecuted and imprisoned by the Nazi authorities on many occasions.

Born on June 4, 1876, into a poor family, Lore Agnes did not have the opportunity to go beyond an elementary-school education. She overcame these social barriers, however, educating herself and becoming a highly articulate, persuasive political leader. Always independent, she disagreed with the prowar leadership of the German Social Democratic Party (SPD) during World War I and joined the Independent Social Democratic Party, which advocated a radical social and economic democratization of Germany as well as the signing of a peace treaty without annexations and indemnities. Elected in January 1919 to the Constituent Assembly that hammered out the Weimar Constitution, Agnes was highly respected by her largely working-class constituency and was reelected in June 1920 as a regular delegate to the German Reichstag. In 1924, with the demise of the Independent Social Democratic movement, she rejoined the majority Social Democrats and was placed on their electoral ticket for the Düsseldorf district. Regularly reelected throughout the 1920s, she had become a prominent parliamentarian by the early 1930s, serving as a member of the Reichstag presidium. Hated by the local Nazis, she was high on their list of democrats, Marxists, feminists, pacifists, and others professing "un-German" ideals who were to be eliminated with the coming of a fascist Third Reich.

Two days before the elections of March 5, 1933, in which the Nazis used the burning of the Reichstag as a pretext for unleashing a reign of terror throughout Germany, Lore Agnes was arrested. As the most prominent Social Democrat in Düsseldorf, she was a prime target of the local Nazis, who regarded her as a key enemy leader and as a "dangerous Red agitator." Although many Social Democrats and other anti-Nazis would follow her into prisons and concentration camps, she was the first SPD official in Düsseldorf to be placed in "protective custody," the Nazi euphemism used to create a pseudo-legal justification for the arrest and imprisonment of their political foes. Still recuperating from a recent gall-bladder operation, Agnes spent almost a month in custody, part of the time in harsh conditions at the women's prison in Derendorf, a suburb of Düsseldorf. After her release, she was admitted to a hospital because her poor health had been shattered by Nazi brutality. In 1934, she was once again briefly imprisoned, and on many occasions over the following years her home would be searched by Gestapo officials seeking evidence of illegal political activities. Despite the great danger of discovery, she remained loyal to her beliefs and comrades, distributing illegal literature, and attending banned meetings. Not only did she and her husband Peter fear renewed arrest and imprisonment but they also lived in the shadow of economic insecurity. On several occasions, she was unable to secure work because of her political record.

On August 22, 1944, as a result of the reign of terror unleashed by the failed assassination attempt on Adolf Hitler's life a month earlier, Lore Agnes was once more arrested. She was returned to the women's prison in Derendorf, but was scheduled to be moved to the notorious women's concentration camp of Ravensbrück. A doctor's report detailing serious cardiac and circulatory problems prevented this possibly fatal transfer. Nazi officials found and confiscated in her home subversive materials, including books by *Angelica Balabanoff, Eva Broido, and *Clara Zetkin. Released in October 1944, she survived the defeat of Nazi Germany and, in 1950, received compensation for the sufferings she had endured as an anti-Nazi. A few days after her 77th birthday, Lore Agnes died in Cologne on June 9, 1953, in a Germany more interested in the achievement of material prosperity and personal happiness than in tales of heroism in the face of a bloody dictatorship.

John Haag, Associate Professor of History,
University of Georgia, Athens, Georgia

Agnes, Mere (1593–1671).

See Arnauld, Jeanne Catherine in entry titled "Port Royal des Champs, abbesses of."

Agnes, Saint (d. possibly c. 304)

Christian martyr. Name variations: Formerly Annes, Annis, Annice; (French) Agnès. Born in Rome, though date of birth unknown; some historians place her death around 254 (under emperor Decius), some about 304 (under Diocletian); daughter of a noble Roman family; foster sister of St. Emerentiana (d. around 305).

Legend has it that Agnes was 12 when her beauty excited the desires of wealthy suitors who vainly sought her in honorable marriage. When she refused them, saying she wanted to devote her life to Christ, they denounced her to the Roman governor as a Christian. Unmoved by threats of torture, she was sent to the public brothel. There, only one man dared touch her, and he was stricken blind until his sight was restored in answer to the young girl's prayers. Though scholars disagree as to the date of Agnes' death, it is thought that she was beheaded in Rome by order of the emperor Diocletian who, in an attempt to wipe out Christianity, had decreed in 303 that churches be torn down, sacred writings be destroyed, Christians be removed from public office, and all Christians be subject to torture. Through the centuries, young girls observed St. Agnes' Eve (January 20–21) with rites that supposedly divined the form of their future husbands. John Keats used this superstition as *mise en scène* for his poem "The Eve of St. Agnes" (1819). Another poem, "Saint Agnes' Eve," was written by Alfred Lord Tennyson.

Agnes, Saint (1274–1317).

See Agnes of Monte Pulciano, Saint.

Agnes Capet (1260–1327)

Duchess of Burgundy. Name variations: Agnes of Burgundy; Agnes of France. Born in 1260; died on December 19, 1327, in Chateau de Lanthenay, France; daughter of Louis IX, king of France, and *Margaret of Provence (1221–1295); married Robert II, duke of Burgundy, in 1279; children: John of Burgundy (1279–1283); *Blanche of Burgundy (1288–1348); *Margaret of Burgundy (1290–1315, first wife of Louis X of France); *Jeanne of Burgundy (1293–1348, who married Philip VI of France); Hugh V, duke of Burgundy; Eudes IV, duke of Burgundy; Louis (1297–1316), king of Thessalonica; Marie of Burgundy (1298–c. 1310), who married Edward I, count of Bar); Robert (1302–1334), count of Tonnerre.

Agnes de Castro (c. 1320–1355).

See Castro, Inez de.

Agnes de Dampierre (1237–1288)

Ruler of Bourbon. Name variations: Agness. Born in 1237; died on September 7, 1288 in Bourbon; daughter of Count of Guy (or Gui) II de Dampierre and Mahaut I (r. 1215–1242); sister of Mahaut II (ruler of Bourbon, 1249–1262, ruler of Nevers, 1257–1266); granddaughter of *Mahaut de Courtenay (ruler of Nevers, 1182–1257); married Jean de Bourgogne, also known as John of Burgundy, in February 1247; children: Beatrix de Bourgogne (1257–1310), ruler of Bourbon (r. 1287–1310).

Born into the French nobility, Agnes was the younger daughter of Guy II de Dampierre and *Mahaut I, countess of Bourbon. Her parents arranged a marriage for her with Sir John of Burgundy, a petty noble. Her older sister, another Mahaut, married John's brother Eudes. Agnes' mother left no male heirs when she died in 1259, and the barony of Bourbon passed to Mahaut, who succeeded as *Mahaut II. Mahaut II ruled until 1262, then Bourbon passed to Agnes, who held it until her death in 1287. Her daughter *Beatrix de Bourgogne ruled Bourbon from 1287 to 1310.

Agnes de Nevers (r. 1181–1192)

Countess and ruler of Nevers. Reigned from 1181 to 1192; married Pierre de Courtenay; children: Mahaut de Courtenay (r. 1192–1257).

Succeeding Count Guillaume V, also known as William V, Agnes de Nevers became the ruler of Nevers, located in central France, in 1181. Her daughter *Mahaut de Courtenay succeeded her in 1192.

Agnes de Poitiers (fl. 1135)

Queen of Aragon. Name variations: Agnes of Aquitaine. Flourished around 1135; daughter of William IX, duke of Aquitaine, and Philippa de Rouergue (daughter of William IV of Toulouse); married Ramiro II (c. 1075–1157), king of Aragon (r. 1134–1157), in 1135; children: *Petronilla (1135–1174), queen of Aragon.

Agnes of Anjou (c. 1005–1068).

See Agnes of Aquitaine.

Agnes of Aquitaine (c. 995–1068)

French noblewoman who became duchess of Aquitaine. Name variations: Agnes of Anjou; Agnes of Burgundy; Agnes, countess of Burgundy. Born around 995 in Burgundy; died on November 10, 1068, at the convent of Notre Dame des Saintes, France; daughter of Otto William, duke of Burgundy, and Ermentrude de Roucy; married William V the Grand or the Pious (d. 1030), duke of Aquitaine, in 1019; married Geoffrey Martel, count of Anjou, around 1032 or 1040 (marriage dissolved, 1050); children: (first marriage) William VII, duke of Aquitaine; another son; *Agnes of Poitou (1024–1077), Holy Roman empress.

Born into the Burgundian ruling house, Agnes of Aquitaine was extremely well-educated as a girl, not only in the accomplishments considered suitable for a noblewoman but also in the web of loyalties and enmities between the ruling feudal families of France. She showed an ambitious, politically motivated nature and was pleased when her father arranged a marriage for her to the powerful lord Duke William V the Grand of Aquitaine in 1019. She and William had two sons and a daughter. Upon William's death in 1030, Agnes was left to struggle to gain control of the duchy for her children, because William's eldest son (William VI) from his previous marriage had inherited the title of duke. Agnes' eldest son, also William, inherited the duchy upon William VI's death in 1038, but Agnes retained her title as duchess and became regent of Aquitaine in his name. Even after he came of age to rule, Agnes played a principal role in the administration of the large duchy.

Two years later, Agnes married Geoffrey Martel, count of Anjou. The two continued their maneuvers for increased political power for ten years, the highlight of which was the alliance of the House of Anjou with the Holy Roman Empire in 1043, when Agnes' daughter *Agnes of Poitou married Emperor Henry III. However, Agnes of Aquitaine and Geoffrey had no children together, and the marriage was dissolved in 1050. When Geoffrey remarried and attempted to bestow Agnes' dower lands on his new wife, Agnes refused to give up the territory that was rightly hers. A small civil war ensued, during which Agnes' son William VII died in battle.

After William's death, Agnes more or less withdrew from politics. Within a few years, she had turned from the temporal realm of land and power to more spiritual endeavors, using her personal wealth to found the abbey of Notre Dame des Saintes and the Abbey of the Trinity. She retired to Notre Dame des Saintes a few years before her death in 1068.

Agnes of Assisi (1207–1232).

See Clare of Assisi for sidebar.

Agnes of Austria (fl. 1100s)

Hungarian queen and German princess. Married Stephen III, king of Hungary (r. 1161–1173).

Agnes of Austria (1281–1364)

*Hungarian queen and German princess. Born in 1281 (some sources cite 1280); died on June 11, 1364, in Konigsfelden; daughter of German king Albert I of Habsburg (1255–1308), Holy Roman emperor (r. 1298–1308), and Elizabeth of Tyrol (c. 1262–1313); sister of Frederick the Handsome, king of Germany, *Anna of Habsburg (d. 1327), Rudolf III, king of Bohemia and Poland, and *Elizabeth of Habsburg (1293–1352); married Andrew III, king of Hungary (r. 1290–1301), in 1296.*

Agnes of Austria was the wife of Andrew III, king of Hungary, who began his reign in 1290. When Andrew died young without an heir in 1301, it was the end of Hungary's Arpad dynasty and the nation was thrown into turmoil. Seven years later, Agnes' father Albert I, whose harsh rule gave rise to the legend of William Tell (a legendary Swiss patriot forced by the Austrian governor to shoot an apple off his son's head with a bow and arrow), was murdered by a nephew (May 1, 1308), not far from his Habsburg domain. Around the same time, Meister Eckhart, the European mystic, wrote one of his best known tracts, *Book of Divine Consolation* (1308–11), for Agnes.

Following her father's death, Agnes pursued all connected with his murder. She also backed her brother, Frederick the Handsome, in his long war with Ludwig of Bavaria for the imperial crown, until Frederick's death in 1330.

As a widow, Agnes lived with her mother ❧▶ Elizabeth of Tyrol in Vienna, acting as her secretary, adviser and deputy. After Elizabeth's death, Agnes continued her mother's charities from the convent Elizabeth had founded at Königsfelden. Agnes resided at the convent for the last 50 years of her life. One of the richest German princesses of her day, Agnes lived simply while heaping gifts on the church and the poor. She also directed a successful peace campaign, as Friedrich Heer tells us in *The Holy Roman Empire*: "Nearly all the arbitrations agreed to in the Swabian possessions of the house of Austria between 1314 and 1360 can be traced to her influence." Agnes brought an end to the war over Laupen (1340), and concluded alliances for the house of Austria with Berne (1341) and Strassburg, Basel, and Freiburg (1350).

Agnes of Bavaria (1024–1077).

See Agnes of Poitou.

Agnes of Beaujeu (d. 1231)

French noblewoman. Died on July 11, 1231; daughter of Richard IV of Beaujeu; became second wife of

> ❧▶ **Elizabeth of Tyrol** (c. 1262–1313)
> *Queen of Germany. Name variations: Elizabeth of Carinthia; Elisabeth of Gorz-Tyrol. Born in 1262 or 1263; died on October 10 or 28, 1313, in Konigsfelden (Aargau, Switzerland); married Albrecht also known as Albert I of Habsburg (1255–1308), king of Germany (r. 1298–1308), Holy Roman emperor (r. 1298–1308, but not crowned); children: Rudolf III (1281–1307), king of Bohemia and Poland (r. 1306–1307); *Agnes of Austria (1281–1364); Friedrich also known as Frederick I (III) the Fair of Austria (1289–1330), king of Germany (r. 1314–1322), (co-regent) Holy Roman emperor (r. 1314–1325); *Elizabeth of Habsburg (1293–1352, who married Frederick IV of Lorraine); Leopold I (1293–1326), duke of Austria and Styria; Catherine (1295–1323); Albrecht also known as Albert II of Austria (1298–1358), duke of Austria; Heinrich also known as Henry (1298–1327); *Anna of Habsburg (d. 1327, who married Hermann of Brandenburg); Otto (1301–1339), duke of Austria, Steiermark and Karten; Guta, also known as Jutta, Jutha, Jeutha, or Bonitas (1302–1329).*

*Teobaldo or Theobald I also known as Theobald IV of Champagne (1201–1253), king of Navarre (r. 1234–1253), in 1222 (divorced 1227); children: probably *Blanche of Navarre (fl. 1239), duchess of Brittany.*

Agnes of Bohemia (1205–1282)

Hungarian princess who popularized the Franciscan order in Bohemia. Born in Prague in 1205; died in 1282; daughter of Otakar or Ottokar I, king of Bohemia and Hungary (r. 1198–1230), and Constance of Hungary (d. 1240); sister of Wenceslas I (1205–1253), king of Bohemia (r. 1230–1253); joined the Order of the Poor Clares.

Revered as a saint but never canonized, the German princess Agnes was renowned for her piety and for popularizing the Franciscan order in Bohemia. The daughter of King Ottokar I of Bohemia and ◄♣ **Constance of Hungary**, Agnes was born in Prague. When she was three, a marriage was arranged for her with the son of the duke of Silesia, and the child was sent to be brought up with her future husband's family.

Agnes returned to Bohemia at age six after the death of the duke's son, at which time her parents arranged for her to be educated in the cloister. The son of Emperor Frederick II was her next betrothed, and Agnes was moved to Vienna to complete her education at the emperor's court. At this time, Agnes began to show a great interest in charitable work; she often visited and cared for the poor, but did so in secret to escape notice. When this second arranged marriage was broken off, she returned once more to Bohemia.

Two more offers of husbands came for Agnes: one from Henry III of England and the other from the now-widowed Emperor Frederick II. While these were being discussed, Agnes' brother Wenceslas I inherited his father's throne.

Agnes, now in her 20s and determined not to marry, wrote to the pope to ask for permission to pursue a religious life. The pope agreed and wrote to Wenceslas, who, concerned for his sister's happiness, ended all marriage prospects about 1233.

Agnes had already adopted an ascetic lifestyle, including sleeping on a hard pallet, but in 1234 she joined the Franciscan order of the Poor Clares. She cut off her hair and gave up her sumptuous wardrobe for a simple grey habit. Her property was divided between the church, the poor, and the nuns of the order. Although the pope commanded that she be the abbess of the newly established convent, Agnes maintained that she was not superior to the other nuns and insisted on performing all menial tasks.

Her growing fame as a pious and virtuous abbess was heightened when she managed to reconcile her brother with his rebellious son Ottokar II. The Franciscan order was spread throughout Bohemia because of Agnes' personal popularity; in addition, she founded several convents as well as a monastery and a hospital at Prague. Agnes of Bohemia was so revered that after her death at age 77, many sick people wore her relics and prayed to Blessed Agnes in the belief that her spirit could effect miracles of healing.

Laura York, Anza, California

Agnes of Bohemia (1269–1297)

*Princess of Bohemia and duchess of Austria. Name variations: Anezka. Born in September 1269; died on May 17, 1297, in Prague (some sources cite 1290 or 1296); daughter of Otakar or Ottokar II (b. 1230?), king of Bohemia (r. 1253–1278), duke of Austria and Styria (r. 1252), and *Cunigunde of Hungary (d. 1285); married Rudolf II (1270–1290, son of Rudolf I, Holy Roman emperor, and *Anna of Hohenberg), duke of Austria (r. 1282–1290); children: John the Parricide (1291–1313).*

Agnes of Brandenburg (d. 1304)

*Queen of Denmark. Died on October 1, 1304; daughter of *Jutta of Saxony (d. 1267) and John I, margrave of Brandenburg; married Erik V Klipping or Clipping (1249–1286), king of Denmark (r. 1259–1286), on November 11, 1273; children: daughter Regitze also known as *Richeza Eriksdottir (who married Nicholas II von Werle); Erik VI, king of Denmark (r. 1286–1319); Christopher I, king of Denmark (r. 1319–26, 1330–32); *Martha of Denmark (c. 1272–1341); Valdemar; Katherina (1283–1283); Elizabeth (1283–1283).*

♣► **Constance of Hungary** (d. 1240)

*Queen of Bohemia. Name variations: Constantia. Died in 1240; daughter of *Anne of Chatillon-Antioche (c. 1155–1185) and Bela III (1148–1196), king of Hungary (r. 1173–1196); sister of Emeric I, king of Hungary (r. 1196–1204), and Andrew II (1175–1235), king of Hungary (r. 1205–1235); second wife of Ottokar I (d. 1230), king of Bohemia (r. 1198–1230); children: Wenzel also known as Wenceslas I, king of Bohemia (r. 1230–1253); *Agnes of Bohemia (1205–1282).*

Agnes of Burgundy (c. 995–1068).

See Agnes of Aquitaine.

Agnes of Burgundy (1260–1327).

See Agnes Capet.

Agnes of Burgundy (d. 1476)

Duchess of Bourbon. Died in 1476; daughter of *Margaret of Bavaria (d. 1424) and John the Fearless, duke of Burgundy (r. 1404–1419); sister of Philip the Good (1396–1467), duke of Burgundy (r. 1419–1467); married Charles I, duke of Bourbon (r. 1434–1456); children: *Isabelle of Bourbon (d. 1465); Charles (c. 1434–1488), archbishop of Lyons; Peter II also known as Pierre de Beaujeu (who married *Anne of Beaujeu); Louis, prince-bishop of Liege; *Marie de Bourbon (who married John II of Calabria); John II (1426–1488), duke of Bourbon (r. 1456–1488, who married *Jeanne of Bourbon [1434–1482]); *Catherine of Bourbon (d. 1469); *Jeanne of Bourbon (d. 1493).

Agnes of Courtenay (1136–1186)

Syrian-Frank royal who held sway in the Frankish principality of Jerusalem. Born in 1136; died in 1186; daughter of Joscelin II and ✤ Beatrice; sister of Joscelin III and Sibylla; first wife of Amalric I, king of Jerusalem (r. 1162–1174); married Hugh of Ramleh also known as Hugh of Ibelin (died 1169); married Reginald also known as Reynald of Sidon, lord of Sidon; children: (first marriage) Baldwin IV, king of Jerusalem (r. 1174–1183) and Sibylla (1160–1190). Amalric's second wife was *Maria Comnena.

Agnes of Courtenay was a dynamic politician who greatly influenced events in the Frankish principality of Jerusalem. She was born a princess in Edessa when the Holy Land was controlled by the Christian knights who had remained to build their fortunes after the successful First Crusade. Married as a young girl to a crusader knight who died soon after the wedding, Agnes moved to Jerusalem in 1149 at age 13. There, in 1157, she was married again, this time to Prince Amalric of Jerusalem. The prince and princess had one son, Baldwin, and a daughter *Sibylla; however, their marriage was annulled on grounds of consanguinity soon after Amalric assumed the throne in 1163.

Undaunted, Agnes married twice more, first to Hugh of Ramleh, then to Reynald of Sidon upon Hugh's death in 1169. Upon Reynald's death, Agnes began to regain power as the mother of Baldwin IV, who had succeeded to his fa-

ther's throne despite his parents' annulment. Agnes became a major participant in the politics of the royal court, arranging, among other accomplishments, her daughter's marriages and securing the loyalty of Jerusalem's nobles and churchmen to her son. When Baldwin's leprosy incapacitated him, she became ruler of Jerusalem in practice if not in name. Finally, Agnes arranged the coronation of her grandson as Baldwin V before her son's death in 1185, thus ensuring a peaceful succession. She died the following year at age 50.

Agnes of France (c. 1170–?).

See Agnes-Anne of France.

Agnes of Germany (1024–1077).

See Agnes of Poitou.

✤ **Beatrice** (fl. c. 1100s)

Countess of Edessa. Married Joscelin II, count of Edessa; children: Joscelin III; Sibylla; *Agnes of Courtenay (1136–1186).

Agnes of Germany (1074–1143)

German princess. Born in 1074; died on September 24, 1143; daughter of Holy Roman emperor Henry IV (r. 1056–1106) and Bertha of Savoy (1051–1087); sister of Henry V and Conrad, both Holy Roman emperors; granddaughter of *Agnes of Poitou (1024–1077); married Frederick I, duke of Swabia, in 1089; married Leopold III, margrave of Austria of the Babenberg line; children: (first marriage) Frederick (d. 1147), duke of Swabia (who married *Judith of Bavaria [fl. 1120s]); Conrad III (first emperor of the Hohenstaufen line); *Gertrude of Swabia (c. 1104–1191, who married Hermann, pfalzgraf of Lotharingen); (second marriage) Leopold IV, margrave of Austria; Henry Jasomirgott, 1st duke of Austria; the historian Otto, bishop of Freising.

The German princess Agnes was the daughter of the Holy Roman Emperor Henry IV (r. 1056–1106) and *Bertha of Savoy. Agnes married Frederick, duke of Swabia, and lived in the castle of Swabia, located in the Black Forest in southwest Germany. The couple was responsible for the beginnings of a German dynasty, the House of Hohenstaufen. Their son, Conrad III, ruled Germany from 1138 to 1152. Their grandson, Frederick I Barbarossa (r. 1152–1190), unified Germany.

Agnes of Guienne (1024–1077).

See Agnes of Poitou.

Agnes of Habsburg (c. 1257–1322)

*Electress of Saxony. Name variations: Gertrud. Born around 1257; died on October 11, 1322, in Wittenberg; daughter of *Anna of Hohenberg (c. 1230–1281) and Rudolph or Rudolf I of Habsburg (1218–1291), king of Germany (r. 1273), Holy Roman emperor (r. 1273–1291); married Albert II, elector of Saxony.*

Agnes of Hesse (1527–1555)

*Electress of Saxony. Born on May 31, 1527; died on November 4, 1555; daughter of *Christine of Saxony (1505–1549) and Philip I the Magnanimous, landgrave of Hesse; married Maurice, elector of Saxony, on January 9, 1541; married John Frederick II, elector of Saxony, on May 26, 1555; children: (first marriage) *Anna of Saxony (1544–1577).*

Agnes of Huntingdonshire
(fl. 13th c.)

English doctor.

Agnes of Huntingdonshire was one of numerous medieval women doctors. Unfortunately, all we know about her life is that she was well-respected for her healing abilities in Huntingdonshire, England, and that she practiced medicine without university training—a privilege denied most medieval women. Given the often nonsensical theories taught to male medical students, a lack of university education could be an advantage for a woman practicing healing (usually illegally), as she would rely more on empirical than theoretical knowledge; it has been argued that this could have made women doctors of the day better healers than their formally trained male counterparts.

Agnes of Jouarre (fl. early 13th c.)

French abbess.

A learned and pious woman, Agnes entered the religious life as a young girl and eventually became abbess at the convent of Jouarre, France. Not content with the decreasing power of abbesses and convents in the increasingly centralized church hierarchy, Agnes of Jouarre worked to secure specific rights for her abbey. She successfully petitioned Pope Innocent III (1198–1216) for independent status for Jouarre,

which meant that the abbey was no longer responsible to local bishops and other church officials, but had to answer only to the pope himself. This substantially increased her own authority as ruler and greatly increased the freedom of Jouarre's nuns to conduct their lives and affairs without interference from male superiors. Saint **Balda** was the third abbess of Jouarre.

Agnes of Looss (fl. 1150–1175)

*Duchess of Bavaria. Flourished between 1150 and 1175; married Otto I (b. around 1120), duke of Bavaria (r. 1180–1183); children: Otto (d. 1181); Ludwig also known as Louis I (b. 1174), duke of Bavaria (r. 1183–1231, who married *Ludmilla of Bohemia and was assassinated in 1231).*

Agnes of March (1312–1369).
See Dunbar, Agnes.

Agnes of Maurienne (1092–1154).
See Adelaide of Maurienne.

Agnes of Meissen (1184–1203).
See Agnes of Quedlinburg.

Agnes of Meran (d. 1201)

*Queen of France. Name variations: The White Lady; Agnes of Neran; Agnes de Méranie or Meranie. Died on July 20, 1201, in Paris, France; daughter of Berthold III of Andrechs, marquis of Meran, count of Tirol, and duke of Carinthia and Istria, and Agnes of Dedo; sister of *Gertrude of Andrechs-Meran, queen of Hungary, and Saint *Hedwig of Silesia (1174–1243); married Philip II Augustus (1165–1223), king of France (r. 1180–1223), in 1196; children: Philip Hurepel (1200–1234), count of Boulogne; Marie of France (1198–c. 1223).*

Born into a German noble family, Agnes of Meran became the mistress of the French king Philip II Augustus. After his first wife died, Philip contracted a marriage with *Ingeborg of Denmark (c. 1176–c. 1237) in 1193, but he repudiated her soon after the wedding. The king apparently loved Agnes and made her his queen in all but title, since neither the church nor the Danish or French people accepted his divorce from Ingeborg as legitimate. Instead of returning to Denmark, Ingeborg remained at a French convent, appealing to the pope to force Philip to reinstate her as his rightful wife. But Philip refused to give Agnes up, even after the pope placed him under interdict. Philip and Agnes had a wedding ceremony performed in 1196, although they seem to have been the only ones who felt their marriage was valid. Agnes acted as queen and presided over the French Court, much to the scandal of the rest of Europe. She gave him a son, Philip Hurepel (literally "bristling hide," because his hair, like his father's, was always bristling), and a daughter, *Marie of France. After Agnes' death in 1201, Philip finally reinstated Ingeborg, but managed to have Agnes' son Philip legitimized as heir to the throne.

Laura York, Anza, California

Agnes of Monte Pulciano

(1274–1317)

Italian abbess thought to have gifts of prophecy and healing. Name variations: Agnese, Agnes of Montepulciano, Agnes of Procena. Born around 1274 in Monte Pulciano, Italy; died in 1317 at the convent of Monte Pulciano.

Saint Agnes of Monte Pulciano entered a Franciscan convent at the age of nine. The order she joined (known as the Sackins) was dedicated to poverty; its members wore only coarse sackcloth. Well-respected for her devotion to the poor and sick, Agnes had a reputation for piousness that earned her the position of abbess at the convent of Procena, probably around age 20. She remained there for some years but later answered a call to establish her own religious foundation. Returning to Monte Pulciano, Agnes started a Dominican double monastery, again acting as abbess. Her renown spread throughout Italy, and she was soon known for having the gifts of prophecy and healing. After the venerable abbess died about age 43, her many supporters campaigned successfully for her canonization. Her feast day is April 20.

Agnes of Poitou (1024–1077)

*Holy Roman Empress and regent whose court attracted Europe's most creative minds to Germany. Name variations: Agnes of Aquitaine; Agnes of Bavaria; Agnes of Germany; Agnes of Guienne. Born in 1024 in Poitou, France; died on December 14, 1077, in an Italian convent; daughter of William V the Pious, duke of Aquitaine, and *Agnes of Aquitaine (c. 995–1068); became second wife of Henry of Germany (1017–1056) also known as Henry III, Holy Roman emperor (r. 1039–1056), on November 1, 1043; children: Henry IV (b. 1050), Holy Roman emperor (r. 1056–1106).*

Daughter of the ruling family of Aquitaine, Poitou, and later Anjou, Agnes of Poitou grew up expecting to marry a foreign noble. Her betrothal to Prince Henry of Germany was a tri-

umph for her parents, since he would eventually be crowned Holy Roman emperor. Three years after Agnes' marriage and move to Germany, Henry succeeded to the throne and had Agnes crowned empress with him by Pope Clement II. Agnes did not play a large role in the administration of the empire, but she presided over a brilliant court and became known as a generous patron of writers, painters, and poets, attracting Europe's most creative minds to Germany.

She had been empress for ten years when Henry died suddenly; their son Henry succeeded his father as Henry IV, but, as he was only six years old, Agnes became regent of the empire in his name. Her previous lack of experience in ruling became apparent as she attempted to manage the extensive German kingdom. Her husband, although a powerful monarch, had extended his power too far, in the view of his many vassals; they believed he had infringed on their property rights in his attempts to consolidate his own power. Thus, Agnes suffered from both the lasting enmity towards Henry III and her own ignorance of the mood of the German people. She was not a skilled negotiator nor was she well-advised by her councillors, and soon the empire was threatened by both foreign armies and internal religious strife. Her alliances against the religious reform movements spreading through Germany proved unwise, and ambitious invaders wrested control of several imperial territories away from the empress. Finally, her son the emperor was kidnapped by supporters of Anno, archbishop of Cologne, in May 1062. Agnes then abandoned the regency to the archbishop and left politics altogether. She retired to an Italian convent where she died at about age 53.

Laura York, Anza, California

Agnes of Poitou (1052–1078)

*Queen of Castile and Leon. Name variations: Ines of Poitou or Pointou. Born in 1052; died on June 6, 1078; daughter of Guillaume also known as William VIII (or VI), duke of Aquitaine; became first wife of Alphonso VI (c. 1030–1109), king of Leon (r. 1065–1070, 1072–1109) and Castile (r. 1072–1109), in 1069 (divorced 1077). Some sources claim that Agnes was the mother of *Teresa of Castile, though most historians believe Teresa was the illegitimate daughter of *Jimena Muñoz.*

Agnes of Poland (1137–after 1181)

*Princess of Kiev. Born in 1137; died after 1181; daughter of *Salomea (d. 1144) and Boleslaw III Krzy-*

wousty also known as Boleslaus III the Wrymouthed (1085–1138), king of Poland (r. 1102–1138); married Mstislav II, prince of Kiev, in 1151.

Agnes of Procena (1274–1317).

See Agnes of Monte Pulciano.

Agnes of Quedlinburg (1184–1203)

German abbess and artist. Name variations: Agnes of Meissen. Born in 1184 in Meissen, Germany; died in 1203 at the abbey of Quedlinburg.

It is not clear if Agnes of Quedlinburg felt a strong religious calling or if her parents could not afford a wedding dowry and so sent her to be cloistered, but she entered the large, wealthy convent of Quedlinburg at a young age. At the convent, Agnes received an exceptional education as well as artistic training. Quedlinburg housed a major scriptorium (where manuscripts were copied and illustrated), and so its abbess ensured that many of its nuns learned calligraphy, miniature painting, and other aspects of manuscript production. Agnes' artistic abilities garnered her much attention. Not only was she a talented writer familiar with the works of the ancient pagan philosophers as well as those of contemporary writers, but she painted both miniatures and scenes from Greek mythology for the abbey, as well as contributing to the abbey's tapestry production. Her deep piety led her to be chosen abbess of Quedlinburg before she was 20, a very rare occurrence, though she died only a short time later.

Laura York, Anza, California

Agnes of Saarbrucken.

See Siege Warfare and Women.

Agnes of Saxony

Countess Palatine and duchess of Bavaria. Flourished in the 1200s. Married Otto II, count Palatine and duke of Bavaria (r. 1231–1253); children: *Elizabeth of Bavaria; Ludwig also known as Louis II the Stern (b. 1229), duke of Bavaria (r. 1255–1294); Henry I, duke of Lower Bavaria (r. 1255–1290).

Agnes Sorel (1422–1450).

See Sorel, Agnes.

Agnes-Anne of France (b. 1171)

Byzantine empress. Name variations: Agnes of France. Born in 1171; died after 1240; daughter of Louis VII (1120–1180), king of France (r. 1137–1180), and *Adele of Champagne (1145–1206); sister of Philip II Augustus, king of France (r. 1180–1223); became childbride of Alexius II Comnenus (1167–1183) Byzantine emperor (r. 1180–1183), on Easter 1179 (Alexius was killed in 1183); married Andronicus I Comnenus, Byzantine emperor (r. 1183–1185), in 1183; married Theodor Branas in 1204; children: (second marriage) possibly Manuel.

Byzantine emperor Manuel I Comnenus had a predilection for Frankish ways. Both his wives were Western princesses. His first was the German *Bertha-Irene of Sulzbach, who gave him two daughters. Following her death, he married *Marie of Antioch, the mother of his legitimate son Alexius II. When Manuel died in 1180, Marie of Antioch assumed the regency for the 11-year-old Alexius, who was growing up with his intended bride Agnes-Anne of France. Intentions went astray in 1182, when Andronicus Comnenus, a cousin of the imperial family, arrived in Constantinople. Convincing Alexius to sign a death warrant for his mother Marie of Antioch, Andronicus had himself crowned co-emperor. Andronicus' henchmen strangled Alexius, whose widow, the 12- or 13-year-old Agnes-Anne of France was made to marry Andronicus. Despite his ruthless usurpation, Andronicus I was a popular ruler at the beginning of his reign; he rooted out corruption and tried to improve the administration of the empire. It is said that when he was killed by the mob during a revolt three years later (1185), his wife Agnes-Anne mourned his loss deeply.

Agnese.

Variant of Agnes.

Agnesi, Maria Gaetana (1718–1799)

Italian mathematician credited with calculating the bell-shaped curve known as the "Witch of Agnesi" and the first woman in Europe to distinguish herself in the field of mathematics. Name variations: Agnese. Born Maria Gaetana Agnesi on May 16, 1718, in Milan, Italy; died on January 9, 1799, in Milan, Italy; daughter of Pietro Agnesi (a wealthy merchant with ties to the University of Bologna) and Anna Fortunata (Brivio) Agnesi; sister of Italian composer Maria Teresa Agnesi (1720–1795); tutored privately; no formal education; never married; no children.

Awards: Gold medal and a gold wreath adorned with precious stones presented by Pope Benedict XIV in honor of her publication of Instituzioni Analitiche

(1749); Crystal box with diamonds and a diamond ring given by Empress Maria Theresa of Austria to whom Instituzioni Analitiche *was dedicated (1749).*

Participated in debates at her father's house with learned guests from the age of nine until 1739, when she withdrew from public life to concentrate on the study of mathematics; member of Academia della Scienze (Bologna); published Instituzioni Analitiche *(Foundations of Analysis), a systematic compilation of developments in algebra, calculus, differential equations and analytic geometry (1748); appointed by Pope Benedict XIV as honorary chair of Mathematics and Natural Philosophy at the University of Bologna (1750–52); devoted herself to the study of theology and to charity work (after 1752); made director of women at Pio Instituto Trivulzio (1771), where she took up residence (1783) and lived until her death (1799).*

Maria Gaetana Agnesi, one of the earliest pioneers in the field of mathematics, was the oldest of 21 children of Pietro Agnesi, a wealthy merchant who prized culture and learning and moved among the highest circle of the Milanese intelligentsia. Maria's mother, Anna Fortunata Brivio, died in 1732 after giving birth to eight children; Pietro remarried twice.

Maria Gaetana exhibited great potential for learning from early childhood. By the age of five, she spoke French fluently, and by the age of eleven she could converse in Latin, Greek, German, Spanish, and Hebrew. Pietro Agnesi used his wealth and influence to secure for Maria the finest tutors available in Italy, including Carlo Belloni and two future university professors, **Francesco Manara** (in Pavia) and **Michele Casati** (in Turin). After 1740, Maria studied almost exclusively with Ramiro Rampinelli, a professor of mathematics at the University of Pavia.

From the time Maria was nine years old, Pietro put her on display at his "academic evenings," during which he hosted a gathering of local celebrities and learned men from all over Europe. At age nine, Maria presented, in Latin, a scholarly address defending the study of liberal arts by women. Typically, at these gatherings Maria would recite a series of theses in Latin and engage distinguished guests in debates on mathematics, logic, mechanics, chemistry, botany, and a variety of other scientific topics. Visitors to Pietro Agnesi's home were deeply impressed by Maria's linguistic fluency and the breadth of her knowledge. Monsieur De Brosses, first president of the parliament of Dijon and a member of the Royal Academy of Inscriptions and Belles Lettres of Paris, called her facility with languages "prodigious" and described her usage of Latin as "with such purity, ease and accuracy that I do not recollect to have ever read any book in modern Latin that was written in so classical style as that in which she pronounced these discourses." He recalled that later in the evening "the conversation became more general, every one speaking to her in the language of his own country, and she answering him in the same language."

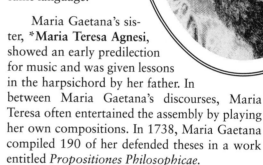

Maria
Agnesi

Maria Gaetana's sister, ***Maria Teresa Agnesi**, showed an early predilection for music and was given lessons in the harpsichord by her father. In between Maria Gaetana's discourses, Maria Teresa often entertained the assembly by playing her own compositions. In 1738, Maria Gaetana compiled 190 of her defended theses in a work entitled *Propositiones Philosophicae*.

As Maria Gaetana neared adulthood, she expressed a strong preference for studies in mathematics, geometry, and ballistics. Always shy and retiring, she began to express displeasure at being put on display in her father's soirees. When she was 20, she declared her desire to enter a convent, preferably that of the Blue Nuns, an Augustinian order that earned their nickname because of the color of their habits. When her father objected to her desire to take the veil, Maria struck a compromise wherein Pietro agreed to excuse her from public display, to allow her to dress simply and modestly, and to attend mass whenever she desired. Maria thereafter remained at home and dedicated the next decade of her life to the study of mathematics.

The result of Agnesi's systematic study of the new mathematical discoveries of the 17th and 18th centuries was the publication of the *Instituzioni Analitiche* (Foundations of Analysis). A two-volume work of over 1,000 pages, the *Instituzioni Analitiche* was a compilation of the most recent developments in the study of algebra, analytic geometry, calculus, and differential equations. The first volume dealt with finite processes, while the second concentrated on infinitesimal analysis. Agnesi supervised the publication of the *Instituzioni Analitiche,* which was printed in late 1748 on presses installed in the Agnesi house. It was published in Italian, instead of the more traditional Latin, in an effort to encourage its study by the *gioventu* (youth) and to avoid the necessity of translation.

Although Agnesi intended the *Instituzioni Analitiche* to be a compilation of previous discoveries rather than a presentation of new theories, the process of weeding through and organizing such a large mass of material prompted her to include some of her own theories and developments. She described her attempts to put the material into its "natural order," although much of it was "scattered here and there in the works of many authors, and principally in the *Acta* of Leipzig, in the *Memoires* of the Academy of Paris and in other journals." She modestly admitted that "in the act of handling the various methods, there occurred to me several extensions and a number of things, which by chance are not without novelty and originality."

Despite the publication of several of her own discoveries, the "discovery" with which Agnesi has been popularly accredited was actually developed earlier by both Pierre de Fermat and Isaac Newton. It is the curve known in English as the Witch of Agnesi, so called because of a mistranslation of the word *versiera,* derived from the Latin word *versoria* (a rope that guides a sail), which was translated by the English scholar John Colson as the Italian word for "female goblin or witch." The Witch of Agnesi is a bell-shaped curve, which she described using the equation $x(a^2+y^2)=a^3$, where the x-axis is vertical and the y-axis is horizontal:

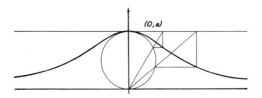

In the *Instituzioni Analitiche,* Agnesi used the curve as an exercise in analytic geometry, and she utilized algebraic formulae to illustrate the method of deriving points of inflection on the curve.

Agnesi's *Instituzioni Analitiche* won immediate acclaim within the academic community. The French Academy of Sciences proclaimed: "The work is characterized by its careful organization, its clarity, and its precision. There is no other book, in any language, which would enable a reader to penetrate as deeply, or as rapid-

ly, into the fundamental concepts of analysis. We consider this treatise the most complete and best written work of its kind." The Academy subsidized the translation of the second volume into French in 1749. The entire work was later translated into English by John Colson, Lucasian professor of mathematics at Cambridge University, who "found her work to be so excellent that he was at the pains of learning the Italian language at an advanced age for the sole purpose of translating her book into English, that the British Youth might have the benefit of it as well as the Youth of Italy." The English edition was published in 1801.

Agnesi dedicated the *Instituzioni Analitiche* to Empress *Maria Theresa (1717–1780) of Austria, who had a reputation for enlightenment and patronage of scholarship. In her dedication, Agnesi noted, "For, if at any time there can be an excuse for the rashness of a woman who ventures to aspire to the sublimities of a science which knows no bounds, not even those of infinity itself, it certainly should be at this glorious period." Maria Theresa acknowledged the dedication with a crystal box with diamonds and a diamond ring. Pope Benedict XIV recognized Agnesi's achievement with a gold wreath set with precious stones and a gold medal. In 1750, he also named Agnesi an honorary professor of mathematics and natural philosophy at the University of Bologna, a position she held until 1752.

Although Agnesi was often entreated by her contemporaries to lecture publicly, she always declined, and after her father's death in 1752 she withdrew from the scholarly world and dedicated herself to charity work, the study of theology, and supervising the education of her many brothers and sisters. Her withdrawal from the outside world was noticeable enough to encourage rumors that she had finally entered the order of the Blue Nuns. Although there is no evidence to that effect, the rumor was strong enough to survive in accounts of Agnesi's life into modern times.

For a while after 1752, Agnesi resided in separate apartments in her family home, where she took in the poor and the sick. In 1759, she secured a house for herself and her wards. Despite her great wealth, Agnesi lived in the simplest quarters, spending the money set aside for her food, clothing, and books on the poor of her parish of San Nazaro. When she was in need of money to finance her charitable activities, she sold the gifts sent to her by Maria Theresa to a rich Englishman and later even sold the crown given by Benedict XIV. Her earliest biographer, **Luisa Anzoletti,** wrote: "To her it is not enough to make the daily pilgrimage as a nurse inside and outside the poorest huts, so that she asked from her father for some rooms to live in, separate from the rest of the family and little by little she transformed them into something like a private hospital."

In 1771, Archbishop Pozzobonelli opened the Pio Albergo Trivulzio in the palace given for this purpose by Prince Antonio Trivulzio. It became a home for the elderly, sick, and poor. He persuaded Agnesi to take the position as director of women there, and within a few years the number of inhabitants had increased to over 450, forcing her to close her own little hospital to concentrate exclusively on this institution. In 1783, she took up residence in two of the rooms at the Pio Albergo Trivulzio, where she insisted on paying rent in order to avoid diminishing the resources available for the poor. Agnesi was described by her colleagues there as "an angel of consolation to the sick and dying women until her death at the age of 81 years on January 9, 1799." In Agnesi's later years, she grew blind and deaf, and developed hydrothorax, which eventually caused her death.

At her request, Maria Agnesi's body was buried in a common grave, without a monument. In 1833, Lorenzo Prinetti, honorary director of the Pio Albergo Trivulzio, placed a small monument on the stairway of the institute to which was later added a marble bust of Agnesi, which he inscribed:

> To Maria Gaetana Agnesi
> Treasure of knowledge
> Most pure flower of virtue
> Well known all over Europe
> In the serious sciences of computation
> Here
> where, having repudiated the comforts and honours of
> the world she lived XV years with the poor of Jesus
> happy till her last day
> for the joys of charity.

At the centennial of her death in 1899, a street in each of three towns—Milan, Monza, and Masciago—was named in her honor and a cornerstone was placed in the facade of the Luogo Pio with the inscription:

> Maria Gaetana Agnesi
> erudite in Mathematics
> glory of Italy and of her century
> most acknowledged in asylums of poor and old
> humble servant of charity
> died in the year 1799.

Two scholarships were set up in Agnesi's honor, which have served to keep her name as an inspiration for future generations.

The curve known as the Witch of Agnesi was studied merely as a curiosity by the scientific community until the 20th century, when physicists discovered that the curve could be used to represent the spectral energy distribution of x-ray lines, optical lines, and the power dissipation in sharply tuned resonant circuits. The discovery of practical applications for the Witch of Agnesi has served to bring the work of this remarkable woman back to light. As a personification of the best ideals of the Enlightenment period, and as an example to women of their capacity to equal men in academic endeavor, Agnesi still provides a stunning example of brilliance, determination, and uncommon devotion to the cause of those less fortunate than herself.

SOURCES:
Jur, Barbara A. "An Abnormal Witch," in *Mathematics Teacher*. Vol. 85. October 1992, pp. 584–87.
Kennedy, Hubert. "Maria Gaetana Agnesi (1718–1799)," in *Women in Mathematics*. Edited by Louis S. Grinstein and Paul J. Campbell. NY: Greenwood Press, 1987.
———. "The Witch of Agnesi—Exorcised," in *Mathematics Teacher*. Vol. 62, 1969, pp. 480–82.
Lowe, Roger. "The Witch of Agnesi," in *Historical Topics for the Mathematics Classroom*. Washington, DC: National Council of Teachers of Mathematics, 1969.
Spencer, Roy C. "Properties of the Witch of Agnesi: Application to Fitting the Shapes of Spectral Lines," in *Journal of the Optical Society of America*. Vol. 30, 1940, pp. 415–19.
Thomas a Kempis, Sister Mary. "The Walking Polyglot," in *Scripta Mathematica*. Vol. 6, 1939, pp. 211–17.

Kimberly Estep Spangler, Assistant Professor of History, Friends University, Wichita, Kansas

Agnesi, Maria Teresa (1720–1795)

Italian harpsichordist, singer, and librettist who was also one of the first female opera composers. Name variations: Maria Theresa. Born in Milan, Italy, on October 17, 1720; died in Milan on January 19, 1795; daughter of Pietro Agnesi (a wealthy merchant with ties to the University of Bologna) and Anna Fortunata Brivio; sister of Maria Gaetana Agnesi (1718–1799, a mathematician); married Pier Antonio Pinottini on June 13, 1752.

Maria Teresa Agnesi, sister of *Maria Gaetana Agnesi, was one of the first female opera composers. Her portrait hangs in the theater museum of La Scala, a testament to her contributions to the musical world. As a girl, she performed and sang her own compositions. In 1747, her first theatrical work, *Il ristoro d'Arcadia*, was successfully presented in Milan's ducal theater. Her next opera, *Ciro in Armenia*, produced in 1753, used her own libretto. She wrote *Insubria consolata* in 1766 to honor the engagement of Beatrice d'Este and the Archduke Ferdinand and it was performed that year. According to Simonetti, the Empress *Maria Theresa of Austria-Hungary sang from a collection of arias Agnesi had given her. A composer, harpsichordist, singer, and librettist, whose collections of arias were widely known in Italy and German-speaking Europe, Maria Teresa Agnesi was a forerunner of the great Italian opera composers.

SUGGESTED READING:
Anzoletti. *L. Maria Gaetana Agnese.* Milan, 1900.

John Haag, Athens, Georgia

Agness.

Variant of Agnes.

Agnodice (fl. 4th c. BCE)
Athenian and first woman of her city to be trained in midwifery and to practice as a professional, who successfully fought for the right to continue to practice before the court of Areopagus.

Agnodice was an Athenian woman (that is, not only an inhabitant of Athens, but also of a citizen family) of the 4th century BCE. She is attested to have been a virgin in the ancient literature, and thus she must have been unmarried, unlike most adult women of her citizenship status. Since she found it necessary to financially support herself, Agnodice almost certainly was too poor for anyone associated with her family to offer a dowry for her marriage. Seeking a congenial profession, she decided upon a career in midwifery at a time when most practitioners of medicine of any sort were men. Disguised as a man, Agnodice attended a course in midwifery taught by the noted physician Hierophilus. Thereafter, she continued in her disguise until she had successfully discharged her duties, whereupon she would disclose her gender to her patient. So successful did Agnodice become that her fame eventually led to her being unmasked as a woman.

Her secret disclosed, some of her male rivals sued her before the court of the Areopagus. This was a body composed of ex-magistrates, which, by the 4th century, was concerned mostly with cases of a religious nature, especially those involving homicide or wounding (that is, in cases involving the letting of blood [itself firmly associated with divine power by the Athenians]). The exact charge against Agnodice is unclear, for it perhaps was not the case that women were ex-plicitly debarred from her occupation, although it would have been very unusual for any free-born woman to have been so employed on her own in the Athens of the day. Since there were allegations of "corruption" aimed at Agnodice, it is possible that she was accused of some sort of professional incompetence in connection with a case gone bad. Regardless, in court Agnodice both admitted her gender and then defended herself so vigorously, with so many witnesses testifying on her behalf, that the Areopagus not only dismissed all charges, but also proceeded to support a law—which subsequently passed—explicitly permitting free-born women to learn and practice midwifery.

William S. Greenwalt, Associate Professor of Classical History, Santa Clara University, Santa Clara, California

Agostina (1788–1857)
Spanish heroine. Name variations: The Maid of Saragossa or Zaragoza; Augustina. Born in 1788; died in 1857.

In 1808, during the French siege of the city of Saragossa, Spain, a Spaniard named Agostina moved through the streets. Dressed in white with flowing hair, she wore a cross and urged resistance. When Napoleon's army broke through a hole in the ancient walls protecting the city and the Spaniards were ready to desert, Agostina seized a flaming torch from the hand of a dying artillery soldier, took his place at the cannon, and shouted, "For so long as French are near, Saragossa has one defender!" Her courage rallied the men, the French were driven back, and the city was saved. Later, offered the rank of artillery soldier with pay and pension, Agostina gained the right to dress as a member of the military and bear arms. She was immortalized as "The Maid of Saragossa," in the first canto of Lord Byron's *Childe Harold*:

> Her lover sinks—she sheds no ill-timed tear;
> Her chief is slain—she fills his fatal post;
> Her fellows flee—she checks their base career;
> The foe retires—she heads the sallying host.

Agostina has also been the subject of a poem by Southey and a painting by Goya.

Agoult, Marie de Flavigny, Comtesse d' (1805–1876).
See Wagner, Cosima for sidebar.

Agreda, Sor María de (1602–1665)
Spanish writer of religious books. Name variations: Coronel de Jesú;s. Born María Coronel y Arana at

Agostina, the
maid of
Saragossa.

Agreda, Spain, in 1602; died at Agreda, on May 24, 1665; never married; no children.

Selected works: The Mystical City of God *(1670);* Spiritual Ladders of the Soul; The Spouse's Laws.

It is said that without leaving her homeland of Agreda, Spain, Sor (Sister) María de Agreda carried a missionary message to the Aboriginal people of the New World. A 17th-century religious woman of great mystery and sectarian debate, she claimed that she was directed in part by a personal revelation from the *Mary the Virgin.

Born into a devoutly Catholic family, María de Agreda became a nun at age 17 when her family turned their home into a convent, and her parents and siblings all took vows of the order. For the three years following, María was in poor health both emotionally and physically. During this time, she experienced trances in which she traveled to areas of New Mexico, Arizona, and Texas. María admitted these trances to her mother and her confessor, and, though she pre-

ferred that her experiences be kept secret, word spread quickly. A man with contacts in the New World sought confirmation from Native Americans to whom she preached while in her trances, and they claimed that Sor María had been among them.

María also believed that the Virgin Mary had imparted her life story in a revelation. Based on this, María wrote the biography *Mystical City of God*. The original manuscript was burned, apparently at the command of María's confessor, who disapproved of women writing. A second draft was completed at the command of yet another confessor, though it would not be published until 1670, five years after María de Agreda's death.

In 1643, aware of the growing legend surrounding María de Agreda, King Philip IV of Spain went to meet the nun. Through hundreds of letters, the two maintained a strong friendship. Indeed, María is acknowledged as one of Philip's most influential political and spiritual advisors. Though most of her time and energies were dedicated to writing, Sor María held the position of abbess until the time of her death.

SOURCES:
Colahan, Clark. *The Visions of Sor María de Agreda.* Tucson: The University of Arizona Press, 1994.

Agrippina I (14 BCE–33 CE).
See Agrippina the Elder.

Agrippina II (15–59 CE).
See Agrippina the Younger.

Agrippina Major (14 BCE–33 CE).
See Agrippina the Elder.

Agrippina Minor (15–59 CE).
See Agrippina the Younger.

Agrippina the Elder (c. 14 BCE–33 CE)

Popular Roman whose independence and ambition for her children annoyed Tiberius and led to her exile and subsequent suicide by starvation. Name variations: Agrippina I; Agrippina Major; Vipsania Agrippina. Born around 14 BCE; died in exile in 33 CE in Pandateria; daughter of Julia (39 BCE–14 CE) and Marcus Agrippa; granddaughter of Caesar Augustus; sister of Gaius (b. 20 BCE), Lucius (b. 17 BCE), Julia (b. 15? BCE); married Germanicus in 5 CE (died 19 CE); children: nine, including Nero Julius Caesar (d. 31 CE); Drusus III Julius Caesar (d. 33 CE); Gaius (12–41 CE, the future emperor Caligula); Drusilla (15–38 CE); Agrippina the Younger (15–59 CE, mother of the future emperor Nero); Julia Livilla (b. 16? CE).

Agrippina was the granddaughter of Augustus and the daughter of Marcus Agrippa, Augustus' closest political associate. Two of Agrippina's brothers had been named as Augustus' heirs to the Roman Empire before their premature deaths. Agrippina was married to Germanicus, himself recently named as an heir of Augustus' successor, Tiberius. Theirs was a loving marriage, producing nine children before Germanicus died of a sudden illness (19 CE) Since Germanicus' relationship with Tiberius had been deteriorating for some time before Germanicus' death, Agrippina accused Tiberius of having her husband poisoned. Thereafter, Agrippina remained Tiberius' implacable foe, even after the aging emperor named her two oldest sons as his political heirs (23 CE). Tragically, neither son lived long enough to inherit the empire, for Sejanus (the commander of Rome's Praetorian Guard) conspired against them and convinced Tiberius to punish their "treason" with exile and execution. Agrippina herself died in exile before she saw the ultimate accession of her youngest son, Caligula.

Agrippina the Elder was the daughter of *Julia (daughter of Caesar Augustus) and Marcus Agrippa (Augustus' closest political associate and one of his best friends). Agrippina was born about 15 years into her grandfather Augustus' transformation of the Roman Republic into the Roman Empire. This metamorphosis was very popular with the vast majority of those living under Roman authority, because the political and military excesses of the late Republic's Senatorial aristocracy had led to constant and debilitating war. However, peace came to the Roman world at the cost of political liberty, for Augustus had slowly accumulated an unparalleled concentration of power.

Augustus did not alter the infrastructure of the Republic, for it largely continued to function in the old way, with one exception: Augustus personally came to hold all of the important offices of the state. Thus, no other potential rival could marshal the resources to challenge Augustus' status. This led Augustus into a conundrum. On the one hand, he claimed to be no more than a beloved servant of the people who had elected him to all his offices. On the other hand, he could not allow any but a chosen successor to approach his status, lest the anarchy of the past—so associated with unfettered freedom—return. While espousing the virtues of a "free" political state, Augustus sought to control the choice as to who would succeed to his collection of powers—technically a role that should have been entirely left to the Roman people. Had Augustus had a biological son, it is certain that he would have been Augustus' choice as a political heir (after all, this was traditional in all Roman Senatorial families); however, despite having two stepsons in Tiberius and Drusus the Elder (the sons of Augustus' last wife *Livia from her former marriage), Augustus' only child was his daughter Julia.

As a result, Julia's marriages were politically manipulated by Augustus. After each marriage, Augustus campaigned to get Julia's husbands elected to the various powers that would eventually elevate them to a successor's prestige. A simple plan, but one that was continuously foiled by their premature deaths.

Julia's first husband, Marcellus (a son of Augustus' sister, *Octavia, and thus Augustus' nephew) died in 23 BCE before their marriage produced children. Next, Julia wed Marcus Agrippa in 21 BCE and remained married to him until his death in 12. In the nine years of their marriage, Julia gave Marcus Agrippa two sons, Gaius (20 BCE) and Lucius (17 BCE), and two daughters, ***Julia** (15? BCE) and Agrippina the Elder (14 BCE). In addition, Julia was pregnant with a third son, Agrippa Postumus, when the elder Marcus Agrippa died.

The oldest two grandsons of Augustus were adopted by him as his legal sons and heirs, but both died (Lucius in 2 CE and Gaius in 4 CE), leaving Augustus to seek yet another successor. (Agrippa Postumus appears to have been too roguish to be considered. Before Augustus died in 14 CE, Postumus was exiled from Rome at Augustus' command.)

The death of Julia's husband Marcus Agrippa saddened Augustus and reminded him of his own mortality. Fearing that he would not see his grandsons live to politically replace him, in 11 BCE, Augustus forced his stepson, Tiberius, to divorce the woman he loved (***Vipsania Agrippina**, daughter of the now dead Marcus Agrippa and his first wife ***Pomponia**) in order to marry a woman he did not love, Augustus daughter, the recently widowed Julia. Tiberius hated Augustus for so abusing him, especially since it was clear that Tiberius was not intended as Augustus' heir, but only as a kind of insurance policy lest Augustus die before his chosen heirs could assume public responsibilities.

Although the relationship between Tiberius and Augustus was rocky after Tiberius' marriage to Julia, Tiberius, more often then not, grudgingly did what Augustus required of him—even as Julia became a public embarrassment to both father and husband, rebelling against her own marital status by sleeping with many of Rome's most important men, and a few who were not so important. For her adultery, which flew in the face of her father's cherished moral legislation, Julia was exiled from Rome in 2 BCE.

In the long run, weathering these unpleasant responsibilities paid off for Tiberius. In 4 CE, Augustus (resentfully to be sure) finally named Tiberius his heir. Over the next ten years, Tiberius received the necessary advancement, so that when Augustus died in 14 CE, Tiberius stood alone as Rome's new emperor. But before Augustus had named Tiberius as his successor, he had forced Tiberius to adopt Germanicus—the son of Tiberius' brother Drusus the Elder—as his son. Both Tiberius and Drusus the Elder had become Augustus' stepsons when he married their mother Livia. The elder Drusus was esteemed by Augustus as his best general (although Tiberius was no incompetent along these lines), and he campaigned extensively in Germany. Before Drusus the Elder fell ill after a fall

from a horse and died in 9 BCE, he married ***Antonia Minor** (36 BCE–37 CE) and had three children with her: Germanicus, ***Livilla** and Claudius (who would eventually become an emperor, 41–54 CE).

Tiberius also had a son, Drusus the Younger, from his marriage to his beloved Vipsania. Thus, Germanicus was now on a par with Drusus the Younger when it came to the succession. Many reasons may have motivated Augustus' demand (for example, Germanicus' connections with the Senatorial aristocracy were impeccable and proceeded along kinship lines, which would have broadened the political base of the imperial family), but Augustus must have known how much such a step nettled Tiberius. Part of Augustus' motivation was probably spite towards the man who may have become his heir, but who had never become his friend.

When Tiberius' heirs came to be of appropriate ages, so as to intertwine the fortunes of the imperial family even further, the younger Drusus married Germanicus' sister, Livilla, while, in 5 CE, Germanicus married Agrippina the Elder, daughter of Marcus Agrippa and Julia.

> Since [Agrippina] seemed scared of tasting an apple which [Tiberius] handed her at dinner, the invitation to his table was never repeated. . . . [H]e said that she had charged him with attempted poisoning.
>
> —Suetonius, *Life of Tiberius*

When Augustus' death in 14 CE led his legions along both the Rhine and Danube to rebel against their current working conditions, Tiberius dispatched Drusus the Younger to put down the mutiny along the Danube, while Germanicus acted similarly along the Rhine. Both commanders succeeded in the primary missions, but Germanicus—remembering Augustus' one-time intention of conquering Germany between the Rhine and the Elbe—spent the years between 14 and 17 campaigning in free Germany. Although Germanicus believed himself close to subduing this region, in 17 Tiberius recalled him to Rome where Germanicus was given a triumph. The reason for the recall resulted in a bone of contention. Germanicus and his supporters became convinced that Tiberius acted out of petty jealousy, not wanting Germanicus to win his due mead of glory.

One of Germanicus' chief supporters was his wife, Agrippina, with whom he had nine children, four of whom outlived their parents: Gaius (the future emperor Caligula); *Agrippina the Younger (mother of Nero), ◄ Drusilla, and *Julia Livilla. Two other sons, Nero Julius Caesar and Drusus III, would receive temporary honors but would die before their mother Agrippina. While Germanicus was in Germany, his wife and family had accompanied him. In fact, when the Rhine mutiny was still in full swing, the presence of Germanicus' family helped break the determination of the mutinous soldiers. (When it was pointed out that the soldiers themselves posed a greater danger to a "helpless" woman and her children than did the Germans across the frontier, the soldiers' will broke and reconciliation became possible.) Agrippina adored her husband, holding him as vastly superior to his "father" Tiberius and his "brother" Drusus the Younger. However, it is probably *not* the case that she so revered him for the "republican" sentiments that would later be attributed to him.

By the end of the 1st century CE, a somewhat romantic view of the defunct Republic would begin to circulate among some of the Senatorial order (including the historian Tacitus). When this movement flourished, it desecrated the memories of those of the empire who were held chiefly responsible for the establishment of the imperial institutions, which were now said by some to have seduced the Roman people from their traditional love of freedom. Historically, Tiberius was a special target for the neo-republicans, while Germanicus—primarily because his relationship with Tiberius deteriorated after the year 17—came to be painted as a republican "hero." It was said that had Germanicus ever come into power, which only the jealous Tiberius had prevented, Germanicus would have restored true Roman liberty. This was a fanciful notion at best, supported by little evidence, but it came to be believed largely because of the resentments and accusations against Tiberius that would one day be aired by Agrippina.

Although Tiberius probably resented the pompous airs Germanicus is said to have assumed, Tiberius continued to honor his adopted son. In 18, Germanicus held a second consulship and began a tour of the East as Tiberius' special envoy. Of particular sensitivity were Roman relations with Armenia, Cappadocia, and Commagene, but Germanicus was being sent to settle Rome's eastern frontier. Along with Germanicus and his family (including Agrippina), Tiberius sent an old friend and colleague, Gnaeus Calpurnius Piso, as the governor of Syria. Although subordinate to Germanicus, Piso was sent to provide a sober reign to Germanicus' transit of the East. Although Tiberius intended to reaffirm his ties with Germanicus with this appointment, Germanicus believed the assignment grew out of Tiberius' fear of his growing popularity.

From his base in Syria, in 19 Germanicus made the mistake of visiting Egypt without Tiberius' prior permission. Although his intentions seem to have been innocent—Germanicus wanted to see Egypt's antiquities, and what Germanicus wanted to do, he did—Egypt was nevertheless a touchy matter as far as Tiberius was concerned. Since the days of Augustus, Egypt (and more important its wealth) was the private possession of the emperor and off-limits to all senators, to which order Germanicus technically belonged. This ban on Egyptian travel was imposed because Egypt's potential for isolating itself from the rest of the world (the primitive state of ancient technology made Egypt inaccessible if a strong power held it aloof) made it a dangerous base from which to assault imperial authority. As a result, any unauthorized entry into Egypt could be construed as an act of treason—and Germanicus certainly knew this. Yet, he traveled there with impunity, holding himself apart from the conventions that shackled other men.

When Germanicus returned to Syria, Piso's loyalty to Tiberius and his anger over Germanicus' tourism led to an open break between the two, and Germanicus, pulling rank, ordered Piso to leave his province. Piso did so, but soon after his departure from Syria Germanicus fell mysteriously ill and died at Antioch, convinced, as was Agrippina, that Piso had had him poisoned. Piso made the mistake of returning to Syria before being recalled to Rome to face charges of murder and of reentering his province against the orders of a superior. Probably innocent of murder, Piso nevertheless understood that he was likely to become a scapegoat in light of his Syrian reentry. Protesting his innocence and maintaining his personal loyalty to Tiberius, Piso committed suicide—a deed that did Tiberius no good, for it intimately linked the allegations of murder against Piso to the emperor himself in many people's minds.

Agrippina greatly lamented the loss of her husband and was as convinced as Germanicus had been that Piso—on Tiberius' orders—had been an assassin. As did Germanicus, Agrippina seems to have believed that the growing awareness of Germanicus' greatness would soon have toppled Tiberius once and for all. It made sense to Agrippina that Tiberius, knowing this, was led to the rash act of removing his rival with poi-

Drusilla. See *Agrippina the Younger* for sidebar.

son. Carefully honoring Germanicus, Agrippina provided a heroic cremation. Thereafter, in a procession intended to win sympathy for the memory of Germanicus and undermine the popularity of Tiberius, Agrippina made her way home, displaying pious grief in the most public fashion, with her children and her husband's ashes. Once in Rome, Agrippina continued a vendetta against Tiberius for the rest of her life.

Although Agrippina truly believed (almost certainly incorrectly) that Tiberius was behind the death of her husband, it is possible that her campaign to associate Germanicus' death with Tiberius had a more Machiavellian rationale. Her return to Rome with Germanicus' ashes caused a sensation, and her charges against Tiberius clearly turned public sentiment in her favor and embarrassed the emperor. As a result, since he maintained his innocence against all such charges, the one thing that Tiberius could not do was dispossess the children of Germanicus from the succession—for if he did so, everyone would be convinced of his complicity in Germanicus' death. How much Agrippina might have been campaigning on behalf of her children is unknown, but having grown up in a highly charged political atmosphere, it is not beyond the realm of possibility that she had such a purpose.

Nevertheless, for the time being, Tiberius' son Drusus the Younger became his sole heir. In 23, however, this Drusus died of another mysterious illness. It was later revealed that Drusus had been poisoned by his wife (Germanicus' sister), Livilla, and her lover, the monstrous Captain of the Praetorian Guard, Sejanus. It is clear that Livilla was convinced to remove her husband by her seducer Sejanus, who promised marriage. In fact, Sejanus hoped to turn his fortuitous command of the Praetorian Guard—the only troops stationed on Italian soil (with a camp just to the east of the city of Rome)—into a bid for imperial power. Sejanus had not been born into Rome's most prestigious social class, the Senatorial Order. As a result, no one (not even Tiberius) considered him as a potential emperor. To overcome the many obstacles before him, Sejanus realized that he needed to (a) eliminate all possible successors to the imperial majesty from within the imperial family and to (b) become associated himself with the imperial family through marriage. With Germanicus gone, the obvious focus of his ambitions was Livilla, the wife of Tiberius' only heir. Remove Drusus, thought Sejanus, and (after a suitable period of mourning) marry Drusus' widow while continuing to ingratiate himself with Tiberius.

Unfortunately for Sejanus, Tiberius would not agree to his and Livilla's marriage when it was first proposed to him (25 CE). Initially rebuffed, Sejanus continued to plot in silence, reasoning that, if Tiberius was truly desperate for an heir, Tiberius would turn to him. Unfortunately for Agrippina's two oldest sons, Nero Julius Caesar and Drusus III, they lay between Sejanus and his dream. Soon after Tiberius' son died, Tiberius named these sons of Germanicus as his imperial successors (23). How much Tiberius' mother, Livia, might have been behind these adoptions is unknown. Even after Agrippina's sons attained their status as Tiberius' successors, Agrippina continued to lambast Tiberius over Germanicus. Sejanus' dream may have been set back by these adoptions, but they did not prove to be insurmountable obstacles, especially after Livia died in 29.

Tiberius had long maintained a love-hate relationship with his mother Livia. She had acted to mitigate the influence such figures as Sejanus could exercise over Tiberius, and it is clear that she shielded Agrippina from Tiberius' anger. But when Livia died in 29, Tiberius became increasingly susceptible to Sejanus' accusations that Nero Julius Caesar and Drusus III were falling into the sins of their father, arrogantly parading their disregard for Tiberius' authority, while flirting with out-and-out treason. These allegations were made all the more believable by Agrippina, who acted as a rallying point for those Senators who opposed either Tiberius or Sejanus, or both. Agrippina's role in this regard intensified as Sejanus' influence grew, and especially blossomed after Tiberius refused to allow Agrippina to remarry (26), undoubtedly reasoning that the husband of the mother of his heirs would be in a good position to offer serious political opposition.

Once Livia was no longer there as ballast, Tiberius' relations with Agrippina and her sons immediately deteriorated, again under Sejanus' artful prompting. Before the end of 29 CE, Nero Julius Caesar and Agrippina were exiled to Pandateria. In the following year, Drusus III was imprisoned in Rome. Both of Agrippina's sons were executed: Nero Julius Caesar in 31 and Drusus in 33. Given the intensity of Agrippina's hatred of Tiberius and the closeness of her ties with her sons, there may have been something behind the suggestions of treason, brought to Tiberius' ear by Sejanus. Whether true or not, however, Agrippina shared her sons' fates, for, after four years in exile, learning of her son Drusus' assassination, she starved herself to death in 33.

Sejanus, however, did not benefit from the destruction of these rivals. In 31, Tiberius (tipped off by Antonia) learned of Sejanus' complicity in the death of his own son, Drusus. This led to Sejanus' well-planned fall and execution. Though it was too late to restore the fortunes of Agrippina or her two oldest sons, she would have a kind of reaffirmation and revenge through her youngest son, Gaius (nicknamed "Caligula," meaning "Little Boots," by her husband's Rhine legionaries, from the little army boots Agrippina had made for her young son so that he could parade around his father's camp). Caligula became not only Tiberius' proposed heir, but also his actual successor in 36. All other possible heirs to the imperial authority having been exterminated by one hand or another, the empire was about to know evil in its most irresponsible form.

SOURCES:
Suetonius. *The Twelve Caesars*. Penguin Press, 1957.
Tacitus. *Complete Works*. Modern Library, 1942.

SUGGESTED READING:
Balsdon, J.P.V.D. *Roman Women*. London: Bodley Head, 1962.
Scullard, H.H. *From the Gracchi to Nero*. 5th. ed. London: Methuen, 1978.

William S. Greenwalt, Associate Professor of Classical History, Santa Clara University, Santa Clara, California

Agrippina the Younger (15–59 CE)

Prominent woman intimately involved in power politics in the Roman Empire, who was often designated by her relationship to three emperors: sister of Caligula, wife of Claudius, and mother of Nero. Name variations: Julia Agrippina (often designated "Agrippina Minor"); Agrippina II. Pronunciation: ag-rih-PEE-nuh. Born at Ara Ubiorum (modern-day Cologne) on November 6, 15 CE; slain at Baiae by order of her son, Emperor Nero, 59 CE; eldest daughter of Germanicus (the great Roman general), and Agrippina the Elder ("Major," granddaughter of the great Augustus); sister of Drusilla (15–38), Caligula (12–41), and Julia Livilla; married Gnaeus Domitius Ahenobarbus (died 40 CE), in 28; married C. Sallustius Passienus Crispus (died 47 CE); married Claudius (died 54 CE), Roman emperor, in 49; children: (with Gnaeus Domitius Ahenobarbus) Emperor Nero.

Received various formal honors along with her sisters (37 CE); accused of treachery by Caligula and exiled (39); recalled by the succeeding Emperor Claudius (41); married Claudius (49); succeeded in having Nero adopted by Claudius and received the prestigious title "Augusta" (50); poisoned Claudius and succeeded in having Nero made emperor (54).

Published an autobiography, no longer extant, which was used by other classical historians as a source for Roman imperial history.

The life of Agrippina the Younger is recorded only in connection with the powerful men of her day, yet she was considered—even by those men—a potent political force. She was never able to hold public office simply because she was a woman, but she pushed the bounds of acceptable feminine behavior, using all possible means and methods to achieve her goals. In doing so, she proved that, for good or for ill, a woman could be both as ruthless and as capable as the men of her time.

Agrippina was born on November 6, 15 CE, only one year after the death of Caesar Augustus, the great founder of the Roman Empire and her own great-grandfather. Her mother, *Agrippina the Elder, gave birth to her in Ara Ubiorum (modern-day Cologne) rather than Rome, because she had accompanied her husband, the popular Roman general Germanicus, to his site of command on the Rhine. The Roman historian Tacitus characterizes Agrippina the Elder as "outshining generals and commanders" and documents her active role in maintaining the morale of the troops. In one famous incident, for example, she stood at a bridgehead to congratulate the troops returning from a bloody but victorious battle with German tribes. At a time when Roman men viewed women as naturally inferior and excluded them entirely from military matters, her actions provoked both admiration and criticism. Clearly, she provided a strong role model for her daughter.

Agrippina the Younger, despite her privileged status, spent her formative years in an atmosphere of suspicion and fear. The family's very prominence forced the Emperor Tiberius to perceive it as a potential threat to his power. Germanicus, who was the emperor's adopted son and blood nephew, died suddenly under mysterious circumstances, and, although she had no proof, Agrippina the Elder believed Tiberius had a hand in her husband's death. The populace, who held Germanicus' family in high esteem, prayed in response to the misfortune that the Elder Agrippina's "children might live to survive their enemies" and called her "the only true descendent of Augustus." This only emphasized the threat. Some years later, she and two of her sons were accused of treason; all three eventually died demeaning deaths, Agrippina the Elder of starvation in exile in 33.

In the meantime, the Emperor Tiberius had chosen a man of respectable heritage,

Gnaeus Domitius Ahenobarbus, for Agrippina the Younger to marry. Domitius was a blood-relation to the founding Caesars, but Suetonius, the ancient biographer, describes him as a "wholly despicable character" marked by cruelty and dishonesty. At the age of 13, in the year 28, Agrippina became his wife, and in 37 she gave birth to her only child, the future emperor, Nero. Domitius is said to have remarked: "It is impossible for any good man to be sprung from me and this woman." But from Agrippina's standpoint, life had taken a positive turn.

Up to this time, she had had little opportunity to exercise her formidable political skills, apart from managing to survive. Yet now she set a goal that superseded everything else in her life: the greatest prize of the empire, emperorship for her son Nero. When astrologers prophesied that Nero would both become emperor and kill his mother, Agrippina is said to have responded, "Let him kill me, but let him rule."

Nero was born the same year that Caligula (Gaius), Agrippina's brother, succeeded Emperor Tiberius. Caligula restored Germanicus' house-

Agrippina
the
Younger

hold to prominence and good fortune, bestowing great public honors on Agrippina and her two sisters, ❦▶ **Drusilla** (15–38) and ***Julia Livilla**. All received the privileges of the vestal virgins (without the corresponding responsibility to live celibate lives or to perform ritual religious duties); all received the right to sit in the royal family enclosure at public games; all were included in the annual vows of allegiance to the emperor and for his safety. Oaths included the statement, "I will not value my life or that of my children less highly than I do the safety of the Emperor Gaius and his sisters." The three sisters were placed on the obverse of a coin which portrayed Caligula: Agrippina represented "Security" personified. Cumulatively, these honors were unprecedented.

Yet Agrippina's good fortune soon vanished. Despite the public prominence Caligula had originally accorded his family, his favor turned to suspicion. In 39, he killed his former brother-in-law Lepidus, accusing him of incest with Agrippina and her sister Julia Livilla, and of involvement in a treasonous plot. Declaring that members of his family should not be given any more honors, Caligula auctioned off his sisters' belongings and sent Agrippina back to Rome in disgrace with orders to carry Lepidus' ashes in an urn for the entire journey. He then sent her and Julia Livilla into exile on the Pontian islands. Nero, only a small child, was separated from his mother and given into care of his aunt, ❦▶ **Domitia Lepida**. His father Domitius died during this negative period as well.

It was I who made you emperor.

—**Agrippina, to her son Nero**

After Caligula's death and the accession of Claudius in 41, Agrippina was recalled from exile. Immediately, she began casting about for a husband who would further her goals. She first pursued Galba, a wealthy man with good future prospects (a later emperor). Although he was married, Agrippina made advances toward him, provoking his mother-in-law to slap her publicly. She next turned her eyes to the literary figure C. Sallustius Passienus Crispus, who was also exceedingly wealthy and politically prominent. Passienus, like Galba, was already married, but he left his wife for Agrippina. Only a few years after their marriage, he died, having designated Agrippina and Nero his heirs. The ancient biographer Suetonius alleges that Passienus' death resulted from Agrippina's intrigues.

In 49, Emperor Claudius' wife ***Valeria Messalina** (c. 23–48) was discovered in a treasonous plot and put to death. Although Claudius vowed he would never marry again, he immediately reconsidered, focusing on several women, Agrippina among them. Arguments in Agrippina's favor were her youth and beauty, her availability, and her proven fertility. Additionally, because she was his niece, a marriage with her would retain control of the empire in the Claudian family. Agrippina, never one to overlook an opportunity, profited by a niece's privilege of kissing and caressing Claudius "with a noticeable effect on his passions," according to Suetonius. This advantage, however, was simultaneously an obstacle, for both Roman law and custom considered such a marriage incestuous. The problem was resolved when the Senate passed legislation specifically allowing a marriage between a man and his brother's daughter. Once enacted, the marriage took place. Tacitus asserts, "From this moment the country was transformed. Complete obedience was accorded to a woman."

And, indeed, Agrippina was finally able to maneuver more effectively to position Nero for the succession. She persuaded Claudius to appoint men who were favorable to her into positions of power. For example, she convinced him to recall Seneca, the philosopher and writer, from exile and to appoint him to public office. More important, Agrippina gave Seneca the task of tutoring Nero, forbidding him to teach philosophy, because it was "no proper study for a future ruler." She further determined to place a loyal man as commander of the Praetorian Guard, a powerful military position. Whereas there had previously been two commanders, she argued that dividing the rule led to disharmony, while a single commander would alleviate the problem. Claudius yielded to her arguments and appointed Afranius Burrus, ever after loyal to Agrippina, to the position.

In addition to buttressing her position by key appointments, Agrippina worked ruthlessly to rid herself of potential threats. In one notorious case, she accused ❦▶ **Lollia Paulina**, previous wife of Caligula and then rival for Claudius' hand, of engaging in the treasonous crime of consulting astrologers about the emperor's marriage. Lollia Paulina's property was confiscated and she was exiled, where she was forced to commit suicide. When Lollia's head was brought back to Agrippina, since she did not recognize it, "she opened the mouth with her own hand and inspected the teeth, which had certain peculiarities," according to Cassius Dio. Another woman was banished merely because Claudius remarked favorably on her beauty.

But Agrippina's most significant accomplishment during the early years of marriage to Claudius was to contrive her son's adoption by the emperor. Claudius already had two children, Britannicus and *Octavia (39?–62), from his previous ill-fated marriage, and Britannicus was expected to succeed Claudius. Agrippina pointed out that the great Augustus had always had two candidates primed and adopted in case of his demise, and her argument worked. In the year 50, Claudius adopted Nero, and since Nero was three years older than Britannicus and the son of the now powerful Agrippina, he became the expected heir to the empire.

After Nero's adoption, Agrippina's influential position was publicly confirmed by formal honors, some unprecedented, that were bestowed on her. Among other things, she was given the title of "Augusta"—the first time a living spouse of a presiding emperor was so honored. A veteran colony was established at Agrippina's birthplace and named for her: Colonia Claudia Augusta Agrippinensium. Claudius allowed her to sit on a separate tribunal and greet foreign and visiting dignitaries with him, an innovation considered culturally inappropriate for a woman but one that emphasized her powerful position in the empire. Although Claudius seems to have appreciated her talents, the ancient historians are less understanding. Cassius Dio asserts, "No one attempted in any way to check Agrippina; indeed, she had more power than Claudius himself."

As Agrippina had arranged, Nero married Octavia, Claudius' daughter, further solidifying Nero's claims to the empire and highlighting the fact that he was nearly an adult and able to rule. But as Nero reached his 17th year, Claudius seems to have taken a new attitude toward his wife. According to Tacitus, he alarmed Agrippina by "remarking in his cups that it was his destiny first to endure his wives' misdeeds, and then to punish them." Claudius began to shift his attention to Britannicus, declaring, according to Suetonius, that even though Britannicus was young, he would give him the *toga virilis* (a symbol of passage to adulthood) "so that the Roman people might at last have a genuine Caesar."

All these factors spurred Agrippina to action. To solidify her control over her son, she first determined to rid Nero of his aunt Domitia Lepida, who had cared for Nero during Agrippina's exile. Domitia Lepida indulged and doted on Nero, while Agrippina, by contrast, maintained the strict

---

❧ Drusilla (15–38 CE)

*Roman noblewoman. Born in 15 CE; died in 38 CE; daughter of Germanicus Caesar and *Agrippina the Elder; sister of Agrippina the Younger and Julia Livilla; sister and mistress of Caligula.*

Several plots to end Caligula's rule were formed and discovered before the conspirators could carry out their plans, including one involving his own sisters. In that particular incident, he banished his sisters to exile and executed the other conspirators. Even so, Caligula decreed great honors for his sisters Drusilla, *Julia Livilla, and *Agrippina the Younger: they were included in oaths, while on coins they personified "Security," "Peace," and "Prosperity." When his sister Drusilla died, Caligula "made it a capital offence to laugh, to bathe, or to dine with one's parents, wives, or children while the period of public mourning lasted," writes Suetonius. Though, in the Roman past, only Julius Caesar and Augustus had been deified, Caligula deified Drusilla, setting up a shrine for her, complete with priests, and gave her the name "Panthea" to show that she had the qualities of all goddesses.

❧ Domitia Lepida (c. 19 BCE–?)

*Roman matron. Flourished at the time of Nero; born around 19 BCE; daughter of *Antonia Major (39 BCE–?) and L. Domitius Ahenobarbus (d. 25 CE); sister of Gnaeus Domitius Ahenobarbus; married M. Valerius Messalla Barbatus (both members of the dynastic Julio-Claudian family); children: *Valeria Messalina (c. 23–48).*

When Nero was three and his mother *Agrippina the Younger was exiled, Roman emperor Caligula confiscated the boy's estate. As a result, Nero lived with his aunt Domitia Lepida until Claudius' accession to the throne of Rome restored Nero's fortune. Domitia, sister of Nero's deceased father Gnaeus Domitius Ahenobarbus, was also alleged to be Nero's lover. (*See also entry on Messalina, Valeria.*)

❧ Lollia Paulina (fl. 30 CE)

Roman noblewoman. Third wife of Caligula.

---

expectations of a Roman mother. Agrippina's advantage in this rivalry for Nero's affection and compliance was her access to the workings of the justice system. Domitia Lepida was charged with employing black magic against Agrippina and with not controlling her bands of slaves in Italy. Nero, now that the choice was forced, sided with his mother and offered evidence against his aunt, who was sentenced to death.

The chief obstacle remaining to threaten Nero's succession was Claudius, the emperor

---

himself. Though accounts of Claudius' death vary in some details, all agree he died by poison and that Agrippina was responsible. In perhaps the most colorful narrative, recounted by Cassius Dio, Agrippina put poison on a mushroom, one of Claudius' favorite foods. "Then she herself ate of the others, but made her husband eat of the one which contained the poison; for it was the largest and finest of them." When the astrologically propitious hour arrived, Agrippina had Claudius' death publicly announced, along with a simultaneous announcement of Nero's accession. She buried Claudius with great pomp, and, like the great Augustus, he was posthumously pronounced a god. Agrippina made sure that Claudius' will was not read, and—since there was no one powerful enough to contest the accession—Nero was immediately accepted as emperor. On October 13, 54, Agrippina had achieved her goal, only one month before her 39th birthday.

Agrippina had identified her own interests with Nero's for so long that she now expected to share in ruling the empire. The ancient sources agree that at first Nero was little more than a figurehead, with Agrippina ruling in his name. Symbolic of her early political prominence was the first password given to the Praetorian Guard: *Optima Mater* (The Best of Mothers). She was appointed priestess of the newly established cult to honor the deified Emperor Claudius. She was represented on coins with Nero, sometimes as a goddess.

When a motion was introduced into the Senate aimed at changing some of Claudius' legislation, because Agrippina was cult priestess of the newly deified Claudius, she objected. She claimed that since Claudius had been deified, none of his decrees should be rescinded. The Senate gave Agrippina's objections due consideration. Although women were never admitted into the Senate chambers, the Senate accommodated her by meeting in a building where Agrippina could listen to the proceedings from behind a curtain. Though she did not win her cause, the fact that she had been allowed to witness proceedings of the Senate broke with tradition and demonstrated her eminence to all of Rome.

Agrippina's power, however, was not unlimited. Nero held the formal authority, while she could control matters only indirectly through her relationship to him or by calling in favors from those who were indebted to her. This reality was illustrated graphically when a visiting delegation was given an imperial audience and Agrippina, going farther than she had during Claudius' reign,

attempted to join Nero on the same tribunal. Seneca prevented this by advising Nero to step down to greet his mother—thus displaying filial piety while denying her "unwomanly" assertion of formal authority. Gradually, Nero turned more and more to Burrus and Seneca for guidance. As Tacitus observed, Agrippina "could give her son the empire, but not endure him as emperor."

Her influence declined even more with Nero's coming of age. Nero fell in love with *Acte (fl. 55–69 CE), an imperial freedwoman far below his social station. When Agrippina discovered their relationship, she had enough authority to force Nero to hide his liaison but not to cut it off. When Nero, as a result of his mother's opposition, began turning ever more to Seneca for counsel than to her, she switched tactics and admitted she had been in error, going so far as to offer the couple the use of her own bedroom.

But the problems were not resolved. Nero, attempting to ameliorate their relations, sent Agrippina a valuable jewelled garment as a present. She responded by claiming that he was only giving her a fraction of what he owed her. She began to rebuff Nero by turning her attention to Britannicus, letting Nero overhear her say that "Britannicus was grown up and was the true and worthy heir of his father's supreme position—now held . . . by an adopted intruder, who used it to maltreat his mother." Nero responded by having Britannicus poisoned at dinner, calmly pretending that his stepbrother was merely having an attack of epilepsy.

As Agrippina's and Nero's hostility escalated, she gave attention to Nero's wife Octavia, to whom Nero was little attached, and began courting other nobility as well. Nero, in a countermove, deprived his mother of her military guard and moved her from the palace to another house. He ended the great receptions she hosted, undermining her influence with other nobility. When Nero visited her in her new quarters, he came with an armed guard and stayed only briefly.

At this crucial juncture, Domitia Lepida, Agrippina's still surviving former sister-in-law, determined to get revenge. She sent reports to Nero that Agrippina was planning to marry a man who could represent a dynastic challenge and that together they were planning to incite a revolution. Nero, going to unexpected extremes, decided he had to get rid of his mother and began to talk of killing her, although, in the Roman view, parricide was the ultimate sacrilege. Burrus offered Nero the convincing argument that all have a right to be heard in self-defense and that this right should be extended to the emperor's own mother in particular. Nero allowed Burrus to bring the charges to her in person.

Agrippina defended herself admirably, charging that those accusing her had tainted motives, while claiming a mother's loyalty to her son, Nero. She demanded to see him personally. As a result of their interview, she obtained benefits for her own supporters and punishments for those who had accused her. Their relationship, however tenuous, was restored.

But in the year 58 another crisis appeared in the form of a new infatuation for Nero: ✥➤ **Poppaea Sabina**. Poppaea, though married, was wealthy, beautiful, aristocratic, and determined—possessing "every asset except goodness," as she is characterized by Tacitus. Poppaea soon had Nero under her influence and went so far as to mock him, implying that he was still under guardianship rather than a man ruling as emperor. She asserted that Agrippina would not allow him to marry Poppaea for fear that his mother's avarice, pride, and control of the Senate would come to light. No one voiced opposition to Poppaea, in part because many wanted Agrippina's influence undermined.

According to several accounts, Agrippina played her last card when, in desperation, she tried to seduce Nero. Other sources argue that Nero tried to seduce her. All agree, however, that Seneca enlisted Nero's earlier lover Acte to dissuade him from this wicked course of action. Nero again began to avoid meeting his mother and even encouraged people to bring lawsuits against her, among other small harassments.

Again, Nero began to toy with possible methods of murdering his mother. Eventually, he settled on a ship with a section that could collapse and drop her into the sea. With the trap set, he invited her for dinner, displaying great filial devotion, as if their differences were resolved, and afterwards sent her off to her own villa across the Bay of Baiae. The ship collapsed as planned, and Agrippina was hurled into the sea. Ever the survivor, she swam until picked up by a small boat.

Pretending she did not know Nero's intent, Agrippina sent a message to him about her narrow escape. Nero in consternation sent for Burrus and Seneca to ask their advice. Both agreed that since the Praetorian Guard was under oath to protect the royal house, it would not consent to kill her. Finally, Nero ordered one of his freedmen, who held personal grudges against Agrippina, to kill her, using as justification the lie that

---

✥➤ **Poppaea Sabina** (d. 65 CE)

Empress of Rome from 63–65. Birth date unknown; died in 65 or 66 CE because of a kick by Nero; daughter of ***Poppaea Sabina*** *(d. 47); granddaughter of Poppaeus Sabinus, governor of Moesia; married Rufius Crispinus; married Marcus Salvius Otho; married Nero (37–68), Roman emperor (r. 54–68), in 63.*

As Nero's hedonism grew, so did his lechery. One affair of note was that with Poppaea Sabina, beginning in the year 58. Poppaea was not just another of Nero's playthings—she was of senatorial background and married to Marcus Salvius Otho, who would briefly reign as emperor after Nero's death. Beautiful and ambitious, Poppaea supposedly seduced Nero, who ordered her husband to Lusitania so as to facilitate their adultery. Shortly after Nero divorced *Octavia (c. 39–62), he married Poppaea. Though Nero seems to have cared for her as much as he ever cared for anyone, in 65 he killed her by kicking her in the stomach (while she was pregnant with their child), reputedly after she complained about his spending too much time at the racetrack.

---

she had sent a messenger to assassinate the emperor. Tacitus reports that the freedman broke into her bedroom with two other officers. Spirited to the end, Agrippina exclaimed, "If you have come to visit me, you can report that I am better. But if you are assassins, I know my son is not responsible. He did not order his mother's death." As they closed around her, she bared her abdomen crying, "Strike here, for this bore Nero!" and then died under their blows.

Nero is said to have coldly observed her body afterward, commenting, "I did not know I had such a beautiful mother," though some skepticism at this final filial degeneracy is voiced by the ancient authors. Agrippina was cremated that same night and buried without honor in an uncovered and unenclosed grave.

After the murder, Seneca helped Nero contrive excuses for her death: she had tried to usurp power over the Roman people; she had engineered deaths of prominent men; she had barely been kept from entering the Senate; she was behind all the wrongs of Claudius' rule. The people responded by decreeing Thanksgivings, establishing annual games to celebrate the discovery of Agrippina's plot against Nero, and designating Agrippina's birthday as an inauspicious day. Agrippina still retained the loyalty of the popular classes, however, and graffiti and ditties expressed an alternate view: "Nero, Orestes, Alcmeon—O, matricides all."

Nero was briefly haunted with remorse for this great breach of Roman morals. It was said that the coast echoed from the neighboring hills with wails from his mother's grave, and Nero left that area of the country to escape his feeling of horror.

Tacitus claims that after Agrippina's death Nero "plunged into the wildest improprieties, which vestiges of respect for his mother had hitherto not indeed repressed, but at least impeded." In this way, the historian divides the periods of Nero's rule (as he did with Claudius') by Agrippina's influence over him and then the lack thereof. But, ultimately, Tacitus designates her merely in relationship to the men over which she exerted such great influence: "A woman who to this day remains unique as the daughter of a great commander and the sister, wife, and mother of emperors."

SOURCES:

Barrett, Anthony A. *Caligula: The Corruption of Power.* NY: Simon and Schuster, 1990.

Bauman, Richard A. *Women and Politics in Ancient Rome.* NY: Routledge, 1992.

Dixon, Suzanne. *The Roman Mother.* Norman, OK: University of Oklahoma Press, 1988.

Griffin, Miriam T. *Nero: The End of a Dynasty.* New Haven, CT: Yale University Press, 1984.

ANCIENT SOURCES:

Cassius Dio. *Roman History.*

Suetonius. "Life of Gaius"; "Life of Claudius"; "Life of Nero."

Tacitus. *Annals of Imperial Rome.*

Sylvia Gray Kaplan, Adjunct Faculty, Humanities, Marylhurst College, Marylhurst, Oregon

Aguilar, Grace (1816–1847)

English novelist whose writings educated the general public about Judaism. Pronunciation: ah-gee-lär. Born at Hackney, London, England, on June 2, 1816; died in Frankfort-on-Main, Germany, on September 16, 1847; eldest child of Emanuel Aguilar (a merchant); mother's name unknown; both parents were Jews of Spanish origin; educated at home; family moved to Devon in 1828; never married, no children.

Born on June 2, 1816, at Hackney, near London, Grace Aguilar was the youngest child in a rich and refined household. Her Spanish-Jewish ancestors were refugees from persecution, and it is likely that her family's personal history inspired much of her faith. A semi-invalid, Aguilar was educated at home by her cultivated father and mother, and by the age of 12 she had written a heroic drama about her favorite hero, Gustavus Vasa. By 14, she had published a volume of poems.

Upon the death of her father, Aguilar took up writing as a profession to support herself. At 24, she accomplished her chief work on the Jewish religion, *The Spirit of Judaism* (1842), a controversial attack on the formalities of institutionalized theology. Republished in America with preface and notes by a well-known rabbi, Isaac Leeser of Philadelphia, the book insists on the importance of the spiritual and moral aspects of the faith delivered to Abraham and condemns a superstitious reverence for the mere letter of the law.

Four years later, in 1846, Aguilar published *The Jewish Faith: Its Spiritual Consolation, Moral Guidance, and Immortal Hope.* She published as well *The Women of Israel*, a series of essays on Biblical history, which was followed by *Essays and Miscellanies*. Her writings were so influential that the Jewish women of London gave her a public testimonial, addressing her as "the first woman who had stood forth as the public advocate of the faith of Israel."

While on her way to visit a brother then residing at Schwalbach, Germany, Aguilar was taken ill at Frankfurt. Unable to speak for some time before her death, she learned to talk with her hands. It was reported that her last hand movement spelled out, "Though He slay me, yet will I trust in Him." She died in Frankfurt at the early age of 31.

Aguilar's work has helped to educate the general public about Judaism and to voice concerns regarding the place of women in Judaism. Her lasting popularity, however, came from her domestic and sentimental novels—all but one of which were edited and published posthumously by her mother. The earliest and best known, and the only one to appear in her lifetime, was *Home Influence* (1847), which quickly passed through 30 editions, and remained a favorite with young girls for many years.

Among her other titles are: *Mother's Recompense, Woman's Friendship, The Days of Bruce,* and *The Vale of Cedars* (1850), a historic tale of the persecution of the Jews in Spain under the Inquisition, which is said to contain pieces of Aguilar's family traditions.

Aguirre, Mirta (1912—)

Cuban poet and essayist. Born in Cuba in 1912. Wrote largely political and revolutionary verse, as well as essays; publications include Juegos y otros poemas *(Games and Other Poems, 1974) and* Ayer de hoy *(Yesterday Today, 1980).*

In Stalinist Cuba, Mirta Aguirre wrote poetry and essays that protested the established political climate. She utilized *criollismo*—the pointed exaggeration of local customs, people, and language—as a tool of political and social criticism in her poetry; she also used the Gypsy ballad, made famous by García Lorca, to sing the praises and demonstrate the detriments of opposing factions and people. Perhaps due to the subversive nature of her work, Aguirre is little known outside Cuba. In her country, her writing is presented in journals and newspapers, and in several collections of verse and essay.

Ahat-milki or Ahatmilku (fl. 1265 BCE).

See Akhat-milki.

Ahern, Lizzie (1877–1969)

Australian socialist. Born Elizabeth Ahern in Ballarret, Victoria, in 1877; died in 1969; daughter of an Irish goldminer and a radical; married Arthur Wallace (a radical, later a Member of Parliament), in 1905; children: a son.

Lizzie Ahern left school at 14 and went to work as a pupil-teacher, then as a cook in Melbourne. By 1905, she was a member of the Social Questions Committee (forerunner of the Victorian Socialist Party). An eloquent orator, she was a conspicuous member of the Free Speech Campaign in Prahra, Melbourne, and was imprisoned in 1906 for defending the right to speak in public places. In 1909, Ahern founded the Women's Socialist League; she and her husband also led the anti-draft campaign during World War I. Despite the couple's activities, their son enlisted, contracted disease, and died while in uniform. In later life, Ahern worked for the Australian Labour Party. She also became a justice of the peace and a children's court magistrate.

Ahhotep (r. 1570–1546 BCE)

Queen-regent of Egypt. Name variations: Ahotep. Ruled around 1570–1546 BCE (there is some debate concerning the chronology of this period of Egyptian history as dates are dependent upon data derived from lunar observations; three separate chronologies have been put forth); children: Egyptian rulers King Kamose (d. 1570); Ahmose I (Ahmosi or Amasis), who is generally credited with founding the 18th Dynasty in Egypt; and daughter Ahmose-Nefertari (reigned around 1570–1546 BCE).

While her son Ahmose I drove the Hyksos kings (rulers of ancient Egypt between the 13th and 18th dynasties) out of Egypt, Ahhotep ruled Thebes in Upper Egypt (modern-day Luxor), together with her daughter ❧ **Ahmose-Nefertari** (r. c. 1570–1546 BCE). An 18th dynasty inscription of Ahhotep claims: "She assembled her fugitives. She brought together her deserters. She pacified her Upper Egyptians. She subdued her rebels." When Ahmose I returned, he married his sister Ahmose-Nefertari; they had a daughter **Ahmose**, mother of *Hatshepsut, and a son Amenhotep I.

Ahinoam (fl. 1020 BCE)

*Biblical woman. Flourished around 1020 BCE; daughter of Ahimaaz; wife of Saul (first king of the Jewish nation); children: Jonathan and others; including two daughters, one of whom was *Michal.*

Ahinoam was the wife of King Saul and the mother of Michal, first wife of David, the greatest Israelite king in the Old Testament.

Ahinoam of Jezreel (fl. 1000 BCE)

Biblical woman. Second wife of King David (Israelite king who unified Israel and Judah; r. 1010–970 BCE); children: Amnon.

Ahlgren, Ernst (1850–1888).

See Key, Ellen for sidebar on Benedictsson, Victoria.

Ahmad, Fathiyya.

See Egyptian Singers and Entrepreneurs.

Ahmose-Nefertari (c. 1570–1535 BCE).

See Hatshepsut for sidebar.

Aholibamah.

See Judith.

Aichinger, Ilse (1921—)

Austrian short-story and fiction writer. Born in Vienna, Austria, in 1921; studied medicine for two years; married Günter Eich (a poet), in 1953 (died); lives in Bayrisch Gmain, Upper Bavaria.

Selected works: The Greater Hope *(1948);* Speech Beneath the Gallows *(1952);* Der Gefesselte *(The Bound Man, 1953);* Knöpfe *(Buttons, 1953);* Zu keiner Stunde *(At No Hour, 1957);* Besuch im Pfarrhaus *(Visit at the Parsonage, 1961);* Wo ich wohne *(Where I Live, 1963);* Eliza, Eliza *(1965);* My Language and I *(1968);* Auckland *(1969);* Nachricht vom Tag *(News of the Day, 1970);* Dialoge, Erzählungen,

Ahmose-Nefertari. See *Hatshepsut for sidebar.*

Gedichte *(Dialogues, Stories, Poems, 1970); Advice Freely Given (1978).*

Ilse Aichinger was born in Vienna to a Jewish mother and an "Aryan" father who divorced by the time Aichinger was five. Her life changed radically in March 1938 with the Anschluss, the annexation of Austria by Nazi Germany. Despite her parents' divorce, Aichinger's father sheltered his daughter and ex-wife when they were threatened with deportation. Aichinger was required, however, to do forced service in Austria until the end of the war. As a result, she matriculated late at the University of Vienna, where she began medical studies. Shortly thereafter, Aichinger left school to work as a reader for a publisher, who later represented her work. In 1947, critic Hans Werner Richter invited a group of mostly young German writers to meet. Aichinger, now a novelist and poet, was included. Richter challenged these writers, dubbed *Gruppe 47* (Group of '47), to define a new, post-Nazi literary voice. They met twice annually and supported one another's work. Since Aichinger's novella, *Speech Beneath the Gallows*, won the Gruppe 47 prize in 1952, she has received countless other literary awards. Aichinger married writer Günter Eich in 1953.

SOURCES:

Aldridge, J.C. *Ilse Aichinger*. Chester Springs, PA: Dufour Editions, 1969.

Crista Martin, Boston, Massachusetts

Aikaterini.

Variant of Catherine.

Aikaterini of Bulgaria

(fl. 1050).

See Anna Comnena for sidebar on Catherine of Bulgaria.

Aiken, Anna L.

(1743–1825).

See Barbauld, Anna.

Aikenhead, Mary

(1787–1858)

Founder of the Irish Sisters of Charity. Born Mary Stackpole Aikenhead on January 19, 1787, in Cork, Ireland; died on July 22, 1858, in Dublin, Ireland; daughter and one of four children of David (a physician and chemist) and Mary (Stackpole) Aikenhead.

When David Aikenhead, a Scottish Protestant, married Mary Stackpole, an Irish Catholic, he allowed her to practice her religion but demanded that the children be brought up in the established church. In accordance with his wishes, their daughter Mary Stackpole Aikenhead, born in Cork, Ireland, in 1787, was baptized a Protestant.

For the first six years of her life, however, Aikenhead was nursed in a poor but loving Catholic home, where she went to mass and said the rosary nightly. Returning to the privileged home of her parents, she grew up attempting to reconcile with Ireland's religious split along socio-economic lines, which left Protestants holding much wealth and power, while Catholics comprised the bulk of the working poor. Although she received a private-school education and wanted for nothing, Aikenhead felt the pull of a strong conscience and spent much of her time administering to the sick and those in need. By age 16, she made her solemn profession to the Catholic faith. At 17, she received her calling into religious life, which she later recounted as a "mysterious and elusive call, so like the gentle whisper of the soft summer breeze." Above the din of the world around her, she caught the sound of the mystic words: "Follow Me."

While visiting Dublin, in the home of a wealthy philanthropist who gave money to the city's sick and poor, Aikenhead met Father Daniel Murray, then coadjutor bishop of Dublin, who would later become archbishop. Murray wanted to establish a body of religious women to do for the poor in Ireland what the Sisters of Charity were doing in France. Seeing potential in Aikenhead, he persuaded her to prepare for the religious congregation. In 1815, after a three-year noviceship at the Bar Convent of the Institute of the Blessed Virgin Mary, in York, England, Aikenhead returned to Dublin with one associate to establish the Sisters of Charity in the William Street Orphanage. Modeling themselves after the Jesuits, members took simple vows—temporary for three years, and then perpetual. A fourth vow of dedication to the poor was added. The congregation was governed by a superior general, elected for a six-year term that could be renewed. Aikenhead resided at the motherhouse, which was established at Mount St. Anne's, Milltown, Dublin.

The sisters began by caring for the orphans, establishing a day school, and visiting poor families in the neighborhood. As the number of re-

Mary Aikenhead

cruits grew, more houses were established, enabling them to teach religion in parochial schools and to staff additional free schools, vocational colleges, and a Magdalen refuge. In 1826, Aikenhead fulfilled a long-time desire to see the Sisters of Charity established in her hometown of Cork.

In 1834, the same year the congregation received papal approval, Aikenhead opened St. Vincent's Hospital in Dublin, the first Catholic hospital in Ireland and a pioneering effort in the staffing and management of hospitals by religious women trained in nursing. Later, the sisters established other health facilities: convalescent homes, institutions for people with physical disabilities, homes for the elderly, maternity welfare centers, homes for widows, recreational centers, and hostels.

In 1838, the sisters went to Australia and were the first religious women to take vows in that country. They later developed a separate congregation there, the Daughters of Mary Aikenhead. After Aikenhead's death, the congregation spread to England, Scotland, the United States, Zambia, and Nigeria. (By 1965, there were 811 sisters, 61 novices, and 9 postulants in 66 Australian houses. Their primary- and secondary-school enrollment was over 30,000 pupils. In the United States, the Sisters of Charity have been associated with the Archdiocese of Los Angeles, California, since 1953.)

Suffering from chronic spinal problems for much of her life, Aikenhead was in pain and had difficulty walking. In her final years, as superior general, she often managed from her bed. Her mind and spirit, however, remained intact. Aikenhead's last words reflected her lifetime devotion to the poor. On the evening before her death, sisters from a neighboring convent sent a woman, who often acted as messenger, to inquire as to Aikenhead's condition. Aikenhead worried about her. "I think that poor creature would badly need a new pair of boots, won't you get them for her." That same night, she also expressed concern that she might die the next day, on the Feast of St. *Mary Magdalene, a time of great celebration. "If I die tomorrow," she said, "do not tell the poor penitents until the day after, as it would spoil their pleasure." She died the following afternoon, July 22, 1858. A group of Dublin's working men were granted their request to carry her coffin to the grave.

SOURCES:
The Life and Work of Mary Aikenhead: Foundress of the Congregation of Irish Sisters of Charity 1787–1858. NY: Longmans, Green, 1924.

Barbara Morgan, Melrose, Massachusetts

Aikin, Anna Letitia (1743–1825).

See Barbauld, Anna Letitia.

Aikin, Lucy (1781–1864)

English historian and biographer. Name variations: edited under the pseudonym Mary Godolphin. Born at Warrington, Lancashire, England, on November 6, 1781; died at Hampstead, England, on January 29, 1864; daughter of John (a physician and author) and Martha (Jennings) Aikin; niece of Anna Letita Barbauld.

Lucy Aikin received a thorough classical education from her father John Aikin (1747–1822), a physician and author who taught in a nonconformist academy. After assisting her father and her aunt, *Anna Letitia Barbauld, in their literary work, Aikin published a poetical volume in 1810, under the title *Epistles to Women*, modelled after the style of Alexander Pope. A staunch Unitarian and feminist, Aikin protested the view of women's roles in 19th-century England.

Under the name Mary Godolphin, Aikin also edited many children's books. Her most acclaimed works, however, are her memoirs of the courts of *Elizabeth I (1818), James I (1822), and Charles I (1833), and her *Life of Addison* (1843). Regarded as one of the most accomplished literary women of her time, Aikin was also a celebrated socialite. After living in London for five years, she moved to Stoke Newington until her father's death in 1822. Her last 12 years were spent in Hampstead, where she lived with a niece.

SUGGESTED READING:
Le Breton, P.H., ed. *Memoirs, Miscellanies and Letters of the Late Lucy Aikin.*

Ailing Soong (1890–1973).

See Song Ailing in entry on The Song Sisters.

Aimée, Anouk (1932—)

French actress, best known for her work in A Man and a Woman. Name variations: Anouk. Born Françoise Sorya Dreyfus in Paris, France, on April 27, 1932; daughter of actors; studied acting and dancing in France and England; married Nico Papatakis (a director), 1952 (divorced 1954); married twice more; married Albert Finney (an actor), in 1970 (divorced 1978); married once more.

Selected filmography: La Maison Sous La Mer *(1947);* Les Amants de Vérone *(The Lovers of Verona,*

1949); The Golden Salamander *(U.K., 1950);* Le Rideau cramoisi *(1951);* The Man Who Watched the Trains Go By *(also titled* The Paris Express, *U.K., 1952);* Les Mauvaises Rencontres *(1955);* Pot-Bouille *(1957);* Montparnasse 19 *(also titled* Modiliani of Montparnasse, *1958);* La Tête contre les Murs, Les Dragueurs *(also titled* The Chasers, the Journey, *United States, 1959);* La Dolce Vita *(1960);* Lola *(1960);* L'Imprevisto *(1961);* Il Giudizio Universale *(1961);* Le Farceur *(*The Joker, *1961);* Sodoma e Gomorra *(1961);* Les Grands Chemins *(*Of Flesh and Blood, *1963);* 8½; *(*Otté e Mezzo, *1963);* Le Voci bianche *(*White Voices, *1964);* La Fuga *(1965);* Un Homme et une Femme *(*A Man and a Woman, *1966);* Justine *(1969);* The Model Shop *(1969);* The Appointment *(1969);* Si c'était à refaire *(*Second Chance, *1976);* Mon Premier Amour *(*My First Love, *1978);* Salto nel Vuoto *(*Leap Into Void, *1980);* Tragedia di un Uomo ridicolo *(*The Tragedy of a Ridiculous Man, *1981);* Qu'est-ce qui fait courir David *(1982);* Le Général de l'Armée Morte *(1983);* Vive la Vie *(1984);* Success is the Best Revenge *(U.K., 1984);* Flagrant Desire *(1985);* Un Homme et une Femme: 20 Ans déjà *(*A

Man and a Woman: 20 Years Later *(1986);* Arrivederci e Grazie *(1988);* La Table tournante *(1988);* Bethuen: The Making of a Hero *(1990);* Il y a des jours . . . et des lunes *(1990).*

Originally known only as Anouk, Anouk Aimée made her film debut at age 14 in *La Maison Sous La Mer* (1947). Two years later, in a Juliet-like role created for her by poet Jacques Prévert, she was brought to the attention of the French public in André Cayette's *Les Amants de Vérone* (*The Lovers of Verona*). A few undistinguished films followed before her international breakthrough as the nymphomaniac in *La Dolce Vita* (1960), Federico Fellini's view of decadent life in the high society of postwar Rome. Aimée followed that with the giggling, flighty Lola in Jacques Demy's new-wave film *Lola*. In 1963, she performed once again for Fellini in his autobiographical mixture of fact and fantasy, *8½* (*Otté e Mezzo*).

In 1966, Aimée starred with Jean-Louis Trintignant in Claude Lelouch's *Un Homme et*

Anouk
Aimée

une Femme (*A Man and a Woman*), a romantic drama that gleaned most of its power from the performances of its leads. For her performance, Aimée was nominated for an Oscar and was awarded Britain's Academy Award for Best Foreign Actress. (The film won an Academy Award for Best Foreign Film.) The two actors reprised their roles in *Un Homme et une Femme: 20 Ans déjà* (*A Man and a Woman: 20 Years Later*) in 1986. Aimée was also named Best Actress at Cannes for her role in *Salto nel Vuoto* (*Leap Into Void*), 1980. Anouk Aimée has worked for a string of prominent international directors, including Anatole Litvak, Vittorio de Sica, Robert Aldrich, Sidney Lumet, Bernardo Bertolucci, George Cukor, and Jerzy Skolimowski.

Aimery, Aenor (d. 1130).

See Eleanor of Aquitaine for sidebar.

Airy, Anna (1882–1964)

British painter and etcher, known for her artistic versatility, including depictions of industrial scenes noted for their unexpected power. Born in London in June 1882; died in Playford, England, on October 23, 1964; daughter of Wilfrid Airy; studied at the Slade School; exhibited as a young artist at the Royal Academy (1905); married Geoffrey Buckingham Pocock (a painter and etcher).

Anna Airy was born in London in June 1882, the only daughter of Wilfrid Airy, M.I.C.E. Her distinguished family lineage included her grandfather Sir George Biddell Airy (1801–1892), Astronomer Royal of Great Britain, who determined the earth's mean density. Anna's artistic talents were revealed early in life, and she studied at the Slade School, where she was regarded as a brilliant student, winning a scholarship and a number of prizes. The precocious young artist began to exhibit at the Royal Academy in 1905. Over the years, she became proficient in figure subjects, portraits and flowers in oils, watercolors and pastels, and etchings. Married to the painter and etcher Geoffrey Buckingham Pocock, Airy exhibited not only in the British Isles but on the Continent of Europe as well. She participated in international exhibitions in Rome and elsewhere. Her works were often seen at exhibitions sponsored by the Royal Society of Portrait Painters, the Royal Institute of Painters in Water Colours, the Royal Society of Painter-Etchers and Engravers, as well as the Pastel Society.

Airy probably inherited an interest in technology from her chemist father. This interest is demonstrated in an impressive series of five paintings she produced in 1918, on commission from the British Ministry of Munitions, which were placed in the Imperial War Museum. One of these oils, titled *Women Working in a Gas Retort House,* depicts a work scene at the South Metropolitan Gas Company of London and demonstrates the significant role women's labor played in the national war effort. Three of these commissioned works made such a strong impression at the time that they were shown at the Royal Academy in 1919, receiving positive critical comments. One of these, entitled *A Shell Forge,* depicts work at the National Projectile Factory, Hackney Marshes, London. The other canvas, *The "L" Press,* presented on a heroic scale of 72' x 84', depicts the forging of the jacket of an 18-inch gun with a hydraulic press at the Armstrong-Whitworth Works at Openshaw. While part of the unfinished gun remains in the furnace, Airy shows the moment when the great crane suspended from overhead beams gently withdraws the whole mass of metal. Many were surprised that these powerful and impressive works were produced by a woman known for painting flowers.

During and immediately after World War I, Airy also received commissions from the Canadian War Memorials Fund. Her work was represented in a number of important exhibitions in Great Britain and the British Commonwealth. In the 1920s, she returned to more peaceful scenes.

Airy was never enticed by abstractionism or other Modernist trends. To the end of her long and productive life, she continued her realistic painting. Anna Airy died at her home in Playford, England, on October 23, 1964. In the 1990s, her works reappeared in gallery sales and auction catalogues as a positive reappraisal of her *oeuvre* began to take place.

SOURCES:
"Miss Anna Airy," in *The Times* [London]. October 24, 1964, p. 10.

> **John Haag**, Associate Professor of History, University of Georgia, Athens, Georgia

Aisenberg-Selove, Fay (b. 1926).

See Ajzenberg-Selove, Fay.

A'ishah bint Abi Bakr (c. 613–678)

Third and favorite wife of Muhammad, Prophet of Islam, whose prominence in early Islamic history is testimony to the high position held by women in Ara-

bian society, before the suffocating atmosphere that began to prevail in the Middle East led to their seclusion from public life. Name variations: Aisha or Ayesha; also known as Umm al-Mu'minin ("Mother of Believers"). Born A'ishah bint Abu Bakr (daughter of Abu Bakr) at Mecca (Makka) around 613 or 614 CE; died at Madinah on July 8, 678; daughter of a prominent family of the city; married Muhammad, in 623 or 624.

Betrothed to her relative, Jubair ibn Mutimi; taken by her father on the flight of Muhammad and his followers to Madinah (622); married to Muhammad (623 or 624); suspected of unfaithfulness and accused by Muhammad's son-in-law, `Ali, but exonerated (627); death of Muhammad (632); reign of her father, Abu Bakr, as caliph "successor" (632–634); protested assassination of Caliph `Uthman, moved from Madinah to Mecca (June 656); joined forces with Talhah and al-Zubayr against the new caliph, `Ali; together they seized Basrah, Iraq (autumn, 656); Battle of the Camel (December 636), Talhah and al-Zubayr killed, `Ali victorious, A'ishah captured, retired to Madinah.

A'ishah bint Abi Bakr was the third and favorite wife of the Prophet Muhammad, founder of the Islamic Faith. Her life can only be understood against the backdrop of the momentous period in Middle Eastern history in which she lived. Although the heartland of the Arabian peninsula is a vast desert, the so-called "Empty Quarter," the provinces of Hijaz and Yemen—the southcentral and southwestern parts of the western Red Sea coastal region—are fertile and were the sites of a flourishing civilization, which in the Hijaz was centered at the trading and religious center of Mecca (Makka). The site of the fall of a great meteorite, which thereafter was kept in a large cubical temple called the *Ka`aba,* surrounded by the temples of the pre-Islamic Arab deities, Mecca was not only a flourishing commercial hub but had long been the center of a great annual pilgrimage to its numerous shrines.

It was in this curious, out-of-the-way city, far removed from the great centers of the Mediterranean and Middle Eastern worlds, that Muhammad was born around 570 CE, a member of a poor branch of the Kuraysh (or Quraysh), one of the great clans of the city. Orphaned while still a small child, he was raised first by his grandfather and then by his uncle, Abu Talib. At an early age, he became a camel driver and, while still a youth, went traveling with the great caravans linking the Hijaz with Yemen and with the Byzantine provinces of Egypt and Syria. Eventually, although he was illiterate, Muhammad be-

came the business manager of a rich widow named *Khadijah, 15 years his senior, who was also his third cousin once removed. Muhammad found favor with his employer and in a short time they were married. He was 25; she was 40. Six children were born to this marriage but only three daughters, **Umm Kulthum, Ruqaiyah** (or Ruqayyah) and *Fatimah, survived, and only the last left descendants. All of the many families claiming descent from the Prophet today trace this descent through Fatimah.

At the age of 40, Muhammad underwent a religious experience, the exact nature of which is a matter of faith alone but the sincerity of which has never been seriously doubted. He began claiming to be receiving revelations from God through the agency of the angel Jabril (Gabriel). The essential integrity of Muhammad's character is attested to by the fact that his wife and his uncle, Abu Talib, the two people who probably knew him best, were his first converts. An examination of the principle doctrines of Islam or the Muslim Faith, by both of which terms Muhammad's religion is known, reveal little that is original, his chief influences being Judaism, Christianity, and Zoroastrianism. Nevertheless, his revelations took on a unique form embodied in an anthology known as the *Qur'an (Koran,* meaning the recitation). Soon Muhammad was preaching an uncompromising monotheism to his fellow Meccans based on *islam* (submission) to the one true God. This God he called Allah from Arabic *al-lah* (the God), as opposed to the idols of Mecca, which he denounced as false.

Monotheism was a religious concept whose time had come in Arabia. By this period, virtually the entire Mediterranean world, including most of the Middle East save Persia, had become Christian, and even Persia boasted a substantial native church; some of the northernmost Arab peoples had become Christian, and at least one Arab tribe had embraced Judaism. Muhammad's teachings were ill-received in Mecca, however, where a considerable number of the population made its living from the annual pilgrimage. Opposition to his preaching steadily increased until it reached dangerous proportions. Thus, Muhammad, a handful of his followers, his wife and children, and his chief companion Abu Bakr and his family, including the child A'ishah, were forced to flee northwards to the city of Yathrib. There, his movement had already made converts. Since there was no economic basis for the continued support of paganism in the city as there was in Mecca, Muhammad and his companions were warmly received by the local population. Thereafter, Yathrib would become the second most sacred city of Islam after Mecca and would be known by the honorific al-madinah (the city), while the year of the *hijrah* (flight, 632 CE) would become the first year of the Muslim calendar.

At Yathrib/Madinah, Muhammad was soon able to assemble an army of believers, which rode from victory to victory (Badr, Uhud, etc.) until Mecca itself was obliged to accept Islamic rule (629). In return for the city's peaceful submission, Muhammad allowed the Meccans to retain the *Ka`aba* and the annual pilgrimage to it but insisted that the pagan temples be closed and the worship of idols abandoned. All of Arabia was soon under Islamic rule and, by the time of the Prophet's death in 632, Muslim armies were poised to attack the Byzantine and Persian empires. The death of Muhammad caused a brief crisis in the Islamic community. It was clear that while he could not be replaced in his unique role as Prophet of God, it was necessary that he be replaced in his capacity as head of the community. Thus the institution of the *caliphate* (successorship) was established. The first *caliph* (successor) was Muhammad's devoted friend and colleague Abu Bakr, the father of A'ishah, the third of the Prophet's 12 wives.

Despite the differences in their ages, there is no question that Muhammad had been deeply devoted to Khadijah and, although both pre-Islamic law and his own teachings permitted polygamy, Muhammad took no other wife while she remained alive. When Muhammad was around 49, however, Khadijah died in 619 CE, and he began to choose and to accumulate wives with great zest. It is often thought that Muhammad encouraged his followers to take four wives. Actually, Muhammad limited his followers to *no more* than four wives in contrast to the pagan religion of Arabia that had permitted an unlimited number. Muhammad further decreed that his followers must treat all their wives equally, a task seemingly so impossible that it became almost a discouragement to polygamy if not a practical prohibition.

A'ishah bint Abi Bakr (which means A'ishah, the daughter of Abu Bakr), came from one of the most distinguished families of Mecca. Her father was the Prophet's closest companion; her mother, &▶ **Umm Ruman**, was a woman of the Kinana tribe. As an infant A'ishah was, following Arab custom, sent to a family of the Makhzumite tribe for nursing. She was a small child when Khadijah died and was already betrothed to a relative, a wealthy pagan of Mecca,

Jubayr ibn Mutimi. We are told that the suggestion that the Prophet remarry came on the initiative of **Khawla bint Maz `un**, his maternal aunt, who seems to have tended to his household affairs after Khadijah's demise. It was she who suggested as a suitable spouse either the six-year-old A'ishah or the 30-year-old **Sawdah bint Zama**, a Muslim widow. After some deliberation, Muhammad decided to marry both, taking Sawdah as his second wife and A'ishah as his third. There was a complication in the fact that A'ishah had already been betrothed, but everyone concerned agreed to set this previous arrangement aside so that the Prophet might marry the bride of his choice.

A'ishah was no more than ten at the time of her wedding, and tradition has it that she brought her dolls and other toys to her husband's home, which consisted of a number of rooms set up as living quarters adjoining the newly constructed mosque in Madinah. Bright and vivacious, A'ishah was dearly loved by Muhammad, who occasionally played with her and waited until she was suitably mature before consummating the marriage. While there seems little doubt that the marriage to Sawdah was governed by the need to find a mate to replace Khadijah, the marriage to A'ishah was dictated at least in part by the fact that her father, Abu Bakr, was important to Muhammad in the spread of his movement. This fact, coupled with A'ishah's undoubted beauty, wit, and charm, led her to become not only his favorite wife but also, despite her youth, the chief wife in his growing menage. A'ishah was devoted to her husband, sensitive to his moods, and never lost the first place in his heart.

But, while A'ishah may have been Muhammad's favorite wife, she was by no means his last. Not long after their marriage in 623 or 624, the Prophet wedded: 4) Hafsah (625); 5) **Umm Salamah** (626); 6) *Zaynab bint Jahsh (627); 7) `Juwairiyah (627); 8) `Raihanah bint Zaid (c. 628); 9) Safiyah (c. 628); 10) **Maryam (Mary) the Egyptian** (629); 11) **Ramlah**; and 12) **Maimu-**

&▶ **Umm Ruman**
Mother of *A'ishah bint Abi Bakr; wife of Abu Bakr who had at least three other wives. Thus, A'ishah, besides her full brother `Abd al-Rahman, had a half-brother Muhammad by her father's wife Asma, a half-sister Umm Kulthum by his wife Habibah, and another half-sister Asma by his wife Quitailah.

See Wives of
Muhammed
below.

nah bint al-Harith (629). Of these wives A'ishah, Zaynab, and Umm Salamah were his favorites; Sawdah, Safiyah, and Hafsah, however, were distinguished for being partisans of A'ishah. Curiously, although Muhammad had no difficulty siring children by the middle-aged Khadijah, he had no children by any of his other wives.

Contrary to common belief, women held a more open position in Arabian society in the early days of Islam than is generally associated with the Islamic world. Indeed, much of the subjection, seclusion, and shrouding of women in the Middle East was alien to pre-Islamic Arabia, and was much more the result of the impact of Syrian and Iranian influence on the Arabs after the Arab conquests of their lands than the other way around. One hears of pre-Islamic Arabian poetesses and of women—including A'ishah's own niece, the beautiful, spirited and vivacious younger **A'ishah bint Talhah**—who went about in the presence of men with their faces unveiled. The harem does not appear to have been a native Arabian institution and was apparently a borrowing from Persia as was the institution of the eunuchs used to guard the harems. Nevertheless, there is no question that Muhammad's attitude towards the position of women was based to no small extent upon his experience with the elaborate household that he established after Khadijah's death, and it is in connection with Muhammad's increasing number of wives that we find him turning his attention to the question of the relations between men and women in the Islamic faith.

Within three years of his marriage to Zaynab, for example, he issued a number of directives regarding the conduct of the proper Muslim woman and spelling out in some detail the position and proper behavior expected of his own wives, stating, in particular, that none of them was to remarry after his death. Some of these stipulations were no doubt due to his own personal experiences. Others, however, were certainly issued in response to what Muhammad perceived to be the laxness in such matters that prevailed in Arabia in his time. In the *Qur'an*, chap. 24:31–32, men and women among believers are both enjoined to "cast down their gaze," i.e. not look lustfully upon one another. In 33:53, "The Curtain," Muhammad proffers a revelation in which he specifies that no guest of the Prophet may outstay his welcome and that if any one of them wishes to address the Prophet's wives, he must do so with the wives hidden behind a curtain. In 33:59, women are required to "let down their mantles over them," i.e. cover their heads with their cloaks, lest they be subject to improper and disrespectful attentions. Muhammad was especially concerned with what became known as the *munafiqun* (hypocrites), who were supposedly believers but who resented the privilege and status of the *Muhajirun* (fleers or refugees), i.e. those who had accompanied Muhammad on his flight from Mecca to Madinah. It is in connection with these hypocrites that the most famous incident in the life of the young A'ishah took place.

On the return to Madinah from Muhammad's expedition against the Banu 'l-Mustalik tribe there occurred "the affair of the slander," an event around which the Prophet ultimately built a large portion of chapter 24 of the *Qur'an*, where-

Wives of Muhammad

Khadijah. *See separate entry.*

A'ishah bint Abi Bakr.

Sawdah bint Zama. *A 30-year-old Muslim widow; married Muhammad around 621* CE.

Hafsah. *Name variations: Hafsa. Daughter of `Umar ibn al-Khattab (who would succeed Muhammad as caliph `Umar [634–644]); widow who had lost her husband at the Battle of Badr; married Muhammad in 625.*

Umm Salamah. *Name variations: Hind bint Abi `mayyah. Sixth cousin of Muhammad; married Abu Salamah (who died of wounds suffered earlier at the battle of Uhud); married Muhammad in 626; children: (first marriage) several.*

Zaynab bint Jahsh. *See separate entry.*

Juwairiyah. *An Arabian woman taken captive at the campaign against the tribe of the Banu `l-Mustalik; married Muhammad in 627* CE.

`Raihanah bint Zaid. *Widow of Jewish origin; married Muhammad around 628* CE.

Safiyah. *Widow of Jewish origin; married Muhammad around 628* CE.

Maryam the Egyptian. *Name variations: Mary the Egyptian. Christian slave sent to Muhammad by the Byzantine governor of Egypt, and who may have been one of Muhammad's chief sources for Christianity his knowledge of which betrays a superficial acquaintance of the faith as it was practiced in Egypt; married Muhammad in 629* CE.

Ramlah. *Name variations: Umm Habibah. Daughter of Abu Sufyan, a distant cousin of Muhammad; married Muhammad in 629* CE.

Maimunah bint al-Harith. *Sister-in-law of Muhammad's uncle Abbas; widowed; married Muhammad in 629.*

in he emphasizes the seriousness and vicious nature of gossip and slander. When the caravan departed from one of its encampments, A'ishah stayed behind to search for a valuable necklace. Since the litter atop her camel was heavily shrouded and A'ishah was yet quite small, no one noticed she was missing until the army reached the next camping place. Returning to the site of the original encampment and finding the caravan gone, A'ishah sat down to await the arrival of whoever would be sent out to find her. Falling asleep, she was discovered the following morning by Safwan ibn al-Mu`attal al-Sulami, a young *Muhajin* (fleer), who had been left behind specifically to retrieve anything that might have been accidentally forgotten. Placing A'ishah on his camel, he led it by his own hand back to the caravan. Upon their arrival the following morning, however, certain enemies took it on themselves to accuse A'ishah of unfaithfulness, their leader being the chief Meccan hypocrite `Abdullah ibn Ubai. A serious scandal ensued with Muhammad temporarily sending A'ishah back to her family, while his son-in-law `Ali, husband of his third daughter, Fatimah, publicly accused her of adultery and urged Muhammad to divorce her. Infuriated, Muhammad questioned his associates and his other wives for their opinions on the truth of the accusations and afterwards claimed a revelation from God attesting to the innocence of his favorite. Then, while leaving `Abdullah to "the punishment of God," he imposed penalties upon `Abdullah's associates, who were, however, allowed to repent. This incident is referred to obliquely in chapter 24:11–16 in the following words:

11. Those who proffered the lie are a clique among the rest of you: don't think that it is unfortunate for you [that this incident happened]; on the contrary, it is good for you [to see the consequences of sin]: to everyone among them [will come the penalty] of the sin that he has earned, and to him who took it on himself to be the leader among them, his penalty will be [especially] severe.

12. [But] why did not the believers—men and women—when they heard of this affair—put the best construction on it in their own minds and say, "this charge is an obvious lie?"

13. Why didn't they bring four witnesses to prove it? When they failed to do so they [stood] in the sight of God as liars!

14. If it weren't for the grace and mercy of God on you in this world and in the next, a heavy penalty would have overtaken you that you rushed glibly into this affair.

15. Look, you received it on your tongues, and spoke about things of which you knew nothing about; and you thought it would be a light matter, whereas it was very serious in the eyes of God.

16. And when you heard of it, why didn't you say "it is not right for us to talk about this: Glory to God! this is a very serious slander!"

To Muslims, the revelation in 24:11–16 remains the Deity's testimony to the innocence of A'ishah. To non-believers who seek a more worldly explanation for the text, it has seemed that Muhammad valued his relationship to Abu Bakr too greatly to allow it to be jeopardized by an accusation that by its nature could neither be proved nor disproved. In any case, A'ishah never forgave `Ali for his attack upon her and would take revenge in years to come.

If I say I am innocent—and Allah most high knows that I am—you will not believe me. But if I confess to anything—and Allah most high knows that I am innocent—you will surely believe me. There remains nothing for me to do but say nothing. . . . Patience is becoming and Allah's help implored.
—A'ishah, quoting *The Holy Qur'an* (12.18) in her defense

The difficulty of maintaining harmony among Muhammad's increasing number of wives was obvious almost from the beginning of his burgeoning household. Muhammad undertook to provide each with gifts of equal value, to assign each one her allotted day and night with him, and to cast lots to determine which among them would be taken along on his annual pilgrimage or current military expedition. Despite his best efforts, after the Prophet's marriage to the Makhzumite Umm Salamah, his wives separated into two factions, each representing the earliest political parties in the Islamic movement. A'ishah and Hafsah were the partisans of both Abu Bakr and `Umar, and they held the upper hand. Fatimah, the Prophet's daughter, supported the cause of her husband `Ali. Finally, Umm Salamah and Ramlah represented the aristocracy of Mecca, which, having finally accepted Islam, now hoped to regain the position of privilege they had held in pagan times. As for Zaynab, she had taken A'ishah's part at the time of

A'ishah bint Talhah
Niece of A'ishah bint Abi Bakr. Daughter of Umm Kulthum (half-sister of A'ishah bint Abi Bakr) and Talhah; sister of Zakariya; married `Abd Allah.

"the affair of the scandal," and A'ishah held her in high regard.

As Muhammad entered his final illness and realized that he was dying, he requested that his wives permit him to retire to the quarters of A'ishah and that she alone be allowed to attend him. This wish was respected and when Muhammad died in her arms on June 8, 632 CE, he was buried in the floor of her room. A'ishah was thus left a widow without children at the age of no more than 18. Respecting the Prophet's command, she never remarried, and there is no suggestion that she was ever suspected of taking a lover, though she by no means lived in anything approaching real seclusion. In the decades that followed, she busied herself arranging family marriages and receiving guests of every description. Highly intelligent, she kept herself well-informed of what was going on in her world, taking an active part in public affairs for a considerable time.

A small woman with a strong voice and a strong personality, A'ishah was a presence, and we are told that her words were taken seriously. Though she could be jealous, and prided herself perhaps too much on having been the Prophet's only virgin bride, A'ishah appears to have been a warm, generous, and kind-hearted woman who inspired great devotion in those who knew her. In regard to her relatives, A'ishah was most attentive, and, though her relations with them were not without disagreements and quarrels, she was ever ready to defend her family against outside harm.

She looked after her youngest half-brother Muhammad (b. 632) after her father's death when the child was but two, and refused to allow her younger half-sister Umm Kulthum to marry the caliph `Umar because of his notorious severity to his wives. Instead, A'ishah gave her to her own first cousin Talhah; they became the parents of her half-niece and namesake: the vivacious younger A'ishah. It was A'ishah who arranged for her namesake to marry her first husband, her own nephew `Abd Allah, and the bride's first cousin; when this marriage soured, she first took the younger A'ishah into her home and then effected a reconciliation. Her other half-sister **Asma** was married to al-Zubayr ibn al-`Awwam, whom she later supported against her cousin `Ali in the struggle for control of the caliphate. Their son, `Abd Allah, was her favorite nephew. After Talhah's death following the Battle of the Camel, A'ishah took his widow, her half-sister Umm-Kulthum, under her protection and watched over the rearing of their son,

Zakariya. Childless herself, she was, by all accounts, a doting aunt.

The death of Muhammad left his surviving wives with the status of widows of the Prophet, but the title by which they each came to be known, especially A'ishah, was "mother of believers." Although all of Muhammad's widows, over half a dozen of them, shared this title, A'ishah's personal stature was no doubt increased by the fact that it was her father, Abu Bakr, the Prophet's closest colleague, who succeeded him as caliph or head of the community of believers. Although Abu Bakr only ruled for two years before his own death (634), this was sufficient time for A'ishah's special status to become established, especially as she remained on good terms with the succeeding caliph, `Umar (634–644), father of Muhammad's fourth wife, Hafsah, and his very distant cousin. In the register of `Umar, dividing the net revenues of the state among the various believers, A'ishah was accorded the first rank and given a pension of no less than 12,000 dihrems. So close was she to `Umar that after his assassination at the hand of a Persian slave, he, like Abu Bakr, was laid to rest next to the Prophet, beneath the floor of A'ishah's former chamber.

Although there is a tradition that A'ishah influenced Muhammad in his later years and her father as well, this seems unlikely in view of her extreme youth at the time. As the years passed, however, and she grew into a mature and sophisticated woman close to the seat of power, A'ishah became increasingly drawn into the politics of the nascent Muslim state. Her relations with `Uthman (644–656), the third caliph (third cousin of the Prophet, once removed, and husband of two of his daughters by Khadijah, Umm Kulthum, and Ruqaiyah), were cool. As opposition grew against his rule, A'ishah took a part in it although she did not actually support his rival, her old foe, `Ali; when `Uthman was murdered (June 656 CE), she publicly protested the crime. Immediately thereafter, for reasons that are not clear but which may have had to do with organizing opposition to `Ali, A'ishah, now a formidable woman of 43, journeyed to Mecca (657) ostensibly to take part in the annual pilgrimage but undoubtedly, given what was to follow, with more worldly concerns in mind.

Four months after the assassination of `Uthman, having been joined by his opponents and rivals, her brothers-in-law Talhah and al-Zubayr, A'ishah left Mecca for Basrah, Iraq, with a force of 1,000 men of the Kuraysh clan seeking revenge. `Ali, setting out from Madinah to Kufa in

Iraq, went out to meet his opposition and, in December, the opposing armies clashed in the celebrated Battle of the Camel (much of the fiercest fighting took place around the prize camel `Askar [warrior], bearing A'ishah's litter). `Ali triumphed in the battle, and although the rebel forces rallied around A'ishah, she was captured after the slaughter of her corps of 70 bodyguards; her camel was killed beneath her. Talhah and al-Zubayr were both killed shortly after their defeat, but `Ali wisely chose to treat A'ishah with the respect due her position as the Prophets' widow and allowed her to return in state to Mecca under the care of her brother, Muhammad, who had been a partisan of `Ali. For her part, A'ishah found it politic to be conciliatory and agreed to retire to Madinah, where she lived in peace and circumspection for the rest of her days.

The experience of defeat and the executions of Talhah and al-Zubayr appear to have sobered A'ishah in regard to the perils of partisanship, and she took no further part in public affairs. The expedition against `Ali had been ill-conceived and was further weakened by the absence of many associates of the Prophet as well as by the rivalry between Talhah and al-Zubayr. In later years, `Ali's supporters maintained that A'ishah had been duped by Talhah and al-Zubayr and that she had had no role in the murder of `Uthman or in the causes of the civil war that ensued. Other contemporaries of the event were not so generous, and there is considerable evidence that, rightly or wrongly, A'ishah was held by many, including some of those close to the Prophet, to have been implicated in the plot to murder `Uthman.

Despite the controversy surrounding her role in the death of Caliph `Uthman and the events that followed it, most Muslims accepted the general opinion that she was innocent of any crime. In her last years, A'ishah became an increasingly revered figure in the Islamic world, one of the last links with the Prophet and a font of knowledge concerning his views and practices. Pilgrims of every social, economic, and political rank came to consult her at her home in Madinah and, though she no longer concerned herself with political affairs, distinguished men still sought her advice. She appears to have accepted these visits with good will, receiving the humble along with the mighty with equal graciousness. She continued to receive her generous pension and was undoubtedly able to offer at will the lavish hospitality dictated by Arab custom. In time, her niece, the younger A'ishah, came to compete with **Sukainah**, granddaughter of `Ali, for the leading

social position in the easy-going and light-hearted society of the Meccan aristocracy. Both were rich and known as patrons of art and literature. Eventually, both were married to Mus'ab ibn al-Zubayr. A'ishah also arranged for the marriage of her brother `Abd al-Rahman's daughter, Hafsah, to Mundhir, another son of al-Zubayr and her sister Asma. Apart from her concerns with these family activities, there are some indications that A'ishah, like many aristocratic Arabian women, was involved in some real-estate transactions, and she is said to have been in some way involved in the slave trade. We know, however, that she often freed slaves as well, an act of virtue highly recommended in the *Qur'an*. As the years passed, she seems to have increasingly rued her participation in the campaign against `Ali and regretted that she had not followed the Qur'anic injunction that women remain in their homes.

A'ishah bint Abi Bakr died at Madinah on July 13, 678, at about the age of 64, having survived her illustrious husband by 46 years, a revered and honored link with the very origins of the Islamic Faith. The cause of her death is not known, but she had time to make the most careful arrangements for her own funeral, specifying in particular that she was not to be buried with the Prophet, but rather in the cemetery of Baqi with his other wives. A curious pall seems to hang over the descriptions of the death of A'ishah, the sources avoiding any suggestion that she died in glory or filled with the expectation of the world to come or of a reunion with Muhammad. A'ishah herself was extremely careful to avoid anything that might be called self-righteousness. That she sincerely felt herself unworthy of celebration is one of the most compelling aspects of her character, though how much of this self-abnegation was due to the guilt she felt over her participation in the campaign against `Ali can never be known. Her funeral, however, was attended by a great throng of people with her nephews and grandnephews as the chief mourners, and among Muslims it was early considered an act of merit to visit the site of her grave. Even today, it is still visited annually by the thousands of pilgrims passing through Madinah to Mecca for the annual pilgrimage that remains after 13 centuries at the very core of Islamic practice.

That A'ishah was an extraordinary woman of remarkable intelligence seems certain. Although she never learned to write, she was able to read and tradition has it, probably with some exaggeration, that she had memorized the *Qur'an* itself. She was especially familiar with poetry, of which the Arabs were inordinately fond, and often regaled her visitors with quotations from classical Arabian verse. She had a good knowledge of Arab history and genealogy, so important to a tribal society, and she is reputed to have had some learning in astronomy and even in medicine. Over the centuries, her intellectual gifts were increasingly exaggerated until there were those who claimed that she was the most learned woman of all time. Later tradition also credited her with an extraordinary asceticism but, though she doubtless lived a simple and modest life, she certainly lived comfortably, entertained freely, and maintained a rich and varied social life. Altogether, however, the Muslim memory of A'ishah is that of a woman who was both a sage and a saint and there must undoubtedly have been a large kernel of truth at the core of both of these traditions. Among Muhammad's wives, only Khadijah holds a higher place in Islamic regard, and it was the apparent slander of both of them in the novel *The Satanic Verses* that brought down the wrath of the Iranian mullahs, whose chief, the Ayatollah Ruhollah Khomeini, passed a death sentence upon the author, Salman Rushdie. Not all Muslims, however, hold A'ishah in such unqualified high regard. The sect known as the *Kharajites* (seceders) reproached her after her death for having gone to war against `Ali and cursed her in their public prayers.

The prophet's wives are among the sources for the *hadith* or traditions concerning the Prophet's acts, practices and sayings that serve to supplement the *Qur'an*. The latter is a small book, shorter than the *New Testament*, and does not attempt to cover every aspect of Muslim life. Thus, the consensus of the Believers (*ijma*), the use of analogies (*qiyas*), and the traditions concerning the Prophet (*hadith*) serve to supplement the *Qur'an* and, taken together, are the four sources upon which has been erected the Islamic law code (*shari'yah*). The *hadith* or traditions, to be acceptable, must be capable of being traced back, mouth-to-mouth, to a firsthand witness of the Prophet's words or deeds in a given circumstance. Thus, for example, we may be told that so-and-so, had it from such-a-one, who had it from someone else, who heard it from yet another person, who was told by Abu Bakr that the Prophet said or did such-and-such in regard to the issue at hand. In this connection, some 2,210 *hadith* have been traced back to A'ishah (1,210 taken by her directly from Muhammad himself, the rest supposedly received by her at second hand from his close associates). And, even though the greatest Islamic specialists in *hadith*

accepted only 174 of the traditions accredited to Muhammad, himself, and between 54 and 68 of the rest attributed to A'ishah, she still remains a source, however modest, for Islamic life and practice. In Arab countries, her name is one of the most common still given to daughters, and she is the most renowned Muslim woman in the non-Muslim world.

In the Islamic world, in which women have been traditionally subordinate to men and where feminist movements have a difficult task earning legitimacy or even being taken seriously, the high position of the women of the Prophet's family—his first wife Khadijah, his daughter Fatimah, his widow A'ishah, and her niece the younger A'ishah—serve as powerful role models for Muslim women who would increase their sphere of action in the modern Islamic world and as arguments justifying their attempts to do so.

SOURCES:

Abbot, Nadia. *Aishah the Beloved of Mohammed.* Chicago, IL: University of Chicago Press, 1942.

The Holy Qur'an. English translation by Abdullah Yusuf Ali. Washington: American International Printing, 1946 (Cambridge, 1967).

Spellberg, D.A. *Politics, Gender and the Islamic Past: The Legacy of `A`isha Bint Abi Bakr.* NY: Columbia University Press, 1994.

SUGGESTED READING:

Hitti, Philip K. *History of the Arabs from the Earliest Times to the Present.* NY: Macmillan, 10th ed., 1970.

Robert H. Hewsen, Professor of History at Rowan University, Glassboro, New Jersey, author of a book and several articles relevant to late Roman, Middle Eastern, and Byzantine history

Aissa Koli (1497–1504)

Queen of Kanem-Bornu. Born in 1497; died in 1504; daughter of Ali Gaji Zanani, ruler of Kanem-Bornu, located in West Africa; her mother was a Bulala.

The family of Aissa Koli was left with no male heirs following the death of Ali Gaji Zanani, the ruler of Kanem-Bornu, and that of another relative, Dunama, in 1497. Taking her father's place, Aissa Koli ruled Kanem-Bornu for seven years—the fixed term of rule in many African nations. In 1504, when a brother who had been put in protective exile was discovered and became king, Aissa Koli continued as his advisor.

Aisse (c. 1694–1733)

Circassian slave. Pronunciation: Ah-EE-say. Name variations: Mlle Äisse or Aïsse (originally Haïdé). Born in the Caucasus, Russia, in 1694; died in Paris, France, in 1733; daughter of a Circassian chief; given the name Charlotte-Elisabeth Aïcha.

The daughter of a Circassian chief, five-year-old Aisse was carried off from her Russian home by Turkish rovers and sold at Constantinople to the French ambassador, Baron de Ferriol, who took her to Paris and educated her. She was raised at court by his sister-in-law, **Madame de Ferriol**, sister of ❧➡ **Madame de Tencin**.

Aisse gained celebrity for her beauty and accomplishments. Her *Letters* to her friend **Madame Calandrini** in Geneva was published in 1787 with notes by Voltaire. They contain anecdotes about the social life in Paris at the beginning of the 18th century, critical reactions to novels read, and the despairing saga of her relationship with Chevalier d'Aydie. The collection was said to have prefigured *Marie Riccoboni's epistolary novels.

Ajzenberg-Selove, Fay (1926—)

German-born American nuclear physicist. Name variations: Aisenberg. Born in Berlin in 1926; daughter of Moisei Abramovich Aisenberg and Olga (Naiditch) Aisenberg; married Walter Selove.

Escaping a certain death in Europe in 1940, Ajzenberg-Selove began studying physics in the United States, the only woman in her class; with a collaborator, produced an immensely valuable annual compilation, Energy Levels of Light Nuclei; *first woman elected to a leadership position in the American Physical Society; forced to sue to obtain a full professorship at the University of Pennsylvania; author of many scientific articles and an autobiography,* A Matter of Choices: Memoirs of a Female Physicist.

In 1926, Fay Ajzenberg was born in Berlin. Both of her parents were Jews who had fled Soviet Russia soon after the 1917 Bolshevik revolution. Her father, Moisei Abramovich Aisenberg, born in Warsaw, Russian Poland, climbed out of extreme poverty by being, in the words of his admiring daughter, "tough, smart and adaptable." He studied mining engineering at the St. Petersburg Mining Academy and spoke several languages other than Polish and Russian, including German, French, and English. Fay's mother, Olga Naiditch, was born in Pinsk into a wealthy Russian-Jewish family. Although musically educated—she was a mezzo-soprano and pianist—Olga never pursued a career. Beautiful and highly emotional, **Olga Aisenberg** was often engaged in noisy conflicts with her husband, and Fay was much closer to her father. Despite what has been described as a psychologically unstable home environment, Fay's talents were encouraged by her father, who had become a successful manager of

a sugar refinery in Lieusaint, a small town 20 miles south of Paris. He prompted his daughter to be intellectually independent as well as confident and open-minded. Fay grew up assuming that she would one day have an engineering career. She resolved to emulate the feats of *Amelia Earhart and to "live a life that I would not regret as I lay dying."

As Jews, Fay and her parents were threatened by the rise of Nazism in Germany. The May 1940 German invasion of Belgium and France transformed their lives. They fled to Brittany, then to Toulouse, and then out of immediate danger to Lisbon, Portugal. On several occasions, Fay, an attractive teenager, used her language skills and lively personality to convince authorities to add her family to the short list of those authorized to leave the war zone. Along their path of escape, she and her parents slept in cars and underground garages. They were briefly jailed, stood in lines with frightened refugees waiting for food, and were dismayed to discover that their bodies were infested by lice. German warplanes strafed them, adding to their terror. Finally the Aisenbergs arrived in Cuba, which they soon left for New York.

Once in America, Fay changed her name from Aisenberg to Ajzenberg. Grateful to have escaped the killing fields of Europe, she was determined to succeed academically, enrolling as an engineering student at the University of Michigan. She was the only woman in a class of 100 men. Although sometimes treated like a younger sister, Ajzenberg generally held her own. Her grades in her physics courses were mediocre, but she found the subject intriguing and intellectually stimulating. A summer spent at the cosmic ray observatories in the European Alps (she was the first woman to work at these research facilities) convinced her that physics, not engineering, would be her life's work.

After completing some courses at Columbia University, Ajzenberg enrolled as a doctoral student at the University of Wisconsin, Madison. She earned her doctorate in 1952 and was confronted by the dual problem of finding a job as a woman physicist in a poor job market. Ajzenberg considered herself fortunate to get a one-year position at Smith College and began her research career by commuting between Smith and Cambridge, Massachusetts, where she worked at the Van de Graaff Laboratory of the Massachusetts Institute of Technology. Most important, she began to collaborate with Thomas Lauritsen of the California Institute of Technology. Together, they produced an immensely valuable

➤❧
Madame de Tencin. *See* *Salonnieres.*

annual compilation, *Energy Levels of Light Nuclei,* which appeared in a number of professional journals, primarily in *Nuclear Physics,* for several decades. These annual reviews presented the best of the year's research on the energy levels of nuclei. Yale University physicist D. Allan Bromley has praised these review articles as "the nuclear scientists' bibles."

Hoping to move from temporary to permanent work, Ajzenberg applied for a tenured position at Boston University. Here, she quickly discovered the sexist nature of academic life in the 1950s when the dean of the university cut the already agreed-upon salary by 15% after he learned that the new faculty member was a woman. Infuriated, Ajzenberg was joined by the chair of her department, and the egregious pay cut was rescinded. At this time, one of her friends, **Marietta Bohr**, told Ajzenberg that she should consider marriage; Bohr also said that a suitable partner was already available for her—a physicist at Harvard University, Walter Selove. But the difficulties that a married female physicist would likely face on the career path were pointed out at a meeting of the American Physical Society. The noted physicist *Maria Goeppert-Mayer invited Ajzenberg to her room and, after pouring her a stiff scotch, told her: "While it is hard to be a woman physicist, it is almost impossible to be a married woman physicist." Goeppert-Mayer gave this advice not only in light of deep-seated prejudice but also because of rigidly enforced nepotism rules. Ajzenberg refused to be discouraged, however, and continued her relationship with Walter Selove. Their marriage in 1955 became a successful, mutually supportive partnership. Walter eventually discovered a particle that he named for Fay, the f-zero, known among their friends as the faon.

Fay and Walter managed dual careers acceptably. She took a tenured position at Haverford College while he became an associate professor at the University of Pennsylvania. Fay loved teaching at Haverford despite some signs of gender discrimination that probably slowed down her promotion. In 1964, she was awarded a Guggenheim fellowship for a year's research at the Lawrence Berkeley Laboratory. Uncomfortable with the politicization of academic life at Haverford, Ajzenberg-Selove accepted an untenured position at the University of Pennsylvania in 1970. During this same time, she underwent surgery for breast cancer. Despite the setback, she organized the first session ever scheduled by the American Physical Society on women in physics, a meeting that began the process of sensitizing the physics community to the issue of gender discrimination. She was also the first woman elected to a leadership position in the American Physical Society.

In 1972, the University of Pennsylvania physics department announced it would hire three new tenured physicists. Knowing her credentials to be strong, Ajzenberg-Selove applied for one of these positions and was shocked and disappointed when her colleagues voted against her, citing "inadequate research publications" and age (at 46, she was evidently "too old" for the position) as reasons for her rejection. The charge that she was no longer an active scientist was absurd—with the exception of her Penn physics department colleague J. Robert Schrieffer (a Nobel laureate), she had more publication citations than any other department member.

Several months later, Ajzenberg-Selove was elected chair of the division of nuclear physics of the American Physical Society. Determined not to bow to blatant discrimination, she lodged complaints with the Federal Equal Opportunity Commission as well as the Pennsylvania State Human Relations Commission. In due course, the discriminatory actions of her colleagues were exposed and the university was required to offer her a tenured professorship in physics, retroactive to July 1, 1973. She became the second female professor in the University of Pennsylvania School of Arts and Sciences.

In 1982, Ajzenberg-Selove fought a new bout with breast cancer. Again, she regained her health, supported by her husband. Though she faced the threat of cancellation of the Department of Energy research grant that had enabled her to continue her *Energy Levels of Light Nuclei* reviews after the death of her longtime collaborator Thomas Lauritsen, outraged letters from leading scientists brought about a reversal of the negative decision. Later, she passed the responsibility for this time-consuming project to other, younger scientists. Ajzenberg-Selove's autobiography, *A Matter of Choices: Memoirs of a Female Physicist* (Rutger's University Press, 1994), was enthusiastically received for its candor, wit, and perspective on the life and achievements of a remarkable scientist.

SOURCES:

Ajzenberg-Selove, Fay. *A Matter of Choices: Memoirs of a Female Physicist.* NJ: Rutgers University Press, 1994.

Bromley, D. Allan. "A Woman's Journey in Physics: Seldo," in *Physics Today.* Vol. 47, no. 7, July 1994, pp. 61–62.

Finkbeiner, Ann K. "Women Who Run With Physicists," in *The Sciences.* Vol. 34, no. 5, September-October 1994, pp. 40–44.

John Haag, Associate Professor of History, University of Georgia, Athens, Georgia

Akeley, Delia J. (1875–1970)

American explorer, hunter, author, and first Western woman to cross equatorial Africa. Born Delia Julia Denning in Beaver Dam, Wisconsin, on December 5, 1875; died in Daytona Beach, Florida, on May 22, 1970; daughter of Margaret (Hanbury) Denning and Patrick Denning; married Arthur J. Reiss, on October 17, 1889 (divorced 1902); married Carl Ethan Akeley, on December 2, 1902 (divorced 1923); married Dr. Warren D. Howe (died 1951), in 1939; children: none.

Left home (1888); moved to Chicago (1895); began first expedition to Africa (August 13, 1905); returned to United States (January 29, 1907); made second expedition to Africa (1909); met Theodore Roosevelt's expedition (1910); returned to United States (1911); traveled to France (1918); her ex-husband Carl Akeley married Mary Jobe (October 18, 1924); made third expedition to Africa (October 1924), reaching the west coast of Africa (September 3, 1925); death of Carl Akeley in Belgian Congo (November 17, 1926); made fourth expedition to Africa (November 1929).

Selected publications: "Monkey Tricks" (Saturday Evening Post, September 18, 1926); "Jungle Rescue" (Collier's, February 11, 1928); "The Little People" (Saturday Evening Post, March 3, 1928); J.T., Jr.: The Biography of an African Monkey (NY: Macmillan, 1929); Jungle Portraits (NY: Macmillan, 1930).

The life of adventurer-naturalist Delia Akeley tells us as much about early 20th-century America as it does about Africa. Like many naturalists of the period, Akeley's career reflects a Darwinian concept of the world in which humanity was seen as the sole engine of destiny. Indeed, the naturalist's impulse to destroy nature, in order that it might be preserved, is one of the most striking aspects of her story.

Born of immigrant Irish parents, Delia Akeley spent her childhood in rural poverty. Devout Catholics, Patrick and Margaret Hanbury Denning arrived in the United States during the 1850s and took up farming near Beaver Dam, Wisconsin. Delia, the last of nine children, rarely spoke of her growing-up years. Nicknamed Mickey, she grew from an energetic child into a rebellious teenager. Like many girls of the period, her early life was dominated by the drudgery of washing dishes, cooking, sewing, and housekeeping. At age 13, Delia ran away from home after an argument with her father. When she reached Milwaukee, she was befriended by Arthur J. Reiss, a local barber. Several months later, they married. In later life, Akeley rarely alluded to the union.

How and when Delia met her second husband, Carl Ethan Akeley, is uncertain. One story suggests that he and Reiss were hunting companions, another that Reiss was Akeley's barber. Whatever the truth, after divorcing Reiss, Delia married Carl Akeley on December 2, 1902. She was 27; he was 38. Photographs show a pretty, slender woman, 5'5", with soft eyes and delicate skin.

Carl Akeley had also grown up on a farm. As a boy, he was an avid hunter and naturalist. At 19, he secured employment at Ward's Natural Science Establishment in Rochester, New York. Ward's supplied mounted specimens to most of the museums in America. Carl learned taxidermy under Augustus Ward, whom he referred to as "the father of American museums." But Carl Akeley felt that Ward's animals looked upholstered. Seeking ways to improve traditional methods of taxidermy, Carl used his skills as a sculptor to shape lifelike *papier-mâché* models of animals. He then stretched the skins over the models. The results were a vast improvement over conventional techniques and allowed the animals to be posed realistically.

With Delia's help, Carl perfected his technique and revolutionized taxidermy. As a result, he was offered a position at the Chicago Field Museum of Natural History in 1895. By this time, Delia Akeley had developed considerable skill as a taxidermist herself. Determined and ingenious, Carl dreamed of an ambitious project. As Delia later recalled:

> For some time Mr. Akeley had been developing plans for a series of habitat animal groups which he believed would revolutionize such work in museums. Taking deer for his subject he planned four groups which would show a family of deer just as they looked in the forest in summer, spring, autumn, and winter.

Delia undertook several expeditions to the surrounding countryside, collecting samples of flora and fauna. She made wax replicas of these, which where later incorporated into Carl's display for the Chicago Field Museum. Appropriately, the display was entitled "The Four Seasons."

Impressed with Carl's work, the museum commissioned him to travel to East Africa and collect examples of the African elephant. Unlike its Indian cousin familiar to circus audiences across the country, the larger, more aggressive African elephant was virtually unknown in the United States. The couple set sail for Kenya on August 13, 1905. Colonized only a few years previously, Kenya was still an unspoiled wilderness. Having stopped over in London to purchase supplies and collect the necessary permits, the Akeleys arrived late in the year. It was Delia's first trip to Africa; her husband had made a similar trip in 1896.

Though she had never fired a gun before, Delia Akeley quickly became an accomplished markswoman and hunter. She did so for reasons of personal safety and to assist her husband with his work. As **Elizabeth Olds** noted, however, "so in disrepute is big-game hunting today that it is with a certain queasiness that one hails a woman as an uncommonly fine hunter."

I'm always frightened in the jungle—always prepared for a violent death.

—Delia J. Akeley

The safari moved in a long column, roaming the savanna and collecting specimens. A year from the day of their departure, Delia Akeley and her husband arrived at Fort Hall, near Mount Kenya. In the foothills, elephants abounded. By the end of their first week, Delia Akeley had brought down two of the finest elephants collected on the expedition. Photographs show her in a safari jacket, standing beside an elephant whose tusks alone dwarfed her. It was an enthralling experience for her and not a one-sided contest as one might assume. As Akeley pointed out, "Odds are all in favor of the elephant." Many elephants stand over 12 feet tall and weigh several tons.

After five weeks on Mount Kenya, the expedition moved to the Tana River to hunt water buffalo. Returning to Fort Hall on November 22, they then proceeded to the capital Nairobi. Here the fruits of the expedition were packed for shipment to the United States. The 84 crates that arrived safely on January 29, 1907, caused a sensation at the Chicago Field Museum. The Akeleys were welcomed home in February. Their superb collection of elephants, buffaloes, birds, and gazelles were seen by thousands.

In 1909, the couple jumped at the opportunity to collect elephants for the American Museum of Natural History in New York. That year, they set sail for Africa once more. While in Kenya, the expedition joined up with one led by Theodore Roosevelt. The former president was in Africa to collect animals for the Smithsonian Institution. Many of these specimens continue to be displayed.

After a few weeks, the expeditions parted company. Delia Akeley and her husband struck out in search of a bull elephant to be the centerpiece of the American Museum exhibit. If elephants had been plentiful on their first visit, the couple soon discovered that they were a rapidly vanishing commodity. For weeks, they searched in vain for a perfect specimen.

The physical and psychological toll of the odyssey soon began to tell on Carl's health. In quick succession, he contracted meningitis, black water fever, and spirillum fever. Delia passed her days alternately nursing her patient and hunting. As their funds began to dwindle, she despaired of their chances of success. Carl Akeley's health finally improved. With new funds from the sale of his small family farm in the United States, the expedition returned to Mount Kenya, where elephants had been plentiful in the past.

One day, when Carl was out shooting photographs, a guide suddenly appeared in the camp and sadly informed Delia that her husband had been killed by an elephant. After a long and anxious trek, she found the spot were her husband had been attacked. Knocked unconscious, Carl's guides had assumed he was dead. Refusing to touch the body, according to tribal custom, they left him lying unconscious in the sun for five hours. By the time Delia arrived, he was alive but severely wounded. Roy Chapman Andrews recalled the story:

> Mickey told me that Carl was a dreadful sight. The elephant's trunk had scalped his forehead, closed one eye, smashed his nose and torn open one cheek so that it hung down and exposed the teeth in a horrible grin. Many of his ribs were broken. Several had punctured his lung and blood was running out of the corners of his mouth. She knew what that meant and it scared her worst of all.

Fortunately, at Delia's summons, a doctor arrived the next day. During the next three months, she took charge of the expedition, hunting every day, both for specimens and to supplement the camp's food supply.

It was during this expedition that Delia Akeley began observing the behavior of monkeys, and she was soon attempting to communicate with them. Her pioneering efforts presaged the research of such notable female scientists as *Jane Goodall and *Dian Fossey. After Akeley adopted a vervet monkey that she named J.T., her experiences with the creature became the basis of a book published in 1930 under the title *J.T., Jr.: The Biography of an African Monkey.*

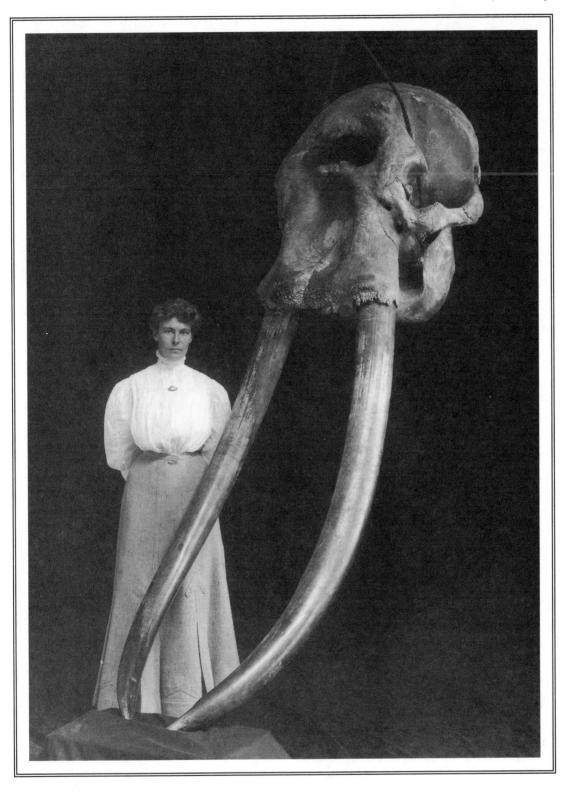

Delia J. Akeley

During the years following their second expedition and his accident, Carl Akeley worked on the African Hall at the American Museum of Natural History. The dioramas he created, his most ambitious project, can still be seen today. They present a view of nature that is a mystical simile of the contemporary American social order. The division of species emulates the division of race, the position of the animal groups in the hall mimics the division of labor, and the family groupings speak of a society steeped with a strong patriarchal sensibility. Carl Akeley's

African Hall is a Darwinian morality play set against a Hollywood backdrop. It says volumes about the United States, but little about Africa.

As her reputation grew, Delia Akeley's marriage began to falter. In 1918, she traveled to Europe to assist with the war effort. The couple divorced on March 23, 1923. The following year, Carl married *Mary Jobe (Akeley). Within two years, he was dead from fever in the Belgian Congo.

Shortly after Carl and Delia divorced, George Englehardt of the Brooklyn Museum announced that Delia Akeley would lead another expedition to Africa. In her mid-50s, grey-haired and bespectacled, she was hardly the stereotype of an intrepid explorer. The *Brooklyn Times* reported that she looked like a "gracious private-school mistress." Despite the condescending press coverage, Delia Akeley landed in Africa in October 1924.

Unlike previous trips, Akeley's expedition was small. With only a handful of native porters, she set off to hunt and photograph specimens for the museum. Having completed that task, she decided to study the Pygmies of the Belgian Congo. Little was known of Pygmies, and the reason for their small stature was the subject of considerable speculation. Akeley dispatched a cable to the *New York World* summarizing her intentions:

> I plan to go north to Kilo and from there to pygmy country, then northwest into the French Congo, then northeast to Nigeria and Lake Chad. From here I shall either cut across to the railway or come out by way of the Niger River.

The telegram brought relief to friends back home. For two months, Akeley had not been heard from, and the *Brooklyn Eagle* was reporting that she was lost and presumed dead.

Crossing into the Belgian Congo, Akeley discovered a new face of Africa. The interior was inhospitable, with frequent downpours and treacherous topography. She was appalled by the use of slave labor to construct roads and bridges. In a prescient statement, she noted, "It is an inexpensive way as far as money is concerned to develop the country. But on the other hand, isn't it expensive after all?" Indeed, the ill-will engendered by Belgian administration of the colony led to a bitter civil war and its independence under the name Zaire in 1960.

After a long and exhausting search, Akeley finally located a Pygmy village. Even though its inhabitants were indifferent to her, if not hostile at times, she remained with them for several months, studying their hunting practices, diet, and culture. She had expected to find a people stunted by poor nutrition and a lack of sunlight. Instead, she discovered a well-nourished society, happy and well-suited to their hunter-gatherer existence in the jungle. Akeley dispatched her findings to the Brooklyn Museum. Though not a scientist, her work did much to further the field of ethnology. She took measurements of average weight and height, described facial and body types, and shot hundreds of photographs.

Sick with fever, Akeley decided to abandoned her original route and instead chose to travel down the Congo River to Angola. She reached the west coast on September 3, 1925, the first Western woman to cross equatorial Africa. Returning to the United States, she regaled reporters at a news conference with tales of her adventures. During the next few years, Akeley published a string of magazine articles, as well as two books.

In November 1929, intent on further study of the Pygmies of the Belgian Congo, Akeley undertook her second expedition for the Brooklyn Museum. After five months of continuous rain, however, she was forced to abandon the project. Nevertheless, she shot 5,000 feet of film, as well as 1,500 stills. Upon her return, *The New York Times* ran a full-page spread of her photographs.

Akeley married Dr. Warren D. Howe in 1939. For many more years, she remained a popular author and speaker on the lecture circuit. In 1951, Howe died. It was not until 1970, however, that Delia Akeley died at age 95. Ironically, the cause of her death was neither disease nor injury that she had suffered in Africa but simply old age.

Although not a scientist, Delia Akeley helped to pioneer the study of the primates and the indigenous peoples of the African continent. She explored previously unmapped regions of the world. Though her writings were often moralistic (in the tone of the times, they were filled with references to "boys" when referring to the Africans who helped make her expeditions possible), nevertheless, she did much to popularize the African continent in the American mind. Her numerous speaking engagements and writing helped raise awareness about the plight of endangered species.

SOURCES:

Bohlander, Richard E., ed. *World Explorers and Discoverers.* NY: Maxwell Macmillan, 1992, pp. 3–4.

Haraway, Donna. *Primate Visions: Gender, Race, and Nature in the World of Modern Science.* London: Routledge, 1989.

Tinling, Marion. *Women into the Unknown: A Sourcebook on Women Explorers and Travellers.* CT: Greenwood Press, 1989.

SUGGESTED READING:

Olds, Elizabeth Fagg. *Women of the Four Winds: The Adventures of Four of America's First Women Explorers.* Boston, MA: Houghton Mifflin, 1985.

Hugh A. Stewart, M.A., University of Guelph, Ontario, Canada

Akeley, Mary Jobe (1878–1966)

American explorer, author, and photographer. Name variations: Mary Lee Jobe. Born Mary Leonore Jobe in Tappan, Ohio, on January 29, 1878; died in Stonington, Connecticut, on July 19, 1966; daughter of Sarah Jane Pittis and Richard Watson Jobe; granted Ph.B., Scio College, 1897, A.M., Columbia University, 1909; married Carl Ethan Akeley, on October 18, 1924; children: none.

Awards: Canadian government named Mount Jobe in her honor, 1925; awarded Belgium Cross of the Knight, 1929, made trustee of the American Museum of Natural Science, 1938.

Mary Jobe Akeley undertook her first journey of exploration to Canada in 1909. Subsequent expeditions led to the naming of one of that nation's highest peaks, Mt. Jobe, in her honor. From 1916 to 1930, Mary operated Camp Mystic in Mystic, Connecticut. In 1924, she married Carl Ethan Akeley, a year after his divorce from *Delia Akeley. His death two years later in Africa forced Mary to return to the United States. A writer and photographer, Mary Akeley was a popular staple on the lecture circuit. In later years, she continued to travel in Africa and Canada. She died of a stroke at her home in Stonington, Connecticut, in 1966.

Akers, Dolly Smith (1902—)

Assiniboine tribal leader and first Native woman elected to Montana state legislature. Born in 1902 in Wolf Point, Montana; educated in southern California at Sherman Institute.

Dolly Smith Akers was the first woman in the history of the Assiniboines to be elected chair of the tribal council, an extraordinary accomplishment considering the Assiniboines—a Siouan tribe of the northern Montana plains—are not by tradition a matriarchal society. Akers was already an active organizer on behalf of her tribe by the early 1930s. In 1934, at the behest of the governor of Montana, she lobbied the Roosevelt Administration in Washington, D.C., to request that all Native tribes in Montana be involved in the new public-welfare act. Later, Akers became the first Native woman to be elected to the Montana state legislature, and served with distinction as chair of the Federal Relations Committee. In 1960, she was the Montana governor's delegate to the White House Congress on Children and Youth. After the death of her husband, Akers retired from public life in order to manage the family's 1,400-acre Montana ranch.

Deborah Jones, freelance writer, Studio City, California

Akesson, Sonja (1926–1977)

Swedish poet. Name variations: Akeson or Åkeson; (full name) Sonja Berta Maria Hammarberg Akesson. Born in Buttle, Gotland, Sweden, in 1926; died in 1977; grew up on the island of Gotland; married.

Upon moving to Stockholm in 1951, Sonja Akesson began writing of her childhood and everyday domestic conditions. Her first collection of poems *Situationer* (*Situations,* 1957) was published six years later. It was followed by *Leva livet* (*Living Life,* 1961), *Husfrid* (*Peace in the House,* 1963), *Pris* (*Prize,* 1968), and *Sagan om Siv* (*The Saga of Siv,* 1974). Known for her sizzling critiques of society, she disparaged the role of a housewife in "Be White Man's Slave" (1963). Her major poem "Autobiography (reply to Ferlinghetti)" was written in 1963.

Akhat-milki (fl. 1265 BCE)

Wife of Niqmepa, king of Canaanite Ugarit, who managed affairs of state as dowager queen for a short time after his death. Name variations: Ahat-milki, Ahatmilku, Sharelli. Born probably in mid-late 1200s BCE in Amorite Amurru; date of death in Ugarit unknown; daughter of King DU-Teshub of Amurru; married King Niqmepa of Ugarit at an unknown date; children: Khishmi-Sharruma, ARAD-Sharruma, Ammishtamru II.

The small city-state of Ugarit (present-day Ras Shamra in Northern Syria) was located on the Mediterranean coast just opposite the northeastern tip of Cyprus. Founded in the 19th or 18th century BCE, it fell repeatedly under the hegemony of the competitive empires of Egypt and Mesopotamia, but its excellent location at the juncture of commercial routes by land and sea seems to have ensured its relative peace, prosperity, and autonomy until its destruction in

1230 BCE by a band of the marauding "Sea Peoples," the Biblical Philistines. In 1928, some of ancient Ugarit's tombs were accidentally uncovered by a Syrian farmer. Since then, excavation of the old port, city, and royal palace has been extensive. In addition to some fine artifacts and architectural remains, thousands of cuneiform tablets have been discovered, many in a hitherto unknown alphabetic script. Decipherment of this script has demonstrated that the language of Ugarit is a close cognate of Hebrew, and the various religious and mythological texts have advanced scholarly understanding of Biblical Hebrew and ancient Canaanite religion enormously.

Akhat-milki ("sister of the king") was the daughter of King *DU*-Teshub of Amurru, an Amorite kingdom to the east of Ugarit. She was married at some point in the late 1200s BCE to King Niqmepa of Ugarit, probably to seal a political and military alliance between the two states. There is evidence to suggest that Niqmepa was placed forcibly on the throne by the city's Hittite overlord after his brother and predecessor participated in a Syrian revolt against Hittite control of the region. Nevertheless, he seems to have enjoyed a long and fairly peaceful reign of more than 60 years. Though his son and successor, Ammishtamru II, would have been in middle age at the time of Niqmepa's death in 1265, his accession to the throne was apparently not immediate, and Akhat-milki ruled briefly in his place.

Akhat-Milki's reign was probably marked by the plot of her sons Khishmi-Sharruma and *ARAD*-Sharruma against their mother and brother Ammishtamru. One of the Ugaritic tablets explains how the case was submitted to the arbitration of the king of Carchemish (a city-state on the Euphrates) and the Hittite court. The tablet shows that Akhat-milki then brought her errant sons to Cyprus, where they were made to swear before the goddess Ishtar that they would not ask anything of the king of Ugarit or his son. It is probable that the two lived thenceforth in exile, for Ammishtamru went on to rule Ugarit alone and chose his son as his successor. He had two unhappy marriages with princesses of Amurru, the first of whom was a grandniece of Akhat-milki.

It is not known when Akhat-milki died, but several of the tablets found in Ugarit indicate that she lived a life of luxury with the king and wielded some measure of power while he was alive. A tablet found in 1953 records the trousseau of Akhat-milki as consisting of various pieces of gold jewelry, vessels and boxes of precious metals, perfumes, cosmetics, and fine clothing. Several tablets comprise letters from dignitaries addressed to Akhat-milki asking for her intervention or intercession with the king in important matters. The apparent stature of this woman makes it highly desirable that we learn more about her. Given the relatively recent date of the excavation of Ugarit, and the even later date of the publication of the Ugaritic tablets, it may be reasonable to hope that more information will come to light in the future.

SOURCES AND SUGGESTED READING:

Catling, H.W. "The identification of Cyprus with Alashiya," and "Ugarit" by Margaret S. Drower in *The Cambridge Ancient History.* 3rd ed. Vol. 2, part 2, *The Middle East and Aegean Region c. 1380-1000 B.C.,* edited by I.E.S. Edwards, C.J. Gadd, N.G.L. Hammond, and E. Sollberger, 201–205. Cambridge: Cambridge University Press, 1975.

Curtis, Adrian. *Ugarit (Ras Shamra): Cities of the Biblical World.* Grand Rapids: William B. Eerdmans, 1985.

Peter H. O'Brien, Boston University, Boston, Massachusetts

Akhmatova, Anna (1889–1966)

Russian poet, translator, and literary scholar, who was perhaps the most famous 20th-century Russian poet. Name variations: Axmatova, Achmatowa, Akhmátova, Anna Andreevna Akhmatova, Anna Gorenko. Pronunciation: AHN-na An-DRAY-ev-na Akh-MAH-toh-va (Gah-RYEN-kuh). Born Anna Andreevna Gorenko on June 11, 1889, in Bol'shoi Fontan, Russia; died in Domodedovo, a sanatorium outside Moscow, on March 5, 1966; daughter of Andrei Gorenko and Inna Stogova; married Nikolai Gumilyov, in 1910 (separated 1916; divorced 1918); married Vladimir Shileyko, in 1918 (separated 1921); lived 15 years with Nikolai Punin; children: (first marriage) son Lev Nikolaevich Gumilyov (b. 1912). Awarded honorary degree from Oxford University, 1965.

Selected poetry: Evening (St. Petersburg, 1912); Rosary (St. Petersburg, 1914); White Flock (Petrograd, 1917); Plantain (Petrograd, 1921); By the Very Sea (1921); Anno Domini MCMXXI (Petrograd, 1922); From Six Books (Leningrad, 1940); Selected Works (1943); Selected Verses (Moscow, 1946); Verses (Moscow, 1961); The Flight of Time (Moscow-Leningrad, 1965); Requiem (Munich, 1965). Major poem: "Poem Without a Hero." Criticism: On Pushkin (1977).

After her son was arrested for the second time in 1938, Anna Akhmatova spent over 300 hours standing in line outside prisons in Leningrad. Since she frequently ate only black bread and tea without sugar, she was often feverish with illness or hunger. The lines contained mostly women, grey with exhaustion and the horror of their relatives' arrests, their legs swollen and aching with the long hours of standing. Some carried packages they hoped to get to their husbands, brothers or sons; others just wanted to learn where their men were and how long their sentences would be. One day when Akhmatova's name was called, the woman behind her recognized it and burst into tears. Indeed, 20 years earlier the name Anna Akhmatova had symbolized the height of grace and elegance in Russian poetry, and a whole generation conducted their romances with her love poems. The contrast underlined the tragic changes in Russia through which Akhmatova's generation lived.

When she mentioned this episode as part of the introduction to her long poem "Requiem," Akhmatova changed the details, writing that the woman behind her had never heard her name before. In this version, the woman, upon hearing Anna was a writer, gestured toward the line and asked, "Can you describe this?" Akhmatova answered, "I can." She had grown into a very different poet.

Anna Akhmatova was born Anna Gorenko near the Black Sea port of Odessa; her father Andrei Gorenko was a naval engineer with a Ukrainian last name. Akhmatova's mother **Inna Stogova** was an aristocrat with some radical political activity in her past, distantly related to the early Russian poet ❧▶ **Anna Bunina**. Akhmatova had five brothers and sisters; one sister died at the age of four, the first of many premature deaths among the siblings. The Gorenko family moved in 1890 to Tsarskoe Selo ("Tsar's Village"), located outside the capital city of the Russian Empire, St. Petersburg. This royal residence was later renamed Pushkin after the great poet Alexander Pushkin, who studied at the elite lyceum there in the early 19th century: the town was a showplace for palace architecture, gardens, and statuary. Akhmatova received a good education, was fluent in French, and later in life learned Italian and English so as to read Dante and Shakespeare. She started writing poetry at 11, though poetry was not yet widely in fashion when she was a girl.

Akhmatova's parents separated in 1905, and she moved with her mother and siblings to live in the Crimea. She continued studying with tutors at home and then, in 1907, finished the *Gymnazia* (high school with a demanding classical curriculum) in Kiev. She later recalled a day when she and her mother were walking home to their summer cottage and Akhmatova absent-

---

❧▶ **Bunina, Anna Petrovna** (1774–1829)

Russian poet. Name variations: *Bú;nina. Born in 1774; died in 1829; sixth child born into a gentry family.*

Anna Bunina was Russia's first major woman poet. When her father died in 1801, she moved to St. Petersburg where she used her small inheritance to educate herself and to support her writing. Having composed poetry from childhood, she gained immediate prominence with her first volumes *An Inexperienced Muse* (Vol. 1, 1809, Vol. 2, 1812). In 1815, to seek treatment for breast cancer, she journeyed to England, but, because of illness and pain, wrote very little after 1817. See Barbara Heldt's biography *Terrible Perfection*.

---

mindedly said: "Some day there will be a memorial plaque on this house." Her mother answered, "I've brought you up so badly!"

Akhmatova studied briefly at the Faculty of Law in Kiev, largely because it was one of the places a woman could receive a higher education, but she found the Latin and history courses more interesting than the law itself. She moved to St. Petersburg to advanced courses in the study of literature; the city and its rich literary history would become one of the major themes of her writing.

Anna had met the poet and critic Nikolai Gumilyov in Tsarskoe Selo, and he had been courting her for years. In 1910, she finally agreed to marry him. Though Gumilyov thought she should become a dancer—since she had the build and was flexible enough to touch the back of her head with her foot—he also took her seriously as a poetic talent. Since her husband liked to make long trips to exotic places, which he then used as material for his poems about pirates and safaris, Akhmatova was often alone during their marriage, which was not very stable or happy, as both partners were strong-willed and seemed to thrive on crisis and discord. In the end, they loved each other more as fellow poets, though Gumilyov's writing had hardly any influence on Akhmatova's work. It seems, rather, that her poems, much simpler than the ornate Symbolist style of the time, served as a model for his "Acmeist" literary theories and manifestos. The only literary influence Akhmatova acknowledged was the poetry of Innokentii Annenskii, who died in 1909.

Akhmatova had published her first poem in 1907, in a small journal edited by Gumilyov. Her father disapproved of her writing and did

*Anna
Akhmatova*

details about her personal experiences tended to come scattered in conversations.

Gumilyov helped found a group of young writers called the Guild of Poets, and Akhmatova was its "secretary"; eventually the group was better known as Acmeists. Their theoretical articles demanded a literature of greater simplicity and freshness—very much what Akhmatova was writing, though she preferred poetry to criticism or theory. Another Acmeist was Osip Mandelstam, a great poet and Akhmatova's good friend until his arrest and death in the Stalinist purges of the late 1930s. In 1912, Akhmatova's only child was born, her son Lev Nikolaevich Gumilyov, who was raised mostly by Akhmatova's mother-in-law until he was 16. The same year, Akhmatova published her first book of poems, *Evening.* She published her second book, *Rosary,* in 1914, and despite the beginning of World War I, it was a huge success. Poetry lovers spent evenings "telling the Rosary"—reciting the poems in order, one by one, around their circle. Akhmatova's fame was something like the fame of rock stars: well-known, avant-garde artists wanted to paint her portrait, postcards were sold with her photographs, other poets tried to imitate her writing style, and her less sophisticated readers assumed they knew all about her, since they had read what seemed like intimate details in her poems.

Akhmatova and her friends favored the Stray Dog, a fashionable basement nightclub. She had a good theatrical sense and knew how to make the most of her exotic profile (the amazing nose), slender height, pale skin, dark hair, and clear blue eyes, all of which went well with the Oriental-sounding pseudonym. Before long, the best-known older poets in St. Petersburg recognized her talent, inviting her to readings and writing poems to her, or scorning her in a way that proved their envy. Akhmatova was the first Russian woman poet to gain such widespread fame; for other women writers, she was both an inspiration and a threat.

not want her to shame the family, so she chose her Tatar great-grandmother's beautiful maiden name Akhmatova as a pseudonym.

Traveling abroad with Gumilyov in 1910 and 1911, she became friends with the artist Amadeo Modigliani in Paris before he was famous, and he drew her portrait. Akhmatova loved French culture and poetry, but it was the architecture of northern Italy that left the most lasting impression. Back in Russia, St. Petersburg was the major center of literary activity at the time, and Akhmatova and her husband were soon very much in fashion. Akhmatova was self-possessed and cool about her own attractiveness and growing reputation, which made her all the more irresistible to her admirers. She eventually became famous for the number and variety of her lovers, though many of the affairs she reportedly had were imagined by her friends and readers. She remained reticent about her private life until her death; her "autobiographical sketches" were brief, and the most interesting

Her early poems are simple but psychologically nuanced, based on the psychological realism of the great 19th-century Russian novel. So much of the story is left out that what is given gains extra resonance and mystery. Many of the poems are about love, but they also include elements of nature, religion, and a concern with poetic creation. Certain poems celebrate the lively Petersburg cultural scene, while others treat it as a fallen, sinful city, far from what real, old-fashioned Russians would approve of.

When the Great War began in the summer of 1914, Gumilyov immediately enlisted as a cavalry officer, and in 1916 the couple separated. Akhmatova later called World War I the beginning of "the real twentieth century," and her poems of anxiety and mourning started the expansion of the poetic voice that would eventually speak for all Russia's people. In the war years, one of Akhmatova's sisters died in her 20s of tuberculosis, a disease that killed many otherwise privileged young people. Indeed, Akhmatova herself suffered from bouts with tuberculosis for decades, but she had a thyroid condition that seemed to balance the tuberculosis, keeping it in check.

In 1918, after the epochal October Revolution, Akhmatova officially divorced Gumilyov and married Vladimir Shileyko, a scholar of ancient Assyrian cuneiform script. She disliked Lenin's Bolsheviks but chose not to emigrate, though her brother and some of her closest friends did leave Russia for Western Europe. The power of her poetic denial suggests that she was strongly tempted to leave and foresaw the difficulties ahead, but felt even more deeply that she must stay with her people. She mourned Gumilyov's execution in August 1921 (he was supposedly involved in a monarchist counter-revolutionary plot) both as a former husband and as an artistic colleague. Many other important poets died or emigrated, changing the literary geography of Russia drastically. Akhmatova published three more books to continuing acclaim, but then the growing Soviet literary bureaucracy moved to put an end to her publishing career, because her great popularity and increasing moral authority made her a threat. She was condemned as a petty-bourgeois writer, a survivor from the old days, an "internal émigrée." The government granted her a meager pension, and even readers who loved her work assumed she was no longer writing. Only *Alexandra Kollontai, herself a thoughtful writer as well as a feminist politician, defended Akhmatova's work for its presentation of women's adaptation to conditions of life in the new society.

Both religion and female sexuality were taboo topics under the new revolutionary puritanism, and Akhmatova, as her critics noted, did write a great deal about religion and love, both of them traditionally associated with women in Russian culture. Akhmatova's new husband Shileyko burned her poetry so she would stop writing, and the two separated in 1921; very few poems survive from these years. Instead, the poet made a living by working in the library of the Institute of Agronomy, and more and more by literary translating. From 1925 until 1940, Akhmatova lived with the art critic Nikolai Punin, in a communal apartment in the former Sheremet'ev Palace, where his ex-wife, also named **Anna,** was also living.

The mass arrests of the late 1930s included Akhmatova's son and Punin, both arrested in 1935 and both released after a few months. But Lev was arrested again in 1938 (his father, after all, had been executed for alleged involvement in a monarchist plot, and Lev had the same dangerous surname). Akhmatova waited in those long lines and begged people to intervene. At the same time, she wrote more, composing simple poems about the horrifying tragedy her society was undergoing. Eventually, she completed the long poem "Requiem," containing sections written from 1935 to 1940, in its way the Stations of the Cross of a prisoner's mother. The poem runs from the arrest, through the endless lines, to the final blow of the sentencing, where the mother becomes Christ's mother at the crucifixion. The poet takes on the role of mourning mother, the feminine voice of Russia itself, and the full stature of the poet as conscience and recorder of national tragedy. "Requiem" powerfully condemns the crimes of Stalinism; it was not printed in Russia until 1987, two decades after her death.

*S*he was accused of being both nun and whore, of concentrating on the personal to the exclusion of the (approved) political, of talking too much about "love," of being too "subjective." From this point in time it all sounds rather familiar, but Akhmatova was not permitted to counter with "the personal is political," that slogan then being some thirty years in the future.

—Margaret Atwood, 1989

Akhmatova always feared police surveillance, and in these years she worked out a special ritual for her writing: *Lidiya Chukovskaya recalled that Akhmatova would talk loudly about something trivial while scribbling a new poem on a scrap of paper. Once her friend had memorized the lines, Akhmatova would burn the paper over her ashtray. From time to time, she would meet with the friends who had memorized her work and tell them what changes she had made, or check to make sure that they still remembered everything properly. It was not safe to keep any writing that was at all critical of Stalinist rule or of Stalin himself. Akhmatova's poems from this period survived only because they had been memorized. Her other strategy was using so-called "Aesopic language," which made things sound innocent but gave enough of a hint of the true meaning that knowledgeable readers would understand it. Even without that practice of concealment, her poetry in the 1930s becomes difficult to decode without knowing the historical and political background. For example, calling a cycle "Poems from a Burned Notebook" could sound like romantic posing, but the writer often felt compelled to burn her papers or notebooks so that the secret police would not find them while searching her room, use them to harass her and her friends, or cause more trouble for her son. Akhmatova was convinced that her room was searched when she was away and complained that someone kept cutting the bindings of precious books to look in them for hidden documents. At this time, Akhmatova began to spend more time with friends in Moscow, and these visits went on until the end of her life. The pressures of her son's arrest, bad health, poverty, and real or imagined surveillance made Akhmatova fear that she would lose her sanity. By staying with friends, she could escape some of the unwelcome attention from the secret police, and her friends would make sure she was well fed and cared for.

When World War II began for the Soviet Union with the surprise German invasion in June 1941, Akhmatova was in St. Petersburg (then known as Leningrad), and she witnessed the terrible bombardment there before she was evacuated to Tashkent. There she was often sick, worried about the fate of her beloved city during the siege of nearly three years. At the same time, as the government relaxed many of its restrictions on religion and culture in order to encourage all-out participation in the war effort, Akhmatova's poetry was suddenly hot property again because of its resonant patriotism. She combined her wrath at the tragedy of the war with an artist's concern for the survival of the Russian language. Her son Lev was released from camp so he could join the army, and he later told her that fighting at the front was much easier than life in the prison camp. In fact, many Soviet citizens felt a new sense of hope and freedom during the war, as if the lifting of restrictions promised that things would be different after victory. In 1944, Akhmatova returned to Leningrad; on her return trip, she gave a poetry reading in Moscow, where she was greeted by a standing ovation.

One day in 1946, Akhmatova opened the package of salted herring she had just brought home from market and glanced at the newspaper in which it was wrapped. That is how she first learned that Stalin's literary hatchet man Andrei Zhdanov had just denounced her in the crudest terms, as "half-nun, half-whore," a sign of the postwar return to cultural restriction and repression in the Soviet Union. She was expelled from the Writers' Union and lost her ration card. Worst of all, Lev was rearrested in 1949, and Akhmatova became desperate enough to write and publish a cycle of 15 poems praising the dictator Stalin, called "Glory to Peace," in a futile attempt to free her son. She continued her own reading and work in literary scholarship, especially on Pushkin, and earned what she could by doing literary translation. Though she eventually published several whole volumes of translations, she complained that, for a poet, translating was like eating your own brain.

Akhmatova's poor health was not improved by her grinding poverty and forced dependence on friends and well-wishers. Partly as a strategy to protect her working time, she cultivated a kind of helplessness in everyday matters, but she was also terrified of the large, anonymous cities and the speeding, sinister cars of police and political figures. She had to borrow money to send to her son in prison and had no place of her own for decades. The squalid rooms where she lived retained only a few leftovers of past luxury: a fine wood-framed mirror and Modigliani's portrait of her on the wall. Her appearance seemed to depend on her mood: she could look ancient, puffy, and bad-tempered one day, but the next day she could be as charming and imposing as ever, even in very old age.

Like her friend Boris Pasternak, Akhmatova outlived Stalin and saw the "thaw," the relative expansion of freedom in the years when Nikita Khrushchev was at the head of the Soviet government. Her son Lev was finally released from camp in 1956, but he returned home very scarred. (He had been told that his mother was to blame for his arrest and continuing imprisonment, which may have reinforced childhood memories of being left at his grandmother's house.) Akhmatova was never officially "rehabilitated" after Zhdanov's denunciation of her writing, but she was able to publish her own original poetry again. In the new atmosphere, she was acknowledged as the grand old lady of Russian literature and attracted a fresh generation of readers and young poets who sought her advice and blessing. She had become a legend in her lifetime, a living link with the great literary culture of the Silver Age. Her admirers took care of the everyday tasks that she had always, half-intentionally, been unable to do for herself. Akhmatova preferred the young male poets; she liked beautiful women but perhaps did not want any to compete with her verbal preeminence. She also continued to write love poems, always in very good taste, which shocked some of her readers, who evidently did not think such things possible at her advanced age. She continued to write and publish poems with clear Aesopic content of protest and criticism, and she petitioned the authorities directly to help persecuted poets such as Joseph Brodsky.

Most Russian women writers have been forgotten in their old age, but the elderly Akhmatova was renowned throughout the world. In 1965, she was the third Russian ever to be invited to Oxford University in England to receive an honorary doctorate in literature. She relished the position of senior poet and took the role seriously, using her memories to teach about the history of Russian literature. Her intricate and often-revised work "Poem without a Hero" also served to teach. It is full of musical and cultural references and comments on its own difficulty for the unqualified reader. Learning what is needed to read and understand this poem quite thoroughly introduces the reader to the Russian Silver Age in St. Petersburg and the historical events that followed it. As the last major poet of her generation to survive, Akhmatova was anxious to preserve her view of literary history, and her own role in it, which she felt had often been distorted. She enjoyed judging the literary value of the young poets who came, or did not come, to hear her opinions, and she also made caustic, clever comments about the many famous contemporaries who had not lived to contradict her. She finally received a *dacha* (summer house) outside Leningrad from the Writers' Union and spent a great deal of time there in the last decade of her life.

Akhmatova's health had always been bad, and she spent many weeks in hospital or bedridden at home. She died in Domodedovo, a sanatorium outside Moscow, on March 5, 1966, at the age of 76. Her funeral was a major event, and hundreds of mourners came to the cathedral in Leningrad to view her body. As the last great Russian poet of that generation, her death marked the end of an era.

Akhmatova is one of the best-known Russian poets abroad, both for her writing and for the civic courage that sustained her work through personal and national tragedies. Her early poetry, spare and simple, and the later, opaque long poems with their baffling musical complexity all make her a challenge to the poetic or scholarly translator, but she is one of the most-translated 20th-century Russian writers. In the world, as in Russia, her reputation is secure.

SOURCES:

Atwood, Margaret. "Two Poems," in *Canadian Studies*. Winter 1989.

Chukovskaya, Lidiya. *Zapiski ob Anne Akhmatovoi* (Notes on Anna Akhmatova). 2 vols. Paris: YMCA Press, 1976, 1980.

Haight, Amanda. *Akhmatova: A Poetic Pilgrimage.* New York and London: Oxford University Press, 1976.

SUGGESTED READING:

Akhmatova, Anna. *Poem Without a Hero and other poems.* Trans. by Lenore Mayhew and William McNaughton. Oberlin, OH: Oberlin College Press, 1988.

———. *Selected Poems.* Ed. and intro. by Walter Arndt. Trans. Walter Arndt, Robin Kemball, and Carl Proffer. Ann Arbor, MI: Ardis, 1976.

———. *Selected Poems.* Trans. and intro. by Richard McKane. London: Oxford University Press, 1983.

———. *Way of All the Earth.* Trans. by D.M. Thomas. Athens, OH: Ohio University Press, 1979.

———. *Anna Akhmatova: Poems-Correspondence-Reminiscences-Iconography.* Comp. by Ellendea Proffer. Ann Arbor: Ardis, 1977.

———. *The Complete Poems of Anna Akhmatova.* (Bilingual edition.) Trans. by Judith Hemschemeyer. Ed. and intro. by Roberta Reeder. Somerville, MA: Zephyr Press, 1990.

———. *Poems.* Selected and trans. by Lyn Coffin. NY: W.W. Norton, 1983.

———. *Poems of Anna Akhmatova.* (Bilingual edition.) Selected, trans. and intro. by Stanley Kunitz, with Max Hayward. Boston, MA: Little, Brown, 1973.

Chukovskaya, Lydia. *The Akhmatova Journals, Vol. I, 1938–41.* Trans. by Milena Michalski and Sylva Rubashova. NY: Farrar, Straus, 1994.

Sibelan Forrester, Assistant Professor of Russian, Swarthmore College, Swarthmore, Pennsylvania

Akhyaliyya, Layla al-.

See Layla al-Akhyaliyya (fl. 650-660).

Akins, Zoe (1886–1958)

American playwright and screenwriter who was awarded the Pulitzer Prize for her stage adaptation of Edith Wharton's novella The Old Maid. *Born Zoe Akins on October 30, 1886, in Humansville, Missouri; died of cancer on October 29, 1958, in Los Angeles, California; daughter of Thomas J. Akins and Elizabeth (Green) Akins; attended Monticello Seminary in Godfrey, Illinois, and Hosmer Hall in St. Louis, Missouri; married Hugo C. Rumbold, in 1932 (Rumbold died a few months later); children: none.*

Selected plays: The Magical City *(1916);* Papa *(1919);* Declasse *(1919);* Footloose *(1920);* Daddy's Gone a-Hunting *(1921);* The Varying Shore *(1921);*

Greatness *(published as* The Texas Nightingale, *1923);* A Royal Fandango *(1924);* The Moon-Flower *(1924);* First Love *(adaptation, 1926);* The Crown Prince, Thou Desperate Pilot *(1927);* The Furies *(1928);* The Love Duel *(adaptation, 1929);* The Greeks Had a Word For It *(1929);* The Old Maid *(1935);* O Evening Star *(1936);* The Human Element *(adaptation, 1939);* Mrs. January and Mr. X *(1948);* The Swallow's Nest *(1950).*

Selected screenplays: (with **Doris Anderson**) Anybody's Woman *(1930);* Sarah and Son *(1930);* Working Girls *(1931);* Women Love Once *(1931);* Girls About Town *(1931); (with Samuel Hoffenstein)* Once A Lady *(1931);* Morning Glory *(1933);* Christopher Strong *(1933);* Accused *(1936); (with Joseph Anthony)* Lady of Secrets *(1936); (with* ***Frances Marion** *and James Hilton)* Camille *(1937);* The Toy Wife *(1938);* Zaza *(1938);* The Old Maid *(film adaptation of her play, 1939); (with* **Marguerite Roberts**) Desire Me *(1947);* How to Marry a Millionaire *(1953);* Stagestruck *(remake of* Morning Glory, *1958). Novel:* Forever Young *(1941).*

Stagestruck from childhood, Zoe Akins left an affluent life in the Midwest to pursue a career as an actress. After several years of struggling in New York without success, she turned to writing. What had been a youthful avocation soon developed into a lucrative career that spanned several decades and, in 1938, garnered Akins the Pulitzer Prize for her stage adaptation of ***Edith Wharton**'s novella, *The Old Maid.*

Ironically, Akins' life was not unlike that of novelist Wharton. Akins spent much of her adult years in Pasadena, California, living in an opulently furnished Edwardian mansion complete with British servants. In 1932, she had married the son of Sir Hugo Rumbold, former British ambassador to Austria-Hungary. The marriage had ended sadly with Rumbold's early death that same year. Wharton, born to a well-to-do New York family, also lived a pampered life and, like Akins, married a man of considerable wealth, though her marriage ended in divorce. Neither women remarried and both were childless.

Wharton and Akins also created similar characters. Each wrote about unorthodox or rebellious women who struggled with society's conventions. Compare Wharton's *House of Mirth* with Akins' film adaptation of Gilbert Frankau's novel *Christopher Strong* (starring ***Katharine Hepburn** and directed by ***Dorothy Arzner**). Each story concerns a heroine struggling with social norms that eventually destroy her.

From 1916, when the Bandbox Theater produced her first play, *The Magical City,* through the late 1940s, Akins was a solid presence in the New York theater. In 1928, though she claimed to have moved to the West Coast for her health, she quickly launched a second career as a screenwriter. Beginning with Dorothy Arzner's *Sarah and Son,* Akins wrote or co-wrote such classics as *Camille,* starring ***Greta Garbo**, *Zaza,* starring ***Claudette Colbert**, and *Morning Glory,* which served as a vehicle for Katharine Hepburn's first Academy Award.

Critically, Akins received decidedly mixed reviews for both stage and screen. When ***Ethel Barrymore** starred in Akins' 1919 hit, *Declasse, The New York Times* reviewer wrote that it was "the richest and most interesting play" that had fallen to Barrymore in "all her years upon the stage." *Accused,* the film that starred Douglas Fairbanks and ***Delores Del Rio**, was hailed by *Variety* as having "brilliant, incisive dialogue." But of the 1931 film, *Women Love Once, Variety* cracked that it "heaves too much in the clinches." And though *Christopher Strong* secured Hepburn's place as a star, Akins' script was taken to task by *Variety* as "overloaded with playwright device and nothing more."

Akins' happiest professional collaboration was probably with director George Cukor. The two met in New York in the early 1920s, when Cukor was a stage manager and Akins had already made her reputation as a prominent playwright. Within five years, Cukor's career as a director was in full swing. In 1928, he directed Akins' play, *The Furies,* starring Broadway legend ***Laurette Taylor**. Cukor followed Akins to Hollywood where he became one of the motion picture industry's most legendary figures.

Akins was important to Cukor's budding Hollywood career and would often consult with him on the scripts for his films. Though Cukor eventually eclipsed Akins in his overall contribution to the screen, he remained a loyal friend, despite his feelings that the mercurial Akins could be troublesome. (It was common for Akins to call at all hours and read an entire play over the phone to him.)

No doubt the pinnacle of the Akins-Cukor collaboration was the wildly successful *Camille,* the story of courtesan ***Alphonsine Plessis**, which starred Garbo. Though three writers are credited on *Camille,* it is reputed that the script Cukor shot was written entirely by Akins. Cukor and Akins also worked together on *Zaza, Pride and Prejudice,* and *Desire Me,* though on the latter, Cukor was replaced by director Mervyn Leroy.

Though Akins' career continued into the 1950s, her last plays, *Happy Days, Another Darling,* and *Mrs. January and Mr. X,* did not do well at the box office. At the time of her death from cancer in 1958, Akins was working on *Heller With A Gun,* a screenplay for producer Carlo Ponti and Paramount Pictures. Said fellow screenwriter *Sonya Levien, Akins "was brilliantly young and vital to the very last."

SOURCES:

McGilligan, Patrick. *George Cukor: A Double Life.* NY: St. Martin's Press, 1991.

Slide, Anthony. *American Screenwriters.* Edited by Robert E. Morsberger, Stephen O. Lesser, and Randall Clark. Detroit, MI: Gale Research, 1984.

Variety Film Reviews: 1930–1933 (Vol.4) and *1934–1937* (Vol. 5). NY: Garland, 1983.

Obituary. *Variety.* November 5, 1958.

Deborah Jones, freelance writer, Studio City, California

Akiyoshi, Toshiko (1929—)

Japanese-American jazz pianist, composer, and bandleader. Born in Darien, Manchuria (a province of China then controlled by the Japanese), on December 12, 1929; daughter of a Japanese owner of a textile company and steel mill; married Stan Kenton (the bandleader and saxophonist; divorced in the mid-1960s); married Lew Tabackin (a sax player), in 1969.

Toshiko Akiyoshi's career established the international nature of jazz. Born in Manchuria of Japanese parents in 1929, she fled the area with her family when the Chinese reclaimed the region in 1945. Her father, who had owned steel and textile mills, was financially destroyed; thus, at age 16, Akiyoshi had to find work playing for a dance band for four dollars an hour. Though she had had training in classical music, her knowledge of jazz improvisation was mainly empirical. Akiyoshi recounts the day a friend played her a Teddy Wilson record: "A whole new world opened up for me. I said, 'Oh, jazz can be beautiful!' I had really dumb luck as a pioneer in the jazz field: if you were just a little bit better than the next guy, you got the job. I became the highest paid studio musician in Japan."

Akiyoshi played piano with three symphony orchestras and ten Tokyo jazz groups before she decided to form her own jazz combo in 1952. Oscar Peterson heard her play in a club and arranged for her to be recorded. When that recording was played in America, Akiyoshi was offered a scholarship at Berklee, Boston's jazz college. Despite great luck as a musician, establishing a career wasn't easy: "In the early years in America, I dealt with both racial and sexual prejudice," said Akiyoshi. "I played clubs and TV wearing a kimono, because people were amazed to see an Oriental woman playing jazz." As a composer, Akiyoshi was a genius at weaving rich, complex tone colors. She composed a fascinating update of the classic swing-band tradition of brass and saxes. Her style was unique, however, because of its cross-pollination of cultures. Lew Tabackin said of her work, "Toshiko is not one of those foreign musicians who try to be ultra American. Through her attitude, she achieves a very special kind of oneness." For example, in *Kogun* she combined pretaped percussion sounds with vocal cries from Japanese Noh drama as well as a brass section pitted against a Noh actor's piercing tones. *Children in the Temple Ground* begins with long, vocal wails in Japanese blended with a flute and orchestra accompanied by piano.

Akiyoshi's music often reflects social themes. In *Tales of a Courtesan,* she drew on the lives of women who employed sexual favors in order to survive and prosper. "The European concept of the courtesan is too happy," she explained. "For three centuries under the shoguns, poorer families had to sell their daughters into slavery. Though some courtesans were highly educated, they had no freedom; attempted escape meant punishment by death. My music expresses the contrast between the superficially luxurious life of some of these women and the tragic denial of human rights they suffered." Another example is *Minamata,* a work that some regard as Akiyoshi's crowning achievement. This piece was named for the small Japanese fishing village poisoned by industrialization, pollution, and the dumping of mercury that killed the fish and, ultimately, many people. The suite begins with Akiyoshi's teenage daughter **Michiru** intoning an introduction that is repeated by a Noh action at the end. Two *tsuzumi* drummers commence, followed by the band, and a wild climax is reached through the effects of a bizarre, writhing sax section. Such creative use of jazz is typical of Toshiko Akiyoshi's work.

In America, Akiyoshi married Stan Kenton, the bandleader, but the union dissolved in the mid-1960s. She began to divide her time between New York, where she played with Charlie Mingus, and Tokyo, where she played with her own trio. In 1967, while she was organizing a Town Hall concert with her own big band, she met Lew Tabackin who played the tenor sax. "I had reservations about the relationship," she said. "Lew is

Toshiko
Akiyoshi

the only son in a very tight Jewish family. But finally I decided that Buddha knew we were meant for each other." They were married in 1969 and moved to California in 1972 where she organized an orchestra and Lew became a sideman in Doc Severinsen's *Tonight Show* band.

Akiyoshi's reputation continued to grow in jazz circles. She won the 1977 Readers' Poll in Japan's *Swing Journal*. In 1976 and 1977, her albums were nominated for Grammy awards, and her band appeared at the Monterey and Newport jazz festivals. In 1978, her band played at the First Annual Women's Jazz Festival in Kansas City and went on to play at the Village Gate in New York. Appearances in Europe and Japan followed. A pioneer in the field of jazz as both an Asian and a woman, Akiyoshi received rave reviews for her unique style as well as her compositions and won great acclaim as an extraordinary musician.

SOURCES:

Feather, Leonard. "Music: Toshiko Akiyoshi—The Leader of the Band," in *Ms.* Vol. 7, no. 5. November 1978, pp. 34–35, 40.

———. "The Passion for Jazz. Interview with Akiyoshi and Lew Tabackin," in *Ms.* Vol. 7, no. 5. November 1978, pp. 109–119.

John Haag, Associate Professor of History, University of Georgia, Athens, Georgia

Akselrod, Liubo (1868–1946)

Russian Marxist philosopher and literary critic. Name variations: Lyubov Axel'rod, Axelrod; (pseudonyms) Ortodox, Orthodox; Born Liubo Isaakovna Akselrod in Russia, where she lived until her exile to France in 1887; earned a Ph.D., University of Berne, Switzerland; returned to Russia in 1906.

Member of the Social Democratic Party (1906–18); teacher at the Institute of Red Professors (1906–21); professor at the University of Sverdlov (1921–46).

Selected works: Against Idealism; Marx as a Philosopher; Critique of the Foundations of Bourgeois Sociology and Historical Materialism; In Defense of Dialectical Materialism; Against Scholasticism; The Idealist Dialectic of Hegel and the Materialist Dialectic of Marx.

Long before she became a Marxist scholar, Liubo Isaakovna Akselrod was a political Marxist. As an activist from 1884, 33 years before the Russian Revolution, her insurrectionist activities led to her exile from Russia in 1887 after Alexander III was attacked. Akselrod went to France and then Switzerland, where she completed her Ph.D. on Leo Tolstoy at the University of Berne. In 1906, an amnesty was reached, and she returned to Russia. Generally considered to have been involved in the Russian Revolution of 1917, Akselrod belonged to the Social Democratic Party until 1918, but she is better known for her academic Marxism. Although her Ph.D. was in literature, and she was known as a literary critic, she is particularly noted for her work in Marxist philosophy.

Considered an orthodox Marxist—not someone seeking to revamp Marx's work but to understand and apply his thinking—Akselrod

was given a teaching position at the Institute of Red Professors after the Revolution. A professorship at the University of Sverdlov followed, where she gained a reputation for her position that existence is independent of consciousness. Within orthodox Marxism, this placed her—with her teacher Georgi Plekhanov—among the mechanists who advocated an understanding of reality much like that of Immanuel Kant. They argued that materialism must be explained scientifically, rather than in terms of consciousness (so de-emphasizing the influence of Hegel on Marx). This placed them in opposition to the Deborinists, who believed different types of matter have different essences. Despite her position in this debate, Akselrod took pains to emphasize that a Kantian epistemology, or theory of knowledge, is not part of Marxism. She argued that Marxism is an independent philosophy that provides its own epistemology based on history, thus contrasting with the metaphysical foundations (a characterization of reality) in Kant's system.

SOURCES:

Wetter, Gustav. *Dialectical Materialism; a Historical and Systematic Survey of Philosophy in the Soviet Union.* Translated from the German by Peter Heath. London: John M. Watkins, 1926.

Catherine Hundleby, M.A. Philosophy, University of Guelph, Guelph, Ontario, Canada

Akte, Claudia (fl. 55–69 CE).

See Acte.

al-.

For Arabic names that begin with al-, see the second component (e.g., al-Khaizaran. See Khaizaran).

Alacoque, Marguerite Marie (1647–1690)

French nun. Pronunciation: ah-lah-COKE. Born in Lauthecour, Saône-et-Loire, in central France, on July 22, 1647; died at Paray-le-Monial, France, on October 17, 1690.

Marguerite Marie Alacoque attributed a recovery from paralysis to the intercession of the Virgin Mary and entered the convent at Paray. Her visions of Christ provided the origin of the Catholic practice of worshipping the Sacred Heart of Jesus. She was beatified in 1864 and canonized in 1920 by Benedict XV; her feast day is celebrated on October 17.

Alacseal, Virgili (1869–1966).

See Albert, Caterina.

Alain, Marie-Claire (1926—)

French organist. Born in St. Germain-en-Laye, France, on August 10, 1926; daughter of Albert Alain (an organist); her brother Jehan Alain (1911–1940), the composer and organist, was killed in World War II; student of Durflé, DuPré, and Plé-Caussade; won the Bach Prize of the Amis de l'Orgue (1951).

The organ was the center of existence to the Alain family. Marie-Claire Alain's father was an organist as was her brother, Jehan. At age 18, Alain entered the Paris Conservatoire where she studied with Durflé, Dupré, and Plé-Caussade. She won an organ prize at the Geneva International Competition in 1950 and gave her first recital at St. Merri in Paris that same year. The following year, she won the Bach Prize of the Amis de l'Orgue in Paris. She then spent two years studying with Litaize. Marie-Claire Alain was especially interested in 17th- and 18th-century music and in reproducing its sound. When recording or playing, she sought out organs from the era of the composer: Schnitger or Marcussen organs when she performed Bach, Clicquot, Gonzalez or Haerpfer; Erman organs for Couperin and De Grigny. In addition, she performed the complete works of her brother, Jehan, who was killed in World War II. A scholar as well as a concertizer and composer, Alain wrote many articles about the organ.

Alais.

Variant of Alice.

Alais (fl. 12th c.)

French troubadour.

Unfortunately, almost nothing is known about Alais, one of the few female troubadours of southern France. Her only known work is a poem composed with two other women. Alais and her co-authors, **Iselda** and **Carenza**, were opposed to the idea of marriage and refer in their poem to the anguish of being someone's wife and to their distaste for the idea of bearing children. The overall message of the work is that becoming a nun is infinitely preferable to marriage.

Alais of France (1160–?)

*Princess of France. Name variations: Alix or Alice. Born on October 4, 1160; death date unknown; daughter of *Constance of Castile (d. 1160) and Louis VII, king of France (r. 1137–1180); half sister of Philip II Augustus (1165–1223), king of France; be-trothed to Richard the Lionheart; possibly married William II of Ponthieu, count of Ponthieu, around 1195; children: possibly *Joanna of Ponthieu, countess of Aumale (d. 1251).*

Alais was a French princess, the daughter of King Louis VII and his second wife, *Constance of Castile**. In an arrangement made to secure peace between her family and the family of Louis' first wife, *Eleanor of Aquitaine**, and her new husband, England's King Henry II, Alais was betrothed to Eleanor and Henry's son Richard the Lionheart and sent to the English royal court for her upbringing. Despite the marriage arrangement, Louis still held a grudge against Eleanor for divorcing him, and he agreed to the betrothal only on condition that Eleanor not be allowed to supervise Alais' upbringing.

Unfortunately for Alais, the serious conflicts that arose between the English princes and their father Henry kept her marriage from occurring as planned. There was a popular rumor that Alais became the mistress of Henry, although this is not fully substantiated. One chronicler even wrote that Henry planned to have his marriage to Eleanor annulled and then marry Alais himself. At any rate, Richard refused to marry the French princess after he succeeded Henry in 1189, supposedly because she was not chaste, but possibly because she was his estranged father's choice; he later married *Berengaria of Navarre**.

After Henry's death Alais became the virtual prisoner of Eleanor and Richard, as the new king and his mother did not want to lose her dower lands of the county of Berry by returning her to the French king. They installed her at the fortress of Rouen under guard. At age 33, Alais was released as part of a truce in the war that had erupted between Richard and Philip II Augustus, Alais' younger half brother and now king of France. After a 24-year absence, she returned to Paris. With few options open to her, Alais might have entered a convent, but Philip arranged a marriage for her in 1195 to one of his supporters, Count William of Ponthieu. Little is known of her life after this.

Laura York, Anza, California

Alarie, Pierrette (1921—)

French-Canadian soprano. Born Marguerite Alarie in Montreal, Canada, on November 9, 1921; daughter of Sylva (a choirmaster) and Amanda Alarie (a soprano and actress); studied with Jeanne Maubourg, Salvator Issaurel, and Albert Roberval; married Léopold Simoneau, in 1946.

Won the Metropolitan Opera Auditions of the Air (1945); made her Metropolitan debut (1945); appeared on opera stages in San Francisco, Philadelphia, New Orleans, and Vancouver.

Pierrette Alarie was born into a musical family. Her father was the Montreal choirmaster and assistant conductor of the Société canadienne d'opérette and her mother **Amanda Alarie** was a soprano and actress. Following in their footsteps, Alarie made her first appearance on the radio at age 14. She studied voice with Salvator Issaurel from 1938–43 when she met Léopold Simoneau whom she married in 1946. From 1943–46, Alarie had studied with ***Elisabeth Schumann** at the Curtis Institute in Philadelphia while she was on scholarship. After winning the Metropolitan Opera Auditions of the Air in 1945, she made her debut at the Met. In 1949, she and her husband were engaged by the Paris Opera and the Opéra Comique for three years. Alarie appeared in opera houses throughout Europe and concertized widely in North America. In 1961, her recording of Mozart arias made with her husband won the Grand Prix du disque of the Académie Charles-Cros. Alarie appeared in a number of opera productions made for television. During the 1960s, she began teaching at the École Vincent d'Indy. In 1959, she and Simoneau were awarded the Prix de musique Calixa-Lavallée, and in 1967 Pierrette Alarie was made an Officer of the Order of Canada.

John Haag, Associate Professor of History, University of Georgia, Athens, Georgia

Albanese, Licia (1913—)

Italian soprano. Born on July 22, 1913, in Bari, Italy; studied with Emanuel De Rosa in Bari and Giuseppina Baldassare-Tedeschi in Milan; married Joseph Gimma (an Italian-American businessman), in 1945.

Debuted at the Teatro Lirico in Milan (1934); debuted at the Metropolitan Opera (1940); final Metropolitan Opera performance (1966); received the Lady Grand Cross of the Equestrian Order of the Holy Sepulchre from Pope Pius XII.

Licia Albanese was born the fifth of seven children into a close-knit Italian family on July 22, 1913. All members of her family had excellent voices, and Licia was no exception. She began to study singing in her teens, flourishing under the tutelage of **Giuseppina Baldassare-Tedeschi** in Milan. At 22, Albanese won the first Italian government-sponsored vocal competition in a field of 300 entrants.

In the first five years of her career, Albanese sang at Teatro alla Scala, Covent Garden, and the Rome Opera. In 1939, when Benito Mussolini would no longer let distinguished Italian artists leave the country, Albanese managed to escape to Portugal and board a ship bound for the United States. During her debut at the Metropolitan Opera on February 9, 1940, as Cio-Cio-San, she established a special rapport with the audience, and it is said that no singer was ever more believed by the Italian-American opera audience. She performed there until 1966. Though Albanese's voice was bright, penetrating, and emotionally charged, it was not large enough to fill a huge theater as have some historically great voices. Rather, it was her artistry that made Albanese a great favorite with audiences. After her retirement, she worked for the Puccini Foundation, founded by her husband, to further the survival of opera as an art form. In 1995, Albanese was awarded the President's Medal by Bill Clinton for her work in the arts.

John Haag, Associate Professor of History, University of Georgia, Athens, Georgia

Licia Albanese

Albanesi, Meggie (1899–1923)

*English actress. Born in Kent, England, on October 8, 1899; died on December 9, 1923; daughter of an Italian violin teacher at the Royal Academy of Music and **Maria Albanesi** (a novelist); studied piano, attended Royal Academy of Dramatic Art (RADA), and trained under Helen Hayes; winner of the Bancroft Medal.*

Meggie Albanesi made her stage debut as an understudy in *Dear Brutus*. Discovered by Basil Dean, she was then given the lead role of Jill in *The Skin Game*, followed by a triumphant opening night in ***Clemence Dane**'s *A Bill of Divorcement* in 1921. Six years later, while in rehearsal for *A Magdalen's Husband*, Albanesi collapsed. She died of a severe hemorrhage a few days later, age 25, in a Broadstairs nursing home. Whereas her mother attributed her death to peritonitis caused by overwork, she was more commonly thought to have died from a botched abortion.

Wrote John Galsworthy: "She had real devotion to her art, great quickness to seize shades of meaning, and a brain which she did not hesitate to use. She was not limited. She would have gone very far. Not often does Death so wastefully spill."

SOURCES:
Morley, Sheridan. *The Great Stage Stars.* London: Angus & Robertson, 1986.

Albani, Emma (c. 1847–1930)

French-Canadian soprano and first Canadian artist to achieve international fame. Born Marie Louise Cécile Lajeunesse in Chambly near Montreal, Canada, on September 27 or November 1, probably in 1847; died in London, England, on April 3, 1930; eldest daughter of Joseph Lajeunesse and Mélinda Mignault; studied with Gilbert-Louis Duprez and François Benoist; married Ernest Gye, in 1878; children: one son, Frederick Ernest (b. 1879).

Sang for the Prince of Wales (1860); debuted in Milan (1870), Covent Garden (1872), and at the New York Academy of Music (1876); sang Elisabeth at the London premiere of Tannhäuser; *sang the leading role in Franz Liszt's oratorio* The Legend of Saint Elisabeth *in his presence (1886); debuted at the Metropolitan Opera (1891); retired from the opera (1894); received the Royal Philharmonic Society's gold medal known as the Beethoven Medal (1897); continued concertizing in North America, Europe, India, South Africa, Australia, and New Zealand; sang at a private family funeral service for Queen Victoria (1901) at Windsor Castle; made last public appearance at Royal Albert Hall (1911); made Dame Commander of the British Empire (1925).*

Born Marie Louise Lajeunesse, Emma Albani was the first Canadian-born artist to achieve international fame. She belonged to the seventh generation of the musical Lajeunesse family, who had been among the first to settle Canada. Albani began studying piano with her mother at age four, and a year later she was studying harp, piano, and singing with her father. From 1852 until the death of Emma's mother in 1856, the family lived in Plattsburgh, New York; they then moved to Montreal. There, Albani was a student at Sacré Coeur Convent in Montreal where her father taught music. A talented young singer, she was asked to perform for the prince of Wales during his visit to Canada. Though Emma's father wanted to send her for further study in Europe, he did not have the means. Thus, after graduation in 1865, she was engaged as a soloist at St. Joseph's Catholic Church in Albany. Three years later, in 1868, the congregation raised funds to send her to Europe where she studied with Gilbert-Louis Duprez and François Benoist in Paris.

She first appeared as Emma Albani on stage in Milan in 1870, and not long after at Covent Garden where she was to remain a perennial favorite. Albani enjoyed triumphs in Florence, St. Petersburg, and Moscow before returning to Covent Garden in 1874. She sang Elsa in the English premiere of *Lohengrin* and the following year was Elisabeth in the London premiere of *Tannhäuser.* In 1877, as her popularity continued to grow, she performed before an audience of 20,000 at the Crystal Palace. Albani met Ernest Gye, who had just taken over the management of Covent Garden, in 1872 and married him on August 6, 1878. A son, Frederick Ernest, was born on June 4, 1879. When Albani finally returned to Montreal in 1883, a delirious crowd of 10,000 admirers turned out to greet her. In 1886, she performed for Franz Liszt in his oratorio, *The Legend of Saint Elizabeth.* She appeared at the Metropolitan in 1891. Albani always returned to Covent Garden. Describing a performance of *Tristan and Isolde,* Herbert Klein wrote in 1896: "Never before at Covent Garden has the wondrous beauty of this scène d'amour been so totally realized." She was asked to sing at Windsor Castle at a private family funeral for Queen *Victoria in 1901. An operatic superstar, Albani was awarded the Royal Philharmonic's gold medal in 1897. She retired in 1911 after a farewell performance at London's Royal Albert Hall.

Her last years were not easy due to financial difficulties after her husband's death in 1925. A grand benefit concert was arranged at Covent Garden on May 25 of that year, and the proceeds allowed her to live in relative comfort until her death in 1930. In 1925, she was made a Dame Commander of the British Empire. A street was named for her in Montreal and a plaque marks her birthplace in Chambly. In 1980, a postage stamp was issued in Canada to commemorate the 50th anniversary of her death. Much beloved in her lifetime, Emma Albani is remembered as one of opera's finest performers.

SUGGESTED READING:
MacDonald, Cheryl. *Emma Albani: Victorian Diva.* Toronto: Dundurn Press, 1984.

John Haag, Associate Professor of History, University of Georgia, Athens, Georgia

Albany, countess of.

See Louise of Stolberg-Gedern (1752–1824).

Albany, duchess of.

See Keith, Muriel (d. 1449).
See Isabel, Countess of Lennox (d. 1457?).
See Anne de la Tour (d. 1512).
See Anne de la Tour (c. 1496–1524).
See Frederica of Prussia (1767–1820).
See Helen of Waldeck & Pyrmont (1861–1922).
See Victoria Adelaide of Schleswig-Holstein (1885–1970).

Alberghetti, Anna Maria (1936—)

Italian singer and actress. Born on May 15, 1936, in Pesaro, Italy; eldest of three children of Daniele (a cellist) and Vittoria Alberghetti (a pianist); married Claudio Guzman (a producer-director; now divorced); children: Alexander and Pilar.

As a child, Anna Maria Alberghetti sang for candy from American troops who were marching through Italy in 1944. At age 12, she made her first European concert tour. Two years later, she made her U.S. debut at Carnegie Hall (1950). "When it was over, the audience stood up and cheered," wrote *Time*, "famous singers stepped forward to congratulate her, and surprised music critics for the Manhattan press dashed off to write enthusiastic pieces for the morning papers."

That same year, she made her film debut as Monica in Gian-Carlo Menotti's opera *The Medium*. Groomed by Paramount for parts once played by *Deanna Durbin, Alberghetti gave a "standout" rendition of the "Caro Nome" aria from *Rigoletto* in *Here Comes the Groom* (1951), which featured Bing Crosby. Her other films include *The Stars Are Singing* (with *Rosemary Clooney, 1953), *The Last Command* (1955), *10,000 Bedrooms* (1957), *Duel at Apache Wells* (1957), and *Cinderfella* (1960). After starring on Broadway in the musical *Carnival*, for which she won a Tony Award, Alberghetti retired in 1961.

Albers, Anni (1899–1994)

German-born textile and graphic artist, who taught in the United States. Born Anni Farman on June 12, 1899, in Berlin-Charlottenburg, Germany; died in 1994 (some sources cite 1993); daughter of S. and T. (Ullstein) Farman; student at Bauhaus in Weimar and Dessau, Bauhaus diploma 1922–30; married artist and teacher Josef Albers, in 1925.

Hired as assistant professor of art, Black Mountain College, North Carolina, (1933–49); awarded

Anna Maria Alberghetti

Medal of American Institute of Architects in the Field of Craftsmanship (1961); awarded citation by the Philadelphia Museum College of Art (1962).

Anni Albers first made her artistic reputation as a weaver during the Bauhaus days at the famous design school founded by Walter Gropius in Weimar Germany in 1919. It was the Bauhaus approach she had in mind when she wrote, "The more we avoid standing in the way of the material and in the way of tools and machines, the better chance there is that our work will not be dated, will not bear the stamp of too limited a period." An art teacher at the time, she had little idea of the materials and tools she was yet to master.

The Bauhaus design school was formed amid the economic and political chaos pervasive in Germany at the end of World War I. In his four-page prospectus, Gropius proposed to break down the "arrogant barrier between craftsman and artist" in order to achieve a new unity of industry and art and crafts, while conceiving and creating the "new building of the future."

Anni Albers

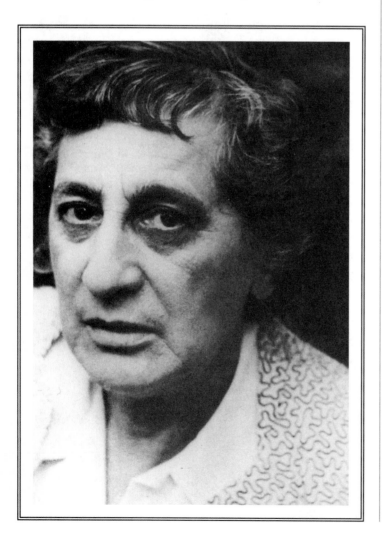

As a 23-year-old student entering the Bauhaus in 1922, Albers found gender barriers little changed when school authorities steered women toward weaving, because textiles were considered to be "women's work." Uninspired by wallpainting or work in metal, wood, or glass, Albers reluctantly settled on weaving to fulfill her requirement for a workshop. Her teacher was the great contemporary artist Paul Klee, nicknamed "the heavenly father," and, under his guidance, working with threads caught the imagination of Albers and a number of other women, including **Gunta Stölzl**, **Benita Otte**, and **Marli Ehrman**. With their designs ranging from the severely geometrical to riotously colorful and free, the women turned the Bauhaus weaving workshops into an innovative laboratory that set standards for textile production worldwide.

Fascinated with the possibilities of the straight line and abstraction in her chosen medium, Anni Albers became a leader in abstract textile design. For the next 16 years, she concentrated on "a weaver's concern with threads as an artistic vehicle." Believing that "there is no medium that cannot serve art," she experimented with the uses of textiles in industry, and bridled against the distinction generally made between works done in thread, and thus accepted only as craft (with a few notable exceptions, including the great tapestries of the Middle Ages and the Renaissance), and works on paper, which found much easier acceptance as art.

In 1933, when the Nazis were taking political control of Germany, they closed the Bauhaus school for its support of "cultural bolshevism." Albers, along with her artist-husband Josef, joined others from the school in moving to the United States to continue to work. Gropius went to Harvard, Mies van der Rohe became head of the architectural school at the Illinois Institute of Technology, and Laszlo Moholy-Nagy founded the New Bauhaus in Chicago. Albers joined her husband in teaching art at Black Mountain College in North Carolina, where she became an assistant professor; four years later, in 1937, she became a naturalized U.S. citizen. In 1950, the couple moved to New Haven, Connecticut, where Josef was appointed chair of the department of design at Yale, and Anni freelanced.

In the 1960s, when Josef was invited to work at the Tamarind Lithography Workshop in Los Angeles, California, Anni tagged along at first as a self-described "useless wife," until workshop director **June Wayne** encouraged her to try printmaking. In lithography, Albers noted, the "image of threads could project a freedom I had never suspected," as she learned to make drawings on paper, then transfer them to stones or zinc plates in order to produce a succession of prints. The duplication of lithographic images opened a more accessible path for the presentation of her creative ideas and gained her a wider audience, giving the artist "the longed-for pat on the shoulder" she freely acknowledged.

In 1964, when Tamarind published an edition of Albers' first lithographs and she was offered a fellowship to return the following year, the artist was hooked on her new process. Returning to New Haven, where she found no suitable workshops for lithographic reproduction, she transformed her enthusiasm into the similar working mode of silkscreen printing; from then on, graphic techniques, particularly screenprinting, remained her medium of choice.

SOURCES:

Albers, Anni. *On Designing*. New Haven, CT: Pellango Press, 1959.
———. *On Weaving*. Middletown, CT: Wesleyan University Press, 1965.
———. *Pre-Columbian Mexican Miniatures*. NY: Praeger, 1970.
Baro, Gene. *Anni Albers*. The Brooklyn Museum, 1977.
Welliver, Neil. "A Conversation with Anni Albers," in *Craft Horizon*. July-August 1965.
Weltge, Sigrid Wortmann. *Textile Art from the Bauhaus*. Chronicle, 1993.

COLLECTIONS—PICTORIAL WEAVINGS:

The Art Institute of Chicago; Baltimore Museum of Art; Bauhaus-Archiv, Berlin, Germany; Busch-Reisinger Museum, Cambridge, Mass.; Cranbrook Academy of Art, Bloomfield Hills, Michigan; Currier Gallery of Art, Manchester, New Hampshire; Jewish Museum, New York.

COLLECTIONS—GRAPHIC WORK:

Art Gallery of Ontario, Toronto, Ontario; Brooklyn Museum, Brooklyn, New York; Busch-Reisinger Museum; Fort Worth Art Museum; Israel Museum, Jerusalem; Kunstmuseum der Stadt Düsseldorf; Metropolitan Museum of Art, New York; Museum of Modern Art, New York; New York Public Library; St. Louis Art Museum; Seattle Art Museum; University of California, Los Angeles; Wadsworth Atheneum, Hartford, Connecticut; Westfälisches Landesmuseum für Kunst und Kulturgeschichte, Münster, Germany; Yale University Art Gallery, New Haven, Connecticut.

Albert, Caterina (1869–1966)

Catalonian author. Name variations: Catarina; Víctor Català; Virgili Alacseal. Born Caterina Albert i Paradís on September 11, 1869, in L'Escala, Spain, on the Costa Brava; died in L'Escala in 1966; daughter of Lluis Albert i Paradeda and Dolors Paradís i Farrés. Selected works: Solitud *(1905);* Caires vius *(1907).*

Growing up in the village of L'Escala, Caterina Albert rarely attended school. Instead, she studied mostly with her maternal grandmother, **Caterina Farrés i Sureda**, with whom her family lived. In 1890, Albert's father died; in 1899, her grandmother Caterina died. From this point forward, the family lived intermittently in Barcelona until they took up permanent residence there in 1904.

Albert had interests in both writing and art, but her poetry and theatrical pieces were the most cultivated. She adopted the pseudonym Virgili Alacseal and in 1898 won the Jocs Florals Prize for her first monologue, "La Infanticida" (The Infanticide). In 1901, she assumed the identity of Víctor Català, the name of a main male character in a novel she was writing. Though the novel was never completed, in 1901, as Català, she published three more dramatic pieces and a collection of poetry, *El cant dels messos* (*Song of the Months*), all of which won critical praise (though none of the dramas were actually performed until 1967).

As Català, Albert wrote of stark subjects with a masculine voice. She corresponded with admirers and critics as Català and was praised as one of the leading male writers of Catalan. Not until 1902, following publication of her second volume of poetry, did she reveal her true gender in correspondence with the male critic Joan Maragall. Though Maragall received the revelation well and admired her talents, not everyone was so generous. By and large, Albert was chided for her unladylike subject matter. Subsequent works nevertheless retained their earlier tone. Beginning in 1905, Albert's first novel, *Solitud* (*Solitude*), was serialized in 46 segments by the journal *Joventut*. Her talent for the visual arts was not recognized until 1955 with the publication of a book showing her drawings, paintings and sculpture.

Considered the greatest Catalonian woman writer, Albert was so private that in interviews she was unwilling to reveal even her favorite authors. Therefore, little of her adult life—except that of her male personas as depicted in correspondences—is known. After the Spanish Civil War, Albert returned to her home in L'Escala where she lived until her death in 1966.

Crista Martin, Boston, Massachusetts

Albert, Octavia V.R. (1853–c. 1899)

African-American historian. Born Octavia Victoria Rogers in Oglethorpe, Georgia, on December 24, 1853; died around 1899, in Houma, Louisiana; stud-

ied at Atlanta University; married Reverend A.E.P. Albert, in 1874; children: Laura T.F. Albert.

Selected works: The House of Bondage: or Charlotte Brooks and Other Slaves *(1891).*

Octavia Albert was born into slavery but was emancipated at the end of the Civil War. Devoutly African Methodist Episcopal, she attended school in Oglethorpe, Georgia, before attending Atlanta University, where she studied education. She then took a teaching post in Montezuma, Georgia. There she worked with A.E.P. Albert, whom she married on October 21, 1874. The Alberts moved to Houma, Louisiana, and in 1877 A.E.P. was ordained a minister in the Methodist Episcopal church. In 1888, Octavia was converted to her husband's church and baptized by him.

Their home in Louisiana became a gathering place for former slaves. Albert was known to feed, house, read to, and teach anyone who needed her assistance. In the process, she gathered oral histories of those men, women, and children who passed through her home and told her stories of slavery and freedom. Albert's intentions were twofold: she hoped to create a history of slavery and post-abolition that would accurately represent African-American experiences; and she believed that Christians—hearing and recognizing the mistreatment of blacks—would prevent it from happening again. Albert's preface to the small book of personal stories caused some concern because she had addressed an audience that she did not perceive as exclusively black women. Instead, the book was intended for readers regardless of gender or race, a hitherto unheard of concept. It is perhaps for this reason that the book was not published until 1891.

SOURCES:
Albert, Octavia V.R. *The House of Bondage: or Charlotte Brooks and Other Slaves.* NY: Oxford University Press, 1988.

Alberta Five.

See individual entries on Henrietta Muir Edwards, Nellie McClung, Louise McKinney, Emily Murphy, and Irene Parlby.

Albertina Agnes (d. 1696)

*Princess of Orange. Name variations: Albertina Orange-Nassau. Born Albertina Agnes; died in 1696; daughter of Frederick Henry, prince of Orange (r. 1625–1647), and *Amelia of Solms (1602–1675); married William Frederick of Nassau-Dietz (died 1664); children: Henry Casimir (1657–1696), cousin*

of King William III).

Albertina of Baden-Durlach
(1682–1755)

*Duchess of Holstein-Gottorp. Born on July 3, 1682; died on December 22, 1755; daughter of *Augusta Maria of Holstein-Gottorp (1649–1728) and Frederick VII, margrave of Baden-Durlach; married Christian Augustus, duke of Holstein-Gottorp, on September 3, 1704; children: 12, including Sofie, abbess of Herford (1705–1764); Karl (b. 1706); Anna (1709–1758, who married Wilhelm of Saxe-Gotha); Adolphus Frederick (1710–1771), king of Sweden; *Johanna Elizabeth of Holstein-Gottorp (1712–1760, mother of *Catherine II the Great); Friederike (1713–1713); Wilhelm Christian (b. 1716); Friedrich Konrad (b. 1718); George (b. 1719).*

Albia Domnica

Byzantine empress. Married Valens, Byzantine and Roman emperor (r. 364–378).

Albin-Guillot, Laure (c. 1880–1962)

French photographer, specializing in portraits, nudes, and photomicrography. Born around 1880, presumably in France; died in Nogent-sur-Marne, France, in 1962; married Albin Guillot (a scientific researcher), in 1901.

Head of Photography, Archives Service Beaux-Arts, Paris (1932); president of French Société Artistes Photographes (1935).

In addition to gaining recognition for her soft-focus portraits and nude studies, Laure Albin-Guillot and her husband, scientific researcher Albin Guillot, spent 30 years amassing a collection of micrographic specimens, including crystallizations, plant cells, and animal organisms. Continuing their research after his death in 1931 as a tribute to her husband, Albin-Guillot created a book of photogravures of 20 photomicrographs, some on colored metallic papers. The book, *Micrographic décorative,* was published in 1931, in an edition of 305 copies. She also wrote articles on photomicrography.

Albin-Guillot was at the center of Parisian photographic circles during the 1920s and '30s, with her portraits and nude studies frequently appearing in magazines. In 1922, she received a gold medal in a contest sponsored by *La Revue française de photographic.* In 1925, she had a solo exhibition in Paris, which included 40 prints. She also provided illustrations for two books: Paul Valéry's *Le Narcisse* in 1936, and Pierre Louÿs' *Douze Chansons de Bilitis* in 1937.

Alboni, Marietta (1823–1894)

Italian contralto. Name variations: Contessa Pepoli. Born Maria Anna Marzia on March 6, 1823, in Città di Castello, Italy; died on June 23, 1894, in Ville d'Avray, France; married Count Pepoli (died 1867), in 1853; married Charles Ziéger, in 1877; studied with Mombelli in Bologna and with Rossini (1841).

Debuted in Bologna (1842) and at the Teatro alla Scala; performed in Russia, Germany, Great Britain, France, and the United States.

Marietta Alboni was born in Città di Castello, Italy, on March 6, 1823. At age 19, she appeared in performances of Rossini's *Stabat Mater* in Parma after studying with the composer that same year. Rossini regarded Alboni as his protégé and helped arrange her debut at the Teatro Communale in Bologna in 1842 as well as her first appearance at the Teatro alla Scala, where she appeared in his *Siege of Corinth*. Starting her career at the top, she remained one of the 19th century's outstanding contralto voices and appeared widely in Italy until her performance in Turin in 1851, which proved to be her last in Italy.

In 1844–45, Alboni sang in St. Petersburg and then went to Vienna, Prague, Paris, and London. Covent Garden became a permanent opera house after she made her first appearance there in 1847 and was a first-night sensation. "A greater sensation," wrote Hogarth, "probably was never produced by a debutante." She sang in 10 of 17 operas performed in Covent Garden's first season. During 1852–53, Alboni appeared in North America.

The great music critic Henry Chorley described her sound as a rich, deep contralto "as sweet as honey . . . and with that tremulous quality which reminds fanciful speculators of the quiver in the air of the calm, blazing summer's noon." She sang soprano roles such as Amina in *La sonnambula* and Zerlina in *Don Giovanni* and was constantly developing new repertory, which she felt eventually damaged her voice. Still, those who heard her in concert after she left the opera stage thought her voice as "fresh, rich, and powerful as that of a woman half her age"; she did not, however, return to the international opera houses in which she had become so well-known.

SUGGESTED READING:
Pougin, A. *Marietta Alboni*. Paris, 1912.

John Haag, Associate Professor of History, University of Georgia, Athens, Georgia

Albrecht, Bertie
(d. 1943).

See Aubrac, Lucie for sidebar.

Albrecht, Sophie
(1757–1840)

German actress and author. Born Sophie Bäumer in Erfurt, Germany, in 1757; died in 1840; daughter of a professor of medicine who died when she was 15; married J.F.E. Albrecht (a doctor).

Sophie Albrecht's acting career flourished when her doctor husband turned to writing and managing theater productions. On tour with him, she became a successful figure on the German stage. During her late 20s, she also produced three volumes of fiction, drama and verse.

Crista Martin, Boston, Massachusetts

Albret, Jeanne III d' (1528–1572).

See Jeanne d'Albret.

Albright, Tenley (1935—)

American figure skater and surgeon, five-time winner of U.S. women's championship, and first American to win an Olympic gold medal in figure skating. Name variations: "Dr. Tenley." Born Tenley Emma Albright on July 18, 1935, in Newton Center, Massachusetts; daughter of Hollis L. (a surgeon) and Elin Peterson (a housewife) Albright; graduated from Radcliffe College, 1957, and Harvard Medical School, M.D., 1961; married Tudor Gardiner, in 1962 (divorced); married Gerald W. Blakeley; children: (first marriage) three daughters, Lilla Rhys Gardiner; Erin Albright Gardiner; Elee Emma Gardiner.

Earned regional championship figure-skating title for age 12 and under (1947); winner of the U.S. Ladies Novice championship at age 13; winner of the U.S. Ladies Junior title at 14, and the U.S. Ladies Senior title at 16; winner of the U.S. National figure-skating championships five times (1952–56); first

Marietta Alboni

Tenley
Albright

American woman to win the World amateur women's free-skating title (1953); first American to capture an Olympic gold medal in figure skating (1956); first woman to be named to the U.S. Olympic Committee (1976); first woman to be admitted to the Harvard University Hall of Fame (1974); also admitted to U.S. Figure Skating Hall of Fame (1976) and Olympic Hall of Fame (1988).

On July 18, 1935, Tenley Emma Albright was born into a well-to-do family in Newton Center, Massachusetts, just outside Boston. Her father was Hollis Albright, a prominent surgeon, and her mother was **Elin Peterson Albright** who scheduled the family's generally busy life. Tenley began skating the year she was eight and received her first pair of ice skates at Christmas; the following year, they were replaced by skates with the curved blades used in figure skating. Albright was so enthusiastic about the sport that her father flooded part of the backyard to create ice where she could practice. He also enrolled her at the Skating Club of Boston where she caught the eye of a well-known coach, *Maribel Vinson Owen, the 1932 Olympic singles bronze medalist. At first, Tenley preferred free-skating to mastering the 68 figures basic to figure skating. But after Owen explained that the figures counted for 60% of competition scores, Albright applied herself to performing them with precision. She would later admit that she found them fascinating.

Tenley Albright was 11 when she contracted polio in September 1946. Fortunately, it was a mild case of the virus, and she was out of the hospital in three weeks, but her leg and back muscles were left weakened. At the encouragement of her father and other doctors, she returned to the ice to regain her strength, and the following year, in 1947, she attended the Eastern figure-skating championships in Philadelphia. There, she won the title for girls 12 and under—the first of many championships.

Her life was disciplined. Motivated to become a surgeon like her father, she was an excellent student at Manter Hall School in nearby Cambridge, rising each morning at 4 AM to practice skating at an indoor rink. "I had to listen to my music over and over while working out my routines," she said. "I couldn't do that with other skaters present, all wanting to play their music, or at least getting very sick of mine." After three or four hours on the ice, she went home to breakfast and then to school. In summer, she traveled to Lake Placid, New York, Denver, Colorado, and California for more skating practice at rinks.

As Albright continued competitive skating, her expenses continued to escalate, rising from $400–$500 a year to $4,000–$5,000 (an enormous sum for the period) and finally to $30,000 as she neared the Olympic level. Fortunate to have well-to-do parents who could meet such expenses, Albright wanted their investment to pay off. At the Oslo Olympics in 1952, she placed second behind ⚘➤ Jeanette Altwegg of Great Britain in the Winter Games. In 1953, Albright became the first American woman to win the World amateur women's figure-skating championship title, in Davos, Switzerland. From 1952–56, she won the U.S. National figure-skating title five times. In 1956, age 21 and recognized as one of the best skaters in the world, she began to prepare for the next Olympics. Albright was intent on being the first American woman to capture a gold medal in women's figure skating.

In the meantime, she had become an undergraduate student at Radcliffe College, carrying the academic schedule typical of students in premed. Studying physics and chemistry as well as preparing for the Olympics, she still rose early every morning to skate and averaged seven hours a day on the ice. The little blue Porsche given to her by her father was used mostly for ferrying herself between classes and the skating rink. Following her father's example, she never touched coffee or tea, much less alcohol or cigarettes.

For many years, Albright's main competitor had been *Carol Heiss, who would win the U.S. Nationals from 1957–60. In contrast to Albright's poised and fluid, classical style, Heiss was a fiery whirling figure who skated with complete abandon. The media reported a rivalry that the two women never considered personal; they regarded each other instead as worthy opponents, accepting the fact that only a few points separated them in any competition. Two

---

⚘➤ **Altwegg, Jeanette**

English figure skater. Won the World Championship (1951); won the Olympic gold medal in figure skating (1952) and the bronze (1948).

Jeanette Altwegg beat out *Tenley Albright for the gold medal at the Oslo Games in 1952. Four years earlier, Altwegg came in third behind gold medalist *Barbara Ann Scott of Canada. Foregoing the Ice Capades route, Altwegg retired immediately after the 1952 Games to work at the Pestalozzi Children's Village in Trogen, Switzerland.

weeks before the Olympics, it looked as if Albright's chances for a medal might be shattered when she struck a hole in the ice during practice and fell, cutting a gash in her right leg with the sharp edge of her left skate. Albright, however, was soon back on the ice.

At the beginning of the 1956 Olympic competition in Cortina D'Ampezzo, Italy, Albright beat Heiss by a slim margin in the school figures and free-figure trials. Despite her recent injury, Tenley was in top form for the final competition, performing a spectacular mazurka, witches' jump followed by a drag, and an Axel Paulsen jump. She became the first American woman figure skater to win the gold medal. Heiss took the silver; **Ingrid Wendl** of Austria took the bronze. On March 4, a crowd of 50,000 turned out to greet the champion on her return to Newton, Massachusetts.

But the fierce Heiss-Albright rivalry continued. Three weeks later, while competing in the World Championship in Garmisch-Partenkirchen, West Germany, Albright lost to Carol Heiss by a few points. In the next U.S. National competition in Philadelphia, it was Albright's turn to defeat Heiss by the same slim margin. Afterward, the two young women posed arm-in-arm for the cameras. Albright told reporters, "I think we both know how the other feels."

With medicine in mind, but with many offers to turn professional as a skater, Albright decided to put the glamour of the sport behind her. She refused a $100,000 contract for an exhibition tour and the offer of a Cadillac if she would skate on occasion for General Motors. "I've wanted to be a doctor since I was a little girl," she said. "The skating offers were flattering. But the only thing that would have kept me from medicine would have been not getting into medical school." Since both her college record and medical-aptitude test scores were outstanding, she was accepted into Harvard Medical School after only three undergraduate years, one of six women admitted into a class of 140.

With the approach of the 1960 Olympics, Albright thought briefly of competing. When she asked for permission to leave school for a few weeks of training in Squaw Valley, she was told that she would have to lose a full year of medical studies. The cost too high, she no longer considered competitive skating. Albright did, however, continue to skate for pleasure.

Interested initially in pediatrics, Albright became fascinated with surgery. Few American hospitals accepted women as surgical residents at the time, and the male monopoly on the profession had not yet been broken in Boston, but she was attracted by its precision and concentration:

> There isn't any real exercise or practicing you do, apart from operating, except perhaps cutting with your left hand or tying knots. You begin by holding a retractor for five hours. My first operation I held a retractor, and I was so far back I couldn't even see the operating field. Then they let you sponge, and then they let you put in one skin stitch, and by the time they let you really do something you can't *wait* to get in there. Surgery, I think, is all of medicine, plus a little bit more, and I love the idea of being able to do something well technically. Like working on a jump and then doing it higher.

In 1962, when she was 26, Albright had completed medical school and begun her residency at Beverly Hospital, 17 miles outside Boston, when she married 43-year-old Tudor Gardiner, a classical philologist from a socially distinguished Boston family. The original wedding date had to be changed because Albright, a young resident, was on duty. She recalled:

> You know the honeymoon is supposed to be different from what your life will be like so we stayed home for two weeks. Then I was on duty at the hospital every other night and every other weekend. For six months I commuted, and for six months Tudor commuted, and then for six months we lived in Beverly, in four rooms in an abandoned pediatrics ward. Lilla had been born and I wanted to be able to look in on her during the day.

Through the birth of two more daughters, Tudor continued to cooperate with his wife's erratic schedule. Describing the dominance of her medical practice in the marriage, Albright recounted, "There was an emergency one night and I called Tudor and said, 'I won't be finished in time. Can you feed the baby?' I called later and asked, 'Did you give her her bottle?' and Tudor said, 'Yes. Now I am going to give her her cereal. If she doesn't eat it, I am going to.'"

It was no surprise when Albright entered general surgical practice with her father. One of the first women in surgery in the Boston area, she performed appendectomies, amputations, thyroidectomies, and complex gastrectomies, which involve partial removal of the stomach. Before reporting to the operating theater, she would wake her daughters, give them breakfast, and get them off to school, but the rigors of her practice were a strain on the marriage.

In 1964, Albright attended the Winter Olympics in Innsbruck, Austria, where she donated a silver cup for the best free-skating performance by a woman. That year, the women's title went to *Sjoukje Dijkstra of the Netherlands; Regine Heitzer of Austria won the silver, and Petra Burka of Canada took the bronze. American chances in figure skating had been shattered before the games even began. On February 15, 1961, 72 persons boarded a plane to attend the world figure-skating championships in Prague, Czechoslovakia, including 18 members of the U.S. figure-skating team, five coaches, and the team manager. When the jetliner crashed at Berg, near Brussels, Belgium, all the passengers were killed. Five of the skaters had participated in the 1960 Winter Games at Squaw Valley. They were *Laurence Owen in women's singles, and the pairs teams of *Maribel Owen and Dudley Richards and Ray and Ila Hadley. Another victim was Maribel Vinson Owen, mother of Laurence and Maribel, and coach of Tenley Albright.

While in Innsbruck, Albright also visited clinics for sports medicine and interviewed doctors from all over the world. After becoming a general surgeon at Boston's Deaconess Hospital, she showed increased interest in sports medicine and eventually founded Sports Medicine Resource, Inc., in Brookline, Massachusetts, an early attempt to focus on the specialized medical care of athletes. She also showed up three times a week at the Skating Club of Boston for short sessions on the ice.

Tenley Albright became the first woman officer on the U.S. Olympic Committee (1976), was named to the International Women's Sports Hall of Fame (1983), and organized a seminar on fitness for older Americans (1989). After a divorce from her first husband, Albright married Gerald W. Blakeley, a real-estate developer. In winter, "Dr. Tenley" (as she prefers to be called) continues to skate on a neighborhood pond or rink when her schedule allows. For her, the disciplines of skating and medicine have been closely linked. "You're always preparing for something," she said, "it really matters if you pay attention."

SOURCES:

Bingham, Walter. "Figure Skating," in *Sports Illustrated*. Vol. 67, no. 17. October 19, 1987, pp. 57–59.

Bock, Jean Libman. "Father-Daughter Surgical Team," in *Good Housekeeping*. Vol. 151, no. 3. September 1960.

Candee, Marjorie Dent, ed. *Current Biography Yearbook 1956*. NY: H.W. Wilson, 1956.

Dietz, Jean. "Senior Set: Rediscovering the Secret to Fitness," in *Boston Globe*. January 29, 1989, p. A13.

"Formula for Titles," in *Newsweek*. Vol. 41, no. 14. April 6, 1953, pp. 76–77.

Gross, Leonard. "Champion's Dawn," in *Collier's*. Vol. 137, no. 4. February 17, 1956, pp. 26–27.

Keerdoja, Eileen, and Jacob Young, *et al.* "Gold Medalists Still Skating Through Life," in *Newsweek*. Vol. 101, no. 5. January 31, 1983, pp. 10–12.

LaFontaine, Barbara. "There Is a Doctor on the Ice," in *Sports Illustrated*. Vol. 22, no. 6. February 8, 1965, pp. 28–30.

"Mothers and Daughters," in *Time*. Vol. 76, no. 13. March 26, 1956, p. 72.

"Victory Over Polio," in *Life*. Vol. 31, no. 9. March 2, 1953, pp. 78–80.

Karin Loewen Haag, freelance writer, Athens, Georgia

Albrizzi, Isabella Teotochi, Contessa d' (1770–1836)

Italian writer and patron of the arts. Pronunciation: ahl-BREET-tsee. Name variations: Isabella Teotochi-Albrizzi. Born on the Greek island of Corfu in 1770; died in Venice, Italy, on September 27, 1836; daughter of a Greek father and Venetian mother; married a Venetian at 16 (annulled); married a noble of Venice.

A Venetian patron of literature and art, Isabella Albrizzi was also an articulate memorialist. She authored a study of the works of Canova (*Descrizione delle opere di Canova*, 1821–25), wrote essays on celebrated contemporaries, which were published as *Ritratti* (*Portraits*), and completed a biography of *Vittoria Colonna (1836). Her home was a gathering place for the literati, including the dramatist Vittorio Alfieri, the writer Ugo Foscolo, and the poet Lord Byron who dubbed her "the Madame de Staël of Venice."

Alcantara, Dolores Jimenez (b. 1909)

Spanish Flamenco singer. Name variations: La Niña de Puebla. Born Dolores Jimenez Alcantara in La Puebla de Cazalla, near Seville, Spain.

Blinded during childhood, Dolores Alcantara took the name "La Niña de Puebla" ("Girl of the Town") and made her singing debut in 1931. Her specialty was fandangos and zambras.

Alcayaga, Lucila Godoy (1889–1957).
See Mistral, Gabriela.

Alcipe (1750–c. 1839).
See Alorna, Marquesa de.

Alcoforado, Mariana (1640–1723)

Portuguese nun whose love for Noël Bouton, the Marquis of Chamilly, reportedly led her to write five love letters, which gained fame as the Lettres portugaises (1669). Name variations: Mariana Alcoforada. Baptized in the Portuguese city of Beja on April 22, 1640; died on July 28, 1723; daughter of Francisco da Costa Alcoforado and Leonor Mendes.

Her paramour Noël Bouton de Chamilly born (April 6, 1636); her parents married (1637); Portugal rebelled against Spain (December 1, 1640); her brother Baltazar born (1645); Mariana placed in Our Lady of the Conception convent in Beja (1652); her stepmother died and Peregrina Maria joined her in convent (1663); Bouton arrived in Portugal (February 8, 1664); Bouton promoted to captain of cavalry by Count of Schomberg (April 30, 1664); Mariana met Bouton when his detachment quartered in and around Beja (mid-1666); Bouton departed for France (late 1667); Mariana allegedly wrote five letters to Bouton (December 1667 to June 1668); Claude Barbin published first edition of Lettres portugaises in Paris (January 4, 1669); Mariana lost election to serve as abbess of convent (July 30, 1709); Bouton died (January 6, 1715); French scholar Jean François Boissonade claimed Mariana authored the letters (1810).

Mariana Alcoforado was born in 1640, baptized on April 22 of that year in the Portuguese city of Beja, and lived in relative obscurity for 83 years until she died in 1723. Almost a century after her death, fame was unexpectedly attached to her name by Jean François Boissonade, a French literary scholar. Writing under the pseudonym "Omega" in the *Journal de l'Empire*, Boissonade reported his discovery of a marginal notation written in his first edition of *Lettres portugaises traduites en français*. The book, first published in 1669, is a series of five letters allegedly written by a Portuguese nun to her lover, a French military officer. An immediate sensation for their desperate passion and scandalous theme, the letters went through five editions during the seven months following their first appearance and had won lasting renown as celebrated examples of amorous correspondence. Yet the identity of the nun had remained unknown, until Boissonade revealed the marginalia: "The nun that wrote these letters was named Mariana Alcoforada, a nun in Beja, between Extremadura and Andalusia. The gentlemen to whom these letters were written was the Count of Chamilly, then called the Count of Saint-Léger."

The literary world had never heard of Mariana Alcoforado, nor did it have any proof of her existence. But Boissonade's report caused researchers to seek verification. Had there been a nun named Mariana Alcoforado in Beja during the 1660s? Had the Count of Chamilly's military career taken him there, and might he have known Sister Mariana? In short, was there documentary evidence to substantiate the marginal note?

Investigation revealed Mariana to public view. In 1652, her parents, Francisco da Costa Alcoforado and **Leonor Mendes** placed Mariana in the Our Lady of the Conception convent of Beja. Her father was a public official, administering royal properties in the region, and descended from an old noble family. He possessed enough property and had sufficient political connections to establish an entailed estate and stipulated that no monk or nun could inherit it. Mariana was one of his eight children by two wives. Her parents lied about her age when they put her in the convent. Rather than 12 they said she was 16, the minimum age at which a young woman could take vows. The few documents that mention her give no indication of her spiritual vocation for life in the cloister. Perhaps she had shown a preference for prayer and meditation, but many families used convents as a dumping ground for daughters, "the general situation of woman" in the words of one Portuguese writer. Mariana's condition was, wrote Humberto Delgado, another of Mariana's compatriots: "A human tragedy. A tragedy of women. A tragedy of the poor girls cast against their will into the monotony of the cloister, and against nature into meaningless chastity."

A Carmelite institution founded in 1467 by *Beatrice of Beja and Ferdinand, duke of Beja and Viseu, parents of King Manuel I, the convent was a large urban establishment without gardens or orchards. But it had a verandah from which the sisters could see the outside world, barred to them by the convent's high walls. Silence and discipline ruled within. By 1660, Mariana had taken her final vows. Her sister **Catherine** was a novice within the same house. In 1663, Mariana's stepmother died, and her father placed three-year-old **Peregrina Maria** in the convent in the nun's care. Mariana raised the child, the two apparently living at times in a small house outside but close by the convent.

If Mariana Alcoforado wrote the *Lettres portugaises*, 1664 was a crucial year, for that was when Noël Bouton de Chamilly arrived in Portugal. Having achieved some reputation for valor in France, Chamilly joined Louis XIV's forces in Portugal, which were supporting, since 1640, that nation's struggle to assert its independence from Spain and restore the Portuguese monarchy. Chamilly served as a cavalry captain under the command of the Count of Schomberg, a Prussian officer in French employ. How Mariana and Chamilly became acquainted, if indeed they did, is a mystery, except for inferences from the *Lettres*. They record that from the verandah of the convent, she was "thrilled by the sight of you passing by, and I was on that verandah that fatal day when I first grew conscious of my unhappy love." Excited by his horsemanship, she convinced herself that Bouton was purposely parading before her to catch her eye. Mariana's brother, Baltazar Vaz Alcoforado, served with Bouton in the siege of Alcaria de la Puebla in 1666, and some scholars have speculated that he introduced his sister to the French officer. Their only evidence stems from the fact that Baltazar took vows to become a monk in 1669: perhaps, they speculate, he did so motivated by a sense of guilt over his role in his sister's scandal.

The letters indicate that for a cloistered nun Mariana had surprising access to the officers. If, contrary to monastic rules and royal law, she was allowed to live outside the convent while raising Peregrina Maria, she would have had opportunity. Such a living arrangement would have been irregular but not necessarily unheard of. Within the convent, it would have been impossible for her to have had an affair with the French officer without some complicity on the part of the other nuns. Even after Bouton's departure for France, during the period the letters were allegedly written, she continued to receive visits from French officers. The second of the *Lettres*, for example, records that one morning she spent three hours talking to a French officer about her beloved. On other occasions, Bouton's compatriots picked up letters from her to send on to him. Sometimes, they waited impatiently while she wrote. Through them, she also seems to have returned all but the last two of Bouton's letters to him. Those brief missives she kept as proof of his faithlessness and as an antidote against her violent passion for him.

The *Lettres* portray a woman consumed by her obsession, a "frenzy," more in love with her passion than with the French officer. "I consecrated my life to you the first time I saw you, and it gives me some pleasure to be sacrificing it to you," she writes, ". . . and yet I feel that I should not altogether wish to be free from sorrows of which you only are the cause." She accuses him of deceit, of bringing her to love him, all the while knowing he would desert her. He intended little more than a vulgar affair; she loved him "so much that no such suspicion ever occurred to me." Mariana pleads for him to re-turn and take her away to France. She complains that he does not write, but when he does, his perfunctory letters prove her worst fears. "Why could you not leave me my love?" she weeps. "You had only to keep from writing to me." Determined by then to write him no more, she makes arrangements to return his portrait. Her love has turned to hate: "I have proved that I loved my passion more than I loved you; and I have had a bitter struggle to fight it down, after your insulting behaviour made you personally hateful to me."

> One should love
> like the Portuguese nun,
> with a soul on fire.
> —Stendahl

Such emotions did not go unnoticed within the convent, according to the *Lettres*. The abbess chastised her but then treated her kindly, perhaps recognizing the futility of Mariana's passion and her inability to escape the convent. Her love, Mariana reported, touched her sister nuns, and even the most austere of them showed pity for her. Some talked to her about her lover and her hopeless condition. Perhaps for that reason, she kept to her room as much as possible.

Little is known about her life after 1668, when she would have written the last of the *Lettres*. In one, she mentions that she had been named doorkeeper, a rather strange appointment in light of her liaison with Bouton. Thereafter, she lived in near anonymity, at least as far as surviving documents are concerned. In 1709, she was a candidate for abbess of the convent but lost the election 48 votes to 58. When she died, a sister nun, **Antónia Sophia Baptista de Almeida**, duly registered the death in the convent records: "On the 28 of the month of July of 1723, Mother D. Mariana Alcoforada passed away in this Royal Convent of the Conception; of 87 years of age; she spent them all in the service of God; . . . she was very benign with everyone; for thirty years she did severe penance; she suffered great infirmities . . . desiring to have more to suffer." Her age, based on the deception perpetrated when she was placed in the convent, was incorrect: she was really 83 when she died.

Mariana's scholarly partisans consider the unusual reference to 30 years' penance as an implicit confirmation of her affair with Bouton. Meanwhile, Bouton had died eight years earlier, in 1715, promoted to marshal of France and grown so stout that the Duke of St. Simon, the renowned observer at Versailles, wrote: "He was

Maria Isabel Barreno, Maria Teresa Horta, and *Maria Velho da Costa.* See *The Three Marias.*

a tall and fat man, the best man of the world, the most brave, filled with honor, but so stupid and heavy that it is not to be understood how he could have any talent for war."

In light of what the Portuguese documents showed, there was no doubt that Mariana Alcoforado lived. Nonetheless, research failed to prove her authorship. Lacking definitive proof, authorship of the *Lettres portugaises* largely depended on scholars' prejudices. Some of her compatriots patriotically defended Mariana as making one of the "most decisive Portuguese contributions to European sensibility." For them the *Lettres* were the "psychological document most truly felt, that represents the Portuguese soul in the seventeenth century." They asserted that the letters' syntax showed that they had been translated in a literal fashion from Portuguese. The nun's despair and solitude resonated with the melancholy and passion experienced by a nation of mariners, often separated from lovers and family by the sea.

Yet others, including Portuguese writers, rejected her authorship. This was especially true of conservative Catholics, who denied that a nun would have succumbed to seduction. They claimed the *Lettres* were nothing more than exotic French fiction. Other critics dismissed Mariana on the grounds that the original letters in Portuguese had never surfaced, that the letters' precious style, supposed internal contradictions, and lack of direct connection with Mariana Alcoforado showed them to be French literary creations. American literary scholar F.C. Green argued in 1926, based on study of Claude Barbin's royal license to print the letters, that they were written by Gabriel Joseph de Lavergne Guilleragues, traditionally thought to have been their translator. Decades earlier, before Boissonade first revealed Mariana Alcoforado's name with the *Lettres,* Jean Jacques Rousseau had pronounced them fakes written by a man: "That celestial fire which warms and kindles the soul, that genius which consumes and devours, that burning eloquence, those sublime transports which plunge their raptures to the depths of human hearts, will always be lacking in women's writings: these are all cold and pretty like their authors. For women are incapable of either describing or feeling love. . . . I would wager anything in the world that the *Portuguese Letters* were written by a man."

In the end, however, the question of authorship is moot. The *Lettres portugaises* have brought Mariana Alcoforado to life from her anonymous cell in the convent, and she in turn has given new life to Portuguese women. In 1972, during the final shudders of the Salazar dictatorship in Portugal, **Maria Isabel Barreno, Maria Teresa Horta,** and **Maria Velho da Costa** published the *Novas Cartas Portuguesas* (*New Portuguese Letters*). They had written in homage to Mariana Alcoforado, whom they had taken as their champion in the struggle to liberate Portuguese women. The regime found their feminism offensive to public morality, and the "Three Marias" were arrested and put on trial, to the dismay of human rights organizations around the world. But the Salazar dictatorship fell in 1974, and the new government dropped all charges against the women. The *Novas Cartas* quickly became "a milestone in the fight for freedom for women." To the "Three Marias," Portuguese society imposed marriage, motherhood, and submissiveness on women, comparable to the convent walls that held Mariana's aspirations in check. In one of their poems, they shared Mariana's grief: "For a daughter put in a convent/ is not loved in her house."

SOURCES:

Aveline, Claude. . . . *Et tout le reste n'est rien.* Paris: Mercure de France, 1986.

Barreno, Maria Isabel, Maria Teresa Horta, and Maria Velho da Costa. *The Three Marias: New Portuguese Letters.* Translated by Helen R. Lane. Garden City, NY: Doubleday, 1975.

Cordeiro, Luciano. *Soror Marianna, a freira portugueza.* 2nd ed. Lisbon: Livraria Ferin e Cia., 1891.

Delgado, Humberto. *O infeliz amor de Sóror Mariana: a freira de Beja.* Rio de Janeiro: Editôra Civilização Brasileira S.A., 1964.

Fonseca, Antonio Belard da. *Mariana Alcoforado: a freira de Beja e as Lettres Portugaises.* Lisbon: Imprensa Portugal-Brasil, 1966.

Garcia, Ápio. *Camilo e Sóror Mariana por detrás das grades.* Porto: Livraria Simões Lopes de Domingos Barreira, 1945.

Letters of a Portuguese Nun. Lisbon: Arcádia Travelling and Culture, 1973.

Rodrigues, Antonio Augusto Gonçalves. *Mariana Alcoforado: história e crítica de uma fraude literária.* 2nd ed. Coimbra, 1943.

SUGGESTED READING:

Beauvois, Eugène. "La jeunesse de Maréchal de Chamilly. Notice sur Noël Bouton et sa famille de 1636 a 1667," in *Memoires de la Société d'Histoire . . . de Beaune.* 1885.

Guilleragues, Gabriel Joseph de Lavergne, vicomte de. *Lettres portugaises, Valentins et autres oeuvres.* Frédèric Deloffre and Jacques Rougeot, eds. Paris: Garnier, 1962.

Lassalle, Jean-Pierre. *Un manuscrit des lettres d'une religieuse portugaise: leçons, interrogations, hypotheses.* Seattle: Papers on French Seventeenth Century Literature, 1982.

Kendall W. Brown, Professor of History, Brigham Young University, Provo, Utah

Alcorta, Gloria (1915—)

Argentinean author and sculptor. Born in 1915 in Argentina; daughter of a French diplomat; granddaughter of the author Eduarda Mansilla de García. Works include nine books of poetry, fiction or drama, as well as sculpture.

Born the daughter of the Argentinean diplomat to France, Gloria Alcorta studied French, which became her second language. In Paris, she was a student of the dramatic arts from 1932 to 1938. She launched her career first as a sculptor, however, winning prizes in both Buenos Aires and Paris. Alcorta published her first volume of verse, written in French, when she was just 20. Illustrated by Héctor Basaldú;a, *La prison de l'enfant* (*The Child's Prison*) included an introduction by Jorge Luis Borges, who remained an advocate of her work. Two of her plays were written in French and produced in Paris. The novel *El hotel de la luna* (*The Moon Hotel,* 1958), penned in Spanish, is Alcorta's most recognized work.

Crista Martin, Boston, Massachusetts

Alcott, Amy (1956—)

American golfer and LPGA champion. Born in Kansas City, Missouri, on February 22, 1956; lives in Santa Monica, California.

Won the Orange Blossom Classic (1976). Won the LPGA Classic and the Colgate Far East Open (1977); won the Peter Jackson Classic (1979); won the U.S. Women's Open and the Vare Trophy (1980); took the Nabisco-Dinah Shore title (1983, 1988, 1991); won the Lady Keystone Open (1984).

As a young golfer, Amy Alcott won the U.S. Junior Girls' title in 1973 and came in second in the Canadian Amateur in 1974. While still a teenager, she won a tournament at the difficult Pebble Beach course, her score of 70 breaking an earlier record set by *Babe Zaharias. Before turning pro, Alcott supported herself as a short-order cook at the Butterfly Bakery in Los Angeles. In January 1975, she joined the Ladies' Professional Golf Association (LPGA) Tour. By February, on her 19th birthday, Alcott had won the Orange Blossom Classic. That first year, she was named Rookie of the Year, and she would continue to win a tournament in each of her first 12 years on the Tour, a record she shares with *Louise Suggs and *Betsy Rawls.

In 1980, Alcott was the U.S. Women's Open champion, shooting 280 despite the 100° temperatures; she was also voted Player of the Year by America's *Golf* magazine and was the recipient of the coveted Vare trophy with a yearly average of 71.51. In 1983, 1988, and 1991, she won the prestigious Nabisco-*Dinah Shore Invitational. In 1984, Alcott took first place and $200,000 in the Lady Keystone Open with a score of 65. Asked what she would do with her winnings, she replied that a downpayment on a bakery might provide a secure future once she retired from the links.

Karin Loewen Haag, freelance writer, Athens, Georgia

Alcott, Anna Bronson (1831–1893).

See Alcott, Louisa May for sidebar.

Alcott, Louisa May (1832–1888)

American author whose best-known work is the classic Little Women. *Name variations: (pseudonyms) Flora Fairfield; A.M. Barnard. Born in Germantown, Pennsylvania, on November 29, 1832; died in Dun-*

Louisa May Alcott

reath Place, Roxbury, Massachusetts, on March 6, 1888; second child of Bronson (a writer, educator, and Transcendentalist) and Abigail (May) Alcott; never married; no children.

Selected works: Flower Fables (1855); Hospital Sketches (1863); Moods (1865); Little Women (1868); Little Men (1871); Jo's Boys (1886); and over 30 others.

Louisa May Alcott's best-known work, Little Women, is often said to have its basis in the author's own life. The novel is set in Concord, Massachusetts, in the 1800s, where a band of four sisters rally 'round their parents as all conspire to do good for their neighbors and be gentle, kind souls to one another, providing enough familial warmth to ward off even the harshest, sparsest winters. The vision was idyllic. It was, however, far from reminiscent of Louisa May Alcott's life, which was neither warm nor reassuring. The sights were perhaps similar, but Alcott's view was different: dominated by her father and bearing the financial weight of her sisters and mother, Louisa often disliked her life. She sequestered herself at home and journeyed out only as required to make a living for the Alcotts. She did not enjoy many people, and in fact was afraid of men. Her journals display a disappointment in self that is both unbending and unfair.

Louisa was the second child of Bronson and **Abigail May Alcott** (known as Abba). In 1830, the newly married couple had moved to Germantown, Pennsylvania, where Bronson, a writer and educator, became principal and teacher in the Germantown Academy. ❧ **Anna Bronson Alcott** was Bronson and Abba's first born, arriving on March 16, 1831. Bronson was fascinated by the child and watched her keenly. He kept a journal, starting from her first day. "Observations on the Life" recorded both Anna's physical and emotional development. She was a peaceful child and he showered her with adoration. On Bronson's 33rd birthday, November 29, 1832, Louisa May was born. Unlike her older sister, Louisa was a temperamental baby who cried often. She was instantly less favored, a fact based partially on Bronson's financial and personal reverses. He saw Louisa as less pleasant than her sister Anna and viewed her behavior clinically: "Louisa required authoritative measures in a few instances," he wrote. "She yields with less reluctance than yesterday." Meanwhile Anna "is generally quite docile and happy." By the summer of 1834, Bronson's educational efforts in Pennsylvania foundered. His teaching methods, based in the transcendental ideal—ascension to higher being by forsaking worldly material and physical pleasures—had caused parents to withdraw their children from all his schools. Destitute, the Alcotts sold their belongings and headed to Boston (both Bronson and Abba had grown up in New England). That fall, Bronson opened the Temple School and the small family took lodgings near Boston Common.

In June of 1835, the family increased to five with the birth of **Elizabeth (Beth) Sewall Alcott.** Though they enjoyed a brief period of financial success (Bronson was well-received and lauded in his efforts in the progressive Boston society), by 1837 his reputation and enrollment at Temple School had fallen. The family moved to cheaper rooms in the South End and subsisted on bread and vegetables, while Bronson believed that a diet not dependent on the sacrifice of animals purified them spiritually. On the rare occasions when Abba saved enough to buy meat, Bronson either refused to run the errand or conveniently forgot and spent the money otherwise. Abba and Bronson clashed frequently, as she tried to provide for the well-being and health of her children while he tried to further their spiritual growth. The marriage was unhappy, and Abba was forced to ask for charity from her more well-to-do family and friends. Bronson considered the arrangement mutually beneficial: while people supported him, he brought them closer to God.

On March 23, 1839, the Temple School closed. It was to be the end of Bronson's consistent, if meager, contribution to supporting his family. Two weeks later, an Alcott son was born, but he did not live. On the encouragement of Ralph Waldo Emerson, Bronson's closest friend (and often financial benefactor), the family moved in 1840 to Concord, where the cost of living was much reduced. They continued to lean heavily on the aid of others. On July 26, 1840, ❧ **May Alcott** was born.

For Louisa, the move to Concord, at age six, was a perfect fit. Her rambunctiousness and energy—traits that Bronson deemed unfeminine

❧ **Alcott, Anna Bronson** (1831–1893)

Sister of Louisa May Alcott and caretaker of Orchard House. Name variations: Anna Alcott Pratt. Born Anna Bronson Alcott on March 16, 1831; died in July 1893; daughter of Bronson (a writer, educator, and Transcendentalist) and Abigail (May) Alcott; sister of *Louisa May Alcott and *May Alcott; married John Pratt (an insurance firm employee), in 1860; children: two sons.

and therefore improper—needed space. She preferred solitude to the constant company of others, including her sisters. She ran through the woods and explored nature. She wrote her first known poem there, in wonder of winter giving way to spring. She also met Henry David Thoreau, who was to be her lifelong, unvoiced love. Henry and his brother John ran the Concord Academy, where Anna and Louisa were enrolled. Louisa adored Thoreau's withdrawn behavior. He was more like herself than anyone she had ever met. They often went on walks, exploring the woods and hillsides. She felt she understood him.

The Alcotts were journal keepers. While Bronson dedicated much of his time to recording each day's thoughts, Abba also wrote in a diary, and the couple instructed their daughters to do the same. By 1843, Louisa kept a regular journal. She was, by her own admission, an angry child, though it is apparent that this self-denunciation was in part caused and reinforced by years of her father's chiding and shunning of his wilder, second daughter. "[Father] asked us all what faults we wa[n]ted to get rid of," went an early entry. "I said Impatience." The following month, she wrote, "I was cross to-day, and I cried when I went to bed. I made good resolutions, and felt better in my heart. If I only *kept* all I make, I should be the best girl in the world. But I don't and so am very bad." She was not yet 11. A note appended to the entry by Alcott at a much later date reads, "*Poor little sinner! She says the same at fifty.*—L.M.A."

By 11, Alcott had already taken refuge in books, frequently withdrawing to her room to read and think. But there was much work to perform around the house, in addition to regular lessons from Bronson. He referred to his children as "living manifestations of my intellect" and insisted on keeping a heavy hand in their lessons. Both he and Abba also read their children's journals and commented on them. Abba wrote small notes to Louisa, wishing that she could be a "happier child" or praising the bits of poetry there. Bronson noted that Anna's journal was filled with thoughts of others. Louisa's, he observed with displeasure, was almost purely self-absorbed.

In the spring of 1842, the Alcott women were briefly alone when Bronson sailed to England, a nation more receptive to his transcendental ideas. He returned in the fall buoyed by his success there, and the lives of the Alcott women grew even poorer. Bronson had been accompanied to England by Charles Lane and Henry

Wright, and they had conceived a new household arrangement: communal, agricultural living. In a home that incorporated several families, they could work the land and pool their labors without depending so heavily on money. Of course, they needed money to launch the endeavor, so Abba turned, as she had often done before, to her brother. Sam May had grown tired of supporting his sister and brother-in-law. He complained of Bronson's unwillingness to work, and grudgingly gave more money. Lane paid the other half of the Alcott debts, and, in June 1843, the Alcotts, Lane and his son, and Wright moved from Concord to a farmhouse in Harvard, Massachusetts. They called the house "The Fruitlands," not for the fruit grown there, since there was none, but for its spiritual promise. The experiment lasted six months. Abba and her daughters were the only women in the household, which accepted whomever chose to pass through and share Bronson's vision. The men did little work, except occasional attention to the gardens. While the men discussed philosophy, Abba and her daughters cleaned, sewed, and prepared the food—a strictly vegetarian

---

❧➤ **Alcott, May** (1840–1879)

American artist. Born Abby May Alcott on July 26, 1840; died in December 1879, about a month after giving birth; daughter of Bronson (a writer, educator, and Transcendentalist) and Abigail (May) Alcott; sister of ***Louisa May Alcott*** *and* ***Anna Bronson Alcott***; *studied art in Paris; married Ernest Nieriker (a Swiss businessman), on March 22, 1878, and settled in a Parisian suburb; children: daughter* **Louisa May Nieriker** *(b. November 8, 1879).*

While studying in Paris, May Alcott wrote home and described a tea party in *Mary Cassatt's studio: "We sipped our chocalat [sic] from superior china, served on an India waiter, upon an embroidered cloth of heavy material. Miss Cassatt was charming as usual in two shades of brown satin and rep, being very lively and a woman of real genius, she will be a first-class light as soon as her pictures get circulated and known for they are handled in a masterly way."

But Alcott was just one of many fighting the art world's closed-door policy toward women artists. Writing home of the Julian academy, which charged more for women and offered less in the way of instruction, she complained, "The lower school as it is called, or male class, no longer opens its doors to women, for the price, being but one half of the upper [women's] school, attracted too many."

SUGGESTED READING:

Ticknor, Caroline. *May Alcott: A Memoir.* Boston: Little, Brown, 1927.

diet, the bulk of which was cooked or raw apples, sparse breads and grains, and any vegetables they could cultivate. Exhausted and ill, and watching her children grow sicker, Abba put forth an ultimatum: she and her children were returning to a more normal life. Though Bronson considered staying put or moving in with a Shaker community up the road, he did not abandon the family. He did, however, hold them responsible for his spiritual stagnation and retreated even further from his wife and daughters.

In the five years following The Fruitlands experiment, as the family moved from Harvard to Still River to Concord, Louisa grew to adolescence, a time that went virtually unnoticed by her parents. Abba was overwhelmed with keeping the family together, while Bronson continued his communal ways. In 1845, at age 13, Louisa wrote in her journal, "More people coming to live with us; I wish we could be together, and no one else. I don't see who is to clothe and feed us all, when we are so poor now." Her moods were erratic, and, at a time when boys might have been a fascination, Louisa's long exposure to her father made her largely afraid of any real romance. She continued to do battle with her disposition as well. "I have made a plan for my life, as I am [13], and no more a child. . . . People think I'm wild and queer; but Mother understands and helps me. . . . Now I'm going to work really, for I feel a true desire to improve and be a help and comfort, not a care and sorrow, to my dear mother." For the next several years, as she bent to the task of remolding herself, her journals were blank.

By 1848, Abba had grown miserable in Concord. The employment opportunities for women were few, and she was humiliated by having begged assistance for so long (other children even shared their school lunches with Anna and Louisa). That summer, the family moved to Boston. Louisa hated to leave the open expanses of Concord and found the Common, once a haven from people, no longer satisfying. Boston had grown more populated and citified, and the waters around the city were being filled in to make more space. Louisa stayed inside the dingy rooms the family rented and wrote plays that she and her sisters acted for their parents. Abba took a position, for $25 a month, collecting and handing out charitable donations and items. Anna and Louisa helped Abba teach a group of black children to read—the city provided no schools for blacks—as well as taking other teaching, nursemaid, or governess posts. They pooled their finances to be sure that daughters Beth and May could continue school.

Bronson, meanwhile, offered to give "conversations" with anyone who would listen. He occasionally traveled but never brought home more than a pocketful of change. In September of 1851, after dreaming about fame, Louisa saw her first poem published in *Peterson's Magazine*. "Sunlight" was printed under the name Flora Fairfield. Three years later, the *Saturday Evening Gazette* printed another Fairfield piece, the story "The Rival Prima Donnas." Alcott was paid the sum of $10. All the while, Anna and Louisa continued to work but found their most stable employment as teachers of their own small school. Though Bronson occasionally stopped by to lecture, the curriculum was standard and therefore enrollment remained steady. Louisa viewed teaching as a boring but necessary evil.

In December of 1854, the tables began to turn. Her first novel, *Flower Fables,* a series of moral tales written for a friend, was published. Recognizing her potential for providing a steady living, the family saw to it that 22-year-old Louisa spent more time writing, and they relieved her of most of her teaching duties. She continued to print pieces in the *Saturday Evening Gazette* at five dollars an item. Her writing wages were not enough, though, and, in July of 1855, the family moved north to Walpole, New Hampshire. Louisa returned to Boston in November to be near her publishers. Anna went to Syracuse to work as a governess, but the employment was brief; her sensitive nature made her easily tired or easily offended.

Louisa Alcott grew more confident in her 20s. She was 5'6" tall, dark-haired and eyed, and accustomed to hard work, which gave her a sturdy, stern look. Her rising status as the family breadwinner gave Louisa immeasurable pleasure. As she finally outgrew her position in the family as the troublesome one, the earnings from her writing made her the glue that kept the Alcotts together. "My book came out; and people began to think that topsy-turvy Louisa would amount to something after all," she wrote. She took in sewing to supplement her writing income. While patching her own clothes, she noted happily the gifts of new dresses for her sisters or ribbons for her mother's bonnet that she sent home. Bronson's absences or time in the garden were no longer a nuisance but commented on with cheer or encouragement. He became an innocent for whom Louisa cared and provided. It was a niche that gave her great purpose and satisfaction.

In June 1856, when she traveled to Walpole to be with the family, Alcott found her youngest sisters ill from scarlet fever. Abba had caught the germs from a charitable visit to a nearby family. May shortly recovered, but Louisa spent the bulk of the summer nursing Beth, who rose from bed for only brief periods. Louisa returned to Boston in the fall, and the family endured as they had before. By late 1857, it was apparent that Beth would not recover. The Alcotts decided to return to Concord, purchasing a house next door to Nathaniel and ✥➤ **Sophia Peabody Hawthorne** (who had three children, including daughter *Rose Hawthorne Lathrop). The Alcotts spent the winter repairing the house, and planned to move in come springtime. Beth Alcott died on March 14, 1858, before the family was installed at Orchard House. Louisa had nursed Beth diligently and had slept at her bedside. Initially at peace with the loss, she later grew depressed. Her mood was exacerbated the following month by Anna's announcement of her intention to marry John Pratt, an insurance firm employee and acquaintance from local plays in which both Pratt and Anna had performed. Though Louisa liked John, he was taking her confidant, just after she had lost Beth. The family moved into Orchard House in July, but by October Louisa had gone to Boston for the year to earn wages to keep Orchard House running. In the fall of 1859, Louisa had her greatest publishing success to date. *The Atlantic Monthly*, a new and elite journal of literary work, accepted her story "Love and Self-Love." It earned Alcott $50 and praise from both her parents. Another story, "A Modern Cinderella," appeared in the *Atlantic* in 1860, shortly before Anna and John Pratt married and moved to Chelsea, Massachusetts.

After years of toiling at short stories, Alcott sat down in August of 1860 with an idea for a book called *Moods*. In her journal, she wrote, "Genius burned so fiercely that for four weeks I wrote all day and planned nearly all night, being quite possessed by my work. I was perfectly happy, and seemed to have no wants. Finished the book, or a rough draught of it, and put it away to settle." By December, she was the only daughter left at Orchard House. Sister May had gone, first to Boston, then to Syracuse, New York, to study and teach painting. "A quiet Christmas; no presents but apples and flowers," wrote Alcott. "No merry-making; for [Anna] and May were gone, and [Beth] under the snow." The bulk of the household chores rested on her. Abba, often sick, became her frequent patient, neglected only in times of Alcott's writing fits. She took up *Moods* again in February of 1861. "It was very pleasant and queer while it

lasted; but after three weeks of it I found that my mind was too rampant for my body. . . . So I dropped the pen, and took long walks, cold baths, and had [Anna] up to frolic with me. Read all I had done to my family. . . . So I had a good time, even if it never comes to anything; for it was worth something to have my three dearest sit up till midnight listening with wide-open eyes to Lu's first novel."

Concord was an intellectual center, the most famous of its inhabitants being Bronson Alcott, Emerson, Thoreau, and Hawthorne. It was therefore also the site of the most current political and social debates. The abolitionist movement found a supportive audience, and among them was Louisa. The war highlighted for her another of the inequities of her gender. She felt prepared to fight for the abolition of slavery, yet women's participation was unwanted, except for their sewing skills. Alcott stitched unflaggingly, but at the end of the year noted, "Wrote, read, sewed, and wanted something to do." The dull duty was broken up only by the death of Thoreau that May. She took it well, considering her long unrequited love for the writer. As she had never expected his attentions in return, his death merely made him more perfect in her mind. The event went unnoted in her journal. (Shortly before her death, Alcott's daily journals were destroyed by the author, as was most of her personal correspondence. What remains is a summary journal, usually limited to several sentences describing a month or a special event. At the end of each year is another short summary, plus an accounting of money earned. Thoreau's death most probably garnered some writing, but Alcott, tremendously private and aware of the likelihood that her journals would one day be read, seems to have eliminated any mention of his death.)

By September, her attentions returned to the war. She remarked that she liked "the stir in the air, and longed for battle like a warhorse when he smells powder." In November, the opportunity for a deeper involvement arose. A call had gone out for middle-aged women to serve as nurses in Army hospitals around Washington, D.C. Though Alcott was shy of the age requirement, she submitted her application and was called to the capital in late December. Granted train fare, accommodations, and 40 cents a day, she reported to the Union Hotel Hospital in Georgetown on December 13, 1862. Washington was in chaos. The city and its hospitals were raging with disease. Clean water was rare, and epidemics of pests, typhoid, diarrhea, and pneumonia ravaged patients more than the frequent

◀✥
Hawthorne, Sophia Peabody.
See Lathrop, Rose Hawthorne for sidebar.

amputations of their limbs. Alcott was responsible for a ward of male patients. The days were long and the prospects for the men seemed dismal. Despite her homesickness, she was thrilled at finally making a more important contribution to the abolition efforts.

Before she had served a month, however, Alcott was ill with what a doctor diagnosed as typhoid pneumonia. "Sharp pain in the side, cough, fever and dizziness. A pleasant prospect for a lonely soul five hundred miles from home!" she wrote. "Dream awfully and wake unfreshed, think of home and wonder if I am to die here." Doctors treated Alcott with calomel, an emetic used in massive doses. The intent was to induce enough vomiting and diarrhea to clear the patient's body of all illness. Calomel was prescribed for nearly any ailment, but the mercury-based medication had side effects. In those times, doctors dosed patients to the point of early acute mercury poisoning. Their other ailments were overshadowed or replaced in the short term with sore gums; loss of hair, teeth, and voices; swollen tongues (to four times normal size); and poisonous mucus that oozed from the mouth. Alcott, like countless others, was permanently poisoned. When her father was called from Concord to take her home, he found his daughter in delirious hysteria. They returned to Orchard House on the 23rd of January. The rest of her life would be marred by the effects of mercury poisoning.

When I had the youth I had no money; now I have the money I have no time; and when I get the time, if I ever do, I shall have no health to enjoy life.

—Louisa May Alcott

By mid-February, Alcott regained consciousness but could hardly stand, let alone walk. Because her hair had fallen out raggedly, she had it shorn off. Eating was difficult due to mouth sores, so she was wasting away. In March, she was able to resume minor movement around the house, but she had not regained enough strength to be present when Anna gave birth, at the end of the month, to Louisa's first nephew. Slowly, Alcott resumed her writing and standing as financial supporter. The family was glad of her return to health and therefore work. In particular, she had found that her more literary writing was not as good a source of money as the passionate and somewhat racy stories she seemed able to write with little effort. "Pauline's Passion and Punishment" earned the author her largest payment—$100. In fact, it exceeded Al-

cott's combined payments from teaching, nursing, and the publication of one other story that year by $30. Aware that such stories would earn her no praises at home or around Concord, Louisa stipulated that "Pauline's Passion" and others be published under the name A.M. Barnard. It was a secret she kept for many years, but a source of income that was both easy and rewarding. The fantastic, imaginative writing was truly enjoyable for her.

Late that spring, Alcott organized her letters home from her aborted stay in Washington, D.C., into a three-part series called "Hospital Sketches," to be published in the *Commonwealth*. Much to her surprise, they were a huge hit, reprinted nationally and finally collected as a book. The letters, slightly fictionalized, described the men who came through Union hospital from the perspective of Nurse Periwinkle. By year's end, the effort had earned her a surprising and welcome $200. Encouraged by the success, Alcott spent much time over the next several months touching up *Moods* and another book in progress, *Work*. She found that her strength waned quickly, however, and, for the once vigorous and active woman, exhaustion was frustrating. In January, finally feeling ready to share the novel nearest to her heart, Alcott submitted *Moods* to two editors. It was rejected by both, with the complaint that it was twice as long as they wanted. Dejected, Alcott put *Moods* away. Late that spring, Nathaniel Hawthorne, Alcott's next-door neighbor, died.

In the fall, still dutifully writing stories to pay the family bills, Alcott struck upon the solution for *Moods*, which would cut it by ten chapters. She wrote without pause for a month, and when she was finished the book was accepted. By December, it was published and Alcott was gratified to find people, wherever she went, talking about it or reading it. Though its first edition sold out, interest waned and her brief fame faded. The stories continued to be more lucrative, and therefore earned more of Alcott's attention.

In June of 1865, Anna gave birth to a second son. While visiting her sister, Louisa was offered the opportunity to go to Europe as the nursemaid for shipping merchant William Weld's daughter Anna, an invalid. Rather abruptly, and against her own doubts, Louisa set sail with the young woman and her brother for an intended year abroad. The sea voyage made Alcott ill, and she was "heartily glad to set [her] feet on solid earth again." They arrived in England in August and began with a rapid tour through that country, France, and into Bavaria, where they stopped so Anna could receive a watercure from a local doctor. Before September was over, Alcott was annoyed by the dullness of the trip, which was slowed considerably by the onset of Anna's illness. While Anna's brother was able to explore during the delays, Alcott was housebound, keeping Anna company. In October, Alcott wrote, "I missed my freedom and grew very tired of the daily worry." By February, she "decided to go home in May though A. wants me to stay. I'm tired of it and as she is not going to travel my time is too valuable to be spent fussing over cushions and carrying shawls." Alcott left Weld's service and traveled on her own to Paris and London. When she returned home in July, Orchard House and its inhabitants were in great need of her administration. Abba and Anna were both ill, the house was in disrepair, and debts had sprung up anew. Louisa spent the entire fall writing and tending to the mess. Abba was to have surgery to restore part of her sight, but by the time it came around Louisa was too ill to accompany her. The mer-

cury had seized her body again, and its fevers, restlessness, and rheumatic-like pain stayed with her until May of 1867.

For Alcott, the next 20 years were predictable, lifeless, and sad. Her arrangement with her parents formed new patterns. Bronson, who had previously hurt her and condemned them to poverty with his arrogance, now seemed to Louisa a wise yet childlike figure who depended on her wholly. She could think of him with less anger because his actions no longer weighed so on his wife and children. Louisa cared for her family, and saw that they were fed and clothed as best she could provide. She could afford to feel indulgent about her father's philosophies and way of life. For Abba, she had less patience. Once the matriarch, Abba had become rather an unseemly character. In part, she was losing her faculties, growing senile and sightless. She tended to preach to her daughters and neighbors—to anyone who would listen—and had even alienated Sophia Hawthorne, once a close friend. (Several years before, Abba had literally driven

Little Women, starring Katharine Hepburn, Frances Dee, Joan Bennett, and Jean Parker. RKO, 1933.

Sophia into a such a nervous state that she began to avoid the Alcotts.) Abba had also become a tough critic. She was more reluctant to praise her daughter and cheer her efforts, when once she had been Louisa's greatest champion. Louisa settled into a grim regimen of caring for them and Orchard House while she churned out stories to pay the family bills. All the while, she periodically succumbed to the effects of the calomel, and had stretches of illness and debilitation.

Needing to focus on her writing in order to earn money, Alcott moved out of Orchard House to downtown Boston. In January of 1868, she accepted $500 to serve as a contributing editor for *Merry's Museum,* and the fee was more than enough to pay housekeepers in Concord and rent in the city. In the spring, Thomas Niles, a former employee of one of Alcott's editors, approached her about writing a children's story. He had been speaking with Bronson, who hoped to resume his own writing. Niles agreed to publish them both if Louisa would take on the assignment. In May, with the promise of lucrative earnings, Alcott returned to Concord to begin work on *Little Women.* "Marmee [Abba], Anna, and May all approve my plan. So I plod away, though I don't enjoy this sort of thing." She sent the first volume of the manuscript off by July, and, though she did not much like it, young girls loved it. The book appeared in October to quiet praise, and Alcott, joined by her sister May, went back to Boston to live and work for the winter. Volume II of *Little Women* was released in the early spring of 1869. Alcott and her sister returned to Concord in May to tend to their parents, and Louisa was alternately ill and jittery. Needing rest, she went to Canada and Maine with cousins. She returned in August to find that the author of *Little Women* had become famous. Though she did not yet know it, never again would the Alcotts want for money. Louisa no longer wrote what she wanted, but what the world wanted, and they clamored for each new book. *An Old Fashioned Girl* followed *Little Women* and was an immediate success.

There was another trip to Europe, this time with her sister May, in April of 1870, but Alcott was unwell often. Still, it was a more engaging and restful trip than the previous one, though they experienced some delay in their travels due to the Franco-Prussian War. Finally, in September, they were able to proceed to Italy. There, in December, Louisa and May learned that their brother-in-law, John, had died the month before. Like Louisa, John had received calomel treatments for an ailment, but had not withstood the

poisoning. The loss shocked Alcott again into worries of how she would support them all. Her response was to produce yet another children's book, *Little Men,* "that John's death may not leave A[nna] and the dear little boys in want." In May of 1871, receiving encouraging paychecks and reports of success from America, Louisa prepared to go home. "A very pleasant year in spite of constant pain, John's death, and home anxieties. Very glad I came, for May's sake. It has been a very useful year for her." Alcott returned alone, while May, funded by her sister, stayed on to study her art.

It was Concord for the summer, Boston for the fall, writing again. In 1872, Alcott rewrote *Work* and copied it in three impressions. The carbon copies required her to bear down so hard on her pen that she experienced permanent paralysis in her right thumb. She learned to write left-handed to compensate. May came back from Europe in the fall, returned to Paris in April of 1873, and arrived back home in November. Louisa went to Concord and back to Boston in the fall with Abba in tow, while Bronson was on a lecture tour. Fame was not what Alcott had imagined as a child; most upsetting was the disruption of her privacy. People sought her autograph and her company regularly, often stopping by Orchard House. She found her name in gossip columns more than once, prompting her to complain that they should read the books and leave the person alone.

Abba's health continued to slide as her daughters maintained round-robin bedside care. In September of 1876, Alcott rewarded May for her long stay at home with another trip to Europe. May had not returned by November of 1877 when, on the 25th, Abba died. Having worn herself out caring for her mother, Alcott was near death herself. They buried Abba next to Beth in Concord's Sleepy Hollow Cemetery, and both Louisa and Bronson suffered from the loss of direction that Abba had given them. Determined to put a memoir of her together, they began reviewing her years of letters and journals. Bronson, reading in Abba's daily entries the pain he had so often inflicted, felt a new awareness of his effect on his family. He regretted having caused his wife so much difficulty. Hovering over the papers together, Louisa and Bronson grew closer.

In February, the Alcotts received word from May that she was engaged to a Swiss businessman. On March 22, 1878, May married Ernest Nieriker in London, and they settled in a Parisian suburb. Alcott's letters and journal en-

From the movie Little Women, *starring June Allyson and Peter Lawford (MGM, 1949).*

tries express pleasure at their whirlwind romance, touched by a hint of desperation for her own situation. "How different our lives are just now!—I so lonely, sad, and sick; she so happy, well and blest. She always had the cream of things, and deserved it. My time is yet to come somewhere else, when I am ready for it." The spring was busied with cleaning and, to a degree, clearing out Orchard House. Anna had her own home, but Louisa and Bronson felt lost and unwilling to live where Abba had been so much a fixture. Instead, they boarded with Anna, and Bronson planned a Concord School of Philosophy. Informally, the school began at Orchard House that summer, receiving students from around town and fans of Bronson's from his western tours. The school gave Bronson new purpose and a renewed glory; for Louisa and Anna, it proved to be more work than fun. That fall, they mostly stayed at Anna's home, noting the one-year anniversary of Abba's passing. Louisa went into Boston for a brief stay and an attempt at writing, but she was back shortly. Depression and a weak body allowed her little energy to write. Visiting doctors frequently, Alcott questioned the quality of such a life.

On July 15, 1879, Bronson's school officially began at Orchard House. For one month, more than 400 people swarmed through and around Concord. "[T]hey roost on our steps like hens waiting for corn," Alcott wrote. "Father revels in it, so we keep the hotel going and try to look as if we like it. . . . [S]peculation seems a waste of time when there is so much real work crying to be done. Why discuss the Unknowable till our poor are fed and the wicked saved?"

Alcott continued to churn out stories and publications slowly. She had no strength for impassioned work, and mostly continued that which was popular and paid the bills. What energy she had she turned to the community or the ongoing effort for women's right to vote. Her patience was short for those who resisted changing the status quo. Plans to visit May and meet her new husband were permanently set aside. Alcott recognized that her health would never withstand the trip. Deeply disappointed, she went to Boston, where she received news that on November 8th, May had given birth to a daughter, **Louisa May Nieriker**. The joy was brief. Within two weeks of the birth, May grew suddenly ill. On the 31st of December, 1879, Ralph Waldo Emerson received a telegram from Nieriker, who hoped he could more gently break the news. Alcott was alone at home in Concord when Emerson arrived to tell her that another sister had gone. She was devastated not to have been with May.

In the months following, the Alcotts received frequent letters from Nieriker and his mother, describing May's last days, her burial in a cemetery outside the city, and the child Lulu. May had earlier extracted a promise from Louisa to care for the baby. That spring, trunks of May's diaries, clothing, and artwork arrived, and heightened Alcott's grief. She wrote little, read more, and began preparations for her niece's arrival. Lulu's trip to America was delayed from spring until fall, so Alcott took rooms in Boston. Bronson was to join her there after the School of Philoso-

From the 1995 movie Little Women, *starring Claire Danes, Trini Alvarado, Winona Ryder, and Kirsten Dunst (Columbia).*

phy had finished. In late August, a nanny was dispatched to pick Lulu up, and they returned in mid-September. Alcott watched the baby's every step. At year's end, Louisa had only one publication, but finances were no longer pivotal. She had invested well.

For several years, all were absorbed by Lulu's progress. She was a happy and strong-willed child, and she adored her new "mother." For her part, Alcott finally seemed to have a reason for living that did not center on making money. Comfortable in finances, she could simply enjoy her days. Her journal entries are sparse. In the spring of 1882, Emerson, Alcott's strongest friend and supporter, also died. That fall, Louisa separated from Lulu for the first time, leaving her with Anna. Again, she went into Boston to work, and again her time there was cut short. On the 24th of October, 1882, Bronson had a stroke that paralyzed him and, for several months, robbed him of speech. Alcott returned home to help care for him, but by early spring of 1883 the sisters were back to routine. Anna cared for her father while Louisa went to

Boston to write. Lulu moved back and forth between the two homes, and Louisa went through a series of nannies, never finding an adequate caretaker for Lulu and often caring for her herself. The sisters took turns with Bronson so each could have their rest.

In December of 1884, Alcott began work on *Jo's Boys,* the last of the March family trilogy, which included *Little Women* and *Little Men.* She also set to work editing her letters and journals. *Jo's Boys* was completed in July of 1886, and the effort took the last of Alcott's strength. In January of 1887, she moved into a convalescent home in Roxbury, Massachusetts, just outside Boston, as Anna was unable to nurse both her sister and father. Alcott ate poorly and often slept restlessly, both the effects of mercury. She missed her family and noted their visits or absences often. On March 1, 1888, knowing her father's end was near, Alcott traveled to Boston to visit him. "Very sweet and feeble. Kissed me and said 'Come soon.' Smelt my flowers and asked me to write him a letter." The following day, Alcott wrote her final diary entry. "Fine. Better in mind but food a little uneasy. Write letters. . . . Sew. L[ulu] to come."

On March 4, Bronson passed away. And on March 6, at 3:30 in the morning, Louisa May Alcott died in her sleep, at age 55. While her father was being buried that day in Sleepy Hollow, mourners were greeted with news of her death. She followed him to Sleepy Hollow on the 8th. Final notes in her diary, including remarks about her funeral, are written by her sister. Alcott left her family well endowed. Anna and the boys received the bulk of her estate, with a provision for Lulu of $500. The little girl was sent back to Europe to live with her father. Anna returned to Concord, where Orchard House became a museum and memorial for Louisa May Alcott. Anna oversaw it until her death, in July of 1893. The responsibility then went to her sons.

Louisa May Alcott's writing was so prolific that her death did not prove to be the end of her publishing career. In the 1940s, biographer **Madeleine Stern** and historian **Leona Rostenberg** discovered, among the Alcott family papers and letters kept at Harvard University, the A.M. Barnard pseudonym. While the "blood and thunder" stories were some of Alcott's personal favorites, and certainly well written, Alcott had not considered them reputable. They are gothic, romantic, and fantastic. In 1975, four were published, with Stern as editor, under the title *Behind a Mask: The Unknown Thrillers of Louisa May Alcott.* Alcott's manuscripts continue to be discovered by collectors. *The Inheritance,* believed to be her first novel, written in 1849 when Alcott was 17, was unearthed at a Harvard University library in 1996.

The previous year another came to publication. Kent Bicknell, a New Hampshire school principal, purchased the handwritten pages of *A Long Fatal Love Chase,* the writing of which receives no mention in Alcott's diaries. Intended as a magazine serial, it was apparently rejected. Bicknell's literary agents negotiated a $1.5 million advance for the book. Bicknell stipulated that he was to receive only 25% of whatever proceeds the book earned. The remainder of the advance, and 75% of royalties, was to be split between Bicknell's school, three Pratt brothers (grandnephews of Louisa), and the Louisa May Alcott Memorial Fund, which provides for the upkeep and operation of Orchard House. Said Bicknell: "My sense was that if I could do my best to follow her expectations for the book, to bring it to the public in the form she wanted, to use the income properly, including the support of her family and her house, it would all come together."

SOURCES:

Cheney, Ednah D., ed. *Louisa May Alcott: Her Life, Letters, and Journals.* Boston, MA: Roberts Brothers, 1889.

Montgomery, M.R. "An Alcott Story's Surprise Ending," in *Boston Globe.* September 12, 1995, p. 25.

Myerson, Joel, and Daniel Shealy. *The Journals of Louisa May Alcott.* Boston, MA: Little Brown, 1989.

Saxton, Martha. *Louisa May Alcott: A Modern Biography.* Boston: Houghton Mifflin, 1977.

Stern, Madeleine, ed. *Behind a Mask: The Unknown Thrillers of Louisa May Alcott.* NY: William Morrow, 1975.

Crista Martin, Boston, Massachusetts

Alcott, May (1840–1879).

See Alcott, Louisa May for sidebar.

Alda, Frances (1879–1952)

*New Zealand soprano. Born Frances Jeanne Davis on May 31, 1879, in Christchurch, New Zealand; died on September 18, 1952, in Venice, Italy; studied with *Mathilde Marchesi in Paris; married Giulio Gatti-Casazza (director of Metropolitan Opera House), on April 3, 1910 (divorced 1928).*

Made debut as Manon at the Opéra-Comique in Paris (1904); appeared in Brussels (1905–08), Covent Garden (1906), and Teatro alla Scala (1908); debuted at the Metropolitan Opera in Rigoletto (1908) where she performed 250 times until 1930; premiered Damrosch's Cyrano as Roxanne (1913), Herbert's Madeleine (1914), and Hadley's Cleopatra's Night (1920).

Frances Jean Davis, who would be known on international opera stages as Frances Alda, was born in Christchurch, New Zealand, on May 31, 1879, into one of Australia's most notable operatic families. Alda, whose beautiful head tones were acquired when she studied with *Mathilde Marchesi in Paris, learned piano and violin thoroughly before studying voice. She debuted at the Opéra-Comique in 1904. An early recording star, Alda made 130 gramophone recordings for the Victor Company between 1909 and 1923. Although she performed throughout Europe and America, she was best known on the stage of the Metropolitan Opera where she appeared 250 times from 1908 until 1930. When she married the Metropolitan's general manager, Giulio Gatti-Casazza, she worked much harder to maintain her position so as not to cause any hint of favoritism.

*Frances
Alda*

During the Metropolitan's golden age of sopranos, Alda was one of the leading lyric sopranos of her day, though she did not attain the status of superstar *Geraldine Farrar. Known as outspoken and acerbic, Alda did not always win the hearts of colleagues and critics, despite the fact that she was better schooled in musicianship than many of them. Her technical security, in addition to forward voice production and clean style, made her performances memorable. Avoiding musical tricks, her technique was marked by subtle musical feeling rather than passion. With foresight, Alda recognized the role recordings would play in the musical world. She also believed that only films would ultimately be able to present the perfect opera presentation. Her roles were many, including Desdemona in Verdi's *Otello;* Manon in Massenet's *Manon* and Puccini's *Manon Lescaut;* Marguerite in Gounod's *Faust;* and Mimi in *La Bohème,* which was her favorite. In 1937, Alda wrote her biography, *Men, Women, and Tenors,* which employs a lively style to express contemporary views on singers and singing; it continues to be a worthwhile read for its observations on the world of opera.

John Haag, Associate Professor of History,
University of Georgia, Athens, Georgia

Aldebarán, Olga or Bertilda
(1833–1903).

See Acosta de Samper, Soledad.

Aldecoa, Josefina R. (1926—)

Spanish educator and author. Born Josefina Rodriquez in La Roba (León), Spain, in 1926; earned doctorate in philosophy from University of Madrid; married Ignacio Aldecoa (d. 1969, a writer), in 1952; children: Susanna (b. 1954).

Selected works: El arte del niño (The Art of the Child, 1960); A ningune parte (Going Nowhere, 1961); Los niños de la gueraa (Children of Wartime, 1983); La enredadera (The Clinging Vine, 1984); Porque éramos jóvenes (Because We Were Young, 1986); El vergel (The Orchard, 1988).

In the late 1940s, Josefina Aldecoa earned her doctorate in philosophy from the University of Madrid. Though she wrote articles and stories for the reviews *Espadaña* and *Revista española,* and published a volume of short stories in the 1960s, Aldecoa would remain less interested in her own literary career than in education and in her husband's writing.

In 1950, Josefina met Ignacio Aldecoa at the High Council of Scientific Research. They were married two years later and in October of 1954 had a daughter, Susanna. Socially the Aldecoas were among the literati of Madrid's café society. Between 1951 and 1953, they made over 100 missions to less privileged regions of Spain to spread education and culture. In 1956, they moved to Blasco de Garay, and then to America in 1958, when Josefina received a grant to study education in the States. Upon their return to Spain in 1959, Josefina founded Estilo, a private school for children from two to seventeen years of age. Ignacio died in 1969. In the years following, Aldecoa's publications resumed, including her memoirs and her first novel.

SOURCES:
Fiddian, Robin. *Ignacio Aldecoa.* Boston: Twayne Publishers, 1979.

Crista Martin, Boston, Massachusetts

Aldegund (c. 630–684)

*Frankish abbess. Name variations: Aldegundis. Born around 630; died of cancer in 684; daughter of St. Walbert and St. Bertilia; sister of St. *Wandru; aunt of *Madelberte and St. Aldetrude, abbess of Maubeuge.*

Aldegund came from a wealthy noble family of Hainault. Rather than marry, she dedicated herself to a religious life as a young woman. She felt she could best serve God by establishing religious institutions, and used her personal fortune to build a double monastery-abbey at Hautmount, where she took vows of poverty, chastity, and obedience. Soon, she was elected abbess. Aldegund's commitment to assisting individuals who wanted to seclude themselves in holy studies and writing, and her efforts to help feed and house the poor, influenced many of her fellow noble Franks to use their wealth for charitable purposes.

Laura York, Anza, California

Alden, Isabella (1841–1930)

American religious author. Name variations: (pseudonym) Pansy. Born Isabella Macdonald in Rochester, New York, on November 3, 1841; died in Palo Alto, California, in 1930; daughter of Myra (Spafford) and Isaac Macdonald; married Gustavus R. Alden (a Presbyterian minister).

Selected works: Helen Lester *(1866);* An Interrupted Night *(1929).*

In 1866, "Pansy" Macdonald found lifelong direction with her marriage to Presbyterian minister Gustavus Alden and with the publication of her first book, *Helen Lester,* which won that year's Christian Tract Society prize. Thereafter, Alden's work was dedicated primarily to religious writing, encompassing over 120 books that she wrote, edited, and organized. She also founded and edited the Sunday School magazine *Pansy* as well as the *Presbyterian Primary Quarterly* in 1874. During the 1870s, her novels about the Chautauqua region helped found the Chautauqua movement and the Christian summer camp. Alden died in 1930, leaving her autobiography, *Memories of Yesterday,* incomplete. Her niece, novelist *Grace Livingston Hill, finished the work and published it in 1931.

Crista Martin, Boston, Massachusetts

Alden, Priscilla (c. 1602–c. 1685)

American colonist who arrived on the Mayflower. Name variations: Mollins or Mollines. Born Priscilla Mullens or Mullins in Dorking, Surrey, England, around 1602; died around 1685; daughter of William Mullens (a shopkeeper); married John Alden (1599–1687, an American colonist and barrelmaker), probably in 1622; children: at least 11.

Priscilla Mullens came to America on the *Mayflower.* (The rest of her family, as well as 14 of the 18 mothers who shared the ocean cross-

Priscilla Alden

ing, died within a few months of arrival in that first, rugged winter of the Plymouth Colony.) One of the first passengers to be married in the colonies, Priscilla wed John Alden, probably in 1622 or 1623. The Aldens lived in Plymouth until around 1631; they then moved north to settle the town of Duxbury. Descendants of John and Priscilla Alden include William Cullen Bryant, President John Quincy Adams, and Henry Wadsworth Longfellow who wrote of Priscilla and John Alden in *The Courtship of Miles Standish*. The site of the Alden home in Duxbury, Massachusetts, has been preserved.

Aldgyth.
Variant of Edith.

Aldona of Lithuania
*Polish royal. Name variations: Anna of Lithuania; Anna Aldona. Died in 1339; daughter of Gediminas, duke of Lithuania; became first wife of Kazimierz also known as Casimir III the Great, king of Poland (r. 1333–1370), in 1325; children: possibly *Elizabeth of Poland (d. 1361); possibly *Cunegunde (d. 1357, who married Louis VI the Roman, duke of Bavaria); possibly Anna.*

Aldrich, Bess Streeter (1881–1954)
American author who wrote ten novels and more than 150 short stories. Name variations: (pseudonym) Margaret Dean Stevens. Born in Cedar Falls, Iowa, on February 17, 1881; died in Lincoln, Nebraska, on August 3, 1954; daughter of James and Mary Anderson Streeter; married Charles S. Aldrich, in 1907; children: one daughter, three sons.

Bess Streeter Aldrich's ancestors were pioneers, traveling throughout the Midwest before her parents James and **Mary Streeter** settled in Iowa. There, Aldrich was born and raised to understand the harshness of frontier life. Though her family had left the poverty behind, she heard detailed stories of her history from her grandparents, and this tradition was to be the subject of much of her writing.

Bess was just 17 when her first story was published. It would not be followed by another Aldrich work until 1911, when she wrote under the pseudonym Margaret Dean Stevens. After attending the State Teacher College in Iowa, she taught for six years. In 1907, she married Charles S. Aldrich, a lawyer and one-time captain in the Spanish American War. The Aldrichs stayed in

Iowa, and Bess returned to writing. Not until 1925, when Charles Aldrich died, did Bess consider writing as a profession to support her four children. In that year, she published *The Rim of the Prairie*. Her 1928 book, *A Lantern in Her Hand*, became a bestseller (both were reprinted by the University of Nebraska Press, 1994).

In 1946, Aldrich moved from Elmwood to Lincoln, Nebraska, to live next to her daughter. By the time of her death eight years later, Aldrich had produced 10 novels and more than 150 stories.

Aldrich-Blake, Louisa (1865–1925)
English surgeon. Name variations: Dame Louisa Aldrich Blake. Born Louisa Brandreth Aldrich in Essex, England, in 1865; died in 1925; graduated from London University, 1892, M.D., 1894; master in surgery, 1895.

The first woman to be qualified as an English surgeon, Louisa Aldrich-Blake was named dean of the London School of Medicine for Women in 1914.

Aldrude (fl. 1172)
Italian countess.

As the countess of Bertinoro in Italy, Aldrude was an efficient military leader. She commanded the army that fought to lift an imperial siege of the town of Aucona in 1172. The siege was indeed lifted and the successful countess saw the emperor's troops flee Aucona in defeat. Following that victory, she disappeared from history.

Alegría, Claribel (1924—)
Nicaraguan writer of poetry, narrative, and testimony about political upheaval in Central America from the perspective of popular resistance. Pronunciation: Clar-ee-BEL Al-eh-GREE-uh. Name variations: Alegria. Born on May 12, 1924, in Estelí, Nicaragua; daughter of Dr. Daniel Alegría and Ana Maria Vides; attended George Washington University, B.A., 1948; married Darwin B. Flakoll (a journalist), in December 1947, in Wendte, South Dakota; children: daughters Maya, Patricia, and Karen; son Erik.

Family forced into political exile in El Salvador because of father's opposition to U.S. Marine occupation of Nicaragua (1925); published first poems in Repertorio Americano (Costa Rica, 1941); admitted to George Washington University (1944); graduated and published Anillo de silencio, first book of poetry, in

Mexico (1948); moved with husband and three children to Mexico; moved with family to Santiago, Chile, to work with husband on anthology of Latin American writers and poets (1953); returned to U.S. (1956); moved to foreign service post in Uruguay (1958); posted to Argentina (1960); moved with family to Paris and began collaboration on a novel (1962); moved to Majorca (1966); San Salvador's university closed and remaining copies of Aprendizaje *burned by army (1972); won the Casa de las Américas Prize (1978); after the Sandinista rebels gained power in Nicaragua, began research with husband for history of the Sandinista movement (1979); delivered eulogy at the Sorbonne for assassinated Monsignor Arnulfo Romero, archbishop of San Salvador, resulting in exile (1980); co-authored history of the Sandinista revolution.*

Selected writings: Anillo de silencio *(Ring of Silence, Mexico, 1948);* Suite *(Argentina, 1951);* Vigilias *(Vigils, Mexico, 1953);* Acuario *(Aquarium, book of poems, 1953);* Huésped de mi tiempo *(Guest of My Time, Argentina, 1961); (edited with Darwin B. Flakoll),* New Voices of Hispanic America *(Beacon Press, 1962);* Via Unica *(One-Way Traffic, Uruguay, 1965); (edited with Flakoll)* Cenizas de Izalco *(Ashes of Izalco, novel, Spain, 1966, English trans. in United States, 1989);* Luisa in Realityland *(prose-verse novel, 1966, published in United States by Curbstone Press, 1987);* Aprendizaje *(Apprenticeship, poetry collection, Editorial Universitaria, San Salvador, 1970);* Pagaré a cobrar *(Installment Payments, Barcelona, 1973);* El detén *(The Talisman, Barcelona, 1977);* Sobrevivo *(I Survive, Havana, 1978);* Suma y sique *(Add and Carry, Spain, 1981); (edited with Flakoll)* Nuevas Voces de Norteamerica *(New Voices of North America, Spain, 1981);* Flowers from the Volcano *(a poetry collection translated by* **Carolyn Forché**, *University of Pittsburgh Press, 1982); (edited with Flakoll)* Nicaragua: La Revolucíon sandinista: Un crónica politica 1955–1979 *(Nicaragua: The Sandinista Revolution, a Political chronicle, Central America, 1982);* Karen en barque sur la mer *(French version of novel* El detén *and poetry* Petit pays, *Paris, 1983);* Despierta mi bien despierta *(Awake, My Love, Awake, El Salvador, 1986);* Woman of the River *(poetry trans. by Flakoll, United States, 1989);* Y este poema-rio *(And This River Poem, Nicaragua, 1989); (edited with Flakoll)* On the Frontline *(guerrilla poetry, Curbstone, 1990);* Album familiar *(Family Album, three-novella collection, Women's Press, England, 1990, Curbstone, United States, 1991);* Fugas *(Fugues, Curbstone, 1993). Also edited with Flakoll,* Cien poemas de Robert Graves *(One Hundred Poems of Robert Graves).*

Following the climax of the Cuban revolution in 1959, the 1960s ushered in what the writer Arturo Arias has called a "golden decade of Latin American narrative [boom literature]," during which it became evident to a number of writers living in Central America that those who were politically committed could employ new narrative methods in order to blend their personal and political concerns. At the forefront of this movement was Claribel Alegría, who initiated what Arias has described as a "generic transition from poetry to narrative" that led to "the transformation of Central American literature."

Alegría's most singular achievement is the novel *Cenizas de Izalco* (*Ashes of Izalco*), co-written with her journalist husband Darwin (Bud) Flakoll, and widely recognized today as a seminal work in Central American literature. Rooted in Alegría's childhood memories of the *matanza*, it is the story of the 1932 massacre of 30,000 peasants in Izalco, El Salvador, by members of the Salvadoran army, as the country's military dictatorship sought to quell an uprising led by the revolutionary hero Farabundo Martí. Since the book's first publication, in 1966, it has become an instrument for Salvadoran school children to learn about a chapter in their history that the dictator Maximiliano Hernández Martínez had sought to excise, performing what Alegría has called a "cultural lobotomy" on her people by means of censorship.

Indeed, all of Alegría's writing is rooted in the historical and social history of her region, as well as in its spiritual life and its "magical reality." It is the work of a woman who knows the pain of exile, but who, first and foremost, as she writes in her experimental prose-verse novel, *Luisa In Realityland,* believes in "the resurrection of the oppressed/ in the Church of the people/ in the power of the people."

This writer who was to become a voice for the oppressed was born into a well-to-do family in Estelí, Nicaragua. Her mother was a member of the oligarchy of neighboring El Salvador, and her father was a physician with liberal views who had fought against "yanqui invaders" as a boy. Before Alegría's first birthday, the family was forced to flee to El Salvador because of her father's active opposition to the 1925 occupation of Nicaragua by U.S. Marines. Alegría remembers being told by her mother that when she was eight months old and in her mother's arms in front of her house, a bullet narrowly missed the two of them and lodged in the wall.

In El Salvador, Alegría's childhood was enriched by various storytelling uncles, by her

Claribel
Alegría

grandmother's reciting of Biblical passages, and by the family's well-stocked library. The house was frequented by Salvadoran intellectuals—**Claudia Lars**, Alberto Guerra Trigueros, Serafin Quiteño, and José Vasconcelos, who eventually wrote the prologue to her first book of poems, *Ring of Silence*. In 1929, Alegría entered the progressive school of her uncle Ricardo, where she learned regional history, mythology, and geography. In 1932, after the *matanza,* her teacher, Chico Laura, explained the reason for the uprising, describing the conditions of the country in which the vast majority of Salvadorans lived in abject poverty, while the wealth of the country was in the hands of a privileged few. Alegría's sense of injustice grew steadily after the *matanza,* reinforced by her view of the squalid lives of the children in the *meson,* or tenement, across the street from her house. She has related that she began to understand "the cruel reality in which the majority of my countrymen were immersed," and the knowledge opened in her "a deep psychic wound that has never healed."

Alegría has often spoken of the encouragement received from her mother regarding her literary ambitions, and the complicity of her father and grandfather, as well as family friends like Trigueros and Quiteño. But she has also acknowledged the difficulties in Central America for a woman wishing to become a writer in a social atmosphere where women who wrote were regarded as "pedantic" or "crazed." From an early age, she consciously sought out women poets as role models: Claudia Lars, *Sor Juana Inez de la Cruz, *Gabriela Mistral, *Alfonsina Storni, and others. Alegría revealed in an interview that she feels that "women poets of this generation—the Sandinista women—are better than their male contemporaries," and that the women writers of the region, by bearing witness to their own experience, are educating people around the world about "the position of women in Central America, about the importance of women in the liberation movements, about the many women who have died under torture." Alegría points to the stereotypical gender roles reinforced by male *machismo* that support the oppression of women in her culture, with a political awareness that draws on memories of her own youth. Though she finished secondary school before her 16th birthday, her father initially refused to send her abroad to study, stating that it was a "woman's place" to stay beside her mother, learning from her until marriage. He also refused to allow Alegría to study medicine at the University of San Salvador, consigning her instead to a regimen of sewing, piano, and cooking lessons. During this interval, Alegría read and wrote extensively, biding her time. Her father finally realized her misery when she admitted that she had been weeping because she found herself praying for him to die and set her free. Shortly thereafter, she was sent with her brother to study in the United States.

Alegría first attended a preparatory school for women in Hammond, Louisiana, repeating her senior high school year in order to learn English, the language in which she preferred to study. She was successful enough to win a scholarship to Loyola University, but after attending a summer session there in 1944, she followed the advice of Juan Ramón Jiménez and his wife **Zenobia**; they recommended that she study at George Washington University in Washington, D.C., where she could be tutored by Jiménez in poetry. The resultant volume of her poems, *Anillo de silencio* (*Ring of Silence*), came out in Mexico in 1948, the year after she met and married Bud Flakoll, and the year in which she graduated from the university, conspicuously pregnant with her first child.

During the ensuing years, especially after twin daughters were born in mid-1950, Alegría had little time for writing, with the exception of a book of children's stories, *Tres cuentos* (*Three Stories*). In 1951, however, after Flakoll accepted a job as managing editor of the *Daily News* in Mexico City, she was able to hire household help and proceed with her writing; she has said, "For me, Mexico was a rebirth." Soon she had produced two new collections of poetry, *Suite,* which was published in Argentina in 1951, and *Vigilias* (*Vigils*), written mostly in sonnet form, in which Alegría feels that she came into her own poetic voice. At this time, she also forged friendships with prominent Latin American writers Augusto (Tito) Monterroso, Juan José Arreola, and Juan Rulfo.

In 1953, *Vigilias* was published in Mexico, and Alegría and Flakoll moved their family to Chile, where they were supported by a Catherwood Foundation grant while they worked together, compiling an anthology for English-speaking readers of Latin American writers who were part of the new literary "boom." Among the writers introduced to the English-speaking world by their *New Voices of Hispanic America,* published in 1962, were Ernesto Cardenal, Juan Rulfo, *Rosario Castellanos, Mario Benedetti, Julio Cortázar, and Octavio Paz.

In 1953, after giving birth to her son Erik, Alegría completed a new book of poems,

Acuario (*Aquarium*), in which she emerged from her more personal perspectives of the past into social awareness and the characteristic humor that marks her later work. The years 1956–59 were trying on a personal level, however, as she and Bud returned to Washington so that he could train for the foreign service; they were subsequently posted in Montevideo, Uruguay. In 1958, despite her completion of the poems that would later appear as *Huésped de mi tiempo* (*Guest of My Time*), Alegría felt her poetic expression blocked.

After another diplomatic transfer to Argentina in 1960, Alegría, inspired by the overthrow of the dictatorship in Cuba, published *Vía Unica* (*One Way Traffic*), a volume of poetry that embodies her newly confirmed belief in political self-determination in Latin America. The Cuban revolution established Havana as a haven for Latin American artists and offered them the opportunity for cross-cultural communication. In 1962, when Flakoll resigned from the foreign service to resume a journalistic career, the family moved to Paris, where their apartment became a gathering place for prominent Latin American writers—Julio Cortázar, Carlos Fuentes, Saul Yurkievich, Mario Benedetti, and Mario Vargos Llosa. It was Fuentes who suggested that Alegría write a historical novel about the *matanza,* and eventually Flakoll suggested that they write it together. Although the plan was for Flakoll to write from the male protagonist's point of view and Alegría to write from that of the female protagonist, the collaboration was so close that today neither can remember who wrote which part of the novel. The project took two years, and publication was initially delayed by Spanish censorship. According to Alegría, *Ashes of Izalco* was eventually allowed to be published in El Salvador, when the dictator, General Arturo Armando Molina, decided to "leave office with a liberal image." Since then it has become a secondary school text, has gone through many editions, and is widely acknowledged as one of the most important Central American novels of the 20th century. Nominally a love story, it captures the spirit and essence of an event that shaped the character of El Salvador for years to come. Into the novel Alegría has poured her outrage and grief for the peasants and Indians whom she saw marched by her house with their thumbs tied behind their backs, and the painful memory of the shots she heard that marked their execution.

In 1966, Alegría and Flakoll decided to move to the island of Majorca and devote their full time to writing, and in 1968 they bought a house, Ca'n Blau Vell ("the old blue house") in Deyá. For Alegría, the Deyá years were highly productive, covering the time that she wrote *Pagaré a cobrar* (*Installment Payments*); *Sobrevivo* (*I Survive*), which won the Casa de las Américas Prize in 1978; *Suma y sigue* (*Add and Carry*); and three short novels: *El detén* (*The Talisman*), *Album familiar* (*Family Album*), and *Pueblo de Dios y de Mandinga* (*Village of God and the Devil*). The latter novella evokes the magical reality of Deyá, and its protagonist is based on Robert Graves, a close friend of Alegría and Flakoll's. During this time, they were collaborating on an anthology of Graves' poems, as well as on another anthology of poems by young U.S. poets, *Nuevas Voces de Norteamerica* (*New Voices of North America*). Also in Deyá, at the urging of Cortázar and his wife **Carol Dunlap,** Alegría wrote *Luisa in Realityland,* an experimental prose-verse novel that contains reminiscences of her childhood.

In 1979, rejoicing at the flight of the dictator Anastasio Somoza II and his son El Chiguín from Nicaragua, and the ascendancy to power of the Sandinista rebels, Alegría and Flakoll returned to Nicaragua for six months to do the research for an historical account of the Sandinista revolution, using interviews of the *comandantes* and soldiers who had finally triumphed after 20 years of struggle against the Somoza dynasty. They were on their way back to Deyá to write their account when they stopped in Paris to visit their daughters, and were told by the Salvadoran writer Roberto Armijo that Monsigñor Oscar Arnulfo Romero, archbishop of San Salvador, had been assassinated by a member of the government's death squad while saying mass in a hospital chapel. Alegría, who had been preparing for a poetry reading at the Sorbonne, stayed up all night with Flakoll preparing a statement of outraged protest against the Salvadoran government and its death squads, which she delivered instead of her poems. Shortly afterward, Alegría reports, her cousin, who was director of the national guard of El Salvador and later minister of defense, told her that she should not return to that country, as he could not guarantee her safety. Viewing this event as her moment of "awakening," the poet has said: "I felt that I had to do something for my people, that I had to have the courage to speak out about what was happening. I was frequently invited to the United States and Europe, and I felt it would be self-betrayal if I didn't speak out."

Thus began a long period of political exile. When her mother died in El Salvador in 1982,

Alegría was warned by her brother not to return, or "there would most likely be two burials." Since the signing of the peace agreement, in 1992, she has returned to the country once, on the anniversary of her mother's death, to lay flowers on her grave. In the interim, she has received threatening letters, one of which "bore the letterhead of the Women's Auxiliary of ARENA," the death squad party in power. The letter said that as Alegría was "senile" and "crazy," they wouldn't "bother" to kill her but would revenge themselves on her children. Not even that threat could silence her.

In *Contemporary Authors Autobiography Series*, Alegría states that she writes her poetry "under obsession's spur." And though the political and social turmoil in Latin America began to obsess her in 1982, she says, "The poems that I began to write then are not political, as some have said. To me, they are love poems to my people, to my America. . . . But if a situation or event moves me, that event can sometimes be translated into poetry, just as love or death or a tranquil evening can be so translated."

Nicaragua: La revolutión sandinista: Una crónica politica, 1955–1979 (*Nicaragua: The Sandinista Revolution, a Political Chronicle*) was published in 1982, and the years since then have been productive ones for Alegría. Her growing political awareness has been manifested, in part, in her collaboration with Flakoll in recording a number of testimonies, or eyewitness accounts, of the *comandantes,* soldiers, and political prisoners in El Salvador and elsewhere in Latin America. Among these works are *La encrucijada salvodoreña* (*Salvadoran Crossroads*), *No me agarran viva* (*They Won't Take Me Alive:* the story of Comandante Eugenia's life and death), and *Para romper el silencio* (*To Break the Silence:* the history of El Salvador's political prisoners). Because most of the people who could tell these stories were in Nicaragua, Alegría and Flakoll decided in 1983 to make their principal residence in Managua, Nicaragua, and to vacation occasionally in Deyá.

Besides the remarkable testimonies, Alegría continued in the mid- to late-1980s to publish poetry and fiction in France, Mexico, England, El Salvador, and the United States. *Flowers from the Volcano*, poetry translated by **Carolyn Forché**, was published by the University of Pittsburgh Press in 1982, and *Woman of the River*, translated by Flakoll, in 1989. In 1990, *On the Frontline*, an anthology of Salvadoran guerrilla poetry, edited with Flakoll, was published in the United States by Curbstone Press, which also

brought out three novellas written at Deyá under the collective title *Family Album*. Another short novel, *Despierta mi bien despierta* (*Awake, My Love, Awake*) was published in El Salvador in 1986, and *Y este Poema-río* (*And This River Poem*) was published in Nicaragua in 1989. Many other poems and stories have appeared in journals and have been anthologized.

> *B*ecause I want peace
> and not war
> because I don't want to see
> hungry children
> squalid women
> men whose tongues
> are silenced
> I have to keep on fighting
> —Claribel Alegría

Claribel Alegría's joy in life, her creativity, her political commitment, and her courage endure. She and Flakoll wrote yet another testimony, covering the account of 48 political prisoners in Lima, Peru, who tunneled to safety through a 345-meter cavity dug secretly over a period of three years at the maximum-security detention center, Canto Grande, from a safehouse operational base outside the walls to a point within the prison. On the basis of their previous testimonies, Alegría and Flakoll were invited by some members of the MRTA (Peruvian Tupac Amaru Revolutionary Movement) to go to Lima and spend a week in a much hunted-for clandestine safehouse, interviewing escapees and the people who had planned and dug the tunnel. In addition, a new book of poems, *Fugas* (*Fugues*), was published by Curbstone Press in 1993, whose themes, Alegría says, are "love, death, and the encounter with old age." This volume incorporates the perspectives of such female mythological figures as Penelope, Pandora, Persephone, and Demeter in light of contemporary feminism and psychology.

Alegría has said in many interviews that she writes "letras de emergencia" or "urgent literature." Her sense of urgency, as well as her humor and ebullience, pervade her fiction, her poetry, and her testimonies. As **Marjorie Agosín** has said in the Foreword to *Claribel Alegría and Central American Literature*, "By means of this woman's furious, fiery, tender and lovesick words, the marginalized, the indigenous recuperate spaces, resuscitate their dead, and celebrate life by defying death."

SOURCES:

"Alegría, Claribel," in *Contemporary Authors Autobiography Series*. Vol. 15. Detroit, MI: Gale Research, 1992.

Boschetto-Sandoval, Sandra M., and Marcia Phillips McGowan, eds. *Claribel Alegría and Central American Literature*. Ohio University.

SUGGESTED READING:

Beverley, John, and Marc Zimmerman. *Literature and Politics in the Central American Revolutions*. Austin: Texas University Press, 1990.

Center for International Studies: Monographs in International Studies, 1993. (This anthology contains 13 critical essays on Alegría's work, as well as a bibliography and an interview with the author.)

Hopkinson, Amanda. *Lovers and Comrades: Women's Resistance Poetry from Central America*. London: The Women's Press, 1989.

Sternbach, Nancy Saporta. "Remembering the Dead: Latin American Women's 'Testimonial' Discourse," in *Latin American Perspectives*. Vol. 18, no. 3. Summer 1991, pp. 91–102.

Marcia Phillips McGowan,
Professor of English and director of Women's Studies,
Eastern Connecticut State University,
Willimantic, Connecticut, and author with
Sandra M. Boschetto-Sandoval
of *Claribel Alegría and Central American Literature*

Aleksandrovna, Vera (1895–1966)

Russian émigré literary critic, historian, and editor. Born Vera Aleksandrovna Mordvinova in 1895; died in New York in 1966; married S.M. Shvarts, who introduced her to Marxist theories, in 1919.

Exiled to Germany (1921), to France (1933), to the United States (1940) where she worked with Margaret Mead, the anthropologist; served as editor-in-chief of the Chekhov Publishing House, making important contributions to Soviet literature.

When Vera Aleksandrovna Mordvinova was born, tsarist Russia was in its final decline, a fact that would shape the whole of her life. Her family was politically patriotic and intellectually conservative, beliefs Vera soon rejected. She studied in Odessa and Moscow, where she spent much of her time in artistic and literary circles centering around religious and mystical ideals. In 1919, she married the Menshevik activist S.M. Shvarts who introduced her to Marxist theories. Strongly opposed to Lenin's concept of a proletarian dictatorship led by the Bolsheviks, she became a Menshevik with beliefs similar to that of the Social Democratic movements of Western Europe. This break with Leninist party doctrine had immediate consequences, as the new Soviet regime was aggressively purging Soviet Russia of dissidents. In 1921, she and her husband went into exile in Germany.

Throughout the next dozen years, she contributed numerous articles to leading German and Austrian Social Democratic publications under the name Vera Aleksandrovna. By the late 1920s, she had also become a respected contributor to the émigré Menshevik magazine *Sotsialisticheski vestnik* (*Socialist Herald*). In 1933, politics again intervened in Aleksandrovna's life with the advent of Nazism in Germany; she and her husband fled to Paris, which had a large and intellectually vibrant Russian émigré community. For several years, she continued her journalistic work and deepened her knowledge of the history of Russian literature. In June 1940, Hitler's troops invaded France, and leftists like Aleksandrovna and her husband were targeted for extinction. The couple's last flight was to New York in 1940. Virtually penniless but full of hope for the future, she was soon a regular contributor to the respected émigré journals *Novoe russkoe slovo* and *Novyi zhurnal*. As her reputation in New York intellectual circles grew, she also wrote for a number of English-language periodicals.

Vera Aleksandrovna became involved with many literary projects in the United States. Her contributions to the magazine *Amerika* from 1946 through 1948 gained a widening audience. She also worked on a research project concerning human behavior led by *Margaret Mead at Columbia University. From 1951 to 1956, Aleksandrovna was editor-in-chief of the Chekhov Publishing House, one of the leading voices of the Russian émigré intelligentsia. During the last years of her life, she worked on English-language editions of histories of Soviet literature, which gained wide critical acclaim.

Vera Aleksandrovna's vision of the future was not Stalin's harsh socialism or Hitler's cruel fascism. She believed the modern state could provide jobs, health care, and retirement benefits for all its citizens, while allowing them to function in a democratic state.

SOURCES:

Aleksandrovna, Vera. *A History of Soviet Literature, 1917–1962*. Garden City, NY: Doubleday, 1963.

——. *A History of Soviet Literature, 1917–1964: From Gorky to Solzhenitsyn*. Garden City, NY: Doubleday, 1964.

Terras, Victor, ed. "Aleksandrovna, Vera," in *Handbook of Russian Literature*. New Haven, CT: Yale University Press, 1985, pp. 18–19.

John Haag, Associate Professor of History,
University of Georgia, Athens, Georgia

Alekseeva, Lidiya (1909—)

Russian émigré poet. Name variations: Lidiia Alekseevna Alekseeva. Born Lidiya Alekseeva Devel in

Dvinsk, Russia, in 1909; began to write poetry at age seven; continued her mystical writing despite exile and displacement.

Lidiya Alekseeva Devel was born into a military family in Dvinsk, Russia, in 1909. Her family traced its ancestry back to a French émigré from the Napoleonic period. Growing up in the Crimea, Alekseeva began to write poetry at age seven. The advent of Bolshevism disrupted her life and, in 1920, she left Russia for Yugoslavia, where she spent the next two decades. Displaced by the war in 1945, she immigrated once more, in 1949, to the United States.

Alekseeva appeared in print by the time she was in her early 20s. In many ways a traditionalist, she never attempted to create new techniques that did not necessarily enhance the emotional core of a poetic statement. Some of her major themes depicted humans as frightened, lonely pilgrims in the universe, enduring the burdens of freedom in an age alienated from God. Though much of her work expresses despair, strains of optimism appear in her descriptions of the beauty and wisdom of nature. Alekseeva is a significant poet of the Russian literary emigration, whose poetry was held in high regard by her maternal relative, the great Russian poet *Anna Akhmatova. Although virtually all of her major work is in verse, Lidiya Alekseeva also published a number of delicately tinted, lyrical prose miniatures.

John Haag, Associate Professor of History, University of Georgia, Athens, Georgia

Alekseyevna, Sophia (1657–1704).

See Sophia Alekseyevna.

Alençon, Emilenne d'.

See Uzès, Anne, Duchesse d' for sidebar.

Aleotti, Raffaella (c. 1570–c. 1646)

Italian composer. Probably born in 1570; probably died in 1646; daughter of Giovanni Battista (architect to Alphonso II d'Este, duke of Ferrara); elder sister of Vittoria Aleotti; studied harpsichord and composition with Alessandro Milleville and Ercole Pasquini; entered the Augustinian convent of San Vito, Ferrara; wrote some of the earliest Italian music in the concertante style.

After entering the Augustinian convent at a very young age, Raffaella Aleotti took her vows in 1590. She was the elder sister of *Vittoria Aleotti, who was also a composer. Raffaella's musical talents were already greatly developed in the flourishing atmosphere of the San Vito, Ferrara, convent. About 1593, she took over the direction of the *concerto grande,* the convent's main ensemble that consisted of 23 singers and instrumentalists who played the harpsichord, lute, bass viol, flute, cornet, and trombone. In 1598, the ensemble performed in the presence of Pope Clement VIII and the queen of Spain ❧➤ **Margaret of Austria** (c. 1577–1611) who unsuccessfully urged Aleotti to return to Spain with her. Aleotti probably composed a great deal of music but only her *Sacrae cantiones . . . liber primus* for five, seven, eight and ten voices has survived.

John Haag, Associate Professor of History, University of Georgia, Athens, Georgia

Aleotti, Vittoria (c. 1573–c. 1620)

*Italian composer. Probably born in 1573; probably died in 1620; daughter of Giovanni Battista (architect to Alphonso II d'Este, duke of Ferrara); younger sister of *Raffaella Aleotti; studied harpsichord and composition with Alessandro Milleville and Ercole Pasquini; entered the Augustinian convent of San Vito, Ferrara, where she assisted her sister with the convent ensemble as well as with composing.*

Vittoria Aleotti came from a musical family, as both her father and older sister were composers. After entering the San Vito convent at Ferrara, she assisted her sister Raffaella with the musical ensemble, writing many pieces for the group. One of her madrigals for five voices was included alongside leading Ferrarese madrigalists in the famous anthology *Il giardino de musici ferrarsei* published in 1591. Her father published *Ghirlanda de madrigali,* which included a collection of four-part madrigals Vittoria had written, that same year. In the latter work, there are two spiritual madrigals and 19 secular ones. Aleotti's music is known for its grace and passion.

Aleramo, Sibilla (1876–1960).

See Pierangeli, Rina Faccio.

Alexander, Annie Montague
(1867–1949)

American naturalist who devoted her life to the fields of paleontology, botany, ornithology, and mammology. Born in Honolulu, Hawaii, in 1867; died in 1949; lived with Louise Kellogg.

Founded the Museum of Vertebrate Zoology and the Museum of Paleontology at the University of California, Berkeley.

Margaret of Austria. *See Anne of Austria (1601–1666) for sidebar.*

Annie Montague Alexander seems to have developed her wanderlust early in life. Born in Honolulu, Hawaii, she spent her childhood on the exotic island of Maui, then moved with her family to Oakland, California, when she was 15. Her education included private schools and a tour of Europe, as was the prescribed path of most privileged young women around the turn of the century. Her father, a wealthy real-estate investor and avid traveler, often took his daughter along on his trips and tours. He was killed in an accident while on safari in East Africa, leaving a considerable fortune.

A friend, *Martha Beckwith, an instructor at Mount Holyoke College, first interested Alexander in science. She began to attend lectures on paleontology at the University of California at Berkeley, and, by 1903, Alexander was heading up her own expeditions. These included a series of trips to Alaska, where she collected a large number of skulls of different mammal species. On one trip, she discovered a new subspecies of grizzly bear, *Ursus alexandrae,* which was named after her.

In 1909, Alexander collaborated with naturalist Joseph Grinnell to establish a natural history museum on the Berkeley campus, the first of its kind on the West Coast. She provided the funds while Grinnell became the museum's permanent director. That same year, Alexander also established the university's Department of Paleontology.

At the age of 41, Alexander met and began traveling with *Louise Kellogg, then 28, and the two would remain close companions for the rest of Alexander's life. From 1911 to 1922, they lived on a farm on Grizzly Island in the California Suisun Marshes, raising asparagus and cattle. When Alexander was 53, the pair undertook another series of collecting trips, exploring the desert regions of California, Nevada, New Mexico, Utah, Colorado, Idaho, and Arizona, often enduring primitive living conditions and intense heat, sometimes as high as 136 degrees.

In 1939, Joseph Grinnell died, and the two women turned their attention to botany, collecting over 17,851 botanical specimens for the University of California Herbarium, including a new and rare species of grass, named *Swallennia alexandrae.* Their further contributions to the Museum of Vertebrate Zoology included specimens of 6,744 different animals, some new to science.

Alexander continued her travels into the wild with Kellogg until she suffered a debilitating stoke at 81. She died several months later. Kellogg continued to make collecting trips until her own death, 17 years later.

SUGGESTED READING:

Bonta, Margaret Meyers. *Women in the Field: America's Pioneering Naturalists.* College Station, TX: Texas A&M Press, 1991.

Reifschneider, Olga. *Biographies of Nevada Botanists.* Reno: University of Nevada Press, 1964.

COLLECTIONS:

Alexander's papers reside at the Bancroft Library at the University of California at Berkeley; her field notebooks are located at the Museum of Vertebrate Zoology at the University of California at Berkeley.

Barbara Morgan, Melrose, Massachusetts

Alexander, Cecil Frances

(1818–1895)

Irish children's hymn writer and poet. Name variations: C.F. Alexander; Mrs. Cecil Frances Alexander. Born Cecil Frances Humphreys in County Wicklow in 1818; died in Londonderry, on October 12, 1895; daughter of Major John Humphreys; married William Alexander, Protestant bishop of Derry (afterwards archbishop of Armagh and primate of all Ireland), in 1850; children: four—two boys and two girls, including Robert, who was awarded the Newdigate Prize for English Verse while at Oxford.

Cecil Frances Alexander started writing poetry at age nine, spurred on by a sister who could be counted on to request a reading. She grew up in the countryside of Strabane on the borders of Donegal and Tyrone, the daughter of Major John Humprey, an agent for the Duke of Abercorn. The family was active in the Church of Ireland, aiding the sick, the poor, and establishing a school for "deaf and dumb" children. Early in her career, Alexander came under the influence of Dr. Hook of Leeds, the dean of Chichester, and John Keble, who edited her *Hymns for Little Children.*

Following her marriage to William Alexander, Cecil Frances lived with her husband in the

WOMEN IN WORLD HISTORY

remote community of Termonamongan in County Tyrone. From there, they moved to the parish of Fahan, on Lough Swilly, and then returned to Strabane, when William was appointed rector.

All things bright and beautiful,

All creatures great and small,

All things wise and wonderful,

The Lord God made them all.

—Cecil Frances Alexander

With her close friend **Lady Harriet Howard**, Alexander wrote tracts for the Oxford Movement. Her poetry, celebrating the rugged beauty of rural Ireland, has been the impetus for many hymns, including "Once in Royal David's City," "Roseate Hue of Early Dawn," "There is a Green Hill Far Away," and "All Things Bright and Beautiful." Her most famous poems were "The Siege of Derry" and "The Burial of Moses," the latter of which appeared anonymously in 1856 in the *Dublin University Magazine*. Alfred Lord Tennyson admitted it was one of the few poems that made him envious of its authorship. Following her death, in 1895, her husband, also a poet, collected and edited her works. Alexander wrote 400 hymns and was favorably compared to Rudyard Kipling. "The best of her hymns were neither new nor old," writes Stephen Gwynn, "just as Shakespeare's songs are neither new nor old—and the best of them were written when she was a girl under twenty."

SOURCES:
Lazell, David. "The Children's Hymn Writer," in *This England*. Winter 1985, pp. 12–13.

Alexander, Hattie (1901–1968)

American microbiologist, pediatrician, and researcher, who was an early pioneer in DNA research. Born Hattie Elizabeth Alexander in Baltimore, Maryland, on April 5, 1901; died in New York City on June 24, 1968; daughter of William B. and Elsie M. (Townsend) Alexander; graduated A.B., Goucher College, 1923; M.D., Johns Hopkins, 1930; never married; no children; lived with Elizabeth Ufford.

First woman to serve as president of the American Pediatric Society; discovered the first cure for pediatric influenza meningitis; one of the first researchers to note bacterial resistance to antibiotics; collaborated with Grace Leidy, noting changes in DNA, which was very early research in this field; received the E. Mead Johnson Award for Research in Pediatrics (1942), the prestigious Stevens Triennial Prize (1954), and the Oscar B. Hunter Memorial Award of the American Therapeutic Society (1961).

Hattie Alexander was born in Baltimore, Maryland, on April 5, 1901. Her ancestors on both sides of her family were Scottish. Energetic and curious, she was determined to continue her education after graduating from high school. At Goucher College, Alexander was an average student, more interested in athletics than in intellectual pursuits. Nonetheless, the Goucher yearbook of 1923 summed up what would be her lifetime attributes: "Ambition fires her; hygiene claims her; kindness portrays her." Alexander's strong interest in hygiene led her to study bacteriology and physiology. After graduation, she worked as a bacteriologist for several years to save money for medical school. At the Johns Hopkins Medical School, she was a brilliant student, graduating with an M.D. in 1930.

Alexander's first job was at the Harriet Lane Home in Baltimore, where she developed a lifelong interest in influenza meningitis. In 1931, she interned at Babies Hospital of the Columbia-Presbyterian Medical Center, and upon completion of her service she accepted an appointment in the pediatrics department. A superb teacher as well as a researcher and medical doctor, Alexander emphasized skepticism and disbelief as a prerequisite to medical progress. She made her students defend their diagnostic decisions. At bedside discussions, she frequently used recurring questions such as, "What is your evidence?" or "What makes you think so?" Alexander's remarkably successful professional life at Columbia-Presbyterian culminated in her promotion to full professor in 1958.

Alexander's first research studies at the Harriet Lane Home in Baltimore dealt with the diagnosis and treatment of bacterial meningitis, a disease that had caused great frustration because it did not respond to anti-influenza serum prepared in horses. Knowing that researchers at the Rockefeller Institute had prepared a highly effective serum for the treatment of pneumonia in rabbits, Alexander applied this technique to the previously intractable problem of developing an effective therapy for meningitis. Working with the immunochemist Michael Heidelberger, she immunized rabbits with large doses of influenza bacilli. In this way, she developed a complete cure for infants critically ill with influenza meningitis. Her work, published in 1939, was the first successful treatment of this previously fatal disease. After this success, Alexander began experiments to discern how various drug treatments would combat influenza meningitis. First she worked with sulfa drugs before moving on to other antibiotics. After years of painstaking research, she also produced therapeutic strategies that significantly reduced the death rate of patients with influenza meningitis.

Alexander was one of the first medical researchers to note the rapid development of resistance of influenza bacilli cultures to antibiotic drugs. Her scientific curiosity led her into an intensive study of the new area of microbiological genetics. Unlike many others who responded with skepticism or indifference, Alexander immediately recognized the great importance of the 1944 Rockefeller Institute report detailing artificial changes in hereditary characteristics of pneumococci by means of the genetic constituent that would later be known as DNA. Collaborating with **Grace Leidy**, she developed techniques that produced hereditary changes in the DNA of *Hemophilus influenzae* in 1950. This research provided a highly successful confirmation and served as an extension of the work done in microbiological genetics at the Rockefeller Institute in the 1940s.

Hattie Alexander

After her retirement in 1966, Alexander continued to lecture and serve as a consultant to the Presbyterian Hospital. She remained impressively productive, incorporating the latest insights in genetic research into her investigations of several bacterial species and a number of viruses. She also continued teaching in the wards, where she passed on her vast store of clinical knowledge to a generation of pediatricians. Her clinical studies in this stage of her career included tuberculosis, then regarded as a disease about to disappear from modern civilization.

Alexander published over 150 papers during her lifetime. The merit of her work was widely recognized and she was awarded the E. Mead Johnson Award for Research in Pediatrics in 1942, the prestigious Stevens Triennial Prize in 1954, and the Oscar B. Hunter Memorial Award of the American Therapeutic Society in 1961. In 1964, Hattie Alexander was chosen the first woman to serve as president of the American Pediatric Society.

Alexander had many interests outside medicine. She was especially fond of music, travel, and the growing of rare, exotic flowers. She lived in Port Washington, New York, with her companion of many years, Dr. **Elizabeth Ufford**. Both women loved boating, and the residents of Port Washington were used to seeing the two zoom past in their speedboat. Having made important scientific contributions to the 20th century, Hattie Alexander died of cancer in New York City on June 24, 1968.

SOURCES:

McIntosh, Rustin. "Hattie Alexander," in *Pediatrics*. Vol. 42, no. 3, September, 1968, p. 544.

Turner, Lenore. "From C Student to Winning Scientist," in *Goucher Alumnae Quarterly*. Winter, 1962, pp. 18–20.

Vare, Ethlie Ann, and Greg Ptacek. *Mothers of Invention: From the Bra to the Bomb: Forgotten Women & Their Unforgettable Ideas*. NY: William Morrow, 1988.

John Haag, Associate Professor of History, University of Georgia, Athens, Georgia

Alexander, Leni (1924—)

German-born Chilean composer. Born on June 8, 1924, in Breslau, Germany (today Wrocław, Poland); lived in Hamburg, Germany, until 1939 when forced by Nazi racial and political persecution to flee with her family to Chile; continued her musical studies in Santiago, concentrating on piano and cello; began to study composition (1949); became Chilean citizen (1952); studied in France and Italy (1954–55); returned to France (1969).

Had Adolf Hitler not seized power in Germany in 1933, Leni Alexander would likely have had a successful musical career in one of Germany's great cities. Instead, she grew up in a refugee culture in South America and returned to Europe as a mature artist on the threshold of an international career. By her early 20s, Alexander had decided to become a composer, and she studied with some of Chile's finest teachers. But Europe always beckoned, and a scholarship from the French government in 1954 enabled her to study in Paris with such eminent composers as René Leibowitz and Olivier Messiaen. During this period, she studied as well with other members of the European avant-garde, the Italian composers Luigi Nono and Bruno Maderna. Returning to Chile, she reviewed her earlier work and attempted to incorporate her European experiences into her new compositions. By 1959, Alexander was receiving commissions to compose ballet scores and other works. A Guggenheim fellowship in 1969 enabled her to return to France for further study. Because of the bloody military coup in Chile in 1973, Alexander was to remain in Europe, dividing her time between Paris and Cologne. As a modernist, she did not expect her compositions to become popular, but many of them gained her respect from fellow composers and small but growing circles of listeners. Her work included preparing programs for Radio France and teaching.

John Haag, Associate Professor of History, University of Georgia, Athens, Georgia

Alexander, Mrs. (1825–1902).

See Hector, Annie French.

Alexandra (r. 76–67 BCE)

Queen of Judea. Name variations: Salome Alexandra; Alexandra Salome. Birth date unknown; died in 67 BCE; married King Alexander Jannaeus (or Jannæus) of the Asmonean, also known as the Hasmonean or Hasmonian, dynasty (Syria) who ruled from 103–76 BCE; children: John Hyrcanus II (d. 30 BCE); Aristobulus II.

Succeeding her husband Alexander Jannaeus, Alexandra was the ruler of the Maccabees in Judea from 76 to 67 BCE (some sources cite 78 to 69 BCE) during the continued conflict between the Sadducees and Pharisees. In a reversal of her husband's policies, she supported the Pharisees. After her death, her eldest son, the high priest John Hyrcanus II, succeeded her in name only, as he was engaged in a civil war against his brother Aristobulus II. Hasmonean power ended with Pompey's seizure of Jerusalem in 63 BCE.

Alexandra (d. 27 BCE)

*Hasmonian royal. Died in 27 BCE; daughter of John Hyrcanus II (d. 30 BCE); granddaughter of *Alexandra (r. 76–67 BCE); married her cousin Alexander (d. 49 BCE, son of Aristobulus II); children: *Mariamne the Hasmonian (d. 29 BCE); Aristobulus III (d. 36 BCE).*

Alexandra (1921–1993)

*Queen of Yugoslavia. Name variations: Alexandra Oldenburg; Alexandra of Greece. Born in Athens, Greece, on March 25, 1921; died at her home outside London on September 30, 1993; daughter of Alexander I, King of the Hellenes, and *Aspasia Manos (daughter of a royal equerry); great-grandchild of Queen *Victoria; married Peter II, the last king of Yugoslavia, on March 20, 1944, at the Yugoslav Legation in London; children: Alexander Karadjordjevic (b. July 17, 1945).*

Alexandra was born into Greek royalty in 1921, five months after her father Alexander I, king of Greece, died of blood poisoning from the bite of a pet monkey. Though formally recognized as a princess when she was 18 months old, she was exiled in England the following year because of shifting Greek politics. Alexandra did not reappear in Greece until 13 years later, when her uncle, King George II, returned to rule in 1935. When the Germans overran Greece during World War II, Alexandra and her mother again traveled to London. While there, she met King Peter II, who was studying at Cambridge. The Yugoslavian king was also in exile, having fled his country after the 1941 invasion of German troops. A year after their marriage in 1944, Peter was formally deposed when Marshal Tito established a communist regime in Yugoslavia. The royal property was confiscated, leaving the couple virtually penniless. Peter died in Denver, Colorado, in 1970 following a liver transplant. Alexandra was seriously ill with cancer for several years before her death in 1993.

Alexandra, Queen of England (1844–1925).

See Alexandra of Denmark.

Alexandra Feodorovna (1798–1860).

See Charlotte of Prussia.

Alexandra Feodorovna (1872–1918)

*Empress of Russia who played a major role in undermining the stability of the Russian monarchy during the first part of the 20th century. Name variations: Alix or Alexandra of Hesse-Darmstadt; christened Princess Alix Victoria Helena Louise Beatrice, Princess of Hesse-Darmstadt, changed her name to the Russian form and took a Russian title of nobility, becoming Grand Duchess Alexandra Feodorovna at the time of her marriage. Born on June 6, 1872, in the city of Darmstadt in the German principality of Hesse-Darmstadt; murdered along with her family by Communist authorities on the night of July 16–17, 1918, at Ekaterinburg in western Siberia; daughter of Prince Louis of Hesse-Darmstadt and Princess Alice Maud Mary (1843–1878) of Great Britain; granddaughter of Queen Victoria; educated by private tutors; married Nicholas II, tsar of Russia, in 1894; children: ✤ Olga (1895–1918); ✤ Tatiana (1897–1918); ✤ Marie (1899–1918); *Anastasia (1901–1918); Alexis (1904–1918).*

Her mother and younger sister died (1878); made first trip to Russia and had first meeting with future husband (1884); her father died (1892); on the death of Tsar Alexander III, Nicholas became Tsar Nicholas II (1894); Nicholas and Alexandra married (1894);

✤➤ **Olga** (1895–1918)

Russian grand duchess. Name variations: Olga Nicholaevna. Born Olga Nicholaevna Romanov (Romanoff or Romanovna) on November 15, 1895, in St. Petersburg, Russia; executed by the Bolsheviks on July 16–17, 1918, at Ekaterinburg, in Central Russia; daughter of Alexandra Feodorovna (1872–1918) and Nicholas II (tsar of Russia).

✤➤ **Tatiana** (1897–1918)

Russian grand duchess. Name variations: Tatiana Nicholaevna. Born Tatiana Nicholaevna Romanov (Romanoff or Romanovna) on June 10, 1897, in St. Petersburg, Russia; executed by the Bolsheviks on July 16–17, 1918, at Ekaterinburg, in Central Russia; daughter of Alexandra Feodorovna (1872–1918) and Nicholas II (tsar of Russia).

✤➤ **Marie** (1899–1918)

Russian grand duchess. Name variations: Mary Nicholaevna. Born Marie Nicholaevna Romanov (Romanoff or Romanovna) on June 26, 1899, in Peterhof, Russia; executed by the Bolsheviks on July 16–17, 1918, at Ekaterinburg, in Central Russia; daughter of Alexandra Feodorovna (1872–1918) and Nicholas II (tsar of Russia); never married; no children.

coronation held (1896); her grandmother, Queen Victoria, died (1901); outbreak of Russo-Japanese War (1904); outbreak of revolution and Rasputin entered entourage of imperial family (1905); Rasputin expelled from St. Petersburg despite Alexandra's objections (1911); Rasputin seemingly saved life of Alexis (1912); 300th anniversary of Romanov dynasty (1913); outbreak of World War I (1914); Nicholas left Petrograd to command the Russian army (1915); Miliukov gave speech of accusation in Russian Duma and Rasputin assassinated (1916); March Revolution, tsar abdicated, Romanov family arrested and exiled to Siberia, November Revolution (1917); Alexandra, Nicholas, and their children executed (1918).

On November 26, 1894, the strikingly beautiful Princess Alix of Hesse-Darmstadt, granddaughter of Queen *Victoria, married the 26-year-old Nicholas Romanov who had just become Nicholas II, tsar of Russia. His first decree as tsar, only three weeks before, had declared that Alix was now the Russian Grand Duchess Alexandra Feodorovna and a member of the Russian Orthodox Church. Her cousin *Alexandra of Denmark, the princess of Wales, remarked that "she looked too wonderfully lovely" in her wedding costume of silver, gold, and ermine. Nonetheless, the occasion was marked by sadness instead of joy.

The young couple had faced the disapproval of the Russian imperial family during their brief courtship. But the overshadowing tragedy of the moment was the sudden passing of Nicholas' father, Alexander III, dead of kidney failure at the age of 49. Now, both painfully young and utterly inexperienced in the problems of government, Nicholas and Alexandra found themselves monarchs of the largest and most troubled of the great powers of Europe. He and Alix had planned a gala wedding. Instead, the young couple married in haste only a week after his father's funeral. Struck by the gloomy atmosphere in St. Petersburg, Alexandra described the marriage ceremony as "a mere continuation of the masses for the dead."

The Russia over which Nicholas and Alexandra ruled as unlimited monarchs was a

Alexandra Feodorovna surrounded by her husband Nicholas II and (back row, left to right) Grand Duchess Anastasia, Tatiana, Olga, and Marie. Tsarevitch Alexis is at her feet.

country in a state of calm, but it was a calm preceded by painful turmoil, and the turmoil was soon to resume. The coronation festivities for Nicholas II led to a particular horror. Half a million Russians, many of them peasants from distant parts of the empire, had come to Moscow at the tsar's invitation to help celebrate the coronation. They gathered for a feast at Khodynka Field, five miles out of Moscow. There were too few police to control the crowd, and no one in authority had remembered that Khodynka Field was covered with ditches and trenches left over from military maneuvers. When the great horde of people rushed across the field to the food stalls awaiting them, at least 1,300 people died, trampled to death.

Although Nicholas visited the injured in the hospital and established a generous fund to aid the families of the dead, his reputation among the Russian population was hurt by the memory of Khodynka Field. Why, people asked, had he and Alexandra attended a party at the residence of the French ambassador the night following the tragedy? How could he hold a giant military review at Khodynka Field little more than a week after so many of his unfortunate subjects had been killed there?

An empire of 150 million people, Russia was tormented by the poverty of its peasant population and the pain of an industrialization pro-gram forced ahead at breakneck speed by the government. There was unrest among its ethnic minorities (who made up half the population), and a recent history of political violence. In 1881, as a boy of 16, Nicholas had witnessed the death of his grandfather, Alexander II, at the hands of assassins.

Alexandra had been born in the small German principality of Hesse-Darmstadt on June 6, 1872. In the previous year, Prime Minister Otto von Bismarck of Prussia had succeeded in creating a united Germany that included Hesse-Darmstadt. During the last years of her life, Alexandra was to bear the heavy burden of being identified with Germany, Russia's most dangerous opponent in World War I.

The young princess was a child with a happy disposition—her childhood nickname was "Sunny," and Nicholas used it in writing to her throughout their 24-year marriage. But tragedy entered her life in 1878 when first her small sister, then her mother ◄✥ **Alice Maud Mary**, died of diphtheria. Alix was raised by governesses, but a constant presence in her life was her grandmother, Queen Victoria of Great Britain. In 1884, Alix accompanied Victoria to Russia for the marriage of her sister *Ella to a member of the Russian imperial family. On a second trip to visit Ella in 1889, she and Nicholas fell in love.

Following her marriage, Alexandra plunged into much of Russian life: she enthusiastically practiced the Eastern Orthodox version of Christianity, which was the official religion. She appointed herself her new husband's "guardian angel" in commenting on how he led his country. At the same time, the new empress kept herself aloof. She disliked most members of the court, and she equally disliked appearing in public.

Despite her isolation, Alexandra was confident of her understanding of the Russian people's wishes. She took advantage of her ability to dominate her vacillating husband and urged Nicholas—who did not need urging—to resist any moves to change the top heavy political system. But her focus was on her family duties and the pressing need to provide heirs to the throne. Her first four children were girls, all of whom grew to be attractive young women. The male heir, needed for political reasons, came only in 1904, and the boy, Alexis, suffered from a dreadful illness—hemophilia—for which his mother felt deeply responsible. Hemophilia was a hereditary disease passed down to a child by its mother. Alexandra searched desperately for people outside the regular medical community

---

✥► **Alice Maud Mary** (1843–1878)

*Princess of Great Britain and Ireland, duchess of Saxony, and grand duchess of Hesse-Darmstadt. Name variations: Alice Saxe-Coburg. Born on April 25, 1843, at Buckingham Palace, London, England; died of diphtheria on December 14, 1878, in Darmstadt, Hesse, Germany; second daughter of Queen *Victoria and Prince Albert; married Prince Louis of Hesse-Darmstadt (1837–1892), also known as Grand Duke Louis IV, in 1862; children: seven, including *Victoria of Hesse-Darmstadt (1863–1950, who married Louis Alexander of Battenberg, marquis of Milford Haven, and was the mother of Lord Mountbatten); *Ella (1864–1918, who married Grand Duke Serge of Russia and became Elizabeth Feodorovna); Irene (1866–1953, who married Prince Henry of Prussia); Ernest (who married *Victoria Melita of Edinburgh); Alix (1872–1918, who became empress *Alexandra Feodorovna of Russia and married Nicholas II); Mary Victoria (b. May 1874–1878, who died of diphtheria in infancy, the same year as her mother). Princess Alice founded the Women's Union for Nursing Sick and Wounded in War.*

---

who could help her imperilled son. A cavalcade of unlicensed healers found they were welcomed at the palace.

Outside the palace, popular unrest was rising. The economic strains of the Russo-Japanese War and the failure of the government to lead the nation effectively were having their effect. In January 1905, on "Bloody Sunday," crowds of Russians tried to petition the tsar to help them. As hundreds were shot down in front of Nicholas' Winter Palace, Nicholas and Alexandra isolated themselves at the Tsarskoe Seloe palace outside St. Petersburg. The country was shaken by strikes, peasant unrest, and a growing call for political change. By the fall of 1905, the empire was paralyzed by a general strike. Everyone from bakers to ballet dancers refused to work.

The tsar found himself compelled to issue the "October Manifesto," granting the two concessions he had always rejected: the creation of a *Duma* with the power to make laws, and a Constitution. The Revolution of 1905 had apparently overturned much of the old order, but Nicholas remained stubbornly committed to the outmoded ways. Almost from the moment he issued the October Manifesto, Nicholas showed his distaste for the changes that had been forced upon him. In early 1906, ridding himself of Finance Minister Sergei Witte, the architect and first prime minister under the new system, Nicholas insisted on keeping the title of "autocrat" (or unlimited monarch). He repeatedly restricted the power of the Duma and frequently spoke of eliminating it entirely.

As Russia remained torn by internal divisions after the Revolution of 1905, the tsar's prestige continued to decline. Exerting an important influence on him, the Empress Alexandra strengthened Nicholas' own conservative inclinations, in particular his view that restrictions on his power violated Russia's political and religious heritage. She insisted to her "Nicky" that he play the role of a strong, unmovable monarch, a fitting descendant of Peter the Great in the 18th century.

Finally, in a way that tied the troubles of the imperial family to the looming tragedy of the Russian state, a Siberian peasant and self-proclaimed holy man named Rasputin was introduced to the empress and her husband in late 1905. Rasputin's ability to treat Alexis' hemophilia gave him increasing psychological control over the empress. Russia's more capable political leaders, like the Prime Minister Peter Stolypin, became alarmed when word of Rasputin's scandalous sexual behavior became the talk of the capital. Inevitably, the smutty stories grew to stain Alexandra's reputation. Stolypin managed to expel Rasputin from St. Petersburg in 1911, but, the following year, the holy man gained an unshakable hold over Alexandra and the imperial family by seeming to save young Alexis from a critical attack of hemophilia.

In August 1914, Alexandra's adopted country went to war with Germany, the country of her birth. Rumors swirled about what loyalties the empress, who had removed herself from public view for years, really held. Alexandra gave the Russian people no answer that might have alleviated their concerns. Along with her daughters, she qualified as a nurse and tended the wounded during WWI, but she was careful to do this away from the public eye. At the same time, she went on playing guardian angel to stiffen and supervise her "Boysy," her indecisive husband. Ironically, Nicholas, who was so vulnerable to his wife's wishes, held political powers that made him the most significant monarch in Europe.

As the war went on and Russia's military catastrophes grew, Alexandra moved toward the center of political life. She showed no grasp of her country's desperate realities. She had greeted the conflict as a "healthy war" that would raise the nation's spirits. Always suspicious of Russia's leading officials—and most suspicious when they were talented—the empress continually urged Nicholas to send away the most gifted and confident ones.

Alexandra's dependency upon Rasputin grew in two measurable ways. First, her references to him no longer stopped at calling him a holy man: she now identified him as a Christ figure. Second, Rasputin's likes and dislikes, especially toward the country's key leaders, determined who would rise and for how long, and who would lose power.

In the fall of 1915, Alexandra persuaded her husband to leave St. Petersburg (which had been renamed Petrograd) to take personal command of the defeated Russian armies at the fighting front. The tsar had no real desire to direct the war and, when Alexandra and the children came to visit him at the front, he had no difficulty forgetting about military decisions in order to find time for them. In reality, General Mikhail Alexeev, the army chief of staff, ran the war.

The irreparable harm in Nicholas' absence came as Alexandra, with Rasputin at her side, took over the role of ruling monarch. Alexis Polivanov, the capable war minister, Serge

Sazonov, the foreign minister, and a host of others were removed from office to be replaced by political naifs acceptable to Rasputin. Alexandra was particularly hostile to the weak parliament, the Duma. Its leaders were distressed by the disastrous course the war was taking, and they were trying to find an expanding role for themselves in directing Russia's affairs.

In November 1916, the tensions that had been building up for years came out in a dramatic Duma speech. Paul Miliukov, head of the Cadet (Constitutional Democratic) Party and one of the country's most important liberals, implied that there was a lack of patriotism at the top of Russian political life. Miliukov pushed beyond the previous boundaries of propriety by listing the failures of the government and, after each instance asking, "Is this stupidity or is this treason?" To most of his listeners, his attacks were directed in the first instance at Boris Sturmer, an inept prime minister appointed at Rasputin's insistence. But at least indirectly, the attacks reached up to stain the empress.

In late 1916, as the country approached the third winter of the war, rumors swirled in Petrograd about a coming revolutionary change. Informed observers thought that perhaps the army's leaders would take power. Meanwhile, Alexandra's faith in Rasputin continued to grow—she scorned members of the imperial family who criticized him—and she labeled any talk of political unrest as "high treason."

The empress was crushed when conservative plotters murdered Rasputin in December 1916. But even more catastrophic events soon descended on Russia's rulers. In March 1917, food riots, military mutinies, and railroad strikes in and around the capital could not be put down. In despair and desperation, Nicholas tried to pass his throne to another member of his family but no one would accept it. The monarchy limped to its close, and the monarch, now a private citizen, stole back to Petrograd to join his family.

Alexandra spent the last year of her life in worsening conditions of confinement. There was no easy way out of revolutionary Russia for the former empress and her loved ones. The country's wartime allies—even Great Britain whose royal family had numerous blood ties to the Romanovs—would not help. In the crucial wartime atmosphere of 1917, politics meant more than family ties among royalty. To aid Alexandra, her husband, and her children meant risking Britain's wartime alliance with the new revolutionary Russian government. Russia had to be kept fighting at all costs.

Alexandra and her family were sent for safe keeping to western Siberia by Russia's post-revolutionary leaders. When the more radical Bolsheviks led by V.I. Lenin and Leon Trotsky came to power in November 1917, hope that the Romanovs would survive faded. The outbreak of civil war in the spring of 1918 sealed their fate.

White forces, opposed to the Bolsheviks, approached the city of Ekaterinburg in the Ural Mountains where the former monarchs, their family, and a small retinue were held. If anti-Bolshevik forces were to save Nicholas, the former tsar would be a rallying point for counter-revolution. Lenin and Trotsky would not permit this to happen. During the night of July 16–17, 1918, Nicholas, Alexandra, their four daughters and son, and several members of their household, were roused from their sleep. Escorted to the cellar by a local commissar, they were executed by a firing squad. The 11 victims were buried in an abandoned mineshaft, then reburied in an open field.

SOURCES:

Crankshaw, Edward. *The Shadow of the Winter Palace.* NY: Viking Press, 1976.

Lincoln, W. Bruce. *In War's Dark Shadow: The Russians before the Great War.* NY: Dial Press, 1983.

———. *Passage through Armageddon: The Russians in War and Revolution, 1914–1918.* NY: Simon and Schuster, 1986.

Massie, Robert K. *Nicholas and Alexandra.* NY: Atheneum, 1967.

Pipes, Richard. *The Russian Revolution.* NY: Alfred A. Knopf, 1990.

SUGGESTED READING:

Buxhoeveden, Baroness Sophie. *The Life and Tragedy of Alexandra Feodorovna, Empress of Russia: A Biography.* London: Longmans, Green, 1929.

Ferro, Marc. *Nicholas II: Last of the Tsars.* Translated by Brian Pearce. NY: Oxford University Press, 1993.

King, G. *The Last Empress.* Birch Lane, 1995.

Lincoln, W. Bruce. *The Romanovs: Autocrats of All the Russias.* NY: Dial Press, 1981.

RELATED MEDIA:

"Nicholas and Alexandra," film starring Michael Jayston and **Janet Suzman** (183 min.), Columbia Pictures, produced by Sam Spiegel, directed by Franklin Schaffner, 1971.

"Rasputin," film (in Russian) starring **Velta Linei** and Alexei Petrenko (104 minutes), Mosfilm Studios, produced by Semyon Kutikov, directed by Elem Klimov, 1985.

Neil M. Heyman, Professor of History, San Diego State University, San Diego, California

Alexandra Guelph (1882–1963)

Grand Duchess of Mecklenburg-Schwerin. Born in Gmunden, Austria, on September 29, 1882; died in

*Glucksburg, Schleswig-Holstein, Germany, on August 30, 1963; daughter of Ernest Augustus, third duke of Cumberland and Teviotdale, and *Thyra Oldenburg (sister of *Alexandra of Denmark and Empress *Marie Feodorovna of Russia); married Frederick Francis IV, grand duke of Mecklenburg-Schwerin, on June 7, 1904; children: four, including Christian Louis, duke of Mecklenburg-Schwerin.*

Alexandra Nikolaevna (1825–1844)

*Landgravine of Hesse-Cassel. Name variations: Alexandra Nicholaievna; Alexandra Romanov. Born on June 12, 1825; died on August 10, 1844; daughter of *Charlotte of Prussia (1798–1860) and Nicholas I (1796–1855), tsar of Russia (r. 1825–1855); married Frederick William, landgrave of Hesse-Cassel, on January 28, 1844. Frederick William was also married to Anne Frederica (1836–1918).*

Alexandra of Denmark

(1844–1925)

*Queen-consort of King Edward VII of Great Britain, remembered for her classical beauty and her interest in charities and social relief programs. Name variations: Princess Alexandra of Schleswig-Holstein-Sönderborg-Glücksborg; Alexandra Oldenburg; Queen Alexandra; Alix, Princess of Wales. Pronunciation: AL-ig-ZANdra. Born Alexandra Caroline Marie Charlotte Louise Julia on December 1, 1844, at Gule Palace in Copenhagen, Denmark; died at Sandringham, Norfolk, England, on November 20, 1925; eldest daughter of Prince Christian of Schleswig-Holstein-Sönderborg-Glücksborg (future Christian IX) and Louise of Hesse-Cassel (daughter of the Landgrave William of Hesse-Cassel); sister of *Thyra Oldenburg and *Marie Feodorovna (1847–1928, Russian empress and wife of Tsar Alexander III of Russia); her education was simple; she was taught foreign languages including English, and had a marked aptitude for music; married Albert Edward, prince of Wales (and heir to the British throne as Edward VII), on March 10, 1863; children: (two sons) Albert Victor (duke of Clarence, who predeceased his father), and George (duke of York, prince of Wales, and King George V); (three daughters) *Louise Victoria (1867–1931, princess royal and duchess of Fife); *Victoria (1868–1935); *Maud (1869–1938, queen of Norway).*

Met the Prince of Wales (1861); betrothed (1862); married (1863); official trips with her husband to several countries (1864–81); became queen-consort to King Edward VII on his accession to the throne (1902); granted Order of the Garter (1902); established Queen Alexandra Imperial Military Nursing Service (1902); became dowager queen following Edward VII's death (1910); "Alexandra Day" established in her honor (1913).

Princess Alexandra of Denmark was carefully selected to marry Albert Edward, crown prince of Great Britain (the future Edward VII). The time had passed when a princess was chosen for a large dowry or to satisfy diplomatic necessities, but it was essential that she be beautiful, cheerful, and dignified. Alexandra was a breathtakingly handsome woman with a graceful demeanor that even impressed a dour Queen *Victoria when she first met her in 1862. Alexandra became an immediate and lasting favorite of an admiring British public.

Alexandra Caroline Marie Charlotte Louise Julia was born on December 1, 1844, at Gule Palace, Copenhagen, Denmark. She was the eldest daughter and second of six children of Prince Christian of Schleswig-Holstein-Sönderborg-Glücksborg and Princess *Louise of Hesse-Cassel, daughter of landgrave William of Hesse-Cassel. Alexandra's parents lived in modest surroundings in Copenhagen, but Louise's mother, a niece of King Christian VIII (r. 1839–1848), was the natural heiress to the Danish throne, one step removed from her childless cousin, King Frederick VII (r. 1848–1863). When a succession struggle became imminent, several European nations reached an agreement in 1852, known as the London Protocol, which established the borders of Denmark and named Prince Christian and Princess Louise as heirs to the crown of Denmark.

Alexandra spent her youthful years living in the Yellow Palace, an unpretentious home provided by her maternal grandfather, on a street lined with similar houses near the Copenhagen harbor. She shared a room with her sister, Dagmar, who later married the crown prince of Russia and became *Marie Feodorovna (1847–1928). Prince Christian, only a captain in the Danish Guards, had a small income. To make ends meet, the girls sewed their own clothes and knitted their own stockings. Though they were taught foreign languages and learned English from English nannies, to save money on their education their mother taught them music and religion and their father looked after their physical training. Sometimes the girls spent the summers at the 18th-century château of Bernstorff, ten miles from Copenhagen. Hans Christian Andersen was a family friend and visitor whom Alexandra and her siblings knew well.

Alexandra of Denmark on Royal Yacht Osborne.

Alexandra was a beautiful young lady. She had blue eyes, light brown hair, and a tanned, dark complexion. Possessing an excellent, athletic figure, she was an outstanding equestrian and a graceful dancer. A pleasant child of good temperament, affection, honesty and tact, Alexandra was also impulsive, somewhat unsophisticated, and passionate. Her beauty and personality offset her weaker qualities, which included an inherited deafness, a lack of clever intelligence, and a proclivity to be late for ceremonies or appointments.

In 1858, while Alexandra was still a child, the British royal family was intent on selecting a bride for Albert Edward, prince of Wales. King Leopold I of Belgium, on whose advice the English monarchs, Queen Victoria and Prince Albert, heavily relied, provided a list of seven eligible and prospective brides. Leopold, who was Victoria's uncle, strongly favored Alexandra and even underlined her name on the list. The desire of the royals to procure a suitable bride for Prince Albert Edward was a pragmatic deci-

sion. Bertie, as he was known, was extremely well-educated in a formal way, fluent in three languages, had traveled extensively and was an avid, competent sportsman. Though he was charming and handsome, he had a gourmet's love of food and was highly susceptible to women's charms with a careless attitude towards the consequences of scandal. His parents concluded that marriage would curb his overexuberant appetites. The prospective bride must be of royal blood, Protestant, attractive, healthy, and of good disposition. After discarding several European princesses for a variety of reasons, Alexandra, not highly considered at first, gained in status after it was learned that her photograph had been forwarded to the Russian court as a possible bride for Alexander III, the Romanov heir. On viewing her picture, Queen Victoria and Bertie were impressed, and Bertie declared that he would immediately marry Alexandra. Much of the matchmaking was performed by Bertie's older sister, Vicky (***Victoria Adelaide**, 1840–1901), wife of the crown prince of Prussia, who arranged a secret meeting for Alexandra and Bertie in Speyer, Germany, on September 24, 1861, and a few days later in Heidelberg.

Following the German gatherings, Bertie, who had been impressed with Alexandra's beauty, hedged on the marriage plans. Prior to their rendezvous, the fickle Bertie had entered a liaison with **Nellie Clifton** (or Clifden), an actress he had met at Curragh, Ireland. Because Clifton bragged about their affair, the story spread throughout London and left Prince Albert heartbroken over his son's behavior. In the midst of this family crises, Prince Albert died of typhoid fever on December 14, 1861. Queen Victoria would always blame Bertie and the Clifton affair for his death. Determined to carry out her late husband's wishes, Victoria set in motion the plans for Bertie to marry Alexandra. More inquiries were made about the young woman, and Queen Victoria traveled to Brussels to meet her on September 2, 1862. In sympathy to the queen's mourning, Alexandra wore a plain, black dress without jewels to the engagement. Her loveliness and simplicity captivated the queen and formal arrangements were made with Alexandra's parents. The betrothal was announced at Laeken Palace near Brussels on September 9, 1862.

The wedding took place on March 10, 1863, in St. George's Chapel, Windsor, amidst uniformed officers, diamonds, robes, feathers, and lace. Bertie wore the uniform of a general and the robes of the Order of the Garter. Alexandra wore a silver-tissue dress, trimmed in an ornate Honiton lace, and the skirt was garlanded in orange blossom loops. It took eight bridesmaids to bear her long train. Queen Victoria, who had taken Bertie and Alexandra to Prince Albert's mausoleum at Frogmore for her deceased husband's approval the day before, wore black widow's weeds and watched the service from the privacy of *Catherine of Aragon's closet. The newlyweds honeymooned at Osborne on the Isle of Wight for a week before returning to Buckingham Palace.

The self-imposed seclusion of the queen at Windsor gave the young prince and princess of Wales the only available sway over the social world of Britain. The aristocracy flocked to this new younger circle of court gaiety and youthful excitement that had been missing since Prince Albert's death. Both of the royals delighted in entertaining, but their court was unrecognizable from previous entourages. Prior to this time, the aristocracy had been one of political ambition and power, but those surrounding Alexandra and Bertie were the "idle rich" pursuing a life of ease and pleasure. The young couple had the Norfolk estate of Sandringham, their elegant London home of Marlborough House, and were well off financially. Although they had the revenues from the duchy of Cornwall and a sizable stipend voted to them by Parliament, they often overspent their incomes. Bertie showered Alexandra with jewels and generally spent money extravagantly with his wealthy friends. Alexandra wildly donated to charities and exhibited no money sense at all.

During the first year of her marriage, in 1863, Alexandra's father became king of Denmark as Christian IX (r. 1863–1906) and her brother was elected king of Hellenes (Greece) as George I. By the end of the year, Alexandra's happiness was shattered by the outbreak of war between Denmark and Prussia over the duchies of Schleswig-Holstein, which were claimed not only by her father, but also by Wilhelm I of Prussia on behalf of his son, who was Bertie's brother-in-law. Alexandra's emotions were divided between sympathy for her family and the Danish people or loyalty to her new family and the strong-willed mother-in-law who forcefully supported Prussia. Denmark eventually lost the war and its territorial claims. When the conflict ended, Alexandra and Bertie, while on a tour of Europe, visited her family in Denmark. On Queen Victoria's insistence, the visit had to be private, because a state visit would have suggested support for the Danes. An added insult by Queen Victoria was the arrangement of a marriage between her daughter, ❧ **Helena**, and the duke of Schleswig-Holstein, who had fought Alexandra's parents in the recent war. Bertie joined Alexandra in an unsuccessful opposition to the marriage. Alexandra refused to attend the wedding, but Bertie, who had initially refused, gave in to his mother and family and reluctantly showed up.

During the time of the Danish war, Alexandra had been pregnant with her first child. On January 7, 1864, after two days of watching ice-hockey and attending skating parties on frozen ponds, she went into labor two months early. The baby, weighing only three and three-quarter pounds was wrapped in flannel purchased from a draper in Frogmore. The child, named Albert Victor, managed to survive, but the premature birth resulted in oxygen deprivation to the brain. As he grew, he had learning disabilities and was unable to concentrate, which would raise doubts about his suitability to serve as king of England. Alexandra's other four children—George (born in 1865), ❧ **Louise Victoria** (in 1867), ❧ **Victoria** (in 1868), and *Maud (in 1869)—suffered no complications and were normal.

❧ *Helena.* See Queen Victoria for sidebar.

❧ *See sidebar on the following page*

Alexandra was a religious woman and her interest in the church increased as she grew older and sought comfort. Her deafness, probably hereditary, worsened as her life progressed. She tried unsuccessfully to learn lip-reading but shunned the rather obvious devices of the time such as ear-trumpets. Following the birth of Louise, Alexandra became very ill with leg pains and high fever. Diagnosed as having rheumatic fever but possibly polio, she took months to recover from the excruciating pain and would remain permanently lame in one leg. Bertie continued to live a luxurious life and never lost his eye for women. Alexandra could do little but ignore the gossip about his numerous affairs, which included actresses like *Sarah Bernhardt, *Lillie Langtry, and the Moulin-Rouge cancan dancer, *La Goulue. Others were with society women such as *Frances Evelyn Greville, countess of Warwick, *Alice Keppel, and Miss Chamberlayne, the daughter of a millionaire from Cleveland. Bertie was once involved, though not as co-respondent, in the Mordaunt public divorce case. He was also accused, but found not guilty, in a card-sharking scandal and was even threatened by a prominent politician with blackmail for his earlier affair with Lady Aylesford. Alexandra tolerated his many liaisons and even stood by his side in scandals. She never forgave him for his insensitive neglect of her when she was ill but never tried to beat him at his own promiscuous game. Bertie was rapidly destroying all public support for the royal family when a near-fatal typhoid fever attack swung popular support back to him.

❧▸ **Louise Victoria** (1867–1931)
*Princess Royal and duchess of Fife. Born Louise Victoria Alexandra Dagmar Saxe-Coburg on February 20, 1867, in London, England; died on January 4, 1931, in London; daughter of Edward VII, king of England (r. 1901–1910), and *Alexandra of Denmark (1844–1925); married Alexander Duff, 1st duke of Fife, in 1889; children: three, including *Alexandra Victoria (1891–1959, Princess Arthur of Connaught) and *Maud Duff Carnegie.*

❧▸ **Victoria** (1868–1935)
*Princess Royal. Name variations: Victoria Saxe-Coburg. Born Victoria Alexandra Olga Mary on July 6, 1868, in London, England; died on December 3, 1935, in Iver, Buckinghamshire, England; daughter of Edward VII, king of England (r. 1901–1910), and *Alexandra of Denmark (1844–1925).*

Alexandra turned to her children for solace and emotional satisfaction. She continued to fulfil her social obligations and even accompanied her husband on four state visits to Ireland and a foreign tour to Egypt and Greece in 1868–69. As the years passed, she made several state trips abroad. She refrained from foreign policy statements unless it involved Denmark or Greece. She fearlessly traveled to St. Petersburg, Russia, in March 1881 to be at the side of her sister, Empress Marie, following the assassination of Tsar Alexander II.

Meanwhile, Alexandra's children were growing up. In 1889, her eldest daughter, Louise, was married to Alexander, earl of Fife. Alexandra's major concern, however, was finding a suitable bride for Prince Albert Victor, duke of Clarence. Eddie, as he was called, was very charming but was overly interested in sexual matters and very fickle toward women. Feeling that marriage might be a positive experience for him, Alexandra and Bertie selected Princess *Mary of Teck, an Englishwoman by upbringing who was related to the English ruling family. Eddie and Mary became engaged in December 1891 but a few weeks before the scheduled wedding, Eddie died of influenza on January 13, 1882. His death at the age of 28 was a crushing blow to Alexandra who had held his hand as he died.

Feeling that Mary of Teck had been the ideal wife for one son, it seemed logical to the family that she would be an excellent choice for George, duke of York. The wedding took place in 1893 and Alexandra entered a new phase of her life. Still beautiful, although much older, deaf and partially lame, she was now caught in a situation between the elderly Queen Victoria and the young Mary, duchess of York. Though Alexandra and Bertie were still heirs to the throne, Alexandra withdrew more and more to Sandringham. Bertie continued his profligate and lavish lifestyle while being totally excluded by his mother from national affairs and politics.

Queen Victoria died on January 22, 1901, with Alexandra, Bertie and the family in attendance. At Westminster Abbey, on August 9, 1902, Bertie succeeded to the throne as Edward VIII and Alexandra was crowned as queen consort. In one of his first acts as monarch, Edward bestowed upon Alexandra the Order of the Garter. Always interested in charity, improved medical care, and helping the poor, Alexandra doubled her efforts in those matters. She was instrumental in founding the Queen Alexandra Imperial Military Nursing Service in 1902. She raised large amounts of revenue to help the unemployed workmen during the economic crisis in 1906.

Alexandra was queen for a very short time. Edward VII died on May 6, 1910. Her devotion to her husband was so complete that she even invited Edward's current mistress, Alice Keppel, to visit him during his fatal illness. Alexandra withdrew into virtual retirement at Sandringham but returned to comfort her people and the wounded soldiers during the First World War. In 1913, the 50th anniversary of her arrival in Britain, "Alexandra Day" was established for the sale of roses to benefit British hospitals.

The last two years of Alexandra's life were quietly passed at Sandringham. She actively followed the lives of her grandchildren and her favorite was King George's son Edward VIII. It is doubtful that she would have approved of his love affair and abdication for Mrs. *Wallis Warfield Simpson (duchess of Windsor) in 1936. Alexandra died suddenly and peacefully of a heart attack at Sandringham on November 20, 1925, and was interred beside her husband in St. George's Chapel at Windsor. She was solemnly mourned by a nation that remembered her for her charity, beauty, and patience.

SOURCES:

Battiscombe, Georgina. *Queen Alexandra.* Boston, MA: Houghton Mifflin, 1969.

Cook, Petronelle. *Queen Consorts of England.* NY: Facts on File, 1993.

Fisher, Graham, and Heather Fisher. *Bertie and Alix: Anatomy of a Marriage.* London: R. Hale, 1974.

St. Aubyn, Giles. *Edward VII: Prince and King.* NY: Atheneum, 1979.

SUGGESTED READING:

Argy, Josy, and Wendy Riches. *Britain's Royal Brides.* London: David & Charles, 1975.

Arthur, George C.A. *Queen Alexandra.* London: Chapman & Hall, 1934.

Gernsheim, Alison, and Helmut Gernsheim. *Edward VII and Queen Alexandra: A Biography in Word and Picture.* London: Muller, 1962.

Madol, Hans Roger. *The Private Life of Queen Alexandra As Viewed by Her Friends.* London: Hutchinson, 1940.

Trowbridge, William R.H. *Queen Alexandra: A Study of Royalty.* London: T.F. Unwin, 1921.

Phillip E. Koerper, Professor of History, Jacksonville State University, Jacksonville, Alabama

Alexandra of Hesse-Darmstadt
(1872–1918).

See Alexandra Feodorovna.

Alexandra of Kent (1936—)

Princess. Name variations: Princess Alexandra Windsor. Born Alexandra Helen Elizabeth Olga Christabel on December 25, 1936, in London, England; daughter of George Windsor, 1st duke of Kent, and *Marina of Greece (1906–1968); studied at Heathfield School, 1947, first British princess to attend a public school; married Angus Ogilvy, on April 24, 1963; children: James Ogilvy (b. 1964); *Marina Ogilvy (b. 1966).

Alexandra of Oldenburg
(1838–1900)

Russian royal. Born Alexandra Fredericka Wilhelmina on June 2, 1838; died on April 25, 1900; daughter of Peter (b. 1812), duke of Oldenburg, and *Therese of Nassau (b. 1815); granddaughter of Duke William of Nassau and Louise of Saxe-Altenburg; married Nicholas Nicholaevitch (son of Nicholas I of Russia and *Charlotte of Prussia), on February 6, 1856; children: Nicholas Nicholaevitch (b. 1856, who married *Anastasia Petrovitch-Njegos); Peter Nicholaevitch (b. 1864, who married *Militza of Montenegro).

Alexandra of Saxe-Altenburg
(1830–1911)

Russian royal. Name variations: Elizabeth Alexandra of Saxe-Altenburg. Born Alexandra Fredericka Henrietta Pauline Marianne Elizabeth on July 8, 1830; died on July 6, 1911; daughter of Joseph, duke of Saxe-Altenburg, and *Amelia of Wurttemberg (1799–1848); married Constantine Nicholaevitch (son of Nicholas I of Russia and *Charlotte of Prussia), on September 11, 1848; children: Nicholas (b. 1850); *Olga Constantinovna (1851–1926, who married George I, king of the Hellenes); *Vera Constantinovna (1854–1912); Constantine Constantinovitch (b. 1858); Dmitri (b. 1860); Vladislav (b. 1862).

Alexandra Oldenburg (1844–1925).

See Alexandra of Denmark.

Alexandra Oldenburg (1870–1891)

Greek princess. Name variations: Alexandra of Greece. Born on August 18, 1870; died at age 21, six days after the birth of her son, on September 12, 1891; daughter of George I, king of Hellenes, and *Olga Constantinovna; married Paul Alexandrovitch (son of Alexander II of Russia and *Marie of Hesse-Darmstadt), grand duke, on June 5, 1889; children: *Marie Pavlovna (1890–1958); Dmitri Pavlovitch (b. 1891).

Alexandra Pavlovna (1783–1801)

Archduchess of Austria. Born on August 9, 1783; died on March 16, 1801; daughter of *Sophia Dorothea of Wurttemberg (1759–1828) and Paul I (1754–1801), *tsar of Russia (r. 1796–1801); married Joseph, archduke of Austria, on October 30, 1799; children: Alexandrine (1801–1801).*

Alexandra Saxe-Coburg
(1878–1942)

Princess of Hohenlohe-Langenburg. Name variations: Alexandra of Saxe-Coburg. Born Alexandra Louise Olga Victoria on September 1, 1878, in Coburg, Bavaria, Germany; died on April 16, 1942, at Schwabisch Hall, Baden-Wurttemberg, Germany; daughter of Alfred Saxe-Coburg, duke of Edinburgh (son of Queen Victoria) and *Marie Alexandrovna (1853–1920); sister of *Marie of Rumania; married Ernest, 7th prince of Hohenlohe-Langenburg, on April 20, 1896; children: Godfrey (b. 1897), 8th prince of Hohenlohe-Langenburg; Marie-Melita of Hohenlohe-Langenburg (b. 1899); Alexandra of Hohenlohe-Langenburg (b. 1901); *Irma of Hohenlohe-Langenburg (1902–1986); Alfred (b. 1911).

Alexandra Victoria (1891–1959)

Princess Arthur of Connaught, duchess of Fife. Name variations: Alexandra Duff and Countess of Macduff. Born Alexandra Victoria Alberta Edwina Louise Duff on May 17, 1891, in Richmond-upon-Thames, Surrey, England; died on February 26, 1959, in London, England; elder daughter of Alexander Duff, first duke of Fife, and of *Louise Victoria (1867–1931, daughter of Edward VII); married Arthur Windsor, Prince Arthur of Connaught, in 1913; children: Alastair Windsor, 2nd duke of Connaught and Strathearn.

In 1912, Alexandra succeeded her father Alexander Duff, becoming duchess of Fife. She took up nursing and practiced at St. Mary's Hospital in Paddington (1915–19), while with her husband in South Africa (1920–23), and at University College and Charing Cross hospitals. She also ran the Fife Nursing Home in London from 1939 to 1949.

Alexandra Victoria of Schleswig-Holstein (1887–1957)

German royal. Name variations: Alexandra of Schleswig; Alexandra Victoria of Schleswig-Holstein-Sonderburg-Glucksburg. Born Alexandra Victoria Augusta Leopoldine Charlotte Amelia Wilhelmina on April 21, 1887, in Grunholz, Germany; died on April 15, 1957, in Lyon, France; daughter of Frederick Ferdinand, duke of Schleswig-Holstein-Sonderburg-

Glucksburg, and *Caroline Matilda of Schleswig-Holstein (1860–1932); married Augustus William (son of Kaiser Wilhelm II and *Augusta of Schleswig-Holstein), on October 22, 1908 (divorced 1920); married Arnold Rumann, on January 7, 1922 (divorced 1933); children: (first marriage) Alexander Ferdinand (b. 1912), prince of Prussia.

Alexandrina of Baden (1820–1904)

Duchess of Saxe-Coburg and Gotha. Name variations: Alexandrine. Born Alexandrina Louise Amelia Fredericka Elizabeth Sophia Zahringen on December 6, 1820; died on December 20, 1904; daughter of Leopold, grand duke of Baden, and *Sophia of Sweden (1801–1865, daughter of Gustavus IV Adolphus of Sweden); married Ernest II, duke of Saxe-Coburg and Gotha, on May 3, 1842.

Alexandrina of Mecklenburg-Schwerin (1879–1952)

Queen of Denmark. Name variations: Alexandrine Augustine, Duchess of Mecklenburg-Schwerin. Born Alexandrina Augusta von Mecklenburg-Schwerin on December 24, 1879; died on December 28, 1952; daughter of Frederick Francis III, grand duke of Mecklenburg-Schwerin, and *Anastasia Romanova (1860–1922, granddaughter of Nicholas I of Russia and *Charlotte of Prussia); married Christian X, king of Denmark (r. 1912–1947), on April 26, 1898; children: Frederick IX, king of Denmark (r. 1947–1972), who married *Ingrid of Sweden); Knud also known as Canute (b. 1900).

Alexandrine of Prussia (1803–1892).
See Louise of Prussia (1776–1810) for sidebar.

Alexeevna, Sophia (1657–1704).
See Sophia Alekseyevna.

Alexiou, Elli (c. 1898–1986)

Greek novelist, playwright, and teacher. Name variations: Elly Alexioy. Born in Herakleion, Crete, around 1898; died in 1986; daughter of a prominent journalist; sister of Galateia Kazantzaki (a Greek novelist); studied at Sorbonne in Paris, France; married Vasso Daskalakios (a Greek writer).

Selected novels: Hard Struggles for a Short Life *(1931);* The Third Christian School for Girls *(1934);* Louben *(1940);* Tributaries *(1956);* Spondi *(1963);* And So On *(1965);* That He May Be Great *(1966);*

The Reigning One *(1972)*; Demolished Mansions *(1977)*. *Play:* A Day in the Secondary School *(1973)*.

Elli Alexiou was a Greek writer and teacher whose work spanned the greater part of the 20th century. In addition to the fact that Alexiou spent much of her time devoted to various educational committees, her literary accomplishments are impressive. She frequently combined a deep understanding of human psychology with a critical eye toward the social climates of her surroundings. Her collective works are contained in a series of ten volumes, and the collection spans a variety of topics.

Alexiou was born around 1898 in Herakleion, Crete, to a literary family. Early in her life, she traveled to Athens where she studied for a career in education and interacted with a variety of progressive writers. After securing her qualifications as a teacher, she worked at a girls' high school and gathered the material for one of her early novels, *The Third Christian School for Girls* (1934). In 1928, Alexiou became a member of the Greek Communist Party and remained involved with various left-wing enterprises throughout her life.

During World War II, she participated in a Communist resistance group. In 1945, she received a scholarship to study at the Sorbonne in Paris, France. While there, she taught her native language to the Greek community in Paris. During the 1950s, Alexiou, deprived of her Greek citizenship, lived in several countries of Eastern Europe. A theme of exile is reflected in a great deal of her literature. In 1962, she returned to Greece and lived there for the remainder of her life. Elli Alexiou died in 1986, although some dispute about the actual date remains.

M.C. English, M.A., Boston University, Boston, Massachusetts

Alexsandra.

Variant of Alexandra.

Alexseyevna, Yekaterina or Catherine (1684–1727).

See Catherine I.

Alfifa (c. 1000–1044).

See Elfgifu of Northampton.

Alford, Marianne Margaret (1817–1888)

English artist. Name variations: Lady Marian Alford, Viscountess Alford. Born in 1817; died in 1888; daughter of Spencer Compton, 2nd marquis of Northampton; married John Hume Cust, Viscount Alford (son of Earl Brownlow), in 1841.

Friend to leading artists of her day, Lady Alford helped found the Royal School of Art Needlework in Kensington and published *Needlework as Art* in 1886.

Alianora.

Variant of Eleanor.

Alice.

Variant of Alix.

Alice (1201–1221)

Duchess of Brittany and Richmond. Name variations: Alice de Thouars; Alice of Brittany. Born in 1201; died on October 21, 1221; daughter of Guy, viscount of Thouars, and *Constance of Brittany (1161–1201); married Pierre also known as Peter I, duke of Brittany, around 1211 or 1213; children: John I, duke of Brittany.

Alice, countess of Blois (1150–c. 1197).

See Eleanor of Aquitaine for sidebar.

Alice, princess of Greece and Denmark (1885–1969).

See Alice of Battenberg.

Alice de Bryene (d. 1435)

The life of Alice de Bryene of England typifies the lives of many moderately wealthy noblewomen of her era. Her history has been preserved by the correspondence and household accounts she left, providing a look into the day-to-day life of a woman. Alice married a petty noble as a young girl and was widowed in 1386. She led an active widowed life, moving to be near her family in Suffolk after her husband's burial. Alice managed her estates carefully, overseeing all aspects of her financial affairs herself. She negotiated good marriages for her two daughters, and was also in correspondence with King Richard II over the marriage plans of two young noblewomen being raised in her home. She was also a busy hostess, planning meals and lodging for her noble visitors, who numbered in the hundreds during the holidays.

Laura York, Anza, California

Alice de Condet (fl. 12th c.).

See Adelaide de Condet.

Alice de Courtenay (fl. 1170–1190).

See Isabella of Angoulême for sidebar.

Alice de Joinville

*Countess of Lancaster. Second wife of Henry (1281–1345), 3rd earl of Lancaster. Henry's first wife was *Maud Chaworth.*

Alice de Lusignan.

See Isabella of Angoulême for sidebar on Alice le Brun.

Alice de Warrenne (d. around 1338).

See Fitzalan, Alice.

Alice le Brun.

See Isabella of Angoulême for sidebar.

Alice Maud Mary, princess of Great Britain and Ireland (1843–1878).

See Alexandra Feodorovna (1872–1918) for sidebar.

Alice of Athlone (1883–1981)

Princess of Great Britain and Northern Ireland, countess of Athlone, and one of the monarchy's most popular royals. Name variations: Princess Alice; Alice Saxe-Coburg. Born Alice Mary Victoria Augusta Pauline, princess of Great Britain and Ireland and the countess of Athlone, at Windsor Castle, Berkshire, England, on February 25, 1883; died at Kensington Palace, London, on January 3, 1981; daughter of Prince Leopold Albert, duke of Albany (Queen Victoria's fourth and youngest son) and Princess Helen of Waldeck-Pyrmont; last surviving grandchild of Queen Victoria; great-aunt of Queen Elizabeth II; married Prince Alexander of Teck, earl of Athlone (younger brother of Mary of Teck), in February 1904; children: four, including May Helen Emma (1906–1994, who married Henry Abel Smith); Rupert Alexander George Augustus, Viscount Trematon (1907–1928); Maurice (1910–1910).

Her long life spanned the reigns of six British sovereigns, and she personally attended four coronations; one of the most popular members of the royal family for many decades, she was outspoken, independent and public-spirited, particularly in her role of highly successful fundraiser as chancellor of the University of the West Indies; active in public life until her final months.

On February 25, 1883, Princess Alice was born as Alice Mary Victoria Augusta Pauline,

princess of Great Britain and Ireland and the countess of Athlone, at Windsor Castle. Her father Prince Leopold Albert, duke of Albany, was Queen *Victoria's fourth and youngest son and the younger brother of the prince of Wales who would succeed Victoria in 1901 as King Edward VII. Alice's mother was Princess *Helen of Waldeck-Pyrmont of the small German principality of Waldeck-Pyrmont.

The first of several tragedies in Alice's life struck little more than a year after her birth, when her father died of hemophilia. From this point, the infant princess was raised by her mother at Claremont House, near Esher. In her childhood, Alice rode in the carriage procession for Queen Victoria's Diamond Jubilee of 1897 (in the final years of her extraordinarily long life, Alice would be part of the 1977 Silver Jubilee procession of Queen *Elizabeth II). In Alice's 1966 memoirs, *For My Grandchildren*, she somewhat idealized the aristocratic world of the 1880s and 1890s, in which she grew up, as a society in which "class distinctions permeated the whole social structure and could be as rigid in the servants hall and in the village as they were in the castle. These distinctions were, however, tempered by gracious manners; and, in general, a courteous consideration for others, alas so rare today, governed the relationship between all ranks of society."

In February 1904, Alice was married to Prince Alexander of Teck, younger brother of the future Queen *Mary of Teck. Alexander was a serving officer in the British Army and had—like all members of the reigning British royal family whose family name was Saxe-Coburg-Gotha—deep blood and historical ties to the German aristocracy. Not until the third year of World War I, in 1917, would he become the earl of Athlone (with the family name of Cambridge) after abandoning his German title of nobility. For Princess Alice, the familial and personal ruptures brought on by the war were even more traumatic than for her husband. Her cousins, including Empress *Alexandra Feodorovna of Russia (1872–1918) and Kaiser Wilhelm II of Germany, were on opposite sides of the terrible conflagration. In the early years of the new century, Alice spent extended periods of time at the German court in Berlin and Potsdam. Her brother Prince Charles Edward, duke of Albany, had left Eton at the age of 16 to be brought up in Germany as heir to his uncle, the reigning duke of Coburg. Upon succeeding to his inheritance in 1900, Charles Edward also became a general in the German army and fought for his adopted country in the war. With the German defeat and proclamation of a republic in November 1918, he was deposed and stripped of his title. The following year, he also lost his British title of duke of Albany. Alice's brother became an embittered man who soon succumbed to the siren calls of Adolf Hitler and became a fervent Nazi supporter of the Third Reich. One can only speculate how much grief these events caused Princess Alice, torn as she was between her strong British patriotism and her deep affection for an ill-starred only brother.

The postwar era began auspiciously for Princess Alice when her husband was appointed governor-general of South Africa in 1923, a post he held until 1931. She was in no way eclipsed by him, becoming a memorable proconsul in her own right who displayed grace, sympathy, and enthusiasm in the countless public activities that accompanied the governor-generalship. The princess more than compensated for her less than average height with an unmistakably patrician presence. Stylishly dressed, she commanded respect with her aquiline features and intelligent eyes. But all was not carefree during these years. In 1910, her second son died at the age of six months, leaving a daughter born in 1906 and a son born in 1907. In 1928, Princess Alice and Prince Alexander lost their remaining son, Rupert, Viscount Trematon. Due to the hemophilia inherited from his grandfather, Prince Leopold Albert, Rupert died as the result of injuries suffered in an automobile accident. After a period of mourning, Princess Alice reentered the swirl of public life, returning to Britain in 1931 when her husband's term as governor-general ended.

At the start of World War II, Prince Alexander was called upon once more to serve as governor-general, this time of Canada. Starting in the grim year of 1940, Princess Alice served with great distinction as a hostess until this tour of duty ended in 1946. Known as an engaging conversationalist, she enjoyed recounting colorful tales of life at Windsor Castle in the days of Queen Victoria, whose mannerisms she could recall with vivid detail. Alice also remembered incidents that could not, in her mind, be forgiven. One such event was the decision of Prime Minister William Gladstone to deny a substantial royal allowance to Alice's mother in view of the fact that Alice's father had died a few days before the start of a new fiscal year. The decision left the bereaved family in a state of relative penury, and, even after a half-century or longer, Princess Alice would not forgive Gladstone for his "cruelty." During the war years, Alice and

her husband were hosts to a number of highly distinguished Allied visitors to Canada, including Franklin D. Roosevelt and Winston Churchill. Alice never forgave Churchill for his behavior during the 1943 Quebec Conference, when the prime minister filled her drawing room with clouds of pungent cigar smoke.

In 1946, the couple returned to London, where they lived either in an apartment in Kensington Palace or at their country place at Brantridge Park, Sussex. Although a staunch believer in the institution of monarchy and the utility of class distinctions, Alice was, like her cousin King George V, quite free of racial prejudice. Thus, in 1950, she accepted with enthusiasm the job of chancellor of the recently created University of the West Indies. Determined to do more than serve as a figurehead, she quickly set about turning the institution—which in the early 1950s was little more than great hopes and a collection of shacks—into a major educational center for an impoverished island population seeking independence from Great Britain. The princess made

Alice of Athlone

numerous trips to the Caribbean, for many years traveling there not by airplane but by commercial freighters ("banana boats"). Back in Britain, she was for two decades an indefatigable and usually irresistible fundraiser for the University of the West Indies. Her advanced years, and the rise of militant politics in the Caribbean, led to her retirement as chancellor in 1971.

After the death of Prince Alexander in 1957, the princess remained active in public life, not only continuing with her educational fund-raising work, but branching out into television interviews and writing. Her 1966 memoirs, *For My Grandchildren,* became an unexpected bestseller in the British Isles. For decades, she was a familiar sight to Londoners as she left her apartment in the Clock House of Kensington Palace, boarding the public bus on the corner. She would often return on the same bus route carrying a shopping bag. Spry into the ninth decade of her life, it was not until she entered her 90s that the princess began to consider making concessions to her advancing years. Acceding to the wishes of friends, she started using a walking stick, though at first her strategy was to disguise it as an umbrella.

Throughout her long life, Princess Alice retained a strongly independent personality. From her earliest days, she rarely minced words. Unafraid of being ahead of public opinion, she was the first member of the royal family to speak out publicly in favor of birth control. Physically, too, she was quite fearless; in her early years, she developed an intense interest in hunting big game, and once shot a tiger as it sprang at her.

As Princess Alice grew older, she grew more eccentric but also reportedly more lovable. She worked in her garden and exchanged gossip and risqué stories with old friends, and she was popular with Queen Elizabeth II, who telephoned her often to invite her to royal events. On one occasion, Charles, Prince of Wales, her great-great-grandnephew, took her as his date to an opera party with his friends. A woman of great dignity and verve, Princess Alice died in her sleep at her London home, Kensington Palace, on January 3, 1981. The queen received the news "with great sadness," according to a representative for Buckingham Palace. She was the last of the Victorians.

SOURCES:

Alice, Princess, Countess of Athlone. *For My Grandchildren.* London: Evans, 1966.

Aronson, Theo. *Princess Alice, Countess of Athlone.* London: Cassell, 1981.

"At 94, Princess Alice Pursues a Regally Active Life," in *The New York Times Biographical Service.* November 1976, p. 1503.

"Princess Alice, at London Home; A Grandchild of Queen Victoria," in *The New York Times Biographical Service.* January 1981, p. 1.

John Haag, Associate Professor of History, University of Georgia, Athens, Georgia

Alice of Battenberg (1885–1969)

*Princess of Greece and Denmark, mother of the duke of Edinburgh, and a "Righteous Gentile" as rescuer of Greek Jews in World War II. Name variations: Princess Andrew, Princess Alice. Born Victoria Alice Elizabeth Julia Mary at Windsor Castle, Berkshire, England, on February 25, 1885; died in London's Buckingham Palace on December 5, 1969; daughter of Prince Louis Alexander Battenberg, 1st marquess of Milford Haven, and Princess Victoria of Hesse-Darmstadt (1863–1950); sister of *Louise Mountbatten (1889–1965) and Earl Mountbatten of Burma; married Prince Andrew of Greece (1882–1944), on October 7, 1903; children: *Margaret Oldenburg (1905–1981, who married Godfrey, 8th prince of Hohenlohe-Langenburg); *Theodora Oldenburg (1906–1969, who married Berthod, margrave of Baden); *Cecily Oldenburg (1911–1937, who married George Donatus of Hesse); *Sophia of Greece (b. 1914, who married Christopher of Hesse-Cassell and George Guelph); Prince Philip (b. 1921, also known as Philip Mountbatten, duke of Edinburgh, husband of Queen Elizabeth II of England).*

After her husband's family's expulsion from Greece (1923), lived in exile; during WWII, returned to Greece and hid Jewish refugees in her home at the risk of her own life, protecting them from certain death in Nazi-occupied Greece; named a "Righteous Gentile" by Yad Vashem, Israel's Holocaust memorial museum and research center (1994).

Born in Windsor, England, on February 25, 1885, Alice of Battenberg, princess of Greece, was one of Queen *Victoria's many grandchildren. Her father was Prince Louis Alexander Battenberg, and her mother was Princess *Victoria of Hesse-Darmstadt. Alice was the eldest sister of Earl Mountbatten of Burma.

After she married Prince Andrew of Greece in 1903, Alice spent most of her life in that country. Known as Princess Andrew, she shared in many of the tragic events that afflicted Greece in the 20th century. Her husband Prince Andrew was commander of a Greek army corps in the ill-fated war against Turkey, which ended catastrophically in a Greek military rout in 1922. As politicians searched for scapegoats, they targeted Prince Andrew, arresting him for a show trial.

Foreign pressure saved his life, but he and his family were banished when a republican regime overthrew the Greek monarchy in 1923.

Living in exile with her husband and children near Paris, Princess Alice remained indignant over the shabby treatment her husband had received in Greece, and she vowed that their son, Prince Philip, would never suffer the same humiliations. Philip was sent to school in England, effectively preparing him for his later life as an exemplary British officer and gentleman. Living as exiled royalty, Princess Alice became a businesswoman, opening up an embroidery and jewelry boutique in Paris.

Toward the beginning of World War II, the German occupation of Greece in April 1941 strengthened her resolve to render assistance to her adopted country, and Princess Alice returned to Greece. The country endured a Nazi occupation regime that imposed terror and starvation on hundreds of thousands of civilians. While her husband lived in Monte Carlo (where he died in 1944), the princess worked to alleviate Hellenic suffering. Volunteering with the Swedish and Swiss Red Cross organizations, she struggled to bring relief supplies to the populace. World War II also brought private agony to Alice, as it divided her family. While two of her three daughters were married to Germans, her son, Prince Philip, was on active duty in the British Royal Navy.

In several instances, Princess Alice saved lives. In 1942, Nazi occupation forces began to round up all of Greece's Jewish population for deportation to the death camps of German-occupied Eastern Europe. Risking her life, Alice hid several members of a Jewish family in one of her Athens residences, and facilitated the escape of other members of the same family.

After World War II, Princess Alice founded the monastic society of Martha and Mary in 1949. Its goal was to train sisters to care for poor children and the sick. As the society's mother superior under the name of Alice-Elizabeth, she raised funds to buy two houses, one to house convalescents and the other to train nurses. The plan was to use funds derived from the rest home to pay for the nurses' training, but unfortunately too few suitable candidates were available at the time for the sisterhood, and, after a time, the project had to be abandoned.

When her son, Prince Philip, married Princess Elizabeth, who became *Elizabeth II, queen of England, Alice could have returned permanently to her native country, but she did not. For many years, the princess lived in a small

apartment in Athens, often traveling abroad to visit her children, with whom she remained close. When she became ill in Germany in 1966, Prince Philip flew to accompany her on her return trip to Greece. Until the last years of her life, she preferred to stay in a hotel for her London visits, rather than at one of the royal palaces. Greek political turmoil continued to intervene in Alice's life when military dictatorship was imposed on Greece in 1967. Alice was forced to flee Athens, leaving her beloved adopted country forever. Finally, with the onset of old age and increasingly fragile health, Alice consented to take up residence in one of the British royal family's palaces. She died in London's Buckingham Palace on December 5, 1969, at age 84.

Many of Princess Alice's heroic deeds were not recognized until after her death. In October 1994, Prince Philip accepted the award of "Righteous Gentile" from Yad Vashem, Israel's Holocaust memorial museum and research center, on his mother's behalf. Visiting her memorial, located on Jerusalem's Mount of Olives, he noted, "It never occurred to her that her action was in any way special. She was a person with a deep religious faith, and she would have considered it to be a perfectly natural human reaction to fellow beings in distress."

SOURCES:

Brozan, Nadine. "Chronicle. Prince Philip accepts an award on behalf of his mother," in *The New York Times*. November 1, 1994, section B, p. 20.

Cathcart, Helen. *The Royal Bedside Book*. London: W.H. Allen, 1969.

"Princess Andrew of Greece, 84, Mother of Prince Philip, Dead," in *The New York Times*. December 6, 1969, p. 37.

John Haag, Associate Professor of History, University of Georgia, Athens, Georgia

Alice of Champagne (1145–1206).

See Adele of Champagne.

Alice of Champagne (fl. 1200s)

*Queen of Cyprus. Flourished in the 1200s; daughter of *Isabella I of Jerusalem (d. 1205) and Henry II of Champagne, king of Jerusalem (r. 1192–1197); married her stepbrother Hugh I, king of Cyprus (r. 1205–1218); children: Henry I, king of Cyprus (r. 1218–1253); Isabella (who married John of Lusignan).*

Alice of France (c. 1160–?).

See Alais of France.

Alice of Jerusalem (c. 1106–?).

See Melisande for sidebar.

Alice of Normandy (fl. 1017–1037)

*Countess of Burgundy. Name variations: Adelaide, Adeliza, and Judith. Born before 1017; died after 1037; daughter of Richard II the Good (d. 1027), duke of Normandy, and *Judith of Rennes (c. 982–1018, daughter of Conan I, duke of Brittany); married Renaud I, count of Burgundy.*

Alice of Saluzzo (fl. 1285).

See Fitzalan, Alice.

Alice of Vergy.

See Alix of Vergy.

Alicia of Parma (1849–1935)

*Grand duchess of Tuscany. Name variations: Alice of Bourbon-Parma; Alice of Parma; Alix of Parma. Born Alice Maria on December 27, 1849, in Parma; died on January 16, 1935, in Schwertberg, Upper Austria; daughter of *Louise of Bourbon-Berry (1819–1864) and Charles III, duke of Parma; became second wife of Ferdinand IV (1835–1908), titular grand duke of Tuscany (r. 1859–1908), on January 11, 1868; children: Leopold Ferdinand (1868–1935, who married Wilhelmine Adamowic); *Louisa Toselli (1870–1947); Joseph Ferdinand (1872–1942); Peter Ferdinand (1874–1948, who married *Maria Cristina of Sicily); *Anna Maria Theresa (1879–1961); Agnes Maria (1891–1945); and five others.*

al-Idlibi, `Ulfah.

See Idlibi, `Ulfah al-.

Alienor or Aliénor.

Variant of Eleanor.

Aliger, Margarita Iosifovna (1915–1992)

Soviet Russian journalist and lyrical poet who depicted Soviet life in universal terms and took great risks in speaking out against Stalinism. Born in Odessa, Russia, on October 7, 1915; died in 1992; married Konstantin Makarov-Rakitin, in 1936; children: one son (who did not survive infancy), and two daughters.

Margarita Iosifovna Aliger was born into a poor Jewish family in Odessa on October 7, 1915. Although her parents had little in the way of material possessions, their lives were culturally rich. The Aligers had assimilated Russian culture, retaining an unquenchable thirst for the arts. Aliger's father was an excellent amateur violinist, while her mother, who had a deep love for Russian literature, often read the poetry of Pushkin and other classic works to her young daughter. Margarita's poetic impulse emerged early, and, at age 16, she went to Moscow to seek literary recognition. Two years later, in 1933, her first poems appeared in print.

Working as a librarian, Aliger constantly strove to improve her poetic skills. Her life in Moscow became more settled in 1936 when she married Konstantin Makarov-Rakitin. Determined to find her personal literary voice, she enrolled in a program of night classes for aspiring writers (which later became the Gorky Literary Institute). Soon, she published her first book-length works. Among these early publications were *God rozhdeniya* (*Year of Birth*), a verse collection, which appeared in 1938, praising Socialist construction and the triumphs of Stalinist industrialization. These early, relentlessly optimistic works pleased Joseph Stalin who personally saw to it that Aliger was awarded a Soviet decoration in 1939, the first of many she would receive in her long literary career. The same year, she published *Zima etogo goda* (*The Winter of that Year*), based on a personal tragedy, the death of her infant son as a result of meningitis at the age of 18 months.

As was true for countless millions of Soviet citizens, the war years were marked by tragedy for Margarita Aliger. After her husband died in combat in 1941, she had the responsibility of raising two daughters by herself. Aliger's life became a never ending struggle of privations and loss of family and friends to war, starvation, disease, and exhaustion. Not long after the Nazi attack on the Soviet Union in June 1941, it became clear that Hitler's policy of genocide would result in the death of all Jews in German-occupied territory. Aliger became increasingly active in Soviet organizations, including the internationally known Jewish Antifascist Committee. These groups actively assisted the threatened Jewish population, bringing their plight to the attention of the Soviet Union's Western wartime allies. Her most important activity was editing a *Black Book* of eyewitness accounts of Nazi mass murder on Soviet territory for later publication.

As both a Russian and a Jew, Aliger hated German Fascism. She wrote a number of patriotic works, including *To the Memory of the Brave* and *Zoya* (both published in 1942). *Zoya* was a long narrative poem honoring *Zoya Kosmodemyanskaya, the young woman executed by the Nazi invaders in 1941 for her guerrilla exploits. Aliger's play *Tale about Truth* also dealt with

patriotic wartime themes. These works, which reflected the intense patriotism of the struggle against the invaders of the Soviet Union, earned Aliger a State Prize of the USSR; later, she also received the Stalin Prize. Though she was aware at the time of the terrors perpetrated by the Stalin regime, her work reflected the shared privations and suffering, as well as hope for a better future, which characterized the Soviet Union during the war. Decades later, Aliger would describe the war years as a "time when all our people were together, and knew they were fighting an enemy *outside* that was evil." Full of such optimism, Aliger joined the Soviet Communist Party in 1942.

After victory over Nazi Germany in May 1945, the latent anti-Semitism of Joseph Stalin and his inner circle began to reassert itself. The *Black Book* project was shelved and the volume never published. Now, Soviet Jews began to be accused of shirking their wartime duties and enriching themselves behind the front lines while others fought and died. From the outset, Aliger became acutely aware of the radically changed attitudes that now made anti-Semitism acceptable in the Soviet Union, despite the fact that it was officially banned. In her narrative poem, *Your Victory,* published in 1946, she boldly fought this campaign of vilification, speaking of the Jewish people not as loafers or deserters but as "doctors and musicians/ Workers small and big/ Descendants of the brave Maccabees/ Sons of their fathers/ Thousands of fighting Jews— Russian commanders and soldiers." Banned by Stalin's censors, these lines were not printed in *Your Victory* but circulated widely in manuscript form. Aliger vigorously fought anti-Semitic slander, asking in her poetry: "Answer my question/ Haven't we shared everything/ With which we were rich?/ Why do millions think we're guilty?"

As the attack on Jews continued, escalating in the late 1940s with the systematic murder of a number of prominent Jewish intellectuals, Aliger continued to write and publish. Her works were cautious and deliberately nonpolitical, for she recognized the new reign of terror taking hold in her country. Her defiance of Stalinist hatred was poetically subtle: a glorification of the renewal of human life and love after years of war and destruction. Often in poor health in the postwar years, she was deeply concerned about the safety and survival of her two daughters. On several occasions, she was denounced in public for alleged "pessimism" and other ideological transgressions, although it was obvious that some of the criticism was thinly veiled anti-Semitism. When the paranoid Stalin demanded that Jewish intellectuals sign a letter justifying a bloody purge of Soviet Jews in the last months of his regime, a fragile and sickly Aliger felt that she had no alternative but to comply. Years later she explained, "It was very terrifying, and not everyone is capable of being a suicidal hero." Massive purges were planned for 1952–53, but these were averted with the death of Joseph Stalin in March 1953.

Stalin's death brought a political and cultural "thaw" that lightened the burden of millions of people. Margarita Aliger also began to feel a sense of rebirth and hope. She began writing in a new burst of energy and won a number of medals and awards, including the Order of the Red Banner of Labor in 1965 and the Order of Friendship of the Peoples in 1975. Increasingly, her fellow poets regarded her as a venerable figure of Russian literature. In 1962, following the publication of Yevgeny Yevtushenko's poem *Babi Yar*—which for the first time brought up the issue of the Holocaust and Jewish deaths in World War II in the Soviet Union—Aliger wrote and privately circulated a poem bitterly condemning the continuation of anti-Semitism in the post-Stalinist USSR. Yevtushenko reciprocated by publishing a poem about Aliger, *Poet na rynke* (*A Poet at the Market*). He movingly describes her as buying honey for her extremely ill older daughter (who later died), a frail figure unrecognized by other shoppers standing among the "cabbages and the pork/ That, nearing sixty, forgotten by all/ The poet was writing as never before."

In the final decades of her life, Aliger wrote of the powerful moral struggles she and her generation faced during the years of bloody Stalinist dictatorship and terrible suffering during World War II. One of her finest poems, "House in Meudon," is dedicated to the poet *Marina Tsvetaeva (1892–1941), who committed suicide. Tsvetaeva's works were not printed in the Soviet Union until years after the death of Stalin, when Aliger determined to rehabilitate Tsvetaeva's reputation.

To the end of her life, Margarita Aliger struggled with the great moral problems of her country and century. She resigned from the Communist Party in 1990 and died in 1992. Aliger kept alive a great literary tradition, maintaining a spirit of lyrical simplicity in a harsh world bent on destroying itself. She summed up her artistic credo in her own words, "Lyrics are my soul, myself as I am."

SOURCES:
Feinstein, Elaine. "Poetry and Conscience: Russian Women Poets of the Twentieth Century," in *Women Writing and Writing about Women*. Edited by Mary Jacobus. London: Croom Helm/Oxford University Women's Studies Committee; NY: Barnes and Noble Books, 1979, pp. 133–158.
Vaksberg, Arkady. *Stalin Against the Jews*. Translated by Antonina W. Bouis. NY: Alfred A. Knopf, 1994.

John Haag, Associate Professor of History, University of Georgia, Athens, Georgia

Ali Khan, Begum Liaquat (d. 1991).

See Khan, Begum Liaquat Ali.

Aline Sitoe (c. 1920–1944)

Queen of Diola Tribe, Casamance, who rebelled against the French. Born around 1920 in Kabrousse, West Africa (a section of modern-day Senegal); died of scurvy on May 22, 1944; reigned from around 1936 to 1943.

Early in 1942, when Aline Sitoe incited her people to rebel against their French rulers with the declaration, "The white man is not invincible," her challenge was heard as far away as Mauritania and Mali. She fomented a boycott of French goods, discouraged use of the French language, and encouraged her people to revive their own culture. When Diola warriors ambushed a truck and killed three French soldiers, the French held Kabrousse under siege for 16 days in January of 1943. Finally, the queen surrendered to avoid watching the town destroyed by fire. Taken into custody, she was condemned to a ten-year exile in Timbuktu. The following year, she died of scurvy and was buried in Timbuktu's Sidi el Wafi Cemetery. Nineteen years after her death, her nation ceased being a French protectorate. In 1983, plans were made to return her remains to Senegal.

Alisia of Antioch

Ferrarese noblewoman. Third wife of Azo also known as Azzo VI d'Este (1170–1212), 1st lord of Ferrara (r. 1208–1212); children: Azzo VII Novello (d. 1264).

Alix.

Variant of Alice.

Alix, countess of Blois (1150–c. 1197).

See Eleanor of Aquitaine for sidebar.

Alix, princess of Wales (1844–1925).

See Alexandra of Denmark.

Alix de Vergy.
See Alix of Vergy.

Alix of Burgundy.
See Alix of Vergy.

Alix of France (c. 1160–?).
See Alais of France.

Alix of Hesse-Darmstadt (1872–1918).
See Alexandra Feodorovna, empress of Russia.

Alix of Vergy (d. after 1218)

Duchess of Burgundy. Name variations: Alice de Vergy; Alix of Burgundy. Died after 1218 in Burgundy, France; daughter of Count Hugues de Vergy; married Eudes III (d. 1218), duke of Burgundy, in 1199; children: one son.

Alix of Vergy was a member of the lesser nobility of France. In 1199, her father arranged a marriage for her with Eudes III, duke of Burgundy, a match designed to increase the prestige of the House of Vergy by aligning it with one of the most powerful feudal families of Western Europe. Although Alix was not much involved in the administration of the duchy during Eudes' life, upon his death in 1218 she became regent of Burgundy for their young son. Alix proved a competent regent, taking an active role in bettering the lives of her people. She passed laws to strengthen the Burgundian economy, aided the growth of towns by confirming charters protecting their right to some self-rule, and in addition preserved peace by forming an alliance with the powerful overlord of Champagne, Count Theobald. Alix remained an important part of Burgundian government even after her son came of age.

Laura York, Anza, California

Alix of Vergy (r. 1248–c. 1290)

Countess, ruler of Burgundy. Name variations: Alix de Vergy. Born in 1248; died sometime before 1290; daughter of Count Otto II, count of Burgundy, and Countess Beatrix (daughter of Count Otto I); sister of Otto III, count of Burgundy; married Hugh of Chalon; children: son Otto IV (d. 1302).

Alix of Vergy inherited Burgundy (present-day Eastern France) in 1248 upon the death of her brother Otto III. She ruled for over 40 years.

Aliya, Fatima (1862–1936).
See Aliye, Fatima.

Aliye, Fatima (1862–1936)

Turkish author who wrote novels and translated French textbooks from multiple disciplines into Turkish. Name variations: Fatma Aliye, Fatima Aliya. Born in 1862 in Turkey; died in 1936 in Turkey; daughter of Ahmad Cevdet (or Gaudat) Pasha; educated at home; married a Turkish army officer.

Selected works: Muhadarat *(1892);* History of Women of Islam *(1892);* Mercy *(1898);* Udi, the Lute Player *(1899);* Biographies of Philosophers *(1900).*

As the daughter of statesman and historian Ahmad Cevdet Pasha, Fatima Aliye was privileged to receive a superior education at home, which included a thorough study in the language and literature of France. As a teenager, she married a Turkish army officer, with whom she traveled to his various postings. She translated French texts from the sciences and arts and used her position as a member of the governing class to impress upon others the need to educate men and women alike. While Aliye wrote in Turkish, her own well-received work was of the French tradition and encompassed fiction and nonfiction. Among her publications were a biography of her father and a *History of Women of Islam* (1892). Though Aliye continued to write and speak out through the early 1900s, with the fall of the Ottoman Empire in 1919 her literary voice was silenced. She lived in Turkey until her death in 1936.

Crista Martin, Boston, Massachusetts

al-Khaizuran (d. 790).
See Khaizuran.

al-Khansa (c. 575–c. 645).
See Khansa, al-.

Allan, Elizabeth (1908–1990)

English actress, best known for her performance in **David Copperfield.** *Born in Skegness, England, on April 9, 1908; died in 1990; married W.J. O'Bryen (d. 1977, a theatrical agent and her manager), in 1932.*

Selected filmography: Alibi *(1931);* Michael and Mary *(1931);* Service for Ladies *(*Reserved for Ladies, *1932);* The Lodger *(1933);* The Shadow *(1933);* David Copperfield *(1934);* Java Head *(1934);* Men in White *(1934);* Mark of the Vampire *(1934);* The Mystery of Mr. X *(1936);* A Tale of Two Cities *(1936);* A Woman Rebels *(1936);* Camille *(1937);* Michael Strogoff *(1937);* Slave Ship *(1937);* Inquest *(1940);* 48 Hours *(1942);* The Great Mr. Handel *(1942);* He Snoops to Conquer *(1944);* No Highway *(*No Highway in the

Sky, 1951); Folly to be Wise (1952); The Heart of the Matter (1954); Front Page Story (1954); Grip of the Strangler (1958).

After making her stage debut with the Old Vic in 1927 and appearing in several British movies, Elizabeth Allan played the lead in more than a dozen Hollywood films. Her American career was cut short when she sued MGM for replacing her in the lead of *The Citadel* with *Rosalind Russell. Rebellious actresses were rare and quickly stifled in the movie industry, and Allan was barred from further studio work. Best remembered as the mother of Freddie Bartholomew in George Cukor's 1934 film adaptation of *David Copperfield*, she returned to England in 1937 and continued her career in movies, theater, and television. Popular in British television from 1955 to 1960, Allan had her own program "Swap Shop." She retired in 1977.

Allan, Stella (1871–1962)

New Zealand-born Australian journalist. Name variations: Vesta. Born Stella May Henderson on October 25, 1871, at Kaiapoi, South Island, New Zealand; died in Melbourne on March 1, 1962; seventh child of Alice (Connolly) Henderson and Daniel Henderson (a clerk); graduated Canterbury Girls' High School and Canterbury University College, B.A., 1892, M.A., 1893, LL.B., 1896; married Edwin Frank Allan (d. 1922, leader-writer for the Wellington Evening Post*), in 1900; children: four daughters.*

Despite laws prohibiting women from practicing law in New Zealand, Stella Allan entered law school in 1893. She completed her degree in 1896, when the New Zealand legislature relaxed the ban. In 1903, she married the journalist Edwin Frank Allan and moved to Melbourne. Like her husband, Stella Allan worked as a freelance journalist, authoring a column for the *Argus* under the name Vesta called "Women to Women," while raising four daughters. She wrote about women's issues, such as child care and "domestic feminism."

Allard, Marie (1742–1802)

French ballerina. Born Marie Allard in 1742; died in 1802; children: (with balletmaster Gaëtan Vestris) Marie-Jean-Augustin Vestris (b. March 27, 1760; d. 1842), a major ballet dancer known as Auguste Vestris.

It was the fashion in 18th-century France for a man of means to have a mistress or four.

(The title went to Prince de Conti who, as reported by **Parmenia Migel,** "kept sixty recognized mistresses, without counting the 'minor,' the 'occasional,' and the 'imperceptible' ones.") Ballet mothers of the day aimed to keep their daughters from marrying young so as to profit from the attentions of these aristocrats. But a rule remained in effect until 1775, limiting the power of the mothers: once a ballerina was "on the list" of the Paris Opera, she was no longer subject to the authority of her parents, police, or husband. To obtain a young girl, rakes only had to get her signed up with the Opera, then elope. When parents complained, they were informed that the police could do nothing; their daughters belonged to the Opera.

Ten-year-old Marie Allard was caught in this system. She was born in Marseille to poor parents who offered her to the Comédie de Marseille and a certain Monsieur V who had the means to pay for her. When her mother died two years later, Marie went to the Lyon opera and was engaged among the *premieres danseuses* (first dancers). By 1756, at age 14, she was settled in a small apartment in Paris with a job at the Comédie-Française. Allard capitalized on the attentions of her lovers. Her first amour paid the rent, her second offered her a larger apartment, her third was a duke, her fourth was balletmaster Gaëtan Vestris with whom she had just begun to study. While with Vestris, she also enjoyed the affections of another dancer named Jean Bercher, known as Dauberval. On March 27, 1760, she gave birth to a young Vestris.

At 18, Allard made her Paris Opera debut in June 1761 in *Zaïs* by Cahusac and Rameau. The audience, along with a large number of young rakes—including the Duc de Mazarin and Monsieur de Bontems—fell in love with her. At one point, Mlle Allard's contract was temporarily suspended "on the ground that her deplorable habit of producing two children every eighteen months caused her to be constantly in a condition which was destructive of all stage effect."

But Allard was a serious dancer, who danced 35 roles in her first 10 years at the Opera, and was lauded for her *pas de deux* with Dauberval in *Sylvie* (1766 and 1767). Meanwhile, she helped Vestris train their son Auguste who would become the dance marvel of the age. As her son's career was on the rise, hers began to decline, chiefly because of her burgeoning weight, and the committee requested her retirement in 1781. Marie Allard died of a stroke in 1802, brought on by her excessive weight.

SOURCES:
Migel, Parmenia. *The Ballerinas: From the Court of Louis XIV to Pavlova.* NY: Macmillan, 1972.

Allart, Hortense (1801–1879)

French feminist, novelist, and essayist. Name variations: Allart de Meritens. Born in 1801; died in 1879.

Selected works: Lettres sur les Ouvrages de Mme de Staël *(Letters on the Work of Madame de Staël, 1826);* Settimie *(1826);* Gertrude *(1827);* L'Indienne *(The Indian Girl, 1832);* La Vie Rose *(1833);* La Femme et la Démocratie de Notre Temps *(Women and Democracy Today, 1836);* Histoire de la République de Florence *(History of the Florentine Republic, 1837);* Novum Organum, ou Saintete Philosophique *(1857);* Essai sur l'Histoire Politique depuis l'Invasion des Barbares jusqu'en 1848 *(Essay on the Political History from the Barbarian Invasion to 1848, 1857);* Les Enchantements de Prudence *(The Delights of Prudence, 1872).*

With her aristocratic background, Hortense Allart was wary of the socialism of many of her contemporaries, but she was very involved in the women's movement of 19th-century France. An established novelist and essayist, she was an integral part of the *Gazette des Femmes*—a "Journal of Legislation, Jurisprudence, Literature, Theater, Art, Commerce, Law, Music, and Fashion" for women—especially aimed at analyzing French law as it pertained to the rights of women. Allart attended the weekly editorial meetings held to keep the journal in touch with the women's movement of the time. The journal became particularly devoted to encouraging individual women to set up petitions, which they held on file for other women to sign; subjects of petition included reestablishing a divorce law and abolishing capital punishment. Allart also attempted to set up an association for the improvement of the status of women, which was approved by an editorial meeting of the *Gazette*, but which failed to materialize.

Allart's *La Femme et la Démocratie de Notre Temps* (Women and Democracy Today), published in 1836, is particularly noted for its argument for free love and for improving the social status of women. Indeed, Allart is notorious for her many love affairs, including one with the writer Chateaubriand. Her last work, a novel, *Les Enchantements de Prudence* (The Delights of Prudence), is largely autobiographical, detailing the life of a woman who flouts the sexual and social conventions of the time.

Her writing was not limited to feminist topics, however. As well as several essays on history, Allart is noted for *Novum Organum, ou Saintete Philosophique,* a 300-page philosophical work published in 1857. She argued for a common foundation for religion and science: "an attempt to understand natural religion as an object of science. The understanding of God and holiness, knowing God as we know life, and being pious as we are mortal." Allart believed that religion should help solve philosophical problems, such as the nature of knowledge in metaphysics. She argued that there is an almost universal belief in a higher being and that we get closer to understanding the mind of God, initially understood through scriptures, through the progression of scientific knowledge.

Allart apologized for the inadequacies of previous philosophies in their failure to prove the existence of God and the importance of religious morality, and she attacked Francis Bacon for his fear of sensory illusions. Although she agreed with him that human experience should be examined in terms of spirit, rather than matter, she held that, like the ancient Greek philosopher Democritus, we can only ascertain natural laws by examining how we act within nature.

Catherine Hundleby, M.A. Philosophy, University of Guelph, Guelph, Ontario, Canada

Allen, Adrianne (1907—)

English actress. Born in 1907; married Raymond Massey (an actor), in 1929 (divorced 1939); married William Dwight Whitney, in 1939; children: (first marriage) Daniel Massey (an actor, b. 1933) and Anna Massey (an actress, b. 1937).

Adrianne Allen made her screen debut in 1930 with *Loose Ends;* she also appeared in *The Night of June 13th, Merrily We Go to Hell, The Morals of Marcus, The October Man, Vote for Huggett, The Final Test,* and the 1954 movie *Meet Mr. Malcolm.* In 1958, she made her final stage appearance in London in *Five Finger Exercise.* Allen's daughter **Anna Massey**, born in Thakeham, Sussex, on August 11, 1937, is a noted stage and film actress in England.

Allen, Dede (1923—)

American film editor, one of the few to receive star billing, who was the first to bring attention to film editing as an art. Born Dorothea Carothers Allen in 1923 in Cleveland, Ohio; attended Scripps College; married Steve Fleischman (a television writer and producer); children: two.

Dede
Allen

Day Afternoon *(1975)*; Night Moves *(1975)*; The Missouri Breaks *(1976)*; Slapshot *(1977)*; The Wiz *(1978)*; Reds *(1981)*; Mike's Murder *(1984)*; Harry and Son *(1984)*; The Breakfast Club *(1985)*; Offbeat *(1986)*; The Milagro Beanfield War *(1988)*; Let It Ride *(1989)*; Henry and June *(1990)*; The Addams Family *(1991)*.

On a warm day in 1943, while attending Scripps College in Claremont, California, Dede Allen drove into nearby Los Angeles to meet her grandfather's friend, theatrical director and producer Eliot Nugent, who was in Hollywood directing his first feature film. When she told Nugent of her lifelong dream of becoming a film director, he replied: "Young lady, if you want to be a director, get a job in the cutting room." She never forgot that advice. Rather than becoming a director, Allen became one of the top five film editors in the business and the first to win a solo credit board on screen.

Dede Allen began her Hollywood film career as a messenger, apprentice, and assistant editor. Though she came out of a period when "you just didn't take a job away from a man," World War II sent the men to war, providing Allen with a shot at sound editing. Still, when the men returned, she was "bumped back to the bottom."

In 1950, she moved to New York and began editing film. Nine years later, Robert Wise gave Allen her first big break on a major motion picture, *Odds Against Tomorrow*. "In those days," she told **Ally Acker**, "editing was done primitively. We couldn't Scotch-tape film the way we do now. So every time I wanted to make a cut, I literally needed to melt a piece of film away. But the black slugs were distracting, so editors tried *not* to make too many changes if they could help it."

Among other films, she edited six pictures for Arthur Penn, three for Sidney Lumet, two for George Roy Hill, two for Paul Newman, and one each for Wise, Elia Kazan, and Robert Rossen. She recalls being a one-woman operation in New York: "There was no studio system, no post production departments. The editor did it all; supervising sound editing, ADR, Foley, rerecording, labs, prints—all the elements of post-production. You were lucky if you had an accountant to help you with the books."

As she grew confident in her craft, Allen began to experiment with the encouragement of some of her directors, including Wise. In the '50s, when she started pre-lapping sound (the sound track coming in ahead of the picture on a cut), she had to remind her sound editors not to

Nominations and awards: British Academy Award for Dog Day Afternoon *(1975); American Academy Award nominations for* Dog Day Afternoon *(1975) and* Reds *(1981); Ace Eddie nominations for* The Hustler *(1961),* Dog Day Afternoon *(1975), and* Reds *(1981); Crystal Award from Women in Film (1982); American Film Institute: Doctor of Fine Arts, Honorary Degree (1990); Ace Lifetime Achievement Award (1994).*

I was never afraid of breaking the rules.

—Dede Allen

Filmography: Story of Life *(1948);* Endowing Our Future *(1957);* Terror from the Year 5,000 *(1958);* Odds Against Tomorrow *(1959);* The Hustler *(1961);* America, America *(1963);* It's Always Now *(1965);* Bonnie and Clyde *(1967);* Rachel, Rachel *(1968);* Alice's Restaurant *(1969);* Little Big Man *(1970);* Slaughterhouse Five *(1972);* Visions of Eight *("The Highest" segment, 1973);* Serpico *(1974);* Dog tamper with her work. "I had to say, 'don't change that. It's not out of sync. That's the way I want it.'" Later, the startling transitions of her energetic cutting on *Bonnie and Clyde*—with unmatched cuts, fade-outs and cut-ins—would be imitated many times over. But during filming of the movie in 1966, Jack Warner was unhappy with the way Allen was cutting the movie and wanted to replace her. Producer Arthur Penn and star-producer Warren Beatty refused, and Beatty continued to pay Allen's salary with his own funds.

Sometime mid-shoot, she was having dinner with Beatty when he asked her if she had ever heard of John Reed. When she replied that she was aware of the author of *Ten Days that Shook the World*, Beatty announced that one day he was going to do his story. Neither one of them forgot that conversation, and 15 years later Allen edited Beatty's ambitious production, *Reds*. She worked on *Reds* in London and New York for two and a half years, longer than she had worked on any other film, and received an executive-producer credit as well as her editor credit. Other films edited by Allen for prominent actors-turned-directors include *Rachel, Rachel* for Paul Newman and *The Milagro Beanfield War* for Robert Redford. In 1992, Allen returned to Los Angeles to become a creative executive in theatrical production for Warner Bros., where she consults on films from dailies to post production.

SOURCES:
Correspondence with Dede Allen.
Acker, Ally. *Reel Women*. NY: Continuum, 1991.

Allen, Florence Ellinwood

(1884–1966)

American pacifist and champion of women's rights, who was the first woman on the Ohio Common Pleas Court, the Ohio Supreme Court, and the U.S. Court of Appeals. Born Florence Ellinwood Allen on March 23, 1884, in Salt Lake City, Utah; died of a stroke on September 12, 1966, in Cleveland, Ohio; daughter of Clarence Emir (a classical scholar, congressional delegate, and mining company executive) and Corinne Marie (Tuckerman) Allen; attended New Lyme Institute in Ashtabula County, Ohio, 1895–97, and Salt Lake College, 1897–99; graduated from Western Reserve University, Cleveland, Ohio, Phi Beta Kappa, 1904; studied music in Berlin, Germany, 1904–06; granted A.M. in political science, Western Reserve, 1908; LL.B. New York University Law School, 1913; never married; no children.

Admitted to Ohio bar (1914); campaigned for municipal suffrage for women; appointed assistant county prosecutor of Cuyahoga County, Ohio (1919); elected to common pleas court (1920); elected to Ohio Supreme Court (1922), re-elected (1928); appointed to Sixth Circuit Court of Appeals (1934–59), chief judge (1958); member of various professional associations, serving on several committees and attending numerous international conferences. Awards: Albert Gallatin Award, New York University (1960), and 25 honorary degrees.

Selected publications: Patris *(poems, 1908);* This Constitution of Ours *(1940);* The Treaty as an Instrument of Legislation *(1952);* To Do Justly *(memoirs, 1965).*

Florence Allen was born into a family of pioneers. While subsequent generations had been settlers in Ohio and Pennsylvania, her parents moved to Utah when it was still a territory and brought up their six children in an adobe house. Her mother had been the first woman to enroll in Smith College, and her father was the first U.S. representative from the state of Utah, so it was natural for Florence Allen to blaze trails. She became the first woman assistant county prosecutor in Ohio, the first woman to preside over a first-degree murder trial and to pronounce the death sentence, the first woman to sit in a court of general jurisdiction (the Ohio Court of Common Pleas), the first woman to preside as a judge in a court of last resort (the Ohio Supreme Court), the first woman appointed to a Federal Court of Appeals, and the first woman to serve as chief judge of such a court. Though *Eleanor Roosevelt wrote, "If a president of the United States should decide to nominate a woman for the Supreme Court, it should be Judge Allen," Allen correctly supposed, as early as 1934, that she would not see such an appointment in her lifetime.

Florence Allen's earliest memory was of sitting on the lap of her father, Clarence Emir Allen, at the age of four while he taught her a sentence in Greek from the book he was reading. A year later, for his birthday present, she recited the Greek alphabet. Clarence Allen tutored the children in Latin, starting when Florence was seven. He had been a professor of classics at Western Reserve University in Cleveland, Ohio, when he contracted tuberculosis and moved to Utah. His wife followed after his recovery, and he resumed teaching at Hammond Hall, one of the New West Congregational Schools, where Florence was born on March 23, 1884. Her father's health worsened again; advised to seek a less sedentary occupation, he became a mine assayer. The rapidly growing family (six children survived to adulthood) lived in a miner's cabin, where the children enjoyed the attentions of the lonely miners, the Chinese cook, and the mine donkey. The versatile Clarence studied law, was admitted to the bar, and served in the Utah territorial legislature; he was also the state's first representative to the U.S. Congress in 1895.

Her mother, too, had an important influence on Florence's education. **Corinne Allen** had helped establish a free public library in Salt Lake City, was president of the Ladies' Literary Club and a member of the Daughters of the American Revolution, president of the State Federation of Women's Clubs, and one of the founders of the Mothers' Congress, later the P.T.A. Corinne had played piano in college, and after her husband was able to bring one out West for her, she taught Florence to play. She also coached her daughter to participate in a girls' debating society, advising her to "make your point and then sit down."

While her father served in Congress, Florence attended the New Lyme Institute in Ashtabula County directed by her maternal grandfather, Jacob Tuckerman. Her father returned to Utah after one term, and she attended Salt Lake City College. In 1900, at the age of 16, Allen entered Western Reserve University in Cleveland, Ohio, where she was elected president of the freshman class. She wrote verse, performed in plays, and played the piano, but showed her early concern for social justice by writing an editorial calling for the abolition of sororities (even though she belonged to one) and resigning her post as chair of Democratic Women for Newton Baker (later Woodrow Wilson's secretary of war) because he advocated compulsory military service. Allen graduated Phi Beta Kappa in 1904.

That year her family moved to Germany where her father attended the University of Berlin. Until a nerve injury to her arm put an end to a career in music, Florence was studying piano and wrote music reviews for the *Musical Courier* and the *Continental Times*. Back in Cleveland by 1906, she taught at the Laurel School for Girls. In addition to classes in Greek, German, geography, grammar and American history, she directed the drama and glee clubs, was music editor for the *Cleveland Plain Dealer*, and published a book of poetry, *Patris*, in 1908. Apparently indefatigable, Allen also studied political science and constitutional law at Western Reserve, receiving her M.A. in 1908. At that point, she determined to make law her career.

Western Reserve did not admit women to the law school, so she matriculated at Chicago University, one of only two women in a class of 100. After meeting activist *Frances Kellor, Allen left Chicago to work with her at the New York League for the Protection of Immigrants, where Allen served as legal investigator. She transferred to New York University (NYU) Law School, but had to interrupt her studies for a time because of eye problems. Reluctant to accept more money from her father, she lectured on music in the New York City public schools and later accepted a better-paying position offered by *Maud Wood Park as secretary of the College Equal Suffrage League. Allen abhorred discrimination on any grounds and declined to join the legal sorority because Jewish students were not admitted. She received a Bachelor of Law degree in 1913, graduating second in her class; later she was awarded an honorary LL.D., the first awarded by NYU to a woman.

After graduation, Allen continued to work for suffrage. In 1912, she campaigned for a suffrage bill in Ohio, speaking 92 times in 88 counties, and organizing the women in each locale. When the bill was defeated, she worked for municipal suffrage in charter cities, a strategy that proved more successful. Admitted to the Ohio bar in 1914, she gained experience as a volunteer counselor for the Legal Aid Society, as well as for the Woman Suffrage Party. In 1919, she represented women streetcar conductors who had been dismissed from their jobs to make way for returning World War I veterans. When her name was included on memorials to suffrage work in the Ohio State House and the Capitol in Washington D.C., Allen professed herself more pleased by that recognition than by any other tributes she later received.

The year 1919 saw the beginning of Allen's public career, with her appointment as assistant prosecutor of Cuyahoga County, the first woman in Ohio so named. She overcame the prejudice of the Grand Jury, mostly composed of retired police officers, who were at first opposed to a woman in the post. They later acknowledged her to be "as good as any of the men and better than some." The following year, when she campaigned for election to the Cuyahoga County Court of Common Pleas, the police as well as her suffrage contacts were important allies; she was not only the first woman elected to a court of general jurisdiction, a scant ten weeks after passage of the national woman suffrage amendment, but received the largest vote ever given to a candidate for that bench. She celebrated by climbing Mount Katahdin in Maine, where her daring impressed her guide.

Judge Allen refused to take the divorce division, and was amused when the *Cleveland News* applauded her decision to "decline appointment as a judge of a court of marital relations on the ground that she was ignorant of the subject." Allen's interest was in greater efficiency in the courts, believing that speed was essential to justice. In 20 months, she disposed of 892 cases, only three of which were reversed. Her actions were popular, as was her belief that while rehabilitation of the criminal was important, the "all-important purpose of the criminal law is the protection of the community." As the first woman judge to preside over a first-degree murder trial, she did not shrink from imposing the death sentence, though she received "black hand" threats on smudged letters and even on the walls of her basement. More controversial was her decision to deny the suit of an African-American woman who claimed she had suffered discrimination in college housing, and her decision to uphold the right of the state to award a contract to a non-union shop.

Judge Allen resigned from the court in the fall of 1922 to campaign for election to the Supreme Court of Ohio, touring the state in a Model-T Ford. She ran on a non-partisan platform, which irritated members of both parties; the new women voters rallied to her support by forming Florence Allen clubs throughout Ohio. Elected by a huge majority, Allen was the first woman to preside over a court of last resort, and, though she sensed apprehension among her fellow judges on the first day, she quickly put them at ease by urging them to feel free to smoke. She handled problems arising out of increased industrialization, such as workers compensation and crowded housing, as well as constitutional questions of authority. She maintained: "Justice is not, as certain people believe, a system under which they get what they want. Justice is a system under which they get the thing that they are entitled to." Allen was elected in 1928 to a second term. A penetrating and original thinker, her opinions establishing the constitutionality of the city manager plan for Ohio cities were widely appreciated, and her dissenting opinions were much admired by other lawyers and the press.

During the 1920s, Allen became active in the movement to outlaw war, seeing a need for more substantive international law. Both her younger brothers had died of wounds received in active service during World War I. She spoke to the Conference on the Cause and Cure of War

chaired by *Carrie Chapman Catt in 1925. The following year, Allen was moved to run for the U.S. Senate, convinced that she might do more as a senator to outlaw war, but she lost in the primary.

Florence Allen was appointed by President Franklin D. Roosevelt to the Sixth Circuit Court of Appeals in 1934, where she would serve for 25 years, the first woman justice to sit on a national bench of general jurisdiction. "Allen was not appointed because she was a woman," commented U.S. Attorney General Homer Cummings. "All we did was to see that she was not rejected because she was a woman." The Sixth Circuit included Ohio, Michigan, Kentucky, and Tennessee; one judge from each state sat on the federal court. Although her three colleagues originally disapproved of the appointment, they eventually came to offer her grudging respect. Of ten circuit courts in the United States, the Sixth ranked fourth in volume of work handled in the mid-1930s.

The Circuit Court cases included patents, taxes, civil suits, personal injuries, forgeries, stolen cars, narcotics, admiralty law, contracts, interstate commerce, conflicts between federal and state authority, and crime in all its branches. At first, Allen was assigned no patent cases, but when she protested, explaining her family's association with industry, she was assigned to many and became recognized as an expert in patent law.

Florence Allen was able to accomplish prodigious amounts of work due to her ability to extract information from a printed page with almost a single glance and to her formidable powers of concentration. Her passion for punctuality was key to coordinating a busy schedule, which included a hike at dawn, during which she memorized poetry, and a swim at noon. At night, she relaxed by playing from memory the piano music of Schumann, Beethoven, Brahms, and Chopin. Allen saved time by delegating housework and even the purchase of her clothes to other people.

Judge Allen's most notable case was a suit brought in 1937 against the Tennessee Valley Authority (TVA) by 19 private utility concerns; one of the lawyers representing the utilities was Wendell Willkie, later Republican candidate for president. They argued that the TVA, in using its dams to generate electricity, was forcing private companies out of business and accused the TVA and the Public Works Administration of conspiracy. In preparation, Allen, one of a three-judge panel, moved to Tennessee with her cousin, put in hours of study broken only by walks on the mountain with her dogs, and found it a "fascinating and grueling experience." She would not leave even when Eleanor Roosevelt invited her to dinner at the White House. "Toward the close of the case," Judge Allen wrote, "I found myself unable to sleep, and often got up at night to work over the opinion." The other judges accepted the opinion as she had written it, insisting that her name be signed to it. The decision found that the statute creating the authority was constitutional. It was later upheld by the Supreme Court.

Although Allen ceased active participation in politics after her appointment to the federal bench, her interest in international relations continued throughout her life. Beginning in 1930, she attended seminars in Mexico to promote understanding and ease tensions between the two North American countries. From 1948 to 1956, she attended several international conferences of lawyers, believing that international arbitration and the new United Nations would make it possible for countries to settle disputes without warfare. She also served as chair for the International Bar Association's Human Rights committee and traveled to many different countries to support women lawyers and women's equal rights. She was one of the first to call for an international law to govern space exploration.

Florence Allen also traveled around the United States lecturing on the U.S. Constitution at various colleges. These talks were collected and published in 1940 as *This Constitution of Ours*. In 1952, under the auspices of the Kappa Delta Pi educational honor society, she published *The Treaty as an Instrument of Legislation* in which she pointed out that the United Nations, with no legislature, was dependent on treaties ratified by individual nations. In the United States, unlike other countries, those treaties were binding on judges in every state, and Allen was concerned that UN proposals might encroach on the domestic jurisdiction of member states. She believed the UN needed constructive criticism as well as support. After her retirement at the age of 75 in 1959, she worked on her memoir, *To Do Justly*, published in 1965.

Throughout her long life, Florence Allen was greatly admired and was awarded many honors. She was named the outstanding professional woman in the United States by the National Federation of Business Women's Clubs in 1926, and received the National Achievement Award from Chi Omega, the national women's sorority, in 1938. In 1960, she was the first woman to receive the Albert Gallatin Award from New York University, an honor conferred on Dr. Ralph Bunche and Dr. Jonas Salk among others. She was granted honorary degrees by 25 universities, and the Florence Allen Award for outstanding women lawyers was established in 1966.

Accounted a genial friend, Allen was also close to her family. Her parents lived with her in their old age, and she also supported a sister and a niece, despite financial strains from loss on a note she co-signed for friends just before the Depression of the 1930s.

Florence Allen's guiding principle was a quotation from Micah: "What doth the Lord require of thee but to do justly, to love mercy, and to walk humbly with thy God." She believed that "to do justly is one of the highest human endeavors, and happy are they who share in it."

SOURCES:

Allen, Florence. *To Do Justly*. Cleveland, OH: Press of Western Reserve University, 1965.

Izant, Grace. "The Life Story of Ohio's First Lady," in *Cleveland Plain Dealer*. October 6, 1935, p. 4.

Roosevelt, Eleanor, and Lorena Hickok. *Ladies of Courage*. NY: Putnam, 1954.

COLLECTIONS:

The Florence E. Allen Papers at the Western Reserve Historical Society, Cleveland, Ohio, include diaries, papers, scrapbooks and clippings. Some duplicates in the Schlesinger Library, Radcliffe College, Cambridge, MA. Appellate opinions in the *Ohio Reports*, 1923–28, and the *Federal Reporter*, 1935–65.

Kristie Miller, author of *Ruth Hanna McCormick: A Life in Politics 1880–1944*, University of New Mexico Press, 1992

Allen, Frances S. (1854–1941) and Mary E. (1858–1941)

American photographers. Frances S. Allen was born in Wapping, Massachusetts, in 1854; died on February 14, 1941, in Deerfield, Massachusetts. Mary E. Allen was born in Wapping, Massachusetts, in 1858; died on February 18, 1941, in Deerfield, Massachusetts.

Growing up on the family farm in Wapping, Massachusetts, Mary Allen and her older sister Frances attended State Normal School in Westfield and obtained jobs as teachers. In the early 1890s, both sisters began going deaf, probably as the result of a childhood illness. With their teaching future in jeopardy, they turned to photography in order to make a living, specializing in portraits, genre, and scenic views. When their father died in 1895, they moved to scenic Deerfield, where they enjoyed considerable success selling souvenir views of "Old Deerfield" and typical scenes of New England life. It is believed that most of their portraits of children were posed and photographed by Frances.

The sisters were first published in 1891, when some of their early pictures appeared in a publication about Franklin, Massachusetts, *Picturesque Franklin,* edited by Charles Warner. Four of their photographs were in **Frances Benjamin Johnston**'s exhibition of 1900–1901, and Johnston also wrote about them in a series for *Ladies' Home Journal* called "The Foremost Women Photographers of America."

The sisters remained active until the early 1930s, when Frances became almost totally blind. They died just four days apart, Frances on February 14, 1941, and Mary on the 18th.

Allen, Gracie (1902–1964)

American comedian, smart enough to play the dumbest woman in show-business history. Born Grace Ethel Cecile Rosalie Allen on July 26, 1902, in San Francisco, California; died on August 27, 1964; one of five children of George and Margaret (Darragh) Allen (both vaudevillians); married George Burns (a comedian), on January 7, 1926; children: (adopted) Sandra Jean and Ronald Jon.

Made her show business debut (1909); teamed up with George Burns (1923); began hosting radio show with Burns (1932); ran for president of United States (1940); "The Burns & Allen Show" aired on television (October 12, 1950); filmed final television show (June 4, 1958).

Filmography: The Big Broadcast *(1932);* College Humor *(1933);* International House *(1933);* Six of a Kind *(1934);* We're Not Dressing *(1934);* Many Happy Returns *(1934);* Love in Bloom *(1935);* Big Broadcast of 1936 *(1935);* Here Comes Cookie *(1935);* Big Broadcast of 1937 *(1936);* College Holiday *(1936);* A Damsel in Distress *(1937);* College Swing *(1938); (without Burns)* The Gracie Allen Murder Case *(1939);* Honolulu *(1939); (without Burns)* Mr. and Mrs. North *(1942);* Two Gentleman and a Sailor *(1944).*

When Gracie Allen teamed up with George Burns on the vaudeville circuit of 1923, magic happened, and it lasted for 40 years: on radio, film, television, and in an offstage marriage that endured the rigors of show business and a probing public. At the height of their success, the tough, proud Irish lass with the quick, nasal, birdlike voice was on a first-name basis with the entire country. Burns described her as, "lovable, confusing Gracie, who once claimed to have grown grapefruits so big it took only eight of them to make a dozen," or as "Gracie, who confessed to cheating on her driver's test by copying

from the car in front of her." By his own admission, she was the truly gifted half of the union, known for her impeccable timing and a convincingly sincere delivery, regardless of how nonsensical or "malapropistic" her remarks were. She didn't try to be funny, and seemed honestly surprised when the audience laughed. Adds Burns, "She had the talent onstage, and I had the talent offstage."

Born on July 26, 1902, Gracie Allen was the youngest daughter of George Allen, a well-known song-and-dance man, who deserted the family when she was five. Her mother **Margaret Darragh Allen** would later remarry. Gracie, who had three sisters and a brother George, was hooked on show business from the age of three, when she made her debut performing an Irish dance at a church social. Almost daily on her way home from the Star of the Sea Convent School in San Francisco, Allen would detour downtown and stroll by the theaters to stargaze at placards in the lobbies. When she was 14, she left school to join her sisters—Hazel, Bessie, and Pearl—in a vaudeville act. The girls later became members of the Larry Reilly Company, in which Gracie was featured in Irish colleen parts, complete with a fake Irish brogue to cover a real Irish brogue that for some reason didn't sound real enough on stage. Her sisters left the company one-by-one and before long Gracie Allen became a headliner. She eventually quit the company in a dispute over billing, and, unable to find another booking, enrolled in a secretarial school with every intention of becoming a stenographer. Allen lasted three months. On a backstage visit at the Union Hill Theater in New Jersey in 1923, she met George Burns. She was 21; he was 27 and looking for a partner.

Originally, Allen was the singer-dancer of the act, while Burns was the comedian, dressed in baggy pants, a short coat, and a trick bow tie that twirled to signify a joke. As the "straightman," Allen appeared in a lovely dress. When Burns noticed that people were laughing more at her straight lines than his "toppers," he changed the routine. Gracie started delivering the punch lines.

After three years of performing together, Burns and Allen were married in Cleveland on January 7, 1926. Though George had been secretly in love with Gracie throughout, it was no easy job getting her to agree to more than friendship. When she first met Burns, she had been engaged to vaudeville star Benny Ryan and almost married him in 1925. Years later on their show, she announced, "I just want everyone to know one thing. I was courted by the handsomest, most charming, most sought-after star in show business." "Thank you very much," Burns interrupted. "But I married George because I loved him."

Barely five feet tall and under a hundred pounds, Gracie Allen had long brown hair with curls to her shoulders, and intriguing eyes of two different colors: one blue, one green. Her skin, as described by Burns, was "that Irish peach-bloom." When she was not performing, she was nothing like the ditsy character she portrayed. Rather, she was a beautiful, perfectly groomed, and elegant woman, who always performed in long-sleeved dresses and blouses, or with full-length gloves. Fashion was not, however, the dictator.

When Allen was a small child, she had pulled a boiling pot of tea off the stove, scalding her left arm and shoulder. For a while, doctors thought the arm might have to be amputated. Though they finally managed to save it, it was badly scarred and could never be completely straightened out. Embarrassed, Allen kept it hidden. Once, long after she had retired and was quite ill, Burns asked her if there was anything she wanted to do that she hadn't done before. She thought for a moment and replied that yes, there was one thing: she had always wanted to spend one evening wearing a strapless, sleeveless evening gown.

Throughout her life, Allen also suffered from severe migraine headaches, though she never let them interfere with a performance. Her work ethic was such that if she had a show scheduled, nothing kept her from it. Once, after breaking her nose when a taxicab stopped suddenly and threw her into the partition, she did three shows the following day.

After their days on the road, radio and films introduced Burns and Allen to a larger audience who had read of them but had never seen them perform. In January 1931, they signed a movie contract with Paramount Studios. Following their first full-length film *The Big Broadcast of 1932*, they would make close to 20 films together, while Gracie would appear without George in *The Gracie Allen Murder Case* (1939) and *Mr. and Mrs. North* (1942).

On February 15, 1932, Burns and Allen gave the first performance of their radio show, which would also continue for close to 20 years and attract an audience of 45 million. The characters and routines were the same as the vaudeville act, with the plot typically revolving around Gracie's illogical logic. Allen had a minimal role in script preparation. Three or so writers would submit the weekly script to Burns, who would decide what to cut and what to keep. In 1932, while the country was in the middle of the Depression, Burns and Allen were an unqualified success and were making as much as $10,000 week.

Much of their material had to do with Gracie's numerous relatives. There was her nephew who went to the doctor with a cold; when the doctor told him to take something warm, the nephew took the doctor's overcoat. Gracie's missing brother George, in particular, was the subject of a running exchange that usually started with Burns asking, "Gracie, how's your brother?" or:

Burns: What does your brother call himself?
Allen: Don't be silly; he doesn't have to call himself—he knows who he is.
Burns: What I mean is: if your brother was here, what would you call him?
Allen: If my brother was here, I wouldn't have to call him.
Burns: No, listen to me. If I found your brother, and I wanted to call him by name, what would it be?
Allen: It would be wonderful.

In 1933, this stunt was launched into a nationwide search for Gracie's lost brother. Allen made surprise guest appearances on other popular radio shows to ask if anyone had seen her brother George. The search rapidly spread beyond radio. Stores around the country vied for shoppers with promises of bargains and the prospect of finding Gracie Allen's missing brother in aisle nine. *Time* magazine commented that big game hunter Frank Buck had joined the search, while one newspaper reported that a man had been arrested who claimed to be Gracie's missing brother. "You look like Gracie Allen's brother" became a popular catch phrase. Unfortunately, Gracie's real brother George, an accountant in San Francisco, was eventually forced into hiding until public interest in him subsided.

Two other promotional stunts were successful. In 1938, when surrealist art was new and controversial, Gracie claimed to have done about ten paintings in this style, and convinced the posh Julian Levy Gallery in New York to sponsor a one-woman exhibition to benefit the Chinese Relief Fund. People paid 25 cents to see such unlikely works as, "Behind the Before Yet Under the Vast Above, the World is in Tears and Tomorrow is Tuesday."

During the 1940 election year, five men sought the presidency—Franklin Delano Roosevelt, John Nance Garner, Thomas E. Dewey, Robert A. Taft, and Arthur Vandenberg—as well as one woman, Gracie Allen. Running on a new third party ticket, the Surprise Party, she made the rounds of other radio programs such as "The Texaco Star Theater," "Fibber McGee and Molly," and "The Jack Benny Program," bursting in unannounced to offer her views on the burning issues of the day. Asked if she would recognize Russia, she said, "I don't know. I meet so many people." She appeared in D.C. as the guest of honor before the Women's National Press Club at the special invitation of First Lady *Eleanor Roosevelt, and was endorsed by students of Harvard.

Gracie Allen pioneered the idea of a sew-on campaign button to discourage her supporters from changing their minds. She wrote an article for *Liberty* entitled "Why America's Next President Should Be a Woman," and a book, *How To Become President,* was prepared through the "Gracie Allen Self-Delusion Institute." Key provisions were to put Congress on a commission basis—whenever the country prospered, Congress would get 10% of the take—and to extend Civil Service to all branches of government because "a little politeness goes a long way." In May of that year, her entourage whistle-stopped from Hollywood to Omaha, making more than 30 stops, culminating in a three-day convention at which she was unanimously nominated. Her speech was carried live on NBC.

On November 5, 1940, FDR was re-elected with more than 27 million votes. Republican Wendell Willkie received 22 million. Gracie Allen had a few hundred write-ins but claimed she had actually won and was prepared to do what Oliva Dionne, father of the famous *Dionne quintuplets had done—ask for a recount. She concluded, "I realize the president of today is merely the postage stamp of tomorrow."

One of the great sorrows of Gracie's early married life was that she could not get pregnant. Coming from a large family, she missed having children. In the 1930s, when many of their show-business friends were adopting, the couple contacted a foundling home in Illinois and added their names to the list of those wanting babies. Sandra Jean came first, followed about a year later, by Ronald Jon, a premature, sickly two-month old, who spent most of the first year of his life in doctor's offices. Allen was a devoted mother. Though she couldn't spend as much time with the children as she would have liked, she tried hard to make up for it, rushing home from work, racing into the nursery before taking off her coat. She even took on the role of disciplinarian. According to Burns, her rules consist-

ed basically of, "Watch Dad and don't do what he does." He said there were three things she wanted her children to be able to do: speak French, play the piano, and swim. On the grounds of their ranch house in Beverly Hills, she had a pool built; though she disliked spending time in the sun because of her fair complexion, she took private swimming lessons without telling anyone. One day, she dove into the pool and swam a lap. "See," she told the kids, "your mother can swim, too." Burns says he never saw her near the pool again.

In October 1950, Burns and Allen made their television debut for the Columbia Broadcasting System in a biweekly series of live programs that were described as "a carefully done replica of the radio show." The plots revolved around Burns and Allen as two performers at home, but, in an innovative touch, Burns was able to step out of the story, speak directly to the audience, and then step back into the action. Nothing like that had been seen before. At the end of most shows, Burns and Allen would come back on stage and do some of the old vaudeville routines. After the first few shows were broadcast from New York, they moved to the General Service Studio in Los Angeles.

> But let me tell you that women are getting very tired of running a poor second to the Forgotten Man. . . . The Constitution doesn't say anything about "he" or "him"; it refers only to "the person to be voted for." And if women aren't persons, what goes on here?
>
> —Gracie Allen

In 1952, they began filming the weekly show, shooting 39 episodes a season. It was an exhausting schedule with long hours in wardrobe and rehearsing. On Wednesdays, filming day began early and sometimes ended well after midnight. For Gracie, who frequently had to memorize 26 pages of dialogue in a 40-page script, it came at a time when she wanted desperately to ease up. (In fact, she had started talking to Burns about retiring while they were still doing the radio show). The strain began to take its toll; the migraines increased, and she sometimes became tense and withdrawn. Unlike her husband, reported her friend *June Allyson, Gracie was never *on* at parties, and "anyone who tried to get her to be funny got a dirty look." But sometimes, there were exceptions, wrote Allyson:

> George liked to make the point that he *had* to marry Gracie because he owed her $200

Gracie
Allen and
George
Burns

"wrap," there was a bottle of champagne on the set and a standing ovation from the crew. Gracie took one sip of champagne and said, "Okay, that's it." She paused for just a second, took a look around the set, and added, "And thank you very much, everyone." She then walked off the set and never looked back.

In the eight seasons the show aired, Gracie Allen received six nominations as Best Actress-Comedienne, and the show received four nominations as Best Comedy Series. When she retired, Allen thought the television industry would finally vote her an Emmy, but it never did. Although she said she didn't care about awards, Burns knew she felt slighted.

Allen truly enjoyed the first few years of retirement. Despite some bad bouts of chest pains and the continued migraines, she shopped, saw friends, played cards, and took up a new hobby—gambling. "She had a gambling problem," Burns confessed. "She was bad at it." When someone asked Gracie if she missed the good old days, she laughed. "They're always talking about the good old days. Believe me, the really good days are right now." The only thing that made her unhappy was the fact that each of her sisters, to whom she had remained close, had been put in rest homes. She worried that the same thing would happen to her.

In early 1964, as Gracie's heart condition grew worse, she began spending more time in confinement. When she died on August 27 of that year, at age 62, she was buried in Forest Lawn Cemetery in Glendale, California, where Burns, well into his 90s, still visited once a month to tell her what was going on in his life. "Marrying Gracie was the best thing that ever happened to me," he said. "I have a feeling she felt the same way—that marrying her was the best thing that ever happened to me."

and didn't know how else to pay it off. Once he added, "And I've been working it off ever since, right Gracie?" Gracie . . . turned to him and said, in her sweetest voice, "Oh really, George? I wasn't sure. I thought *I* was working it off."

She kept the pace, however, not only for her husband, but for all those whose jobs depended upon her. As always, she worked, no matter how she felt, even after she suffered her first heart attack.

Burns was amazed that Gracie, who seemed to have more energy than any woman in the world, would wind up with a bad heart. After her first attack in the early 1950s, she had several minor episodes over the next few years. It may have been inherited from her mother, who also died from heart trouble. Today, it would be called *angina*. Then, it was called a *heart condition* and treated with nitroglycerin pills. Whatever it was, it was time to quit working.

Burns and Allen filmed the final episode of their television show on June 4, 1958. At the

SOURCES:

Allyson, June, with Frances Spatz Leighton. *June Allyson by June Allyson.* NY: Putnam, 1982.

Burns, George. *Gracie: A Love Story.* NY: Putnam, 1989.

Coville, G.W. "Gracie Allen's 1940 Presidential Campaign," in *American History Illustrated.* November-December 1990.

Hubbard, K., and D. Mathison. "George Burns Writes a Final Loving Tribute to Gracie Allen," in *People Weekly.* October 31, 1988.

Leerhsen, C. "Grace after Gracie," in *Newsweek.* December 1988.

Rothe, Anna, ed. *Current Biography.* NY: H.W. Wilson, 1951.

Stoddard, M.G. "Amazing Gracie," in *The Saturday Evening Post.* March 1989.

SUGGESTED READING:

Mordden, Ethan. *Movie Star: A Look at the Women Who Made Hollywood.* St. Martin's Press, 1983.

Unterbrink, Mary. *Funny Women: American Comediennes, 1860–1985.* McFarland, 1987.

RELATED MEDIA:

"The Burns & Allen Show" (Radio & Television), Museum of Television and Radio, New York, New York.

Susan Slosberg, freelance writer, New Rochelle, New York

Allen, Mary E. (1858–1941).

See joint entry under Allen, Frances S.

Allen, Mary Sophia (1878–1964)

British police administrator and pioneer of women's police work whose many contributions were forgotten because of her support for fascism in the 1930s. Born Mary Sophia Allen on March 12, 1878; died in Croydon, England, on December 16, 1964; educated at Princess Helena College, Ealing, London.

Mary Sophia Allen was born on March 12, 1878, into a family of comfortable circumstances. Her father was a manager of the Great Western Railway. Educated at Princess Helena College, Ealing, London, Allen was a militant suffragist, serving three terms of imprisonment for her activities. Along with **Margaret Damer Dawson**, she was a co-founder of the women's police service in London in 1914 and was appointed to the rank of sub-commandant in that year. In 1919, she was promoted to commandant of the service, a position she held until her retirement in 1938. In addition to increasing the number and quality of her staff over a period of more than two decades, Allen argued persuasively for women's expanded role in police work, publishing three books on the subject. She also founded and served as editor of *The Policewoman's Review* from 1927 through 1937. Because of the pioneering nature of her work, she was invited to a number of foreign countries to lecture and give advice on the training of women's police forces.

Foreign contacts eventually brought Mary Allen into a swirl of bitter controversies in the 1930s. Visits to Germany led to meetings with Adolf Hitler, Hermann Goering and other Nazi

Mary Sophia Allen (center) with members of the Women Police. Photograph by *Christina Broom.

leaders. Favorably impressed by the "restoration of order" in Nazi Germany, she openly disseminated such views upon her return to Great Britain. She was also a strong supporter of the Fascist rebellion in Spain led by Francisco Franco. Needless to say, such viewpoints created heated controversy regarding her suitability as a leading police executive in a democratic society threatened by dictatorial regimes. Her views were attacked by several members of Parliament, and the fact that she was also director of the Voluntary Women's Auxiliary Service raised the question of her suitability for heading that organization, which had ties to the national civil-defense system. Her pioneering achievements momentarily eclipsed, Allen retired in 1938 under a cloud of controversy and criticism. In 1953, she converted to the Roman Catholic faith. Mary Sophia Allen died in Croydon, England, on December 16, 1964. Though her political instincts were misguided, Allen helped pave the way for women in the police force.

SOURCES:

Allen, Mary Sophia. *Lady in Blue: Reminiscences, and a Study of the Status of Women Police.* London: Stanley Paul, 1936.

———. *The Pioneer Policewoman.* Edited by Julie Helen Heyneman. London: Chatto & Windus, 1925.

———, and Julie Helen Heyneman. *Woman at the Cross Roads: Reminiscences of Mary S. Allen.* London: Unicorn Press, 1934.

"Miss Mary Allen, A Pioneer of Women's Police Service," in *The Times* [London]. December 18, 1964, p. 15.

John Haag, Associate Professor of History, University of Georgia, Athens, Georgia

Viola Allen

Allen, Sadie (c. 1868–?)

American daredevil. Born around 1868; death date unknown.

On November 28, 1886, along with her partner George Hazlett and 500 pounds of sand, Sadie Allen had a successful and memorable ride over Niagara Falls in a barrel. The 18-year-old from Buffalo suffered only slight bruises.

Allen, Viola
(1867–1948)

American actress. Born on October 27, 1867, in Huntsville, Alabama; died on May 9, 1948, at her home in New York; daughter of actors Charles Leslie Allen and Sara Jane (Lyon) Allen; married Peter Cornell Duryea (a Kentucky horse breeder), in 1905; children: none.

Performed on stage for 35 years, appearing in over 80 different roles, including her debut in the title role of Esmerelda *on July 4, 1882.*

While Charles Leslie Allen and **Sara Jane Allen** performed in the major Eastern theater cities of New York, Boston, and Toronto, as well as with touring companies, their four children traveled with them. Viola Allen was born in Huntsville, Alabama, while her parents were on their road. As preteens, Viola, her sister, and two brothers appeared as needed in their parents' plays and attended schools wherever the family stayed. At home, Viola's father studied Shakespeare with her, hoping to further his daughter's literary interests and refine her rhetorical talents. In 1882, when Viola was 14, Charles presented her to the director of the play *Esmerelda,* in which he was performing. She was chosen as an understudy to *Annie Russell (1869–1936), who held the title role. On July 4 of that year, Viola made her New York debut and did not stop working for the next 35 years. Her 80-plus roles included several of those Shakespearean characters studied with her father, including Lady Macbeth and Ophelia. On December 1, 1918, at age 51, Viola Allen retired from the stage.

Allen had married Peter Cornell Duryea, a wealthy Kentucky horse breeder, in 1905, and the couple divided their time between homes in America and Europe. Though Allen made occasional appearances in charity benefits and war relief efforts, she was largely removed from public life. In 1944, her husband died. Two years later, Allen made her last public appearance in a ceremony during which she donated her large collection of theater memorabilia—much of it related to her roles and travels—to the Museum of the City of New York. In 1948, Viola Allen died at her home, at age 80.

Crista Martin, Boston, Massachusetts

Alleyne, Ellen (1830–1894).

See Rossetti, Christina.

Allfrey, Phyllis Shand (1915–1986)

Dominican author and politician. Born Phyllis Byam Shand in Dominica, West Indies, on October 24, 1915; died in Dominica in 1986; daughter of Francis Byam Berkeley Shand and Elfreda (Nicholls) Shand; married Robert Allfrey; children: five, including Philip

and Josephine Allfrey (d. 1977); three of her children were adopted.

Selected works: In Circles *(1940);* Palm and Oak *(1950);* The Orchid House *(1953);* Contrasts *(1955);* Palm and Oak II *(1974).*

Phyllis Shand, the second of four daughters born to Francis and Elfreda Shand, was a descendent of early settlers who formed Dominica's white ruling class. Nevertheless, the family had fallen in financial standing. Though Francis Shand later became crown attorney of Dominica, in the early years the family was fortunate to have a large home that Elfreda had inherited. There, Phyllis and her sisters, Celia, Marion, and Rosalind, were educated by a series of tutors, including their mother's sister, Aunt Mags, and an Anglican rector. Phyllis often wrote plays that she and her sisters performed, and she sold her first story at age 13.

When Phyllis was 17, she studied and traveled in England, France, Belgium and Germany, finally returning to London, where her sister Celia had settled and married. There Phyllis met and married Robert Allfrey, her brother-in-law's younger sibling. The couple moved briefly to America and lived in New York State, where daughter Josephine and son Philip were born, until the Depression made it impossible for them to stay. Returning to England, Allfrey went to work as a secretary for novelist and historian *Naomi Mitchison. Mitchison introduced Allfrey to several politicians, and Allfrey subsequently worked for the Parliamentary Committee for West Indian Affairs. She also joined the Labour Party and the Fabian Society.

Allfrey's publishing career began in England. She produced two volumes of poetry and, in 1953, her first novel, *The Orchid House,* which was based on her childhood home. The novel made her homesick and, in 1954, the Allfreys returned to Dominica. That same year, Allfrey founded the Labour Party to help tropical fruit workers command fair pay. In 1958, she was elected minister for labour and social affairs. The family moved to Trinidad during this tenure but returned to Dominica in 1962 when the federal government faltered. She assumed an editorial position at the *Dominican Herald* and with her husband founded and edited the *Dominican Star* in 1965. The Allfreys also expanded their family with three adopted children.

The late 1970s held serious misfortune. In April of 1977, her daughter Josephine was killed in Botswana, and Allfrey in her grief abandoned her novel in progress, *In the Cabinet.* In 1979,

Hurricane David badly damaged the Allfrey home and ruined many of their possessions, including her books and manuscripts. Later that year, Allfrey's long-time friend, correspondent, and countrywoman, author *Jean Rhys, died. Financially devastated, the Allfreys had to give up the *Star* in 1982. At the time of her death in 1986, *In the Cabinet* lay unfinished.

Crista Martin, Boston, Massachusetts

Allgood, Molly (1885–1952).

See O'Neill, Máire.

Allgood, Sara (1883–1950)

*Irish character actress. Born in Dublin, Ireland, on October 31, 1883; died in Hollywood, California, on September 13, 1950; sister of actress Molly Allgood whose stagename was *Máire O'Neill (1885–1952); apprenticed to an upholsterer; joined Inghinidehe na hÉireann, founded by *Maude Gonne MacBride; married Gerald Henson (d. 1918, an actor), in September 1916; children: one daughter who died at birth (January 1918); became an American citizen in 1945.*

Filmography: Just Peggy *(Australia, 1918);* Blackmail *(1929);* Juno and the Paycock *(The Shame of Mary Boyle, 1930);* The World, the Flesh, and the Devil *(U.K., 1932);* Irish Hearts *(also titled* Nora O'Neale, *U.K., 1934);* Peg of Old Drury *(U.K., 1935);* Riders to the Sea *(U.K., 1935);* The Passing of the Third Floor Back *(U.K., 1935);* It's Love Again *(U.K, 1936);* Sabotage *(The Woman Alone; U.K., 1936);* Storm in a Teacup *(U.K., 1937);* On the Night of the Fire *(The Fugitive, U.K., 1939);* That Hamilton Woman *(Lady Hamilton, 1941);* Dr. Jekyll and Mr. Hyde *(1941);* Lydia *(1941);* How Green Was my Valley *(1941);* Roxie Hart *(1942);* This Above All *(1942);* It Happened in Flatbush *(1942);* The War Against Mrs. Hadley *(1942);* Life Begins at 8:30 *(1942);* City Without Men *(1943);* The Lodger *(1944);* Jane Eyre *(1944);* Keys of the Kingdom *(1944);* Between Two Worlds *(1944);* The Spiral Staircase *(1945);* Uncle Harry *(1945);* Kitty *(1946);* Cluny Brown *(1946);* Ivy *(1947);* The Fabulous Dorseys *(1947);* Mourning Becomes Electra *(1947);* Mother Wore Tights *(1947);* My Wild Irish Rose *(1947);* The Girl From Manhattan *(1948);* One Touch of Venus *(1948);* The Man From Texas *(1948);* The Accused *(1948);* Challenge to Lassie *(U.S, 1949);* Cheaper by the Dozen *(1950);* Sierra *(1950).*

Legendary character actress Sara Allgood began her career in 1904 at Dublin's Abbey Theatre, then known as the Irish National Theatre

Society; Allgood was a founding member. She made her debut as Cathleen in John Millington Synge's *Riders to the Sea*. Playing at the Irish National for the next decade, she originated such great roles as Mrs. Fallon in *Lady (Augusta) Gregory's *Spreading the News* (1904), the Widow Quin in J.M. Synge's *The Playboy of the Western World* (1907), Lavarcham in *Deirdre of the Sorrows* (1910), and the title role in *Cathleen ni Houlihan* (1913). Allgood was also involved with the inception of the Liverpool Repertory Theatre and *Annie Horniman's company at Manchester. In London, Allgood created the role of Nannie Webster in James M. Barrie's *The Little Minister*.

In 1916, she toured Australia in *Peg o' My Heart* and, that September, married her leading man, Gerald Henson, in Melbourne. In January 1918, she gave birth to a daughter who lived only one hour, and, in November of that same year, her husband died during an influenza epidemic in Wellington. The year 1920 found Allgood back in London reprising her role in *Playboy of the Western World*, while also creating the roles of Juno Boyle in Sean O'Casey's *Juno and the Paycock* and Bessie Burgess in *The Plough and the Stars*. Allgood also portrayed Mrs. Henderson in the Court production of *Shadow of a Gunman*. Arriving in America in the 1920s, Allgood reprised all her O'Casey roles on stage, which she would do again in London in the 1930s. Now in her 40s, she began to be typecast as a loveable Irish mother or grandmother.

Her film career began in England when she teamed with Alfred Hitchcock for two roles: the 1929 *Blackmail* and the 1930 filming of her greatest stage success in *Juno and the Paycock* (also titled *The Shame of Mary Boyle*), with screenplay by Hitchcock and *Alma Reville. In 1940, Allgood was off to Hollywood. Though she continued to be cast as the kindly Irish mother, she added heft to the parts and was nominated for best supporting actress for her role in Richard Llewellyn's *How Green Was my Valley* (1941). She died in Hollywood on September 13, 1950.

Alliluyeva, Svetlana (1926—)

Writer and sole surviving child of Soviet dictator Joseph Stalin. Name variations: Svetlana Stalin, but for most of her life she used her mother's maiden name Alliluyeva (also spelled Allilluyeva). Born Svetlana Iosifovna Stalina on February 28, 1926, in Moscow, USSR; youngest child and only daughter of Joseph and Nadezhda Alliluyeva-Stalin; graduated Moscow University, 1949; graduate study, Academy of Social Sciences, Moscow; married Grigory Morozov, in 1943 (divorced 1947); married Yury Zhdanov, in 1949 (divorced); reportedly married Mikhail L. Kaganovich, 1951; married, in common law, Brijesh Singh (d. 1966), around 1963; married James Wesley Peters, 1970 (separated 1971); children: (first marriage) Joseph Alliluyev (b. 1945); (second marriage) Ekaterina (Katya, b. 1950); (fourth marriage) Olga.

Selected writings: Dvadsat pisem k drugu (translation by Priscilla Johnson McMillan published as Twenty Letters to a Friend, *Harper, 1967); Tol'ko odin god (translation by Paul Chavchavadze published as* Only One Year, *Harper, 1969); also author of a pamphlet,* Borisu Leonidoichu Pasternaku.

Svetlana Alliluyeva, the sole surviving child and only daughter of Soviet dictator Joseph Stalin, might never have gained notice in the Western World had it not been for her well-publicized defection to the United States in 1967. In an escape from the Indian Embassy, where she was being held for deportation back to Moscow, Alliluyeva slipped out to the American Embassy, setting in motion a journey to Switzerland, Rome, and, finally, freedom in the United States. A year later, Alliluyeva announced that she had burned her Soviet passport and, regretting only her separation from her children, had decided to apply for U.S. citizenship. She bought a house in the university town of Princeton, New Jersey.

Born in 1926, in post revolutionary Moscow, Alliluyeva was the youngest of three children. Both of her brothers died prematurely: Yakov, Stalin's son by an earlier marriage to **Ekaterina Keke Svanidze**, died in a Nazi prison camp during World War II after his father refused to intercede for his release; and Vasily, a Soviet air-force flyer, died of alcoholism in 1962.

Alliluyeva, apparently shielded from many of the political forces swirling around her at the time, characterized her early years as idyllic. Her father, known to the world as a ruthless dictator, was evidently an affectionate and doting father. Alliluyeva described her mother *Nadezhda Alliluyeva-Stalin (1901-1932) as the acknowledged head of the household, who was respected and loved by everyone. "She was intelligent, beautiful, extraordinarily gentle and considerate in every relationship. At the same time she could be firm, stubborn and unyielding when she felt that a conviction could not be compromised." Like most Bolshevik women, Nadezhda left the children in the care of a nurse while she pursued her own political and intellectual interests. Alliluyeva attended music school as a preschooler and was tutored by a governess. Later, in addition to tutoring, she attended public school in Moscow. The family had an apartment in the Kremlin and summered in the country.

In 1932, Alliluyeva's world shattered when her mother, apparently tortured by Stalin's merciless political activities and his frequent verbal and physical abuse, shot herself. Alliluyeva was told and believed that her mother had died of a burst appendix, until she read of the suicide in an American magazine ten years later. Stalin, apparently angered over his wife's suicide, refused to stay in the home they had shared and moved the family to a new apartment. The children continued to summer with his wife's family, with whom Stalin had little interaction. Eventually, several members of the family fell victim to his purges.

Alliluyeva evidently remained close to her father until her girlhood affair with Jewish filmmaker Alexei Kapler, who was 40 at the time. The rabidly anti-Semitic Stalin was enraged at the romance and had Kapler banished to Lubianka Prison in Siberia for ten years. From then on, Alliluyeva saw little of her father, although he exerted rigid control over her life.

After her graduation from Moscow University, Alliluyeva entered into a series of marriages about which little is known. Her first husband, Grigory Morozov, was a fellow student at the university and, like Kapler, was Jewish. (Stalin, for some reason, appeared to endure this union, although he refused to meet or have anything to do with his new son-in-law.) After having a son Joseph, born in May 1945, they divorced in 1947. Two years later, this time with her father's blessing, she married Stalin's second in command, and they had a daughter Ekaterina (Katya) in 1950. When they, too, divorced, Alliluyeva took an apartment in Moscow, outside the Kremlin, where she lived quietly with her two children, receiving a modest allowance from the state. In 1953, the year of her father's death, there were unconfirmed reports that she had married Mikhail Kaganovich, the son of a high Soviet official.

In 1963, she met Brijesh Singh, an Indian Communist 17 years her senior. Their warm and loving relationship, which developed while they were both confined in a hospital, is detailed in her book *Only One Year*. Unable to legally marry because of Singh's foreign status, and denied permission to accompany him to India when he became seriously ill in 1966, it was only after his death that she received permission to return his ashes to his native village. She remained

Svetlana
Alliluyeva

there for two months, fully embracing the Hindu culture. Outspoken in her criticism of the Soviet Union, through friends she inquired about remaining in India, but the Indian government, fearing a threat to Soviet-Indian relations, did not encourage her. She was summoned to the Soviet Embassy in New Delhi, where she was told to stay until a flight back to Moscow could be arranged. It was then that she made her fateful escape to the American Embassy. She called her defection an attempt to "salvage the spirit."

Alliluyeva held various jobs in Moscow, occasionally teaching at the university and working as an English translator. In 1963, she wrote her memoirs "for the drawer," as they could not be published in Russia because of the strict censorship laws. Her literary career in America was considerably more successful. Her much heralded and long awaited *Twenty Letters to a Friend*, the story of her mother's family, which has been called "an allegory of the sufferings of the Soviet people as a whole," brought unprecedented offers and made her a great deal of money, most of which she gave to charity. Although the book was not acclaimed as a great work of art, it was favorably reviewed by critics. William Henry Chamberlin's review in the *Wall Street Journal* praised her "excellent gift of conveying personalities and recalling dramatic scenes." The Soviet government, which had earlier charged that CIA agents were helping her rewrite her memoirs, was relieved that the book "divulged no new secrets nor did it deviate from the Soviet view of Stalin's regime."

In 1984, Alliluyeva returned to her homeland, in a well-publicized visit with her 14-year-old daughter, **Olga Peters**. Although she had been stripped of her Soviet citizenship following her defection, it was restored after she criticized the West, claiming a lack of freedom. She returned briefly to the United States in 1986. Since 1986, she has avoided the news media, but there have been many Svetlana sightings. In 1995, one newspaper claimed she was destitute and living in London, frequenting a charity hostel that catered to indigents with severe emotional problems. In 1996, an Italian priest said that she had stayed for a year in a Roman Catholic convent near Rugby, England, in 1993. Alliluyeva had told him that she thought religion might give her peace.

SOURCES:
Alliluyeva, Svetlana. *Only One Year.* NY: Harper and Row, 1969.
——. *Twenty Letters to a Friend.* NY: Harper and Row, 1967.
Moritz, Charles, ed. *Current Biography Yearbook, 1968.* NY: H.W. Wilson, 1968.

Barbara Morgan, Melrose, Massachusetts

Alliluyeva-Stalin, Nadezhda

(1901–1932)

Soviet writer and wife of Joseph Stalin. Name variations: Nadya or Nadejda Alliluieva, Allilueva, or Allileyevna. Born in the Caucasus, Russia, in 1901; committed suicide in Moscow, USSR, on November 8, 1932; daughter of Sergei Alliluyev and Olga Fedorenko (a Georgian); younger sister of **Anna Alliluyeva Redens**; *married Joseph V. Stalin, in 1918 (his first wife was Ekaterina [Keke] Svanidze, who died in 1907 and gave birth to his son Yakov); children: Vassily and* *Svetlana Alliluyeva (1926—).*

Joseph Stalin's second wife, Nadezhda Alliluyeva, was the daughter of a political colleague. Nada, as she was known, worked as a secretary in the Commissariat of Nationalities. Her mother was opposed to the marriage with Stalin because of his reputation for being cold and driven, but Alliluyeva married the rising po-

litical star, and they moved to an apartment on the grounds of the Kremlin. She worked briefly for the journal *Revolution and Culture,* and gave Stalin a son, Vassily (c. 1920), and a daughter, Svetlana (1926). As Stalin was rarely home, Alliluyeva began study at the Industrial Academy in 1930 as a means of battling depression and boredom.

In part influenced by her fellow students, she began to turn from Stalin's ideas and policies. On November 8, 1932, Stalin and Alliluyeva argued publicly at a formal dinner. The fight seems to have been politically motivated. "Hey, you. Have a drink!" Stalin yelled at her. "Don't you dare 'hey' me!" retorted Alliluyeva before she stormed out. On the morning of November 9, she was found dead in their apartment, apparently of a self-inflicted gunshot wound. She left a suicide note that was both personally and politically critical of Stalin. He viewed the suicide as treachery against him and did not attend the civil funeral ceremony. At the private ceremony, he approached the casket but made a dismissive gesture toward his dead wife and walked away.

SOURCES:
Tucker, Robert C. *Stalin in Power.* NY: Norton, 1990.
Ulam, Adam B. *Stalin.* Boston, MA: Beacon Press, 1973.
Volkogonov, Dmitri. *Stalin: Triumph and Tragedy.* NY: Grove Weidenfeld, 1988.

Crista Martin, Boston, Massachusetts

Allingham, Helen Patterson

(1848–1926).

See Greenaway, Kate for sidebar.

Allingham, Margery (1904–1966)

British mystery novelist best known for her Albert Campion mystery-thrillers. Born Margery Louise Allingham in London, England, in 1904; died in 1966; daughter of Herbert and Emily Jane (Hughes) Allingham; educated at Perse High School, Cambridge; married Philip Youngman Carter (an artist), in 1927.

Margery Allingham was born into a British family of writers: her grandfather was the owner of a religious newspaper, and her father Herbert (known as H.J. Allingham) wrote a popular weekly serial. Following their example, Margery began writing at an early age. Her father assigned her a plot, then helped her edit and revise the piece, sometimes for up to a year, before he considered the story finished. As a result, when Margery was eight her first paid piece appeared in a magazine her aunt edited. Allingham attended the Perse School in Cambridge, where she focused on drama, as well as the Regent Street Polytechnic. Leaving school at 15, she wrote fiction for Britain's *Sexton Blake* and *Girls' Cinema*. Her first novel appeared in 1922.

In 1929, she introduced her meek, bespectacled detective Albert Campion in *The Crime at Black Dudley*. In her next novel, *Mystery Mile*, she created Campion's manservant Lugg (1930). Though she wrote a small number of plays, nearly 150 articles and book reviews, 60 short stories, and four novellas—*Flowers for the Judge* (1936), *The Tiger in the Smoke* (1952), *The Beckoning Lady* (1955), and *Cargo of Eagles*, completed by her husband after her death in 1966—it is the Campion stories for which she is remembered. As the series progressed, Allingham began to explore the psychology of crime, the darker underbelly of her characters. She defied those who demanded she stay within the confines of the accepted mystery format. "I would like to say here and now," she wrote a friend, "that under Margery Allingham I shall write the sort of book I believe in and no other." In breaking the rules, Allingham expanded the genre.

At age 23, she had married artist and journalist Philip Youngman Carter. They lived in a Queen Anne house on the edge of the Essex Marshes, in Tolleshunt D'Arcy.

SOURCES:

Allingham, Margery. *The Tiger in the Smoke.* Harmondsworth, England: Penguin Books, 1952.

Crista Martin, Boston, Massachusetts

Margery Allingham

Allison, May (1895–1989)

American actress and one of MGM's greatest box-office stars of the 1920s. Born on a farm in Rising Fawn, Georgia, on June 14, 1895; died in 1989; educated in Birmingham, Alabama; married Robert Ellis (divorced); married James R. Quirk (a Photoplay *editor, who died in 1932); married Carl N. Osborne (a businessman).*

Before working as a silent-screen actress, May Allison had a successful career on stage, starring in *Everyman* and *The Quaker Girl* on Broadway. In 1915, the 5'6" blue-eyed, Southern blonde beauty made her first film, *A Fool There Was.* That same year, Will Rogers convinced her to play a leading role in his movie *David Harum.* From 1915 to 1917, Allison and Harold Lockwood became a romantic duo on screen, shooting eight movies together. She also co-starred with her first husband Robert Ellis in *Peggy Does Her Darndest* and *In for Thirty Days.* A popular actress throughout the 1920s,

Allison's films include *The Great Question* (1915), *The End of the Road* (1915), *One Increasing Purpose, The Testing of Mildred Vane* (1918), *Fair and Warmer* (1919), *The Woman Who Fooled Herself* (1922), *Flapper Wives* (1924), *I Want My Man* (1925), *Wreckage* (1925), *The Greater Glory* (1926), *Men of Steel* (1926), *The City* (1926), and *Mismates.* Allison, whose other pursuits included flying her own plane, made her last movie, *The Telephone Girl*, in 1927. She retired to care for her ailing husband James R. Quirk, a *Photoplay* editor, who died five years later.

Allyn, Ellen (1830–1894).

See Rossetti, Christina.

Allyson, June (1917—)

American actress, popular in the 1940s and 1950s. Born Kathryn Ann Eleanor "Ella" van Geisman on October 7, 1917, in the Bronx, New York; daughter

of Arthur van Geisman (a building superintendent) and Clare van Geisman; attended public schools in New York and in Pelham in Westchester County, and Theodore Roosevelt High School in the Bronx; married Dick Powell (1904–1963, actor-director), on August 19, 1945; married Alfred Glenn Maxwell (Dick Powell's barber), 1963 (divorced 1965, remarried 1966, divorced); married David Ashrow (a dental surgeon), October 30, 1976; children: (first marriage) Pamela (adopted on August 10, 1948); Richard, Jr. (b. December 24, 1950); (stepchildren) Ellen Powell and Norman Powell.

Filmography: Girl Crazy (MGM, 1943); Best Foot Forward (MGM, 1943); Thousands Cheer (MGM, 1943); Two Girls and a Sailor (MGM, 1944); Meet the People (MGM, 1944); Music For Millions (MGM, 1945); Her Highness and the Bellboy (MGM, 1945); The Sailor Takes a Wife (MGM, 1945); Two Sisters From Boston (MGM, 1946); Till the Clouds Roll By (MGM, 1946); The Secret Heart (MGM, 1946); High Barbaree (MGM, 1947); Good News (MGM, 1947); The Bride Goes Wild (MGM, 1948); The Three Musketeers (MGM, 1948); Words and Music (MGM, 1948); Little Women (MGM, 1949); The Stratton Story (MGM, 1949); The Reformer and the Redhead (MGM, 1950); Right Cross (MGM, 1950); Too Young to Kiss (MGM, 1951); The Girl in White (MGM, 1952); Battle Circus (MGM, 1953); Remains to Be Seen (MGM, 1953); The Glenn Miller Story (Univ., 1954); Executive Suite (MGM, 1954); Woman's World (20th, 1954); Strategic Air Command (Par., 1955); The McConnell Story (WB, 1955); The Shrike (Univ., 1955); The Opposite Sex (MGM, 1956); You Can't Run Away From It (Col., 1956); Interlude (Univ., 1957); My Man Godfrey (Univ., 1957); Stranger in My Arms (Univ., 1959); They Only Kill Their Masters (1972); Blackout (Can.-Fr., 1978). Television: "The June Allyson Show" (1960).

June Allyson, the husky-voiced actress with the tiny lisp and the Peter Pan collar, was born Ella Geisman in the Bronx, New York, on October 7, 1923. Her alcoholic father Arthur left home when Allyson was six months old, taking a brother with him. Mother Clare, with babe in arms, moved in with her parents and scrambled for work in a printing plant; she also worked as a switchboard operator and restaurant cashier, anything that would help pay the bills. The death of Allyson's grandmother in those early years left the future actress inconsolable.

A freak accident at age eight added to the family woes. In 1925, while Allyson was riding her tricycle with a neighborhood boy, a dead tree limb fell on both of them. The tricycle was crushed, her friend was killed, and the branch broke "half the bones" in her body. Allyson spent that summer learning to walk again; she went from a wheelchair to crutches to a corrective back brace that she wore for four more years. Eventually, she swam for therapy, once winning a Greater New York City free-style championship. Though the cause of the accident had been negligence on the part of the city, they were only reimbursed $100 for medical costs. Under the weight of medical bills, June and her mother were destitute. On those days when there was only food for one, her mother would claim a lack of appetite.

Life changed for the better when Allyson's mother remarried and the family moved to 1975 Bryant Avenue. Despite her brace, the young girl began to dance. June plunked down a hard-to-come-by $20 to enroll in a dance school, but it went bankrupt before she had her first lesson. She learned to dance by watching Fred Astaire and *Ginger Rogers in The Gay Divorcee, attending the local bijou 17 times. Flying Down to Rio served as advanced training. On a dare, at age 21, Allyson auditioned for the chorus line in a musical and landed her first Broadway show, Sing out the News (1938). "They hired me for laughs," she said. Professionally naive, she hadn't known to bring her own sheet music to the audition, so when they asked what she was prepared to sing, she answered, "What do you wanna hear?" Even so, the show was a hit, and the choreographer gave her a new name—June Allyson.

Following a turn in Jerome Kern-Oscar Hammerstein II's less-than-successful Very Warm for May, where she shared the chorus line with *Vera-Ellen, Allyson joined the cast of the even-less-successful Higher and Higher. "I've been in more flops than you can imagine," she commented. "I couldn't dance, and Lord knows I couldn't sing, but I got by somehow. It was Richard Rodgers who was always keeping them from firing me, as every dance director wanted to do." Finally, she managed to snag another chorus part in *Ethel Merman's Panama Hattie, which included understudying *Betty Hutton. When Hutton came down with measles, Allyson had her big break; during one of those five performances, George Abbott was in the audience and hired her for Best Foot Forward, starring *Rosemary Lane. In that hit musical, Allyson shared a showstopper "The Three B's" with *Nancy Walker and Erlene Schools. One night backstage, in the celebrity crush, she was introduced to Dick Powell, while somewhere in the crowd was his wife *Joan Blondell.

At age 26, in 1943, Allyson arrived in wartime Hollywood, having been signed for the movie of *Best Foot Forward,* which also starred *Lucille Ball. The first day on the set Allyson was told to go home and come back after she had shaken her cold. "But I haven't got a cold," she claimed, "I talk like this all the time." She then landed a part in *Girl Crazy,* starring Mickey Rooney, followed by *Thousands Cheer* and *Meet*

the People, both again with Ball. *Meet the People* also starred the still-married Dick Powell.

By now, Powell had become a sort of precise mentor. For example, when offered the part of the pretty sister next to **Gloria De Haven**'s plain sister in *Two Girls and a Sailor,* Allyson notes in her autobiography that she sought out Powell for advice. "There are two lines in the script that absolutely negate your doing the role of the beautiful sister," declared Powell, "and they are when the grandfather asks Gloria, 'Is your sister as pretty as you?' and she says, 'Oh, prettier,

June
Allyson

much prettier.' Nobody is going to believe that. Gloria is a real beauty. So what I want you to do is go in and tell Mr. Mayer that you want to test for the role of the plain sister. . . . And when he agrees, which you will make him do, I want you to go home and cut off your hair. Just straight across bangs and short, straight sides and don't use any makeup in the test." The rest, as they say, is movie history.

When Powell separated from Blondell, the Allyson-Powell courtship started, despite Louis B. Mayer's demands that she date her frequent co-star Van Johnson. Powell was a take-charge kind of guy, a professor Higgins. When he asked Allyson what her philosophy of life was, she replied, "If you see someone without a smile, give him yours." Powell addressed the heavens, "Oh God, don't ever let her change." They were married on August 19, 1945. He was 41; she 22.

Allyson, who quickly became typecast as the girl-next-door in the MGM musicals of the 1940s, made movie after movie in rapid succession: *Music for Millions, Her Highness and the Bellboy, The Sailor Takes a Wife, Two Sisters from Boston, Look for the Silver Lining.* She and **Margaret O'Brien** began to be known as the Town Criers. If the part called for tears, they could cover two age groups. It was wartime in Hollywood, a time when the character of the "virtuous woman left behind to wait for her soldier" was in vogue. "New personalities, such as *Jane Powell, June Allyson, **Debbie Reynolds**, and, in the early fifties, *Doris Day and *Janet Leigh, brought a disarming naïveté to the screen," writes **Marjorie Rosen** in *Popcorn Venus,* "a novel scrubbed kind of heroine, one without pretense, without maturity, and without the womanly stature that had been so distinctive of the greatest stars of the past two decades." They were dubbed bobby-sox films.

In 1949, the remake of *Louisa May Alcott's *Little Women* was released, starring *Elizabeth Taylor, Janet Leigh, Margaret O'Brien, and Allyson. Despite press comparisons to *Katharine Hepburn who had starred as Jo in the 1933 version, Allyson's performance as Jo was deemed authentic. Leaving MGM, her "all powerful and benevolent crutch," in 1954, she signed on for the highly successful *Glenn Miller Story* opposite Jimmy Stewart at Universal. Allyson teamed with Stewart for two more pictures: *The Stratton Story,* in which her performance was praised by Bosley Crowther, and *Strategic Air Command.* More noble wives followed. Generally cast, says Rosen, as the "perfect, selfless martyr," one of the many who "sobbed and suffered for their men

rather than themselves," June Allyson stayed home and waited for her man in *The Stratton Story, The Glenn Miller Story, Executive Suite, Woman's World, Strategic Air Command,* and *The McConnell Story.* It was not until 1955, when José Ferrer asked her to play his insanely possessive wife in *The Shrike,* that Allyson defied the sweet-wife casting trap and played the opposite stereotype: in the shrike world, the female bird preys upon the male and destroys him. Some thought her performance was spine-chilling; others found it strident.

After undergoing a kidney operation and throat surgery in 1961, momentarily causing her voice to rise to a high soprano, Allyson learned that her husband had cancer of the lymph glands. When Powell died on January 2, 1963, her world fell apart, and it would take many years before she shook her lethargy and depression. In later years, she returned to the stage, replacing **Julie Harris** in *40 Carats,* and undertaking the national tour of *No No Nanette.* Remarried, Allyson moved to Ojai, California.

"I never did feel quite right about the roles I was called upon to portray," she once commented, "the gentle, kind, loving, perfect wife, who will stand by her man through 'anything.' In real life I'm a poor dressmaker and a terrible cook; in fact, anything but the perfect wife."

SOURCES:
Allyson, June, with Frances Spatz Leighton. *June Allyson.* NY: Putnam, 1982.

Parish, James Robert, and Ronald L. Bowers. *The MGM Stock Company.* New Rochelle, NY: Arlington House, 1973.

Rosen, Marjorie. *Popcorn Venus.* NY: Coward, McCann, 1973.

Almada, Filipa de (fl. 15th c.)

Portuguese poet and noblewoman. Lived in Portugal.

Her nobility and stature in the Avis dynasty afforded Filipa de Almada the luxury of being an educated woman in 15th-century Portugal. She lived and wrote under the rule of Portuguese kings Alphonso V (1438–1481) and John II (1481–1495). Almada's poetry appeared in Garcia de Resende's *Cancioneiro Geral (General Songbook,* 1516), an anthology of Spanish and Portuguese poetry of the time, which is called "palace poetry" because its audience and authors were largely royalty.

Almania, Jacqueline Felicie de (fl. 1322).

See de Almania, Jacqueline Felicia.

Almedingen, E.M. (1898–1971)

Russian author. Name variations: Edith Martha Almedingen. Born Martha Edith von Almedingen in 1898 in St. Petersburg, Russia; died in 1971 in England; educated in St. Petersburg private schools, Xenia Nobility College, and University of Petrograd. More than ten books to her credit, including Out of Seir *(1943),* Storm at Westminster *(1952),* The Empress Alexandra, 1872–1918 *(1961), and* Anna *(1972).*

Martha Edith von Almedingen's extensive education in her homeland of St. Petersburg included a private early education, and work at two institutes of higher learning, the Xenia Nobility College and the University of Petrograd. Specializing in medieval history and philosophy, Almedingen lectured at Petrograd in English medieval history and literature from 1920 until her departure from Russia two years later. By 1923, she had moved to England where her writing career began.

Almedingen, who could read in seven languages, authored poetry, plays, novels, and biographies for both children and adults, using St. Petersburg and the Russian landscape as her setting. Drawing upon her history background, she wrote biographies of Russian nobility, including the Empress *Alexandra Feodorovna (1872–1919) and the Emperor Alexander I (publications in 1961 and 1966 respectively). In 1951, she reentered teaching at Oxford University as a lecturer on Russian history and literature. In her final years, she wrote *Anna,* the story of her great-grandmother's childhood in a wealthy Russian family, and the book was published posthumously. Though identified as a Russian, Almedingen lived in England for nearly two-thirds of her life.

SOURCES:

Almedingen, E.M. *The Emperor Alexander I.* NY: Vanguard Press, 1966.

Crista Martin, Boston, Massachusetts

Almeida, Brites de (fl. 1385)

Portuguese heroine whose courage in battle helped win her country's independence. Name variations: Portuguese Joan of Arc. Lived in Aljubarotta, a small town in Portugal, about 63 miles north of Lisbon.

Known as the Portuguese Joan of Arc, Brites de Almeida gained national prominence during the Battle of Aljubarotta. Fought on August 14, 1385, the conflict was between the Portuguese under John I of Avis (illegitimate son of Peter I of Portugal) and the Castilians under John I of Castile, who was supporting the claim of his new wife *Beatrice of Portugal to the throne of Portugal. During the battle, Brites de Almeida led her townspeople against the Castilians, seven of whom she killed with her own hand. With her help, the Portuguese inflicted a crushing defeat upon the Spaniards, and John I was compelled to withdraw his troops and renounce his wife's claim. This was a decisive event in the history of Portugal: the battle established the country's independence beyond all possible challenge, and Portugal, under the Avis dynasty, entered the greatest period of its history.

Almeida, Filinto de (1862–1934).

See Almeida, Julia Lopes de.

Almeida, Julia Lopes de (1862–1934)

Brazilian novelist. Name variations: (pseudonyms) A. Jalinto, Filinto de Almeida, Eila Worns. Born Julia Lopes in 1862 in Brazil; died in 1934; married Filinto de Almeida (a Portuguese author); children: three sons.

Selected works: A viuva Simões *(The Widow Simões, 1987);* Ansia eterna *(Eternal Desire, 1903);* A intrusa *(The Intruder, 1908); and* A família Medeiros *(The Medeiros Family, 1919).*

Considered one of Brazil's most prolific and important novelists in the period before modernism, Julia Lopes de Almeida came from a family of productive writers. Under her own name and several pseudonyms, she produced more than 40 books, the majority of which are highly romantic and present a woman's view of Brazilian life. Her sister, her three sons, and her husband, Portuguese novelist Filinto de Almeida (whose name was one of her pseudonyms), were also authors. With Filinto, Julia wrote *A casa verde (The Green House),* which was published in 1896. In addition to her impressive pace of one novel a year, Almeida contributed frequently to a number of newspapers. *A família Medeiros (The Medeiros Family,* 1919) was her most respected work.

Crista Martin, Boston, Massachusetts

Almeria (1758–1816).

See Hamilton, Elizabeth.

Almon, Baylee (1994–1995)

American child killed in the Oklahoma City terrorist bombing. Born in Oklahoma City, Oklahoma, on

April 18, 1994; killed in Oklahoma City on April 19, 1995; daughter of Aren Almon (who married Stan Kok in 1997 and gave birth to a daughter, Bella Almon Kok, in 1998).

On Wednesday, April 19, 1995, one day after the celebration of her first birthday, Baylee Almon became a painful symbol of the 17 children and 165 adults killed in the bombing of the Alfred P. Murrah Federal Building in Oklahoma City, Oklahoma, as a result of a terrorist attack by right-wing extremist Timothy McVeigh.

Less than 30 minutes after the 9:04 AM explosion of a 5,000-ton bomb directly in front of the building's America's Kids day-care center, Oklahoma City police sergeant John Avera eased himself through a window of the second floor into the wreckage of the day-care facility. Under two inches of rubble, he found Baylee Almon. Avera dug the baby free and raced out of the building. From across the street, amateur photographer Charles H. Porter IV captured the moment with a zoom lens as the infant was handed to Oklahoma City firefighter Chris Fields who checked for a pulse.

That day two photos were downloaded from the Associated Press into newsrooms around the world: the first was of the infant, covered with insulation and dust, being rushed by a policeman into the waiting arms of Fields; the second was of Fields cradling the body, his right elbow uplifted, as he gazed down at the lifeless child. The following day, a third photograph appeared worldwide: a dimpled 10-month-old Baylee in pink headband and Minnie Mouse overalls, laughing for the camera. Through these pictures, Baylee Almon became a symbol, noted *Time*, "of catastrophe all over the world." When photographer Porter was asked: "What do you think when you see your name below the photo on the cover of *Newsweek?*," he replied, "I don't see my name, I see the baby."

SOURCES:
Gibbs, Nancy. "The Blood of Innocents," in *Time*. May 1, 1995, pp. 56–64.
"Tiny Symbol of Life and Death," in *People Weekly*. May 8, 1995, p. 56.
"Why the Children?" in *Newsweek*. May 1, 1995, pp. 48–54.

Almond, Linda (1881–1987).

See Potter, Beatrix for sidebar.

Almucs de Castelnau (fl. 12th c.)

French noblewoman. Probably born in Provence, France, about 1140; married Guiraut de Simiane, lord of Castelnau; children: four sons, including Raimbaut.

A noblewoman of Provence, Almucs de Castelnau composed poetry and was a patron of troubadours. As a young teenager, she became the second wife of Guiraut de Simiane, who was lord of Castelnau. The couple had four sons, one of whom, Raimbaut, became a troubadour and patron of troubadours. The one extant poem by Almucs is a *tenson* (a poem in the form of a dialogue or debate) written with Iseut de Capio, in which Iseut begs Almucs to have pity on a dying knight who was Almucs' lover but then betrayed her.

Laura York, Anza, California

Almy, Mary Gould (1735–1808)

American diarist who wrote Mrs. Almy's Journal. *Born Mary Gould in Newport, Rhode Island, in 1735; died in Newport in March 1808; daughter of James and Mary (Rathbone) Gould; married Benjamin Almy in Newport Rhode Island, in 1762; children.*

In 1735, Mary Gould was the fourth child of eight born to James and **Mary Gould** of Newport, Rhode Island. The wealthy and elegant homes of Newport are renowned in New England, and schoolteacher James Gould, who had a substantial inheritance and lavish spending habits, was among the well-to-do. When he died, however, huge debts were attached to his estate, and his children saw little of the money.

At age 27, Mary married Benjamin Almy at the Trinity Church in Newport. Though a Loyalist at heart, she supported her husband's revolutionary ideals. When the British invaded the American colonies, Benjamin enlisted as a Patriot on the side of the colonies. As loyalties were made apparent, those with dedication to England were persecuted and their belongings confiscated. Jahleel Brenton was among those forced to return to England, and his mansion on Thames Street was taken over by the Almys. With Benjamin often away at battle, Mary took in boarders to help pay the expenses.

In December of 1776, British troops invaded Rhode Island and encamped in Newport, taking over the Colony House, only blocks away from the Almy home. The British seized all weapons and fishing boats; supplies were scarce for the citizens of the town. When the French allied with the colonies and came to assist the Americans, they halted their ships off the Rhode Island coast. Again Benjamin took up arms and left home. *Mrs. Almy's Journal* is Mary's diary, which begins on July 29, 1778, with the French arrival. Her entries detail the hardships of the

Revolution, as well as her Loyalist tendencies. Still, a number of entries address her husband and her hopes that he find success and health.

After the Battle of Rhode Island in late 1779, Almy concluded her journal, sealed it, and gave it to a friend, with directions that only her sister could read it. When Almy died in 1808 at the age of 73 and was buried at the same church where she had married, her husband left the Thames Street mansion. It had several inhabitants in the succeeding years but was razed in the 1920s.

SOURCES:

Evans, Elizabeth. *Weathering the Storm: Women of the American Revolution.* NY: Scribner, 1975.

Crista Martin, Boston, Massachusetts

A.L.O.E. (1821–1893).

See Tucker, Charlotte Maria.

Aloni, Shulamit (1931—)

Israeli government official. Born in Tel-Aviv in 1931; daughter of Russian parents; educated at the Ben Shemers school; received a law degree, 1956; married a civil administrator; children: three.

In 1948, Shulamit Aloni fought with the Haganah, the underground Jewish defense force. She was a member of parliament for the Labour Party (1965–69), chaired the Israeli Consumer Council (1966), founded the Civil Rights Party (1973), was appointed Minister without Portfolio (1974), and became Civil Rights MP in the Knesset (1977—). Her books include *The Citizen and His Country, The Rights of the Child in Israel,* and *Woman as a Human Being.*

Alonso, Alicia (1921—)

Cuban ballet dancer and ballet troupe director of international reputation, who danced despite visual impairment. Born Alicia Martinez in Havana, Cuba, on December 21, 1921; daughter of Antonio Martinez and Ernestina (Hoyo) Martinez; studied ballet with Alexandra Fedorova, Leon Fokine, Anatole Vilzak, and Vera Volkova; married Fernando Alonso, in 1937; children: Laura Alonso (a ballerina).

Alicia Alonso was born in Havana, Cuba, on December 21, 1921, the daughter of Antonio Martinez and **Ernestina Hoyo Martinez**. Her father was an army officer, and Alicia grew up in comfortable circumstances in a fashionable section of the Cuban capital. Her love of dance revealed itself when she was still a very small child. Alicia's mother kept her occupied for long periods of time by simply putting the little girl in a room with a phonograph, some records, and a scarf. As Alicia recalled years later, "That would keep me quiet for a few hours, doing what I imagined was dancing." At the age of nine, she began taking ballet lessons, and a year later she gave her first public performance dancing a waltz in an abridged version of Tchaikovsky's *The Sleeping Beauty.*

Alicia made excellent progress the next few years, but her future became an open question when a fellow student, Fernando Alonso, fell in love with her and she became pregnant. Though she was only 16, Alicia married Fernando in February 1937. Soon after, the couple moved to New York City to continue their dancing careers in one of the great centers of ballet and modern dance. The Alonsos lived with relatives in Spanish Harlem, attempting to raise their newborn daughter Laura and find success in a city that could be cold and indifferent. Fernando joined the newly organized Mordkin Ballet Company, while Alicia continued her training at the School of American Ballet. She studied privately as well with **Alexandra Fedorova**, Leon Fokine, and Anatole Vilzak. Alicia also went to London to study for a period with *Vera Volkova. Ironically, it was not in ballet but in musical comedy that Alonso made her American professional debut. She appeared in the chorus line of two musicals. One of these, *Great Lady* (1938), ran for only 20 performances despite a score by Frederick Loewe, while the other, *Stars in Your Eyes* (1939), was somewhat more successful, perhaps because it boasted the talents of *Ethel Merman and Jimmy Durante and was choreographed by George Balanchine.

Grimly determined to be a great success, Alicia sent her little daughter back to Cuba to be raised by her family. Meanwhile, she and her husband hardened their bodies, improved their techniques, and looked for the big break. Her regimen was grueling. According to *Agnes de Mille, few dancers would put themselves through such sacrifice and unrelenting pain. In 1941, Alicia was chosen by the newly formed Ballet Theater as a dancer in its corps de ballet. At 11 o'clock every morning, she did 90 minutes of demanding work in the company class. Then she would take a second class at another school for another two hours. Every night, just before her performance, Fernando coached her lengthy warm-up. Wet with perspiration, she went to her dressing room, dried off, got into her costume, and went on stage to give a brilliant performance. Concerned about Alicia's health, her

Alicia
Alonso

friend de Mille voiced concern about the toll exacted by such a harsh regimen ("Alicia, you will be exhausted"). Alicia responded in her Spanish accent, "Ahnes, I must do this . . . or I won't get strong. I must get strong."

In time, the constant exercise significantly changed Alonso's body, so she was capable of carrying out the immense physical demands ballet makes on those who practice the art. Her feet, which had been described by some observers as "more like spoons," changed; dance critics described them as strong as steel, yet "soft and caressing." Rave reviews from critics clearly indicated she was on the threshold of becoming a great star when disaster struck. In March 1941, she was diagnosed with a detached retina. After an operation, she was ordered to lie in bed absolutely motionless for three months while her eyes healed. With her eyes bandaged, and her body lying quite still, her feet moved under the covers throughout her convalescence as she did *battements tendus,* pointing and stretching her toes without moving her body. One of her fellow ballet dancers cautioned her not to move, but she responded, "I have to keep my feet alive."

After three months, the bandages were removed. Soon it was clear the operation had been only a partial success. A second operation also failed, and Alicia would always lack peripheral vision. A third operation, which took place in Havana, proved a brutal test; her physician told her that she would have to lie completely still for one year with her eyes in bandages. For 12 months, she could not move her head one-sixth of an inch, neither laugh nor cry, chew her food hard, or play with her daughter. Every day, Fernando sat with her, teaching her the great roles of classic ballet with her fingers. She would later recall that it was torture for her to "lie still, feeling my body gain weight and become flabby. I saw all the steps I had done and how often I had done them wrong. I danced in my mind. Blinded, motionless, lying flat on my back, I taught myself to dance Giselle." After a year in bed, Alicia was finally allowed to get up but was not yet permitted to dance. She took walks with her dog, and, against doctor's orders, visited the ballet studio two blocks down the street where she began daily practice to regain her technique.

When a hurricane bore down on Cuba while Alonso was still recovering her dancing skills, she went outside to help her dog, who had just given birth to puppies. Fierce winds shattered the glass door on the porch, showering her head and face with glass splinters. Fernando found her there screaming. Miraculously, her eyes were unhurt, and she escaped with only cuts and bruises. After the hurricane, her doctor allowed her to dance again, reasoning that if she could survive a shattered glass door, a resumption of dancing would probably do no harm.

An impatient Alonso returned to New York, her head still bandaged from the broken glass. With dramatic suddenness, she was asked to take the place of an indisposed *Alicia Markova in *Giselle.* Her brilliant performance was praised to the skies, and a new ballet star was born. The next five years were extremely busy ones for Alonso and her husband, and in 1946 she was promoted to principal dancer of Ballet Theater. Besides dancing the title role in *Giselle,* which she alternated with Alicia Markova, many new roles came her way during these years, including that of the Accused in *Fall River Legend,* Agnes de Mille's dramatic ballet based on the *Lizzie Borden case.

In 1948, Alonso returned to Havana in order to found her own company, the Ballet Alicia Alonso. Composed largely of Ballet Theater personnel temporarily out of work because of reorganization in New York, the new company was headed by Fernando Alonso as general director and his brother Alberto, a choreographer, as artistic director. Following a brief debut in Havana, the company undertook a successful South American tour. Using the money she had earned in recent years, Alonso kept her new ensemble alive, working all the while to improve its artistic standards by bringing some of the world's best ballet teachers to Cuba to train her young dancers. As usual, her life was a hectic one of commuting between Havana and New York. Her eyesight remained a serious problem, but she rarely, if ever, complained, dancing superbly even though objects on stage did not present themselves as they would to a person enjoying healthy sight. With partial sight in one eye but no peripheral vision, she had to learn how to move independently on an open stage. Her solution was to arrange for two very strong spotlights in different colors that were focused on the front of the stage a safe distance from the edge. Since she could sense these, she knew that if she stepped in their glow, she was in great danger of plunging into the orchestra pit. A wire was also stretched at waist height across the footlights as a further precaution. Usually she danced within the cage of her dance partner's arms or was led, so the audience did not notice. An extraordinary artist, Alicia Alonso entered the annals of dance history in the late 1940s, a woman nearly sightless yet one of the greatest dancers of the 20th century.

In 1950, Alonso opened her own dance school in Havana, the Alicia Alonso Academy of Ballet, thanks to a modest subsidy from the Ministry of Education and donations from a number of wealthy patrons. Unfortunately, by the mid-1950s, Alonso's dance company was in serious trouble as much for political as for artistic reasons. The Cuban dictator, Fulgencio Batista, was supported by most members of the island's financial oligarchy, American business interests, and the Mafia, but the majority of Cubans opposed his regime. He retaliated with bloody repression. Deciding that all artists and intellectuals had left-wing sympathies, Batista slashed the budget of Alonso's ballet troupe as well as that of her dance academy. To keep the company alive, the dancers worked in nightclubs and were exhausted the next day when they arrived for ballet practice.

When Alonso began to verbally flay Batista and his dictatorship in the best circles, the regime decided to deal with this potentially embarrassing artist in time-honored fashion, namely by bribery. Alonso was offered a monthly "subsidy" of $500 for the rest of her life, "in exchange for . . . keep[ing] my mouth shut." Outraged by such a crude effort to silence her, Alonso disbanded both her dance company and ballet school in 1956.

For the next three years, Alonso danced with the famed Ballet Russe de Monte Carlo, the successor to the fabled Diaghilev company of a generation earlier. During these years, she became the first dancer from the West ever invited to dance in the Soviet Union. A ten-week tour of the USSR in the winter of 1957 gave her the opportunity to dance *Giselle* in Moscow, Leningrad, and other Soviet cities, to perform several pieces that were broadcast on Moscow television, and to star in the Leningrad Opera Ballet's three-act *Path of Thunder,* a strong artistic denunciation of the injustices of South Africa's system of apartheid. When she returned to the United States, she received the prestigious *Dance Magazine* Award in 1958.

In 1959, Alonso's world changed forever. On January 1, 1959, Fidel Castro's revolutionary movement overthrew the Batista dictatorship. Although she was a superstar in New York with a bright future, Alonso felt increasingly isolated and "very lonely" in a gilded cage of fame. She returned to Cuba, and, in March 1959, she received $200,000 from the revolutionary government to form a new ballet company and re-open her dance school. In 1960, her Ballet Nacional de Cuba became an official entity with a guarantee of annual financial support. Encouraged both financially and emotionally by the new popular regime, Alonso began to recruit and train a corps of highly motivated, superbly trained dancers. Within a few years, Alicia Alonso's company began taking top honors in numerous international dance competitions.

Alonso was a dedicated supporter of the new Cuban government, who believed fervently that she and her dancers were "very much part of the Cuban revolution." Devoted to the notion "ballet for everyone, with all the trimmings," Alonso saw that her task was to bring the beauty and exhilaration of dance to the vast number of workers and farmers in Cuba who had never been exposed to such an artistic experience. Indeed, for countless Cubans in fishing villages, factories, schools, parks and youth camps, Alicia Alonso's Ballet Nacional de Cuba was their first exposure to the art of the dance. A true believer in the revolution, she and her troupe actively participated in the harvest, bringing in the crops in the broiling sun. Alonso wore a huge Vietnamese hat that was as much a bold political statement as a practical piece of agricultural garb in the 1960s.

American hostility to the Castro regime guaranteed Alicia Alonso's virtual disappearance from cultural consciousness in the United States, where the remarkable achievements of her dance troupe were also unknown. She and her ensemble appeared in Western and Eastern Europe from 1960 to 1990. Occasionally, she performed in Canada (1967 and 1971), and American critics like Clive Barnes concluded that she remained a great dancer in whom "the elegant line of the truly classical ballerina was never missing." The end of the Vietnam War and the Nixon era made it somewhat easier for her to visit the United States, and her performances in 1975 and 1976 received highly positive reviews including one by Frances Herridge of the New York *Post* who noted that she triumphed in *Carmen*: "At fifty-four she creates more sexual promise than ballerinas half her age." By the time this review was written, Alonso was a grandmother with several grandchildren and her daughter Laura had been dancing as a soloist with the Ballet Nacional de Cuba for several years. The state-subsidized Cuban film industry did document Alonso's entire repertory on film, but otherwise her remarkable achievements were lost on the United States. Apparently ageless, Alonso continued to appear on stage as a solo dancer into her 70s. Her near-blindness remained a basic fact of her personal as well as artistic life, even though a 1972 operation had briefly provided hope for a genuine restoration of her eyesight.

A May 1995 performance in San Francisco offered a bittersweet commentary on the times and opportunities wasted for Alicia Alonso. She and her company, many of them also aging, performed *In the Middle of the Sunset,* which many felt was an allegory about the vanished hopes of the Cuban revolution and perhaps even of the Ballet Nacional as well. At this point, the 73-year-old Alicia Alonso's "virtual blindness [was] uneasily apparent." Nonetheless, an extraordinary artist, Alonso triumphed "as a theatrical presence through sheer nerve and determination, showing that she can still do a pirouette . . . and that her personality can still be magnetic."

SOURCES:
"Alonso, Alicia," in *Current Biography 1977.* NY: H.W. Wilson, pp. 17–20.

Barnes, Clive. "Alicia Alonso," in *The New York Times Biographical Service.* June 1976, p. 798.

De Mille, Agnes. "Cuba's National Treasure: ¡Viva Alicia!," in *Dance Magazine.* Vol. 64, no. 8. August 1990, pp. 32–43.

————. *Portrait Gallery.* Boston: Houghton Mifflin, 1990.

Ehrmann, Hans. "Ballet Nacional de Cuba, Teatro Municipal, Santiago, Chile, June 15–18, 1991," in *Dance Magazine.* Vol. 65, no. 11. November 1991, pp. 88 and 90.

Gámez, Tana de. *Alicia Alonso at Home and Abroad. With an Appreciation of the Artist by Arnold L. Haskell.* NY: Citadel Press, 1971.

Kisselgoff, Anna. "San Francisco Festival Presents a Legend," in *The New York Times.* May 15, 1995, p. B3.

Kumin, Laura. "Alonso Surfaces in Madrid," in *Dance Magazine.* Vol. 66, no. 10. October 1992, pp. 22–23.

Terry, Walter. *Star Performance: The Story of the World's Great Ballerinas.* Garden City, NY: Doubleday, 1954.

John Haag, Associate Professor of History, University of Georgia, Athens, Georgia

Alonso, Dora (1910—)

Cuban author. Name variations: (pseudonyms) Nora Lin, D. Polimita. Born Dora Alonso on December 22, 1910, in Máximo Gómez, Cuba. Selected works of fiction and drama include Tierro adentro *(1944),* Cain *(1955), and* Once caballos *(Eleven Horses, 1970).*

Dora Alonso studied at the Cárdenas High School in Cuba before withdrawing to continue studying and writing on her own. In 1931, her first publication was "Humildad," a story that won top prize from the journal *Bohemia.* Both political and writing interests led Alonso to move to Havana in 1935, where she was a contributor to a number of Latin American journals. Her first novel, *Tierro adentro,* appeared in 1944. A dedicated member of the Communist Party, Alonso traveled throughout Mexico, Europe, and the former Soviet Union. Her work includes children's books and fiction of the working class in Cuba, as well as depictions of her political and social views. Her 1955 play *Cain* attacked racism.

Crista Martin, Boston, Massachusetts

Alorna, Marquesa de (1750–c. 1839)

Portuguese poet. Name variations: (pseudonym) Alcipe. Born Leonor de Almeida Portugal de Lorena e Lencastre in Portugal in 1750; died around 1839; married the count of Oeynhausen, in 1779.

In 1758, eight-year-old Marquesa de Alorna was confined, along with her mother and sister, at the convent of Chellas, while her father was imprisoned for conspiring against King Joseph I Emanuel. Alorna was 27 before she was released from the convent upon the death of the king. Two years later, she married the count of Oeynhausen, a diplomat, and moved to Vienna, where he was stationed and would later become minister of Vienna. When the count died in 1793, Alorna and her two children moved to England, then Lisbon. Though she wrote and published poetry, Alorna is best remembered for her salon and her influence on young writers such as Manuel Bocage and Alexandre Herculano. In 1814, she returned to Portugal and reclaimed the titles and properties that had been stripped from the family by the king in 1758.

Crista Martin, Boston, Massachusetts

Alós, Concha (1922—)

Spanish novelist. Name variations: Alos. Born María Concepción "Concha" Alós Domingo in Valencia, Spain, in 1922; daughter of Francisco Alós Tárrega and Pilar Domingo Pardo; married Eliseo Feijóo, in 1943.

Selected works: Los enamos *(The Dwarfs, 1963);* Los cien pájaros *(Bonfires, 1964);* Os habla Electra *(Electra Speaking, 1975).*

When she was three months old, Concha Alós' adoptive father Francisco and her mother Pilar moved the family from Valencia, Spain, to Castellón de la Plana. A shy, only child, Alós made up stories and games to play alone. Enrolled in a private school for girls that focused on sewing, cooking, and manners, Alós was ill-prepared for the academically based high-school entrance exam and failed on her first try.

Though she passed on a later attempt, her high-school education was interrupted in 1935 by the Spanish Civil War when her family fled Castellón. Subsequently, her mother Pilar suffered a mental breakdown, her father Francisco was imprisoned, and the family often went without food. When they returned home in 1939, their house had been destroyed. Pilar died shortly thereafter and Francisco married a woman whom his daughter did not like. In 1943, Alós married journalist Eliseo Feijóo. They moved to Palma de Mallorca where Alós enrolled at the local teachers college, graduating in 1953. After several years of teaching in neighboring areas, she separated from Feijóo and in 1959 moved to Barcelona. Although Alós had been writing for some time, recognition came in 1962 when she entered her novel *The Dwarfs* for the prestigious Planeta Prize and won. Her book *Electra Speaking* (1975) is perhaps her best-known work.

Crista Martin, Boston, Massachusetts

Alpaida (c. 654–c. 714).

See Alphaida.

Alpar, Gitta (1903—)

Hungarian soprano. Born in Budapest, Hungary, on March 5, 1903; married twice, the second time to Gustav Frölich (a German actor who would later marry *Lida Baarova).

Gitta Alpar

Gitta Alpar was among a generation of Central European musicians forced to flee Europe because of the Nazi menace. Alpar studied with **Laura Hilgermann** before launching her singing career in Budapest in 1923. She sang in Munich, Berlin, and Vienna. Though she sang Gilda, Rosina, and the Queen of the Night, her greatest success was in operetta. She was particularly remembered for her appearances in Millöcker's *Der Bettelstudent* at the Meropolteater in Berlin and for premiering in Lehár's *Schön ist die Welt* in 1930. A year later, she sang the title role in Millöcker's *Gräfin Dubarry*. By 1936, Gitta Alpar left Europe for America as Nazi crusades against Jews and leftists increased. In America, she reestablished her operetta career and also appeared in several movies.

John Haag, Athens, Georgia

Alphaida (c. 654–c. 714)

Noblewoman of the House of Pepin. Name variations: Alpaida; Alpoide or Alpoïde; Chalpaida; Elphide. Born around 654; died around 714; second wife of Pepin II of Herstol or Heristal, mayor of Austrasia and Neustria (r. 687–714); children: Charles Martel (c. 690–741), mayor of Austrasia and Neustria (r. 714–741); Hildebrand (Chilebrand).

Alphonsa, Mother (1851–1926).

See Lathrop, Rose Hawthorne.

Alpoide (c. 654–c. 714).

See Alphaida.

Alsop, Mary O'Hara (1885–1980).

See O'Hara, Mary.

Alston, Theodosia (1783–1813).

See Burr, Theodosia.

al-Taymuriyya, 'Aisha 'Esmat (1840–1902).

See Taymuriyya, 'A'isha 'Ismat al-.

Altwegg, Jeanette.

See Albright, Tenley for sidebar.

Alvarez, Lili d'.

See Aussem, Cilly for sidebar.

al-Zayyat, Latifa (b. 1923).

See Zayyat, Latifa al- in Egyptian Feminists.

Amalasuntha (c. 498–535)

Regent of Ostrogothic Italy. Name variations: Amalswinthe, Amalaswintha, Amalasontha, Amalasuentha. Born around 498 in Italy; killed in 535 (or 534) in Italy; daughter of Theodoric the Great, king of Italy, and ❧ Audofleda (sister of King Clovis); married Eutharic (d. 522), in 515; married her cousin Theodat also known as Theodahad or Theodatus; children: (first marriage) son Athalaric or Athalric; daughter Matasuntha.

Amalasuntha was the daughter of the powerful Theodoric the Great, who had conquered Italy with his Ostrogothic armies and declared himself king. Despite his barbarian tradition, Theodoric had immense respect for the culture and government of ancient Rome, and he encouraged his daughter to study its literature and history. When Theodoric died in 526 without a male heir, the kingdom fell to Amalasuntha, then age 28, as guardian of her son. Intelligent and cultured, she reigned for nine years and earned the enmity of her Ostrogothic nobles for her conciliatory foreign policies to Justinian and *Theodora of the later Roman capital at Byzantium (Istanbul), who were viewed as enemies of Italy. Aware of her risky position, Amalasuntha promised the Byzantine emperor that if her throne were lost, she and her entire Ostrogothic treasury would move to Constantinople.

Amalasuntha's desire to stay on good terms with both Rome and the Church brought about plotting by her people. In 533, after successfully thwarting a rebellion of her nobles, she put to death three of its instigators. In 534, when her 17-year-old son died, Amalasuntha married and became co-ruler with her cousin Theodat to gain support against her rebellious subjects. Some sources say that Justinian, in an attempt to arrange the peaceful addition of Italy to the Byzantine Empire, also married Amalasuntha. Theodat, fearing for his own position (and encouraged by Byzantine empress Theodora who feared for hers), overthrew Amalasuntha in 534 and banished her to an island in the lake of Bolsena (Tuscany, Italy). In 535, while in her bath, Amalasuntha was strangled to death by relatives of the three nobles she had put to death. Some say the assassins acted on orders of Theodat who feared she would escape and regain control of Italy; others say they acted on orders of Theodora.

The death of Amalasuntha, the rightful queen, provided Justinian with the necessary pretext for invasion. He could both avenge her and save the Orthodox Church in Italy, which was in danger of being overthrown by the Goths. The emperor sent an army against her murderers under the celebrated general Belisarius, who defeated and dethroned Theodat.

SOURCES:

Tuck, Stephen L. "Justinian," in *Historic World Leaders.* Edited by Anne Commire. Detroit: Gale Research, 1994.

Klapisch-Zuber, Christiane, ed. *A History of Women in the West: Silences of the Middle Ages.* Cambridge, MA: Belknap/Harvard, 1992.

Laura York, Anza, California

Amalaswintha or Amalswinthe (c. 498–535).

See Amalasuntha.

Amalia.

Variant of Amalie.

> **Audofleda** (c. 470–?)
>
> *Queen of Italy. Born around 470; daughter of Childeric; sister of King Clovis I (c. 466–511); married Theodoric the Great, king of the Ostrogoths; children: *Amalasuntha (c. 498–535).*

Amalia, Anna, duchess of Saxe-Weimar (1739–1807).

See Anna Amalia of Saxe-Weimar.

Amália, Narcisa (1852–1924)

Brazilian poet. Name variations: Narcisa Amalia. Born Narcisa Amália de Oliveria Campos in São João de Barra, Brazil, in 1852; died in 1924; daughter of Joaquim Jácome de Oliveria Campos Filho (a writer); married twice.

Selected works: Nebulosas *(Starry Skies, 1872);* Flores do Campo *(Flowers of the Field, 1874).*

Narcisa Amália, daughter of writer Joaquim Jácome de Oliveria Campos Filho, moved from São João de Barra to Resende when she was 11 years old. There, in her 20s, she wrote and published two volumes of poetry and edited the literary magazine *A Gazetinha de Resende* (*The Resende Gazette*). In 1888 Amália moved to Rio. She worked as a teacher and was an outspoken advocate for change in the social and political status of women. Amália is viewed as a foremother in her country's feminist movement.

Crista Martin, Boston, Massachusetts

Amalia of Bavaria (1801–1877)

*Queen of Saxony. Born in 1801; died in 1877; daughter of Maximilian I Joseph, elector of Bavaria (r. 1799–1805), king of Bavaria (r. 1805–1825), and *Caroline of Baden (1776–1841); twin sister of *Elizabeth of Bavaria (1801–1873); married Johann also known as John (1801–1873), king of Saxony (r. 1854–1873); children: Albert (1828–1902), king of Saxony (r. 1873–1902); George (1832–1904), king of Saxony (r. 1902–1904); *Anna Maria of Saxony (1836–1859); *Margaret of Saxony (1840–1858).*

Amalia of Oldenburg (1818–1875).

See Amalie.

Amalie (1818–1875)

Queen of Greece and princess of Oldenburg. Name variations: Amalia. Born Marie Friederike Amalie on

December 21, 1818; died on May 20, 1875; eldest daughter of Grand Duke Augustus of Oldenburg and Adelheid of Anhalt-Bernburg-Schaumburg (b. 1800); married Otho also known as Otto I (1815–1867), king of Greece (r. 1833–1862, deposed), on November 22, 1836.

Amalie, princess of Oldenburg, and her husband King Otto I were unpopular during their reign. Taxation, the king's attempt to establish a central bureaucratic system, his use of German advisors, and the queen's interference contributed to their unpopularity. The 17-year-old Otto had been imposed as King of the Hellenes by the London Conference in 1832, when the Greeks were given their independence. After an uprising forced Otto to grant Greece a constitution and a bicameral parliament in 1843, the couple was deposed by a revolutionary government in October 1862.

Amalie Auguste (1788–1851)

*Duchess of Leuchtenburg. Name variations: Princess Amalie Auguste of Bavaria; Augusta of Bavaria; Auguste, princess of Bavaria. Born on June 21, 1788; died on May 13, 1851; daughter of Maximilian I Joseph, king of Bavaria (r. 1805–1825), and *Wilhelmine of Darmstadt (1765–1796); married Eugène de Beauharnais, duke of Leuchtenburg, on January 4, 1806; children: August or Auguste (1810–1835); Maximilian (1817–1852), duke of Leuchtenburg; Josephine Beauharnais (1807–1876); Eugénie Hortense (1808–1847); Amelia of Leuchtenburg (1812–1873); Theodelinde (1814–1857).*

After Amalie Auguste married Eugène de Beauharnais in 1806, her French husband purchased title and lands from her father Maximilian I Joseph, king of Bavaria. In 1817, he also purchased the principality of Eichstätt. As duke and duchess, the couple were now the founders of the landgraviate of Leuchtenburg in Bavaria, and their children formed connections with several royal families. Their son August of Leuchtenburg married Queen *Maria II da Gloria of Portugal but he died two months later. Maximilian married *Maria Nikolaevna (1819–1876), eldest daughter of Nicholas I, tsar of Russia. Eldest daughter *Josèphine Beauharnais married Oscar I, king of Sweden, in 1823. The second daughter *Eugénie Hortense married Frederick-William, a prince of Hohenzollern-Hechingen. Their daughter *Amelia of Leuchtenburg married Pedro I, emperor of Brazil in 1829, and the

fourth daughter *Theodelinde married Count William of Württemberg.

Amalie of Hesse-Darmstadt
(1754–1832)

*Princess of Padua and Baden. Born on June 20, 1754; died on July 21, 1832; daughter of Louis IX, landgrave of Hesse-Darmstadt, and *Caroline of Zweibrucken-Birkenfeld (1721–1774); married Charles Louis of Padua (b. 1755), prince of Padua and Baden, on July 15, 1774; children: *Caroline of Baden (1776–1841); *Elizabeth of Baden (1779–1826), empress of Russia; *Frederica Dorothea of Baden (1781–1826), queen of Sweden; *Mary-Elizabeth of Padua (1782–1808); Karl Friedrich (b. 1784); Karl Ludwig also known as Charles Louis (b. 1786); *Wilhelmine of Baden (1788–1836).*

Amalie of Saxe-Coburg-Gotha
(1848–1894)

*Duchess of Bavaria. Born on October 23, 1848, in Coburg, Germany; died on May 6, 1894, in Schloss Biederstein, Munich; daughter of *Clementine of Orleans (1817–1907) and Augustus, prince of Saxe-Coburg-Gotha; married Maximilian (1849–1893), duke of Bavaria, on September 20, 1875; children: Sigfrid August of Bavaria; Christopher Joseph of Bavaria; Leopold of Bavaria.*

Amalie of Saxony (1794–1870)

*German composer, harpsichordist, singer, author, and duchess of Saxony. Name variations: (pseudonyms) Amalie Heiter and Amalie Serena. Born Amalie Marie Friederike Auguste on August 10, 1794, in Dresden, Saxony; died in Dresden on September 18, 1870; daughter of Maximilian, duke of Saxony, and *Caroline of Parma (1770–1804); sister of King Frederick Augustus II and King John of Saxony; studied with private tutors and lived her entire life in Pillnitz Castle in Dresden.*

Composed mostly operas and liturgical works; highly educated and intellectually curious, also composed an operetta to a French-language libretto and wrote comedies under the pseudonyms Amalie Heiter and Amalie Serena.

In 1816, Princess Amalie of Saxony began to compose over a dozen operas, mainly to Italian libretti, that for a number of years delighted the inner circles of Dresden society. The princess also composed some chamber music and several fine works of liturgical music, including an impressive *Stabat Mater* (a hymn commemorating the sorrows of the Virgin Mary at the Cross). She tried her hand at composing an operetta in 1819 to a French text. When she tired of music, she wrote a number of comedies, publishing them under pseudonyms. Amalie of Saxony was one of the last representatives of a culture that tried to justify aristocratic privileges in terms of serious artistic endeavors on the part of an educated and serious elite who remained amateurs in the best sense of the word. She was the author of *Die Fürstenbraut, Der Majoratserbe*, and *Der Oheim*.

John Haag, Athens, Georgia

Amanishakhete (r. c. 41–12 BCE)

Influential queen of the kingdom of Meroe who negotiated peace with the Roman Empire after an ill-conceived raid into Egypt brought a Roman punitive expedition upon Meroe. Name variations: Candace. Born in Meroe, an extensive kingdom ranging from just south of Aswan and the First Cataract of the Nile in the north to well into modern Ethiopia in the south.

Amanishakhete's "reign" in Meroe (whatever precisely that may have meant in her kingdom) is most often set between 41 and 12 BCE. Little is known about her except that literary and archaeological sources imply that she was one of four major figures to dominate the kingdom of Meroe shortly before the onset of the Christian era. The other attested major figures of her time include another woman, **Amanirenas**, and two men, Akinidad and Teriteqas. These four probably can be thought of as having constituted Meroe's royalty in the second half of the 1st century BCE, but their exact relationships with one another cannot be established on current evidence.

During Amanishakhete's day, Meroe was an extensive kingdom ranging from just south of Aswan and the First Cataract (meaning "falls") of the Nile in the north to well into modern Ethiopia in the south. Thus, the heartland of Meroe was the modern Sudan. Its capital city, Meroe, lay between the fifth and sixth of the Nile's cataracts, and its ruins today give testimony to the kingdom's once extensive authority. Meroe at the end of the 1st century BCE was no military match for the Roman Empire, which had annexed Egypt in 30 BCE. However, when Roman attention to Egypt's southern frontier flagged for one reason or another, raids frequently could and did sweep out of the south as Meroe sought booty. The first official contact between Rome and Meroe came in 29 BCE when the Roman praefect of Egypt, Gaius Cornelius Gallus, briefly campaigned to the south of the First Cataract where he seems to have established diplomatic contact with the rulers of Meroe. However, Gallus immediately thereafter campaigned in Arabia, taking with him some of his Egyptian garrison. When this occurred, a Meroan raid struck north and plundered southern Egypt (among the booty then claimed seems to have been a statue of Augustus, which archaeology has unearthed at Meroe).

There followed in 23 BCE under Gallus' successor, Publius Petronius, a punitive expedition that ravaged the Meroan countryside at least as far south as the Meroan city of Napata (a city that apparently hosted Meroan royalty for at least a part of the year, and which the Romans razed). As a result of this show of strength, in 21 or 20 BCE a weathered, "manly," and one-eyed "candace" (meaning "queen mother") of Meroe—probably Amanishakhete—made her way to the Aegean island of Samos where she negotiated with Roman emperor Augustus a more permanent peace between Meroe and Rome. Satisfactory terms between the two powers were arranged, frontiers were established, and garrisons withdrawn from their forward positions. In short, a fairly stable arrangement resulted, which permitted the establishment of a more profitable relationship between the states based on the trade of exotic products.

Archaeology has uncovered at Meroe Amanishakhete's palace, as well as her funeral pyramid, the latter being one of the most imposing to have been constructed in this ancient capital. In addition, we know that Amanishakhete was actively involved in the construction of temples, with a particularly impressive dedication to Amun-Re being perhaps the most important of these to have been rediscovered. Hence, Amanishakhete's status within her kingdom is made manifest.

But exactly what was the nature of that status? Meroan epigraphy makes it clear that Amanishakhete bore at least two official titles during her ascendancy: those being *qere* and *candace*. The second of these seems to have been the most traditional for royal Meroan woman, for the term means "queen mother." Thus, it is likely that Amanishakhete was married to an acknowledged king, and that she bore another. This hardly does her status of *candace* justice, however, for it seems most probable that the kingdom of Meroe was a matriarchy, with royal legitimacy passed down from generation to generation through the *candaces* whose religious potency seems to have legitimized the eventual accession of their sons. Although a king normally exercised political and military sovereignty, it seems that he achieved legitimacy not through his father but through his mother, the *candace*. Moreover, the practice of matriarchy in Meroe is complicated and made all the more interesting by the fact that it seems to have been customary for the sitting *candace* to adopt as her "daughter" the wife of her son, thus setting that woman up as the *candace* of the next generation, although she was not necessarily of any blood relation to the *candace* who preceded her.

Above and beyond her status as a *candace*, Amanishakhete also was referred to in inscriptions as a "qere," a title, which implies more than religious potency and political succession. A *qere* appears to have been a ruler in the position of actually exercising political sovereignty. Since even in Meroe this seems to have been a status normally held by a king, it would be interesting to know by what process Amanishakhete came to be so honored. Perhaps the disaster brought upon Meroe in 23 and Amanishakhete's successful diplomacy in bringing peace to the northern frontier tipped the domestic scales against the perpetrator of the original Meroan raid of Egypt in Amanishakhete's favor. Regardless, Amanishakhete seems to have been recognized as a *qere* from some point in her adult life until the time of her death, for the pyramid erected in her honor implies that her people remained grateful to her memory even in death.

William S. Greenwalt, Associate Professor of History, Santa Clara University, Santa Clara, California

Amathila, Libertine Appolus

(1940–)

Namibian political leader and health expert. Born Libertine Appolus in 1940 in Fransfontein, South West Africa (today Namibia); married Namibian political activist, Ben Amathila.

Director of the Women's Council of SWAPO; named to the new cabinet as minister of local government and housing after the founding of Namibia.

Libertine Appolus was born in 1940 in Fransfontein, South West Africa, and completed her secondary education in South Africa. After returning to South West Africa, she joined the growing Namibian independence movement, becoming increasingly a target of the South African authorities that ruled Namibia at that time. In 1962, Libertine Appolus went into exile and lived for some time in Tanzania, where she ap-

plied for, and received, a scholarship to study in Poland. In the 1960s, while becoming a leading SWAPO activist in Europe, she completed a medical education in Poland, Sweden, and London. Instead of specializing, she covered several broad areas that would be useful in developing a nation when the time came for her to return: public health, nutrition, pediatrics and tropical medicine. During her exile years, Libertine Appolus married another prominent Namibian political activist, Ben Amathila (1930—), who was treasurer general of SWAPO and also the organization's deputy secretary for education and culture.

In the late 1960s and early 1970s, Libertine Amathila served as director of the Women's Council of SWAPO. In 1970, she was appointed to the position of the party's assistant secretary for health and social welfare. She began serving on the central committee of SWAPO in the late 1960s and was a universally recognized national figure by the time Namibian independence was achieved in 1990. As number ten on the SWAPO election list of 1989, she was easily elected to the Assembly of a newly independent Namibia and was named to the new cabinet as minister of Local Government and Housing. In the same election her husband also won an Assembly seat and joined his wife in the cabinet as minister of Trade and Industry.

SOURCES:

Grotpeter, John J. *Historical Dictionary of Namibia.* Metuchen, NJ: Scarecrow Press, 1994.

John Haag, Associate Professor of History, University of Georgia, Athens, Georgia

Amaya, Carmen (1913–1963)

Spanish flamenco dancer of great renown. Born in Barcelona, Spain, in 1913; died in Bagur, Spain, on November 19, 1963; daughter and granddaughter of dancers; married Juan Antonio Aguero (a guitarist).

From her first public appearance at age seven, Carmen Amaya enjoyed a successful career and a reputation as one of Spain's greatest flamenco dancers. At the outbreak of the Spanish Civil War in 1936, the Amaya family fled to Mexico and then to Buenos Aires, Argentina, where Carmen was such a sensation that a theater was named after her. In 1941, she made her U.S. debut, where she appeared in night clubs and toured with her group, comprised of her father and two sisters. She appeared in the movie *Los Tarantos,* which was released in the United States in 1964. In the summer of 1963, Amaya began to suffer from a kidney ailment and was hospitalized in Barcelona. Following her release in early November, she returned to her home in Bagur where she died on November 19. A week before her death, the Spanish government granted her the Medal of Isabela la Catolica.

Amazon Army of Dahomey
(1818–1892)

An army of women in West Africa who fought a war against French expansionism.

The West African nation of the Dahomey was formed in the 17th century and owed its rapid growth to an advanced military structure. In the early 18th century, because of encroachments of neighboring tribes and European colonizers, King Agadja began to form an army that included women. They became a permanent part of the Dahoman force in 1818, when the usurping King Gezo, anxious to maintain his position, enlisted his many wives to form a permanent phalanx to defend him in civil war. Michael Crowder has called the Amazon Army of the Dahomey, an army of women, "one of the most impressive armies in West Africa." These women helped secure the independence for the people of Dahomey, called the Fon, between 1818 and 1822.

Though the actual fighting force numbered about 1,700, there were about 2,500 Amazons, most of whom were official wives of the king. Their weapons were muskets, blunderbusses, bows and arrows, duck-guns, and short swords that were used in close fighting. They were especially fond of the military tactic of ambush. "When still a few days' march from the town or village to be attacked they lit no fires and observed silence," wrote the Mackseys in the *Book of Women's Achievement.* "Avoiding trodden paths, they made their own way through the bush and (barefoot) through the thorny acacia defences, noiselessly surrounding the objective by night to attack in mass just before dawn." Since their aim was to capture slaves or fodder for the king's 500 annual human sacrifices, they killed only in self-defense.

The Amazons enjoyed the privileges of royalty. They lived and were fed in the palace, and passing sojourners on the road made way for them. But as the king's wives, they were also restricted. Except for the king, any involvement with another man brought death. Thus, more frequently than not, depending on the energy of their king, they were forced to live in an almost perpetual state of chastity.

Though originally the legion had been made up of loyal non-Dahoman captives, after King Gezo died in 1858, Amazons were recruited throughout the kingdom, even from important Fon families. They were involved in the war with the Egba in the 1840s, and attacks on Yoruba towns in 1851, 1864, 1883, and 1885. The British explorer Sir Richard Burton visited them in 1863 and offered his European view of the women: "They were mostly elderly and all of them hideous. The officers were decidedly chosen for the size of their bottoms. . . . They manoeuvre with the precision of a flock of sheep." It is interesting to note, in light of his account, that the Amazons soon became "the most warlike, and the most feared, of all the Dahoman troops," as stated by David Ross in *West African Resistance.* "It was they who bore the brunt of the fighting in a number of the most important of the nineteenth-century Dahoman wars. It was they who tended to suffer most severely when the Fon either won a Pyrrhic victory or sustained a costly defeat."

Dahomey occupied the southern third of what is today the republic of Dahomey, flanked by the rivers Ouéme and Cuffo. Its capital was

An Amazon warrior.

Abomey. Around 1820, the Dahoman army, which included the Amazons, had captured and annexed the kingdoms of Allada and Whydah to the south. They headed east, incorporating the kingdoms of Cotonou and Agony. Fortunately, all these peoples spoke a common language and shared many traditions, and the regions quickly banded into one state. As the kingdom grew, so did the notion that the territory of Dahomey was sacred and had to be preserved at all costs by its people. Theirs was a sacred trust: a mandate that the territory and institutions they had inherited from their ancestors be passed on to their heirs.

Throughout the 19th century, vigorous trading went on between the Europeans and the Fon; at first, it was slaves at the busy port of Whydah; later, palm oil at the port of Cotonou. Produced on the plantations in the interior, the palm oil was transported by way of the River Ouéme, a strategically important river of commerce, to Cotonou.

In the 1870s, trading between France and the Fons was friendly. But in the 1880s, the French began to assert that the port of Cotonou had been given to them in the trading treaties of 1868 and 1878. In truth, French merchants had inserted forged clauses. It didn't help the Fons' cause when the boundary kingdom of Port Novo—which had been a tributary to Dahomey—became a French protectorate and repudiated Dahomey's hold on it. Nor did it help that the Fon leader King Behanzin had been recently installed and lacked the power of earlier kings.

In November 1889, the French sent Dr. Jean Bayol, a zealous champion of French expansion, to settle the affair. Bayol arrived in Abomey and met with Crown Prince Kondo to demand Cotonou. Kondo balked. Then on February 22, 1890, Bayol sent 360 French soldiers to occupy Cotonou and put its Fon administrators under arrest. With the two countries now at war, the Dahoman army began to mobilize. By the 1880s, about half of the Dahoman's 4,000 standing army was comprised of the famous Amazons who had developed into one of the most important units in the Dahoman army. In this emergency, about 12,000 regional warriors were also conscripted.

As the men and women of Dahomey marched toward Cotonou in February of 1890 in their formal four-division formations (a flexible structure that changed in combination depending on circumstances), they carried either flintlock rifles or rapid-firing rifles, acquired in trade with the Germans. Most of their experience, however, was in attacking and controlling border towns. A

dawn attack, on March 4, 1890, left 127 of the Fon dead inside the French lines, including the she-Gaou (or *Khetungan*), the leader of the left division of the Amazons. (The right was led by the she-Kposu [or *Akpadume*].) Regrouping, the Dahoman army began to lead raids on palm oil plantations around Port Novo, hoping to weaken the French economically.

It only fueled Bayol, who saw his chance and justification to take over the entire Dahoman coast. The French Cabinet, however, disagreed and recalled him to France. Though his successor was instructed to hold Cotonou but effect an honorable peace, the wishes of the French Cabinet were obstructed by colonial officials and the Fons' unwillingness to hand over Cotonou. Fighting did not cease, and the French claimed a major victory near the village of Atchoupa. Finally, a peace settlement was agreed upon on October 3, 1890. Though the French flag now flew over Cotonou, the French also had to reimburse the Fon annually 20,000 francs, compensation for loss of customs revenue. More important, Dahoman authorities could return to the town to cater to the need of Fon inhabitants. Thus, in their eyes, it was still under Dahoman hegemony.

But no one was happy with the peace. The Fon began to equip their army with more efficient weapons. They bought 1,700 rapid-firing rifles, six Krupp cannons, five machine guns, and amassed 400,000 cartridges and shells. For their part, the French were sorry that they had negotiated a peace before acquiring more territory. By November 1891, colonial administrators had convinced the French parliament to resume hostilities under the first pretense. On March 27, 1892, the Resident of Port Novo, while making a trip up the River Ouéme in the gunboat *Topaz*, was fired upon by Fon soldiers. It didn't matter that the Resident was threatening deep into Dahoman territory; the *Topaz* incident became the rallying cry.

Colonel Alfred-Amedée Dodds, commander of French troops in Senegal, arrived in Cotonou on May 20. Within three months, he had assembled an expeditionary force of 2,000, and they began to move up the River Ouéme in late September with the intention of attacking Abomey. The entire Fon army, knowing this was where they were the most vulnerable, sat waiting between the river and their capital. One month later, though they had fought bravely and with ferocity, the Dahoman army was completely destroyed. They had been short of provisions, less disciplined, unschooled in modern fighting techniques, and unused to a steady advance. It is estimated that 2,000 Fon were killed, 3,000 wounded, while the French lost 10 officers and 67 men. The Amazon army was effectively wiped out.

SOURCES:

Macksey, Joan, and Kenneth Macksey. *Book of Women's Achievements.* NY: Stein & Day, 1975.

Ross, David. "Dahomey," in *West African Resistance: The Military Response to Colonial Occupation.* Edited by Michael Crowder. NY: Africana Publishing, 1971.

Ambapali (fl. c. 540 BCE)

Indian courtesan who became a holy follower of Siddhartha. Born in Vaisali, India, in the 6th century BCE; lived during the time of Siddhartha Gautama, the Buddha (c. 563–483 BCE).

It is said that Ambapali was the greatest courtesan of her time, capable of charging exorbitant prices. By the time of Siddhartha's passing through Vaisali, she owned a large home with mango groves. But Siddhartha impressed her deeply, and Ambapali retired from her lucrative profession, began to study his teachings, and offered him her groves. She became an *arhat* (holy one), a state so high that it is achieved by few. This was a major accomplishment, since it was believed at the time that only men could attain such a place of nirvana. Ambapali seems to have been the basis for Kamala the courtesan in Hermann Hesse's *Siddhartha*.

Ambler, Mary Cary (fl. 1700s)

American diarist.

While living in Jamestown, Virginia, Mary Cary Ambler discovered that doctors in Baltimore, Maryland, had learned how to inoculate children against smallpox. With her children in tow, she headed north, keeping a journal of her three-month trek. *The Diary of M. Ambler* (1770) details the trip and the early history of the smallpox vaccine.

Crista Martin, Boston, Massachusetts

Amboise, Francise d' (1427–1485)

French founder and duchess of Brittany. Born in 1427; died in 1485; daughter of Louis Amboise; married Peter II, duke of Brittany.

French noblewoman and founder, Francise d'Amboise was the daughter of the powerful lord Louis d'Amboise. Like many young nobles of her time, she longed to pursue a religious calling but was unable to escape a political marriage. Francise became duchess of Brittany when she married Duke Peter II. Despite the fact that she could not enter a convent, she managed to use her position to accomplish some of her religious goals. The duchess founded the first Carmelite monastery in Brittany; thus, she popularized that order, which led to its diffusion into other areas of northern France. Francise's keenly felt obligation to help feed and shelter the poor gained her a reputation for sincere piety. She died at about age 58, greatly respected for her charity.

Laura York, Anza, California

Ambree, Mary (fl. 1584)

Captain who fought to liberate Ghent from the Spanish.

In 1584, when the Spanish captured Ghent in the Netherlands, Dutch and English volunteers moved in to liberate the city. Among them was a captain named Mary Ambree. She was said to be avenging the death of her lover, a sergeant major slain in the siege. Frequently mentioned in old ballads, Ambree is the subject of one preserved by Thomas Percy.

> Then Captain Courageous, whom death could not daunt,
> Had roundly besiegéd the city of Gaunt,
> And manly they marched by two and by three,
> And foremost in battle was Mary Ambree.

Ben Jonson refers to Ambree in the *Epicoene,* as does Jonathan Swift in *Tale of a Tub,* and John Fletcher in *The Scournful Lady.* The ballad in Percy's *Reliques* is often quoted by the writers of Jonson's time, and, like him, they frequently gave the name of Mary Ambree to any extraordinary virago who adopted man's attire. Over time, the name was so commonly used in this manner that, in 1931, P.C. Wren, author of *Beau Geste,* wrote the novel *Sowing Glory* about a woman French Legionnaire and gave her the name Mary Ambree to protect the identity of the actual woman upon whom, he maintained, his book was based.

Ambrose, Alice (1906—)

American philosopher and author of the "Blue and Yellow Books" based on Wittgenstein's lectures. Name variations: Alice Lazerowitz. Born on November 26, 1906; graduated, B.A., Millikin University (1928); M.A., University of Wisconsin (1929), Ph.D. (1932); attended Cambridge University, 1932–1935; awarded Millikin University Honorary L.L.D., 1958; married Morris Lazerowitz.

Smith College assistant professor (1943–51); professor (1951–64); Sophia and Austin Smith professor of philosophy (1964–72); professor emeritus (1972—). Edited Journal of Symbolic Logic *(1953–68).*

Selected works: among the contributors of notes from the lectures of Ludwig Wittgenstein called "The Blue and Yellow Books" (sometimes "The Blue and Brown Books") that are published as Wittgenstein's Lectures, Cambridge 1932–35; *(with Morris Lazerowitz)* Fundamentals of Symbolic Logic *(1948);* Logic: The Theory of Formal Inference *(1961); (ed., with Morris Lazerowitz)* Essays in Analysis *(1966);* G.E. Moore: Essays in Retrospect *(1970);* Ludwig Wittgenstein: Philosophy and Language *(1972); (with Morris Lazerowitz)* Philosophical Theories *(1976); (with Morris Lazerowitz)* Essays in the Unknown Wittgenstein *(1984); and many articles in philosophical journals.*

Alice Ambrose belongs to the tradition of analytic philosophy that has predominated in North America and England in the 20th century. In contrast with continental philosophy, which tries to characterize ways of being, this tradition is concerned with providing philosophical analyses of the problems of knowledge, language, logic, and the mind. After receiving her undergraduate and graduate education in the United States, culminating in a Ph.D. from the University of Wisconsin in 1932, Ambrose went to study with G.E. Moore and Ludwig Wittgenstein at Cambridge University from 1932–35. Her work has been influenced by both of these great philosophers. She adopts the problems of Moore, concerned with the clarity of philosophical issues, and uses the approach advocated by Wittgenstein, the analysis of ordinary language.

Ambrose has published many books and articles in the analytic tradition, some with her husband Morris Lazerowitz, and she edited the *Journal of Symbolic Logic* for 15 years. She is also noted historically for her part in the production of "The Blue and Yellow Books," or "The Blue and Brown Books," so called because they are based on notebooks hidden under the blue and yellow (or brown) skirts of Ambrose and her fellow student, *Margaret MacDonald, during Wittgenstein's lectures. Professor Wittgenstein had prohibited the taking of notes during lectures, but Ambrose and MacDonald were defiant, scribbling down his thoughts during class breaks. Eventually, they persuaded him that the lectures should be recorded, so he allowed them to notate in the open, then publish their notes. The notebooks were widely distributed, then

edited by Ambrose and published in 1958 as *Wittgenstein's Lectures, Cambridge 1932–35.* Wittgenstein's later philosophy opposed the views that he had published as the *Tractatus Logico-Philosophicus,* which had been very influential, and Ambrose's notes helped spread awareness of the details of Wittgenstein's new thought, as yet unpublished. Eager to receive reports of his nascent theories, philosophers in the analytic tradition took the "Blue and Yellow Books" to be more reliable than word-of-mouth.

Catherine Hundleby, M.A. Philosophy,
University of Guelph, Ontario, Canada

Ambrosius, Johanna (b. 1854)

German poet. Born at Lengwethen, a parish village in East Prussia, on August 3, 1854; death date unknown; daughter of an artisan; married a peasant's son by the name of Voigt, 1874.

Johanna Ambrosius led the life of a peasant woman until she began to write verse in middle age. Her work became known when she started submitting poems to a German weekly and attracted the attention of Dr. Schrattenthal, who collected her verses and published them in one volume. The book went through 26 editions. This initial success led to the publication of other poems and stories that were also extremely popular.

Amelia (1783–1810)

*English princess. Name variations: Amelia Guelph. Born on August 7, 1783, in Buckingham House, London, England; died on November 2, 1810, in Windsor, Berkshire, England; buried at St. George's Chapel, Windsor, Berkshire; 15th and youngest child of George III, king of England, and *Charlotte of Mecklenburg-Strelitz; possibly married to Charles Fitzroy.*

Amelia of Anhalt-Dessau (1666–1726)

*Princess of Nassau-Dietz. Name variations: Henriette Amalie von Anhalt-Dessau. Born on August 26, 1666; died on April 17, 1726; daughter of John George II, prince of Anhalt-Dessau, and *Henrietta Catherine of Nassau (1637–1708); married Henry Casimir of Orange-Nassau (1657–1696, cousin of King William III), prince of Nassau-Dietz; grandmother of William IV, prince of Orange; children: John William Firso of Orange-Nassau (1686–1711, who married *Louise of Hesse-Cassel).*

Amelia of Cleves (1517–1586)

*English noblewoman. Born in 1517; died in 1586; daughter of John III, duke of Cleves, and *Maria of Julich-Berg; sister of *Anne of Cleves (1515–1557).*

Amelia of Denmark (1580–1639)

*Duchess of Holstein-Gottorp. Name variations: Augusta Oldenburg. Born on April 8, 1580; died on February 5, 1639; daughter of *Sophia of Mecklenburg (1557–1631) and Frederick II (1534–1588), king of Denmark and Norway (r. 1559–1588); married John Adolphus, duke of Holstein-Gottorp, on August 30, 1596; children: Frederick III (b. 1597), duke of Holstein-Gottorp.*

Amelia of Leuchtenburg (1812–1873)

*Empress of Brazil. Name variations: Amelie or Amélie; Amalie von Leuchtenberg. Born on July 31, 1812, in Milan; died on January 26, 1873, in Lisbon; daughter of *Amalie Auguste (1788–1851) and Eugène de Beauharnais, duchess and duke of Leuchtenburg; became second wife of Dom Pedro I, emperor of Brazil (r. 1822–1831), on October 17, 1829; children: Maria Amelia Augusta (1831–1853), princess of Brazil. See also *Maria II da Gloria.*

Amelia of Orleans (1865–1951).

See Marie-Amelie of Orleans.

Amelia of Solms (1602–1675)

*Princess of Orange. Name variations: Amalia or Amelia von Solms-Braunfels. Born on August 31, 1602; died on September 8, 1675 (some sources cite 1667); married Frederick Henry, prince of Orange (r. 1625–1647); children: William II (1626–1650), prince of Orange (r. 1647–1650); *Louisa Henrietta of Orange (1627–1667); *Henrietta Catherine of Nassau (1637–1708); *Albertina Agnes (d. 1696).*

Amelia of Wurttemberg (1799–1848)

*Duchess of Saxe-Altenburg. Name variations: Amalie von Wurttemberg. Born Amelia Theresa Louise Wilhelmina Philippina on June 28, 1799; died on November 28, 1848; daughter of Louis Frederick, duke of Wurttemberg (brother of King Frederick I) and *Henrietta of Nassau-Weilburg (1780–1857); married Joseph, duke of Saxe-Altenburg, on April 24, 1817; children:*

*six, including *Mary of Saxe-Altenburg (1818–1907); *Elisabeth of Saxe-Altenburg (1826–1896); *Alexandra of Saxe-Altenburg (1830–1911); *Therese of Saxe-Altenburg.*

Amelia Sophia (1711–1786).

See Charlotte of Ansbach for sidebar.

Ameling, Elly (1938—)

Dutch soprano, winner of the Hertogenbosch and Geneva competitions as well as the Edison Prize. Born Elisabeth Sara in Rotterdam, The Netherlands, on February 8, 1938.

Elly Ameling garnered many prizes in her singing career. In 1956, she won the Hertogenbosch Prize; in 1957, the Geneva Prize; and, in 1965, and again in 1970, the Edison Prize. Ameling studied with Pierre Bernac before debuting in London in 1966 and in New York in 1968. After a brief foray into opera, she decided to focus on the concert stage. Ameling was particularly known for her French songs as well as for her Schubert *lieder*. Her fresh, pure voice was especially suited to Mozart and Handel. However, she also performed works of more modern composers like Satie, Mahler, Ravel, Stravinsky, and Britten. In 1971, Ameling was made a Knight of the Order of Oranje Nassau for her contributions to music.

John Haag, Athens, Georgia

America³ Team

*Crew of the first all-women America's Cup Team in 1995. Pronunciation: America Cubed. Team members: Jenifer (J.J.) Isler (San Diego, California); Ann Nelson (San Diego, California); Elizabeth (Lisa) Charles (Provincetown, Rhode Island); Hannah Swett (Jamestown, Rhode Island); Joan Lee Touchette (Newport, Rhode Island); Shelley Beattie (Malibu, California); Stephanie Armitage-Johnson (Auburn, Washington); *Dawn Riley (Detroit, Michigan); Merritt Carey (Tenants Harbor, Maine); Amy Baltzell (Wellesley, Massachusetts); Courtenay Becker (The Dalles, Oregon); Sarah Bergeron (Middletown, New Jersey); Sarah Cavanagh (Denver, Colorado); Leslie Egnot (born in South Carolina but moved to Auckland, New Zealand); Christie Evans (Marblehead, Massachusetts); Diana Klybert (Annapolis, Maryland); Susanne (Suzy) Leech Nairn (Annapolis, Maryland); Linda Lindquist (Chicago, Illinois); Stephanie Maxwell-Pierson (Somerville, New Jersey); Jane Oetking (Rockwell, Texas); Merritt Palm (Fort Lauderdale,*

Florida); Katherine (Katie) Pettibone (Coral Gables, Florida); Marci Porter (Oarton, Virginia); Melissa Purdy (Tiburon, California).

The ship Mighty Mary *(America³) and its all-women crew in the America's Cup race.*

The first all-women team to compete in the 144-year history of the America's Cup race was the brain child of millionaire businessman Bill Koch, who in 1992 skippered the winning boat. Hoping to pique the interest of an increasingly blasé American audience, Koch put together his 23-member team (16 would sail the boat during a race) from more than 650 applicants. The women who made it through the rigorous two-week final tryouts included veteran sailors, world-class rowers, and weight lifters. One third were married and a few had small children. **Ann Nelson**, the team navigator and winner of at least 50 sailing titles, apprised reporters of the additional challenges: "I'll bet none of those men are worrying about the laundry or making sure there's milk in the fridge or Pampers in the cupboards."

Since 1990, two all-female crews have sailed the 33,000-mile Round-the World Whitbread,

but only a handful of women have sailed in the America's Cup since it began in 1851. **Hope Goddard Iselin** sailed in 1895, 1899, and 1903. In 1934, Britain's **Phyllis Brodie Gordon Sopwith** held the stopwatch for her husband T.O.M. Sopwith. They were defeated that year by Harold S. Vanderbilt, who was also sailing with his wife **Gertie Vanderbilt**. Since then, women have been relegated to alternates during trial races, but have never actually raced in an America's Cup final series.

The women's team began a rigorous training program six months earlier than the men, under a former San Diego Padres trainer, one of some 90 top-level coaches hired to get the women in shape. Enduring 13-hour days that included a morning aerobic and weight-lifting work-out, intensive tacking and jibing training, and an evening strategy meeting, the women prepared for the Defense Trials, a series of round-robin races running from January to April. (The winning defender then raced the foreign challenger in a best-of-nine series held in May.) The fierce competition came from the two

other U.S. syndicates vying for a chance to defend the Cup: the Stars & Stripes crew headed by world-famous sailor Dennis Conner, who skippered three Cup Champions, and PACT '95, a hotshot team skippered by Olympic sailing gold medalist Kevin Mahaney. The women endured their share of jabs from the opposition, some good-natured, others less so.

In a remarkable first showing in January, the America3 team defeated the highly touted *Stars & Stripes,* with Conner at the helm, by one minute nine seconds. Although Conner was favored to annihilate *America³,* the *Stars & Stripes* made a crucial mistake during the pre-start maneuvering and had to take a penalty turn just off the starting line. Taking advantage of the situation, the women took the lead, which they retained, even with a slight falter in the fourth mark of the six-leg course. The win was a huge confidence builder.

The women stayed in contention until March, when they were beset by a number of problems. Difficulty with the 3-year-old yacht *America³* forced her retirement, and, despite the introduction of a new boat, *Mighty Mary,* the women lost their sixth straight race. By the middle of the month, hoping to ward off elimination in a pending semifinal round, Koch broke his pledge to stay with the all-women team and added a man, David Dellenbaugh, who was the tactician on Koch's 1992 team. **Jennifer Isler,** the tactician for the women, was devastated by the replacement, although Koch, who was bombarded by incredulous reporters and angry sponsors, made the decision at the request of several women on the team, whose overwhelming desire to win evidently overshadowed their desire to further the cause for women.

Despite Dellenbaugh's best efforts, and a flawless 10th race of the round-robin with **Leslie Egnot** at the helm, the dream was not to be. The women ultimately lost their opportunity in a final race against *Stars & Stripes.* The first 15 miles of the determining round looked like an easy victory for the women. At the top of the final leg, however, with a comfortable lead, *Mighty Mary* suddenly encountered a wind shift that required a sharp move. By the time the two covering jibes had been straightened, Conner had made his move. In the last mile of the round, *Mighty Mary* simply could not maintain momentum, and *Stars & Stripes* crossed the finish 52 seconds ahead of the women's team. In the final series held in May, the America's Cup was eventually captured by the New Zealand team, whose boat was skippered by Russell Coutts.

Bill Koch remained confident that the women had what it took to win, telling reporters, "We had a top team that can compete with anyone. . . . Next time an all-women's team sails in the top of the competition, they can go all the way. That's what this team has meant to the sport."

SOURCES:

Chamberlain, Tony. "A Lost Cause Ends in Conner Triumph," in *Boston Globe.* April 27, 1995.

———. "At End of Rope, Mighty Mary Cries Foul on Conner," in *Boston Globe.* March 30, 1995.

———. "Controversy Swirls on America," in *Boston Globe.* March 20, 1995.

———. "Kiwi Effort Brought New Zealand to Cup," in *Boston Globe,* May 15, 1995.

Hornblower, Margot. "Will They Blow," in *Time.* January 16, 1995, pp. 66–67.

Lloyd, Barbara. "Women to Conner: Take That!" in *The* [New London] *Day.* January 14, 1995.

Starr, Mark. "A New Crew Rocks the Boat," in *Newsweek.* January 16, 1995, pp. 70–71.

Wilson, Bernie. "All-women Cup crew named," in *The* [New London] *Day.* June 2, 1994.

Barbara Morgan, Melrose, Massachusetts

Ames, Blanche (1878–1969)

Botanical illustrator, inventor, and crusader for women's rights. Born February 18, 1878, in Lowell, Massachusetts; died in North Easton, Massachusetts, in 1969; daughter and fourth of six children of Adelbert (a Civil War general, U.S. Senator, and governor of Mississippi during Reconstruction) and Blanche (Butler) Ames; graduated Rogers Hall School, Lowell, Massachusetts; awarded B.A., Smith College, 1899; married Oakes Ames, on May 15, 1900; children: Pauline (Mrs. Francis T.P. Plimpton); Oliver; Amyas; Evelyn (Mrs. John Paschall Davis).

The talent and accomplishments of Blanche Ames were overshadowed by her husband's more famous career as a renowned botanist. She was not only wife, mother, and a valued collaborator in her husband's work, but she also made her own distinctive mark on the world.

One of six children of a prominent and wealthy old New England family, Ames delighted her demanding parents by excelling in everything she attempted. She was a natural athlete, mastering tennis, golf, and yachting, and even played some football (out of the public eye, of course). Her career at Smith College, beginning in 1895, included art studies and a variety of extracurricular activities. She played basketball and was president of her class. A year after graduation, she married Oakes Ames, a young botany instructor at Harvard University. In a letter sent before their marriage, he wrote, "You and I are forming a contract . . . we have an equal voice." The couple made their home in a large estate in North Easton, Massachusetts, and began their collaboration with four children.

Her husband's study of orchids provided the perfect outlet for Ames' artistic talent, and she became involved in precisely illustrating the various species he identified. Over a period of 17 years, the couple published a definitive seven-volume series, *Orchidaceae Illustrations and Studies of the Family Orchidaceae.* Oakes Ames went on to become the leading orchidologist of his day. He was the Arnold Professor of Botany at Harvard, the director of the Botanical Museum, and the supervisor of the Arnold Arboretum.

In addition to her painstaking, time-consuming work over a drawing board, Ames devoted hours to her own oil painting, some of which is displayed at Phillips Exeter Academy, Columbia University, and Dartmouth College. She was also active on the political front. As a staunch suffragist, she set her artist's pen to a number of political cartoons. As a co-founder of the Birth Control League of Massachusetts, she wrote and illustrated pamphlets describing methods for homemade diaphragms and spermicidal jelly. Oakes Ames took up the political banner as well, heading a men's suffrage league and lobbying at the 1914 Republican National Convention for suffrage.

Ames' interests and imagination were wide-ranging. She invented and patented several unlikely devices, including an antipollution toilet, a hexagonal lumber cutter, and a snare for catching low-flying enemy planes during World War II. "For her to have an idea was to act," said her daughter Pauline, "no matter how difficult or how impossible."

Ames outlived her husband by 19 years. One of her final accomplishments before her death at age 91 was the completion of a book about her father's career, *Adelbert Ames, 1835–1933: Broken Oaths and Reconstruction in Mississippi,* which she published in 1964.

SOURCES:
Bailey, Brooke. *The Remarkable Lives of 100 Women Artists.* Holbrook, MA: Bob Adams, 1994.

SUGGESTED READING:
Plimpton, Pauline. *Oakes Ames: Jottings of a Harvard Botanist, 1874–1950.* Cambridge, Botanical Museum and the Arnold Arboretum of Harvard University, distributed by Harvard University Press, 1908.

COLLECTIONS:
Ames' papers are in the Schlesinger Library at Radcliffe College.

Barbara Morgan, Melrose, Massachusetts

Ames, Fanny Baker (1840–1931)

American reformer. Born in Canandaigua, New York, in 1840; died in Barnstable, Massachusetts, in 1931; attended Antioch College; married Charles G. Ames.

In 1873, along with her Unitarian minister husband Charles, Fanny Baker Ames founded the Relief Society of Germantown, Pennsylvania; it was the first visiting social-worker service in the United States.

Ames, Jessie Daniel (1883–1972)

Founding president of the Association of Southern Women for the Prevention of Lynching, who succeeded in increasing positive race relations and decreasing lynching in the South. Name variations: Daniel Ames, Jessie. Born Jessie Daniel on November 2, 1883, in Palestine, Texas; died on February 21, 1972, of crippling arthritis in an Austin, Texas, nursing home; daughter of Laura Leonard (a teacher and nurse) and James Malcolm Daniel (a railroad worker); attended Southwestern College, B.A., 1902; married Roger Post Ames (d. 1914), on June 28, 1905; children: Frederick (b. 1907); Mary (b. 1912); Lulu (b. 1915).

Entered college at age 13; graduated (1902); helped make Texas the first Southern state to ratify 19th Amendment (1918); was founding president of the Texas League of Women Voters (1919); appointed executive director of the Texas Commission on Interracial Cooperation and field representative for the Southwest (1922–25); appointed first president of the Texas Interracial Commission (1922); helped found and was the first president of the American Association of University Women (1926); appointed director of the women's program for all Commission on Interracial Cooperation branches, which resulted in a move to Atlanta (1929–37); was founding president of the Association of Southern Women for the Prevention of Lynching (1930–42); served as general field secretary of Commission on Interracial Cooperation for 13 Southern states (1937–44).

Determined to correct social injustices, Jessie Daniel Ames believed that the key to change was local action and regional organization—an early interpretation of "think globally, act locally." Her method of leadership, unique to the times, contributed to positive changes in women's suffrage and race relations in the South. Only a decade before her birth in 1883, the Ku Klux Klan had ruled her tiny town of Palestine, Texas. Years later, she would play a key role in lessening the South's racial violence.

Months after her birth, the Daniel family moved from Palestine to the small railroad town of Overton, Texas. Ames recalled her ten years in Overton as a dismal time beset by death. Her mother worked as a nurse during the diphtheria, smallpox, and typhoid fever epidemics, leaving Ames well acquainted with death and disease. Surrounded by human suffering, she joined the church against the wishes of her outspoken, non-believer father; this was only one of many times she would stand up for her beliefs in the face of opposition.

The third of four children, Ames fought feelings of unworthiness throughout her youth. Her older sister Lulu was her father's favorite child in what Ames has characterized as an incestuous relationship. Feeling unwanted by her father, who treated her as both unintelligent and unattractive, she had no desire to fit the expected role of a "young lady" by playing with dolls. Instead, she crossed the railroad tracks and found friendship among poor children, both black and white.

The Daniel family's 1893 move to Georgetown (30 miles south of the University of Texas at Austin) dramatically escalated Jessie's standard of living and opportunities for education. She entered Southwestern College's private primary school, and, in 1897, the 13-year-old enrolled in the local college. Author **Jaquelyn Dowd Hall** quotes Ames' recollection of her father's words: "Young lady, I am sending you to college because there is nothing else to do with you. But I want you to understand right now that . . . I do not expect you to graduate." These words fueled her determination to succeed. Since her father refused to let her attend social functions until senior year, Ames turned to books to escape feelings of inadequacy as a woman.

In 1902, she graduated from Southwestern. Two years later, the Daniel family moved to Laredo, Texas, where Roger Post Ames, an army surgeon 13 years her senior and a friend of her father, began to court her. In June of 1905, Ames was married. But her husband's family disapproved of the marriage, viewing her as socially inferior and fearing the loss of Roger's financial contribution to the family. In addition, the marriage suffered from sexual incompatibility. Shortly after they were wed, Roger left for New Orleans to work with a yellow-fever epidemic and sent his wife back to Texas feeling as though she had failed her husband and the marriage. This separation became the norm, with Ames claiming they were together only ten months of the nine-year marriage.

Despite the separation, and Roger's opposition, she gave birth to three children.

Her father died in 1911, her husband in 1914. A widow at age 31, with three children, Ames began her life as an independent woman. With her mother Laura, she began managing a telephone company. Soon, she found her way to feminist activism. In 1916, she organized a county suffrage association in reaction to the business discrimination she encountered. Through this organization, she met her mentor, *Minnie Fisher Cunningham, president of the Texas Equal Suffrage Association. With Cunningham's support, Ames began writing and speaking on women's rights, helping to secure suffrage for women in primary elections and to make Texas the first Southern state to ratify the 19th Amendment, which guaranteed women the right to vote.

Ames took a formal role in the suffrage movement by becoming the founding president of the Texas League of Women Voters in 1919, serving as representative to the Pan-American Congress of 1923, and by acting as a delegate-at-large to the national Democratic Party conventions in 1920 and 1924. During her work for suffrage, women were voting in increasing numbers; however, a female voting bloc did not emerge. She continued working for women's rights by founding and serving as president of the American Association of University Women (AAUW). In keeping with Ames' belief that there should be no difference in professional training or pay between women and men, the AAUW urged colleges to offer equal opportunities to women and to create equality in pay scales.

Troubled by the exclusion of black women from the women's movement and by the rising racial violence, Ames campaigned for **Mary Shipp Sanders**, a Georgetown University English instructor who in 1921 became the first woman to be elected county school superintendent. Ames worked with Sanders to investigate and fight for better conditions in the black county schools. Their work raised funds and secured a grant to erect a new building, replacing the shack that black students had been using as a school. Also in 1921, Ames took her first formal position in the civil-rights movement as chair of the Texas Federation of Women's Clubs Committee on the Condition of Our Colored People. In 1922, **Carrie Parks Johnson**, director of Woman's Work for the Atlanta based Commission on Interracial Cooperation (CIC), called a meeting of Texas women during which the outspoken Ames emerged as the obvious choice for president of the new Texas Interracial Commission. Her active role in the movement led her to Georgia in 1929 to become director of the Woman's Committee of the CIC. She remained in this position until 1937, when the number of women equalled the number of men in the CIC, at which point the women's division was dissolved.

I have never learned in all the fifty-six years of my life to keep my mouth shut when something arises which offends either my sense of justice and fair play or violates the principles of democracy and Christianity.

—Jessie Daniel Ames

Although she began her work fighting for women's suffrage, Ames was most influential and active working to stop lynchings in the South. Despite the 1892–95 anti-lynching movement led by *Ida Wells-Barnett, and the follow-up 1921–22 NAACP campaign organized by *Mary Morris Talbert and *Mary Church Terrell, in 1938 Ames could still write in *Public Opinion Quarterly:* "Newspapers and Southern society accept lynching as justifiable homicide in defense of society."

While the desire to maintain white power was at the core of lynchings, there was a false, though pervasive, belief that lynchings were conducted to save white womanhood. Representatives and senators defended lynching in Congress on the grounds that it was the only way to stop black crimes against women. In the *Congressional Record,* Senator Ben Tillman of South Carolina told the U.S. Senate that white men in the South would "not submit to [the Negro's] gratifying his lust on our wives and daughters without lynching him." Though, according to author J.R. McGovern, "the chance of a white woman in the South being raped by a black male was probably not much greater than of her being struck dead by lightening," the threat of interracial rape preserved white male chivalry and power over white women and all blacks. Sexism was justified under the guise of racism, and vice-versa. Like the black women before her who had led, and were still leading, anti-lynching campaigns, Ames was outraged that the crime of lynching was widely "justified in the name of white Southern womanhood."

The central problem she faced was that a large number of white women accepted the myth and believed that lynchings were committed to protect them. Viewing race and gender problems as interrelated, Ames felt that a coalition of white Southern women could successfully correct this falsehood and put a stop to lynchings. In November of 1930, she led a meeting of 12 women in Atlanta to form the Association of Southern Women for the Prevention of Lynching (ASWPL). As the church was the central influence in the South, she believed that the ASWPL could be most successful if organized through the churches; however, this would not prove an easy prospect. As Ames said in a speech to the women of the Presbyterian Church: "Racial superiority and white supremacy were so bound up with our emotional concepts of religion that our traditions were untouched by the simple words of Jesus." Believing that the church justified racism, and thus lynching, she also believed that the church had the strength to combat both social problems.

One obstacle Ames faced was that most Southern women were so involved in the church that they had time for little else. The solution was to work through existing groups of small-town church women who were experts at running organizations, were familiar with the gospel and local issues, and were sensitized by the prohibition and suffrage movement's arguments about law enforcement and social order. Her strategy thus was to organize regionally and act locally. Ames felt that if each of these women introduced the issue of lynching to her constituency on every occasion, and got signatures on anti-lynching pledges from women and men at their meetings, the organization could have an impact.

In the first five years, the ASWPL received 58 official endorsements from national and state organizations. By 1936, the ASWPL had secured signatures of sheriffs and officers in every state on anti-lynching petitions. Whenever a lynching occurred, the local ASWPL organization investigated, sent a telegram to the governor of the state and the sheriff of the county, and notified the press. By 1939, 43,000 anti-lynching pledges had been signed. Each signature, thought Ames, represented another person educated.

Indeed, it was this strong belief in education as the key to improving race relations that motivated her refusal to endorse federal anti-lynching legislation. In 1934, and again in 1938, the Costigan-Wagner Act was introduced defining lynching as a breach of 14th-Amendment rights. Despite the negative backlash, Ames did not support legislation to make lynching a federal crime. She believed lynching was already illegal and feared that, with federal legislation, the members of the ASWPL would consider the battle won and would stop educating, which was the measure she considered vital to improving long-term race relations. Her insistence, however, that the ASWPL not support the legislation led to ill feelings towards her and would affect her later career.

During the 40 years of anti-lynching movements before the ASWPL, black women had tried to get white women involved with no success. Ida Wells-Barnett had made efforts to bring white women into the NAACP crusade against lynching at the turn of the century; however, it would take a separate organization to secure substantial white Southern involvement. The ASWPL included black women in their movement but did not allow them to join. In the *Chattanooga Sunday Times Magazine,* Ames expressed her firm belief that "white women alone could remove the halo of chivalry from the heads of lynchers by repudiating the claim that lynchers acted in defense of white women." Hall points out that black women of the CIC had long been saying that lynching would be stopped only when white women were ready to stop it. By 1939, of the three lynchings that occurred, not one was justified by protection of white womanhood. Beyond the primary goal of stopping lynchings, the ASWPL empowered white women. Though it was segregated, the organization helped to bring the races together and open lines of communication.

Through the ASWPL, Ames helped reform the image of the "white Southern lady" from that of a dependent creature to an outspoken woman with the ability to effect social change. Equally important, politicians began to recognize this power. In addition to working with white women to end lynching, Ames sought to bring white and black women together to break down racial mistrust. Clubs were started throughout the South during which black and white women studied, taught, played, and prayed together for ten days each year. The idea was that, after these clubs mingled, racial cooperation among the women would continue in their respective communities. And, indeed, it did. Both races came together to help establish community centers for working mothers and to improve schools.

Ames continued as head of the ASWPL until its dissolution in 1942. The following year, the Interracial Commission, of which Ames was a part, was replaced by the Southern Regional Council. Much to her dismay, she was not included in the new organization. This exclusion was apparently due to dissent surrounding her position on federal lynching legislation and personality conflicts with male colleagues. Though she wanted to remain with the new organization, she delivered a farewell address to the Interracial Movement on February 16, 1944, making a final plea for black and white women to continue spearheading work for improved race relations.

From 1944 until her death in 1972, Ames resided in the Blue Ridge Mountains of western North Carolina. During her retirement, she organized women's study groups on world affairs, worked in the Methodist Church, and registered black voters. In her last years, she realized that through her decades of work, her relationships with family and friends had become strained, if not severed. While working for suffrage and to stop lynchings, Ames had remained distant but dedicated to her children. Her son Frederick and daughter Mary became medical doctors. Her youngest daughter Lulu, crippled with polio at a young age, became a leading figure in Texas politics and owned and operated a successful business. Recognizing that she had isolated herself and that she longed for companionship, Ames lived with Lulu her final four years in Texas.

Jessie Ames was active at a time when women had virtually no political or economic power and racial violence was rampant, yet she succeeded in spearheading organizations that began to open doors for women and African-Americans. In a speech to the Morehouse student body, she said:

> If you can accomplish a thing in your life time it really is not very big. It is not big at all. The thing you are working for should be bigger than anything you could possibly see come true in your life time. . . . Of those women assembled at Seneca Falls in 1848, not one lived to see the franchise given to the women. But they started it.

SOURCES:

Ames, Jessie Daniel. "Editorial Treatment of Lynchings," in *Public Opinion Quarterly 2.* 1938, pp. 77–84.
———. Speech presented to the Morehouse student body, Atlanta, 1934. Special Collections/Archives division of the Robert W. Woodruff Library, Atlanta University Center.
———. Speech presented to women of the Presbyterian Church. Summer, 1935. Southern Historical Collection of the Manuscripts Department, University of North Carolina, Chapel Hill.
———. "Women War on Lynching," in *Chattanooga Sunday Times Magazine.* October 18, 1936, p. 1.
Congressional Record. March 23, 1900.
Ellis, Ann Wells. "Jessie Daniel Ames," in *Dictionary of Georgia Biography.* Edited by Kenneth Coleman and Charles Stephen Gurr. Athens, GA: University of Georgia Press, 1983.
Hall, Jaquelyn Dowd. *Revolt Against Chivalry: Jessie Daniel Ames and the Women's Campaign Against*

Lynching. New York: Columbia University Press, 1979.

McGovern, J.R. *Anatomy of a Lynching: The Killing of Claude Neal.* Baton Rouge: Louisiana State University Press, 1982.

COLLECTIONS:

Papers of Jessie Daniel Ames while head of the ASWPL, including personal correspondence, publications, and association records from 1932 to 1940, are held at the Special Collections Department, Robert W. Woodruff Library, Emory University in Atlanta, Georgia.

Boxes of papers, including personal correspondence, speeches, publications, and CIC and ASWPL records from 1930 to 1944, are part of the Southern Historical Collection of the University of North Carolina Archives of the Manuscripts Department, University of North Carolina, Chapel Hill.

Correspondence, ASWPL records, speeches, publications, copies of anti-lynching pledges, and news clippings from 1930 to 1944 are on microfilm at the Special Collections-Archives division of the Robert W. Woodruff Library, Atlanta University Center (formerly Trevor Arnett Library).

Kimberly A. Powell, Assistant Professor of Communication, Luther College, Decorah, Iowa

Amicie de Courtenay (d. 1275)

Countess of Artois. Name variations: Amicia de Courteney. Daughter of Peter de Courtenay; died in 1275; married Robert II (1250–1302), count of Artois, in 1262; children: *Mahaut (c. 1270–1329), countess of Artois.

Amina (c. 1533–c. 1598)

Queen of Zaria and sovereign ruler of the Hausa Empire in what is today the northern region of Nigeria, who was one of the most important leaders of West Africa in the last third of the 16th century. Born in the early 16th century; daughter of Queen Turunku Bakwa; sister of Zaria.

Oral tradition places Amina's birth around 1533, during the reign of the Sarkin Zazzau Nohir. The region she was born in, Zazzau, occupies a plain about 60 miles to the south of Kano and has been inhabited for at least the past millennium by Hausa-speaking peoples. Two cities, Turunku and Kufena, dominated the Zazzau region and provided it with political stability, economic security, and a strong sense of cultural continuity. Just before or around the time of her birth, the state of Zazzau was ruled by a queen (*sarauniya*) named *Turunku Bakwa. Turunku Bakwa appears to have come to power during an interregnum in the city of Kufena. Her reign began a period of expansion by force of arms by the Zazzau state, and her daughter

Amina, whose reign began in the mid-1570s, brought this period of energetic state-building to its height.

Legend tells us that Amina spent her childhood at the court of her grandfather. The precocious infant was said to be present whenever court was in full session, appearing as early as the age of two at the dais of the king. Her grandfather often carried her, placing her on his lap before proceeding with the royal business of the day. Frequent interaction at court gave Amina political knowledge, skills, and personal confidence that would prove immensely useful in later years. She learned countless details of political and military life directly from her grandfather and other members of the Zazzau noble class. She became *magajiya* (heir apparent) at age 16 when political and military affairs became an even greater part of her daily existence.

The death of King Karama around the year 1576 brought Amina to power as *sarauniya*. From the outset of her reign, her policies were based on warfare and a political strategy of unambiguous expansionism. Among her first messages to her subjects was one imploring the leading warriors to resharpen their weapons. After only three months on the throne, she began her first military campaign. Soon she was known in much of West Africa as the fearsome ruler who personally led a well-trained army of 20,000 warriors. Tradition holds that for the rest of her reign her kingdom was at war, expanding its territories. The frontiers of the new state of Zaria eventually expanded to the Atlantic coast and to the River Niger. New cities and walled encampments were established, including the wall around Katsina and the impressive Zaria Wall that remains standing today. While she received tributes from the defeated and intimidated tribal chiefs bordering on her expanding state, it is not certain whether she ever married. Oral tradition states that she took on new lovers whenever warfare ceased, disposing of them when the campaign resumed.

By the end of Amina's reign, Zaria was recognized as the leading state of the Hausa people. She had established the economic as well as military foundations of a great state, introducing and encouraging the spread of the cola nut as a crop. In modern Nigeria, an equestrian statue of Amina has been erected on the grounds of the National Theater in Lagos. She is depicted with sword in hand.

SOURCES:

Abubakr, Sa'ad. "Queen Amina of Zaria," in Bolanle Awe, ed., *Nigerian Women in Historical Perspective.* Lagos and Ibadan: Sankore Publishers Ltd./Bookcraft, 1992, pp. 11–23.

John Haag, Associate Professor of History,
University of Georgia, Athens, Georgia

Amlingyn, Katherine (fl. late-15th c.)

Erfurt merchant. Flourished in the late-15th century.

Merchants in the city of Erfurt, Katherine Amlingyn and her daughter ran a trading company specializing in woad, a plant of the mustard family from which blue textile dye was made. Erfurt was an important woad center at the time. Apparently Katherine Amlingyn was quite successful and ran a large operation, dealing with buyers in cities all across southern Europe. The mother-daughter trading firm even involved other outside merchants as partners. Although this kind of business arrangement was unusual, the Amlingyns reveal that it was possible for women to form independent mercantile businesses in the late Middle Ages.

Laura York, Anza, California

Ammers-Küller, Johanna van (1884–1966)

Dutch novelist and playwright who enjoyed her great success in the 1920s and 1930s. Born Johanna Küller on August 13, 1884, in Delft, Holland, the Netherlands; died in 1966 in Amsterdam, Holland; married in 1904; children: two sons.

Selected works: The House of Joy *(1929);* Tantalus *(1930);* No Surrender *(1931);* Masquerade *(1932);* The House of Tavelinck *(1938). Her novel* The Rebel Generation *(1925) was translated into ten languages.*

Johanna van Ammers-Küller, who would become known as the foremost interpreter of Dutch middle-class life after World War I, was born into a family of prominent lawyers and doctors. Known as Jo, she was an only child born and raised in the town of Delft where the Küllers had long resided. At an early age, she was attracted to the stage, writing and performing stories and plays for her family and friends, sometimes drawing others into the act. When she was 14, she saw her first publication.

At 20, Ammers-Küller married and moved to London. For the next eight years, as she raised two sons, she did not submit work for publication. In 1912, she reemerged with a play, and within the next nine years she wrote two more dramas and a novel. She also returned to Amsterdam. It was not until 1925, with her depiction of Holland's youth in *The Rebel Genera-tion*, that she received international attention. Fame afforded her the opportunity to travel throughout Europe as well as the United States where she met President Franklin Roosevelt. With the advent of World War II, Ammers-Küller faded from international view. In Holland, she remained a foremost fiction writer and recorder of Dutch life, and an activist with Holland's P.E.N. She died in 1966 at the age of 82.

Crista Martin, Boston, Massachusetts

Amor, Guadalupe (1920—)

Mexican poet. Born in 1920 in Mexico.

Selected works: Yo soy mi casa *(I Am My House, 1946);* Circulo de anguista *(Circle of Anguish, 1948);* Polvo *(Dust, 1949);* Antologia poética *(Poetry Anthology, 1956);* Como reina de barajas *(Queen of Cards, 1966);* A mí me ha dado en escriber sonetos *(I Have Taken to Writing Sonnets, 1981);* Soy dueña del universo *(I Am the Mistress of the Universe, 1984).*

Before she discovered poetry, Guadalupe Amor longed for fame and material things. She did not begin to publish until three events forced her to reexamine her values: her attempts at a stage and screen career failed, her mother died, and she lost her home. Amor looked for spiritual guidance. Through her metaphysical poetry, widely read in Mexico, she explores the human condition. Her work is included in anthologies, journals, periodicals, and more than 12 books of her own.

Crista Martin, Boston, Massachusetts

Amrouche, Fadhma Mansour (1882–1967)

Algerian-born Berber poet and folksinger. Name variations: Fadhma Aith Mansur. Born in the Kabylia region of Eastern Algeria in 1882; died in Brittany on July 9, 1967; an out-of-wedlock child, she was raised by French nuns; married Belkacem-ou-Amrouche, in 1899; children: eight, including Marie-Louise Amrouche (1813–1976) and Jean Amrouche (a poet).

One of the first, if not the first, women educated in colonial Algeria; uneasily suspended between Berber and French culture, Amrouche recorded the vicissitudes of her life in her autobiography My Life Story: The Autobiography of a Berber Woman.

Fadhma Aith Mansour was born in a remote mountain village in the Kabylia region of Eastern Algeria in 1882, the illegitimate daughter of a young widow. Because she was born out of wedlock, Fadhma's life was at risk, as was her mother's, for the patriarchal code of honor stipulated that such "immoral" behavior must be punished in the harshest possible terms. To avoid violence against her daughter as well as herself, Fadhma's mother walked for six days to entrust the endangered child to the care of French nuns, the White Sisters who lived in a convent at Ouadhias. From 1887 to 1897, the bright young girl attended a secular school at Taddert-ou-Fella. Fadhma Mansour was one of the first, and possibly the very first, Berber girl to receive a Western-style education in colonial Algeria. Upon graduation, she began working in the linen room of the Saint-Eugénie Hospital in the town of Aîth-Manegueleth.

In 1899, Fadhma was baptized into the Roman Catholic Church and simultaneously married a young Berber schoolteacher, Belkacem-ou-Amrouche. The Amrouches had eight children and lived in the often precarious cultural region between Algerian life and that of the dominant European colonial regime. Despite her European upbringing, Fadhma remained deeply immersed in the rich cultural traditions of the Berber people, fiercely independent tribes of the Barbary Coast and the Sahara who had never been completely absorbed by the dominant Arab language and folkways.

In order to support a growing family, Belkacem-ou-Amrouche took a job with the Tunisian Railway Company and moved his family to Tunis. Soon after, they lost their son and fourth child, baby Louis-Marie, who died in October 1909. Because her husband was a loyal civil servant of the French colonial regime, in 1913, Fadhma's entire family was granted French naturalization papers. Fadhma gave birth to *Marie-Louise Amrouche, her sixth child and only daughter, not long after. The onset of World War I meant increasing assimilation of French colonials like the Amrouches, as France drew upon the people of Algeria and Tunisia to replenish troops lost in the trenches. In 1918, Fadhma's first son, Paul-Mohand-Saîd, was called to the colors; fortunately, however, the carnage ended in November of that year and he never served.

Throughout her life, Fadhma Amrouche continued to expand her Berber legacy in song and poetry, a polestar for a woman caught in a cultural crossfire. The large Amrouche family, which now included Belkacem's aged father, Ahmed-ou-Amrouche, continued to live in Tunis and to be both Berber and French, Catholic and Algerian. But these divided loyalties often caused problems. For example, Amrouche's son Paul left his wife and child to seek his fortune in Paris, while her father-in-law left Tunis for the traditions of his home region of the Kabylia in 1923. It was difficult to know which path to choose.

Fadhma Amrouche lost three sons in quick succession. In 1939, her son Louis-Mohand-Seghir died of tuberculosis at the age of 29. The next year, 1940, France was utterly defeated by the Nazi armed forces in June, and Amrouche's first-born son Paul committed suicide at only 40. Before the year was over tuberculosis claimed another son, Noël-Saâdi, not yet 24. During these tragic years, Fadhma Amrouche overcame her grief by writing folk poetry and singing the wild, plaintive songs of her beloved Kabylia. At first, these stirring renditions of age-old laments and sagas were known only to her family and friends, but, with the passage of time, it became clear that Fadhma possessed an extraordinary gift and her fame grew. In 1946, she wrote down the fascinating story of her life (*My Life Story: The Autobiography of a Berber Woman*). For a time, it appeared that she would be granted a serene old age.

But traumatic and bloody events continued to plague Amrouche's final years. The savage, atrocity-ridden Algerian war of independence began in 1954, the same year in which Fadhma's aged father-in-law died after a life of dramatic changes. For Christian families like the Amrouches, the war was catastrophic as they were regarded as traitors and puppets of the alien French Europeans. In 1956, Fadhma and her husband fled to France, taking refuge with their son Jean-El-Mouhouv and his wife Marie-Louise. What would prove to be only a temporary amelioration in the military situation prompted them to return home in 1957, but, in January 1959, her beloved husband died at their home in Ighil-Ali, and five weeks later Fadhma closed up the house to return to France. When her son died in April 1962, she wrote a new introduction to her autobiography. Although written earlier, the book now received a wider audience and rave reviews. Critics recognized the simple, moving chronicle as a classic account of determination and one woman's call to keep her cultural roots alive.

When Fadhma Amrouche died in Brittany on July 9, 1967, her lifetime achievement of preserving the Berber culture of her ancestors was increasingly recognized not only in France but in Algeria. This legacy of poetry and song was passed on to her daughter, Marie-Louise Amrouche, who recorded many of her own versions of the ancient poems and songs of the Kabylia. Both mother and daughter drew sustenance from the powerful traditions of their Berber past that continue to speak to the eternal concerns of humankind.

SOURCES:

Amrouche, Fadhma A.M. *My Life Story: The Autobiography of a Berber Woman.* Translated with an introduction by Dorothy S. Blair. London: The Women's Press, 1988.

John Haag, Associate Professor of History,
University of Georgia, Athens, Georgia

Amrouche, Marie-Louise

(1913–1976)

Algerian folklorist and first Algerian woman to publish a novel, who brought her mother's work to publication as well. Name variations: Taos Amrouche; Marguerite Taos Bourdil. Born Marie-Louise Taos Amrouche in 1913 in Tunisia, Algeria; died in 1976 in France; daughter of Fadhma Mansour Amrouche (an author) and Belkacem-ou-Amrouche; sister of Jean Amrouche (a poet).

Selected works: Jacinthe noir *(Black Hyacinth, 1947);* Rue des Tambourins *(1960);* Le grain magique *(The Magic Grain, 1966);* L'Amant imaginaire *(The Imaginary Lover, 1975); and three recorded interpretations of Berber folk songs.*

In the then French-occupied nation of Algeria, Marie-Louise Amrouche was born into a life suspended between two worlds. In her native Berber culture, she was given the name Taos by her parents, both native Algerians. But her family converted to Christianity, and under Christian French rule she also bore the name Marie-Louise. The dichotomies of religion and national alliance left her feeling as though she had no home—a common feeling among women in colonial-occupied countries.

Amrouche, who lived in Tunisia, rose to fame around 1937 with her translation and performance of traditional Berber (Kabylia) songs in French. Despite this attempt to connect the two cultures, she still felt at odds in Algeria. In 1945, she moved to France and assumed French nationality. While there, she wrote and published *Jacinthe noir (Black Hyacinth)*, the first novel released by an Algerian woman. (Subjugated in their native land, Algerian women have been denied many opportunities.) Amrouche's brother, poet Jean Amrouche, is credited with helping his sister find peace with the diverse cultures influencing her. Written in native Kabylia and translated to French, *Le grain magique (The Magic Grain)* was published in 1966; its poems

and songs explored Amrouche's resolution with her French and Algerian influences.

The year 1967 brought the death of Amrouche's mother, *Fadhma Mansour Amrouche.* One year later, despite her father's objections, Amrouche saw to it that her mother's autobiography, *The Story of My Life,* was published. In her later years, Amrouche was instrumental in the creation of a chair of Berber literature and sociology at the University of Algeria. She died in 1976 in France, where she had lived for 31 years.

Crista Martin, Boston, Massachusetts

Amrouche, Taos (1913–1976).

See Amrouche, Marie-Louise.

Anable, Gloria Hollister

(1903–1988)

American zoologist and explorer. Name variations: Gloria Hollister. Born in 1903; died in 1988.

American zoologist Gloria Hollister Anable worked with William Beebe in exploring the sea in his bathysphere. She set the women's record for depth in August 1931 at 1,208 feet. In 1936, while flying a light plane in British Guiana, she discovered 43 as yet unmapped waterfalls, including Kaieteur Falls, which is five times the elevation of Niagara. Anable was a fellow with the New York Zoological Society and the Geographical Society.

Anacáona (fl. 1492)

Indian princess of Haiti. Name variations: Anacaona; name means "Golden Flower." Flourished around 1492; sister of Behechio; married Caonabo (cacique of Haiti).

An Indian princess, Anacáona was the sister of Behechio and wife of Caonabo; both were caciques of Haiti when it was discovered by Christopher Columbus in 1492. After the capture and death of Caonabo, Anacáona advocated submission to the Spaniards, and she received Bartholomew Columbus with great hospitality in 1498. Anacáona succeeded her brother Behechio as ruler of his tribe, and friendly relations with the whites continued until 1503. In that year, she entertained Ovando and his Spanish forces, but in the midst of a festival in their honor, the Spanish attacked her village, massacred a great number of her people, and carried Anacáona to Santo Domingo where she was hanged.

Anagnos, Julia Rowana (1844–1886).

See Howe, Julia Ward for sidebar.

Anastaise (fl. 1400)

French manuscript illuminator. Flourished in Paris around 1400.

Anastaise worked as a professional illuminator of manuscripts in 15th-century Paris. Although few details about her life are known, her fame as an artist is documented in a book by her internationally known contemporary, the poet and author *Christine de Pizan. Pizan's *Book of the City of Ladies* mentions Anastaise as an example of a talented female artist. Anastaise was reportedly one of the most sought-after manuscript illuminators in Paris, specializing in painting borders and flowers.

SOURCES:

Christine de Pizan. *The Book of the City of Ladies.* Translated by Earl Jeffrey Richards. NY: Persea Books, 1982.

Laura York, Anza, California

Anastasia (fl. 600s)

Byzantine empress. Flourished in the 600s; married Constantine IV Pogonatus (r. 668–685); children: Justinian II Rhinotmetos, Byzantine emperor (r. 705–711).

Anastasia (fl. 800s)

Byzantine princess. Daughter of Theophilus and Empress *Theodora (fl. 842–856); sister of Pulcheria, Mary, *Thecla, Anna, and Michael III.

Anastasia (1902–1984).

See Anderson, Anna.

Anastasia (1901–1918)

Russian grand duchess who was the youngest daughter of Russia's last tsar. Name variations: Anastasia Romanov. Born Anastasia Romanov (Romanoff or Romanovna) on June 18, 1901, in Peterhof, Russia; executed on July 17, 1918, at Ekaterinburg, in Central Russia; youngest daughter of Tsar Nicholas II and

(from left) Grand Duchess Olga, Tatiana, Marie, and Anastasia, 1906.

Alexandra Feodorovna (1872–1918, known also as Alix of Hesse-Darmstadt).

In March 1917, the abdication of Tsar Nicholas II became one of the precipitating events of the Russian Revolution and made the deposed ruler, his wife, Empress *Alexandra Feodorovna, and their five children pawns in the tumult that overtook their country until their deaths the following year. When Civil War broke out, the Grand Duchess Anastasia, the youngest daughter in the family, was moved in the spring of 1918—along with her parents, sisters *Tatiana (b. 1897), *Olga (b. 1895), and *Marie (b. 1899), and her brother, Alexis (b. 1904)—to Ekaterinburg, east of the Ural Mountains. As White Russian armies, including tsarist supporters, approached the Urals, orders came down from the opposing Bolshevik leader Vladimir I. Lenin to execute the royal family. On the night of July 16, the tsar, his wife, the five children, and several members of their household were roused from their beds and escorted by a local commissar to the cellar, where they fell to the shots of a firing squad. The 11 victims were buried in an abandoned mineshaft, then reburied later in an open field.

For a long time, as rumors circulated that the 17-year-old Anastasia had survived the death squad, theories abounded as to her subsequent whereabouts. The most convincing conjecture was that she reappeared in Germany under the name *Anna Anderson. In 1993, DNA tests were conducted in Britain to identify remains found under railroad ties in a deep pit in the Ural mountains. The remains were identified as those of the tsar, Empress Alexandra, and three of their four daughters. Though DNA comparisons finally debunked Anderson's claim, speculation continues around the "missing children" whose remains have not been found—Alexei and either Anastasia or Maria.

Inevitably, the myth of the lost princess led to dramatization. A play by Marcelle Baurette, loosely based on Anna Anderson's claim, became the basis for the 20th Century-Fox movie *Anastasia,* starring *Ingrid Bergman, Yul Brynner and *Helen Hayes. The story of the impostor-duchess proved auspicious in drawing the legendary Bergman back to American screens after a long absence and won her an Academy Award. A later movie version of the Anastasia story starred **Amy Irving**.

Anastasia, Saint (d. 304)

Christian saint. Name variations: Anastasia of Sirmium.

A Roman of noble birth, Anastasia suffered martyrdom during the persecution of Christians in Sirmium (modern-day Yugoslavia) under the Roman emperor Diocletian. Her mother was a Christian; her father a pagan. When her mother died, her father demanded that she marry a pagan. Her new husband, learning belatedly that she was a Christian, treated her cruelly and squandered her property until his death a few years later. Free of him, Anastasia devoted herself to secret works of charity, using what remained of her fortune to relieve the Christian poor, many of whom were in prison. After her works caused suspicion, she and three female servants were arrested and ordered to sacrifice to idols. When they refused, the servants were immediately executed, and Anastasia was banished for a time. She was then brought back to Rome and burned alive. In the Orthodox Church, her feast is celebrated on December 22; in the Roman Catholic Church, she is the only saint to be celebrated on a major feast day, receiving a special commemoration in the second Mass of Christmas Day.

Anastasia, Saint (d. about 860)

Christian saint. Name variations: Athanasia. Born and lived on the island of Aegina.

Though Anastasia had looked forward to the life of a religious from childhood, her wealthy parents forced her into an advantageous marriage. But when the island of Aegina was attacked by Moors from Spain, her husband was killed in its defense. As a series of wars had depopulated the island, the government issued edicts against celibacy, and Anastasia was forced to marry a second time. Her new husband was as wealthy and generous as she, and their home became a refuge for the poor. He stayed home to minister to the unfortunate, while Anastasia sought out the poor who were too proud to request help. Eventually, her husband became a monk and left her all his possessions. Anastasia gathered companions to her home and trained them for the religious life; then, with the help of a priest called Matthias, she went with them into the wilderness of Timia. There, she built her convent, which she directed until her death around 860. Reputedly, Anastasia corresponded with the empress *Theodora the Blessed (fl. 842–856). Anastasia's feast day is August 14th.

Anastasia and Basilissa, Saints (fl. 54–68)

Christian martyrs. Pronunciation: An-as-TAY-shi-a. Slain during the reign of Nero (r. 54–68).

Anastasia and Basilissa are said to have been two Roman women of the 1st century who were beheaded for burying the bodies of their teachers, St. Peter and St. Paul. Their martyrdom is commemorated on April 15.

Anastasia and Comitona (fl. 500s)

*Byzantine courtesans. Name variations: (for Comitona) Comito. Born on the island of Cyprus, or more likely in Syria, in about the year 500; daughters of Acacius (guardian of the bears for the Greens at the Hippodrome in Constantinople) and an unnamed actress; sisters of the Empress Theodora. Comitona married Sittas, around 528, and was the mother of *Sophia (c. 525–after 600 CE).*

Empress *Theodora (c. 500–548) had two sisters, Anastasia and Comitona. Upon the death of their father when they were children, Theodora began to work on stage as a mime with her older sister Comitona. By her late teens, Anastasia was also a favorite both on the stage, where she "undraped the beauty of which she was so proud," and off, where she followed in the footsteps of Comitona as a prostitute or courtesan. In the context of the time, actress was synonymous with prostitute.

Anastasia of Montenegro (1868–1935).

See Anastasia Petrovitch-Njegos.

Anastasia of Russia (c. 1023–after 1074)

*Queen of Hungary. Name variations: Anastasia Agmunda of Kiev. Born around 1023 in Kiev, Ukraine; died after 1074; daughter of Yaroslav I the Wise (b. 978), grand prince of Kiev (r. 1019–1054), and *Ingigerd Olafsdottir (c. 1001–1050); married Andrew I (c. 1001–1060), king of Hungary (r. 1047–1060), around 1046; children: Salamon also known as Solomon, king of Hungary (r. 1063–1074, deposed); *Adelaide of Hungary (d. 1062).*

Anastasia of Sirmium (d. 304).

See Anastasia, Saint.

Anastasia Petrovitch-Njegos (1868–1935)

Russian royal. Name variations: Anastasia of Montenegro; (nickname) Stana. Born on January 4, 1868; died on November 15, 1935; daughter of Nicholas, king of Montenegro, and *Milena (1847–1923); married Nicholas Nicholaevitch (grandson of Nicholas I of Russia and *Charlotte of Prussia), on May 12, 1907.*

Fond of psychics and faith healers, Anastasia Petrovitch-Njegos had a hand in introducing Rasputin into the Romanov household of Empress *Alexandra Feodorovna (1872–1918).

Anastasia Romanova (d. 1560)

Russian empress. Name variations: Romanovna. Died on August 7, 1560; daughter of Roman Yurievich, a non-titled landowner (d. 1543) and Juliane Feodorovna (d. 1550); sister of Nikita Romanov (d. 1586); became first wife of Ivan IV (1530–1584), tsar of Russia (r. 1533–1584), on February 3, 1547; children: Anna (1548–1550); Dmitri (b. 1552, drowned in 1553); Maria (1551–1554); Ivan Ivanovich (b. 1554, killed by his father in 1581); Eudoxia (1556–1558); Fyodor also known as Theodore I (1557–1598), tsar of Russia (r. 1584–1598).

Anastasia Romanova (1860–1922)

*Russian royal and grand duchess of Mecklenburg-Schwerin. Name variations: Grand Duchess Anastasia; Romanov. Born Anastasia Michaelovna Romanov on July 28, 1860; died on March 11, 1922; daughter of Michael Nicholaevitch (son of Nicholas I of Russia and *Charlotte of Prussia) and *Cecilia of Baden (1839–1891); married Frederick Francis III, grand duke of Mecklenburg-Schwerin, on January 24, 1879; children: *Alexandrina of Mecklenburg-Schwerin (1879–1952); Frederick Francis IV, grand duke of Mecklenburg-Schwerin; *Cecilia of Mecklenberg-Schwerin (1886–1954).*

Anastasia the Patrician (d. 567)

Christian saint.

Anastasia the Patrician was lady-in-waiting to Empress *Theodora (c. 500–548). To escape the attentions of the emperor Justinian I, Anastasia fled from the court of Constantinople and, for 28 years, dressed as a male, lived the life of a hermit in the desert of Scete.

Ancelot, Marguerite (1792–1875)

French author. Born Marguerite Louise Virginie Chardon in Dijon, France, in 1792; died in 1875; married Jacques Arsène Polycarpe Ancelot (1794–1854, a French dramatist).

Selected works: Un mariage raisonable *(A Sensible Marriage, 1835);* Marie ou les trois époques *(Marie or the Three Epochs, 1836);* Renée de Varville *(1853);* The Banker's Niece *(1853).*

Marguerite Ancelot's published writing appears either in conjunction with and as part of her husband's work or as chronicles of salon life. She is remembered as a kindly but insistent force in the work of her husband and those who visited her Paris salon, which was one of the most fashionable during the period of the July monarchy (1831–1848). The salon is mentioned in letters or memoirs of the time, and Ancelot is cited as being influential in the works of Prosper Merimée and Stendhal.

Crista Martin, Boston, Massachusetts

Ancher, Anna (1859–1935)

Danish painter of portraits and interiors, known for her masterful use of color and light. Pronunciation: AN-ker. Born Anna Kirstine Bröndum in Skagen, the northernmost village in Denmark, in 1859; died in 1935; daughter of Erik and Anna (Hedvig) Bröndum; attended public school there; studied under Professor Vilhelm Kyhn, 1875–78; studied under Pierre Puvis de Chavannes in Paris, 1888–89; married Michael Ancher (a painter), in 1880; children: **Helga Ancher** *(a painter, b. 1883).*

Made debut at the Spring Exhibition of Paintings at Charlottenborg in Copenhagen (1880); elected a member of the Copenhagen Academy (1904); house inaugurated as a museum (June 23, 1967).

"Among European painters, Anna Ancher is one of the few women of consequence," writes Walter Schwartz in his work on the village of Skagen and its importance to Nordic painting. "She is the exception to the rule that great artistic innovators are men. In Nordic painting she stands alone. . . . She has inspired no school of painting; her specific talent was a sense of color, an inborn gift which can as little be transferred to others as can red hair or personal charm." Schwartz is not alone in his opinion of women's contributions to painting. In **Geraldine Norman's** *Nineteenth-Century Painters, and Painting,* published in 1977, she includes merely six women in more than 700 entries: *Elisabeth Vigee-Le Brun, *Rosa Bonheur, *Mary Cassatt, *Berthe Morisot, the Norwegian *Harriet Backer, and Anna Ancher. While these sources speak to the remarkably scant attention often paid to women artists, they also make Anna Ancher's mark on art history quite clear.

Anna Bröndum was born at Skagen, Denmark, in the summer of 1859. Her grandfather was considered the most influential member of the village, a political dictator who determined who would sit on the Council. Her mother had married the grocer and innkeeper Erik Bröndum and worked in the kitchen of what gradually became a nationally known hotel and, from the 1870s, a famous gathering place for artists. A mild and generous woman, the senior **Anna Bröndum** wore herself out but stayed by her stove until she was too old to work any longer. Her daughter describes her as:

> a poetic nature and very bright, but she took on the guise of servant and strove from morning till night by the stove. She was very beautiful. Yet I remember her dressed up only once in a grey silk dress with a grey hat and red carnations. She had made a promise to God on one occasion when she feared the family would go bankrupt that if He would help, she would always work in her kitchen to His honor, and she did. First up, last to bed, dressed in the humblest of clothes, providential to the poor, she struggled on till she was eighty years old.

The children would sit around the kitchen table fighting over the light from a single candle. As they played with their toys, the boys would sometimes invite Anna's participation, but mostly they discounted their sister "who understood only colors." Throughout her life, she would draw and paint the things and people surrounding her inside and outside the hotel, rarely venturing beyond those environs.

Anna spent the winters between 1875 and 1878 in Copenhagen at the drawing academy for women directed by Vilhelm Kyhn, a landscape painter. He appears to have had little appreciation for his student's talent and offered little encouragement. As a wedding present, Kyhn would send her a set of china accompanied by a note suggesting that she go down to the beach with her painting box and all her painting equipment and set them "to sail the seas, because now, as a married woman, she would no longer want to be an artist but a housewife."

Ancher's only other formal training was a six-month stay in Paris where she studied drawing at the school of Pierre Puvis de Chavannes. Given that rather sporadic instruction and the fact that she was mostly self-taught, perhaps she would have become a painter no matter where she lived. It was her fate, however, to have been born at a place where painters, writers, actors, and composers gathered to visit or to set up permanent residency. They came to the small fishing village on the northernmost tip of the Jutland peninsula, surrounded by water: the North Sea to the northwest, the Skagerak to the north, and the Kattegat to the east. Then as now, Skagen gets more sunshine than anywhere else in Denmark, and the light reflected from the sea intensifies the daylight. From the time Ancher was ten years old, she could observe painters arriving in her hometown and at her parents' hotel to paint the sea and the fishing population, and to capture the unusual light and the limpid colors.

In an essay, Anna Ancher describes the arrival of the man she would marry in 1880. "In the summer [of 1874] a young, long haired painter came dragging his paint box and asking for room and board. He ate three pigeons and could have eaten more. He looked like one of the Pharaoh's lean cows. I was permitted to bring him tea and took a good look at him; he wasn't too bad. His name was Michael Ancher."

Anna made her debut as a painter at the Spring Exhibition of 1881 at Charlottenborg in Copenhagen, but before then she had already painted *Lars Gaihede Whittling a Stick*. Gaihede was a member of a large Skagen family and many of his relatives posed for other Skagen painters as well. Anna Ancher's painting is a close-up of the peasant concentrating on his whittling. It has a heavier, darker quality than that of her later works, which suggests a temporary influence of her husband's teachings. Even here, however, the play of light on the figure's face and hands shows the direction her painting would take. She would credit other influences, such as fellow Skagen painters Christian Krogh and P.S. Kroyer, but Ancher developed and refined an outstanding sense of color all her own, thereby becoming a pioneer of modern Danish art.

In 1884, the Anchers, with their one-year-old daughter Helga, moved into the house, which today is the best preserved artist's house in Denmark. For the first 15 years, they were relatively poor. Though Michael became known as Skagen's most authentic painter of fishermen, his works did not sell until around the turn of the century. Even so, the Anchers were generous and hospitable hosts, and their doors were open to fishermen as well as artists, local residents, and visitors. They set a modest table, but their cordial manner and helpful demeanor had no limits. Anna was spontaneous, open to life and people; Michael always put the guests ahead of himself. Understandably, their house became the image of Skagen to locals and strangers alike.

Michael and Anna Ancher were of different dispositions. Though Michael understood and respected his wife's work and admired her, he could not comprehend her artistic views and habits. He was hardworking to a fault, passionate and persistent. His daughter describes him with a paintbrush in hand from the time he got up until he went to bed, ever trying to reach the goal he had set for himself as an artist. Anna, on the other hand, painted as if in play, with a seemingly organic matter-of-factness, an unconscious absorption and enjoyment that was evident in her work. "She was like sunshine," wrote the leading painter among the Swedish contingent, Oscar Björck, who admired Anna Ancher both as a painter and as a person. "Her paintings had something which none of ours had to the same degree, a quiet devotion to the task and a coloring so mellow we enjoyed it as we would ripened fruit. She had none of our aggression. She painted slowly and surely, and we had the impression she enjoyed working that way." Anna consistently found her subject matter in things and people around her, but a seemingly casual glimpse into everyday life in a fisherman's house or a room at the hotel gains importance and significance in her rendition. Her sense of humor and strong empathy show especially in her portraits of children.

Unlike her male colleagues, Anna Ancher painted mostly indoor scenes and portraits. She loved Skagen's sun but liked it best when filtered through curtains or a row of green plants on a windowsill. Her famous *The Maid in the Kitchen* shows bright sunlight flooding the room through yellow curtains while a standing woman has her back to the viewer. A mellower light comes in from the side through a half-open door. As Ancher developed her style, light became the major feature of her paintings, demonstrated in the series featuring the blue room of Bröndum's Hotel, which was her mother's quarters. *Sunshine in the Blue Room* shows window light making shadows on the back wall. The dominating colors are blue and yellow and the entire scene is filtered through a golden mist. Between the two windows sits a little girl—Helga Ancher—whose round, blonde head is placed in the beam of sunlight, which also highlights the back of her apron.

Anna Ancher painted her mother in the same way she wrote about her, in a series suggesting an allegorical representation of the passage of life. From the earlier realistic and naturalistic portrayals to the last, the series depicting an old woman sitting in her chair suggests the development in Ancher's work as she moved toward a symbolic representation of images, a dis-

Anna Ancher,
The Maid in the
Kitchen,
1883–1886.

solution of the weights of objects or people in favor of colors and light. The old woman sits wrapped in light, covered by a rose-colored blanket, her head resting against a white pillow, her hands folded. She gives the impression of being ready for the final journey—out of life and out of the picture. Again, the sun shining through the window makes shadows on the blue wall. The viewer recognizes the blue room and the old lady, but the contours are fainter than in earlier renditions; color and light are becoming figures in their own right and point in the direction of modern abstract painting. In terms of composition and use of color as motifs, it is a picture ahead of its time.

Anna Ancher never moved far away from her mother's hotel. With the exception of her studies in Copenhagen and Paris and a trip to Vienna with her husband in 1882, she lived and died where she was born. She was unique in her use of color and, like Matisse, she could make much of little, give an ordinary event or object depth and significance with a simple yet sophisticated juxtaposition of colors. Tied to her time and milieu, she unknowingly crossed from the prevailing naturalism into art, which makes the interplay of light and color the subject matter of a painting.

SOURCES:

Berg, Knut, ed., *et al.* *1880-tal i nordiskt maaleri.* Stockholm Nationalmuseum, 1986.

Greer, Germaine. *The Obstacle Race.* NY: Farrar, Straus & Giroux, 1979.

Schwartz, Walter. *Skagen I Nordisk Kunst.* Copenhagen: Carit Andersens Forlag, 1968

Varnedoe, Kirk. *Northern Light.* New Haven, CT: Yale University press, 1988.

Voss, Knud. *Skatte fra Skagen.* Copenhagen: Herluf Stockholms Forlag, n.d.

Wivel, Ole. *Rejsen til Skagen.* Copenhagen: G.E. Gad, 1978.

Inga Wiehl, Yakima Valley Community College, Yakima, Washington

Anckarsvard, Karin (1915–1969)

Swedish author of 14 books for children, all translated from Swedish to English. Pronunciation: Ank-er-sord. Born Karin Inez Maria Olson on August 10, 1915, in Stockholm, Sweden; died on January 16, 1969; daughter of Oscar Emil (a doctor) and Iris (Forssling) Olson; married Carl M. Cosswa Anckarsvard, on January 20, 1940; children: Marie Christine, Marie Cecile, Marie Madeleine, Mikael, Carl Henrik.

Selected works: Bonifacius den groene (*Bonifacius the Green, 1952*); Aunt Vinnie's Invasion *(1962);* Aunt Vinnie's Victorious Six *(1964).*

Though she began writing as a child and had her first story published when she was just eight years old, Karin Anckarsvard experienced most of her success late in life. She was born in Stockholm on August 10, 1915, the daughter of a medical doctor, and educated largely in Sweden, except for a brief turn at Oxford University from 1934 to 1935. On her return from Oxford, she took a secretarial position, which she held until her marriage in 1940, at age 24, to Carl Anckarsvard. Following the births of their five children, she began writing for young people in her native Swedish. The first of her books, *Boni-*

facius the Green, was translated from Swedish to English by her husband. Thirteen others followed, including the "Aunt Vinnie" series, written for young girls. Anckarsvard was also a journalist, contributing to Sweden's daily newspaper *Expressea.* She died in 1969, age 54.

Crista Martin, Boston, Massachusetts

Anders, Beth (1951—)

American field hockey player and coach. Born on November 13, 1951, in Norristown, Pennsylvania; graduated Ursinus College, 1973.

Won the bronze medal with her team at the 1984 Olympics; voted Amateur Athlete of the Year for Field Hockey by the U.S. Olympic Committee (1981, 1984); voted Co-Athlete of the Year in 1982 with Charlene Morett *by* Olympian *magazine.*

At the dawn of the 20th century, field hockey was wildly popular in the United States; it was also one of the first sports in which large numbers of American women participated. Introduced by *Constance Applebee in 1901, it would become an Olympic sport for women in 1980. Beth Anders joined the U.S. national field hockey team in 1969. Beginning in 1971, she played on every World Cup team. An experienced player, whose specialty was penalty corner goals, Anders scored six of them in seven matches in the 1983 World Cup competition. In 1984, when the United States won a gold medal in the Four Nations Competition, defeating New Zealand, Australia, and Canada, Anders' scoring of four penalty corner goals was crucial to the victory.

Anders was also an excellent defensive player. Assisted by goalkeeper **Gwen Cheesman** and left-wing forward **Charlene Morett,** Anders led her team to a third-place finish and a bronze medal at the 1984 Olympic Games in Los Angeles. (The team was coached by Field Hockey Hall of Famer **Vonnie Gros.**) In addition to playing in national and international competition, Anders also coached. As head coach at Old Dominion, she long held the most impressive win-loss record of any field hockey program. Her teams won four NCAA Division I titles, three of them consecutively (1982–84).

Karin Loewen Haag, Athens, Georgia

Andersen, Astrid Hjertenaes (1915–1985)

Norwegian writer and one of the foremost postwar poets. Born on September 5, 1915, in Horten, Norway; died on April 21, 1985. Author of 14 poetry col-

lections, including De ville traner *(1945) and* Samlede dikt *(1985).*

In the post-World War II era, Astrid Andersen emerged as a prolific, acclaimed poet. A Norwegian author of verse and short prose, as well as translations from English and German, she penned 14 collections of poetry in a career that spanned more than 40 years. From her first book (*De ville traner*, 1945) to her last (*Samlede dikt*, 1985), she used her interest in the visual arts to create an imagery in words that was called her strongest poetic gift. Andersen, who traveled extensively in the United States, died four months shy of her 70th birthday.

Andersen, Dorothy Hansine

(1901–1963)

American pathologist and pediatrician who discovered and named the hereditary disease cystic fibrosis. Born Dorothy Hansine Andersen in Asheville, North Carolina, on May 15, 1901; died in New York, New York, on March 3, 1963; only child of Hans Peter and Mary Louise (Mason) Andersen (a descendant of Sir John Wentworth, colonial governor of New Hampshire, and of Benning Wentworth, for whom the town of Bennington, Vermont was named); graduated from Saint Johnsbury Academy, 1918; graduated from Mount Holyoke College, 1922; graduated from Johns Hopkins Medical School, 1926; interned at Strong Memorial Hospital in Rochester, New York; received M.D. degree from Columbia University, 1935; never married; no children.

By the time Dorothy Hansine Andersen reached the age of 19, both of her parents had died and she could not claim a single close relative. Even so, she graduated from Mount Holyoke College and set her sights on a medical career. Living and working according to her own dictates and often flaunting convention, Andersen would leave an indelible mark on the field of pediatric medicine.

While still in medical school at Johns Hopkins University, Andersen had two research papers published in *Contributions to Embryology*. After graduation in 1926, she taught anatomy for a year before beginning an internship in surgery at Strong Memorial Hospital in Rochester, New York. Denied both a residency in surgery and an appointment in pathology because she was a woman, Andersen took a position in the department of pathology at the College of Physicians and Surgeons at Columbia

University. There she began research on the relationship of the endocrine glands to the female reproductive cycle. In 1930, she was appointed an instructor in pathology, and, in 1935, received her M.D. degree.

𝒟orothy 𝒜ndersen

From Columbia, Andersen moved to Babies Hospital at the Columbia-Presbyterian Medical Center, where as a pathologist she researched congenital heart defects in infants. Studying cardiac embryology and anatomy by analyzing infants' hearts with various defects, she later shared her expertise with the pioneers in open-heart surgery. By 1950, the innovative training program she devised, utilizing her collection of heart defects as illustrations, was mandatory for all pediatric heart surgeons at Babies Hospital, and was also presented in seminars at other hospitals.

In 1935, Andersen's work found new direction with the discovery of lesions in the pancreas of a child who had died of celiac disease. Exhaustive research into medical literature and autopsy files for similar cases finally produced a clear picture of a previously unrecognized disease, which she named cystic fibrosis. In 1938, she presented a paper on her findings at a joint meeting of the American Pediatric Society and the Society for Pediatric Research. She later received the E. Mead Johnson Award for her discovery.

Andersen went on to research methods for diagnosing cystic fibrosis and search for a way to save young patients from what, at that time, was almost certain death. Using self-acquired skills as a chemist and a clinical pediatrician, she mastered techniques for obtaining duodenal fluid and analyzing its enzymes, which ultimately allowed her to diagnose the disease. She published a number of papers during the 1940s on treating respiratory tract infections in cystic fibrosis and on the genetics of this hereditary disease. Her research group also developed a simple, definitive test to diagnose the disease, which replaced the more complicated one she had pioneered.

In her personal life, Andersen was a controversial figure. With hair and clothing usually askew, a cigarette dangling permanently from the corner of her mouth, she eschewed prescribed feminine behavior and enjoyed canoeing, swimming, skiing, and hiking. She did much of the work at her farm in the Kittatinny range of northwest New Jersey with her own hands, adding a chimney and fireplace, replacing the roof, and building some of the furniture. Although not formally associated with any feminist organizations, she fought for professional equality and spoke out forcefully against sex discrimination.

In 1952, when she was named chief of pathology at Babies Hospital, her colleagues were split in their loyalties. Some were almost fanatical in their devotion, citing her outstanding teaching skills and the support she provided for research projects. Detractors criticized her disregard for convention, her lack of personal grooming, and the untidy condition of her laboratory. Controversy aside, in 1958, Andersen became a full professor at the College of Physicians and Surgeons. In 1959, she published her last paper on cystic fibrosis in a new category of patients— young adults. Formerly, all patients of the disease had died in childhood. Her final years also included more research on cardiac malformations.

Andersen's numerous honors included the Borden Award for research in nutrition, a citation for outstanding performance from Mount Holyoke College, and the distinguished service medal of the Columbia-Presbyterian Medical Center. She died of lung cancer in New York City on March 3, 1963.

SOURCES:

Olsen, Kirsten. *Remember the Ladies.* Pittstown, NJ: Main Street Press, 1988.

Sicherman, Barbara, and Carol Hurd Green, eds. *Notable American Women: The Modern Period.* Cambridge, MA: The Belknap Press of Harvard University Press, 1980.

Barbara Morgan, Melrose, Massachusetts

Andersen, Greta (1927—)

Danish long-distance swimmer. Born in Copenhagen, Denmark, on May 1, 1927.

Won the gold medal in the 100-meter freestyle relay in London Olympics (1948); holder of 24 national titles and four European championships; repeatedly beat men in long-distance swimming; elected to the International Swimming Hall of Fame (1969).

Though her father taught gymnastics, Greta Andersen enrolled in swimming school when she was a teenager. Soon she was a national champion, easily qualifying for the 1948 Olympics in London, where she won the gold medal in the 100-meter freestyle relay. (Her Danish teammate **Karen-Margrete Harup** took the 100-meter backstroke and was runner-up in the 400-meter freestyle.) Not long after the games, with a time of 58.2, Andersen set a world record for the 100 meters that would stand for seven years.

In 1950, she came to the United States, eventually becoming a swimming instructor in California. After she retired from indoor-pool races, Andersen began to enter long-distance meets. Though several men arrived ahead of her in the 1956 Salton Sea competition, she was the only woman to swim the 10½ miles, finishing in 4 hrs. and 25 min. The following year, Andersen decided to cross the English Channel with 23 other swimmers; she was one of only two who completed the swim.

Noting that in long-distance swims she usually placed second to a man, she was determined to take first. In 1958 she did just that, defeating 27 swimmers in the 26 miles along the coast of Guaymas, Mexico. She swam the English Channel again, arriving ahead of four men, with a time of 11 hrs. and 1 min. In 1958, she swam 18-mile Lake St. John in Quebec with a time of 8 hrs. 17 min., beating all comers. She also crossed Catalina Channel twice, swimming the 19 miles over in 10 hrs. 49 min., with a total time of 26 hrs. 53 min. In 1959, she swam the English Channel a third time. She also swam from the U.S. mainland to Catalina in 11 hrs. 7 min., breaking *Florence Chadwick's record. In 1962, Andersen swam across Lake Michigan, a distance of 50 miles, further than any long-distance swimmer had gone. During her long-distance career, Greta Andersen beat every male she competed against at least once.

Karin Loewen Haag, Athens, Georgia

Andersen, Lale (1910–1972)

German singer whose recordings of "Lilli Marlene" and "Never on Sunday" made her one of the 20th century's best-known recording artists. Born in Bremerhaven, Germany, in 1910; died in 1972.

Born in Bremerhaven, Germany, Lale Andersen was a talented singer who became a moderately successful cabaret performer. She traveled the circuit, appearing in small clubs throughout Germany and Central Europe. One song, "Lilli Marlene," recorded by Andersen in 1939, propelled her to international fame and would shape the whole of her life, though the song was not successful when it was originally released.

Hans Leip was a lyricist who had a longterm affair with **Lilli Freud Marlé** (a niece of Sigmund Freud), who inspired him to write this song. Leip merged his lyrics with a tune composed by Rudy Link. When the song went nowhere, Leip coupled the lyrics with a waltz composed by Norbert Schulze, which caught perfectly the melancholy mood that was settling over wartime Europe. Initially, however, Lale Andersen's 1939 Electrola recording of the song was ignored.

In 1941, German forces conquered Yugoslavia and set up a military radio station in Belgrade. One of the few German records on hand was Lale Andersen's recording of "Lilli Marlene," which the station's music director played frequently. Within days of being broadcast, this recording became a super-hit, as German soldiers in Radio Belgrade's broadcasting range requested repeat performances. Lale Andersen was not pro-Nazi; in fact, the Nazi minister of propaganda and public enlightenment, Dr. Joseph Goebbels, had expressly forbidden broadcasts of her recordings because she had a reputation of being openly critical of the regime. But Goebbels was forced to swallow his personal animosities and allow broadcasts to continue because her performances were so popular that they buoyed German military morale in a time of increasing defeats.

Allied troops, too, picked up German broadcasts, and soon "Lilli Marlene" was as well known among Allied soldiers as among their German counterparts. During World War II, everyone hummed this "enemy tune," whose lyrics were translated into more than 40 languages. The anti-Nazi émigré *Marlene Dietrich performed the best-known version of the song. "Lilli Marlene" became a shared wartime experience for women and men who fought and died on both sides.

After the war, Lale Andersen sank back into obscurity. For some years, her career was in eclipse, a second hit song forever eluding her. Then in 1960, she recorded the theme from *Never on Sunday*, a poorly funded film made in Greece, which starred *Melina Mercouri. It was a smash hit both as a movie and as a song. Mercouri became an international star, and Lale Andersen was back on top after years of obscurity. In 1961, Andersen won the Eurovision Song Contest. Her autobiography was published in 1972, the year she died. Two films about "Lilli Marlene" were made, one released in 1950, the other, a movie by Rainer Werner Fassbinder, was released in 1982.

SOURCES:

Andersen, Lale. *Der Himmel hat viele Farben: Leben mit einem Lied*. Stuttgart: Deutsche Verlags-Anstalt, 1972.

"Lale Andersen," *The Times* [London], August 30, 1972, p. 14.

Marlé, Anne. "Lilli Freud Marlé," *Jewish Chronicle* [London], No. 6575, April 28, 1995, p. 27.

John Haag, Associate Professor of History, University of Georgia, Athens, Georgia

Anderson, Anna (1902–1984)

Impersonator of Russia's Grand Duchess Anastasia, who maintained until her death that she had survived the execution of the family of the last tsar. Name variations: mistakenly, Anastasia; allegedly, Franziska Schanzkowskia; Anna Anderson Manahan. Born in 1902; died in Charlottesville, Virginia, in 1984; married John E. "Jack" Manahan (a retired university lecturer who backed her case for a decade); identity probably that of Franziska Schanzkowskia, the daughter of Polish peasants.

Two years after the murder of Russia's royal family, a one-time Polish factory worker was rescued from a suicide attempt in a Berlin canal and brought to a German mental hospital. At first, she refused to give her name. After learning of the rumor that 17-year-old **Anastasia**, youngest daughter of Russia's Tsar Nicholas II and Empress *Alexandra Feodorovna, had escaped the execution of her family in July 1918, the patient began to call herself Anna Anderson and declared she was the surviving grand duchess. She would hold to this claim for the rest of her life.

The possibility was kept alive because the bodies of only three of the tsar's four daughters were ever identified among those found in the royal family's mass grave, and many Russian exiles continued to believe her. In 1970, a high court in Germany refused to acknowledge any validity to Anna Anderson's claim, and she died in 1984. In September 1994, scientists used DNA tests to compare her remains with those from the family of Anastasia and confirmed that Anderson was an impostor. Said exiled Russian prince Nicholas Romanov: "I am certain at the end of her life she believed in her own story, and in a confused way she forgot her own life. But history is brutally effective in its solutions, and brutally simple."

Anderson, Anne (1874–1930)

British-Argentinean illustrator of children's books. Born in 1874; died in 1930; married Alan Wright (a painter), with whom she collaborated.

During the height of her career, Anne Anderson was one of the most popular illustrators for children, following in the tradition and style of *Jessie M. King and Charles Robinson. Accomplished in both black-and-white line drawing and watercolor, she also was successful as a greeting-card designer.

Raised in Argentina, Anderson married the painter Alan Wright in 1912, and they collaborated on a number of children's books including, *The Busy Bunny Book* (1916), *The Bold Sportsmen* (1918), *The Cuddly Kitty* (1926), and *The Podgy Puppy* (1927). They often worked on the same picture at the same time. On her own, Anderson wrote and illustrated *The Funny Bunny ABC* (1912) and *The Patsy Book* (1919). She also illustrated such children's classics as **Ethel Eliot**'s *The House Above the Trees* (1921), **Agnes Herbertson**'s *Sing-Song Stories* (1922), **Madeleine Barnes**' *Fireside Stories* (1922), Charles Kingsley's *The Water Babies* (1924), Hans Andersen's *Fairy Tales* (1924), *Johanna Spyri's Heidi* (1924), and *The Old Mother Goose Nursery Rhyme Books* (1926).

Barbara Morgan, Melrose, Massachusetts

Anderson, Caroline Still (1848–1919).

See Zakrzewska, Marie for sidebar.

Anderson, Doris (1921—)

Canadian journalist, novelist, and editor of the magazine Chatelaine. *Born Doris Hilda McCubbin on November 10, 1921, in Calgary, Alberta, Canada; daughter of Thomas and Rebecca (Laycock) McCubbin; educated at the University of Alberta; married David Anderson (a lawyer), on May 24, 1957 (divorced 1972); children: three sons, Peter, Stephen, and Mitchell.*

Selected works: Two Women *(1978);* Rough Layout *(1981);* The Unfinished Revolution: The Status of Women in Twelve Countries *(1991). Editor of the magazine* Chatelaine *from 1958 to 1977.*

Born and raised in Western Canada, Doris Anderson was educated in public schools, then attended the University of Alberta, graduating in 1945. Though she had begun publishing in magazines at the age of 16, her first job came the year after her graduation, as a journalist for *Star Weekly*. She then worked as a copywriter for a publishing company until 1951, when she joined the staff of *Chatelaine*, a magazine of fashion and opinion for women. By 1958, she was the magazine's editor, a position she would hold for

18 years, through her marriage to and divorce from David Anderson and the birth of their three sons.

In 1977, she left *Chatelaine* and worked for a brief period as president of the Canadian Advisory Council on the Status of Women. Her disappointment with the literary heroines available to women inspired Anderson's first novel *Two Women* (1978). After another novel, *Rough Layout*, in 1981, she turned her attention to nonfiction. Her interest in the status of women throughout the world led to the writing of *The Unfinished Revolution*, an examination of the personal, professional, and cultural places of women in 12 countries.

Crista Martin, Boston, Massachusetts

Anderson, Elizabeth Garrett
(1836–1917)

First British woman doctor and founder of the New Hospital for Women, the first hospital in England to be staffed entirely by women, and dean of the London School of Medicine for Women, England's first women's medical school. Name variations: Elizabeth Garrett. Born on June 9, 1836, in London, England; died on December 17, 1917, in Aldeburgh, England; second daughter of Newson Garrett (a successful merchant) and Louisa Dunnell Garrett (a housewife); attended Miss Browning's School for Girls, London, 1849–51; studied medicine privately and at various hospitals in Britain, 1860–65; received MD degree from the Sorbonne, 1870; married James Skelton Anderson (a successful ship owner and businessman), on February 9, 1871; children: Louisa Garrett Anderson; Margaret Skelton Anderson; Alan Garrett Anderson.

Moved to Aldeburgh, Suffolk, England (1841); attended lectures by Elizabeth Blackwell, an American doctor, and resolved to pursue a medical career (1859); passed examinations for London Society of Apothecaries, allowing her to practice medicine in Britain, and became the second woman (after Blackwell) listed on the British Medical Register (1865); helped found the Women's Suffrage Committee and opened a dispensary for women and children in London (1866); became first woman to receive an MD degree from the Sorbonne and became one of the first two women to be elected to the newly established London School Board (1870); opened the New Hospital for Women, the first hospital in Britain staffed entirely by women (1872); elected to the British Medical Association (1874); helped found the London School of Medicine for Women, the first medical school for women in Britain, and served as a lecturer and board member for the school (1874), and, as its dean (1883–1902); elected mayor of Aldeburgh, becoming the first female mayor in Britain (1908); published numerous articles on women in medicine, education for girls, and various medical subjects in publications such as The Edinburgh Review, The British Medical Journal, and The Times of London (1867–1910).

On March 2, 1859, the crowd filling the Marylebone Hall in London eagerly awaited the first in a series of lectures on "Medicine as a Profession for Ladies" to be delivered by the celebrated *Elizabeth Blackwell, an American and the first woman doctor of modern times. For one young woman in the audience, however, Blackwell's talk would provide more than an evening of informative entertainment. Inspired by the lecture, Elizabeth Garrett, searching for a meaningful occupation to divert her from an idle life as a wealthy merchant's daughter, made the momentous decision to pursue a career in medicine. After many years of struggle and study, marked by rebuffs from the medical establishment and from virtually every British university and medical school, Garrett became the first British female doctor, opening the field for the thousands of women who followed.

Although born in London, Garrett grew up in the small coastal town of Aldeburgh in Suffolk, England, where her family moved when she was five. She was the second child of **Louisa Dunnell Garrett**, a devoutly religious housewife, and Newson Garrett, a merchant who started his career as a pawnbroker and gradually amassed a small fortune from his shipping enterprise. The young Elizabeth's education was typical for the mid-Victorian period, when girls were expected to acquire a smattering of accomplishments (such as needlework and singing), marry young, and settle down to raise a large family, with no thought of higher education or a career. For several years, her mother taught Elizabeth and her older sister **Louisa** at home. When Elizabeth was ten, the family, by then prosperous, hired a governess whom, according to family legend, Elizabeth and Louisa teased mercilessly. The two then attended Miss Browning's School for Girls in London where they received solid training in writing and the French language. After a brief trip abroad and a visit to the famous Crystal Palace Exhibition in London, Elizabeth returned to Aldeburgh in 1851 to assist with housekeeping duties and supervision of her brothers and sisters.

Victorian girls were not expected to strive for academic achievements—indeed, the colleges

Elizabeth Garrett Anderson (from a painting by John Singer Sargent, 1901).

and universities of England were closed to women. Nor could an active and intelligent young woman of the middle class pursue a career; it was considered disgraceful for women to work outside the home. The only occupation open to respectable ladies was to serve as a governess, an underpaid and often degrading employment undertaken only in cases of dire financial need. Thus, like thousands of Victorian girls, Elizabeth Garrett seemingly had no choice after the completion of her brief formal education but to live quietly with her parents, awaiting the inevitable marriage proposal. Garrett later wrote of her years as a dutiful daughter, "I was a young woman living at home with nothing to do in what authors call 'comfortable circumstances.' But I was wicked enough not to be comfortable. I was full of energy and vigour and of the discontent which goes with unemployed activities."

The years after 1851 were not completely idle, however. Garrett attempted to round out her uneven education, studying on her own and reading widely. On Sunday evenings, she held informal "Talks on Things in General" for her younger siblings in which she discussed current political topics. Garrett's own growing sense that women must play a larger role in the wider world may have rubbed off on the youngsters during these sessions, for several followed in their older sister's footsteps as pioneers for women's rights. *Millicent Garrett (Fawcett, 1847–1929) became the preeminent leader of the women's suffrage movement in Britain and the president of the National Union of Women's Suffrage Societies. Agnes and her cousin Rhoda Garrett became the first female interior decorators in Britain, thus opening another career to women. Alice followed Elizabeth onto the London School Board as one of the first women to hold public office. And Sam, the youngest brother, grew up to be an attorney who worked vigorously for women's admission to the legal profession.

It is indeed far more wonderful that a healthy woman should spend a long life in comparative idleness, than that she should wish for some suitable work.

—Elizabeth Garrett Anderson, with tongue in cheek

Perhaps the most important event of these otherwise quiet years in Aldeburgh was Garrett's meeting with *Emily Davies, a young woman six years her elder. Davies was passionately committed to expanding educational and professional opportunities for women. (Indeed, she later founded Girton College, Cambridge, one of the first women's university colleges in England.) The two young women became fast friends, and Davies was to prove instrumental in Garrett's struggle to enter the medical profession. Davies proffered encouragement, along with level-headed, if a bit conservative, advice, and much practical assistance.

Elizabeth Garrett and Emily Davies were not the only people in England in the 1850s who believed that women must enter into a wider sphere of employment. In London, a group of women known as "The Ladies of Langham Place," after the location of their organization's offices, advocated women's academic and professional advancement through their magazine, *The Englishwoman's Journal,* and through their activities with the Society for Promoting the Employment of Women. Garrett's sister Louisa, now married and living in London, was actively involved with this group of pioneering women and Emily Davies, too, had friends among the Langham Place circle. Through *Barbara Bodichon, one of the founders of the Langham Place group, Gar-

rett secured an invitation to the fateful lecture by Elizabeth Blackwell and received a personal introduction to the famous medical woman.

Although immediately impressed by Dr. Blackwell, Garrett felt no immediate calling to enter the medical profession herself. She only knew that she needed to find some worthwhile employment, preferably an occupation that would also lead to greater opportunities for other women as well. It was only after many serious discussions with her close friend Davies that Garrett decided the medical field should be opened to women and that she would be the one to attempt it. She later wrote:

> It seemed to us that the duty of ministering as a physician does to the care of women and children would be work not unsuitable to a woman, and also that it was work they ought to be free to take up if they chose. Naturally neither of us knew much of the details of medical education, nor did we realize how long and sustained an effort would be needed before our end could be reached.

The general public, including Garrett's parents, were not quite so receptive to the idea of female doctors as Elizabeth and her friend had naively assumed. In mid-Victorian England, Ray Strachey noted in an early history of the women's emancipation movement, "the idea of women doctors was revolting to every sense; it was indecent, dangerous, and brazen, as well as new." Louisa Garrett vehemently objected to her daughter's novel career plans, citing the "disgrace" that it would bring down on the family. Indeed, it was not until Elizabeth achieved worldwide professional recognition in the medical field, as well as considerable financial success, that Mrs. Garrett became reconciled to her daughter's unorthodox lifestyle. Newson Garrett, too, initially resisted his daughter's entreaties to pursue medical studies, exclaiming that he found the whole idea of women doctors "disgusting." He abruptly changed his mind, however, after every prominent London physician canvassed by Garrett and his daughter refused to assist Elizabeth in her medical studies simply because she was a woman. Newson Garrett became so incensed that his beloved daughter had been rejected that he resolved not only to lend moral support to her efforts but also to provide her with whatever financial assistance she needed. Thereafter, Elizabeth Garrett's father was one of her most active and ardent supporters.

In 1860, following the advice of friends, Garrett began a six-month training period as a nurse at Middlesex Hospital in London. Only a few years earlier, the heroic work of *Florence

Nightingale and her "lady nurses" in the Crimean War had made nursing a respectable occupation for middle-class women like Garrett. Indeed, many people had suggested that Garrett abandon her plans to open the medical profession to women and become a nurse instead. (Garrett's rather flippant response to those who suggested the nursing option was that she preferred "to earn a thousand, rather than twenty pounds a year.") She entered Middlesex Hospital with no intention of becoming a nurse; rather, she hoped to prove that she had the physical, mental, and emotional stamina to withstand the rigors of medical practice. After three short months, Garrett had adapted so successfully to the hospital routine that she became, in effect, an unofficial medical student, receiving tutoring in various subjects from several doctors at the hospital and attending them on their rounds. However, Garrett's intelligence and medical skill made several male students uneasy, and they petitioned to eject Garrett from the medical training program. Fearing the loss of revenue if its male students withdrew, the powers of Middlesex Hospital reluctantly complied.

Garrett now faced a perplexing dilemma if she wished to continue her medical studies. Like many other occupations, medicine was becoming increasingly professionalized in the 19th century, with practitioners seeking to heighten their status by regulating training and professional conduct. Under the Medical Act of 1858, Britain set up a register of qualified doctors and established minimum criteria for registration as a medical professional. Although the Act did not specifically bar women from entering the profession, it did not require either that women be admitted to universities or medical schools offering the necessary training or that they be allowed to sit for the qualifying examinations to establish their credentials. Additionally, although Elizabeth Blackwell had successfully presented her American medical diploma to be listed on the British Medical Register, the Medical Council had subsequently decided to exclude holders of foreign medical degrees from registration. Garrett realized that she would need to obtain a British medical degree in order to practice medicine in the United Kingdom.

After an exhaustive search, Garrett discovered that the only medical examining body that could not legally exclude her from its examinations by virtue of her sex was the Society of Apothecaries, perhaps the least prestigious of the several examining boards. In order to meet the prerequisites laid down by the Apothecaries'

Society, however, Garrett would need further medical training. Her efforts were stymied by the wholesale ban on women in institutions of higher learning. After the difficulties at Middlesex Hospital, no other hospital medical school would accept her. The University of London refused to accept women, claiming that it was forbidden under their charter, and the University of St. Andrew's in Scotland also rebuffed her attempts to enroll. When all options seemed to be closed off, the Society of Apothecaries finally agreed to recognize a private course of lectures, which Garrett easily arranged with medical men friendly to the cause of women doctors. In 1865, she passed the examination of the London Society of Apothecaries and was listed on the British Medical Register. The examiners were apparently quite relieved that they had not been compelled to rank the examination candidates because, they later explained, they would have been forced to put Elizabeth Garrett first.

Garrett then set to work to employ her hard-won skills and professional recognition. Although she certainly felt qualified to treat patients of both sexes, she realized that accepting male patients could create a scandal and damage the cause of female medical practitioners. In 1866, therefore, with the financial assistance of her father, Garrett opened a dispensary for women and children in a poor area of London. This small office, which would eventually grow into a hospital for women, was to remain the heart of Garrett's medical work until her retirement from practice. The services provided by Garrett—as well as the fact that she was a woman ministering to other women—clearly answered a need in the community. In its first five years of operation, Garrett's dispensary served 40,000 patients.

Garrett had realized from the beginning of her endeavors that opening the medical profession to women was merely one facet of the campaign to integrate women more fully into the public and professional life of Britain. Although busy with her medical practice, she also continued to work for women's emancipation in other areas. In 1866, she was one of the founding members of the Women's Suffrage Committee, established to secure the vote for women on the same terms as men. She and her good friend Emily Davies personally handed a massive women's suffrage petition to John Stuart Mill, an ardent supporter of women's rights, for presentation in Parliament (where it was defeated). In 1870, with certain municipal positions opened to women, Garrett ran for election to the London School Board, winning by a large majority.

Despite her active involvement in other facets of the women's movement, Garrett had not abandoned her role as pioneer in the medical profession. Her qualification to practice medicine through the Apothecaries' Society did not entitle Garrett to claim the designation "Medical Doctor" or "M.D." Although acknowledging that all avenues to the M.D. designation were closed to women in Britain and that a foreign M.D. degree would not be recognized by the British medical profession, Garrett nonetheless decided to sit for the M.D. exams at the Sorbonne in Paris, believing that "it would command more respect than the license from the [Apothecaries' Society] alone." Without taking time away from her busy medical practice to attend additional classes, Garrett took the series of examinations necessary for the degree in 1869 and 1870 and became the first woman to receive an M.D. degree from the Sorbonne.

While pursuing her medical studies, she had neglected the social life normal for a woman of her position in Victorian England. She had received a marriage proposal from Henry Fawcett, a Cambridge economics professor who later became a member of Parliament and Cabinet official. Because Fawcett was blind, Garrett felt that she would have to abandon her own career in order to support his professional ambitions. She reluctantly refused his offer and Fawcett subsequently married Garrett's younger sister, Millicent. In 1869, however, through her volunteer work for a children's charity hospital in London's poor East End, Garrett met a fellow hospital board member, James Skelton Anderson, a businessman and shipping entrepreneur. Garrett and Anderson worked together on the board to ensure the efficient administration of the children's hospital and the proper qualifications of its practitioners. The two became good friends, and Anderson served as Garrett's campaign chair in her run for the London School Board.

When Anderson and Garrett became engaged late in 1870, however, many of her supporters, including her father, lamented the match, believing that Garrett would be forced to abandon her medical work once she was a married woman. Neither Garrett nor her fiance, however, felt that Garrett's marriage should compromise her professional role in the least. Shortly after her engagement, Garrett wrote to her sister Millicent Fawcett:

> I do hope my dear you will not think I have meanly deserted my post. I think it need not prove to be so and I believe that [James] would regret it as much as I or you would. I am sure that the woman question will never be solved in any complete way so long as marriage is thought to be incompatible with freedom and with an independent career and think there is a very good chance that we may be able to do something to discourage this notion.

Garrett's marriage, and the birth of three children in 1873, 1874, and 1877, did not hamper her continuing work in medicine and in opening the profession to women. In 1872, she established the New Hospital for Women in London, an innovative institution staffed entirely by women in all its medical and administrative positions. In 1874, her professional accomplishments were recognized by her election to the British Medical Association, in which for many years she was to be the sole female member.

Securing the necessary education for a medical career continued to prove difficult for women, despite Garrett Anderson's pioneering work. In 1869, *Sophia Jex-Blake and six other women had been allowed to matriculate at the University of Edinburgh Medical Faculty. However, the facilities available to women were still slender in relation to the growing demand for female medical education. Critics of women doctors raised numerous objections to women's medical studies, arguing that women students would distract the men from their work, that lecturers would not be able to discuss the details of human anatomy in mixed company without offending propriety, and that any serious intellectual work for women would impair their reproductive abilities.

In 1874, in response to the continued resistance to the admission of women to British medical schools, Jex-Blake and others proposed the founding of a medical school exclusively for women. Garrett had previously argued that, so long as British institutions barred female medical students, women should pursue their medical education abroad in countries that recognized a woman's right to medical training, although women with foreign degrees would not legally be allowed to practice medicine in Britain. Realizing, however, that the movement that was so important to her would be damaged by any signs of internal division, Garrett agreed to support the new school, which became The London School of Medicine for Women. She served on the school's board and as a lecturer and in 1883 was elected dean, a position she held until her retirement in 1902. Under her leadership, the school greatly expanded its facilities and the size of its student body, contributing to the increasing respectability of the female medical professional. One of Garrett's daughters, Louisa, joined the growing contingent of women doctors, receiving her MD degree in 1900. To her mother's satisfaction, **Louisa Garrett Anderson** was among the first contingent of medical women to volunteer for work in France at the outbreak of World War I.

After her retirement, Garrett continued to work for women's educational and professional advancement, writing articles on women in medicine and on the benefits of regular physical exercise and more rigorous academic training for girls. Her interest in women's rights continued throughout her later years as well. For many years, Garrett supported the work of her sister, Millicent Fawcett, in pursuing constitutional reform to secure the suffrage for women. In 1908, however, believing that constitutional reform was proceeding too slowly, Garrett joined the radical suffragist organization, the Women's Social and Political Union (WSPU), and was actively involved in their suffrage marches and other activities. She resigned from the WSPU in 1911 when their tactics became more militant and violent. A pioneer for women to the end, Garrett was elected mayor of her girlhood hometown of Aldeburgh in 1908, becoming the first female mayor in Great Britain. During the last three years of her life, Garrett's mental capabilities slowly declined. She died on December 17, 1917, at her home in Aldeburgh.

SOURCES:

Anderson, Louisa Garrett. *Elizabeth Garrett Anderson.* London: Faber and Faber, n.d.

Manton, Jo. *Elizabeth Garrett Anderson.* London: Methuen, 1964.

Mitchison, Naomi. "Elizabeth Garrett Anderson," in *Revaluations.* 1931 (reprinted by Haskell House, 1976).

SUGGESTED READING:

Rubinstein, David. *A Different World for Women.* Columbus: Ohio State University Press, 1991 (biography of Anderson's younger sister, Millicent Garrett Fawcett, that includes information on the youth of the Garretts).

Strachey, Ray. *The Cause.* London: G. Bell, 1928.

COLLECTIONS:

Correspondence and papers mainly in the Anderson Library, Jersey, Great Britain, and the Fawcett Library, London, Great Britain.

Mary A. Procida,
University of Pennsylvania, Philadelphia, Pennsylvania

Anderson, Elizabeth Milbank

(1850–1921)

American philanthropist. Born Elizabeth Milbank in New York, New York, in 1850; died in 1921; married Abram A. Anderson (a portrait painter), in 1887.

With her brother Joseph Milbank, Elizabeth Milbank Anderson made liberal contributions to Teachers College and Barnard College ($3 million), to the Children's Aid Society of New York ($500,000), and to many other social-welfare agencies. She also established the Milbank Memorial Fund, with interest income to be used to "improve the physical, mental, and moral condition of humanity." Milbank Memorial Chapel at Teachers College and Milbank Hall at Barnard are named in honor of Elizabeth and her brother.

Anderson, Erica (1914–1976)

Austrian-born American filmmaker who influenced the medium of documentaries. Born Erika Kellner in Vienna, Austria, on August 8, 1914; died in Great Barrington, Massachusetts, in September 1976; daughter of Eduard Kellner and Ilona Rosenberg Kellner; married Dr. Lawrence Collier Anderson (a British physician), in June 1940 (divorced 1942).

Made documentaries of important 20th-century figures such as *Grandma Moses, Henry Moore, and Albert Schweitzer.

Erika Kellner was born in Vienna, Austria, on August 8, 1914, to Eduard and **Ilona Rosenberg Kellner**. Despite the economic chaos that descended upon the Habsburg Empire after its dissolution in 1918, Erika grew up in a home that was emotionally and economically stable. Her father was a physician who wanted both of his daughters to choose medicine as their careers. Erika's older sister Anita took pre-medical courses but terminated her studies when she married a doctor. Meanwhile Erika became interested in photography after she received her first camera. When the depression hit Central Europe in the early 1930s, she decided not to attend the university. Instead, she worked in a photography studio by day and took advanced classes in photographic theory and practice at night.

Throughout the 1930s, Nazism became increasingly dominant in Austria, and in 1936 Erika's parents immigrated to the United States while she moved to London. Working in picture galleries, she continued to take photographs in her free time. In London, Erika, who by now had changed the spelling of her name to Erica, met and married Dr. Lawrence Collier Anderson, a British physician, in June 1940.

While Erica was in London, her father, no longer young, experienced great difficulties in resuming his medical career in New York City.

Her parents wrote often about their desperate financial and emotional situation, and Erica grew increasingly concerned about them. Indifferent to the danger of an Atlantic Ocean filled with German U-Boats, she left her husband and joined her parents in New York City.

As soon as she was settled in New York, Anderson enrolled in the New York Institute of Photography to continue her film studies. At the same time, she took a job with a small firm, United Specialists, quickly proving to her superiors just how multitalented she was. Within a year, she earned enough to support her parents. Anderson was divorced in 1942, not long after her new career was established. For the next three years, she produced documentary films for United Specialists, a shoestring firm with an impressive name but little else. She not only shot films, but also researched them, wrote the scripts, and then matched, cut, and edited them for release. Anderson was also the first cinematographer to work in color at the firm. The documentaries she created during this period include: *They Need Not Die* (for the American Red Cross), *The Capitol* (for the Coordinator of Inter-American Affairs), and *Animals in the Service of Man* (for the American Humane Society).

In 1944, Anderson resigned from United Specialists to do freelance work, a courageous and perhaps reckless decision, as she had no capital. She quickly landed an important job producing a documentary film on the Girl Scouts of America. During the next few years, her commissions included films of General Dwight Eisenhower's visit to New York, the Duke of Windsor's stay in Washington, D.C., and a travelogue of Pennsylvania for the Standard Oil Company. Anderson also produced a documentary of the exhibit of the works of the British sculptor Henry Moore at New York's Museum of Modern Art, which was released in 1947 as *Henry Moore, Sculptor.* Another major work was the 1948 film *French Tapestries Visit America,* which documented an exhibition of magnificent tapestries at New York's Metropolitan Museum of Art and the Art Institute of Chicago. This work was particularly effective because early French music was used for the soundtrack.

In 1947, Erica Anderson decided to interview *Grandma Moses, the famous folk painter who had produced her canvases only in extreme old age. This color film, with script and narration by Archibald MacLeish, was finally released to rave reviews in 1950. Over the next few years, Anderson combined her bread-and-butter work of producing films for corporate and industrial sponsors with more artistically oriented projects. One of the most important of these was a documentary about the controversial Swiss psychologist and student of myths, Carl Gustav Jung. Anderson showed Jung working at his studio in Bollingen and with patients in Zurich.

In 1952, Anderson interviewed Dr. Albert Schweitzer (1875–1965) both in his home province of Alsace and in his mission hospital in Lambaréné, French Equatorial Africa (modern-day Republic of Gabon). At first, Schweitzer was reluctant to participate in a film project, but Anderson's Viennese charm worked its magic on the venerable medical missionary. During five trips to Africa, Anderson collected a large body of film that was released in January 1957. This documentary received generally positive reviews, although some critics noted that the quality of color was often uneven. Anderson's visual biography was a reverential work that revealed the essence of Schweitzer's powerful yet aloof personality.

While in the process of filming Schweitzer in his jungle hospital, Anderson published a collection of photographs that was also well received by critics. Some of her conversations with him, as well as recordings of him playing the organ, were released at the time by Columbia Records. Writing in the New York *Herald Tribune,* Herbert Kupferberg praised Anderson for capturing the "sunlight and shadows of the strange world" where Schweitzer built his jungle hospital complex. Anderson's work came to international attention because of her Schweitzer documentary. Later, when Schweitzer was criticized as a racist who harbored colonial attitudes toward the natives, her films began to be seen as apologies for Schweitzer's medical and cultural paternalism and faded from view. Schweitzer brought modern medical care to large numbers of people who had previously lived and suffered without it, and in recent years his contributions have begun to be reassessed in terms of the times in which he lived and worked. A comparable reassessment of the film achievements of Erica Anderson has yet to take place.

Erica Anderson never again found a subject comparable to Albert Schweitzer to film. She moved from New York City to the Berkshires in 1965. She died at her home in Great Barrington, Massachusetts, in September 1976, having made significant contributions to the evolution of the modern documentary film.

SOURCES:
Anderson, Erica. *The World of Albert Schweitzer.* NY: Harper and Brothers, 1955.
———. *The Schweitzer Album.* NY: Harper & Row, 1965.

"Anderson, Erica (Collier)," in *Current Biography 1957*. NY: H.W. Wilson, pp. 15–17.

Ennis, Thomas W. "Erica Anderson, 62, a Film Maker and Schweitzer Associate, Is Dead," in *The New York Times Biographical Service*. September 1976, p. 1223.

John Haag, Associate Professor of History, University of Georgia, Athens, Georgia

Anderson, Ernestine (1928—)

American jazz singer. Born in Houston, Texas, on November 11, 1928.

Starting out in the 1940s with the bands of Russell Jacquet and Johnny Otis, Ernestine Anderson had her first hit in 1947 while singing with Shifty Henry's band. She then worked with Lionel Hampton (1952–53) and recorded with **Gigi Gryce** (1955). While on a 1956 tour of Sweden with Rolf Ericson's group, Anderson recorded "Hot Cargo" with Harry Arnold's band. Three years later, she was named New Star in *Downbeat*'s critic's poll. After that, little was heard of Anderson for a decade, except her voice on the soundtrack of Sidney Poitier's movie *The Lost Man*. She had moved to England in 1965, returning in 1976 to sign with Concord Records. Her albums include: *Hot Cargo* (1958), *Live from Concord to London* (1976), *Hello Like Before* (1976), *Never Make Your Move Too Soon* (1980), and *Be Mine Tonight*. In 1984, with her own quartet, she recorded the album *When the Sun Goes Down*.

Anderson, Eugenie Moore

(1909–1997)

U.S. ambassador to Denmark who was the first American woman to achieve a high diplomatic posting. Born Helen Eugenie Moore on May 26, 1909, in Adair, Iowa; died in Red Wing, Minnesota, on April 14, 1997; daughter and one of five children of the Reverend Ezekiel Arrowsmith Moore (a Methodist minister) and Flora Belle (McMillen) Moore (a former school teacher); attended Stephens College (Columbia, Missouri), Simpson College (Indianola, Iowa), and lastly, Carleton College (Northfield, Minnesota); married John Pierce Anderson, on September 9, 1930; children: Johanna and Hans Pierce.

In 1949, when Eugenie Anderson was sworn in as U.S. ambassador to Denmark—the first woman in the history of her country to achieve that high diplomatic rank—the press was not yet accustomed to dealing with women of worldly accomplishment. An article for the New York *Post* began: "Mrs. Anderson was a pretty brunette as a college girl, and she's still a pretty brunette as a diplomat." The most widely published news photograph of Anderson showed her standing at a kitchen stove. In an attempt to make the best of this less-than-official likeness, another article suggested that instead of picturing Anderson in the kitchen, it might be more accurate to envision her as a smartly dressed hostess, in whose living room "scientists, physicians, lawyers, artists, educators and semanticists congregate."

Helen Eugenie ("Genie") Moore, a minister's daughter, was raised in parsonages in various Iowa cities and was influenced early by her father's and grandfather's political discussions. Her mother nurtured her considerable musical talent with piano lessons that began before she turned six. In 1925, Moore graduated from high school with hopes of becoming a concert pianist and taught piano for a year before going to work for the telephone company to put herself through college. At Carleton College, she met young University of Chicago and Yale art student, John Pierce Anderson. They married in 1930, at the end of her junior year, and settled in her husband's family estate, "Tower View," located on a 400-acre farm in Red Wing, Minnesota, where their two children were born. Anderson returned to school to pursue yet another interest, child psychology, and later taught nursery school. Her earliest experience in public office was as the first woman member of the Red Wing school board.

When a trip to Germany in 1937, part of a European tour, gave Anderson a glimpse of what she described as "the totalitarian state in action," she began an intensive study of international relations. She became a member of the board and of the speakers' bureau of the Minnesota League of Women Voters, and, for six years, gave speeches to various area groups on the United Nations, the Baruch plan for atomic energy control, and on other aspects of American foreign policy, including the Atlantic Pact and the Marshall Plan. As a delegate to the Democratic State convention in 1944, her efforts in unifying Democratic and Farmer-Labor parties gained her appointments as Democratic-Farmer Labor Party chair for Goodhue County, party chair for the First Congressional District, and member of the State central committee. Her organizational skills and ability as a persuasive speaker won her state recognition, and, in 1946 to 1947, she was instrumental in the expulsion of Communist elements from the combined Democratic-Farmer Labor Party. By that time, she concurrently held posts as vice-chair of the central committee and member of its Minnesota executive committee. As one of the organizers of Americans for Democratic Action, Anderson served as state chair and member of the national executive board during 1947 to 1948.

In 1948, as Minnesota's delegate-at-large to the Democratic National Convention, Anderson became a Democratic National Committeewoman and campaigned for the reelection of President Harry S. Truman and for election of Hubert H. Humphrey to the Senate. Humphrey said of her, "Everyone respects her judgment, responds to her suggestions for action."

After his election, Humphrey urged the appointment of Anderson to an appropriate post, and her nomination as U.S. ambassador of Denmark was announced by President Truman on October 12, 1949. She served in that post from 1949 to 1953, often using a bicycle as a mode of transportation as most Danes did. In 1951, she signed a treaty between the United States and Denmark announcing agreements of friendship, commerce, and navigation, becoming the first woman to sign such a pact.

From 1955 to 1960, Anderson served as chair of the Minnesota Commission for Fair Employment Practices, and later under President John F. Kennedy was named U.S. envoy to Bulgaria (1962 to 1965), the first American woman to function as chief of a mission to an Eastern European country. While there, she openly defied the secret police. Anderson served as U.S. representative on the Trusteeship Council of the United Nations from 1965 to 1968, when she was appointed special assistant to the secretary of state. Leaving that post in 1972, she served as a member of the Commission on the Future of Minnesota until her retirement.

SOURCES:

O'Neill, Lois Decker, ed. *The Women's Book of World Records and Achievements.* NY: Anchor Press, 1979.

Rothe, Anna, ed. *Current Biography 1950.* NY: H.W. Wilson, 1951.

Barbara Morgan, Melrose, Massachusetts

Anderson, Evelyn (1907–1994).

See Baker, Josephine for sidebar.

Anderson, Evelyn N. (1909–1977)

German-born British journalist. Name variations: Lore Seligmann. Born Lore Seligmann on May 13, 1909, in Frankfurt am Main, Germany; died in London, England, on January 8, 1977; daughter of a prosperous bourgeois family; married Paul Anderson, in 1934.

Joined the German Communist Party (KPD, 1927), but was quickly disillusioned by its rapidly developing spirit of Stalinism and intellectual regimentation; joined the Social Democratic Party (SPD, 1929), but noted the near-paralysis of the SPD leadership when confronted by a growing and increasingly aggressive Nazi movement; following a brief attempt to launch a career in journalism in Berlin (1932–33), emigrated to Great Britain (1933); became a successful journalist in London (late 1930s), taking part in the propaganda war against Nazi Germany (1940s).

Evelyn N. Anderson was a highly regarded journalist who made an impressive transition from one language and culture to another. Born May 1, 1909, on the eve of World War I, into a middle-class German-Jewish family in the commercial city of Frankfurt am Main, Anderson would witness many of the most dramatic events in modern European history. From 1927 through 1932, she studied economics and sociology at several German universities and at the Sorbonne, ending her studies in 1932 with a doctorate in political science. A lifelong commitment to social justice led her to Marxism, first to its dogmatic, revolutionary Communist version, then to a more flexible and democratic Social Democratic variety.

Despite her solidly bourgeois origins, Anderson developed a deep, intuitive understanding of German working-class history and aspirations. As a woman, a socialist, and a Jew, she had multiple reasons to hate the Hitler dictatorship in her native Germany and join in the European struggle against Fascism. After working briefly in the anti-Nazi underground in Berlin, she fled to Great Britain in May 1933. In 1934, she married Paul Anderson, a fellow refugee from Nazi Germany.

Her journalistic activities in London attempted to warn the English-speaking world of the imminent threat of Nazi aggression. During World War II, Anderson worked as an editor and announcer for anti-Nazi radio broadcasting stations in England. The first of these stations, "Sender der Europäischen Revolution," employed her from the fall of 1940 through September 1941. Though financed by the British government, this station called on the German people to overthrow Hitler and replace his regime with a revolutionary socialist society led by the working class. Starting in 1942, she worked as an announcer for the German-language broadcasts of the BBC beamed at Nazi

Germany. Her history of the German working class, *Hammer or Anvil* (London 1945; German edition published 1948), was a well-received critical overview of successes and failures that helped to explain the collapse of German democracy and the rise of Nazism.

During World War II, she was a member of the circle of advisors around the British Labour Party leader Aneurin Bevan. She contributed articles to the newspaper *Tribune* from 1943 through 1952, and also worked as BBC editor for Eastern European questions from 1953 until 1976, as well as making BBC broadcasts from Germany in 1946, 1952 and 1963. Evelyn Anderson died in London on January 8, 1977.

SOURCES:

Pütter, Conrad. *Rundfunk gegen das "Dritte Reich": Ein Handbuch.* Munich: K.G. Saur, 1986.

Röder, Werner, and Herbert A. Strauss, eds. *Biographisches Handbuch der deutschsprachigen Emigration nach 1933.* 4 vols. Munich: K.G. Saur, 1980.

Walk, Joseph. *Kurzbiographien zur Geschichte der Juden.* Munich: K.G. Saur, 1988.

John Haag, Associate Professor of History, University of Georgia, Athens, Georgia

Anderson, Ivie (1904–1949)

African-American jazz singer. Born in Gilroy, California, on July 10, 1904; died in Los Angeles, California, on December 28, 1949; received vocal training at the local St. Mary's Convent; studied with **Sara Ritt** in Washington, D.C.

Ivie Anderson's first professional booking was at Tait's Club in Los Angeles. Before becoming a featured vocalist, she toured as a dancer with Fanchon and Marco, a revue that then starred *Mamie Smith. In 1925, Anderson worked at the Cotton Club, then toured with the "Shuffle Along" revue. After an Australian tour with the Sonny Clay revue, she teamed up with bands led by Earl Hines and Paul Howard, before a highly successful stint with Duke Ellington from February 1931 to August 1942. An elegant stylist, Anderson recorded "It Don't Mean a Thing," "I Got It Bad," "Mood Indigo," and "Solitude." When chronic asthma put a crimp in extensive tours, she opened her own restaurant, the Chicken Shack, in Los Angeles and continued entertaining on the West Coast. Anderson also appeared in the Marx Brothers' movie *A Day at the Races.*

Anderson, Judith (1898–1992)

Australian-born actress who was considered one of the greatest of her day, though the popular acclaim enjoyed by many of her contemporaries eluded her. *Name variations: first performed as Frances Anderson and finally as Judith Anderson in 1923; Dame Judith Anderson as of 1960. Born Frances Margaret Anderson-Anderson in Adelaide, Australia, on February 10, 1898; died in Santa Barbara, California, on January 3, 1992; daughter of James Anderson-Anderson and Jessie Margaret Saltmarsh; attended Rose Park School (1908–12) and Norwood School (1913–16); married Benjamin Harrison Lehman (a professor of English at the University of California), on May 18, 1937 (divorced, August 23, 1939); married Luther Greene (a producer-director), on July 11, 1946 (divorced, June 36, 1951); no children.*

Awards: The Donaldson Award for acting, the New York Critics' Award, and the American Academy of Arts and Sciences Award for the best diction—all three for her performance as Medea (1948); honorary doctorates from Northwestern University (1953) and Fairfield University in Connecticut (1964); Emmy awards for her two television performances as Lady Macbeth (1954, 1961); made Dame Commander of the British Empire (1960); the Dickinson College Art Award (1960).

Made stage debut in Australia (1915); arrived in America (1918); appeared in New York as Elise Van Zile in The Cobra *(1924); as Dolores Romero in* The Dove *(1925–26); as Antoinette Lyle in George Kelly's* Behold the Bridegroom *(1927); as Anna Plumer in* Anna *(1928); replaced Lynn Fontanne as Nina Leeds in Eugene O'Neill's* Strange Interlude *(1928–29), and with tour (1930–31); as Lavinia Mannon in O'Neill's* Mourning Becomes Electra *(1931), and with tour (1932); as the Unknown One in Pirandello's* As You Desire Me *(1932); as Helen Nolte in* Conquest *(1933); as Valerie Latour in* The Drums Begin *(1933); made first film* Blood Money *(1933); as Mimeas Sheller in* The Female of the Species, *as Savina Grazia in* The Mask and the Face, *as The Woman in Clemence Dane's* Come of Age *and as Lila in* Divided by Three *(all 1934); as Delia Lovell in* **Zoe Akins'** The Old Maid *(1935); as Gertrude opposite John Gielgud in* Hamlet *(1936); first appearance on radio as Mary in Maxwell Anderson's "Mary of Scotland" (1937); made her London debut at the Old Vic as Lady Macbeth opposite Laurence Olivier (1937); as the Virgin Mary in* Family Portrait *(1939); as Gertrude opposite Maurice Evans in* Macbeth; *as Clytemnestra in Robinson Jeffers'* The Tower Beyond Tragedy *and as Olga in Chekhov's* The Three Sisters *(all 1942); toured with USO entertaining troops in Hawaii, New Guinea, and the Caribbean (1942–45); starred in* Medea *(1947), and with tour (1948–49); as Clytemnestra in* The

Tower Beyond Tragedy *at American National Theater and Academy (ANTA, 1950); in Berlin with* Medea *(1951); in a revival of* Come of Age *at the N.Y. City Center (1952); toured with Raymond Massey and Tyrone Power in a dramatic reading of* John Brown's Body, *and appeared as Gertrude Eastman-Cuevas in* **Jane Bowles**' In the Summer House *(both 1953); second radio debut (April 1954); appeared in* Medea *in Paris in the Salute to France Festival (June 14, 1955); toured as Miss Madrigal in* The Chalk Garden *(1956–57); as Isabel Lawton in* Comes a Day *(1958); performed in* Medea *at the Sarah Bernhardt Theater in Paris and at the Old Vic in London (1960); toured in scenes from* Macbeth, The Tower Beyond Tragedy, *and* Medea *(1961–63); as Alice Christie in* Black Chiffon *at the Sombrero Playhouse, Phoenix, Arizona (1964); toured Australia in excerpts from* Medea *and* Macbeth *(1966); as Clytemnestra in the* Oresteia *at the Greek Theater, Ypsilanti, Michigan (summer, 1966); as Elizabeth the Queen at the New York City Center (1970); played Hamlet at Carnegie Hall (January 1971).*

Filmography: Blood Money *(1933);* Rebecca *(United Artists, 1940);* Forty Little Mothers *(MGM, 1941);* Lady Scarface *(RKO, 1941);* Free and Easy *(MGM, 1941);* Kings Row *(Warner Bros., 1941);* All Through the Night *(WB, 1941);* Edge of Darkness *(WB, 1943);* Stage Door Canteen *(United Artists, 1943);* Jane Eyre *(20th Century-Fox, 1944);* Laura *(20th Century-Fox, 1944);* And Then There Were None *(Fox, 1945);* The Diary of a Chambermaid *(UA, 1946);* Specter of the Rose *(Republic, 1946);* The Strange Love of Martha Ivers *(Paramount, 1946);* The Red House *(UA, 1947);* Pursued *(WB, 1947);* Tycoon *(RKO, 1950);* The Furies *(Par., 1950);* Don't Bother to Knock *(Fox, 1952); (as Queen Herodias)* Salome *(Columbia, 1953);* The Ten Commandments *(Par., 1956);* Cat on a Hot Tin Roof *(MGM, 1958);* Cinderfella *(Par., 1960);* A Man Called Horse *(1970);* Inn of the Damned *(Australian 1974);* Star Trek III: The Search for Spock *(1984).*

Television: "Black Chiffon" *(ABC, April 1954);* "Macbeth" *("Hallmark Hall of Fame," NBC, Nov. 28, 1954);* "Yesterday's Magic," *("Elgin Hour," NBC, Dec. 14, 1954);* "Caesar and Cleopatra" *("NBC Showcase," Mar. 4, 1956);* "The Cradle Song" *("Hallmark Hall of Fame," NBC, May 6, 1956);* "The Circular Staircase" *("Climax," CBS, June 21, 1956);* "The Clouded Image" *("Playhouse 90," CBS, Nov. 7, 1957);* "Abby, Julia and the Seven Pet Cows" *("Telephone Time," CBS, Jan. 7, 1958);* "The Bridge of San Luis Rey" *("Dupont Show of the Month," CBS, Jan. 21, 1958);* "Medea" *("Play of the Week," WNTA,*

Oct., 12, 1959); "The Moon and Sixpence" *(NBC, Oct. 30, 1959);* "Macbeth" *("Hallmark Hall of Fame," NBC, Nov. 20, 1960);* "The Chinese Prime Minister" *(1974); and as a regular on the soap opera* "Santa Barbara" *(1984).*

One of the greatest actresses of the 20th century and arguably the greatest tragedienne of the American theater, Judith Anderson was born Frances Margaret Anderson-Anderson in Adelaide, Australia, on February 10, 1898. The youngest of four children, she was the daughter of an English mother, Jessie Margaret Saltmarsh, and a Scottish father, James Anderson-Anderson. Her father had made a fortune in silver mining but, after gambling most of it away, he deserted the family when Frances was five; her mother was forced to open a grocery store to support her children. Nevertheless, Jessie was able to finance a good private-school education for her daughter, who attended both the Rose Park and Norwood schools (1908–12, 1913–16). Anderson, who had a good voice, decided to become a singer after attending a performance of the great Australian singer Dame *Nellie Melba, but when she failed at this (as well as at her attempt to master the piano) she turned to elocution, receiving Australia's highest award for recitation. She made her stage debut in Julius Knight's production of *A Royal Divorce* at the Theatre Royal, Sidney, 1915. Thereafter, she toured Australia in Knight's company in such plays as *Monsieur Beaucaire, The Scarlet Pimpernel, The Three Musketeers*, and *David Garrick*, and later in Australia and New Zealand with E.J. Tait in *Turn to the Right*.

In 1917, carrying a letter of introduction to Cecil B. DeMille, Anderson and her mother set out for Hollywood. After four months of seeking work in films without success, they moved on to a shabby, furnished room in New York, where Jessie made a meager living as a seamstress. Both skipped meals so that Anderson could seek work. As a result of malnutrition, she fell victim to the influenza epidemic of 1918 but recovered sufficiently to resume job hunting. Still weak, Anderson was discovered when she paused to rest in an agency waiting room by the manager of the **Emma Bunting** Fourteenth Street Stock Company, where she was immediately engaged to play supporting roles at $40 a week. Following a year of successful performances, she was promoted to major roles at $50 per week and afterwards went on tour with the famed actor William Gillette in *Dear Brutus* (1920), later playing leading roles with stock companies in Boston and Albany, New York (1921). She made her Broadway debut under the name Frances Anderson as Mrs. Bellmore with Arnold Daly in *On the Stairs* (Sept. 25, 1922).

Dissatisfied with her stage name and still an unknown, Frances Anderson became Judith Anderson, first appearing under this name in *Crooked Square, Peter Weston,* and *Patches* (1923). Acclaim first came to her as Judith Anderson with her performance as Elise Van Zile in Martin Brown's *The Cobra* (1924), a poor play that she turned into an unforgettable evening in the theater. Following this critical success, An-

derson returned to Australia, where she toured in *The Cobra, Tea for Three,* and as Iris March in Michael Arlen's *The Green Hat,* one of the most popular plays of her day.

Returning to New York, Anderson appeared in several plays, including *The Dove* (1926), which cemented her reputation as a young actress to be watched. She replaced *Lynn Fontanne** as Nina Leeds in Eugene O'Neill's *Strange Interlude* (1928–29), and then starred as Lavinia Mannon in his *Mourning Becomes Electra* (1931), a long and solemn reworking of the

Judith Anderson

Oresteia trilogy of Aeschylus, in which she toured for much of 1932. Both of these appearances in O' Neill productions confirmed her as a major actress on the New York stage. By 1935, she was considered by many drama critics to be the finest actress of the day.

In 1933, Judith Anderson made her motion-picture debut in the unlikely role of a gangster's moll in the film *Blood Money*. Though she admitted that she hated making movies, unlike many Broadway performers she made no pretense of despising either Hollywood or her work in motion pictures and, after a gap of seven years, she continued to make films for the rest of her career. Of all her film roles, there is no question that her meatiest, the one for which she is best remembered, was that of Mrs. Danvers, the villainous housekeeper in *Daphne du Maurier's Rebecca*, directed by Alfred Hitchcock, a performance that earned her a seven-year contract at MGM and enabled her to purchase her first real home in 1940, a house with three acres in Pacific Palisades, after 30 years of living out of a trunk. In her more than two dozen films, no matter how small the part, Judith Anderson never gave a bad or even poor performance except, perhaps, in *Cat on a Hot Tin Roof* (in which, some say, she was unbelievably miscast). She is remembered well as the malevolent aunt in the opening scene of *The Strange Love of Martha Ivers* (1946), as the disfigured and discarded older woman in *The Furies* (1950), as Queen *Herodias in the otherwise undistinguished *Rita Hayworth vehicle *Salome* (1953), and as the nurse in Cecil B. DeMille's remake of *The Ten Commandments* (1956), in which she finally got to perform under the director to whom she had first applied for a job as a film actress in 1917.

> [She is] perhaps the greatest tragedienne of our time.
>
> —John Mason Brown

One of Anderson's greatest assets as an actress was her voice—a deep, throaty instrument of great power; another was her striking appearance. Anything but beautiful, with her hard rugged face, and large, irregular nose, she was nonetheless a striking woman, with blue eyes and light brown hair, her face punctuated by an interesting mole high on the right side of her chin just below the corner of her mouth. Although only 5'4", she could command magnificence of stature and appearance whenever the part called for them. She remarked in 1924: "I wish I had a beautiful face. An unattractive

woman has to work doubly hard. Some tell me I have a mobile, interesting face which would never grow monotonous."

Something of a clothes horse on the stage (on the order of *Gloria Swanson, another diminutive actress who could get away with clothes no other woman could wear), Judith Anderson was very attentive to her appearance as a part of the creation of the characters that she played; she changed her hair style for every role and, in the film *Salome*, she positively luxuriates in the trappings of an oriental half-barbarous queen. At the end of a performance, Anderson, not for an instant stepping out of character, was remarkable for her long, deep, solemn bows.

In 1934, Anderson appeared as The Woman in *Clemence Dane's *Come of Age*, which she later revived more than once and which she always considered her favorite role. Then in 1936, still only 38, she played Gertrude to the Hamlet of John Gielgud, himself but six years her junior. Although the production (with *Lillian Gish, also 38, as a rather overaged Ophelia) was criticized for its overblown sets and excessively elaborate costumes, and Anderson did not get the best reviews of her career in her first Shakespearean role, the production helped clinch Gielgud's reputation. Anderson and Gielgud would appear together again and remain good friends throughout their lives.

The following year, she made her London debut playing Lady Macbeth to critical acclaim opposite Laurence Olivier in his production of *Macbeth*, thereby establishing herself as a performer on the English stage in a role that she repeated opposite Maurice Evans in New York in 1941. (Writing of her television performance of the same role in 1960, *New York Times* critic James Gould called it "nothing short of a masterpiece . . . alternatingly vibrant, calculating, cruel, regal and pitiful.")

Between the two Shakespearean productions, Anderson appeared in New York in the extremely difficult role of the Virgin Mary in *Family Portrait* (1939), for which she received considerable acclaim. The New York Macbeth was followed by the role of Clytemnestra in Robinson Jeffers' reworking of Aeschylus' *Agamemnon*, a verse play that he titled *The Tower Beyond Tragedy*. She also played Olga in *Katharine Cornell's revival of Chekhov's *The Three Sisters* (1942). As a result of her work up to this time, Anderson was cited by George Jean Nathan—the acerbic and most difficult-to-please New York drama critic—as second only to *Helen Hayes as the greatest actress in the American theater (second place being accorded to her only because of her inability to excel in comedy). By now, the Second World War was raging, and, though hardly an actress known to young soldiers, Anderson toured with the USO, entertaining troops in Hawaii, New Guinea, and the Caribbean.

As a person, Anderson was remarkably different from the roles she played. Anything but solemn in her daily life, she was lively, vivacious, and humorous. Speaking of herself and her home in 1941, she said: "I'm a sleepy, lazy girl, and I love the earth. I love the space. I love the sunshine. I love the trees. Eucalyptus, mimosa, pepper trees, daphne, vegetables—marvelous!"

Judith Anderson was the favorite actress of the American poet Robinson Jeffers. Beyond question, her greatest triumph occurred in his adaptation of Euripides' great tragedy *Medea*, which he wrote expressly for her to perform. Directed by John Gielgud (who, at Anderson's urging, played Jason to less than critical ac-

claim), *Medea* opened to rave reviews at the National Theater in New York on October 20, 1947. The play, never performed on the modern stage since *Fanny Janauschek had toured with a German troupe a century before, ran for an astonishing six months (214 performances) and toured the United States from coast to coast for the next eight months, winning extraordinary praise. Anderson's performance electrified Broadway, and she was heaped with honors for her acting, with the General Federation of Women's Clubs calling her "the First Lady of the Theater." Of this play, a critic for *Theater Arts* said, "It seems to cry out with the anguish of the world in torment," and, a month later, **Rosamond Gilder**, after classing Judith Anderson with Edmund Kean, *Rachel, Tommaso Salvini, and *Sarah Bernhardt, said of her performance in the same magazine, "Her interpretation evokes more terror than pity." The *New Republic* called it, "a full cavalry charge across an open plain."

Speaking of her interpretation of this, her greatest, role, Anderson remarked:

From the movie Rebecca, starring Judith Anderson and Joan Fontaine (20th Century-Fox, 1940).

I see her as a great barbarian, purely animal, all her reactions fiercely primitive in contrast to the smooth and cultured Greeks. . . . I love the part because it is such a challenge. Lady Macbeth with her few telling scenes is simple compared to Medea.

After Medea's New York triumph, Judith Anderson took the play to Paris and Berlin, and then to Australia with the Elizabethan Theater Trust, afterwards performing the role at the famed Old Vic in London (1960) as well as that of Madame Arkadina in Chekhov's The Seagull with the Old Vic at the Edinburgh Festival in Scotland. Never having renounced her Australian citizenship, that same year she was eligible for and received the order of Dame Commander of the British Empire, the feminine equivalent of a knighthood, from *Elizabeth II as a part of the queen's annual Birthday Honors (July 12, 1960). Thereafter, she was referred to as Dame Judith Anderson.

Meanwhile, she appeared on tour in scenes from her great plays (Macbeth, Medea, and The Tower Beyond Tragedy) in 1961–63, and then as Alice Christie in Black Chiffon at the well-known Sombrero Playhouse in Phoenix, Arizona. Returning to her native Australia, Anderson did dramatic readings at Elder Hall in her hometown of Adelaide (March 1966); she then starred as Clytemnestra in a revival of Euripides' Oresteia trilogy at the Ypsilanti Greek Theater in Michigan; and played *Elizabeth I in Maxwell Anderson's Elizabeth the Queen in New York at the City Center, both performances in 1966. Finally, as her theatrical career drew to a close, she ventured a comparison with Sarah Bernhardt by becoming the second woman ever to attempt the role of Hamlet (Santa Barbara, 1968; Chicago, 1970; Carnegie Hall in New York, 1971). She regretted that she had not been the first.

Judith Anderson made her radio debut as early as 1937, when she performed in "Mary of Scotland" on the prestigious "Lux Radio Theater" and first appeared on television in "Black Chiffon" on ABC in April 1954. She received an Emmy Award for her performance as Lady Macbeth on ABC in November of the same year, and a second one for a repeat of the performance in 1961. All of these, as well as her many other brief television appearances, serve as a better record of Anderson's greatness than her film roles, in which she was always a supporting actress, often in undistinguished roles. Besides her Emmys and other awards, in 1985, 70 years after her debut in Australia, the Lion Theater on West 42nd Street was renamed The Judith Anderson Theater in her honor.

In 1974, at age 76, Anderson appeared again in Medea, reviving the play in 1982 for a final time with Zoe Caldwell in the title role and Anderson, now 84, performing the less demanding role of the nurse but nevertheless achieving great acclaim; The New York Times called her performance "harrowing." This was her last Broadway appearance. In 1984, she appeared regularly on the TV series "Santa Barbara." Though Anderson never formally retired, these performances in her mid-80s would be her last.

As an actress, there is no question that Judith Anderson excelled in tragic roles and performed least successfully in light plays and comedies. As time went on, she ceased to appear in anything but serious drama and played, in films, one sinister or malevolent role after another. As early as 1924, she remarked: "I love emotional roles because they permit unleashing of one's feelings. A character can be complex and difficult but she must be plausible." That she never achieved the public fame of Helen Hayes or Katharine Cornell was largely due to her less outgoing nature but also partly because she never drew around herself the cloak of glamour that was expected of a Broadway star in her time. Although she tackled the roles of Gertrude, Medea, and Lady Macbeth, she never essayed many of the other great female roles.

As to Anderson's attitudes towards her art, she commented during an interview at the end of her career in 1984: "We live, we breathe, we experience, we die; we love, we hate, we experience beauty and tragedy, and we find it in the parts we play. . . . [W]hatever I do I am passionate about."

Up at dawn when making a film, she was at the studio by 6:45 and stayed as late as 7:00 in the evening. Her recreations were riding, reading, music, and gardening. Highly intelligent (all the men in her life were highly educated intellectuals), she never got around to writing her memoirs. In her later years, she lived in Santa Barbara when she was not on tour or working on location. Rose Hadleigh devoted an entire chapter to her in the book Hollywood Lesbians, but Anderson was twice married, first to Benjamin Harrison Lehman, a professor of English at the University of California, on May 18, 1937 (they divorced on August 23, 1939), and, second, to the producer-director Luther Greene on July 11, 1946 (whom she divorced on June 36, 1951). Apart from her two husbands, she maintained a long-term relationship with John Broadus Watson, founder of the behaviorist school of psychology, who was 20 years her senior.

Judith Anderson fell ill in the autumn of 1991, lingered a few weeks, and finally died in her home in Santa Barbara, on January 3, 1992. Ninety-three at the time of her death, she had been an actress for just under 70 years. Judith Anderson will be remembered as one of the great ladies of the American theater.

SOURCES:

"Judith Anderson," in *Current Biography*. NY: H.W. Wilson, 1941.

Hadleigh, Rose. *Hollywood Lesbians*. NY: Barricade Books, 1994.

"Portrait as Mary in Family Portrait," in *Theater Arts Monthly*. May 1939.

"They Stand Out from the Crowd," in *Literary Digest*. March 2, 1935.

Wallsten, R. "Shakespeare on the Jungle Circuit," in *Collier's*. December 9, 1944.

SUGGESTED READING:

Brown, John Mason. *Dramatis Personae*. NY: Viking, 1963.

Young, William C. *Famous Actors and Actresses on the American Stage*. Vol. I, 1975.

Robert H. Hewsen, Professor of History,
Rowan University, Glassboro, New Jersey

Anderson, Lucille (1897–1948).

See Bogan, Lucille.

Anderson, Lucy (1797–1878)

English pianist and famous English concert artist of her era. Born Lucy Philpot on December 12, 1797, in Bath, England; died in London on December 24, 1878; married George Frederick Anderson (1793–1876).

Performing Hummel's B minor Concerto, Lucy Anderson was the first woman pianist to play at a concert of the Royal Philharmonic Society in London. While her husband George Frederick Anderson served as Master of the Queen's Musick from 1848 to 1870, Lucy taught piano to Queen *Victoria and her children. Anderson had a long and successful career, appearing the last time at the Royal Philharmonic concerts in 1862 as soloist in Beethoven's Choral Fantasia. A contemporary critic noted her "delicate touch and legitimate style."

John Haag, Athens, Georgia

Anderson, Margaret Carolyn (1886–1973)

American founder, editor, and publisher of the avant-garde literary magazine the **Little Review** *between 1914 and 1929. Born Margaret Carolyn Anderson on November 24, 1886, in Indianapolis, Indiana; died from emphysema on October 15, 1973, at Le Cannet,* France; *daughter of Arthur Aubrey (an electric railway executive) and Jessie (Shortridge) Anderson; attended high school in Indianapolis, and two-year junior preparatory classes at Western College in Miami, Ohio; lived with Georgette Leblanc (the French singer, 1922–41); never married; no children.*

Moved frequently with family throughout Midwest; book critic of the Chicago Evening Post *(1912); made editor of* The Continent *and founded* Little Review *in Chicago (1914); moved magazine to New York (1916); began serialization of James Joyce's* Ulysses *in the* Little Review *(1918); convicted, along with editor Jane Heap, on obscenity charges for publishing* Ulysses *(1921); published final issue of the* Little Review *in Paris (1929).*

Selected works: The Fiery Fountains *(1951);* The "Little Review" Anthology *(1953);* The Unknowable Gurdjieff *(1962);* My Thirty Years' War *(1969);* The Strange Necessity *(1969).*

Margaret Carolyn Anderson reached the pinnacle of her career during and immediately following World War I—a period that brought with it a distrust of foreigners, the Espionage Act of 1917, and a dread of communism that became known as "the red scare." In this atmosphere of national angst, Anderson and others like her turned to art as a defense against a world in chaos. Out of this avant-garde movement in the American Midwest emerged a group known as the Chicago Renaissance. According to Dale Kramer, "The Renaissance had sprung from the freshness of hope and idealism and dedication which the war largely strangled." Along with Floyd Dell, Theodore Dreiser, Sherwood Anderson, and *Harriet Monroe, Kramer also includes the editor and writer Margaret Anderson among the ten figures named as the chief Renaissance makers.

Anderson's childhood was spent mostly in Indianapolis, Indiana. Born into a family of substantial means, she was the daughter of a socially ambitious mother and a charming but ineffectual father who was unable to take a stand against his wife. Jessie Anderson wanted only the finer things for her daughters, but the life of bridge games and country clubs that attracted her were never meaningful to her eldest daughter. The daughter's relationship with her mother remained strained throughout their lives, and Margaret and her two younger sisters referred to their home as "The Great Divide" because it was filled with their mother's "taunts, threats, misinterpretations and revilings."

Soon after her return home from two years at Western College in Ohio, boredom with her family's bourgeois values led Anderson to write to ⬥ **Clara Laughlin**, who conducted the "So You're Going to Paris" department at *Good Housekeeping* magazine, pleading for advice on "how a perfectly nice but revolting girl could leave home." In reply, Anderson received an invitation to meet Laughlin, and in November 1912 she headed for Chicago, accompanied by her sister Lois.

There is nothing stronger than the force of a conviction. It will drive you to success.

—Margaret Anderson

Laughlin, who was also editor of *The Continent,* a religious weekly, hired Anderson to write book reviews, and she soon found a second job reviewing for the *Chicago Evening Post* under literary editor Francis Hackett. While the sisters lived at the YWCA, Margaret never missed the Saturday night and Sunday afternoon concerts of the Chicago Symphony. In April 1913, the sisters were caught not only smoking but introducing other young women to the practice, and were forced to leave the Y; since they were also deeply in debt, they returned home.

By June 1913, Margaret Anderson was back in Chicago alone, working as a clerk at Browne's Bookstore in the Fine Arts building for eight dollars a week. Shortly thereafter, she became chief literary assistant for Francis F. Browne at *The Dial,* a literary review originally founded by Edgar Allan Poe, and began to learn about proofreading, magazine make-up, and composition.

⬥ **Laughlin, Clara E.** (1873–1941)

American author and lecturer. Born Clara Elizabeth Laughlin in New York City on August 3, 1873; died on March 3, 1941; daughter of Samuel Wilson and Elizabeth (Abbott) Laughlin; attended Chicago public schools; graduated from North Division high school; never married.

Clara Laughlin, the author of a well-known series of travel guides, also founded the Clara Laughlin Travel Services in Chicago, New York, Paris, and London. Her first book, *So You're Going to Paris* (1924), met with instant success. She followed this with travels guides for other countries, including Italy, England, France, and was a frequent contributor to magazines and newspapers. Her 1934 memoirs were appropriately entitled *Traveling Through Life.*

In 1914, when Laughlin left her position at *The Continent,* Anderson took over as literary editor, ready by this time to declare her views on the sterility of the current art scene. When she wrote a complimentary review of Theodore Dreiser's *Sister Carrie* and was lambasted by readers because she had not prefaced her observations with a disclaimer on the book's immoral content, Anderson's first reaction to the uproar was to respond, "How was I to know what is immoral?" Her next was to decide to start her own magazine.

The aim of her new publication, as she saw it, was to subvert literary oppression by filling the magazine "with the best conversation the world has to offer." It was an act born out of the kind of naive confidence she described 15 years later when she wrote in the final issue: "There was no creative opinion in Indianapolis, Indiana, in 1912. So I went to Chicago and tried to produce it, in 1914, by founding the *Little Review.*"

The same confidence allowed her to ignore issues like money, backing, and contributors. After persuading Dewitt Wing, editor of *Breeders Gazette,* to become her original financial backer by announcing she was "going to publish the best art magazine in the world," she concerned herself with its goals, about which she wrote:

> My conviction in founding the *Little Review* was that people who make Art are more interesting than those who don't; that they have a special illumination about life; that this illumination is the subject-matter of all inspired conversation; that one might as well be dead as to live outside this radiance. I was sure that I could impose my conviction by creating a magazine dedicated to Art for Art's sake.

Her slogan for the publication was, "The Little Review, making no compromise with the public taste." (Ezra Pound later wanted to change it to, "The magazine that is read by those who write the others.") In the first issue, launched in March 1914, Anderson declared its high purpose with a spirited editorial:

> If you've ever read poetry with a feeling that it was your religion, your very life; if you've ever come suddenly upon the whiteness of a Venus in a dim, deep room; if you've ever felt music replacing your shabby soul with a new one of shining gold; if, in the early morning, you've watched a bird with great white wings fly from the edge of the sea straight up into the rose-colored sun—if these things have happened to you and continue to happen till you're left speechless with the wonder of it all, then you'll understand our hope to bring them near to the common experience of the people who read us.

Contributors were not paid, but over the next 15 years the Little Review would help to change the course of American literature by introducing the world to such artists as *Amy Lowell*, *Djuna Barnes*, H.D. (*Hilda Doolittle*), *Dorothy Richardson*, Sherwood Anderson, Carl Sandburg, Vachel Lindsay, *Gertrude Stein*, Ernest Hemingway, Ezra Pound, James Joyce, and William Butler Yeats. The publication was never profitable, but it gained wide respect for its editorial willingness to take risks.

As early as May 1914, the magazine took on an anarchist tone after Anderson became acquainted with *Emma Goldman*. The radical and controversial Goldman, sent to prison for saying that "women need not always keep their mouths shut and their wombs open," eventually led Dewitt to pull his financial support, but Anderson and her magazine managed to persevere.

Choice combined at times with economic circumstance to draw Anderson into a truly bohemian lifestyle. A lack of funds as well as her sense of adventure led Anderson, in the spring of 1915, to persuade both her sisters, as well as **Harriet Dean**, Caesar Awaska, Lois' children, and their housekeeper, to move into tents with

Margaret
Carolyn
Anderson

wood floors set up on the beach at Braeside, near Lake Bluff outside Chicago. Anderson swam every morning before work, ate by campfire in the evenings, and slept under the stars at night. The *Chicago Tribune* did a full-page Sunday story with color photos of the gathering, while Sherwood Anderson, Lawrence Langner of the New York Theatre Guild, and others would frequent their camp in the evenings to extol group action and socialism, share stories, and intoxicate themselves on ideas. The camp lasted for six months before it was declared illegal and burned down by the police. "It is marvelous," Anderson wrote in her autobiography, *The Strange Necessity,* "to be more in imagination than in abundance."

In 1916, she hired ❧ **Jane Heap** to become editor for the *Little Review.* Heap was a gifted conversationalist, and their friendship developed into an intimate relationship that lasted for three years and a close professional relationship that lasted until 1922. By 1916, they had moved the magazine to New York; Anderson's infatuation with anarchism came to an end that year after an argument between Heap and Goldman. Also in 1916, Ezra Pound became the magazine's foreign editor, working out of London, and responsible for introducing both Yeats and Joyce to the *Little Review.*

In March 1918, Anderson and Heap launched a literary controversy when the *Little Review* began the serialization of James Joyce's *Ulysses.* In October 1920, John S. Sumner, secretary for the Society for Suppression of Vice, served papers on the publisher and her editor. Their conviction on an obscenity charge on February 21, 1921, resulted in a fine of $100 and a prohibition against publishing any part of *Ulysses.*

The charges focused specifically on the book's Episode XIII. According to Assistant District Attorney Joseph Forrester, quoted in a *New York Times* interview in 1921, "Some of the chief objections had to do with a too frank expression concerning a woman's dress when the woman was in the clothes described." In *Four Lives in Paris,* Hugh Ford points out that the passages deemed "obscene" were never actually read aloud during the trial, apparently because one of the judges refused to allow the material to be read in the presence of a lady—Margaret Anderson. The fact that Anderson had been the publisher of the work did not appear to be germane, in his opinion, because "she probably did not understand the 'significance' of what she was publishing." The case, which was to go to the U.S. Supreme Court, resulted in suspension of publication of the *Little Review* from 1926 until the final issue, in 1929.

Anderson, meanwhile, had met ❧ **Georgette Leblanc,** the French singer and ex-companion of the Belgian writer Maurice Maeterlinck. In 1922, Anderson moved to Paris, where the two would live together for almost 20 years, until Leblanc's death in October 1941. From the time Leblanc showed the first signs of illness with a bout of pneumonia in 1934, until she died of cancer, Anderson would see to her welfare with loving care. Of their relationship, Anderson wrote, "Someone who inspires great love gives you so much to think about that you never come to the end of your remembrances."

In 1923, after she had moved to France, Anderson turned over the editorship of the *Little Review* to Jane Heap. By 1924, Anderson, Leblanc, and Heap were all living at the institute established by the philosopher and spiritual leader George Gurdjieff at Fountainebleau-Avon. Anderson never became totally committed to his influence, and, in 1962, she would write about her faltering spiritual journey in *The Unknowable Gurdjieff.* From 1936–38, Anderson experienced a period of depression, which she would describe in her first full-length book, *The Fiery Fountains,* published in 1951. During this time, she also kept intimate ties with journalist and poet *Solita Solano, who occasionally provided her with financial help.

In June 1942, on a voyage back to America to escape the onslaught of war in France, Anderson met **Dorothy Caruso** widow of the opera star Enrico Caruso. "She was the last great friendship of my life," said Anderson, after the death of Caruso in 1955. "She was 62, young, lovely, handsome and strong; and I couldn't believe she would die." Margaret Anderson, who lived to be 82, died of emphysema on October 15, 1973, at Le Cannet, France. She was buried in Notre Dame des Anges Cemetery beside Georgette Leblanc.

Ezra Pound once described Margaret Anderson as the only editor in America who "ever felt the need of, or responsibility for, getting the best writers concentrated in an American periodical." According to her *New York Times* obituary, because of Margaret Anderson, "contemporary art had 'arrived'; for a hundred years perhaps, the literary world would produce repetitions only."

SOURCES:

Anderson, Margaret. *Forbidden Fires.* Edited and with an introduction by Mathilda Hills. Naiad, 1996.

🎵 Heap, Jane (1887–1964)

American philanthropist and publisher. Name variations: jane heap. Born in 1887; died in 1964.

Though *Margaret Carolyn Anderson founded the *Little Review,* Jane Heap doubled as cook and editor in their cramped office in the Fine Arts Building on Michigan Avenue in Chicago as well as in Greenwich Village; as a confirmed modernist, she also exerted a profound influence on the contents of the journal. When the *Review* folded in 1929, Heap was convinced they had published nothing of lasting value, except for their serialization of James Joyce's *Ulysses,* which prompted the obscenity trial of 1920. Jane Heap also presided over a small group of Gurdjieff disciples in Montparnasse in the studio of *Georgette Leblanc.

🎵 Leblanc, Georgette (c. 1875–1941)

*French opera singer and actress. Name variations: Le Blanc. Born around 1875; died in October, possibly the 26th, 1941; grew up in Rouen, France; daughter of an Italian father and Norman mother; educated by her older brother Maurice Leblanc (author of the detective novels of Arsène Lupin); married at 17 to escape her father's household; companion of Belgian poet and playwright Maurice Maeterlinck, 1895–1918; lived with *Margaret Carolyn Anderson (editor of* Little Review*), 1922–41.*

Entered a sanitarium at 18 to escape an unhappy marriage; created the role of Thaïs at the Théâtre de la Monnaie, Brussels; inaugurated the new Opéra-Comique, appearing as Carmen (December 15, 1898); appeared as Ariane in Ariane and Bluebeard *(1907); sang Mélisande in* Pélléas and Mélisande *at the Boston Opera (1912).*

Growing up in Rouen, France, Georgette Leblanc "sang madly, anything at all, provided it dealt with a broken heart." Her mother, whom she adored, died when she was 13. "Dressed for a ball," recalled Leblanc, "lighted by her jewels beneath the great chandelier, she fell dead in my arms." That same year, her only friend killed herself. After a disastrous ten-month marriage, Leblanc made her debut at Paris' Opéra-Comique and, "dazzled by my liberty," began to hold *soirées* in her studio apartment.

In 1895, she met the poet and playwright Maurice Maeterlinck (1862–1949) and was his inspiration and companion for 20 years. Leblanc fitted up an apartment at the Villa Dupont in the rue Pergolèse in Paris in what she called "Island of Walkeren" style, hired a Belgian cook, and established a brilliant salon where the great artists of the period were guests. There, and at their presbytery at Gruchet-Saint-Siméon, she entertained Octave Mirabeau, Anatole France, Rodin, Jules Renard, *Judith Gautier, *Colette, Mallarmé, Oscar Wilde, Saint-Saëns, and Rachilde (pseudonym of *Marguerite Vallette).

Though Maeterlinck wrote several of his plays for Leblanc, including *Aglavaine and Sélysette, Monna Vanna,* and *Mary Magdalene,* they agreed marriage was not for them and swore they would give each other—her favorite word—liberty. "I kept my word," Leblanc wrote, "without understanding that a man does not wish liberty that is authorized. He prefers simply to take it and is even offended if the woman doesn't mind." After their breakup and his subsequent marriage to actress **Renée Dahon** in 1919, Leblanc left for America where she remained for four years. She began living with Margaret Anderson in 1922, and their relationship would continue until LeBlanc's death in 1941. In 1932, LeBlanc published Souvenirs: *My Life with Maeterlinck* (translated from the French by *Janet Flanner.) She also adapted Maeterlinck's *The Blue Bird* into *The Children's Blue Bird.*

———. The "Little Review" Anthology. NY: Horizon Press, 1953.

———. My Thirty Years' War. NY: Horizon Press, 1969.

———. The Strange Necessity. NY: Horizon Press, 1969.

Blau, Eleanor. "Margaret Anderson dies at 82," in *The New York Times.* October 19, 1973, p. 34.

Ford, Hugh. *Four Lives in Paris.* San Francisco, CA: North Point Press, 1987.

"Improper novel costs women $100," in *The New York Times.* February 22, 1921, p. 13.

Kramer, Dale. *Chicago Renaissance.* NY: Appleton-Century, 1966.

"*Little Review* in court," in *The New York Times.* February 15, 1921, p. 4.

Sicherman Barbara, and Carol Hurd Green, eds. *Notable American Women.* Vol. IV. Cambridge, MA: Harvard University Press, 1980, pp. 21–23.

SUGGESTED READING:

Goldman, Emma. *Living My Life.* NY: Alfred A. Knopf, 1931.

Leblanc, Georgette. *La Machine à Courage.* Paris, 1947.

Scott, Thomas L., and Melvin J. Friedman, eds. *Pound/The Little Review.* NY: New Directions Books, 1988.

Carla Stoner, freelance writer in American literature, San Diego State University, California

Anderson, Marian (1897–1993)

African-American concert singer who was widely acclaimed as the world's greatest contralto in the 1930s and 1940s. Born Marian Anderson on February 27, 1897, in Philadelphia, Pennsylvania; died in Portland,

Oregon, on April 8, 1993; daughter of John Anderson (a laborer) and Anna Anderson (erstwhile school-teacher); graduated from South Philadelphia High School; married Orpheus H. Fisher (an architect), in 1943. Concert performer, 1925–65.

On Easter Sunday, 1939, some 75,000 Americans gathered at the mall in Washington, D.C., to hear a free open-air concert. Millions more listened on the radio. The performer was a prominent African-American contralto, who began with "My Country 'Tis of Thee," then moved to such works as "America," Franz Schubert's "Ave Maria," and Gaetano Donizetti's "O mio Fernando," from the opera *La Savorita*. Three spirituals were included: "Gospel Train," "Trampin'," and "My Soul is Anchored in the Lord." Overnight, Marian Anderson had become an international figure of the highest importance.

Anderson's impresario, Sol Hurok, had originally hoped to rent Washington's Constitutional Hall for the event. Its auditorium, which seated 4,000 and opened in 1929, was the city's foremost concert platform. Washington was a segregated city, but blacks could sit in a restricted section and there was no color bar for performers. Indeed, the black tenor Roland Hayes had performed there. Yet, in 1935, a new clause for performance in the hall was introduced: "Concert by white artists only." The Daughters of the American Revolution (DAR), which owned and operated the hall, sought to fudge the issue by telling Hurok that no dates were available. When, however, a rival manager subsequently asked about the very dates for which Anderson had been turned down, he was told they were open. The hall's director finally leveled with Hurok, telling him just before he slammed down the phone, "No Negro will ever appear in this hall while I am manager."

Immediately, there was public outrage. Protests were made by famous musicians, such as violinist Jascha Heifetz. America's first lady *Eleanor Roosevelt announced in her newspaper column that she was resigning from the DAR. Anderson was genuinely embarrassed by the incident:

> What were my own feelings? I was saddened and ashamed. I was sorry for the people who had precipitated the affair. I felt that their behavior stemmed from a lack of understanding. They were not persecuting me personally or as a representative of my people so much as they were doing something that was neither sensible nor good. Could I have erased the bitterness, I would have done so gladly.

Hurok and Walter White, secretary of the National Association for the Advancement of Colored People (NAACP), came up with the idea of a concert at the Lincoln Memorial. Secretary of the Interior Harold Ickes arranged the performance, which was given on April 9. Anderson had some trepidation before the event:

> I said yes, but the yes did not come easily or quickly. I don't like a lot of show, and one could not tell in advance what direction the affair would take. I studied my conscience. In principle the idea was sound, but it could not be comfortable to me as an individual. As I thought further, I could see that my significance as an individual was small in this affair. I had become, whether I like it or not, a symbol, representing my people.

So she sang on the steps of the Lincoln Memorial, while a sea of people watched from below. (A mural depicting the event was placed on a wall in the U.S. Department of the Interior.)

Four years later, in 1943, Anderson finally performed at Constitution Hall, doing so at a benefit for Chinese relief. She insisted that the DAR suspend its segregation policy for her concert. "I felt no different than I had in other halls," she later noted. "There was no sense of triumph. I felt that it was a beautiful concert hall, and I was happy to sing in it."

According to her birth certificate, Marian Anderson was born on February 27, 1897, in South Philadelphia. (Throughout her life she would give the date as February 17, 1902.) Soon two sisters were added to the family. Her father John Anderson was a loader at the Reading Terminal Market. Her mother **Anna Anderson** had been a licensed teacher in Virginia.

John Anderson died in 1912. He had suffered a head wound while working and was later found to have a tumor. Her mother, fearing it would take too long to obtain a teacher's license in Philadelphia, supported the family as a cleaning lady, laundress, and floor-scrubber in Wanamaker's department store. The family resided with Anderson's paternal grandparents, living, she later recalled, in modest dignity in a racially mixed neighborhood. "We had enough to eat and we dressed decently. We were not so poor that we had nothing, and our neighbors were in the same situation." Later in her life, she told a television audience that she had never consciously made up her mind to be a singer: "I don't know that I had to decide. It was something that just had to be done. I don't think I had much say in choosing it. I think music chose me."

Anderson's start was an early one. As a child, she later remembered, she would sit "at the table or on a little bench, beating out some sort of rhythm with my hand and feet and la-la-la-ing a vocal accompaniment." At six, she joined the junior choir of the Union Baptist Church, where her father had been a lay leader. The parish was known in the black community for its excellent musical programs. At age eight, she was already appearing in neighborhood concerts. Obviously a prodigy, she was soon billed as "the ten-year-old contralto."

Though Marian's father had bought a piano when she was about eight, the family could not afford lessons. Originally, she had a yen for the violin. As a child, she scrubbed the steps of neighbors' houses, each set of steps yielding a nickel, so as to purchase a violin at what was for her the stiff price of $3.45.

Her real strength, however, was her voice. By age 13, Anderson was admitted to Union Baptist's adult choir. She impressed the congregation's music director by learning all the parts—soprano, alto, tenor, and bass. By then Marian was experiencing the color line:

> In some stores we might have to stand around longer than other people until we were waited on. There were times when we stood on a street corner, waiting for a trolley car, and the motorman would pass us by. There were places in town where all people could go, and there were others where some of us could not go. There were girls we played with and others we didn't. There were parties we went to, and some we didn't. We were interested in neither the places nor the people who didn't want us.

Segregation really hit home for the first time when, on a railroad journey, Marian and her mother had to move to a Jim-Crow car once the train reached Washington, D.C. [Jim Crow is a term derived from the title of a song sung in a minstrel show, which denotes the practice of discrimination against blacks, as well as places for blacks only.] Another insult came when she applied for voice lessons at a Philadelphia conservatory, only to be told by the receptionist that the institution did not accept blacks.

As a student at William Penn High School, Anderson found that her vocation was music, not the regular commercial course. She transferred to South Philadelphia High School for girls, from which she graduated at age 18. Her remarkable voice gained the attention of John Thomas Butler, a distinguished black actor, who invited her to appear on his programs. Anderson's real role model, however, was black tenor

*Marian
Anderson*

Marian Anderson singing before a crowd of 75,000 at the Lincoln Memorial.

When Anderson was 19, her high school principal, Dr. **Lucy Wilson**, helped her meet Guiseppe Boghetti, who had taught many of the nation's finest concert performers. Her audition came at the end of a hard day's teaching for Boghetti. Weary of singing and singers, he found himself listening to a tall calm young woman whose rendition of "Deep River" was so moving that it made him cry. Boghetti was a stern taskmaster but permitted Anderson, who was often broke, to defer payments. She studied under his direction for many years.

When Anderson first began her tours, they centered on black colleges and churches in the South. She was accompanied by William ("Billy") King, a popular and skilled black musician who also served as her manager. Soon she was drawing $100 per concert. One initial professional effort, however, met with failure. On April 23, 1924, she gave a concert in New York's Town Hall. Not only was the event poorly attended, but critics found her voice lacking, one writing that she sang Johannes Brahms as if by rote. She was so discouraged that she considered abandoning music as a career.

Yet the seeds of her success had already been planted. Anderson had won a singing contest run by Philadelphia's Philharmonic Society. Then, in 1925, she entered the Lewisohn Stadium competition. After defeating some 300 rivals, she had the privilege of singing in the New York's amphitheater accompanied by the city's Philharmonic Orchestra. Her concert, held on August 26, was a triumph. Francis D. Perkins, critic for the *New York Herald Tribune,* called it "the voice in a thousand—or shall we say ten thousand or a hundred thousand," though Perkins did see a need for further progress concerning some lower notes, her upper register, and one incident of a harsh timbre.

In one sense, the Lewisohn concert achieved its goal. An important impresario, Arthur Judson, placed Anderson under contract. In 1926, she toured the eastern and southern United States, developing her repertoire. On March 2, 1930, she performed at Carnegie Hall, the first black female to do so. Judged *The New York Times* critic, "A true mezzo-soprano, she encompassed both ranges with full power, expressive feeling, dynamic contrast, and utmost delicacy." However, aside from invitations from various glee clubs, choirs, and black organizations, she received relatively few engagements. Finding her career stagnating and desiring further training, she went to Britain on a scholarship granted by the National Association of Negro Musicians.

Roland Hayes, whose repertoire included both classical songs and spirituals. One of her proudest moments was performing with Hayes at a Union Baptist concert. Hayes in turn was impressed by her talent. He aided her in finding engagements, for as a teenager she was already singing solo in the city's black schools and churches. Sometimes Anderson was so popular that she would appear at three different places in a single evening. She broke with tradition by not limiting herself to spirituals but by drawing upon such classical composers as Antonin Dvorak and Sergei Rachmaninoff. After many appearances, she had the temerity to ask for five dollars per performance.

Butler had sent the 15-year-old Marian to receive voice lessons from **Mary Saunders Patterson**, a prominent black soprano. Butler had also paid the fee: a dollar per lesson. Some months later, the Philadelphia Choral Society gave a benefit concert that netted her $500, thereby enabling her to study for two years with leading contralto **Agnes Reifsnyder**.

On September 16, 1930, she performed at London's Wigmore Hall. Famed composer Roger Quilter had arranged the concert.

Almost immediately after her return to the United States, Anderson journeyed to Europe again, this time on a scholarship from the Julius Rosenwald Fund. She not only sought concert engagements, thinking—quite correctly—that an African-American might be more accepted overseas, but she also desired to perfect her language skills and study the art of lieder singing. A German manager agreed for her to debut in Berlin's Bachsaal. The concert cost her $500, the last time she ever paid to perform. (A fee was standard practice for novice singers there.) Most reviews were flattering. Moreover, the Berlin concert caught the eye of Norwegian manager Rule Rasmussen and his Swedish counterpart Helmer Enwall, who immediately arranged a tour of the Scandinavian countries. (Enwall soon became her general manager throughout Europe.) Oslo, Stockholm, Helsinki, and Copenhagen—all were part of her itinerary.

In 1933, after more concerts in the United States, Anderson returned to Europe, thanks again to the Rosenwald Fund. For the next two years, her engagements took her through the Continent. From September 1933 through April 1934, she gave 142 concerts in the Scandinavian countries alone. She sang before King Gustav in Stockholm and King Christian in Copenhagen, and received a rare invitation from the 70-year-old Jean Sibelius, the great Finnish composer. He was so impressed that he dedicated his song "Solitude" to her. "The roof of my house," he said, "is too low for your voice." She appeared in Paris and London in May 1934, Belgium and Holland that summer. Her tour continued with visits to such nations as Poland, Latvia, Switzerland, Hungary, Italy, and Spain. At the finale of her first concert in Leningrad, the audience rushed to the platform, pounding on it with their fists—a Russian indication of exceptional enthusiasm. Anderson suspected that dictator Joseph Stalin might have watched her performance from a special box.

The tour concluded in the summer of 1935 with an engagement at the Mozarteum, a great international festival held in the Weiner Konzerthaus, Salzburg. It was there that Arturo Toscanini, the most prestigious conductor of his time, heard her sing. Embracing Anderson, he told her that one hears such a voice once in a hundred years. She was too awestruck upon meeting him to hear the remark, but it was overheard by a friend, **Madame Charles Cahier**, who

was an instructor at Philadelphia's Curtis Institute, and it was because of Cahier that the comment was frequently repeated.

In June 1935, the famed impresario Sol Hurok heard Anderson perform in Paris. He was so impressed that he made an exclusive contract for her American appearances. That December 30, Anderson gave her first homecoming recital at New York's Town Hall. As her foot had been fractured during the voyage home, she had to stand on one foot, which was hidden by her gown, during the entire recital; the other was in a cast. At the end of each group of songs, the curtain was lowered. The audience did not know of her injury until the intermission. Music critic Harold Taubman of *The New York Times* began his review with the words: "Let it be said at the outset, Marian Anderson has returned to her native land one of the great singers of our time. . . . She was mistress of all she surveyed."

> *Y*ours is a voice such as one hears once in a hundred years.
>
> —Arturo Toscanini to Marian Anderson

Two additional concerts were given in New York that season, both at Carnegie Hall before a capacity audience, followed by a coast-to-coast American tour. June 1936 saw her again in Vienna, performing with conductor Bruno Walter. She sang Brahms' difficult "Alto Rhapsody" without a score. Until 1938, she frequently toured Europe and Latin America. At this point, she was giving about 70 concerts a year.

In 1939, several weeks after her famous Easter concert at the Lincoln Memorial, Anderson was asked to give a solo concert at the White House. President Franklin D. Roosevelt was entertaining British king George VI and Queen *Elizabeth Bowes-Lyon. When the president said to her, "Oh, hello, Miss Anderson, you look just like your pictures, don't you?" she had one of the few attacks of stage fright in her life. By 1940, Anderson was the most popular concert singer in America, possibly the world. During World War II, she entertained troops in hospitals and bases. She would do the same during the Korean War—a hospital ship off Inchon, a hospital on shore, a facility for troops of the Republic of Korea. By 1956, she would have performed over a thousand times.

In July 1943, she married Orpheus H. ("King" or "Razzle") Fisher, an architect of Wilmington, Delaware, whom she had known as a schoolgirl. They lived on her 105-acre "Marianna Farm" near Danbury, Connecticut.

On January 7, 1955, Anderson made her debut at the New York Metropolitan Opera. Its director, Rudolph Bing, invited her to sing Ulrica in Guiseppe Verdi's *Un Ballo in Machera* (*The Masked Ball*). She was the first black to sing as a regular member of the company. Past her vocal prime, she was not pleased with her first performance, feeling she "overdid" out of sheer nervousness. "I trembled," she recalled, "and when the audience applauded and applauded before I could sing a note, I felt myself tightening into a knot." When, however, she sang the part in Philadelphia, she was satisfied.

In 1957, Anderson toured India and the Far East as goodwill ambassador, sponsored by the U.S. State Department and the American National Theater and Academy. Her instructions were: "You are not a propagandist. Just be yourself." In a CBS film of her tour, "The Lady from Philadelphia," narrator Edward R. Murrow spoke of a trip that ranged from "the thirty-eighth parallel to the Equator." It was no exaggeration. Anderson traveled 35,000 miles in 12 weeks, giving 24 concerts. During the trip, she became the first foreigner invited to speak at the Mahatma Gandhi memorial statue in India. Such honors were just beginning. A year later, President Dwight Eisenhower appointed her delegate to the United Nations Human Rights Committee. She sang at Eisenhower's 1957 inauguration as well as that of John F. Kennedy in 1961. Even at the outset of the 1960s Anderson did not slow down. In 1962, she toured Australia. In 1963, she sang at the March on Washington for Job and Freedom. Her last concert was given on April 19, 1965, Easter Sunday, in Carnegie Hall as the culmination of a yearlong farewell tour.

Anderson always conveyed an aura of dignified calm. In 1945, Arthur Bronson, a writer for the show-business journal *Variety*, described her as "a cultured, thoughtful woman, graceful, and unaffected, with deep-set eyes and a generous mouth." A year later, *Time* staffer Whittaker Chambers wrote, "Manifest in the tranquil architecture of her face is her constant submission to the 'Spirit, that dost prefer before all temples the upright heart and pure.'" Music critics frequently praised her voice for its unique combination of power, gentleness, depth, and range, some saying that it had never been duplicated. If there was any real criticism, it centered on a reedy stridency in some high notes and a "blues" quality in some lower ones—more criticized by purists than by her audiences.

Anderson never liked singing into a microphone, always preferring a live audience. She made an exception for the "Telephone Hour," a program on which she appeared regularly. Furthermore, her records were extremely popular, her rendition of Schubert's "Ave Maria" selling 750,000 by 1955. Her recordings included lieder by Schubert, Brahms, Robert Schumann, and Richard Strauss; sacred arias by Johann Sebastian Bach; some George Frederick Handel and Felix Mendelssohn; old American songs; spirituals; and operatic arias.

Anderson's stage manner—closed eyes and few gestures—conveyed dignity, stateliness and, above all, inner serenity. Her repertoire was varied—200 songs in nine languages. No program of hers was complete without spirituals. Favorites included "Crucifixion," "Trampin'," and "My Lord, What a Morning." Even when performing in the Soviet Union, where she was not supposed to sing any religious songs, she insisted upon "Ave Maria" and several spirituals. She said:

> They are my own music, but it's not for that reason that I love to sing them. I love the spirituals because they are truly spiritual in quality; they give forth an aura of faith, simplicity, humility and hope.

Anderson was deeply spiritual. She wrote in her autobiography, "I believe that I could not have had my career without the help of the Being above." Or, as *Time*'s Chambers put it: "With a naturalness impossible to most people, she says: 'I do a good deal of praying.' For to her, her voice is directly a gift from God, her singing a religious experience."

In her lifetime, Anderson received many awards. In 1939, Eleanor Roosevelt presented her with the Spingarn Medal, given annually to the black American who "shall have made the highest achievement during the preceding year or years in any honorable field of endeavor." A year later, she was awarded the prestigious Finnish decoration, the Probenignitate Humana. When in 1941 she was given the Bok award, bestowed each year upon an outstanding Philadelphia citizen, she used the $10,000 prize money to establish the Marian Anderson Scholarships. Each year, three trustees allocate funds to help young people, irrespective of race, creed, or color, to pursue an artistic career.

Various medals followed. In 1963, President Lyndon Johnson awarded her the American Medal of Freedom. In 1977, Congress awarded her a gold medal in honor of what was thought to be her 75th birthday. In 1980, the U.S. Treasury Department coined a half-ounce gold commemorative medal with her likeness. In 1986, President Ronald Reagan presented her with the National Medal of Arts.

For many years, Anderson's American tours were marked by racial discrimination. Unlike Europe, where she was welcomed to the Continent's finest hotels, cafes, and parlors, she found that the racial barrier made the most elementary of tasks difficult: taking a train, obtaining an auto, choosing a restaurant, booking a hotel room, arranging for laundry, finding a place to practice. She was often shunted to third- or fourth-class accommodations, although in the North she did break the color line at some first-class hotels. In the South, she would have to stay with friends. She preferred to take her meals in her hotel room rather than be the cause of any incident. She avoided Jim Crow restrictions by traveling in drawing rooms on night trains. She once said:

> If I were inclined to be combative, I suppose I might insist on making an issue of these things. But that is not my nature, and I always bear in mind that my mission is to leave behind me the kind of impression that will make it easier for those who follow.

At first, in cities where there was segregation, she demanded "vertical" seating, which meant that black ticket purchasers, though seated apart from others, must be allotted seats in every part of the auditorium. Her concerts often marked the first time that blacks could be seated in the orchestra of an auditorium. By 1950, she was refusing to sing where the audience was segregated. Marvin Feinstein, a former vice president of Hurok Artists, recalled, "In her own quiet way—there was really no civil rights movement at that time—Miss Anderson was already breaking barriers for artists that followed her."

In 1949, a *Newsweek* writer noted that she used the first person plural when speaking of her singing, a phenomena attributed to "the humility with which she has always approached her great gift of song, and to the fact that she looks upon her accompanist as a full partner." Her autobiography, *My Lord, What a Morning* (1955), devoted a chapter to her gifted accompanists. From 1933 to 1940, her accompanist was Kosti Vehanen, a respected Finnish pianist, and, from 1940 to 1965, Franz Rupp, a German refugee from Nazism. She also praised Isaac Alexander Jofe, her touring factotum since 1937. Of the ego involvement experienced by any artist, she once commented:

> There was a time when I was very much interested in applause and the lovely things

they said. But now we are interested in singing so that somebody in the audience will leave feeling a little better than when he came.

In 1992, six years after the death of her husband, Anderson moved to Portland, Oregon, to live with her nephew and only survivor, conductor James DePreist. The son of her sister Ethel, James had been raised by Anderson as a son. In her last years, she was restricted to a wheelchair. On April 4, 1994, Marian Anderson died in Portland.

SOURCES:

Anderson, Marian. *My Lord, What a Morning*. NY: Viking, 1956.

Dickey, Richard C. "Marian Anderson," in *Research Guide to American Historical Biography*. Edited by Suzanne Niemeyer. Vol. 4. Washington, DC: Beacham, 1990, pp. 1783–1788.

Vehanen, Kosti. *Marian Anderson: A Portrait*. NY: McGraw-Hill, 1941 (reprinted by Greenwood Press, 1970).

SUGGESTED READING:

Bronson, Arthur. "Marian Anderson," in *American Mercury*. Vol. 61. September 1945, pp. 282–288.

[Chambers, Whittaker]. "In Egypt Land," in *Time*. Vol. 48. December 30, 1946, pp. 59–65.

Newman, Shirlee P. *Marian Anderson: Lady from Philadelphia*. Philadelphia, PA: Westminster, 1966.

Sims, Janet L., ed. *Marian Anderson: An Annotated Bibliography and Discography*. Westport, CT: Greenwood, 1981.

"Singer and Citizen," in *Newsweek*. Vol. 33. April 25, 1949, pp. 84–86.

COLLECTIONS:

The papers of Marian Anderson are located in the Van Pelt Library, University of Pennsylvania. Other Anderson papers are found in the Trevor Arnett Library of Atlanta University; the Julius Rosenwald Fund Records at the Amistad Research Center, Tulane University, New Orleans; the Schomburg Collection, New York Public Library; and the Moorland-Spingarn Research Center, Howard University, Washington, D.C.

RELATED MEDIA:

"Portrait of Marian Anderson" (1 hour), produced by Dante J. James, Greater Washington Educational Telecommunications Association, 1991.

Justus D. Doenecke, Professor of History, New College of the University of South Florida, Sarasota, Florida

Anderson, Mary (1859–1940)

American actress. Name variations: Mary de Navarro, Madame de Navarro. Born Mary Antoinette Anderson in Sacramento, California, on July 28, 1859; died in Worcestershire, England, on May 29, 1940; educated at the Ursuline Convent in Louisville, Kentucky; studied elocution with Vandenhoff; married Antonio F. de Navarro, in 1890; children: one son.

Mary
Anderson
(1859–1940)

Rosalind, Lady Macbeth, Bianca, Pauline, Meg Merrilees, and Juliet.

Illness in 1889 forced her to retire. The following year, she married Antonio de Navarro and made her residence in the village of Broadway, Worcestershire, England, nestled at the foot of the Cotswold Hills, in Shakespeare country. After World War I broke out, Anderson frequently appeared at special performances for the benefit of wounded soldiers and, later, in support of the poor. Working with composer and friend *Maude Valerie White, she also developed her singing voice. On a bitterly cold winter evening, Anderson appeared in a benefit for the poor in the East End of London, as described in a 1905 edition of *Munsey's Magazine*: "It seemed probable that the West End folk who had paid high prices for their seats would not face the storm; it even seemed possible that the poor people for whom the entertainment was provided would prefer to crouch in the shelter of their poverty-stricken homes. Yet when the time came the great hall was packed." When Mary Anderson appeared, she was greeted "with a demonstration of applause so terrific that it seemed to tear the building. . . . When she was allowed to begin, she held her hearers in absolute thrall." Anderson gave two more performances in that hall, once to 4,000 children. She wrote two autobiographies, including *A Few Memories* (1896), and co-authored, with Robert Hichens, the long-running play *The Garden of Allah*.

At age 13, Mary Anderson began to study for the theater. Three years later, on November 25, 1875, she made her first appearance on the American stage as Juliet in an amateur production at Macauley's Theater in Louisville, Kentucky, and scored an immediate success. During the following ten years, she played in all the principal cities of the United States and was immensely popular with all classes. Her beauty and magnificent voice made her the most famous actress of her day.

From 1885 to 1989, Anderson appeared in England, where she repeated her American triumphs. She had wanted to make her debut there in the part of Juliet but had been warned against it by American critic William Winter. "Your Juliet will be compared to that of the reigning favorite, Ellen Terry. Try Parthenia." In 1883, Anderson opened as Parthenia in *Maria Anne Lovell's *Ingomar* at the Lyceum and was once again successful. As a result, she was later accepted in any part she chose. Her most notable portrayals were Perdita, Hermione, Galatea,

Anderson, Mary (1872–1964)

Swedish-born American union leader who fought for acceptance of the principles of collective bargaining and arbitration and became the first director of the Women's Bureau of the U.S. Department of Labor. Born Mary Anderson on August 27, 1872, on her parents' farm outside of Lidköping, Sweden; died of a stroke at her home in Washington, D.C., on January 29, 1964; daughter of Magnus and Matilda (Johnson) Anderson (both farmers); graduated from a Lutheran grammar school at the top of her class; never married; no children.

Immigrated to America (1889); worked as a domestic and briefly in the garment trade before finding work as a stitcher in a shoe factory outside Chicago; joined the International Boot and Shoe Workers Union (BSWU, 1899); elected president of women's stitchers Local 94 (Chicago, 1900); member, BSWU national executive board (1906–19); joined the Women's Trade Union League (WTUL, 1905); appointed full-time WTUL organizer (1911); named as-

sistant director, Women in Industry Service (1918), appointed director (1919); appointed director of the Women's Bureau of the U.S. Department of Labor (1920–44); named WTUL delegate to both the Paris Peace Conference and the International Congress of Working Women (1919); organized Bryn Mawr Summer School for Women Workers (1921); given honorary degree, Smith College (1941), and Award of Merit, U.S. Labor Department (1962).

Selected publications: (autobiography) Woman at Work *(1951), as well as numerous articles.*

Mary Anderson arrived in the United States in 1889, speaking no English and possessing few skills. "I had the idea that America was a promised land," she would later recall, "because I felt that there might be something other than housework that a person like me could do." In fact, the industrial growth under way in her adoptive country would both shape and be shaped by her career. It took some years for her to escape the low wages and domestic work that many working-class women of this period hoped to avoid. As a skilled factory worker, Anderson found industrial work beset with its own problems, and she became involved in serving the interests of laboring women through trade unionism and, later, government protection. Rising through the ranks of the Boot and Shoe Workers Union and then the Women's Trade Union League, Anderson eventually became the first director of a federal agency devoted to the issues of women's employment, a position she held until she was in her 70s.

Mary Anderson was born outside the small Swedish village of Lidköping on August 27, 1872, the youngest of seven children born to Magnus and Matilda Anderson, prosperous farmers living in the southwestern area of the country. A sturdy child, Anderson preferred playing outside or doing farm chores. Unlike her sisters, she avoided housework or assisting her mother with the family weaving. Anderson attended the local Lutheran grammar school for several years and graduated at the head of her class. By her own account, she was at times painfully shy, but her childhood was a pleasant one.

In the late 1880s, a severe agricultural depression hit Sweden, and Magnus Anderson lost his farm. Unable to support their children still living at home, and with no employment opportunities for women nearby except domestic work, the Andersons reluctantly allowed their youngest daughter to emigrate to America. In 1889, 16-year-old Mary departed with her older sister Hilda; they were to join their sister Anna, who had left two years earlier and found work as a domestic in Pentwater, Michigan.

Like most working-class immigrants at that time, the Anderson sisters traveled to the United States in the steerage section of the ship and suffered from seasickness for days. From New York, they had several more days of travel to Michigan on the train. In the town of Ludington, Mary Anderson found a job washing dishes in a boarding house for lumberjacks. A month later, she was hired by a Norwegian family as a housemaid. Paid $1.50 a week, she was responsible for the housework, the laundry, the cooking, and serving dinner each night, with no time off. Over the next few years, she held domestic jobs, some better than others in terms of time off and salary, for several other families. Meanwhile, she taught herself to speak English.

In 1892, when her sister Anna, now married, wrote that she and her husband were moving to Chicago, Mary Anderson jumped at the chance to join them. She worked briefly in a garment factory, then as a shoestitcher in a small company outside Chicago. After that company failed during the depression of 1893, Anderson found a job with Schwab Company, a much larger shoe manufacturer in Chicago. At age 22, Anderson had been in the United States for six years, and gone from earning $1.50 a week as a domestic worker to $14 a week as a skilled shoeworker.

At the end of the 19th century, it was considered difficult to organize women for membership in trade unions. Women were usually viewed as temporary workers who would leave their occupations once they married. They also tended to take the low paying, unskilled jobs that most of the established unions did not represent. In reality, however, many women were lifelong self-providers, and often responsible for supporting other dependent family members as well. And at a time when mechanization was changing the methods of production, women increasingly moved into skilled occupations such as printing, bookbinding, and shoemaking.

In 1899, when most locals in Chicago and elsewhere had memberships that were primarily male, Anderson joined Chicago Local 94 of the International Boot and Shoe Workers Union (BSWU), an all female local that was 150 members strong. Mary Anderson did not follow the radical political views of her day, nor did she see marriage as the ultimate source of economic security for working-class women like herself. In her words, "Through union negotiations with the employer . . . conditions were improved for a great many people and not just for the one person who changed to a better job." Throughout her career, her approach was pragmatic.

Within one year of joining Local 94, Anderson was elected its president. Shortly thereafter, she was elected to serve as the Local's representative to the Chicago Federation of Labor, a citywide council comprised of both men and women labor leaders. When not on the job as a shoestitcher, she began to spend her time doing union work. As she would later recall, "My life outside the factory was devoted almost entirely to meetings."

In 1905, Anderson followed the suggestion of her friend and fellow shoeworker, **Emma Steghagen**, in joining the local chapter of the Chicago Women's Trade Union League (WTUL). Founded at the 1903 convention of the American Federation of Labor (AFL), the organization was a cross-class alliance of women workers and middle-class allies to provide financial assistance and day-to-day support in organizing working-class women. The Chicago branch of the WTUL was closely associated with Hull House and its leader, *__Jane Addams__, and Anderson's BSWU Local 94 was one of many of the women's unions

*Mary
Anderson*

(1872–1964)

that held meetings at the settlement house. Anderson soon became friends with ✿➤ **Margaret Dreier Robins** (1868–1945), WTUL president and Chicago reformer, who according to Anderson was "the mainspring of our work." By 1906, Anderson's efforts in Chicago had brought her to the attention of the BSWU leadership. That year, she was elected to the national union's executive board, filling the seat left vacant when Steghagen became secretary of the Chicago WTUL. Anderson was to hold this position until 1919.

In 1910, hundreds of women garment workers in Chicago, though not members of a union, went out on strike against Hart, Schaffner, and Marx, the city's largest clothing manufacturer, over the issues of dangerous work conditions and low wages. The Chicago WTUL joined with the United Garment Workers and the Chicago Federation of Labor to assist the striking employees. After working all day at her job in a shoe factory, Anderson joined others each night in organizing relief funds for the strikers, and also led meetings to explain the principles of trade unionism to the strikers. When the strike ended after several weeks, part of the settlement involved the company's recognition of the women's right to collective bargaining and the establishment of methods of arbitration between the company and the workers.

Within a year of the settlement, however, it was evident that the women at Hart, Schaffner, and Marx were not functioning effectively as a union. Many were young, speaking little if any English, and without experience in trade unionism. When WTUL president Robins decided that a full-time organizer was needed, she turned to her good friend Mary Anderson.

In July 1911, Anderson quit her job as a shoestitcher to become a paid organizer for the WTUL. For two years, she worked to shore up the garment workers union among the hundreds of Hart, Schaffner, and Marx employees. She would later devote a chapter to this period in her autobiography, *Woman at Work.* She was particularly proud of establishing an arbitration board that forestalled, or quickly ended, several wildcat strikes in the early years of the union. For her, a strike was always to be used as a last resort, not because of the upset caused to business but due to the economic hardship it brought to workers. From 1913 to 1917, Anderson organized countless other women workers—waitresses, department store clerks, and corset makers—always stressing the function of a trade union as a vehicle of negotiation and arbitration.

In 1917, with the United States' entry into World War I, Anderson joined the war effort in Washington. In April of that year, she was appointed by AFL president Samuel Gompers, the labor representative of the Advisory Commission of the United States Council of National Defense, to a subcommittee to address the concerns of women in industry. Also serving on the subcommittee was ✿➤ **Mary Van Kleeck**, then director of industrial studies for the Russell Sage Foundation. By January 1918, Van Kleeck had been appointed to direct the women's branch of the Army's Ordinance Department and invited Anderson to join her staff. Anderson, who had been commuting back and forth from Chicago to Washington, moved to the capital, where she was to reside for the rest of her life. By June 1918, she was appointed assistant director of the Women in Industry Service, a wartime agency of the Department of Labor.

➤✿
Margaret Dreier Robins. See *Dreier Sisters.*

✿➤ **Van Kleeck, Mary Abby** (1883–1972)

American reformer. Born in 1883; died in Woodstock, New York, in 1972; grew up in New York City; graduated from Smith College, 1904.

In 1908, Mary Van Kleeck began her studies on the status of working women, sponsored by the Russell Sage Foundation. Her conclusions, and her own activities for minimum wage and protective legislation, exerted a powerful influence on labor reform. Van Kleeck's first book, *Artificial Flower Makers* (1913), which concerned immigrant women, was followed by *Women in the Bookbinding Trade* (1913), *Wages in the Military Trade* (1914), *Working Girls in Evening Schools* (1914), and *A Seasonal Industry* (1917). In 1917, hired to advise the army Ordnance Department and to serve as a member of the War Labor Policies Board, she helped form the Women's Bureau of the Department of Labor, which she headed briefly; in 1919, she turned the task over to her assistant *Mary Anderson and returned to her work with the Russell Sage Foundation.

Over the years, Van Kleeck also served on two presidential commissions on unemployment; chaired the National Interracial Conference (1928); co-authored *The Negro in American Civilization* (1930); and presided over the International Conference of Social Work in Germany (1932). As she grew older, she swung more to the political left, putting forth her views in *Creative America* (1936) and *Technology and Livelihood* (1944). A non-violent Socialist, she made trips to the Soviet Union following World War II and championed the presidency of Henry Wallace in 1948. In 1953, after the 70-year-old was summoned to appear before the McCarthy hearings, she retired from public life to Woodstock, New York. She died there a few days before her 89th birthday.

Anderson was now able to put her skills as an organizer and her personal experiences as an industrial worker to use on the national level. At the same time, she learned a great deal from Van Kleeck's years of experience as an administrator and social investigator. When Van Kleeck resigned in August 1919, Anderson succeeded her as director of the Women in Industry Service. Not yet 47, she was in charge of the only federal agency overseeing the concerns of working-class women.

Despite her full-time government work, Anderson also remained active in the WTUL. In early 1919, she accompanied fellow WTUL leader *Rose Schneiderman to the Paris Peace Conference as a female labor delegate. Out of that conference came the International Congress of Working Women, which held its first meeting in Washington in the fall of that year, sponsored by the WTUL, with Anderson as the union league's representative.

When World War I ended in 1918, the WTUL and other women's groups began lobbying for a permanent agency to represent the interests established under the Women in Industry Service. In June 1920, Congress created the Women's Bureau as a permanent part of the Department of Labor, and President Woodrow Wilson appointed Mary Anderson as the Bureau's first director. For the next 24 years, she held the position, through Republican and Democratic presidential administrations.

Under Anderson's leadership, the Women's Bureau collected masses of data regarding the conditions of women and labor and coordinated legislative efforts aimed at addressing the worst abuses. As the WTUL turned increasingly to legislation to meet the needs of working women, Anderson maintained her association with the league. During her earlier years in Chicago, Anderson had been too busy to take advantage of the various courses offered at Hull House, but she understood the importance of education, which remained a significant focus of the work of both the WTUL and the Women's Bureau. In 1921, she was one of the organizers of the Bryn Mawr Summer School for Women Workers through the Women's Bureau.

During the 1920s, Anderson had cordial relations with the Republican secretaries of labor, but, in 1933, she eagerly anticipated working with the first woman labor secretary, *Frances Perkins, appointed by President Franklin Roosevelt. Unfortunately, Perkins and Anderson never established a close working relationship. Part of the difficulty stemmed from the challenge faced by Perkins as the first woman to hold the position of a cabinet officer. She felt that she could not be associated with issues that were seen as primarily concerned with women. Anderson had good relations with the president, however, whom she had met during World War I, and with *Eleanor Roosevelt, whom she had known for years through the WTUL. Over the objections of Perkins, the president appointed Anderson chief of the U.S. delegation to the International Labor Conference of 1933.

The problems between Anderson and Perkins came to a head during World War II. As thousands of women became employed in wartime production, the responsibilities of the Women's Bureau were greatly expanded. In 1944, when Perkins refused to support an increase in the bureau's budget, Anderson resigned. At the age of 72, after 40 years of effort for the rights of women workers but lacking the support of her immediate supervisor, she felt it was time to retire.

Before and after her retirement, Anderson received many honors. In 1941, she was awarded an honorary degree from Smith College, which recognized her as a "leader in the field of industrial relations." According to Anderson, "I did not make myself a leader. If I became a leader it was only because of the support and cooperation of the hundreds of friends and colleagues with whom I had worked for so many years." In 1962, at the age of 90, Anderson received the U.S. Department of Labor's Award of Merit. Two years later, on January 29, 1964, Mary Anderson died of a stroke at age 92, in her Washington home.

In 1915, Anderson had become a U.S. citizen because she heard that Illinois was about to pass a state law granting woman suffrage. While eager for the opportunity to vote, she remained opposed to the passage of an Equal Rights Amendment throughout her life, for fear it would negate the years of hard work she had spent in securing protective labor legislation for women. After decades of union activity, Anderson understood how difficult it was to organize women workers. She came to believe that government protection was needed to ensure both the rights and the safety of women workers.

SOURCES:

Anderson, Mary. *Woman at Work: The Autobiography of Mary Anderson as told to Mary Winslow.* Minneapolis, MN: University of Minnesota Press, 1951.

Conn, Sandra. "Three Talents: Robins, Nestor, and Anderson of the Chicago Trade Union League," in *Chicago History.* Vol. 9, 1980–1981, pp. 234–247.

SUGGESTED READING:

Payne, Elizabeth Anne. *Reform, Labor, and Feminism: Margaret Dreier Robins and the Women's Trade Union League.* Urbana, IL: University of Illinois Press, 1988.

Ware, Susan. *Beyond Suffrage: Women in the New Deal.* Cambridge, MA: Harvard University Press, 1981.

COLLECTIONS:

Correspondence, papers, and memorabilia located in the Schlesinger Library, Radcliffe College.

Kathleen Banks Nutter, Department of History, University of Massachusetts at Amherst

Anderson, Mary Reid (1880–1921).

See Macarthur, Mary Reid.

Anderson, Regina M. (1901—)

African-American librarian, playwright, and arts patron. Name variations: Regina Anderson Andrews; (pseudonym) Ursula Trelling. Born in Chicago, Illinois, on May 21, 1901; daughter of William Grant (an attorney) and Margaret (Simons) Anderson; attended Normal Training School and Hyde Park High School in Chicago; studied at Wilberforce University in Ohio, the University of Chicago, and City College of New York; received library science degree from Columbia University Library School; married William T. Andrews, in 1926; children: one daughter, Regina.

Regina M. Anderson was instrumental in launching the careers of countless black artists who, in turn, gave rise to the Harlem Renaissance of the late 1920s and 1930s. She had moved to New York from Chicago because of Manhattan's "liberating atmosphere," and first came in contact with the young artists through her job as assistant librarian at Harlem's 135th Street branch of the New York Public Library (later renamed the Schomburg Center for Research in Black Culture). Meeting the writers, singers, dancers, painters, and actors of her time, she was in the center of Harlem's artistic life and became a crucial member of the movement for black arts.

Before her marriage in 1926, Anderson used her apartment in Harlem's posh Sugar Hill, shared with **Ethel Ray Nance** and **Louella Tucker**, as a "sort of Harlem Renaissance USO" for newcomers to the area. Anderson and Nance, who worked for the National Urban League, had the power to launch an artist's or writer's career from their own living room.

The two helped instigate and plan the famous Civic Club dinner, held in March 1924, with guests like Jean Toomer, Countee Cullen,

and Langston Hughes, as well as other writers of the time. Speeches were given by members of the older black generation, such as W.E.B. Du Bois and James Weldon Johnson. The younger writers, in turn, gave readings to an audience that included white editors and publishers, who then became their patrons and advisors. These contacts resulted in publications devoted exclusively to black writing.

Sharing W.E.B. Du Bois' hope for serious black theater, Anderson became involved with the fledgling Krigwa Players, under the direction of Du Bois and housed in the 135th Street library basement. The Players served as the parent group of the Negro Experimental Theater (also known as the Harlem Experimental Theater), which was founded in 1929. In 1931, the group moved to Saint Philip's Parish House, where they produced a number of original scripts, including several by Anderson. Her *Climbing Jacob's Ladder,* presented in 1931, was a serious folk drama written under the pseudonym of Ursula Trelling. Anderson claimed the need for the pen name because of her professional connection with the 135th Street Library, but others cite modesty. The play met with great success and led to Broadway roles for many of the cast members.

The Negro Experimental Theater was instrumental in helping to bring the Federal Theater (WPA) to New York and Harlem. It was also an inspiration to theater groups across the country, and Anderson and Du Bois were credited with paving the way for future black playwrights such as Langston Hughes, **Lorraine Hansberry, James Baldwin, and Imamu Amiri Baraka (LeRoi Jones). Among the ten black women recognized by the 1939 World's Fair in New York City, Anderson viewed her efforts as only a beginning. "It gives me a great deal of personal satisfaction," she said, "to have lived to see much of what we and other pioneers worked to achieve becoming a reality. However, we need more and more opportunities for our actors, writers, and directors."

Before her retirement in 1967, Anderson had become second vice president of the National Council of Women as well as National Urban League representative to the U.S. Commission for UNESCO; she also worked with the State Commission for Human Rights. Anderson received countless awards, including an Asian Foundation grant that enabled her to visit India, Hong Kong, Japan, Iran, Thailand, and Afghanistan, to meet with visiting scholars who had been guests in the programs she directed at the library. She settled in upstate New York after her retirement, and in 1971 she and Ethel Ray Nance coedited a book titled *Chronology of African-Americans in New York, 1921–1966*.

SOURCES:

Smith, Jessie Carney, ed. *Notable Black American Women*. Detroit, MI: Gale Research, 1992.

SUGGESTED READING:

Anderson, Jervis. *This Was Harlem: A Cultural Portrait, 1900–1950*. NY: Farrar Straus Giroux, 1981.

Kellner, Bruce, ed. *The Harlem Renaissance: A Historical Dictionary for the Era*. Westport, CT: Greenwood Press, 1984.

Mitchell, Loften. *Black Drama: The Story of the American Negro in the Theater*. NY: Hawthorn Books, 1967.

Roses, Lorraine E., and Ruth E. Randolph. "Regina M. Anderson" [Ursula Trelling]. *Harlem Renaissance and Beyond: 100 Black Women Writers 1900–1945*. Boston: G.K. Hall, 1990.

COLLECTIONS:

Books from her private library as well as papers, a scrapbook, and an oral history videotape of Regina Anderson Andrews are in the Schomburg Center for Research on Black Culture.

Barbara Morgan, Melrose, Massachusetts

Andics, Erzsebet (1902–1986)

Hungarian Communist militant. Born in Hungary in 1902; died in Hungary in 1986.

Joined the Communist Party of Hungary at its inception (1918); narrowly escaped imprisonment or death (1919) and fled to Soviet Russia; arrested (early 1920s) and imprisoned by Hungarian regime but exchanged for Hungarian captives; returned to Hungary after World War II and served as one of the few women ever elected to the Politburo; even after the failed revolution of 1956, remained a hard-line Marxist-Leninist up to the time of her death (1986), a scant three years before the collapse of Communism in Hungary.

During World War I, the teenaged Erzsebet Andics discovered the Marxism that would sustain her both intellectually and emotionally the rest of her life. The horrors of the world conflagration and the incalculable suffering she witnessed at first hand were explained for her by the Marxist theory of class struggle and the inevitability of proletarian revolution. As it did to many of her generation, to Andics the Bolshevik revolution led by Lenin in Russia in November 1917 represented a beacon of hope for a world mad with war and nationalistic frenzy. The ideal of international working-class solidarity was for Andics and other idealists a solid foundation on which to build their lives. She joined the Hungarian Communist Party at its birth in the fall of 1918 and, despite her extreme youth, was an active participant in the Hungarian Soviet Republic that ruled Hungary briefly in the spring and early summer of 1919. With the collapse of the Soviet regime, a bloody anti-Communist reaction took place, and Andics was fortunate in escaping the wrath of a White Terror that took vengeance against the Reds. Andics took refuge in Soviet Russia, which was struggling to survive against foreign troops, internal anti-Bolshevik armies, famine, and general chaos.

After a course of indoctrination and training, Andics was sent back to Hungary by the Communist International as an underground operative. The time for revolution had already passed, however, and the workers were much less receptive than they had been a year or two earlier. More important, the secret police of the right-wing regime was highly efficient and soon arrested her as a Bolshevik agent. The charge of Marxist subversion was a serious one in the Hungary of the early 1920s. While Erzsebet did not get a death sentence, she received 15 years but spent only one of them in prison. She was released in exchange for several Hungarian military officers who had been imprisoned in Russia since World War I and retained as hostages by the Bolsheviks. A grateful Andics went immediately to Soviet Russia, where she witnessed the drama of collectivization, Stalinization, the bloody purges of the 1930s, and the near collapse of the Soviet Union during World War II. During these decades, she remained a dedicated Communist, believing that one day she would return to Hungary.

Her opportunity came in 1945, when she returned with the Soviet forces that liberated Central Europe from Nazi rule. One of the few women among the cadre of veteran Communists, she quickly joined the inner circle. Between 1948 and 1956, Andics was a member of the Hungarian Politburo. Although she wielded little, if any, substantive power, her prestige as a proven "party veteran" shielded her from some of the stresses of internal party factional struggles. Surprised and shocked by the national uprising that convulsed Hungary in October and November 1956, Andics approved of its suppression by Soviet forces and, in the aftermath of the crisis, accepted the position of departmental chair of humanities at Budapest's Eotvos Lorand University.

In the next decades, she continued to lecture and publish in defense of the Socialist system as it evolved in Hungary. As an old-line prewar Communist, Andics took a hostile position toward new ideas, including the flexible and pragmatic "Goulash Communism" that appeared in Hungarian political life in the 1960s as the government of Janos Kadar asserted itself. After growing up in the revolutionary age of Lenin and surviving the terrors of Stalinism, Erzsebet Andics died in 1986 still believing in the historical correctness of her lifelong Marxist beliefs. Three years after her death, Communism in Hungary simply collapsed of its own contradictions.

SOURCES:

Aczél, Tamás, and Tibor Meray. *The Revolt of the Mind: A Case History of Intellectual Resistance behind the Iron Curtain.* NY: Frederick A. Praeger, 1959.

Held, Joseph. *Dictionary of East European History Since 1945.* Westport, CT: Greenwood Press, 1994.

John Haag, Associate Professor of History, University of Georgia, Athens, Georgia

Andilly, Angelique de Saint-Jean Arnauld d' (1624–1684).

See Arnauld, Angelique in entry titled "Port Royal des Champ, abbesses of."

André, Valerie (1922—)

Military physician and the first French woman to achieve the rank of general. Name variations: Andre. Born Valerie Marie André in Strasbourg, France, on April 21, 1922; daughter of Philibert André (a professor at the Strasbourg Lycée); married Alexis Santini, in 1963.

After receiving a medical doctorate, served in Vietnam; became a helicopter pilot and flew over 150 medical missions; named commanding officer of helicopter pilots at the Gialam air base in Tonkin province; became a lieutenant-colonel in the Medical Corps (1965); achieved rank of colonel (1970); achieved rank of Médecin général (1976), thus becoming a general officer—the first female general in the history of France; received equivalency of the rank and prerogatives of a major general (1976); became a founding member of the French National Air and Space Academy (1983); received many awards.

Valerie Marie André was born in Strasbourg, France, on April 21, 1922, the daughter of Philibert André, a professor at the Strasbourg Lycée. With an early interest in medicine, Valerie André received a doctorate from the University of Paris Faculty of Medicine in 1948. In 1946, France had become embroiled in a bloody war with the Communist-led Vietminh nationalists whose goal was complete independence from European rule. In 1948, André joined the military and went to Vietnam at the rank of captain. Assigned to the hospital at My Tho, she was directly transferred to the staff of the French women's infirmary in Saigon.

Her skills were quickly recognized, and she was soon working as an assistant neurosurgeon at the Coste Military Hospital.

In 1950, she received a commission as a helicopter pilot, and, in the next four years, she flew over 150 medical missions. These took place under dangerous combat conditions, including the months-long siege of the fortress at Dienbienphu. In 1952, she became commanding officer of helicopter pilots at the Gialam air base in Tonkin province. André left Vietnam in 1953 to serve as research physician at the Brétigny-sur-Orge aviation test center, a position she held for the next five years. In 1954, France was defeated and withdrew from Indochina.

By the late 1950s, the bloody colonial war escalated in Algeria, and Valerie André was once again actively involved in military operations, serving as medical chief of the 23rd Helicopter Squadron, as well as chief medical officer at the Reghaïa air base. When the Algerian war was also lost in 1962, André returned to France where she became medical commander at the Villacoublay base. In December 1963, she took time off from foreign colonial wars and married Alexis Santini, a fellow officer in the aviation service.

André's military career continued to flourish. In 1965, she became a lieutenant-colonel in the Medical Corps and in 1970 achieved the rank of colonel. In 1976, she was promoted to the rank of *Médecin général,* thus becoming a general officer—the first female general in the history of France. Further distinctions in the final years of Valerie André's distinguished military career included her promotion in 1976 to director of health services of the Fourth Air Region. In 1980–81, she also directed medical services of the Second Air Region and received the rank of physician inspector-general, which gave her the equivalency of the rank and prerogatives of a major general. In 1983, she became a founding member of the French National Air and Space Academy.

General André wrote several books, including her autobiographical *Madame le Général (Madame General),* published in 1988, which documents her colorful career. Her many awards and decorations include the Grand Officer of the Legion of Honor, the Grand Cross of the National Order of Merit, the Combat Cross, the Aeronautics Medal, the Gold Medal of the Aero Club of France, and the United States Legion of Merit.

SOURCES:

André, Valerie. *Physio-pathologie du parachutisme.* Thesis, Université de Paris,1948.

———. *Ici, Ventilateur! Extraits d'un carnet de vol.* Paris: Calmann-Lévy, 1954.

———. *Madame le Général.* Paris: Librairie académique Perrin, 1988.

John Haag, Associate Professor of History, University of Georgia, Athens, Georgia

Andreas-Salomé, Lou (1861–1937)

Russian-born author, biographer, novelist, and essayist, who was a celebrated figure in the cultural and intellectual life of turn-of-the-century Central Europe. Name variations: Louise von Salomé, Lelia, Lyolya, Frau Lou; (pseudonym) Henri Lou. Pronunciation: Loo Ahn-DRAY-us Saa-low-MAY. Born Louise Salomé on February 12, 1861, in St. Petersburg, Russia; died of uremia on February 5, 1937, in Göttingen, Germany; daughter of Gustav Ludwig Salomé (a Russian noble and general) and Louise (Wilm) Salomé (daughter of a sugar refiner); tutored and attended small English private school, as well as the Petrischule (all in St. Petersburg); university study in Zurich; married Fred Charles (later changed to Friedreich Carl) Andreas, in June 1887; children: none.

Selected publications: Ibsen's Heroines *(ed. and trans. by Siegfried Mandel, 1985); (under name Henri Lou)* Im Kampf um Gott *(A Struggle for God, 1885);* Friedreich Nietzsche in seinen Werken *(Friedreich Nietzsche in His Work, 1894);* Rainer Maria Rilke *(1928);* Mein Dank an Freud *(My Thanks to Freud, 1931);* Looking Back *(ed. by Ernst Pfeiffer, 1991);* "Anal und Sexual," in Imago *(1915).*

All but forgotten when she died in 1937, Lou Andreas-Salomé experienced an operatic rebirth with the 1981 performance of Giuseppe Sinopoli's *Lou Salomé.* The story of that opera, her encounter with German philosopher Friedreich Nietzsche, distorted her true place in the cultural and intellectual history of turn-of-the-century Central Europe. Her brief relationship with Nietzsche formed only a small part of a much more complex life.

That life began on February 12, 1861, with the birth of Louise Salomé in Russia. Her father Gustav was a Baltic German of Huguenot ancestry who, following distinguished service during the Polish rebellion of 1830, rose quickly through the ranks to general. The baby girl was named for her mother **Louise (Wilm) Salomé** who was the daughter of a Danish sugar refiner. The youngest of six children, Louise had five brothers, two of whom died in childhood.

The family enjoyed an affluent lifestyle and lived close to the tsar's Winter Palace in St. Petersburg. Summers were spent in a house in Peterhof, where the tsar also owned a residence. In her memoirs, Lou Salomé remembers growing up "in the midst of officers' uniforms." Even though Gustav Salomé was a member of the Russian nobility, the family's identity was formed by the close-knit Protestant German expatriate community. German and French were the languages spoken at home. Lyolya, as she was affectionately known to her family, also read some Russian. At age eight, she attended, by her own account, an unchallenging English private school in St. Petersburg; this was followed by two years, 1876 and 1877, in the German Lutheran Petrischule, which she again considered a waste of time. Indeed, much of her youth was spent in a fantasy world of her own construction.

Lyolya spent much of her time alone and confided in a cousin Emma and in an Aunt Caro. Caro, according to biographer Rudolph Binion, was "uncannily clever and charming." She impressed on Lyolya the need for a woman to choose between "freedom," defined as the acting out of deep "unconscious needs" that governed the mind and will, and "independence," or having a mind of her own. She wrote in her diary that her "earliest memory" was "my acquaintance with God . . . wholly for me alone and wholly secret." One day, when her God refused an answer to a direct question, her belief was shattered. "Like lightening, unbelief entered my heart." Yet God and religion—and father-God figures, such as her earthly father, Pastor Hendrik Gillot, Friedreich Nietzsche or Sigmund Freud—would remain central to her life.

Gillot, a liberal and unorthodox Protestant preacher in St. Petersburg, brought 17-year-old Louise out of her fantasy world. Introduced to Gillot by Aunt Caro, Louise seized upon the young and brilliant preacher as a substitute for her lost God. Together they explored the history of philosophy, studied comparative religion and the place of ritual in primitive societies, and discussed French literature. When Gillot, who had a wife and children, impulsively proposed marriage to Louise, she again lost "God." "With one blow what I had worshiped . . . became alien." But she had learned well and was prepared for the world beyond Russia. According to biographer Biddy Martin, Lou Salomé as she began to call herself, was not much different from other young women who decided to pursue their university studies in Zurich. "Most of these women . . . intended to use what they learned in the service of the Russian people and their revolution [against tsarist authority]. For Salomé . . . the passage to Europe opened up worlds of possibilities for the intellectual, psychological, and emotional life she sought." In 1879, she obtained her passport and, in 1880, traveled to Zurich with her mother for study.

In Zurich, Salomé audited classes in logic, metaphysics, and the history of religion and joined the literary circle of the minor, but revered, Swiss poet Gottfried Kinkel. For some years, she had suffered from poor health, which the climate in Zurich did nothing to improve. In 1882, she and her mother traveled to Italy and spent three months in Rome. Bearing a letter of introduction from Kinkel to *Malwida von Meysenburg (1816–1903), Salomé was welcomed into her salon. Meysenburg was a celebrated feminist and author of the bestselling *Memoirs of an Idealist* (1876) and offered Salomé, in the words of biographer **Angela Livingstone**, "just what she was looking for: 'great friendship'." Livingstone notes that Meysenburg saw in Salomé a woman who "could further the emancipation of the female intellect" and develop a "new kind of relationship" between men and women. But Salomé would never identify herself as a feminist.

Lou
Andreas-
Salomé

In Rome, Salomé made the acquaintance of Paul Rée, a positivist philosopher, who knew Friedreich Nietzsche. Rée arranged for a dramatic meeting between Salomé and Nietzsche in St. Peter's cathedral. Nietzsche was immediately attracted to her and felt himself "in the presence of a female intellect." Their friendship was intense in an intellectual sense but was to founder on the rocks of a jealous Paul Rée and the suspicion and hostility of Nietzsche's sister, *Elisabeth Förster-Nietzsche. At one point Salomé suggested that she and Rée and Friedreich Nietzsche live together in a small intellectual circle jokingly cast as an "unholy trinity." Meysenburg was distraught by the flouting of convention; Gillot wrote and suggested that she had returned to a fantasy world. Her reply to Gillot was succinct and said that she could "neither live according to models nor . . . ever be a model for anyone at all; on the contrary—what I shall most certainly do is make my own life according to myself, whatever may become of it." Even though Salomé's relationship with Nietzsche was brief and, in the end, rancorous, she left a lasting impression on him as a "presence and catalyst." Martin wrote that Nietzsche's "exasperation with Lou and his own sister and mother translated itself into ambivalent pronouncements on women in *Thus Spoke Zarathustra*, while Salomé brought the reflections and perceptions gained through the Nietzsche encounter into her autobiographical novel, *Im Kampf um Gott* (*A Struggle for God*), published in 1885 under the pseudonym Henri Lou. Indeed, according to Livingstone, Nietzsche's "views and high standards, his unparalleled evocation of the struggles and rewards of the life of the mind—all corroborated her intellectuality and her self-confidence as a thinker, and the romantic habit of being enraptured by thoughts." In the book, the heroine, in biographer Martin's words, "speaks out for intellectual and psychological equality for the sexes and against the imposed double standards of morality and the confinements of home and marriage."

I can neither base my life on models nor make of my life a model for anyone; instead, I will most certainly fashion my life in my own way, whatever may come of it.

—Lou Andreas-Salomé

Salomé and Rée lived together in a passionless intellectual relationship during the years 1883–86. Salomé's unexpected marriage to Fred Charles Andreas, a specialist in Oriental languages, abruptly ended her friendship with Rée, who had always expected he might win Salomé's hand. The union with Fred Andreas was curious in that it was never consummated. It was a marriage that sprang from an inner sense of her destiny. Livingstone noted that it was as if she had "submitted to something greater than the human" and that it was "an irrational compulsion to give and bind herself forever, as though being forced by something much more mysterious than love . . . and yet at the same time an absolute *self* will in her refusal to sleep with him."

Salomé's first work of sustained scholarship, *Hendrik Ibsens Frauengestalten* (*Ibsen's Heroines*), published in 1892, was instrumental in calling attention to the Norwegian playwright. Martin argues that Salomé's essays "are especially valuable in that they represent the view of the first woman writer to tell us if Ibsen came at all close in his objective to capture the dimensions of the female psyche." Even though Salomé wrote about female emancipation, she did not take part in the growing women's movement in Germany. There is no doubt that she was aware of the issues and believed firmly that marriage, for women, was a trap. As for differences between the sexes, Salomé not only affirmed them but was their advocate. One radical feminist, *Hedwig Dohm (1831–1919), complained in 1899 that Salomé, in Livingstone's words, "was a reactionary who felt that males were superior intellectually and was opposed to women engaging in professional and active life." Self-centered, Salomé never showed any real interest in political or economic issues.

Attracted by the avant-garde intellectuals of the Naturalist movement, Salomé penned numerous articles for *Die Freie Bühne* (*The Free Theater*) and, in 1894, published her second scholarly book entitled *Friedreich Nietzsche in seinen Werken* (*Friedreich Nietzsche in His Works*). It was an important book when it was first published and has stood the test of time. Intellectual historian Crane Brinton wrote: "It was by no means a bad book, rather pretentious philosophically, but sensible about Nietzsche as a person." Rudolph Binion, who used Salomé's life as a psychological case study and who is her harshest critic, also praised the book: "For the bulk of it she sorted out Nietzschean thematic threads and tied them together expertly—authoritatively."

The 1890s were a period of great productivity for Lou Salomé. Psychological novels patterned more often than not on her own experiences appeared in rapid succession and, for the most part, were well received: *Ruth* (1895), *Aus fremder Seele* (*From a Troubled Soul*, 1896), *Fenitschka* (1898), *Menschenkinder* (*Children of*

Man, 1899), *Ma* (Mom, 1901), and, in 1902, *Im Zwischenland* (*The Land Between*) all furthered her reputation and gave her the financial resources to travel.

In the same decade, Salomé wrote a number of influential essays on the experience and psychology of religion. Even though she concluded that God was a human "fabrication," she felt that religion helped people evolve, that it was a positive force in the lives of humans. One of her essays, "Jesus der Jude" ("Jesus the Jew"), published in the *Neue Deutsche Rundschau* (New German Roundtable) in 1896, attracted the attention of the young poet René Maria Rilke. They met in Munich the following year and became lovers. "No one," writes Walter Sorrell, "ever understood Rilke better than Lou and no one ever seems to have been closer to him, a man who was always in great need of love and human sympathy." At her urging, he changed his first name to the more masculine "Rainer." Twice they traveled to Russia; he began an extraordinarily creative and productive phase of his life while Salomé assembled her Russian reminiscences in a book, *Im Zwischenland.* Rilke and Salomé parted in 1903, but she would remain a confidant and friend until his death in 1926.

During the first decade of the 20th century, Lou Salomé enjoyed celebrity as an established essayist and novelist. She and her husband moved to Göttingen where she began work on several new novels, including *Das Haus* (*The House,* 1919) and *Rodinka* (1923), and collected several of her earlier essays into a book, *Die Erotik* (*Eroticism,* 1910). In her novels and books, she had always dealt with psychological themes and began to read avidly into this rapidly developing field.

Lou Salomé's career took a dramatic turn after 1911. In that year, she met Sigmund Freud and throughout 1912 and 1913 immersed herself in the study of psychology. Livingstone argues that psychoanalysis "in particular suited her for it promised to systematise, to make 'scientific' many of her own cherished ideas." Her ideas about the erotic, of which she had written a good deal, were reformulated within the context of "libido." "Her interest in the phenomenon of idealization was rearranged in the vocabulary of 'sublimation' and 'sexual over-esteem'." Especially attractive to Salomé was Freud's idea of narcissism, for here she found, in Livingstone's words, "the formulation for the ideal she envisaged, which combined self-love with the glorious unity of person and cosmos." When she left Vienna to return to Göttingen in 1913, she wrote in her journal that she was delighted that "I had met [Freud] on my journey and was permitted to *experience* him: as the turning-point in my life."

When war broke out in Europe and revolution tore Russia apart, she noted, in Binion's words, the "surge of mass hate and crude propagandizing throughout the Old World." While she initially welcomed the profound changes that occurred in Russia after 1917, she later rejected Bolshevik rule. Throughout the period, she continued to write. Her articles entitled "Anal und Sexual" and "Narzissmus als Doppelrichtung" ("Narcissism as Dual Orientation") appeared in Freud's journal, *Imago,* in 1915 and 1921 respectively. Taken together, they comprise Salomé's main contribution to psychological theory. Her ability to synthesize material impressed Freud, even though he was critical of synthesis. His feelings are best expressed in a letter to her:

> [N]othing has changed in our respective ways of approaching a theme. . . . I strike up a—mostly very simple—melody; you supply the higher octaves for it; I separate the one from the other, and you blend what has been separated into a higher unity; I silently accept the limits imposed by our objectivity, whereas you draw express attention to them. Generally speaking, we have understood each other and are at one in our opinions. Only, I tend to exclude all opinions except one, whereas you tend to include all opinions together.

The 1920s were difficult times financially for Salomé and her husband as the runaway inflation of the Weimar period destroyed Germany's currency. Freud helped with gifts of money. Declining health also began to take its toll. She was frequently sick and in 1929 was hospitalized with diabetes. Cancer took her husband in 1930; she lost a breast to cancer in 1935. But Lou Salomé remained productive. Her book on Rainer Maria Rilke appeared in 1928 to mixed reviews, and, in 1931, she published *Mein Dank an Freud* (My Thanks to Freud), which Freud called her best book. Salomé's remaining years were spent rewriting her memoirs in which she recast her life within the context of a personal destiny. Uremic poisoning ended her life on February 5, 1937.

SOURCES:

Andreas-Salomé, Lou. *Ibsen's Heroines.* Ed. and trans. by Siegfried Mandel. Redding Ridge, CT: Black Swan Books, 1985.

———. *Looking Back: Memoirs.* Ed. by Ernst Pfeiffer. NY: Paragon House, 1991.

Binion, Rudolph. *Frau Lou: Nietzsche's Wayward Disciple.* Princeton, NJ: Princeton University Press, 1968.

Livingstone, Angela. *Salomé: Her Life and Work.* Mt. Kisco, NY: Moyer Bell, 1984.

Martin, Biddy. *Woman and Modernity: The (Life) Styles of Lou Andreas-Salomé.* Ithaca, NY: Cornell, University Press, 1991.

Peters, H.F. *My Sister, My Spouse: A Biography of Lou Andreas-Salomé.* NY: W.W. Norton, 1962.

Pfeiffer, Ernst, ed. *Sigmund Freud and Lou Andreas-Salomé: Letters.* NY: Harcourt Brace Jovanovich, 1972.

Sorrell, Walter. *Three Women: Lives of Sex and Genius.* Indianapolis, IN: Bobbs-Merrill, 1975.

SUGGESTED READING:

Bergmann, Peter. *Nietzsche: "The Last Antipolitical German."* Bloomington, IN: Indiana University Press, 1987.

Brinton, Crane. *Nietzsche.* Cambridge: Harvard University Press, 1941.

Masur, Gerhard. *Imperial Berlin.* London: Routledge & Kegan Paul, 1971 (chapters 6 and 7).

Paul B. Goodwin, Jr., Professor of History, University of Connecticut, Storrs, Connecticut

Andree, Elfrida (1841–1929)

Swedish composer and organist. Born in Visby, Sweden, on February 19, 1841; died in Stockholm on January 11, 1929; daughter of W. Sohrling; sister of the noted opera singer **Fredricka Stenhammar;** *studied at the Stockholm Conservatory under L. Norman and H. Berens.*

Elfrida Andree was a modernist who broke many barriers that had limited women's musical activities. A pioneer of women's rights, she was the first woman telegraphist in Sweden. Music, however, was her initial love, and she was taught by her father before studying with Niels Gade. Though she was trained as a singer, Andree hoped to be an organist—a difficult feat since Swedish law forbade women organists. Eventually she was appointed organist of the Finnish Reformed Church from 1861 to 1867 and of the French Reformed Church in Stockholm from 1862 to 1867. Elected cathedral organist in Göteborg, she was then put in charge of its people's concerts, directing 800. Andree was the first woman to write an organ symphony; she also composed for the orchestra, piano, and chamber groups. In 1879, Elfrida Andree was one of the first women elected to the Swedish Academy of Music.

John Haag, Associate Professor of History, University of Georgia, Athens, Georgia

Andreeva, Maria Fedorovna
(1868–1953)

Russian actress, theatrical manager, and one of the founders of the Bolshoi Drama Theatre in St. Petersburg. Name variations: (stage name) Maria Andreeva; also known as Maria Fyodorovna or Feodorovna Andreyeva; (real name) Maria Yurkovskaya. Born Maria Yurkovskaya in 1868; died in Moscow on December 8, 1953; studied at the Moscow Conservatory; married A.A. Zhelyabuzhsky, though she left him in 1903 for the playwright Maxim Gorky.

In a family that was part of the theatrical community, Maria Yurkovskaya grew up surrounded by artists. Changing her name to Andreeva, she joined the Russian Society of Art and Literature in 1894, and was an actress at the Moscow Art Theatre (MAT) from 1898 to 1905 where she worked with Constantin Stanislavski.

Andreeva was married to A.A. Zhelyabuzhsky, a state official who worked for the railroad department, when she met the playwright Maxim Gorky, in 1900, while touring with the MAT. A relationship grew as the theater rehearsed his play *The Lower Depths.* In 1903, Andreeva left her husband, Gorky left his wife **Ekaterina Peshkov,** and the two began living together. At this point, Andreeva put her artistic career on hold to work with him and to spend time on her factional goals.

Andreeva's politics had always been radical; she donated money to various underground organizations and helped in the distribution of illegal brochures. But in 1904, she settled down to work with one party, the Marxist Bolshevik Party, led by Vladimir Ilyich Lenin, for which she had done sporadic work since 1902. During the Russian uprising of 1905, she edited the party paper *Novaia zhin'* (New Life).

In 1906, she and Gorky left Russia in an effort to raise funds for underground groups. They first went to Europe, then the United States, where Andreeva—conversant in several languages—served as Gorky's interpreter. When their status as an unmarried couple was discovered in the United States, it caused a scandal, and they were unceremoniously booted out of their hotel. More important, those from whom they had hoped to solicit money shunned the couple, and their fundraising trip was not nearly as successful as they had hoped.

In September 1907, they left the United States for Italy, where they settled on the island of Capri. Andreeva served as Gorky's secretary and translator as he continued to write. Remaining on Capri until 1913, they then returned to Russia, and Andreeva resumed her acting career in Kiev and elsewhere, performing with, among others, the Nezlobin Theatre. She later did other work for the Bolsheviks and earned the nickname "Phenomenon."

After the February 1917 Revolution, she was made chief of Municipal Theatres under the State Duma. Her relationship with the Bolsheviks cooled somewhat after the October Revolution, though only for a brief time. In 1918, she was appointed the commissar of Theatre and Entertainment of the Northern Commune as well as chief of the Commission of Experts of the Commissariat of Foreign Trade.

Still pursuing her acting career, she portrayed Lady Macbeth at the Alexandrinsky Theatre in 1918. The success of the production led Andreeva, Gorky, and their two partners (Fedor Chaliapin and Yuri Yurev) to found a theater for the purpose of producing classical repertory suitable for revolutionary times. Together, they founded the Bolshoi Theatre of Drama in Petrograd (St. Petersburg) in 1919, with which she also acted. Prominent figures of the art world joined them, including poet Alexander Blok, who became the theater's manager. The Bolshoi Theatre opened on February 15, 1919, with Schiller's *Don Carlos*, and continued until 1926.

In 1920, Andreeva was made chief of the Petrograd section of the Commissariat of Enlightenment. In April of the following year, her relationship with Gorky ended when the Bolsheviks sent her abroad on a cultural mission for the new government. One of her duties was the international sale of art, which included both articles from museums and pieces found by the Bolsheviks after they had liquidated the houses and the owners of the bourgeoisie.

In 1922, Andreeva was part of a trade delegation that the Soviets sent to Berlin; she handled film negotiation on behalf of the Commissariat of Enlightenment. Returning to Russia in 1930, she directed the Moscow House of Scholars until 1948, when she retired from active political life. Maria Andreeva died in Moscow on December 8, 1953, at the age of 85.

SOURCES:

Fitzpatrick, Sheila. *The Commissariat of Enlightenment: Soviet Organization of Education and the Arts Under Lunacharsky October 1917–1921.* Cambridge: Cambridge University Press, 1970.

Stanislavski, Constantin. *My Life in Art.* Moscow: Foreign Languages Publishing House, 1925.

Troyat, Henri. *Gorky: A Biography.* NY: Crown Publishers, 1989.

von Geldern, James. *Bolshevik Festivals, 1917–1920.* Berkeley, CA: University of California Press, 1993.

Wieczynski, Joseph L., ed. *The Modern Encyclopedia of Russian and Soviet History.* Vol. 1. Academic International Press, 1976.

SUGGESTED READING:

Voloxova, Nina. *Fenomen* (Phenomenon). Leningrad: (Russian-language biography), 1982.

Susan Brazier, freelance writer, Ottawa, Ontario, Canada

Andresen, Sophia de Mello Breyner (1919—)

Portuguese author of poetry, children's books, and short stories. Born in 1919 in Oporto, Portugal; educated at the University of Lisbon; children: five.

Selected works: Poesia *(1944);* Dia do Mar *(Day of the Sea, 1947);* Coral *(1950);* Mar Nova *(New Sea, 1958);* Contos Exemplares *(Exemplary Tales, 1962);* Histórias da Terra e do Mar *(Stories of the Earth and the Sea, 1984).*

Sophia Andresen was a student of philosophy at the University of Lisbon before she became one of Portugal's most respected poets. She arrived on the literary scene at age 25, with her collection *Poesia.* Over the next 50 years, Andresen produced 11 more volumes of verse, as well as short stories and children's books. In addition to her own writing, she is known for her translations, including works of Shakespeare. Andresen's preoccupations greatly influenced her poetry; she wrote frequently about religion, social injustice, inhumanity, and nature, especially the sea. An intensely private figure, sometimes referred to as hermetic, Andresen has five children.

Andrew, Princess (1885–1969).

See Alice of Battenberg.

Andrews, Eliza Frances (1840–1931)

American author and botanist. Name variations: (pseudonym) Elzey Hay. Born in Washington, Georgia, on August 10, 1840, a member of the Southern landowning class; died in Rome, Georgia, on January 21, 1931; daughter of Garnett Andrews and Annulet Ball Andrews; had two sisters and five brothers.

Her family escaped the devastation of the Civil War (1861–65), but became impoverished after her father died (1873); her diary of the Civil War became a classic chronicle of the conflict, compared by some historians to the famous diary of *Mary Boykin Chesnut; wrote novels, taught in public schools, and became a noted botanist whose scientific knowledge was self-taught; unafraid of espousing new ideas and indifferent to peer pressure, proclaimed herself a Marxian Socialist in a region hostile to any form of social or political radicalism.

Born in Georgia when "Cotton was king," Eliza Frances Andrews grew up in a large family that had considerable influence in Wilkes County. Her father Garnett Andrews, a lawyer, judge, and politician, was a loner, fiercely independent and honest. Though he owned 200 slaves, he supported the Union. Both before and during the Civil War, he criticized vehemently the folly of secession while his eight children, including Eliza, fervently supported the Rebel cause. The Andrews children were raised in an environment of intellectual excitement, which included lively discussions and debates on the arts and current events. As a young woman, Eliza wrote intermittently for various Southern newspapers, usually submitting her pieces anonymously or pseudonymously.

When war came, Andrews did not write about it at first. But by 1864, surrounded by death and devastation, she began to keep a diary. Not published until 1908 when she permitted an edited version to appear in print, her *War-Time Journal* is considered one of the Civil War's best. In part, it describes tensions at Haywood, the family home and plantation near Washington, Georgia, between Garnett Andrews and his children. The journal also vividly describes Sherman's March to the Sea. Though her home was spared, Eliza and her younger sister were sent for safety to a brother-in-law's plantation in southwest Georgia near Albany as Sherman's troops burned their way to the coast. Andrews' journal gives a detailed account of the collapse of her traditional agrarian world.

The financial crisis of 1873, and the death of her father the same year, brought severe financial reverses for the formerly affluent Andrews clan, and they lost Haywood due to the reckless speculations of a trusted family adviser. At age 33, Eliza Andrews was confronted with the necessity of earning a living for the first time. She left home to become principal of the Girls' High School in Yazoo City, Mississippi. Working under an African-American superintendent of education, she experienced a perceived loss of status: a planter's daughter was now an employee of former slaves. After only a year in Yazoo City, she returned home in 1874 to Washington, living with one of her married sisters and serving for almost a decade as principal of the local girls' school. After several years of forced idleness due to illness, Andrews taught literature and French at Wesleyan Female College in Macon, Georgia, from 1885 to 1896. From 1898 until her retirement in 1903, she was once again in her hometown of Washington, where she taught botany at the local public high school.

Andrews supplemented her income with the publication of several novels. She also published serialized stories in magazines and for a time was a lecturer on the Chautauqua circuit. Her most substantial writings were three novels. In her 1876 novel *A Family Secret,* she described the physical devastation and psychological stresses of the post-1865 South, whereas *A Mere Adventurer* (1879) and *Prince Hal* (1882) celebrated the Old South's antebellum culture. Although not considered great literature, these novels are still of considerable interest. Eliza Andrews' writings breathe a deep and abiding contempt for the crude, money-grasping mores that replaced the leisured semi-feudal culture she had known in her youth.

Andrews' philosophical approach to these changes was innovative—she embraced the doctrines of Marxian Socialism. She defined the hated Yankee capitalists as the ruling class fated for destruction in Marxist thought. In her view, the system imposed by carpetbaggers was doomed and would soon be replaced by a revolutionary upheaval led by the exploited industrial proletariat. Andrews was serious about her political beliefs. From 1899 to 1918, she was listed as a Socialist in *Who's Who in America.* As late as July 1916, she wrote an article entitled "Socialism in the Plant World," which appeared in the *International Socialist Review.*

In an 1865 diary entry, Andrews had vowed never to marry but to pursue "the career that I have marked out for myself." Though she enjoyed parties, dances and flirtations, she did indeed remain single. As she grew older, she became more freespirited, venturing forth into new fields as she entered the seventh decade of her life, including the publication of a textbook in 1903, *Botany All the Year Round.* Entirely self-taught, Andrews absorbed a vast amount of information on botany, developing an ability to communicate these ideas to a general audience. A positive response to her first botany book led to further research, much of it conducted at the Alabama Polytechnic Institute in Auburn. In 1911, she published *A Practical Course in Botany,* a book that remains remarkably fresh despite many advances in factual knowledge in the field. Not simply a plant taxonomy, *A Practical Course* places plants in an organic, universalistic context of interdependence between the natural and man-made environments. Written by an individual who was an autodidact in an impoverished and war-devastated region, it is an amazing achievement and an astonishingly modern work. The intellectual quality of Andrews' book was recognized at the time and it was translated for school use in France.

Eliza Andrews' political and scientific judgments were bold to the end of her extraordinarily long and productive life. In her introduction to the first edition of her diary, she explained how the Civil War had radically transformed the role of women in Southern life, stating, "The exigencies of the times did away with many conventions." Although she found some of these changes difficult to accept, Andrews became an assertive, independent woman who left her mark on her state and region. She died in Rome, Georgia, on January 21, 1931, and was buried alongside her family at the Rest Haven Cemetery in Washington, Georgia.

SOURCES:

Andrews, Eliza Frances. *The War-Time Journal of a Georgia Girl, 1864–1865.* Edited by Spencer Bidwell King. New reprint edition. Atlanta, GA: Cherokee Publishing, 1976.

Patton, James W. "Eliza Frances Andrews," in *Notable American Women 1607–1950: A Biographical Dictionary.* 3 vols. Edited by Edward T. James *et al.* Cambridge, MA: The Belknap Press of Harvard University Press, 1971, vol. 1, pp. 45–46.

Reitt, Barbara B. "Andrews, Eliza Frances," in *Dictionary of Georgia Biography.* 2 vols. Edited by Kenneth Coleman and Charles Stephen Gurr. Athens, GA: University of Georgia Press, 1983, Vol. 1, pp. 29–31.

John Haag, Associate Professor of History, University of Georgia, Athens, Georgia

Andrews, Laverne (1911–1967).
See Andrews Sisters.

Andrews, Maxene (1916–1995).
See Andrews Sisters.

Andrews, Patti (b. 1918).
See Andrews Sisters.

Andrews, Regina Anderson (b. 1901).
See Anderson, Regina M.

Andrews Sisters (1932–1953)

American singing sisters who were among the nation's most popular entertainers in the 1930s and 1940s, especially known for their appearances at morale-boosting USO shows during World War II.

LaVerne (1911–1967). *Name variations: Laverne. Born on July 6, 1911, in Minneapolis, Minnesota; died of cancer in Hollywood, California, on May 8, 1967; first daughter of Peter Andrews (of Greek descent) and Olga "Ollie" (Sollie) Andrews (a Norwegian); married Louis Rogers, in 1948.*

Maxene (1916–1995). *Name variations: sometimes mistakenly spelled Maxine. Born on January 3, 1916, in Minneapolis, Minnesota; died of a heart attack while vacationing in Hyannis, Massachusetts, on October 21, 1995; second daughter of Peter Andrews (of Greek descent) and a Norwegian mother Olga "Ollie" (Sollie) Andrews (a Norwegian); married Lou Levy (their manager), on July 28, 1941 (divorced 1950); children: Peter and Aleda Anne.*

Patti (1918—). *Born on February 16, 1918, in Minneapolis, Minnesota; third daughter of Peter Andrews (of Greek descent) and a Norwegian mother Olga "Ollie" (Sollie) Andrews (a Norwegian); married Martin Melcher (an agent and future husband of *Doris Day*), in October 1947 (divorced 1950); married Walter Wescheler (the group's accompanist), on December 25, 1951.*

First appeared professionally as the Andrews Sisters (1932); toured with vaudeville shows (1930s); released their first hit record (1937); appeared on national radio shows and in feature films (1940–53); with the country's entry into World War II and the subsequent formation of the United Services Organization (USO), began touring military facilities in the United States and abroad as part of the effort to entertain the troops and keep morale high (1941); dissolved their act (1953).

Selected discography: "Bei Mir Bist du Schön," "The Hut Sut Song," "Three Little Fishies," "Hold Tight-Hold Tight," "Beer Barrel Polka," "Well, All Right," "Oh Johnny," "Ferryboat Serenade," "Boogie Woogie Bugle Boy," "In Apple Blossom Time," "Aurora," "Elmer's Tune," "Chattanooga Choo Choo," "Pennsylvania Polka," "Sonny Boy," "Beat Me Daddy, Eight to the Bar," "Oh! Ma-ma!," "Rum and Coca Cola."

Filmography: Argentine Nights (1940); Buck Privates (1941); In the Navy (1941); Hold That Ghost (1941); What's Cookin'? (1942); Private Buckaroo (1942); Give Out Sisters (1942); Always a Bridesmaid (1943); How's About It? (1943); Swingtime Johnny (1943); Follow the Boys (1944); Moonlight and Cactus (1944); Hollywood Canteen (1944); (dubbed vocals only) Make Mine Music (1946); Road to Rio (1947); (dubbed vocals only) Melody Time (1948); (cameo for Patti) The Phynx (1970).

One cold winter's day in 1941, when the dust-coated old Studebaker drew up outside Cincinnati's largest theater, its occupants knew something was wrong. The street was deserted. By this time of day, there were generally long lines at the box office window to see them perform. But once inside the theater, the reason for the lack of business could be heard on the radio around which the stagehands were clustered. It was December 7, 1941, and the nation was just learning about the disaster at Pearl Harbor. The fact that the Andrews Sisters were appearing in town that night suddenly seemed unimportant. For LaVerne, Patti, and Maxene Andrews—and for their parents who trooped them from city to city, cooked their meals, and washed their clothes—America's entry into World War II would be a turning point in their careers, just as it would be the defining moment for the next 50 years of the nation's history.

It wasn't that the sisters weren't already famous from coast to coast. "The Andrews Sisters are said to be the most popular singing trio that ever came down the pike," *The New York Times* observed in 1940, and the first audiences that heard them sing in their native Minneapolis back in 1932 would have predicted such success. Born between 1911 and 1918 to Greek-Norwegian parents who ran the successful Pure Food Cafe on Hennepin Avenue, the three girls were ardent

fans of the ***Boswell Sisters**, a popular 1920s group, and pooled their allowance to buy nearly every song their idols performed. It was mother Olga who came from a musical background and instilled the love of song and dance; it was LaVerne who learned to read music and took up the piano. The Andrews house was filled with the young girls' effort to mimic the Boswells, with blonde Patti singing lead, brunette Maxene taking the soprano line, and red-haired LaVerne as the alto. Much to their credit, the girls' parents recognized their daughters' talent and encouraged them to appear at small social gatherings around Minneapolis. Olga also recognized that there were fewer sisterly squabbles. Among several other awards, the Andrews Sisters took first prize at the city's Orpheum Theater on the same bill with a ventriloquist named Edgar Bergen. Their act became so popular that it attracted the interest of RKO, which had not yet forsaken its dying vaudeville business for its burgeoning movie studios.

By the early '30s, the Andrews Sisters hit the road with an RKO "unit show," featuring band-

Andrews Sisters (from left to right, LaVerne, Patti, and Maxene).

leader Larry Rich. The unit shows were the last gasp of the old vaudeville days of the 'teens and 'twenties, and everyone knew it. "We must have closed every RKO theater in the Midwest," recalled Maxene many years later, but no one could deny that the Andrews Sisters were developing a new kind of singing style that would survive vaudeville's demise. By then, the family had sold the restaurant to finance a move to New York to further show-business ambitions.

The girls, like most teenagers in the 1930s, were listening to the "new music"—Swing. An outgrowth of the jazz bands of the 1920s, the Swing bands added strong rhythm and reed sections and expanded to 20 or more players. Benny Goodman, Tommy Dorsey, Glenn Miller, all were forming bands that were giving the "kids" what they wanted to hear and, even more, wanted to dance to: expressive percussion, vigorous horns, and swooping, velvety reeds in tightly woven harmonies. It was just this layered, seamless vocalizing the Andrews Sisters were perfecting that would prove to be the perfect complement to the Big Bands. At the same time, Patti Andrews brought her two sisters' attention to a kind of swing everyone was calling "boogie woogie." It was derived from the old South and was characterized by a jumpy, foot-tapping eight beats to the bar. (The Andrews Sisters would, in fact, record a boogie-woogie hit some years later called "Beat Me Daddy, Eight to the Bar.") Patti was the youngest of the three, and it came as no surprise that she was the one to discover the new style. "Patti was the fun one of the group," Maxene later wrote, "the clown who kept us laughing during those endless periods of backstage boredom between shows, when we were doing five or six shows a day."

It was, however, a traditional Yiddish song that set the girls on a recording career that would bring them nationwide fame. The song was "Bei Mir Bist Du Schön" ("For Me You Are Always Beautiful"), and the girls' swing arrangement of it was released by Decca Records in 1937; it sold over a million copies for which they received $50, no royalties. "Nice Work If You Can Get It" was on the flip side. The following year, they had another hit, again taking an old vaudeville tune from 1916 and dressing it up in swing. "Oh Johnny, Oh Johnny, Oh!" was quickly followed by "The Beer Barrel Polka" (which was recycled after the war broke out as "Here Comes The Navy," with different lyrics). Given a more lucrative contract, the group would stay with Decca for almost 17 years, recording over 400 songs, selling over 80 million records.

By 1940, vaudeville was officially dead, but the Andrews Sisters were perfectly positioned to make the transition to its mass entertainment successor, radio. Radio was now big business, and it wasn't long before the major networks (Mutual, NBC, and CBS) realized the audience potential for Swing. Glenn Miller had agreed to a 15-minute, once-weekly radio show, but the sponsor—Chesterfield cigarettes—wanted to hedge its bet on the "new music" and began searching for an added attraction that would increase the show's chances for success. Patti, Maxene, and LaVerne had already been appearing on "Your Hit Parade" to good notices, and they were soon added to the Miller show. Audience response was so enthusiastic that the show was soon expanded to three nights a week. It was on Glenn Miller's show that the Andrews Sisters introduced what would become their signature tune, "In Apple Blossom Time." They were also the first group to literally move on stage; other groups had always stood still and harmonized.

The world changed for everyone with the outbreak of war in 1941. Only six people attended the afternoon show at that Cincinnati theater on December 7th in 1941. Only a few dozen showed up for the evening show, in a theater that could hold 2,000. But it would not be long before Patti, Maxene, and LaVerne would be performing before some of the largest and most enthusiastic audiences they had ever encountered.

The USO (United Services Organization) was born in April of that year. Spearheaded by Broadway impresario Billy Rose, the USO was a collaboration between show business professionals and the military, with the goal of bringing morale-boosting entertainment to the troops. Funded entirely by public donation at first, the USO brought "draftee shows" to military bases around the country where America's young men and women were in training before heading overseas to fight. The shows were mounted on the backs of flatbed trucks, packed up and driven from base to base, and featured some of the top talent of the day: Bob Hope, Bing Crosby, *Ginger Rogers, *Betty Grable, Abbott & Costello, *Dorothy Lamour, and Clark Gable, along with the music of Dorsey, Miller, Goodman and, of course, the Andrews Sisters.

Thanks to their vaudeville background, the girls could troop with the best of them and over the next four years would be on the road almost continuously. For the armed forces' men and women, the Andrews Sisters represented home and family, the security and comforts of a youth they had so quickly lost. When the three sisters, still in their 20s themselves, began singing "I'll Be With You In Apple Blossom Time," a hush fell over an audience about to leave sweethearts behind for distant battles in Europe or the Pacific; and when they launched into "Boogie Woogie Bugle Boy of Company B," the crowd would be on their feet, clapping and dancing and ready to take on anything the war could throw at them. Many years later, Maxene would remember singing the lyrics to another of their hit tunes, "Don't sit under the apple tree/ With anyone else but me/ 'Til I come marching home," on the docks of Seattle to young men about to leave for the Pacific. "We stood down there on the pier," Maxene recalled, "looking up at all those young men leaning over the ships' rails, waving and yelling and screaming. . . . One thought nagged at you: how many of the young men shipping out wouldn't come back?"

Andrews Sisters (from left to right, LaVerne, Patti, and Maxene).

From 1941 to 1945, the Andrews Sisters sang in USO shows, at war bond rallies, and in the "canteens" set up in major cities by the USO, where the entertainers also waited tables. In 1944, they went overseas, performing in Italy and North Africa, sometimes only a few miles from the front lines. By war's end, the USO had staged some 293,000 performances and played to a combined audience of some 16 million servicemen and women. It was the biggest production in show business history, and the entertainers earned their title of "soldiers in greasepaint."

In addition to their USO duties, the three women played to civilian audiences (setting attendance records during a national tour in 1942), had their own half-hour radio show, "The Eight-to-the-Bar Ranch," on Sunday nights, appeared in more than a dozen films, and continued to record for Decca, selling 30 million records by 1944. *Time* called them "the queens of the jukebox," and *The New York Times*' Jack Gould observed that "the Andrews Sisters are in a class by themselves."

With the war over in 1945, the sisters began thinking about a future that lacked the USO. They formed a corporation to handle their finances and permanently relocated to Los Angeles, settling their parents in a home in Brent-

wood. Maxene had married their manager, Lou Levy, in 1941 (although she kept it a secret from everyone but Patti for some time); LaVerne married musician Lou Rogers in 1948. Compared to the hectic pace of the war years, the girls' lives seemed to be settling down by the late 1940s. There were still tours and recording dates, to be sure, and newspaper reporter **Mary Morris**, who came to one of these studio sessions to interview them, found that the Andrews Sisters remained every bit as energetic when it came to their music. "They made faces," she wrote, "beat their feet while their bodies jumped and swayed. Even the arranger's derriere wriggled wildly in the piano seat. The whole room jumped."

"They were as different as three sisters could possibly be," wrote Bernie Woods. "Patti, very outgoing, devil-may-care. LaVerne, quiet and unassuming. Maxene was the main gear and handled most of the trio's business dealings with Levy. . . . And she drove a car like a racer." "Music is the one thing we had in common," said Maxene, who was always the group rebel. "We never agreed on hair styles or clothes, but we were always together" on material and arrangements.

By the early 1950s, though, the strains were beginning to show. "Everything seemed to catch up with us at once," said Maxene. Their mother had died in 1948; their father soon after. They had split with their arranger Vic Schoen. Patti separated from her agent-husband Marty Melcher (who would marry *Doris Day the following year); Maxene divorced her husband. Patti, who had a solo hit in 1949 with "I Can Dream Can't I," began complaining that her older sisters still treated her like a baby, and disputes broke out over the corporation and the salaries it paid to each of the girls. In 1951, Maxene underwent major surgery, and LaVerne and Patti finished their commitments as a duet. In 1953, the corporation was dissolved, along with the act itself. The Andrews Sisters were officially retired, and Patti went solo in 1954, signing with Capitol records. When Patti sued her sisters, demanding proper settlement of their mother's estate, Maxene made the headlines on December 21, 1954, with a suspected suicide attempt because of the conflict. Maxene denied it, and LaVerne maintained that Maxene "loves life too much to want to end it." LaVerne also told reporters that more than 2,000 letters had poured in begging them to reconsider the breakup, and in 1956 the Andrews Sisters did, indeed, revive the act for a few appearances. But the times were different. The Korean War was being fought, but it inspired nothing like the national pride and enthusiasm of the Second World War. The enemy was no longer a man called Hitler, but an ideology called Communism. People were listening to radio less and watching television more, and the great Swing bands were giving way to bebop and a quirky new sound called rock-and-roll.

> *A*mericans could beat anything and anybody, and if you didn't believe it, the Andrews Sisters would make a believer out of you.
> —Maxene Andrews

Even so, no one completely forgot the Andrews Sisters. There were occasional solo television and film appearances for each of the sisters and, after LaVerne died of cancer in 1967, interviews and articles about the sisters and what they had meant to a generation of Americans. Maxene was then teaching in the drama and speech department at Tahoe Paradise College in Lake Tahoe, Nevada, where she became dean of women for two years beginning in 1968. It was reported that Patti and Maxene had become estranged and rarely spoke to one another. Both were closed mouth as to the reasons why.

In 1973, when **Bette Midler** re-recorded "Boogie Woogie Bugle Boy of Company B" with enormous success, there was renewed interest in the original act that had performed it. Before long, a Broadway musical opened, called *Over Here*—a nostalgic recreation of the war years starring Maxene and Patti and a third "sister," actress ✥▶ **Janie Sell**. Produced by Kenneth Waissman and **Maxine Fox**, it opened on Broadway on March 6, 1974. After a near-fatal heart attack in 1982 and quadruple bypass surgery, Maxene recorded a solo album in 1985, moved to Nevada in 1989, appeared briefly in a dance

---

✥▶ **Sell, Janie** (1941—)

American actress. Name variations: Jane Trese. Born in Detroit, Michigan, on October 1, 1941; attended University of Detroit; graduated from Hunter College, 1989; married in 1965 and divorced; married Patrick Trese, around 1990; children: (first marriage) one son.

Janie Sell made her debut in *Mixed Doubles* in 1966; she was also featured in *Dark Horses, Dames at Sea, George M, Irene, Pal Joey, Happy End, I Love My Wife*, and *Over Here*, for which she received a Theater World Award.

show called "Company B" created by choreographer Paul Taylor in 1991, and published a memoir of the USO years in 1993. Before she died in October 1995, she had also become interested in group therapy, forming a foundation to work with drug addicts and delinquents.

Following a solo appearance in Florida in 1991, Maxene had encountered a WWII veteran waiting for her outside her dressing room. He shook her hand warmly, and then told her, "I don't know if you think this is a compliment or not, but to me and my buddies, the Andrews Sisters are synonymous with World War II." Maxene thought it was one of the best compliments she had ever been paid.

SOURCES:

Andrews, Maxene, with Bill Gilbert. *Over Here, Over There: The Andrews Sisters and the USO Stars in WWII.* NY: Kensington Publishers, 1993.

Clarke, Donald. *The Rise and Fall of Popular Music.* NY: St. Martin's Press, 1995.

Katz, Ephraim. *The Film Encyclopedia.* NY: The Perennial Library, 1990.

Lamparski, Richard. *Whatever Became of . . . ?* Third Series. NY: Crown, 1971.

Parish, James Robert, and Michael R. Pitts. *Hollywood Songsters.* NY: Garland, 1991.

Woods, Bernie. *When the Music Stopped.* NY: Barricade Books, 1994.

Norman Powers, writer/producer,
Chelsea Lane Productions, New York, New York

Andreyeva, Maria Fyodorovna

(1868–1953).

See Andreeva, Maria Fedorovna.

Andrezel, Pierre (1885–1962).

See Dinesen, Isak.

Andriesse, Emmy (1914–1953)

Dutch photographer. Born at The Hague, the Netherlands, in 1914; died in Amsterdam, in 1953; attended Koninklijke Academie voor Beeldende Kunsten, The Hague, 1932–37; married Dilck Elffers, in 1941.

Primarily known for her portraits, especially of artists, as well as commercial advertising and fashion work, Emmy Andriesse studied graphic design and photography with Dutch avant-garde teachers Gerrit Kiljan, Paul Schuitema, and Piet Zwart. Her early career also included work with *Eva Besnyö, Carel Blazer, and Cas Oorthuys. During the German occupation, from 1940 to 1945, Andriesse was a member of a group of photographers using disguised cameras (*Ondergedoken Camera*).

In 1951, while in Paris photographing artists and singers, Andriesse was invited by the director of the Stedelijk Museum in Amsterdam to photograph 13 sculptors in Paris and Belgium. That same year, she also began photography for a book on the artist Vincent Van Gogh, which was published posthumously in 1953 as *The World of Van Gogh.* Andriesse's photographs were seen in the United States in periodicals like *U.S. Camera,* and, in 1955, two of her photographs appeared in Edward Steichen's show, *The Family of Man* (Museum of Modern Art, New York) and the accompanying book. In 1975, there was an exhibition of her work at the Van Gogh Museum in Amsterdam. Her archives are housed at the Printcabinet of University of Leiden, the Netherlands.

Andrus, Ethel Percy (1884–1967)

American reformer and founder of the AARP. Born on September 21, 1884; died in Long Beach, California, in 1967; graduated from the University of Chicago, 1903; granted an M.A. (1926) and Ph.D. (1930) from the University of Southern California at Los Angeles (UCLA).

Taught at Lewis Institute (1903–10), Abraham Lincoln High School in Los Angeles (1910–44).

In 1944, upon retiring from over 40 years as a teacher and public-school principal, Ethel Percy Andrus found, to her dismay, that her retirement pay was $60 a month. Working to improve the lot of teachers, she founded the National Retired Teachers Association (NRTA) in 1947. In 1956, the group sponsored the first health-insurance plan for all people over 65, which led to Andrus' founding of the American Association of Retired Persons (AARP) two years later. In 1961, she was asked to join the national advisory committee for the White House Conference on Aging. She was also a founder and editor of *Modern Maturity*, the magazine of the AARP.

Anezka.

Variant of Agnes.

Angela, Mother (1824–1887).

See Gillespie, Mother Angela.

Angela of Brescia (1474–1540)

Founder of the Ursuline nuns, a Roman Catholic order focused on teaching young girls and young women. Name variations: Angela Merici. Pronuncia-

tion: Mer-EE-chi. Born Angela Merici on March 21, 1474, at Grezze on Lake Garda in Italy, though a local legend persists that she was born in the town of Desenzano, a few miles away; died on January 27, 1540, in Brescia; daughter of John Merici (a well-to-do vintner), and Signora Merici (of the Biancosi merchant family from Salo); never married, no children.

Orphaned in early teens and moved to Salo; became a member of the third Order of St. Francis, a lay order dedicated to charitable works and teaching; experienced a vision that told her to found an order of women in Brescia (c. 1495); dedicated to St. Ursula, the order was formally approved as an unenclosed group of women devoted to teaching children, especially young girls (August 8, 1536).

The end of the 15th century was a time of change and innovation. Christopher Columbus opened the sea route to the Americas, Henry VII ended the War of the Roses in England and re-united the ruling houses of Lancaster and York, and the Jews were expelled from the Iberian peninsula during the joint reign of Ferdinand and *Isabella I (1451–1504) of Spain. The age of new invention and new art included the novel idea of the printing press and the works of the Renaissance artists Raphael and Michelangelo. It was an age that found women with generally low status, tied to their male relatives for both rank and survival. Bracketed between the birth years of two famous men, Nicholas Copernicus (1473), the Polish astronomer who popularized the heliocentric theory of the universe, and Michelangelo Buonarroti (1475), the painter of the Sistine Chapel, was the birth of Angela Merici, the founder of the teaching order of the Ursuline nuns, on March 21, 1474.

The fate of a woman in the society of 15th-century Italy was linked to her dowry and to her husband. History notes the name of Angela's father as John Merici, a well-to-do farmer and vintner, who owned the farm and the house called Grezze. There, Angela was born, a scant two miles outside the town of Desenzano on the shores of Lake Garda in Italy. Angela's mother, on the other hand, is remembered only as Signora Merici, whose family was comprised of wealthy merchants from Salo. Signora Merici gave birth to at least one other child besides Angela. Biographers know of the existence of one verifiable sister who influenced Angela's life in many ways. The number of other children is difficult to assess; there may have been another sister or two, and as many as three brothers, all of whom would have died during childhood, and perhaps before Angela was born.

The two surviving children, Angela and her sister, grew up on the farm. Portraits of the family show the group reading from the lives of the saints, *Legenda Sanctorum*, a book printed in 1475. Reading and home-teaching formed the basis of Angela's education. Her later knowledge of Latin was, in fact, seen to be miraculous due to a lack of formal schooling. Probably in her childhood, at the knee of her father, she developed a strong devotion to Saint *Ursula, a British princess martyred by marauding Huns in the 5th century. According to legend, Angela and her sister enacted the stories of the saints and practiced the penances they read about, including fasting and hours of long prayer.

They were the closest of friends. The two little girls with the fair hair, clear complexions, and short stature were a regular sight in the town and on the farm. However, at the time Angela was about ten years old, her sister died. (The exact date is unknown; some biographers place it about five years later, after Angela's move to Salo.) Her death affected Angela greatly. She missed her sister and prayed for her so intensely that her first recorded vision is attributed to this period: Angela had a mystical vision at Barchetto of her sister in heaven, with angels bearing her happily to her eternal reward. Whether this vision served to put Angela at ease is uncertain, but undeniably her life during the next few years was one of sadness and loss. Within a year of her sister's death, her father died, leaving Angela and her mother to run the farm. Within the passage of yet another year, her mother died and Angela was an orphan. Though there is no exact date, it is reasonable to assume that Angela was orphaned before she was 15 years of age. As a young girl, she required a guardian, so her maternal uncle moved her to the Biancosi family home in Salo. There Angela spent her remaining teen years.

By the time she was 20 years old, Angela joined the Third Order of Saint Francis. The Franciscan Tertiary was the lay branch of the Franciscans who lived at home, wore simple dress (neither white nor black) and a veil. They did not attend banquets, social functions, or dances, and spent their time in charitable works, such as visiting the sick, daily prayer, and teaching the catechism. This was evidently not enough for Angela, and she attempted to run away from Salo to become an anchorite. Her uncle, however, brought her back and put an end to that scheme.

Angela's 20th year, 1495, was a year of fighting in northern Italy between Francis I of

France and Charles V of Spain, heir to the title of Holy Roman emperor. War was not uncommon in northern Italy where inter-city warfare was led by men like the condottieri Francesco Sforza in Milan and the Medici in Florence whose one-time advisor Niccolo Machiavelli preserved the ideology of the era in his work, *The Prince.* Amid civil strife, Angela left Sola to return to Grezze, her paternal inheritance. There, she became well-known for teaching young girls their catechism, caring for the sick, and aiding the needy. With a group of young women, she spent her time traveling around Lake Garda to the local towns doing good works. It was at Brudazzo during this period of her life that Angela had her second mystical experience. A vision of stairs or a ladder stretching from heaven to earth is said to have filled her soul. Upon the stairs were angels and young women moving down in groups playing music. The vision told her, "Before you die, you are to found, in Brescia, a company like these virgins."

Traveling around the lake, Angela made many contacts. One of the most influential was **Caterina Patengula**, a wealthy woman who had come to spend time at her summer home on Lake Garda after the death of her sons. Angela consoled her, and they became such good friends that Angela left Grezze in 1516 and moved in with Patengula in Brescia. She continued to lodge there for some months before she took a room in the home of Antonio Romano, a room she kept for 14 years.

The years of Angela's young adulthood were years of disarray, both in her homeland and in Western Europe. Brescia itself was troubled with warring families within the confines of the town, and warring city-states threatened the city repeatedly from the outside. Furthermore, the influence of the Inquisition was seen in the district surrounding Brescia between 1516 and 1524. During that time, a number of young adolescent girls were tried and convicted of witchcraft. Angela felt the girls were acting young, naive, and dangerously silly, but that was not grounds for burning as a witch. At the height of the scandal, some 2,500 persons were involved, and in July 1518 eight girls were sentenced to burn. The Inquisition used innuendo and torture to obtain the confessions. To Angela, this was just one more example of how young women lacked education and were exploited by society. Young girls without the chance of a good dowry had few choices, and many became caught up in fads and illusions, some of which ended with the witchcraft trials.

The fears of the Inquisition were reinforced by the heresy of the monk Martin Luther in Germany. In 1517, he had attacked certain money-making schemes of the Catholic Church, including the selling of indulgences to augment the Vatican treasury. Luther had valid objections and probably never intended to leave the Church. However, a number of German princes thought less Vatican control would be an ideal way to increase their own power. Rapidly, Luther's message swept northern Europe and the "heresy" began to filter into northern Italy through the words of street-corner preachers. This "Reformation," and the general plight of young untutored girls, strengthened Angela's resolve to develop a new type of education to combat the doctrinal disputes of the Reformation and to offer women another choice beyond the convent.

The next 16 years of Angela's life were dedicated to her new mission and new ideal. She envisioned a company of lay women from all socio-economic groups. There was to be no social stratification among the sisters who were to take quiet vows and live uncloistered among the people they served through nursing, teaching, and catechizing. There was to be no formal dress or formal rituals. In part, Angela planned this type of life for the young girls, and widows who embraced it, as an alternative to the convent. Some dowerless girls found the convent an unwelcome option, which led to scandal and excesses within the convents themselves.

In her search for the right method for her congregation, Angela made a series of pilgrimages. Her first was to Blessed **Osanna Andreasi** in Mantua in early 1524. After her return, she embarked for Jerusalem in late May. As Angela toured the Holy Land and the sites where Jesus had walked, she suffered a loss of vision that was not restored until she neared Italy on the voyage home. After a difficult passage, she reached the coastline of Italy and stayed in Venice that autumn. Though asked by the doge's council to remain in the city and administer the Hospital of Incurables, Angela returned home. After a brief stay, she journeyed to Rome in 1525 where she had an audience with Pope Clement VII, who blessed her mission.

Angela returned to Brescia in the midst of a plague year. The plague was not only of disease, but of mercenaries left behind by warring armies to overrun the cities of northern Italy. Angela had a reputation as an arbitrator in cases of civil unrest. This function may have brought her to the attention of the young duke Francesco Sforza who had been exiled from Milan in 1521, when the duchy was attacked by Charles V of France. Angela listened and lent advice to the duke.

In 1529, Angela took one of her last major pilgrimages to Varalla, Italy, or the "New Jerusalem." On the way home, she visited Sforza in Milan. Perhaps through his intercession, she met and spoke to **Stefana Quinzani**, prioress at the convent of Dominican Tertiaries at Soncino. Entering what was to be the last decade of her life, Angela returned to Brescia to organize her congregation only to find the city beset by new difficulties and new threats. The people of Brescia moved into exile in Cremona where Angela stayed with a new sponsor Agostino Gallo and his sister **Hippolyta**. That year, the usually hearty Angela fell ill and nearly died.

Fortunately, her health and peace returned in 1530. When Charles V of France was crowned by Pope Clement VII in Bologna on February 24, Sforza was once again returned to Milan, and Angela returned to Brescia where she occupied an apartment next to the church of Saint *Afra's. Making her last pilgrimage to Varallo, she returned home to finish work on her Rule for the congregation and to organize it formally. By this time, a group of young women and widows followed her and kept her company, no doubt influenced by the tales of her sanctity, which were enhanced by reports that she levitated during prayer.

By 1531, Angela had the basic structure of her company. It derived its sense of mission from the lives of three Catholic saints, Saint *Paula (347–404), a Roman widow; Saint *Elizabeth of Hungary (1207–1231), the queen of that nation and a woman devoted to aiding the poor and sick; and finally, Saint Ursula. On November 25, 1535, Angela and 28 companions received communion and initiated their new order. Between 1534 and 1537, the congregation chose its leadership and organized itself through democratic elections. Finally, on August 8, 1536, the congregation was approved by Cardinal Cornaro's vicar-general.

As the congregation was originally envisioned, maidens, matrons, and men made up the group. Angela's secretary was a man named Gabriel Cozano, but further involvement of men never materialized. The women devoted themselves to good works, nursing, and charity. Their special mission, however, was to educate young girls and young women. Girls had had little chance for education unless a widow opened up a school in her home. The Ursulines entered the homes of the girls to teach them and to mold them. Angela's philosophy permeated her work:

"The teacher only a care-taker? Perish the thought! The teacher's office must be to foster, to direct, to instruct. . . . Inquire into their conditions . . . in fact their whole being."

Disorder in society is the result of disorder in the family.

—Angela of Brescia

In order to carry out this work, the city was divided into quadrants, and the teachers were encouraged not to try to instill a vocation for religious life but to teach the girls and listen to them. Just as her mission was beginning to succeed, Angela fell ill in 1539. Nursed through the summer and fall, she died on January 27, 1540, and was interred at St. Afra's Church beside which she had lived for so long. Her body still resides there, below the high altar. The Catholic Church beatified her in 1768, and she was canonized in 1807; her feast day is celebrated on May 31.

Angela's congregation, which numbered around 100 at the time of her death, did not endure for as long as she had planned. Under pressure from the Reformation, the Catholic Church began a Counter-Reformation to remove all vice from the Church or anything that might be considered a temptation. Virgins unenclosed and in contact with the world were seen as one such temptation. The Council of Trent (1545–63) affirmed the Catholic Church's strict ideas on enclosure for women. Under the "reforms" of Saint Charles Borremeo, the Ursulines found themselves living in cloisters and wearing traditional habits. However, they were allowed to continue their work as teachers of young girls. By 1576, the order spread into France and on into the Benelux countries by 1611. From there, the Ursulines migrated to the Americas by the mid-17th century where they continued to teach girls in convent-based schools.

The movement that Angela of Brescia founded began as a response to the plight of young women and the hazards of unprotected life without education. Living through the early throes of the Reformation, Angela offered a way to reform both female monasticism and female education. In many ways, she was before her time in her conception of the Ursulines as unenclosed lay workers.

As a saint, her mission is traditionally explained by her vision of inspiration; as a woman, her vision was an intelligent response to the societal problems around her. If women were the center of the home, she reasoned, the most effective way to reform society was to reform the role of women and, concomitantly, their educational opportunities. In that way, both the family and society would be reformed for the good of all concerned.

SOURCES:

Bridenthal, Renate, Claudia Koonz, and Susan Stuard, eds. *Becoming Visible.* Boston, MA: Houghton-Mifflin, 1987.

Boulding, Elise. *The Underside of History.* Vol. II. Newbury Park, CA: Sage Publications, 1992.

Caraman, Philip. *Saint Angela: The Life of Angela Merici, Foundress of the Ursulines.* NY: Farrar, Straus, 1963.

Monica, Sister Mary. *Angela Merici and Her Teaching Idea (1474–1540).* Saint Martin, OH: The Ursulines of Brown County, 1945.

Ruether, Rosemary, and Eleanor McLaughlin, eds. *Women of Spirit.* NY: Simon and Schuster, 1979.

SUGGESTED READING:

Anderson, Bonnie S., and Judith P. Zinsser. *A History of Their Own.* NY: Harper and Row, 1988.

Michaela Crawford Reaves, Department of History, California Lutheran University, Thousand Oaks, California

Angela of Foligno (1249–1309)

Saint and author of Divine Consolation. *Born in Umbria in 1249; died in 1309; married with several children. Beatified in 1693.*

Angela of Foligno was revered as a woman of exceptional piety, who dictated a work about her life, which came to be called the *Divine Consolations of the Blessed Angela of Foligno*; her emphasis on true humility and the importance of prayer made her a spiritual inspiration to other holy women, like Saint *Teresa of Avila. Born into an affluent Umbrian family, Angela received little education except some religious instruction from her mother. She married young, as was usual, and had several children.

As revealed in her later writings, Angela considered herself self-indulgent and fun-loving as a wife and mother. She enjoyed life and was as kind and generous as her wealthy social position allowed her to be. Though at times she became fearful about her salvation, she did not have the courage to alter her lifestyle.

Pier Angeli

Early in her adult life, however, death took her husband, her children, and her mother within a short span of time. At this point, Angela's immense grief led her to join the Third Order of Saint Francis, but it would be several years before she found peace by repenting her past and giving up worldliness.

Believing poverty to be the basis for virtue and wisdom, Angela then sold all her property. She and an equally devout companion, **Pasqualina**, regularly went to visit the poor and the ill to bring comfort to the less fortunate. They also worked in hospitals, washing lepers and consoling the patients. At age 60, Angela of Foligno died. She was beatified in 1693.

Laura York, Anza, California

Angelberga (c. 840–890).

See Engelberga.

Angeli, Pier (1932–1971)

Italian actress. Born Anna Maria Pierangeli in Cagliari, Sardinia, Italy, on June 19, 1932; daughter of a construction engineer and architect father and an amateur actress mother; committed suicide on September 10, 1971; twin sister of Maria Luisa Pierangeli, who performed under the screen name **Marisa Pavan***; married Vic Damone (a singer), on November 24, 1954 (divorced 1959); married Armando Travajoli (an Italian bandleader), in 1962 (separated 1963); children: (first marriage) Perry Rocco Damone (b. 1955); (second marriage) Howard Andrea (called Popino, b. 1963).*

Selected filmography: Domani é troppo Tardi *(Tomorrow is Too Late, 1949);* Domani é un altro Giorno *(1950);* Teresa *(MGM, 1951);* The Light Touch *(MGM, 1951);* The Devil Makes Three *(MGM, 1952);* The Story of Three Loves *(MGM, 1953);* Sombrero *(MGM, 1953);* The Flame and the Flesh *(MGM, 1954);* The Silver Chalice *(WB, 1955);* Santarella *(French-Italian, 1954);* Somebody Up There Likes Me *(MGM, 1956);* Port Afrique *(Columbia, 1956);* The Vintage *(MGM, 1957);* Merry Andrew *(MGM, 1958);* S.O.S. Pacific *(U.K., 1959);* The Angry Silence *(U.K., 1960);* Musketeers of the Sea *(Italian-French, 1962);* White Slave Ship *(AIP, 1962);* Sodoma e Gomorra *(1961);* Battle of the Bulge *(WB; 1965);* Spy in Your Eye *(AIP, 1966);* Per Mille Dollari al Giorno *(Spanish-Italian, 1966);* Rose Rosse Per Il Führer *(Italian, 1968);* Every Bastard a King *(Israel, 1968);* Addio, Alexandra *(International Arts, 1971);* Nelle Pieghe della Carne *(In the Folds of the Flesh, 1971);* Octaman *(1971).*

Pier Angeli was the daughter of a father who opposed a show-business career for his girls and a mother who carefully trained and nurtured a movie career for them. Angeli made her debut opposite Vittorio de Sica in Leonide Moguy's *Domani é troppo Tardi* (*Tomorrow is Too Late*, 1949). A year later, she filmed the sequel, *Domani é un altro Giorno*. Both films dealt with the pain of adolescence and the need for sexual guidance. Fred Zinnemann then hired her for the title role of his soulful Italian bride *Teresa* (MGM, 1951), which was filmed in Italy. At this time, she met singer Vic Damone who was stationed as a soldier there. Moving to Hollywood with her mother and sister, Angeli became a close friend of **Debbie Reynolds** (who taught her American slang), dated James Dean and Kirk Douglas, and surprised everyone by marrying Damone in 1954.

During the 1950s, Angeli played the lead in many Hollywood films, generally as the fragile innocent. She also struggled with injuries in her personal life. In 1955, she fell aboard an airplane while pregnant and broke her pelvis; fortunately, a healthy son was born that August. The following year, she broke her ankle and had a miscarriage. In addition, her marriage to Damone was little more than a series of separations and reconciliations; Damone blamed their problems on a meddling mother-in-law, and they were divorced in 1959. The next six years were taken up with custody battles over their son.

Except for her appearance in two prestigious television productions, as *Bernadette of Lourdes** in "Song of Bernadette" (1958) and as the Tahitian girl opposite Laurence Olivier in "The Moon and Sixpence" (1959), Angeli's career began to stall. After her breakup with Damone, she returned to Italy, remarried, made a few more movies, and ended up penniless. Returning to Hollywood in 1971, she was feted by her friend Reynolds and their mutual friend *Agnes Moorehead**; both women were determined to reignite her career. On September 10, 1971, while living with drama coach **Helen Sorell**, Angeli died of an overdose of barbiturates at age 39, unaware that she had just been offered a guest-starring role on the then hugely popular *Bonanza*.

Angelique, Mere (1591–1661).

See Jacqueline Arnauld in entry titled "Port Royal des Champ, abbesses of."

Angelique de Saint-Jean, Mere (1624–1684).

See Angelique Arnauld in entry titled "Port Royal des Champ, abbesses of."

Angelou, Maya (1928—)

African-American author, actress, and dancer. Born Marguerite Annie Johnson on April 4, 1928, in St. Louis, Missouri; daughter of Bailey and Vivian Baxter Johnson (divorced 1931); married Tosh Angelos (an ex-sailor), around 1950 (divorced around 1952); married Vusumzi Make (a South African freedom fighter), around 1960 (divorced 1963); married Paul Du Feu (a builder and writer), 1973 (divorced around 1981); children: Guy Johnson.

Selected works: I Know Why the Caged Bird Sings *(1970);* Just Give Me a Cool Drink of Water 'Fore I Diiie *(1971);* Gather Together in My Name *(1974);* Oh Pray My Wings Are Gonna Fit Me Well *(1975);* Singin' and Swingin' and Gettin' Merry Like Christmas *(1976);* And Still I Rise *(1978);* The Heart of a Woman *(1981);* Shaker Why Don't You Sing *(1983);* All God's Children Need Travelling Shoes *(1986); (with Tom Feeling)* Now Sheba Sings the Song *(1987);* I Shall Not Be Moved *(1990);* On the Pulse of Morning *(1993);* Wouldn't Take Nothing for My Journey Now *(1993).*

While growing up in the racist South of the 1930s, eight-year-old Maya Angelou stopped speaking for five years after she was brutalized by her mother's boyfriend. During her silence, she came to understand the importance of words and to love writing. She played many roles, both on and off stage, before her autobiography *Why the Caged Bird Sings* brought her to the fore of American literature and consciousness. On January 20, 1993, Angelou, now a teacher and poet, was called upon to deliver an inaugural poem intended to characterize the presidency of William Jefferson Clinton and a renewed American attitude. To the ears of millions, she raised the unmistakable Angelou voice and read "On the Pulse of Morning," including the lines:

> Lift up your eyes upon
> This day breaking for you.
> Give birth again
> To the dream.

Angelou was born Marguerite Annie Johnson, the second child of Bailey and **Vivian Johnson**, in St. Louis, Missouri. She was soon called Maya, her brother Bailey's version of "mine" or "my sister." The Johnsons' marriage was stormy, and when Maya was three she and four-year-old Bailey were sent to Stamps, Arkansas, to live

Maya
Angelou

with their grandmother **Annie Henderson**. Though her grandmother owned a grocery store, the family lived in a segregated shanty area and thought white people were "ghosts." At age eight, Maya made her first visit to her mother in St. Louis. While there, she was raped by her mother's boyfriend, and he was lynched the following day. Maya returned to her grandmother shattered and silent; she refused to talk, other than to Bailey, for the next five years. During this time, said Angelou, she learned the value of words and came to adore writing.

In 1940, after Maya had graduated from the Lafayette County Training School, her grandmother shipped the siblings to San Francisco, where their mother had relocated, remarried and become a professional gambler. Coming from a devoutly religious and quiet life in Stamps, they found San Francisco and the family there jubilant and loud. Maya was enrolled at Mission High School. By the time of her graduation in 1945, she was the mother of a boy named Guy whose father was a neighbor's son. To support Guy, Maya moved out of her mother's home and took various jobs around San Francisco. She was the city's first black streetcar toll-taker and conductor, but also made ends meet with work as a Creole cook, a prostitute, a singer, and a dancer. In the early 1950s, she met a white ex-sailor, Tosh Angelos, who managed a record store. Angelos provided an isolated and sheltered environment for Maya and her son. For several years, she stayed at home and wrote, tended to her child, and "recovered," as she called it, from the difficulties of her life. When she felt well enough to face the world again, she divorced Angelos to gain her freedom.

Angelou was selected to study dance with dancer-choreographer *Pearl Primus in 1952, and later with *Martha Graham and Ann Halprin. Throughout the 1950s and '60s, she worked in nightclubs and with stage shows, including the touring company of *Porgy and Bess*, which took her across America and Europe. She lived in New York and interacted with Malcolm X and Martin Luther King, Jr., which led to her post from 1960 to 1961 as the northern coordinator for King's Southern Christian Leadership Council. Still looking for a place that felt like home, Angelou headed for Africa. There she met Vusumzi Make, a South African freedom fighter and politician, after a week's courtship, the two married. Because Africa was neither safe for, nor politically welcoming to, Make, they lived primarily in Europe, but by 1963 their marriage had collapsed and Angelou moved on to Ghana.

She served as a writer and editor for the *Ghanian Times* and the *African Review,* and as an assistant administrator for the School of Music and Drama at the University of Ghana in Legon-Accra. The experience of "returning home," as she referred to her time in Ghana, nurtured Angelou. She raised her language proficiencies to six, wrote and developed several dramatic projects, including *Black, Blues, Black,* a ten-part television series on African traditions in America, which Angelou brought with her back to the States in 1966 (the series was produced in 1968). Angelou returned in part to work with Malcolm X, but their association was never to come to fruition. Two days after she arrived in New York, she spoke with him on the phone. The next day, he was assassinated. The event marked the end of an era and with it Angelou's political involvement. The political arena, she determined, was too crazy.

> *I* decided many years ago to invent myself. I had obviously been invented by someone else—by a whole society—and I didn't like their invention.
>
> —Maya Angelou

Before Angelou left New York for California, where she would join the Theatre of Being in Hollywood, she had dinner with Jules and **Judy Feiffer** and her friend, writer James Baldwin. The four drank scotch late into the night and told stories, including much of Angelou's life history. The following morning, Judy Feiffer called Robert Loomis, an editor at Random House, and recommended that the story of Angelou's life be published. Initially, Angelou rejected Loomis' interest in her autobiography. In an effort to win Angelou, he told her that she probably wouldn't be up to the writing involved. Angelou did not refuse the challenge. Published in 1970, *I Know Why the Caged Bird Sings* was nominated for the prestigious National Book Award, and Angelou's literary career was launched. In 1971, her first volume of poetry, *Just Give Me a Cool Drink of Water 'Fore I Diiie,* was published and nominated for a Pulitzer Prize. She became the first black woman to have an original screenplay produced (*Georgia, Georgia* in 1972) and made her Broadway acting debut the following year in *Look Away,* which brought her a 1973 Tony nomination.

Angelou's literary and dramatic prominence earned her teaching posts and residency-fellowships at the University of Kansas, Yale, and Wake Forest, among others. She made her home in California, where she married the writer and former builder Paul Du Feu. Angelou used her popularity to advocate on behalf of feminist and race issues, and was recognized by several presidents with posts to committees and organizations. From volumes of interviews, her honed public persona emerged: tough, determined, loving. She largely reserves herself from political discussions, which she regards as less fruitful than examinations of people and their passions. She considers herself less a black advocate than a people advocate.

In 1982, when she was offered the Reynolds Chair at Wake Forest University, Angelou moved to North Carolina having "worn out" both the state of California and her marriage. The Reynolds Chair is a lifetime post that allows her the freedom to travel, lecture, and write, which she does in bursts of total absorption. When writing, Angelou is known to work in hotel rooms in which she keeps no reading material other than the Bible. Her works include five autobiographies, five collections of poetry, and a book of essays, *Wouldn't Take Nothing for My Journey Now*, which she calls "some lessons in living, which I had learned over many years."

SOURCES:

Angelou, Maya. *On the Pulse of Morning*. NY: Random House, 1993.
———. *Wouldn't Take Nothing for My Journey Now*. NY: Random House, 1993.
Davidson, Cathy N., and Linda Wagner-Martin, eds. *Oxford Companion to Women's Writing in the U.S.* NY: Oxford University Press, 1995.
Elliot, Jeffrey M., ed. *Conversations With Maya Angelou*. Jackson: University Press of Mississippi, 1989.
Page, James A. *Selected Black American Authors*. Boston: G.K. Hall, 1977.

Crista Martin, Boston, Massachusetts

Angelus, Muriel (b. 1909).

See Lupino, Ida for sidebar.

Anger, Jane (fl. c. 1580)

British essayist. Selected work: "Jane Anger, Her Protection for Women" (1589).

In 1588, the pamphlet "Boke, his Surfeyt in love" chided the moral corruption of women. A response, "Jane Anger, Her Protection for Women," claimed that females were the purer sex, corrupted only by men who drew them astray. The gender of the author, listed as Ja. A., Gent., came into question despite the feminine voice of the text. Though several Jane Angers are known to have lived at that time, there is no record of any of them authoring the pamphlet. If indeed the author was female, she would have

been the first Englishwoman to enter the debate on gender issues of the Renaissance. Only one copy of the original pamphlet still exists.

Anges, Jeanne des.

See French "Witches" (14–17th centuries).

Angeville, Henriette d' (1795–1871).

See D'Angeville, Henriette.

Angharad (d. 1162)

Queen of Wales. Pronunciation: ANG-hairid. Died in 1162; married Gruffydd ap Cynan, king of Gwynedd, around 1095; children: eight, including Owen Gwynedd, prince of Gwynedd, and Susan.

Angharad (fl. 13th c.)

Princess of Wales. Daughter of Llywelyn II the Great, 1173–1240), prince of Gwynedd and ruler of All Wales, and Tangwystl (once his mistress); married Maelgwn Fychan.

Anglin, Margaret (1876–1958)

Canadian-born American actress. Born in Ottawa, Canada, in 1876; died in 1958; daughter of Honorable Timothy Warren Anglin (speaker of the Canadian House of Commons); sister of Francis A. Anglin, a Canadian supreme court judge; studied in New York; married Howard Hull, in 1911.

Margaret Anglin scored her first success as Roxane in Richard Mansfield's presentation of *Cyrano de Bergerac*. After playing in a number of important American productions, including *Camille* (1903–04), *Zira* (1905–06), and *The Great Divide* (1906–07), she toured Australia in 1908, appearing in Shakespearean roles. In her later years, her revivals of the Greek tragedies distinguished her as a dramatic artist of rare ability. She also played the lead in *Margaret Deland*'s *The Awakening of Helena Richie*.

Angoulême, countess of.

See Isabella of Angoulême for sidebar on Alice de Courtenay (d. 1211).
See Isabella of Valois (1389–1410).
See Louise of Savoy (1476–1531).
See Margaret de Rohan (fl. 1449).
See Margaret of Turenne.

Angoulême, duchess of.

See Marie Therese Charlotte (1778–1851).
See Medici, Catherine de for sidebar on Diane de France (1538–1619).

Angoulême, Marguerite d'.

See Margaret of Angoulême (1492–1549).

Anguissola, Anna Maria, Elena, Europa, and Lucia.

See Anguissola, Sofonisba for sidebars.

Anguissola, Sofonisba (1532–1625)

Italian artist known for her portraits, who was court painter to Philip II of Spain and the first professional woman artist of the Italian Renaissance. Name variations: Sephonisba or Sophonisba Angussola or Anguisciola. Pronunciation ang-GWEE-sho-la or ang-GOOS-so-la. Born Sofonisba Anguissola in 1532, in Cremona, Italy; died in Palermo, Sicily, in 1625; daughter of Amilcare Anguissola (a noble) and Bianca Ponzone; married Don Fabrizio de Moncada, around 1570 (died 1578); married Orazio Lomellino, in 1580; children: none.

Drew Self-Portrait with Old Woman (c. 1545); began training with Bernardino Campi (c. 1546); became painter at the Spanish court (1560); painted last known self-portrait (c. 1620).

Paintings and drawings: Self-Portrait with Old Woman, Gabinetto dei Disegni, Uffizi Gallery, Florence (c. 1545); Bernardino Campi Painting Sofonisba Anguissola, Pinacoteca Nazionale, Siena (c. 1550); The Chess Game or Three of the Artist's Sisters Playing Chess, Museum Narodowe, Poznan, Poland (1555); Boy Pinched by a Crayfish or Asdrubale Being Bitten by a Crab, Galleria Nazionale de Capodimonte, Naples (1557); Portrait of a Lady, Hermitage, St. Petersburg (date unknown); Madonna Nursing her Child, Museum of Fine Arts, Budapest (1588); Self-Portrait, Nivaagaards Art Museum, Niva, Denmark (c.1620). Signed works: "Sofonisba Anguissola" and (on occasion after marriage) "Sofonisba Lomellino Anguissola."

Although the Italian Renaissance is often regarded as a time of opportunity, adventure, and change, for women it marked a reduction in many of the social rights enjoyed since medieval times, a tightening of the rules surrounding girls' education, and a growth in misogynistic attitudes. The merging of arts and crafts with the subsequent control by the Guild system, coupled with a new emphasis in artistic training upon the study of the human body, made entry into this world hugely difficult for women: where once art had been made in convents or monasteries, it was now the product of a working-class artisan. For women of the higher social classes, writes historian **Wendy Slatkin**, "all the advances of

Sofonisba Anguissola, Self-Portrait with Old Woman.

Renaissance Italy . . . worked to mold the noblewoman into an aesthetic object: decorous, chaste, and doubly dependent—on her husband as well as the prince." With the publication of *The Courtier*, by Castiglione, in 1528, an influential framework was established for the education of upper-class girls where the skills of painting and drawing, along with musical talents, were regarded as desirable and attractive attributes, to be mastered sufficiently to entertain and amuse a husband and his guests, but certainly not to be practiced outside the home. Given the prevailing ideology, the decision of the noble Amilcare Anguissola to allow, even encourage, his daughters to become professional painters becomes even more surprising.

It is now generally accepted that Sofonisba Anguissola was born in Cremona in 1532 to Amilcare Anguissola, a noble, and **Bianca Ponzone**, his second wife. Five more daughters would follow before the desired son and heir arrived, causing many art historians to speculate that the true reason for Amilcare's encouragement of serious art training for women had less to do with a liberal conscience than with a fear of the burden of all those dowries. From an early age, Sofonisba demonstrated a talent for drawing, some examples of which still exist: *Self-Portrait with Old Woman* (c. 1545), a chalk sketch, shows the artist in her early teens with a woman who, by dress, appears to be a servant of the household. Although unpolished, the skill evidenced by the sketch is, by any standard, precocious for such a young, untrained girl.

At the age of 14, Sofonisba was sent, with her younger sister, ◄❧ **Elena**, to study painting with Bernardino Campi, a successful proponent of Mannerism—a style often defined by its multifigured, garishly colored compositions featuring elongated bodies. Since their gender prohibited them from the usual workshop training, Sofonisba and Elena lived and worked as paying guests in the Campi house, chaperoned by Bernardino's wife. When not drawing or copying the master's works at his home or in the churches where they were displayed, the girls learned the key techniques of contemporary art practice. As well as demonstrating their representational skills, artists of the time had to be able to mix natural pigments to make their own oil paints, having first prepared an oil base by a laborious cooking process. The canvas or panel that was to be painted upon also demanded tedious preparation, involving the boiling of dried rabbit skins to make a type of glue that was applied in thin layers before painting took place.

A copy of Campi's Pietà by Sofonisba, now held in the Pinacoteca di Brera, Milan, shows that his pupil was not overwhelmed by his artistic in-

---

❧▶ **Anguissola, Elena** (c. 1525–after 1584)

Italian painter. Name variations: Angussola or Anguisciola. Pronunciation ang-GWEE-sho-la or ang-GOOS-so-la. Born around 1525 in Cremona, Italy; died after 1584; second daughter of Amilcare Anguissola (a noble) and Bianca Ponzone; sister of *Sofonisba, *Anna Maria, *Europa, and *Lucia Anguissola.

Elena Anguissola trained with her sister, Sofonisba, under the mannerist artist Bernardino Campi, from 1546–49; she then joined the Convent of the Holy Virgin at San Vincenzo in Mantua as a Dominican nun; her entry into the order is commemorated by Sofonisba's painting, *Portrait of a Nun*. Little is known of her life after this date, and, although it is thought that she continued to paint (in the tradition of convent artists), no works remain.

---

fluence, instead demonstrating a softer style that incorporates hints of Leonardo and Michelangelo. Ilya Perlingieri writes, "Comparing the Pietàs of both teacher and student, it is evident that Anguissola not only simplified the composition and muted the colors, but she also chose to portray it in an atmosphere of calm resignation. Her homage to her teacher incorporates only similar facial features (but done more delicately) and the elongation of the figures." Towards the end of her training with him, Sofonisba painted *Bernardino Campi Painting Sofonisba Anguissola*, the only known image of her teacher, in which she presents Campi, half turned towards the viewer, in the act of portraying his pupil. This style of portraiture was extremely unusual: the subject was routinely represented seated or standing, perhaps surrounded by some identifying or significant objects. The concept of presenting an active subject was as yet unknown, making this one of the earliest examples of the type. Of the content, **Germaine Greer** notes: "This painting . . . seems to be Sofonisba's painterly joke. The head of Campi is subtly expressive, in her own best manner, while her version of his version of herself is blank and moon-faced, larger than life." Whether this irony [painting him well, while having him paint her poorly] was intentional is not entirely clear. Still, Sofonisba had begun to demonstrate the inventiveness of composition, which would be evidenced throughout her career.

When Campi went to Milan in about 1549, Sofonisba's tuition was taken over by another Cremonese painter, Bernardino Gatti, with whom she trained for a further three years. Meanwhile her sister, Elena, following the conventional path of a second daughter, entered a convent.

Of the 50 or so securely attributed paintings of Sofonisba Anguissola, at least 13 are self-portraits—a remarkably large number for her day. However, since she could not do paintings with representations of the naked male form—ruling out most of the popular themes of the time—portraiture became, for her, the most accessible mode of work: painting herself was a method of both advertising and honing skills. The 1552 self-portrait (inscribed "Sofonisba Anguissola, Cremona, painted this at twenty"), which hangs in the Uffizi Gallery, Florence, depicts the young woman in the typical style of dress, a boned dark bodice with a high collar worn over a white, lace-edged chemise, which features in other portraits. Seated, she holds a piece of paper in her right hand, and in her left, the tools of her trade—a palette and paintbrush. The final self-portrait, some 70 years later, completes the range, which offers a fascinating picture of this Renaissance woman's journey through life.

In 1554, Sofonisba made the long trip southward to Rome, the center of the Italian art world and home to its most influential practitioner—Michelangelo. The city, with its ruins and churches, had become a mecca for artists who now regarded a working visit there as an indispensable part of their training. Michelangelo, though by now an old man, was sufficiently impressed with the skills of the young woman from Cremona to offer her his advice and guidance, a service he continued upon her return home, sending sketches for her to copy and return for his critique. As Sofonisba began to display the benefits of his mentoring, Amilcare sent gushing letters of gratitude to the great master: "I assure you that I am more grateful for the favor I receive for your most honorable affection than all the riches that any Prince could give." Legend has it that, having seen a sketch by Sofonisba of a girl smiling, Michelangelo challenged her to depict the more difficult subject of a boy crying; the result, modelled on her young brother, was *Asdrubale Being Bitten by a Crab*, which successfully combined both themes. A friend of Michelangelo's later sent the sketch to Cosimo de Medici, duke of Florence, from where it was widely copied and circulated, and is believed to have been a major influence on the later Caravaggio painting *Boy Bitten by a Lizard*.

After her time in Rome, Sofonisba began to receive commissions for portraits from the nobility and clergy, but still continued to use her family as models for new compositions, both to advertise and practice her skills. She also devoted time to developing the already substantial artistic skills of her younger sisters ❧ **Lucia**, ❧ **Anna Maria** and ❧ **Europa**. (Another sister **Minerva**

❧ Anguissola, Lucia (c. 1536–1565)

*Italian painter. Name variations: Angussola or Anguisciola. Pronunciation ang-GWEE-sho-la or ang-GOOS-so-la. Born around 1536 or 1538 in Cremona, Italy; died in 1565; daughter of Amilcare Anguissola (a noble) and Bianca Ponzone; sister of *Sofonisba, *Elena, *Europa, and *Anna Maria Anguissola.*

Paintings: Dr. Pietro Maria, *Prado Museum, Madrid (early 1560s)*; Self-Portrait, *Civico Museo D'Arte Antica, Castello Sforzesco, Milan (c. 1557)*; Self-Portrait, *Borghese Gallery, Rome (early 1560s)*.

Lucia Anguissola received her artistic training at home, from Sofonisba, and hence her work displays the influences of her sister. Two signed paintings are in existence: the portrait of Dr. Pietro Maria was seen by the writer Vasari on his visit to the Anguissola household; the *Self-Portrait* of around 1557 portrays her in a three-quarter-length seated pose, one hand on the bodice of her dress, the other holding a book. Perlingieri attributes the Borghese *Self-Portrait*, on stylistic grounds, to Lucia, not Sofonisba, as previously given. It is not known if she married or how she died.

❧ Anguissola, Anna Maria (c. 1545–?)

*Italian painter. Name variations: Angussola or Anguisciola. Pronunciation ang-GWEE-sho-la or ang-GOOS-so-la. Born around 1545 or 1546 in Cremona, Italy; date of death unknown; daughter of Amilcare Anguissola (a noble) and Bianca Ponzone; sister of *Sofonisba, *Elena, *Europa, and *Lucia Anguissola; married Giacopo Sommi, around 1570.*

Paintings: Holy Family with Saint Francis, *Museo Civico ala Ponzone, Cremona*; Holy Family with Saint John, *Church of Sant'Agata, Cremona*.

Anna Maria Anguissola received her formal art training from her sister Sofonisba, though, according to Perlingieri, she displays greater influence of Bernardino Gatti in her two extant religious works. It is known that she collaborated with Sofonisba on a *Madonna with the Christ Child and Saint John*, and that she painted a portrait of her mother. The whereabouts of both are unknown.

❧ Anguissola, Europa (c. 1542–?)

*Italian painter. Name variations: Angussola or Anguisciola. Pronunciation ang-GWEE-sho-la or ang-GOOS-so-la. Born around 1542 or 1544 in Cremona, Italy; date of death unknown; daughter of Amilcare Anguissola (a noble) and Bianca Ponzone; sister of *Sofonisba, *Elena, *Anna Maria, and *Lucia Anguissola; married Carlo Schinchinelli, in 1568; children: Antonio Galeazzo.*

Although it is known that Europa painted (the writer Vasari mentions that a portrait of her mother, completed in Europa's youth, was sent to Spain, probably to Sofonisba), no secure attributions have been made and no signed paintings are known to exist.

SOURCES:

Perlingieri, Ilya Sandra. *Sofonisba Anguissola: The First Great Woman Artist of the Renaissance.* NY: Rizzoli International, 1992.

Diane Moody, freelance writer, London, England

was alone in her dedication to writing.) *The Chess Game*, probably one of Sofonisba's most famous works, dates from this time and was praised by the writer Vasari, who, having heard of the talented Anguissola daughters, went to see the evidence for himself. He later wrote, "I have this year seen a picture in [Sofonisba's] father's house at Cremona, most carefully finished, representing her three sisters playing at chess, in the company of an old lady of the house, making them appear alive and lacking speech only." The painting shows Lucia, Minerva and Europa Anguissola, dressed in brocade and velvet finery and adorned with gold jewelry, playing chess on a small table that is covered by an oriental carpet. A servant woman watches the proceedings and an imaginary landscape fills the background. The girls are animated: Minerva is gesticulating, as if to concede defeat, lending a palpable sense of social interplay to the scene. This work is unusual in many ways: its dynamism presents a strong contrast to the usual stiff poses of the time; the inclusion of a domestic servant in any type of portrait of nobility was rare; and the interaction between the sisters leads art historians to mark it as possibly the first "conversation piece" painting, a genre that was popularized by Dutch artists in the following century. Perlingieri notes that the limited range of subject matter generally available to her did not hinder Sofonisba's success: rather, "because she did not have access to the usual avenues of artistic studies, [she] capitalized on what she did have, her family, and in so doing . . . inadvertently pioneered a new style."

Sometime around 1558, possibly with her sister, Lucia, Sofonisba went to Milan, a city now part of the Spanish Empire, where she was commissioned to paint the portrait of the Duke of Alba, commander of the Spanish troops in Italy, and adviser to King Philip II of Spain. The result was favorably received and three more portraits ordered. Soon afterwards, Amilcare Anguissola received a request from the king to send his eldest daughter to the Spanish court, and so, in the winter of 1559, Sofonisba began the long and arduous journey to Madrid.

Whether Anguissola was invited as a painter or as a lady-in-waiting is not clarified by documents of the time, though it is certain that she came to Philip's attention through her work. The king of Spain was a renowned collector, not only of painting, but of books, maps, and other artifacts, and was an established patron of the arts. The year of Sofonisba's arrival in Spain coincided with that of his new queen from France, *Elizabeth of Valois, who, at 18 years his junior, brought a lively youthfulness to the previously dour Spanish court. Sharing tastes in fashion, music and art, the queen and the Cremonese noblewoman evidently spent much time together, as a contemporary wrote: "The Queen, who shows much ingenuity, has begun to paint, and Sofonisba, who is a great favorite of hers, says that she draws in naturalistic way [sic] in a fashion in which it appears that she knows well the person whom she is painting." When she died in 1568, at the age of 23, the Spanish queen recognized Sofonisba in her will with a bequest of money and valuable brocade.

Though very few signed works remain from Sofonisba's period at the Spanish court, writings of the time refer to her paintings of the king, his sister, and his son, along with other paintings of Queen Elizabeth. Documents also attest that Pope Pius IV commissioned a painting of the Spanish queen from the young artist, writing upon receipt, "we thank you and assure you that we shall treasure it among our choicest possessions, and commend your marvelous talent which is the least among your numerous virtues." The painting is thought, by Perlingieri, to be in the Piacoteca de Brera, Milan, misidentified as a later Flemish *Portrait of a Woman*. The art historian also contends that many extant court paintings of the time were by Sofonisba, and not the male painters to whom they are currently given. Unfortunately, fires in later centuries destroyed much of the royal family's collection or resulted in poor reconstructive work for others, making accurate attribution difficult.

Philip of Spain was married again, to *Anne of Austria (c. 1550–1580), two years after Queen Elizabeth's death, and Sofonisba became the governess of his elder daughter, *Isabella Clara Eugenia. By now marital considerations had become important for the artist also, so she requested that the king, her effective guardian, find her a husband. Around 1570, she married Don Fabrizio de Moncada, a suitably noble Sicilian, chosen by Philip who provided a generous dowry. After a journey back to Italy to visit family, the couple returned to the Spanish court where Sofonisba resumed her work, teaching and painting. *Portrait of a Lady* dates from this period, depicting the right profile of a woman holding a vase of flowers—an unusual combination of still-life and portrait. Like many of her other works, great attention has been paid to every detail of the woman's costume: a black velvet gown, embroidered and inlaid with real beaten gold appears almost tangibly luxurious.

In 1578, on another trip to their homelands, Don Fabrizio died in Sicily, leaving Sofonisba to face a lonely journey back to Spain. Happily for her, fate intervened and, on her return to the north of Italy by sea, she met, and shortly afterwards married, the ship's captain, Orazio Lomellino. Much has been made of this maritime romance, with some commentators finding such a speedy remarriage distasteful, especially given Sofonisba's mature years. Greer, however, offers a different reading: "Life for an unattached foreign woman in the Spanish court cannot have been easy. . . . Her long employment at the Spanish court may have been less a matter of choice than commentators usually suppose. Marrying Lomellino may have been less an indication of how 'buoyant' she was in her private life than how keen a sense of self-preservation she had." Whatever the case, all of the evidence supports the view that, unlike the first, this marriage truly was a love match and the couple were to spend many happy years together, their childlessness increasing their mutual devotion.

Though no firm evidence of commissions exists, Sofonisba's letters of the period suggest that she was working for the grand duke of Tuscany, Francesco I de Medici, a leading patron, and founder of the Uffizi Gallery in Genoa. In Orazio's *palazzo* in Genoa, Sofonisba painted and welcomed other artists to her home, where she established a type of "salon" to exchange ideas and receive advice. Only two paintings signed in her married name, "Sofonisba Lomellino Anguissola," survive, both on religious themes. *Madonna Nursing her Child*, painted in 1588, depicts Mary looking down at her son who turns away from the breast towards the viewer. The colors are vibrant and rich, dominated by the red of Mary's dress and the blue of her cape, and the sense of togetherness, warmth, and comfort are accentuated both by the oval shape of the picture and its composition. It is known that she carried out other commissions, particularly portraits of the nobility and clergy, in addition to self-portraits. And when Isabella Clara Eugenia was to be married to her cousin, the Archduke Albert of Austria, it was to Sofonisba she came for her commemorative portrait in 1599.

By the turn of the century, Sofonisba's longevity was so remarkable for the time that she was required to prove her continuing existence at regular intervals in order to collect her stipend from the Spanish court. As her eyesight failed, she worked less, but continued to represent herself, without sentimentality, as in the *Self-Portrait*, now in the Gottfried Keller Collection, Bern, Switzerland. Perlingieri describes it: "Here Anguissola portrays herself in a three-quarter-length pose as the older stateswoman of

the Renaissance: seated as an elegant septuagenarian." Painted as a commission for King Philip III of Spain, Sofonisba is shown holding in her right hand a piece of paper inscribed (in Italian), "To his Catholic Majesty, I kiss your hand, Anguissola." Her final self-portrait of around 1620 gives a sense of her increasing frailty as she approaches her ninth decade.

In 1624, the artist Anthony Van Dyck visited Anguissola at her home in Palermo, where he sketched and painted the final representations of her, noting, "When I drew her portrait, she gave me several hints. . . . She also talked to me about her life and that she was a wonderful painter of nature. Her greatest sorrow was not to be able to paint any more because of her failing eyesight." The following year, with a plague raging through the city, Sofonisba died.

𝒮ofonisba Anguissola stood as the pioneering model for late 16th- and early 17th-century women artists.

—Ilya Sandra Perlingieri

Sofonisba Anguissola was in the vanguard of women artists: as a successful professional painter of widespread fame, she paved the way for other women artists such as *Lavinia Fontana and *Artemisia Gentileschi. Her compositions were recognized in her own lifetime, as today, for their unique and imaginative qualities, and, in her role as court painter, she brought many Italian influences to Spain for the first time. With a career of almost constant commissions spanning 70 years, she continues to be regarded as one of the great painters.

SOURCES:

Greer, Germaine. *The Obstacle Race.* NY: Farrar, Straus, 1979.

Perlingieri, Ilya Sandra. *Sofonisba Anguissola: The First Great Woman Artist of the Renaissance.* NY: Rizzoli International, 1992.

Slatkin, Wendy. *Women Artists in History.* NY: Prentice-Hall, 1985.

Tufts, Eleanor. "Sofonisba Anguissola, Renaissance Woman," in *Artnews.* October 1972.

Diane Moody, freelance writer, London, England

Aníchkova, Anna (1868–1935)

Russian author and translator. Born Anna Mitrofanovna in 1868 in Russia; died in 1935 in Russia; married E.V. Aníchkov (a literary critic).

Selected works: La pensée russe contemporaine (*Contemporary Russian Thought, 1903*); L'ombre de la maison (*The Shadow of the House, 1904*).

With her husband, literary critic E.V. Aníchkov, Anna Aníchkova moved from Russia to Paris in the late 1890s. There, she created a literary salon that was frequented by writers such as Anatole France and Viacheslav Ivanov. Aníchkova wrote novels in French, the most popular of which, *L'ombre de la maison* (1904), was translated into English as *The Shadow of the House*. She also contributed to several French periodicals (*Revue de Paris, Revue Bleu,* and *Figaro*), and penned a collection of essays on contemporary Russian intellectuals. In 1909, the Aníchkovs returned to Russia, where Anna began contributing short fiction to "thick journals," voluminous literary journals of essay, fiction, and verse, which often represented political views and were unique for their regular female contributors. Though her fiction was critically well received, after the 1917 revolution Aníchkova turned her literary talents to other efforts. From 1917 until her death in 1935, she devoted her writing exclusively to translation.

Anisimova, Nina (1909—)

*Soviet dancer and choreographer. Born in USSR in 1909; studied under *Maria Romanova, *Agrippina Vaganova, and Alexander Shiryayev at the Leningrad ballet school, 1919–26.*

Nina Anisimova created many notable roles in the dramatic ballets of the 1930s, including Therese in Vassily Vainonen's *Flames of Paris*. One of the first Soviet women choreographers, she worked on *Gayané* for the Leningrad Kirov Theater (1945). For her long association with the Maly Opera Theater in Leningrad, she created *The Magic Veil* (1947), *Coppélia* (new version, 1949), *Schéhérazade* (new version, 1950), and *Willow Tree* (1957). Anisimova retired as a dancer in 1957, when she began to focus solely on choreography.

Anker, Nini Roll (1873–1942)

Norwegian novelist. Name variations: (pseudonyms) Jo Nein and Kaare P. Born Nicoline Magdalen Roll in Molde, Norway, in 1873; died in 1942; daughter of Ferdinand Roll; married Peter Anker, in 1892 (divorced 1907); married Johan Anker, in 1910.

Selected works: I blinde *(Blind,1898);* Benedicte Stendal *(1909).*

Born into an aristocratic Norwegian family, Nicoline Roll produced novels depicting the lives of the less advantaged. Her father, an associate justice of the Supreme Court, stationed his family in Molde where Nicoline lived until the age of 18 or 19. In 1892, she married an estate owner named Peter Anker and moved to Halden. (Fifteen years later, she would divorce Anker, then marry Johan Anker, an engineer and cousin to her first husband, in 1910.)

Anker's first novel *I blinde* (*Blind*) was published in 1898 under the pseudonym Jo Nein. *Benedicte Stendal,* a novel in diary form, was published in 1909. In all, she produced 29 books and many articles and essays, the most successful of which were the dairy-novels. Her credits include several books for adolescents, published under the name Kaare P., which critics long believed to be the work of a young man.

Crista Martin, Boston, Massachusetts

Ankers, Evelyn (1918–1985)

English actress. Born in Valparaiso, Chile, on August 17, 1918; died in 1985; daughter of British parents; married Richard Denning (an actor), in 1942; children: daughter Dee.

Known as the screamer or the queen of the horror movies, Evelyn Ankers made her debut in England before coming to the United States. Her films include *The Villiers Diamond* (U.K., 1933), *Rembrandt* (1936), *Fire Over England* (1937), *Hold that Ghost* (1941), *Burma Convoy* (1941), *The Wolf Man* (1941), *The Ghost of Frankenstein* (1942), *The Great Impersonation* (1942), *Eagle Squadron* (1942), *Sherlock Holmes and the Voice of Terror* (1942), *Captive Wild Woman* (1943), *Son of Dracula* (1943), *Pearl of Death* (1944), *Pillow of Death* (1945), *Queen of Burlesque* (1946), *Black Beauty* (1946), *Spoilers of the North* (1947), *Flight to Nowhere* (1946), *The Lone Wolf in London* (1947), *Tarzan's Magic Fountain* (1949), *The Texan Meets Calamity Jane* (1950). In 1968, she moved with her actor husband Richard Denning to Maui.

Anna.

Variant of Anne or Hannah.

Anna

Biblical woman. Born into the tribe of Asher; daughter of Phanuel.

While an aged woman, Anna was a prophet like *Miriam the Prophet, *Deborah, and *Huldah. After seven years of marriage, her husband died; during her long widowhood, she attended daily temple services. When she was 84, Anna entered the temple at the moment when the aged Simeon uttered his memorable words of praise and thanks to God for sending his Son into the world; thus, Anna recognized the infant Jesus as the Messiah (Luke 2:36, 37).

Anna, Saint (fl. 1st c.).
See Anne, Saint.

Anna Amalia of Prussia
(1723–1787)

*German composer of military band music, a genre rarely adopted by women of the 18th century. Name variations: Princess Anna Amalia. Born on November 9, 1723, in Berlin, Germany; died on March 30, 1787, in Berlin (some sources cite 1788); daughter of *Sophia Dorothea of Brunswick-Lüneburg-Hanover (1687–1757) and Frederick William I (1688–1740), king of Prussia (r. 1713–1740); youngest sister of Frederick II the Great; aunt of *Anna Amalia of Saxe-Weimar (1739–1807); studied harpsichord and piano under Gottlieb Hayne and counterpoint with Johann Philipp Kirnberger.*

Princess Anna Amalia was born in a Berlin castle where she would spend her entire life. The youngest sister of Frederick II the Great, she was a product of the Enlightenment, a period when women played an important role in public affairs. She grew up in a rich cultural environment and was trained by court musicians. Most accounts agree that Anna Amalia did not begin composing until her mid-40s. Interestingly, she concentrated on composing marches for military regiments for certain generals, a genre rarely adopted by women. In addition, she founded a music library collection, which includes autographed scores of Johann Sebastian Bach and other composers. Known as the Amalien Bibliothek, it exists today in its entirety. This collection reveals her high level of musical education and her conservative musical taste. Anna Amalia was also a patron of music, and musicians throughout Germany were employed by the court. Under her influence, music flourished in the Prussian court, a rich heritage from which all Germany would benefit.

Anna Amalia of Saxe-Weimar
(1739–1807)

German composer, patron of the arts, and duchess of Saxe-Weimar who created the Musenhof, or court of muses, known throughout Europe for its rich musical and cultural life. Name variations: Amalia, Duchess of Saxe-Weimar. Born at Wolfenbüttel on October 24, 1739; died in Weimar on April 10, 1807; daughter of

*Charles (Karl) I, duke of Brunswick-Wolfenbüttel, and Duchess *Philippine Charlotte (1716–1801); niece of Frederick II the Great and Anna Amalia of Prussia (1723–1787); married Ernst August Konstantin (Ernst Wilhelm Wolff), duke of Saxe-Weimar, in 1756 (died 1758); children: two sons, including Charles Augustus.*

Studied with Friedrich G. Fleischer, organist and composer, and Ernst Wilhelm Wolff; regent of Saxe-Weimar after her husband's death (1758); known for her work in the new German opera genre of the Singspiel; created the Musenhof, or court of muses, known throughout Europe for its rich musical and cultural life.

Duchess Anna Amalia was the namesake and niece of *Anna Amalia of Prussia and grew up in the musical court of Brunswick, which was greatly influenced by the Prussian court where her aunt was a composer. At age 18, Anna Amalia married Ernst Wilhelm Wolff, the duke of Saxe-Weimar. Shortly thereafter, she employed the duke to give

Anna Amalia of Saxe-Weimar

her private lessons. Composer of 20 Singspiels, a new German opera genre, Wolff influenced the young princess to compose these comic operas, which were a forerunner of 19th-century German Romantic opera. Her entry into composition marked the creation of the Musenhof, or court of muses. Throughout Europe, Saxe-Weimar was known for its rich musical and cultural life. Christoph Martin Wieland (1733–1813), Johann Gottfried von Herder (1744–1803), and Johann Wolfgang von Goethe (1749–1832) were all members of the court of muses and supplied libretti or poetry for some of Anna Amalia's compositions. So influential was Anna Amalia in the creation of Singspiel that Johann Adam Hiller (1728–1804), the composer credited with creating the first German Singspiel, dedicated his initial work to her.

Anna Amalia's husband died in 1758, leaving her as regent for their infant son, Charles Augustus. During his protracted minority, she administered the affairs of the duchy with great prudence, strengthening its resources and improving its position despite the troubles of the Seven Years' War.

With these additional duties, she still continued to compose. In 1776, she wrote *Erwin und Elmire* based on a text by Goethe, and two years later she wrote *Das Jahrmarksfest zu Plunderweisen* also based on a text by the celebrated poet. By 1775, she had retired into private life, her son having attained his majority. In 1788, she set out on a lengthened tour through Italy, accompanied by Goethe. A memorial of the duchess is included in Goethe's works under the title *Zum Andenken der Fürstin Anna-Amalia*. As a composer and patron, Anna Amalia was widely known and respected.

SUGGESTED READING:

Bornhak, F. *Anna Amalia Herzogin von Saxe-Weimar-Eisenach*. Berlin, 1892.

John Haag, Associate Professor of History, University of Georgia, Athens, Georgia

Anna Anachoutlou (r. 1341–1342)

Queen of Trebizond. Reigned as queen of Trebizond (in present-day Turkey) from 1341 to 1342; daughter of King Alexius II (r. 1297–1330).

The empire of Trebizond arose on the southeast coast of the Black Sea under Byzantium's Alexius I, Grand Comnenus, and David Comnenus, grandsons of Andronicus I. With support from queen *Tamara the Great, the Comneni captured Trebizond in April 1204. Alexius became emperor, founding a dynasty that lasted 250 years.

Following the removal of **Irene Palaeologina** from the throne, Anna Anachoutlou was crowned in 1341. That same year, she was deposed in favor of Michael, son of former King John II (r. 1280–1284). She was then, however, restored to the throne and ruled for one more year.

Anna Angelina (d. 1210?).

See Irene Lascaris for sidebar.

Anna Carlovna (1718–1746).

See Anna Ivanovna for sidebar on Anna Leopoldovna.

Anna Catherina of Brandenburg (1575–1612)

*Queen of Denmark and Norway. Name variations: Anna Catherine of Brandenburg; Anne Catherine Hohenzollern. Born on June 26, 1575; died on March 29, 1612; daughter of *Catherine of Custrin (1549–1602) and Joachim Frederick (1546–1608), elector of Brandenburg (r. 1598–1608); married Christian IV (1577–1648), king of Denmark and Norway (r. 1588–1648), on November 27, 1597; children: Christian or Christiane (1603–1647); Elizabeth (1606–1608); Frederick III (b. 1609), king of Norway and Denmark (r. 1648–1670); Ulrich (b. 1611). Christian IV's second wife was *Kirsten Munk (1598–1658).*

Anna Comnena (1083–1153/55)

Byzantine princess, first known woman historian, and perhaps the best-educated woman in the entire Mediterranean world between the 5th and the 15th centuries. Name variations: (Greek) Anna Komnena, called "The Tenth Muse" and the "Pallas of Byzantine Greece." Born on December 2, 1083; died at age 70–72, sometime between 1153 and 1155; daughter of Alexius I Comnenus, emperor of Byzantium (r. 1081–1118), and Irene Ducas or Ducaena (c. 1066–1133); married Byzantine noble, Nicephorus Bryennius, in 1098 (died 1138); children: Alexius Comnenus (b. 1098); John Ducas (b. 1100); Irene Ducas or Ducaena (b. ca. 1101/1103); and a daughter whose name is unknown.

Little is known of the education of Anna Comnena beyond the fact that it was profound. As the daughter of an emperor, she surely had the best tutors available but much of what she learned undoubtedly came from a lifelong devotion to classical learning on the very highest levels. She read Homer, the great writers of Greek tragedy, Aristophanes and the lyric poets, the works of the philosophers Plato and Aristotle, those of the orators Isocrates and Demosthenes but, above all, those of the great historians, Thucydides and Polybius. In her own words, she had gone "to the end of the end of Hellenism." Works of theology were less to her taste and, though she read them, she admitted that they made her "dizzy."

Born and immediately proclaimed heir to the Byzantine throne (December 2, 1083); birth of brother John (1085); John proclaimed heir to the throne and Anna lost the right of succession (1091); Anna Dalassena, mother of Alexius I and grandmother of Anna, retired to the convent of Pantepoptes (1100); brother John married Princess Priska of Hungary, daughter of St. Ladislav (1103); twin sons born to John and Priska (1104); death of Anna Dalassena (1105); death of Adrian Comnenus, brother of Emperor Alexius (1105); death of Isaac, brother of Alexius (c. 1106); Anna joined her father and mother at Phillipopolis in Bulgaria (1114); death of father, Alexius I, whose son John succeeded with his empress, Priska, who now took the name Irene (August 15, 1118); Anna's brother, Andronicus, killed in battle against the Turks (1129); death of Anna's mother, Empress Irene, widow of Alexius I (February 19, 1133); death of Anna's sister-in-law, Empress ❧▶ Priska-Irene (August 13, 1133); death of Anna's husband, Nicephorus Bryennius (1138); death of her brother, Emperor John II (1143); Anna completed The Alexiad *(1148).*

At the death of the Emperor Basil II in 1025, the Byzantine Empire was at the highest peak of its power and glory since the days of Heraclius (610–642); its frontiers extended to Lake Sevan in Eastern Armenia and as far south as Palestine, and its treasury was filled. After Basil's death, however, a period of 56 years of incompetent and unstable rule followed at precisely the time when the empire, struck by the onrushing wave of the Turks, needed the best leadership it could find. During the years immediately following Basil's death, the Turks conquered the newly established Byzantine provinces in Armenia. At the famed Battle of Manzikert (Manazkert) in 1071, the Byzantine armies were overwhelmed, the Emperor Romanus IV Diogenes was killed, and the Romano-Byzantine occupation was swept from Armenia (where it had been a reality for 999 years) and from central Anatolia (where it had been installed for almost 12 centuries). An era had ended in the East, and the Turkish presence would eventually erase the age-old Hellenic influence in this part of the world.

The effects of the disaster of 1071 were felt throughout Byzantine civilization, especially in

❧▶ Priska-Irene of Hungary (c. 1085–1133)

*Byzantine empress. Name variations: Princess Prisca of Hungary; Irene of Hungary. Born around 1085; died on August 13, 1133; daughter of St. Ladislaus also known as Ladislav or Ladislas, king of Hungary (r. 1077–1095) and *Adelheid of Rheinfelden (c. 1065–?); married John II Comnenus, emperor of Byzantium (r. 1118–1143), in 1103 (died as the result of a poisoned arrow on April 8, 1143); children: four sons and four daughters, including twin sons Alexius (1104–1142) and Andronicus (1104–1142), and Manuel I Comnenus (1120?–1180), emperor of Byzantium (r. 1143–1180).*

When Priska-Irene of Hungary died young, her husband John II vowed to remain true to her memory. By all accounts, he did just that. Among the most famous mosaics of Hagia St. Sophia in Istanbul is a panel depicting John and the sandy-haired Priska-Irene on either side of the Virgin Mary and the Christ child. Their son Manuel I Comnenus reigned from 1143 to 1180 and married *Bertha-Irene of Sulzbach and *Marie of Antioch.

art and literature, which thereafter became largely sterile. In the words of **Rose Dalven**: "The springs of progress dried up; there was no longer any power of organic growth; the only change now possible was the passive acceptance of external forces." Though badly mauled by the Turks, and culturally stagnant, the empire survived the initial onslaught for another four centuries, largely due to the efforts of the Comnenid Dynasty and in particular of Anna's father Alexius I and her grandmother *Anna Dalassena. In the general decay of Byzantine civilization, Anna Comnena's history of her father's reign shines like a lamp in the gathering darkness.

The Comnenids were of a Greek family first mentioned in the time of Basil II. Originally from a village near Hadrianople in Thrace (modern Edirne in European Turkey), they later became a part of the large, landowning rural aristocracy in Asia Minor. Neither Anna nor her husband dwell on the origins of the Comneni, which may thus have been rather humble; attempts, however, to ascribe the family a Vlach (Wallachian, i.e. Rumanian) origin have been unsuccessful. Nicephorus Comnenus was governor of the new Byzantine province of Asprakania or Basprakania (Vaspurakan) in Armenia under Basil II, while another Comnenus, Manuel, great-grandfather of Anna, was a close friend of the same emperor and his representative in the negotiations with the rebel Bardas Sclerus.

At Manuel's death, he left two sons, Isaac and John II Comnenus, whom, their mother having died, he had placed under the emperor's care. Basil saw to the education of the boys and trained them for military careers; he then gave them high positions in his military guard. Isaac married ◄❧ **Catherine of Bulgaria**, daughter of King Samuel of Bulgaria, and briefly became emperor (1057–59); John, Anna's paternal grandfather, married Anna Dalassena, daughter of Alexius "Charon" Dalassenus, Byzantine governor of Italy. John Comnenus and Anna Dalassena had eight children, five sons of whom Alexius, Anna's father, was the third, and three daughters. Anna thus had, in addition to her seven siblings, a large number of uncles, aunts, and cousins of varying degrees. Through her paternal grandfather, Anna was at least partly Armenian; through her paternal grandmother, one-quarter Bulgarian. Despite its size and public position, the Comnenus family was an unusually devoted one, so much so that it would manage to survive the upcoming treason.

When Anna's father Alexius came to the throne in the revolution of 1081, his ascension represented the triumph of the growing power of the provincial aristocrats over that of the civil bureaucracy centered in Constantinople and brought the period of disaster and chaos (1056–81) to an end. It also led to the establishment of the norms that were to guarantee the survival of the empire, in its new truncated form, as a Greek national state, thereby rolling back time as if Alexander the Great had never lived and his dream of a combined Hellenic and Oriental world empire had never been. From then on—instead of dominating the entire east Mediterranean world as it had until the 7th century, and the northern half until 1071—the Byzantine "Empire" would be no more than another of many states in the increasingly fragmented Middle East. Alexius stabilized the surviving empire after the Turkish onslaught, resisted the invasion of the Patzinaks (a major Turkish tribe),

Cumans, and Seljuk Turks, and established a fruitful, if costly, alliance with Venice.

At home, Alexius reorganized the provincial administration, restored the empire's defensive system, used the higher clergy as a check on the growing power of the great landowners while appeasing the latter with high-ranking titles and other honorifics. In addition, he vigorously fought the adherents of the Bogomil faith, a sect largely imported into the Balkans by Armenian heretics settled there by his predecessors. With the coming of the First Crusade, Alexius had to deal with numerous conflicts between the rough-hewn leaders of these armies from Western Europe and the cunning officials of his own bureaucracy. Distrusted by the Westerners, he is today regarded as one of the ablest rulers, military commanders, and diplomatists that the empire ever produced. All of these activities and accomplishments are detailed by Anna in the history of her father's reign.

Anna was born on December 2, 1083. At the time, her father had been emperor for two years, making her, in the eyes of the Byzantines, a *porphyrogenete,* i.e., one born to the purple, the reference being to the purple-hung chamber where the consorts of the reigning emperor gave birth to their children. Her father, Alexius, who was to be the subject of her historical work, was born in 1048, the nephew of the Emperor Isaac I Comnenus (r. 1057–59) and the son of the extraordinary Anna Dalassena. Her mother was *Irene Ducas (1066–1133) of the great Byzantine house of Ducas. Anna appears to have loved both her parents and siblings deeply, the exception being her brother John, toward whom she developed a great animosity that may have been at least partly due to sibling rivalry for, until his birth, she had been the heir to the throne. In her childhood, and indeed until she was 17, the house of Comnenus, the Byzantine court, and, at times, even the empire were dominated by her paternal grandmother, the remarkable Anna Dalassena. Daughter of a high official of a distinguished Asiatic family, Anna Dalassena was a woman of great gifts and a high intellect. Pious and virtuous, she steadied the morals of the court and was so capable in public affairs that her son not only credited her with his having successfully attained the throne (thus earning her the title "Mother of the Comneni"), but thought nothing of leaving her as regent with full power to act in his stead when he was absent from the capital. Educated and well-read, Anna Dalassena played a dominant role in the politics of the empire, the life of the court, and in the up-

❧➤ **Catherine of Bulgaria** (fl. 1050)

Byzantine empress. Name variations: Aikaterini. Daughter of King Samuel of Bulgaria; married Isaac I Comnenus, emperor of Byzantium (r. 1057–1059).

A princess of Bulgaria, Catherine married Isaac Comnenus long before he became emperor of Byzantium. On his illness and abdication, Isaac took monastic vows.

bringing of her children and grandchildren alike. It seems more than likely that Anna Comnena inherited much of her intellect from Anna Dalassena, who may have served as her great role model as she grew to maturity.

Although devoted to her father, with whom her life was totally intertwined, and loyal to his family, Anna seems to have actually been closer to the family of her mother, Irene Ducas. The Byzantine house of Ducas was one of the most illustrious of the great families of the empire. Indeed, Anna, while silent on the origins of the Comneni, claims for the Ducas family a Roman origin tracing it from a cousin of the Emperor Constantine I (280?–337) and asserting that the family name was derived from the title that Constantine granted to his cousin: "Duke of Constantinople." Anna's maternal grandmother, **Marie of Bulgaria**, another relative of King Samuel, was descended on her mother's side from Greek families including the house of Phocas. Maria married Andronicus Ducas, by whom she had two sons and three daughters, the eldest of whom was Irene, the mother of Anna Comnena. Andronicus was a distinguished military man but his desertion of the Emperor Romanus Diogenes at the Battle of Manzikert was in part responsible for the disaster that ensued. His failure to stand firm and Romanus' capture led to the defection of the Armenian general Philaretos, which guaranteed the triumph of the Turks.

Anna's mother, Irene Ducas, was devout and retiring, and Anna, who loved her dearly, inherited her reverence for the Orthodox faith. Irene, on her part, was devoted to her daughter and used her influence to try to have Anna's husband named as heir to the throne. Since the emperor, by definition, was supposed to be able to command the army, women—Roman or Byzantine—had never been permitted to ascend the imperial throne; this accepted norm, however, had been violated by the empress *Irene of Athens** (c. 752–803) as early as 797, while, much more recently, Basil II had been successively followed by his two daughters. The short, but recent, reigns of these last two empresses doubtless served as Irene's models for her ambitions for her daughter.

Despite their intrigues, piety ran in the women of both sides of Anna's family: in 1100, Anna Dalassena retired from public life to become a nun in the Convent of Pantepoptes, which she had founded; she died there five years later. As for Irene, she entered the convent of Kecharitomene, which she had founded, dying there in 1133. Anna Comnena would retire there

as well, and there she too would die. Anna's piety, however, did not deter her from intriguing nor, as we shall see, from an attempt at fratricide.

As a young girl, Anna Comnena was closely involved with both sides of her family and, indeed, was early engaged to her second cousin, Constantine Ducas, the son of the Emperor Michael VII (r. 1071–1078) and ☙ **Maria of Alania**, a daughter of the king of Georgia. Constantine, however, died when Anna was still a child, and she was then betrothed to Nicephorus Bryennius, a youth of noble birth, whose father was a leader of the conspiracy that had put Isaac on the throne in 1067, and whose grandfather was in rebellion against the emperor in 1068–71. They were married in 1098, when Anna was 15.

The two appear to have been well-matched. Born in 1081, Nicephorus was but two years older than his bride, and both of them were well-educated and steeped in the classics. He, too, was a historian, and this may have influenced Anna in her choice of the same occupation. We know that he had planned to write a history of Alexius' reign and had actually gathered materials for it. He had even written a chronicle of the events of the period 1070–79 before he died. It is likely that these papers were available to his widow and would have been incorporated in some way into her own text. At least four children were born to this marriage: Alexius Comnenus, John Ducas, *Irene Ducas** (born between 1101 and 1103), and a second daughter whose name is not known. Under Anna's attentive supervision, all of them married well.

Anna was remarkably devoted to her father, whom she called "The Whole Sun," "The Great Lighthouse," and even "The Thirteenth Apostle." Sleepless, she attended him in his last illness—along with her mother and her sisters **Maria Comnena** and **Eudocia Comnena**—preparing his food, consulting with the physicians, and disputing their diagnoses and methods of treatment. Her profound knowledge of medicine is readily apparent from her detailed description of the progress of his final illness, and at one point in her narrative she offers the observation:

> It seems to me that if the body is sick, the illness is often aggravated by external influences, but that sometimes too, the causes of an illness may arise of themselves, although we are apt to blame the irregularities of the weather, faulty diet, or perhaps, also, the humors of our animal fluids, as the cause of our fever.

Hostile to her father's designation of her brother John as his successor, Anna worked as-

☙ *Maria of Alania.* See Anna Dalassena for sidebar.

siduously to secure the throne for her own husband, developing an elaborate, though unsuccessful, scheme to get her father to name Nicephorus his heir in her brother's place. On her side were her mother, her husband, and her brother Andronicus; on her brother John's side were the patriarch of Constantinople, head of the Greek Church, and his brother Isaac, whom the patriarch supported almost as a co-ruler with John.

I, Anna, daughter of Emperor Alexius and Empress Irene, born and reared in the purple, not inexperienced in the sciences and having devoted myself pre-eminently to the study of all that is Greek, well acquainted with the system of Aristotle and the Dialogues of Plato . . . wish in this work to describe my father's deeds, which should on no account be passed over in silence.

—**Anna Comnena, opening lines of** *The Alexiad.*

Anna more than dabbled in politics and even went so far as to organize and launch a plot to assassinate her brother less than a year after his accession to the throne. The plot was supposed to transpire while he was spending the night at the hippodrome of Philopation, an imperial residence outside the city walls near the Golden Gate, the ceremonial entrance to the capital. The guards had been duly bribed, but when Anna's husband was supposed to give the signal to storm the residence and effect the murder, Nicephorus could not go through with it. The plot thus failed and the details were all shortly discovered. Anna, enraged, lamented: would that Nicephorus had been the woman and she the man. The conspirators benefitted enormously, however, from the mild character of John II Comnenus. In a milieu in which horrible deaths or at least the cruelest mutilations were imposed upon would-be usurpers, the heaviest punishment meted out was the confiscation of property. Anna's wealth was given to John Axuchus, a Turk in the Byzantine service, but he declined to accept it, and at his urging everything eventually reverted to Anna.

Although treated with almost astonishing leniency by her brother, there is no evidence that Anna and John were ever reconciled. Forced from the court, even though her husband was welcomed and continued to hold high office there, she appears to have retired from public life, spending much of her time at the convent of Kecharitomene overlooking the Golden Horn. After the death of her husband in 1138, she retired there permanently in the company of her daughter Irene.

At Kecharitomene, Anna surrounded herself with a circle of philosophers and men of letters, forming a kind of salon of which she was the director and chief inspiration. She was particularly drawn to the works of Aristotle and encouraged the writers of commentaries upon them, in particular Michael of Ephesus, who is said to have ruined his eyes writing treatises on Aristotle's *Politics and Rhetoric,* and on his zoological and anthropological works. It was during her long years at this convent that Anna found the peace and tranquility to compose her history of her father's reign, the work for which her name has become famous. She died at Kecharitomene in either 1153 or 1155. On her deathbed, she is said to have taken the veil (obviously, her vaunted religiosity was in sharp contrast to her attempt to murder her own brother and the bitterness that she held toward him after his generosity when the plot was revealed). Although no portraits of Anna Comnena survive, in physical appearance, she was said to have resembled her father, with large, dark, lively eyes, a nose slightly turned down, a round face, an agile figure, and a white skin that retained a rosy hue until late in life.

The *Alexiad* of Anna Comnena, openly modelled after Homer's *Iliad,* is not only one of the most original works of Byzantine historiography, it also began the Byzantine classical renaissance, which lasted for 300 years until the empire's demise. Consisting of a prologue and 15 books (i.e. chapters), the work begins with the year 1069 and ends with the death of her father, the Emperor Alexius, in 1118. It thus follows up the work of her late husband and is itself followed up by the history of Choniates. The text is written in the stilted imitation of Classical Greek, which was utilized as the literary language of Byzantine literature and which forced the Byzantines, Anna included, to write, in effect, in a foreign tongue. She calls the Patzinaks the "Scythians," the Danube the "Ister," and apologizes to the gentle reader for having to introduce into her Hellenic prose the barbarous names of her father's enemies. Only Anna's superb education and thorough knowledge of Classical Greek made it possible for her to rise above the artificiality that characterizes so many other medieval Greek writers. Though rambling, gossipy, filled with exaggeration and naturally biased, her history is remarkable for its detachment, with Anna preferring to pass over embarrassing topics in silence rather than to misrepresent what actually occurred. She has the outlook of her class (the landed aristocracy), is credulous in matters of religion, and frequently refers to visions and oracular dreams in a way that shows that she takes them seriously. A devout Orthodox Greek, Anna attacks heresy and rails against the plots and machinations of the Catholic and Muslim enemies of the empire. Extolling the empire and her family's role in its affairs, she regards all outsiders as more or less barbarous and, a true Byzantine, she praises the wiles and ruses of her father whereby these enemies were duped, tricked, and otherwise outsmarted. In particular, she detests the Latins of the West, calling them: "by nature brazen-faced and insolent, greedy for money, incapable of resisting any whim, and, above all, more talkative than any other men on earth."

The most important contributions of her work are her account of the First Crusade, the detailed description of the expansion of the Turks into the empire, and her telling of the history of the Patzinaks, a major Turkish tribe of the Russian steppes that loomed large in this period and were destroyed by two Cuman chieftains in the Byzantine pay. Indeed, Anna is extremely well-informed about the Seljuk Turks and tells us much of their character, internal affairs, and methods of warfare. Her descriptions of life at the Byzantine court are vivid as are her accounts of the intrigues and struggles within it. She also has much to say about the religious situation of her day and preserves for us the texts of several important documents and letters. More forthright than Michael Psellus, whom she freely imitates and occasionally borrows from (to the point of plagiarism), Anna's chief model is Thucydides and, though she can be vitriolic when she wishes to be (she describes Bohemond, her father's Norman nemesis as "of insignificant origin, in temper tyrannical, in mind most cunning, brave in action, very clever in attaching the wealth and substance of great men, [and] most obstinate in achievement, for he did not allow any obstacle to prevent the execution of his will"), she is generally fair in her assessments.

Hostile to her brother, John, her father's successor, Anna has little to say about him and nothing at all about his reign, though she completed her history after his death when his reign had long been over. There are problems with her chronology, her geography is not at all clear, her descriptions of battles (which she had probably never witnessed) are poor, her work has several lacunae and minor contradictions, and she leaves many loose ends and questions unanswered. A sense of gloom hangs like a pall over the entire narrative. Yet, for all this, she is easy to read, vivid and urbane, and her work is a far more cultivated and sophisticated piece of literature than anything written in the West in her time. The *Alexiad* was not Anna's only work. She has left us a ten-line poem dedicated to the Logos, two seals and a four-page prologue to her will.

Anna Comnena is one of the most remarkable women in history prior to the emergence of the Western World. Her history of her father's reign is an important historical document and is invaluable for our understanding of the period in which she lived. The first woman historian, and one of the best educated women before modern times, she came close to sitting on the throne of the Caesars, and there appears to be little doubt that she would have worn the crown with distinction.

SOURCES:
Anna Comnena. *The Alexiad.* English translation by E.R.A. Sewter. Baltimore: Penguin Books, 1969.
Buckler, Georgina. *Anna Comnena: A Study.* London: Oxford University, 1929 (reprinted 1968).
Dalven, Rose. *Anna Comnena.* NY: Twayne, 1972.
Psellus, Michael. *Chronographia.* English translation by E.R.A. Sewter as *Fourteen Byzantine Rulers.* New Haven, CT: Yale University Press, 1953.

SUGGESTED READING:
Charanis, Peter. "The Byzantine Empire in the 11th Century," in *A History of the Crusades.* Edited by K.M. Sutton. Philadelphia: 1955.
Ostrogorsky, George. *The History of the Byzantine State.* New Brunswick, NJ: Rutgers University Press, 1957.

Robert H. Hewsen, Professor of History, Rowan University, Glassboro, New Jersey, and author of a book and several articles relevant to late Roman and Byzantine history

Anna Constancia (1619–1651)

Electress of the Palatinate. Name variations: Anna Katherina Constance. Born on August 7, 1619; died on October 8, 1651; daughter of *Constance of Styria (1588–1631) and Sigismund III, king of Poland (r. 1587–1632), king of Sweden (r. 1592–1599); married Philip William of Neuburg, elector of the Palatinate, on June 8, 1642.

Anna Dalassena (c. 1025–1105)

Byzantine empress, and mother of the Comneni, who helped found the Comnenid Dynasty. Birth date unknown, possibly around 1025; died around 1105; daughter of Alexius "Charon" Dalassenus (Byzantine governor of Italy); married John Comnenus or Kom-

nenos (d. 1067, brother of Isaac Comnenus, r. 1057–1059); children: eight, including Manuel; Isaac (d. ca. 1106); Alexius I Comnenus (1048–1118), Byzantine emperor (r. 1081–1118); Adrian (d. 1105); Nicephorus; and three daughters (names unknown: one married Michael Taronite; another married Nicephorus Melissenus; the youngest married Constantine Diogenes); grandmother of Anna Comnena.

Two years after he had ascended the Byzantine throne, Isaac Comnenus became dangerously ill and discouraged over his inability to effect reforms; he decided to abdicate. Isaac longed to turn the empire over to his brother John, whom he had already raised to the rank of Curopalates and Grand Domestic. But John Comnenus adamantly refused the throne—much to the disgust of his wife Anna Dalassena. Instead, in November 1059, Isaac nominated Constantine X Ducas. From that time on, Anna determined to win back the throne and the power that her family was meant to wield. "The coup d'etat of 1081, which set the Comnenian dynasty upon the throne for more than a century," writes Charles Diehl, "was the indirect but certain and logical result of her tenacious energy, of her passionate desire for the glory of her house, and of the deep, unalterable devotion for her children which she displayed in every juncture." Fortunately, Anna Dalassena's extraordinary qualities proved equal to her lofty ambitions.

We were two bodies with one soul.

—Alexius I, writing of his mother Anna Dalassena

Charitable and deeply religious, Anna Dalassena enjoyed the company of priests and monks and longed to end her days in a convent. She was an aristocrat, a somber woman who spent her nights in prayer and her days in devotion to her children. Her son Alexius I wrote:

> Nothing can be compared to a tender mother who loves her children. In all the world there is no stronger support, whether against annoyance or against impending danger. If she gives advice, her advice is good; if she prays, her all-powerful prayer is an invincible protection to its object. Such has been to me since my earliest youth my revered mother and sovereign, who in every circumstance was my teacher and my guide. We were two bodies with one soul.

Born into a powerful family, she married into an even more powerful family and spent her life at court. There, she learned the art of royal intrigue, acquired a thorough grasp of politics, and became skilled in navigating the corridors of Byzantine power. With an easy eloquence and first-rate intellect, she possessed "a powerful mind, truly royal, and worthy of the throne," wrote her granddaughter *Anna Comnena*. "It was extraordinary to find so old a head on such young shoulders; and all her earnestness and worth were obvious at a glance."

Anna Dalassena exercised enormous influence over her sons. When her husband John died in 1067 and she was left a widow with eight children, this influence increased. "It was she who really brought up all her sons, and made them the remarkable men they were," writes Diehl. At the time of her husband's death, five of the children were grown: Manuel was in the imperial army; Isaac and Alexius were 19 or 20; one daughter had married Michael Taronite; the other daughter married Nicephorus Melissenus.

While Anna Dalassena was raising her children, *Eudocia Macrembolitissa* (1021–1096), the widow of Constantine X Ducas, was ruling Byzantium as regent for her young son Michael VII Ducas (r. 1071–1078). Eudocia was intelligent, talented, and well-educated. She too had a passion for power and intended to "die on the throne." In exchange for her succession and joint rule with their son Michael, the not quite 40-year-old Eudocia had promised her husband, upon his death, that she would never marry again. The promise had been put in writing, and the document resided with Patriarch John Xiphilin. But Eudocia fell in love with Romanus Diogenes, a general who had fomented an uprising on the death of her husband. When Romanus was brought to Constantinople as a prisoner, Eudocia surprised the court and granted him a pardon. In time, she wanted to marry her general, but first she would have to wangle the contract out of the hands of the prelate. Claiming to be in love with the prelate's brother, Eudocia so pleased Patriarch John that he agreed to give back the paper. When he did, she married Romanus Diogenes and proclaimed him emperor, much to the dismay of her teenaged son Michael. The patriarch, Eudocia's brother-in-law Caesar John Ducas, and ex-minister Michael Psellus (who was now tutor to Michael VII) were furious over the deceit. The accession of Romanus IV Diogenes literally meant the accession of the army and the end of the reign of the Ducae.

Delighted at the downfall of her old nemesis, the family Ducas, Anna Dalassena stood by Eudocia, and married her youngest daughter to Constantine Diogenes, a near relative of Romanus. As a result, the Comneni family was in great favor at court. Anna's son Manuel was made commander-in-chief of the Army of the East where he distinguished himself. When he fell dangerously ill, his worried mother rushed to see him in Bithynia. On her arrival, Manuel used his last effort to rise and receive her, then fell into her arms. Writes Diehl: "After expressing the wish to be buried in the same tomb in which later his beloved mother would rest, he grew weaker and expired."

The revolution of 1071 weakened Anna's courtly influence. In August, Romanus IV was defeated by the Turks near the Armenian town of Manzikert and captured by the sultan Alp Arslan. With Romanus in bondage, the Ducae saw their chance. Announcing that Romanus was now dethroned, they made war upon his release from captivity. Because Anna Dalassena remained faithful to Romanus, she was summoned before a tribunal that was predisposed to condemn her. When she appeared before them, she pulled a crucifix from beneath her cloak and waved it in their faces, saying, "Here is my Judge and yours. Think on Him when you sentence me, and take care that your sentence be worthy of the Supreme Judge who knoweth the secrets of the heart." Taken aback, some jurists were in favor of acquittal. Others were adamantly opposed. In the end, they compromised, and Anna Dalassena was banished with her sons to one of the Princes' Islands.

Before long, however, Caesar John Ducas had a falling out with his nephew Michael VII and was forced to leave court and retire to his estates. The new ministers, hoping for the cooperation of the still powerful Comneni, returned Anna and her sons from banishment. In another conciliatory gesture, Michael and his Empress ❧▶ Maria of Alania offered one of her cousins to Anna's son Isaac in marriage. Isaac was also offered his brother Manuel's old position as commander-in-chief of the Army of the East.

When Isaac took up his post at his mother's encouragement, he brought along his 23-year-old brother Alexius as his lieutenant. Soon, both were considered brave soldiers, but whereas Isaac could be foolhardy, Alexius was even tempered. The unacknowledged favorite of his mother, Alexius was intelligent, strong, and tenacious; he preferred to gain by diplomacy rather than force.

During the years 1072–73, the Byzantine Empire was seriously vulnerable. On the Asiatic front, the Turks were threatening; there was also a revolt by Roussel de Bailleul, the Norman leader of the mercenaries. The brothers Comneni, though outnumbered, accomplished military miracles and, in so doing, became venerated by the populace of Constantinople on their return. So much adoration proved threatening to the Ducae. Isaac was dispatched to Syria as duke of Antioch. Alexius, given few soldiers and little money, was sent to fight Roussel de Bailleul. In 1074, Alexius returned to Constantinople with the Norman in tow.

By then, Alexius was one of the most renowned citizens of Byzantium. His enormous popularity stood in sharp contrast to the unpopularity of Michael. The emperor's prime minister had exhausted the finances of the kingdom, causing famine; the army, having received no

❧▶ **Maria of Alania** (fl. 1070–1081)
*Byzantine empress. Name variations: Mary of Alania, Maria Ducas. Born into the tribe of Alan, located in what is now southern Russia; daughter of the king of Georgia; married Michael VII Ducas, emperor of Byzantium (r. 1071–1078); married Nicephorus III Botaneiates (Botoniates), emperor of Byzantium (r. 1078–1081), in 1708; children: (first marriage) Constantine Ducas (who was at one time betrothed to *Anna Comnena).*

When Michael VII Ducas abandoned his throne to Nicephorus III Botaneiates, he took monastic vows, which meant that he had to give up his wife, Maria of Alania. Nicephorus was an elderly man who had been married to a woman named **Verdenia** in his youth. As emperor, now twice a widower, he wanted a third wife to shore up his claim to the throne. After rejecting a proposal from *Eudocia Macrembolitissa, he chose the "beautiful Maria" of Alania, she of the red hair, the alabaster skin, and the bright blue eyes. "Neither Apelles nor Phidias," wrote *Anna Comnena, "ever created anything so beautiful. . . . She was a living statue whom lovers of the beautiful could never weary of admiring; or, rather, she was Love incarnate descended to earth." Though Maria was less than enthusiastic, she agreed to the marriage to safeguard the possible succession of her son Constantine, then age four.

Alexius I Comnenus was also infatuated with the Empress Maria, to the consternation of his wife *Irene Ducas. Historians claim the attraction was mutual and rumors spread throughout the capital of Constantinople. It must have been scandalous when Maria officially adopted Alexius Comnenus, making him a member of the royal family, which allowed him to enter the inner sanctum of the palace. When Nicephorus named his nephew Synadenus successor instead of her son Constantine, Maria was furious. She threw her energy to the Comneni and aided Alexius' and *Anna Dalassena's royal ambitions.

pay, spoke of mutiny. In Europe, Nicephorus Bryennius (future husband of Anna Comnena) proclaimed himself emperor. In Asia, Nicephorus Botaneiates (Botoniates) did the same. Throughout the confusion, all sides courted Alexius and sought the backing of the Comneni.

Alexius had recently lost his first wife, and it was now time to marry for a new alliance. Emperor Michael offered him the hand of his sister Zoë, while Caesar John Ducas was proposing his granddaughter *Irene Ducas. When Alexius chose the granddaughter there was an outcry, not only from the Emperor Michael but from Anna Dalassena who found it difficult to swallow the marriage of her favorite son to her old enemy. Using all his diplomacy, and with the assistance of his future mother-in-law **Marie of Bulgaria**, Alexius managed to break down his mother's resistance, and Anna Dalassena finally gave her consent. Though she would never totally come to terms with her daughter-in-law, Anna soon saw that Alexius was right, and the alliance between the Comneni and the Ducae was to prove too powerful for the existing government.

In the beginning, Alexius backed Michael, defeating Nicephorus Bryennius in Macedonia in 1078. Shortly thereafter, however, when Nicephorus Botaneiates dethroned Michael, Alexius backed Botaneiates. For his support, Alexius was created Grand Domestic of the Scholae with the title of Noblissimus. Because of his brilliant victories, he grew even more celebrated by the people and was adored by his soldiers. Through his marriage, Alexius had won over most of the aristocracy; he had also won the backing of the patriarch. Meanwhile, Emperor Nicephorus Botaneiates was unpopular. Old and apathetic, he had corrupt ministers who were squandering the Byzantine treasury, and the army continued to be poorly paid.

The revolt of Anna Dalassena's son-in-law Nicephorus Melissenus, who had just ascended the throne in Asia, posed another threat to the empire. When Alexius refused to lead the forces sent against his rebellious brother-in-law, the ministers tried to warn Nicephorus Botaneiates that Alexius might make trouble. But Botaneiates had married Maria of Alania, the wife of his predecessor Michael, and she was partial to Alexius. While Anna Dalassena also maneuvered and abetted Alexius, her other son Isaac, who was related to Maria by marriage, furthered their cause with his easy access to her. The surprising result was the official adoption of Alexius Comnenus by Maria of Alania.

Alarmed, Emperor Botaneiates chose his nephew Synadenus for his successor while his ministers made plans to put out the eyes of both brothers, Isaac and Alexius. Warned of the plans, doubtless by Maria of Alania, the brothers made plans of their own. On the night of February 14, 1081, Isaac and Alexius fled Constantinople and made their way to the army of Thrace (modern Edirne in European Turkey). In the dawn hours, Anna took her daughters, her daughters-in-law, and her grandchildren, and sought sanctuary at the Hagia St. Sophia. When Nicephorus Botaneiates commanded that she come to the palace, she refused. Clinging to the iconostasis (the screened partition that separates the altar from the nave of the church), she warned that they'd have to cut off her hands to take her away. Instead, the emperor negotiated with her, promising to spare all their lives no matter the outcome. He then imprisoned them in the Petrion convent for safekeeping. Marie of Bulgaria, who was the daughter-in-law of Caesar John Ducas and the mother-in-law of Alexius Comnenus, soon joined them.

Alexius and his armies advanced on Constantinople. Upon taking the city, he immediately had himself crowned alone, and he bestowed on his mother, Anna Dalassena, the title of empress. His wife Irene and all her relatives were assigned to live in the Lower Palace, while Alexius, his mother, and all his relatives, lived in the Upper Palace. Thus, the Ducae and the Comneni were symbolically separated. Amid the grumblings of the Ducae and the strong urging of Patriarch Cosmas, Alexius reluctantly agreed to have Irene crowned seven days later. Alexius increased the power of his mother day by day; keeping her thoroughly informed, he requested her counsel on all occasions. When in August 1081 he had to leave Constantinople and go to Illyria to fight the Normans under Robert Guiscard, Alexius issued a golden bull, giving his mother absolute power during his absence. "Whatever she may decree, whether in writing or by word of mouth, is to be considered final." Anna was also given her own seal, still extant, on which was written: "Lord, protect Anna I, Dalassena, the mother of the Basileus." For 20 years, she ruled jointly with her son, and she governed well. Wrote Anna Comnena, "She gave orders, and her son obeyed like a slave. He had the trappings of power, but she the substance." Anna Dalassena brought order to the government and reformed the indifferent morality within the confines of the palace. "Part of her nights she spent in prayer," wrote Diehl; "the morning was given up to audiences and to the signing of dispatches; in the afternoon she followed the Divine Office in the chapel of *St. Thecla, after which, until evening, she devoted herself once more to public affairs."

As she aged, Anna Dalassena became more imperious and inflexible. Sensing that her time had come, in 1100, she retired voluntarily from public life to become a nun in the convent of Pantepoptes, which she had founded. "Without her intelligence and acumen," wrote Alexius, "the monarchy would have been lost."

SOURCES:

Diehl, Charles. *Byzantine Portraits.* Translated by Harold Bell. NY: Knopf, 1927.

Head. Constance. *Imperial Byzantine Portraits.* New Rochelle, NY: Caratzas Brothers, 1982.

Ostrogorsky, George. *History of the Byzantine State.* New Brunswick, NJ: Rutgers University Press, 1969.

Anna de Medici (b. 1616).

See Medici, Anna de.

Anna Ioannovna (1693–1740).

See Anna Ivanovna.

Anna Ivanovna (1693–1740)

Russian empress who ruled from 1730 to 1740 in a reign characterized by the continuation of the Westernization of Russia initiated by Tsar Peter I. Name variations: Anny Ioannovny; Ioannovna; Anne of Courland. Pronunciation: I-va-NOV-na. Born Anna Ivanovna on January 28, 1693, in Moscow, Russia; died in St. Petersburg, Russia, on October 17, 1740; second daughter of Ivan V (Alekseevich) and Praskovya Saltykova (1664–1723); niece of Peter the Great; secular education by Western tutors and religious training from the church; married Frederick-William Kettler, duke of Courland (a nephew of the king of Prussia), in 1710 (died 1711); no children.

Her father Ivan V died (1696) and her family became dependent on Tsar Peter I; widowed on wedding trip (1710); resided in Mitau, capital of Courland (until 1730); succeeded Peter II as tsar (1730); overthrew the Supreme Privy Council and re-established autocracy; succeeded by Ivan VI at her death (1740).

On February 25, 1730, Anna Ivanovna, with the support of the clergy and lower nobility, repudiated the limitations on her monarchical power and overthrew the Supreme Privy Council of Russia. She had been selected by the Privy Council in January and had signed the "Conditions," which made her tsar but deprived her of all real power. After her arrival in Moscow, she shrewdly professed her amazement that the general public had not approved of the limitation and dramatically tore up the Conditions. Her reign began in controversy and remains controversial. Historians have depicted her absolutist reign as a dark page in Russian history in which German favorites exploited the policies, resources, and interests of Russia. The reappraisal of both Russian history and the role of women in history has led to new evaluations of Anna's reign. Some now believe that foreign domination has been overemphasized, and that the German advisors were actually capable and loyal servants of Russia who improved many aspects of Russian society.

Anna Ivanovna was born in Moscow on January 28, 1693, into a Russia where men wore beards and heavy robes and women wore veils and lived in seclusion in an almost oriental society. She was the fourth daughter of Ivan V (1682–1696), co-tsar of Russia with his half-brother Peter I. Her mother, *Praskovya Saltykova, was a woman of the old Russian order of piousness and hospitality who descended from a powerful aristocratic family. Ivan V, a man more suited to monastic life, suffered from retardation and ruled in name only. He died in 1696 when Anna was three years old and her uncle, Peter I the Great (1682–1725), acted as her parent-guardian.

Anna and two of her sisters grew up in the old wooden palace of Ismailovo near Moscow. It was like a small isolated kingdom of stewards, grooms, and watchmen. Their mother filled the palace with tumblers, buffoons, dwarfs, jesters, and the severely deformed to entertain their free hours. Peter, whose goal was to bring Western culture to Russia, insisted on introducing Anna's family to secular ideas through French and German tutors. Anna's worldly education was counterbalanced by a rigorous religious training supervised by her tradition-minded mother. Anna learned all of the social graces and courtly conduct, but her personality was a cultural confusion of Eastern Orthodox Christianity, Western secular culture, and the barbaric and superstitious atmosphere of her mother's household. The constant bickering and turmoil of her home life left Anna with a spiteful, stubborn, and temperamental personality.

Anna was a minor figure at Peter's court but, after the age of 13, was sometimes invited to court functions. In 1708, she was summoned by Peter to accompany the family to St. Petersburg where she soon enjoyed the status and respect society paid to her. Peter found a match for his niece and on October 31, 1710, Anna was

Anna Ivanovna,
painting by
Caravaque.

married to Frederick-William Kettler, duke of Courland, a nephew of the king of Prussia. The newlyweds remained in St. Petersburg until the new year, when they left for Mitau, the capital of Courland. Less than 30 miles from St. Petersburg, the duke took ill and died. Anna, a 17-year-old widow, promptly returned to Peter's court where she resided until Peter ordered her to take up residence in Mitau. His hope that Anna could strengthen Russian influence in Courland was disrupted by an antagonistic political faction that forced Anna to leave. She resided in Danzig until she was permitted to return to Mitau in 1717 as a *de facto* sovereign. During her 13 years in Courland, Anna lived an unhappy existence, receiving little attention from her homeland. Her one opportunity to remarry was prevented by Prince Alexander Menshikov in 1726 because her marriage to the count of Saxony would have frustrated his desire to claim Courland for himself one day.

During Anna's years in Courland, Russia entered a period of instability when Peter the Great died in 1725. In 1722, Peter had issued a decree allowing the tsar to designate his successor rather than continue the primogeniture succession of Muscovite Russia. This procedure rested upon the tsar's ability to publicly declare his successor and for the principle constituency of Russian society to accept that choice. The emergence in 1726 of the Supreme Privy Council as an independent political institution comprising nobles further complicated the succession method. Peter himself had failed to designate a successor before his death and his wife Catherine, with the support of Prince Menshikov and his pro-Western faction, succeeded him as ruler. *Catherine I (1684–1727) reigned for two years with little interest or talent for the business of absolutist government. Menshikov and his supporters dominated her reign but fell from power when she died in May 1727. The anti-Western *boyar* (noble) faction led by the Golitsyn and Dolgoruky families purged the Supreme Privy Council and chose Peter Alexevich, grandson of Peter I, to succeed to the throne. During his brief reign, Peter II (r. 1727–30) was dominated by the Dolgoruky-controlled Council, which returned Russia to the old ways. In a symbolic gesture, they moved the capital from St. Petersburg back to Moscow. On January 18, 1730, the day of his intended wedding to **Catherine Dolgoruky**, the 14-year-old Peter II died of smallpox. For the third time in five years, the succession method devised by Peter I failed at designating an heir on the death of a tsar.

The Supreme Privy Council, dominated by the Dolgoruky and Golitsyn families, met during the night of January 18–19, 1730, to discuss the pressing issue of succession. The Dolgorukys offered Peter II's proposed bride as the new ruler, but the Council narrowly refused to accept her. They passed over *Elizabeth Petrovna, the daughter of Peter I and Catherine I, on the grounds of illegitimacy because she was born three years before her parents' marriage. The most appealing of the remaining candidates was Anna Ivanovna, duchess of Courland, because

she was widowed and without children. Thus, the Council could decide the succession again at her death. That same night, the Council dispatched to Anna at Mitau the offer and conditions under which it was prepared to raise her to the throne. The document, called the "Conditions," stipulated that Anna must pledge neither to marry nor name a successor, alter the Council, declare war or peace, impose new taxes, disburse public funds, confiscate property, impose death penalties, create new *boyars,* or exercise any control of the regiments unless the Council gave its unanimous consent. Although Anna was forewarned of the "Conditions," she welcomed the official delegates and signed the document. She left for Moscow three days later and entered the city on February 15, 1730.

Before entering Moscow, Anna had met a delegation of boyars and representatives from the Preobrazhensky Guards and concluded that the Council did not enjoy universal support. She proclaimed herself colonel of the Guards, an infringement of the conditions, and forced the Council's hand by entering the city. On February 25, about 800 angry boyars petitioned Anna to publicly review the "Conditions" with the Assembly. When the Privy Council protested this request, the Guard officers loudly requested that Anna abolish the Council and assume absolute power. With theatrical flair, Anna professed her amazement that the "Conditions" lacked the support of the "generality." She sent for the documents and, in full view of the public, tore up the signed "Conditions" and expressed her intention to rule Russia in the autocratic tradition of the past. The Supreme Privy Council was abolished, and the principal members were eventually punished with prison, exile, or death.

Anna Ivanovna's experiences before her accession to the throne had a significant influence on her reign. Her years of existence on paltry allowances controlled by others heightened her desire for luxuries as tsar of Russia. Anna's past had given her a harsh and distrustful outlook on life, and the political intrigues she encountered at the Russian court reinforced her suspicious nature. During her years in Courland, Anna had developed a Western outlook, and her high regard for German administration and government made her seem heavily partial to German advisors. Her unhappy life of widowhood led her to depend on her secretary and paramour, Ernst Johann Biron. Anna's behavior and appearance did little to ingratiate herself to her people. She was a boorish, obese woman with a sullen disposition and appalling manners who enjoyed pursuits such as hunting, horse riding, and firearms. Possibly in revenge for her earlier treatment, Anna treated her relatives with disdain. Although indifferent to religion, she occasionally pretended to be zealously devoted to the Eastern Orthodox Church. Like her mother and Peter I, Anna surrounded herself with idiots, jesters, giants, and miscreants in a court that often presented a circus-like atmosphere. Her luxurious living led to a courtly budget five times that of Peter I and resulted in higher taxes throughout the realm.

She liked magnificence in keeping with her imperial rank, but only in so far as this was consistent with the good government of the state.

—Prince M.M. Shcherbatov

Anna was shrewd in her political action and used her absolutism to play one contending side against another while consolidating her own position. She had little interest in the details of governmental affairs and relied heavily on many favorites, most of them German, from Courland. The empress moved the capital back to the more progressive and Western environment of St. Petersburg. With her suspicious nature toward the boyars, she placed her confidence and authority behind her handful of foreign courtiers. Together, they created a small executive committee called the Cabinet in 1731. It replaced the Supreme Privy Council, and the conduct of the Russian state emanated from this body appointed by Anna. Biron, though created a count in 1730, acquired the highest honors and power and effectively controlled the administration of the government. Count Burkhard Cristoph von Münnich, a native of Oldenburg and a servant of the Russian court since 1721, became commander of the Russian military. Count Andrei I. Ostermann, a native of Westphalia, dominated the Cabinet and ran foreign affairs. Additional principal officials, such as Artemi Volynski and Alexis Bestuzhev-Ryumin, were drawn from the lesser Russian nobility. Other Germans, many favorites of Anna, had no qualifications for their positions and simply acted in their self-interest while disdaining everything Russian. To provide more positions for her favorites and to counterbalance the Preobrazhensky Guards, Anna formed the Ismailovsky Guards whose officer ranks were composed solely of Baltic Germans. Despite these appointments and the powerful personalities of Anna's chief ministers, no definable "German Party" can be discerned during this time.

Historians, particularly nationalistic Russian scholars, have portrayed Anna Ivanovna's reign as a dark period of German exploitation of Russia. It would be injudicious to deny the distasteful appearances of Anna's reign, but it would also be misleading to assign all of the negative aspects to foreign influence, or to the empress. Germans did dominate the Cabinet, but the Senate and many other administrative bodies remained Russian. Germans like Ostermann and Münnich had served Russia many years before Anna's accession and proved to be honest and loyal to Russia. Many important members, such as Prince Alexis M. Cherkassky and Vasily F. Saltykov, were associates of Peter the Great. Biron was the most hated figure of Anna's reign and "Bironism" referred to the police persecutions, spying, executions of thousands of Russians, and the exile of nearly 30,000 to Siberia. Many of these were old Believers (religious heretics) and common criminals rather than members of the political opposition. The cruelties of Biron and his minions were not exceptional for that time, but the persecutions were idealistically exaggerated by romantic imaginations when compared to Anna's successor. To emphasize this point, General Andrei I. Ushakov, who headed the secret investigative body that carried out the policies of Biron, learned his skills from Peter the Great.

During Anna's reign, Ostermann directed Russia's foreign policy. With her approval, he intervened in the War of Polish Succession (1733–35), which placed the pro-Russian Augustus III of Saxony on the Polish throne. In the Russo-Turkish War (1735–39), the Russian army under Münnich won several great victories and eventually secured the Black Sea region of Azov by the Treaty of Belgrade in 1730. The elevation of Biron to duke of Courland in 1737 increased Russian authority in that duchy and strengthened Russian power in the Baltic Sea region.

In cultural matters, Anna Ivanovna's reign was a continuation of the policies of Peter the Great. The emergence of a new literary tradition conforming to the literary trends of Western Europe can be traced to those years. Many authors had lived and studied in the West and were influenced by the classical and pseudo-classical styles of the time. Alexander P. Sumarokov, Mikhail V. Lomonosov, and Vasily K. Trediakovsky published their poetry and dramatic works. Antiockh D. Kantemir translated the works of Baron Montesquieu but was best known for his satires. Historians were also affected by Western culture. Vasily Tatishchev in his critical *Istoriia Rossiiskaia* (History of Russia) even questioned the ancient chronicles and the influences of the Russian church in history. Gerhard Muller, a German scholar, traveled in Siberia and wrote the first definitive history of that region. Another of Anna's favorites from Courland, Reinhold Loewenwolde, brought a great love for the arts to Russia and encouraged the development of Italian theater and chamber music. Loewenwolde also persuaded Anna to establish Russia's first school of ballet and brought an Italian opera company for a performance at Anna's court in 1736. The Academy of Arts was established in 1757 by Ivan Shuvalov to encourage painting, sculpture, and architecture. Under the Academy's patronage, Count Bartholomew Rastrelli applied his Russian Baroque style to many of St. Petersburg's 18th-century buildings, including the Smolny Convent and the Winter Palace.

The Academy of Sciences, founded during the reign of Peter the Great, continued to flourish under the directorship of Baron I.A. Korf. During Anna's reign, the first native Russians were admitted to Academy membership. In 1735, the Russian Society was established as a branch of the Academy to refine and study the Russian language. The Academy also appointed Vitus Bering to lead the second Kamchatka expedition in 1732 to explore the region between Asia and North America. In 1731, Anna established the Shliakhetsky Korpus, a school for noble children whose graduates were commissioned as officers. In 1736, she redefined the obligations of nobles by limiting the period of required service to 25 years. She also permitted one brother in each family to be released from obligatory service to manage the family estates.

Anna continued the economic policies initiated by Peter the Great. Business growth was brisk in metallurgy and textiles in a state regulated market. Exports grew because of commercial treaties with the West, and tariffs protected the fledgling industries in Russia. While the nobility and businessmen made some gains under Anna's reign, peasants continued to lose their remaining rights. Peasants were barred from purchasing real estate in 1730, forbidden to negotiate contracts in 1731, and prohibited from operating cloth industries in 1734.

Having no children or direct heirs, Anna was determined that the succession pass through the line of Ivan V, her father, rather than that of Peter the Great. Shortly before her death, Anna named a two-month-old infant to be her successor, a grandson of Anna's elder sister, *Catherine of Mecklenburg-Schwerin, who had married Charles Leopold, duke of Mecklenburg, in

1716. A daughter from this marriage, ❦➤ **Anna Leopoldovna**, married Duke Anton Ulrich of Brunswick-Bevern-Lüneburg in 1739. Their marriage produced Ivan Antonovich, who was born on August 12, 1740. Under the provisions established by Peter the Great but never used, Anna Ivanovna designated the infant, Ivan VI (r. 1740–41), as her heir on October 5, 1740. In a controversial action, Anna passed over the parents and named Biron as regent. This arrangement was doomed to failure. Biron was overthrown within a month by Münnich, and Anna Leopoldovna became regent. By the end of 1741, Ivan VI, Anna Leopoldovna, and the German court were overthrown by Elizabeth Petrovna, daughter of Peter the Great and Catherine I.

Anna's reign ended with the same confusion as her accession. Her intemperate life had undermined her health, and she suffered from gout. After several days of torment, Anna Ivanovna died at the age of 46 on October 17, 1740.

❦➤ Anna Leopoldovna (1718–1746)

Russian regent for a few months during the minority of her son Ivan. Name variations: Anna Carlovna or Karlovna. Born Elisabeth Katharina Christine on December 18, 1718; died in exile on March 18 or 19, 1746; daughter of *Catherine of Mecklenburg-Schwerin (1692–1733) and Charles Leopold, duke of Mecklenburg-Schwerin; married Anton Ulrich (b. 1714), duke of Brunswick, in 1739 (died 1775); children: Ivan VI (b. 1740), emperor of Russia (r. 1740–1741); Catherine of Brunswick-Wolfenbuttel (1741–1807); Elizabeth of Brunswick-Wolfenbuttel (1743–1782); Peter (b. 1745); Alexei (b. 1746).

In 1740, Anna Leopoldovna's son Ivan was adopted by Empress *Anna Ivanovna and proclaimed heir to the Russian throne. A few days following the proclamation, the empress died, leaving directions regarding the succession, and appointing her favorite Ernst Johann Biron, duke of Courland, as regent. Biron, however, was hated by the Russian people, and Anna Leopoldovna had little difficulty in overthrowing him. Assuming the regency, she then took the title of grand-duchess, but she knew little of the character of the people with whom she had to deal, was ignorant of the approved Russian mode of government, and quarrelled with her key supporters. In December 1741, *Elizabeth Petrovna, daughter of Peter the Great and a favorite with the soldiers, incited the guards to revolt, overcame the meager opposition, and was proclaimed Empress Elizabeth I. Ivan VI was thrown into prison, where he soon died. Along with her husband, Anna Leopoldovna was banished to a small island in the river Dvina, where on March 18, 1746, she died in childbirth.

SOURCES:

Bain, Nisbet. *The Pupils of Peter the Great: A History of the Russian Court and Empire from 1697 to 1740.* London: Constable, 1897.

Curtiss, Mina. *A Forgotten Empress: Anna Ivanovna and Her Era, 1730–1740.* NY: Frederick Ungar, 1974.

Lipski, Alexander. "A Re-examination of the 'Dark Era' of Anna Ivanovna," in *Slavic Review.* Vol. 15, 1956, pp. 477–488.

———. "Some Aspects of Russia's Westernization During the Reign of Anna Ivanovna." *Slavic Review.* Vol. 18, 1959, pp. 1–11.

Longworth, Philip. *The Three Empresses: Catherine I, Anne and Elizabeth of Russia.* NY: Holt, Rinehart and Winston, 1972.

Wieczynski, Joseph L., ed. *The Modern Encyclopedia of Russian and Soviet History.* Gulf Breeze, FL: Academic International Press, 1976.

SUGGESTED READING:

de Manstein, C.H. *Memoirs of Russia from the Year 1727–1744.* London: n.p., 1770 (reprint 1968).

Kluyuchevsky, V.O. *A History of Russia.* Vol. 4. Translated by C.J. Hogarth. NY: Russell & Russell, 1960.

Miliukov, Paul, C. Seignobos, and L. Eisenmann. *History of Russia.* Vol. 2: *The Successors of Peter the Great.* Translated by C.L. Markmann. NY: Funk & Wagnalls, 1968.

Morfill, W.R. *A History of Russia from the Birth of Peter the Great to the Death of Alexander II.* London: Methuen, 1902.

COLLECTIONS:

Ukases (edicts) located in the European Law Division, Library of Congress, Washington, D.C.

Historical documents in the Georgi M. Kiselevskii Papers, Bakhmeteff Archive, Columbia University, New York City.

Phillip E. Koerper, Professor of History, Jacksonville State University, Jacksonville, Alabama

Anna Jagello (1523–1596)

Queen of Poland. Name variations: Jagiello, Jagiellonica or Jagiellonka. Born in 1523; died in 1596; daughter of *Bona Sforza (1493–1557) and Zygmunt I Stary also known as Sigismund I the Elder (1467–1548), king of Poland (r. 1506–1548); married Istvan also known as Stefan Batory or Stephen Bathory (1533–1586), king of Poland-Lithuania (r. 1575–1586).

Anna Juliana of Saxe-Coburg-Saalfeld (1781–1860)

Russian royal. Name variations: Anna Juliane. Born on September 23, 1781; died on August 15, 1860; daughter of Francis Frederick, duke of Saxe-Coburg-Saalfeld, and *Augusta of Reuss-Ebersdorf (1757–1831); married Constantine Pavlovich Romanov (1779–1831, son of Paul I, tsar of Russia, who renounced his succession), on February 26, 1796 (divorced 1820). Constantine Romanov also entered into a morganatic marriage with Johanna von Grudna-Grudczinski, princess of Lowicz (1799–1831), on May 24, 1820.

Anna Karlovna (1718–1746).

See Anna Ivanovna for sidebar on Anna Leopoldovna.

Anna Leopoldovna (1718–1746).

See Anna Ivanovna for sidebar.

Anna Maria de Medici (d. 1741).

See Medici, Anna Maria de.

Anna Maria Ludovica (1667–1743).

See Medici, Anna Maria Luisa de.

Anna Maria Luisa de Medici (1667–1743).

See Medici, Anna Maria Luisa de.

Anna Maria Luisa of the Palatinate (1667–1743).

See Medici, Anna Maria Luisa de.

Anna Maria of Saxe-Lauenburg (d. 1741).

See Medici, Anna Maria de.

Anna Maria of Saxony (1836–1859)

Grand duchess of Tuscany. Name variations: Anna of Saxony; Maria Anna of Saxony. Born on April 1, 1836, in Dresden, Germany; died on February 10, 1859, in Florence, Italy; daughter of *Amalia of Bavaria (1801–1877) and Johann also known as John (1801–1873), king of Saxony (r. 1854–1873); became first wife of Ferdinand IV (1835–1908), titular grand duke of Tuscany from 1859 to 1908, on November 24, 1856; children: Antonia (1858–1883). Ferdinand IV's second wife was *Alicia of Parma (1849–1935).

Anna Maria of the Palatinate (1561–1589)

Swedish royal. Name variations: Maria of the Palatinate. Born on July 24, 1561; died on July 29, 1589; daughter of Louis of the Palatinate; became first wife of Charles IX (1550–1611), king of Sweden (r. 1604–1611); children: *Catherine, countess Palatine (1584–1638, who married John Casimir of Zweibrücken, count Palatine); Margaret Elizabeth (1580–1585); Elizabeth Sabine (1582–1585); Ludwig or Louis (b. 1583); Gustav (1587–1587); Marie (1588–1589); Christine (1593–1594).

Anna Maria Theresa (1879–1961)

Princess of Hohenlohe. Born on October 17, 1879, in Lindau; died on May 30, 1961, in Baden-Baden, Germany; daughter of Alicia of Parma (1849–1935) and Ferdinand IV (1835–1908), titular grand duke of Tuscany from 1859 to 1908.

Anna of Bohemia (fl. 1230s)

Duchess of Silesia. Flourished in the 1230s; married Henry II the Pious, duke of Silesia (r. 1238–1241); children: Boleslaw II Lysy of Legnica; Henry III of Breslaw; Conrad I of Glogow; Ladislas, archbishop of Salzburg; *Elizabeth of Silesia (fl. 1257).

Anna of Bohemia (fl. 1318)

Bohemian princess. Name variations: Anne. Flourished around 1318; daughter of Wenceslas II, king of Bohemia (r. 1278–1305) and *Judith (d. 1297); married Henry of Carinthia (d. 1335), king of Bohemia (r. 1306–1310); children: *Margaret Maultasch (1318–1369).

Anna of Bohemia and Hungary (1503–1547)

Holy Roman Empress. Name variations: Anna of Hungary. Born in 1503 in Prague; died in 1547 in Prague; daughter of Vladislav or Wladyslaw also known as Ladislas II of Bohemia, king of Bohemia (r. 1471–1516), and *Anne de Foix; sister of Louis II, king of Hungary (r. 1516–1528); married Ferdinand I, Holy Roman emperor (r. 1556–1564), in 1521; children: *Elizabeth of Habsburg (d. 1545); Maximilian II (1527–1576), Holy Roman emperor (r. 1564–1576); *Anna of Brunswick (1528–1590, who married Albert V of Bavaria); *Mary (1531–1581, who married William V, duke of Cleves); Magdalena (1532–1590); *Catherine of Habsburg (1533–1572); *Eleonora of Austria (1534–1594); Margaretha (1536–1566); Charles of Styria (1540–1590); Ferdinand, count of Tyrol; Helen (1543–1574); *Joanna of Austria (1546–1578, who married Francis I de Medici, grand duke of Tuscany).

Anna of Brandenburg (1487–1514)

Danish royal. Name variations: Anna von Brandenburg. Born on August 27, 1487; died on May 3, 1514, in Kiel; daughter of *Margaret of Saxony (1449–1501) and John Cicero (1455–1499), elector of Brandenburg (r. 1486–1499); became first wife of Frederick I, king of Denmark and Norway (r. 1523–1533), on April 10,

1502; children: Christian III (1503–1559), king of Denmark and Norway (r. 1534–1559); Hans; *Dorothea Oldenburg (1504–1547, who married Albert, duke of Prussia).

Anna of Brandenburg (1507–1567)

Duchess of Mecklenburg-Schwerin. Name variations: Anna Hohenzollern. Born in 1507; died on June 19, 1567; daughter of *Elizabeth of Denmark (1485–1555) and Joachim I Nestor, elector of Brandenburg (r. 1499–1535); married Albert V (1488–1547), duke of Mecklenburg-Schwerin (r. 1519–1547), on January 17, 1524; children: John Albert (b. 1525), duke of Mecklenburg-Gustrow; Ulrich III (b. 1528), duke of Mecklenburg-Gustrow; Christof (b. 1537).

Anna of Brunswick (fl. 1400s)

Duchess of Bavaria. Married Albert III the Pious (1401–1460, sometimes referred to as Albert II), duke of Bavaria (r. 1438–1460); children: John IV (b. 1437), duke of Bavaria (r. 1460–1463); Sigismund (b. 1439), duke of Bavaria (r. 1460–1467; abdicated in 1467); Albert IV (1447–1508, sometimes referred to as Albert III), duke of Bavaria (r. 1465–1508).

Anna of Brunswick (1528–1590)

Duchess of Bavaria. Name variations: Anna Habsburg or Hapsburg. Born on July 7, 1528, in Prague; died on October 17, 1590, in Munich; daughter of *Anna of Bohemia and Hungary (1503–1547) and Ferdinand I, Holy Roman emperor (r. 1558–1564); married Albert V (d. 1579), duke of Bavaria; children: William V the Pious, duke of Bavaria (r. 1579–1597, abdicated); *Mary of Bavaria (1551–1608).

Anna of Byzantium (fl. 901)

Holy Roman empress. Daughter of Leo VI the Wise, Byzantine emperor (r. 886–912) and one of his four wives, possibly *Zoë Carbopsina (c. 890–920); married Louis III the Blind of Provence, Holy Roman emperor (r. 901–905); children: Charles Constantine of Vienne (b. 901), count of Vienne.

Anna of Byzantium (963–1011).

See Theophano (c. 940–?) for sidebar.

Anna of Cumin (d. 1111)

Princess of Kiev. Died on October 7, 1111; became second wife of Vsevolod I, prince of Kiev (r.

*1078–1093), in 1067; children: Anna of Kiev, abbess of Janczyn (b. around 1068); *Adelaide of Kiev (c. 1070–1109); Katherine of Kiev (a nun). Vsevolod's first wife was *Irene of Byzantium (d. 1067).*

Anna of Denmark (1532–1585)

Princess of Denmark and electress of Saxony. *Born on November 22, 1532; died on October 1, 1585; daughter of Christian III, king of Denmark and Norway (r. 1535–1559), and Dorothea of Saxe-Lauenburg (1511–1571); married Augustus (1526–1586), elector of Saxony on October 7, 1584; children: Christian I (b. 1560), elector of Saxony; *Dorothea of Saxony (1563–1587).*

Anna of Denmark was the daughter of *Dorothea of Saxe-Lauenburg and Christian III, king of Denmark, who consolidated the gains of the Lutheran Reformation in Denmark by imprisoning all Catholic bishops until they agreed to cease their resistance. Through her influence, her husband Augustus turned to Lutheranism in 1574. As elector of Saxony from 1553–86, Augustus then helped secure the adoption of *Formula Concordiae*, a Lutheran creed of orthodoxy, in 1580.

Anna of Egmont (1533–1558)

Countess of Egmont. *Name variations: Anne. Born in 1533; died on March 24, 1558; daughter of Max, count of Egmont and Büren; became first wife of William I the Silent (1533–1584), prince of Orange, count of Nassau, stadholder of Holland, Zealand, and Utrecht (r. 1572–1584), on July 8, 1551; children: Philip William (d. 1618).*

Anna of Habsburg (d. 1327)

German princess. *Born in the late 1270s; died in March 1327; daughter of *Elizabeth of Tyrol (c. 1262–1313) and Albrecht also spelled Albert I of Habsburg (1255–1308), king of Germany (r. 1298–1308), Holy Roman emperor (r. 1298–1308, but not crowned); married Hermann of Brandenburg.*

Anna of Hohenberg (c. 1230–1281)

Holy Roman empress. *Name variations: Gertrud of Hohenberg became Anna of Hohenberg at her crowning at Aachen in 1273. Born Gertrud of Hohenberg between 1230 and 1235; died on January 16, 1281, in Vienna; married Rudolph or Rudolf I of Habsburg (1218–1291), king of Germany (r. 1273), Holy*

*Roman emperor (r. 1273–1291); children: Albert I (1250–1308), king of Germany (r. 1298–1308), Holy Roman emperor (r. 1298–1308, but not crowned); Hartmann (c. 1263–1281); *Matilda of Habsburg (1251–1304, who married Louis II of Bavaria); *Catherine of Habsburg (c. 1254–1282, who married Otto III of Bavaria); *Hedwig of Habsburg (d. 1286, who married Otto of Brandenburg); *Clementia of Habsburg (d. 1293, who married Charles Martel of Hungary); *Judith (1271–1297, who married Wenceslas of Bohemia); *Agnes of Habsburg (c. 1257–1322, who married Albert II of Saxony); Rudolf II (1270–1290, who married *Agnes of Bohemia).*

Holy Roman Empress Anna of Hohenberg was the wife of Rudolf I and mother of eight. The first of the Habsburg line to achieve the crown, Rudolph and Anna established a political power base in Austria where the family ruled for nearly seven centuries until 1918. They skillfully arranged for the marriage of their offspring to other royal houses, thereby establishing a resourceful Habsburg tactic and solidifying the Habsburg claim to preeminence in European affairs. Later generations would coin the phrase that best described the House: "Oh fortunate Austria! You gain by marriage what others must get by war." Anna's son Albert's harsh rule gave rise to the legend of William Tell.

Anna of Hungary (fl. 1244)

Hungarian princess. *Flourished around 1244; daughter of *Salome of Hungary (1201–c. 1270) and Bela IV, king of Hungary (r. 1235–1270); married Rastislav of Chernigov (b. around 1225), prince of Novgorod, prince of Kiev, in 1244; children: *Cunigunde of Hungary (d. 1285, who married Ottokar II, king of Bohemia).*

Anna of Hungary (d. around 1284)

Byzantine empress. *Died young, around 1284; daughter of Stephen V, king of Hungary (r. 1270–1272), and *Elizabeth of Kumania; became first wife of Andronicus II Paleologus (1259–1332), emperor of Nicaea (r. 1282–1328), in 1274; children: Michael IX Paleologus (d. 1320), Byzantine co-emperor (r. 1295–1320); Constantine. Andronicus II's second wife was *Irene of Montferrat.*

Anna of Moscow (1393–1417)

Russian royal. *Born in 1393; died of the plague in 1417; daughter of Basil I, prince of Moscow, and *So-*

phie of Lithuania (b. 1370); became first wife of John VIII Paleologus (1391–1448), emperor of Nicaea (r. 1425–1448), in 1411.

Anna of Prussia (fl. 1590s)

Electress of Brandenburg. Flourished in the 1590s; daughter of *Maria Eleanora and Albert Frederick, duke of Prussia; married John Sigismund (1572–1619), elector of Brandenburg (r. 1608–1619); children: *Maria Eleonora of Brandenburg (1599–1655); George William (1595–1640), elector of Brandenburg (r. 1619–1640); Catherine (who married Bethlen Gabor of Transylvania).

Anna of Russia (1795–1865).

See Anna Pavlovna.

Anna of Savoy (c. 1320–1353).

See Anne of Savoy.

Anna of Savoy (1455–1480)

Noblewoman of Savoy. Born in 1455; died in 1480; daughter of *Yolande of France (1434–1478) and Amédée also known as Amadeus IX, duke of Savoy (r. 1465–1472); married Frederick IV (1452–1504), king of Naples (r. 1496–1501, deposed), on September 11, 1478. Frederick's second wife was *Isabella del Balzo (d. 1533).

Anna of Saxony (1420–1462)

Landgravine of Hesse. Born on June 5, 1420; died on September 17, 1462; daughter of Fredrick I the Warlike (b. 1370), elector of Saxony; sister of *Catherine of Saxony (1421–1476); married Louis II the Peaceful, landgrave of Hesse, on September 13, 1436; children: Henry III the Rich (b. 1440), landgrave of Hesse; Louis III the Frank (b. 1438), landgrave of Hesse.

Anna of Saxony (1544–1577)

Princess of Orange and countess of Nassau. Name variations: Anne of Saxony. Born on December 23, 1544; died on December 18, 1577; daughter of *Agnes of Hesse (1527–1555) and Maurice, elector of Saxony; became second wife of William I the Silent (1533–1584), prince of Orange, count of Nassau, stadholder of Holland, Zealand, and Utrecht (r. 1572–1584), on August 24, 1561 (divorced in 1574); children: Maurice, prince of Orange, count of Nassau (r. 1584–1625); *Emilia of Orange (1569–1629).

William I the Silent's second wife Anna of Saxony caused him constant distress through her "poor, deranged, deluded and unhappy" behavior. Defying him publicly, denying him access to his children, Anna tormented the Dutch lord. She eventually had an affair with an older German lawyer in the Rhineland. When it was discovered, Anna confessed her part and pleaded that William kill both her and her lover; the lawyer asked only that he be beheaded like a gentleman. But William was "notoriously compassionate" in an age that was often barbaric. He quietly divorced Anne and pardoned the lawyer.

Anna of Schweidnitz (c. 1340–?)

Holy Roman empress. Born around 1340; daughter of Henry II, duke of Schweidnitz; third wife of Charles IV, Holy Roman emperor (r. 1347–1378); children: Wenceslas IV (1361–1419), duke of Luxemburg (r. 1383–1419), king of Bohemia (r. 1378–1419), and Holy Roman emperor as Wenceslas (r. 1378–1400).

Anna of Silesia

Duchess of Bavaria. Second wife of Louis II the Stern (1229–1294), count Palatine (r. 1253–1294), duke of Bavaria (r. 1255–1294); children: Louis (d. 1290).

Anna of Styria (1573–1598)

Queen of Poland and Sweden. Name variations: Anna of Austria. Born on August 16, 1573; died on February 10, 1598; daughter of Charles (1540–1590), archduke of Austria, and *Mary of Bavaria (1551–1608); sister of *Margaret of Austria (c. 1577–1611) and Constance of Styria (1588–1631); became first wife of Sigismund III (1566–1632), king of Poland (r. 1587–1632), king of Sweden (r. 1592–1599), on May 31, 1592; children: Karol Ferdinand, bishop of Breslau; Alexander Karol; Wladyslaw also known as Ladislas IV (b. 1595), king of Poland (r. 1632–1648); Anna Marie (1593–1600); Katherina (1596–1597). Following Anne of Styria's death in 1598, Sigismund married her younger sister *Constance of Styria.

Anna of the Palatinate

Holy Roman empress. Daughter of Rudolf, elector Palatine; second wife of Charles IV Luxemburg, Holy Roman emperor (r. 1347–1378).

Anna of Tyrol (1585–1618).

See Gonzaga, Anna.

Anna Paleologina (d. 1340)

Regent of Epirus. Name variations: Palaeologina. Birth date unknown; died after 1340 in Thessalonica (Greece); married John Orsini, despot of Epirus (r. 1323–1335); children: Nicephorus, later Nicephorus II of Epirus.

A princess of the Byzantine ruling family, Anna Paleologina married John Orsini, despot of the northwest Greek principality of Epirus. Anna, who despised her husband, arranged to have him murdered by poison in 1335. Then she and her son Nicephorus became the acting rulers of Epirus. Anna remained in power for only five years, during which time she tried to appease the Byzantine emperor Andronicus III Palaeologus, whose extensive empire and powerful army posed the greatest threat to her throne and the independence of the Eprian people. The emperor, however, wanted Epirus under Byzantine control, and, in 1340, Anna was overthrown and forced to flee Epirus with Nicephorus. She died in exile in Thessalonica, though her son continued to wage war in an ultimately unsuccessful attempt to regain his inheritance.

Laura York, Anza, California

Anna Paleologina-Cantacuzene (fl. 1270–1313)

*Regent of Epirus. Name variations: Palaeologina-Cantacuzena, Palaiologina. Born before 1270 in Byzantium; died after 1313 in Epirus; daughter of Princess *Eulogia Paleologina (fl. 1200s); married Nicephorus I of Epirus (died 1296); children: Thomas of Epirus; *Tamara (fl. 1300s, who married Philip of Tarento).*

Anna was born into the Palaeologi house, the imperial family of Byzantium. Her mother was the princess Eulogia, and her uncle was Emperor Michael VIII Paleologus. Anna's royal birth led to her marriage to the despot Nicephorus I, ruler of the principality of Epirus. On Nicephorus' death in 1296, Anna took over the government of Epirus in her infant son's name. As regent, she quickly became embroiled in the civil struggles between those favoring stronger ties to the Greek emperor, whom Anna supported, and those seeking to ally Epirus with neighboring kingdoms against the Byzantine Empire. During the 17 years that she retained the regency, Anna successfully repelled invasions and threats to her power, both from inside Epirus and from foreign states. She turned over the reins of government to her son Thomas when he came of age in 1313.

Laura York, Anza, California

Anna Pavlovna (1795–1865)

*Grand duchess of Russia and queen of the Netherlands. Name variations: Anna of Russia; Anne Romanov. Born on January 18, 1795, in St. Petersburg, Russia; died on March 1, 1865, at The Hague, Netherlands; daughter of *Sophia Dorothea of Wurttemberg (1759–1828) and Paul I (1754–1801), tsar of Russia (r. 1796–1801); sister of *Marie Pavlovna (1786–1859) and Nicholas I, tsar of Russia; grandmother of *Wilhelmina (1880–1962), queen of the Netherlands; married William II, king of the Netherlands, on February 21, 1816; children: William III (b. 1817), king of the Netherlands (r. 1840–1849); Alexander (b. 1818); Henry (b. 1820); Ernest (b. 1822); *Sophia of Nassau (1824–1897).*

Anna Petrovna (1708–1729).
See Elizabeth Petrovna for sidebar.

Anna Petrovna (1757–1758).
See Catherine II the Great for sidebar.

Anna Sophia of Denmark (1647–1717)

*Electress of Saxony. Name variations: Anne Sophia Oldenburg. Born on September 11, 1647; died on July 1, 1717; daughter of *Sophie Amalie of Brunswick-Lüneberg (1628–1685) and Frederick III (1609–1670), king of Denmark and Norway (r. 1648–1670); married John George III (1647–1691), elector of Saxony (r. 1680–1691), on October 19, 1666; children: John George IV (1668–1694), elector of Saxony (r. 1691–1694); Frederick Augustus I the Strong (1670–1733), elector of Saxony (r. 1694–1733), king of Poland (r. 1697–1704, 1709–1733).*

Anna Sophia of Prussia (1527–1591)

*Duchess of Mecklenburg-Gustrow. Born on June 11, 1527; died on February 6, 1591; daughter of *Dorothea Oldenburg (1504–1547) and Albert (1490–1568), duke of Prussia (r. 1525–1568); married John Albert, duke of Mecklenburg-Gustrow, on February 24, 1555; children: John V (b. 1558), duke of Mecklenburg-Schwerin.*

Anna Victoria of Savoy

Princess of Savoy-Carignan. Probably the daughter of Emmanuel Philibert (d. 1709) and Catherine d'Este.

Opposite page

𝒜nnabella

Because he never married and had no children, Eugene of Savoy (1663–1736), prince of Savoy-Carignan, was succeeded by his niece Anna Victoria of Savoy.

Anna von Munzingen (fl. 1327)

German abbess and biographer. Name variations: Anna of Adelshausen. Birth date unknown; died after 1327 at convent of Adelshausen, Germany.

Born into the German nobility, Anna von Munzingen entered the Dominican convent of Adelshausen, probably as a young girl. There, she was highly educated by the convent nuns, and her social rank led her to become abbess of Adelshausen. Although she was not a mystic, Anna was acquainted with many nuns who experienced visions and heard prophetic voices. She gathered their stories in her *Chronicle of the Mystics of Adelshausen*, composed of 34 biographies of the mystical nuns over whom she presided as abbess.

Annabella (1909–1996)

French actress. Born Suzanne Georgette Charpentier in La Varenne-Saint-Hilaire, near Paris, France, on July 14, 1909; died on September 18, 1996, in Neuilly-sur-Seine, France; daughter of a publisher; married Jean Murat (an actor; divorced); married Tyrone Power (an actor), in 1939 (divorced 1948); children: (first marriage) **Anna Murat** *(who was married to German actor Oskar Werner).*

Selected filmography: Napoleon *(1926);* Maldone *(France, 1928);* Le Million *(1931);* Un Soir de Rafle *(France, 1931);* Paris-Mediterranée *(France, 1932);* La Quatorze Juillet *(July 14th, France, 1933);* La Bataille *(France, 1933);* Caravan *(United States, 1934);* L'Equipage *(Flight into Darkness, France, 1935);* Veille d'Armes *(1935);* La Bandera *(Escape from Yesterday, France, 1935);* La Citadel du Silence *(The Citadel of Silence, France, 1937);* Under the Red Robe *(1937);* Dinner at the Ritz *(1937);* Wings of the Morning *(1937);* Hôtel du Nord *(France, 1938);* The Baroness and the Butler *(United States, 1938);* Suez *(United States, 1938);* Bridal Suite *(United States, 1939);* Tonight We Raid Calais *(United States, 1943);* Bomber's Moon *(United States, 1943);* 13 Rue Madeleine *(United States, 1947);* Dernier Amour *(France, 1949);* Don Juan *(Spain, 1950).*

In 1926, Annabella made her film debut at 16 with a small role in Abel Gance's *Napoleon*. Her first break came in 1931, when she was

hired by René Clair for the lead in his *Le Million*, because, he said, she bore a striking resemblance to silent star *Bessie Love. Annabella was featured once again in his 1933 movie *La Quatorze Juillet* (July 14th). In 1935, by then one of France's most celebrated young performers, she was voted best actress at the Venice Biennale for her performance in *Veille d'Armes*. She journeyed to England for three movies in 1936: *Under the Red Robe*, *Dinner at the Ritz*, and the first color film made in Britain, *Wings of the Morning* (all released in 1937).

By the late 1930s, Annabella was one of the most sought-after actresses in continental filmmaking, working in Britain, France, Hungary, Germany, and Austria. Though Hollywood beckoned, it offered her little. She interspersed her Los Angeles sojourns with stage work, appearing in Chicago in *Blithe Spirit* and on Broadway in *Jacobowsky and the Colonel* (1944) and Jean-Paul Sartre's *No Exit* (1946), which was directed by John Huston. Following her divorce from Tyrone Power in 1948, she returned to Europe to nurse her mother. She then retired to her farm in the French Pyrenees and volunteered for prison welfare work.

SOURCES:
Lamparski, Richard. *Whatever Became of . . . ? 1st and 2nd Series*. NY: Crown, 1967.

Anne (fl. 1st c.)

Saint. Name variations: Ann, Anna; (Hebrew) Hanna or Hannah. Born in the 1st century into the tribe of Juda; married Joachim; children: Mary. In the apocryphal gospels, the mother of Mary (the names of Mary's parents are not found in the New Testament).

According to tradition, Anne was the wife of St. Joachim and mother—after 21 years of barrenness—of *Mary the Virgin, mother of Jesus. Wrote *María de Agreda:

> St. Joachim had his family and his house at Nazareth. Illumined by heavenly light, he constantly implored God to Fulfil his promises. He was humble, proud, pure, and deeply sincere. For her part, Anne asked that a spouse be given her who would help her to keep the divine law. Joachim addressed the same prayer to the Lord. Their union in marriage was destined by God, and that from them should be born the mother of the Incarnate Word.

Although she is not mentioned in the Scriptures, Anne's cult was popular as early as the 4th century. In the year 550, Emperor Justinian built a basilica in her honor in Constantinople.

St. Anne is invoked as the patron of women in labor. In art, she is usually represented as an elderly woman, almost always accompanied by her tiny daughter. Her principal shrines, Ste. Anne d'Auray in Brittany, France, and Ste. Anne de Beaupré in Quebec, Canada, are famous places of pilgrimage. It is said that Anne appeared to Yves Nicolazic de Keranna near Auray from 1623 to 1625. The feast of St. Anne—once suppressed by Pope Pius V, reestablished by Gregory XIII in 1594, and ordained a public holiday by Gregory XV in 1622—is celebrated on July 26.

Anne (1665–1714)

Queen of Great Britain and Ireland and the last Stuart monarch, whose devotion to the Church of England and adherence to the Act of Settlement of 1701 undid much of the harm of the earlier Stuart kings. Name variations: Mrs. Morley. Born Anne Stuart on February 6, 1665, at St. James's Palace in London, England; died at Kensington Palace in London on August 1, 1714; daughter of King James II, king of England (r. 1685–1688), and Anne Hyde (1638–1671); sister of Mary II (1662–1694); married Prince George of Denmark, on July 28, 1683; children: 17, including Anne Stuart-Oldenburg (May 12, 1686–February 2, 1687), but only William, duke of Gloucester, survived infancy.

Death of her uncle, Charles II (1685); Glorious Revolution overthrew her father James II in favor of her sister Mary II and her husband William III (1688); Anne succeeded William III (1702); War of Spanish Succession (1702–13); Queen Anne's Bounty established (1704); Union of Scotland Act (1707); Treaty of Utrecht (1713).

Queen Anne secured the English throne nearly a decade after she should have succeeded her sister *Mary II. Instead, Anne had spent those years bearing children, while her brother-in-law, William III, ruled England. William had no blood right to the throne, but it had been understood when he and his wife Mary jointly accepted the crown that he would reign upon Mary's death. Anne's opportunity came when the "little gentleman in the velvet coat" met with an accident—a mole, which caused William's horse to stumble, hastened William's death. Constantly ill, this conscientious, pious woman effectively coped with the religious tensions and sweeping events that threatened her nation and reign.

Anne Stuart was born on February 6, 1665, at St. James's Palace in London, England. She was the second daughter and third of eight children of James, duke of York, and *Anne Hyde.

Only Anne and her older sister Mary survived to become adults. Anne's life was complicated by the politics surrounding the English crown. In 1660, her uncle, Charles II (1660–1685), was restored to the English throne, which the Stuarts had lost in the English Civil War (1642–49). Because Charles and his queen *Catherine of Braganza** were unable to provide an heir, Anne's father, as duke of York, was next in line for the throne. James, however, had brought scandal to the royal family in 1660 when he married Anne Hyde, daughter of a prominent commoner, Sir Edward Hyde. Despite his transgressions, James would become king as James II (1685–1688) at his brother's death, but widespread discontentment over his Catholicism and behavior would result in his quick removal.

Anne Stuart grew up during these complicated succession struggles within the Stuart dynasty. She and Mary spent much of their youth in the company of female relatives and servants. Because of her poor eyesight, five-year-old Anne spent some time in France with her paternal grandmother *Henrietta Maria** while receiving treatment from a noted oculist. She returned to England and lived in the rooms at St. James's Palace provided to her family by King Charles II. In the aristocratic tradition of the time, Anne was confined to a nursery and secluded from the adult courtiers. As her prospects of becoming queen were unlikely, she received an extremely narrow education. Though she studied French, elocution, and religion, Anne was more accomplished in music, dance, and playing the guitar. She had no practical studies in history and government, nor did she gain any lessons of life that would benefit a future monarch.

When Anne was six, her mother died of cancer. Rather than leave his nieces and heirs under the exclusive supervision of his brother, Charles II arranged for Colonel Edward Villiers and **Frances Villiers** to raise and supervise the education of the young girls. Although their parents had accepted the Roman Catholic Church, Anne and Mary were raised as Protestants, upon the acquiescence of their father James and the insistence of King Charles. As the Villiers were staunch Protestants, and Bishop Henry Compton also provided religious guidance to the girls, the princesses became fervent defenders of the Protestant faith. In the Villiers' household, Anne first met *Sarah Jennings (Churchill)**, the woman who would dominate much of Anne's early reign as queen.

In 1673, Anne's father married a 15-year-old Catholic Italian princess, *Mary of

Anne
(1665–1714)

Modena. The English were resigned to the future succession of the Catholic James to the throne, but they had believed that his Protestant daughters, Mary and Anne, would follow him. Thus, the possibility that this marriage could produce a Catholic heir created a clamor in Parliament and the revival of anti-Catholic feeling. In 1678, the anti-James hysteria produced rumors that the pope had planned the murder of Charles II and the succession of his Catholic brother. Known as the "Popish Plot" and based on the perjury of the adventurer Titus Oates, several Catholics were executed before the conspiracy was discredited.

In the Plot's aftermath, a political movement arose aimed at excluding James from the throne, under the direction of a group of men who were derisively referred to as *Whigs,* a name given to Scottish outlaws. They in turn called their opponents *Tories,* or Irish rebels. The party labels lasted beyond the unsuccessful Exclusion Crisis, and bickering between the two political parties blighted later reigns.

Throughout the political events dominating English society, Anne—considered dull and ordinary by nearly everyone—lived away from court and estranged from her father. It was now imperative that suitable Protestant mates be found for Mary and Anne. In November 1677, Mary married their Lutheran first cousin, William of Orange, ruler of Holland. Bedridden with smallpox, Anne could not even visit Mary before her departure for Holland and did not attend the wedding. A year later, Anne was to feel more isolated when her dearest friend, Sarah Jennings, married John Churchill.

In 1683, 18-year-old Anne married a Lutheran prince, George of Denmark, an amiable but uninspiring nonentity who became her devoted companion. He was a handsome and pleasant prince but soon settled into a phlegmatic life of obesity and apathy. They loved each other, and George would sustain Anne through the births, illnesses, and deaths of 17 children. Anne's first child was stillborn, and two later pregnancies ended in miscarriages. In 1687, smallpox would claim the lives of her two daughters, Mary and Anne Sophia. Her son William, duke of Gloucester, the longest surviving child, was hydrocephalic; following a sickly life, he would die of scarlet fever in July 1700, at 11 years of age.

When Charles II died in 1685 and her father James II was crowned king, Anne became heir presumptive behind her sister Mary, who now resided in Holland and had failed to conceive in eight years of marriage to William of Orange. Mary of Modena had also failed to produce a male heir in 12 years of marriage to James II, and many assumed her childbearing years were over. Anne, once again pregnant at James' coronation, seemed to hold the key to the future of the Stuart family. She became a rallying point for militant Anglicans, who opposed James' pro-Catholic policies.

Anne's life was dominated by the loss of her children and her own poor health. She suffered from gout, obesity, and premature aging from porphyria, a blood infection found in the Stuart line. When Anne sought an intimate friend and confidante, she found one in her old childhood friend Sarah Jennings Churchill. Sarah was beautiful, ambitious, intelligent and, at times, arrogant. Anne on the other hand was tall, lacked confidence, and, though attractive, not really beautiful. The shy, reserved Anne was captivated by her confident, blunt, and spirited companion, but the friendship meant much more to Anne than it did to Sarah. Anne's emo-

tional reliance on, and devotion to, Sarah made Anne a perfect vehicle for her friend's ambition. In a note to Sarah apologizing for James' initial refusal to give her a position in Anne's household, Anne revealed her characteristic insecurity:

> I will try once more, be he never so angry; but oh do not let this take away your kindness from me, for I assure you 'tis the greatest trouble in the world to me and I am sure you have not met a faithfuller friend on earth nor that loves you better, than I do.

Eventually James backed down and Anne appointed Sarah as first lady of the bedchamber. To create a more intimate relationship, Anne suggested that they use private names for each other. Sarah and her husband John Churchill were called Mrs. and Mr. Freeman, another intimate advisor, Sidney Godolphin, was called Mr. Montgomery, and Anne was known as Mrs. Morley.

James II exacerbated fears that he intended to reestablish Catholicism in England by handing down a Declaration of Indulgence, which allowed non-Anglicans to hold public office. He also launched a campaign to remove strong anti-Catholic Anglicans from all government positions, including Anne's own household. The final straw for many Anglicans was the announcement in late 1687 that 30-year-old Mary of Modena was pregnant. Because of the queen's age, many, including Anne, doubted the pregnancy and later the legitimacy of the son, James (who would be known as James Francis Edward Stuart, the Old Pretender), born the following June. Anne vigorously denied that the child was her stepmother's, and, consequently, it was rumored that Mary of Modena had faked her pregnancy and that the baby had been smuggled into the royal bedchamber. Public displeasure with King James for his Catholicism and absolutist exercise of royal power was already widespread in England. The prospect of another Catholic heir and an unending dynasty of Stuart Catholic monarchs led to open discontent. When James II was deposed in November 1688, Sarah Churchill convinced Anne to reject her father and support her sister Mary and brother-in-law William of Orange when they landed at Torbay at the invitation of the English nobility. Anne deserted the Court and escaped in disguise into the countryside. On hearing of his daughter's flight, James was devastated: "God help me," he was reported to have cried, "even my children have forsaken me." He then fled to France.

At William's insistence, he and Mary were established as joint rulers of England, Scotland, and Ireland in the revolution settlement of 1689.

As William III, he was made coequal with Mary II, and, should Mary predecease him, William was to be made sole monarch of England. Although Anne reluctantly agreed to this settlement, she later referred to it bitterly as her "abdication." Anne was recognized as their successor if they left no heirs. The bloodless nature of the transfer of power caused the English to hail William's arrival as the "Glorious Revolution." Loyalists to James, called Jacobites, awaited an opportunity to bring James back to the throne.

During the early years of William and Mary's reign, Anne received an income of £50,000 a year voted to her by Parliament. She lived at her own residence on Downing Street that was called the Cockpit. But the unique political circumstances of the Glorious Revolution fostered a change in the structure of politics. Loyalty to the "Crown" became more abstract and less vested in the person of the monarch, and so a kind of "loyal opposition" to the monarch emerged, centered around Anne, and continued to shape British politics throughout the 18th century. Drifting into opposition to William and Mary soon after the revolution settlement was made, Anne attracted a number of politicians to her camp who looked forward to reaping the benefits of office as soon as she succeeded to the throne.

Antipathy between Anne and the new monarchs centered around the volatile issues of succession, money, and the Churchills. William resented and feared Anne's hereditary claim to the throne and tried to keep Anne financially dependent on his own generosity; she was given no share of her father's personal estates and no guaranteed personal income. The major problem faced by Anne was her sister's disapproval of Sarah Churchill. When Anne refused to dismiss her closest friend, a rift developed between the sisters. This breach widened in 1691 when charges of treason were brought against Sarah's husband John Churchill. The ambitious Churchill had been a brilliant supporter of William in the Irish campaign, but became involved with dissident elements when he felt his services had been inadequately rewarded by the king. John Churchill, for a short time, was deprived of all offices and confined to the infamous Tower of London. When Anne bluntly refused to part with Sarah, Anne's husband was relieved of all his government offices. Outraged, Anne left the Palace of Whitehall, assuring Sarah: "I am more yours than can be expressed and had rather live in a cottage with you than Reign Empress of the world without you." In

her letters, Anne referred venomously to William as "that Monster" or "that Dutch abortive."

An atmosphere of outright hostility persisted between Anne and William until, in 1694, Mary died suddenly of smallpox. Anne and William were devastated by their loss, and both reached an uneasy truce that lasted for the rest of his reign. The king also restored Churchill to his favor. While Anne bided her time until she would succeed her childless brother-in-law, she made a reconciliation by letter with her exiled father before his death on September 6, 1701.

After creating the alliance leading to the War of Spanish Succession to block the territorial ambitions of his French archenemy Louis XIV (1643–1715), William III died of complications from the riding accident on March 8, 1702. Anne's coronation was held in London on April 23. She was 37-years-old, and her health was so precarious that she had to be carried to her coronation on a low canopied chair of state with the six-yard train flowing over it. Her coronation gown was velvet, the petticoat of gold tissue, and both were embroidered with jewels and diamonds. The coronation crown was covered with diamonds and diamonds overlaid the cross at the top of the dome. The motto on the coronation favors stated that: God has sent our hearts content.

> [Anne's] passionate affection for Sarah Churchill . . . was to give her much pleasure and later much pain. Sarah's voluminous writings have been largely relied upon by Anne's biographers as a basis for assessing her character, but it has to be remembered that what Sarah recorded was chiefly written after they had quarreled. The fact was that Anne was an extremely conscientious Queen.
>
> —Antonia Fraser

Two weeks later, England declared war on France. Having dominated European affairs for half a century, Louis XIV now intended to place his grandson, Philip of Anjou, on the throne of Spain, as the Spanish king had died without heir. England determined to put a check on Louis' aggression, which threatened to upset Europe's delicate balance of power. When Louis was told of Anne's move, he jokingly replied, "It means I'm growing old when ladies declare war on me." Louis' overconfidence was soon deflated by a series of setbacks on the field.

The War of Spanish Succession catapulted Sarah's husband John Churchill, duke of Marlborough, into the international spotlight. An able military strategist, Marlborough routed the French at the Battle of Blenheim (1704) and continued to achieve surprising gains against them throughout the war. Sarah Churchill had been appointed groom of the stole, keeper of the privy stole, and mistress of the robes. Her intimacy and closeness to Anne guaranteed John his command and a free hand over the entire British army. While John served as Anne's emissary abroad, another old friend, Sydney Godolphin, served Anne at home as lord treasurer. A nominal Tory, Godolphin was an able financier and administrator whose first loyalty was to Anne. The junior member of Anne's inner circle of ministers was Robert Harley, later earl of Oxford, another moderate Tory. Harley was indispensable to Anne because of his ability to manage the House of Commons and to preserve good relations between Anne and her parliament.

Despite her physical problems, Anne attempted to attend all cabinet meetings, read all petitions, made all necessary religious and political appointments, and performed a myriad of other monarchial duties. She was politically astute in never totally trusting either the Whig or Tory political factions. She constantly shuffled her government leaders and often utilized "mixed ministries" composed of ambitious but capable officials.

In time, Anne realized that she disagreed with the Tories' war strategy. Despite the spectacular victories by Marlborough, the Tories believed that England should only engage the enemy at sea, but Anne, Marlborough, and the Whig Party favored the utilization of ground forces in continental Europe. Godolphin's government became progressively more Whig. Sarah's relationship with Anne developed a breach when Sarah exerted excessive pressure to remove ministers unsympathetic to her husband's war policies. An ardent Whig, Sarah had become even more arrogant and sometimes abusive to Anne. By 1707, her affectionate relationship with the queen had been usurped by ❧▶ **Abigail Masham**, Sarah's relative, whom Anne had placed in the royal household.

In 1710, Godolphin went too far in his sympathies, unwisely impeaching the cleric Henry Sacheverell for preaching sermons against the Whig faction. Abigail Masham, pro-Tory in her politics, convinced Anne to dismiss Godolphin and to appoint an antiwar Tory government. Their leaders, Harley and Henry St. John, later

Lord Bolingbroke, immediately opened peace negotiations with France, dismissed Marlborough in 1711, and, with Anne's approval, restructured the cabinet to secure support for a treaty. The Treaty of Utrecht, signed in 1713, gave England several naval bases (Gibraltar, Newfoundland, Nova Scotia, Hudson Bay) and trading privileges in Spanish America, while Philip of Anjou ascended the Spanish throne as Philip V. Following the conclusion of the war, Harley and St. John's rivalry split the cabinet. Anne finally dismissed Harley, but under St. John the cabinet would remain in a state of confusion through Anne's reign.

While Sarah Churchill had always been abrasive, Anne had accepted that as part of her energetic and exciting personality. Sarah was also known to absent herself from her courtly duties for long periods and return to request favors or to champion political causes. The death of Anne's beloved George in October 1708 left the queen with few personal allies. With a growing suspicion about the wealth and power of the Marlboroughs, and advice from Abigail Masham and other enemies of Sarah, Anne finally realized that Sarah's contempt was genuine and her cruel words were deliberate. She stripped Sarah of all offices and compensations in April 1711, eight months before Sarah's husband John was relieved of his military command. This decision remained painful to Anne until the day she died.

From the beginning of her reign, Anne was motivated by her intense devotion to the Anglican Church. She detested Dissenters and Catholics and favored the High Church Tories over the Low Church Whigs. During her reign, she built 50 churches in the new suburbs of London. The Queen Anne's Bounty was established from her private revenues for the benefit of the poorer clergy. Deeply religious, Anne was the last English monarch to practice healing her subjects by touch.

During Anne's reign, a beneficial political settlement was finally achieved with Scotland. The Scots had refused to accept the Act of Settlement (1701), which legally arranged for the Hanoverian succession should both William III and Anne die without heirs. The English were fearful that the Scottish throne might be occupied by a monarch hostile to English interest. To assuage these fears, Anne's government began negotiations to create a union between the two countries. The Scots saw little that was politically advantageous in union, but they astutely saw the possibility of economic advantages previously restricted to the English. Out of these negotiations came the parliamentary union in 1707 that created the Kingdom of Great Britain. A single monarch would rule throughout Britain, as before, but there would be only one Parliament, at Westminster, in which the Scots would be represented. Scotland would gain the desired commercial equality but would retain her Presbyterian faith and distinctive legal and judicial system. In May 1707, Anne gave her royal assent for the Act of Union in a state ceremony in the House of Lords. The first Parliament of Great Britain met on October 23, 1707.

Although Anne demonstrated little interest in the art, drama, and literature of her time, she did provide a receptive climate for the arts. In architecture, Christopher Wren completed the English Renaissance renovation in 1710 of St. Paul's Cathedral, which had been damaged in the Great Fire of London. Sir John Vanbrugh designed the grandest mansion of the time, Blenheim Palace, near Oxford for the duke of Marlborough. Other beautiful buildings from Anne's reign include Greenwich Hospital, Trinity College Library at Cambridge, and the Sheldonian Theater at Oxford. In art, Sir Godfrey Kneller was an accomplished painter who left numerous portraits of the famous people of her reign.

Literature was influenced by the Whig and Tory political arguments. Jonathan Swift wrote devastating articles against the Whigs. Writing in a simple but polished style, Daniel Defoe started a paper called the *Review,* which was critical of the Tories. Joseph Addison and Richard Steele, in their *Tatler* and *Spectator* essays, wrote elegantly of correct manners and behavior in all elements of English society. Alexander Pope's *The Rape of the Lock* illustrated how a cultivated society depended upon proportion, good humor, and good sense. While Anne's friend Lady *Mary Wortley Montagu was busy writing provocative letters, *Mary Astell was examining the education of women and the institution of marriage, and poet *Anne Finch was holding literary court at her estate in Eastwell Park.

Queen Anne had accepted the principle of a constitutional monarchy, which helped to end the abuse of monarchial authority by placing parliamentary restrictions on the sovereign. She was the last ruler to veto an act of Parliament or to attend the majority of cabinet meetings. Her advancing age and health made the succession her last crucial issue in government. Anne personally leaned toward continuing the Stuart succession. Leading Tories, including Secretary of State St. John, were in constant communication with Anne's exiled half-brother, James, the Old Pretender, who claimed to be James III. Anne distrusted St. John and relied in her last months on her Whig Lord Treasurer, the Earl of Shrewsbury. She also listened to her new woman friend, the moderate Whig Duchess of Somerset. Although she disliked her Hanoverian relatives, Anne refused to support her exiled brother. Her vague references to James in her will, and her reliance on Shrewsbury's advice, left little doubt that she saw her Hanoverian cousin as a guarantee that her beloved Anglican Church would be preserved. In her last days, she refused assistance to the Tory plan to support James. Following her death, Tory efforts to find papers supporting James were fruitless, and George of Hanover succeeded her on the throne as King George I (1714–1727).

On Thursday, July 29, 1714, the queen's fragile health had turned suddenly critical. After a brief improvement, she went into convulsions

✤ Masham, Abigail (1670–1734)

English confidante of Queen Anne. Born Abigail Hill in 1670; died in 1734; daughter of a wealthy merchant of London named Hill; married a page at Court named Masham, in 1707. Favorite of queen Anne of England.

*Sarah Churchill's relationship with Queen *Anne began deteriorating soon after Anne's succession. An ardent Whig, Sarah's tactless insistence on converting Anne to her point of view did little to endear her to the new queen, and Sarah also became lax in her attendance at Court. In her absence, Anne began to turn more and more for solace and support to Abigail Hill Masham. A poor relation of Sarah's, Abigail had been given a position in Anne's household at Sarah's request, and Abigail proved attentive and eager to please. When Sarah discovered that she had been supplanted as royal favorite, she was furious to "see a woman whom I raised out of the Dust put on such a Superior air." Anne and Sarah's relationship degenerated into constant bickering. In 1711, Anne finally dismissed Sarah and Sarah's husband John Churchill, duke of Marlborough, from her Court appointments.

Plain in appearance and delicate in health, Abigail Masham was the daughter of a wealthy merchant of London named Hill. When her father filed for bankruptcy, she had no choice but to take employment as attendant of **Lady Rivers**, before becoming waiting maid to Queen Anne. Masham was not accomplished, but she did possess great powers of mimicry and shared her taste in music with the queen. With the ouster of the Marlboroughs, Masham's husband was raised to the peerage, and Lady Masham became involved in the intrigues of Court, especially those in favor of the Tories and the exiled House of Stuart.

the following day. All efforts, pitiful as they were in 18th-century medicine, were used to save the queen. Although they placed garlic at Anne's feet and bled her, she went into a coma. She died in Kensington Palace at 7:30 in the morning of Sunday, August 1, 1714, at the age of 49. Anne had a private funeral and was buried beside her husband Prince George, in a vault with Charles II and William and Mary, in Westminster Abbey on August 24, 1714.

SOURCES:

Brown, Beatrice Curtis. *The Letters and Diplomatic Instructions of Queen Anne*. London: Cassell, 1935.

Churchill, Winston S. *Marlborough: His Life and Times*. 2 vols. London: George G. Harrap, 1947.

Fraser, Antonia, ed. *The Lives of the Kings and Queens of England*. London: Weidenfeld & Nicolson, 1975.

Green, David, *Queen Anne*. NY: Scribner, 1970.

———. *Sarah, Duchess of Marlborough*. London: Collins, 1967.

Gregg, Edward. *Queen Anne*. London: Routledge & Kegan Paul, 1986.

Holmes, Geoffrey. *British Politics in the Age of Queen Anne*. London: Macmillan, 1967.

Trevelyan, G.M. *England Under Queen Anne*. 3 vols. London: Longmans, Green, 1930–1934.

SUGGESTED READING:

Butler, Iris. *Rule of Three*. London: Hodder & Stoughton, 1967.

Connell, Neville. *Anne, the Last Stuart Monarch*. London: Thornton Butterworth, 1937.

Curtis, Gila. *The Life and Times of Queen Anne*. London: Weidenfeld & Nicolson, 1972.

Herbert, Paul. *Queen Anne*. London: Hodder & Stoughton, 1912.

COLLECTIONS:

Queen Anne's correspondence with the Duke and Duchess of Marlborough, Lord Godolphin, and the Earl of Sunderlin are the property of Blenheim Palace.

Queen Anne's papers are scattered about several archives: the British Library, Public Record Office, Longleat, and other locations.

Phillip E. Koerper, Professor of History,
Jacksonville State University, Jacksonville, Alabama

Anne, Princess (1950—)

British princess and equestrian champion. Name variations: Anne, Princess of the United Kingdom. Born Anne Elizabeth Alice Louise on August 15, 1950, in Clarence House, London, England; second child and only daughter of Queen Elizabeth II (b. 1926), queen of England (r. 1952—) and Prince Phillip (b. 1921); attended Benenden School in Kent; married Mark Phillips (captain of the Queen's Dragoon Guards and twice a medalist in three-day eventing at the Olympic games), in 1973 (separated 1989; divorced, April 1992); married Tim Laurence (a naval commander), on December 12, 1992; children (first marriage) Peter Mark Andrew (b. 1977) and *Zara Phillips (b. 1981).

First royal rider to win the Raleigh Trophy; president of the British Olympics Association; declared Princess Royal, 1987.

Princess Anne was born into a royal family that was dotty over horses. Her mother Queen *Elizabeth II owned some of the finest thoroughbreds in Great Britain, and her father Prince Phillip was president of the International Equestrian Federation. As she watched her mother review the troops astride a mount, Anne longed to be a horsewoman; she rode as a child through the trails surrounding Windsor Castle.

At 17, Anne started training with **Allison Ower**, determined to compete in the Equestrian Championships of Europe. Though it was unusual for royalty to enter competitions with commoners, in Anne's view horses were a leveling influence, a bond between her and the British people.

In September 1971, when the Three Day Event was held in Burghley, England, 20,000 subjects watched 21-year-old Anne perform on her favorite horse, Doublet. Though she had not been rated expert enough to make the British team, to everyone's surprise she soon held the lead. When the championships ended, Anne was 37.8 points ahead of the next British rider; she was also ahead of riders from eight other countries. The Raleigh Trophy was hers, and Princess Anne became the first member of royalty to win the European Equestrian Championships.

The public was enthralled by the sight of the young princess jumping her horse over high hedges and fences. Closer at hand, Anne captured the attention of fellow competitor, Lt. Mark Phillips, who finished sixth at the championships. They married in 1973. Mark had been a reserve member of the British Equestrian Team in the 1968 Olympic games in Mexico, and after the two married it became their combined goal to perform in the 1976 Montreal Olympics.

In 1974, Anne lost Doublet when he broke his leg and had to be put down. A year later, she was selected for the official British team to compete in the European Championships in the Federal Republic in Germany. Hers was the first all-woman British team and the first ever to boast a member of the Royal family. The princess won silver medals in both individual and team competitions.

Just three months before Olympic team selection, Anne was hospitalized with a serious hairline fracture of a vertebrae after a bad fall during horse trials at Durweston, Dorset. Through sheer will and intense physiotherapy, she was well enough to win her place on the team, though in a final trial her husband Mark was named only as a reserve. Unfortunately, the games proved somewhat of an anticlimax. The team started poorly, with one horse going lame and another pulling a tendon. Princess Anne suffered another serious fall in the cross-country and crossed the finish line in a daze, though Olympic watchers were impressed with her determination. In subsequent years, she continued to compete throughout Britain and Europe, including the Horse of the Year Show at Wembley, and was successful as a jockey in horse racing.

Though in her youth Anne acquired a reputation for being brusque with the media, she slowly changed British perceptions with her avid support of charities and overseas relief work, including travel in Third World countries as president of the Save the Children Fund. Scandal surrounded her separation from Mark Phillips in 1989, after disclosure of a relationship with Lt. Tim Laurence, whom she met during his tour of duty on the Royal Yacht Britannia. In April 1992, Anne divorced Phillips and, in December of that year, married Laurence.

SOURCES:

Cooper, Jonathan. "Princess Anne Clears a New Hurdle: The Steeplechase," in *People Weekly*. March 30, 1987, pp. 36–37.

Parker, John. *The Princess Royal*. London, England: Hamish Hamilton, 1989.

Karin Loewen Haag, Athens, Georgia

Anne, Princess of Orange (1709–1759).

See Caroline of Ansbach for sidebar.

Anne Boleyn (1507?–1536).

See Boleyn, Anne. See also entry titled "Six Wives of Henry VIII."

Anne de Bretagne (c. 1477–1514).

See Anne of Brittany.

Anne de Foix.

See Foix, Anne de.

Anne de France (c. 1460–1522).

See Anne of Beaujeu.

Anne de Gonzaga (1616–1684).

See Simmern, Anne.

Anne de la Tour (d. 1512)

Duchess of Albany. Died on October 3, 1512, at La Rochette Castle, Savoy; interred at the Carmelite

Monastery de la Rochette in Savoy; daughter of Bertrand de la Tour, count of Auvergne, and **Louise de la Tremoille**; *married Alexander Stewart (c. 1454–1485), 1st duke of Albany, on January 19, 1480; married Louis, count de la Chambre, on February 15, 1487; children: (first marriage) John Stewart (b. 1484), 2nd duke of Albany.*

Anne de la Tour (c. 1496–1524)

Duchess of Albany and countess of Auvergne. Born around 1496; died in June 1524 at Castle of St. Saturnin, France; daughter of John de la Tour (b. 1467), count of Auvergne, and ***Jane Bourbon-Vendome** (d. 1511); married John Stewart, 2nd duke of Albany, on July 8, 1505.*

Anne-Eleanor of Hesse-Darmstadt (1601–1659)

Duchess of Brunswick. Born on July 30, 1601; died on May 6, 1659; daughter of ***Magdalene of Branden-***

𝒫rincess 𝒜nne (1950—)

burg (1582–1616) and Louis V, landgrave of Hesse-Darmstadt; married George of Brunswick-Luneberg, duke of Brunswick, on December 14, 1617; children: Christian Louis (b. 1622), duke of Brunswick-Zelle; George William (b. 1624), duke of Brunswick-Zelle; John Frederick (b. 1625), duke of Brunswick; *Sophia Amelia of Brunswick-Lüneberg (1628–1685); Ernest August (b. 1629), duke of Brunswick-Lunen.

Anne Hyde (1638–1671).

See Hyde, Anne.

Anne-Marie d' Bourbon-Orleans
(1669–1728).

See Henrietta Anne for sidebar.

Anne Marie Louise d'Orleans
(1627–1693).

See Montpensier, Anne Marie Louise d'Orleans.

Anne Marie of Brunswick
(1532–1568)

Duchess of Prussia. Born in 1532; died on March 20, 1568; daughter of *Elizabeth of Brandenburg (1510–1558) and Erik I the Elder, duke of Brunswick; became second wife of Albert, duke of Prussia, on February 26, 1550; children: Albert Frederick (b. 1553), duke of Prussia.

Anne-Marie Oldenburg (1946—)

Queen of Greece. Name variations: Anne Marie of Denmark; Anne Marie of Greece. Born Anne Mary Dagmar Ingrid Oldenburg on August 30, 1946, in Copenhagen, Denmark; daughter of Frederick IX, king of Denmark (r. 1947–1972), and *Ingrid of Sweden (b. 1910); married Constantine II, king of the Hellenes (r. 1964–1973, deposed 1973), on September 18, 1964; children: Alexia (b. 1965); Paul (b. 1967); Nicholas (b. 1969); Theodora (b. 1983); and Philip (b. 1986).

Anne Neville (1456–1485).

See Anne of Warwick.

Anne of Austria (1432–1462)

Duchess of Luxemburg. Born in 1432; died in 1462; daughter of *Elizabeth of Luxemburg (1409–1442) and Albert V (1404–1439), duke of Austria, king of Germany, also known as Albert II as Holy Roman emperor (r. 1438–1439), on June 20, 1446; married William III the Brave of Saxony, duke of Luxemburg; children: *Margaret of Saxony (1449–1501).

Anne of Austria (c. 1550–1580).

See Elisabeth of Habsburg (1554–1592) for sidebar.

Anne of Austria (1601–1666)

Spanish princess who ruled France as regent and gave birth to its most famous king, Louis XIV. Name variations: Anne d'Autriche; Anne Hapsburg or Habsburg. Born Ana Maria Mauricia on September 22, 1601, in Valladolid, Castile and Leon, Spain; died of breast cancer on January 20, 1666, in Paris, France; daughter of Philip III, king of Spain (r. 1598–1621), and Margaret of Austria (c. 1577–1611); educated at Spanish royal court; married Louis XIII, king of France (r. 1610–1643), on November 24, 1615; children: Louis de Dieudonne (1638–1715), later Louis XIV, king of France (r. 1643–1715); Phillipe I, duke of Orleans (1640–1701).

Became queen of France at age 14 (1615); acted as regent for Louis XIII (1620); suffered miscarriage (1622) and was estranged from Louis; accused of treason but pardoned (1637); governed France as regent for Louis XIV (1643–52).

On May 14, 1643, Louis XIII died, leaving a boy who was not yet five years old as heir to the French throne. Like his predecessors, however, Louis had appointed his wife, Anne of Austria, to the regency council. The newly widowed queen was following a long line of women who, since 1483, had ruled France until their sons were declared old enough to govern independently. Although she was unused to wielding political power, 42-year-old Anne of Austria quickly rose to the challenge.

Born on September 22, 1601, Ana Maria Mauricia was the eldest daughter of King Philip III of Spain and ☙➤ Margaret of Austria. Interestingly, her future husband, Louis XIII of France, was born five days later. Contemporaries regarded this coincidence as an omen and concluded that the two royal children should marry. Anne's formative years were heavily influenced by her mother. Margaret of Austria was a pious woman who engaged in charitable work and took responsibility for her children's religious upbringing. Although the royal children lived in a separate household, Anne began to see more of her mother once her father's favorite courtier, the duke of Lerma, lost his influence over the king. Historian Ruth Kleinman has concluded that Anne learned two things from her mother: "reliance on the pillar of religion and resistance to royal favourites."

There is little information about Anne's early years after her mother's death in 1611. In appearance, she was blonde, with green eyes and an oval-shaped face. Aside from a bout of smallpox in 1613, Anne was a healthy child who, from all accounts, led a quiet life and remained close to her family. As a royal princess, however, she was expected to marry, and negotiations for her union with the French dauphin began as early as 1609. Like most royal children, Anne was given no choice as to who she would wed. Instead, her marriage was guided by political motivations. It was hoped that a marriage alliance between France and Spain would be a major factor in maintaining peace between the two most important Catholic kingdoms of early modern Europe.

In August 1612, the contracts were signed and three years later, on November 25, 1615, Anne of Austria married Louis XIII at Bordeaux. They had both just turned 14 years old. Although she was homesick, Anne made a concerted effort to adjust to her new life as queen of France. After a triumphant entry into Paris, the royal newlyweds took up residence in the Louvre. As queen, Anne had her own household with her own servants and household officials, many of whom she had brought from Spain. As a result, she rarely saw her husband except on formal occasions. Though her routine was not busy, it was varied by religious holidays and visits to country palaces. In addition, Anne maintained a steady correspondence with her family.

Life at court, however, was never dull. Anne's mother-in-law, *Marie de Medici, continued to dominate the royal council. In April 1617, Louis XIII, under the influence of his favorite Charles d'Albert, duke of Luynes, declared his independence and banished the queen mother Marie to Blois while purging the council of her supporters. Louis also indulged his dislike of Spain and Spaniards by dismissing the majority of Anne's Spanish servants. The young queen was thus becoming increasingly isolated. Her uncertainty was encouraged by Louis' refusal to engage in marital relations with his wife. Although it was believed that they had consummated the marriage on their wedding night three years previous, they had not slept together since. Both Anne and her father were becoming increasingly alarmed by this state of affairs since the most important duty of a royal wife was to produce an heir to the throne.

Fortunately, and for reasons unknown, Louis finally slept with Anne in late January 1619. From that moment on, it was clear to everyone that the young king was deeply in love with his wife. He grew frantic when she fell seriously ill during the spring of 1620, but by August, when she had fully recovered, he left her to run the government while he went on a military campaign against his mother. Eventually reconciled, Marie de Medici was welcomed back to court and, two years later, to the royal council.

The queen, my mother, was not only a great queen but she deserved to be ranked among the greatest kings.

—Louis XIV

Although Louis was still in love with his wife, he gave no additional opportunities to obtain experience in governing. Consequently, she relied on religion and a close circle of female friends. Like her mother, Anne was a pious woman, and she spent much of her time visiting churches and convents. She was also a fastidious woman whose insistence upon cleanliness and fine fabrics was unusual for the time. In March 1622, her prayers were answered when she became pregnant. The joy was limited, however, as she suffered a miscarriage shortly thereafter. Even more unfortunate was Louis' reaction—he blamed her, and their marriage suffered.

Margaret of Austria (c. 1577–1611)

*Queen of Spain. Name variations: Archduchess Margarete of Styria; Margaret Habsburg. Born around 1577 (some sources cite 1584); died of puerperal fever in 1611; daughter of Karl also known as Charles (youngest son of Emperor Ferdinand I, founder of the Austrian branch of the House of Habsburg), archduke of Styria (located in southeastern Austria and Slovenia) and *Mary of Bavaria (daughter of the duke of Bavaria); sister of Holy Roman emperor Ferdinand II (1578–1637); cousin of Rudolf II, Holy Roman emperor, king of Hungary and Bohemia (present-day Czech Republic) and archduke of Austria; married Philip III (1578–1621), king of Spain (r. 1598–1621), in 1599; children: seven, including *Maria Anna of Spain (1606–1646, who married Ferdinand III, king of Bohemia and Hungary); *Anne of Austria (1601–1666); Philip IV (1605–1665), king of Spain (r.1621–1665).*

After crossing Europe in 1599 to meet and marry the king of Spain, the Archduchess Margaret of Austria was soon adored by her husband Philip III. In 13 years of marriage, the Austrian Habsburg gave birth to six children but was stricken with foreboding during her seventh confinement; though she survived the birth, she died of puerperal fever soon after.

Anne of
Austria
(1601–1666)

Changes at court occurred over the next several years. In 1624, Louis admitted Cardinal Richelieu to the royal council and for the remainder of Louis' reign, the cardinal dominated French foreign and domestic policy. In May 1625, Louis' sister, *Henrietta Maria (1609–1669), married Charles I, king of England, by proxy. Included in the English king's delegation was the handsome and virile duke of Buckingham. During the weeks of marriage celebrations, Anne engaged in a mild, yet public, flirtation with the duke. While Buckingham later declared his passionate love for her, it is generally felt that Anne did not reciprocate. Louis, however, was intensely jealous.

His anger was not alleviated when, a year later, a plot to depose him and assassinate Richelieu was discovered. Louis suspected Anne's involvement since part of the plot included her possible marriage to the king's brother Gaston. Although she disliked the cardinal intensely, it is unlikely that Anne was involved. Louis, unfortunately, was never convinced of her innocence, and the rift between them widened considerably.

For the next ten years, Anne lived in what historian Kleinman has described as "an atmosphere of suspicion and constraint." The king, instead of depending upon his wife for advice and companionship, continued to keep her out of the political arena while his chief minister, Cardinal Richelieu, grew increasingly influential. Anne, for her part, blamed Richelieu for her unsuccessful marriage and chose to surround herself with people who disliked him. This was an unwise policy since Louis viewed enmity towards the cardinal as animosity towards himself.

Opposition towards Richelieu centered upon his domestic and foreign policy. Many people were critical of his toleration for the Huguenots (French Protestants) as well as the alliances he made with Protestant countries against Spain. Since 1618, most of Europe had been involved in the Thirty Years' War. Animosity between France and Spain was renewed, and Richelieu abandoned religious solidarity for French expansion and domination. This was a difficult situation for Anne as she still maintained close ties with her family. In addition, she was becoming increasingly concerned over her failure to bear an heir to the throne. The relationship of the king and queen was characterized by mutual misunderstanding—Louis saw a disobedient wife who did not support his admiration of Richelieu; Anne, on the other hand, resented Louis' reliance upon the cardinal.

By 1635, relations with Spain had deteriorated to the point that Louis declared war. Although the marriage alliance of Anne and Louis had been an attempt to ensure peace between the two countries, French foreign policy now concentrated upon lessening, rather than maintaining, Spanish domination in Europe. This state of affairs was troubling for Anne who feared that Louis might repudiate her. Furthermore, she endangered herself by continuing to write to her brother, King Philip IV of Spain. Richelieu, who knew of her secret correspondence, allowed it to continue until August 1637 when he formally accused her of treason. Anne made a full confession although there is little to suggest that her letters contained anything that would have endangered the safety of the realm. Nonetheless, Louis reacted by sending her a memorandum in which he outlined the behavior she was to exhibit in the future. This, of course, included submissiveness and obedience to his wishes. She was also assigned a separate residence. Visibly upset by the entire affair, Anne wept often.

Despite their estrangement, the king and queen resumed marital relations sometime in the fall of 1637 and by February it was announced publicly that Anne was pregnant. Many contemporaries, and indeed Anne herself, were convinced that her pregnancy was the result of divine mercy. On September 5, 1638, after 22 years of marriage, 36-year-old Anne of Austria gave birth to a son, Louis de Dieudonne (later Louis XIV). The dauphin was soon referred to as "the gift of God." For Anne, he became the center of her life. She was an extremely devoted mother and, although she gave birth to another son, Phillipe, two years later, it was Louis who remained her favorite. Her devotion to the dauphin was noted by contemporaries. An attendant wrote in 1639 that the queen "hardly leaves him. She takes great pleasure in playing with him and taking him out in her carriage whenever the weather is fine; it is the whole of her amusement."

For the next five years, Anne was preoccupied with motherhood while others renewed their attempts to topple Richelieu from power. Each of these attempts failed and on December 4, 1642, the plots ceased when Richelieu died. Louis, who was also suffering from ill-health, soon found a replacement for the cardinal, however. Giulio Mazarini, or Jules Mazarin, as he came to be called in French, was born in 1602 and was raised and educated in Rome. He took priestly orders and worked as a diplomat for the pope. Hard-working and affable, Mazarin entered French service in 1636 where he worked under Richelieu. He became a cardinal in 1641 and, after Richelieu's death, was appointed minister of state by Louis XIII. More significantly, in April 1643 the king chose Mazarin to be his son's godfather.

During that spring, it became clear that the king was dying. Since the dauphin was not yet five years old, Louis appointed Anne regent, although he attempted to restrict her powers by creating a council of regency whose members included the king's brother, Gaston, the Prince de Condé, and Mazarin. Finally, on May 14, 1643, suffering from intestinal tuberculosis, Louis XIII died. Anne, though grief-stricken, was already planning for the future. She succeeded in having the last wishes of her late husband quashed when the French Parlement agreed to disband the council of regency. Anne was now the governor of France and could choose whom she wished to serve as her advisors. She chose Mazarin.

For the next nine years, Anne of Austria and Jules Mazarin ruled France together. He helped her to gain confidence and experience in running the kingdom by meeting with her nightly to discuss the affairs of state. Many of his policies reflected those of his predecessor, Richelieu, and his personal theory of governing centered upon a strong, absolute monarchy. Mazarin was able to pass on these theories to Louis XIV when Anne entrusted the young king's education to the cardinal in March 1646.

During the early years of the regency, Anne continued to visit churches and convents. As thanks for the birth of Louis, she had a church, the Val-de-Grace, built in which there were rooms set aside for her own use. In October 1643, she and her sons moved from the Louvre to Richelieu's palace, now known as the Palais-Royal. Mazarin moved in shortly after, making the royal "family" complete. Anne was also fond of the theater and had plays frequently performed at court. This happy state of affairs was soon shattered as resentment towards Mazarin's governance and jealousy of his influence over the queen came to the fore.

From 1648 until 1653, France was engaged in civil warfare. Known as the Fronde, the rebellion was the product of grievances that stretched back into the reign of Louis XIII and Richelieu. The main participants were members of the aristocracy and the royal family who rebelled against Anne's authority on the pretext of defending young King Louis against Mazarin.

Rather than advocating revolution, the rebels were ambitious royalists who wanted greater involvement in government. A steady increase of taxes and the continuation of the war with Spain also contributed to the rebels' disenchantment with the regency government.

During the rebellion, Anne maintained her loyalty to Mazarin even though it damaged her reputation. Since contemporaries could not understand why she continued to support him, they assumed that their relationship was sexual. Scurrilous pamphlets and rumors that Anne and Mazarin were lovers circulated constantly during the regency and even afterwards. Surviving letters between them indicate that they held strong feelings for one another and were emotionally close. It has never been proven, however, that their relationship was sexual.

By 1651, the rebels were gaining the upper hand and succeeded in demanding Mazarin's exile. Though he left Paris on February 4, Mazarin maintained contact with the queen from Germany. Still loyal, Anne replied to the many complaints about him, saying, "I believe I have an obligation to defend a minister who is being taken from me by force." Fortunately, the rebels were unable to maintain any kind of solidarity, as conflicting ambitions and allegiances soon divided them. More important, in September 1651, Louis turned 13 years old and, according to French law, proclaimed his majority. The regency was now officially over, though Louis named his mother as head of his council. The king also invited Mazarin back to France, and, by the summer of 1653, the Fronde was finally over.

One year later, on June 7, 1654, Louis was crowned king of France. His policy was one of reconciliation. For Anne, it meant a more settled routine, though she maintained her position on the king's council and often met with Louis and Mazarin. She did, however, begin to visit churches and convents more frequently, often accompanied by her younger son, Phillipe. She also concentrated on arranging Louis' marriage. After 24 years of war, peace with Spain was finally declared in 1659. Like her own marriage to Louis XIII so many years before, Louis XIV cemented the peace treaty by marrying Philip IV's daughter, *Maria Teresa of Spain (1638–1683). At the marriage ceremony on June 3, 1660, Anne met her brother Philip for the first time since 1615. When he mentioned the late war, she replied: "I think your Majesty will pardon me for having been such a good Frenchwoman: I owed it to the King, my son, and to France."

After Mazarin's death in March 1661, Anne's governmental responsibilities lessened. As the queen mother, she now spent much of her time with Louis' young wife. At Easter in 1663, Anne fell seriously ill, and by May 1664 she was diagnosed with breast cancer. There was no known treatment for the disease and she suffered from much pain. Her faith, however, was her sustenance: "What I shall suffer will no doubt help my salvation; I hope that God will give me the strength to endure it with patience." Anne was not immediately bedridden and throughout the following year she continued to visit churches and convents. By September 1665, her health began to deteriorate rapidly, and Louis XIV arrived to take her to the Louvre. In mid-January, it became clear that her time remaining was short. On January 19, the clergy were called in to administer the last rites. Louis had fainted and was absent when Anne of Austria died in the early morning of January 20, 1666.

SOURCES:

Buchanan, Meriel. *Anne of Austria, the Infanta Queen.* London: Hutchinson, 1937.

Freer, Martha Walker. *The Regency of Anne of Austria.* London: Tinsley Brothers, 1866.

Kleinman, Ruth. *Anne of Austria: Queen of France.* Columbus, OH: State University Press, 1985.

SUGGESTED READING:

Bluche, Francis. *Louis XIV.* Oxford: Basil Blackwell, 1990.

RELATED MEDIA:

The Three Musketeers (90 min.), adapted from the novel by Alexander Dumas, starring Walter Abel, with **Rosamond Pinchot** as Anne of Austria, RKO, 1935.

The Three Musketeers (126 min.), starring *Lana Turner and Gene Kelly, with **Angela Lansbury** as Anne of Austria, MGM, 1948.

The Three Musketeers (105 min.), starring Oliver Reed and **Raquel Welch**, with **Geraldine Chaplin** as Anne of Austria, 20th Century-Fox, 1974.

Margaret McIntyre,
Trent University, Peterborough, Canada

Anne of Beaujeu (c. 1460–1522)

*French princess who ruled France for her brother Charles VIII. Name variations: Anne de Beaujeu, Anne de France, Anne of France. Pronunciation: bo-ZHU. Born in April of 1460 or 1461; died on November 14, 1522; daughter of *Charlotte of Savoy (c. 1442–1483), queen of France, and Louis XI (1423–1483), king of France (r. 1461–1483); sister of Jeanne de France (1464–1505) and Charles VIII, king of France; married Pierre de Bourbon also known as Peter II, lord of Beaujeu also known as Peter II, lord of Beaujeu, on November 3, 1473; children: of an un-*

known number only one, ❧▶ *Suzanne of Bourbon (1491–1521), survived to adulthood.*

Since her brother, the future Charles VIII, was too young to rule at the time of her father's death, Anne was named regent of France (1483); regency ended (1492).

The France of 1483 was a land of turmoil and tension. The Hundred Years' War, over for a mere 30 years, had pitted France against its powerful enemy, England. Much of what we now call "France" was not at that time a single country under the rule of the French king. Instead, Brittany (on the northwestern shore), Burgundy (south of Paris), and several other regions were independent nations. King Louis XI had managed to keep his kingdom together by various means, one of which was strategic marriage: he had his daughter ❧▶ **Jeanne de France** marry his chief rival claimant to the throne, his second cousin Louis, duke of Orléans. He also used diplomacy and often resorted to armed battle to keep France safe from its neighbors. But many strong enemies were ready to pounce at his death.

❧▶ **Jeanne de France** (c. 1464–1505)
*Queen of France and saint. Name variations: Jeanne of France; Jeanne de Valois; Joan de Valois; Joan of France; duchess of Orleans or duchess of Orléans. Born around 1464; died in 1505; daughter of *Charlotte of Savoy (c. 1442–1483) and Louis XI, king of France; sister of *Anne of Beaujeau (c. 1460–1522) and Charles VIII, king of France; married Louis, duke of Orléans (later Louis XII, king of France), on September 8, 1476 (annulled 1498). Jeanne de France was canonized in 1950.*

After Louis XII repudiated his marriage to Jeanne de France in order to marry *Anne of Brittany** in 1499, Jeanne retired to Bourges and was given a dowry for the rest of her life. Protesting that he had married Jeanne against his will at the behest of her father Louis XI, the king claimed he had never lived with her as man and wife. The pope at the time was Alexander VI, formerly Cardinal Rodrigo Borgia, who was open to bribes from a monarchy. The divorce decree was brought to France by Caesar Borgia, the pope's illegitimate son, to whom Louis granted the title and duchy of Valentinois. Considered a saint by contemporaries, Jeanne de France has come down through history as either deformed, in the vernacular of the time, or, notes historian Thomas E. Watson, as a woman whose "only defect was an extreme ugliness." Following the divorce, she spent the rest of her years in prayer and serving the poor.

Suzanne of Bourbon (1491–1521). See *Louise of Savoy* for sidebar.

Unfortunately, when Louis died in 1483, his only son, Charles, was merely 13 years old, and in any case did not show much evidence of strength of either mind or spirit. Concerned that his fierce struggles on France's behalf would be wasted if Charles were to become king, and aware that he was dying, Louis had named his oldest daughter Anne of Beaujeu regent: that is, she would rule in Charles' place until he was old enough to take the throne. The French parlement had decided on 14 years as the age of majority, but, instead of yielding her power after the year was up, Anne would manage to keep hold of the reins until 1492, when her strong-minded sister-in-law, *Anne of Brittany, forced her to take a much lesser role in the governance of the country.

Anne was 22 years old when her father died; Louis had grudgingly admitted that she was the "least stupid woman in France," adding, "there is none that is wise." Despite this lukewarm evaluation, Anne proved to be an able administrator who strengthened not only the power of the royal family in France, but the position of France itself. The 16th-century biographer Brantôme called her "a shrewd and clever woman if ever there was one, and the true image in everything of King Louis her father." Frederic Baumgartner, in a more recent appraisal, says that she was "a more attractive version of her father, combining the same iron will, political sagacity, and tightfistedness with greater tact, better humor, and a more gentle nature."

And Anne desperately needed all these qualities of shrewdness, willfulness, and sagacity. With the occasional help of her husband, Pierre de Beaujeu, she plunged straight into affairs of state after her father's funeral. In an effort to forge new political ties with England, still smarting from the enmity engendered through their long conflict, she supplied troops to Henry VI. She lowered the taxes of the common people, who had been burdened for so long during the war years, ordered troops to the borders of the country to repel foreign invaders, and managed successfully to crush several attempted internal revolts.

Threatened by their powerful French neighbor, the leaders of Orléans and Brittany decided to put aside their own differences and forged an alliance to unite against this mighty force. Anne's French troops engaged in several skirmishes with the armies of Brittany and Orléans until July of 1488, when her troops defeated them in a decisive battle. Among the prisoners taken by the French was Anne's brother-in-law and distant cousin, Louis d'Orléans. Fearing his increasing political power, she had him confined to prison for three years, apparently not even answering her sister Jeanne's letters pleading that he be released.

Anne's political competence was matched by her capabilities in running her own life. She and her husband managed their estates so shrewdly that they amassed a great fortune, including much land and several castles. The people, among whom she was wildly popular, called her "Madame la Grande."

During the years of the regency, Anne ruled France skillfully. The 17th-century historian de Jaligny said, "Madame de Beaujeu his sister was with the king all the time . . . nor was anything touching the king and the kingdom done except with her knowledge, approval, and consent." Her control over the French government was so complete that she probably would have continued ruling in fact, if not in name, if her brother Charles had not married Anne of Brittany in 1491. This Anne was at least as strong, proud, and intelligent as her sister-in-law, and resented Anne de Beaujeu's involvement in politics. Charles also began to express resentment (after all, he had been king since 1484 but entirely under the control of his older sister), and Anne quietly withdrew.

She did not intend to be pushed aside entirely, however. When Louis d'Orléans inherited the throne from Charles as Louis XII, Anne and her husband asked that he grant them the right to leave their property to their daughter Suzanne, as they had no son (in certain parts of 15th-century Europe, including France, women were not allowed by law to inherit property). Despite the fact that he must have resented his three years' imprisonment ordered by Anne, Louis allowed them to do so. Anne was 62 years old when she died on one of her estates.

SOURCES:

Baumgartner, Frederic J. *Louis XII*. NY: St. Martin's Press, 1994.

Bearne, Catherine Mary Charlton. *Pictures of the Old French Court*. NY: E.P. Dutton, 1900.

Echols, Anne, and Marty Williams. *An Annotated Index of Medieval Women*. Oxford, UK; Berg Publishers, 1992.

Griffiths, Ralph, and Roger S. Thomas. *The Making of the Tudor Dynasty*. NY: St. Martin's Press, 1985.

Guérard, Albert. *France: A Modern History*. Ann Arbor, MI: University of Michigan Press, 1969.

Guizot, M., and Madame Guizot de Witt. *The History of France from the Earliest Times to 1848*. Vol. II. Translated by Robert Black. Chicago, IL: Belford, Clarke.

Kitchin, G.W. *A History of France*. Vol. II. Oxford, UK: Clarendon Press, 1896.

Tracy Barrett, Department of French and Italian, Vanderbilt University, Nashville, Tennessee

Anne of Bohemia (1366–1394)

Queen of England. Name variations: Anne Limburg. Born on May 11, 1366, in Prague, Bohemia; died on June 7, 1394, in Sheen Palace, Richmond, Surrey, England; daughter of Charles IV, Holy Roman emperor (r. 1347–1378), and *Elizabeth of Pomerania (1347–1393); became first wife of Richard II (1367–1400), king of England (r. 1377–1400), on January 22, 1383; no children.

Born into the royal family of Germany, Anne of Bohemia was 13 years old when an alliance between England and the Holy Roman Empire resulted in a contract for her marriage to King Richard II of England. The English ambassadors reported to Richard that his future bride had a fair complexion, possessed a keen intelligence, was gentle, well educated (she knew Latin, German, Bohemian and also came to know English), and already quite tall. Due to civil unrest in England, and the fact that Anne's mother, the Empress ❧➤ Elizabeth of Pomerania, refused to allow Anne to leave until she turned 15, the royal wedding was postponed for two years.

Anne's journey to England proved a hazardous one. Charles V, king of France, had previously asked the Empress Elizabeth for a marriage alliance between Anne and his son; however, for political reasons Elizabeth had refused. As Anne and her large entourage arrived in Brussels in the fall of 1381, they learned that the French king had no intention of allowing England to enjoy the economic and political advantages of the Bohemian alliance that France had been denied. French ships patrolled the English Channel, waiting for a chance to kidnap the princess and take her to Paris. However, as the bridal party waited in Brussels in confusion, envoys sent to the French king found he had become suddenly ill with little hope of recovery. On his deathbed, King Charles agreed to recall his ships and let Anne pass safely to England.

Anne and Richard were married January 14, 1382, in Westminster Cathedral, and Anne was crowned queen a week later. Richard and Anne, both 15 years old, proved to be well suited for one another and quickly grew close, sharing a love that would last the length of their married lives. Anne also became popular with the English people during the 12 years of her reign and was remembered by her subjects as "Good Queen Anne." She became known as a generous patron of writers and poets, including Geoffrey Chaucer.

It is possible that Queen Anne indirectly influenced the emerging religious reformation in

❧➤ **Elizabeth of Pomerania** (1347–1393)

Holy Roman Empress. Name variations: Elizabeth von Pommern; Elzbieta of Slupsk. Born in 1347 (some sources cite 1335 or 1345); died on February 14, 1393; daughter of Boleslav V, duke of Pomerania, and Elizabeth of Poland (d. 1361); became fourth wife of Charles IV (1316–1378), Holy Roman emperor (r. 1347–1378), in May 1363; children: *Anne of Bohemia (1366–1394); Sigismund I (b. 1368), king of Hungary and Bohemia, Holy Roman emperor (r. 1387–1437).

Europe, for historians speculate that when her Bohemian entourage returned to their native land, they took with them the writings of John Wycliffe, one of the earliest Reformation leaders. These works were translated into Bohemian and found a receptive audience, which included Jan Hus, who is now recognized as one of the most important voices in spreading the new Protestant ideas in Germany. Anne owned one of Wycliffe's Bibles among many other works, indicating at least an intellectual interest in the radical religious ideas sweeping across Europe.

On June 5, 1394, Anne suddenly took ill. Richard was at her bedside when she died only two days later, probably of plague, about age 28. Overcome with grief, Richard ordered that Shene Palace, which had been their favorite residence, be completely destroyed, as he could not bear to have it remind him of Anne. He also ordered the preparation of an extravagant funeral and commanded all the peers of the realm to attend with their wives. At the service, the king actually struck down the earl of Arundel, his longtime antagonist, when the earl asked permission to leave early, and thus failed to show proper respect for the deceased queen.

SOURCES:

Costain, Thomas B. *The Last Plantagenets.* NY: Popular Library, 1962.
Lofts, Norah. *Queens of England.* NY: Doubleday, 1977.

Laura York, freelance writer in medieval and women's history, Anza, California

Anne of Bourbon-Parma (b. 1923).

See Pauker, Ana for sidebar.

Anne of Brittany (c. 1477–1514)

French queen, patron of the arts, and a powerful force in her brief lifetime. Name variations: Anne de Bretagne; duchess of Brittany. Born in Nantes, France, on January 26, 1477 (some sources cite 1476); died after

*childbirth on January 9, 1514 (some sources cite 1512); daughter of *Marguerite de Foix (fl. 1456–1477) and François also known as Francis II, duke of Brittany; married Charles VIII (1470–1498), king of France (r. 1483–1498), in 1491; shortly after his death, married his successor, Louis XII (1462–1515), king of France (r. 1498–1515), on January 8, 1499; children: (second marriage) Charles-Orland (1492–1495); and two daughters who survived infancy, Claude de France (1499–1524), queen of France, and Renée of France (1510–1575), duchess of Ferrara, Italy.*

By the age of 22, Anne of Brittany had been engaged countless times, married twice, divorced once, and finally widowed. Since her birth it had been obvious that her father (the duke of Brittany), the Breton nobles, and the rulers of France and other European countries saw her as a means to forge alliances between their countries, through betrothals and marriages. Yet working within the legal and customary restraints of her time, Anne forced the European leaders to recognize her as a powerful force in her own right. And when her first husband, Charles VIII, left her a widow at 22, more than just personal happiness depended on her next actions. What she did, including her second marriage, would decide whether France, and indeed much of Europe, still recovering from the long, bitter conflict known as the Hundred Years' War, would remain in its fragile state of peace.

In the 15th century, the country we call France was made up of several small, independent states. These nations sometimes united against a common enemy, but more often were hostile toward each other. The Hundred Years' War, waged only a few decades before, had increased the enmity between some of the states.

One of the most fiercely independent of these separate countries was Brittany, on the northwest corner of France. At times controlled by England, at times by France, at times independent, in 1477, the year of Anne's birth, Brittany was struggling to maintain its autonomy. Anne's father, Duke Francis II, was a popular ruler whose leadership enabled him to keep his small country out of the control of the French. Aside from his political abilities, he was a cultured man who encouraged the arts, literature, and commerce in his duchy. He must have recognized his daughter's intelligence, for he had her well educated. Like him, she knew both Greek and Latin, and later in life became a passionate collector of books.

But even if he acknowledged her gifts, he could not leave his land and his title to her: Breton law did not allow women to inherit either. So he decided to use her instead as a means to unite his country's interests with those of a neighbor. Anne of Brittany was at one time engaged to a son of England's Edward IV, and at another time to the crown prince of Spain. One of the Breton nobles mentioned that Francis was wise in having each of his two daughters engaged five or six times, providing a multitude of alliances. Many of the nobles of Brittany urged Francis to force Anne to marry a certain Breton lord named Albret; this he refused to do, perhaps seeing little political advantage.

Before he could marry either daughter to his liking, however, Francis was defeated by the French and forced to promise that his children would not wed without the permission of France's king Charles VIII. Francis died shortly after, leaving Anne, a contemporary noted, "the greatest heiress in Christendom."

Only 14 years old, Anne knew she had to marry someone of political importance, and quickly, if she was to retain any kind of control of Brittany at all. The nobles again urged her to consider Albret, but she replied that she would rather become a nun. Her chancellor and some nobles supported her in this refusal, but the situation was proving difficult when Charles sent a messenger to remind them that his permission was needed before any marriage could take place. He further stated that he would have two of his nobles marry Anne and her sister. The Breton nobles did not want to see both of their princesses married to Frenchmen, assuming that these unions would destroy forever Brittany's autonomy. They suggested several other possible matches, but Anne refused them all.

Finally, in 1490, without Charles' consent, Anne contracted a "proxy marriage" with Maximilian I, the son of the Holy Roman emperor. In this form of marriage, both parties need not be present at the wedding ceremony. Anne exchanged vows with a representative of the Holy Roman government, then lay down in a bed fully dressed after the ceremony, while her proxy "husband" slid his naked leg into the bed next to her. This satisfied the legal requirement that a husband and wife share the same bed in order to be considered married.

Charles, however, refused to recognize the validity of this marriage and sent his army to besiege the town of Rennes in Brittany. He then offered to lift the siege and give Anne a large pension if she would marry one of his lords and hand over the duchy to him. Once again she re-

fused, placing the Bretons and French in jeopardy of a long and exhausting war. Charles made one last offer: Anne was to have her marriage to Maximilian annulled and marry him. Many on both sides supported this proposal, but Anne was undecided. Finally, when her priest convinced her

that this marriage would work for the good of her soul and the country, she accepted Charles.

Her divorce from Maximilian caused few problems. The marriage had been by proxy, which was never considered as binding as a real ceremony; and, in any case, the union broke the contract her father had made to secure Charles' permission before allowing her to marry. With these two circumstances, it was easy to declare the marriage invalid. Charles, too, was married, but in his case the wedding ceremony had also been a formality. He had been married to the young princess *Margaret of Austria (1480–1530), daughter of *Mary of Burgundy (1457–1482) and the same Maximilian with whom Anne had had the proxy marriage. Margaret was a small child and the marriage had never been consummated, so Charles had sent her back to her father with many gifts to ease the insult.

Anne, now 15, and Charles, 20, had a magnificent wedding in 1491. Contemporary accounts say that the royal crown was too large and heavy for the young bride, so it was carried through the ceremony by Charles' distant cousin, Louis, duke of Orléans. By this marriage, Brittany was annexed to France, but Anne did not give up all rights to her throne; she stipulated in the marriage contract that if she survived her husband, Brittany would revert to her. Further, she would marry the next king of France to avoid a repetition of the conflict between the two states.

Charles had been only 13 when his father Louis XI died; since that time, his older sister *Anne of Beaujeu had been running the country as its regent. An extremely able administrator who strengthened the country both domestically and externally, Anne of Beaujeu was supposed to release control of France when Charles had turned 14 but had continued to run matters with his apparent consent. She met her match, however, in her new sister-in-law. Anne, as duchess of Brittany, was used to being obeyed in all things, and, in any case, her husband had been of legal age to rule for six years. She stood her ground against Anne of Beaujeu, and her sister-in-law was forced to step down.

Anne of Brittany involved herself in every aspect of court life. She was a great patron of the arts, and had many tapestries, paintings, and sculptures made in France and imported from other countries to decorate the royal family's palaces, especially her favorite, the Château of Amboise. She also continued dealing in matters of state, often serving as scribe for her illiterate husband. Many of her contemporaries thought it odd that the king would allow her so much power and freedom; he replied that "one must surely put up with something from a woman when she loves her honor and her husband." She also received ambassadors from different European states. One

of them, the Venetian Zacharia Contarini, saw her in 1492 and left this description:

> The queen is short, . . . thin, lame of one foot and perceptibly so, though she does what she can for herself by means of boots with high heels, a brunette and very pretty in the face, and, for her age, very knowing; in such sort that what she has once taken into her head she will obtain somehow or other, whether it be smiles or tears that be needed for it.

The marriage of the king and queen was evidently a happy one. They had their first child, Charles-Orland, in 1492. He died in 1495. Philippe Comines noted that the queen:

> conceived the greatest sorrow from this that any woman might experience, and it lasted with her for a long time. . . . The king her husband . . . wanted to comfort her by having a dance performed before her; and several young lords and gentlemen came there in their doublets to dance at the king's invitation. And among them was the duke of Orléans . . . and at this the lady was extremely sad, for indeed it seemed to her that he was happy about this death, since he was closest in line to the crown after the king. And for this reason [Anne and Louis] did not speak to each other for a long time afterwards.

They had three more children over the next several years, but all died within weeks of their birth. Charles assumed that their deaths were punishment for some sin of his.

It appears that the marriage was successful. Charles had previously been known for his love affairs, but after the wedding Anne began to accompany him on many of his longer trips—to keep an eye on him, some suspected. Despite differences in their interests—Anne was a devout Catholic, Charles less so; Anne was a passionate book-collector, Charles could not read—they spent much time together at their lively court. They sponsored constant jousts, balls, and other celebrations. Fond of hunting, Anne kept a stable with horses and mules, as well as a large collection of hawks and dogs. She also strictly supervised her ladies-in-waiting and made sure they were educated.

Jousting was not the only spectator sport at the royal court. A very popular game of the day was the *jeu de paume*, a kind of handball that is the ancestor of tennis. The royal couple held many tournaments of this game, and Charles in particular was said to be passionate in his devotion to the sport. One day in 1498, Charles and Anne were walking hand-in-hand through a rarely used corridor to watch a game of *paume*. Charles, unaccustomed to this hall, struck his head hard on a low arch. Despite the concerns of their attendants, he insisted on continuing on to the game. After a short time, however, he complained of a violent headache, and he and Anne, with some servants, began walking back to their rooms. As he passed under the same arch on which he had hit his head, he fell to the floor in a faint. Terrified, the attendants slid a straw mattress under him—no one dared move him. He lay there unconscious for several hours, and then died.

Anne fled. Her servants, who could not convince her to come out of her room, could hear her sobbing hysterically. She then refused meals until the bishop managed to console her, urging her to eat. She reluctantly agreed, and in a few hours she appeared to return to her old self. Her first thought was of Brittany. She immediately signed a decree restoring the ruling Council to the land, freeing it from France's control once again, and started directing Brittany's affairs of state.

Meanwhile, the question of the succession to the throne of France was raised. Among several contenders, the one that had the most legitimate claim was Louis, duke of Orléans. Popular among his people, he had fought bravely for Orléans against France, even spending three years in prison at the command of Anne's sister-in-law, Anne of Beaujeu. At the time of his succession, he was married to Charles' sister ❧ **Jeanne de France**, a pious woman who was said to be deformed. Aware of the legal requirement that Anne marry the man who inherited the crown after Charles, Louis immediately started divorce proceedings. So in 1499, Anne of Brittany married Louis (now Louis XII) of France—the same man who had carried her crown at her wedding, and whom Anne had resented for his seeming lightheartedness at the death of her son.

Anne's second marriage mirrored, in many ways, her first. Perhaps the most important difference was that this time she retained control over Brittany; at 22, she was able to defend her position more capably than she had at 15. But otherwise, she maintained a similar role to the one she had held when married to Charles. She remained active in politics, even at one time joining her Breton troops with Louis' French soldiers in an unsuccessful campaign against the Turks. Like Charles, Louis was uninterested in books; Anne continued her book-collecting until she had amassed one of the most impressive libraries in Europe. She also commissioned magnificent religious books, some of which survive today as outstanding examples of late medieval illumination.

Just as in her first marriage, Anne had four children with Louis. Their two sons died, but the two daughters survived. Their daughter ***Claude de France** married the French prince Francis who later became France's King Francis I. By this marriage, Brittany was once more allied with France. Their younger daughter ***Renée of France** married the duke of Ferrara, one of the Italian peninsula's most powerful rulers. In 1514, Anne gave birth to her last child. He died almost immediately, but Anne of Brittany lingered a few months before dying herself. She was 37 years old.

SOURCES:
Bearne, Catherine Mary Charlton. *Pictures of the Old French Court*. NY: E.P. Dutton, 1900.

Comines, Philippe de. *The Memoirs of Philippe de Commynes*. Vol. II. Edited by Samuel Kinser, translated by Isabelle Cazeaux. Columbia, SC: University of South Carolina Press, 1969.

Echols, Anne, and Marty Williams. *An Annotated Index of Medieval Women*. Oxford, UK; Berg Publishers, 1992.

Galliou, Patrick, and Michael Jones. *The Bretons*. Oxford: Blackwell, 1991.

Griffiths, Ralph, and Roger S. Thomas. *The Making of the Tudor Dynasty*. NY: St. Martin's Press, 1985.

Guizot, M., and Madame Guizot de Witt. *The History of France from the Earliest Times to 1848*, Vol. II. Translated by Robert Black. Chicago: Belford, Clarke.

SUGGESTED READING:
Sanborn, Helen H. *Anne of Brittany; The Story of a Duchess and Twice-Crowned Queen*. Boston, MA: Lothrop, Lee, and Shepard, 1917.

Tracy Barrett, Department of French and Italian, Vanderbilt University, Nashville, Tennessee

Anne of Byzantium (c. 1320–1353).
See Anne of Savoy.

Anne of Chatillon-Antioche
(c. 1155–c. 1185)
*Queen of Hungary. Name variations: Agnes Chatillon. Born around 1155; died around 1185; daughter of *Constance of Antioch (1128–1164) and Reynald of Chatillon; first wife of Bela III (1148–1196), king of Hungary (r. 1173–1196); children: Emeric I, king of Hungary (r. 1196–1204); Andrew II (1175–1235), king of Hungary (r. 1205–1235); *Margaret-Mary of Hungary (c. 1177–?, who married Emperor Isaac II Angelus, Eastern Roman Emperor); *Constance of Hungary (d. 1240, who married Ottokar I, king of Bohemia).*

Anne of Cleves (1515–1557).
See Six Wives of Henry VIII.

Anne of Courland (1693–1740).
See Anna Ivanovna.

❧ *Jeanne de France. See Anne of Beaujeu for sidebar.*

Anne of Cyprus (b. around 1430).

See Louise of Savoy for sidebar on Anne of Lusignan.

Anne of Denmark (1574–1619)

Danish princess, queen of Scotland, first queen consort of Great Britain, and patron of the arts. Name variations: Anna of Denmark. Born Anna at Skanderborg Castle, Jutland, Denmark, on December 12 (some sources cite October 14), 1574; died at Hampton Court, near London, on March 2 or 4, 1619; interred at Westminster Abbey, London; daughter of Frederick II (b. 1534), king of Denmark and Norway (r. 1559–1588), and Sophia of Mecklenburg (1557–1631); sister of Christian IV, king of Denmark and Norway, Elizabeth of Denmark (1573–1626), and Hedwig of Denmark (1581–1641); married James VI (1566–1625), king of Scotland (r. 1567–1625), later king of England as James I (r. 1603–1625), on November 23, 1589; children: Henry Frederick (1594–1612); *Elizabeth of Bohemia (1596–1662); Margaret (1598–1600); Charles (Charles I, king of England, 1600–1649); Robert (1601–1602); Mary (1605–1607); Sophia (1606–1606).

Crowned queen of Scotland (1590); crowned queen of England (1603).

Shortly after James Stuart, king of Scotland, ascended the wealthier and more powerful throne of England as James I, a foreign visitor to the English Court sized up the new queen: "She is very gracious to those who know to promote her wishes; but to those whom she does not like, she is proud, disdainful—not to say insupportable." Another observer put the contrast another way, noting that her luminous white skin, much admired in her day, was "far more amiable than the features it covered."

Born to greatness as a princess, Anne of Denmark was nevertheless a woman possessed of little education, a common measure of intellect, and ample indiscretion and willfulness. Her own meager accomplishments and capabilities notwithstanding, however, Anne lived her life on a grand stage surrounded by the spectacular pageantry and brilliant culture of Renaissance courts in their most splendid age. Anne (or Anna as she always styled herself) played a considerable role as a patron of some of England's greatest artists.

Anne was born on December 12, 1574, at Skanderborg in Jutland, the second child of Frederick II, king of Denmark and Norway, re-

puted one of the wealthiest princes in Europe, and ❧▶ Sophia of Mecklenburg, the daughter of Duke Ulrich III of Mecklenburg. Frederick and Sophia presided over an enlightened royal court that fostered the arts and sciences, the royal couple supporting such luminaries as the astronomer Tycho Brahe and the historian Anders Sorensen Vedel. Sophia was also admired for the attention she bestowed on her children. According to a spy in Lord Burleigh's pay, Sophia was "a right virtuous and godly princess, who, with a motherly care and great wisdom, ruleth her children." Apart from this, almost nothing is known about Anne's rearing. A story alleges that she did not walk until age nine, before then being carried around by her attendants. Anne seems to have been taught French and Italian, then the international languages of court, but she appears to have received little formal education otherwise—a curious fact, given her parents' intellectual cultivation and the prevailing custom in Renaissance courts to educate royal children to a very high standard. Certainly the letters she wrote later in life, invariably short and to the point, bear no scholarly flourishes, though they are written in a beautiful clear hand. It may simply be that Anne's educational deficiencies resulted from a want of aptitude.

By the time Anne reached the age of 11, negotiations regarding her marriage and that of her elder sister *Elizabeth of Denmark (1573–1626) had already begun. In 1585, Frederick sent an embassy to Scotland with the express aim of arranging for the redemption of the Shetland and Orkney islands, which had been pledged to Scotland as security in an earlier marriage settlement the previous century. The Scots were loathe to part with these strategically important territories, and Frederick's ambassadors hinted that a new Danish alliance, embodied in James' marriage to one of Frederick's daughters, whichever "suld be the maist comely, and the best for his princelie contentment," would allow a more effectual transfer of the islands to be made as part of her dowry. James had to balance the advantages of this marriage prospect, however, with the opposition he faced both from his mother, *Mary Stuart, Queen of Scots (1542–1587), then a prisoner in England, who favored a match with Spain, and also from her captor, the powerful *Elizabeth I of England, who desired a Swedish alliance. These twin obstacles led James to delay until, in 1587, Frederick forced his hand by threatening war if James failed to marry one of his daughters. A commission thereupon sent by James to open marital negotiations was scuttled by Elizabeth's machinations in offering to James the hand of a princess of Navarre. By this time, however, anti-English feeling in Scotland was running high following Elizabeth's execution of Mary Stuart, and James was emboldened to accept the Danish match. He sent proxies to marry the 14-year-old princess, the ceremony being performed on August 20, 1589.

The story of Anne's voyage to Scotland and her first encounter with James seems taken rather from the pages of a romance novel than from the historical record. A Danish fleet assembled to transport Anne to her new kingdom embarked in September but encountered persistent strong storms. Twice the fleet came within sight of the Scottish shore only to be blown back to sea. After another tempest dispersed the fleet, some of the ships returned to Denmark, but the admiral's ship in which Anne sailed found safe haven on the coast of Norway. From Opsloe, Anne sent James word of her whereabouts, since the approach of winter now made it difficult for her to reach Scotland.

Once news of Anne's predicament reached him, James resolved to fetch his bride himself and immediately organized an expedition to sail to Norway. He landed at Slaikray on October 28 and then went overland to Opsloe, which he finally reached on November 19. James greeted his bride with a kiss, which she at first refused, "as not being the forme of hir cuntrie," but the royal pair quickly gained familiarity with each other. They were married again (this time in person) on the 23rd by James' favorite chaplain, David Lindsay, and the morning afterward James bestowed on Anne the lordship of Dunfermline, in conformity with the Scottish custom of making a "morrowinggift."

James intended to return to Scotland forthwith, but the continued stormy weather precluded westward sailing. Accordingly, James and Anne accepted her mother's invitation to spend the winter with her in Copenhagen. After making a mid-winter crossing of the Norwegian Alps and passing through Swedish territory, James and Anne arrived at the castle of Kronenburg on January 21, 1590. There they passed several months in revelry, "drinking and driving" as James wrote home, "in the auld manner," and were married for yet a third time according to the rites of the Lutheran Church. On April 21, the pair finally set sail for Scotland, landing at Leith ten days later.

Anne was crowned queen of Scotland on May 17 and was legally invested with her three lordships of Falkland, Dunfermline, and Linlith-

&➤ **Sophia of Mecklenburg** (1557–1631)

Queen of Denmark and Norway. Name variations: Sophia of Mecklenburg-Gustrow. Born on September 4, 1557; died on October 4, 1631, in Nykobing; daughter of Ulrich III (b. 1528), duke of Mecklenburg, and *Elizabeth of Denmark (1524–1586); married Frederick II (1534–1588), king of Denmark and Norway (r. 1559–1588), on July 20, 1572; children: *Elizabeth of Denmark (1573–1626); *Anne of Denmark (1574–1619); Christian IV (1577–1648), king of Denmark and Norway (r. 1588–1648); Ulrich (b. 1578); *Amelia of Denmark (1580–1639); *Hedwig of Denmark (1581–1641); Johann (b. 1583).

gow. These holdings provided her with some independent means, but Anne—still a girl of 16—faced the formidable challenges of reviving the long-dormant position of queen-consort in a strange country, and of negotiating her way through the minefield of Scottish politics. The Scottish crown was fairly weak. Through a succession of seven royal minorities (rulers too young to assume control), feudal lords had competed with one another for control over the young monarch. Added to this dynastic rivalry were rifts that pitted Calvinist presbyterians, Roman Catholics, and adherents of the episcopal but Protestant Church of Scotland against one another. The king and queen were vulnerable to noble intrigues: the Gowrie brothers almost succeeded in assassinating James in 1600, and in the early 1590s both he and Anne had endured a desultory insurrection by the earl of Bothwell.

The birth of Anne's first child, Henry Frederick, on February 19, 1594, at once secured the royal dynasty but also placed Anne and James in even greater political jeopardy. James correctly perceived that, given the tradition of kidnapping and controlling royal minors, the birth of an heir posed a threat to his authority and perhaps even a danger to his life. Accordingly, James arranged that his closest allies, the Earl of Mar and &➤ **Lady Mar**, should raise his infant son at Stirling Castle. Anne opposed this move, pleading with her husband that she not be forced to relinquish her newborn child. Even in the face of her appeals and grief, however, James remained adamant. But in the summer of 1595, with James absent in the country, Anne hatched a plot to seize her son through armed force. James was tipped off beforehand and successfully forestalled any action, but felt that Anne's willfulness required a formal confirma-

◄➤
*Lady Mar
(fl. 1594).*
Countess of Mar.
Flourished
around 1594;
married John
Erskine, 2nd or
7th earl of Mar
(1558–1634).

tion of the earl of Mar's authority over the heir apparent. James therefore issued a written declaration in the presence of the queen at Stirling Castle in which he strictly instructed Mar to retain custody of Henry even "in case God call me at any time," and to "see that neither for the queen, nor the estates their pleasure, you deliver him till he be eighteen, and that he command yow himself."

Anne's frustrations over the control of her son were temporarily diverted by the birth of her second child, *Elizabeth of Bohemia, on August 15, 1596, and by the short-lived Margaret in 1598. But relations between Anne and James were further strained in the aftermath of the Gowrie plot when Anne continued to harbor her favorite attendant, **Beatrice Ruthven**, and refused to believe that her brothers, the Gowries, acted treasonably despite the fact that they had been slain during their attempt on James' life. The ill-feeling that this incident generated was abbreviated, however, by the joyous birth of a second son, Charles, on November 19, 1600, the same day that the carcasses of the Gowrie brothers were drawn and quartered.

The fortunes of the House of Stuart soared in March of 1603 when Elizabeth I died and James was proclaimed King James I of England, a far wealthier and more powerful realm than Scotland. There could be no question that James and Anne would rule from London, and in April James set out for England with a retinue including the earl of Mar, leaving Anne to follow once it became clear that his English subjects would accept a Scottish king as their own. With James and the earl of Mar departed, Anne again attempted to gain possession of her elder son. In the company of a faction of anti-Mar nobles, Anne descended upon Stirling Castle and demanded custody of Henry from Lady Mar. Although much perplexed, Lady Mar held firm and refused to surrender the boy. At this, Anne flew into a rage so intense that she became ill and miscarried a son. Writing from England, James succeeded in calming his wife. Eventually, he transferred custody of Henry to Anne and summoned both to England, where the royal family stood in much less danger of over-mighty nobles.

On July 24, 1603, Anne and James were crowned at Westminster, although their official entry into the city of London was delayed until the following spring due to a serious outbreak of the plague. At her coronation, it was noted that Anne refused to take the sacrament according to the English rite, giving rise to speculation that she secretly harbored Roman Catholic sympathies, though it is equally possible that she had Lutheran scruples about doing so. Anne's religious convictions are, in fact, difficult to plumb. Ambassadorial reports repeatedly referred to the queen's Catholicism, and the fact that she pursued a pro-Spanish policy at court, at least until her last years, lent credence to this belief. Anne supported the idea of a Spanish match for her son Charles in 1613, and even carried out exploratory negotiations with the pope and the grand duke of Florence for Henry, the prince of Wales, to marry the grand duke's sister. Whatever Catholic feelings Anne may have had seem to have ebbed after 1613, however, when one of her attendants, a **Mrs. Drummond** who was in the pay of Spain and allegedly encouraged the queen's beliefs, married and moved away from court. We do know that on her deathbed Anne "renounced the mediation of all saints and her own merits, and relied only upon her Saviour," a definitively Protestant formula.

Anne's accession to the English throne meant acclimating again to a new political environment, one less exposed to the manipulation and factionalism that characterized Scottish court life. Moreover, the court personnel were almost all drawn from the English aristocracy since James and Anne brought few of their Scottish attendants with them. And again Anne had to reinvent her role as queen-consort, a position that had been vacant in England for nearly 60 years. The practical effect of these changes was that Anne found herself more politically circumscribed than she had been in Scotland. As a result, she indulged her passion for court pageantry, and to this end she was helped by the considerable reservoir of talent to be found at court. Anne's inner circle consisted in large part of women who had been members of the Essex connection and who, together with their male kin, comprised a formidable source of artistic production and patronage. Indeed, partly under Anne's influence the Jacobean Court became the site of theatrical masterworks and lavish entertainments. Of particular note are the elaborate court masques that Anne commissioned England's premier dramatists to compose and in which she sometimes acted, including Ben Jonson's *Mask of Blackness* (1604), his *Mask of Queens* (1609), and Samuel Daniel's *Tethys Festival* (1610). Anne also patronized Inigo Jones, England's foremost architect, in a series of rebuildings and renovations of Greenwich House and of Somerset House (renamed Denmark House during her tenure) in London.

All of these projects involved considerable expense and put a severe strain on Anne's finances, made worse by her appetite for fine jewels and extravagant dress. By 1609, James was forced to make her a present of £20,000 in order to settle her debts and to add a further £3,000 to her annuity of £13,000. Such was the scale of her spending, however, that by the following year she still owed in excess of £17,000 to her jeweller and other creditors. In this respect, Anne contributed to the nation's growing dissatisfaction with the profligacy of the Stuart Court, which it compared unfavorably with the frugality of the late Queen Elizabeth.

Anne suffered a severe shock in November 1612 when her beloved son, Henry, prince of Wales, died of typhoid fever. Compounding her sense of loss was the marriage of her daughter, Elizabeth, to Frederick V, the Elector Palatine, in February 1613, a match Anne initially opposed as being beneath the dignity of her daughter. About this time Anne's own health began to fail. A condition that was at first believed to be gout gradually worsened and was eventually recognized as dropsy. While Anne's life was brightened by a surprise visit to England of her brother, Christian IV of Denmark, in 1614, she increasingly suffered from her illness, though as late as 1617 she danced in one of the court masques of which she was so fond. Politically, Anne found her position improved by the replacement in November 1614 of Robert Carr, earl of Somerset, by the king's handsome new favorite, George Villiers, the future duke of Buckingham, with whom the queen maintained warm relations. Villiers was careful to cultivate the queen's favor and performed useful service for her in governing the king's sometimes uncouth behavior.

In late 1618, Anne's health worsened, and she remained confined at Hampton Court through the following January and February. James was also ill at this time, confined at Newmarket and hence prevented from visiting his wife. She was attended by Charles, heir to the throne, in her last hours and died early on March 2, 1619. Anne of Denmark lay in state at Somerset House until May 13, when she was interred in Westminster Cathedral.

SOURCES:

Barroll, Leeds. "The court of the first Stuart queen," in *The Mental World of the Jacobean Court.* Edited by Linda Levy Peck. Cambridge: Cambridge University Press, 1991.

Lancelott, Francis. *The Queens of England and their Times.* NY: D. Appleton, 1894.

Strickland, Agnes. *Lives of the Queens of England.* Vol. VI. Philadelphia, PA: Blanchard and Lea, 1859.

SUGGESTED READING:

Akrigg, G.P.V. *Jacobean Pageant.* Cambridge, MA, 1962.

Strong, Roy. *Henry Prince of Wales, and England's Lost Renaissance.* London, 1986.

Williams, E.C. *Anne of Denmark.* London, 1971.

Geoffrey Clark, Assistant Professor of History, Emory University, Atlanta, Georgia

Anne of Ferrara (1531–1607).

See Morata, Fulvia Olympia (1526–1555) for sidebar.

Anne of France (c. 1460–1522).

See Anne of Beaujeu.

Anne of Kiev (1024–1066)

Queen of France. Name variations: Anne of Russia. Born in 1024; died in 1066 (some sources cite after 1075); daughter of Jaroslav also known as Yaroslav I the Wise (978–1054), prince of Kiev (r. 1019–1054), and *Ingigerd Olafsdottir (c. 1001–1050); became second wife of Henry I (1008–1060), king of France (r. 1031–1060), in 1051 (some sources cite January 29, 1044); married Raoul II de Crépi, in 1061 (divorced); children: (first marriage) Philip I (1052–1108), king of France (r. 1060–1108).

Anne of Lusignan (b. around 1430).

See Louise of Savoy for sidebar.

Anne of Savoy (c. 1320–1353)

Empress of Byzantium. Name variations: Anna; Anne of Byzantium. Born around 1320 in Savoy, Italy (modern-day southeastern France); died in 1353 in Byzantium; daughter of Count Amadeus V of Savoy; became second wife of Andronikos also spelled Andronicus III Paleologus (d. 1341), emperor of Byzantium (r. 1328–1341), in 1326; children: John V Paleologus (b. 1331), Byzantine or Nicaean emperor (r. 1341–1347, 1355–1391); Michael; Maria (who married Francesco Gattilusio). Andronicus III's first wife was *Irene of Brunswick.

Born into an important Italian noble family, Anne was the daughter of Count Amadeus V of Savoy, a region in what is now southeastern France, bordering on Italy. She was betrothed and married to Emperor Andronicus III of Byzantium at the age of six, a not-uncommon age for royal brides. She grew up in the imperial castles and palaces, where she was educated in Greek language and tradition. About age 16, she became empress of Byzantium. When Andronicus died in 1341, Anne was named regent for her nine-year-old son John, who succeeded his father as John V Paleologus.

However, as was common during a long royal minority, enemies of the imperial family saw an opportunity to increase their own power and wealth by rebelling against the emperor and his regent-mother. Thus, Anne of Savoy was forced to struggle to keep herself and her son in power, even appealing to Pope Clement VI for aid against her enemies. She faced opposition from her husband's chief minister, John Cantacuzene (John VI), who claimed the regency as well. When this John became involved in a foreign war, Anne took advantage of his absence to arrest his supporters and consolidate her own power.

The seven years of her regency were marked by a constant civil war against John Cantacuzene, who even declared himself emperor in 1346. Anne faced increasing unpopularity with the Byzantine people during her years of rule due to the civil unrest and her efforts to reunite the Eastern and Western Christian churches. Her lack of popular support led to her gradual loss of power, and she surrendered the throne in 1347. John Cantacuzene ruled as regent-emperor with Anne's son until he came of age. Anne died in 1353.

Laura York, Anza, California

Anne of Saxony (1437–1512)

Electress of Brandenburg. Born on March 7, 1437; died on October 31, 1512; daughter of *Margaret of Saxony (c. 1416–1486) and Frederick II the Gentle (1412–1464), elector of Saxony; became second wife of Albert Achilles (1414–1486), elector of Brandenburg as Albert III (r. 1470–1486), on November 12, 1458; children: Frederick V of Ansbach (b. 1460), margrave of Ansbach.

Anne of Velasquez (1585–1607)

Duchess of Braganza. Born in 1585; died on November 7, 1607, at Villa Vicosa, Evora; daughter of John de Velasco or Velasquez, duke of Frias; married Teodosio also known as Theodosius II (1568–1630), 7th duke of Braganza (son of *Catherine of Portugal), on June 17, 1603; children: Joao also known as John IV (1604–1656), king of Portugal (r. 1640–1656, house of Braganza).

Anne of Warwick (1456–1485)

Queen of England. Name variations: Anne Neville. Born on June 11, 1456, at Warwick Castle, Warwickshire, England; died of tuberculosis on March 16, 1485, at Westminster, London; daughter of Richard Neville, count of Warwick (the Kingmaker), and *Anne Beauchamp (1426–1492); married Edward Plantagenet, prince of Wales (son of Henry VI), on July 25, 1470 (killed 1471); married Richard, duke of Gloucester, later Richard III, king of England, on July 12, 1472; children: (second marriage) Edward of Middleham, prince of Wales (d. 1484).

Anne was the heiress of the titles and extensive estates of Warwick during the turbulent years of the English civil war, the War of the Roses. Given her high rank and wealth, it is not surprising that in her teens she was married to Edward Plantagenet, prince of Wales, the son of the Lancastrian king Henry VI. Anne had been married to Edward only a brief time when both Henry and Edward were killed by partisans of the enemy House of York in 1471.

In the meantime, Anne's father Richard Neville had changed his allegiance from the Lancasters to the Yorks, and, within a year after Anne was widowed, he arranged a second marriage for his daughter to one of the Yorkist leaders, Duke Richard of Gloucester (the future Richard III). It was reported that Anne spent that year working as a maid at a London inn, although the reasons are unclear; possibly, she was resisting her father's marital plans. However, she could not remain in hiding forever, and she and Richard were married at Westminster Abbey in 1472.

Their marriage was a loveless union, evidenced by the popular belief that sprang up after Anne's death that Richard had poisoned her. The duchess of Gloucester finally saw her coronation as queen of England in 1483, when Richard seized the crown on the death of his brother, Edward IV.

Richard's succession was not without bloodshed, as well as the imprisonment and possible murder of his brother's young sons, Edward V and Richard, duke of York. Ruthless and often cruel, Richard was fated to hold the throne for only two years. During this time, Anne attempted to create a court for her royal husband, but the constant intrigues, battles, and unstable conditions made normal royal life impossible. To add to the instability of the realm—and especially of Richard's hold on the throne—their only child Edward died in March 1484, leaving the king without an heir. Richard had not yet been defeated and killed at the Battle of Bosworth in 1485 when Queen Anne of Warwick died after a long illness (possibly tuberculosis) and was buried at Westminster Abbey. She was portrayed by **Claire Bloom** in the 1955 film *Richard II*.

SOURCES:
Cannon, John, and Ralph Griffiths. *The Oxford Illustrated History of the British Monarchy.* NY: Oxford University Press, 1988.
Lofts, Norah. *Queens of England.* NY: Doubleday, 1977.

Laura York, Anza, California

Anne of York (fl. 13th c.)
English doctor.

Anne of York was a respected doctor in England. Although she probably had no formal training, she served the poor and ailing with distinction at Saint Leonard's hospital in York for many years. Little else is known about her life.

Anne Petrovna (1708–c. 1729).

See Elizabeth Petrovna for sidebar.

Anne Plantagenet (1383–1438)

*Countess of Stafford. Name variations: Anne Stafford. Born in April 1383; died on October 16, 1438 and buried at Llanthony Priory, Gwent, Wales; daughter of Thomas of Woodstock, 1st duke of Gloucester, and *Eleanor de Bohun (1366–1399); married Thomas Stafford, 3rd earl of Stafford, in 1392; married Edmund Stafford, 5th earl of Stafford, in 1398; married William Bourchier, count of Eu, in 1404; children: (second marriage) Humphrey Stafford, 1st duke of Buckingham; *Anne Stafford (d. 1432); Philippa Stafford (died young); (third marriage) Henry Bourchier, 1st earl of Essex; Thomas Bourchier (cardinal archbishop of Canterbury); John Bourchier (1st Baron Berners); William Bourchier (Lord Fitzwarren); *Anne Bourchier (d. 1474).*

Anne Plantagenet (1439–1476)

*Duchess of Exeter. Name variations: Anne Holland. Born on August 10, 1439, at Fotheringhay, Northamptonshire, England; died on January 14, 1476; buried at St. George's Chapel, Windsor, Berkshire; daughter of Richard Plantagenet, 3rd duke of York, and *Cecily Neville; married Henry Holland, 2nd duke of Exeter, on July 30, 1447 (divorced, November 12, 1472); married Thomas St. Leger, around 1473; children: (first marriage) Anne Holland; (second marriage) one.*

Anne Romanov (1795–1865).

See Anna Pavlovna.

Anne Stuart (1637–1640).

See Henrietta Maria for sidebar.

Anne Valois (c. 1405–1432)

*Duchess of Bedford. Name variations: Anne of Burgundy. Born around 1405 in Arras, Burgundy, France; died in Paris, France, on November 14, 1432; interred at Chartreuse de Champnol, Digon, Burgundy; daughter of John the Fearless (1371–1419), duke of Burgundy, and *Margaret of Bavaria (d. 1424); married John Plantagenet, duke of Bedford, on April 17, 1423; children: one (b. 1432 and died in infancy).*

Anneke, Mathilde Franziska (1817–1884)

German-born American author and early advocate of women's political and social rights. Name variations: Giesler-Anneke. Born Mathilde Franziska Giesler on April 3, 1817, in Lerchenhausen, Westphalia; died in Milwaukee, Wisconsin, on November 25, 1884; daughter of Karl and Elisabeth Hülswitt Giesler; married Alfred von Tabouillot, in 1836 (divorced and retained her maiden name after a long court battle); married Fritz Anneke, in 1847; children: (first marriage) one daughter, Fanny.

Fought alongside her husband in the German revolution of 1848; fled to the United States after the revolution failed; began publishing a militant monthly newsletter about women's rights, the Deutsche Frauenzeitung *(1852); addressed the women's rights convention held in New York City (1853); opened a progressive girls' school, the Milwaukee Töchter Institut; founded a women's suffrage association in Wisconsin (1869).*

Mathilde Franziska Giesler was born the eldest of 12 children on April 3, 1817, in Lerchenhausen, Westphalia, the daughter of Karl and **Elisabeth Giesler**. Because Mathilde's father was a wealthy mine owner, she received her education from private tutors at home. In 1836, at age 19, she was married to a considerably older man, the French-born wine merchant Alfred von Tabouillot. The marriage was a disaster and was dissolved after little more than a year. Mathilde fought for custody of her daughter Fanny and to retain her maiden name in the long court battles that followed. Memories of this unhappy marriage played a significant role in Anneke's crusade for women's full legal equality in marriage.

At the time of these difficulties, Mathilde found solace in the Roman Catholic faith in which she had been reared. Her first significant literary efforts, two prayer books, one in verse and the other prose, appeared intended for the edification of pious Catholic women. In 1840, a volume of verse, *Heimatgruss (Greetings from Home)*, was published; it was a curious compilation of her own poems as well as her translations of verse by Lord Byron and Petrarch and selections from the works of Ferdinand Freiligrath and Nikolaus Lenau. Emboldened by the moderate success of this work, she followed it with two collections of contemporary poetry. In 1844, her drama *Othono, oder die Tempelweihe* was staged to lukewarm reviews in Münster. It did, however, achieve considerable success in the last years of her life, when in 1882 it was performed in Milwaukee before a German-speaking audience of immigrants.

In 1847, Mathilde's life changed dramatically. Her father died in that year, and, in June, she married Fritz Anneke, a Prussian artillery officer whose political and social radicalism distinguished him from the majority of his fellow officers. The 1840s were a decade of great intellectual, social, and political ferment in the various states that comprised the yet to be created united Germany. Mathilde's husband quickly introduced her to the newest and most radical ideas, including socialism. Her enthusiasm focused on the issue of women's social oppression. By the end of the year, she had published a fiery pamphlet, *Das Weib im Konflikt mit den sozialen Verhältnissen* (*Woman in Conflict with Social Conditions*).

Fritz and Mathilde Anneke were far to the left of the majority of the bourgeois revolutionaries of 1848. Fearful of a social revolution led by the working class, German middle-class liberals retreated into a state of political impotence, failing to unify Germany or purge it of authoritarian feudalism and militarism. As Mathilde Anneke became increasingly convinced that German society oppressed both workers and women, she developed an open, defiant radicalism. Meanwhile, her husband's passionate advocacy of communism lost him his army commission and resulted in a jail sentence of 11 months. During this time, Mathilde became publisher of the revolutionary communist newspaper *Neue Kölnische Zeitung*. Nervous local officials quickly banned the paper, but a determined Anneke simply founded a new journal, the *Frauenzeitung*, which championed the ideal of a united Germany based on a social revolution that would expand women's social, economic and political rights.

Throughout the exhilarating months of revolution that convulsed Germany and Austria in 1848 and 1849, Mathilde Anneke was at the center of events. She often acted as her husband's deputy, meeting with revolutionaries like Karl Marx and Michael Bakunin. Fritz Anneke was an idealist, extraordinarily well-read in literature, philosophy and history, but he was also known to be argumentative, overly sensitive, and incapable of compromise. A brave military commander, he was idolized by many of the 1,200 men in his unit. During the revolutionary battles, Mathilde Anneke joined Fritz in the front lines and was as brave as she was stunning. The tall, blue-eyed Mathilde, an accomplished horsewoman, rode to the battle lines with her black hair cut short and a determined look on her face.

Unfortunately, the revolution collapsed in the summer of 1849, defeated by newly energized monarchies, particularly the Prussian. When the Prussian army captured the fortress of Rastatt, Fritz and Mathilde, along with many thousand "Forty-Eighters," fled Germany. After a brief stay in Switzerland and France, the Annekes decided to cross the ocean to the United States.

Young and optimistic despite the defeats, Fritz and Mathilde settled in the German-dominated city of Milwaukee in 1849. At first, they supported themselves by lecturing on the recently defeated German revolution, but soon they had to find more permanent occupations. Mathilde became a correspondent, working for German-language newspapers both in Europe and the United States. Fritz taught swimming and horseback riding; he also found work as a typesetter and as a draftsman for a railroad. In 1852, Mathilde began publishing a militant monthly journal of women's rights, the *Deutsche Frauenzeitung*. That same year, Fritz received a tempting job offer from New Jersey, so the couple moved to Newark where Fritz became editor of the *Newarkerzeitung*.

Mathilde continued to publish her militant journal, one of the first feminist periodicals in North America, despite the difficulties that accompanied this publishing venture. Because the journal never evolved into an economically viable enterprise, the only way to keep the *Deutsche Frauenzeitung* alive was to subsidize it with money she earned from extensive lecture tours. The hostility of the vast majority of German-American males to the *Deutsche Frauenzeitung's* demands for total emancipation of women made economic viability more difficult. In addition, Mathilde Anneke's undisguised animosity to middle-class morality and traditional religion also offended many German-American women, the majority of whom remained tied to traditional beliefs and assumptions.

By 1852, the *Deutsche Frauenzeitung* suspended publication, but Mathilde was not discouraged. By this time, her marriage to the brilliant but unstable Fritz was in crisis, and he returned to Europe to work as a foreign correspondent for a number of German-language newspapers. Mathilde remained in the United States, rapidly forging alliances with American-born members of the women's movement. In 1853, she addressed the women's rights convention that was held in New York City and from this point forward was a familiar figure at women's rights meetings. Invariably, Anneke's speeches were broadly conceived analyses of women's inferior role in society. She advocated female equality and also attacked nativism and clericalism.

Mathilde's myriad activities had led to a serious deterioration of her health by 1860, and she traveled to Switzerland to convalesce and to be with her husband. Her sparse income during these years was supplemented by articles she wrote for the *Illinois Staatszeitung* and New York City's *Belletristisches Journal*. A number of her short stories written during the Civil War remain powerful even after more than a century. The main theme of many of these is the double burden borne by America's black women, who faced oppression on the basis of both race and gender.

The unconventional and often troubled Anneke marriage continued its erratic course when Fritz returned to the United States at the start of the Civil War. Like his wife, he was an ardent abolitionist determined to lead a holy crusade against slavery. Although he easily secured an officer's commission in the 35th Wisconsin Regiment of the Union Army, Fritz's uncompromising ideals and flinty personality soon landed him in trouble with his superiors. By 1863, he was dismissed from military service for insubordination. When he died in 1872, he and Mathilde had long been separated although they never officially divorced.

An impoverished but determined Mathilde Anneke returned from Switzerland to the United States in 1865, after another attempt to improve her health. The following year, she opened a progressive girls' school, the Milwaukee Töchter Institut, in association with **Cecilia Kapp**. Although it would always operate on a financial shoestring, the school had high intellectual standards. It rapidly gained the respect of the Milwaukee German community, attaining a peak enrollment of 65 pupils. Anneke managed the Töchter Institut and taught many of its classes in a wide variety of subjects. Now middle-aged, she still retained the ability to draw upon almost limitless sources of energy needed to keep her school alive, though funding remained a constant problem. Besides giving lectures on current cultural and political themes, she sold insurance policies to the German community and wrote articles for the *Illinois Staatszeitung*.

In addition, Anneke somehow found the time and energy to continue to work for the women's movement. In 1869, she helped found a women's suffrage association in Wisconsin, and she attended conventions of the National Woman Suffrage Association. In her final years,

Mathilde Anneke remained a formidable personality, respected even by those who did not agree with her radical feminism. Few who encountered her ever forgot this "portly figure, robed in black," observed one writer, "who walked with a . . . military stride." Mathilde Anneke died in Milwaukee on November 25, 1884, and was buried in that city's Forest Home Cemetery.

SOURCES:
Anneke, Mathilde Franziska. *Gebrochene Ketten: Erzählungen, Reportagen und Reden 1861–1873.* Edited by Maria Wagner. Stuttgart: Akademischer Verlag, 1983.
Faust, Albert B. "Mathilde Franziska Giesler-Anneke: 'Memoiren einer Frau aus dem badisch-pfälzischen Feldzug', and a Sketch of Her Career," in *German-American Annals.* New Series. Vol. 16, 1918, pp. 73–140.
Heinzen, Henriette M., and Hertha Anneke Sanne. "Biographical Notes in Commemoration of Fritz Anneke and Mathilde Franziska Anneke." Unpublished two-volume manuscript, Archives of the State Historical Society of Wisconsin, Madison, Wisconsin.
Henkel, Martin, and Rolf Taubert, eds. *Das Weib im Konflikt mit den sozialen Verhältnissen: Mathilde Anneke und die erste deutsche Frauenzeitung.* Bochum: edition égalité, 1976.
Marzolf, Marion. *Up from the Footnote: A History of Women Journalists.* NY: Hastings House, 1977.
Möhrmann, Renate. *Frauenemanzipation im deutschen Vormärz.* Stuttgart: Reclam Verlag, 1978.
Poore, Carol J. *German-American Socialist Literature 1865–1900.* Bern and Frankfurt am Main: Peter Lang, 1982.
Stuecher, Dorothea Diver. *Twice Removed: The Experience of German-American Women Writers in the 19th Century.* New York and Bern: Peter Lang, 1990.
Tolzmann, Don Heinrich. *German-American Literature.* Metuchen, NJ: Scarecrow Press, 1977.
Ward, Robert E. *A Bio-Bibliography of German-American Writers 1670–1970.* White Plains, NY: Kraus International Publications, 1985.
Wittke, Carl Frederick. "Anneke, Mathilde Franziska Giesler," in *Notable American Women 1607–1950: A Biographical Dictionary.* Edited by Edward T. James. 3 vols. Cambridge, MA: The Belknap Press of Harvard University Press, 1971, vol. 1, pp. 50–51.
———. *Refugees of Revolution: The German Forty-Eighters in America.* Philadelphia: University of Pennsylvania Press, 1952.
Zucker, Adolf Eduard. *The Forty-Eighters, Political Refugees of the German Revolution of 1848.* NY: Columbia University Press, 1950.

John Haag, Associate Professor of History, University of Georgia, Athens, Georgia

Annenkova, Julia (c. 1898–c. 1938)

Soviet activist and journalist, appointed editor-in-chief of Moscow's **Deutsche Zentral-Zeitung.** *Name variations: Julia Gamarnik. Born Julia Ilyishchna Annenkova in Riga, Latvia, around 1898; killed herself*

in a labor camp after her son denounced her, around 1938; married Yan Borisovich Gamarnik.

Julia Annenkova, who was born in Riga, Latvia, joined the Communist Party in her teens, at the time of the Bolshevik Revolution, and became a zealous activist. Her husband Yan Borisovich Gamarnik (1894–1937), a leading Communist, played a decisive role in the Bolshevik Revolution as a leader of the Reds' seizure of power in Kiev in November 1917. Gamarnik distinguished himself in the Russian Civil War of 1918–1920, rapidly advancing to the post of deputy people's commissar of defense in June 1930.

Annenkova wrote and edited many articles explaining the Revolution. After several promotions, she was appointed editor-in-chief of Moscow's *Deutsche Zentral-Zeitung,* the central organ for the Soviet Union's German-speaking minority, in 1934. Hers was an extremely sensitive position, because, while the Stalin regime proclaimed itself anti-Fascist, it was increasingly interested in reaching a rapprochement with Nazi Germany. As editor-in-chief, Annenkova was caught between two forces. The political refugees who had fled the Third Reich for sanctuary in the USSR wanted to use the *Deutsche Zentral-Zeitung* to warn of the peril German National Socialism presented. Joseph Stalin, on the other hand, did not want to convey this message at this particular time. While hewing faithfully to the Stalinist party line, Annenkova raised the quality of the *Deutsche Zentral-Zeitung,* transforming it into an attractive, readable newspaper. By Soviet standards, the paper provided its readers with significant amounts of news and intelligent commentary.

Annenkova's work gained respect in Moscow's intellectual circles. She included among her close friends the journalist Mikhail Koltsov and his companion, the German refugee writer **Maria Osten** (1909-1942). German exile intellectuals visiting Moscow, including Bertolt Brecht, Erwin Piscator, Franz Carl Weiskopf, Ernst Busch and Gustav von Wangenheim, never failed to drop by the editorial offices of the *Deutsche Zentral-Zeitung* to visit Annenkova. She was respected for her passionate hatred of Fascism, lively intellect, and journalistic achievements.

In 1936, Stalin began massive purges of Soviet Communist leaders. Although he was a hero of the Revolution, Yan Gamarnik was charged with being the leader of a "Fascist conspiracy" to destroy the Red Army. He committed suicide on May 31, 1937. Already seriously ill with a heart condition, Annenkova was summarily removed from her editorial position at the *Deutsche Zentral-Zeitung* and arrested on a trumped-up charge of anti-Soviet activities. In the infamous Butyrka prison, she told fellow prisoner **Evgenia Ginzburg** that her arrest was a mistake. Believing it necessary to purge the Soviet Union of traitors and doubters, Annenkova asserted that she and a few other innocent individuals had been falsely accused, a mistake that would be rectified.

Julia Annenkova was sent to the Magadan labor camp. Here, she learned that her ten-year-old son had denounced her publicly as a traitor. With her belief in the justness of the Soviet system shattered, she committed suicide, probably sometime in 1938. Throughout her life, Julia Annenkova had worked for a better society in which resources would be shared by all. She and the dream both perished at Joseph Stalin's hands.

SOURCES:

Ginzburg, Evgenia. *Journey into the Whirlwind.* NY: Harcourt, Brace and World, 1967.

Huppert, Hugo. *Wanduhr mit Vordergrund: Stationen eines Lebens.* Halle-Saale: Mitteldeutscher Verlag, 1977.

Jarmatz, Klaus, Simone Barck, and Peter Diezel. *Exil in der UdSSR.* Frankfurt am Main: Röderberg-Verlag, 1979.

Müller, Reinhard, ed. *Die Säuberung: Moskau 1936: Stenogramm einer geschlossenen Parteiversammlung.* Reinbek bei Hamburg: Rowohlt Taschenbuch Verlag, 1991.

Pike, David. *German Writers in Soviet Exile 1933–1945.* Chapel Hill: University of North Carolina Press, 1982.

Suggs, William H. "Gamarnik, Yan Borisovich (1894–1937)," in *The Modern Encyclopedia of Russian, Soviet and Eurasian History.* Edited by Joseph L. Wieczynski. 58 vols. Gulf Breeze, FL: Academic International Press, 1979, vol. 12, pp. 74–76.

John Haag, Associate Professor of History, University of Georgia, Athens, Georgia

Annenkova-Bernár, Nina Pávlovna (1859/64–1933)

Russian stage actress and author of plays and short stories. Name variations: Nina Annenkova-Bernard. Born Ánna Pávlovna Bernárd between 1859 and 1864 in Russia; died in Orenberg, Russia, in 1933; married twice, first to Druzhinina, second to Borisova.

Selected works: Noose *(1896);* Daughter of the People *(1903).*

The daughter of a tax assessor, Anna Pávlovna Bernárd studied gymnastics and theater as a child. In 1880, she made her debut on the Russian stage as an actress in a provincial theater. For the next eight years, she worked in these smaller venues until she won a place in a Moscow theater company. Between 1889 and 1893, recognized as a charismatic talent, she performed primarily in Moscow and St. Petersburg, before she left the stage to devote herself to writing.

Bernárd's romance with actor Modest Pisarev, with whom she lived during the 1890s, helped launch her literary career. Under the pen name Nina Pávlovna Annenkova-Bernár, her short story "Noose" was published for the first time in 1896 in a journal edited by one of Pisarev's friends. For the next four years, her stories appeared regularly in journals. Her frequent subjects were the least considered figures of Russian society: women, children, the poor and the elderly. It is a common belief that Pisarev's influence was not limited to publishing contacts; he also did a good deal of the stories' writing, often editing and adding whole pages to drafts presented to him by Bernárd for review.

Though Bernárd also wrote for the stage, only one of her dramas experienced any critical success. *Daughter of the People*, about *Joan of Arc, was written and staged in 1903, with Bernárd in the leading role. In 1917, she retired to Orenberg, where she ran a theater studio for children. She married twice, though neither union is thought to have influenced her as much as her relationship with Pisarev. Bernárd died in 1933.

Crista Martin,
Boston, Massachusetts

Annes.
Variant of Agnes.

Annia Aurelia Galeria Lucilla (b. 150 CE).
See Faustina II for sidebar on Lucilla.

Annia Galeria Faustina I (c. 90–141 CE).
See Faustina I.

Annia Galeria Faustina II (130–175 CE).
See Faustina II.

Annice.
Variant of Agnes.

Anning, Mary (1799–1847)

English fossil collector. Born at Lyme Regis, England, in May 1799; died on March 9, 1847; daughter of Richard Anning (a cabinetmaker and one of the earliest collectors and dealers in fossils).

In 1811, Mary Anning was only a 12-year-old child when she discovered the first skeleton of an ichthyosaur, bringing her to scientific attention. In 1821, she found the remains of a new saurian, the plesiosaurus. Seven years later, she unearthed the remains of a pterodactyl (Dimorphodon), the first time such a discovery had been made in England.

Annis.
Variant of Agnes.

Annora de Braose (d. 1241).
See Braose, Annora de.

Annunciata of Sicily (1843–1871).
See Marie Annunziata.

Anny Ioannovny (1693–1740).
See Anna Ivanovna.

Anois, Marie (c. 1650–1705).
See Aulnoy, Marie Catherine, Comtesse d.

A Nong (c. 1005–1055)

Powerful shaman and leader of the Zhuang/Nung minority peoples of the Sino-Vietnamese frontier, who led her people in resisting the encroachment of both the Chinese and Vietnamese states. Pronunciation: Ah Nung. Born A Nong around 1005, in the area now bordering the northernmost region of Vietnam and southern China; executed by the Chinese in 1055; daughter of a noted chieftain of the Nong clan of the minority people known today in China as the Zhuang, and in Vietnam as the Nung; married Nong Quanfu (a leader of the Nong clan), around 1020; children: several, the most famous of whom was her son Nong Zhigao (b. 1025).

In concert with her father, husband, and son, led her people in attempting to found a Zhuang/Nung kingdom, (1035); escaped with her son, Nong Zhigao, at the time of her husband's capture and execution (1039); after years of political strategy and warfare, she declared a second independent state (1052); captured by the Chinese and executed (1055).

In the early 11th century, ethnic identities and boundaries of rule were far more fluid than they are today in the frontier region lying along what is now the Sino-Vietnamese border. But the dominant ethnic group at that time was largely the same as the largest minority still found there, the Zhuang/Nung, who now number more than 15 million people. Identified in China as the *Zhuang*, and in Vietnam as the *Nung*, they are usually referred to as the Zhuang/Nung. At a time of crisis during the 11th century, their ancestors were led by A Nong in a valiant war that briefly established an independent state under her son, the group's most famous leader, King Nong Zhigao.

The land of the Zhuang/Nung was a region of great natural wealth, making it attractive for encroachment by the more powerful Chinese from the north and the Vietnamese from the south. Gold was easily mined or gleaned from stream beds, and the ancient Chinese chronicles mention chieftains who kept baskets of gold to "ward off evil influences." The broken terrain was also rich with other mineral resources, while flourishing plant and animal life supplied timber, sugar, ivory, and rare birds and animals for trade, as well as medical herbs that were highly prized in both China and Vietnam.

The region's dramatic limestone crags, crisscrossed by numerous large and small streams, made communication and transport difficult, helping to protect it from outside invaders. But the roughness of the terrain also increased the difficulties of indigenous peoples trying to establish a unified political organization, and their relative isolation from each other often kept their associations tenuous. Although the Zhuang/Nung people spoke a common tongue, a member of the Thai family of languages, there were distinct dialect differences.

Life for A Nong's people was centered upon the region's high mountain valleys, where landowners applied skillful and intensive farming techniques to the raising of rice and other grains, augmented by the periodic cultivation of mountain-side fields, according to "slash-and-burn" agriculture. Some larger valleys, with a good water supply, could support a population of tens of thousands, and the powerful lords who controlled them commanded many armed men and plentiful resources. A Nong was the daughter of such a lord. A noted warrior, he was a clan chieftain who accepted administrative titles under both the Chinese and the Vietnamese, who were then in dispute for control of the prosperous high grounds, which threatened the rice-raising lowlands of their neighbors.

When the Chinese first pushed into the area, the Zhuang/Nung peoples still had no written language, but they quickly adapted written Chinese to suit their own needs. Since Chinese characters do not carry any fixed pronunciation, it was simple to assign their own pronunciation to given Chinese words, as did the Koreans, the Japanese, and the Vietnamese. Unfortunately, because the Zhuang/Nung had no earlier written

history, our earliest knowledge of them is through the eyes of the Chinese chroniclers, who often viewed the mountain culture with prejudice. They were scandalized, for example, by the strong social role of Zhuang women, and viewed Zhuang shamanesses as terrifying witches.

Compared to the strict hierarchical family of traditional China, gender roles of the local peoples were usually quite open and egalitarian, perhaps because of the regional terrain. Men engaged in child-care and frequently moved in with their wive's families rather than establish their own. Women had great power, reflected in the region's number of famous female warriors, including the Vietnamese *Trung Sisters. And while the Chinese, and to a lesser extent the Vietnamese, worshipped primarily male figures, the high status of females among the Zhuang and Nong is suggested by the number of their religious cults involving goddesses and powerful female demons, often watched over by a shaman like A Nong.

The Barbarian Nong clan . . . loved to fight and struggle and regarded death lightly.
— *The Song History*

In an open gender system, women tend to be powerful members of the family structure. In A Nong's time, many families traced their descent through both female and male lines, mothers were as important as fathers, and a marriage was a complicated alliance between two families or "clans," both of whom jealously guarded the rights and powers of their family member.

Among the Zhuang/Nung, women were particularly noted as shamanesses, or "Wu," a Chinese word meaning witches. They were knowledgeable about an amazing pharmacopeia of herbs, used as both medicines and poisons. The Zhuang (as well as Chinese) men believed that their wives regularly dosed them with a powerful elixir, the *Wu-gu*, which would kill them horribly the moment they were unfaithful, and Zhuang/Nung soldiers were particularly feared because of the poisons they applied to their edged weapons. The Zhuang/Nung are also known to have practiced ritual cannibalism and human sacrifice.

The people of A Nong lived in a difficult and dangerous land, inhabited by crocodiles, tigers, panthers, wolves, and many varieties of poisonous snakes. The region is also subject to high winds, thunderstorms, and the sudden onset of great typhoons. The fearful power of nature was sometimes personified as dark and fierce gods.

But the lives of these peoples also had an easier side. Where the power and influence of women was strong, their household labor usually had significant value. A Nong's people were noted for their textiles: fibers spun and woven into beautiful cloth, then dyed in brilliant colors and richly embroidered. Zhuang/Nung brocades were highly prized at both the Chinese and Vietnamese courts.

These people also loved to sing, and courting was carried out as a bawdy songfest between gaily dressed ranks of young men and women who competed in sung verse, responding to their intended marriage partners in complicated rhyme and meter. Even today, some older women of the region are said never to speak in prose, but to communicate only in poetic verse. The Chinese likened the Zhuang/Nung's beautiful spoken language to the twittering of birds. The importance of song in courting, as well as in transmitting shared culture and history, is probably one of the primary factors that have contributed to their lasting ethnic cohesion and relatively egalitarian gender system. In their important singing ceremonies, still held today, the wit and verbal fluency of the women is usually more than a match for that displayed by the men.

As a child, A Nong probably learned spinning and weaving from her mother as most girls did, and most likely spent a great deal of time in company with young women of her age, sometimes living with them communally. Girls learned the beautiful traditional songs and ballads of their peoples and flirted with young men who were practicing their warriors' skills. Some women, too, learned to use spears, swords, and cross-bows, and became noted warriors in their own right. Many young men served as mercenary soldiers in the armies of both China and Vietnam, observing a strict warrior code of resolute loyalty to their employers. Their indigenous terrain developed powerful limbs and strong lungs, making these men celebrated for physical endurance and ferocious courage for more than 2,000 years. (Nung men were famous fighters during the war between the United States and Vietnam. While Americans like to think that they were usually on the side of the United States, they in fact fought on both sides. Vietnamese graveyards have extensive sections allotted to the Nung who fought in that war. In the Sino-Vietnamese war of 1978, the Zhuang/Nung probably constituted the majority of forces on both sides.)

At some point, probably at puberty, A Nong was separated from the other girls to begin her studies as a shaman. We cannot know precisely how she was selected, but a combination of heredity and ability probably led to her choice within the clan for this important but demanding role. Under the guidance of older shamanesses, she learned the names and histories of the gods and goddesses of the region, of the fearful demons that had to be propitiated, and how their protective powers could be invoked in spells. She also studied plant and animal life and learned the healing powers of herbs, as well as those that could be compounded into subtle poisons.

The status A Nong thus achieved, as well as the political power of her family, prepared her for the role of a leader, but since few other such women ever obtained power comparable to hers, we assume that she was also unusually intelligent, brave, and determined. She was also born at a critical historical moment, and it fell to her family to take the lead in resisting the encroaching Chinese and Vietnamese.

Once A Nong married Nong Quanfu, who was also a member of the extensive Nong clan, she became his primary political advisor. She gave birth to several children, the most famous of whom was Nong Zhigao, born in 1025. Ten years later, in 1035, Quanfu and A Nong, seeing the power and political cohesion gained by both the Chinese and Vietnamese peoples through state organization, declared the founding of their own kingdom.

As the power located closest to the Zhuang/Nung lands, the Vietnamese found this a challenge they could not ignore. In 1039, Ly Thai-tong, the king of the Vietnamese state of Dai Viet, or Great Vietnam, led his armies into the region, seized Quanfu, and executed him. A Nong escaped with Nong Zhigao, her oldest son and Quanfu's heir.

A Nong's ability now came to the fore, as she rallied the survivors among her people and planned for the future. Zhigao proved a worthy student under his mother's tutelage, and continued to expand the power of the Nong clan, while shrewdly paying costly tributes to both the Chinese and the Vietnamese, as he grew to adulthood. Gold, silver, and trained war elephants were all sent to the Chinese court, buying time for the Zhuang/Nung to rebuild their military and economic base. They migrated north into the lands of the Chinese Song dynasty (960–1279), people who were weaker than the Vietnamese in the frontier region.

In 1052, A Nong and Zhigao were ready. They declared another independent state, invoked the blessings of heaven, and attacked the major Chinese towns and fortifications all along their border. With their skilled soldiers moving more quickly, they rapidly occupied them. For almost two months, they besieged the great southern port city of Canton, but were finally forced to withdraw in the face of terrible weather and massive Chinese reinforcements. Their superior military machine, however, allowed the Zhuang to defeat five successive Chinese armies and execute each of their commanding generals.

After many defeats, the Chinese resolved to end the threat of the insurgents. They selected the best commanders in their vast empire and assembled their most experienced troops, including a large contingent of northern nomadic cavalry. In 1054, the Chinese attacked the capital city of the Zhuang, who fought bravely and were initially victorious but were eventually outweighed by the enemy's numbers. The effect of the crack cavalry forces of the Chinese Song was decisive, the capital fell, and A Nong and Nong Zhigao were forced to flee west into the isolated highlands.

The Song pursued the rebels relentlessly, offering huge rewards for the heads of A Nong and Nong Zhigao, and carrying out intrigues to split the Zhuang clans' alliance. In 1055, aided by the Zhuang who resented the power of the Nong clan, Chinese forces captured A Nong, and executed her summarily, believing her too dangerous to try to hold in prison. Nong Zhigao escaped and disappeared. The *Song History* says simply: "His death cannot be known."

For a brief period, the fate of the Zhuang/Nung people as a unified nation was held in the balance by the determination of A Nong and the military talent of her son. Today their descendants are a substantial minority in the lands that were formerly theirs. Divided by Vietnamese and Chinese authorities, their culture eventually diverged to the point where they are now usually thought of as two distinct peoples. Eventually, however, both the Chinese and the Vietnamese learned that they had to give these people a measure of independence, or face continual conflict. Zhuang women have continued to act as leaders in the region, some of them worthy successors to A Nong, including the remarkable Zhuang woman *Wa Shi.

A Nong led a long struggle to preserve the unity of her people, but the forces arrayed against her were too great. Today, the Zhuang/Nung people have made their peace with both the Chinese and the Vietnamese and are regarded by both states as the best guardians of the frontier between them. But whenever the youth of her people gather and sing their lovely songs in the high mountains she protected, A Nong is remembered.

SOURCES:

Barlow, Jeffrey G. "The Zhuang Peoples of the Sino-Vietnamese Frontier in the Song Period," in *Journal of Southeast Asian Studies*. Vol. XVII, no. 2, September 1987.

Eberhard, Wolfram. *China's Minorities, Yesterday and Today*. Belmont CA: Wadsworth, 1982.

Schafer, Edward. *The Vermillion Bird: Tang Images of the South*. Berkeley: University of California, 1967.

SUGGESTED READING:

Taylor, K.W. *The Birth of Vietnam*. Berkeley: The University of California Press, 1983.

Ma Yin, ed. *China's Minority Nationalities*. Beijing: Foreign Languages Press, 1989.

Jeffrey G. Barlow, Professor of History, Lewis & Clark College, Portland, Oregon

Anor of Châtellerault (d. 1130).

See Eleanor of Aquitaine for sidebar on Aénor of Châtellerault.

Anouk (b. 1932).

See Aimée, Anouk.

Anscombe, G.E.M. (1919—)

English philosopher who edited and translated the work of her friend Ludwig Wittgenstein. Born Gertrude Elizabeth Margaret Anscombe in 1919; daughter of Allen Wells and Gertrude Elizabeth Anscombe; attended St. Hugh's College, Oxford, 1941; married Peter Geach (a Wittgenstein scholar), in 1941; children: three sons and four daughters.

Obtained research fellowships at Oxford and Newnham College, Cambridge (1941–44); named research fellow, Somerville College, Oxford (1946–64); named fellow, Somerville College (1964–70); became professor of philosophy, Cambridge (1970–86); named fellow, New Hall, Cambridge (1970–86). Honorary fellow, Somerville College, Oxford (1970); honorary fellow, St. Hugh's College, Oxford (1972); foreign honorary member, American Academy of Arts and Sciences (1979); Ehrenkruez Pro Litteris et Artibus (Austria, 1978); Forschungspreis, Alexander von Humbolt Stiftung (1983); honorary J.D., Notre Dame University (1986).

Selected works: Intention *(1957);* An Introduction to Wittgenstein's Tractatus *(1959); (with Peter Geach)* Three Philosophers *(1961); "Thought and Action in Aristotle: What is 'Practical Truth'?" in* New Essays on Plato and Aristotle *(1965);* Causality and

Determinism *(1971); The Collected Papers of G.E.M. Anscombe: 1. Parmenides to Wittgenstein; 2. Metaphysics and the Philosophy of Mind; 3. Religion and Politics (1981); translator and coeditor with G.H. Von Wright of posthumous works of Ludwig Wittgenstein, and wrote over 40 articles in philosophical journals.*

Elizabeth Anscombe has been called the most distinguished woman philosopher England has produced, for her work in logic, semantics, semiotics, and philosophy of language, as well as in the development of the tradition of analytic philosophy that has dominated England and North America in the 20th century. She has also argued for the importance of Aristotle in analytic philosophy.

Anscombe is particularly famous for *An Introduction to Wittgenstein's Tractatus*, which is the classic exposition of the views in her friend Ludwig Wittgenstein's *Tractatus Logico-Philosophicus*. With G.H. Von Wright, she edited and translated Wittgenstein's manuscripts and notebooks posthumously, thus making his later work accessible to the philosophical community. Wittgenstein had published only one book in his lifetime, the *Tractatus*. Although this work was influential and adopted as a text by philosophers in Vienna who were developing the views of logical positivism (the view that meaning depends on the possibility that something is true or false), Wittgenstein rejected these ideas in his later life. Anscombe's work on Wittgenstein's later writing served to provide access to his revised thought, which had only been accessible before by word of mouth and through the notes taken by some of Wittgenstein's students, *Alice Ambrose and Margaret MacDonald.

SOURCES:
Kersey, Ethel M. *Women Philosophers: a Bio-critical Source Book.* NY: Greenwood Press, 1989.

Catherine Hundleby, M.A. Philosophy,
University of Guelph, Ontario, Canada

Anselmi, Tina (1927—)

Politician and Italy's first female cabinet minister.
Born in Castelfranco Veneto, Italy, in 1927.

Elected to the Italian Parliament in 1968, Tina Anselmi became Italy's first woman cabinet minister when she was appointed minister of labor, 1976–78, and then minister of health, 1978–79. Her career in politics began at the age of 16, during the Second World War, when she worked with the Cesare Battista Brigade in the Resistance movement, for which she later received the military cross for valor. Joining the

Christian Democratic Party in 1944, she was head of the local textile trade union from 1945 to 1948, and then local party representative. As party spokeswoman on youth (1960–68) and national women's representative, she concentrated her efforts on industrial relations, family issues, and the status of women. She became vice president of the European Feminist Union in 1966.

Barbara Morgan,
Melrose, Massachusetts

Ansgard (fl. 863)

*Queen of France. Name variations: Ansgarde; Ansgarde of Burgundy. Flourished around 863; daughter of Count Harduin; became first wife of Louis II the Stammerer (846–879), king of France (r. 877–879), in 862; children: Louis III (863–882), king of France (r. 879–882); Carloman (866–884), king of France (r. 879–884); Gisela (who married Robert, count of Troyes). The name of Louis the Stammerer's second wife was *Adelaide Judith, mother of Charles III the Simple (879–929), king of France (r. 898–923).*

Anstei, Olga Nikolaevna (1912–1985)

Author and translator who was considered Russia's most visible émigré poet. Name variations: Ol'ga. Born Olga Shteinberg on March 1, 1912, in Kiev, Russia; died on May 30, 1985, in New York City; married Anglaia Shishova (divorced); married Ivan Elagin, in 1937 (divorced); married Boris Filippov (divorced).

Selected works: Door in the Wall *(1949); (translator) Stephen Vincent Benet's* The Devil and Daniel Webster *(1960);* In the Way *(1976).*

Born and raised in Kiev, Russia, Olga Nikolaevna Anstei was trained extensively in foreign languages, and her fluency would carry her across Europe and to a new home in America. After secondary school in her hometown, Anstei was admitted to the Institute of Foreign Languages, where she specialized in English and French. When she graduated at age 19, she took positions as a secretary and translator. She was briefly married and divorced before she met author Ivan Elagin, whom she married in 1937. When Russia, in the throes of World War II, became politically uncomfortable for Anstei and Elagin, they were forced to emigrate in 1943, spending time in Prague and Berlin.

Anstei had been writing since childhood, and, though she did not publish in Russia, her work had been known and admired there by poet Maksim Ryl'skii. In Berlin, she submitted poetry written at age 18, and it was published. When she and Elagin moved to Munich in 1946, they lived in a barracks for displaced persons (DP) and produced a collection of DP poetry. Anstei's poetry also began to appear regularly in Russian émigré journals, which led to the publication of her first collection *Door in the Wall* in 1949.

The following year, Anstei and Elagin made their way to New York City, where Anstei found a position in the United Nations as a secretary and translator. In New York, the Russian-American publication *New Review* was eager for her writings, but the poet's output was intermittent and interspersed with translations of such authors as Housman, Tennyson, Rilke, and Benét. During this time, Anstei's marriage to Elagin faltered and was followed by a brief and unsuccessful union with Boris Filippov, another émigré writer and scholar.

When Anstei visited the Ukraine in 1973, her reputation in Russia as one of the most visible émigré poets of her time was well established. But America had become her home, and she returned to live in New York City, where she died at age 73.

Crista Martin,
Boston, Massachusetts

Anstrude of Laon (fl. 7th c.)

Frankish abbess. Flourished in 7th century; daughter of Blandinus Boson and Salaberga of Laon (Frankish nobles).

Anstrude of Laon, daughter of the Frankish nobles Blandinus Boson and *Salaberga of Laon, served as one of early medieval Europe's great abbesses. After her husband's death, Salaberga entered a convent in Laon and eventually became its abbess. Anstrude followed her mother into the religious life, taking a nun's vows at age 12. Highly educated, she showed a considerable depth of piety. After Salaberga's death, Anstrude was chosen to act as abbess of Laon, supervising the spiritual and material well-being of both the convent and the monastery. She earned widespread admiration for her faith and great administrative skills. During Anstrude's term, Laon became one of France's most important learning centers; the nuns were educated in both ancient and contemporary studies, and Anstrude also managed a scriptorium where books were copied and illustrated.

Laura York, Anza, California

Antarjanam, Lalitambika (1909—)

Indian author. Born in 1909 in Kerala, India; daughter of poets.

Though her formal education was limited, Lalitambika Antarjanam received a literary upbringing from her parents, both poets, in their hometown of Kerala, a southern state of India. As an adult, Antarjanam was active in the Indian effort for independence from Britain, working with both the Indian National Congress and the Marxist Party of Kerala. Her poetry and fiction bear her political and social reformist ideas and are written primarily in her native language of Malayalam. The author's only novel, *Agnisaksi* (*Testimony of Fire*), received the Kerala Sahitya Akademi Award in 1976 as the best literary work of the year. Antarjanam's credits also include nine collections of short fiction, six volumes of verse, and several children's books.

Anthony, Katharine Susan
(1877–1965)

American writer and feminist. Born Katharine Susan Anthony in Roseville, Arkansas, on November 27, 1877; died in 1965; daughter of Ernest Augustus Anthony (brother of suffragist Susan B. Anthony) and Susan Jane (Cathey) Anthony; niece of Susan B. Anthony; attended Peabody College for Teachers in Nashville, Tennessee, for two years; granted B.S. from University of Chicago; spent one year abroad studying at the universities of Frieburg and Heidelberg; never married; no children.

After teaching at Wellesley College, Katharine Susan Anthony moved to New York to take up writing; she also did some social research and editorial work for the Russell Sage Foundation. Influenced by her aunt, *Susan B. Anthony, and her mother, Susan Jane Anthony, both pioneers in the woman suffrage movement, Katharine continued working in that area with books and articles. She wrote *Mothers Who Must Earn* (1914); *Feminism in Germany and Scandinavia* (1915); *Margaret Fuller: A Psychological Biography* (1920); *Catherine the Great* (1925); *Queen *Elizabeth I* (1929); *Marie Antoinette* (1923); *Louisa May Alcott* (1937); and *Susan B. Anthony: Her Personal History and Her Era* (1954). Her last book, on *Mercy Otis Warren, was published in 1958, when she was 81.

Anthony, Saint (1684–1706).
See Beatrice, Dona.

Anthony, Sister (1814–1897).
See O'Connell, Mary.

Anthony, Susan B. (1820–1906)

American women's rights activist, educator, and reformer whose lifelong effort on behalf of women culminated in passage of the 19th "Anthony" Amendment, which enfranchised women in the United States. Name variations: "Aunt Susan." Born Susan Brownell Anthony on February 15, 1820, at Adams, Massachusetts, a small village in the Berkshire Mountains; died on March 13, 1906, at her home in Rochester, New York; daughter of Daniel Anthony (a prosperous Quaker mill owner and merchant) and Lucy Read Anthony (a Baptist homemaker and mother of seven children, one of whom died in infancy); attended Deborah Moulson's Female Seminary in Hamilton, Pennsylvania, in 1837–38; never married; no children.

Taught school (1838–52); organized New York State Woman's Temperance Association (1852); meeting with Elizabeth Cady Stanton began lifelong collaboration (1852); attended first women's rights convention (1852), beginning of lifelong commitment to woman suffrage; spearheaded petition drive for abolition of slavery during Civil War, resulting in 400,000 signatures; co-founded and edited The Revolution, a weekly paper devoted to women's rights (1868–70); founded the Working Woman's Association (1868); co-founded and led National Woman Suffrage Association (1869–90); president National American Woman Suffrage Association (1892–1900); arrested and tried for voting in presidential election (1872); organized International Council of Women (1888).

Alternately exhorting, pleading, planning, begging, and borrowing on behalf of women's suffrage, the cause that consumed her life, Susan B. Anthony met repeated disappointments with the resilience that led her to say, "Failure is impossible." Progress in the 72-year battle for voting rights for women was measured not in feet, but in inches. No one appreciated the military analogy better than Anthony, who stood at the head of the shock troops of women's suffrage from its 19th-century inception until her death in 1906. Anthony was indefatigable in her efforts; her dedication to women's suffrage was her *raison d'etre*, and the amendment to the Constitution that at last enfranchised women came to be known as "the Anthony Amendment."

Anthony was born into a family of reformers in Adams, Massachusetts. Her father Daniel, a Quaker, and her mother Lucy, a Baptist, were both champions of temperance, women's rights, and the abolition of slavery. They insisted on providing equal educations for their two sons and four daughters. In 1826, Daniel Anthony relocated the family to Battenville, New York, where he became a partner in a large-scale cotton manufactory.

Despite severe financial difficulties caused by the Panic of 1837, Daniel and **Lucy Anthony** sent Susan, the second oldest, to board at **Deborah Moulson**'s Female Seminary in Hamilton, Pennsylvania, in order to continue her education beyond the district public school in Battenville. At Miss Moulson's, along with algebra, literature, chemistry, and philosophy, Anthony was taught "the principles of Humility, Morality, and a love of Virtue." Following the bankruptcy auction of Daniel Anthony's assets, Susan and her older sister **Guelma** went to work as schoolteachers.

In 1846, Susan was offered a position as headmistress of the female department of the Canojoharie Academy, a prestigious private school in upstate New York. There she remained until 1849, enjoying a full and demanding professional and social life. By 1849, Anthony had

Susan B. Anthony

grown restless, and she returned to the family, now relocated to a farm near Rochester, New York. Here she began to devote herself to the cause of reform.

Although Anthony had been at Canojoharie when the historic 1848 gathering of women at Seneca Falls, New York, took place, her parents and her younger sister **Mary** had heard of it and had made the trip to the follow-up meeting that took place two weeks later in Rochester. Though Daniel, Lucy, and Mary Anthony all signed the petition demanding the right of suffrage for women, Susan B., while committed to anti-slavery and temperance causes, was slower to embrace the call for women's suffrage. The events of 1852 would change her mind and alter the course of her life. In January of that year, Anthony attended a convention of the Sons of Temperance in Albany, New York. Her attempt to speak at the meeting was rebuffed with the warning that the women "were not invited there to speak but to listen and learn." Incensed, Anthony—showing the genius for publicity that would mark her career—met with the editor of the powerful *Albany Evening Journal,* Thurlow Weed, and persuaded him to write a story on the silencing of the women at the convention.

After this incident, Anthony undertook the organization of the Woman's State Temperance Society. This too would prove a turning point, for it was as an organizer that Anthony found her life's work. For the temperance society's first convention, Anthony wrote hundreds of letters, raised money, held a series of meetings throughout the state, secured speakers, and arranged for publicity. The convention, held in Rochester in April of 1852, was a huge success. When the women's organization was again rebuffed at the Men's Temperance Society convention held later that spring, Anthony surrendered the last of her reservations about women's rights reform. Thus, in a single year, Anthony tapped into what would prove a genius for organization and found the cause that would consume her life.

It was also in 1852 that Anthony met *Elizabeth Cady Stanton**—the woman who would provide a "partnership of head and heart" that enriched both women's lives. Both later agreed that from the first there was an "intense attraction" between them. For more than half a century, they would be "Mrs. Stanton and Susan" to each other—intellectual partners, reform collaborators, and fast friends.

Stanton agreed to accept the presidency of the Woman's State Temperance Society, and in

their subsequent meetings convinced Anthony of the need for women's organized activity on behalf of political, social, and legal rights. Anthony agreed to attend the 1852 Syracuse, New York, National Woman's Rights Convention (NWRC). There, Anthony displayed the plain-spoken honesty that would characterize her throughout her life. The report of the Syracuse convention furnishes an early example of Anthony's style. First, she spoke out boldly against electing the fashionably dressed ❦▶ **Elizabeth Oakes Smith** to the presidency of the convention, saying that no one who dressed so elegantly could possibly represent the hard-working women of the country. Oakes was defeated, and the conservatively clad Quaker, *Lucretia Mott,* was elected instead. Anthony also interrupted the speech of a soft-voiced woman orator, saying, "Mrs. President, I move that hereafter the papers shall be given to some one to read who can be heard. It is an imposition on an audience to have to sit quietly through a long speech of which they can not hear a word." Audiences came to expect such plain truths from Anthony, who could be blunt and cantankerous even as she earned the respect and affection of her fellow reform workers.

Following the Syracuse convention, though still committed to temperance, Anthony found

❦▶ Smith, Elizabeth Oakes (1806–1893)

American author. Born Elizabeth Prince in the vicinity of Portland, Maine, in 1806; died in 1893; descended from distinguished Puritan ancestry; married Seba Smith (an American satirist who founded and edited the Portland [Maine] Courier).

Elizabeth Oakes Smith was married at an early age to Seba Smith, who was then editing a newspaper in Portland, Maine; he would go on to enjoy a national reputation writing under the pseudonym Jack Downing. Though Elizabeth Smith's earliest poems were contributed anonymously to various periodicals, she took to writing openly as a means of support for her family in order to offset her husband's business disasters. An early collection of poems published in New York was followed by *The Sinless Child and Other Poems* in 1843, which had originally appeared in the *Southern Literary Messenger.* Smith also wrote *The Western Captive* (1842), *Bald Eagle: Or, The Last of the Ramapaughs* (1867), *The Newsboy, Sagamore of Saco, The Two Wives, Kitty Howard's Journal, Destiny: A Tragedy, Jacob Leisler, The Salamander: A Legend for Christmas,* and a tragedy in five acts entitled *The Roman Tribute.* A prominent advocate of women's rights, Smith occasionally lectured on the issue; her book *Woman and Her Needs* was published in 1851.

herself drawn ever more strongly to women's rights. That autumn, Anthony, Stanton, and the third of the great suffrage pioneers, *Lucy Stone, met at Stanton's home to plan for the organization of a co-educational university. Though the institution would fall short of the women's dreams, merging before its inception with Cornell University, the partnership formed around Stanton's dinner table would prove a formidable force for change in the half-century to come. They were a powerful trio of women—Stone, the charismatic orator and canny politician; Stanton, the brilliant philosopher; and Anthony, the woman who more than any other would come to be identified with the movement for women's suffrage.

From the early 1850s through the outbreak of the Civil War, Stanton, Stone, and Anthony led the suffrage movement through a period of explosive growth. Each national women's suffrage convention met with huge crowds, and a series of small conventions took place throughout the country and into Canada. Anthony took on the thankless and necessary task of raising funds to keep the movement alive and of arranging publicity for the meetings, while Lucy Stone, as chair of the executive committee, made the convention arrangements and published the various tracts. Both Stone and Stanton wrote and delivered a series of major addresses on women's rights at large and small gatherings throughout the country. Anthony, at first reluctant to lecture, grew more at home on the platform in later years; in the early years of her public life, she was more comfortable traveling from town to town, holding women's suffrage meetings.

The work of traveling and organizing was often hazardous in the 1850s. Letters quoted in *Ida Husted Harper's biography of Anthony detail some of the difficulties: "Mercury 12 degrees below zero, but we took a sleigh. . . . Trains all blocked by snow . . . yet we had a full house and good meeting"; in another letter, "we floundered through the deepest snowbanks I ever saw." Such determination paid off; interest in women's suffrage grew steadily.

By the middle of the 1850s, women's suffrage had become Anthony's passion, although her opposition to slavery remained strong. She made abolitionist speeches, and she and her family sheltered fugitive slaves. For a while, she considered becoming a paid lecture agent for an antislavery society, but her devotion to women's rights won out. As the ranks of suffragists swelled, and as attendance at the local and national conventions grew year by year, Anthony

began to believe that victory was not far off. However, with the outbreak of the Civil War, organized women's suffrage activity came to a halt.

In the early years of the war, Anthony continued to make abolitionist speeches, decrying the gradualism of Abraham Lincoln and calling for immediate emancipation of all slaves. Following Lincoln's issuance of the Emancipation Proclamation, Anthony determined to work toward the complete abolition of slavery through a Constitutional amendment. Along with Stanton and Stone, Anthony convened the Women's Loyal National League in 1863. At its first convention, those present agreed to labor to establish the "civil and political rights of all citizens of African descent and all women."

With Anthony as its driving force, the League began a massive petition campaign for a Constitutional amendment prohibiting slavery. The work devolved largely on Anthony, who raised more than $5,000 for the effort. Under her direction, thousands of letters went out, and more than 25,000 petitions were circulated and collected. By August of 1864, Anthony's efforts had resulted in more than 400,000 signatures on the petitions that then were carried by the armload and presented in the Senate. When in February of 1865, Congress passed the 13th Amendment, thereby abolishing slavery, an exhausted Anthony could be satisfied that her efforts had contributed to its passage.

After the war, the women's effort to be included in a postwar push for civil and political rights was thwarted when the 14th Amendment introduced the word "male" as a qualification for voting. Abolitionist allies were unwilling to risk adding women to the call for Constitutional protections and guarantees for former slaves. Though freed by the Constitution, African-Americans found themselves increasingly imperiled by harsh and punitive Black Codes throughout the South. Fearful that adding women to the call for enfranchisement would doom their cause, reformers voted to labor for freedmen's rights, not women's rights.

Within the next four years, the decision to work only for freedmen's rights would split the women's rights movement. Tensions were exacerbated in 1867 by the alliance of Anthony and Stanton with an eccentric, racist demagogue, George Francis Train. Train offered them financial support in return for a share of the speakers' platform; he and Anthony first toured Kansas together in the fall of 1867, and then went on a joint speaking tour of the Midwest and East in late 1867 and early 1868.

Reports of Train's anti-black rhetoric alienated most suffragists, but Anthony held firm to her belief in the rectitude of her course. Her diary entry for January 1, 1868, reads: "All the old friends, with scarce an exception, are sure we are wrong. Only time can tell, but I believe we are right and hence bound to succeed." Stanton, less sure of their course, nevertheless justified their actions by saying that she "would take money from the Devil himself" if it would further the cause of women's suffrage. At the close of their lecture tour, Train furnished the women funds to begin a weekly women's suffrage newspaper, *The Revolution*. Within a year, he had withdrawn his financial support and ceased to fill pages of the newspaper with his eccentric political views. *The Revolution* carried news of women's political, social, and economic gains. It also printed the text of *Mary Wollstonecraft*'s 1792 manifesto, *The Vindication of the Rights of Woman*. The paper ceased publication in 1870, leaving a debt of $10,000. Anthony vowed to repay every creditor; although it took years of hard work, she eventually settled every debt. Among its causes, *The Revolution* had championed the plight of working women,

Susan B. Anthony

whose attempts to integrate male-dominated trade unions often failed. Anthony founded the Working Woman's Association, hoping to combine woman's rights with increased power for employed women.

At the 1869 national convention of women suffragists, an impassioned Anthony, joined by Stanton, attempted to pass a series of resolutions committing the women's rights organization to opposing the 15th Amendment (freedmen's rights) unless it should include men and women in its guarantee of the right of suffrage. The majority of women's rights activists, aware of the amendment's already precarious chances for ratification, spurned this position, but Anthony held to her convictions with the same indomitable resolve that had marked each stage of her life.

And when we shall have our amendment to the Constitution of the United States, everybody will think it was always so. . . . They have no idea of how every single inch of ground . . . has been gained by the hard work of some little handful of women of the past.

—Susan B. Anthony, February 15, 1894

Certain of her course, Anthony joined Stanton in forming a separate organization, calling it the National Woman Suffrage Association (NWSA). Known for years afterward as "Miss Anthony's organization," the National pressed first for a Constitutional remedy—claiming that the 14th Amendment guaranteed women's rights as citizens, rights that included the right to vote. While a series of court cases based upon this strategy were being considered, Anthony took matters into her own hands. On November 5, 1871, she wrote triumphantly to Stanton, "Well, I have been and gone and done it, positively voted this morning at 7 o'clock, and swore my vote in at that."

Anthony's triumph was short-lived; on November 28th, she was arrested by federal marshals. At the trial, the judge directed the jury to bring in a verdict of guilty. Asked if she wished to speak before sentencing, the record of the trial reports Anthony as saying:

> Yes, your honor, I have many things to say; for in your ordered verdict of guilty you have trampled under foot every vital principle of our government. My natural rights, my civil rights, my political rights, my judicial rights, are all alike ignored. Robbed of the fundamental privilege of citizenship, I am degraded from the status of a citizen to that of a subject.

When the judge fined Anthony $100, she announced that she would not pay, concluding with the revolutionary maxim, "Resistance to tyranny is obedience to God." Anthony's trial was widely reported, and her remarks appeared in newspapers throughout the nation.

Anthony's conviction and the subsequent failure in the courts of the other cases based upon the 14th Amendment led her to conclude that a women's suffrage amendment was the only available remedy for women's disfranchisement. The NWSA began a highly organized push for a federal amendment to the Constitution. Each January, Anthony arranged a convention in Washington, at which the women lobbied federal legislators on behalf of a women's suffrage amendment.

What gains Anthony and her organization made were balanced by a deluge of negative publicity in the 1870s. The 1871 alliance with the notorious *Victoria Woodhull, whose Congressional testimony and subsequent pledge of $10,000 to the NWSA won her a place of honor on the speakers' platform, brought widespread association of women's suffrage with "Freeloveism." Though Anthony would sever the tie a year later, the accusations would cling stubbornly for more than a decade. When Woodhull's newspaper accused the renowned preacher Henry Ward Beecher of an adulterous liaison with *Elizabeth Tilton, wife of a suffrage activist, the sensational court trial that followed played up the women's suffrage ties of all the participants, to the detriment of the cause. Faced with such adversity, Anthony redoubled her efforts.

By 1883, Anthony's unceasing work had earned her the affection and esteem of suffragists and the respect of those who opposed the reform. When she sailed for Europe, the nation's newspapers reported the lavish sendoff as befitting a head of state. Her fame had preceded her, and she was met warmly in England, Italy, France, Germany, and Ireland. On the Continent, an international congress on women's rights had been held in 1878. The subject of political rights had not been on the agenda, and upon her return to the United States, Anthony laid the groundwork for an International Council of Women, which met in Washington in 1888, the 40th anniversary of the Seneca Falls convention that had launched the movement.

In 1890, the two rival suffrage organizations merged to form the National American Woman Suffrage Association. Though Stanton was the titular head, Anthony continued to provide the energy and leadership. Beginning in 1892, when Stanton retired from active suffrage work, Anthony presided over the national organization for eight years. Following the death of Lucy Stone in 1893, Anthony alone remained to remind women of how far they had traveled.

In 1896, while conducting a suffrage campaign in California, Anthony met and felt an immediate liking for Ida Husted Harper, an Indiana reporter. She commissioned Harper to write her official biography, and the cooperation resulted in a three-volume biography that offers the most complete sourcebook of information on Anthony's life. She also persuaded Harper to write the last two volumes of the *History of Woman Suffrage.* Anthony herself continued to work on behalf of women's suffrage until the end of her life. She celebrated her 86th birthday at the NAWSA convention in Washington. Leaning heavily upon *Anna Howard Shaw, a leader of the younger generation of suffragists, the visibly enfeebled Anthony responded to a lengthy birthday congratulatory message from President Theodore Roosevelt by saying, "When will men do something besides extend congratulations? I would rather President Roosevelt say one word to Congress in favor of amending the Constitution to give women suffrage than to praise me endlessly." When it was time for her closing remarks, she encouraged those present to carry on the struggle, concluding with: "Failure is impossible."

Within a month, Anthony succumbed to pneumonia. With her sister Mary at her side, and her good friend Anna Shaw holding her other hand, Anthony softly spoke the names of the women in her life—the long parade of helpers, colleagues, and reformers whose lives had touched, and been touched, by her own. To Anna Shaw, she said, "They are still passing before me—face after face, hundreds and hundreds of them. . . . I know how hard they have worked. I know the sacrifices they have made." These would be her last words; she died on March 13, 1906.

Ten thousand mourners filed past Anthony's casket in Central Presbyterian Church of Rochester, New York. Anthony's death marked the close of a heroic era, even as it came at the beginning of the final push to suffrage. Though the 19th Amendment that had come to be known as the "Anthony Amendment" would not be ratified for another 14 years, much of the groundwork had been laid by the indomitable efforts of the feisty former schoolteacher who had believed to the last that failure was impossible.

SOURCES:

*Anthony, Katharine Susan. *Susan B. Anthony: Her Personal History and Her Era.* Garden City, NY: Doubleday, 1954.

Barry, Kathleen. *Susan B. Anthony: A Biography of a Singular Feminist.* NY: New York University Press, 1988.

*Dorr, Rheta Childe. *Susan B. Anthony: The Woman Who Changed the Mind of a Nation.* NY: Frederick A. Stokes, 1928.

DuBois, Ellen Carol, ed. *The Elizabeth Cady Stanton-Susan B. Anthony Reader: Correspondence, Writings, Speeches.* Rev. ed. Boston, MA: Northeastern University Press, 1992.

Harper, Ida Husted. *Life and Work of Susan B. Anthony.* 3 vols. Indianapolis, IN: The Hollenbeck Press, 1898.

Sherr, Lynn. *Failure Is Impossible: Susan B. Anthony in Her Own Words.* NY: Random House, 1995.

SUGGESTED READING:

Anthony, Susan B., Elizabeth Cady Stanton, and Ida Husted Harper. *History of Woman Suffrage.* vols. 1–3. Fowler and Wells, 1881 (reprint, NY: Arno and The New York Times, 1969).

Flexner, Eleanor. *Century of Struggle: The Woman's Rights Movement in the United States.* NY: Atheneum, 1970.

Wheeler, Marjorie Spruill, ed. *One Woman, One Vote: Rediscovering the Woman Suffrage Movement.* Oregon: New Sage Press, 1995.

COLLECTIONS:

Susan B. Anthony papers, Library of Congress; NAWSA Collection, Library of Congress; Susan B. Anthony papers, Schlesinger Library of Radcliffe College; The Papers of Elizabeth Cady Stanton and Susan B. Anthony, microfilm edition edited by Patricia G. Holland and Ann D. Gordon.

RELATED MEDIA:

One Woman, One Vote. Annandale, Virginia: Educational Film Company, 1995.

Andrea Moore Kerr, women's historian and author of *Lucy Stone: Speaking Out For Equality,* Washington, D.C.

Anthony, Susan B., II (1916–1991)

*American writer and feminist. Born in Pennsylvania in 1916; died in Boca Raton, Florida, in 1991, a few days short of her 75th birthday; great niece of *Susan B. Anthony (1820–1906).*

A journalist and one of the first women to be hired by the *Washington Star,* Susan B. Anthony II was born ten years after the death of her famous great-aunt. The author of eight books, she is best known for *Out of the Kitchen—Into the War* written in 1943, during World War II. In her last years, after successfully battling her own alcohol addiction, Anthony retired in Florida where she co-founded Wayside House in Delray Beach for women alcoholics and wrote for the *Key West Citizen.*

Anthusa (c. 324/334–?)

Mother of John Chrysostom, the Father of the Eastern Church. Born in 324 or 334; death date unknown; married Secundus (a high-ranking military officer in the Roman army of Syria), around 343; children: John Chrysostom (c. 344/354–407).

Anthusa takes her place in history as a young widow whose son John would become the Father of the Eastern Church and patriarch of Constantinople. She nurtured his Christian character, provided his classical education, and molded him into the man who would become one of the great reformers and ascetics in the church. So renowned would John become for his preaching that he would earn the name Chrysostom, meaning "Golden-Mouthed."

A contemporary of *Nonna (329?–374), Anthusa was a resident of Antioch, one of the four chief cities of the Roman Empire. Founded in 300 BCE and predominantly Greek in influence, the city had been visited by Christian missionaries quite early. By the 4th century, when Anthusa gave birth to her son, the city's population of 150,000 to 300,000 was composed of pagan, Jewish, and Christian communities.

Anthusa was the widow of Secundus, a high-ranking military officer in the Roman army of Syria. Her husband died when she was 20, shortly after the birth of her son, and she never remarried. Although she had misgivings about bringing her son up amid the corruption of Antioch, she had faith in God's support and found great joy in seeing her husband's image reproduced in her child.

Resolute in her Christian piety, Anthusa tended to her son's religious education, acquainting him with the Scriptures and teaching him to love the Bible. John credited his mother's early influence with providing his "enthusiasm for the good, his moral energy, his aversion to ostentation, his zeal for justice and truth and his steadfast faith."

Anthusa used her considerable wealth to pay for John's law education, sending him to study with the celebrated orator Libanius. She later encouraged him to study theology under the noted Diodore of Tarsus, who started him on his career as a preacher and expositor of the Bible. Although John reveled in his classical education, he "drank still more deeply of the things of the spirit from his mother at home."

After completing his education, John embarked on the practice of law. Although he attracted wide attention and could have had a brilliant career as a lawyer, he disapproved of the "fraud and avarice" he saw practiced by the businessmen in Antioch. He withdrew from all activities, fasted, and undertook a life of study and prayer. When he wanted to remove himself still further to a remote hermitage of monks in Syria, his mother pleaded with him not to leave her alone: "Wait for my death—perhaps I shall soon be gone! When you have committed my body to the ground, and mingled my bones with your father's bones, then you will be free to embark on any sea you please."

Honoring his mother's wishes, John stayed in her home until she died. Throughout his life, he remained an impassioned advocate of the church, defending the deity of Christ. His uncompromising reforms, however, brought him into conflict with authorities and caused his eventual exile, where he died a "martyr of the pulpit."

SOURCES:

Becknell, Branan. "John Chrysostom," in *Historic World Leaders*. Detroit, MI: Gale Research, 1994.

Deen, Edith. *Great Women of the Christian Faith*. NY: Harper & Row, 1959.

Barbara Morgan, Melrose, Massachusetts

Antin, Mary (1881–1942).

See Yezierska, Anzia for sidebar.

Antoinette, Marie (1755–1793).

See Marie Antoinette.

Antoinette of Bourbon (1494–1583).

See Mary of Guise for sidebar.

Antoinette of Luxemburg
(1899–1954)

*Princess of Nassau. Born on October 7, 1899; died on July 31, 1954; daughter of *Marie-Anne of Braganza (1861–1942) and William IV (1852–1912), grand duke of Luxemburg (of the House of Nassau); became second wife of Crown Prince Rupprecht also known as Rupert of Bavaria (1869–1955), on April 7, 1921; children: Henry (b. 1922); Irmingard (b. 1923); Editha (b. 1924); Hilda (b. 1926); Gabriele (b. 1927); Sophie (b. 1935).*

Antoinette Saxe-Coburg
(1779–1824)

*Duchess of Wurttemberg. Born in 1779; died in 1824; daughter of Francis, duke of Saxe-Coburg-Saalfeld, and *Augusta of Reuss-Ebersdorf (grandmother of Queen *Victoria); married Alexander, duke of Wurt-*

temberg (uncle of Queen Victoria); children: *Mary of Wurttemberg (1799–1860); Alexander, duke of Wurttemberg; Ernest of Wurttemberg.

Antonia (1456–1491)

Italian painter. Born in 1456; died in 1491; daughter of Paolo Ucello (a painter).

Daughter of Italian painter Paolo Ucello, Antonia was taught by her father and eventually became a painter of renown. After she took the vows of a nun and entered a Carmelite convent, however, most of her paintings were done for the aesthetic and financial benefit of the Carmelite house.

Antonia (1858–1883)

*Tuscan noblewoman. Name variations: Maria Antonia; Antonette. Born on January 10, 1858, in Florence, Italy; died on April 13, 1883, in Cannes; daughter of *Anna Maria of Saxony (1836–1859) and Ferdinand IV (1835–1908), titular grand duke of Tuscany from 1859 to 1908.*

Antonia Augusta (36 BCE–37 CE).

See Antonia Minor.

Antonia del Balzo (d. 1538).

See Gonzaga, Antonia.

Antonia Maior (39 BCE–?).

See Antonia Major.

Antonia Major (39 BCE–?)

Roman imperial and grandmother of Emperor Nero. Name variations: Antonia Maior, Antonia the Elder. Born 39 BCE; death date unknown; daughter of Marc Antony (80–30 BCE) and Octavia (c. 69 BCE–11 BCE); at age two, was betrothed to L. Domitius Ahenobarbus, 37 BCE (they were married much later); children: Domitia Lepida (c. 19 BCE–?); Gnaeus Domitius Ahenobarbus.

Antonia Major's powerful lineage—her mother was *Octavia, sister to the first Roman emperor Augustus, her father Marc Antony, colleague of Julius Caesar and last rival to Augustus for political supremacy—seems not to have touched her in the same degree as it did her younger sister *Antonia Minor. Under the emperors Tiberius, Gaius (Caligula) and Claudius, the younger Antonia became the mother figure for the imperial family and a powerful political patron in her own right. But the Roman historians took notice of the older sister only as wife and mother of relatively insignificant men in the Julio-Claudian dynasty. The Roman biographer Suetonius calls her husband cruel and arrogant, although apparently he was close to Augustus. In addition, Suetonius notes the sadism and dishonesty of her son Domitius, who was also accused of incest with his sister ❧➤ Domitia Lepida. This Domitius was the father of the emperor Nero. The Greco-Roman historian Cassius Dio supplies us with the slim fact that Augustus returned to her (and her sister) property that had been seized from her father. Otherwise, the life, personality and accomplishments of Antonia Major are unknown, as is often the case with Roman women; even the date of her death is a mystery.

SOURCES:

Cassius Dio. *Roman History.*
Suetonius. *Nero.*

Alexander Ingle, Research Assistant, Institute for the Classical Tradition, Boston University, Boston, Massachusetts

❧➤
Domitia Lepida.
See Agrippina
the Younger for
sidebar.

Antonia Minor (36 BCE–37 CE)

*Ranking Roman woman at the center of imperial power under the first Caesars. Name variations: Antonia the Younger, Antonia Augusta (given the title Augusta [Revered] by Caligula posthumously in 37 CE). Born on January 31, 36 BCE, in Rome; died in Rome, either by suicide or was poisoned by grandson Caligula, on May 1, 37 CE; daughter of Marc Antony and Octavia (c. 69 BCE–11 BCE, the sister of Octavian, later Caesar Augustus); married Drusus the Elder (also known as Nero Drusus, brother of the future emperor Tiberius), in 18 BCE; remained a widow after his death in 9 BCE; children: Germanicus (b. 15 BCE–19 CE); Livilla (c. 14/11 BCE–c. 31 CE); and the emperor Claudius (10 BCE–54 CE); grandchildren: the emperor Gaius (Caligula), Drusilla (15–38), *Agrippina the Younger, and *Julia Livilla (c. 16 CE–after 38).*

Reared in Augustus' household (32–18 BCE); accompanied Drusus the Elder to Lugdunum (modern Lyons, 10 BCE); became effective head of her family after Drusus' death; as mother of the heir-apparent, Germanicus, visited her father's former possessions in the Roman East (17 CE); under Tiberius, wielded great influence in the imperial family; voted thanks by Roman senate for helping to convict the conspirator Gnaeus Piso (19 ce); informed Tiberius of the conspiracy of Sejanus (31 CE); executed her daughter Livilla by starvation for her ties to Sejanus; granted public honors by Caligula (37 CE); commemorated on scores of surviving inscriptions, coin-issues, portraits and statues throughout the Roman Empire (12 BCE–74 CE).

Antonia
Minor

five-year treaty between them. At the time of their marriage, Octavia and Antony already had one daughter, *Antonia Major (b. 39 BCE). When the younger Antonia was born in 36 BCE in Antony's house at Rome, Antony was in Syria already consorting with *Cleopatra (VII), the last Ptolemaic queen of Egypt.

Antony officially divorced Octavia in 32 BCE. In the year following, Augustus defeated Antony and Cleopatra's forces at Actium. Antonia Minor was six years old when her father took his life in 30 BCE. She had lived with Augustus' household (familia) since she was four and would spend the next few years there with her older sister, her half-brothers and sisters (among whom were Cleopatra's children), as well as the sons of Augustus' wife *Livia, including Antonia's future husband Drusus the Elder. Like any Roman aristocratic household, Augustus' familia would have included huge numbers of male and female slaves and former slaves. The imperial residence on Rome's Palatine Hill undoubtedly was also crowded with visiting clients, political supporters, and foreign emissaries.

Little is known about the lives of children in the imperial family. One source (Strabo's Geography) tells us that Octavia hired a Greek philosopher to teach her children. Antonia clearly grew up in an environment unique even for a girl of the Roman upper classes. Women in the household, and especially her mother Octavia, held unprecedented influence in the affairs of state: in 35 BCE, Augustus granted Octavia and Livia the equivalent of the special legal protection associated with the political office of the tribunate. Richard Bauman in his Women and Politics in Ancient Rome makes the convincing argument that Octavia played a leading role in the imperial household during its first years, particularly with regard to policies of imperial succession. She died in 11 BCE.

Antonia married her cousin Drusus the Elder in 18 BCE and gave birth to her first child Germanicus on May 24, 15 BCE. Her daughter *Livilla was born between 14 and 11 BCE. During this time, Antonia's husband pursued the traditional political and military career of a Roman senator, although at a more rapid pace than usual because he was the stepson of Augustus. There is some evidence that Antonia accompanied Drusus to Spain in 12 BCE. Her youngest son, the future emperor Claudius, was born while she was with Drusus at Lugdunum (Lyons) on August 1, 10 BCE. The Roman biographer Suetonius says that the couple had children who

Antonia Minor was one of the most powerful individuals alive during the first decades of the Roman Empire. She not only helped educate three generations of the first imperial family but also played an active role in imperial politics for many years. From historical sources, it seems clear that she represented a moral counterbalance to the dissolute practices of some of her relatives. It is no wonder that she came to represent the Julio-Claudian dynasty in official propaganda and perhaps even in the popular sentiment of the times.

Her birth and childhood followed the fortunes of the disintegration of the Roman republic and the formation of a new government of one-man rule under her uncle Octavian, later the emperor Augustus. Her father Marc Antony was Augustus' last serious rival. Marc Antony had married Augustus' sister *Octavia to renew political association with him in 37 BCE. For a time, Octavia functioned as an unofficial mediator between the two rulers. According to the Greco-Roman biographer Plutarch, she negotiated a died in infancy, but no other mention of them has come down to us.

Drusus died while campaigning in Germany in 9 BCE, the same year he had attained the consulship, the highest formal political office in the Roman state and a mark of imperial favor. The cause of his death has been variously laid to a riding accident, illness, and poisoning. A poem attributed to Ovid depicts Antonia as wholly bereft and suicidal at the news of his death. The poem praises the couple as "a pair well suited." Antonia refused to marry again, though her uncle Augustus encouraged her to do so. The historian Flavius Josephus indicates that her obstinacy was a benefit, "she kept her life free of reproach."

For the next 25 years, the details of Antonia's life are obscured. We hear mostly about the fate of her eldest son Germanicus, who was adopted by his uncle Tiberius in 4 CE and became the heir-apparent when Tiberius assumed the imperial power at the death of Augustus in 14 CE. Germanicus, who had married *Agrippina the Elder, was given wide-ranging authority and honors by Tiberius. In 18 CE, he toured Rome's eastern provinces, the former powerbase of his grandfather Marc Antony. Nikos Kokkinos has established that Antonia accompanied her son on part of this journey, and he believes that one of the purposes of this visit may have been to commemorate the 50th anniversary of Antony's defeat at Actium. Germanicus died after a lingering illness in Syria on October 10, 19 CE, believing that he was being poisoned by the senator Gnaeus Piso, according to the historian Tacitus. Tacitus tells us that after Piso's condemnation and execution, the senate voted Antonia, along with the emperor and others, thanks for avenging the death of Germanicus. He also suggests that Antonia was kept from attending her son's funeral by Tiberius and Livia so that their own absences would not seem conspicuous.

It was after Livia's death in 29 CE that Antonia's power reached its zenith. She became the most prominent woman of the imperial house. As such, she supervised the upbringing of many royal children from various client states, such as Armenia and Judaea. As Kokkinos observes, this was an outstanding contribution to the political interests of the empire, as far as it acculturated these princes and princesses to Roman ways. She was later an active patron for at least one young noble, Herod I Agrippa, the future ruler of Judaea. Josephus records that she and Herod Agrippa's mother *Berenice (c. 35 BCE–?) were close friends and that Berenice had entrusted her son to Antonia's care. Herod Agrippa himself "arrived

in the friendship" of the great lady. When he was about to be disgraced in front of Tiberius because of bad financial management, Antonia loaned him 300,000 drachmas. She personally interceded with Tiberius when Herod Agrippa was suspected of treason; since her entreaties did not help, she saw to it that he was given special privileges in prison. Antonia's responsibilities also included supervision of her grandson Gaius, the future emperor Caligula, whom, in a forecast of his abusive and destructive reign, she caught in bed with his sister ❧▶ Drusilla.

According to Josephus, Antonia rose even higher in reputation and esteem when she played a decisive role in the fall of Tiberius' potential usurper Sejanus. After it became apparent to her that Sejanus was conspiring to overthrow Tiberius, she prevented him from succeeding "with greater craft in daring than Sejanus had in evil-doing." She wrote a letter to Tiberius detailing the conspiracy and had it delivered by her loyal slave Pallas (who was later to be influential as an imperial freedman in Claudius' reign). Antonia's daughter Livilla had been seduced by Sejanus and had brought such shame on the imperial family (since Sejanus was not even of senatorial rank) that, as reported by the Greco-Roman historian Cassius Dio, even though Tiberius spared Livilla "out of regard for her mother," Antonia executed her by starving her to death. Such an action was not out of accord with the Roman mentality, but Antonia's legal and emotional ability to starve her own daughter emphasizes the central role Antonia played in the imperial family and her occasional severity. In this vein, the writer Pliny the Elder cites Antonia as an example of a "hard and unbending" personality and says that "she never spat."

A fellow singer of wisdom, her genius saved the whole world.

—Honestus

When Antonia's grandson Gaius became the emperor Caligula after Tiberius' death in 37 CE, he granted her the title of Augusta, previously held only by Livia. He also gave her the privileges of the Vestal Virgins and other honors. Soon, however, the new emperor exhibited less respectful behavior toward his grandmother. He refused to grant her a private audience without a guard. Suetonius believes that Caligula hastened her end and either drove her to suicide or poisoned her. Caligula watched her funeral from his house.

Antonia died on May 1, 37 CE, at age 72. While the historical record shows that she was

▶❧
Drusilla. See Agrippina the Younger for sidebar.

regarded as a temperate and virtuous woman by her contemporaries, the Roman historians paid little attention to her compared with other imperial women. This may be because, as Gunhild Vidén notes about Tacitus, the greatest historian of the Julio-Claudian dynasty: "It seems that when Tacitus cannot say anything negative about a woman he prefers to say nothing at all." Suetonius cares only to mention Antonia's disparaging comments about her son Claudius.

The literature of the Renaissance, basing itself on these sources, was not much kinder to Antonia. Two plays about Tiberius' reign, Ben Jonson's *Sejanus His Fall* (1604) and the anonymous *Claudius Tiberius Nero, Rome's Greatest Tyrant* (1607), fail to create a literary Antonia (a task only fulfilled in this century by Robert Graves in *I, Claudius*), although other women of the imperial family such as Livilla and Agrippina are characters in these works.

Modern scholarship also has too often followed the ancient historians in giving Antonia less than her due. Only with the publication of Nikos Kokkinos' *Antonia Augusta* has evidence from several media, not only literature, been brought to the fore in creating a fuller picture of her. For example, Kokkinos has taken into account papyri (scraps of official, private or literary documents preserved in the dry climate of Egypt), which indicate that Antonia had large-scale land holdings in that province. While the papyri confirm the obvious—that Antonia was one of the richest people in the empire—they also give us a fascinating glimpse as to how and where Antonia derived some of her income.

Kokkinos has also gathered evidence for the wide-ranging influence of members of her household. The most famous was her slave Pallas. More interesting was the role she played as a symbol of the imperial household. Numerous inscriptions, both in state decrees and of dedicatory poetry, attest to her importance. Antonia also appears to have had her own priests in the imperial cult in ancient Caria (modern Turkey) after her death, where, as mother of the imperial family, she was identified with the goddess Aphrodite, mother of Aeneas, the legendary founder of Rome. Kokkinos has tracked down 50 pieces of sculpture likely to be representations of Antonia at various phases of her life. Most come from the reign of Claudius, but a large number seem to have originated in the reigns of Tiberius and Caligula. Finally, Claudius, and perhaps Tiberius, used Antonia's portrait on coins. One depicts Antonia as Ceres,

Opposite page

S. Inkeri

Anttila

the mother-goddess of the harvest, as a reflection of her maternal role in the imperial family.

SOURCES:
Cassius Dio. *Roman History.*
Flavius Josephus. *Jewish Antiquities.*
Pliny the Elder. *Natural History.*
Plutarch. *Life of Antony.*
Pseudo-Ovid. *Consolatio ad Liviam.*
Suetonius. *Claudius 1.* and *Gaius 1.*
Gaius Fannius Strabo. *Geography.*
Tacitus. *Annals.*

SUGGESTED READING:
Kokkinos, Nikos. *Antonia Augusta: Portrait of a Great Roman Lady.* London and NY: Routledge, 1992.

Alexander Ingle, Research Assistant, Institute for the Classical Tradition, Boston University, Boston, Massachusetts

Antonia of Portugal (1845–1913)

Princess of Hohenzollern-Sigmaringen. Name variations: Antonia Saxe-Coburg. Born on February 17, 1845, in Lisbon, Portugal; died on December 27, 1913, in Sigmaringen; daughter of *Maria II da Gloria (1819–1853), queen of Portugal, and Ferdinand of Saxe-Coburg Gotha; married Leopold (1835–1905), prince of Hohenzollern-Sigmaringen, on September 12, 1861; children: William (1864–1927), prince of Hohenzollern; Ferdinand I (b. 1865), king of Rumania (r. 1914–1927); Charles Anthony (1868–1919), prince of Hohenzollern.

Antonia the Elder (39 BCE–?).

See Antonia Major.

Antonia the Younger (36 BCE–37 CE).

See Antonia Minor.

Antonietta of Bourbon-Two Sicilies (1814–1898).

See Maria Antonia of Sicily.

Antrim, Angela (1911–1984)

Irish artist. Name variations: Countess of Antrim. Born Angela Sykes in 1911; died in 1984; educated privately; studied in Belgium under sculptor D'Havlosse; attended British School in Rome; married the 8th earl of Antrim.

Known for her large scale stone sculptures, Lady Angela Antrim was educated privately and studied in Belgium under the sculptor D'Havlosse, before attending the British School in Rome. Her early work was done out of a studio in London. After the outbreak of World War II, she and her husband, the 8th earl of Antrim, moved to Glenarm Castle in County Antrim, where she lived until her death in 1984. Her work included a number of public commissions in stone, including those at St. Joseph's Church, Ballygally, County Antrim, and at the parliament buildings, Newfoundland. She exhibited with the Royal Hibernian Academy and the Irish Exhibition of Living Art. After an injury to her hand put an end to her sculpting in 1962, Antrim turned to working mostly with models cast in bronze.

Anttila, S. Inkeri (1916—)

Finnish criminologist and minister of justice, recognized internationally for her work in professionalizing the study of victimology. Pronunciation: SIL-Vee EN-ker-EE AN-til-AH. Born Sylvi Inkeri Metsämies on November 29, 1916 (some sources cite the 21st or 26th), at Viipuri, Finland; daughter of Veini Ireneus (a lawyer) and Sylvi Airio Metsämies; graduated University of Helsinki, Cand. Jur., 1936, LL.D. in criminal law, 1946, Lic. Sociology, 1954, D. Political Sciences (honorary), 1976; married Sulo Anttila, in December 1934; children: Veini, Liisa, and Mirja.

Qualified for the bar in Finland (1942); made director of the Training School for Prison Service (1949–61); appointed professor of criminal law, University of Helsinki Law School (1961–); made director, Finland's Institute of Criminology in the Ministry of Justice (1963–74); appointed director, Research Institute of Legal Policy, 1974; appointed minister of justice (1975–); elected president, Fifth United Nations Congress on the Prevention of Crime and Treatment of Offenders (1975); named chair of the board of the International Center of Comparative Criminology (1977).

Selected publications: "Loukatun suostumus, oikeudenvastaisuuden poistavana perusteena" (thesis, University of Helsinki, 1946); with Risto Jaakola, Unrecorded Criminality in Finland (Helsinki: 1966); with Patrik Tornudd, Kriminologi i kriminalpolitiskt perspektiv (Stockholm: Norstedt, 1973); "Victimology: A New Territory in Criminology," Scandinavian Studies in Criminology (Vol. 5, 1974, pp. 3–7); with Olavi Heinonen, Pekka Koskinen and Raimo Lahti, Rikollisuus ongelmana: kriminaalipolitiikan perusteet (Helsinki: Tammi, 1974); Incarceration for Crimes Never Committed (Helsinki: Research Institute of Legal Policy, 1975); with Olavi Heinonen, Rikosoikeus ja kriminaalipolitiikka (Helsinki: Tammi, 1977); Papers on Crime Control, 1977–1978 (Helsinki: Research Institute of Legal Policy, 1978); Women in the Criminal Justice System (Helsinki: Research Institute of Legal Policy, 1979); with Patrik Tornudd, Kriminologia ja kriminaalipolitiikka (Porvoo: Soder-

strom, 1983); with Patrik Tornudd, Rikollisuus ja kriminaalipolitiikka: Uudessa Suomessa vuosina 1980–1984 julkaistuista kirjoituksista *(Helsinki: Lakimiesliiton kustannus, 1986).*

In a long and distinguished career, Inkeri Anttila has pioneered a vastly broadened approach to the study of crime and its victims, ranging from the prey of a purse-snatching to Haitian boat people seeking asylum. Through the Finnish lawyer and criminologist's deep analysis and balanced approach, incorporating the issues that surround both the perpetrators of crime and their victims—including the criminal who may be wronged by the judicial system itself—she has raised victimology to the level of a genuine sociological discipline, enhanced her profession, and pioneered judicial reforms with an international reach.

Sylvi Inkeri Metsämies came of age professionally at a time and place when political events across Europe left all crimes subject to scrutiny in terms of the involvement of their participants. She was born on November 29, 1916 (some sources give the 21st or 26th), at Viipuri, Finland, the daughter of Veini Ireneus and Sylvi Airio Metsämies. Not much has been documented about Inkeri's childhood, but the fact that her father was a lawyer likely helped mold her intellectual curiosity in legal issues. Like many Finns, she became fluent in Finnish, Swedish, and English, and, after graduating from high school in 1933, she attended the University of Helsinki. In 1936, she received a degree in criminal law, two years after her marriage to Sulo Anttila on December 8, 1934 (some sources give the date as December 12); they were to have three children: Veini, Liisa, and Mirja.

Juggling family and career, Anttila passed the bar in 1942, while World War II had mainland Europe to the south of Finland in turmoil. In 1946, she earned her doctorate in criminal law; her thesis was an analysis of justification and consent in the legal system, a subject that may have been encouraged by the experience of Finland's military cooperation with German forces to reclaim territory seized by the Russians, and by the Russo-Finnish War, which disrupted her country up to February 1947. Anttila's postgraduate training was to last into the 1950s, when she was licensed as an authority in sociology. By then, she worked in a criminal court, and she served as director of the Training School for Prison Service from 1949–61. In 1949, she became a docent of criminal law at the University of Helsinki Law School, and was a full professor beginning in 1961. From 1953–56, she was president of the Finnish Federation of University Women.

Before Anttila, the work of most criminologists focused on offenders, not victims. "Victimology" is a term coined in 1949 by American psychiatrist Frederick Wertham, who insisted on the need for sociologists to take a scientific approach to the study of victims of crime. This followed the appearance of *The Criminal and His Victim: Studies in the Socio-biology of Crime,* by Hans Von Hentig, in 1948. In what was to become a classic text, the author criticized sociologists for limiting their analysis to the offenders and viewing crime victims merely as passive participants. Von Hentig's suggestion that knowledge of the social background of a victim and time and place of a crime might determine that the victim had actually initiated the crime, would become a major step in encouraging further study of the dynamics of criminal-victim interaction.

Inspired by these seminal works, Anttila set about exploring new issues and establishing new paradigms of research for the study of victimology, and wrote prolifically in her new field. During the 1960s, she chaired Finnish government commissions on juvenile crime (1965–66), abortion (1965–68), and women's rights (1966–70), and directed a committee on sexual crimes that lasted from 1966–69, while she also belonged to groups that sought to improve penal policy, eliminate censorship, and secure expanded social rights. In 1963, she was named director of Finland's Institute of Criminology in the Ministry of Justice, and served there until 1974, when she became director of the Research Institute of Legal Policy in Helsinki. The following year, she was the first woman to be named Finland's minister of justice, a cabinet-level position in the government.

In 1974, Anttila produced what was perhaps her most ground-breaking article, "Victimology: A New Territory in Criminology," published in *Scandinavian Studies in Criminology.* Anttila's position was to stress the criminal-victim relationship as an important factor in crime, but she was vocally critical of books such as *Patterns of Forcible Rape,* by M. Amir, published in 1971, which stated that 19% of "victims of assault have no one except themselves to blame if they deliberately walk in dark alleys after dark." Rather than blaming the victim, she defined victimology as the scientific study of victims and their problems, regardless of their stature as individuals, groups, or societies, and outlined the important issues to be explored within the new discipline.

Anttila's work by this time had led to international recognition in the field of criminology. She sat on the board of directors of the International Association of Penal Law and was vice-president of the International Penal and Penitentiary Foundation. She chaired the Scandinavian Research Council on Criminology from 1970–74, and served at the same time as vice-president of the United Nations Committee on Crime Prevention and Control; in 1975, she was president of the Fifth United Nations Congress on the Prevention of Crime and Treatment of Offenders. She also was director of the International Criminological Institute in Montreal.

By 1977, Anttila was on the council of the International Association of Criminology and chair of the board of the International Center of Comparative Criminology. During that decade, she was active in the National Research Council's social sciences section and a member of the Association Internationale de Droit Penale and the Scientific Council of International Society for Criminology.

Primary victimology research consisted of victim surveys that included the tabulation of statistics estimating what percentage of crimes were reported to police, evaluations of the legal officials' perception of the crime, and their accountability to the victim. As a direct result of Anttila's work, research was expanded to incorporate much more information about the victim. In response to these liberal analyses, a victims' movement emerged in the late 1960s, maturing in the 1970s. It attempted to encourage the criminal justice system to become more victim-oriented.

Recognizing crime prevention as the criminologist's ultimate long-term goal, Anttila kept her sights on the lesser, but perhaps more easily achievable, goal of keeping the consequences of a crime to a minimum for the victims. She was interested in the impact of a crime on the victim's life and how the consequences could be alleviated, while maintaining a balance between the rights of victims and their offenders. She also stressed that crime victims suffered not only from the actions of the criminal but the justice system itself, due to delays in prosecution. She focused on more effective sentencing of offenders through a system of compensations and fines that were appropriate and fair in an effort to reduce recurrence. She challenged courts to reassess their conventional methods of determining penalties according to the severity of offenses, and sought protection for victims of crime from a judicial process that could sometimes seem unsympathetic.

Turning from the sociological to the psychological, Anttila examined the causes of victimization, including assessments of the likelihood of an individual to be victimized or to instigate crimes, hoping thereby to arrive at a means of crime prevention. She researched the fact that victimization could transform victims into offenders, recognizing the pattern among some offenders who responded to the experience of being crime victims by turning to crime or were encouraged toward criminal acts by excessive punishment within the justice system.

Anttila also expanded the perspective on victimization beyond the traditional legal system, recognizing that groups could be vulnerable to becoming victims of governments and organizations. A well-known example is found among the Haitian boat people seeking asylum through migration to the United States. When such groups require aid from emergency mental and health services, negligence or deprivation of such services might well be construed as a form of national victimization.

One aspect of Anttila's research was to assess the relevance of bystanders to the victim of a crime. In examining whether bystanders offered assistance to a victim, she defined the occurrence of "hidden victimization," when onlookers proved unwilling to come to the rescue of a victim. On the other hand, she proposed that bystanders who risked breaking laws to protect a victim should be considered for immunity from prosecution and even compensation.

Writing alone and with colleagues, Anttila eventually produced 80 articles and ten books about criminal law and policy, criminology, and crime control, often sponsored by the Research Institute of Legal Policy. Her *Unrecorded Criminality in Finland,* published in 1966, was an examination of statistics related to unreported crimes. With Patrik Tornudd, she examined criminal justice administration with specific Finnish examples in *Kriminologi i kriminalpolitiskt perspektiv* (1973), *Kriminologia ja kriminaalipolitiikka* (1983), and *Rikollisuus ja kriminaalipolitiikka: Uudessa Suomessa vuosina 1980–1984 julkaistuista kirjoituksista* (1986).

Anttila considered preventive detention techniques in *Incarceration for Crimes Never Committed* (1975) and crime prevention in *Papers on Crime Control, 1977–1978* (1978). With **Olavi Heinonen**, she covered her views on criminal law in *Rikosoikeus ja kriminaalipolitiikka* (1977); one particularly interesting treatise was *Women in the Criminal Justice System* (1979) in which she discussed both the careers and roles of women lawyers and correctional personnel and the sexual discrimination directed against women in these professions.

In September 1983, the First International Symposium in Victimology, held in Jerusalem, brought the study international recognition as a scholarly field. Anttila was a featured speaker discussing new perspectives in victim-centered research and stating the limits and biases that should be considered when studying crime from the victim's perspective.

Concerned with having victimology taken seriously by the intellectual community, Anttila emphasized the lessons of her own research, namely that victims were a source of information otherwise unavailable that could provide insight to the characteristics of offenders and their crimes. She told her audience that such information was therefore crucial, even when an offender was never caught.

Previously, as she explained, offenders had been at the center of investigations, with criminologists seeking causes such as mental illness and character defects to explain their criminal motivations; but to balance criminological research, she urged that victims be asked the same questions. She also protested against stereotypes of offenders as evil deviants and victims portrayed either as innocent law-abiding citizens or guilty crime-precipitants, voicing theories then emerging among some criminologists about stores that tempted thieves by displaying valuables or tourists who became lost in dark alleys and thus invited muggers to take their wallets. Anttila's aim was to eliminate all such stereotypes by presenting a new perspective of both victims and criminals that limited neither category to certain groups or environments. She also suggested that victim-centered research could provide methods for crime control that were an improvement over the previously held view that the risk of capture and threat of punishment could be sufficient to thwart many criminals.

Declaring that all victims could not be considered innocent and unsuspecting, Anttila proposed that some offenders could perhaps be impeded through the alteration of victim behavior. When a potential victim could be identified, for instance, special locks and surveillance might prevent the occurrence of a crime; and as sociology of crime became victim-centered, the emphasis might shift more toward the responsibility of victims for the prevention of crime than the punishment of offenders by the justice system. In determining the severity of offenses, Anttila

stressed that the victim should have some input, noting that middle-class administrators often measured offenses according to a value system different from that of a victim from lower socioeconomic classes, who should be allowed to participate in evaluating compensation for loss.

At the same time, Anttila warned against the potential weaknesses of victim-centered research that could become preoccupied with the individual characteristics of a particular victim or offender while lacking data for broader analysis. She encouraged a shift of emphasis toward understanding aspects of the criminal situation and the criminal-victim interaction before any extensive alteration of legal policy-making.

She warned criminologists not to overemphasize research of criminal behavior where the victim was easily identified—as in cases of assault, larceny, and rape—at the expense of crimes where victims were obscure. In the case of consenting minors, for instance, victims may not consider themselves victimized; and in the case of institutional or governmental policies, entire communities might be considered victims, while criminals might be viewed as victims of society and the justice system. She noted the dangers in an ideology among some criminologists that embraces the belief that crime is an unavoidable aspect of society and criminals are necessary to test legal limits, perpetuating both the acceptance of criminals and the need for increased victimology research in an ongoing cycle.

Anttila concluded that "these observation may, I hope, help us to see the limits of victim-centered research. I have, in particular, wanted to point to the dangers of an atomistic mode of thinking, where sometimes only the offenders, sometimes only the victims are the main targets of interest." She encouraged her peers to expand victim-centered research but advised that "these efforts will not prevent us from seeing the crime problem in its entirety and in all its complexity."

A citizen of Helsinki, where she served on the Helsinki City Council from 1974–76, Inkeri Anttila has been honored for criminological research since 1954, when she was decorated with the Order of the White Cross of Finland; in 1961, she received a Badge of Merit in prison service in Finland, and six years later she was awarded her country's Order of Commander of Lions of Finland. The Emil Aaltonen Foundation recognized her in 1972, and she received an honorary degree in political science from her alma mater in 1976. The study of victims remains her number one priority.

SOURCES:

"Anttila, Mrs. Sylvi Inkeri," in *Who's Who in the United Nations and Related Agencies.* NY: Arno Press, 1975.

"Anttila, S. Inkeri," in *Who's Who in the World.* Chicago, IL: Marquis, 1979.

Drapkin, Israel, and Emilio Viano, eds. *Victimology: A New Focus.* 5 vols. Lexington, MA: Lexington Books, 1973.

SUGGESTED READING:

Joutsen, M. *The Role of the Victim of Crime in European Criminal Justice Systems: A Crossnational Study of the Role of the Victim.* Helsinki, 1987.

Maguire, Mike, Rod Morgan, and Robert Reiner, eds. *The Oxford Handbook of Criminology.* Oxford: Clarendon Press, 1994.

Walklate, S. *Victimology.* London, 1989.

Elizabeth D. Schafer, Ph.D., freelance writer on the history of technology and science, Loachapoka, Alabama

Anula (r. 47–42 BCE)

Queen of Ceylon (modern-day Sri Lanka). Birth date unknown; reigned from 47 to 42 BCE; married King Darubhatika Tissa; children: King Kutakanna Tissa (died 47 BCE); children.

Upon the death of King Kutakanna Tissa in 47 BCE, Ceylon went through a period of unrest, and three people tried to rule. Eventually, the king's wife Anula was asked to govern. After five years, she was succeeded by her son.

Anyte of Tegea (fl. 3rd c. BCE)

Greek poet famous for her elegantly crafted dedications, whose emotional sensitivity looked back to the achievement of Sappho, while her romantic portrayal of animals and pastoral settings looked forward to the urbane sophistication of poets such as Theocritus. Born in Tegea, Peloponnesus, in the 3rd century.

A poet of the early 3rd century BCE, Anyte came from Tegea in the Peloponnesus. Consensus recognizes as extant 19 genuine epigrams in the Doric dialect, but Anyte also wrote lyric poems and versified oracles rendered by the priests of the god Asclepius at Epidarus, the famous sanctuary and sanitarium not far from her native city. Her extant work underscores the profundity of the everyday and is set in an inscriptional form especially suited to funerary dedications. Anyte's muse was simple but eloquent, and she displayed an emotional sensitivity reminiscent of *Sappho's best work. As such, Anyte constituted a bridge between Archaic and Hellenistic poetry, for her Sapphic qualities merged with a fascination for the bucolic in a fashion anticipating the romantic glorification of the countryside that was to appear in many Alexandrian poets, especially Theocritus, a century later. The following translation by **Sally Purcell** is representative of Anyte's poetry:

> Sit down in the shade of this fine spreading laurel
> draw a welcome drink from the sweet flowing stream,
> and rest your breathless limbs from the harvesting
> here, where the West wind blows over you.

William S. Greenwalt, Santa Clara, California

Aoki, Tsuru (1892–1961)

Japanese actress. Born in 1892; died in 1961; married Sessue Hayakawa.

Tsuru Aoki was the first Japanese leading lady in American films. After costarring with her husband, the noted Japanese actor Sessue Hayakawa, in *The Typhoon* in 1914, she starred in *The Wrath of the Gods* (1914), *The Call of the East* (1917), *Five Days to Life* (1922), and *The Danger Line* (1924).

Aoua Kéita (1912–1979).

See Kéita, Aoua.

Apama or Apame (fl. 324 BCE).

See Stratonice I for sidebar.

Apama or Apame (c. 290 BCE–?).

See Berenice II of Cyrene for sidebar.

Apama or Apame (fl. 245 BCE).

See Stratonice II for sidebar.

Apgar, Virginia (1909–1974)

American physician, researcher and administrator known for her contributions in the prevention of birth defects and development of the Apgar Score for Evaluating New-Born Infants. Pronunciation: APP-gar. Born Virginia Apgar on June 7, 1909, in Westfield, New Jersey; died in New York City on August 7, 1974; daughter of Charles Emory (an automobile salesman) and Helen May (Clarke) Apgar; attended Westfield High School, diploma, 1925; Mount Holyoke College, B.A. in zoology, 1929; Columbia University College of Physicians and Surgeons, M.D., 1933; Johns Hopkins University, M.P.H., 1959; never married; no children.

Granted two-year surgical internship at Presbyterian Hospital after receiving her M.D. degree (1933); residency in anesthesiology at the University of Wisconsin and Bellevue Hospital, New York City

(1937); instructor of anesthesiology at Columbia University (1938); assistant professor and clinical director of the Department of Anesthesiology at Columbia-Presbyterian Medical Center (1938); associate professor, Columbia (1942); full professor, Columbia (1949); head of Division on Congenital Malformations, The National Foundation (1967); lecturer in teratology, Cornell University Medical Center (1965); senior vice president for Medical Affairs, the National Foundation (1973); clinical professor of pediatrics, Cornell University (1971); lecturer in genetics, Johns Hopkins University (1973).

Every baby born in a modern hospital anywhere in the world is looked at first through the eyes of Virginia Apgar.

—Anonymous physician

Before 1952, it was routine practice for newborn babies to be whisked away in a blanket and taken to the nursery to be examined at a later time. A young anesthesiologist at Columbia-Presbyterian Medical Center by the name of Virginia Apgar was present during many such births and felt that the practice of deferring examination of newborn infants was dangerous. Many babies, she reasoned, could greatly benefit if early problems, especially those with the heart and lungs, were identified and treated immediately. In an interview with *Women's Day* magazine in 1966, Apgar related that she wondered, "who was really responsible for the newborn." In 1952, she presented her now classic Apgar Scoring System at an International Anesthesia Research Society meeting. In it, she proposed that infants be evaluated in five categories within one minute of birth and then again within five minutes after delivery. The five areas in which infants are observed and rated are: appearance, pulse, grimace, activity, and respiration. Each of these signs is given a numerical value of 0 to 2, with a maximum of 10 points possible for all five categories. This examination was designed to be conducted by a nurse or physician, and in just a few minutes provides an assessment of a child's reflexes, color, heart rate, respiration rate, and muscle tone. A total score of 7 or above is most desirable, with anything less indicating possible problems. The Apgar Scoring System became widely adopted throughout the United States and various other countries.

On June 7, 1909, in Westfield, New Jersey, Virginia Apgar was born to Charles Emory and Helen May Apgar. One of her brothers became a music professor at Earlham College in Indiana, while the other brother had died in 1903. During her childhood, Apgar was exposed to her parents' many interests and hobbies, such as science and music; the musically gifted family enjoyed sharing their talents in concert. Apgar began playing the violin at the age of six, and her love for music continued throughout her lifetime. She was also athletic and participated in sports during both her high school and college years. When she graduated from Westfield High School in 1925, Apgar knew she wanted to enroll in medical school and become a doctor.

Attending Mount Holyoke College from 1925 to 1929, Apgar majored in zoology with minors in both physiology and chemistry, working hard to achieve her B.A. degree. In addition to her rigorous studies, she played violin in the school orchestra and lettered 11 times in athletics. Though she received scholarships to partially finance her education, she was also employed in various jobs, such as librarian and dining-service waitress, to pay expenses. Apgar even found time to serve as a reporter for the college newspaper.

While attending medical school at the Columbia University College of Physicians and Surgeons, she reportedly said that, in many respects, she found medical school easier than her undergraduate program. Graduating in 1933 with her M.D. degree, Apgar went on to do her internship in surgery at Presbyterian Hospital, New York.

Her internship lasted two years; however, Virginia Apgar was not to become a surgeon. Influenced by one of her professors, she became convinced that the surgical field was in many ways inaccessible to women. She was said to have remarked: "Women won't go to a woman surgeon. Only the Lord can answer that one." As a result, she switched to the field of anesthesiology, a specialty in its early stages of development. (Before becoming an area of medical specialization for physicians in the United States, anesthesiology was largely an area of expertise practiced during the early 20th century by nurses.) In 1937, having served her residency at the University of Wisconsin and at Bellevue Hospital, New York, Apgar was the 15th physician certified as an anesthesiologist by the American Board of Anesthesiology.

Upon her return to Columbia University in 1936, Apgar served as an instructor in anesthesiology. Two years later, she was promoted to assistant professor and served as head of the Department of Anesthesiology at Columbia-Presbyterian

Medical Center. She became an associate professor in 1942 and was the first woman to be promoted to full professor on Columbia's medical faculty in 1949. Apgar remained in this position until 1959, assisting in the training of over 250 physicians. During these years, she became in-

tensely interested in obstetrics, finding the delivery room one of the most fascinating places in the hospital. Personally involved in administering anesthesia to thousands of mothers, she also had many opportunities to observe obstetric procedures. Her concern for treatment needs of the newborn culminated in her development of the Apgar Scoring System.

After assisting in over 17,000 births at various New York and New Jersey hospitals, Apgar resigned her position as teacher and practitioner and returned to the classroom, this time as a student at Johns Hopkins University School of Hygiene and Public Health. In 1959, she earned her Master of Public Health degree. That same year, she was approached by The National Foundation-March of Dimes to become the head of its division on congenital malformations. Though she confessed to knowing little about birth defects, the foundation convinced her to accept the position, claiming that she "could learn" anything else she needed to know.

One of Apgar's roles as head of the division on congenital malformations was to distribute over five million dollars annually in the form of research grants to scientists studying birth defects. In addition, she wrote extensively, as well as lectured widely, about congenital malformations. Apgar has been credited with her outspoken views on the importance of good prenatal care, advocating healthy lifestyle choices for the expectant mother, including good diet, avoidance of most drugs and radiation, and protection from exposure to infections such as measles. During this time, she also authored many articles geared toward the general public that appeared in widely circulated magazines such as *Ladies Home Journal, Woman's Day,* and *Today's Health.*

In 1967, Apgar was promoted to vice president and director of basic research at The National Foundation. Her position involved extensive travel and the delivery of presentations throughout the world. In 1972, she co-authored the well-known book *Is My Baby All Right?* with syndicated-columnist **Joan Beck**. In the widely acclaimed publication, the authors discuss children "who are born with defects and disorders occurring before or at the time of birth that are serious enough to require special medical care and/or educational help and that will change the course of their lives and the lives of their families in major or minor ways."

In 1973, Apgar, appointed senior vice president for medical affairs, continued to research, supervise funding, and write prolifically in the areas of birth defects and the need for sound prenatal care. She also authored over 60 articles that appeared in medical journals. During her tenure with The National Foundation-March of Dimes, Apgar lectured in the fields of teratology (the study of abnormal functions) at Cornell Medical School and genetics at Johns Hopkins University. From 1965 to 1971, she was a member of the Methodist Board of Hospitals and Homes and an alumnae trustee of Mt. Holyoke College.

During her lifetime, Apgar received many honors. She was awarded honorary doctorates from Woman's Medical College of Pennsylvania, Mt. Holyoke College, New Jersey College of Medicine and Dentistry, and Boston University. She was a fellow of the American College of Anesthesiology and served as chair in 1951 and 1952. She was also a fellow of the New York Academy of Medicine, the American Public Health Association, and the New York Academy of Sciences. Her other professional affiliations included the American Academy of Pediatrics, American College of Obstetrics and Gynecology, American Pediatrics Society, American Eugenics Society, Congenital Anomalies Research Association of Japan, American Society of Human Genetics, Teratology Society, Pan-American Society for Anesthesiology, Alpha Omega Alpha, Sigma Delta Epsilon, the Irish-American Pediatric Society, and the Drug Information Association.

Apgar's professional accomplishments were extraordinary in both number and quality, yet she was known as a modest, down-to-earth woman who was not comfortable with celebrity. In addition to her professional achievements, she had other interests: stamp collecting, gardening, golf, and photography. Through the years, she never lost her passion for music and was a member of the Amateur Chamber Music Players and the Catgut Acoustical Society. She continued to play violin, viola, and cello, while also studying the art of constructing stringed instruments.

Virginia Apgar died on August 7, 1974, in New York City of an apparent pulmonary embolism. Her obituary in *Time* magazine described her as a "wise, industrious specialist."

SOURCES:

McHenry, Robert. *Liberty's Women.* Springfield, MA: G. & C. Merriam, 1980.

"Milestones." *Time.* August 19, 1974, p. 79.

Moritz, Charles, ed. *Current Biography Yearbook.* NY: H.W. Wilson, 1968.

SUGGESTED READING:

Apgar, Virginia, M.D., M.P.H., and Joan Beck. *Is My Baby All Right?* NY: Pocket Books, 1972.

———. "A Proposal for a New Method of Evaluations of the New Born Infant." in *Curr. Res. Anesth. Analg.* Vol. 32., no. 260, 1953.

RELATED MEDIA:

"Accomplished Women" (25 min.), Films, Inc., 1974.

Denise Hope Amschler, Ph.D., Professor of Health Science, Ball State University, Muncie, Indiana

Apostoloy, Electra (1911–1944)

*Greek Communist militant and anti-Nazi resistance
leader during World War II. Name variations: Ilektra
Apostolou. Born in 1911 in Iraklion-Attikis, a suburb of
Athens; executed on July 26, 1944; received secondary
education in a German-language school in Athens; married briefly to a doctor; children: daughter Agni.*

*A Communist, she was arrested by the political po-
lice and sentenced to two years' imprisonment for disseminating subversive "anti-Greek" literature (1936);
founded EPON (1943), a communist youth group; during final months of the Nazi occupation of Greece in
World War II, was arrested for her resistance activities;
after being tortured, she was executed (1944).*

Electra Apostoloy was born in 1911 in Iraklion-Attikis, a suburb of Athens. She received
her secondary education in a German-language
school in Athens. At age 13, she became a passionate Communist and joined the Greek Communist Youth League, a decision thta shocked
her middle-class parents. Revolutionary sentiments were strong in her generation, and her
brother Lefteris Apostoloy (1903–1981) became
an important Communist leader at the same
time. Electra Apostoloy formed a small group
that sent financial assistance to exiled Communists and their families.

From 1931 to 1933, she gained organizational experience as director of a factory workers' club. Remaining a Communist, she devoted
virtually all her time to revolutionary political
activity. Apostoloy taught classes on Marxism as
well as revolutionary history and theory to
working-class men and women. She also served
as editor of the Young Communist League journal *Youth*. In 1935, she represented the Greek
Communist movement as a delegate for Greek
women at the International Conference against
Fascism held in Paris. She traveled to several European countries to meet with Communists and
other anti-Fascist youth leaders. Back in Greece,
she spread the message that the growing threat
of Fascism was an enemy all working men and
women must fight.

In 1936, General Metaxas established a Fascist dictatorship in Greece, promising its conservative supporters to crack down hard on the
Marxist menace. The anti-Communist intelligence office in Athens regarded Electra Apostoloy as one of the most potentially dangerous
leaders of the younger generation of Communists. Shortly after Metaxas came to power, she
was arrested and sentenced to two years' imprisonment for disseminating subversive "anti-

Greek" literature. Unbroken in captivity, she
gave lectures to her fellow inmates. Apostoloy
had newspapers smuggled into her cell so that
she could remain informed of the worsening political situation in Greece and the world at large.

After a short period of freedom, she was arrested again in 1939 and sent to the distant town
of Anaphi. She had been married briefly to a
doctor who renounced his Communist beliefs
after arrest, ending their marriage. Her daughter
Agni was born in Anaphi during the end of that
relationship. The harsh conditions of her imprisonment exacerbated her deteriorating health,
and Electra was eventually transported to a
prison hospital in Athens. In 1941, she effected a
bold escape from this hospital.

By this time, German forces occupied
Greece, and it was difficult for Apostoloy to
evade capture. In the spring of 1941, patriotic
Greeks—incensed by their harsh treatment at the
Nazis' hands—began to actively resist. From
June 1942 to February 1943, Apostoloy led a resistance organization of young Greek anti-Fas-
cists who called themselves the "New Freedom"
group. A militant Marxist revolutionary, one of
her tasks was to weed out individuals likely to
succumb to Fascist blandishments or torture. In
1943, Apostoloy was instrumental in founding
EPON, the youth movement of EAM or National Liberation Front. The Communist Party created this liberation organization to lead Greeks of
all political colorations in a broad-based struggle
against Nazi occupiers and their Greek stooges.

In 1944, Apostoloy's luck ran out, and she
was arrested by the Greek version of the Gestapo.
Despite horrendous torture, she revealed nothing
about her organization or its members. When it
became obvious that she would never provide intelligence of any value, Apostoloy was executed
on July 26, 1944. Her brother Lefteris, himself a
leader in the Communist resistance movement,
was also arrested by the Germans. He escaped
and was never recaptured, living until his death in
Athens in November 1981 at the age of 78. In
honor of his martyred sister, Lefteris Apostoloy
named his daughter Electra.

SOURCES:

Chiclet, Christophe. *Les Communistes Grecs dans la
Guerre.* Paris: Editions L'Harmattan, 1987.

Eudes, Dominique. *The Kapetanios: Partisans and Civil
War in Greece, 1943–1949.* NY: Monthly Review,
1972.

Fourtouni, Eleni. *Greek Women in Resistance: Journals,
Oral Histories.* New Haven, CT: Thelphini Press,
1986.

Hondros, John Louis. *Occupation and Resistance: The
Greek Agony, 1941–44.* NY: Pella Publishing, 1983.

Judt, Tony, ed. *Resistance and Revolution in Mediter-ranean* Europe, 1939–1948. *London: Routledge, 1989.*

John Haag, Associate Professor of History, University of Georgia, Athens, Georgia

Apphia
Biblical woman.

A Christian at Colossae mentioned in the ad-dress of the letter to Philemon (Philemon 2), sup-posed by some to have been the wife of Philemon.

Applebee, Constance (1873–1981)

English-born coach and promoter of field hockey who founded the U.S. Field Hockey Association, pub-lished and edited the first American magazine devot-ed to women's sports, and advanced the development of women's athletics. Name variations: Connie, "The Apple." Born Constance Mary Katherine Applebee in Chigwall, Essex, England, on June 4, 1873; died in Burley, Hampshire, England, on January 26, 1981; graduated from the British College of Physical Educa-tion in London; never married; no children.

Traveled to United States to study at Harvard University (1901); founded the American Field Hock-ey Association (AFHA, 1901); appointed director of athletics at Bryn Mawr College (1904); founded the U.S. Field Hockey Association (USFHA), superseding the AFHA (1922); edited and published The Sports-woman, *the first sports magazine for American women (1922); inducted into the U.S. Field Hockey Association Hall of Fame and the International Women's Sports Hall of Fame; received the Distin-guished Service Award of the American Association for Health, Physical Education, and Recreation, and the Award of Merit of the Association of Intercolle-giate Athletics for Women.*

Fragile health in childhood may have been responsible for Constance Applebee's lifelong dedication to women's athletics. From the time of her birth, in Chigwall, Essex, England, on June 4, 1873, she was considered a delicate child and kept from attending school with other chil-dren. Applebee studied privately with a neigh-boring cleric whose lessons included Greek and Latin. The notion that physical exercise could improve poor health was considered controver-sial at the time, but as Applebee grew older she took the idea to heart and began to exercise, with such positive results that she became con-vinced of the importance of physical education to women's well being.

In the summer of 1901, Applebee was 29 years old and a graduate of the British College of Physical Education in London when she came to the United States to study with Dr. Dudley A. Sargent at Harvard University. A fellow class-mate, **Harriet Ballintine,** was director of athlet-ics at nearby Vassar College and asked Applebee to demonstrate the game of field hockey to their class. Although practically unknown in the Unit-ed States, field hockey had been wildly popular in the British Isles as a women's team sport since the 1880s, not long after Lady **Margaret Hall** began playing the game. The Moseley Ladies' Hockey Club had been organized in 1887, fol-lowed by the Wimbledon Ladies' Hockey Club in 1889 (the oldest women's hockey club still in existence), and the Irish Ladies' Hockey Union (the first women's national hockey union) in 1894. Shortly after Ballintine's request for a demonstration of the game, Applebee took the group out behind the gymnasium, where she ex-plained that field hockey consisted of two teams of 11 members each, and that the object of the game was to knock the ball into the netted goal of the opposing team. Armed with wands and a dumbbell, the only implements available as sub-stitutes for hockey equipment, Applebee then demonstrated the sport.

When Ballintine's enthusiasm for field hock-ey led her to ask Applebee to remain in the Unit-ed States to introduce the sport to American col-lege women, an 80-year career that would change the public perception of women on the playing field was launched. In 1901, along with ***Senda Berenson,** and **Lucille Eaton Hill,** Apple-bee founded the American Field Hockey Associ-ation (AFHA) to promote the game. Berenson was physical education director at Smith Col-lege, and Hill held the same position at Welles-ley, two of the most prestigious women's colleges in the country. Already a pioneer in American women's sports, having modified Naismith's basketball rules for use by girls and women, Berenson chaired the committee that edited the rules for basketball published by the American Sports Publishing Company in 1901. The three women now teamed up to accomplish the same program for field hockey, drawing up the rules of the game and founding an athletic association to monitor it.

As Applebee began traveling from campus to campus, teaching women to play America's newest competitive sport, her first challenge was to locate equipment. After much searching, she finally found 22 hockey sticks and a cricket ball in A.G. Spalding's New York store, virtually the

Opposite page

*C*onstance
*A*pplebee

only field hockey equipment in the country, which she lugged to Vassar, Bryn Mawr, Wellesley, Smith, Mount Holyoke, and Radcliffe, where many signed up to learn to play the new sport. The involvement of women in team sports was still controversial at the time, even among those who considered themselves open-minded. Luther Halsey Gulick, an educational progressive of the era, summed up the typical attitude toward women's participation in team sports:

> I believe . . . that athletics for women should for the present be restricted to sport within the school; that they should be used for recreation and pleasure; that the strenuous training of teams tends to be injurious to both body and mind; that public, general competition emphasizes qualities that are on the whole unnecessary and undesirable. Let us then have athletics for recreation, but not for serious, public competition.

Applebee, however, believed that if competitive athletics taught men teamwork and sportsmanship while building their character, it would do the same for women. Her coaching outlook was always both enthusiastic and innovative. Before she turned her attention to the students of elite New England women's colleges, she had worked with London street urchins and the uneducated. At a YWCA class comprised of factory women, her charges were a loud and undisciplined mob more interested in talking to each other than doing physical exercise. Facing them cheerfully, Applebee would urge, "Come now, I want all to take hands and run as fast as you can to the other end of the gym, shouting as loud as you can!" She then kept the group running and shouting until they were physically exhausted and ready to sit down and be instructed about participating in sports.

In 1904, Applebee ceased traveling from campus to campus when she was invited to become director of athletics at Bryn Mawr College in Pennsylvania, where her program became a national model for the teaching of physical education throughout America. It was a period of profound social change as well as considerable controversy, much of it revolving around the acceptable behavior of women. While it was generally accepted by then that women benefitted from physical exercise, few supported their public participation in sports. Instructions for constructing a high-school playground sum up the prevailing mindset: "The playground of older girls should, if possible, be screened from public view by building, shrubs, or vines." Meanwhile, technology was changing traditional concepts about women and sports. The bicycle craze that began in the late 19th century brought women as

well as men out in the open air; and the Industrial Revolution was funneling more women into factory jobs, creating the notion that women were as capable as men in industry. The introduction of electricity, canned foods, refrigeration, and household gadgets freed women from some onerous household chores, giving many of them time to participate in sports. Constance Applebee began organizing women's field hockey teams at a time when many were ready to be participants.

At the start, however, a great deal of Applebee's energy went into changing accepted norms, particularly regarding women's hockey uniforms. Most of the first women to participate in sports in the 19th century were upper-class and dressed for playing tennis, hockey, or lacrosse with the same elaborate preparations they spent on attending a cotillion; this meant wearing tight corsets, long skirts, and multiple petticoats. Since such garb could make playing more difficult, if not actually dangerous, Applebee began to promote sensible sports clothes for women, first by concentrating on skirt lengths and doing away with petticoats. The field hockey rules she wrote in 1903 mandated that "the hockey skirt should be plainly made and . . . six inches from the ground all the way round." Furthermore, the rules stated, "Petticoats should not be worn, but knickerbockers . . . fastening at the knee, [should] be substituted." Eventually knee-length bloomers or baggy pants worn with long stockings and a loose-fitting "middy" blouse with a large, navy-style collar became a standard athletic costume. Freed of physical restraints, women were quick to recognize the physical benefits of comfortable social apparel, and the clothing revolution had consequences that reached far beyond the playing field. Applebee's continual lobbying for sensible sportswear ultimately helped change the way women dressed in everyday life—one of the most profound transformations in the 20th century.

In addition to founding 25 hockey teams, Applebee organized 50 teams to play interclass competitive basketball, and she introduced water polo, track, tennis, swimming, fencing, archery, and badminton to the Bryn Mawr campus. "The Apple," as her students fondly called her, wanted students to play from the "varsity to the lowest class team, with all their heart." Testing strength and skill against the abilities of others was important, and fairness was central to any game. Applebee or another instructor umpired every game, assisted by four students. Three whistles on every foul was the rule, and she expected the whistles of all umpires to sound in unison. Applebee particularly excelled as a hockey coach. Wrote **Cynthia Wesson:**

> It is hard to describe for those who have never experienced it, Miss Applebee's genius as a hockey coach. She can take twenty-two players who have literally never seen a game or a stick. She can teach the rudiments of skill in hitting and stopping the ball, and the fundamentals of how a team works to score goals; and in less than half an hour she has her players playing hockey! . . . It is impossible to be coached by Miss Applebee without being stimulated to do one's best, without leaving the field wanting to play more and better hockey.

Applebee's activities on campus were not limited to coaching. For Bryn Mawr's annual Elizabethan May Day program, she trained students in the Morris and country dances, and she sometimes served as festival director, supervising the work of putting on the plays and seeing that hundreds of authentic historical costumes were sewn for the event. In 1910, when Bryn Mawr established one of the earliest college health departments, Applebee worked closely with the college doctor in overseeing the general health and well-being of the students. When a group of students founded the College News in 1915, she served as faculty advisor for five years until the publication was firmly established. To resolve the rivalry existing between two religious groups on campus, Applebee became involved in her students' spiritual welfare, encouraging the groups to disband in order to form a united Christian Association.

Constance Applebee never married, but she had many devoted friends. Shortly after Applebee's appointment as athletic director at Bryn Mawr in 1904, **Mary Warren Taylor** joined her staff, serving as secretary to the Department of Athletics and Gymnastics. Equally enthusiastic about women's sports, Taylor operated as Applebee's assistant and major supporter. When Taylor's health began to fail in 1929, Applebee withdrew from many campus activities to care for her friend until Taylor's death in 1936.

In 1922, Applebee extended her activities beyond the Bryn Mawr Campus by launching *The Sportswoman,* America's first magazine devoted to women's athletics. With articles about lacrosse, fencing, archery, swimming, bowling, skating, and field hockey, the magazine was an innovative step in an era when the public had only recently accepted women's participation in sports. During the ten years Applebee edited and published *The Sportswoman,* it was a thriving publication, reaching a wide audience of college coaches and students as well as women who belonged to sports clubs. Once she no longer had the time to devote to it, the magazine floundered and eventually failed, but not before Applebee had demonstrated that there was a market for sports publications for women.

Throughout her career, Constance Applebee worked to expand field hockey beyond the confines of a few Eastern women's colleges. In 1922, she organized the Pocono Hockey Camp in Pennsylvania, importing coaches from England to teach the sport. This summer camp quickly grew from 300 to include over 1,000 participants. Physical education teachers as well as high school, college, and club players came to learn more about field hockey. During the one- or two-week sessions, athletes enjoyed companionship and competition. The Pocono Hockey Camp provided an opportunity for women to create their own sports world and to form important networks. This was especially true for physical education teachers from small, isolated towns. A model for summer sports camps, the Pocono Hockey Camp played an important role in the development of women's athletics in the United States.

By the 1920s, many colleges sponsored women's hockey. Thousands of junior and senior high-school students also played the game, as well as over 50,000 club sports players. By 1922, Applebee decided the expanded number of players required a new organization. She presided over a meeting of 100 women in Philadelphia that determined that the American Field Hockey Association had outlived its usefulness, and replaced it with the United States Field Hockey Association (USFHA). Because the sport had by then gained worldwide popularity among women, the role of the new association was to promote the game both internationally and nationally, as well as sponsor tournaments and monitor games. Applebee's goal was for the new organization to function as a peacemaker as well as a sports organization, fostering international goodwill, and for this reason she decided that the USFHA would recognize no champions because unbridled competition "might destroy the friendly atmosphere among players and nations."

Although Constance Applebee eventually became an American citizen, she returned to England annually, maintaining close ties with her native country. With the onset of World War II in England, her idealistic notion of sports were sorely tested. In 1939, Adolf Hitler's Blitzkrieg swept across Europe, and Nazi troops occupied country after country; only the English Channel saved Great Britain from a similar fate. Determined to conquer the British Isles, Hitler's Luftwaffe began raining bombs on heavily populated cities, killing thousands. In the United States, a strong sentiment for neutrality prevailed as Americans were not anxious to become involved in another European conflict following the experience of World War I. Unwilling to accept this neutral stance for the USFHA, Applebee determined to employ the sport of hockey in defense of her homeland. In the early fall of 1940, she appealed to all American hockey players, past and present, to help the British. Individuals and clubs rallied to her cause. Applebee's fundraising goal had been to purchase one ambulance to aid her compatriots, but her appeal was so well received that three were sent to Britain, focusing attention on the Battle of Britain during a time when much of American public opinion remained neutral.

When World War II ended, Applebee was in her 70s. She remained active as a hockey coach, tirelessly advocating the sport even in old age. At 90, she was still at summer camp, prodding and scolding players. She continued to return to Britain for annual visits, but during a sojourn there in 1967, at age 94, her doctor ordered her to remain because of failing eyesight. She took up residence in a cottage bordering on the New Forest. In advanced age, Applebee continued to live alone. Though largely confined to an electric wheelchair for the last five or six years of her life, she managed to get around her house and garden until her death at 107.

In her late years, Applebee's contributions to women's sports were increasingly recognized. She was inducted into the U.S. Field Hockey Association Hall of Fame and into the International Women's Sports Hall of Fame. She received the Distinguished Service Award of the American Association for Health, Physical Education, and Recreation, and the Award of Merit of the Association of Intercollegiate Athletics for Women. When Constance Applebee died, on January 26, 1981, *The Times* of London summed up her remarkable life: "She had a strong belief in Christian day to day living and the lessons of give and take, working with others, initiative, concentration, endurance, sportsmanship, friendship, fun, and fitness."

SOURCES:

"Constance Applebee," in *The New York Times.* January 28, 1981, sec. B, p. 5.

Davidson, Judith A. "Applebee, Constance M.K." in *Sports Encyclopedia North America.* Vol. II. Edited by John D. Windhausen. Gulf Breeze, FL: Academic International Press, 1988, pp. 167–168.

Howell, Reet. *Her Story in Sports: A Historical Antholo-gy of Women in Sports.* West Point, NY: Leisure Press, 1982.

Lee, Mabel. *Memories Beyond Bloomers.* Washington: American Alliance for Health, Physical Education, and Recreation, 1978.

"Miss Constance Applebee. Pioneer in women's hockey," in *The Times* [London]. January 28, 1981, p. 16.

Wesson, Cynthia. "Miss C.M.K. Applebee. A Sketch of Forty Years of Service," in *Research Quarterly.* Supplement, vol XII, no. 3, October 1941, pp. 696–699.

Karin Loewen Haag,
freelance writer, Athens, Georgia

Appolus, Libertine (b. 1940).

See Amathila, Libertine Appolus.

Apponyi, Geraldine (1915—)

Queen of Albania. Name variations: Countess Apponyi. Born in Hungary in 1915; daughter of Gladys Stewart Girrault of New York City and Count Julius Nagi-Apponyi of Hungary; married King Zog I, king of Albania (1895–1961), on April 27, 1938; children: one son.

Geraldine Apponyi was working as a clerk in the souvenir shop of the Budapest National Museum before she married King Zog of Albania and became a queen in 1938. One year later, the royals fled their country with their two-day-old son. They lived in England and Egypt during World War II. Deposed by the Communists after the war, the family resided in France.

Apréleva, Elena Ivanovna (1846–1923)

Russian author. Name variations: Apreleva; (pseudonym) E. Ardov. Born in 1846 in St. Petersburg, Russia; died in 1923 in Belgrade, Yugoslavia; married.

Author of short fiction and novels, including Guilty but Guiltless *(1877) and* Quick Sketches *(1893).*

Elena Apréleva was born in 1846 to a Greek mother and a French geodesist (a technique of applied math to determine size, shape, and properties of the earth) in the Russian army, who raised their daughter in an affluent and cultivated St. Petersburg home. In her early 20s, Apréleva began a publishing career, producing books for children. Encouraged by author Ivan Turgenev, who was then experiencing his greatest writing period, Apréleva turned to fiction for adults in the 1870s. Under the pseudonym E. Ardov, her first novel and short story were both published in 1877; over the years, these were fol-lowed by a number of short, moralistic, heavily detailed stories. In 1890, Apréleva moved with her husband to Central Asia, which would be her home until her death. Continuing her writing, in 1893 she saw her stories collected in *Quick Sketches.* Apréleva died in 1923 while visiting Belgrade.

Crista Martin,
Boston, Massachusetts

Aptheker, Bettina (1944—)

American sociologist and feminist. Born in 1944; daughter of Herbert Aptheker (a Marxist historian).

While Bettina Aptheker taught women's studies at San Jose State University and at the University of California at Santa Clara, she gained recognition in the protest and feminist movements in the United States during the 1960s. She was also one of the directors of the American Institute for Marxist Studies. Her early publications were related to protest within the academic world and included *FSM* (Free Speech Movement), with Robert Kaufman and Michael Folson (1965), *Big Business and the American University* (1966), and the bibliography *Higher Education and the Student Rebellion in the United States* (1969). In 1972, she wrote a Marxist appraisal, *The Academic Rebellion.*

Aptheker explored her concern over the radical aspects of the civil-rights movement in a 1971 collaboration with her father, Marxist historian Herbert Aptheker, entitled *Racism and Reaction in the United States.* That same year, she teamed up with *Angela Davis for *If They Come in the Morning: Voices of Resistance.* Later, Aptheker wrote an account and analysis of the Davis trial, *The Morning Breaks* (1975). More recent historical studies include *Woman's Legacy: Interpretative Essays in US History* (1980).

Apulia, duchess of.

See Aubrey of Buonalbergo (fl. 1000s).
See Sichelgaita of Salerno (1040–1090).

Aquash, Anna Mae (1945–1976)

Native American, Micmac activist. Name variations: Anna Mae Pictou; Annie Mae. Born March 27, 1945, in Shubenacadie, Nova Scotia, Canada; murdered on February 24, 1976, on Pine Ridge Indian Reservation, South Dakota; third daughter of Mary Ellen Pictou and Frances Levi; attended Wheelock College; scholarship to Brandeis University (unused); married Jake Maloney (Micmac), in 1962 (later divorced); married

Nogeeshik Aquash (an Ojibwa artist), 1973, at Pine Ridge; children: (first marriage) two daughters.

Anna Mae Pictou Aquash knew from first-hand experience how poverty could devastate Native tribes. Born on the Micmac reserve in Nova Scotia, Aquash became a determined and dedicated worker on behalf of Indian rights at an early age. She attended school in Nova Scotia and, at 17, married tribal member Jake Maloney. They had two daughters before divorcing.

In the early 1960s, Aquash moved to Boston where she became active on the Boston Indian Council, a group established to aid Native American alcoholics. She also was employed as a social worker in the predominately black area of Boston called Roxbury. It was during her early years as an activist that she developed her vision for "A People's History of the Land," an assemblage of the cultural history of Indian people from the Indian point of view.

Aquash's dream was not to be. In 1970, her life took a decided turn when she met Russell Means, a charismatic, outspoken organizer for the American Indian Movement (AIM). Formed in 1968, the organization sought to address problems of Native Americans and to rekindle a sense of tribal identity both in urban Indian centers and on the reservations. Unfortunately, the conservative administration of Richard Nixon took a dim view of AIM and put the group under FBI surveillance.

From 1970 until her murder in 1976, Aquash was a tireless organizer. She crisscrossed the country organizing on behalf of AIM and participating in demonstrations like the Mayflower II Thanksgiving Day protest and the Trail of Broken Treaties, which was staged in 1972. The following year, Aquash left her "day job" as a factory worker at the General Motors plant in Framingham, Massachusetts, to travel to the Oglala Nation's Pine Ridge Reservation at Wounded Knee, South Dakota. There, she married Ojibwa artist and fellow activist Nogeeshik Aquash, in a traditional ceremony performed by Wallace Black Elk.

In 1975, the strain between the FBI and AIM took a deadly turn. Because more than 60 Indians had been mysteriously killed, tensions on the Pine Ridge Reservation ran high. In a final confrontation, with AIM members believing they were under siege, two FBI agents were killed. Because Aquash was among the activists in residence at the time, federal authorities grilled her about the killings. Though later re-leased, she told close friends that she believed herself to be a target. Five months later, Aquash disappeared.

On February 24, 1976, the body of an unidentified female was discovered in a ditch on the Pine Ridge Reservation. Authorities, who originally identified the body, dismissed the case as "routine," claiming the woman had died of "exposure" probably due to alcohol abuse. A second autopsy, however, not only identified the woman as Anna Mae Aquash, but the report also revealed that she had been raped and shot in the head, execution style, with a .38 caliber pistol. Though an investigation was ordered and a grand jury convened to look into links between the FBI and the events surrounding the Aquash murder, the results were never released. The case of Anna Mae Aquash remains unsolved.

SOURCES:

Brand, Johanna. *The Life and Death of Anna Mae Aquash.* Toronto: James Lorimer, 1978.

Matthiessen, Peter. *In the Spirit of Crazy Horse.* NY: Viking Press, 1983 (revised and updated, Penguin Press, 1992).

Weir, David, and Lowell Bergman. "The Killing of Anna Mae Aquash," in *Rolling Stone.* April 7, 1977, pp. 51–55.

Deborah Jones,
freelance writer, Studio City, California

Aquino, Corazon (1933—)

Philippine political leader and president of the Philippines from 1986 to 1992, who led a quiet revolution that overthrew the hated Marcos regime without a single shot. Name variations: Cory. Born Maria Corazon Cojuangco on January 25, 1933, in Tarlac Province, the Philippines; sixth of eight children; daughter of José Cojuangco and Demetria "Metring" Sumulong (daughter of Juan Sumulong, a nationally known Philippine senator; the Sumulongs, were among the wealthiest landowners of Rizal Province); educated at an exclusive girls' school in Manila; finished her education at two Roman Catholic convent schools—Raven Hill Academy in Philadelphia and Notre Dame School in New York City; graduated from Mount St. Vincent College with a major in French, 1953; married Benigno Aquino, Jr. (1932–1983), on October 11, 1954; children: five.

Before becoming a major opponent of Ferdinand Marcos, served as dutiful political wife while husband Benigno Aquino, Jr. served as mayor, senator, and governor; her husband and thousands of the opposition arrested (1972); became speaker for Benigno, lobbying for his release; when her husband was released from prison for reasons of health, family went into exile in

United States (1980); determined to return to his country, Benigno was murdered as he stepped off the plane (August 21, 1983); became her husband's surrogate, leading a revolution in the streets that ousted the Marcos regime; sworn in as president (February 25, 1986); cleaned up corruption, instituted land reform, and rewrote the constitution; opposition to her term of office continued and six coups were staged against her administration; despite immense challenges, brought the Philippines through troubled times leaving a more stable democracy when her term ended (1992).

Corazon Aquino was born into an elite group of landowning oligarchs who have dominated the Philippine Islands since Spanish colonial rule. Her family's wealth was based on commercial and banking interests as well as a vast sugar plantation of over 18,000 acres. Her maternal grandfather, Juan Sumulong, served in the Philippine Senate while her father and brother served in the nation's House of Representatives. Although her early education was at an exclusive girls' school in Manila, she finished her education in America at Raven Hill Academy in Philadelphia and Notre Dame School in New York City. She graduated from Mount St. Vincent College with a major in French in 1953.

During a summer vacation in the Philippines, Cory met Benigno Aquino, Jr. (1932–1983), a dynamic young journalist. "Ninoy," as he was nicknamed, did not initially make an impression on the quiet young woman. He wrote her frequently during her senior year in college, and only after she returned home following graduation did the attraction become mutual. Corazon began studying law at Far Eastern University in Manila before she agreed to marry him. Following the wedding on October 11, 1954, she abandoned her career plans and dropped out of law school. Her life settled into the predictable pattern of a member of the Philippine elite. Five children and social duties occupied her time. A gracious host, Cory Aquino spoke unaccented English, the Philippine national language Tagalog, as well as French, Spanish, and Japanese. One of her close friends characterized her as the "classic Oriental wife." Her favorite pastimes were cooking, knitting, and cultivating bonsai trees. Deeply religious, she frequently attended mass.

From the outset, Corazon Aquino was a political wife. Benigno was elected mayor of his hometown at age 22. Six years later, he became governor of Tarlac Province. In 1966, Benigno was elected to the Philippine Senate, becoming the youngest senator in the nation's history. That same year, he was chosen secretary general of the Liberal Party, which made him a leader of the political opposition to the Marcos administration. A figure of national stature, Benigno was the youngest war correspondent, presidential assistant, mayor, vice-governor, governor and senator in Philippine history. An idealist, he believed his country needed major reforms. Although Benigno was a member of the landowning elite, he thought his country could not prosper when less than 100 families controlled most of the national wealth. Calling himself a "radical rich guy," he gave away pieces of his land to field and factory workers, unusual behavior in a feudal society.

By the late 1960s, rural and urban discontent was growing. The Ferdinand Marcos regime alienated many of the nation's young people, some of whom began to see violent revolution as the only alternative to the existing social and political order. Benigno Aquino was seen as an alternative to the corrupt government. As the 1973 presidential elections drew closer, Ferdinand and *Imelda Marcos felt threatened by the young leader's growing popularity. Using an expanding Communist guerrilla insurgency as a pretext, Ferdinand Marcos declared martial law on September 23, 1972. Benigno Aquino was immediately arrested as a subversive, largely because Marcos feared he would win the upcoming presidential election. Over 6,000 student activists, journalists, broadcasters, politicians, and entrepreneurs were also thrown into prisons and concentration camps.

Her husband's arrest shocked Corazon Aquino, who had only known a life of ease and affluence. Suddenly, she was her imprisoned husband's sole link to the outside world. She began holding press conferences for reporters who were willing to risk their jobs and lives to maintain the semblance of a free press. Her husband suffered a harsh imprisonment. He endured long stretches in solitary confinement, and his clothing hung on a near-skeletal frame. After one of his articles was smuggled out and published in a Bangkok newspaper, Benigno Aquino was transferred to a high-security facility north of Manila where conditions deteriorated. A neon light burned day and night in a room that was completely bare except for a steel bed without a mattress.

Whenever Corazon visited the prison, she was subjected to humiliating strip searches. Friends abandoned her. The outside world, especially the United States, seemed completely uninterested in Benigno's fate. The American govern-

Corazon Aquino

ment regarded the Marcos coup as an anti-Communist measure, justified by the red menace. Locked in mortal combat with North Vietnamese in 1972, Washington was unwilling to risk essential air and naval bases in the Philippines because a few members of the political op-

position were imprisoned. Conventional wisdom held that American interests would best be served if the United States did not attempt to comment on or characterize internal developments in the Philippines. Separated from her husband and abandoned by her friends, Aquino was bitter that the American government turned a deaf ear to her pleas for intervention.

Corazon Aquino did win allies, however. One was Robert Trent Jones, Jr., the renowned American golf-course architect. Jones had met the Aquino family in the Philippines in the 1960s when he constructed a golf course on the family estate. Described by one of his Yale classmates as "a humanist as well as basically conservative," Jones had a strong sense of justice. He began to lobby for Benigno Aquino in Washington even when a Marcos-controlled court sentenced Aquino to death in 1977. Jones was joined in his efforts by **Patricia (Patt) Murphy Derian**, assistant secretary of state for human rights under President Jimmy Carter. A civil-rights activist in the 1960s in the American South, Patt Derian was convinced that major human-rights abuses were commonplace in the Philippines. During a trip there in early 1978, she visited Benigno Aquino, now imprisoned more than five years. His quiet manner dramatically refuted State Department and CIA reports depicting him as a rich playboy who was an adventurer of dubious character. She described him as "somebody of monumental stature. Intellectually and in terms of democracy. Like Churchill. A giant." Patt Derian and Trent Jones' support meant a great deal to Corazon Aquino who despaired that her husband would ever be freed.

When Benigno Aquino's health deteriorated dramatically because of a serious heart problem in 1980, he was finally released. Ferdinand and Imelda Marcos were fearful he might die and become a martyr while in detention, so he and his family were allowed to go to the United States where Benigno had triple bypass surgery. After recovering, he accepted academic positions at both Harvard University and the Massachusetts Institute of Technology. Aquino was greatly relieved to be back in the United States where she resumed her role as wife and mother. For the first two years of their American sojourn, Benigno was happy with his role in academia, but gradually he resumed his interest in politics. By the end of 1982, he was openly discussing the possibility of returning to the Philippines. Parliamentary elections were scheduled for May 1984 and Benigno hoped to return home to restore the democratic institutions destroyed by the Marcos regime. His plan was to act as a mediator and facilitator between the Marcos regime and the opposition, rather than to run for office himself.

Ferdinand and Imelda Marcos did not want the Aquinos back in the Philippines. In May 1983, Imelda Marcos met Benigno Aquino in New York and warned him not to return. When she failed to deter him, she tried bribery, offering to set up a business for the family in the United States. This encounter made Benigno Aquino more determined than ever to return to his country. Corazon supported him, despite the fact that she was quite happy in exile. A few days before his departure in August 1983, he remarked proudly to a friend, "Isn't she a remarkable lady? If it were some women, they would be crying and begging me not to go home. But she hasn't said a word."

Benigno Aquino announced he would return on August 7, 1983. Manila authorities countered by refusing to issue passports to his family and then revived the old charges against him. Determined to return, he booked a flight on China Air Lines flight 811 scheduled to land in Manila on August 21, 1983. He knew he risked his life by returning but believed that the presence of reporters on the plane offered some protection. Just before the plane began its descent, he slipped into a bulletproof vest remarking, "If they hit me in the head, I'm a goner." A squad of uniformed soldiers escorted Benigno off the plane. As he was about to step on Philippine soil, a single bullet penetrated his skull, killing him instantly. A fusillade of bullets followed. The bullet-riddled body of Rolando Galman fell a few feet from Benigno. Later the government claimed that Galman was a notorious subversive with links to the Communists and the insurgent New People's Army and accused him of assassinating the popular leader.

Like her fellow Filipinos, Corazon Aquino was shocked by her husband's murder. She quickly flew to Manila. Few believed the government's story about Galman and many were convinced that the highest echelons of the Marcos government had ordered the killing. Suddenly the streets of Manila were awash in yellow. Traditionally a symbol for the return of prisoners, yellow was transformed into a color of protest. The martyr's body lay in state in his family home in the Manila suburb of Quezon City, and over 100,000 men, women, and children paid their respects. All ages and social classes were represented, the poor arriving in the gaudy jeepneys unique to the Philippines, the rich in their chauffeured cars. The day the casket was taken to a nearby church, despite the oppressive heat and humidity, hundreds of thousands followed the hearse in a solemn procession.

Cory Aquino presided over her husband's funeral with calm and dignity. The housewife who had gratefully slipped into near-anonymity in 1980 now resumed the public role she had played during Benigno's years of imprisonment. In the months that followed, she always wore yellow—a powerful symbol of her husband's tragically aborted struggle for democracy. Speaking frequently before crowds, she gained confidence, and her leadership role increased. In the May 1984 parliamentary elections, she pleaded for all factions to be included. But the Marcos regime with its usual "guns, goons and gold" made a mockery of Philippine democracy, "winning" 89 out of 143 seats. Nonetheless, the opposition under Corazon Aquino's leadership made a surprisingly good showing.

As Corazon Aquino's political leadership grew stronger, Ferdinand Marcos' grew weaker. His health collapsed in 1983; with kidney transplants and dependency on dialysis, his once prodigious energies were permanently impaired. Now Imelda Marcos ruled the country, in close alliance with a group of generals and wealthy landowners. Although martial law had ostensibly been ended in 1981, President Marcos continued to rule arbitrarily by decree. These powers were becoming increasingly irrelevant, however, as economic crisis radicalized middle-class intellectuals and illiterate peasants alike. Increasingly, Filipinos joined the "Parliament of the Streets" or joined the revolutionary New People's Army (NPA). Pressure against the Marcos regime increased. In 1985, a panel investigated Benigno Aquino's murder, implicating General Fabian C. Ver and other military leaders in his assassination. In October, Marcos announced a "snap election" for February 1986 to reestablish legitimacy for his regime.

Corazon Aquino continued her quiet leadership role. Although she did not preside over a tested political machine, she did lead the Laban ("People Power") organization. Over 1.2 million men and women petitioned so that she could run in the snap election against Marcos. At first, Aquino was reluctant to run for the presidency, but the acquittal in December 1985 of General Ver and others implicated in her husband's murder raised public indignation to new heights and forced her hand. She formed a ticket with Salvador Laurel, a politician from the Unido organization who had broken with Marcos in 1980. Aquino's campaign got off to a slow start. She lacked confidence and was poorly informed about basic issues. Marcos and his running-mate Arturo Tolentino began to make patronizing jokes about women running for public office. This disparagement of her attempts to bring about social change galvanized Aquino. She put aside canned speeches provided by her staff and began to speak of her hopes for the future in simple, personal terms. Suddenly this "ordinary housewife" became a formidable opponent.

Election day, February 7, 1986, was marked by both violence (at least 30 died) and fraud. It was immediately apparent that the Marcos forces would steal the election. These plans were thwarted on February 9 when "weeping and fearful," wrote one reporter, "the Government computer workers arose from their terminals and, data disks in hand, darted from the Commission on Elections to make the charge that the Marcos Government was rigging the presidential vote." The frightened electoral workers found refuge in the Church of Our Mother of Perpetual Help, where a crowd soon assembled to support them. Although the Reagan administration had always supported the Marcos regime, this support began to erode. Allies in the U.S. embassy, the State Department, leading members of Congress, and influential conservatives like the columnist George Will began to speak openly of corruption in the Philippines.

This is a land of broken promises.

—Corazon Aquino

When Marcos declared victory with 53.8% of the vote, Corazon Aquino stood firm, declaring she had won 60 to 70% of the vote. Robert Trent Jones, a close friend of Senator Sam Nunn of Georgia, ranking Democrat of the Armed Services Committee, convinced the senator that America must break with the discredited regime. Nunn declared that Aquino had won the election that Ferdinand Marcos was attempting to steal "by massive fraud, intimidation and murder." On February 14, the Roman Catholic Church condemned the tainted, violence-ridden election, pointedly noting that a government that assumed or retained power "through fraudulent means has no moral basis." Task Force Detainees, a Catholic human-rights organization, noted that in 1985 they had tallied at least 276 executions of Marcos' political foes, 1,326 cases of torture, and 602 unexplained "disappearances." The Philippine Bishops' Conference, a conservative body, announced its support for Aquino, calling her campaign a "nonviolent struggle for justice."

On February 22, forces led by Defense Minister Juan Ponce Enrile and Lieutenant General Fidel V. Ramos, deputy chief of staff, seized important military bases. They demanded Marcos resign and turn power over to Aquino. Many feared for Corazon Aquino's safety so she retired to a Carmelite monastery where the nuns assured her that the Marcos troops would have to "kill all of us before they do anything to you." On the following day, February 23, a Sunday, thousands massed outside the two major military bases of Manila, effectively blocking Epifanio de los Santos Avenue (EDSA)—thus giving the revolution its name, the "EDSA Revolution." The large crowd included nuns, priests, young men and women, and a cross section of all classes. It behaved peacefully, bringing food and flowers to the anti-Marcos soldiers. Underscoring that this was not a military coup but the rightful restoration of democracy, General Ramos told the assembled throng that "what is happening is not a coup d'état but a revolution of the people."

Still unwilling to relinquish power, Ferdinand Marcos dispatched General Fabian Ver, implicated in Benigno Aquino's murder, to crush the revolt. But Ver's armored column was prevented from moving forward by thousands of unarmed people, including mothers with infants, women bearing flowers, and nuns and priests kneeling in prayer. Under the surveillance of worldwide television networks, the tanks could not move forward. The next day, February 24, helicopters sent to attack the rebel bases defected, joining the popular uprising. Large numbers of Air Force pilots joined them and soon rebel jets streaked across the sky. Hundreds of thousands of Filipinos continued to pack Manila's major thoroughfares. Sensing victory, Enrile declared the formation of a provisional government under Corazon Aquino. At this crucial moment, the Reagan administration finally abandoned Marcos.

Corazon Aquino was sworn in as president of the Philippines at mid-morning on February 25, 1986, at the Club Filipino, a prestigious social club in Manila's exclusive suburb of Greenhills. Wearing a yellow dress, she declared, "I am taking power in the name of the Filipino people," and pledged to head "a government dedicated to upholding truth and justice, morality and decency, freedom and democracy." Refusing to accept what had happened, Ferdinand Marcos staged a grotesque inaugural ceremony at the Malacanang Palace, which was literally surrounded by the angry people of Manila. Finally, Ferdinand and Imelda Marcos fled to Hawaii, taking large amounts of stolen money and goods.

Now president of the Philippines, Corazon Aquino formed a new government. Working out of a small, makeshift office, she appointed a cabinet of 17 members. As she strove for peace between all factions, her advisers included former Marcos loyalists like Enrile and Ramos as defense minister and chief of staff. Her other cabinet appointees were moderate to conservative businessmen and professionals. At the same time, she restored the right of habeas corpus and released more than 500 political prisoners, some of them linked to the Communist-led New People's Army (NPA). Aquino also released four NPA leaders as a gesture of national conciliation, angering both Enrile and Ramos. Determined to clean up the government, Aquino pressured the resignation of corrupt officials and dismantled entrenched Marcos institutions. Supreme Court justices and half of the nation's generals soon left government service. Mayors and provincial governors were replaced by individuals free of Marcos affiliations. The legal basis of her government also had to be addressed. The authoritarian Marcos constitution of January 1973 remained in force, and the National Assembly was packed with Marcos loyalists. Aquino realized she had her work cut out for her and told Cardinal Jaime Sin, "I can no longer be so humble because people don't take me seriously then, so I have to project my confidence even more than most men would."

On March 25, Aquino proclaimed a new provisional constitution and abolished the National Assembly as well as the office of prime minister. She assumed broad powers and governed by decree. Responding to critics, she argued Philippine society could be healed only by cutting out "the cancer in our political system." A temporary "freedom constitution" was enacted, which included a bill of rights and provisions of judicial review. A commission was appointed to draw up a permanent constitution within three months. By May, the president had met a small group of guerrillas who had responded to her call for national reconciliation and surrendered their weapons. Her initial stated strategy was to court the 20,000 insurgents in the Philippines with an offer of a six-month cease-fire and amnesty. After they laid down their weapons, job training, work on government-owned farms, and a lease on a small plot of land would be offered to the guerrillas. By August, meaningful negotiations were taking place, and, on November 27, a 60-day truce was signed between the government and the NPA. In July 1986, Marcos diehards attempted an uprising and tried to install Arturo Tolentino, Marcos' former vice-president, as "acting president." Although this amateurish coup was easily quashed, Aquino warned that it should "be understood that any incident like this will not be allowed to happen again."

By August 1986, President Aquino felt secure enough in her presidency to visit foreign capitals in Indonesia and Singapore. She then visited Washington, D.C., as well as several other major American cities. Relieved American officials who had shown concern about the stability of the Philippines now noted, "It became pretty clear that this was no ordinary housewife." Rapidly gaining self-confidence as her embattled nation's moral as well as political leader, Aquino compared her new role to the one she had played prior to February 1986: "Being President, when I have so many many forces under my control, is really that much easier. I'm no longer alone with only my friends and relatives helping me. It's really much easier when I compare my life now to what it was when my husband was in prison."

On July 27, 1987, Aquino gave up the power to rule by decree. During the previous months, she had signed 302 decrees, one of the most important was the creation of an Agrarian Reform Council to redistribute land. Despite these positive steps toward reform, the political landscape remained bleak and violent. Three separate military uprisings—in January, July, and August—tried to overthrow Aquino, arguing that she was "soft on Communism." The August 28 coup attempt was a serious rebellion in which more than 50 persons lost their lives. Political murder also reappeared on the scene. On August 2, the cabinet secretary for local government was murdered, while on September 19 a prominent leftist leader was assassinated. In neither case were the killers captured or identified. The efforts to open negotiations with the NPA ended in failure and guerrilla operations increased throughout 1987. NPA ambushes made life uncertain throughout much of the country and their organization was believed to control 20% of the country's 42,000 villages. The foreign debt problem remained acute, inhibiting economic growth, while uncertainty over the future of land reform acted as a damper on investment. A disillusioned Jaime Sin, who had played a key role in the revolutionary "people power" events of February 1986, commented: "We got rid of Ali Baba, but the forty thieves stayed behind."

Local elections in January 1988 gave some hope for future improvement. On June 10, Aquino signed into law a comprehensive agrarian reform program that set limits on the amount of agricultural land an individual could own. In her July 25 state of the nation address, Aquino asserted that 1988 "may be remembered as the year the insurgency was broken." Her optimism

was based on the capture of eight senior NPA commanders. The economy, however, continued to undermine many of Aquino's efforts. Forty-two percent of the national budget went to pay interest on foreign and domestic debts. Thirty million of the nation's population of 59 million lived in conditions of "absolute poverty." Nature was unkind as well. In October 1988, Typhoon Ruby killed about 500 people and destroyed $45 million worth of crops. Vice-President Laurel and Defense Secretary Enrile left the Aquino administration to launch a new opposition party, a move that engendered little popular support.

When Ferdinand Marcos died in exile in Hawaii in 1989, Corazon Aquino denied Imelda Marcos the right to return his body for burial, arguing that disruptive demonstrations might result. In addition to other disruptions, a serious attempt to overthrow her government erupted on December 1, when rebel troops bombed the presidential palace, seized military bases and television stations, and transformed sections of downtown Manila into war zones. Aquino waited until December 6 to declare a state of emergency and reshuffled her cabinet at the end of the month. An insoluble dilemma of her administration was the fact that the military was Aquino's biggest threat, while it was also her sole protector. A growing trade deficit and a double-digit inflation rate, the highest since the overthrow of Marcos, continued to plague the economy. Despite all these problems, Cory Aquino's personal honesty and quiet determination gained her wide public support. Economic growth continued, although wealth distribution was extremely unequal. Since the People Power revolution of 1986, middle-class support for the NPA had diminished and student militancy had significantly declined.

The Iraqi invasion of Kuwait in August 1990 was an economic disaster for the Philippines because of the loss of foreign exchange from Filipino workers in the Gulf as well as a doubling of the price of imported oil. A massive earthquake in July 1990 killed almost 2,000 north of Manila and was held responsible for a rapidly increasing budget deficit. In a last coup attempt against Aquino's rule, two army bases on Mindanao rose against the Manila government in October, a rebellion that was suppressed within two days. In September 1990, a Manila court convicted 16 military men of murdering Benigno Aquino, Jr., sentencing them all to life imprisonment but leaving unresolved the question of who ordered the murder. Nature continued to wreak havoc and in June 1991 Mt. Pinatubo erupted killing at least 800 and destroying the livelihood of 651,000 persons. The Clark Air Base and Subic Bay Naval Station began to close and by the fall of 1992, 80,000 Filipino jobs had been lost. In November 1991, an unrepentant Imelda Marcos returned to the Philippines to face criminal charges of graft and tax fraud. Although all were vexing, none of these crises destroyed Philippine democracy.

After six years as president, Cory Aquino announced she would not run again for office in 1992. Few leaders have faced as many difficulties as she during her term of office. Summing up many disappointments, she noted ruefully, "This is a land of broken promises." But coup attempts, volcanic eruptions, and economic woes did not deter this small, quiet woman during her tenure as president. Without her leadership, the Philippines could easily have lapsed into chaos and anarchy. When the general elections were held on May 11, 1992, they were peaceful and fair. Even the insurgency of the New People's Army appeared to be on the wane. Corazon Aquino brought democracy and the hope of economic reform to her country in troubled times. The Philippines owe much to her quiet decency and steely courage.

SOURCES:
Anderson, Harry. "Mutiny in Manila," in *Newsweek*. Vol. 110, no. 10. September 7, 1987, pp. 26–29.

Aquino, Benigno S., Jr. *Testament from a Prison Cell*. Manila: Benigno S. Aquino, Jr. Foundation, 1984.

"Aquino, Corazon," in *Current Biography Yearbook 1986*. NY: H.W. Wilson, pp. 16–20.

"Benigno Aquino," in Elizabeth Devine, ed. *The Annual Obituary 1983*. Chicago: St. James Press, 1984.

Bonner, Raymond. *Waltzing with a Dictator: The Marcoses and the Making of American Policy*. NY: Vintage Books, 1988.

———. "Washington's Philippines," in *New Yorker*. Vol. 65, no. 37. October 30, 1989, pp. 112–118.

Browne, Ray B., ed. *Contemporary Heroes and Heroines*. Detroit, MI: Gale Research, 1990.

Buss, Claude A. *Cory Aquino and the People of the Philippines*. Stanford, CA: Stanford Alumni Association, 1987.

Clines, Francis X. "Corazon Aquino: Putting It Together," in *The New York Times Biographical Service*. April 1986, pp. 543–545.

"Corazon Aquino," in *The New York Times Biographical Service*. December 1985, p. 1488.

Crisostomo, Isabelo T. *Cory: Profile of a President*. Quezon City: J. Kriz, 1986.

Fallows, James. "A Damaged Culture," in *Atlantic Monthly*. Vol. 260, no. 5. November 1987, pp. 49–54, 56–58.

Goodno, James B. *The Philippines: Land of Broken Promises*. London: Zed Books, 1991.

Harper, Peter, and Laurie Fullerton. *Philippines Handbook*. 2nd ed. Chico, CA: Moon Publications, 1994.

"Here I Am Only Two Days and You Are Expecting Miracles," in *Time*. Vol. 127, no. 10. March 10, 1986, p. 18.

Historic Documents of 1986. Washington, DC: Congressional Quarterly, 1987.

Joaquin, Nick. *The Aquinos of Tarlac: An Essay on History as Three Generations*. Manila: Cacho Hermanos, 1983.

Karnow, Stanley. *In Our Image: America's Empire in the Philippines*. NY: Random House, 1989.

Komisar, Lucy. *Corazon Aquino: The Story of a Revolution*. NY: George Braziller, 1987.

Mydans, Seth. "The Embattled Mrs. Aquino," in *The New York Times Magazine*. November 15, 1987, pp. 42–43.

Stewart, William. "An Interview with Corazon Aquino," in *Time*. Vol. 128, no. 12. September 22, 1986, p. 55.

Wilhelm, Maria, and Peter Carlson. "A Matter of Family Honor," in *People Weekly*. Vol. 25, no. 11. March 17, 1986, pp. 34–39.

John Haag, Associate Professor of History, University of Georgia, Athens, Georgia

Aquino, Iva d' (b. 1916).

See Toguri, Iva.

Aquino, Melchora (1812–1919)

Philippine heroine considered "Mother of the Philippine Revolution." Name variations: known as Matandang Sora or Tandang Sora. Pronunciation: Ah-KEEN-o. Born in barrio Banlat, Caloocan, Rizal (now part of Quezon City), on January 6, 1812; died in Pasong Tamo, in February or March 1919; daughter of Juan Aquino (a farmer) and Valentina de Aquino; married Fulgencio Ramos; children: Juan, Simon, Epifania (also seen as Estefania), Saturnina, Romualdo, and Juana.

Melchora Aquino led a normal life until she was well into her 80s, when she became a political revolutionary. In her early years, she was known in her village as a medicine woman who helped her neighbors with minor illnesses and injuries. Her marriage to Fulgencio Ramos (who would become a barrio captain) produced six children before Fulgencio's untimely death left her a widow. With a large family to support, she took over the management of the family farm and other business interests entrusted to her. Working the farm with 15 tenants, she produced enough rice and sugarcane to sustain her children to adulthood.

In the late 19th century, a movement for independence from Spain was growing in the Philippines after centuries of corrupt and indifferent Spanish colonial rule. Aquino became involved with a secret revolutionary society known as Katipunan (derived from K.K.K., Kataastaasan Kagalanggalangang Katipunan Ng Mga Anak Ng Bayan, or Highest and Most Respected Association of the Sons of the Country). Founded in July 1892 by Andres Bonifacio (1863–1897), a writer who had risen from extreme poverty, its goal was the unification of Filipinos into one nation, liberated from Spanish domination. Bonifacio's *Katipunan* advocated revolution, a concept that Aquino, now an old woman, also endorsed. When she became involved with the group, it had grown to almost 100,000 members.

Melchora Aquino, also known as Tandang Sora, sympathized with the rebels and let them use her store to hold meetings and to stock supplies and weapons. At first, her collaboration was not suspected because she was an old woman and considered harmless. But on an August evening in 1896, Bonifacio's rebel soldiers used her house for a rendezvous to plan the Philippine Revolution, which would free the country from Spanish rule in 1898. While Aquino was feeding the soldiers an evening meal, the *guardias civil*, led by a Filipino spy, invaded the meeting. Aquino and her family managed to escape to nearby Novaliches before the house was torched by the Spanish police, but on August 29 she was captured and jailed at the Old Bilibid Prison in Manila. On September 2, 1896, she and 171 other Filipinos (including one other woman, **Segunda Puentes Santiago**), were charged with sedition and rebellion.

Deported to Guam, she and Santiago were placed in the custody of a wealthy Filipino who had settled on the island some years earlier. In accounts of Aquino's imprisonment and subsequent deportation, she is cited for her bravery under what must have been difficult conditions for a woman of her advanced age. There are reports of grueling prison interrogations by the Spanish inquisitor, during which Aquino held fast and refused to divulge information about Bonifacio and his men.

Aquino was set free in 1898 when the United States defeated the Spanish and established an American colonial regime over the Philippines. Melchora Aquino was 86 years old when the war ended, but she had many years ahead of her. She spent them caring for her surviving children. Declining monetary rewards for her patriotism and sacrifice, she lived in poverty, content with the knowledge that she had contributed to her country's freedom. She died in the home of her daughter Saturnina, in 1919, at the age of 107,

Melchora Aquino

and was interred at the Mausoleum of the Veterans of the Philippine Revolution at the La Loma North Cemetery. Later her remains were transferred to Himlayang Pilipino in Quezon City, overlooking her ancestral home. Greatly revered for her courageous participation in the liberation of her country, Melchora Aquino became known as the "Mother of the Philippine Revolution." The 50th anniversary of her death in November 1969 was commemorated by a series of three postage stamps in her honor.

SOURCES:

Filipinos in History. Vol. I. Manila, Philippines: National Historical Institute, 1989.

Maring, Ester G., and Joel M. Maring. *Historical and Cultural Dictionary of the Philippines.* Metuchen, NJ: Scarecrow Press, 1973.

Soriano, Rafaelita Hilario, ed. *Women in the Philippine Revolution.*

SUGGESTED READING:

Eminent Filipinos. Manila Philippines: National Historical Institute, 1965.

Kalaw, Teodoro M. *The Philippine Revolution.* Kawilihan, Mandaluyong: Jorge B. Vargas Filipiniana Foundation, 1969.

Zaide, Gregorio F. *The Philippine Revolution*. Revised ed. Manila: The Modern Book Co., 1968.

John Haag, Associate Professor of History, University of Georgia, Athens, Georgia

Arabella Stuart (1575–1615).

See Stuart, Arabella.

Aragon, Mme. (1896–1970).

See Triolet, Elsa.

Aragon, queen of.

See Matilda of Portugal (c. 1149–1173).
See Sancha of Castille and Leon (1164–1208).
See Eleanor of Castile for sidebar on Eleanor Plantagenet (1264–1297).
See Eleanor of Portugal (1328–1348).
See Eleanor of Sicily (d. 1375).
See Maria of Castile (1401–1458).

Aragona, Tullia d' (1510–1556)

Italian poet. Born in 1510 in Italy; died in Italy in 1556.

Born into the Italian nobility, Tullia d'Aragona was a highly educated woman who showed great creative ability. Instead of marrying young, as did most of her contemporaries, she moved through Italian aristocratic society as a *cortegiana onesta*, or "honest courtesan." Acquainted with the leading artists and politicians of her time, she traveled extensively across Italy and became a model of the intellectual, artistic courtesan. At age 33, she married, probably to escape the many laws promulgated against courtesans. She continued to write prolifically, and her first book of poetry, *Rhymes*, was published in 1547. In 1552, her *Dialogue on the Infinity of Love* was printed, and her last major book, *Meschino, Otherwise Known as Guerrino*, was published four years after her death.

Aranyi, Jelly d' (1895–1966)

Hungarian-born British violin virtuosa. Name variations: Yelly d'Arányi. Born as Jelly Eva Aranyi de Hunyadvar in Budapest, Hungary, on May 30, 1895; died in Florence, Italy, on March 30, 1966; grandniece of Joseph Joachim (Austro-Hungarian violinist, conductor, and composer); studied with Jenö Hubay at the Hungarian Royal Academy; began public career in 1908.

Jelly Eva Aranyi de Hunyadvar was born in Budapest on May 30, 1895, into an assimilated Jewish family. The grandniece of the great Hungarian violinist Joseph Joachim (1831–1907), she showed musical talent at an early age. Although her first instrument was the piano, in 1903 she switched to the violin, making rapid progress under the instruction of noted musical pedagogues Heinrich Grünfeld and, later at the Budapest Academy, Jenö Hubay. D'Aranyi's career began auspiciously in 1908 in a series of joint recitals with her sister **Adila Fachiri** (1886–1962) in several cities including Vienna, where they received rave reviews. Fachiri, who had been left a 1715 Stradivarius belonging to Joachim, made her Vienna debut in 1906 playing the Beethoven violin concerto. In 1909, the two performed in England to an equally enthusiastic reception. D'Aranyi and her sister settled in Great Britain in 1913 on the eve of World War I. They quickly became known for exquisite performances of works like Johann Sebastian Bach's Concerto for Two Violins and Orchestra. Within a few years, D'Aranyi was able to surpass the musical reputation of her sister, who was ten years older but whose violinistic technique was considerably less impressive.

D'Aranyi's colorful personality made excellent newspaper copy. Her violinistic style was passionate, exhibiting a true gypsy exuberance. The warmth and almost improvisational nature of her playing was suited to works such as Johannes Brahms' Violin Concerto. Her style, often described as rhapsodic, also worked well for many modern compositions, including a number of important works written for and dedicated to her by major contemporary composers. These pieces included both of Bela Bartók's two Sonatas for Violin and Piano, and Maurice Ravel's gypsy-drenched *Tzigane*. D'Aranyi's powerful playing inspired a number of important concert works for violin, including a concerto by Julius Röntgen, the concerto for violin and horn by *Ethel Smyth, and Ralph Vaughan Williams' Concerto Accademico. Recognizing the superb virtuosity of both sisters, Gustav Holst composed his Double Concerto for D'Aranyi and Fachiri. As talented a performer of chamber music as she was an acclaimed concert virtuosa, D'Aranyi formed a piano trio as early as 1914 with the brilliant cellist *Guilhermina Suggia and the pianist *Fanny Davies. Another grouping, this time with cellist Felix Salmond and pianist *Myra Hess, was popular with the public in the 1930s.

One of the more bizarre incidents in the history of music was associated with D'Aranyi's psychic interests and the music of the great German Romantic composer Robert Schumann (1810–1856). In 1853, Schumann, who was rapidly slipping into dementia, had composed his last major work, a violin concerto. After Schumann's death in 1856, his widow *Clara Schumann and Joseph Joachim decided the piece was unworthy of the composer and should not be published or performed. The manuscript was then deposited in the Prussian State Library with a proviso that it was not to be released until 1956, a full century after Schumann's death. There had long been curiosity about the piece but little could be done to effect its release from the dusty archive. In 1933, D'Aranyi announced that her Ouija board had lifted the ban, and sensational stories of her communing with the spirit of the long-dead Robert Schumann appeared in countless newspapers and magazines throughout the world. In Germany, a number of Nazi musicologists and propagandists argued that it was the malignant influence of the long-dead Hungarian Jew Joseph Joachim that had denied public performance of immortal German music. Finally, in 1938, D'Aranyi gave the British premiere of this sometimes disjointedly fragile but poignantly beautiful work. One of the most dynamic musicians of the first half of the 20th century, Jelly D'Aranyi died in Florence, Italy, on March 30, 1966.

SOURCES:

Creighton, James Lesley. *Discopaedia of the Violin, 1889–1971*. Toronto: University of Toronto Press, 1974.

Gill, Dominic, ed. *The Book of the Violin*. NY: Rizzoli International Publications, 1984.

Macleod, Joseph Todd Gordon. *The Sisters d'Aranyi*. London: Allen & Unwin, 1969.

Schwarz, Boris. *Great Masters of the Violin*. NY: Simon and Schuster, 1983.

John Haag, Associate Professor of History, University of Georgia, Athens, Georgia

Araz, Nezihe (1922—)

Turkish author of religious poetry and children's books. Born in Konya, Turkey, in 1922; educated at Ankara's Girls Lycée; graduated from the University of Ankara, 1946, with a degree in philosophy and psychology.

A religious and cultural conservative, Araz was deeply influenced in her work by the teachings of the 13th-century Turkish mystic Jalal al-Din Rumi, the best-known Islamic mystical poet. Despite attempts to create a Western-based secular culture that began in the first decades of the 20th century, Araz represents Islamic traditionalism in Turkish intellectual life.

In 1922, Nezihe Araz was born in the city of Konya, Turkey, the center of a mystical tradition founded 700 years earlier by the Sufi mystic Jalal al-Din Rumi. She was educated at Ankara's Girls Lycée and then enrolled at the University of Ankara, graduating in 1946 with a degree in philosophy and psychology. In the 1950s, Araz published several books of poetry inspired by Islamic history, including the spiritual growth of the Prophet Muhammad and the saints of Anatolia. She also took on journalistic assignments for several of Turkey's conservative pro-Islamic newspapers, including *Yeni Sabah* and *Yeni Istanbul*. As an editor, Araz was in charge of major projects including the Turkish-language edition of the *Larousse Encyclopedia* and a multivolume history of the first 50 years of the Turkish Republic from 1923–1973.

Strongly influenced by Sufic teachings, Araz advocated a fundamentalist Muslim piety that emphasizes love and morality. The Turkish Sufi order of the Mevlevi, which Araz has written about in highly sympathetic terms, played a major role in defining Ottoman culture in the final centuries of that powerful empire. Her writings reflect a growing dissatisfaction with what are widely perceived to be the negative aspects of Westernization. She defended Turkish historical, and Islamic theological, traditions, arguing that these can be valid in a complex and often destructive modern world slavishly following a Western spiritual and social model inappropriate for Turkey. Araz's writings have influenced the resurgence of Islamic fundamentalism in Turkey in the last decades of the 20th century.

SOURCES:

Araz, Nezihe. *Anadolu evliyalari*. Istanbul: Fatis Yayinevi, 1958.

———. *Dertli dolap: Yunus Emre'nin hayat hikâyesi*. Istanbul: Fatis Yayinevi, 1961.

———. *Fatihin deruni tarihi*. Istanbul: Inkilâp kitabevi, 1953.

Elias, Jamal J. "Mawlawiyah," in *Oxford Encyclopedia of the Modern Islamic World*. Vol. 3. Edited by John L. Esposito. Oxford: Oxford University Press, 1995, pp. 77–79.

Mitler, Louis. *Contemporary Turkish Writers: A Critical Bio-Bibliography of Leading Writers in the Turkish Republican Period up to 1980*. Bloomington: Research Institute for Inner Asian Studies, Indiana University, 1988.

Schimmel, Annemarie. *The Triumphant Sun: A Study of the Works of Jalaloddin Rumi*. Rev. ed. London: East-West Publications, 1980.

John Haag, Associate Professor of History, University of Georgia, Athens, Georgia

Arber, Agnes (1879–1960)

English botanist. Born Agnes Robertson in 1879; died in 1960; granted B.Sc., London, 1899; attended Newnham College, Cambridge, 1901–02; was Quain

student in biology, 1903–08; awarded D.Sc., London University, 1905; married E.A.N. Arber, 1909.

Hailed as the most distinguished as well as the most erudite British plant morphologist, Agnes Arber was granted a D.Sc. from London University in 1905 for research on fertilization. She was a lecturer in botany from 1908–09 at University College, London, before researching plant anatomy in Balfour Laboratory, Newnham, from 1909 to 1927. Arber then continued her research at home. Her published works include *Herbals: Their Origins and Evolution* (1912), *Waterplants* (1920), *Monocotyledons* (1935), *Gramineae* (1934), *The Natural Philosophy of Plant Form* (1950), and *The Mind and the Eye* (1954).

Arblay, Madame d' (1752–1840).

See Burney, Fanny.

Arbus, Diane (1923–1971)

American photographer whose work had a profound influence on American documentary photography. Name variations: Diane Nemerov. Surname sometimes pronounced DEE-yan. Born Diane Nemerov on March 14, 1923, in New York, New York; committed suicide on July 26, 1971, in New York City; second child and first daughter of David (a retailer) and Gertrude (Russek) Nemerov; sister of essayist, novelist, and critic Howard Nemerov (1920–1991); sister of Renée Sparkia, a sculptor whose work is in collections at Palm Beach Institute and Lord Beaverbrook's museum in New Brunswick; married Allan Arbus (a photographer), on March 10, 1941 (divorced 1969); children: Doon Arbus (b. 1945, a writer) and Amy Arbus (b. April 16, 1954, a photographer).

Established fashion photography studio with husband Allan Arbus (1947); dissolved partnership with Allan (1957); studied photography with Lisette Model (1958–59); received first Guggenheim fellowship (1963); second Guggenheim (1966); work included in "New Documents" exhibition at Museum of Modern Art, New York (1967); given the Robert Levitt Award from the American Society of Magazine Photographers for outstanding achievement (1970); work exhibited at Venice Biennale (1972); retrospective, Museum of Modern Art (1972).

Diane Arbus was born on March 14, 1923, in New York, New York. "Even as a baby she didn't just look at you—she *considered* you," said her mother. Diane's self-estimate at 16

would be less generous; she maintained that she was "cranky—always crying, yelling, screaming. I can always remember the feeling I had. I always felt warm and tired and there was warm sun on me and I didn't want to wake up."

From about 1930 on, Arbus and her brother, the poet Howard Nemerov, grew up in a Manhattan apartment on the 11th floor of New York's San Remo, 146 Central Park West. Her maternal grandfather, Frank Russek, was a penniless Polish Jew who immigrated to New York and in 1897 established a fur business with his brother in New York City. By 1915, the phenomenal success of Russek's Furs had made the brothers millionaires. Diane's father was David Nemerov, son of a poor Jewish immigrant from Russia, who began working for Russek's Furs as a window dresser but was soon named merchandising director. Although the difference in their social backgrounds caused much disapproval among the Russek family, David married Frank Russek's daughter Gertrude, despite the Russeks' objections.

In 1923, David expanded Russek's Furs into Russek's Fifth Avenue, a department store on 36th Street. "The outside of the seven-story building was imposing," writes **Patricia Bosworth**; "with its balconies and marble columns, it resembled a Venetian palazzo." Inside, "purple velvet carpets covered the floor, and salesmen and salesladies behaved obsequiously." Arbus found her family's affluence "humiliating." At home, there was an army of household help: two maids, a chauffeur, a cook, a nanny for each child. Diane adored Mamselle, her French nanny. As opposed to visits with her mother to Russek's where the clerks fawned ("I was treated like a crummy princess," groused Arbus), Mamselle took her to see some Hooverville shanties—makeshift squatters' homes that were by-products of the Depression—in Central Park. It was a powerful memory for Arbus, "Seeing the other side of the tracks, holding the hand of one's governess."

Her father, who worked 14-hour days at the store while finding time for numerous affairs, was aloof and showed little interest in his children, though, said Arbus, he was "fantastic at giving advice." (His name would later crop up in the red-leather telephone book of Madame **Pat Ward**, who ran a call-girl ring for executives; the book made the front pages of the *Daily News* in 1955). Arbus' chain-smoking, card-playing mother Gertrude was far more attentive, but prone to depression.

Diane and her brother Howard were voracious readers; they also shared rich fantasies and

were both private, prone to fears, and agonizingly shy. Until Howard left for school in 1926, they were inseparable. "Howard doted on Diane," said a cousin. "He kept a photograph of her in his wallet until she died. He was certainly in awe—because even when she was tiny, she never behaved like a little girl. She had innate sophistication—wisdom about things—and she was gorgeously intuitive. Howard turned into a highly critical, precise intellectual. It was some combination." When their younger sister Renée was born, Diane lavished all the affection she wasn't getting on her baby sister.

Though the children attended Temple Emanu-El on the High Holy Days, Arbus did not have a sense of the potential consequences of her Judaism while growing up. "I didn't know it was an unfortunate thing to be! Because I grew up in a Jewish city in a Jewish family and my father was a rich Jew and I went to a Jewish school, I was confirmed in a sense of unreality. All I could feel was my sense of unreality." In later years, she would march into Yorkville to photograph and scrutinize delegates of the American Nazi Party.

At age seven, she was sent to the Ethical Culture School, a private lyceum for New York's elite based on a system of religious humanistic philosophy, which encouraged each pupil's artistic talent. From seventh to twelfth grade, she attended Fieldston School in the Riverdale section of the Bronx (a continuation of Ethical Culture). "The teachers always used to think I was smart and it would torment me because I knew that I was really terribly dumb," she wrote. Contrary to her own opinion, it is clear that Arbus was not only extremely bright but also extremely creative. Her talent both frightened her and made her feel separate from others. "Diane would float away from a group of us—suddenly—no explanation," said a classmate. "Later we'd see her sitting by herself reading a book of poetry in Central Park. She did that a lot."

Arbus took an enormous interest in myths, rituals, quests, and legends. Her favorite book was *Alice in Wonderland;* her favorite artists: *****Käthe Kollwitz** and Paul Klee. While on a class trip visiting a settlement house, she wanted to talk to the derelicts on the street. She identified

Diane Arbus, with her "Child with a Toy Handgrenade in Central Park, NYC," 1962. Courtesy of Stephen Frank, photographer.

with their isolation and their otherness. Feeling overly protected, Arbus regarded herself as insulated from life; she once complained to a friend that at summer camp all the children had been bitten by leeches except her.

Arbus and a schoolfriend rode the subway to observe marks and qualities that set certain people apart—birthmarks, impairments. They mingled with New York's street people: the mutterer, the corner preacher, or the lady dressed to the hilt in infested fur. Desperately curious to see how they lived, the schoolgirls sometimes followed their subjects home. Then Diane returned to her own household, where her mother was playing cards with the well-to-do matrons in a gloomy apartment fringed with thick curtains. "I got the feeling that Diane was as terrified of reentering the bourgeois world of her parents as she was of exploring the world of freaks and eccentrics," said her friend **Phyllis Carton**. "Both worlds fascinated her because they seemed one and the same to her."

A photograph is a secret about a secret.
The more it tells you the less you know.

—Diane Arbus

When Diane was 15, her mother's melancholia increased; Gertrude would sit in silence at the dinner table. "I simply could not communicate with my family," said Gertrude. "I didn't know why. I felt my husband and children didn't love me and I couldn't love them. I stopped functioning. I was like a zombie. My friend May Miller had to take me shopping and help me try on clothes. I wasn't able to take them off the hangers I felt so weak." After a year, however, Gertrude slowly came out of it. Arbus' brother Howard also experienced deep depressions throughout his life.

In 1937, at age 14, Diane met and fell in love with Allan Arbus, a 19-year-old aspiring actor and musician who worked in the art department at Russek's Fifth Avenue. Diane's announcement that she and Allan wanted to marry met with shock from her parents, and they refused permission. Allan came from a poor family, and the Nemerovs would not allow their daughter to "marry beneath her," despite the history of their own contested marriage. The two, however, managed to date regularly, and her parents' opposition only served to increase Diane's determination.

In 1940, she graduated from Fieldston with no future plans other than to marry Allan Arbus.

Her parents relented, and in April 1941, soon after Arbus' 18th birthday, Diane and Allan were married at a small wedding ceremony. When her parents refused to assist the newlyweds financially, Allan worked two jobs to support his wife, who dedicated herself to becoming a homemaker. She continued to read—*Willa Cather, Carl Jung, *Emily Dickinson—and attend plays and concerts. When she went to museums, she tended to ignore the art while scrutinizing the spectators.

In 1943, during World War II, the couple moved to New Jersey, where Allan attended a photography school as part of his service in the Signal Corps. Nightly, he shared his knowledge with his wife; they set up a darkroom, and Diane became fascinated with the possibilities offered by photography for both documentation and creative expression. She began to fill her days by taking pictures, a hobby that turned more serious after Allan was shipped off to Burma with a photographers' unit in 1944. Their first child, Doon, was born on April 3, 1945, while Diane was staying with her parents in New York. Arbus divided her time between her daughter and her cameras until Allan returned in 1946. To make ends meet, Allan gave up his dream of being an actor and, with Diane as his partner, he entered the world of fashion photography. (Arbus would never receive financial help from her father throughout the marriage; they were continually burdened with bills.)

Tina Fredericks, art director at Condé Nast and a close friend of Diane's, gave them a job in January 1947 at *Glamour*. Their first assignment, "The New Sweater is a Long Story," was published in May 1947. The couple eventually achieved success, though they still struggled financially. Throughout the 1950s, they did editorial work for *Vogue*; had accounts from the advertising agencies Young & Rubicam and J. Walter Thompson; shot layouts for vodka, Greyhound Bus, Maxwell House coffee; and worked on the ad campaign known as "Modess Because." The more successful they grew, the more they hated the world of commercial photography, regarding it as shallow and deceitful. The field drew a calculating, hustling, hard-drinking crowd.

Creative perfectionists, the Arbuses—who usually alternated shooting assignments although they both attended each of them—gained a reputation for precision and painstaking detail in the world of fashion photography. In addition to collaborating with her husband on the actual shoot, Arbus was usually the stylist for their assignments; she coordinated the models' wardrobes, hairstyles, makeup, and poses. Observers tell of how closely the Arbuses worked, holding hands, secretive. Many used the phrase "they were like twins."

Allan also encouraged Diane to shoot on her own, to perfect her style. She needed little urging and appeared everywhere with a camera slung around her neck. She wanted to photograph the underbelly of people's lives, the side hidden from the public (she had a fascination for medicine cabinets), but she was too shy to ask strangers to pose, so she continued to ask friends. With a particular interest in photographing children, she enjoyed shooting her older daughter Doon and her younger child Amy, born in 1954. Indeed, throughout her career, children would remain her most common subjects.

As the antithesis of women in the fashion industry, Arbus preferred paper bags to purses and eschewed deodorant, preferring the body's natural smell. At times, she was a lethargic daydreamer who spoke in a husky whisper and faded into the shadows. Like her mother, she felt inadequate and suffered dark moods and depressions that she tried to hide from her own daughters. As her sister Renée pointed out, the camera was like a shield. Diane sometimes wore it around her neck at Friday night family dinners, then she'd point and click. "I think," said Renée, "she imagined that if she was invisible, everybody would forget she was there."

Despite a frenetic work schedule, Allan found her depressions progressively harder to deal with. Episodes had no obvious onset; Diane would grow listless, remote, and dazed, barely responding to life. Once, when asked at a dinner party what her workday was like, she involuntarily broke into rare tears. In 1957, Diane and Allan broke up their business partnership. He would continue to run the studio under their joint name, while pursuing his acting career; Diane would no longer work in fashion photography but was free to go in whatever direction she wished.

She enrolled in Alexey Brodovitch's workshop, walking away with his axiom, "If you see something you've seen before, don't click the shutter." As she studied the history of photography briefly with *Berenice Abbott, she became familiar with the works of *Julia Cameron, Mathew Brady, and Lewis Hine. Arbus was most impressed with *Lisette Model, whose images included portraits of the frail and sickly, subjects rarely seen in photo exhibitions at the time.

In 1958, the 35-year-old Arbus enrolled in Lisette Model's class at the New School. The two formed a close bond. Arbus told *Newsweek*:

> Until I studied with Lisette I'd gone on dreaming photography rather than doing it. Lisette told me to enjoy myself when I was photographing and I began to, and then I learned from the work. Lisette taught me that I'd felt guilty about being a woman. Guilty because I didn't think I could ever understand the mechanics of the camera. I'd always believed that since painters rendered every line on a canvas, they experience the image more completely than a photographer. That had bothered me. Lisette talked to me about how ancient the camera was and how the light stains the silver coating of the film silver so memory stains it too.

Indeed, Model convinced Arbus that she could experience the object of her work as much as any painter.

Arbus gradually ceased taking pictures of ordinary people. She began to seek out circuses and other venues where she found individuals living on the margins of society—transvestites, dwarves, midgets, contortionists, people deformed from birth or by accident. She saw Tod Browning's 1932 movie *Freaks* and began photographing ❧▶ **Stormé Delarverié**, a male impersonator. She began to prowl the city at night, blending into the scenery as she entered the world of Times Square bag ladies, subway bums, and prostitutes. She became fascinated with Moondog, the blind beggar who carried a staff, wore a Viking helmet, and favored traffic islands for his eight-hour catatonic shifts. She followed

---

❧▶ Delarverié, Stormé

American male impersonator. Name variations: De Larverie.

In 1955, Stormé Delarverié joined the Jewel Box Review in which she worked as a male impersonator with 25 female impersonators. The review toured theaters from Mexico to Canada, and during the 1950s and '60s performed across the segregated south. When asked whether she wanted to be referred to as a "he" or a "she," Delarverié responded, "I tell people, 'Use whatever makes you comfortable.'" Repeatedly beaten and a victim during the Stonewall rebellion of 1969, Delarverié went on to tell transgender historian Leslie Feinberg, "It really doesn't matter whether you're male, female, gay, straight—whatever you want your identity to be—no one has the right to try to take your life or to beat you down for it."

SOURCES:

Feinberg, Leslie. *Transgender Warriors: Making History from Joan of Arc to RuPaul*. Boston: Beacon Press, 1996.

---

circuses to small towns and haunted sideshows, enjoying the company of Presto the Fireeater and the tattooed man. She sat by the hour with the manager of a flea circus while he fed his fleas, serving up his arm for dinner as he read the *Daily News*. Throughout, the diffident Arbus was generally frightened. Then again, she was always frightened, she maintained, "crawling forward on her belly," no matter what she was doing. Finally, however, she mustered up the courage to ask strangers to pose.

Arbus approached her subjects cautiously, not using her camera until she had established a trusting relationship with them. Her portraits of this period reveal her ability to capture something beyond the posed, masked smile. Using an intrusive photographic technique, she moved in close and used a bright flash, which startled the subject, often resulting in a less guarded expression in the final image. By all accounts, Arbus was a magnificent listener who concentrated intensely on each individual with whom she conversed. Many people were drawn to her, and many became possessive of her. She was seductive, bisexual. With sex, as with photography, she was constantly experimenting. "Sex was the quickest, most primitive way [for her] to begin connecting with another human being," wrote Bosworth.

The more she learned, the more critical she became of her husband's fashion shoots, though only when asked. As their marriage disintegrated, Allan shut himself up in his room for hours, practicing the clarinet. She began printing her pictures in a borrowed darkroom; he began studying acting under **Mira Rostova**, working on scenes with a young actress. The family became poorer as Diane took photo after photo without knowing how to sell them. There were no magazine outlets for dark, idiosyncratic glossies.

In late 1959, Arbus found a mentor in modernist painter Marvin Israel. Believing that she had a special talent, he used his connections to promote her. His efforts led to an assignment for *Esquire* when the magazine was devoting an entire issue to Manhattan. Arbus spent four months traversing the city; she shot hundreds of rolls of film: of the morgue at Bellevue, of bodies in potter's field, of dancers at Roseland, and of **Flora Knapp Dickinson** of the Daughters of the American Revolution (DAR). The success of her images led to other assignments on a regular basis from the editors of *Esquire*.

Though they remained friends, the Arbuses officially separated in the summer of 1960. She anguished over the loss of the ideal more than the marriage and felt the strain of single motherhood. She always put her children's schedule before her own.

Arbus sold a layout of five eccentrics for the November 1961 issue of *Harper's Bazaar*. Still interested in people with unusual physicalities, she was also intrigued by individuals, often mentally ill, whose cognitions made them unusual, such as a man from Oklahoma who believed he was the rightful emperor of Byzantium and demanded to be treated as royalty. She wanted to dramatize their lives. Wrote Arbus in the introductory essay:

> These are five singular people, who appear further out than we do; beckoned, not driven; invented by belief; each the author and hero of a real dream by which our own courage and cunning are tested and tried; so that we may wonder all over again what is veritable and inevitable and possible and what it is to become whoever we may be.

She adored and respected the talent of her friend Richard Avedon but wondered how he could shoot a portrait in ten minutes and not remember any of his conversation with the subject during the sitting. She had trouble with his "unearned intimacy." Arbus remembered everything that was said by her subjects and shot them over and over for years, like Morales, the Mexican dwarf, and Eddie Carmel, the Jewish giant. She took off her clothes to shoot in a nudist colony and marched in peace marches to shoot the marchers. She revealed herself to her subjects, so that they might reveal themselves to her. What she wanted most was to follow her subjects home, to go into their houses, to shoot them in their bedrooms.

She was finally making a little money, but ashamed that she was making it from her photographs. Arbus was shooting celebrities on assignment like *Mae West, *Jayne Mansfield, Blaze Starr, F. Lee Bailey, *Jacqueline Susann, *Nathalie Sarraute, Jorge Luis Borges, Tokyo Rose (*Iva Toguri), feminists Ti Grace Atkinson and Germaine Greer, even Ozzie and *Harriet Nelson. She also photographed Tricia Nixon's White House wedding for the London *Sunday Times*.

On March 6, 1967, "New Documents" opened at the Metropolitan Museum of Art. The show featured her work along with that of photographers Garry Winogrand and Lee Friedlander. The purpose of the exhibition was to present a new era in documentary photography, an era that contradicted the previous romanticism and provided a more individualized, less generous view of humanity. It contained at least 30 of her photographs. Arbus' technique of photographing in square format with flash would soon be duplicated by hundreds of budding photographers. Wrote Marion Magid in *Arts* magazine: "In the end the great humanity of Diane Arbus' art is to sanctify that privacy which she seemed at first to have violated." Arbus was extremely proud of the show and of the recognition she received as a result of its exposure to the public, though she was secretly depressed by the negative comments she heard from viewers. As with her first exhibition, public reaction was either approving or censorious, but her work always seemed to move its viewers in some way. Remarked one critic: "One does not look with impunity" at a Diane Arbus photograph.

Friends, who included sculptor **Mary Frank**, Anita Steckel, playwright **Rosalyn Drexler**, filmmakers *Shirley Clarke and *Maya Deren told Arbus she would have to grow a thicker skin. She was terrified that her pictures would be misunderstood, and they often were. She was terrified that she'd be known as the photographer of freaks, and she often was. As the public and the art world invaded her world and work, her most enduring terror was that things would now be *expected* of her.

After battling a bout of hepatitis in 1966, her depressions had grown worse. "She fell into a ghastly, unending depression that went on for three years—until her death," said her mother. "Periodically she would call me on the phone in Florida and cry 'Mummy—Mummy—tell me the story of your depression and how you got over it.'" In 1968, Arbus began to suffer from nausea, low energy, dizziness, back pains, and weight loss. Finally diagnosed with "toxic hepatitis ostensibly secondary to the combination of drugs used for depression and birth control," she went off all pills.

In 1969, she and Allan were finally divorced. He married actress **Mariclare Costello**, and they moved to Los Angeles to pursue acting careers. His departure frightened Diane, who had always relied on Allan, even after their separation. Believing that their union would last forever, she had felt that even if they each had other lovers (and Diane had many), they could remain a married couple. Still struggling financially, she moved into the subsidized Manhattan artist community of Westbeth in January of 1970, living near *Muriel Ruckeyser, Merce Cunningham, Tobias Schneebaum, **Thalia Seltz**, and her good friend Mary Frank. She also taught a course out of her apartment.

Summers had been difficult during Arbus' childhood. Her favorite governess Mamselle left abruptly one summer, and her parents went to Europe. In the summer of 1971, when Arbus was 48 years old, friends noticed that she began tying things up. Frequently in tears, she was convinced her work would never sell. She had dinner with her brother and, though cheerful, announced, "You know, I'm going to be remembered for being Howard Nemerov's sister." She could no longer lose herself in her work.

Diane Arbus was last seen alive on July 26th, walking toward Westbeth. She bumped into an acquaintance and confided that she was catching a cold and thinking of moving out of New York. On July 28th, when her friend Marvin Israel could not reach her by phone, he went to Westbeth and found her in the empty bathtub with her wrists slit. On her desk, her journal was opened to July 26th. It read, "The last supper."

SOURCES:
Bosworth, Patricia. *Diane Arbus: A Biography*. NY: W.W. Norton, 1984.

SUGGESTED READING:
Arbus, Diane. *Untitled*. Edited by Doon Arbus and Yolanda Cumo. NY: Aperture, 1995.
Arbus, Doon, and Marvin Israel, eds. *Diane Arbus: An Aperture Monograph*. Millerton, NY: Aperture, 1972.
———. *Diane Arbus: Magazine Work*. Millerton, NY: Aperture, 1984.

Heather Moore, freelance writer in women's studies, Northampton, Massachusetts

Arc, Jeanne d' or Arc, Joan of (c. 1412–1431).

See Joan of Arc.

Arcangela, Sor (1604–1652).

See Tarabotti, Arcangela.

Arceo, Liwayway (1924—)

Filipino author. Born in 1924 in the Philippines.

The prolific Filipino author Liwayway Arceo began writing as a teenager. In more than five decades of work, she has produced on average a novel and 18 short stories a year. In her native Tagalog, the national tongue of the Philippines, she is considered a modernist and a feminist, whose frequent subject is the virtue and importance of women. The weekly journal *Liwayway*, which Arceo edited for many years, has published the majority of her stories and served as a literary model for young writers of the Philippines. In addition to her fiction, Arceo wrote a radio serial, *Ilaw ng Tahanan* (*Light of the Home*), which ran for several years and dramatized the domestic role of women from all walks of life. She is the author of more than 50 novels and 900 short stories.

Crista Martin,
Boston, Massachusetts

Archambault, Mademoiselle

(c. 1724–?)

French feminist essayist. Born around 1724 in Laval, France; died after 1750.

In the spirit of British feminist *Jane Anger, Mademoiselle Archambault, a native of Laval and daughter of a tax collector, wrote in defense of women. The essay *Dissertation sur la question: lequel de l'homme ou de la femme est plus capable de constance?* ("Essay on the Question: Are Men or Women More Loyal?") was published in 1750. Archambault followed with a piece questioning the equality of women and men in intellectual and physical strength; never published, this work can be found in the Bibliothèque de Laval.

Crista Martin,
Boston, Massachusetts

Archer, Maria (1905—)

Portuguese author. Born in 1905 in Portugal.

Selected works: Ida e Volta duma Caixa de Cigarros *(Round Trip of a Cigarette Box, 1938)*; Casa Sem Pão *(House Without Bread, 1946)*; Há de Haver una Lei *(There Ought to be a Law, 1949)*; Os Últimos Dias do Fascismo Português *(The Last Days of Portuguese Fascism, 1961).*

Despite her status as a popular and prolific writer in Portugal, little is written about Maria Archer in either histories or anthologies. The prime of her career coincided with the dictatorship of António Salazar, of whom Archer was critical, and it is assumed that Salazar's regime prevented the dissemination of much information about the author. Archer's primary concern was the subjugation of women in an authoritarian society, an opinion she made clear in nonfiction like *Os Últimos Dias do Fascismo Português* (*The Last Days of Portuguese Fascism*, 1961), published in Brazil, and fiction like *Casa Sem Pão* (*House Without Bread*, 1946), which was banned in Portugal. Her writing has included novels, short fiction, essays, and drama.

Crista Martin,
Boston, Massachusetts

Archer, Violet (1913—)

Canadian composer, pianist, and teacher. Born Violet Balestreri in Montreal, Canada, on April 24, 1913; studied with Douglas Clarke and Claude Champagne at the McGill Conservatory, earning her Bachelor of Music in 1936; studied with Bela Bartók in 1942 and with Paul Hindemith in 1949, both of whom strongly influenced her orchestral and choral works.

Preoccupied with Canadian folksongs and folklore, Violet Archer used folk music as a source of creative material. *The Habitant Sketches, Life in a Prairie Shack*, and *Three Folk Songs from Old Manitoba* all display this influence, as does her opera, *Sganarelle*. Archer won the Woods-Chandler composition prize at Yale, and four scholarships at McGill as well as an honorary doctorate. The anthems, organ voluntaries, piano and choral pieces that comprise much of her output were doubtlessly influenced by Paul Hindemith's musical imagination as she used his system of progressive harmonic weights. Archer taught at McGill (1944–47), at North Texas State University where she was also composer-in-residence (1950–53), at the University of Oklahoma (1953–61), and at the University of Alberta where she became professor and chair of the theory and composition department after 1962. Her Trio No. 2 has been extensively performed abroad. In 1984, Violet Archer was the first woman composer to be chosen as Composer of the Year by the Canadian Music Council.

John Haag, Associate Professor of History,
University of Georgia, Athens, Georgia

Arconville, Geneviève d' (1720–1805).

See d'Arconville, Geneviève.

Arden, Elizabeth (1878–1966)

American cosmetics entrepreneur who introduced a scientific approach to the manufacture of cosmetics and built a multimillion-dollar empire based on her "total woman" approach; she was also one of the nation's top owners of thoroughbreds. Name variations: Florence Graham; Elizabeth N. Graham. Born Florence Nightingale Graham on December 31, 1878, in Woodbridge, Ontario, Canada; died in New York City on October 18, 1966; fourth of five children, third of three daughters of Susan Tadd Graham and William Graham (a market gardener); married Thomas Jenkins Lewis, on November 29, 1915, and became an American citizen (divorced 1934); married Prince Michael Evlanoff (a Russian émigré), on December 30, 1942 (divorced 1944).

Opposite page

Elizabeth

Arden

Left high school out of necessity to seek employment; joined her brother William in New York (1907); began a beauty salon (1909); launched her first branch salon (1914); her business empire began to grow under the name Elizabeth Arden; eventually her products were sold in 78 countries; became interested in thoroughbred racing, a venture in which she also made a great deal of money.

Born into dire poverty near Toronto, Ontario, Canada, on the last day of the year in 1878, the child named Florence Nightingale Graham would become one of America's wealthiest entrepreneurs. But in the village of Woodbridge, as the fourth of five children, she arrived in her family as another mouth to feed.

Florence's parents were both immmigrants to Canada. Her mother, **Susan Tadd Graham**, was born in Cornwall, England. Her father was William Graham, a Scotsman who made his living as a market gardener. Susan Graham died when Florence was six, and the only thing that allowed the Graham children to go to school rather than to work was a small allowance left to them by an aunt. When the allowance ended, Florence had to leave high school and seek employment.

In her first jobs, as a dental assistant, cashier, and stenographer, she approached her positions creatively. Working for the dentist, it was her notion to advertise, bombarding the dentist's patients with clever letters that implied what might happen if they didn't stop by for a checkup; in a year, her employer's business doubled.

In 1907, Florence Graham was 28 when she followed her brother William to New York City; eventually, she went to work for E.R. Squibb & Sons, the chemical manufacturers, as a bookkeeper and stenographer, a job that lasted for only ten days. She found her niche, finally, employed at Eleanor Adair's, a beauty specialist, where she began learning the elementary formulas for manufacturing and selling cosmetics.

At the start of the 20th century, the cosmetics industry was in its infancy, with few manufactured products available on the market. Most cosmetics were made at home. A typical home-style formula for hand lotion was:

10¢ bay rum
10¢ glycerin
10 drops carbolic acid
the juice of one lemon

According to **Margaret Case Harriman**, dressing tables of the time contained "a can of talcum powder, a chamois facecloth, and a little

rosewater and glycerin; face powder was obtainable only in two shades, pink and white." Women who used more than such staples might be considered "loose." Learning the basics of the fledgling industry, Florence would go on to reshape both the cosmetic market and contemporary attitudes.

In 1910, she entered into a partnership with **Elizabeth Hubbard**, establishing a beauty salon at 509 Fifth Avenue. The two women began to mix "nourishing" creams, astringent lotions, youth masks, and muscle oils to sell. The business flourished, but a clash of personalities began to undermine the partnership, and Florence Graham decided to buy out her partner. Planning to register her products under the name "Florence Nightingale," she discovered she was not allowed to use the trademark. Since the name "Elizabeth Hubbard" was already painted on the shop window, she decided to combine her partner's first name with "Arden," which she took from the poem "Enoch Arden." In a bit of early test marketing, Graham mailed herself a letter addressed to "Miss Elizabeth Arden" to decide how it looked, and the sight of the envelope convinced her that she had found her trademark.

$\mathcal{E}$lizabeth Arden has made femininity a science, and probably earned more money doing it than any businesswoman in history.
—*Time*, May 6, 1946

Elizabeth Arden was a perfectionist. When she did not like the hard, slippery texture of a face cream, she told a firm of chemists that she wanted a light, fluffy product, like whipped cream. When her suppliers said her request was impossible, she searched for a firm that would give her what she wanted. In 1914, she met A.F. Swanson, a young analytical chemist at Stillwell & Gladdening; thanks to his efforts, Cream Amoretta was born. According to Arden's specifications, he next created Ardena skin tonic, which sold so well it was difficult to keep in stock. In 1915, Arden opened a salon at 673 Fifth Avenue and a wholesale department at 665 Fifth Avenue to supply the growing demand for her preparations in stores throughout the country. Swanson now worked for Arden full-time, creating the products she envisioned.

On November 29, 1915, at age 43, Elizabeth Arden married Thomas Jenkins Lewis and automatically became an American citizen. Lewis was an advertising man who managed Arden's

wholesale operation. From the outset, the money rolled in to the Arden enterprise. By 1920, demand was so great that a new warehouse at 212 East 52nd Street was supplying Elizabeth Arden merchandise to some 5,000 drug and department stores. The wholesale operation required three floors, and the factory nearby required two buildings and part of a third.

The ingredients for Arden's early cosmetics were simple. Ardena skin tonic, for example, contained water grain alcohol, boric acid, and perfume; her popular muscle oil was nothing but third-grade castor oil and water. What distinguished Arden from her competition was an understanding of the importance of packaging. Paying attention to color, shape, and design, she endowed both her products and her business with a certain aura. When she used some of her first profits to buy a genuine Oriental rug and authentic antique table for her salon, they set the style for props that were to grace many of her enterprises. *Time* magazine would report in 1946, "The grand showcase of the Arden beauty empire at 691 Fifth Avenue is guarded by a grey-liveried doorman and a red door marked simply, Elizabeth Arden." Women who entered her salons felt swept into an exotic world that enhanced their sense of confidence and well-being.

Despite the stock-market crash of 1929 that heralded the Great Depression, Arden remained optimistic about her economic future. "The depression is going to make a lot of manufacturers pull in, economize, cut down," she declared, "and that leaves us a clear field." As sole stockholder in her business, she refused an offer that year of $15 million. That same year, her salons opened in Los Angeles, Palm Springs, and Miami Beach. Her enterprises continued to grow throughout the Depression, while new factories were established in London, Paris, Berlin, Toronto, and Mexico. A sister of Arden's, who had become the **Vicomtesse de Maublanc** through marriage, managed her Paris salon. Although some of her foreign ventures were not as profitable, Arden recognized their value in giving the company an allure that sold well at home. She was involved with every facet of her business empire. Wrote a contemporary:

A driving woman, Elizabeth Arden gets up early every day, even if she's been up late the night before. She okays all her ads, thinks up most of the names for products (Blue Grass, April May, It's You, White Orchid, Winged Victory). . . . She has her own ideas of perfection, and demands it of her employees, even if a chemist has to spend days re-making a color until Arden herself thinks it is "paradise pink." Her competitors say, "Work for Elizabeth Arden and live in a revolving door."

In 1917, Arden had introduced eye shadow and mascara to the United States, and more new products continued to roll off the assembly lines. To test products, she liked to experiment on herself and her employees. Secretaries, stenographers, and file clerks in the company might be spotted trying out a different product on each eye, or with nails painted with different polishes to compare their durability. When a Miss O'Leary began to break out after using a series of experimental creams and lotions, Arden grasped the opportunity to create a profitable new product line for sensitive skin.

Most Arden customers were women over 40, who wanted to retain youth and beauty. Elizabeth Arden was the best advertisement for her beauty products. Only 5'2", she had beautiful skin and maintained her slim figure, appearing much younger than she was; and her vitality was legendary. Arden understood what appealed to her clientele. Judging pink to be the most flattering color in the spectrum, Arden often wore pink, and the color was usually significant in the decor of her many homes and offices. Once, when $100,000 worth of cosmetics deviated from the soft Arden pink that was her trademark, she refused to sell them.

At age 18, Arden had suffered an injury that caused her intense pain throughout life. In an effort to cinch her reputation as the highest kicker in Toronto, she had kicked at a chandelier and fallen, doing permanent damage to her hip. At one point, she was forced to remain bedridden for six months. When doctors wanted to operate, she opted for yoga and meditation, a highly unconventional approach at the time. The yoga exercises and a healthy diet helped her regain her health and strength. This experience later helped her envision other routes to beauty. In 1934, she purchased a farm, which she named Maine Chance, where she set up a treatment center; clients were prescribed low-calorie diets and special exercises tailored to their individual needs. Menus centered on vegetables and fruits, avoiding meats and sugar; and exercises were often performed to music, another innovation. By 1947, Maine Chance had proved so successful, Arden opened the Arizona Maine Chance Farm, promoting her concept of exercise, a healthy diet, and keeping active as the means for women to maintain good health into advanced age.

In 1931, with her beauty empire firmly established, Arden had become involved in horse racing with the purchase of her first thoroughbred. Under the name of Elizabeth N. Graham, she owned as many as 150 horses, many stabled in Lexington, Kentucky, at her Maine Chance Farm. "A beautiful horse," she said, "is like a beautiful woman," and nothing was too good for her horses. She screened their barns to keep out flies, personally massaged their legs if an animal had a limp, sacked a groom whose "mean face" might upset them, and shipped clover from Maine to Kentucky to feed them. During races, jockeys were forbidden to use the whip, and blinders were not allowed on the animals because they didn't "look pretty"; a horse coming off the track would be wrapped in a cashmere blanket. Arden usually visited her horses at least twice weekly, and Blue Grass, her best-selling perfume, was named in honor of her thoroughbreds.

Arden's horses rewarded her for her solicitous care. Her cherry pink, white, and blue racing colors often flashed first over the finish line. In 1946, she was the nation's top winner, with almost $600,000 in earnings. She made the May 6 cover of *Time* that year, as:

> a queen who rules the sport of kings. . . . She rarely hires anyone who is out of a job. She tolerates no tomfoolery or inefficiency in horse trainers or jockeys either. She bubbles into the paddock before a race to tell her jockeys to "get out in front and go, go, go!" When she loses, she is apt to blame anyone but the horse. Many a millionaire has ransomed his kingdom for a race horse, and ended up with a big oat bill. The difference in Millionaire Elizabeth Arden Graham's case, is that Tom Smith spent her gold and brought home silver cups."

The following year, her horse, Jet Pilot, won the Kentucky Derby.

Meanwhile, rivalry in the burgeoning cosmetics industry grew intense. Arden fought to hold the market against all her competitors, but her archrival was *Helena Rubenstein, and their feud lasted 50 years. Arden coaxed many employees away from Rubenstein, including Harry Johnson whom she paid $50,000 a year, then a princely sum, to be her general manager.

Arden resented the fact that her monumental success was sometimes attributed to the business acumen of her first husband Thomas Lewis. In 1934, after their divorce, Rubenstein promptly taunted Arden by hiring Lewis as her sales manager, continuing the feud. After Rubenstein married a prince, Arden married Prince Michael Evlanoff, a Russian émigré, on December 30, 1942, but the union ended in divorce in 1944. In 1959, after Arden lost the tip of her right index finger while feeding an orange to an overeager horse, Rubenstein quipped, "What happened to the horse?"

An exacting employer, Arden was sometimes said to have trained more people for the competition than any other head of the cosmetic business. But she also had a reputation for a certain fairness. She employed a much larger percentage of women than other industries handling similar jobs; she also employed the blind, and her wages and salaries often headed the ranks in the industry. She once paid for the dental work to enhance the smile of a beautiful girl whose appearance was marred by a gold front tooth. Exacting as Arden was, she had many employees who served her loyally for their entire working lives.

In 1943, Arden was in her 60s, when she struck off in a new direction by entering the fashion business, with exclusive collections created for her salons by designers like Oscar de la Renta. In the 1950s, still well ahead of her time, she extended her concept of "total beauty" to men as well as women, when she opened the first men's boutique attached to a beauty salon. Meanwhile, a good diet, meditation, and yoga stood the entrepreneur in good stead. She ran her vast business empire until her death at age 88.

With the advent of the women's movement in the 1960s, some voices condemned the women's cosmetics industry. While there was validity to the criticism that society focused more on women's looks than their abilities, the cosmetics industry gave many women access to entrepreneurial jobs. Elizabeth Arden was not only a businesswoman but head of a major corporation at a time when few women worked. She was also one of the first to extend the limits of attention to beauty beyond women and to create the link between beauty and health. Decades after her death, newspapers and magazines feature diet and exercise advice that originated with Arden.

SOURCES:

Current Biography 1957. NY: H.W. Wilson, pp. 19–21.

Harriman, Margaret Case. "Glamour, Inc.," in *The New Yorker.* Vol. 11, no. 8. April 6, 1935, pp. 24–30.

Hoogenboom, Olive. "Arden, Elizabeth," in *Dictionary of American Biography.* Supplement 8. 1966–1970. John A. Garraty and Mark C. Carnes, eds. NY: Scribner, 1988.

"Lady's Day in Louisville" (cover story), in *Time.* Vol. 47, no. 18. May 6, 1946, pp. 57–58.

Lewis, Alfred Allen, and Constance Woodworth. *Miss Elizabeth Arden.* NY: Coward, McCann & Geoghegan, 1972.

Whitman, Alden. *Come to Judgment.* Harmondsworth, U.K.: Penguin, 1980.

Karin Loewen Haag,
freelance writer, Athens, Georgia

Arden, Eve (1907–1990)

American actress, best known as "Our Miss Brooks," who was nominated for an Academy Award for Best Supporting Actress for Mildred Pierce. *Born Eunice Quedens in Mill Valley, California, on April 30, 1907; died on November 12, 1990; daughter of Lucille (Frank) and Charles Peter Quedens; attended Mill Valley Grammar School and Tamalpais High School; married Edward G. Bergen (a literary agent), 1938 (divorced); married Brooks West (an actor, c. 1916–1984); children: Douglas Brooks West; (adopted) Liza Connie and Duncan Paris West.*

Filmography: (as Eunice Quedens) The Song of Love *(1929);* Oh, Doctor *(1937);* Stage Door *(1937);* Having a Wonderful Time *(1938);* Letter of Introduction *(1938);* Eternally Yours *(1939);* At the Circus *(1939);* A Child is Born *(1940);* Slightly Honorable *(1940);* No, No, Nanette *(1940);* Comrade X *(1940);* Ziegfeld Girl *(1941);* That Uncertain Feeling *(1941);* Manpower *(1941);* Whistling in the Dark *(1941);* Bedtime Story *(1942);* Let's Face It *(1943);* Cover Girl *(1944);* The Doughgirls *(1944);* Pan-Americana *(1945);* Mildred Pierce *(1945);* My Reputation *(1946);* The Kid from Brooklyn *(1946);* Night and Day *(1946);* Song of Scheherázade *(1947);* The Unfaithful *(1947);* The Voice of the Turtle *(1947);* One Touch of Venus *(1948);* My Dream is Yours *(1949);* Tea for Two *(1950);* Three Husbands *(1950);* Goodbye My Fancy *(1951);* We're Not Married *(1952);* The Lady Wants Mink *(1953);* Anatomy of a Murder *(1959);* The Dark at the Top of the Stairs *(1960);* Sergeant Deadhead *(1965);* The Strongest Man in the World *(1975);* Grease *(1978);* Under the Rainbow *(1981);* Pandemonium *(1982);* Grease II *(1982).* "Our Miss Brooks" *was broadcast on radio (1948–56), and ran as a television series (1956–60).*

Eve Arden was born Eunice Quedens in Mill Valley, California, in 1907. Two years later, her mother left her father because of his incessant gambling. "My mother, who was extraordinarily lovely," wrote Arden, "was evidently gifted with talent as well." During a short career as an actress, Lucille Quedens had been chosen out of a group of 20 to play second leads in a theatrical company that starred *Blanche Bates. To make ends meet, Lucille then taught drama to children and ran her own millinery shop.

At seven, Arden was sent to live in a Dominican convent in San Rafael. After two years, she moved in with her father's sister, Aunt Elsie, in Mill Valley, though she and her mother remained extremely close. Eventually, her mother

Eve Arden

bought a tract next to Elsie's and built a home for herself and her daughter. A whiz at finances, Lucille purchased four more lots on an adjacent hillside, sold her business, and oversaw the properties. By the time Arden left grade school, her maternal grandmother was also in residence.

In high school, Arden starred in the senior play and, upon graduation, joined the Henry Duffy Stock Company at the Alcazar Theater in San Francisco. When the company moved to Los Angeles, she moved with it, living in a one-room apartment on $50 a week. In 1933, she toured with the Bandbox Repertory Company, then appeared at the Pasadena Playhouse in the review *Lo and Behold*.

That summer Arden was offered a job in New York with *The Ziegfeld Follies of 1934*, but her mother was ill and Arden was fearful of leaving California. On the strength of Lucille's reassurances, Arden opened at New York's Winter Garden Theater on January 4, 1934, along with *Fanny Brice, *Jane Froman, and *Judy Canova. For her New York debut, Arden did a

take-off on "Major Bowes Amateur Hour." As recalled in her autobiography *Three Phases of Eve*, she stepped before the microphone dressed in a blue satin evening gown, wearing a beautifully coiffed white wig. When Major Bowes asked what her talent was, she replied:

"I am a kazooist, and I accompany myself with two cymbals." And so saying, I hummed the first strains of "Sweet Sue" on the kazoo, ending with a terrific crash on my two large cymbals fastened between my knees, hidden beneath my skirt. It was a complete surprise, and the audience howled. It was the same kind of surprise *Bea [Lillie] had given them in a previous show when, having sung a charming song, leaning against the proscenium, she lifted her long satin skirt and gaily roller-skated across the stage.

Producer Lee Shubert suggested Arden's name change. Quedens, he said, was impossible to pronounce (Qwa-DENZ) and besides, combined with Eunice, it would barely fit his marquee. "Eve" came from the heroine in the book she was reading, and "Arden" came from a package of cosmetics within sight. "Only later did I learn, by seeing it emblazoned in lights on a burlesque house outside of Boston," wrote Eve Arden, "that not only was there an[other] Arden, but an Eve Arden, who appeared nightly adorned in a single white fox fur."

Following a tour with the Follies, Arden was featured in the play *Parade* with Jimmy Savo (1935), as well as a second *Follies,* which opened at the Winter Garden in January 1936; she and Bob Hope sang the duet, "I Can't Get Started with You." During those two years in New York, Arden lost her entire family. First both her grandmother and her Aunt Elsie died, and her mother was hospitalized with cancer. Before Arden could reach her bedside, Lucille Quedens slipped into a coma and never regained consciousness.

In spring 1937, Arden was offered her first film, Universal's *Oh, Doctor.* Shortly thereafter, she was interviewed for the film adaptation of *Edna Ferber's *Stage Door,* which was to star *Katharine Hepburn, *Ginger Rogers, *Gail Patrick, Andrea Leeds, *Lucille Ball, and *Ann Miller. Director Gregory La Cava, who liked to improvise scenes on the set, warned Arden that, though he liked her and wanted to use her, he had no specific part in mind. They mutually agreed that she'd sign on for a couple of weeks, and if they didn't develop a satisfactory character, she could depart with no hard feelings. Arden described the reading on the first day:

> All . . . were assembled, and sheets containing lines were handed around. Lines one, two, three, et cetera, were tossed to us like bones to puppies. I had immediately spotted two lines I was drooling over, but alas, they were not to be mine. When the reading started, however, the first of the juicy lines was greeted by complete silence. Finally, I could stand it no longer, "If no one wants this, I'll take it," I said bravely, read it, and was rewarded with a laugh. Katharine Hepburn hooted from her perch on a ladder looking over us. "She's the one to watch out for, girls."

The next day Arden arrived with her cat Henry as a prop. At one point in the scene she was supposed to be shelling peanuts. Running out of hands, she draped Henry around her neck and her character was born.

Known for her timing and deadpan delivery, Arden began to average three films per year, playing secretaries and friends of secretaries. But theater remained her first love. She appeared in the Kern-Hammerstein musical *Very Warm Day* on Broadway, followed by *Two for the Show,* and *Dorothy Field's 1941 musical hit *Let's Face It* (with Danny Kaye). Arden also starred in the movie of the same name opposite Bob Hope.

Movie followed movie: *A Day at the Circus* (with the Marx Brothers), *Comrade X* (with *Hedy Lamarr and Clark Gable), *Ziegfeld Girl, One Touch of Venus, Cover Girl,* and *Mildred Pierce* for which Arden was nominated for Best Supporting Actress. (The award went to *Anne Revere for her performance in *National Velvet.*)

In 1948, Arden's "Our Miss Brooks" went on CBS radio as a summer replacement; by August, it was the number one show on the air. As schoolteacher Connie Brooks, Arden was surrounded by the whackos of mythical Madison High: Gale Gordon as the persnickety Mr. Conklin, Richard Crenna as the teenaged, squeaky-voiced Walter Denton, and **Jane Morgan** as ditzy Mrs. Davis, her landlady. Wrote Arden:

> I'll never forget my landlady, Mrs. Davis, of the deep gravelly voice, who could always make me laugh. One night we did a scene where the two of us were locked up together in the "pokey" and she picked up a tin cup and ran it across the cell bars, then, in her inimitable voice, called for the guard. She bellowed, "Screw" as I fell apart and couldn't finish the scene the next five times.

When the show was transferred to television in 1956, Robert Rockwell replaced Jeff Chandler as the bashful biology teacher, Mr. Boynton, and Arden won an Emmy. In the fourth televised year, a new executive producer came in, effectively jettisoned the cast, and transformed the show out of all recognition. Arden wagered that they would have the entire cast back in three months; they were, but it was too late. The audience had moved on. "Our Miss Brooks" had run eight years on radio, and four on television. The following year, it went into syndication, and reruns brought it renewed fame. She was then handed "The Eve Arden Show" but, without the benefit of good writers, it lasted only one year. Her other series, "The Mothers-in-Law" with **Kaye Ballard**, had a respectable run.

Following her 1938 marriage to literary agent Edward Bergen, Arden had longed for children but was unable to conceive, so she adopted a daughter Liza. By the time she adopted her second daughter Connie three years later, Arden was a single mother. Some years later, while starring in *Ruth Gordon's play *Over Twenty-One* in summer stock, Arden met actor Brooks West. After they married and adopted a boy Duncan, Eve learned she was pregnant, and Douglas Brooks West was born. She now had four children, a large assortment of animals (lambs, goats, a pinto horse, and a donkey named Molly Bee), and a contented life on a 38-acre farm in Hidden Valley, just outside Los Angeles. Despite West's struggles with drinking, the marriage endured, and the couple did one film together, *Anatomy of a Murder*. Arden was out-of-town doing a show when her husband lapsed into a coma from which he never recovered; he died on February 7, 1984. Eve Arden died six years later, on November 12, 1990.

SOURCES:
Arden, Eve. *Three Phases of Eve.* NY: St. Martin's Press, 1985.

Ardler, Stella (1902–1993).
See Adler, Stella.

Ardov, E. (1846–1923).
See Apréleva, Elena Ivanovna.

Aregunde
*Queen of the Franks. Name variations: Aregunda. Sister of *Ingunde (d. 517); 4th wife of Chlothar also known as Clothaire, Clotar, or Lothair I (497–561), king of Soissons (r. 511), king of the Franks (r. 558–561); children: Chilperic I (523–584), king of Soissons (Neustria).*

Aremburg (d. 1126).
See Ermentrude, countess of Maine.

Arenal, Concepción (1820–1893)
Spanish poet and essayist who worked for prison reform. Name variations: Concepcion. Born on January 30, 1820, in El Ferrol, Galicia, Spain; died in 1893 in Vigo; married Fernando Garcia Carrasco (editor of La Iberia*), in 1848; children: daughter (b. around 1848 and died in infancy); sons Fernando (b. 1850) and Ramón (b. 1852).*

Selected works: 474 articles for the magazine La voz de la caridad; *Fábulas en verso (Fables in Verse, 1854).*

Though the Arenals had once been an affluent and distinguished family in Spain, by the time Concepción Arenal's father, a law student, had taken part in the rebellion against the rule of King Ferdinand VII, they were elite in name only. Imprisoned for his rebellion, her father died in jail in 1829. Concepción, with her two sisters and her mother, moved to Armaño Liábana in the Asturias mountains, where they lived with her paternal grandmother. Arenal left

when she was 15 to begin studies in Madrid. Enrolled at a prestigious school for girls, which taught the feminine virtues, she had to undertake more academic studies such as Italian and French on her own.

Despite her mother's fear that she would ruin the family honor and her chances for marriage, Arenal was determined to attend university and study law. In the fall of 1842, she began to audit courses at the Central University of Madrid. Since women were not allowed to officially enroll, nor were they to be seen in public without a parent or servant, it is believed that Arenal began to disguise herself as a man. When her gender was discovered, the dean demanded that she present herself for academic testing. Her intelligence and learning proved to be on par with or above her male counterparts. She was allowed to resume her attendance, provided that she continue to dress as a man.

At the university, Arenal met Fernando Garcia Carrasco, a student 12 years her senior, and in 1948 they were married. Fernando was a vocal liberal, which endangered his safety, so they briefly sought refuge back in Asturias. They returned to Madrid when Fernando was made editor of the liberal newspaper *La Iberia*. Arenal had three children within the first four years of marriage. The first, a daughter, was hydrocephalic and died at age two. Sons Fernando and Ramón were born in 1850 and 1852, respectively. Ramón's birth left Arenal in poor health. While bedridden, she took up writing, beginning with a series of poems, "Anales de la virtus" (Annals of Virtue). She also wrote several plays, and in 1854 her *Fábulas en verso (Fables in Verse)* was published.

As Arenal returned to health, Fernando fell ill with tuberculosis. While she cared for him, she continued his work at *La Iberia*, including writing articles that the paper published under his name. When Fernando died in 1855, Arenal accepted a salary of half that of Fernando's to continue her writing without a byline. Later that year, a law was passed requiring that articles carry an author credit. *La Iberia* proudly revealed Arenal's identity. Though she continued to write, Arenal retired from the paper, took her children back to Asturias, and contributed most of her energy to ministering to the poor.

At the age of 43, Arenal took the post of inspector of the women's prisons in Galicia and moved to La Coruña. There she met the **Countess Espoz y Mina**, who began to fund the publication of Arenal's writings. A great deal of Arenal's work focused on the position of women in Spanish society, particularly in relation to prison reform. In 1864, Arenal founded Las Magdalenas, an organization to assist women during imprisonment and after their release. Las Magdalenas volunteers visited prisoners, read to and helped educate them, and provided a safe haven when they left the prison. Arenal served as inspector until 1873, when the position was terminated.

With the assistance of the countess, in 1870 Arenal established the magazine *La voz de la caridad*, a frequent forum for her work. Two years later, the countess died, and Arenal fell ill. By the time her health improved, the Carlist war had begun, and Arenal organized a Red Cross corp, serving for five months in a military hospital. When she emerged from service, Arenal saw a wave of liberalism sweep through the country. Many of the ideals for which she had campaigned, most notably prison reform, began to be instituted. In 1875, Arenal and her son Fernando moved to Gijon.

La Voz continued publication until its demise in 1884 due to lack of funding. That same year, Arenal's son Ramón died. Moving to Vigo in 1889, Arenal undertook the revision and compilation of her complete works. In 1893, after burning her correspondence and destroying all but one photograph of herself, Concepción Arenal died of chronic bronchitis. Upon publication, her complete works constituted 23 volumes.

Crista Martin, Boston, Massachusetts

Arendsee, Martha (1885–1953)

German Socialist and Communist leader. Born in Berlin, Germany, on March 29, 1885; died in East Berlin on May 22, 1953; married Paul Schwenk (1880–1960).

Served as one of the few female Communist deputies to the Prussian provincial assembly (1921–24); elected to the Reichstag (1924); arrested by the Nazis (1933), escaped to the Soviet Union (1934); arrested in Stalin's purges but survived with husband (1930s); worked tirelessly against the Nazi invasion of the USSR during World War II; became a founding member of the Central Women's Council of the Berlin municipal government (August 1945); elected a member of the Central Committee of the Communist Party of Germany (KPD, 1946), and served as a member of the first party executive committee of the newly created Socialist Unity Party of Germany (SED, 1946–47).

Martha Arendsee was born into a working-class family in Berlin on March 29, 1885. Poverty attracted her to Marxism, and she joined the Social Democratic Party in 1906. Starting in 1907, she became active in Socialist activities, and by 1910 she was working full-time in the administration of the Socialist Consumer's Cooperative Society, where her talent and energy soon brought her to the attention of the party leadership. In 1915, Arendsee was chosen to participate in the international women's conference in Berne, Switzerland. A strong critic of German imperialism in World War I, she quit the prowar party in 1917 and joined the vehemently antiwar Independent Social Democratic Party (USPD) the same year.

By the end of the war, Arendsee had advanced to the important post of district chair of Berlin's militantly working-class Wedding district (known throughout Germany as "Red Wedding"). An early supporter of the Bolshevik Revolution in Russia, she participated in the abortive attempt of the nascent German Communist movement to seize power in Berlin in December 1918 and January 1919. In 1919, she was elected as an USPD delegate to the Prussian provincial assembly, a seat she held until 1921. Though Arendsee was a militant Marxist, she was at times critical of the orthodox Communist Party of Germany (KPD). In 1920, she held a leadership position in the central committee of the left wing of the USPD, but finally joined the Communists in December of that year.

Martha Arendsee was one of the leading women in the KPD from the time she joined the party in 1921 until the Nazi takeover of Germany in January 1933. From 1921 to 1924, she served as one of the few female Communist deputies to the Prussian provincial assembly. Throughout the next decade, Arendsee was active in propaganda work, serving on the editorial staff of a number of journals including *Die Kommunistin* and *Proletarische Sozialpolitik*. In 1924, she was elected to the *Reichstag*, serving in that national parliamentary body until 1930, when she did not receive a nomination from the KPD leadership due to suspicions of "rightist deviationism" and insufficient enthusiasm for the party's Stalinist course. She remained, however, in the party and, in fact, had been advanced by 1931 to the important position of central committee member of the International Workers' Aid, a Communist-dominated organization to assist imprisoned revolutionaries.

The Nazi seizure of power in Germany in the first months of 1933 radically changed Arendsee's life. As prominent Communists, both she and her husband Paul Schwenk (1880–1960) were considered "notorious Marxists" by the new regime. He was able to escape the Nazi dragnet and fled to Paris in April 1933, but Arendsee was not so fortunate; she was arrested at the same time in Berlin. Held under the pseudo-legal notion of "protective custody," she was incarcerated from April through September 1933 at the Barnimstrasse women's prison. After her release, she received orders from the KPD exile leadership to prepare for an escape from Germany in order to emigrate to the Soviet Union. Getting wind of this, Nazi police officials released flyers with her photograph in July 1934, but the "dangerous enemy of the Reich" had already fled the country that March. Her husband had arrived in Moscow from France in May 1934.

While he worked as a research associate at Moscow's Marx-Engels Institute, Arendsee eventually found a permanent position at International Red Trade Union Federation; she was also involved in the administration of the Foreign Workers' Club in the Soviet capital. Meanwhile, back in Germany, the wheels of the Nazi bureaucracy ground on, pursuing Arendsee and her husband on paper if not in person. The feared Nazi People's Court tried to discover her whereabouts in 1937, and, by early 1941, her name had been placed on a list of dangerous Communists to be liquidated once the Soviet Union was conquered and occupied. Both she and her husband were stripped of their German citizenship by the Nazi regime, he in July 1939 and she in December 1942.

The bloody purges initiated by Joseph Stalin in 1936 nearly proved tragic for Martha Arendsee. Her husband Paul, who had also worked in Moscow at the Communist International headquarters as well as at Moscow Radio and the Foreign Languages Publishing House, ran afoul of Stalinist orthodoxy and was arrested in 1937. As for Arendsee, she was regarded as one of the 504 leading functionaries of the pre-1933 KPD. Of these, 68 had found what they assumed was a safe haven in the Soviet Union. But as it turned out, only 18 of the 68 survived the Stalinist bloodbath. For still inexplicable reasons, Arendsee was one of the fortunate. Even more incredible, her husband was one of the very few individuals from the group of targeted foreign Communist emigrés in the USSR who survived the terrors of the Gulag. He was released from the prison camp on January 13, 1941. Only a few months later, on June 22, 1941, Nazi Germany attacked the Soviet Union. With this violent end to the Hitler-Stalin alliance, German Communist emigrés joined in a full-scale war against the hated Nazi regime in their homeland.

Martha Arendsee

Arendsee worked tirelessly to win over German soldiers and prisoners of war, prophesying that defeat was as inevitable for Hitler's legions as it had been for Napoleon more than a century earlier. Arendsee broadcast to the German lines on Moscow Radio and the German People's Station, and was a signatory to several manifestoes of Soviet policy toward a defeated Germany. She was also a founding member of the National Committee for a Free Germany (NKFD), the Soviet-sponsored organization of German POWs on Soviet territory.

In early June 1945, at war's end, Arendsee returned to Berlin as part of a group of German Communists led by fellow-emigré Wilhelm Pieck (1876–1960), who later became the first and only president of the German Democratic Republic. Arendsee's husband, who was considered politically less important to the KPD, did not return to Berlin until the following year. Arendsee was the most prominent woman among the Communist leadership in 1945 Germany, and thus was chosen as one of the signatories of the revived KPD's June 1945 appeal to the German people, a political document that emphasized a democratic, rather than a Marxist, agenda for the defeated German nation. Immediately immersing herself in Berlin political life, she became a founding member of the Central Women's Council of the Berlin municipal government in August 1945. In 1946, she was elected a member of the Central Committee of the KPD, and until September 1947 served as a member of the first party executive committee of the newly created Socialist Unity Party of Germany (SED). Her husband Paul Schwenk too found a niche in the Soviet Occupation Zone of Germany during these years, working as an editor and serving for a period as acting *Oberbürgermeister* (lord mayor) of East Berlin.

During a difficult period of reconstruction and material privation, Arendsee remained a dedicated Communist. Despite the toll taken by advancing age, she was active in virtually all of the important women's councils and organizations affiliated with the KPD and SED. She also headed the social-political branch of the newly founded Communist-dominated trade union organization Free German Union of Labor Unions (FDGB). In the newly founded German Democratic Republic (DDR)—which was created in October 1949 to finalize the Cold War division of Germany—she served as chief executive of the Social Insurance Organization of East Berlin. She retired in 1950 and died in East Berlin on May 22, 1953. The uprising of the workers of East Berlin, which took place less than a month after her death on June 17, 1953, demonstrated how unpopular the DDR regime and the Marxist faith to which Martha Arendsee subscribed had become. In January 1975, the German Democratic Republic issued a postage stamp in her honor as part of its ongoing "Personalities of the German Working Class" series of commemorative issues.

SOURCES:

Arendsee, Martha. *Kinder hungern! Kinder sterben! Wir klagen an.* KPD flyer, Berlin, 1932.

In den Fängen des NKWD: Deutsche Opfer des stalinistischen Terrors in der UdSSR. Berlin: Dietz Verlag, 1991.

Kommunisten im Reichstag: Reden und biographische Skizzen. Berlin: Dietz Verlag, 1980.

Leonhard, Wolfgang. *Child of the Revolution.* Translated by C.M. Woodhouse. Chicago: Henry Regnery, 1958.

Röder, Werner, and Herbert A. Strauss, eds. *Biographisches Handbuch der deutschsprachigen Emigration nach 1933.* 4 vols. Munich: K.G. Saur, 1980.

Schumacher, Martin. *M.d.R. Die Reichstagsabgeordneten der Weimarer Republik in der Zeit des Nationalsozialismus: Politische Verfolgung, Emigration und Ausbürgerung 1933–1945.* Düsseldorf: Droste Verlag, 1991.

Vier Monate Brüning-Regierung: Auf dem Wege zur faschistischen Diktatur, April bis Juli 1930. Mit Beiträgen von Eduard Alexander, Martha Arendsee, Adolf Ende. Herausgegeben im Auftrage des Zentralkomitees der Kommunistischen Partei Deutschlands. Berlin: Internationaler Arbeiter-Verlag, 1930.

Weber, Hermann. *Die Wandlung des deutschen Kommunismus: Die Stalinisierung der KPD in der Weimarer Republik.* 2 vols. Frankfurt am Main: Europäische Verlagsanstalt, 1969.

———. *"Weisse Flecken" in der Geschichte: Die KPD-Opfer der Stalinschen Säuberungen und ihre Rehabilitierung.* Rev. ed. Frankfurt am Main: isp-Verlag, 1990.

John Haag, Associate Professor of History, University of Georgia, Athens, Georgia

Arendt, Hannah (1906–1975)

German-American political theorist and philosopher famed for her analyses of totalitarianism and the trial of Nazi war criminal Adolf Eichmann. Pronunciation: AIR-ent. *Born October 14, 1906, in Hannover, Germany; died on December 4, 1975, in New York City; daughter of Paul Arendt (an engineer) and Martha Cohn Arendt; attended Universities of Marburg, Freiburg, and Heidelberg; granted Ph.D, University of Heidelberg, 1928; married Günther Stern, in September 1929 (divorced 1936); married Heinrich Blücher, on January 16, 1940 (died, October 30, 1970).*

Used home as underground railroad for fleeing Jewish refugees before moving to France (1933); visited Palestine (1935); worked to help Jewish refugees arriving in Paris (1938); placed in French internment camp (1941); came to United States (1941); worked for the Committee for a Jewish Army (1941–42); co-founded, with Joseph Maier, the Young Jewish Group as a replacement for that committee (1942); served as research director of the Conference on Jewish Relations (1944–46); named chief editor of Schocken Books (1946–48); appointed executive director of Jewish Cultural Reconstruction (1948–52); became a U.S. citizen (1951); won the Sigmund Freud Prize (1957), the Lessing Prize (1959), and the Sonning Prize (1974); taught at the University of Chicago, Princeton, University of California at Berkeley, the Rand school, Columbia University, and the New School for Social Research, among others (1950–74).

Selected works: Eichmann in Jerusalem: A Report on the Banality of Evil *(Harmondsworth: Penguin, 1976);* The Human Condition *(Chicago: University of Chicago Press, 1958);* The Life of the Mind *(London: Secker and Warburg, 1978);* On Revolution *(Harmondsworth: Pelican, 1973);* The Origins of Totalitarianism *(London: Deutsch, 1986).*

Although she found herself a "stateless person" part of her life, Hannah Arendt considered herself to be the inheritor of the best of two worlds—the intellectual traditions of the Old World and the social and political standards of the New. Born and educated in Germany, but transplanted to the United States after the rise to power of Nazism, Arendt provided distinctive and iconoclastic explanations for the disasters that overtook Europe in the first half of the 20th century. Her analyses were often controversial, but they were rarely conventional and never simplistic.

An only child, she was born into a middle-class family in the German municipality of Hannover, a major maritime city. The Arendts

were economically well-off, as a result of her father's salary as an engineer. When Hannah was only four years old, they moved back to the family's traditional city of Koenigsberg, in eastern Prussia, where Hannah's father would be treated for an advanced case of syphilis, which he had contracted before his marriage. Eventually, he would be housed in a psychiatric hospital.

Hannah's mother, who kept a doting record of her child's intellectual and physical progress, noted in the journal that she tried to shield her daughter from seeing the toll wrought by the disease. Yet as an adult, Hannah Arendt recounted memories of watching her father struggle to walk and of hearing her mother play the piano to distract him from pain. She also remembered that her father's illness kept her from inviting playmates to visit. The year her father died, 1913, also saw the death of her beloved grandfather Max Arendt, who had often regaled Hannah with colorful stories during Sunday morning walks and who, with her grandmother, had accompanied her to synagogue.

Although young Hannah heard discussions about the need for a Jewish homeland, the family did not favor Zionist ideas. Her grandfather Max had, however, been a personal friend of Kurt Blumenfeld, the founder of the Zionist Organization of Germany. The sizeable Jewish community of the town served to protect Hannah from anti-Semitism, although she remembered a classmate telling her that her family had murdered Jesus.

Politically, the family favored the German Left—her parents considered themselves socialists—although Arendt would remain relatively apolitical until the late 1920s. Her mother was an admirer of the German Marxist *Rosa Luxemburg; when Luxemburg and other German Marxists attempted to carry out a revolution in the country in 1919, Arendt remembered that her mother took her to a prorevolutionary rally and told her, "This is a historical moment."

World War I forced the family to leave Koenigsberg, which was vulnerable to attack from the nearby Russian border. During the first month of the war, the family moved to Berlin, and Hannah was enrolled in a girls' school in the Berlin suburb of Charlottenburg. When her mother married Martin Beerwald, a wealthy businessman, in 1920, their economic difficulties ended, at least for a time. The money was provided for her to prepare for a university education.

Arendt's chances for college seemed slim after she led a student boycott against a teacher whom she accused of insulting her. When the "independent and rebellious" Hannah was expelled from the girls' school, her mother arranged private study for her to prepare for the *Abitur,* the examination that was the key to entering a German university. A teacher at an all-male school was hired, and it was arranged for Hannah to take some classes at the University of Berlin.

When she completed her *Abitur* in 1924, a year ahead of schedule, Arendt enrolled at the University of Marburg, where she began to study philosophy under the existentialist Martin Heidegger; she also had an affair with him. Later, after he proclaimed Adolf Hitler the savior of Germany in an appearance at a Nazi rally in the mid-1930s, she called Heidegger the "last great Romantic"—a man who feared "modern trends" and had a commitment to the "preindustrial."

After a year at Marburg, she left for a six-month term at the University of Freiburg, so that she could study with Heidegger's mentor, Edmund Husserl. She then moved on to the University of Heidelberg, where Karl Jaspers, another existentialist, would become one of the greatest intellectual influences on her career. An opponent of anti-Semitism (his wife was Jewish and would be in peril during the Nazi period), Jaspers sought to combine thought and action. He called for an emphasis on "the movement of philosophy," or the application of philosophical and ethical ideas in the practical realm, including politics.

The influence of Jaspers was apparent in Arendt's doctoral dissertation. Focusing on the concept of love in the thought of St. Augustine, the dissertation illustrated Arendt's interest in both Jewish and Christian thought, and emphasized such Augustinian concepts as redemption and forgiveness. Her first book, on the same topic, was published to good reviews in 1929.

The year 1933 proved to be pivotal: a year, she wrote, that made the most lasting impression on her. When the National Socialists took power in January, the new government began persecuting political opponents, especially after the Reichstag building was burned. Her first husband, Günther Stern, a socialist, felt so threatened that

he left for Paris. Arendt remained behind for a while, working for the Zionist organization of Blumenfeld. Among her assignments was the job of compiling, from the Prussian State Library, evidence of anti-Semitic actions under way or being planned by German organizations and societies. Her apartment became an "underground railway" for Jews trying to flee Germany or Eastern Europe.

She resisted leaving Germany for part of 1933, telling Jaspers, "For me, Germany is mother tongue, philosophy, and poetry." Her mind was changed when the government arrested her and detained her for eight days. Finally, she left. It was a decision she never regretted, although she did feel some responsibility that so many of her friends who remained behind in Germany ended up in concentration camps. "This was such a shock to me," she wrote, "that I have ever since felt responsible." She resolved no longer to be just an "observer." "When one is attacked as a Jew," she later said, "one must defend oneself as a Jew."

Arendt and her mother traveled first to Prague and then Geneva before settling down in France. Relations with her husband cooled; by the time he left, alone, for the United States in 1936, the marriage was over in spirit if not in fact. They were divorced that same year. Her Paris years were ones of increasing involvement in Zionist causes. She supported herself by working for a French organization, *Agriculture et Artisanat,* which provided job training, including training in farming techniques, to young Jewish emigres who planned to move to Palestine. She visited Palestine in 1935, and in 1938 she became active in helping Jewish refugees from Germany and Eastern Europe settle in Paris.

As World War II approached, Arendt and her mother felt less secure. They worried about anti-Semitism in France. After the German invasion in 1940, they were concerned about the degree to which the French government in the unoccupied part of the country would cooperate with the Nazis in arresting Jews for "deportation" to concentration camps. Her second husband, Heinrich Blücher, a Communist whom she married in January 1940, was sent by the French to an internment camp for a time. Arendt herself was briefly detained.

Arendt and Blücher were among the fortunate few able to obtain American visas. French exit permits were not available, however. Traveling secretly to Marseilles, they were able to obtain the exit permits. But after police questioned the hotel management about the identity of patrons, Arendt staged an angry scene. She ranted that her husband had been taken to police headquarters, and she accused the hotel management of betraying him to the police. Meanwhile, while his wife was distracting hotel clerks with her diatribe, Blücher was fleeing the scene and the country.

Arendt managed to join Blücher in New York City in 1941, and her mother reached the United States a few months later. Arendt became active in World War II debates among Jewish emigres in the United States over the proper role of Jews during the war. She decided to support the idea of raising a Jewish army to fight against Nazism alongside Allied armies, even after the British government had rejected the idea. When it was revealed that the main organization supporting the project, founded by Ben Hecht, was being financed by an extremist and terrorist group, she became co-founder of a replacement organization, the Young Jewish Group. To support herself, she worked as the chief editor of a book publisher. In her columns for a German-language newspaper *Aufbau,* published in the United States, she rejected suggestions that Jews should have nothing to do with Germany when the war was over. For Arendt, there was no German "collective responsibility" for Hitler.

During the mid- and late 1940s, Arendt worked for the Commission on European Jewish Cultural Reconstruction, which sought to identify and locate books and manuscripts by Jewish authors that had been seized by the Nazis, or hidden from them. Her work took her back to Europe, where she had a frosty meeting with Heidegger, whom she labeled "just as much a liar as ever," and a warm and sentimental meeting with Jaspers, who, along with his wife, had been saved from imprisonment in a concentration camp only with the liberation of Heidelberg by American troops in 1945. One of her first postwar articles, entitled "What Is Existenz Philosophy?" was an attempt to introduce the thought of Jaspers to the English-speaking world.

Arendt increasingly assumed the role of mediator between the two worlds she had come to love—the Old World and the New. To Europeans scornful of American conformity, she explained that in the United States, a variety of social lifestyles could actually flourish without in any way endangering the political stability of the country. To Americans puzzled by European uneasiness about the atomic power of the U.S. military, she explained that Europe would probably be the major battleground of a future war. She told Europeans that their anti-Americanism might actually be opposition to modern trends, while she warned Americans that they tended to discount the destructive tendencies of new technologies.

Here was an intensity, an inner direction, an instinct for quality, a groping for essence, a probing for depth, which cast a magic about her. One senses an absolute determination to be herself, with the toughness to carry it through in the face of great vulnerability.

—Hans Jonas

Increasingly, she became involved in academia. She stayed with an American family in New England to try to learn the language better, and in the postwar years she taught at a variety of universities, including Columbia, Berkeley, Princeton, and the New School of Social Research. During these years, she received a number of honorary degrees from U.S. universities and was made a member of the National Institute for Arts and Letters and the American Academy for Arts and Science. The writer *Mary McCarthy became her closest friend and confidant.

Arendt now rejected the label of philosopher, preferring to think of herself as a political theorist. It was in that role that she began, in 1944, a work to try to explain to Americans what had brought about the Nazi catastrophe and the rise of dictators. The book was originally entitled the "Three Pillars of Evil," in reference to anti-Semitism, imperialism, and racism. When the book appeared in 1951, its new title was *The Origins of Totalitarianism.* Arendt was trying to address American concerns about the "spread" of Communism and the power of the Soviet dictator Joseph Stalin.

A major premise of the book was that the European intellectual tradition was not responsible for totalitarianism. Arendt made distinctions between "brilliant" intellectuals who had written on racism, such as the French Count Arthur de Gobineau—the first writer to use the term "Aryan" in a racial sense—and the "men who carried out the murders" in the name of race. Totalitarian regimes had arisen in the 20th century, wrote Arendt, because of causes such as overpopulation, economic expansion, and social restlessness.

There were, she wrote, up to then only two "authentic forms" of totalitarianism: the government of National Socialism after 1938, and the Communist government of Stalin after 1930 (the year of the first purges). In many ways, she conceded, they looked like variations of the same model. The differences between democracies and totalitarian government were not matters of free enterprise or class differences, but "a conflict between a government based on civil liberties and a government based on concentration camps."

The methodology of the *Origins* has frequently been criticized: she wrote from the viewpoint of an observer and political philosopher, rather than as a historian trained in the use of documents or as an empirical social scientist. Such an approach invited controversy. The most controversial section of the book concerned Arendt's attempts to explain to an American audience how European anti-Semitism had resulted in the Holocaust attempt to extirpate European Jews. Anti-Semitism, she wrote, had progressed as nationalism had receded. Political anti-Semitism developed because Jews were a separate body in European society; social discrimination had advanced because of the growing social equality of Jews.

To Arendt's critics, such an analysis raised the possibility that she was partly blaming European Jews for anti-Semitism—excusing rather than explaining. Arendt rejected such criticism, pointing out that her pro-Zionist activities had increased at the end of World War II. She insisted that "should catastrophe befall the Jewish state, this would be perhaps the final catastrophe for the Jewish people." And she added that "I have always regarded my Jewishness as one of the indisputable facts of my life." She supported Israel in the 1967 Arab-Israeli War and worked for the United Jewish Appeal and the Israel Emergency Fund.

Yet Arendt was a very independently minded Zionist, and her ideas regarding Israel were sometimes unconventional. She hoped to transfer the American principle of federalism to the Middle East, perhaps with a successful Israel-Arab confederation. She was just as unconventional in her thoughts regarding the trial in Israel of the Nazi war criminal Adolf Eichmann, who had been captured by Israeli agents in South America and transported to Israel in 1960.

Her critical assessment of the trial was published first as a series of articles in *The New Yorker* magazine and later as a book. She challenged the assumption that Eichmann was a major architect of the Holocaust. She suspected that the trial was a result of a backdoor agreement between the Israeli government and the West German government. In this agreement,

she thought, high West German officials who, as former Nazis, had been just as responsible for the Holocaust (or even more responsible) would escape scrutiny. Arendt also challenged the legality of Eichmann's kidnapping by Israeli agents and questioned whether his trial was based on any international laws.

"Eichmann in Jerusalem" warned against demonizing Eichmann, because Arendt feared the Eichmann and Nazi leaders might somehow be romanticized to heroic status. She strongly rejected the idea that Eichmann should be envisioned as an evil monster. He was an average man, and not even particularly intelligent. This very averageness was what was most chilling about Eichmann, she wrote, since it showed that the potential for evil was present in all persons—the "banality of evil," in her words.

"It is my opinion," she wrote, "that evil is never 'radical': that it is only extreme, and that it possesses neither depth nor any demonic dimensions. It is 'thought defying'. . . because thought tries to reach some depth, to go to the roots, and the moment it concerns itself with evil it is frustrated because there is nothing." Many of Arendt's critics believed that she was minimizing the evil of the Holocaust, and they were particularly offended by her suggestions that Jewish councils in Europe had cooperated with Nazi efforts to "deport" Jews to concentration camps, even if the cooperation was not voluntary.

Although she worried that American intellectuals were too passive during the chilling days of the McCarthy era of the 1950s—when a Wisconsin senator named Joseph McCarthy claimed that Communists had infiltrated almost every aspect of American government and life—Arendt came to love many things in what was, after she became an American citizen in 1951, her adopted country. She was impressed that American intellectuals believed, as a matter of principle, that they should generally oppose many prevailing political or social trends. They did not "worship the God of success." She contrasted that with the opportunism of German intellectuals when Hitler came to power in her native country. Social nonconformism, she said, was the "*sine quo non* of intellectual achievement."

In her book *On Revolution* (1973), Arendt defended the American Revolution, which she thought Europeans failed to appreciate sufficiently. "The sad truth," she wrote, "is that the French Revolution, which ended in disaster, has made World History, while the American Revolution, so triumphantly successful, has remained an event of little more than local importance." She had gained, from her observations of Americans, an assurance that there would always be freedom for the "life of the mind" in the United States.

Politically, she thought of herself as being neither on the Left nor on the Right. When the political scientist and friend Hans Morgenthau, a fellow refugee from Europe, asked her if she was a "conservative" or a "liberal," she replied, "I couldn't care less. I don't think the real questions of this century will get any kind of illumination by this kind of thing."

Her political opinions on events in the United States during the 1960s were, in fact, sometimes on the Left and sometimes on the Right. She praised the Hungarian Revolution directed against Soviet control of that country in 1956, saying that it was "an uprising of oppressed people for the sake of freedom." She looked approvingly on student demonstrations against the Vietnam war, seeing these demonstrations as a "sign of profound change in American political life." She even gave approving speeches to groups of demonstrators.

And the civil-rights movement won her general support. She wrote that "as a Jew I take my sympathy for all oppressed and underprivileged people for granted." She thought integration would not be a simple process, however, and she believed that government could not legislate tolerance and understanding; it could only outlaw legalized segregation. She approved when President Dwight Eisenhower sent federal troops to Little Rock, Arkansas, in 1957, in order to enforce a high-school integration plan. She warned, however, that the power of individual American states should not be ignored, since she thought that a division of political power between the states and the federal government was the best way to guarantee freedom and diversity "in the Republic."

Although she was at times confused by the politics of the Watergate affair, which resulted in the resignation of President Richard Nixon in 1974, she expressed outrage that Nixon was "behaving as a tyrant." It was her last major comment on American politics before she succumbed to a heart attack in 1975.

Arendt's work was the product of her own fierce individuality and the mixture of European and American cultures in which she worked. She expressed gratitude that she had "the freedom of becoming a citizen (of the United States) without paying the price of assimilation." She believed that the great ethical and philosophical ideas of

Europe were important and relevant for the diverse society of the United States. She proudly told European friends that freedom and diversity were *sehr amerikanisch*—"very American."

But her roots, and her sentiment, remained with European culture. Traumatized by the rise of Nazism and the Holocaust, Arendt refused to hold the European intellectual tradition responsible for those disasters. While much of her writing after World War II reflected those traumas, she continued to think of herself as a transplanted European. In replying to one of her critics, she proudly said that "I am not one of the intellectuals who came from the German Left. . . . If I can be said to have come from anywhere, it is from the tradition of German philosophy."

SOURCES:

Kateb, George. *Hannah Arendt: Politics, Conscience, Evil.* Totowa, NJ: Rowman and Allanheld, 1983.
Watson, David. *Arendt.* London: Fontana Press, 1992.
Young-Bruehl, Elisabeth. *Hannah Arendt: For Love of the World.* New Haven, CT: Yale University Press, 1982.

COLLECTIONS:

Papers and documents relating to Hannah Arendt are held in the Library of Congress, Washington, D.C.; the Deutsches Literaturarchiv, in Marbach, Germany; and in the Bard College Library, Annandale-on-Hudson, New York.

SUGGESTED READING:

May, Derwent. *Hannah Arendt.* Harmondsworth: Penguin, 1986.
Whitfield, Stephen J. *Into the Dark: Hannah Arendt and Totalitarianism.* Philadelphia, PA: Temple University Press, 1980.

Niles R. Holt, Professor of History,
Illinois State University, Normal-Bloomington, Illinois

Arete of Cyrene (fl. 4th c. BCE)

Greek philosopher of the 4th century BCE *who followed her father Aristippus as the head of the Cyrenaic school, which came to hold that virtue and pleasure were one. Flourished in the 4th century* BCE; *daughter of Aristippus; married; children: Aristippus.*

Arete of Cyrene was a 4th-century BCE Greek philosopher of the Cyrenaic school. Her father was Aristippus, a wealthy citizen of the Greek city of Cyrene, which was founded in north Africa (modern Libya) as a colony of Thera in the 7th century BCE. Aristippus was attracted to Athens at the end of the 5th century by the fame of Socrates, under whose tutelage he began a career in philosophy. Unlike Socrates, Aristippus accepted large fees from students—a practice for which he was roundly criticized by other disciples of Socrates, although it seems to have been Aristippus' practice to share the fruits of his labors with his beloved philosophical master.

Traveling widely throughout the Greek world, Aristippus was eventually attracted to Syracuse on the island of Sicily, where he reaped substantial wealth from that city's tyrants, so clearly interested in philosophy and the legacy of Socrates. Ultimately, Aristippus returned to his native Cyrene and established a philosophical school blending many of the concerns of Socrates with the work of the Sophists. He and his school flourished. When Arete was born is unknown, but she clearly was raised to a life of philosophical speculation by her father, for when he died she assumed his position as the master of his school. Exactly how long she functioned as such is unknown, but in turn she passed the Cyrenaic school to her son (also named Aristippus), maintaining it as a lucrative family concern at least in its first three generations.

Just as Arete's tenure as the head of the Cyrenaic school is sketchy, so is her personal contribution to its philosophy. However, she would have undoubtedly contributed to the school's most important philosophical tenants. Her father had taken away from Socrates a much different philosophical view of the world than did most of the master's other students. To Aristippus, the wise man was he who pursued instinctual pleasure and the financial wherewithal to satisfy what the heart could desire. Not to do so came to be associated with an unnatural and perverse asceticism, which in its own way was as extreme as the hedonism into which the Cyrenaic school's philosophy could logically fall. The Cyrenaics eschewed metaphysics and science essentially as being fields beyond human ken. They came to argue a kind of absolute relativism: what appeared to the individual became the only, absolute truth. Categories of all kinds were suspected, for, since no being could ever really experience the reality of another, no one could ever "know" beyond a shadow of a doubt that what one person is experiencing has anything in common with what another person is experiencing. Rather, the Cyrenaics determined that all that can be counted on is immediate sensation, the pursuit of which renders pleasure, and the goodness sought from life. Thus a philosophical school spawned by Socrates gave rise to a resurgence of the sophistic notion, "man is the measure of all things."

Whatever inconsistencies and problems the Cyrenaics posed, they prized individual freedom, education, and an ability to be independent of hypocritical convention (especially that which was religious in nature), all strikingly characteristic of many ideas current in the late 20th century. Balancing these notions, perhaps, were others that maintained that the world was all right as it is, and that what is needed by everyone seeking happiness is a passive willingness to accept things as they are, along with a willingness to adapt to current conditions, whatever they might be.

SUGGESTED READING:

Waithe, M.E., ed. *Ancient Women Philosophers*. Dordrecht, Boston, 1987.

William S. Greenwalt, Associate Professor of Classical History, Santa Clara University, Santa Clara, California

Aretz, Isabel (1913—)

Venezuelan composer, ethnomusicologist, and folklorist universally recognized as a leading authority on South American folk music. Name variations: Isabel Aretz de Ramón y Rivera. Born in Buenos Aires, Argentina, on April 13, 1913; studied piano with Rafel González and composition with Athos Palma at the Buenos Aires National Conservatory of Music; instrumentation with Heitor Villa-Lobos in Brazil; and anthropology with Carlos Vega; received her doctorate in musicology at the Argentine Catholic University in 1967; married Luis Felipe Ramón y Rivera.

In 1950, Isabel Aretz was appointed the first professor of ethnomusicology at the Escuela Nacional de Danzas de Argentina, where she continued her role as a scholar and composer. She traveled extensively throughout Hispanic America, collecting folk music that she then analyzed and used as a basis for her research papers. Aretz's scholarly work influenced her composition, which had a highly personal, nationalist style based on Afro-Hispanic folk traditions with avantgarde European elements including electronic music. Among other awards, Aretz received a scholarship from the Argentine National Commission on Culture, a Guggenheim Foundation fellowship, and the Polifonia prize of Buenos Aires. Through her scholarship, she documented South American folk music; through her compositions, she applied older traditions to modern music. Well-known and highly respected in international musical organizations, Aretz serves as a board member of the International Folk Music Council and a council member of the Society for Ethnomusicology. From 1953 on, Aretz lived in Venezuela.

John Haag, Associate Professor of History, University of Georgia, Athens, Georgia

Argentina, La (c. 1886–1936).

See Mercé, Antonia.

Argentinita (1898–1945).

See Lopez, Encarnación.

Argerich, Martha (1941—)

Argentine pianist. Born on June 5, 1941, in Buenos Aires, Argentina; studied with Vincenzo Scaramuzza, Friedrich Gulda, Arturo Benedetti Michelangeli, Nikita Magaloff, and Madeleine Lipatti.

Winner of the Busoni International Competition in Bolzano in 1957 and the prestigious Chopin International Competition in Warsaw in 1965.

After early studies with Vincenzo Scaramuzza, Martha Argerich made her debut in Buenos Aires in 1949. Her later training in Europe included working with Friedrich Gulda, Arturo Benedetti Michelangeli, Nikita Magaloff, and **Madeleine Lipatti**. Argerich achieved world rank by winning the 1957 Busoni International Competition in Bolzano and the prestigious Chopin International Competition in Warsaw in 1965. She was considered by many to be one of the most passionate pianists of the late 20th century. Her restless nature and uninhibited musicality invariably excited audiences while occasionally irritating critics. Her recording of Ravel's *Gaspard de la nuit* is considered by some critics to be close to the definitive reading of this difficult work. Argerich became famous as a master performer of such disparate composers as Brahms, Schumann, and Prokofiev. She showed great talent in projecting, and at the same time skillfully blending, her powerful personality in the ensemble nature of chamber-music performances. Putting her family first, Argerich has become something of a cult figure, jealously guarding her private life, seeming diffident toward performance and marquee success.

John Haag, Associate Professor of History,
University of Georgia, Athens, Georgia

Argyle, Pearl (1910–1947)

English ballerina and actress. Born Pearl Wellman in 1910; died in 1947; studied with *Marie Rambert; married Curtis Bernhardt (an American film producer), in 1938.

Pearl Argyle rose quickly to leading roles after her debut with the Ballet Club (later Ballet Rambert) in 1926, creating La Fille in *Bar aux Folies-Bergère*, Hebe in *Descent of Hebe*, the wife in *Les Masques*, and the title roles in Andrée Howard's *Cinderella* and *Mermaid*. Joining the Sadler's Wells in 1935, she danced *Les Syphides*, *Swan Lake*, and created the Queen in *Le Roi Nu*. Argyle was also seen in many English films as well as revues. Following her marriage in 1938, she lived in America and danced in several Broadway musicals, including *One Touch of Venus*, before her death at age 37. The library of the Royal Ballet School in London was dedicated to her memory.

Argyll, duchess of.

See Gunning, Elizabeth (1734–1790).
See Louise (1848–1939).
See Mathilda (1925–1997).

Ariadne (fl. 457–515)

Fifth-century Byzantine empress and daughter of Leo I, whose two marriages preserved the dynasty until her death. Pronunciation: Ari-AD-nee. Name variations: Aelia Ariadne. Born before February 7, 457; died in Constantinople, late 515; daughter of the future Leo I, Byzantine emperor (r. 457–474), and Empress Verina; married the future Emperor Zeno (Tarasicodissa Rousoumbladeotes) in 466 or 467 (died, April 9, 491); married Emperor Anastasius I Dicorus (r. 491–518), on May 20, 491; children: (first marriage) Leo II (b. around 467).

Son Leo II became emperor (473); Leo II died leaving Zeno as ruler (474); Ariadne styled "Augusta" during reigns of Zeno and Anastasius (474–515); possibly involved in the revolt of Basiliscus (475–76); conspired in unsuccessful plots against the general Illus (477, 478, and 480–81); dominated court after death of her husband (491); chose and married his successor, Anastasius I (491).

Following the death of East Roman Emperor Marcian in 457, the Theodosian dynasty of nearly 80 years came to an end, and the dangerous question of succession commanded the attention of the empire. The most powerful man of the day was General Aspar, the *magister militum per orientem* (Master of Soldiers in the East), the highest military rank in Byzantium. But Aspar was eminently unsuited for imperial dignity: he was by descent a barbarian, and by creed an Arian—literally anathema to the official orthodoxy of the state. In order to preserve his power, he nominated and effected the election of one of his own officers and private attendants. The new Emperor Leo I, to be remembered as *Makelles* (the Butcher), was both Orthodox and of acceptable Dacian origin. The imperial family that he settled in Constantinople consisted of his wife ❧ **Verina,** and a young daughter Ariadne.

See sidebar on the following page ❧

❧▶ **Verina** (fl. 437–483)

Byzantine empress. Name variations: Verina Augusta. Birth date unknown; died before 484; sister of the general Basiliscus; married Leo I, emperor of Byzantium (r. 457–474); children: Ariadne (fl. 457–515); Leontia (b. after 457).

Verina and her husband, the future Leo I, were of humble birth. One legend has it that they once worked together in a butcher shop in Constantinople.

At Leo's accession in 457, he was the creature of his general, and he had made Aspar two promises: that Aspar's son be raised to the secondary imperial rank of caesar, thus designating him the successor to the throne, and that this man should then marry one of his daughters. It is possible that Ariadne was first betrothed to the caesar; later her younger sister **Leontia**, born after her father's coronation, took her place as his betrothed. As events transpired, however, neither daughter actually married Aspar's son. In one of his many attempts to break the barbarian influence at court, Leo took a step that would consign his dynasty to alternating threats of exterior and interior plotting and alliance.

Leo was not as compliant an appointment as Aspar had hoped (tension between the emperor and the general would be strong for over a decade, until Leo had Aspar and one of his sons cut down in 471). To oppose the power of Aspar and his German allies, Leo sought to harness the raw power of the Isaurians, a tribal group from the mountainous Mediterranean coast region of present-day Turkey, opposite Cyprus. Though they were fierce, uncouth, and all but autonomous, their lands had long been contained within the imperial borders, and they were technically Romans. The emperor's most successful overture in bringing the Isaurians to his side was his betrothal of his eldest daughter Ariadne to one of their chieftains, Tarasicodissa Rousoumbladeotes, who, before marrying her in 466 or 467, "exchanged that barbarous sound for the Greek appellation of Zeno," wrote Edward Gibbon.

After a tumultuous reign that saw fires in Constantinople, disastrous foreign wars, and religious upheaval, Leo died in 474. Since he was without male offspring, several months before his death he had designated as his successor the six-year-old son of Ariadne and Zeno. At Ariadne's urging, and with the concurrence of the Senate and the Empress Dowager Verina, the little Leo II elevated his father to imperial distinc-

tion on February 9, 474, by making Zeno regent. Probably also at this point, Ariadne adopted the imperial title of "Augusta." Within nine months, Leo II was dead. Later Latin historians did not hesitate to suggest that he was murdered by his unpopular father, who then became sole ruler of the East.

By delivering a son, Ariadne had seemed to secure the continuity of Leo's dynasty; following the death of the male blood line, she became the sole guarantor of her father's achievement. She was not, however, the only powerful imperial female at court in Constantinople. Leo's widow and Ariadne's mother Verina also wielded influence, and though she had acquiesced in Zeno's elevation, she (and much of the populace with her) came to hate him as a barbarous intruder. Added to this hatred, no doubt, was the fact that, as noted by J.B. Bury, "being a woman of energy and ambition, she found it distasteful to fall into the background, overshadowed by her daughter." Out of this atmosphere grew the conspiracy of 475, by which Verina Augusta, using her brother Basiliscus as general, hoped to place herself and her lover Patricius at the helm of empire. The conspiracy was a success insofar as Zeno, perhaps taking Ariadne with him, fled to his mountain strongholds in Isauria, leaving the throne unguarded. It failed for Verina insofar as Basiliscus seized the throne for himself and had Patricius done to death. After 20 months, Zeno overcame this rebellion and returned to Constantinople.

The varied fortunes of the Basiliscan revolt had been largely in the hands of the general Illus, an Isaurian and former confidant of Zeno who had initially acted with the rebels against the emperor, and then had turned on them to return Zeno to power. At Zeno's reappearance in the palace, Illus was naturally well rewarded. Among other distinctions, he was made *magister militum* and became one of the most powerful figures in the empire. Accompanying his ascendancy however, was the swelling hatred of the Augustae Verina and Ariadne, who resented his influence at court. In 478, Verina originated an attempt to assassinate Illus. It was foiled, and the empress dowager was readily turned over to Illus for safekeeping; there was of course no love lost between the emperor and his mother-in-law after the Basiliscan affair.

After Illus successfully suppressed yet another revolt towards the end of 479, Ariadne approached him with a petition to release her mother, whom he had forced to become a nun and to live in an Isaurian fortress. Johannes Malalas, a chronicler of the next generation, describes the scene dramatically. Ariadne had received secret letters from Verina and besought Zeno to release her. Zeno told Ariadne to refer her plea to Illus. She had Illus summoned, and tearfully asked him to release her mother. "Why do you seek her?" Illus asked, "So that she can again set up another Emperor against your husband?" Returning to Zeno, Ariadne delivered her ultimatum: "Is Illus in the palace, or me?" Shamed into acquiescence, Zeno replied to her, "If you can do anything, do it. I want you here."

Ariadne took action, plotting the death of Illus. Though her intended assassin got close enough to slice off an ear before being slaughtered, Illus escaped with his life. The result was another bout of dynasty-threatening civil discord. Illus was not convinced by Zeno's professions of ignorance about Ariadne's plot, and the general relocated to his native lands once more, where he rallied military support for a new rebellion. Along with Illus this time was the Empress Verina, whose hatred of Zeno had allowed a reconciliation with her jailer. By 484, the rebellion had been crushed and Verina had died, but it was another four years before Illus was finally seized in his fortress and executed.

After the death of Illus, only three years were left for Zeno to rule. By the time of Zeno's death on April 9, 491, he had overcome the two largest problems of his reign: threats from the barbarian Goths on his borders and the series of political revolts inside his dominion. Only the religious tension among the various factions within the church had not been calmed; in fact, Zeno's apparent sympathy for the Monophysite heresy precipitated a schism with the papacy that would last for 35 years. Zeno apparently had the foresight to realize that his death was approaching, and it seems likely that he expected the royal diadem to pass to his unpopular brother Longinus. Superstitious, and perhaps weakening in mind as well as body, Zeno consulted Maurianus, "who was knowledgeable in certain mysteries," as to who would take the throne after him. As Johannes Malalas relates the story, Maurianus replied that "one of the silentiarii would receive both his throne and his wife." The silentiarii were a relatively low-ranking corps of palace officials, whose job nevertheless ensured them access and intimacy with the imperial person: it was their duty to maintain order and silence within the palace. Although Zeno tried to avert the prophecy by having the unfortunate silentarius Pelagius strangled, the prophecy did come true, whether by supernatural or more mundane maneuvers.

Zeno had become emperor because of Ariadne's familial tie with his predecessor. With no son to take his place, Ariadne placed herself in command of affairs at his death, and the choice of the next emperor—and her second husband—came to rest on her shoulders. A 10th-century Byzantine compendium of the rituals of the Byzantine court preserves a detailed account of Ariadne's role in the complex ceremonies and deliberations that followed Zeno's death.

> The daughter, the mother, and the widow of an emperor.
>
> —Edward Gibbon

On the day following (April 10, 491), the people gathered in the Hippodrome (a large stadium attached to the palace for horse racing and other public events) and acclaimed loudly for a new emperor. Summoned by the chief ministers, Ariadne appeared in imperial robes, accompanied by a retinue, and was enthusiastically greeted ("Ariadne Augusta, you conquer! Holy Lord, grant her long life!"). The throng then besought her for "an Orthodox Emperor for the world." Through the lips of one of her officials, she delivered a complimentary and popular speech, in which she informed her people that she had commanded the ministers and Senate, with the consent of the army, to choose "a Christian and Roman Emperor, full of royal virtue, neither given to love of money, nor to any other vice, as far as that is possible for human nature." After more tumultuous applause, she went on to ask the people to allow a brief delay while the funeral of Zeno was performed, and promised that the election for his successor would take place:

> before the Holy Gospels and in the presence of the most reverend and holy Patriarch of this royal city . . . so that no one may give heed to friendship nor enmity nor fortune nor kinship nor any other private concern, but may make the election with a pure and whole conscience before the Lord God.

Concluding her speech, Ariadne returned to the palace while the ministers argued over the choice of the next emperor. After much debate, they were unable to agree on a suitable man, and so one of them proposed that Ariadne be left with the choice. She chose a man called Anastasius—a silentarius. This man met with near universal approval, and on April 11, 491, he was crowned by the Patriarch and proclaimed emperor. On May 20 of the same year, he married Ariadne.

As a convenient vehicle of imperial ambition, Ariadne's marriage to Zeno had seemed destined to serve her father Leo well. The fact that her son had not survived, and that the result was an unpopular Isaurian ascendancy in the capital, did not seem to diminish her own powers of influence; there is indication of this both in the fact that the ministers surrendered to her so important and contentious a decision as the imperial election, and in her evident popularity with her subjects. It should be noted also that she was able to overcome the displeasure of the powerful Patriarch in her choice of new husband (Anastasius was suspected of Monophysitism). There is also testimony of her influence and popularity in the unusual number of portraits of Ariadne (in various media, including statuary) that have survived to the present day.

Anastasius I's first task as emperor was to dampen Isaurian clout in high circles. Ariadne thus outlived the change in court politics she had helped to usher in. Anastasius' reign was not, in later years, a happy one, but we hear no more of Ariadne until her death in 515. Perhaps, with Anastasius' death three years later, we can point to the vicissitude that constitutes Ariadne's only failure: her second marriage (likely entered upon in early middle age) produced no offspring, and so with her died the dynasty begun by her father.

SOURCES:

Bury, J.B. *History of the Later Roman Empire*. Vol. I. London: St. Martin's Press, 1923 (reprint ed., pp. 314–323; 389–404; 429–436). NY: Dover Publications, 1958.

Gibbon, Edward. *The History of the Decline and Fall of the Roman Empire*. Volume 4. Edited by J.B. Bury. London: Methuen, 1901.

Malalas, Johannes. *Chronographia*. Edited by L. Dindorf. Bonn: Weber, 1831.

Martindale, J.R. *Prosopography of the Later Roman Empire*. Vol. 2. S.v. "Aelia Ariadne." Cambridge: Cambridge University Press, 1980.

Porphyrogenitus, Constantine VII. *De Cerimoniis Aulae Byzantinae*. Edited by J.J. Reiske. Bonn: Weber, 1829.

SUGGESTED READING:

Norwich, John Julius. *Byzantium: The Early Centuries*. NY: Alfred A. Knopf, 1989.

Oxford Dictionary of Byzantium. Edited by Alexander P. Kazhdan *et al*. New York and Oxford: Oxford University Press, 1991.

RELATED MEDIA:

Portraits of Ariadne in *Age of Spirituality: Late Antique and Early Christian Art, Third to Seventh Century*. Edited by Kurt Weizman. Pl. 24 & 25. NY: Metropolitan Museum of Art, 1979.

Peter H. O'Brien,
Boston University.

Arignote (fl. 6th c. BCE)

Pythagorean philosopher. Born in Crotona, Italy, to Pythagoras of Samos (philosopher, mathematician, politician, spiritual leader) and Theano of Crotona (Pythagorean philosopher); sister of Myia, Damo, Telauges and Mnesarchus; educated at the School of Pythagoras.

Selected works: several of the Pythagorean Sacred Discourses; Epigrams on the Mysteries of Ceres; *Mysteries of Bacchus; an unnamed work on Dionysius.*

In the 500s BCE, Arignote was born to the philosopher Pythagoras, who established the Pythagorean society, and *Theano, a member of his sect. Arignote was raised with her sisters, *Myia and *Damo, and her brothers, Telauges and Mnesarchus, in a house separate from Pythagorean society. She was, however, educated in the Pythagorean school and adopted that life, which involved the study of mathematics and the contemplation of mathematic's role in the order of the universe, particularly in regard to physical relationships and astronomy. The Pythagoreans were a political body who followed rituals in keeping with the Orphic religion (which included avoiding activities believed to damage the soul or to cause injustice to any living creature, because the soul was believed to go beyond the body and be reincarnated), as well as rituals of their own: observing silence, self-examination, moderation in all things, and not eating meat or beans.

While it is likely that Arignote was central to the development of Pythagorean thought, the extent of her contribution is difficult to ascertain, as it was the practice of the Pythagoreans to attribute all of their work to Pythagoras in recognition of his genius. He was believed to be an incarnation of Apollo, god of moderation. Despite the difficulty, Arignote is recognized to have authored several Pythagorean works. With her brother, Telauges, she is credited as the author of the Sacred Discourses based on the commentaries left by Pythagoras after his death. She is particularly known for this passage:

> The eternal essence of number is the most providential cause of the whole of heaven, earth, and the region in between. Likewise it is the root of the continued existence of the gods and daimones, as well as that of divine men.

Here, Arignote expresses the Pythogorean belief that numbers are part of the order of the universe and the force that sustains it. The numbers 1, 2, 3 and 4—and their relationships to each other and the other natural numbers—were considered to be the origin of all order.

The *Sacred Discourses* were written after the Pythagoreans scattered from their original community at Crotona and set up communities elsewhere. The preservation and continuation of Pythagoras' thought allowed Pythagoreanism to flourish for several hundred years and to influence the thought of Plato in the 4th century BCE.

SOURCES:

Coppleston, Frederick, S.J. *A History of Philosophy.* London: Search Press, 1946.

Guthrie, W.K.C. "Pythagoras and Pythagoreanism," in *Encyclopedia of Philosophy, Vol. 7.* Edited by Paul Edwards. NY: Macmillan, 1967.

Jamblichus, C. *Life of Pythagoras.* London: John M. Watkins, 1926.

Kersey, Ethel M. *Women Philosophers: A Bio-critical Source Book.* NY: Greenwood Press, 1989.

Philip, J.A. *Pythagoras and Early Pythagoreanism.* Toronto: University of Toronto Press, 1966.

Waithe, Mary Ellen, ed. *A History of Women Philosophers, Vol. 1.* Boston: Martinus Nijhoff Publications, 1987.

Catherine Hundleby, M.A. Philosophy,
University of Guelph, Ontario, Canada

Aristarete

Ancient Greek painter who painted an Asclepius. Birth and death dates unknown; born to the painter Nearchus and an unknown mother; taught to paint by her father.

Painting on walls or panels was highly favored in Classical antiquity; a number of testimonials in ancient sources praise painters and record some of their names. Unfortunately, it is also probably the least well-preserved of all the art forms of Greece. Nevertheless, the survival of a fairly large number of Roman frescoes at Pompeii, Herculanum, and elsewhere in the Roman world, many of which reproduce Greek themes and probably had Greek models, allows some insight into the techniques and scope of the genre as a whole.

Pliny the Elder (23/24–79 CE), the Roman scholar and encyclopedist, has left in books 33–37 of his *Naturalis Historiae* (Natural History) a history of art to his day. This portion of his large work contains the most complete extant compendium of the facts and names of ancient painting, for the most part drawn on Greek and Latin sources that are now lost. After listing and briefly discussing the works and careers of several famous male artists, Pliny breaks off at 35.147–8 for a very brief digression on women painters. This passage (some 16 lines) contains little more than the names of five (or possibly six) women artists along with their most notable works, sometimes mentioning their place of birth and their father's or teacher's name.

The note on Aristarete reads in full: "Aristarete, the daughter and pupil of Nearchus, painted an Asclepius." Since this is the sum of our knowledge about this woman, and none of her work has survived, it is clear that there is not a great deal to be said about her character and personal style. Nevertheless, it is interesting to note that she shares the distinction with *Irene (c. 200 BCE?), another woman on the list, of being both daughter and pupil of a painter-father. Of this Nearchus, Pliny tells us a few chapters earlier that he painted an "Aphrodite among the Graces and Cupids" and a "Heracles in Sorrow Repenting his Madness." Since Aristarete's "Asclepius" depicted the Greek god of healing, we might be tempted to say that these titles suggest a family interest in mythological or divine subjects. In truth, however, almost all Classical art was connected with such themes.

There have also been women artists.

—Pliny the Elder

Pliny tells us nothing of the dates or local origins of either Aristarete or her father, though we can infer from their names that they were Greek and lived at some point before the time of his writing. Other than the fact that women did paint, Pliny says little about what might have distinguished a woman's approach to this art; thus, women's painting in antiquity is a dusty corner of an already obscure field. Two preserved wall paintings from Pompeii, however, offer some confirmation of women's participation in the visual arts: one shows a woman painting a statue, another depicts a woman sitting at her easel.

SOURCES AND SUGGESTED READING:

Boardman, John. *Greek Art*. Rev. ed. London: Thames and Hudson, 1985, pp. 158–59; 218–19.

Jex-Blake, K., trans. *The Elder Pliny's Chapters on the History of Art*. Commentary and Historical Introduction by E. Sellers. 1st ed., 1896; reprint ed., with a Preface and Select Bibliography by Raymond V. Schoder, Chicago: Argonaut, 1968.

Paulys Real-Encyclopädie der Classischen Alterumswissenschaft. Edited by Georg Wissowa. S.v. "Aristarete" by O. Rossbach; "Nearchos" by G. Lippold. Stuttgart: J.B. Metzlersche Buchhandlung, 1897.

Pliny. *Natural History*. Trans. by H. Rackham. Vol. 9. London: William Heinemann, 1952.

RELATED MEDIA:

Black-and-white reproduction of a Pompeian painting, "paintress at work" in Ling, Roger. *Roman Painting*. 211. Cambridge: Cambridge University Press, 1991.

FOR REMAINS OF GREEK PAINTING SEE:

Pfuhl, Ernst. *Masterpieces of Greek Drawing and Painting*. Trans. with Foreword by J.D. Beazley. Reprint ed. NY: Hacker Books, 1979.

Robertson, C.M. *Greek Painting*. 2nd ed. NY: Rizzoli International Publications, 1979.

Peter H. O'Brien,
Boston University

Ariyoshi Sawako (1931–1984)

Japanese author whose works, including more than 35 nonfiction, fiction, and dramatic volumes, have been translated into 12 languages. Born Ariyoshi Sawako on January 20, 1931, in Wakayama City, Japan; died in 1984; the second of three children of Shinji and Akitsu; educated at Tokoyo Christian Women's University; married Jin Akira (director), in March 1963 (divorced 1964); children: one daughter, Tamao (b. November 1963).

Selected works: Momoku *(The Blindman, 1954),* Jiuta *(Ballad, 1956),* Masshirokenoke *(White All Over, 1957),* Kinokawa *(The River Ki, 1959),* Arita-gawa *(Arita River, 1963),* Hishoku *(Not Because of Color, 1964),* Hidaka-gawa *(Hidaka River, 1965);* Kōkotsu no hito *(The Twilight Years, 1972),* Kazunomiyasama otome *(Her Highness Princess Kazu, 1978).*

Ariyoshi Sawako was born on January 20, 1931, of an old gentry family in the Wakayama City region of Japan. At the time of her birth, Ariyoshi's father Shinji, a banker, had already left on an assignment to New York City. Returning to his wife Akitsu four years later, Shinji met his daughter for the first time. The family moved to Tokoyo in 1935. Before they were reassigned to Batavia (Java, Indonesia) in 1937, Akitsu gave birth to her second son.

The family spent several privileged years in Batavia. Though she was enrolled in the Japanese Elementary School, Ariyoshi was frequently ill as a child, so her formal schooling was intermittent at best. She was, however, extremely bright and enjoyed reading when illness kept her from school. Her father's bookshelf held the collected works of Japanese authors Natsume Soseki and Arishima Takeo, and Ariyoshi read them diligently. In 1940, Shinji was reassigned to Tokoyo, and, for the following year, the family bounced back and forth between Japan and Batavia, following him. Between 1940 and 1941, Ariyoshi attended five different elementary schools, before the family settled in Tokoyo permanently in 1941.

Her health improved by her teen years, and Ariyoshi attended Takenodai Women's School and Tokoyo Municipal Higher Women's School, from which she graduated in 1949. She subsequently enrolled at the Tokoyo Christian Women's University to study English literature, but her father sparked in her another interest as he instilled in his daughter a love of traditional Japanese Kabuki theater. Kabuki, for Shinji, represented an opportunity to strengthen his daughter's national faith, which her childhood of transience had failed to do. Performed by, and written for, common people, Kabuki theater combines exaggerated visual effects and musical forms to tell moral stories. Ariyoshi's growing interest in the theater was intensified by her father's death in 1950. Graduating from the university in 1952, she worked over the next several years with several Kabuki theater companies and publications.

When her first short story was published in 1955, Ariyoshi began what would become an unrelenting dedication to writing. Short stories and plays earned her numerous prizes and notations as one of Japan's best new writers. In 1959, her first novel, and one of her best known, *Kinokawa* (*The River Ki*), was released. It was followed with an invitation from the Rockefeller Foundation for Ariyoshi to come to America and study drama at Sarah Lawrence College for the winter and spring terms. After nearly a year away from home, she made stops in Europe and the Middle East before her return trip to Japan.

Over the decade between 1962 and 1972, Ariyoshi produced novels or plays, totaling 12, numerous short stories, and a 13-volume set of her selected works. Most of her novels appeared first in serial form in popular Japanese magazines, often running over a six-month period. She paused briefly in March of 1963 to marry Jin Akira, the director of the Art Friend Association. The couple lived with Jin's parents, an arrangement that burdened the marriage. In November of the same year, Ariyoshi gave birth to a daughter, Tamao. By the end of 1964, the marriage was over.

In 1968, Ariyoshi spent four months traveling in Cambodia, Indonesia, and New Guinea. Her trip was cut short by malaria, and Ariyoshi was carried out of the jungles of New Guinea on a hammock. She was hospitalized for all of May and June, but by May she had already begun a written account of the trip, which was serialized until November. This illness likely began Ariyoshi's long struggle with insomnia, which she combatted with sedatives and alcohol, contributing to a slow decline in health.

In 1972, one of Ariyoshi's most controversial works, *Kōkotsu no hito* (*The Twilight Years*), appeared. Within six months of publication, this story of a family's struggle to care for

their aging father sold more than one million copies and earned Ariyoshi $300,000 in royalties. Ariyoshi wanted to donate the entire sum to area nursing homes, but, fearing they would lose the tax money, the government allowed her to give only one-quarter of the sum. She followed this tremendously popular work with a serialization that became the novel *Fukugo osen* (*Compound Pollution*). Ariyoshi's study of both bodily and earthly pollutants led to a reputation as an environmental expert. She was asked to travel and give talks, while researching and writing her next novel. By May of 1977, Ariyoshi had to be hospitalized for exhaustion and overwork. In the following years, she continued to write but was plagued by illness, which encouraged her further use of alcohol and sedatives.

In 1984, Ariyoshi Sawako died in her sleep of cardiac arrest, brought on by her drug dependencies and overwork. She was 53 years old. In January of 1986, her hometown of Wakayama City announced the creation of the Ariyoshi Sawako Memorial Museum, to be placed next to the Wakayama Municipal Library. Ariyoshi's mother Akitsu agreed to contribute the author's belongings and manuscripts to the memorial.

SOURCES:

Lewell, John. *Modern Japanese Novelists.* Tokoyo: Kodansha International, 1993.

Mulhern, Chieko I., ed. *Heroic with Grace: Legendary Women of Japan.* London: M.E. Sharpe, 1991.

———, ed. *Japanese Women Writers.* Westport, CT: Greenwood Press, 1994.

Crista Martin,
Boston, Massachusetts

Arlette (fl. c. 1010)

French noblewoman and mother of William the Conqueror. Name variations: Herleva or Herleve. Born around 1010; death date unknown; daughter of Fulbert (the tanner) of Falaise; liaison with Robert I, duke of Normandy (d. 1035); married Herluin, viscount of Conteville; children: (with Robert I) William I the Conqueror, duke of Normandy (r. 1035–1087), king of England (r. 1066–1087); *Adelicia (c. 1029–1090); (first marriage) Odo, earl of Kent, and Robert, count of Mortain (d. 1091).

Arletty (1898–1992)

French actress, known as "the Garbo of France," who is famed for her work in Les Enfants du Paradis *and* Hôtel du Nord, *and for her brief affair with a German flyer. Name variations: Arlette. Born Léonie Bathiat in Courbevoie, France, on May 15, 1898; died in Paris on July 24, 1992; daughter of a miner and a laundress; never married; no children.*

Filmography: La Douceur D'aimer *(1930);* Un Chien qui rapporte *(1931);* Das schöne Abenteuer *(*La Belle Aventure *with* **Käthe von Nagy,** *French-German, 1932);* Un Idée Folle *(1933);* Walzerkrieg *(*La Guerre de Valses *with* **Madeleine Ozeray,** *Fr.-Germ., 1933);* Le Voyage de Monsieur Perrichon *(1934);* Le Grand Jeu *(directed by Jacques Feyder, 1934);* Pension Mimosas *(1935);* La Fille de Madame Angot *(1935);* L'École des Cocottes *(1935);* Amants et Voleurs *(1935);* La Garçonne *(1936);* Faisons un Rêve *(1937);* Les Perles de la Couronne *(1937);* Aloha le Chant des Iles *(1937);* Mirages *(1937);* Désiré *(1938);* Le Petit Chose *(1938);* La Chaleur du Sein *(1938);* Hôtel du Nord *(1938);* Le Jour se lève *(*Daybreak, *1939);* Fric-Frac *(1939);* Circonstances atténuantes *(*Extenuating Circumstances, *1939);* Madame Sans-Gêne *(1941);* Les Visiteurs du Soir *(*The Devil's Own Envoy, *1942);* Les Enfants du Paradis *(*Children of the Paradise, *1945);* Portrait d'un Assassin *(1949);* L'Amour Madame *(1951);* La Père de Mademoiselle *(1953);* Le Grand Jeu *(*Flesh and the Woman *or* The Big Game, *with* **Gina Lollobrigida,** *directed by Robert Siodmak, 1954);* Huis clos *(*No Exit, *1954);* L'Air de Paris *(1954);* Maxime *(1958);* Un Drôle de Dimanche *(1958);* La Loi des Hommes *(1962);* La Gamberge *(1962);* Tempo di Roma *(1963);* Le Voyage à Biarritz *(1964);* The Longest Day *(United States, 1962);* Les Volets fermés *(replaced by* ***Marie Bell,** *1972).*

One of the immortals of the golden age of French cinema, the actress known as Arletty was born Léonie Bathiat at Courbevoie in the district of Auvergne in 1898, a district that served as a setting for Guy de Maupassant's story "Mont Oriol." She would later borrow her stage name from Maupassant's heroine Arlette. Though Courbevoie was then a Parisian suburb, its occupants considered themselves card-carrying Parisians with a wit and wisdom acquired from the streets.

Arletty came from a large family. When her miner father was killed by a streetcar in 1916, her mother had to take in washing, and they lived in poverty. In those early years, she gave no hint of acting ambitions. At 16, with little schooling, Arletty began work in a factory while living away from home; at 18, she learned shorthand and typing and found a job as a secretary. During World War I, she worked in the Darracq armament plant, which manufactured shells, but the young girl became fascinated with the bohemian life of Paris, frequenting cafes made popular by artists and writers. Spotted among the crowd by Cubist painter and art dealer Paul Guillaume, she was sent to see Armand Berthez, manager of the Capucines, a producer of revues.

By the end of the war, Arletty had been an artist's model (posing for Braque and Matisse), was working as a singer and dancer in music-hall revues, and had become a pacifist when her lover was killed in the war. With her new name, she became a draw for the caustic revues at the Théatre des Capucines. Arletty's dramatic stage work began in 1920 with a small part as a courtesan in *L'École des Cocottes.* She then took on an assortment of roles, most often in the meager costume of a prostitute or a woman of easy virtue, though she was at that time, in her own words, "as thin as a runner bean." "During most of her career she played tarts," writes David Shipman, "but then, it often seemed, so did most French actresses." She broke the casting mold long enough to portray Sacha Guitry's wife in *O Mon Bel Inconnu,* a play that costarred **Jacqueline Delubac,** soon to be Guitry's real wife.

In 1930, with the advent of sound, Arletty began to appear in films. A captivating, dark-haired beauty with a haunting style, she had supporting parts in Jacques Feyder's *Le Grand Jeu* (1934) and *Pension Mimosas* (1935). She had one lead and two bits in the 1937–38 films of Sacha Guitry: *Désiré, Faisons un Rêve* and *Les Perles de la Couronne,* in which she played the queen of Ethiopia in blackface. She made two movies with Michel Simon—*La Chaleur du Sein* and *Circonstances Atténuantes*—but was still playing filmdom's second-woman leads: "the other woman" or "the friend." Thus, the theater remained her principal career; in 1936, Jean Cocteau wrote a successful sketch for her, *L'École des Veuves.* That same year, she starred in the play *Fric-Frac* with Simon and Victor Boucher. She was also involved with its transfer to the screen, though Fernandel replaced Boucher.

Though she was signed to do the first French film in Technicolor, Sardou's play *Madame Sans-Gêne,* the advent of World War II effectively suspended plans for production. It would eventually be shot in 1941, though not in color. Arletty portrayed the washerwoman who becomes the mistress of Napoleon, played by Albert Dieudonné. Dieudonné had assayed the role once before, for Abel Gance's masterpiece.

In 1938, Arletty was teamed up with Marcel Carné for a supporting role in his *Hôtel du Nord,* which starred ***Annabella** and Jean-Pierre Aumont, a tragi-comedy about working-class life in a shabby Paris hotel. Once again, she portrayed a prostitute, Madame Raymonde, "a kind of Mother Courage of the profession," noted the London *Times*. She had one major scene, crossing a bridge over the Canal St.-Martin in northern Paris with her wayward murderous lover Louis Jouvet. He is on his way to go fishing and tells her he prefers going alone. Why? Because she invades his mood, she does not contribute satisfactorily to the "*atmosphère*." "*Atmosphère! Atmosphère!,*" cries Arletty in the accent of the Parisian suburbs, "*Est-ce que j'ai une gueule d'atmosphère?*" ("Have I got a mouth made of atmosphere?") This became one of the most memorable moments in film history, and her line became famous throughout the nation. "Overnight that one word—*atmosphère*—became indelibly associated with Arletty," writes James Lord. "In cafés and châteaux all over France men and women would exclaim to each other, '*Atmosphère! Atmosphère!*' and burst out laughing."

Now a movie star of the first rank and blessed with self-assurance and an extraordinary range, Arletty teamed up with Carné for three more films, with screenplays by Jacques Prévert, a prominent French poet and screenwriter who had been affiliated with the surrealist movement in the 1920s and was influential in injecting "poetic realism" into French films. The triumvirate was responsible for *Le Jour se lève* (1939), *Les Visiteurs du Soir* (1943), and one of the most celebrated films in French cinema: *Les Enfants du Paradis* (*Children of Paradise*). Carné brought his impressionistic realism to the screen, his faithfulness to surroundings, to everyday life, to working people and lower classes; Prévert brought his theme of melancholy, of faded idealism and beauty, and fate-driven lives; Arletty added mystery and elegance.

In the memorable *Le Jour se lève* (*Daybreak*), filmed in 1939 as a metaphor for France's condition on the eve of war, she played the bitter mistress of the sadistic Valentin; as Clara, she falls in love with a kind stranger, played by Jean Gabin. In the movie, writes Roger Manvell, "she stands for profane love, an easy, friendly though somewhat ambivalent and fatalistic acceptance of pleasure as it comes. She plays with a superb casualness, establishing a special presence. . . . But above it all she embodies sheer, mature physical beauty. . . . Whereas most film stars reach their full stature comparatively early, Arletty reached hers only when she was already forty."

Les Visiteurs du Soir was shot in 1943, during the occupation of France by the Germans.

The *mise en scène* is a castle in 15th-century France where two devils dressed as troubadours are intent on destroying a young couple's betrothal feast. As Dominique, Arletty is a seductive companion to one of the troubadours. It was one of her favorite films.

Marcel Carné tapped a strain of melancholy in his leading lady for their next venture, a movie made with difficulty during the last days of the German occupation under the noses of their Nazi occupiers. *Les Enfants du Paradis* (*Children of the Paradise*) took over two years to make. Filming began at the Joinville studio in August 1943, was interrupted, and began again in November. Production was often sabotaged; actors disappeared, roles were recast. Starving extras ate up most of the perishable props before the dinner scenes could be photographed. Actors who were working in the French underground had their scenes shot secretly or briefly came out of hiding. Even Carné and Prévert tried to slow up production, hiding key reels from Nazi supervisors, hoping that their occupiers would be gone by the time the movie was released. But the Nazis—anxious that the French film industry continue—were supportive. Wide in scope, the movie hinted that the drama "could only flourish where men are free, a subtlety of interpretation that eluded the Nazi mind," writes De Witt Bodeen; "otherwise, they would never have authorized production of the film."

This film, Marcel Carné's masterpiece, his tribute to the French theater, is as much a classic as *Casablanca*, and was dubbed by Andrew Sarris France's "*Gone with the Wind* of art films." It too was a movie about a vanishing epoch, with an enthralling woman, adored by many men. It also withstood the *GWTW* test of time: it ran for four hours. "Critically, it was the more highly regarded," writes Shipman, "and, now that the style of both films is extinct, it is, because of the maturity of its dialogue, the more persuasive."

Set in the theater district, Le Boulevard du Temple (more commonly known as the Boulevard of Crime), the film recreates a chaotic world of backstage life in early 19th-century Paris. On one level, the Paradise of the title is the gallery, the cheap upper seats in the second balcony, known by Parisians as "the Gods." Arletty as Garance, an elusive courtesan, is loved by four men—a talented and soulful mime named Baptiste (Jean-Louis Barrault), an ambitious actor (Pierre Brasseur), a philosophical villain (Marcel Herrand), and a haughty aristocrat (Louis Salou). She accepts them all, the good and the bad; she seems to make no distinction. But Garance remains aloof, coveting her independence. Her only love is Baptiste, her Pierrot, a shy mime. "Arletty is supreme in the near-symbolic, feminine character she had by now come to embody," wrote Manvell of her performance, "a character more subtle in its implications than that created by Garbo, but in many ways similar in its projection of a 'feminine mystique.'"

The movie opened in Paris on March 9, 1945, five months before the city's liberation. "Had the then-victorious German Army even faintly realized that in authorizing production of *Les Enfants du Paradis,* they were condoning the exploits of a free woman like Garance, they would have withdrawn their approval of the film immediately," writes Bodeen. "She symbolized the activating spirit of the Free French, a spirit of revolt and independence, a spirit that can never be broken or subjugated, as Hitler's generals soon learned."

Two of the Carné-Prévert-Arletty movies were not seen outside of France during the occupation: *Les Enfants* and *Les Visiteurs.* When they were released internationally in 1946, they would cause a sensation. In France, *Les Enfants* would run nine months, and the French Academy of Cinema Arts and Techniques would name it the Best French Film in the History of Talking Pictures. Not only is the movie visually rich, Jean-Louis Barrault's performance as the lovelorn mime is legendary, and Prévert's screenplay—considered by the *Washington Post* the "finest work . . . ever composed for the screen"—was nominated for an Academy Award for Best Original Screenplay. Arletty was dubbed "the Garbo of France."

Manvell points out other similarities between Arletty and *Greta Garbo.* Self-educated, an unaffected woman of taste, Arletty lived her personal life on her own terms, in style of dress, in style of life. Like Garbo, she did not marry, she often dressed in simple clothes, and she spent many years in reclusive withdrawal. Like her character Garance, Arletty had many friends— some good, some bad—including Louis-Ferdinand Céline, who also came from her Parisian

Arletty, from the movie Les Enfants du Paradis.

suburb of Courbevoie, and ***Josée Laval**, daughter of Pierre Laval, prime minister of France and open collaborator with the Germans.

Arletty was wooed by many: men and women. ("It was no secret," writes Lord, "that Arlette had had lesbian attachments.") By 1939, her admirers were legion "and unrequited," noted *The* [London] *Times.* "The Aga Khan wooed her immensely from afar but never got beyond dinner *à deux* in the private dining room of Larue's restaurant. Sacha Guitry, too, made a stupendous effort and was rewarded with as he ruefully noted, 'everlasting friendship.' For a long time the most admired woman in Paris seemed to have no lover."

When she finally fell in love in 1941, he was Hans Söring, the son of a diplomat, born in Constantinople, fluent in French, and a high-ranking officer in the German *Luftwaffe.* "He was handsome and Arletty fell for him almost at first glance," continued the *Times,* "with a passion which seemed the more violent for having been so long suppressed." Though she was thought a traitor to her country, the affair was open and for all of France to see.

"It was the era of 'politeness,'" writes Lord, "when the French wanted to believe that their enemies, after all, were very well behaved, courteous to ladies, kindly to children, and that military catastrophe might not ravage the integrity of national life." It was tempting for people in the performing arts to "look on the Germans in Paris as no more than a new, cultivated elite," write Beevor and Cooper in *Paris after the Liberation.* German ambassador Otto Abetz "was an ardent Francophile and those who attended his parties at the German embassy in the rue de Lille found it hard to remember that this was the civilized face of a brutal and oppressive enemy." When asked why he had agreed to meet Göring, Sacha Guitry replied, *"Par curiosité"*; he would have been willing to meet Stalin, he said, for the same reason.

It did not help that Arletty put friendship before patriotism; she continued contact with her friend Céline, who was now infamous for his Nazi sympathies and hatred of liberal democracy, and the Lavals. She was apolitical at a time when to be so was unacceptable. In 1944, though she had refused to work for the German-controlled film company, Continental, that operated in France during World War II, she was told that a tribunal in Algiers (the conservative assembly of the French Committee of National Liberation) had condemned her to death.

Directly after the liberation of Paris, the roundup of suspected sympathizers was haphazard, at times unjust, and largely vigilante style. In late August of 1945, Arletty was accused of what was commonly called *collaboration horizontale* (sleeping with the enemy) and before her hearing spent two months in internment at Fresnes; the prison held many of *le Tout Paris,* including Sacha Guitry. There was little or no tolerance for women who slept with Germans, despite the usual French tolerance for *affaires du coeur.* The mood on the street was vicious. After spontaneous kangaroo courts, men were beaten; women had their heads shaved and were paraded through the streets under the fists and spittle of a jeering mob. Old women whose daughters or relatives had been judged guilty were also shaved.

> [Arletty] was outspoken, witty, sometimes inflexibly frank, but never cynical. She bore no grudges, felt no self-pity.
>
> —**James Lord**

On Arletty's arrest, a rumor spread through Paris that she had had her breasts cut off. Though this was untrue, she may have had her head shaved. Her hairdresser attested that a turbaned Arletty asked him to make a wig for her. She is said to have snapped at interrogators: "What is this government which is so interested in our sex lives!" In her memoirs, however, the incident of her arrest is played down. "Two very discreet gentlemen came to fetch me."

There was no trial, only a hearing, where it was decreed that she should be placed under house arrest in some locale 30 miles from Paris for an unspecified length of time. Casual acquaintances, Jacques and **Lelette Bellanger**, stepped forward and offered their château called La Houssaye. Every week, for over 18 months, Arletty walked the four miles to register at the local police station. "It was the best time of my life," she told Lord. "It gave me the opportunity and the initiative to become myself." She lived in the château library, reading Pascal and Proust. "Which is not to say that she became a fatalist," wrote Lord, "but, on the contrary, that she became able to accept a principle of existential commitment which took for granted the responsibility of every human being in his elemental solitude to act in mitigation of the solitude of others. In short, she saw that she had been blind to her own frivolity and failure of imagination."

From prison, under escort, Arletty had been allowed out to reshoot some scenes for *Les Enfants du Paradis.* Despite the film's international success, the untried accusation made it hard for her to get work following her release from house arrest. Though she was hired for three movies, all were abandoned for unrelated reasons. While living in a room at the Plaza Athénée, she waited four more years before she completed her next major film *Portrait d'un Assassin* (with *Maria Montez** and Erich von Stroheim) in 1949, at age 51. In November of that year, she returned to the stage as Blanche in *Un tramway nommé désir,* the French stage production of Tennessee William's *A Streetcar Named Desire,* adapted by Cocteau. Despite some hostile reviews for the production, it was one of the year's hits. This marked a comeback of sorts, since the movie *Portrait* was released in the same month as the play opened. In 1952, she starred on stage in Marcel Achard's *Les Compagnons de la Marjolaine* with *Melina Mercouri**. Arletty would also appear in another play by Williams, *La Descente d'Orphée (Orpheus Descending).*

Arletty played the lesbian Inez in the movie of Jean-Paul Sartre's *Huis Clos* (1945), which was directed by *Jacqueline Audry**. It was a performance, wrote Shipman, that was "scathing and taunting, and horribly fascinating." But in films she had now become a supporting actress: *Maxime* with *Michèle Morgan** and Charles Boyer; *Drôle de Dimanche* with *Danielle Darrieux**; *La Loi des Hommes* with *Micheline Presle**. In 1962, American audiences were given an all-too-brief sample of her exquisite humor in the movie *The Longest Day* when she played a French housewife, hair in nightribbons, on a late-night walk to the privy, who encounters a stream of Allied parachutes wafting into her backyard. In 1968, she would return to the Paris stage in Cocteau's *Montres Sacres.*

By the 1960s, all had been forgotten, or at least forgiven. Arletty had become one of the most admired women in France. She lived at 31, rue Raynouard and owned a small house at Belle-Ile-en-Mer, an island off the southern coast of Brittany. "It was a lonely, solitary dwelling in its windswept location, the residence of a hermit," writes Lord. "And of course that is in a very real sense what by force of circumstances Arlette became." Fifty years earlier, *Sarah Bernhardt** had lived on the island and had retreated to a seat carved out of a cliff that overlooked the sea. Arletty loved to escape there also. Friends gave her money; her benefactors included a wealthy manufacturer, Michel Bolloré, and René de Chambrun, husband of Josée Laval, son-in-law of Pierre.

By the beginning of the 1960s, Arletty had begun to suffer a progressive loss of vision in her left eye. After an unsuccessful operation, she was told to apply different eyedrops nightly to each eye. One solution was to preserve the little sight remaining in the left, the other to prevent deterioration in the right. One night in 1962, returning home late and tired, she inadvertently switched the drops and blinded herself. She could still see, though poorly, and could read only for brief periods at a time. When Italian journalist **Oriana Fallaci** interviewed her in 1963, Fallaci wrote of the "brave Arletty" who was not only blind, but "the loneliest woman I have ever met." Though she continued on stage, Arletty could only accept parts in film requiring little movement. On November 11, 1966, Armistice Day, a couple of years after another operation, the 68-year-old Arletty woke up totally blind. The small house by the sea was sold, and she was moved by friends into a small two-room apartment at 14, rue Rémusat, where she lived the rest of her life with a sketch of *Colette** above her bed.

Though she had written a brief, explanatory memoir *La Défense* in 1948, her autobiography was dictated and published as *Je Suis comme Je Suis (I Am as I Am).* On its publication in 1971, the 73-year-old received enormous attention and experienced a rejuvenated popularity. Her 90th birthday was celebrated in the press; her films were shown on television. But she had no illusions. "Anyone who thinks that in three centuries people will pay to hear her laugh is a dreamer," she said. Asked by interviewers how she wanted to be remembered after her death, she replied, "That broad, she was the real thing." Arletty died on July 23, 1992, at age 94. In accordance with her wishes, she was buried at Courbevoie, but the hearse made a detour, passing the Hôtel du Nord where a large crowd had formed.

Over 40 years earlier, in 1950, her German soldier, who was about to be named an ambassador, had returned to France and asked her to marry him. She had refused. When asked why by her friend James Lord, she replied, "Can you imagine 'Mademoiselle Atmosphère' becoming 'Madame l'Ambassadrice? Not I. . . . He did me a great service by making it possible for me to make so much trouble for myself. Some people say that it ruined my life. It certainly ruined my career and made a mess of my reputation, but thanks to him I discovered the self in myself. And yet when I see him today I can't see what it was that led me to that discovery. The discovery was a marvel, while the man was only an affair."

SOURCES:

"Arletty, 94, French Film Actress and a Legend of 'Hôtel du Nord,'" in *The New York Times Biographical Service,* July 1992, p. 927.

Bodeen, De Witt. "Les Enfants du Paradis," in *The International Dictionary of Films and Filmmakers, Volume I*. Edited by Christopher Lyon. Chicago, IL: St. James Press, 1984.

Lord, James. *Six Exceptional Women: Further Memoirs*. NY: Farrar, Straus & Giroux, 1994.

Manvell, Roger. *Love Goddesses of the Movies*. NY: Crescent Books, 1975.

Shipman, David. *The Great Movie Stars: The International Years*. NY: Hill & Wang, 1980.

The Times [London]. July 25, 1992, p. 17.

Arlington, Lizzie (b. 1876)

First woman to sign a contract in the baseball minor leagues (Atlantic League). Name variations: Stoud; Arlington was a professional name. Born Elizabeth Stride in Pennsylvania, in 1876.

Growing up in the coal-mining hills of Mahanoy City, Pennsylvania, Elizabeth Stride played baseball with her father and brothers. She gained inspiration and pointers on pitching from John Elmer Stivetts, a pitching great who won 35 games for the 1892 Boston world champions.

In 1898, the short, sturdy 22-year-old caught the eye of promoter William J. Conner, who became Stride's manager and paid her $100 a week as a starting pitcher for professional teams. On July 2 of that year, Stride, calling herself Lizzie Arlington, played in her first professional game for the Philadelphia Reserves, pitching four innings and giving up six hits and three unearned runs. At bat, she had two hits off Mike Kilroy and was left at second base at the end of the game in which the Reserves defeated Richmond 18–5.

Though the novelty of a woman pitcher failed to make money for Conner, Edward Grant Barrow, president of the Atlantic League, was intrigued enough to sign Arlington. On July 5, 1898, she pitched in a regulation minor-league game for Reading against Allentown, appearing in the ninth inning when Reading led 5–0. To the cheers of approximately 1,000 spectators, of whom 200 were women, she gave up no runs. An article in the *Reading Eagle* made much of Arlington's "attractive face and rosy cheeks" and the fact that she was very professional, "even down to expectorating on her hands and wiping her hands on her uniform." As to her pitching, the article admonished that "she, of course, hasn't the strength to get much speed on and has poor control. But, for a woman, she is a success."

When Arlington failed to attract an increase in gate receipts, Barrow let her go, but she signed with a bloomer team and went on to play baseball for many years. When minor-league commissioner George Trautman barred women baseball players, George Barrow commented on Arlington's brief career: "The sensible thing, I would think, is to accept or reject a player on merit alone. I admit that I signed Lizzie strictly as a stunt. But I'm not so sure she couldn't win a spot somewhere in organized ball if she were in her prime today."

SOURCES:

Gregorich, Barbara. *Women at Play: The Story of Women in Baseball*. NY: Harcourt Brace, 1993.

Barbara Morgan,
Melrose, Massachusetts

Armand, Inessa (1874–1920)

Russian revolutionary and feminist who was active as an underground propagandist, Bolshevik Party organizer, and champion of women's equality in the early Soviet state. Name variations: Comrade Inessa, Elena Blonina. Pronunciation: In-es-a Ar-mand. Born Elizabeth Stéphane on May 8, 1874, in Paris, France; died of cholera in Nal'chik, Russia, on September 24, 1920; daughter of Théodore Pécheux d'Herbenville (an opera singer who performed under the name Théodore Stéphane) and Nathalie Wild (part-time actress and voice teacher); tutoring at home led to teaching certificate, 1891; auditor, University of Moscow, 1906–1907; license, New University of Brussels, 1910; married Alexander Armand, on October 3, 1893; children: (with husband) Alexander, Fedor, Inna, and Varvara; (with brother-in-law, Vladimir Armand) Andre.

Following death of parents, raised in family of Evgenii Armand outside Moscow; taught in peasant school (1893–98); Russian vice-president, Women's International Progressive Union (1899); president, Moscow Society for Improving the Lot of Women (1900–1903); joined Russian Social Democratic Labor Party (1904); underground propagandist (1904–07); arrested four times and exiled to Mezen in northern Russia (1907–08); escaped, went abroad where she assisted V.I. Lenin in organizing Bolshevik Party (1910–17); lecturer, Longjumeau party school (1911); chair, Committee of Foreign Organizations (1911–12); co-editor, Rabotnitsa (Woman Worker, 1914); Bolshevik spokeswoman at numerous international socialist conferences (1914–16); member, Left Communist opposition (1918); chair, Moscow Provincial Economic Council (1918–19); member, All-Russian Central Executive Committee (1918–19); first director, Women's Section (Zhenotdel) of the Central Committee of the Russian Communist Party (1919–20); editor, Kommunistka (Female Communist,

Inessa Armand

1920); organizer and chair, First International Conference of Communist Women (1920).

Publications: forty journal articles and four popular brochures (all in Russian), most of which are reproduced in I.F. Armand, Stat'i, rechi, pis'ma (Articles, Speeches, Letters), Moscow, 1975.

Inessa Armand was buried in the "Red Graveyard" next to the walls of the Kremlin on October 12, 1920; she had died at the age of 46 of cholera contracted three weeks earlier on a vacation in the Caucasus. The weather on the day of her funeral was crisp and sunny but Moscow itself was bleak, still suffering from six years of civil war, revolution, and world war. The head of the Russian Communist Party and of the new Soviet state, Vladimir Il'ich Lenin, stood next to the freshly dug grave. "I never saw such torment," wrote a fellow Communist *Angelica Balabanoff. "I never saw any human being so completely absorbed by sorrow. . . . Not only his face but his whole body expressed so much sorrow that I dared not greet him. . . . It

was clear that he wanted to be alone with his grief. He seemed to have shrunk . . . his eyes seemed drowned in tears held back with effort."

Lenin listened as various party functionaries eulogized a close family friend. Armand was praised for joining the Bolshevik Party before the 1905 Revolution; for establishing and editing Rabotnitsa, the first Bolshevik paper for women workers; for her work in economic reconstruction as chair of the Moscow Provincial Economic Council; and for her efforts as the first director of the party's Women's Section (Zhenotdel) to attract women to party and state work. No one mentioned that as a young woman she was a Tolstoyan who devoted five years to teaching peasant children or that as a feminist she had sought to rehabilitate prostitutes in Moscow, that she had spent many years as an underground propagandist and had paid for her activity against the tsarist regime by being exiled to the far north, or that she had served as Lenin's assistant in the building of the Bolshevik Party only to quarrel with him as she sought to gain her intellectual and personal independence from his often domineering personality.

While one speaker noted that she had managed to overcome her "rich bourgeois background," no one adequately explained how a person born in Paris and raised in the family of a wealthy Russian textile manufacturer had risen to become one of the two most important women in the Russian Communist Party and the close friend of the leader of that party. It is a unique story but one that touches on many problems encountered by other women of her time: the lack of educational and vocational opportunities open to women; the personal sacrifices often demanded of women by a political career; the frustrations of rarely being taken seriously in a predominantly male environment; and the obsession of later historians with alleged romantic attachments at the expense of a woman's political achievements.

On a superficial level, Inessa Armand was unique in that she was the only Russian Communist of note to have been born in Paris and to have had non-Russian parents. Her father, Théodore Pécheux d'Herbenville, was an undistinguished opera singer who performed on occasion at the Opéra Comique under the name Théodore Stéphane. Inessa, or Elizabeth as she was christened after her birth on May 8, 1874, took her father's stage name of Stéphane. Her mother, **Nathalie Wild**, was half-English, half-French, and made a modest living as an actress and sometime vocal teacher. Before Elizabeth Stéphane was six years old, both of her parents passed away, leaving their three daughters in considerable financial distress. It was decided that Elizabeth, being the eldest, should leave Paris in the company of her English maternal grandmother and her mother's sister, who had secured a position outside Moscow as governess and piano teacher in the family of Evgenii Armand, a wealthy textile manufacturer of French descent.

Evgenii Evgen'evich Armand was the third generation of a family that had moved to Russia late in the 18th century. The firm of E. Armand & Sons owned wool weaving and dyeing factories and employed 1,200 workers in the town of Pushkino, 17 miles northeast of Moscow. He and his wife had a large family of six daughters and five sons. Like many of the Russian aristocracy, they were accustomed to hiring foreign governesses and tutors to educate their children at home. What set Evgenii Armand apart from many of his class was his decision to allow the orphaned niece of his new governess to be reared as part of his own family. As a result, Elizabeth Stéphane, or Inès as her new family called her, grew up "in the nest of gentlefolk," in a manor house looked after by 45 servants.

She, along with the Armand children, received an excellent home education. She learned French and English from her aunt and grandmother as well as German and Russian from other tutors. Her aunt also gave her six years of piano lessons. In later years, Lenin exploited her linguistic skills by having her translate many of his articles and letters and by asking her to serve as his multilingual spokeswoman at several European conferences. Armand got far greater pleasure in impressing her other non-musical revolutionary friends with her skills as a pianist on the rare occasions when time and circumstance gave her an opportunity to play. Her education was surprisingly liberal, given the reactionary climate of late 19th-century Russia. From tutors hired by Evgenii Armand, she and her adoptive siblings were exposed to the ideas of the French Enlightenment, German Romanticism, and the Russian intelligentsia—ideas that called into question their own class privileges, the backwardness of Russian society, and the anachronism of the tsarist autocracy. In part as a result of this education, many of the Armand children acquired a social consciousness, which led at least six of them, as well as three of their cousins and Inessa herself, to join revolutionary parties seeking the overthrow of the economic and political system that had given them their privileges.

One of the privileges she did not have was the right to acquire a higher education since with few exceptions Russian gymnasia and universities were open only to men. This meant that her career opportunities were also decidedly limited. She could become a tutor or home teacher by virtue of the certificate she received at age 17 after concluding her education on the Armand estate or she could marry. On October 3, 1893, she married Alexander Armand, the eldest of Evgenii's sons and five years her senior. As a wedding present from his parents, Alexander was given a small estate at Eldigino, six miles from Pushkino, where for the next several years Inessa spent much of her time having children. A son, Alexander, was born in 1894, followed in short order by Fedor (1896), **Inna** (1898) and **Varvara** (1901). Alexander and his wife also opened a school at Eldigino so that Inessa, an admirer of Leo Tolstoy's efforts to improve the conditions of the Russian peasantry, could use her training to teach peasant children. After five years of this activity, her idealism waned as dealing with the local authorities proved difficult and her sense of personal isolation increased.

> *The conflict between personal and family interests on the one hand, and societal interests on the other, is one of the most serious problems facing the intelligentsia today.*
>
> —Inessa Armand (1908)

She soon found a new outlet for her energies in Moscow. While still in Eldigino, she had entered into correspondence with **Adrianne Veigelé**, the secretary of the Women's International Progressive Union, who invited her to London and suggested that she establish a branch of the Union in Moscow. Although Armand did not go to England, the Progressive Union named her its Russian vice president in 1899 and in July of that year announced the formation of the Moscow Society for Improving the Lot of Women. After a short spell as chair of its Educational Commission, Armand was chosen in 1900 to be the president of the Moscow Society—a post she was to hold for more than three years. The Society had some 643 members—most of them women from privileged backgrounds—who were willing to give either time or money to help their more disadvantaged sisters. One of these endeavors was to set up a "Shelter for Downtrodden Women" where prostitutes and young women from the countryside were given accommodation, moralistic lectures, and limited vocational training in an often futile effort to keep them off the streets. Government authorities were frequently suspicious of these attempts by upper-class feminists to organize and instruct lower-class women. In 1900, they turned down Armand's request that her Society be allowed to open a "Sunday School" that would offer a basic education to often illiterate women workers in the evening or on weekends. In 1902, they denied her application to publish a newspaper that would discuss issues of interest to women. Her efforts to establish a lending library of women's books met a similar fate.

Governmental obstructionism and slow progress caused many Russian feminists to turn away from philanthropic work and to concentrate instead on seeking the right to vote. Inessa chose a different and more radical path. Like the Armand children, she had been exposed at Pushkino to embryonic socialist thought—ideas, which at the turn of the century would find organizational expression in the agrarian Socialist Revolutionary Party and the Marxian Social Democratic Party. Both groups were illegal in tsarist Russia since they sought not just the reform of existing society but the overthrow of the state and the establishment of a new economic and political order. Through her brother-in-law, Vladimir Armand, she later came into contact with Marxist circles at the University of Moscow. Vladimir himself helped to broaden her political horizons. As a result of these influences, in the summer of 1903 she left her position as president of the Moscow Society and a year later started working as an underground propagandist for the Russian Social Democratic Labor Party (RSDRP).

The year 1903 was a pivotal period in her personal life as well. Over time, she had grown apart from her husband. Alexander was often in Eldigino running the estate; she was in Moscow looking after the Moscow Society. He was a liberal by political persuasion; she increasingly was searching for more radical solutions. While in Moscow, she spent considerable time with her brother-in-law Vladimir, who was instrumental in her gradual evolution from feminism to Marxism and who shared, to a greater extent than Alexander, her interests in poetry, the theater, and the arts. This intellectual and political affinity soon became an emotional and personal bond. In January 1903, while on a holiday with Vladimir in Italy, she became pregnant. The Armands' solution to this potentially disruptive family imbroglio was as unique as Inessa's origins. Alexander accepted that his wife was in love with his younger brother and that the two

of them should henceforth live in free union without bothering about divorce and remarriage. He continued to support her and many of her new socialist causes with the profits of his textile mills until her revolution expropriated them. He also raised all five of her children but made sure they visited her abroad as often as possible. For the rest of her life, Inessa corresponded with her estranged husband and not without reason expressed wonder at his "devoted and selfless friendship. . . . What a good relationship we have established," she wrote in the summer of 1905. "What a good feeling our friendship has! Honor and glory to you." Alexander was indeed an "uncommon man" whose generosity and kindness made it easier for Inessa to be an "emancipated woman."

In May 1904, when Armand returned from Switzerland where she had gone to give birth to Vladimir's son Andre and to increase her own appreciation of Marxism, she brought with her a sufficient number of books and pamphlets that she and Vladimir were able to set up an illegal Social Democratic library. Literature from it was loaned to student propagandists who in turn used it to increase the political consciousness of a new generation of Moscow Social Democrats. On the night of February 6, 1905, however, the police burst into their apartment, frightened her children, and seized both illegal literature and a revolver. As a result, Inessa spent the next four months in prison and missed out on much of the unsuccessful Revolution of 1905. In the spring of 1906, she moved back to Pushkino where, with the help of at least six other Armands, she printed illegal leaflets, held agitational meetings with non-party workers, and conducted five propaganda circles for aspiring Social Democrats. In the fall, she tried to combine her duties as chief party propagandist in the Lefortovo District of Moscow with being a student in the Law Faculty of the University of Moscow, which had just opened its doors to women auditors. On three occasions in 1907, her work on behalf of the Social Democratic Party led to her arrest, and, after the third in July 1907, she was sentenced to two years administrative banishment in the north of Russia.

She left for Archangel by train in November accompanied by Vladimir who voluntarily joined her in exile. At Archangel, they switched to a horse-drawn sledge for the five-day journey to Mezen, a small town one degree south of the Arctic Circle. Life in Mezen was bleak: bitterly cold in the winter, swarming with mosquitoes in the summer, isolated from all the material and intellectual comforts of civilization. For a time, she sought to divert herself by organizing propaganda circles for fellow Social Democratic exiles and by giving French lessons. But, as she admitted to her husband at the very beginning of her exile, "I don't know how I shall survive two years without the children." After Vladimir's deteriorating health forced him to leave in September 1908, her loneliness became so acute that she fled Mezen in late October, long before her term was up, and returned illegally to Moscow.

After a brief reunion with her children, Inessa revisited her feminist past by surreptitiously attending the First All-Russian Women's Congress in St. Petersburg. She participated in the sessions on the economic situation of women, was intrigued by the debates over "free love," and for the first time became interested in the possibility of organizing the female proletariat who had been largely ignored by the Russian Marxists. Shortly after the Congress concluded, she received word that Vladimir was dying of tuberculosis at a sanatorium on the French Riviera. She crossed the Finnish frontier illegally and was at his bedside when he died in late January 1909. Inessa was left in a quandary. Her companion was dead; she was estranged from her husband and isolated from her children. She could not return to Russia for fear of immediate arrest for having fled Mezen; and she had no profession to pursue abroad. Her commitment to Social Democracy was still strong, but the party had no need for underground propagandists in Western Europe. After several months of indecision, she resolved to continue her education by enrolling in the New University of Brussels. She chose to study political economy, perhaps in an effort to improve her theoretical knowledge of Marxism. She was well aware that the RSDRP put great store in doctrinal writing and polemical disputation—skills that Russian women, lacking a higher education, rarely possessed; thus, they were never included in the leadership of the party. To be taken seriously by her male colleagues and to be given assignments other than just those of an organizational or secretarial nature, she needed to be able to write and to defend her positions. It was only after receiving her license degree from the New University in July 1910 that she returned to the city of her birth to join Lenin and the Bolshevik emigre colony.

Unfortunately, the chores that Lenin had in mind for her utilized mostly her linguistic and organizational talents. She became the Bolshevik representative to the French Socialist Party; she translated some of his speeches into French; she helped set up and finance (with her husband's money) a school at Longjumeau for underground party workers and was the only woman to lecture at that school; she served as chair of the Committee of Foreign Organizations, which tried to coordinate the activities of all Bolshevik groups in Western Europe; and, in the summer of 1912, she returned illegally to Russia in an attempt to bring the party newspaper *Pravda* (Truth) under Lenin's control and to promote the election of Bolshevik deputies to the Fourth Russian Duma or parliament. This exercise predictably led to her fifth arrest and to six months in solitary confinement until Alexander was allowed to post bail of 5,400 rubles. Then, after four months with her children and on the eve of her trial, she once again fled the country at considerable cost to her husband.

Armand's first stop was Austrian Galicia where Lenin and his wife *Nadezhda Krupskaya were now living. When not attending meetings of the Bolshevik Central Committee, Lenin dragged Armand off on mountain hikes in the High Tatras, and she in turn forced the Bolshevik leader and his wife to accompany her to concerts in Cracow. Armand and Krupskaya also discussed the feasibility of publishing a legal party newspaper in St. Petersburg aimed specifically at women workers. The male leadership of the party did not like the idea. They felt that the grievances of women were related to class, not gender, and that for women Social Democrats to address working women on concerns primarily of interest to women promoted separatism among the proletariat and the party. Moreover, there was a general feeling that women workers were politically backward. As a result, the members of the Central Committee would not finance, write for, or support a venture that they were sure would fail in less experienced female hands. Armand persevered. She raised the necessary money, some of it from the Armand family; she helped to put together an editorial board; and she contributed several articles to the seven issues of *Rabotnitsa*—the party's first attempt to address women workers—which appeared in the six months before the outbreak of the First World War.

Like Lenin, Armand spent most of the war in neutral Switzerland. On the eve of hostilities, he had insisted that she represent his party at the Brussels "Unity" Conference where she took much of the blame for his own schismatic practices. In 1915, he again utilized her linguistic skills and loyalty by instructing her to present the Bolshevik position before international conferences of socialist women and socialist youth (she was then 41) held in Switzerland. She also attended the Zimmerwald and Kienthal conferences of European socialist leaders opposed to the war where Lenin pushed the defeatist views of the so-called Zimmerwald Left. When not attending conferences, Inessa spent much of her time translating Lenin's articles and brochures into French or German. As their correspondence shows, she did not appreciate his hectoring attitude, his insistence on instantaneous service, and his patronizing responses to her suggestions for improvements or changes. Her irritation increased when he did not support her own efforts at writing articles or ridiculed her proposal to write a brochure on marriage and the family. He also altered her plan to resume her education at the University of Bern by sending her off to Paris in a dangerous attempt to find French support for the Zimmerwald Left. When her modest results were received with very faint praise, she chose not to return to Lenin's orbit in Zurich but to try to increase her intellectual and personal independence by studying theoretical questions and by occasionally criticizing the ideas of the great Vladimir Il'ich himself from elsewhere in Switzerland. She did, however, join him and 17 other Bolsheviks on the famous "sealed train" provided by the Germans to get them back to Russia after the overthrow of the tsar in February 1917.

Armand's role in the revolution was modest. She participated in the work of the party's Moscow Committee, and she helped edit another newspaper for working women. In August, however, she returned to Pushkino where she spent the next three months with her ailing son Andre. After the October Revolution had brought the Bolsheviks to power, she joined the Left Communists in an unsuccessful attempt to oppose Lenin's peace of Brest-Litovsk with Germany. This did not prevent her from serving as chair of the Moscow Provincial Economic Council, which sought to regulate and reconstruct the economic life of the province. She also was one of Moscow's representatives to the All-Russian Central Executive Committee of the Soviets, she lectured at the new Sverdlov Communist University, and she served as a delegate on a Red Cross Mission to France, which sought to repatriate Russian prisoners-of-war and at the same time to stir up revolution in the country of her birth.

In August 1919, after her return from France, Armand was named the first director of the Women's Section (or *Zhenotdel*) of the Central Committee of the Communist Party. This was the high point of her career as a revolutionary and a feminist. For the last year of her life, she sought to increase female participation in the labor force by relieving many of the household burdens that normally fell to women, and she fought for female equality in the party and the workplace. Almost single-handedly, she edited *Zhenotdel*'s theoretical journal *Kommunistka* (Female Communist), and she organized and chaired the First International Conference of Communist Women, which met in Moscow in the summer of 1920. These endeavors undermined her health, and at Lenin's insistence she left on a vacation in the Caucasus with Andre in August. One month later, she came down with cholera in that war-torn region and died at the age of 46 on September 24, 1920.

After Armand's burial next to the Kremlin Wall, Krupskaya served as guardian for her younger children, while Lenin sought to promote the careers of her older sons. Krupskaya also edited a collection of reminiscences in honor of her close friend. Time, however, has not been kind either to Armand's works or to her reputation. Many of her pioneering efforts among female factory workers were undone and forgotten when the paternalistic leadership of the Communist Party abandoned in the late 1920s its earlier social experiments, and *Zhenotdel* itself was closed on the spurious excuse that its work was finished. Inessa's name went unmentioned in Soviet history books during Stalin's lifetime, and in the West she is remembered primarily for her unique relationship with Lenin. The fact that she lived in close proximity to him from 1910 to 1917 and received from him more than 135 letters, many of them written in the familiar tense and some left unpublished for unexplained reasons in Soviet archives, has led most recent biographers to conclude that she was Lenin's mistress.

As history proves, the desire to find human interest is frequently stronger than the evidence that supports it. It is more exciting to explain Lenin's distraught state at Armand's funeral in October 1920 by claiming that he was mourning the death of a long-time lover than it is by simply noting that she had been a close family friend for more than a decade and that he was largely responsible for her ill-fated holiday. This attitude may have led writers to ignore Armand's accomplishments as a feminist and a revolutionary before she ever met Lenin in 1909 and to attribute many of her subsequent achievements to others in the party. Little attention has been paid to her attempts to create a meaningful role for herself, to gain intellectual independence from Lenin, and to change the paternalistic attitudes of a male-dominated party. There is no doubt that she was a close personal friend of Lenin and it is difficult to prove that they did not have at some time a romantic attachment. There is, however, little firm evidence that they had a lengthy affair and much to indicate that she was one of the few members of his entourage who had the courage and the ability to oppose him on personal and political matters.

SOURCES:
Armand, I.F. *Stat'i, rechi, pis'ma* (Articles, Speeches, Letters). Moscow, 1975.
Balabanoff, Angelica. *Impressions of Lenin.* Ann Arbor, MI: University of Michigan Press, 1964.
Elwood, R.C. *Inessa Armand: Revolutionary and Feminist.* Cambridge: Cambridge University Press, 1992.
Krupskaya, N.K., ed. *Pamiati Inessy Armand* (Memories of Inessa Armand). Moscow, 1926.
Lenin, V.I. *Polnoe sobranie sochinenii* (Complete Collected Works). Vols. 48 and 49. Moscow, 1964.
"Pis'ma Inessy Armand" (Letters of Inessa Armand), in *Novyi mir.* 1970, no. 6, pp. 196–218. Contains 28 letters written by Armand to friends and relatives, 1899–1909, from which all quotations (unless otherwise identified) have been taken.

SUGGESTED READING:
Bardawil, Georges. *Inès Armand: Biographie.* Paris: J.C. Lattes, 1993.
Podliashuk, P. *Tovarishch Inessa: dokumental'naia povest'* (Comrade Inessa: A Documentary Account), 4th ed. Moscow, 1984.
Stites, Richard. *The Women's Liberation Movement in Russia: Feminism, Nihilism, and Bolshevism, 1860–1930.* Princeton, NJ: Princeton University Press, 1977.

R.C. Elwood, Professor and Chair of History, Carleton University, Ottawa, Canada, and author of *Inessa Armand: Revolutionary and Feminist* (Cambridge University Press, 1993)

Armer, Laura Adams (1874–1963)

American artist and author whose works were influenced by Chinese culture and visits to a Navaho Indian reservation in the Southwest. Born in Sacramento, California, on January 12, 1874; died in 1963; youngest of three children; studied art at California School of Design in San Francisco, 1893; married Sidney Armer (an artist), in 1902; children: one son, Austin, 1903.

Selected writings: (illustrated by the author and Sidney Armer) Waterless Mountain (1931); Dark Circle of Branches (1933); Cactus (1934); (illustrated by the author) Southwest (1935); (illustrated from photographs by the author) The Traders' Children (1937); (illustrated by the author) The Forest Pool (1938); Farthest West (1939); In Navajo Land (McKay, 1962).

Laura Adams Armer, who spent most of her later life living and working in the expansive, undeveloped environment of the Navajos in northern Arizona, grew up in cosmopolitan San Francisco. Her artistic interests were sparked early: "Chinese lacquer boxes held my mother's tea," she wrote. "Japanese paper parasols flaunting the life of the Far East vied with Mexican pottery to create a world of rich fantasy for a little girl of New England ancestry." Influenced by the illustrations of Howard Pyle that appeared in *Harper's Young People,* Armer studied under Arthur Mathews at the California School of Design. She credits Mathews with instilling in her a sense of individual expression with comments like, "Be yourself. Don't touch the system with a ten-foot pole." In 1902, Armer married fellow art student Sidney Armer, who later provided illustrations for many of her books.

Armer was age 50, having raised her son Austin, when she first visited the Navajo region that would eventually figure so prominently in her writings. Inspired by a Navajo song describing the journey of Dawn Boy, translated by Washington Matthews, the Armer family took off from Berkeley, California, in their Buick

Laura Adams Armer

touring car; they were accompanied by a friend who had lived among the Navajos and studied their language and customs. This first trip took them to the Grand Canyon and a chance meeting with some Navajos repairing a road. Enamored with the turquoise earrings worn by the Navajo women, Armer followed them back to their camp to acquire some for herself. Thus began "the turquoise trail which was to lead to the house of happiness among the cliffs."

In the spring of 1925, Armer set up a wilderness camp at the base of the cliffs of Blue Canyon. There, in the most beautiful spot in the Hopi mesas, she lived with only a young Navajo girl to cook and interpret, while she immersed herself in Indian culture, including the religious ritual of sandpainting. The results were a series of books and other projects, which were produced from 1931 to 1939. When asked if she was lonely after spending weeks by herself in the canyon, Armer remarked: "I have learned that one must win his own place in the spiritual world, painfully and alone. There is no other way of salvation."

Armer won the Newbery Medal in 1932 for *Waterless Mountain,* and the Caldecott Medal, in 1939, for *The Forest Pool.* Upon winning the Newbery, she confessed that, as an amateur in the field of literature, she had never heard of it and had never worked consciously for an award. "They made me happy," she said, "in verifying the unconscious approach to art, the unsophisticated passion which lies within us all." Laura Armer's last work, *In Navajo Land,* was published one year before her death in 1963.

SOURCES:

Commire, Anne, ed. *Something about the Author.* Vol. 13. Detroit, MI: Gale Research.

Barbara Morgan,
Melrose, Massachusetts

Armstrong, Anne L. (1927—)

American politician. Born Anne Legendre in New Orleans, Louisiana, on December 27, 1927; daughter of Armant (a coffee importer) and Olive (Martindale) Legendre; attended Foxcroft School in Middleburg, Virginia, valedictorian of 1945 graduating class; graduated Phi Beta Kappa from Vassar College, 1949; married Tobin Armstrong, on April 12, 1950; children: John, Katharine, Sarita, and twin boys, Tobin, Jr., and James.

First woman to be national co-chair of the Republican Party (1971–73); first woman to deliver the keynote speech at a major party's national convention (1972); first woman to have full Cabinet status as counselor to the president (1972).

Anne Armstrong tested the political waters as a campaign worker for Democratic President Harry S. Truman in 1948, while she was still in college. Four years later, she emerged as a Republican, supporting the candidacy of Dwight D. Eisenhower. Insisting that the switch in party affiliation had nothing to do with her marriage to wealthy rancher Tobin Armstrong, she said the decision was prompted by her belief in "freedom and liberty, as against the intrusion of big governments." By 1956, Armstrong was a woman to watch in the GOP.

Committed to her rapidly expanding family (five children, including a set of twins), at first Armstrong attempted to limit her political involvement to the local level, but her speaking and administrative skills soon led to a larger arena. After holding a number of executive positions in the Texas Republican Party, she attended the Republican national conventions of 1964 and 1968 as a delegate and platform committee member, and, from 1968 to 1973, served as Republican national committeewoman for Texas. In 1971, President Richard M. Nixon suggested that she and Delaware national committeeman Thomas B. Evans join with Senator Robert Dole of Kansas to co-chair the Republican National Committee. Interested in recruiting women and young people for the GOP, Armstrong became a champion of women in the Republican Party, lending her support to the Equal Rights Amendment and announcing that the president was interested in appointing women to important jobs.

At the 1972 Republican National Convention, Armstrong was spotlighted as the first woman in either political party to deliver a keynote address. Her tireless campaigning for the Nixon-Agnew team—including a 32-day cross-country bus tour—coupled with a growing dismay among women's groups at Nixon's failure to name women to high-ranking posts, resulted in her appointment as counselor to the president, with full Cabinet status and an annual salary of $42,500. As the first woman ever named to that post, she established the Office of Women's Programs in the White House, which by 1973 boasted 130 women in government policy-making positions, a three-fold increase over the number in previous administrations. In her post, Armstrong also chaired the Federal Property Council.

Fluent in Spanish, Armstrong acted as Nixon's liaison with Hispanic Americans and was a member of the Cabinet committee for opportunities for Spanish-speaking people. She was a member of the Council of Wage and Price Stability, the Domestic Council, and the Commission on the Organization of Government for the Conduct of Foreign Policy. She was also the president's liaison with the American Revolution Bicentennial Commission.

During the dark days of the Watergate crisis, Armstrong defended the president so adamantly that someone remarked that she "sounded like the cruise director on the Titanic." In March 1974, she was still holding firm in her prediction that Nixon would not be impeached. Armstrong did not join the call for his resignation until the tapes directly implicating Nixon were released.

After Nixon left office, Armstrong was mentioned as a prospect for vice president, just as she had been when Vice President Spiro T. Agnew had resigned in October 1973. Though president Gerald Ford did not name her, he did ask her to stay on as counselor. In October 1974, she served as a delegate to the United Nations food conference in Rome. A month later, however, citing "unforeseen and pressing family responsibilities" (her mother's ill health and a suicide attempt by her younger brother), she resigned. Out of office, she served on the boards of several major U.S. corporations, but the excitement and involvement of political life still beckoned. In 1975, *Redbook* magazine, after polling 700 political experts, named Armstrong as one of the women most qualified to serve as president of the United States.

In December 1975, Ford asked Armstrong to become the United States ambassador to Great Britain, an opportunity she almost dismissed because she did not want to leave her husband. But after her eldest son offered to return home to take charge of the Armstrong ranch, she agreed to accept the post. Although Britons knew little about their new ambassador, they were intrigued by her Texas background, as well as her ability to ride a horse and shoot a gun. The *Daily Mail* called her "the most romantic diplomat that America has ever had."

Armstrong was chair of the Advisory Board Center for Strategic and International Studies and chair of the president's Foreign Intelligence Advisory Board. She also served as a member of the board of overseers of the Hoover Institute from 1978 to 1990 and co-chaired the Reagan-Bush presidential campaign in 1980. Armstrong was named to the Texas Women's Hall of Fame in 1986 and awarded the Presidential Medal of Freedom in 1987.

SOURCES:

Moritz, Charles, ed. *Current Biography 1976.* NY: H.W. Wilson, 1976.

Read, Phyllis J., and Bernard L. Witlieb. *Book of Women's Firsts.* NY: Random House, 1992.

Barbara Morgan,
Melrose, Massachusetts

Armstrong, Debbie (1964—)

American skier who won the gold medal in the giant slalom in the 1984 Sarajevo Olympics. Born Deborah Armstrong in Seattle, Washington, in 1964.

In early 1982, Debbie Armstrong, a former high-school soccer and basketball star, earned the right to compete in the world skiing championship though she broke a leg in a training run. When her leg mended, she skied five World Cup giant slalom and downhill races in the 1982–83 season. Her best finish was 5th in the downhill at Le Diablerets, Switzerland. In early 1984, 20-year-old Armstrong placed 3rd in a World Cup supergiant slalom and 5th in a giant slalom. Though her best event was reputed to be the downhill, she took gold in the giant slalom at Sarajevo in the 1984 Olympics. Since her biggest worry before the Olympics had been making the team, Armstrong found it hard to stop laughing. It was her first win in a major ski race. For lack of research and better questions, stunned reporters asked what she had sacrificed. Armstrong replied, "Nothing. Skiing is my life. . . . I knew if I kept my head on straight I'd be OK."

Karin Loewen Haag,
freelance writer, Athens, Georgia

Armstrong, Helen Porter (1861–1931).

See Melba, Nellie.

Armstrong, Lil Hardin
(1898–1971)

African-American jazz pianist, bandleader, composer, and vocalist, who wrote over 150 compositions and led bands that included such illustrious performers as Louis Armstrong, Kid Ory and Johnny Dodds. Name variations: Lillian Hardin Armstrong, Lil Hardin, Lillian. Born Lillian Hardin on February 3, 1898, in Memphis, Tennessee; died of a heart attack on August 27, 1971, in Chicago, Illinois, while performing at a memorial concert for her late former husband, Louis Armstrong; raised by her mother and grandmother; studied classical piano at Fisk University, received a teacher's certificate from the Chicago College of Music, 1924, and a post-graduate diploma from New York College of Music, 1929; married Jimmy Johnson, early 1920s (divorced 1924); married Louis Armstrong, February 5, 1924 (divorced 1938); no children.

Lil Hardin Armstrong

Member of Joe "King" Oliver's Creole Jazz Band (1921–24); recorded nearly 50 tunes with Louis Armstrong's Hot Fives, Hot Sevens, and Lil's Hot Shot (1925–27); led all-woman bands (1932–36); became house pianist for Decca Records, leading many all-star recording sessions (late 1930s); toured Europe, playing with Sidney Bechet and others (1952); played many extended engagements in Chicago until her death (1971).

Selected discography: Lil Hardin Armstrong And Her Swing Orchestra 1936–1940 *(Classics 564);* Forty Years of Women In Jazz *(Jass CD 9/10);* Born to Swing *(Harlequin HQ 2076);* Safely Locked Up in My Heart *(Harlequin HQ 2069);* Women in Jazz: Pianists *(Stash ST-112);* Satchmo and Me *(Riverside 12-120);* The Louis Armstrong Story *(Vols. 1-2, Columbia CL 851 and CL 852);* Young Louis: "The Side Man" *(MCA 1301);* Mean Mothers: Independent Women's Blues *(Rosetta RR 1300).*

At her first audition for work as a musician, the polite student from Fisk University in Memphis asked her prospective employer, "Where's the music?" The leader of the New Orleans-style jazz band explained to the young woman that it was not the habit of his musicians to use sheet music. "Well," she then asked, "what key is it in?" With a look suggesting that her question was not only irrelevant but somewhat eccentric, the bandleader counted off two beats. Lil Hardin, classical piano student, who planned to return south at the end of summer to continue work on her college degree and preparation for a career as a concert pianist, struck a long combi-

nation of notes, figuring that whatever the key and the tune that followed, she would have at least a few notes that fit. But when the band swung into play, she soon got a feel for what it was doing, and was hitting the piano so hard—and with such a swinging sound—she was hired on the spot. Thus began a career that was to last 50 years, with the dreams of a classical career all but forgotten.

Lillian Hardin was born in Memphis, Tennessee, in 1898, and was raised by her mother and grandmother (her father died when she was two.) Musical from the beginning, she was taking organ lessons by age six and studied piano in grade school from a Miss Violet White. At age eight or nine, she was playing for school and church and learning classical music along with marches and hymns at Mrs. Hook's School of Music. She entered Fisk University while still in her teens, planning to get a college degree and then to become a concert pianist. But in an oral history recorded on the Riverside label in 1961, Lil recalled that as far back as the days she played the piano for Sunday school, her music swung.

In 1918, Lil was two years into her studies at Fisk when she paid a summer visit to her mother's new home in Chicago, Illinois. Her mother had become one of the half-million blacks who migrated out of the South between 1915 and 1920, in search of the unprecedented job opportunities opening up in industrial cities to the north as a result of World War I. For the student of classical music, the summer vacation was to change the direction of her life. Describing her first views of the city in *Hear Me Talkin' To Ya*, by Nat Shapiro and Nat Hentoff, "Heaven" was Lil Hardin's word for what she found in Chicago. Wandering up and down the streets of the South Side, with its large brick apartment buildings fronted by lawns and its prosperous businesses owned by blacks, she saw the new surroundings as a veritable oasis of hopefulness. She was also entranced by the music, especially the loud, swinging sounds of the New Orleans-style bands reaching out of Chicago nightclubs into the streets.

Lil had always had an appetite for the popular music abhorred by her mother and her grandmother. Once she received a beating with a broomstick for having a copy of "St. Louis Blues." But a guitar-playing cousin had introduced her to jazz, and she was craving a particular song she had heard people humming when she dropped into Jones' Music Store on 35th and South State Street in search of the sheet music. As the piano was the center of family entertainment in those days, sheet music stores enjoyed enormous popularity. When the proprietor of the shop, **Jennie Jones**, heard Lil play on the store piano, she offered her a job as a music demonstrator or "song plugger." Though Lil's mother did not approve, she was persuaded that the work was appropriate for a future concert pianist because it gave her an opportunity to review all the available sheet music. By the second day on the job, Lil knew all the music in stock, and soon people were coming to the store from all over town to hear the "jazz wonder child." Her salary jumped from three to eight dollars a week.

On one memorable day, the great pianist Ferdinand "Jelly Roll" Morton came into the store and joined the young woman on her piano bench. Initiating an informal "cutting session," in which two musicians compete on the same instrument, Morton would play a few chords in his percussive New Orleans jazz style and Lil would retort with a run of Chopin or Bach. While store patrons declared Lil the winner, the young music student heard something impressive in Morton's style, the likes of which she had never heard before. From that time on, she developed a harder and more vigorous attack on the keyboard.

Since Jennie Jones was also a booking agent, it was not long before Lil was granted her first audition with a band. The group was the New Orleans Rhythm Kings, and they were playing in a Chinese restaurant. When Lil was hired, her mother was not thrilled. She gave up trying to stop her daughter once she realized the money Lil could make, but she did arrange for her to be escorted home at night. All thought of returning to Fisk was soon abandoned. Over the next several years, Lil played with a number of other New Orleans-style bands, including those of the Kansas City-born drummer Curtis Mosby and the celebrated cornet player Freddie Keppard.

By 1921, Lil was pianist for trumpet player Joe "King" Oliver's Creole Jazz Band at the Royal Gardens. As the bands originating in the South had come north in those years, the New Orleans style of instrumentation underwent considerable change (including the addition of the piano), but in the '20s a front line in a Chicago band usually consisted of one trumpet or cornet, one clarinet or saxophone, and one trombone. In 1922, Oliver took the unusual artistic step of hiring a second trumpet player besides himself, a young man from New Orleans named Louis Armstrong.

Louis was immediately impressed by Lil's ability at the piano; he liked the way she played all four beats. But Lil didn't pay much attention to Louis until Oliver admitted to her that his humble new second trumpet player was a great deal better on the instrument than he was. She also began to notice the number of musicians turning up in their audiences to hear the extraordinary young performer play his horn. The scope of his talent became fully apparent to Lil in 1923, at the famous King Oliver recording dates, which produced what James Lincoln Collier has called "the first substantial body of real jazz" on record. By this time, Lil realized that Louis was holding back, careful not to outblow Oliver, whom he loved and admired. When Louis was put further away from the recording equipment than the rest of the musicians, so that they could be heard, Lil saw that the modest trumpeter would never reach his full potential unless he somehow took control of his own career.

I might have known I was gonna end up in jazz, because I played "Onward Christian Soldiers" with a definite beat.
—Lil Hardin Armstrong

Lil ended her brief marriage to singer Jimmy Johnson in 1924 and married Louis Armstrong that February. By 1925, she had convinced him to leave King Oliver and strike out on his own. "I don't want to be married to no second trumpet player," she told him. Although this is the event for which she is best remembered, it is generally not remembered that Lil Hardin Armstrong was making it musically on her own. She was now leading her own band, "The Dreamland Syncopators," at the ornate Dreamland club—one of many African-American women who were successful piano player-band leaders, especially in Chicago, during the 1920s. **Ida Mae Maples**, **Garvinia Dickerson**, ❧▸ **Lovie Austin** and **Lottie Hightower** were among the best known, and during those golden years of Chicago jazz, Lil Hardin Armstrong and Lovie Austin gained national fame.

❧▸

See sidebar on the following page

After Louis quit King Oliver, he briefly joined the band of Ollie Power, and had a short stint with Fletcher Henderson's group. But in 1925 it was Louis' move to Lil's band that launched his independent success. The Dreamland Syncopators became, variously, Louis Armstrong's Hot Five, Hot Seven, and Lil's Hot Shots. On the famous Hot Five and Hot Seven recordings, Lil was both pianist and musical director, and many compositions on these famous recordings, including "Struttin' With Some Bar-

Austin, Lovie (1887–1972)

American pianist, arranger, and leader of Lovie Austin's Blues Serenaders. Born Cora Calhoun in Chattanooga, Tennessee, on September 19, 1887; died in Chicago, Illinois, on July 10, 1972; studied music at Roger Williams' University in Nashville and at Knoxville College; married a Detroit movie-house owner; married a variety artist (who toured with a partner as "Austin and Delaney").

After many years touring with Irving Miller's Blue Babies and The Sunflower Girls, Lovie Austin settled in Chicago and was music director, for 20 years, for the Monogram Theater; she later directed at the Gem and Joyland Theaters. Between 1923 and 1926, her name appeared often on blues releases of the Paramount label, both as pianist and leader of Lovie Austin's Blues Serenaders. At that time, Austin backed Paramount's stars *Ida Cox and *Ma Rainey, and occasionally contributed some group instrumentals on her own. During World War II, she took a job as security inspector at a defense plant. From the late 1940s, she was pianist at Jimmy Payne's Dancing School at Penthouse Studios. She made another recording in 1961.

becue," "Brown Gal," and "Lonesome Blues," are the works of Lil Armstrong. Besides these historic sessions between 1925 and 1927, which produced 50 recordings, some of which are considered among the most important jazz recordings in history, Lil was also recording some excellent sessions on her own.

Louis took a lot of teasing from fellow musicians about working for his wife. By 1931, relations between the couple were strained, and she and Louis separated. They did not divorce until 1938. By that time, Lil had appeared in several Broadway musicals, including *Hot Chocolates* (1929) and *Shuffle Along* (1933). During the late '20s and early '30s, she completed her formal education, earning a teaching certificate and a post-graduate degree. In the 1930s, she led two all-women groups, including one of the first all-female swing bands, the Harlem Harlicans, with included **Leora Mieux** (wife of Fletcher Henderson) on trumpet, **Alma Long Scott** (mother of *Hazel Scott) on reeds, and **Dolly Jones**, one of the greatest solo trumpet players of her time. In 1932, the Harlem Harlicans appeared at the Lafayette Theater in New York City, and they played New York's famed Apollo and Chicago's Regal Theater in 1934.

Also in the mid-1930s, Lil led a highly acclaimed band made up of former members of violinist Stuff Smith's group and featuring trumpet player Jonah Jones. In the depths of these Depression years, the band's manager, who was also manager for her estranged husband, tried to drum up publicity by billing Lil as "Mrs. Louis Armstrong" and by calling Jonah Jones "King Louis II." Despite these humiliations, many of the band's members, including Jones, maintained that it was one of the best sounding bands they ever played in.

In 1936, Lil Armstrong left Chicago to become the house pianist for Decca Records in New York, and she led various all-star band recording sessions until 1940. Many recordings featured her compositions, including "Just for a Thrill," which was recorded 20 years later by Ray Charles and became one of his biggest hits. She had also sued Louis, in 1938, for royalties on songs they had written together and won the case.

In the 1940s, Armstrong returned to Chicago, where she continued to play extended club engagements off and on for the next 30 years. A well-loved solo performer as well as combo musician, she appeared with trumpet player Red Allen and drummer Zutty Singleton. She also pursued other talents. She opened a restaurant called the Swing Shack, which used musical themes in the menu listings, designed clothes, including outfits worn by her ex-husband onstage, and taught music and French. In 1952, she made a tour of Europe, playing with various artists including soprano-sax legend Sidney Bechet and trumpet player Peanuts Holland, as well as giving solo performances and making some recordings.

Despite the fact that the Armstrong marriage had lasted barely 13 years (they had lived together for eight), and despite his subsequent remarriage, Lil and Louis Armstrong remained friends for the rest of their lives. In 1955, she told Shapiro and Hentoff, "My feelings for him haven't changed in spite of all the marriages." She continued to live in the house they had bought together in the 1920s, and when Louis passed away, on July 6, 1971, two months after suffering a heart attack, she was deeply shaken. Six weeks later, on August 27, she was performing at a Louis Armstrong memorial concert in Chicago, playing the "St. Louis Blues," when she suffered a massive heart attack and died. She was 73.

SOURCES:

Chilton, John. *Who's Who of Jazz: Storyville to Swing Street*. Time-Life Records Special Edition, 1978.

Choice, Harriet. "Lil's Last Stand," in *Down Beat*. October 28, 1971, pp. 9–11.

Collier, James Lincoln. *Louis Armstrong: An American Genius*. NY: Oxford University Press, 1983.

Dahl, Linda. *Stormy Weather: The Music and Lives of a Century of Jazzwomen*. NY: Limelight Editions, 1989.

Driggs, Frank. *Women in Jazz: A Survey.* NY: Stash Records, 1977.

Feather, Leonard. *The Encyclopedia of Jazz.* NY: Da Capo Press, 1960.

Giddings, Paula. *When and Where I Enter: The Impact of Black Women on Race and Sex in America.* NY: Bantam Books, 1984.

Handy, D. Antoinette. *Black Women in American Bands and Orchestras.* Metuchen, NJ: Scarecrow Press, 1981.

Peretti, Burton W. *The Creation of Jazz: Music, Race, and Culture in Urban America.* Urbana, IL: University of Illinois Press, 1992.

Placksin, Sally. *Jazzwomen, 1900 to the Present.* London: Pluto Press, 1985.

Ramsey, Frederic, Jr., and Charles Edward Smith. *Jazzmen.* NY: Harcourt, Brace, 1939.

Shapiro, Nat, and Nat Hentoff. *Hear Me Talkin' To Ya.* NY: Dover, 1955.

Williams, Martin. *Jazz Masters of New Orleans.* NY: Macmillan, 1967.

Sherrie Tucker,
Alameda, California

Armstrong, Margaret Neilson

(1867–1944)

American botanist and author. Born Margaret Neilson Armstrong on September 24, 1867, in New York City; died on July 18, 1944, in New York City; daughter of David Maitland and Helen Neilson Armstrong; sister of **Helen Maitland Armstrong** *(a painter and stained-glass artist) and Hamilton Fish Armstrong (author and editor of* Foreign Affairs*).*

Selected works: Field Book of Western Wild Flowers *(1915);* Five Generations *(1930);* Fanny Kemble: A Passionate Victorian *(1938);* Murder in Stained Glass *(1939);* Trelawny: A Man's Life *(1940);* The Blue Santo Murder Mystery *(1941). Wrote fiction and biography, including a history of her family.*

In 1867, Margaret Neilson Armstrong was born at her grandmother's home into a family of New York aristocracy. Her maternal grandfather, Peter Stuyvesant, had been mayor of New Amsterdam before it became New York City. Her father, David Armstrong, was an artist and stained-glass-window maker of old, monied lineage. The Armstrongs lived between a home at West 10th Street in New York City and a Newburgh Bay, New York, estate. Armstrong was two when the family moved temporarily to Italy, where her father served appointments as diplomatic consul to the Papal State and then consul general to Italy. Back in New York, Armstrong and her sister Helen received private education and their talents were encouraged with painting lessons (of which Armstrong's first was in Boston). She was 25 when her brother, Hamilton Fish, was born.

Unmarried, the Armstrong sisters primarily lived at home. Margaret spent several years in the American West as she worked on her *Field Book of Western Wild Flowers*, which was published in 1915; after her study was complete, she returned home. In 1918, her father died, leaving his memoirs unfinished. Armstrong assumed the challenge of completing them and in 1920 *Day Before Yesterday* was published. She followed this with a biography of the Armstrong family, as well as portraits of two popular figures of the time, actress *****Fanny Kemble** and writer and adventurer Edward Trelawny. Her biography *Fanny Kemble: A Passionate Victorian* earned her the greatest praise, though she also authored two mysteries, one of which, *Murder in Stained Glass* (1939), relied heavily on her familiarity with the art of stained glass. Two months shy of her 77th birthday, Armstrong died after a brief illness at the family home on West 10th Street, where she had lived with her sister all her life.

SOURCES:
The New York Times. July 19, 1944, p. L19.

Crista Martin,
Boston, Massachusetts

Armstrong, Nellie (1861–1931).

See Melba, Nellie.

Armstrong-Jones, Margaret (b. 1930).

See Margaret Rose, Princess.

Armstrong-Jones, Sarah (1964—)

English royal. Born Sarah Frances Elizabeth on May 1, 1964, in Clarence House, London, England; daughter of *****Margaret Rose *(b. 1930) and Anthony Armstrong-Jones, earl of Snowdon; sister of David, Viscount Linley; married Daniel Chatto, in 1994.*

Arnaud, Yvonne (1892–1958)

English actress and pianist. Born Yvonne Germaine Arnaud in Bordeaux, France, on December 20, 1892; died in Surrey, England, on September 20, 1958; daughter of Charles Léon Arnaud and Antoinette (de Montegut) Arnaud; educated in Paris; married Hugh McLellan (a theater manager).

In 1905, 13-year-old Yvonne Arnaud was awarded first prize for her piano playing at the Paris Conservatoire and subsequently toured Europe and America as a youthful prodigy. In 1911, with little preparation for the stage, 19-year-old Arnaud made her acting debut as Princess Mathilde in *The Quaker Girl* at London's Adelphi Theater. The following year, she met with success when she opened at the Lyric as Suzanne in *The Girl in the Taxi*. Arnaud advanced her reputation in light comedies and musicals throughout World War I, soon aware that her French accent was a chief asset. Long popular on the British stage, Arnaud managed to maintain her Gallic inflections throughout a nearly 50-year residency in England.

Through the 1930s and 1940s, she added Shaw and Shakespeare to her repertoire, playing the Princess of France in *Henry V* (1934), and Mrs. Frail in *Love for Love* (1943). Her English husband Hugh McLellan had much to do with the creation and management of the Yvonne Arnaud Theatre in Guildford, a repertory playhouse that still bears her name. Starting in 1924, Arnaud also appeared in many films, including *On Approval* (1931), *A Cuckoo in the Nest* (1933), *The Improper Duchess* (1936), *Stormy Weather* (1936), *Neutral Port* (1940), *Tomorrow We Live* (1942), and *The Ghosts of Berkeley Square* (1947).

Arnauld, Agnès (1593–1671).

See Arnauld, Jeanne Catherine in "Port Royal des Champs, abbesses of."

Arnauld, Angelique (1624–1684).

See Port Royal des Champs, abbesses of.

Arnauld, Jacqueline Marie (1591–1661).

See Port Royal des Champs, abbesses of.

Arnauld, Jeanne Catherine (1593–1671).

See Port Royal des Champs, abbesses of.

Arne, Susannah Maria (1714–1766).

See Clive, Kitty for sidebar on Susannah Cibber.

Arnesen, Liv (1954—)

Norwegian athlete and first woman to ski solo from the Antarctic coast to the South Pole. Born in Bærun, outside Oslo, Norway, in 1954; daughter of Finn (a machine contractor) and Berit (an accountant) Arnesen; studied history and literature at the University of Oslo, graduating in 1979; taught school in Norway; married Einar Glestad, in 1990.

Liv Arnesen was 12 when she read Roald Amundsen's account of his 1911 South Pole expedition. "I think it wasn't so much the South Pole that attracted me," she noted, "as it was that long ski trip." After months of preparation, which included gaining 20 pounds, pulling a sled through the mountains, skiing Oslo trails with a 30-pound pack, and dragging 100-pound tires attached to her waist through the forest, Arnesen made her attempt.

On Christmas Day, 1994, she became the first woman to ski solo from the Antarctic coast to the U.S. research base at the South Pole, a 745-mile trek. (Only one man has made the journey: Norway's Erling Kagge in 1993). Setting out from Hercules Inlet on November 5, with high winds and low temperatures, without dog team or backup, Arnesen pulled a sled, called a pulka, containing food, equipment, and a digital transmitter, averaging 15 miles a day. The journey took 50 days. Despite near frostbite in two fingers and a fall into a crevasse, Arnesen felt the adventure went well, though she found her enthusiastic reception by Yanks at the South Pole exhausting. "I was more tired after three or four days at the South Pole," said Arnesen, "than after skiing alone for 50." In 1992, Arnesen and **Julie Maske** traversed the Greenland ice cap in 24 days.

SOURCES:
"Into the Great White Open," in *People Weekly*. March 13, 1995, pp. 109–110.

Arnim, Bettine von (1785–1859)

German writer—best known for her epistolary works published from correspondence with Johann von Goethe, Clemens Brentano, and Karoline von Günderrode—and social activist, whose writings on behalf of the poor, of political agitators, and of social reform annoyed many, including the Prussian King Friedrich Wilhelm IV and the Berlin Magistrate. Name variations: Bettina; Bettina Brentano; Bettine. Pronunciation: AR-neem. Born Elizabeth Catharina Brentano in 1785 in Frankfurt am Main; died in Berlin in 1859; daughter of Maximiliane von La Roche Brentano and Peter Anton Brentano (a Frankfurt merchant); sister of poet Clemens Brentano; granddaughter of Sophie von La Roche; married (Ludwig) Achim von Arnim (1781–1831, a German poet and novelist), in 1811; children: Freimund (b. 1812); Sigmund (b. 1813); Friedmund (b. 1815); Kühnemund (b. 1817); Maximiliane (b. 1818); Armgard von Arnim (b. 1821); Gisela von Arnim (b. 1827).

Published first work Goethes Briefwechsel mit einem Kinde (1835), after her husband had died (1831); through her later political works and deeds, was held partially responsible for the revolt of the Silesian weavers; publication of her work was temporarily stopped, and she was arrested; sympathized with the 1848 revolution and wrote on behalf of imprisoned insurgents; sentenced to three months in prison for lese-majesty; acquitted after trial.

Selected works: Goethes Briefwechsel mit einem Kinde *(Goethe's Correspondence with a Child, 1835);* Die Günderode *(1840);* Clemens Brentanos Frühlingskranz *(Clemens Brentano's Spring Wreath, 1844);* Dies Buch gehört dem König *(1843);* Reichsgräfin Gritta von Rattenzuhausbeiuns *(1843, fairytale co-authored with her daughter Gisela von Arnim);* Das Armenbuch *(Book of the Poor, 1844);* Ilius Pamphilius und die Ambrosia *(1848);* Gespräche mit Dämonen *(1852);* Sämtliche Werke *(Collected Works, 1853).*

Toward the end of her life, Bettine von Arnim told the historian Karl Varnhagen von Ense about the circumstances under which she composed her first published poem. According to her story, her brother, the writer Clemens Brentano, had locked her in a small room, refusing to let her out until she had composed a song. The poem, called "Seelied," or "Sea Song," was published anonymously in the *Zeitung für Einsiedler* of May 11, 1808, the journal of her future husband, (Ludwig) Achim von Arnim.

In many aspects, Arnim's works and life epitomize the romantic spirit of freedom, spontaneity, and individuality. The German philosopher and writer Friedrich Schlegel, in his "Fragment 116," defined romantic poetry as a "universal poetry," one that mixes "poetry and prose, geniality and criticism, artistic poetry and nature poetry." For Schlegel, the romantic makes "poetry lively and social life and society poetic." That interplay between the written word and the lived experience applies to all of Arnim's writings and actions.

"Once upon a time there was a child who had many siblings"; so begins a short autobiography that Bettine von Arnim wrote at the request of her brother Clemens. Her father Peter Brentano, an Italian merchant who had settled in Frankfurt am Main, had had six children in his first marriage. Bettine was the seventh child of twelve from Brentano's second marriage to Maximiliane von La Roche.

Scholars usually connect Bettine von Arnim's name with the famous men she knew: among others, her brother, Clemens Brentano; her husband, the writer Achim von Arnim; her correspondent, the renowned writer Johann von Goethe; and Jakob and Wilhelm Grimm, who dedicated their book of fairytales to her. In doing so, they have largely ignored her place in a long lineage of acclaimed women. Her grandmother, *Sophie von La Roche (1731–1807), was one of the most recognized and renowned woman novelists in Germany. Arnim's mother, Maximiliane von La Roche Brentano, who died at 37, received praise

by those who visited her, including Goethe, as possessing a sensitive, artistic sensibility that also fostered artistic talents in all her children. Arnim's own daughters Armgard and Gisela became artists and writers in their own right.

Bettine von Arnim

Arnim was only eight when her mother died. Her father then placed her and three of her sisters in the Ursuline convent school in Fritzlar. The education the girls received there was a usual one for women of the time—lessons in gardening, stitchery, playing guitar, painting, and singing. Arnim characterizes these early years as happy ones, especially the times when she would sneak out on her own to admire the night moon or to sniff the herbs in the garden. Her knowledge of the medicinal uses of herbs would influence her throughout her life, for she often turned to homeopathic remedies for her own and her friends' illnesses.

When her father died in 1797, her half-brother Franz became her guardian. Franz and his wife Toni tried to socialize her into accepting certain norms of behavior, assigning her household tasks. Arnim's letters to friends during the short time she was there and for a long time afterwards reveal her feelings of confinement.

She was thus pleased when in the middle of the year she moved in with her grandmother, Sophie von La Roche, in Offenbach. Here she was allowed free rein of the library. She engaged in stimulating conversations with her grandmother, who also let her examine old correspondence and papers of her grandfather, who had been a councillor at the courts of various counts and electors, which sparked Arnim's initial interest in biographical writing.

At this time, she also developed a close relationship with her brother, Clemens Brentano. They corresponded while he was at school between the years 1801 and 1803, which was to form the basis for her later book *Clemens Brentanos Frühlingskranz* (*Clemens Brentano's Spring Wreath,* 1844). The education and encouragement Bettine received from her brother had a profound effect on her development. But her recollection of his help often portrays his constant advice about her writing and personal habits as stifling: "I had to promise him to write something before he came back," Bettine confides in her friend, the poet ◄⅜ **Karoline von Günderrode,** "Never, he said, would I learn more about how the world was boarded up than if I tried to write a book. And then he talks about a free future and how, without having written a book, I would never enjoy my future!—A book is thick and has many blank pages, which I can't fill by just grabbing things out of thin air—and that seems like a real chain on my freedom." In her letters to Clemens, there seemed to be tension between his desires to channel her interests into those of a respectable woman and her need to find herself outside of the constraints of society.

To connect her life solely with famous men also ignores the intense friendships she had with women. In 1801, Bettine befriended Günderrode. At this time, Karoline was living in a Lutheran cloister for upper-class, unmarried, and widowed women in Frankfurt. The two met frequently to discuss their active intellectual life. The correspondence she had with Günderrode from 1804 to 1806 was later reworked into *Die Günderode,*

⅜► Günderrode, Karoline von (1780–1806)

German poet. Name variations: Günderode, Gunderode, Gunderrode; sometimes used the pseudonym Tian. Born in Karlsruhe, Germany, on February 11, 1780; committed suicide at Winkel on the Rhine, on July 26, 1806; grew up as one of several daughters of a moderately affluent widow.

Prompted by her mother, Karoline von Günderrode entered a kloster for well-born spinsters but was unhappy there. She soon found that travel and visits to friends, especially her close friend *Bettine von Arnim, freed her. Günderrode's relationships were intense. Before her attachment to Arnim, she'd had a close friendship with **Karoline von Barkhaus,** then **Susanna Maria von Heyden.** An unfortunate love affair with the scholar Friedrich Creuzer, who was married with stepchildren, heightened Günderrode's natural tendency to melancholy and mysticism, which colors her poetry. At age 26, she walked to the bank of her favorite stream and committed suicide with a dagger. Some maintain that a falling out with Arnim caused her early death. *Gedichte und Phantasien* (Poems and Fancies) was published in 1806, the year of her death, as was *Poetic Fragments.* In one of her poems, "Wandel and Treue," she wrote that "there is no certainty save that all is uncertain." *Christa Wolf wrote of her in *Kein Ort, Nirgends* (No Place on Earth, 1979).

---

published in 1840. Unlike her relationship with Clemens, in which Arnim often felt pressured to adhere to certain social and literary norms, her friendship with Günderrode helped transcend them. In their correspondence, she speaks easily to the poet, searching out new methods that enable her to "speak from the heart."

At times, however, the expectations that Bettine placed on the women's relationships seemed almost too demanding for Karoline. The two women grew apart after Günderrode began a relationship with a married man whom Bettine did not like. Despite Arnim's desperate attempts to mend the rift, Günderrode became even more distant from the world in general, showing signs in her letters and poems of an inability to reconcile her passionate desires to write and lead an active life with societal constraints. In 1806, Günderrode committed suicide by stabbing herself on the bank of the Rhine river. Bettine felt the devastating impact of the loss of her friend, and she began a friendship with *Elisabeth Goethe, mother of the admired Johann von Goethe. Bettine von Arnim's correspondence with Elisabeth Goethe showed that Arnim sought out the older woman not only to gain access to the admired Goethe, but also to share her stories with the renowned female story-teller. Arnim's "Report on Günderode's Suicide," which she sends to Elisabeth Goethe in 1808, and then includes in her later publication of *Goethe's Correspondence with a Child,* is a poignant expression of her grief.

In 1807, Arnim's grandmother died and left her without a permanent residence. She stayed with relatives, traveling to Marburg, Kassel, Frankfurt, Berlin, Munich, and Vienna. Through Clemens she met Achim von Arnim, her future husband and Clemens' partner in compiling a collection of folkballads and poems entitled *Des Knaben Wunderhorn.* Bettine anonymously contributed ballads and poems to the collection. Clemens and Achim often encouraged her to lend some of her musical compositions to collections of songs, but because Bettine had insecurities about her talents and fear of ridicule, as her replies indicate, she frequently hesitated to contribute to their projects.

In April 1807, Bettine traveled in men's clothing with her sister and brother-in-law to visit Goethe in Weimar. By early 19th-century standards, this trip was both audacious and aberrant for an unmarried, 23-year-old woman. Bettine was accused of being presumptuous, but for her own personal and literary development, the journey represents a major step toward

---

building her self-confidence. The period after her visit shows much activity as she described her journey to everyone and undertook more travels to visit friends and relatives.

Bettine's marriage to Achim von Arnim took place secretly in 1811, when she was 26. At first the couple lived in Berlin, spending time in Weimar as well, where they were often Goethe's guests. One year after her marriage, she gave birth to her first son, Freimund; six other children would be born in the next 15 years. The family lived in Berlin until 1814, and then moved to a residential estate in Wiepersdorf. In 1817, they struck a compromise whereby Bettine moved to Berlin and Achim stayed in Wiepersdorf. The correspondence between the pair shows how family and financial matters, as well as her constant encouragement of Achim in his literary work, occupied most of Bettine's time.

After Achim von Arnim's death in 1831, Bettine von Arnim began publishing her works. In *Goethe's Correspondence with a Child* (1835), she presented a compilation of letters that she had exchanged with the poet, beginning when she was 17. Goethe had been dead for three years when the book appeared, and the work caused an immediate stir in literary circles for the very erotic way in which Arnim portrayed the relationship between the much older poet and the younger woman. Several critics were quick to point out that Arnim had altered letters to place herself in a more favorable light than Goethe would have wanted. Despite the prevailing gossip, the book was an enormous literary success.

Scholarship has now proven that Arnim did alter many of the original letters between herself and her correspondents when she published her letter books. To try to assemble an exact inventory of those changes, as many scholars attempted in the 19th and early 20th centuries, can lead to condemnation of the works as "untrue" without recognizing the boundaries between truth and fiction, between biography and literature that Arnim was blurring. Such investigations do not consider the innovative literary techniques Arnim was attempting. Arnim's epistolary works are able to stand on their own with their imaginative combination of letters, poetry, dialogue, reflection, and narration. The persona of the child that Arnim adopts in *Goethe's Correspondence with a Child* allows her to enter into discussions on love, friendship, nature, music, and writing. Arnim thought the book so successful that she, as she recounts later, sat down and

translated the entire piece into English herself in just a few days.

Arnim's second book, *Die Günderode* (1840), exemplifies the close, fecund friendship that can and often did exist among women. The two women read works of philosophy, literature, history, and the natural sciences, sometimes together, sometimes separately as they followed their own interests and discussed their views with each other. Arnim's work conveys the two women's differences—Bettine being more prone to spontaneous wanderings in nature and free-flowing bouts of writing, while Karoline preferred contemplative study in her room—and the resulting tolerance they have for each other. Within the confines of their individual houses, they imagined a world in which they could travel together to distant places, sometimes real, sometimes imaginary utopias. Together, they created their own "floating religion" (*Schwebereligion*) that could carry them above the confines of their sometimes stifling lives. *Die Günderode* captured the interest of the American Transcendentalists, as evidenced by a translation of the work into English in 1842 by the philosopher and writer *Margaret Fuller.

*M*y soul is a passionate dancer, it jumps around to an inner dance music that only I hear and not the others. Everyone cries, I should be calm, and you too, but out of the desire to dance my soul does not listen to you, and if the dance were over and done with, then I, too, would be over and done with.

—Bettine von Arnim to her brother Clemens Brentano

Arnim saw many of the proponents of the earlier romantic times die—Friedrich Schlegel in 1829; *Rahel Varnhagen, another famous saloniére and letter-writer, in 1833; Clemens Brentano in 1842. Two years after Clemens' death, she published her earlier correspondence to him as *Clemens Brentanos Frühlingskranz* (1844). The book is both a tribute to his encouragement of her as a young writer as well as a revealing portrait of the constraints his demands represented to her.

Still, in her later years, Arnim did not live for the past, but found new friends and issues in the changing times leading to the 1848 Revolution. The last 20 years of her life are characterized by political struggles, many of which are documented by private correspondence and official reports. Between 1838 and 1840, she wrote her strongest political epistles to the crown prince, later, Prussia's king Friedrich Wilhelm IV, on behalf of acquaintances who had been indicted or dismissed for their subversive actions. From 1838 to 1840, she pleaded the case of Jakob and Wilhelm Grimm, who as members of the dismissed "Göttigen Seven" at the University of Göttigen, had to seek new positions. In 1844, she conducted numerous interviews with poor working families living in the Prussian province of Silesia, published under the title of *Armenbuch* (*Book of the Poor*). In 1845, she defended Friedrich Wilhelm Schlöffel, from whom she had received lists of poor workers for her *Armenbuch*, against accusations that he was a communist. In 1846 and 1847, she wrote on behalf of Ludwig von Mieroslawski who was sentenced to death in 1847 for his involvement in Poland's independence struggle. In 1849, she pleaded against the death sentence of the former Storkow mayor Tschech who had attempted to assassinate the king in 1844. In 1849, she tried to persuade the king to acquit the theologian and art historian Gottfried Kinkel, who was sentenced to life imprisonment for his participation in the 1848 Revolution. From 1846 to 1847, she engaged in an involved correspondence with the Berlin magistrate to defend her actions in publishing Achim von Arnim's and her own works privately. The magistrate had ordered her to purchase her citizenship, which she needed to continue her own private publishing "business" that she had begun in 1846. She stated that she would not pay for the honor of citizenship, but would accept it, if conferred upon her. The magistrate was insulted by her remark and brought suit against her.

Bettine von Arnim's two final books, *Dies Buch gehört dem König* and *Gespräche mit Dämonen*, contain dialogues between Elisabeth Goethe and herself as first-person-narrator as they make an appeal for religious tolerance, freedom of speech, and an improved educational system. During her later political years, Arnim also ran a well-known salon. One of the most famous portraits of her shows a contemplative, white-haired woman in a large easy chair, head leaning into her hand, listening to a string quartet in her living room. Although she appears rather sedate here, we know from letters and documents that her salon offered a lively place where the various political factions sought mediation before and after the failed 1848 democratic revolution.

Bettine von Arnim has not been a forgotten writer, but her works and activities have often been misrepresented. Her connections with famous men have loomed in critical studies and biographies. Questions of truth and fiction have obscured close textual readings of her works and appreciation of her ideas on their own terms. Now and again, however, she has been "rediscovered." Margaret Fuller's captivating studies of *Goethe's Correspondence* and her translation of *Günderode* were the first to recognize the unique intensity of Arnim's emotions and the two women's friendship. Two German women who led the struggle for women's rights in the area of education, *Gertrud Bäumer and *Helene Stoecker, wrote articles on Arnim. Writers and critics in the former German Democratic Republic, such as *Christa Wolf, Ursula Püschel, and Heinz Härtl, have rediscovered and reinterpreted many forgotten and unexamined texts. Recent feminists on both sides of the Atlantic have looked into her writings and salon. Since 1987, the International Bettina-von-Arnim Society in Germany has published a yearbook and newsletter. In 1991, an organization of the "Friends of Wiepersdorf Castle" was founded to commemorate the literary tradition associated with the country estate of Bettine and Achim von Arnim. With a reevaluation of Bettine von Arnim's literary and social works have come analyses of her musical and artistic compositions as scholars delve into more little explored territory in the life of an extraordinary, multitalented woman.

SOURCES:

Arnim, Bettine von. *Bettina von Arnims Armenbuch* (*Bettina von Arnim's Book of the Poor*). Edited by Werner Vortriede. Frankfurt am Main: Insel, 1981.

——. *Goethe's Correspondence with a Child.* Anonymous translation [presumably by Bettine von Arnim]. 3 vols. London: Longman, Orme, Brown, Green, and Longmans, 1839.

——. *Goethe's Correspondence with a Child.* Translation, Anonymous [part of the translation by Bettine von Arnim]. Lowell: D Bixby, 1841.

——. *Die Günderode.* Afterward by Christa Wolf. Frankfurt am Main: Insel, 1983.

——. *Günderode. A Translation from the German by Margaret Fuller.* Boston: Elizabeth Palmer Peabody, 1842.

[——]. "Seelied" ("Sea Song") in Ludwig Achim von Arnim's, *Trost Einsamkeit: alte und neue Sagen und Wahrsagungen. Geschichte und Gedichte.* 1808 rpt. Munich: Meyer & Jessen, 1924, pp. 96.

——. *Werke und Briefe.* (*Works and Letters*). Edited by Gustav Konrad. 4 vols. Frechen: Bartmann Verlag, 1958–1963. *Briefe.* (*Letters*). Edited by Johannes Müller. Vol. 5. Frechen: Bartmann Verlag, 1961.

——, and Gisela von Arnim. *Das Leben der Hochgräfin Gritta von Rattenzuhausbeiuns: Ein Märchenroman.* (*The Life of the High Countess of Rattenzuhausbeiuns: A Fairytale Novel*). Edited by Shawn Jarvis. Frankfurt: Fischer, 1986.

"Bettina von Arnim: Translation of *The Queen's Son* and corrections and amendments to Bettina von Arnim's

(?) translation of *The Report on Günderode's Suicide.*" Translations and introduction by Jeannine Blackwell; bibliography by Edith Waldstein. *Bitter Healing: German Women Writers 1700–1830.* Edited by Jeannine Blackwell and Susanne Zantop. Lincoln: University of Nebraska Press, 1990, pp. 441–472.

Bäumer, Gertrud. *Gestalt und Wandel: Frauenbildnisse.* (*Appearance and Change: Portraits of Women*). Berlin: F.A. Herbig, 1939.

Bettine von Arnim. Romantik und Sozialismus (1831–1859). (*Romanticism and Socialism*: Presentations by Hartwig Schultz, Heinz Härtl and Marie-Claire Hoock-Demarle). Trier: Schriften aus dem Karl-Marx-Haus, 1987.

Fuller, Margaret. "Bettine Brentano and her Friend Günderode," in *The Dial.* Vol. 7. January 1842, pp. 313–357.

Goodman, Katherine R. "'The Butterfly and the Kiss': A Letter from Bettina von Arnim," in *Women in German Yearbook.* Vol. 7. 1991, pp. 65–78.

Goozé, Marjanne Elaine. "Bettine von Arnim, the Writer." Ph.D. Diss., University of California, Berkeley, 1984.

Püschel, Ursula. "Weibliches und Unweibliches der Bettina von Arnim." *Mit allen Sinnen: Frauen in der Literatur. Essays.* ("Feminine and Unfeminine of Bettina von Arnim." *With Full Senses: Women in Literature*). Halle-Leipzig: Mitteldeutscher Verlag, 1980. pp. 48–82.

Schlegel, Friedrich. "Fragment," in *Werke in zwei Bänden.* Ed. Nationale Forschungs-und Gedenkstätten der Klassischen Deutschen Literatur in Weimar. 2 vols. Berlin, Weimar: Aufbau Verlag, 1980. Vol. 1, pp. 204–205.

Stöcker, Helene. "Bettina von Arnim," in *Neue Generation: Zeitschrift für Mutterschutz und Sexualreform.* 25. 1929, pp. 99–105.

Varnhagen, Karl August von Ense. *Aus dem Nachlass Varnhagen's von Ense. Briefe von Stägemann, Metternich, Heine und Bettina von Arnim, nebst Briefen, Anmerkungen und Notizen von Varnhagen von Ense.* (*From the Papers of Varnhagen von Ense. Letters of Stägemann, Metternich, Heine and Bettina von Arnim, with Letters, Remarks, and Notes by Varnhagen von Ense*). Ed. Ludmilla Assing. Leipzig: F.A. Brockhaus, 1865, pp. 272–273.

SUGGESTED READING:

Bäumer, Konstanze. *"Bettine, Psyche, Mignon": Bettina von Arnim und Goethe.* Stuttgart: Verlag Hans-Dieter Heinz Akademischer Verlag Stuttgart, 1986.

Frederiksen, Elke, and Katherine Goodman, eds. *Bettina Brentano-von Arnim: Gender and Politics.* Detroit, MI: Wayne State University Press, 1995.

Herzhaftt in die Dornen der Zeit greifen . . . Bettine von Arnim (1785–1859): Ausstellung 1985. [Exhibition Catalogue]. Edited by Christoph Perels. Frankfurt am Main: Freies Deutsches Hochstift—Frankfurter Goethe Museum, 1985.

Hirsch, Helmut. *Bettine von Arnim.* Reinbek bei Hamburg: Rowohlt, 1987.

Waldstein, Edith. *Bettine von Arnim and the Politics of Romantic Conversation.* Studies in German Literature, Linguistics, and Culture. Vol. 33. Columbia, SC: Camden House, 1988.

COLLECTIONS:

Correspondence and manuscripts auctioned off in 1929 and scattered all over; some locations are unknown. Extant partial collections are in the Goethe Museum Frankfurt am Main; Goethe- and Schiller-Archive Weimar; Staatsbibliothek Preussischer Kulturbesitz Berlin; Varnhagen Collection in the Jagiellonian Library in Cracow, Poland; and Stadt- und Universitätsbibliothek Frankfurt.

Lorely French, Professor of German and Chair of the Humanities Division, Pacific University, Forest Grove, Oregon

Arnim, Elizabeth von (1866–1941)

English novelist, author of Enchanted April. *Name variations: Mary Annette Russell, countess Russell; Elizabeth Mary Russell; (pseudonyms) Elizabeth and Anne Cholmondely. Born Mary Annette Beauchamp in New Zealand on August 31, 1866; died in Charleston, South Carolina, on February 9, 1941; sixth and last child of Henry Beauchamp (an English shipping magnate) and Elizabeth "Louey" Lassetter (an Australian); cousin of* *Katherine Mansfield; *attended Miss Summerhayes' school in Ealing and the Royal College of Music; married Henning August von Arnim-Schlagenthin (a Prussian count), in 1891 (died 1910); married Francis, 2nd Earl Russell (separated 1919); children: (first marriage) five, including daughter Leslie de Charms (a writer).*

Born in New Zealand, Elizabeth von Arnim was three when her family moved to London by way of Switzerland. At 18, while on a European tour with her father, she met and married a Prussian count and moved into his depleted estate in Pomerania, the setting of her best-known book, *Elizabeth and her German Garden*, which was published anonymously in 1898. Employing what would be a continuing theme in her writing, Arnim recounts with humor the restrictions and responsibilities of domestic life, the tyranny of marriage and motherhood, and the autonomy that can be found in nature. Most of her early books were published under the name Elizabeth: *The Benefactress* (1901), *Fraulein Schmidt and Mr. Anstruther* (1907), and *The Caravanners* (1909). In 1917, *Christine* came out under the pseudonym Anne Cholmondely.

When her husband died in 1910, Arnim moved with her five children to a château in Switzerland but returned to England with the outbreak of World War I. Following an affair with H.G. Wells, she married Francis, 2nd earl of Russell, brother of philosopher Bertrand Russell. The marriage was a fiasco, and they separated in 1919. Continuing with the theme of marital tyranny, her books took on a bleaker tone as evidenced by *The Pastor's Wife* (1914), *Vera* (1921), and *The Enchanted April* (1923). In 1936, her memoir *All the Dogs of My Life* was released. With the rumblings of war, Arnim headed for America in 1938, settling in South Carolina. She died there two years later, in 1941, shortly after the publication of her last novel *Mr. Skeffington*. Shortly before, her daughter **Leslie de Charms** had published a biography of Arnim, *Elizabeth of the German Garden*.

Enchanted April, which was filmed by Miramax and produced by **Ann Scott** in 1992, is indicative of Arnim's views. Lottie (played by **Josie Lawrence**) and Rose (**Miranda Richardson**) are two proper, middle-class Englishwomen resigned to their staid lives and passionless marriages. Lottie sees an advertisement for the vacation of a lifetime: a month's stay at a medieval villa overlooking the Italian Riviera. Leaving their inattentive husbands behind, Lottie and Rose rent the villa, sharing expenses with two unlikely companions: an austere dowager (played by **Joan Plowright**) and a beautiful, bored socialite (**Polly Walker**). At first, the ladies are wary of each other and unsure of their roles at the villa. But the idyllic hideaway holds a certain magic, and as friendships flourish and hopes awaken, the visitors find ways to live and love that have long eluded them.

Arnold, Emmy (1884–1980)

German-born leader of the Bruderhof movement. Born Emmy von Hollander in 1884 in Riga, Latvia; married Eberhard Arnold, in December 1909; children.

With her husband, founded a small Christian commune they called the Bruderhof (1920); fled to Great Britain after persecution by the Nazis (1930s); in Britain, the group sheltered Jewish refugees; after the war, members of the Bruderhof immigrated to Paraguay and then to upstate New York.

Emmy von Hollander was born in Riga, Latvia, in 1884. As Germans in the Russian Empire, the von Hollanders lived a comfortable life. Emmy's father was a law professor, and the family was both financially well off and highly respected in the community. But life changed dramatically after the turn of the century when the German minority in the Romanov Empire's Baltic provinces was increasingly subjected to a harsh policy of forced Russification. Determined to maintain their German identity, the family moved to Germany where Emmy's father continued his academic career in the city of Halle an der Saale. In 1908, Emmy von Hollander met her future husband there, an intense young man named Eberhard Arnold.

Eberhard Arnold came from a very religious family. His American paternal great-grandfather, John Arnold, had come under the influence of Charles G. Finney, an American frontier revivalist, who believed that Christianity was a faith that had to be experienced not only in theory but also in practice. Eberhard's grandparents, Franklin Luther Arnold and **Maria Ramsauer Arnold**, had left America to work as missionaries in Africa. His father Carl Franklin Arnold was professor of church history at the University of Breslau. Eberhard himself was born in Breslau (modern-day Wroclaw, Poland) in 1883. While only a child, he criticized what he considered to be his parents' extravagant entertaining. The Salvation Army was his model as an authentic expression of Christian fellowship. At age 16, deeply influenced by his distant relative Ernst Ferdinand Klein, a Lutheran pastor with a strong sense of social justice, Eberhard dedicated his life to creating a more just social order through Christianity.

Emmy fell in love with Eberhard shortly after they met. Both were searching for an experience beyond conventional religion. Both were impressed by the Anabaptist tradition found in the numerically small, but theologically vibrant, Mennonite and Hutterite churches around Halle an der Saale. They were baptized in this tradition, a step that disqualified Eberhard from teaching theology or holding a pastoral office in the Lutheran Church. Dropping his plans to finish a degree in theology, he switched to philosophy and completed a dissertation on Friedrich Nietzsche in November 1909. In December of that year, he and Emmy were married. Eberhard lectured for the Student Christian Movement during the next few years.

World War I convinced these two young idealistic Christians that they were pacifists. By the early 1920s, both were meeting with German, Swiss, and other Christian pacifists with a goal to create a Christian community in a world shattered by four years of war and revolution. In the last months of 1920, Emmy, her husband, and a nucleus of fellow believers founded a small Christian commune in the village of Sannerz-Schlüchtern, near Fulda. By the middle of 1922, this community had grown to 40 members. The Arnolds called their new society the Bruderhof; it would be the focus of their lives from that point forward.

Emmy Arnold played a central role during the Bruderhof's formative years. Busy as a wife and mother, she devoted a great deal of time to molding her life in accordance with the Scriptures and to working to free the community from a life of greed and materialism. Self-sufficiency was the group's first goal. In order to support the community, the society relied on printing, publishing, and providing reliable childcare as a way to pay their expenses. To spread the message of their successful experiment in Christian communal living, Eberhard Arnold went on many lecture trips, including several to the United States in the early 1930s. In his absence, Emmy functioned as the first among equals, providing strong but often unspoken leadership through the power of example. Known in later years as the First Bruderhof, she helped forge a working Christian community.

With the Nazis' ascension to power in 1933, members of the Christian pacifist community were living on borrowed time. Members of the Bruderhof knew Hitler's German Reich would never tolerate a group preaching love and peace, no matter how numerically small that group might be. Increasingly, the Bruderhof's society depended on Emmy's energy and willpower. Eberhard's health was already seriously impaired due to a leg injury that had crippled him, and he was often unable to provide the leadership so desperately needed by his disciples.

At eight o'clock on the morning of November 16, 1933, a contingent of 140 brown-troopers and plainclothes Gestapo officials arrived at the Bruderhof. Emmy held them at bay while her sister Else burned incriminating papers in the stove. During the search, her husband lay on the couch, his injured leg in a cast. After a day spent searching the premises, the Nazis left late that night with a large carload of books and papers.

For several years the Bruderhof had supported itself through its publishing house and printing activities. After the Gestapo raid, this source of income was cut off. Emmy Arnold realized it would not be long before the Gestapo arrived to take the Bruderhof's children, including her own. The children were quickly evacuated to Switzerland, shortly before a new Nazi schoolmaster arrived in the village in January 1934. By this time there were no children for him to indoctrinate. Knowing that members of the religious community soon would be rounded up and sent to concentration camps, Emmy Arnold began plans to relocate the Bruderhof.

In 1935, Eberhard died as a result of complications from surgery. Undeterred by her husband's unexpected death, Emmy made plans to move the community out of Germany, and, by 1936, she had devised a detailed plan for a move to England. In 1937, the Nazis demanded that all eligible male members of the Bruderhof present themselves to authorities for military service, a move totally unacceptable to devout pacifists. In light of recent developments, Emmy decided to move the community to the tiny alpine principality of Liechtenstein, located between Austria and Switzerland. Their sojourn was brief, however, as the Nazis annexed Austria in March 1938, threatening the group's security. On the eve of World War II, led by Emmy Arnold, members of the Bruderhof immigrated to Great Britain as an intact group.

The war years were hard in Britain for the exiles. But despite their difficulties, the Bruderhof managed not only to sustain members of the community but also to provide shelter for many Jewish refugees from the Nazi terror. Later, many Jews who lived with the group said the communal experience was an influence when they founded Israeli kibbutzim.

At war's end, the Bruderhof, led by Arnold, decided to emigrate again. First, they went to Paraguay and later to upstate New York. In the rural environment of Rifton, New York, the group prospered spiritually as well as materially, doubling their population in a single generation. Emmy Arnold remained the group's spiritual inspiration, never abandoning the goal that "Humankind waits for the day when all will be one." The 20th century witnessed many religiously based social experiments; few were as successful as the one led by Emmy Arnold.

SOURCES:

Arnold, Emmy, and Eberhard Arnold. *Seeking for the Kingdom of God: Origins of the Bruderhof Communities.* Selected and edited from earlier sources and memories by Heini and Annemarie Arnold. Rifton, NY: Plough Publishing, 1974.

———. *Torches Together: The Beginning and Early Years of the Bruderhof Communities.* Rifton, NY: Plough Publishing, 1971.

———, and Annemarie Arnold. *From Hitler Germany to Paraguay 1937–1941.* Rifton, NY: Plough Publishing, 1982.

Hüssy, Gertrud. *A Joyful Pilgrimage: Emmy Arnold 1884–1980.* Rifton, NY: Plough Publishing, 1980.

Oved, Yaacov. *Witness of the Brothers: A History of the Bruderhof.* Translated by Anthony Berris. New Brunswick, NJ: Transaction Publishers, 1995.

Yoder, John Howard, and the Hutterian Society of Brothers. *God's Revolution: The Witness of Eberhard Arnold.* Preface by Malcolm Muggeridge. Ramsey, NJ: Paulist Press, 1984.

John Haag, Associate Professor of History, University of Georgia, Athens, Georgia

Arnold, Eve (1913—)

American photojournalist and first woman to join Magnum Photos. Born in Philadelphia, Pennsylvania, in 1913; daughter of Russian immigrant parents (Arnold's maiden name unknown); studied medicine before switching to photography classes at New School for Social Research, 1947; studied under Alexey Brodovitch.

While studying to be a doctor, Eve Arnold received her first camera and began pursuing photography at the New School for Social Research in New York. Training with Alexey Brodovitch, then art director for *Harper's Bazaar,* Arnold's early work—mostly class assignments shot at Harlem fashion shows—was accomplished enough to be published in London's *Picture Post.*

During the 1950s, Arnold became the first woman to photograph for Magnum Photos, an international cooperative of photographers. Joining them in 1951, she became an associate member in 1955, a full member in 1957. Much of her work focused on stories about women, including the poor, elderly, and African-Americans, as well as some celebrities.

In 1961, Arnold moved to London, working mainly for the *Sunday Times* but also frequently contributing to *Life* magazine and other periodicals in the United States and abroad. She took to the road in 1965, making the first of five trips to the then Soviet Union. Her intermittent travels in Afghanistan and Egypt from 1967 to 1971 resulted in the film *Behind the Veil,* which disclosed daily life in a harem. During the '70s, several collections of Arnold's photographs were published, including *The Unretouched Woman* and *Flashback! The '50s* (1978).

A stunning and revealing book, *In China* (1980) was the culmination of two extended trips to China in 1979. After years of unsuccessful attempts to obtain an extended visa, she was finally given free access to travel across and photograph some 40,000 miles of the mainland. Her goal was to present the country as never seen before: "I wanted to make a book about the lives of the people, a book that would go beyond the ubiquitous blue suits and bicycles we had been seeing pictures of for so many years. I wanted to penetrate to their humanity, to get a sense of the sustaining character beneath the surface. I wanted to see as many particulars of China as possible." Traveling with only an interpreter, Arnold photographed everything from a Shanghai millionaire to Tibetan women digging roads to a six-year-old girl enduring the endless process of a permanent wave. In 170 color photographs, Arnold not only provided a never-before-seen glimpse of China but also an extraordinary work of art. Widely acclaimed, *In China* won the National Book Award. For three years, the photographs were also shown in a traveling exhibition, which had originated at the Brooklyn Museum in 1980.

Three years later, *In America,* a book of a similar nature about her own country, was published. Returning from England with the "fresh outlook of a visitor," she had traveled America for two years, through 36 states, capturing a wealth of images that reflect the diversity of U.S. life. The collection, at once both expansive and intimate, explores "the geographical face of America—a kaleidoscope of landscapes so various it is hard to believe they are all aspects of one nation—and a vast array of American faces: striking portraits of simplicity and depth."

Other notable books in the '80s were *All in a Day's Work* (1989) and **Marilyn Monroe—An Appreciation* (1987). Arnold, who through Magnum had photographed Monroe on six occasions from the early '50s, retired many of her photographs after the actress' suicide on August 5, 1962. "I didn't want to exploit the material," Arnold explained. On the 25th anniversary of Monroe's death, Arnold published the pictures as a tribute from a friend, together with a striking narrative.

Eve Arnold shared a Lifetime Achievement Award with *Louise Dahl-Wolfe, presented by the American Association of Magazine Publishers in 1979. In 1991, Arnold's photographs appeared in exhibition at the National Portrait Gallery in London. A retrospective look at her work was published in 1995.

SOURCES:

Arnold, Eve. *In America*. NY: Alfred A. Knopf, 1983.
———. *In China*. NY: Alfred A. Knopf, 1980
———. "I Remember Norma Jean," in *People*. August 10, 1987, p. 72–76.
Rosenblum, Naomi. *A History of Women Photographers*. NY: Abbeville Press, 1994.

SUGGESTED READING:

Arnold, Eve. *In Retrospect*. NY: Knopf, 1995.

Barbara Morgan,
Melrose, Massachusetts

Arnold, Margaret or Peggy (1760–1804).

See Shippen, Peggy.

Arnould, Sophie (1740–1802)

French operatic singer, who performed for two decades. Pronunciation: Ar'-nau. Born Madeleine-So-

phie Arnould on February 13, 1740, in Paris; died on October 22, 1802, in Paris; studied with Marie Fel and Mademoiselle Hippolyte Clarion.

Sophie Arnould was renowned for her beauty and sharp wit, but she also held the diva's place in the spotlight for two decades in the 18th century. Born in Paris, Arnould had the opportunity to study with voice trainers *Marie Fel and Mademoiselle **Hippolyte Clarion**. She joined the Chapelle Royale, and, on December 15, 1757, at age 17, Arnould made her operatic debut. The soprano performed most notably in operas by Raneau and Gluck; Gluck's *Iphigénie en Aulide* is most often associated with Arnould. When she was still only 38, Arnould retired from the stage. Her home in Paris became a salon for writers of the time: Rousseau, Diderot and d'Alembert were known to frequent her rooms. She died in October of 1802, at 62 years of age.

Crista Martin,
Boston, Massachusetts

Sophie Arnould

Arnould-Plessy, Jeanne (1819–1897)

French actress. Name variations: Jeanne Plessy. Born Jeanne Sylvanie Plessy in Metz on September 7, 1819; died in 1897; daughter of a local actor named Plessy; married J.F. Arnould (a playwright), in 1845 (died 1854).

A pupil of Samson at the Paris Conservatoire in 1829, Jeanne Arnould-Plessy made her début as Emma at the Comédie Française in 1834, in Alexandre Duval's *La Fille d'honneur.* She enjoyed instant success. *Mlle Mars, to whom the public compared her, became her benefactor. Though assigned prominent parts in all plays, new and old, Arnould-Plessy suddenly left Paris at the height of her success in 1845 and moved to London, marrying the playwright J.F. Arnould, a man much older than herself. After trying in vain to lure her back, the Comédie Française brought a suit against her and was awarded heavy damages. In the meantime, she accepted an engagement at the French theater at St. Petersburg, Russia, where she played for nine years.

In 1855, following the death of her husband, Arnould-Plessy returned to Paris and was readmitted to the Comédie Française, as *pensionnaire* (resident) with an engagement for eight years. This second half of her career proved even more brilliant than the first. Though she revived some of her old roles, she began to abandon the *jeunes premières* (first ingenue) for the "lead," in which she had a success

unequalled since the retirement of Mars. Her later triumphs were especially associated with new plays by Émile Augier, *Le Fils de Giboyer* and *Maître Guerin*. After her appearance in Edouard Cadol's *La Grand-maman*, Jeanne Arnould-Plessy retired in 1876.

Arnow, Harriette Simpson
(1908–1986)

American author of cultural histories, short stories, and novels, including **The Dollmaker.** *Name variations: H. Arnow, Harriette Simpson Arnow, Harriette Simpson, H.L. Simpson. Born Harriette Louisa Simpson on July 7, 1908, in Wayne County, Kentucky; died in Ann Arbor, Michigan, on March 22, 1986; daughter of Elias Thomas Simpson (a teacher, farmer, and oil driller) and Millie Jane (Denney) Simpson (a teacher and homemaker); attended Berea College, 1924–26; graduated University of Louisville, B.S., 1931; married Harold B. Arnow, on March 11, 1939; children: **Marcella Jane Arnow**; Thomas Louis Arnow.*

Published Mountain Path *(1936);* Hunter's Horn *(1949);* The Dollmaker *(1954);* Seedtime on the Cumberland *(1960);* Flowering of the Cumberland *(1963). Given Berea College Centennial Award (1955); granted honorary degrees from Albion College (1955), Transylvania College (1979), and University of Kentucky (1981); given Outstanding Alumni award from University of Louisville, (1979).*

Harriette Arnow's best novels grow out of the Appalachian hills of Kentucky, just as the author herself had her roots in those Appalachian hills. Her fiction, and the lives of the people in the region were, she said, shaped by the land and the Cumberland River.

Arnow's own ancestors migrated to an area of Kentucky near the Big Sinking Creek in the 18th century. These English and Scotch-Irish pioneers brought their sense of independence and strict religious beliefs across the mountains from Virginia and North Carolina. When Arnow was born, her father Elias was employed as a schoolteacher in rural Wayne County. Her mother, too, had been a teacher before her marriage. Thus, even though Harriette grew up in a provincial setting, she grew up among literate people with a great respect for education and learning. Her father was, however, unable to support a family on a teacher's salary, so when Harriette was four years old, they moved to the town of Burnside, a regional center of lumbering and transportation with approximately 1,000 inhabitants where her father took a position as a bookkeeper.

After only one year, the Simpsons left Burnside for a house with 30 or 40 acres on a hill outside of town. Life on the hill led Harriette to love the outdoors, both the semi-cultivated land of her mother's garden and the unspoiled woods and streams. Days followed no regular routine: meals were prepared when people were hungry and laundry done when everything was dirty.

The Simpson family and Harriette's maternal grandmother were inveterate storytellers. Among her earliest memories, Arnow recalled hearing a kind of ongoing oral history of her forebears, as well as stories of wars and the supernatural. Books were an integral part of life in Harriette's youth, and the happiest time of the year was Christmas when, as Arnow said, "nothing on earth had quite the promise of a new book."

She made her first attempt at writing fiction in the fourth grade. For a class assignment, Arnow was to write of something she had always wanted. She described a big desk with many drawers and pigeonholes, narrated from the point of view of the desk. Her teacher was so impressed that she read the tale aloud to the class, giving Harriette her first public encouragement.

Within the next year, life changed for the Simpsons. Money continued to be scarce, so Elias took a job in the oil fields of Lee County in eastern Kentucky. World War I took many young men from the area, and Harriette would remember her mother reading and writing letters for parents whose illiteracy kept them from communicating with their sons in the service. After the war, the influenza epidemic of 1918 raged through the area, causing Millie Jane to keep her children out of school and to teach them at home. Early the next year, the family moved to Lee County to be with their father.

Schools were poor or non-existent in Lee County, so after a year of being taught at home by her mother, 11-year-old Harriette and her sister were sent to boarding school at St. Helen's Academy. An excellent student, Arnow was ready for high school at 12, and was sent in 1920 to the Presbyterian Stanton Academy. There she participated in the Literary Club and became more interested in writing stories and poems.

Again finances forced the family to move, this time back to the house near Burnside. Arnow left Stanton Academy and somewhat resentfully enrolled in Burnside High School. There, although the curriculum was not as stimulating, she loved her classes in history and agriculture. While in high school, she submitted her first story for publication to *Child Life*. Although the piece was not published, the editors taught the prospective author an important lesson. She had sent the story typed, single-spaced on small pieces of paper. It was returned to her retyped—double-spaced on standard size paper—with a note saying that the editor had inadvertently torn the original copy.

After her graduation in 1924, Arnow followed her parents' decision that she should train to be a teacher and entered Berea College. There the strict religious rules and the requirement that every student work several hours each day at the school's craft industries were difficult for her. She continued with her writing and enjoyed her classes, especially English and science, but after two years her parents insisted that she leave Berea and take a teaching position. She took a job in a remote one-room rural school. The country was beautiful, people were friendly, but Arnow at first felt she had been banished from civilization. Her experiences during that year would become the material for her first novel, *Mountain Path*.

After two years as principal of a small school near her family's home, Arnow was able to return to college at the University of Louisville, where she earned her bachelor's degree in 1931. By this time, she was convinced that her vocation lay in writing. After two more teaching jobs, in Pulaski County and in Louisville, she gave up the classroom. Exhausted and with no money, Arnow left Kentucky for a northern Michigan resort, where she spent the summer of 1934 working as a waitress and beginning serious work on *Mountain Path*. In the fall, she moved to Cincinnati, where, over her family's objections, she continued to wait on tables, to read, to write, and at last, to publish.

Her first short story, "Marigolds and Mules," in which natural beauty contrasts with industrialization, appeared in *Kosmos* in 1934. The following year "A Mess of Pork," about a strong hill woman motivated by vengeance, appeared in *The New Talent*.

After reading the latter story, an editor from Covici Friede publishers contacted Arnow, asking to see more of her work. With some rewriting, she was able to publish *Mountain Path* in 1936. The novel grew from her experience of boarding with a family during her first teaching job. The protagonist, Louisa, is an outsider who comes to respect the mountain people. The novel has been praised for its characterization, which is neither sentimental nor condescending.

Even with her novel in print, Arnow still supported herself with odd jobs and by working for the Federal Writers Project, where she did historical studies of early Cincinnati. In 1938, she met journalist Harold Arnow whom she married the following year. Both wished to retreat to a place where they could write with minimal interruption, so they bought an abandoned farm in Kentucky on Little Indian Creek of the Big South Fork of the Cumberland River. Life there was primitive, and the Arnows nicknamed the place "Submarginal Manor."

Arnow's next novel, *Hunter's Horn*, would not appear until 1949. Developments in her family and in the world delayed her plans to focus on her writing. In 1939, she gave birth to a stillborn child, but two years later on September 22, 1941, her daughter Marcella was born. After Marcella's birth, Harriette and her husband decided that their isolated home was not a practical place to raise a family. Thus in 1944, Harold took a job as a reporter with the *Detroit Times*, and leaving his wife and daughter behind to dispose of their property, moved to Detroit.

Like many industrial cities, Detroit was jammed with people, drawn there to work in the war industries and causing a major housing shortage. The Arnows found a rental in one of the wartime housing projects, hastily constructed to provide temporary shelter for the thousands of migrants. The surroundings—the crowded conditions and the heterogeneous population—were different from anything Harriette had ever experienced. She gave birth to a son Thomas on December 15, 1946, and attempted to continue writing. Her determination to write meant that she rose each day at 4:00 AM to take advantage of a few quiet hours before her family awakened.

In 1949, she published her second novel, *Hunter's Horn*. A segment of the work had appeared earlier in the *Atlantic* as a short story called "The Hunter." Set in the Kentucky hills, *Hunter's Horn* concerns a farmer, Nunn Ballew, and his obsession with hunting a red fox known as King Devil. Critics frequently compare Ballew's chase with Ahab's fixation on the white whale in *Moby Dick*. The characters in *Hunter's Horn* live among limitations imposed by their mountain environment and the narrowness of their fundamentalist religious beliefs. In a sense, Ballew's hunt for the fox provides a rare opportunity for creativity, a chance to rise above the routine of life in Little Smokey Creek. Yet killing the fox ultimately brings tragedy to the hunter and his family. The characters in *Hunter's Horn* include not only Nunn Ballew, Arnow's most powerful male character, but also several outstanding female characters, including Ballew's daughter Suse. Suse is the focus of a parallel plot that concerns the narrow options for women and the inevitability of biology as destiny.

In 1951, the Arnows moved from their crowded quarters in Detroit to a large parcel of land near Ann Arbor, 50 miles away. Harold commuted to the city. She referred to her rather "mixed up life," which did not allow time to review books or to write: "My problems I suppose are like the problems of a great many other women who hope to carry on after marriage and discover they cannot do as they did before," she said.

Her busy life notwithstanding, Arnow published what is generally considered her greatest work, *The Dollmaker*, in 1954. Gertie Nevels, the heroine, and her family move from the Kentucky hills to a housing project in Detroit called, ironically, Merry Hill. It is both a journey from

From the movie The Dollmaker, *starring Jane Fonda, written by Harriette Simpson Arnow.*

the land to the industrialized city and a story of family disintegration. The journey challenges Gertie's strength and values; it presents the dilemmas of work versus integrity and motherhood versus creativity. In the end, Gertie emerges with a new faith in the dignity of human beings but has earned this understanding with the loss of most of the things she loves.

The Dollmaker was both a critical and a popular success. Besides being a bestseller, it was the second place selection for the 1954 National

Book Award. (William Faulkner won the award for *The Fable*.) It also won the Friends of American Literature Award and was chosen best novel of the year by *The Saturday Review*'s national critics' poll. In 1983, the novel was adapted into an Emmy award-winning television film starring **Jane Fonda**. In addition, Arnow was honored with an honorary degree from Albion College, the Berea College Centennial award, and the *Woman's Home Companion* Silver Distaff award for her "unique contribution by a woman to American life."

After the success of *The Dollmaker*, Arnow wrote two works of social and cultural history of her native region. Dealing with southern Kentucky and northern Tennessee during the period from 1780 to 1803, *Seedtime on the Cumberland* (1960) and *Flowering of the Cumberland* (1963) grew from 20 years of research. Her goal was to recreate the life of the ordinary men and women who settled the area. She accomplished this by describing everyday activities—preparing food, washing clothes, making soap—as well as by telling the stories of individual pioneers whose varied motives brought them to the region. In 1961, Arnow won an Award of Merit from the American Association of State and Local History and a commendation from the Tennessee Historical Commission for *Seedtime on the Cumberland*.

In *Flowering of the Cumberland*, Arnow continues the tale of the social institutions of the frontier. Her treatment of the Native American peoples of the area is unrelentingly hostile. She sees the Indians through the eyes of the settlers who lived in fear of massacres. On the other hand, she tells of the vital roles women played in the settlement—in no way inferior to men, but rather as "yoke mates." *Flowering* also includes chapters on the language patterns of the region, on religion, on education, and aspects of popular culture, such as songs, jokes, and games.

During the 1970s, Arnow published several additional books: two novels, *The Weedkiller's Daughter* (1970) and *The Kentucky Trace* (1974); and *Old Burnside* (1978), a work of nonfiction. None of these achieved the critical or popular success of her earlier works. *The Weedkiller's Daughter* is set in the Detroit suburbs and tells the story of a 15-year-old girl who rejects the conservative values of her parents. The plot and the characters who represent the "generation gap" seem trite and unrealistic. The novel seems to lack both the sense of place and the universal themes that distinguish her earlier fiction. *The Kentucky Trace* is set in a familiar geographical setting, but in the time of the American Revolution. Critics have suggested that the novel is a thin vehicle for Arnow's extensive knowledge of the history of the late 18th century.

In her later years, Arnow received recognition from the University of Louisville and Transylvania College (1979) and the University of Kentucky (1981). Those tributes were a sign that Arnow's work was receiving wider attention and recognition. She had suffered during much of her career with being labelled as a "regional" writer. Many would argue that Arnow's work transcends region, as she deals with both rural and urban settings. Others would consider her novels feminist or proletarian literature. Harriette Arnow herself claimed to be neither a novelist nor a historian but, like her ancestors, called herself a storyteller. Harriette Simpson Arnow died of heart disease on March 22, 1986, in Ann Arbor, Michigan.

SOURCES:

Arnow, Harriette Simpson. *Flowering of the Cumberland*. NY: Macmillan, 1963.
———. *Seedtime on the Cumberland*. NY: Macmillan, 1960.
Eckley, Wilton. *Harriette Arnow*. NY: Twayne, 1974.
Hobbs, Glenda. "Harriette Louisa Simpson Arnow," in *American Women Writers: A Critical Reference Guide from Colonial Times to the Present*. Edited by Lisa Mainiero. NY: Frederick Unger, 1979.

RELATED MEDIA:

The Dollmaker, (150 min), starring **Jane Fonda**, directed by Daniel Petrie, 1983.

COLLECTIONS:

A collection of Harriette Arnow's manuscripts and papers is located at the Margaret I. King Library, University of Kentucky in Lexington, Kentucky.

Mary Welek Atwell, Associate Professor of Criminal Justice, Radford University, Radford, Virginia

Arnstein, Fanny von (1758–1818)

Austrian-Jewish patron and philanthropist, known throughout Europe for her Viennese salon that attracted many of the leading composers, musicians, writers, and thinkers of the day, who left a permanent mark on European culture. Name variations: *Baroness von Arnstein. Born Franziska Itzig in Berlin, Germany, on November 29, 1758, into an epoch of rapid emancipation and assimilation for the Jews of German-speaking Central Europe; died in Dreihaus near Vienna on June 8, 1818; daughter of Daniel Itzig (1723–1799, a wealthy banker and court financier) and Marianne (Wulff) Itzig (1725–1788); married Baron Nathan Adam von Arnstein (a Viennese banker), in 1776; children: daughter* **Henriette** *(1780–1879, the Baroness Pereira).*

Entertained artists and political leaders; played a major role in the cultural life of Vienna, supporting Mozart and Beethoven; helped found the Society of the Friends of Music; encouraged many talented artists; her influence was at its height during the Congress of Vienna (1814–15), when "the Congress danced" in her glittering ballrooms; as a leading arbiter of taste, her decisions regarding clothing and entertainment often set new styles, including the introduction of Christmas trees to Vienna; an ardent Austrian patriot, she organized the nursing of soldiers wounded in the Napoleonic wars; she never converted to Christianity, preferring to keep her Jewish faith; as one of Europe's intellectual and social arbiters, she played an important role in the Age of Enlightenment.

Franziska Itzig, later known as Fanny, was born in Berlin, Germany, on November 29, 1758, the eighth child and fourth daughter, of Daniel and **Marianne Itzig**. She came from a large family of 15 children, five sons and ten daughters. The Itzigs did all in their power to develop their large brood's natural talents. Visiting Berlin in 1772, the Danish philosopher August von Hennings wrote of Daniel Itzig's family, "He has sixteen [sic] children of whom some are already in independent positions, while others have just reached the age when beauty begins to unfold. The daughters' loveliness is enhanced by their talents, especially for music, and by their well-refined minds." Family wealth gave Fanny and her siblings the best educational and cultural experience available at the time.

The Itzigs were not "old money." Daniel Itzig was the son of a horse dealer and purveyor to the Prussian court. As a young man, Itzig purchased the right to reside in Prussia and further improved his lot by marrying into the wealthy Wulff family. After a complex business career in which he was known by several names (Daniel Berlin or Daniel Jaffe), he arrived in Berlin in 1750 as a member of the select group of *Schutzjuden* (Protected Jews). Soon Daniel Itzig served as purveyor of silver to the Royal Prussian Mint, a position that led to contracts financing Prussia's involvement in the Seven Years' War. In 1761, he was granted the rights of a Christian merchant. Jews were second-class citizens in most of Europe, so Itzig's ability to achieve equal status was of great importance. His wealth grew as he expanded his activities into banking and manufacturing. In time, he became the richest man in Prussia, perhaps in all of Europe.

The daughter of prominent parents was expected to marry well, an expectation Fanny fulfilled. In 1776, she married the Viennese banker, Baron Nathan Adam von Arnstein. The Arnstein family had played a significant role in Austrian economic life since 1705. Nathan's grandfather, Isaac Aaron Arnstein, was involved in many complex financial transactions, including the redemption of the Spanish crown jewels from pawn. Despite his important position as military purveyor to Emperor Charles VI, the elder Arnstein never forgot his precarious role as a court Jew. In 1736, Isaac used his financial influence to stop the authorities from expelling Vienna's Jews. Isaac Aaron Arnstein's son Adam Isaac Arnstein (1721–1785) continued to expand the family wealth and influence. Also active in Jewish community affairs, he defended the interests of the Jews of Prague, Hamburg, and Saxony. Adam Isaac's son Nathan Adam (1748–1838) made substantial loans to the enlightened Emperor Joseph II, a deeply committed reformer, whose Edict of Tolerance in 1781 and 1782 would grant Jews significant legal rights.

Fanny von Arnstein soon became a star in the Austrian capital's social and intellectual firmament. Fanny loved to put celebrities at ease in the comfort of her many sumptuous homes. She knew how to stimulate and entertain artists and politicians alike. For a generation, she held open house for Europe's most brilliant individuals, receiving all with generosity and graciousness. A contemporary described Arnstein in these terms:

> Tall and slender, radiant with beauty and grace, of elegant manner and tone, of vivacious and fiery expressions, combining a sharp mind and with a gay disposition, well-read and a master of foreign languages as well as of her own, she was a most striking and strange phenomenon in Vienna. Attributes few women in high society possessed were noticed with wonder in a Jewish woman whose refinement and freedom of spirit, nurtured by the beneficial influences of Frederick the Second's reign, seemed all the more effective in a city where these virtues scarcely existed, but where they had begun to be desired and to be esteemed.

Von Arnstein's enthusiasm for music provided her first entree into Viennese society. Soon after her arrival in Vienna, her ardor for music became widely known. She formed a close relationship with *Aloysia Lange, Mozart's former sweetheart and future sister-in-law. Perpetually strapped financially, Mozart often depended upon Fanny and her husband. For a period of months, he even lived with the Arnstein family. Later Fanny von Arnstein also assisted Ludwig von Beethoven financially. Patrons like Arnstein were of critical importance to these artists.

Although she moved in Vienna's highest social circles, Arnstein faced religious prejudice as a Jew. The Empress *Maria Theresa (1717–1780) forbade all unconverted Jews to live in the capital without her permission, stating, "I know of no worse plague of the state than this nation, on account of its frauds, its usury and money deals, its way of reducing people to beggary through evil deeds which other honest men disdain. Wherefore it is to be kept out of here and reduced as much as can be." Although she was anti-Semitic, Maria Theresa was not a racist. She was more than happy to welcome Jews who converted to Christianity to her court with open arms. For example when the great social reformer, Joseph von Sonnenfels, became Catholic, he also became a court favorite.

Despite pressure to convert, Fanny von Arnstein did not choose this path. Her avenue to social success was not dependent on religious conversion. Befriending von Sonnenfels, she gained access to the highest officials of the Habsburg court. She established a close friendship with **Caton von Preissing**, wife of the secretary to the Imperial Court, and gained further influence at court. She frequently attended Mozart's subscription concerts, a strategy that paid rich rewards socially. The chronicler Franz Gräffer described Arnstein as a woman of impressive intellect "whose opinions were rightly considered as much as, and indeed more than, those of an entire Academy of scholars." When Joseph II succeeded Maria Theresa to the throne in 1780, Gräffer noted that he conversed with Fanny "whenever he caught sight of her," a sure sign that she had gained complete acceptance in royal circles.

Like many aristocrats, Joseph II was not immune to Fanny Arnstein's physical and intellectual charms. A remarkably tolerant man, Nathan von Arnstein suffered his wife's involvements, even when scandal threatened. Arnstein had a widely publicized affair with Prince Karl von Lichtenstein, but this did not deter Baron von Weichs from falling in love with her. Determined to have Fanny all to himself, he challenged Lichtenstein to a duel and killed him. The magnanimous Nathan ignored the incident, which only served to heighten Fanny's dominance of the Viennese social scene.

Fanny von Arnstein always offered something new and different. She made frequent visits to her family in Berlin, bringing back the latest trends in the arts, sciences, and philosophy as well as intriguing gossip about the political and cultural elite of the Prussian capital. She also brought a new form of entertaining to the Central European capital. In the past, Vienna's aristocracy had never mixed socially with the bourgeoisie. This, however, had changed in Berlin, a city like Paris, where nobles and merchants intermingled with artists, musicians, writers, and philosophers at political and social events. Fanny Arnstein introduced this novel concept to Vienna, where salons flourished. In fact, her determination to bring nobles and commoners together helped transform the Central European city from a provincial capital to one of Europe's important cultural centers. The sumptuous Arnstein mansion in the heart of Vienna was rivaled in elegance only by the Arnstein villas at Schönbrunn and rural Baden bei Wien. All of these establishments offered superb food, seductive music performed by the city's best artists, and brilliant conversation. Guest lists invariably included the most eminent names of the day. No one in Europe was immune to the lure of Fanny von Arnstein's numerous soirées.

> *Attributes few women in high society possessed were noticed with wonder in a Jewish woman whose refinement and freedom of spirit . . . seemed all the more effective in a city where these virtues scarcely existed.*
>
> **—August Varnhagen von Ense**

Arnstein moved quickly to establish rapport with the new emperor. Determined to implement religious toleration and other Enlightenment ideals, Joseph II worked to harness Jewish talent and energy for the benefit of the Habsburg empire. Arnstein's pleas on behalf of her fellow Jews found a sympathetic ear and may have persuaded him to issue the Toleration Edicts of 1781–82, granting the Jewish minority more civil rights than any other European state. For the first time Jews no longer were required to wear a Star of David, were allowed to wear normal clothing, and were permitted to learn handicrafts. In fact, Joseph II encouraged them to stimulate the national economy by opening shops and factories. In her biography, *Fanny von Arnstein: A Daughter of the Enlightenment, 1758–1818,* **Hilde Spiel** explains how this remarkable woman lobbied on behalf of her fellow Jews.

> How did she manage to succeed in overcoming the difficulties in her path? Her early attempts to vanquish the disadvantages of her origin can be traced, here and there, in contemporary writings. From these isolated references we learn that she was a friend of Joseph von Sonnenfels, the baptized Jew and

great social reformer, that she attended Mozart's subscription concerts in the mixed company of Austrian noblemen, courtiers and wealthy converts formerly of her own faith, and that she won the esteem and admiration of such writers as Alxinger, the pupil of Wieland. We are told that she went to see the Emperor Joseph soon after his succession, while he was preparing his famous "Patent of Tolerance," to plead for her people.

Not only did Fanny von Arnstein gain greater tolerance for Jews in the Habsburg empire, she also benefitted personally from Joseph II's enlightened attitudes. In April 1798, Nathan was elevated to the Austrian nobility as a *freiherr* (baron) of the Holy Roman Empire and Fanny became a *freifrau* (baroness). The witty Prince de Ligne, a refugee from the French revolution who had settled in Vienna called the new *freiherr* "the first baron of the Old Testament." Joseph II was well ahead of his time. It would be a number of decades before the Jewish Rothschilds were elevated to similar noble status in Great Britain, for example.

As a child of the Enlightenment, Fanny von Arnstein had a French soul. Although she was intensely loyal both to her native Prussia and to her adopted nation of Austria, she remained devoted to French culture. Throughout her life, she retained a liberality of spirit, broadmindedness, and a devotion to the French language. Besides German and French, she had a reading knowledge of Italian, English, and Czech. She was most comfortable with French, however, and her intimate diaries were written in that language. One of the many admirers of the Baroness von Arnstein, Gottlieb Hiller, noted the international spirit which predominated at her gatherings stating, "Greeks, Russians, Frenchmen and Dutchmen . . . flow together as it were into one European people, through a common French conversation."

Fanny von Arnstein was soon joined in Vienna by two of her sisters, **Cäcilie von Eskeles** (1760–1839) and **Rebekka Ephraim** (1763–1847), who also became champions of a renascent German culture. In letters to Cäcilie and Fanny, the greatest German writer of the day, Johann Wolfgang von Goethe (1749–1832), expressed gratitude for their tireless efforts to popularize his works in Vienna. The Itzig sisters were quick to recognize young talent, befriending and supporting individuals like the Viennese writer Franz Grillparzer, who did much to establish an autonomous tradition of Austrian literature.

Arnstein's French loyalties were challenged when Napoleon Bonaparte's armies swept across the European continent in the early 19th century. She vigorously argued for a strong Austro-Prussian coalition to challenge Napoleonic hegemony, and her salon served as a clearing house for anti-French sentiment. When French armies occupied Vienna in 1809, she continued to confront the conquerors. Because of her determined resistance, Nathan von Arnstein's banking house subsidized the Tyrolean uprising of 1809. Fanny worked tirelessly to ameliorate the misery of the homeless civilians and wounded soldiers alike. Thanks to her efforts, large amounts of money were raised in Vienna's Jewish community for war-relief efforts. Not only Fanny and Nathan, but other members of their extended family also joined the struggle against the French. Her nephew Moritz Jonathan Itzig (1787–1813) volunteered for the colors and died a hero's death at the battle of Lützen in 1813.

Fanny von Arnstein reached the zenith of her social success at the Congress of Vienna. For many months in 1814–15, Vienna was host to the leading sovereigns and politicians of Europe who labored to sweep away the specter of revolution and redraw the map of the Continent on a stable basis. To lighten the burdens of their geopolitical tasks, Fanny brought all of Europe to her lavish establishments. Her salon and ballrooms glittered with native Viennese and foreigners, emperors, kings, and princes. Diplomats rubbed shoulders with poets while merchants and bankers exchanged gossip with painters and sculptors. The names of her guests during this crucial period in Europe's history were a who's who of power and influence, including Tsar Alexander I of Russia, Arthur Wellesley, duke of Wellington, the Prince of Hardenberg, Count Klemens von Metternich, and the Greek leader Alexander Ypsilanti. The Vatican was represented by Cardinal Ercole Consalvi and the Papal Nuncio Severoli, while the world of letters and ideas had such intellectual luminaries as the brothers Schlegel, *Karoline Pichler, Theodor Körner and Baron Humboldt. When her spacious apartments were too small for guests, Fanny hired one of Vienna's largest ballrooms, decorated it in the most lavish fashion, provided splendid evenings of entertainment, "and the Congress danced."

Tolerance was the hallmark of Fanny von Arnstein's life. A child of the Enlightenment, she believed that all faiths were equal before a reasonable and tolerant Deity. Her biographer Hilde Spiel notes:

For the Baroness von Arnstein, ennobled with her husband in the year 1798, had never been and was never to be baptised. Unlike all other heroines of the Jewish emancipation, *Dorothea Mendelssohn, *Rahel Levin [Varnhagen], *Henriette Herz, Marianne Eybenberg, Sara Grotthuss, and Marianne Saaling, she remained faithful to the creed of her fathers. With the exception of her sister, Cäcilie von Eskeles, who emulated her in every way, she was the only one of their famous generation to be buried, when she died in 1818, according to the ancient rites, and to be laid to rest in the Jewish cemetery at the Währingerlini in a sarcophagus, which stands today in a wilderness of broken tombstones and weeds.

Fanny Arnstein had not eschewed baptism from orthodoxy or bigotry comparable to that shown by Empress Maria Theresa. Throughout her life, she was a pupil of Moses Mendelssohn, a firm believer in his theory of the equality of all religions, as symbolized by the Fable of the Three Rings in Gotthold Lessing's *Nathan,* whose model the philosopher had been. And because she believed that all religions were equal before God, she did not object to her only daughter Henriette's conversion.

It was not by accident that Henriette (1780–1879), her daughter, the Baroness Pereira, continued her mother's salon. Held every Friday, such eminent artists as Franz Grillparzer, Adalbert Stifter, and Heinrich von Schwind were always on hand at Henriette's. In fact, hers was one of the few places where Austrian culture flourished in an atmosphere of tolerance in the decades before the revolution of 1848 when the social order was at its most repressive in the Habsburg monarchy.

Fanny von Arnstein left a permanent imprint on Central European culture. She imported the custom of decorating the Christmas tree from Berlin to Vienna, creating a sensation that caught on throughout the empire. Europe's Age of Enlightenment ushered in many new ideas, the most important being the concept of intellectual, social, and religious freedom. The group that benefitted the most from the Enlightenment were the Jews, who had been kept in ghettoes for centuries, living a way of life very different from that of their Christian neighbors. Jewish acceptance into larger European society was made possible partly through salonniéres like Fanny von Arnstein. These women introduced the musical, literary, and artistic works of Europe's most talented men and women. Women like Arnstein believed a common humanity linked all races in the family of man.

Reason, tolerance, and rational thinking reigned supreme during the Enlightenment, and it is probably not by accident that this period of European history was more influenced by women than any other before or since. In salons from Paris to Vienna and from St. Petersburg to London, brilliant women created a new age. Fanny von Arnstein left a permanent mark on Central European culture. Her patronage gave the world great music by Mozart and Beethoven. Austrian literature also benefitted from her patronage. Arnstein touched almost every facet of European culture. The centuries that followed have not been characterized by enlightened tolerance. Yet wherever tact, kindness, intellectual brilliance, and tolerance thrive, Fanny von Arnstein's legacy still lives.

SOURCES:

Barea, Ilsa. *Vienna.* NY: Alfred A. Knopf, 1966.

Bato, Ludwig. *Die Juden im alten Wien.* Vienna: Phaidon-Verlag, 1928.

Gelber, Nahum N. *Aktenstücke zur Judenfrage am Wiener Kongress 1814–1815.* Vienna: "Esra," 1920.

Gräffer, Franz. *Jüdischer Plutarch.* Vienna: n.p., 1848.

———. *Kleine Wiener Memoiren.* 3 vols. Vienna: F. Beck, 1845.

Grillparzer, Franz. *Grillparzers Briefe und Tagebücher,* ed. Carl Glossy and August Sauer. 2 vols. Stuttgart and Berlin: J.G. Cotta, 1903.

Hertz, Deborah. *Jewish High Society in Old Regime Berlin.* New Haven, CT: Yale University Press, 1988.

Katz, Jacob. *Out of the Ghetto: The Social Background of Jewish Emancipation, 1770–1870.* NY: Schocken Books, 1978.

Mansel, Philip. "Between the ghetto and the *Gotha,*" in *Spectator.* No. 8508, August 10, 1991, p. 27.

Spiel, Hilde. *Fanny von Arnstein: A Daughter of the Enlightenment, 1758–1818.* Translated by Christine Shuttleworth. NY: Berg, 1991.

———. "Fanny von Arnstein: Open House in Vienna," in Peter Quennell, ed., *Affairs of the Mind: The Salon in Europe and America From the 18th to the 20th Century.* Washington, DC: New Republic Books, 1980, pp. 47–54.

———. "Jewish Women in Austrian Culture", in Josef Fraenkel, ed., *The Jews of Austria: Essays on their Life, History and Destruction.* 2nd ed. London: Vallentine Mitchell, 1970, pp. 97–110.

John Haag, Associate Professor of History, University of Georgia, Athens, Georgia

Arquimbau, Rosa Maria (1910—)

Spanish novelist and journalist for leftist periodicals.

Name variations: (pseudonym) *Rosa de Sant Jordi.* *Born in Barcelona, Spain, in 1910.*

Selected works: Historia d'una noia i vont braçalets (*Story of a Girl and Twenty Bracelets,* 1934); Home i dona (*Man and Woman,* 1936); 40 anys perduts (*Forty Years Lost,* 1971).

During Spain's Second Republic, Rosa Maria Arquimbau was a journalist and collaborator on several leftist periodicals. When the Spanish Civil War began, Arquimbau's leanings put her on the side of the Loyalists who, by 1939, had been defeated. Along with approximately 250,000 other Spaniards, Arquimbau was driven into exile after the war. Her fiction had experienced some success in the years leading up to the war, but following it Arquimbau found it difficult to publish her work in Spain. She re-emerged in 1971 with *40 anys perduts* (*Forty Years Lost*).

Crista Martin,
Boston, Massachusetts

Arria Major (d. 42 CE)

Roman matron famous for her conduct during the arrest and death of her husband Caecina Paetus after his participation in a conspiracy against the emperor Claudius. Name variations: Arria Maior; Arria the Elder. Pronunciation: AH-ree-uh. Died 42 CE in Rome by a self-inflicted wound; grandmother of Fannia; married Caecina Paetus (a Roman senator); children: Arria Minor.

Arria Major impressed Roman writers of the 1st and 2nd centuries primarily because of her resolution during the arrest, trial and punishment of her husband, the senator Caecina Paetus. In 42 CE, Camillus Scribonianus, the governor of the province of Dalmatia (which included parts of modern Croatia, Slovenia, Bosnia, Serbia, Macedonia and Albania), attempted to lead a military rebellion against the emperor Claudius. Paetus joined the revolt and was arrested after Scribonianus was killed. According to a letter of the Roman writer Pliny the Younger based on a conversation with Arria's granddaughter **Fannia** some 40 years later, as Paetus was being loaded on a ship bound for Rome, Arria begged his guards to allow her to accompany him and perform the duties of his slaves. After this request was refused, she hired a fishing boat and followed the ship to Italy.

Back in Rome—and in front of the emperor—Arria upbraided Scribonianus' wife **Vibia** for informing on Scribonianus. Paetus was condemned and given the usual choice for senators: execution (and loss of property to his heirs) or suicide. It was clear to her family that Arria, although she had not been convicted of any crime, would commit suicide along with her husband. Pliny tells us that when a guard was placed around her, Arria remarked: "It is possible for you to see that I die badly, but not that I don't die at all." To prove her point, she ran at a wall,

knocked her head against it, and lost consciousness. In the end, Arria set an example for her reluctant husband by stabbing herself in the breast first and handing the dagger to him with the words, *"Paete, non dolet"* ("Paetus, it doesn't hurt"). The Roman poet Martial imagined her telling Paetus that his cowardness hurt her more than the dagger.

By the time of Pliny's letter, *"Paete, non dolet"* seems to have become a byword for courage in adversity. It is likely that to upper-class Romans who had suffered at the hands of the emperors, Arria represented a model of strength and moral conduct. Pliny emphasizes that Arria's whole manner of life was exemplary, not just her death.

Nothing is known of Arria's birth, childhood or youth. The Greco-Roman historian Cassius Dio tells us that she was close to the circle of *Messalina, Claudius' wife. Because she was married to a Roman senator of the highest rank, it is almost certain that Arria also came from the senatorial aristocracy—the most powerful and the wealthiest social order in the Roman Empire. The only other moment of her life we glimpse is the death of her son. Pliny relates that after he died from an illness, she convinced Paetus, who was also gravely ill, that their son was recovering. She even led the funeral services without her husband's knowledge, an unusual act for a Roman wife.

Arria's daughter **Arria Minor** also planned to die with her husband, Thrasea Paetus, when he was condemned by the emperor Nero in 66 CE. Thrasea discouraged his wife, even though, according to Pliny, the elder Arria had told him shortly before her own death that she would want her daughter to die with Thrasea if they lived as long and in as much harmony as had she and Caecina Paetus.

SOURCES:
Cassius Dio, *Roman History* 60. 16.
Martial, *Epigrams* 1. 13.
Pliny the Younger, *Epistles* 3. 16.
Tacitus, *The Annals* 16. 34

SUGGESTED READING:
Vidén, Gunhild. *Women in Roman Literature: Attitudes of Authors under the Early Empire*. Studia Graeca et Latina Gothoburgensia, vol. 57. Göteborg: Acta Universitatis Gothoburgensis, 1993.

Alexander Ingle, Research Assistant,
Institute for the Classical Tradition, Boston University

Arrom, Madame de (1796–1877).

See Böhl von Faber, Cecilia.

Arroyo, Martina (1935—)

*African-American soprano. Born in New York City on February 2, 1935; studied with **Marinka Gurevich** and at Hunter College with Joseph Turnau.*

Co-winner of the Metropolitan Opera Auditions with Grace Bumbry (1958); debuted at the Metropolitan Opera (1959) as the Celestial Voice in Don Carlos; *appeared in Vienna, Frankfurt, Berlin and Zurich (1963–68) and at Covent Garden (1968–80).*

Martina Arroyo was one of several outstanding black singers who rose to prominence at the Metropolitan Opera during the 1960s and 1970s. *Marian Anderson was the first African-American artist to perform at the Met in 1955, and her outstanding performance made the musical world aware of the prejudice that had long denied both singers and music lovers. After studying at Hunter College with Joseph Turnau, Arroyo won the Metropolitan Opera Auditions with **Grace Bumbry** in 1958 and made her debut at the Met in 1959. She excelled in the great Verdi operas that called for a lirico-spinto soprano voice, especially as Aïda, Amelia (in *Un ballo in maschera*), Leonora (in *La forza del destino*), and Donna Anna and Donna Elvira (in *Don Giovanni*).

Arroyo made a number of well-received recordings, displaying an extremely beautiful vocalism with a healthy, rounded tone. A big-voiced soprano, her tone was dark, opulent, and soaring. Critics described Arroyo as a stunning vocalist. Criticism has been reserved for her stage performances rather than her singing as she was considered to be seldom dramatically involved. This might have been due to her own temperament as well as the rounded tone of her voice, which was basically sweet. Her early career was spent in Germany and Austria before she returned to the Met in 1965, where she performed until 1980.

John Haag, Associate Professor of History, University of Georgia, Athens, Georgia

Arsiennieva, Natalia (1903—)

Belarussian poet, especially known in nationalistic circles, who continued writing for émigré journals after coming to the United States. Born in Baku, Azerbaijan, on November 20, 1903; studied at the University of Vilna; married an officer of the Polish Army.

Natalia Arsiennieva studied at the University of Vilna before she married an officer of the Polish Army. She lived in Poland from 1922 to 1940, when Soviet occupation authorities deported her as a "bourgeois nationalist intellectu-

al" to Kazakhstan. She was released from captivity after Belarussian intellectuals protested. In the summer of 1941, Arsiennieva was in Minsk when German forces occupied the city, but she escaped the war zone, and, by 1945, she was in a German displaced persons camp. Emigrating to the United States in 1950, she continued to write and publish in émigré journals. Arsiennieva concentrated on writing highly nationalistic poetry colored by a historical experience of cultural survival despite national tragedy.

John Haag, Associate Professor of History, University of Georgia, Athens, Georgia

Arsinde (fl. 934–957)

French countess and ruler. Born in Carcasonne (southwestern France); died in 957 in Carcasonne; daughter of Acfred II, count of Carcasonne; married Arnaud de Comminges; children: at least one surviving son, Roger (later Roger I of Carcasonne).

Arsinde was born into the ruling feudal house of Carcasonne, in what is now southwestern France. Her father, Acfred II, died in 934. There being no surviving sons, his title and lands passed to Arsinde, his eldest daughter. In the 10th century, Carcasonne was nominally under the dominion of the French royal house; in reality, however, its rulers were generally free to govern as they wished. Thus, Arsinde held complete control of her homeland as countess. She married a local noble, Arnaud de Comminges, and gave birth to at least one son, Roger. Roger succeeded his mother as Roger I, when Arsinde died after 23 years of rule.

Laura York, Anza, California

Arsinoe (fl. 4th c. BCE)

Egyptian princess. Name variations: Arsinoë. Pronunciation: Ar-SIN-o-ee. Born during the 4th century BCE; married Lagus (Loqus); children: Ptolemy I Soter of Egypt.

She was the first Arsinoe of the Ptolemaic dynasty. A concubine of Philip II of Macedon, she was presented by him in marriage to a Macedonian soldier named Lagus shortly before the birth of her son, Ptolemy I Soter of Egypt. Thus, the Macedonians assumed that the Ptolemaic house was actually descended from Philip II and Arsinoe.

Arsinoe I (d. 247 BCE)

Egyptian princess. Pronunciation: Ar-SIN-o-ee. Birth date unknown; died in 247 BCE; daughter of Lysi-

Nicaea. See *Arsinoe II Philadelphus* for sidebar.

machus, king of Thrace, and ◄ Nicaea (who was the daughter of Macedonian general Antipater); became first wife of Ptolemy II Philadelphus (r. 285–247 BCE), around 285; children: Ptolemy III Euergetes; *Berenice Syra (c. 280–246 BCE); and others.

Accused of conspiring against her husband Ptolemy II Philadelphus, who may have already been contemplating a second marriage with his sister (***Arsinoe II Philadelphus**), Arsinoe I was banished to Coptos, in Upper Egypt, around 275 BCE.

Arsinoe II Philadelphus

(c. 316–270 BCE)

Daughter of Ptolemy I (founder of the Macedonian dynasty that ruled Egypt for almost 300 years) and three times a queen. Name variations: Arsinoë II Philadelphos (the name "Philadelphus" was added after her last marriage). Pronunciation: Ar-SIN-o-ee. Probably born in 316 BCE; died in 270 BCE; oldest child of Ptolemy I Soter and Berenice I (c. 345–275 BCE); married Lysimachus (the 60-year-old monarch of Macedonia, Thrace, and Anatolia in order to secure an alliance for her father), in 300 (died 281 BCE); married Ptolemy Ceraunus (her half brother); married Ptolemy II Philadelphus (her full brother, c. 275 BCE); children: (first marriage) three sons, including Ptolemy.

⟨She embraces her husband . . . cherishing him with all of her heart . . . he, who is also her *brother*.

—Adapted from Theocritus, Idyll 17.

Little is known about Arsinoe before c. 283 when she became embroiled in the vicious dynastic struggle that threatened Lysimachus' realm and led to his death (281). With her three sons, Arsinoe fled Lysimachus' Asian domain for the European city of Cassandrea, in which she fortified herself awaiting the opportunity to foster her children's interests. While she was there, Ptolemy Ceraunus offered marriage. This was nothing but a ploy, for this Ptolemy only proposed in order to murder Arsinoe's sons and thus fortify his claim to the dead Lysimachus' realm. Her oldest son escaped (fearing treachery, he fled before the carnage), but Arsinoe witnessed the slaughter of her two other sons (280–279). Immediately thereafter, Arsinoe sought refuge in Egypt. There, she eventually married her full brother, Ptolemy II (c. 275), eight years her junior. Their subsequent joint reign was successful and popular, but it ended with her death (270). Nevertheless, her memory lived on, especially since

she received divine honors while still alive—at that time a novel development in a rapidly changing world.

The civil wars that dismantled Alexander the Great's empire were accompanied by a series of shifting marriage alliances among his Macedonian successors, each seeking to secure through matrimony the assistance of powerful friends who might otherwise become dangerous rivals. One beneficiary of matrimonial politics was Ptolemy I, who had already secured Egypt against all comers when Alexander the Great's 13-year-old son (and the last of his dynasty) was murdered in 310 in Macedonia. Much of Ptolemy's early success came as a result of his marriage to ***Eurydice** (fl. c. 321), the daughter of Antipater (who died in 319, but who was the most respected Macedonian aristocrat in the years following the great Alexander's death in 323).

Ptolemy I had several children by Eurydice, the most notorious of whom was Ptolemy Ceraunus. Despite Eurydice's initial political importance, after the death of Antipater, her status at Ptolemy's court diminished. The woman who took Eurydice's place as Ptolemy I's chief consort was Eurydice's beautiful widowed cousin, ***Berenice I** (c. 345–275 BCE), who had originally come to Egypt at Eurydice's request. Although Berenice replaced Eurydice as Ptolemy I's chief wife, he is unlikely to have bothered with divorce, for Macedonian kings practiced polygamy. Ptolemy I's affection for Berenice proved long-lasting, and their first child, Arsinoe II, was born around 316.

Little is known of Arsinoe's childhood, but it must have been interesting. Among other things, when she was about ten (in 306) her father proclaimed himself king—thus assuming the royal status borne by his line until its extinction in 30 BCE (with the death of the famous ***Cleopatra VII**). Arsinoe received the best education (both in and out of the classroom) available anywhere. Of course, anything less would have diminished Ptolemy I, a political genius who also established in his capital (Alexandria-"near"-Egypt) the famous Museum and Library—the world's then greatest collection of literature.

Arsinoe came to the fore in 300 BCE, when her father brokered her marriage to Lysimachus, his 60-year-old ex-military comrade and recently proclaimed king of Macedonia, Thrace, and Anatolia. This union was arranged so as to frustrate the Aegean ambitions of Demetrius Poliorcetes and the Asian aspirations of Seleucus, both dangerous rivals of Arsinoe's father and new husband. The alliance between Ptolemy I and Lysimachus was critical to both of their foreign policies, a fact that is attested to not only by Arsinoe's marriage, but by two others as well: that between ❧► **Lysandra** (Ptolemy I's daughter with Eurydice) and Agathocles (Lysimachus' son with ❧► **Nicaea**) in around 293; and that between Ptolemy II (Ptolemy I's son with Berenice, and thus Arsinoe II's full brother) and *Arsinoe I (Lysimachus' daughter with Nicaea, and thus Agathocles' full sister) in around 285.

Although Arsinoe II gave Lysimachus three sons, perhaps her most historically significant contribution from this period of her life was her dedication of the "Arsinoeion" on the island of Samothrace. This architecturally significant building (it was the Greek world's largest walled, round building constructed to date) was erected within Samothrace's sacred precinct and thus was associated with the island's famed mysteries, about which, despite their ancient renown, we know little today. Nevertheless, her piety at this pan-hellenic site—and one especially sacred to the Macedonians at that—helped establish Arsinoe's name among her contemporaries. Although we cannot say for certain where Arsinoe got the money needed for her dedication, it probably came from the cities, including Heraclea on the Pontus (and perhaps Ephesus—renamed "Arsinoea" in her honor by Lysimachus—and Cassandrea), which Lysimachus gave to her upon their marriage. Regardless, the Arsinoeion proves that Arsinoe, like other women of her station, privately controlled considerable wealth and willingly spent it to foster their religious and political interests, and those of the dynasties with which they were associated.

In the long run, Arsinoe II's marriage did not achieve everything hoped for, but for 17 years it satisfactorily met all expectations. Serious dynastic rivalries, however, doomed Lysimachus' court, and some of the extant ancient sources attribute the tragedy to Arsinoe. Arsinoe was Lysimachus' third acknowledged wife. With his first wife Nicaea, he had fathered Agathocles, who was slightly older than Arsinoe and, as Lysimachus' only adult son throughout the 290s and 280s, apparently his heir. One tradition has it that in 283, after 17 years of living in close proximity, Arsinoe II could restrain herself no longer and sexually propositioned Agathocles. The story continues by reporting his rejection of the unnatural proposal, thus angering Arsinoe and prompting her, in a fit of jealousy, to plot his ruin. This she is said to have set in motion by accusing him of tendering sexual advances towards her. As a result of the charge, the outraged Lysimachus is reported to have executed his son Agathocles.

❧► **Lysandra** (fl. 300 BCE)

*Macedonian princess. Flourished around 300 BCE; daughter of Ptolemy 1 Soter and *Eurydice (fl. 321 BCE); full sister of Ptolemy Ceraunus; married Agathocles.*

❧► **Nicaea** (fl. 300 BCE)

*Queen of Macedonia, Thrace, and Anatolia. Flourished around 300 BCE; daughter of Antipater (a great Macedonian general); sister of *Eurydice (fl. 321 BCE); first wife of Lysimachus, king of Macedonia, Thrace, and Anatolia (his third acknowledged wife was *Arsinoe II Philadelphus); children: son Agathocles and daughter *Arsinoe I (fl. 280 BCE).*

The truth appears to have been less lurid, but nevertheless revealing of the problems associated with the royal Macedonian custom of polygamy, especially as it affected the reigns of long-lived monarchs. Although by 283 Agathocles was mature enough, qualified enough, and ambitious enough to share with his father the responsibilities of royal rule, Lysimachus (then in his 70s) was as yet unwilling to anticipate his succession by sharing royal authority with his oldest and most experienced son. Undoubtedly, Arsinoe had some role in this decision, for her oldest son (another Ptolemy) was coming of age. Two factions developed at court behind these sons of Lysimachus by different mothers. Since Lysimachus did not stifle their intensifying rivalry, we can assume that he had it in mind to name Arsinoe's 16-year-old Ptolemy as his heir. Why this was the case can only be guessed, but it is likely that with Antipater (the grandfather of Agathocles) long dead and his direct line extinguished, Arsinoe's Egyptian connections (Ptolemy I had recently named her full brother, Ptolemy II, as his heir) were too important for Lysimachus to ignore in his own succession. By 283, Agathocles saw the handwriting on the wall and desperately attempted to assert his claim through a rebellion against the father he thought had betrayed him. The result was his own execution. A baroque sub-plot, however, posthumously offered Agathocles a modicum of revenge.

In Egypt, Ptolemy I's decision to name Ptolemy II as his heir had recently "resolved" a similar rivalry between half brothers. Although Ptolemy I had several sons, the two with the strongest claims to succeed him were Eurydice's oldest son, Ptolemy Ceraunus (meaning the "Thunderbolt"; hereafter, simply, Ceraunus), and Berenice's only son, Ptolemy II (obviously a family with a limited imagination when it came to boys' names), who though younger than Ceraunus, was nevertheless old enough to rule when, in 285, Ptolemy I decided to name his heir. For a number of reasons, Ptolemy I had chosen Ptolemy II (recently married to Lysimachus' daughter Arsinoe I) over Ceraunus, and in early 284 elevated the newly designated legatee to a position of joint kingship. Ceraunus immediately went into exile at Lysimachus' court. Although at first glance Ceraunus' flight to Lysimachus' court might seem odd, in fact, it was clever, for although Arsinoe II (Ptolemy II's full sister) was Lysimachus' wife, Lysandra, Ceraunus' own full sister, was the spouse of Agathocles, who was in 284 still the leading candidate to succeed Lysimachus—especially if the succession could be arranged before Arsinoe's oldest son came of age. As a result, it is likely that Ptolemy Ceraunus' appearance at Lysimachus' court touched off the dynastic tragedy that soon struck there.

Certainly, Ceraunus and his sister Lysandra fought hard for Agathocles, thus making of Arsinoe a bitter enemy. With Agathocles' death and Arsinoe's (temporary) triumph, both Ceraunus and Lysandra fled to the court of Lysimachus' rival, Seleucus, where they were able to incite that opportunistic old monarch to invade Lysimachus' realm. Seleucus responded as quickly as he did in order to exploit the resentment of the many still in Lysimachus' kingdom who had backed Agathocles and who remained disgruntled at the savage turn of events. In early 281, the issue came to a head at the battle of Corupedion, where Seleucus defeated and killed Lysimachus. Sought by assassins, Arsinoe and her sons fled to Cassandrea in Europe (garrisoned by troops loyal to and paid by Arsinoe) by way of the port city of Ephesus (by then called "Arsinoea" in honor of Arsinoe). While still in Ephesus, Arsinoe managed a harrowing escape from the assassins at her heels—for it was only by dressing one of her slaves as herself, while she in turn adopted the slave's attire, that she was able to elude her pursuers. Unfortunately, the slave was not so lucky.

As for Seleucus and Ceraunus, their story was not yet over. Having induced Seleucus to remove Lysimachus, and, after Seleucus had crossed over to Europe to claim Lysimachus' European possessions, Ceraunus personally assassinated Seleucus (fall, 281), so as to put forth his own claim—as Agathocles' avenger—to Lysimachus' realm. Taking his time to secure his newly "won" kingdom, Ceraunus left Arsinoe and her sons alone until late in the next year. By the end of 280, however, Ceraunus began to float the idea of marriage with his half sister, arguing that they should let bygones be bygones for their mutual good. Threatened by many wishing to lay claim to all or some of Lysimachus' kingdom (including Antigonus Gonatus, the son of Demetrius Poliorcetes, in the west and Antiochus I, the son of Seleucus, in the east), Ceraunus made it clear to Arsinoe that neither her first husband's realm nor her royal ambitions for her sons could survive without a mature and able champion of their interests. Arsinoe warily considered Ceraunus' proposal, but eventually (over the strenuous objections of her oldest son, Ptolemy) accepted his offer, if Ceraunus would both promise to accept her children as his heirs and agree to a very public marriage ceremony. The latter was intended to diminish the potential for treachery, since Arsinoe hoped that some sense of public shame would constrain her half brother to live up to his promises. As for their co-sanguinity, although such marriages were rare in the Greek experience they were not taboo, since in this case they shared a common father, not a common mother. Had their relationship been through their mother, most Greeks would have been shocked by their union.

The marriage was thus arranged, but not before Arsinoe's son Ptolemy had escaped Cassandrea for Illyria, fearing that his mother had been duped. Still leery of Ceraunus' intentions, Arsinoe would not admit Ceraunus into Cassandrea until after their vows had been exchanged before her garrison assembled outside of the city's walls. Ceraunus went through with the ceremony and thereafter was admitted into her city with only a token retinue. In the meantime, Arsinoe attempted to assure her own safety and that of her sons by maintaining her garrison on the walls—at least until after the consummation of the marriage had been widely publicized. Unfortunately, no act was too brazen for Ceraunus. At the first opportunity, he personally butchered the two sons who remained with Arsinoe while she looked on in horror, so as to fortify his own claim to Lysimachus' legacy.

Arsinoe immediately fled her butcherous half brother for the haven of Egypt. Ceraunus, meanwhile, lay claim to what had been Lysimachus'—and more. His triumph, however, was short lived for he was cut down within the year trying to protect Macedonia from the ravages of an invading army of Gauls. On the other hand, Arsinoe was about to reach her political acme. In Egypt, Ptolemy II (their father had died in 283) welcomed his sister, Arsinoe II, although her strong personality soon put her at odds with his wife Arsinoe I. Factions formed around each woman, while the pleasure-loving, if diplomatically adept, Ptolemy II did little to encourage harmony. For reasons that were probably more political than personal, eventually Ptolemy II sided with his sister, banishing his wife Arsinoe I (but not his children by her) from court on charges of conspiracy. Not long afterwards, probably after Antiochus I (the Seleucid king in Asia) had dealt Ptolemy II a military defeat in 276, Ptolemy II married his sister. This was the earliest known marriage between politically prominent, full siblings among either the Macedonians or the Greeks, and it shocked most of the Hellenic world.

Although Arsinoe II prospered as a result of the marriage, it is equally clear that Ptolemy II gained much from it as well, and that he set the dynastic terms under which it would be joined. Immediately upon taking Arsinoe II as his wife, Ptolemy II had forced her to adopt his already existing children by Arsinoe I. Whether or not the two truly lived together as man or wife cannot be known, but it should be noted that although both had children from previous marriages, theirs produced no offspring.

But what did Ptolemy gain by the marriage? First, the Greeks thought (whether rightly or not is another matter) that full sibling marriages had been common among Egypt's native pharaohs, and thus the union on one level was an attempt to secure the allegiance of the Egyptians for the newly instituted, foreign dynasty. In this it was successful, for Arsinoe II was especially popular among native Egyptians—as her many statues executed in the local style and scattered throughout the countryside attest.

In addition, the marriage also was an act in a larger policy of dynastic consolidation with Ptolemy II and his children by Arsinoe I at its center. Besides the already dead Ceraunus, Ptolemy II had two other half brothers: one, Meleager, had fled Egypt with Ceraunus and was also killed fighting Gauls in Macedonia; the second, Argaeus was put to death in Egypt on conspiracy charges shortly after Ptolemy II's marriage to Arsinoe II. As a result of these deaths, there were no offspring of Ptolemy I who could themselves produce children who might one day challenge the children of Ptolemy II for the throne of Egypt, *except* Arsinoe II. Once Ptolemy II married this Arsinoe, forced her to acknowledge the dynastic claims of his children by Arsinoe I, and thereafter fathered no children by her, he had virtually eliminated the possibility of a nasty dynastic squabble the likes of which had already

destroyed the realm of Lysimachus. Thus, Arsinoe's third queenship came at the expense of her dynastic ambitions.

Hence it is unlikely that Arsinoe II "forced" herself on Ptolemy II, or that she dominated Egypt as its "true" monarch during the years of their marriage. Nevertheless, although she made some sacrifices to regain the privileges associated with being the wife of a king, it is also true that Ptolemy II treated his sister as a royal colleague, both for propagandistic purposes and to exploit her very real political talents.

In terms of propaganda, ever since the deification of Alexander the Great, there had been a growing tendency among the Greeks of the Hellenistic diaspora to divinize their monarchs. This was largely so as to legitimize the newly established dynasties, which otherwise could only justify their authority by an appeal to military might—an appeal that virtually begged armed challenge.

During Ptolemy II's reign, both of his parents were declared gods and worshipped as such. Of course, having "divine" parents made Ptolemy II somewhat special himself—a status that fit neatly into the Egyptian tradition of recognizing the ruling pharaoh as *Horus* incarnate—that is, as a god in human form. It was a short step for Ptolemy II to elevate himself and his sister to the status of living gods—a status that brought them adoration both individually (Arsinoe II had temples dedicated to her all over Egypt) and as a couple (the divine *Adelphoi,* that is, "brother and sister"—from this both received the cognomen, *Philadelphus,* that is, "sibling lover"). Of course, being widely adored as gods by a population that seldom saw either face to face made rebellion difficult. Also, being gods freed Ptolemy and Arsinoe from the constraints of human morality. Their divinity, therefore, "legitimized" their marriage among their Greek subjects, who might otherwise view it as incestuous. Greek poets at the Alexandrian court, including the famous Theocritus and Callimachus (surely at the request of the royal patrons) glorified the marriage and in the process compared Ptolemy II and Arsinoe II to Zeus and Hera, the king and queen of the gods who were also brother and sister. Few Greeks living beyond Egypt were satisfied by the comparison (although for political reasons Ptolemy and Arsinoe received divine honors at Olympia and Athens in Greece proper), but the mythological parallel helped to define as unique and separate the claims of the Ptolemaic dynasty to rule in Egypt, among both the Greeks and Egyptians living there. In terms of actual cult as opposed to poetic symbolism, Arsinoe was most frequently identified with Aphrodite (for the Greeks) and Isis (for the Egyptians), and was trumpeted as a special protectress of sailors (Egypt at the time ruled over a maritime empire encompassing much of the eastern Mediterranean). In addition, priestesses maintained her cult and there was even a religious festival, the "Arsinoeia," celebrated in her honor.

In secular matters, Arsinoe's influence over her brother was also manifest. On the symbolic level, her image was coupled with Ptolemy's on some of the gold and silver coinages of their joint reign, while hers alone adorned some of the copper. Also, Ptolemy named the area of the Fayum in her honor. Concerning more practical matters, she accompanied Ptolemy on military inspections, and he is known to have showered her with enormous wealth (in one case ceding her the immense revenues from the exploitation of Lake Moeris just to pay for her perfume and jewelry). In addition, her name was linked with his (even after her death) as an equal in the formation of certain diplomatic policies, while throughout Egypt—like Ptolemy—she was designated as a "Pharaoh": that is, as a "God-King."

Many of the domestic and foreign policies pursued by Egypt after 275 have bee attributed to Arsinoe. It is difficult, however, to discern Arsinoe's, as opposed to Ptolemy's, influence in such policies. In particular, it is difficult to know for certain how much Arsinoe may have been behind the First Syrian War (274–271), successfully waged against Antiochus I for control of much of the Syrian and southern Anatolian coast; or, Egypt's political recognition of Rome (272), the first such by an eastern Hellenistic state; or even, Egypt's peripheral involvement in the "Chremonidean" War (268–261), fought in southern Greece after her death in a vain attempt to limit Antigonus Gonatas' (by then the acknowledged king of Macedonia) control of the region. All have been attributed to Arsinoe's influence, with the third particularly tied to a possible attempt to establish her surviving son on the throne of *some* kingdom. Of course, for Ptolemy II to have been active in his nephew's "imperial" interests after he himself had denied Arsinoe's son a piece of Egypt, would be potent testimony to the strength of Arsinoe's influence over Ptolemy II while she was still alive. None of these policies, however, can be proven to have been the product of Arsinoe's ambition alone.

Still, given the recorded vigor of Arsinoe's personality, and given the extreme honors showered upon her by her brother-husband and by

her subjects—proving that she remained a very public and popular figure even after her death in 270—it would be foolish to believe that Arsinoe had no role in the formation of such stratagems after she rose to share her brother's throne. Truly, Arsinoe II seems to have defined for Egypt the model of the strong-willed Ptolemaic queen and to thus have been responsible for a legacy not extinguished until the ambitions of the last of her kind, Cleopatra VII, were crushed by the military might of Rome.

SOURCES:
The sources for the early Hellenistic world are extraordinarily fragmented, so that it is helpful to consult with the modern scholarship as suggested below. Nevertheless, see: Justin. *The History of the World.* Trans. by J.S. Watson. London: Bohn, 1875.

SUGGESTED READING:
Burstein, S.M. "Arsinoe II Philadelphos: A Revisionist View," in *Philip II, Alexander the Great and the Macedonian Heritage.* Edited by W.L. Adams and E.N. Borza. Washington DC: University Press of America, 1982, pp. 197–236.

Macurdy, G.H. *Hellenistic Queens.* Baltimore, MD: Johns Hopkins, 1932, pp. 111–130.

Pomeroy, S.B. *Women In Hellenistic Egypt.* NY: Schocken Books, 1984, pp. 13–40.

William S. Greenwalt, Associate Professor of Classical History, Santa Clara University, Santa Clara, California

Arsinoe III (fl. c. 250–210/05 BCE)

*Egyptian princess. Pronunciation: Ar-SIN-o-ee. Birth date unknown; died between 210 and 205 BCE; daughter of Ptolemy III Euergetes and *Berenice II of Cyrene (c. 273–221 BCE); (following a Pharaonic practice) sister and wife of Ptolemy IV Philopator; children: Ptolemy V Epiphanes.*

The presence of Egyptian royal Arsinoe III greatly encouraged the troops at the battle of Raphia in the 4th Syrian War (217), in which Antiochus III the Great was defeated. The victory restored most of the Syrian coast to the Ptolemies. Arsinoe III's brother-husband Ptolemy IV Philopator put her to death between 210 and 205 BCE to please his mistress **Agathocleia**, a Samian dancer.

Arsinoe IV (d. 41 BCE)

Queen of Egypt. Pronunciation: Ar-SIN-o-ee. Birth date unknown; killed at Miletus in 41 BCE; youngest daughter of Ptolemy XI Auletes; sister of Cleopatra VII, Ptolemy XII, and Ptolemy XIII.

In the year 51 BCE, Ptolemy XI Auletes left his throne to be ruled jointly by his older children *Cleopatra VII and Ptolemy XII. When

Ptolemy XII expelled Cleopatra, Julius Caesar decided to force her restoration. During Caesar's siege of Alexandria (48 BCE) and the subsequent capture and death of young Ptolemy, Cleopatra's sister Arsinoe IV was looked on as sole queen by the Egyptians (47 BCE). As a precaution, Caesar captured Arsinoe and led her triumphantly through Rome. Though Arsinoe was eventually allowed to return to Alexandria, her years were brief. After the battle of Philippi, she was put to death at Miletus (or in the temple of Artemis at Ephesus) by order of Marc Antony, at the request of her sister Cleopatra.

Artemisia I (c. 520–? BCE)

Queen of Halicarnassus (present-day Turkey) who backed Xerxes' invasion of Greece with her own naval contingent. Born around 520 BCE; died after 480 BCE; Artemisia was the daughter of Lygdamis of Halicarnassus.

When Xerxes, the Great King of Persia, set out to conquer European Greece, Artemisia was the ruler of Caria, Nisyrus, Calyndria, Cos, and the Greek cities along their respective coasts, as well as a client-queen of the Persian Empire. A figure of importance, Artemisia personally commanded a contingent of five ships in the armada that supported Xerxes' invasion of Greece in 480 BCE (only one Persian dependent, the Phoenician city of Sidon, contributed more ships to the Persian navy than did she). Her exploits during the naval battle of Salamis were reported by her Halicarnassian compatriot, Herodotus, who took pride in the bravery she displayed during that struggle while simultaneously rejoicing in the defeat of her side. Before Salamis—the battle, which more than any other, ensured that the Persian attempt to subject European Greece would fail—Artemisia advised Xerxes not to attack the Greeks in the narrow channel between Attica and the island of Salamis where the Greek navy had taken refuge. Unfortunately for Xerxes, he did not heed Artemisia's advice, and, consequently, he suffered a devastating naval setback.

During the battle, however, Artemisia proved herself to be so competent a naval commander that Xerxes (whose vantage point allowed him to view the marine struggle from the security of dry land) is said to have remarked that within his fleet, "the men fought like women, and the women like men." Although Artemisia appears to have been an excellent admiral, the incident that provoked Xerxes' comment appears to have occurred when she, in order to prevent being rammed by a Greek ship, rammed and sank the ship of one of her Persian compatriots. Xerxes, recognizing Artemisia's ship but not that which she sank, thus seems to have praised her at a moment when she probably would have preferred not being noticed at all.

Despite the irony of Xerxes' untimely praise, Artemisia fought well enough at Salamis for the Athenians to offer a reward of 10,000 drachmae (about the weekly wage of 2,000 skilled artisans) for her capture; they were especially eager to lay hold of her because she was not only competent, but a woman as well. After Xerxes' defeat at Salamis, his navy was disheveled, and Xerxes' supply lines to Asia were severed, crippling his ability to feed his huge army. Realizing the significance of the defeat, Artemisia was one of the most ardent voices admonishing Xerxes to act expediently by withdrawing from Europe lest his army starve in Greece.

After Xerxes' retreat from Greece, Artemisia returned to her domain within the Persian sphere of influence, where little is heard of her thereafter. If a late source can be trusted, her end came when a much younger would-be lover (Dardanus, from the Greek city of Abydus) rejected her affections, after which she is said to have leaped from the Leucas promontory (not far from Halicarnassus) to her death in the Aegean Sea. It must be pointed out, however, that such romanticism seems out of place for the hard-nosed monarch of one of the Persian Empire's most prosperous districts.

SUGGESTED READING:

Herodotus, *The Histories*, revised edition, Penguin, 1972 (especially Book Eight).

William S. Greenwalt, Associate Professor of Classical History, Santa Clara University, Santa Clara, California

Artemisia II (c. 395–351 BCE)

*Carian daughter of Hekatomnus, who was a devoted wife, co-ruler, and the primary patron behind the construction of the Mausoleum—one of the Seven Wonders of the ancient world. Pronunciation: Ar-te-MIS-i-a. Born around 395; died in 351 BCE; oldest daughter and perhaps primary heir of Hekatomnus (Hekatomnos), the first Carian to rule over his native land as a satrap of the Persian Empire; sister of *Ada (c. 380–323 BCE), Idreus, and Pixodarus; married her full-brother, Mausolus, around 377 BCE.*

Artemisia helped to secure her family's claim to a more independent Caria, albeit without breaking away from the Persian Empire. With her husband, she helped to frustrate the renewal of the Athenian imperial vision, which took concrete form in the Second Delian Confederacy. After Mausolus' death (353 BCE),

Artemisia devoted the rest of her life to glorifying his memory. The primary vehicle for this glorification came in the form of the "Mausoleum," a burial compound so large and magnificent that it became one of the most common tourist destinations in the ancient world. So grandiose and bold were the design and decoration of the Mausoleum, that it came to be incorporated into the ancient world's seven acknowledged wonders. Artemisia died of grief over the loss of her husband in 351 BCE, her reign as the lone satrap of Caria lasting but two years. When she died, her authority passed without incident to the joint reign of her brother and sister—respectively, Idrieus and Ada, who, like Mausolus and Artemisia, were husband and wife. These were followed on the satrapal throne of Caria by Pixodarus, the youngest of Artemisia's siblings.

Artemisia was the daughter of Hekatomnus, who was probably the first native-born Carian (a district in the southwestern part of modern-day Turkey) to be established by Artaxerxes II, the Great King (c. 392 BCE), as the province's satrap (governor), under the authority of the Persian Empire. Before the promotion of Hekatomnus, Caria had been ruled by a Persian appointee of the Great King whose provincial capital had been maintained in the Lydian city of Sardis, to the north of Caria. Hekatomnus seems to have advanced to the position of satrap as a part of a general Persian reorganization of power throughout Anatolia in the late 390s.

> So did Artemisia by flutes and cymbals possess for herself what she had in vain endeavored by force to obtain.
>
> —Polyaenus 8.52.4

Artemisia probably was born shortly before her father's advancement, and certainly grew up in his capital of Mylasa at a provincial court, which not only paid political homage to the Persians, but which also was under the considerable cultural influence of the Greek world and concerned with the fluctuations of Hellenic inter-state relations. The Greeks had been established along the Anatolian seaboard long before the arrival of the Persians (c. 550 BCE). Although these Greeks had known periods of freedom from the Persians in the 400s under the hegemonies of Athens and Sparta, by the time of Artemisia's birth, the Greeks who lived along the Carian shore had been politically subordinated by the Persians, and, hence, fell under Hekatomnus' authority.

Hekatomnus was a reliable servant of Persians until his death around 377–376 BCE, when the mantel of Carian authority passed to his oldest son, Mausolus, who either at this time or shortly thereafter married Artemisia, his full-sister. Although contemporary political documents make it clear that Mausolus was the acknowledged political superior in this marriage, they also indicate that Artemisia wielded public authority at the side of her brother-husband to the extent that she was virtually his co-ruler. Several contemporary fiats and treaties concerned with both domestic and foreign affairs (fragments of which still exist in inscriptional form) make this collegiality manifest, for the public business therein documented was done so under the joint jurisdiction of both Mausolus and Artemisia, albeit with Mausolus clearly indicated as the senior partner. Mausolus and Artemisia are known to have had three (probably younger) siblings: two brothers, Idrieus and Pixodarus, and a sister, *Ada. Duplicating the relationship of Mausolus and Artemisia, Idrieus married Ada.

When Mausolus married Artemisia, unions between full siblings were considered scandalous within the Greek world, and (although not unknown) unusual among non-Greeks as well. There is some justification for assuming that such marriages are indicative of a rare matrilineal tradition among the Carians, for anthropologists know of societies in which property (here an entire realm) is bequeathed not from father to son, but from mother to daughter. In many of these societies, the sons who have no legal claim to a family's legacy reclaim a portion of that legacy for themselves by marrying their sisters. Although our record for Caria is largely fragmentary, the mere fact that Caria had had a ruling queen (*Artemisia I) in the 5th century suggests that women both inherited property and participated in the public sphere to degrees virtually unheard of in the world of the Greek city-state. Whether or not Carian dynasts before Mausolus and Artemisia had engaged in brother-sister marriage is not known. However, even if such unions reflect an ancestral matrilineal system of inheritance, it is probable that in the 4th century brother-sister marriages were employed at least as much for contemporary reasons of policy as for tradition. That is, in the 4th century, beginning with the reign of Hekatomnus, the rulers of Caria were attempting to do two things simultaneously: first, they were attempting to establish their local control of Caria under the umbrella of the Persian Empire; and, second, as the family of Mausolus and Artemisia was establishing its unique claim to rule in

Caria, family members did so in part by maintaining their uniqueness from every other family in the satrapy and beyond. As a result, exogamy (marriage outside of the group) potentially had its drawbacks, for any families related to the Hekatomnid by marriage would have had at least a share of the status that the Hekatomnids desired to hold exclusively.

By and large, the Persian Empire of the 4th century was feudal in its organization and, to a certain extent, decentralized. Individual satraps (provincial governors) usually had a great latitude to act without prior royal approval. They had as well the control of the necessary financial and human resources to do so successfully. Satraps minted coins and collected taxes (some of which stayed in their satrapies), employed mercenaries and occasionally marshalled armies of retainers to maintain order, enforced the law within their provinces, and even maintained diplomatic relations with states beyond the authority of the Great King of Persia. Nonetheless, the extent of their local powers occasionally induced rebellion among these middling potentates, especially if (a) their satrapies were distant from Persis (the heartland of the Persian Empire, located in modern Iran); (b) if affairs were keeping the Great King busy elsewhere; and/or (c) if the competency of the Great King was suspect.

Although Caria generally remained loyal to the rule of the contemporary Achaemenid kings of Persia (Artaxerxes II, 404–359 BCE; Artaxerxes III, 359–338 BCE), during Mausolus' and Artemisia's tenure in Caria (Mausolus 377–353 BCE; Artemisia from the time of her marriage to Mausolus–351 BCE), there were times when the domestic situation of the Persian Empire induced the ruling couple to test the political waters with an eye to establishing Carian independence. The first manifestation of unrest in Asia after the accession of Mausolus occurred in the late 370s when a Datames took possession of Cappadocia (a region of difficult access in what is now the east-central part of Turkey). In Cappadocia, Datames established a dynasty that successfully defied the efforts of the Great King to bring him to heel.

Such brazenness stimulated other breakaways, the second attested led by an Ariobarzanes, the satrap of Hellespotine Phrygia (in the northwest of modern Turkey) in the mid-360s. Mausolus, with other loyal allies, initially mobilized against Ariobarzanes at the command of his king, but broke off the campaign after having cut a deal with the Spartans, who supported Ariobarzanes' rebellion, which allowed

Mausolus to recruit Greek mercenaries for his satrapal army. It was probably at this time that Mausolus became the *xenos* (special guest-friend) of Agesilaus, a king of the Spartans and long one of the Greek world's greatest generals and diplomats. Although Mausolus' rationale for breaking off his attack on the disloyal Ariobarzanes can only be guessed, it is nevertheless probable that he took the opportunity to strengthen his army with Greek recruits in the expectation that he might need a force loyal only to himself, as the Great King's control of Asia Minor appeared to be slipping. What Artemisia thought of this development is unknown, but it is likely that in this, as in virtually everything else, she was one with her husband.

A more serious breach between Artaxerxes II and the ruling couple occurred in the great "Satrap's Revolt" of 362, when Mausolus and Artemisia joined with Orontes (who was both the satrap of Armenia, abutting Cappadocia to the northeast and east, and a member of the Achaemenid royal family), Autophradates (the satrap of Lydia, between Hellespontine Phrygia and Caria, and an ally of Mausolus in the aborted campaign against Ariobarzanes), Datames, Ariobarzanes, and the Spartans in a war against the Great King. Less through military reprisals than through a deft manipulation of the maxim, "divide and conquer," this serious threat to the Persian sovereign was overcome when Artaxerxes drove a wedge between his individually ambitious (if momentarily united) underlings and thus destroyed their common revolt.

Mausolus and Artemisia—who perhaps only joined the revolt so as not to be left behind by their neighboring satraps *if* the uprising were successful—had been among the first to break ranks with the rebels and reconcile with Artaxerxes II. As a result, when the bubble of revolution burst and Artaxerxes' authority was completely reinstated throughout Asia, the Carian dynasts not only suffered no royal retribution for their flirtation with rebellion, but were actually both reaffirmed in their satrapy and allowed to expand their territorial authority at the expense of their neighbors. Thereafter, neither the loyalty of Mausolus nor Artemisia to the Persian king seems to have faltered, even after 357 BCE when Artaxerxes II outlawed the maintenance of mercenary armies by his satraps.

Nonetheless, this was not the end of Mausolus' and Artemisia's diplomatic ambitions, although henceforth their initiatives generally were turned westward. To understand Carian policy after 357 BCE in the west, however, it is important to chronologically retrace events to the very beginning of Mausolus' reign. The year 377 BCE not only witnessed the elevation of Mausolus in Caria, it also marked an attempt by Athens to regain the glory of that city's past, which had been dealt a serious loss when Sparta won the great Peloponnesian War in 404 BCE In short, in an effort to check the growing diplomatic and military arrogance of Sparta, in 377 Athens resurrected an alliance of Greek maritime states. Today this league is known as the "Second Delian Confederacy" to distinguish it from the previous Athenian-led union that Sparta had disbanded after its victory in 404. The very idea of an Athenian-led league, however, aroused anxieties in many states—including those Athens would have invited to join the new confederation—because the first such alliance, although initially a voluntary league formed to expel Persia from the Aegean, had all too quickly evolved into an "Athenian Empire," through which Athens had come to dominate its allies. Despite the nervousness a revived Delian League generated among those asked to join, many enlisted after taking precautions to limit Athens' ability to exploit the union, since Sparta was seen as a greater threat to local autonomy in the 370s than the Athens, which had been humbled and had requested a renewal of friendship.

Mausolus and Artemisia were among the non-members who were very worried by the resurgence of a Second Delian Confederation for, when the First Delian League had been strong, the Greek cities of the Anatolian coast, including those in Caria and currently under Mausolus' and Artemisia's authority, had been controlled by Athens. The implicit threat of a re-generation of Athenian imperial aspirations along the Carian coast seems to have led Mausolus and Artemis to take significant steps. The first of these saw the Carian capital moved from the interior city of Mylasa to the "refounded" and greatly enlarged coastal city of Halicarnassus. The second reaction was the construction of a 100-ship navy, which gave the Carian dynasts a fleet as large as that deployed by Athens. This large navy under the command of a Persian satrap seems to have been unprecedented, but it apparently was tolerated by the Great King since the defense of the Anatolian coast was in his interest as much as it was in the interest of Mausolus and Artemisia. Though the expansion of Carian authority along the coast came at the expense of neighboring Persian officials, again the Great King seemingly permitted this because the resulting naval power prevented the Athenians from adding the Greek cities of the Anatolian coast to their resurrected confederation.

Greater financial and military demands came upon the Second Delian Confederation with the rivalry for control of the eastern Aegean heating up and with Athens' ambitions in Europe. Although restraints had been built into the renewed alliance, ambitious Athenian politicians did what they could to scuttle these so that the old master-servant relationship could be restored. As time went on, alarm grew until this exploded into a rebellion, known today as the "Social" (from the Latin word *socius*, meaning "ally") War against the renewal of Athenian imperialism. In 357 BCE, Byzantium, Chios, Cos, and Rhodes, prompted by Mausolus and Artemisia (who promised the requisite support against Athens), broke away from the Second Delian Confederation—effectively shattering it and destroying forever the imperial dreams of Athens. Perhaps the biggest winner in this conflict was Philip II of Macedon, who took advantage of the Athenian pre-occupation with maintaining control of its Delian League to establish himself firmly in Macedon, which, once achieved, led to Macedon's domination of Athens, all of Greece, Caria, and the entire Persian Empire within three decades.

Though Mausolus and Artemisia fought to stave off a political resurgence of Hellenism in Asia Minor, they (with many others in the western Persian Empire) enthusiastically embraced at least the external rudiments of contemporary Greek culture. During the generation of Mausolus and Artemisia, despite the social problems that had led to prolonged and wide-spread warfare throughout the Greek world, Greek artists continued to be without peer in a variety of disciplines and were extensively employed beyond the limits of Hellas. Over a wide swath of territory encompassing most of the eastern Mediterranean virtually everyone (regardless of ethnicity) with money and social prominence eagerly employed the greatest Hellenic masters in an effort to reinforce social status and political authority. Most of Mausolus' and Artemisia's efforts along these lines were focused upon their window on the Aegean—their new capital, Halicarnassus, itself a city with an ancient Greek heritage.

The most modern city planning available was exploited in rebuilding Halicarnassus, which was developed into a grandiose seat worthy of ambitious oriental potentates. Not only were streets straightened and a grid system laid for a more cosmopolitan arrangement of public space, but also, on a more private level, a palace complex with an access to a restricted harbor was constructed to provide the requisite security for figures who must have appeared almost regal to the local inhabitants. But as much of an opportunity as the reconstruction of the city generally provided, it is clear that from a very early date the nucleus of all was intended to be the space that would come to be filled by the world-famous Mausoleum—a sepulcher first used to bury Mausolus (whose personal name thereafter entered the public domain as a synonym for "tomb"), which was so marvelous as to be included amid the "Seven Wonders" of the ancient world.

Probably begun in 355 BCE (two years before Mausolus' death), the Mausoleum's construction accelerated under Artemisia's sole rule (353–351) and was completed sometime not long after her death. Although the Mausoleum was certainly a tomb, it appears to have been much more for the inhabitants of Halicarnassus and Mausolus' political heirs. As the "founder" of a new Halicarnassus, Mausolus became the city's *oikist,* or, officially designated founding "hero." Custom throughout the Greek world (and apparently in Caria too) rendered such figures *chthonic* honors, which meant that certain religious rituals were offered to the memory of the *oikist* and to his entombed remains. Although of a religious nature, these honors were not the same as those given to the gods of life and the sky. Rather, heroes were more akin to Christian saints in the medieval world. That is, they were considered to have been so special in life that a bit of their unique potency remained even in death. The power that continued to be associated with the remains in the grave was thought an important source of protection for the locality in which these remains lay, as well as a continuing source of strength for those who aspired to the hero's political legacy.

Given the prominence of the Mausoleum's site, it was probably intended from the first to be a *heroon,* or temple-like structure to mark the burial place of a dead hero. Although *heroons* and heroic worship were known before the time of Mausolus, his sepulcher and the rituals staged in his honor after death were nevertheless so extravagant that their very magnitude foreshadowed the age that began with Alexander the Great (born 356 BCE), in which living men, even before their deaths, received not merely *chthonic,* but full-fledged worship—just as if they were immortal gods.

The Mausoleum was designed by two of the era's most famous architects, Pythius and Satyrus. It occupied a central location within the city of Halicarnassus and was of impressive size: its perimeter was 440 feet in circumference and it was, in all, over 140 feet tall. Its lowest three courses (themselves as tall as a five-story building) were rectangular and tiered, and atop these was a temple-like structure surrounded by 36 columns. Capping this story was a pyramid-shaped roof leading to a platform upon which was set a mammoth marble four-horse chariot with rider. Even more impressive than the Mausoleum's size, shape, and surmounting quadriga, however, were the sculpted figures and friezes that graced the lower levels and were integrated into its overall scheme. The four most renowned sculptors of the period each carved the figures adorning the four faces of the lower reaches: Scopas sculpting the eastern facade; Bryaxis the northern; Leochares the western; and Timotheus the southern. Each artist seems to have considered his work on the Mausoleum as his life's greatest achievement. Indeed, whether true or not, it is reported that when Artemisia died before the monument was completed, each artist stayed in Halicarnassus to complete his contribution to the Mausoleum without pay, believing that his reputation through time would depend upon what he there produced.

That Artemisia closely supervised the construction of the Mausoleum, especially after her husband's death, we can be sure. In fact, the only military episode with which she can be directly associated is linked to the building of the Mausoleum. Needing massive amounts of marble to complete the project, but with the only local supplies of a suitable quality found on Mt. Latmus (to the north of Halicarnassus), which was then controlled by a population independent of her authority, Artemisia warred upon these people to secure access to their quarry. Initially unsuccessful in besieging their town, Artemisia resorted to a ruse. Near both the town and the coveted quarry was a sanctuary to a local goddess for whom Artemisia arranged a magnificent ritual celebration, complete with a procession of devotees so grandiose that the inhabitants of Latmus—not used to seeing such magnificent spectacles—came out to wonder at the sight. Distracted by the religious celebrations staged for their benefit, Artemisia sprung an ambush as soon as the Latmians were far enough from their town for the trap to work. Artemisia was thereby able to win her marble quarry by the "marshalling of flutes and cymbals," when before she had been unable to do so with soldiers under arms.

Artemisia's enthusiasm for the construction of the Mausoleum was genuine, as was her grief at the passing of her husband and brother, Mausolus. Her pain at this loss was noted by contemporaries, who not only cited her piety in fostering the completion of the Mausoleum, but who also marked the extravagant funeral games (including athletic competitions, in the Greek manner, to celebrate the uniqueness of human life in the face of death) and artistic competitions (attracting such orators as Isocrates and Theodectes by the size of her purses); the extraordinary rituals she offered to the memory of Mausolus; and her own death from the intensity of her grief (which she never attempted to conceal), after only a two-year reign. Indeed, one story (albeit probably not a true one) maintained that she was so attached to Mausolus that she literally mixed his cremated ashes into her wine, which she then drank. Given her documented reaction to the death of Mausolus, it is inconceivable that she had been anything but his intimate when he was still alive. Thus, it is virtually certain that the diplomatic policies, which the extant literary sources credit to Mausolus, were congenial to Artemisia as well.

SOURCES:

Diodorus Siculus. *Universal History.* Books 15 & 16. Cambridge, MA: Harvard University Press, 1952.

SUGGESTED READING:

Hornblower, Simon. *Mausolus.* London: Oxford University Press, 1982.

Scarre, Chris. "A Tomb to Wonder At," in *Archaeology.* Vol. 46, no. 5. 1993, pp. 32–39.

William S. Greenwalt, Associate Professor of Classical History, Santa Clara University, Santa Clara, California

Arthur, Ellen Herndon (1837–1880)

American philanthropist who died before her husband Chester Arthur took office as president. Born Ellen Lewis Herndon on August 30, 1837, in Culpeper, Virginia; died January 12, 1880, in New York, New York; only child of Frances Elizabeth (Hansbrough) Herndon and William Lewis Herndon (an explorer of the Amazon); married Chester Alan Arthur, on October 25, 1859, in New York, New York; children: William Lewis Herndon (b. 1860, lived only three years); Chester Alan, Jr. (b. 1864); Ellen Arthur (b. 1871).

When Chester Alan Arthur assumed the presidency after the assassination of James Garfield in 1881, he was still mourning the death of his wife Ellen a year earlier. Many grieved with him. A gifted singer, Ellen had lent her talent to countless charities, and her philanthropic efforts were well known and admired.

Ellen Herndon Arthur grew up in an aristocratic Virginia family and was educated in private schools and by tutors. Her father, William Lewis Herndon, was an explorer and naval hero. In 1857, he went down with his ship, the *Central American.* After his death, Ellen and her mother

Frances Hansbrough Herndon took up residence in a New York City townhouse that was given to them as part of a tribute to her father (a monument was also erected at Annapolis Naval Academy). In New York, she met and fell in love with Chester Arthur, then a young lawyer. Two months after her 20th birthday, they were married and made their home with Ellen's mother. A son, William, was born in 1860.

At the onset of the Civil War, Arthur was appointed to the governor's military staff and by 1862 was named brigadier general and quartermaster of New York. With a promising political future in the Republican Party, Arthur moved his family to a new home on Lexington Avenue.

But the following year brought turmoil. When a Democrat took over as governor, Arthur's commission was revoked, and he was forced to return to his law practice. The family was further shaken by the death of three-year-old William from a brain ailment. Ellen managed her grief by keeping busy with her music and charity work. Possessing a beautiful contralto voice, she sang at church and joined the Mendelssohn Glee Club. Before long, she was much in demand as a soloist at charitable events. Two more children, Chester Alan, Jr., and Ellen, were born, and she greatly enjoyed spoiling them.

With an appointment under President Ulysses Grant as collector of the Port of New York, Chester Arthur's political career got back on track, but there is some indication that Ellen resented the time her husband spent away from home with his political cronies. Rumors circulated about a separation. In January 1880, Ellen caught cold waiting for her carriage in the bitter winter air after a benefit concert. By the time Arthur could return from a trip to Albany, pneumonia had set in and she was unconscious. Ellen died three days later, January 12, at the age of 42. Later, when questioned about the separation rumors, Arthur is said to have replied, "I may be President of the United States, but my personal life is my own damned business."

It is reported that during his presidency, Arthur placed a fresh bouquet beside Ellen's photograph each day. He also dedicated a stained-glass window to her in St. John's Church in Washington. With his daughter too young to take on any of the duties of first lady, the president enlisted his younger sister, ❧▶ Mary Arthur McElroy, to act as official hostess. Chester Arthur never remarried.

SOURCES:

Melick, Arden David. *Wives of the Presidents.* Maplewood, NJ: Hammond, 1977.

Paletta, LuAnn. *The World Almanac of First Ladies.* NY: World Almanac, 1990.

Barbara Morgan, Melrose, Massachusetts

Arthur, Jean (1905–1991)

American actress. Born Gladys Georgianna Greene on October 17, 1905, in the Washington Heights section of New York, New York; died in 1991; daughter of a New York photographer; attended a New York City high school; married Julian Anker, in 1928 (divorced 1928); married Frank J. Ross, Jr., in 1932 (divorced 1949).

Filmography—sound feature films: Easy Come, Easy Go *(Par., 1928);* The Canary Murder Case *(Par., 1929);* The Mysterious Dr. Fu Manchu *(Par., 1929);* The Greene Murder Case *(Par., 1929);* The Saturday Night Kid *(Par., 1929);* Half Way to Heaven *(Par., 1929);* Street of Chance *(Par., 1930);* Young Eagles *(Par., 1930);* Paramount on Parade *(Par., 1930);* The Return of Dr. Fu Manchu *(Par., 1930);* Danger Lights *(RKO, 1930);* The Silver Horde *(RKO, 1930);* The Gang Buster *(Par., 1931);* Virtuous Husband *(Univ., 1931);* The Lawyer's Secret *(Par., 1931);* Ex-Bad Boy *(Univ., 1931);* Get That Venus *(Regent, 1933);* The Past of Mary Holmes *(RKO, 1933);* Whirlpool *(Col., 1934);* The Defense Rests *(Col., 1934);* Most Precious Thing in Life *(Col., 1934);* The Whole Town's Talking *(Col., 1935);* Public Hero Number One *(MGM, 1935);* Party Wire *(Col., 1935);* Diamond Jim *(Univ., 1935);* The Public Menace *(Col., 1935);* If You Could Only Cook *(Col., 1935);* Mr. Deeds Goes to Town *(Col., 1936);* The Ex-Mrs. Bradford *(RKO, 1936);* Adventure in Manhattan *(Col., 1936);* The Plainsman *(Par., 1936);* More Than a Secretary *(Col., 1936);* History Is Made at Night *(UA, 1937);* Easy Living *(Par., 1937);* You Can't Take It With You *(Col., 1938);* Only Angels Have Wings *(Col., 1939);* Mr. Smith Goes to Washington *(Col., 1939);* Too Many Husbands *(Col., 1940);* Arizona *(Col., 1940);* The Devil and Miss Jones *(RKO, 1941);* The Talk of the Town *(Col., 1942);* The More the Merrier *(Col., 1943);* A Lady Takes a Chance *(RKO, 1943);* The Impatient Years *(Col., 1944);* A Foreign Affair *(Par., 1948);* Shane *(Par., 1953).*

Hollywood was not always an easy fit for husky-voiced comedienne Jean Arthur, who at the height of her career was one of the least-known stars off screen. Surviving a notorious 12-year climb to her breakthrough part in John Ford's *The Whole Town's Talking* (1935), Arthur played by her own rules, turning down roles she felt were bad for her and refusing to dance to the tune of the usual Hollywood publicity machine. She believed she would rise or fall

McElroy, Mary Arthur (?–1916)

*White House hostess. Born Mary Arthur; died in 1916; daughter of William Arthur (a Baptist cleric); grew up in Fairfield, Vermont; sister of Chester Alan Arthur; schooled at *Emma Willard's Seminary; married John Edward McElroy (an insurance man), in 1861.*

After the death of President Chester Arthur's wife *Ellen, Mary Arthur McElroy became the official White House host. Traveling from Albany to Washington during the social season, she supervised the running of the White House and entertained, often bringing her two daughters with her. At the end of his term, Arthur and his children moved into her home, and he died there in 1886. Mary continued to raise her brother's children. She died in 1916.

on the merits of her performance alone, remarking, "If people don't like your work, all the still pictures in the world can't help you and nothing written about you, even oceans of it, will make you popular."

Jean Arthur grew up in New York, a roughneck who climbed trees, jumped fences, and dreamed of becoming a dancer. As a pretty teenager and the daughter of a photographer, she had no trouble finding employment as a model, once working for Howard Chandler Christy. One of her pictures landed in the lap of a 20th Century-Fox representative and, at 18, she was handed a one-year contract. Arthur was on her way, or so she thought.

Her movie career began auspiciously with a supporting role in John Ford's silent *Cameo Kirby* (1923). But Arthur had no acting experience and was in over her head. Fulfilling her contract playing insignificant parts in minor movies, mostly two-reel comedies and westerns, she continued throughout the 1920s in one forgettable movie after another, mostly for Paramount. The silents were never able to utilize her chief asset as an actress, a unique voice with a zither-like twang. In 1931, dissatisfied with her roles, she left Hollywood and returned to New York, bent on honing her acting skills. The following three years were spent in stock and on Broadway, playing leading roles in short-run stage productions: *Foreign Affairs,* with *Dorothy Gish; The Man Who Reclaimed His Head,* opposite Claude Rains; and, her favorite, *The Curtain Rises.*

Back in Hollywood, Arthur's first solid supporting performance was in the 1934 movie hit

Jean
Arthur

Whirlpool, and she was signed by Harry Cohn at Columbia to a long-term contract. After appearing in back-to-back bombs, she reunited with Ford for *The Whole Town's Talking.* It was here that she firmly realized her screen persona—the cynical, resourceful, wisecracking woman who, wrote Barbara and Scott Siegel, "usually started out taking advantage of an idealist, eventually fell in love with him, and then used her worldly knowledge to help him beat the bad guys by the end of the picture." She starred in three Frank Capra classics: *Mr. Deeds Goes to*

Town (1936), *Mr. Smith Goes to Washington* (1939), and *You Can't Take It With You* (1938).

Other superb performances included, *Public Hero Number One* (1935), *Diamond Jim* (1935), and *The Ex-Mrs. Bradford* (1936). Arthur's husband Frank J. Ross, Jr., was coproducer of the successful *The Devil and Miss Jones* (1941), a comedy-drama about New York "subway society." Teaming with George Stevens, she made *The Talk of the Town* (1942), for which she received rave reviews. *Time* magazine commented on her "expert energy," while Bosley Crowther of *The New York Times* observed: "Miss Arthur is charming, as usual, in her bewilderment." *The More the Merrier* followed in 1943, for which she received her only Academy Award nomination, for Best Actress.

Throughout her career, Arthur's best movies were made on loan-out from Columbia. (Actors signed with a specific studio could not work at another studio, unless they were loaned out; their home studio could then pocket a large percentage of the income.) She often feuded with Cohn over his choice of material, which led to her suspension on a number of occasions. When her contract finally expired in 1944, she not only walked away from Columbia but from her movie career, even though she was still a box-office attraction. She would make only two more movies: *A Foreign Affair* for Billy Wilder in 1948, followed by her masterful swan song, *Shane,* for George Stevens in 1953.

In 1955, Arthur scored a major success on Broadway in *Peter Pan,* though her other vehicles ended in disaster. (At the last minute, *Judy Holliday replaced her in the Broadway-bound *Born Yesterday,* and Arthur's version of *St. Joan* folded in Chicago.) Except for a guest-star appearance in television's "Gunsmoke" and a short-lived series "The Jean Arthur Show," in 1966, Arthur retired to a quiet life out of the limelight. Much of her time, before her death in 1991, was devoted to teaching her craft at several colleges.

From her opening scene in *The Whole Town's Talking,* she "revealed that the key element of the Jean Arthur character was fearlessness—nothing, not Babbitty bosses, tommy-gun-wielding gangsters, or even a national economic crisis was going to faze her," writes Danny Peary. "She exuded those qualities that Depression-era moviegoers liked to think as typically American. Energetic and optimistic, she was guileless enough to utter phrases like 'Gee whiz!' and mean it."

SOURCES:

Peary, Danny, ed. *Close-Ups.* NY: Workman, 1978.

Rothe, Anna, ed. *Current Biography, 1945.* NY: The H.W. Wilson, 1946.

Siegel, Scott, and Barbara Siegel. *The Encyclopedia of Hollywood.* NY: Facts on File, 1990.

Artois, countess of.

See Amicie de Courtenay (d. 1275).
See Jeanne I of Burgundy (c. 1291–1330).
See Jeanne II of Burgundy (1308–1347).
See Mahaut (c. 1270–1329) for sidebar on Agnes of Bourbon (d. 1287).
See Margaret of Artois (d. 1382).
See Maude of Brabant (1224–1288).
See Maude of Brabant (fl. 1240s).

Artôt, Désirée (1835–1907)

Belgian soprano and mezzo-soprano. Name variations: Joséphine Désirée Artôt. Born Marguerite-Joséphine Désirée Montagney in Paris, France, on July 21, 1835; died in Berlin, Germany, on April 3, 1907; daughter of Jean Désire Montagney (1803–1887, a horn player whose professional name was Artôt); married Mariano Padilla y Ramos (a singer), in 1864; children: daughter, Lola Artôt de Padilla (1876–1933), also a well-known singer.

Désirée Artôt appeared throughout continental Europe. She studied with *Pauline Viardot in London and did further study in Paris. The composer Giacomo Meyerbeer promoted Artôt, and, in 1858, she appeared as Fidès. Deciding to concentrate on Italian repertory, she toured France and Belgium as Rosina and Leonora in *Il trovatore.* In 1859, she performed in Italy and at the Victor Theater in Berlin. In 1863, Artôt sang at Her Majesty's Theatre in London, and, a year later, appeared at Covent Garden. After 1866, she no longer appeared in Great Britain. She married Mariano Padilla y Ramos, the Spanish baritone, in 1869, and the couple performed opera together in Germany, Austria, and Russia. Their daughter, **Lola Artôt de Padilla,** continued the family singing tradition on the German stage.

John Haag, Associate Professor of History, University of Georgia, Athens, Georgia

Arundel, Ann (d. 1630)

Countess of Arundel. Name variations: Arundell. Died in 1630; married Philip, earl of Arundel.

Ann, countess of Arundel, was married to Philip, earl of Arundel, who died in the Tower of London in November 1595. When historian Edmund Lodge rescued a copy of verses by Ann, he thought them enkindled by the "melancholy exit of her lord."

Arundel, Anne (d. 1642)

English noblewoman. Name variations: Lady Baltimore; Arundell. Born in England; died in England in 1642; daughter of a Roman Catholic peer; married Cecil Calvert, 2nd Lord Baltimore (1606–1675), in 1629.

Anne Arundel was the wife of Cecil Calvert, 2nd Lord Baltimore, and the first lord proprietor of Maryland; her name still marks Anne Arundel County, Maryland. Until 1694, Annapolis was also called Anne Arundel; then it was renamed in honor of Princess Anne (later Queen *Anne). Neither Anne Arundel, who died at age 34, nor her husband ever set foot on American soil.

Arundel, Blanche (1583–1649)

English noblewoman who fought on the side of Charles I and dislodged Parliamentary forces from Wardour Castle. Name variations: Lady Blanche Arundell; Blanche Somerset, Baroness Arundell of Wardour. Born in 1583 in Worcester, England; died in 1649; sixth of seven daughters of Edward, 4th earl of Worcester, and Elizabeth (third and youngest daughter of Francis Hastings, 2nd earl of Huntingdon); married Thomas, 2nd Lord Arundel of Wardour, in Wiltshire; children: Henry, 3rd Baron Arundel (1606?–1694); Catherine (who married Francis Corwallis); Anne (who married Roger Vaughan); and Clara (who married Humphrey Weld of Lulworth Castle in Dorsetshire).

When James I, the first Stuart king of England, took the throne in 1603, his reign was immersed in conflicts with Parliament over taxes, along with heated debates between sectarians like the Puritans and the leaders of the royalist Church of England over the Protestant makeup of the nation. King Charles I, who succeeded his father James in 1625, pursued his father's policies as he attempted to free the monarchy from Parliament's restraints. Determined to rule without hindrance, Charles dismissed Parliament in 1629, beginning 11 years of "personal rule." In this period, the conflict between king and Parliament deepened, with both sides perfecting their arguments. The center of the debate continued to be the struggle over control of revenue and the levying of taxes. Parliament would not grant Charles the revenue he demanded unless he acknowledged the powers of Parliament. Instead, Charles financed his reign by coerced loans, the sale of offices and titles, confiscation of noble property, arbitrary and, in Parliament's view, illegal tariffs and loans from Catholic France. None of these methods were very popular. By 1640, the king had reached the end of his fiscal rope and was forced to summon Parliament. When Oliver Cromwell was elected to the House of Commons from Cambridge, the great struggle began. Civil war broke out in 1642.

Lady Blanche Arundel was one of many medieval noblewomen who managed a large estate and even took over its defense in these unstable times. She was born into the ruling family of Worcestershire and married Thomas, lord of Arundel. As Lady Arundel, Blanche was responsible for the economic and financial management of her husband's extensive lands, as well as for the health and well-being of all the officials, peasants, servants, and laborers who lived on those lands. Like many married noblewomen, Blanche saw her husband only rarely, as he was absent from home while serving King Charles I at court or at war. However, she had to handle the consequences of her husband's political and military machinations, for his enemies were a constant threat to the safety of her household.

On May 2, 1643, Sir Edward Hungerford approached Blanche's residence, Wardour Castle, with a few soldiers and demanded admittance in order to search for cavaliers and malignants, as the royalists were called. At that time, the castle was occupied by 60-year-old Lady Arundel; **Cecily**, the wife of her only son (and daughter of Sir Henry Crompton, knight of Bath); Cicely's three young children (two boys and a girl); and about 50 servants, of whom, according to the accounts of the time, 25 were fighting men. When Hungerford's demand was contemptuously refused, he then requested a body of neighborhood troops, under the command of Colonel Strode, to come to his aid, augmenting his Parliamentary force to 1,300 men. When Lady Arundel was told to surrender, she answered that "she had a command from her Lord [her husband] to defend the castle to the last extremity, and would obey that command."

On the following day, Hungerford brought up his cannon within musket shot of the walls, then bombarded the castle without a break for six days and nights. For good effect, he also launched two mines; the second landed in a vaulted passage that connected with almost all the lower apartments and shook the building to its foundation. Lady Arundel and her supporters defended the castle with courage: the men constantly on the alert, and the women supplying them with ammunition, loading their weapons, and extinguishing the fiery missiles that the besiegers continually sent over the walls. The besieged, however, were worn down by the unending strain. With the enemy close to entry and all hope of aid failing, Lady Arundel demanded a conference and offered terms of capitulation. The stubborn determination of Lady Arundel and her colleagues had made such a strong impression on the besiegers that they readily agreed to the following terms:

> First that the ladies, and all others in the castle, should have quarter.
> Secondly, that the ladies and servants should carry away all their wearing apparel; and that six of the serving-men whom the ladies should nominate, should attend upon their persons wheresoever the Parliament forces should dispose of them.
> Thirdly, that all the furniture and goods in the house should be safe from plunder: and to this purpose one of the six nominated to attend the ladies was to stay in the castle, and to take an inventory of all in the house, of which the commanders were to have one copy, and the ladies another.

But soon after the victors entered the castle, they broke the treaty. Seizing several trunks, which the castle inmates were packing up, the Parliamentary forces left the servants and ladies only the clothes on their backs. An extraordinary chimneypiece, worth £2,000, was defaced; carved works were demolished with axes; rare paintings were ripped and torn down; outbuildings, including three tenements and two lodges, were burned; 12 great ponds were destroyed as well as "the fish contained therein." All trees on the grounds were cut down and sold, as were the deer they had not already slaughtered, and the horses and cattle. "Having left nothing either in the air or water," adds the Mercurius Rusticus, "they dug under the earth, the castle being served with water brought two miles by a conduit of lead, and cut up the pipe and sold it." The losses were then valued at £100,000.

The violation of the treaty was not confined to plunder and devastation. The ladies and children were led as prisoners to Shaftesbury, where they were confined for some time, and it was proposed that they be sent to the city of Bath—at that time afflicted with the plague. Lady Arundel, health failing under fatigue and anxiety, was then confined to her bed, and her daughter-in-law insisted that they would not leave voluntarily but would have to be removed by force. The rebels, fearful of appearing monstrous by taking such a step in a country where the objects of their persecution were beloved,

Blanche Arundel

gave up their plan. Instead, they wrested the two sons of the younger Mrs. Arundel, one nine and the other seven, from their mother and grandmother, and sent them under guard to Dorchester. Eventually, the attackers were forced to give up and leave the Arundel domains. Blanche's son Henry would have to dislodge Parliamentary forces from Wardour Castle once again the following year.

On July 5, 1644, while fighting at the head of his regiment in the battle of Lansdown, Lord Arundel received two bullets in the thigh and died at Oxford. Blanche Arundel, who died five years later at Winchester on October 28, 1649, was buried with her husband at Tisbury in Wiltshire. A portrait of Lady Arundel, preserved at Wardour Castle, suffered partial decay and only the head remained perfectly intact. Commissioned by the family, *Angelica Kauffmann cut away the damaged parts and copied the head, then added a figure and drapery. Writes Edmund Lodge: "It is a fortunate circumstance that this admirable copy was executed, for it had preserved to the world the only likeness of a heroine who is so eminently distinguished in the dark annals of the rebellion, the small remnant of the original picture being subsequently consumed in the fire which had nearly proved fatal to the splendid edifice of Wardour."

SOURCES:
Lodge, Edmund. *Portraits of Illustrious Personages of Great Britain*. Vol IV. London: William Smith, n.d.

Arundel, countess of.

See Fitzalan, Alice (fl. 1285).
See Fitzalan, Alice (d. around 1338).
See Eleanor Plantagenet (c. 1318–1372).
See Fitzalan, Elizabeth (d. 1385).
See Mortimer, Philippa (1375–1401).
See Beatrice of Portugal (d. 1439).
See Woodville, Margaret (fl. 1450s).
See Percy, Anne (fl. 1470s).
See Neville, Joan (fl. 1480s).
See Fitzalan, Katherine (b. around 1520).
See Fitzalan, Mary (d. 1557).
See Arundel, Ann (d. 1630).

Arusmont, Frances Wright d'
(1795–1852).

See Wright, Frances.

Arvidson, Linda (1884–1949)

American actress. Name variations: Linda Griffith. Born in 1884; died in 1949; married D.W. Griffith (motion-picture director).

As the first wife of movie director David Wark Griffith, Linda Arvidson contributed a valuable look at her husband's early work with her 1925 autobiography *When the Movies Were Young*. Much of her information was gathered while playing leads in many of his early silents. For example, she was playing a customer when Mack Sennett made his comedic debut carrying a long pole through a crowded market (*The Curtain Pole*, 1909): "He succeeded very well," she wrote, "for before I had paid for my cabbage, something hit me and I was knocked not only flat but genuinely out, and left genuinely unconscious in the center of the stage." In 1911, she also starred in her own screenplay of *Enoch Arden*.

Her other films include *The Adventures of Dollie* (1908), *Balked at the Altar* (1909), *After Many Years* (1909), *An Awful Moment* (1909), *The Test of Friendship* (1909), *The Helping Hand* (1909), *The Cord of Life* (1909), *Edgar Allan Poe* (1909), *The Politician's Love Story* (1909), *A Drunkard's Reformation* (1909), *The Cricket on the Hearth* (1909), *The Mills of the Gods* (1909), *Lines of White on a Sullen Sea* (1909), *Pippa Passes* (the first film reviewed by *The New York Times*, 1909), *The Day After* (1909), *The Rocky Road* (1910), *The Converts* (1910), *The Unchanging Sea* (1910), *Fisher Folks* (1911), *The Scarlet Letter* (1913), *A Fair Rebel* (1914), *The Wife* (1914), *The Gambler of the West* (1915), *Charity* (1916).

SOURCES:
Lloyd, Ann, ed. *Movies of the Silent Years*. London: Orbis. 1984.

Arwa (1052–1137)

Yemeni queen. Born in 1052; died in 1137; married al-Mukarram Ahmad (Sulayhid ruler).

In the Middle Ages, the land that is now Israel was known as the Yemen highlands. This region was ruled by a series of dynasties from the area. For several centuries, governments from outside Yemen had attempted to exert a political rule. They were staved off by the dynastic leaders, among them al-Mukarram Ahmad, ruler of the Sulayhid dynasty during the 11th century. Upon the death of his mother, Ahmad turned full rule of Yemen over to his wife, Arwa. At her command, in 1088, the capital of Yemen was moved to Dhu Jibla.

Crista Martin,
Boston, Massachusetts

Arzner, Dorothy (1897–1979)

American filmmaker and the only woman director of the era who developed a substantial body of work within the Hollywood system. Born in San Francisco, California, on January 3, 1897; died in La Quinta, California, on October 1, 1979; only daughter and one of two children of Louis Arzner (a restaurant manager); graduated from the private Westlake girls' school, 1915; studied pre-med at University of Southern California, 1915–1917; lived with Marion Morgan (a dancer and choreographer); never married; no children.

Filmography: Fashions for Women *(1927)*; Ten Modern Commandments *(1927)*; Get Your Man *(1927)*; Manhattan Cocktail *(1928)*; The Wild Party *(1929)*; Sarah and Son *(1930)*; *(co-director with others)* Paramount on Parade *(1930)*; Anybody's Woman *(1930)*: Honor Among Lovers *(1931)*; Working Girls *(1931)*; Merrily We Go to Hell *(1932)*; Christopher Strong *(1933)*; Nana *(1934)*; Craig's Wife *(1936)*; The Bride Wore Red *(1927)*; Dance, Girl, Dance *(1940)*; First Comes Courage *(1943)*.

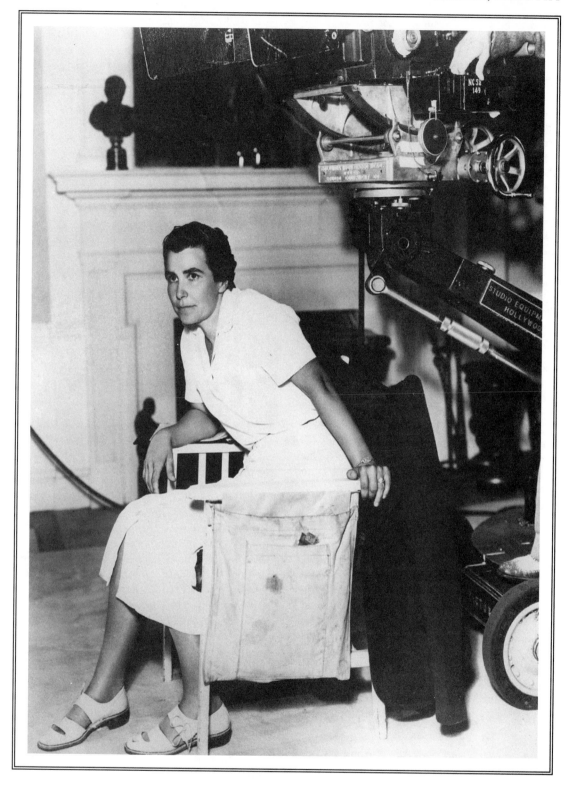

Dorothy Arzner

When not being called a "girl" director ("Girl Film Director Sets New Standards of Beauty" bannered the *Los Angeles Record,* February 10, 1927), Dorothy Arzner was defined by a simple phrase: "woman's director." If one of her movies tended toward the sentimental, it was because, unfortunately, she was a "woman's director." If the movie presented a realistic portrayal of women, it was because, fortunately, she was a "woman's director." The phrase could go either way, as a positive or a pejorative, and gave the press and the male-dominated industry a convenient way to deal with Arzner and her work.

Born into an upper-middle-class household in San Francisco in 1897, Dorothy Arzner moved with her family to the Los Angeles area shortly after the San Francisco earthquake in 1906. By then, her father had remarried, and she grew up with a stepmother. Nothing has been written about what happened to her mother, or about an older brother who died when Arzner was very young. Her father Louis Arzner operated several restaurants, including Hoffman Café, where powerful members of Hollywood's film colony congregated, such as Charles Chaplin, D.W. Griffith, Mack Sennett, and James Cruze. According to Hollywood lore, this whetted the child Arzner's appetite for a film career. She would later deny the claim. If anything, she said, they turned her off; actors were always tossing her up in the air.

Her stepmother, concerned about her "tomboyish ways," sent Arzner to Westlake, a private school for girls. Set on medicine, Arzner underwent two years of pre-med studies at the University of Southern California. During World War I, she left to join the Los Angeles volunteer ambulance corps, then worked in a doctor's office. She was soon convinced that medicine could not give her the immediate gratification she sought. "I wanted to heal the sick and raise the dead instantly."

Unlike many women of her era, Arzner had options. Her father, not only well-off but generous, saw to it that she wasn't dependent on a job. She also invested wisely. Following a chance visit to the studio, her film career began in 1919 at Famous Players-Lasky, which became Paramount. Her first job was typing scripts. She recalled being: "a terrible typist. There was a big, red-headed Irish girl . . . who was a wonder at typing. She took pity on me and did more than half of my work. But for her I wouldn't have lasted a week." Instead, Arzner lasted three months.

From there, she was assigned a continuity job (also known as script girl) on the film *Stronger Than Death* for *Alla Nazimova's production company. Then a friend, **Nan Heron**, who was cutting the Donald Crisp movie *Too Much Johnson*, invited Arzner to cut a reel while she oversaw the work. Arzner cut a second reel unattended. With her career as a cutter and editor now launched, Arzner worked day and night at Realart, a subsidiary of Paramount, cutting 32 movies in one year and becoming chief editor. In 1922, she was brought back to Paramount to edit Rudolph Valentino's *Blood and Sand*, her "first waymark to my claim to a little recognition as an individual." Intercuts between stock and original footage in the bull-fight scenes were masterfully executed. Arzner was efficient and economical, a recipe for Hollywood success.

From there, director James Cruze took her under his wing. Arzner edited several pictures for him and was sometimes scriptwriter: *The Covered Wagon, Ruggles of Red Gap, Merton of the Movies, Old Ironsides*. She also moonlighted, writing scripts for Columbia in the mid-1920s and adapting a seduced-and-abandoned story by *Adela Rogers St. John* into *The Red Kimono* (1925), which was produced by *Dorothy Davenport Reid*. Arzner then threatened to leave Paramount for Columbia unless she were offered a movie to direct, "an A movie." Her first effort, completed in two weeks, was the light comedy *Fashions for Women*, starring *Esther Ralston*. Oddly enough, due to the uniqueness of Paramount's signing its first woman director, it was Arzner, rather than Ralston, who received star billing in the press when the movie was released in April 1927. The reviews were generally good, along with the take at the box office. Arzner was signed to a long-term contract with Paramount and Esther Ralston once again played the lead in Arzner's second film, *Ten Modern Commandments*, released that July.

Arzner's next film *Get Your Man* was a plum assignment starring *Clara Bow*, then Paramount's hottest property. The happy and quite successful collaboration resulted in Arzner's directing Bow once again in Paramount's first talkie *The Wild Party*, for which Arzner cast Broadway star Fredric March in one of his first leading film roles. Throughout her career, Arzner received particular praise for bringing out the best in her actors. Considered a starmaker, she would eventually help launch the careers of *Lucille Ball*, *Rosalind Russell*, *Ruth Chatterton*, *Katharine Hepburn*, *Sylvia Sidney*, and *Irene Dunne*. Because Clara Bow was nervous with the new medium of sound, Arzner reputedly took an ordinarily immovable microphone and put it on a fishpole to give the actress freedom of movement and reduce her fear. Thus, the boom was born.

Arzner's *The Wild Party* was one of the first movies to put a positive face on female bonding. "Perhaps is it the first (certainly it is a rare) case in the cinema where relationships among women are shown to be anything other than catty," writes **Ally Acker**. Whereas the friendship of two women is generally a subplot in films, in *The Wild Party* the women's friendship and the male-female romance are thoroughly intertwined. The novel, *Unforbidden Fruit* by Warner Fabian, from which the movie was adapted, portrayed "all female friendship as pathological," notes Acker. In the book, Fabian emphasized what he called the "peculiar atmosphere of compressed femininity which produces an intellectual and social reaction not unlike the prison psychosis of our penal institutions." This would not be the last time that Arzner, in adapting a book for the screen, would stand the message on its head. The choice of Clara Bow was also a masterstroke; an earlier Fabian book, *Flaming Youth*, had reached the screen as a Bow vehicle, making her the "it" girl. Those with "it" in Fabian's world are seductive and suitably sexual. In short, enchanting to men.

Arzner's next two films, *Sarah and Son* and *Anybody's Women*, both starred Ruth Chatterton who would realize her first taste of extensive praise. They were also the first of many collaborations between Arzner (who continually acknowledged her debt to good writing) and screenwriter *Zoë Akins. *Variety* dubbed them "all-femme" films. Then came *Honor among Lovers* starring *Claudette Colbert and Fredric March (his third film with Arzner), which was a moderate success.

But *Working Girls*, which followed in 1931, with another script by Akins, was a financial disaster. "This was perhaps the most daring and innovative film Arzner ever made," writes **Judith Mayne**, "and its virtual invisibility is a shame. If Arzner rarely took bold artistic risks in her films, *Working Girls* may well provide the rationale, since this effort cost Arzner dearly." Publicity for the film was anemic, and it had no rising stars. Never released nationally, it can only be seen in archival prints. The title is intentionally ambiguous, since 1930s mores deemed women who worked outside the home morally suspect. Arzner had to fight the censors because the story line included an out-of-wedlock pregnancy. Paramount's shabby treatment of the film remains a mystery.

In 1932, Arzner returned to comedy with *Merrily We Go to Hell* starring March and Sylvia Sidney. Though it gathered mixed reviews, it was financially one of the most successful films of the year. After Arzner refused to accept a paycut issued across the board for Paramount employees, it became her last film for the studio.

As a freelancer, she moved to RKO to direct Katharine Hepburn's second film, *Christopher Strong*—Zoë Akins' screenplay about an aviator. (Arzner contended that the protagonist Cynthia Darrington, played by Hepburn, was modeled on Britain's *Amy Johnson, not America's *Amelia Earhart as often thought). The story line centered around the doomed relationship between the flyer and a married Member of Parliament. "It was a no-win situation for the woman of the 1930s," writes Acker, "and Arzner had Hepburn do the only sensible thing a woman in her situation could have done in that time: commit suicide kamikaze style." The film proved weak at the box office. Though some accounts report that Arzner and Hepburn did not get along on the set, Hepburn wrapped up their professional relationship succinctly in her autobiography *Me*: "Dorothy was very well known and had directed a number of hit pictures. She wore pants. So did I. We had a good time working together." Even so, they never collaborated again. When Arzner was offered Hepburn's next starrer *Morning Glory* (script again by Akins), she declined. Except for taking over production of a loose adaptation of Émile Zola's *Nana*, starring *Anna Sten, in 1933, Arzner did not work again until February 1934, when she was signed by Harry Cohn as an associate producer at Columbia and embarked on her most successful film, *Craig's Wife*.

> To be a director you cannot be subject to anyone, even the head of a studio. I threatened to quit each time I didn't get my way.
>
> —**Dorothy Arzner**

George Kelly's Pulitzer Prize-winning play of the same name came with a built-in hazard, an unsympathetic protagonist. Harriet Craig places home, hearth, carpet, and furnishings—and the cleanliness of same—before any human relationship, including those with her husband, sister, and niece. Arzner sidestepped the problem by casting the likeable Rosalind Russell in the lead. She also tempered the character from Kelly's play. Whereas Kelly focused on the failure of a woman, Arzner also focused on the needs of that woman and the failure of the institution of marriage. "This is not to suggest that Arzner presents Harriet as a victim," writes Mayne; "rather, she presents her as a woman with a limited number of choices, whose obsession about her house is in many ways an extension of what is considered a more 'normal' preoccupation for women." As the movie progresses, Russell is found alone in the house. "The audience hated her up to that point," Arzner told **Marjorie Rosen**, "and I only had one close-up left with which to turn their emotion to sympathy. Russell did it so perfectly that in movie theaters handkerchiefs began coming out." With the help of screenwriter **Mary McCall, Jr.,** Arzner had once again turned the tables. Writer and director worked well together. Arzner "had the peculiar notion that a writer might be of some use on the set," said McCall. "This was again all quite new to me. At the end of each rehearsal she turned and said 'how was that for you?' and I couldn't believe it." Edited by **Viola Lawrence,** the movie was another "all-femme film."

Arzner then stepped in to complete the *Joan Crawford vehicle *The Last of Mrs. Cheyney* (1937), which led to her contract to direct *The Bride Wore Red* for MGM. *Bride* would be the beginning of the end. Though intended for *Luise Rainer, the lead went to Crawford who looked forward to working again with Arzner. By the end of the movie, however, they only communicated through written notes. (All must have been forgotten by the 1950s, when Crawford requested that her company hire Arzner to direct some 50 Pepsi commercials.) But there were bigger problems, most notably the death of the film's backer Irving Thalberg and the rise of Louis B. Mayer.

The film was based on *The Girl from Trieste,* a play by Ferenc Molnar about a prostitute who vainly tries to change her profession. Mayer insisted that the prostitute become a cabaret singer and that the movie be given a happy ending. He met his match with Arzner. Soon to become the first woman admitted to the Director's Guild of America, she was one of the first to insist that directors have control over their films. Throughout the shoot, Mayer and Arzner were at loggerheads. He not only interfered, he was also known as a sexist and a homophobe. The poison in their relationship had a great deal to do with Arzner's early retirement. When, in her words, *The Bride Wore Red,* "turned out to be synthetic and plastic," she refused to do the next two or three scripts and was suspended. "Mayer put out the word that I was difficult, and you know how producers talk to each other. I think that was the reason I left." The film was panned by the critics as synthetic and plastic. One noted that it had "no dramatic conviction." They called it a "woman's picture."

In 1940, Arzner took over an RKO production of *Dance, Girl, Dance* (not to be confused with a 1933 clunker of the same name). Though the backstage musical was not a hit in 1940, it is now recognized as Arzner's best-known film.

Based on a story by ***Vicki Baum,** script by ***Tess Slesinger** and Frank Davis, the movie concerns two women dancers (***Maureen O'Hara** and Lucille Ball) and their contrasting roads to success in a troupe led by ***Maria Ouspenskaya.** One pursues burlesque, the other ballet. Burlesque wins. In the plot structure, Arzner avoids the use of easy conflicts; neither woman is villainized, nor do they spend their allotted movie time turning on each other. The conflict instead comes from without, from class expectations and values. The most famous scene in the film takes place when O'Hara, who has become a comedic stooge for stripper Ball, turns on the audience who watches them strip and tells them what she thinks of them. While Arzner allows the man to objectify the woman with his gaze (the most commonly portrayed interaction between men and women), Arzner allows the woman the last look in a crisp reversal of roles. Arzner never went totally against her material; she just did it one better, adding the woman's perspective. As Judy, Maureen O'Hara addresses the audience:

> Go ahead and stare. I'm not ashamed. Go on. Laugh! Get your money's worth. Nobody's going to hurt you. I know you want me to tear my clothes off so's you can look your fifty cents worth. Fifty cents for the privilege of staring at a girl the way your wives won't let you. What do you suppose we think of you up here—with your silly smirks your mothers would be ashamed of? And we know it's the thing of the moment for the dress suits to come and laugh at us too. We'd laugh right back at the lot of you, only we're paid to let you sit there and roll your eyes and make your screamingly clever remarks. What's it for? So's you can go home when the show's over and strut before your wives and sweethearts and play at being the stronger sex for a minute? I'm sure they see through you just like we do.

The theme of working women—from research assistants and telegraph operators to cabaret singers and prostitutes—was often invoked in Arzner's films. Her female characters, notes Mayne, are "active and complex subjects, regardless of what they are subject of or subjected to." Arzner's projects criticized Hollywood films from within and suggested that traditional masculine and feminine roles consist of a series of unnatural poses. She focused on the influence of the social class, on the community of women, and on the frail bond of heterosexual love.

Arzner returned to Columbia in 1943, for *First Comes Courage,* about a female spy in Norway played by ***Merle Oberon.** Based on Elliot Arnold's novel *The Commandoes,* it was to be her last film. With a week to go on shooting,

Arzner contacted pneumonia and Charles Vidor was brought in to replace her. She went into retirement and never directed in Hollywood again—possibly because she was blackballed, possibly because she no longer wanted to put up with the likes of Louis B. Mayer. "I went out with the big studio era," she said, "I wouldn't say that I left it. I think it left me also."

Arzner made training films for the Women's Army Corps during World War II, and developed a short-lived radio show "You Were Meant to be a Star," which presented scenes drawn from life. She taught at Pasadena Playhouse in 1951 and for the theater arts department at University of California at Los Angeles (UCLA) from 1959 to 1963. She also produced plays in California starring *Billie Burke. In the 1970s came recognition. In January 1975, there was a tribute from the Director's Guild of America (*Ida Lupino introduced the film clips). There were also laudatory articles and comments by **Molly Haskell, Nancy Dowd, Francine Parker, Karyn Kay** and Gerald Peary, **Claire Johnston** and **Pam Cook**.

During Arzner's career in Hollywood, the press led off numerous newspaper and magazine pieces with her appearance—short hair brushed back, pants and jackets, comfortable shoes, no make up—and generally treated her as a spinster. When she died at age 82 in her La Quinta home, obituaries all concluded with a variation on this unhappy theme: Never married, she left no known survivors.

But Arzner had shared her home with the same person for 41 years. She was ❧➤ **Marion Morgan**, a dancer and choreographer, who had been married and had a son. For the first 21 years (1930–51), they lived in the Hollywood Hills. In 1951, they moved to the desert in La Quinta, California, where they continued living together until Morgan's death in 1971. Ten years older, Morgan was frequently on the set of Arzner's movies, working on the fashion shows in *Fashions for Women* and the choreography in *Ten Modern Commandments*. Arzner's preference for women was well known throughout the movie colony. "For too long clichés of spinsterhood, of asexuality, of careers managed at the price of any personal satisfactions, have not only rendered lesbianism invisible, but insignificant and meaningless as well," writes Mayne. Arzner not only had a significant other, she left a rich legacy in her motion pictures.

SOURCES:

Acker, Ally. *Reel Women*. NY: Continuum, 1991.

Mayne, Judith. *Directed by Dorothy Arzner*. Bloomington, IN: Indiana University Press, 1994.

❧➤ **Morgan, Marion** (c. 1887–1971)

American choreographer. Born around 1887; died in 1971; grew up in California; graduated from Yale School of Drama, 1934; lived with *Dorothy Arzner from 1930–71; married; children: one son Roderick (died in the 1930s).

In 1910, after teaching physical-education at the Manual Arts High School in Los Angeles, Marion Morgan began directing dance programs for University of California at Berkeley's summer program. She then founded the Marion Morgan Dancers. Her troupe, composed of women students from Berkeley, used interpretive dance to focus on classical legends and history. The Marion Morgan dancers toured on the vaudeville circuit from 1916 to mid-1920s, before they began to be seen on Hollywood soundstages, appearing in *Don Juan* (1926), *Up in Mabel's Room* (1926), *A Night of Love* (1926), *The Masked Woman* (1926), as well as Arzner's first three films: *Fashions of Women, Ten Modern Commandments*, and *Get Your Man*. Morgan was also advisor on the set of *Manhattan Cocktail*.

In 1930, about the same time she moved in with Arzner, Morgan terminated the group and established a dance school, with instruction in all manner of dance. Now in her 40s, she enrolled in graduate studies at the Yale School of Drama. After graduating from Yale in 1934, she collaborated with George Brendan Dowell on two stories that formed the basis of screenplays for *Mae West: Goin' to Town* (1935) and *Klondike Annie* (1936).

Asa (c. 800–c. 850)

Norwegian queen and regent. Born around 800 in Agdir, Norway; died around 850 in Agdir; daughter of King Harald Redbeard of Agdir; married King Gudrod of Vestfold; children: one son, Halfdan "the Swarthy," king of Agdir.

Asa's life has been preserved through traditional Scandinavian sagas, which are often as much fiction as fact. However, the basic facts of the Norwegian queen's career may be ascertained. Born into the royal family of Agdir in the 9th century, Asa was kidnapped and forced to marry Gudrod of Vestfold, rival of her father, Harald Redbeard. Gudrod probably was responsible for Harald's death at the time of Asa's abduction. Asa gave birth to one child with Gudrod, her son Halfdan. After Halfdan's birth, Asa supposedly murdered Gudrod to avenge her father and took her child back to Agdir, where, as heir to his grandfather Harald, the infant was made king. Asa ruled as regent for her son until he came of age.

Laura York,
Anza, California

Asanova, Dinara (1942–1985)

Soviet filmmaker. Born in Kirghizia, one of the 15 republics of the USSR, located in central Asia, in 1942; died in April 1985; attended VGIK (All-union State Institute of Cinematography).

Filmography: Rudolfino *(1970);* Woodpeckers Don't Get Headaches *(Ne bolit golova u diatla, 1975);* The Restricted Key *(Kliunch bez prava peredachi, 1977);* Misfortune *(Beda, 1978);* My Wife Has Left *(Zhena ushla, 1980);* Good-for-Nothing *(Nikudyshnaia, 1980);* Which Would You Choose? *(Chto ty vybral?, 1981);* Tough Kids *(Patsany, 1983);* Dear, Dear, Dearest Beloved *(Mily, dorogoi, liubimyi, edinstvennyi, 1984); and, unfinished,* The Stranger *(Neznakomka, 1985).*

Dinara Asanova began her film career in her national studio, Kirgizfilm, before becoming one of the few non-Russians to be accepted into the prestigious VGIK (All-union State Institute of Cinematography), the former Soviet Union's premiere film school. During her brief career, Asanova made nine feature films that were so critically and financially successful, she must be considered one of the most notable Soviet directors of her time.

Asanova's films often deal with the dark side of the adolescent coming of age: the teenage protagonist is filled with a sense of existential anxiety because the world of adults is insensitive and uncaring. With an interest in the documentary tradition, Asanova often cast non-professionals to play her leads. One of her most important films, *Tough Kids (Patsany,* 1983), is based on episodes from the lives of male teenagers doing time in a juvenile detention center. Her research for this film was also edited into a documentary and aired on television.

Her films neither glorify heroes nor condemn villains. Rather, they are critical of a social system that seems to ignore contemporary problems, especially problems of young people. Strangely, though Asanova's social criticism was often harsh, she apparently never roused the ire of the Soviet censors. In 1985, while shooting her tenth film called *The Stranger,* Asanova died of a heart attack. She was 43.

SOURCES:

Atwood, Lynne. *Red Women on the Silver Screen.* London: Pandora Press, 1993.

Kuhn, Annette, with Susannah Radstone. *The Women's Companion to International Film.* London: Virago Press, 1990.

Lawton, Anna. *Toward A New Openness in Soviet Cinema: 1976–1987.* Indianapolis: Indiana University Press, 1989.

Deborah Jones, freelance writer, Studio City, California

Catherine Parr.

See Six Wives of Henry VIII.

Asantewaa, Yaa (c. 1850–1921).

See Yaa Asantewaa.

Ascarelli, Devora (fl. 1601)

Jewish poet of Italy. Birth and death dates unknown; married Joseph Ascarelli, a merchant. First poetry published 1601–02.

Devora Ascarelli was an active participant in the Italian Renaissance as a translator and as a poet in her own right. Born into the Italian merchant class, Ascarelli was an extremely well-educated and devout woman. Married to the well-to-do merchant Joseph Ascarelli, she devoted much of her time to the religious education of her community by preparing translations of hymns and other religious works from Hebrew into Italian. She gained considerable fame for her translations, yet proved herself a talented poet as well, publishing verse on various religious themes in Italian. Her poetry shows a sense of morality combined with delight in the beauty of nature, a sense of spiritual rapture, and an unfailing devotion to God.

Laura York, Anza, California

Ascham, Margaret Howe (c. 1535–1590)

English letter writer. Born Margaret Howe around 1535 in England; died in England in 1590; married humanist scholar Roger Ascham (1515–1568).

A member of the English aristocracy, Margaret Howe Ascham was a participant in the humanist movement that revolutionized England in the 16th century, emphasizing human potential and placing humanity, rather than God, at the center of philosophy. Highly educated, Margaret married the humanist Roger Ascham and became an important supporter of her husband's work. Hailed as the leading humanist of his day, Roger Ascham was a writer and teacher who served as the tutor of, among others, the princess Elizabeth Tudor, later Queen *Elizabeth I. Through Roger's contacts, Margaret was acquainted with many of her country's greatest figures, including Henry VIII's last queen **Catherine Parr** (1512–1548). After Roger's death in 1568, Margaret arranged for the publication of his final work, a treatise on practical education published as *The Scholemaster (The Schoolmaster)* in 1570. Margaret began the work with a letter of preface, in which she sums up the work and dedicates the book to William Cecil, Lord Burghley, who was Queen

Elizabeth's secretary and one of England's great leaders. *The Schoolmaster* quickly became a seminal text of humanism, and remains one of the most important documents of 16th-century humanist thought.

Laura York,
Anza, California

Asclepignia (c. 375–?)

Greek philosopher and educator. Born in Athens around 375; daughter of Plutarch the Younger of Athens (philosopher and founder of a school following the pagan philosophy of Plotinus who died in 430); sister of Hierius; teacher and then director at Plutarch's school; contemporary of Hypatia, with whom she expounded different versions of Plotinus' teaching; teacher of Proclus, who revolutionized Plotinian doctrine, bolstering it against the popularity of Christianity.

Although works by Asclepignia have not survived, we know of her philosophy through her influence on her pupil Proclus, who developed the philosophy of Plotinus in a manner that sought to merge the pagan tradition with the scientific and philosophic understandings of Plato and Aristotle. This mixture of pagan ritual with study revolutionized the doctrine of Plutarch the Younger, Asclepignia's father, and kept it strong for many years though it suffered with the growing popularity and political power of Christianity.

Plutarch the Younger founded a school at Athens for the continuance of the philosophical program of Plotinus, in the tradition of Plato. Plotinus taught that there were five elements of Reality: the One, intelligence, matter, soul, and nature. For Plotinus, intelligence was of particular importance as it emanates from the One, and human happiness is achieved by using intelligence for self-examination and contemplation of the One. The ultimate ethical goal was union with the One, which could be achieved through using the intelligence for examination of the self, love, truth, and faith.

Asclepignia attended her father's school, taught there, and upon his death in 430 shared the directorship of the school with her brother Hierius and her colleague Syranius. *Hypatia, an older contemporary who probably attended Plutarch's school, taught a very different interpretation of Plotinian doctrine in her school at Alexandria. For Hypatia, contemplation of the One required only the study of math and science, but for Asclepignia—as for Plutarch—knowledge of the One required the observation of pagan rituals.

Asclepignia taught that intellectual understanding was insufficient to achieve the moral goal of unity with the One; psychological involvement and physical practice are also required. Hence, the importance of pagan ritual. Her philosophical program was theurgical, evoking the power of the gods as aids to the practitioners. The first stage of this program was to extract thought from the senses. The second was increasing abstraction to achieve illumination and lead to unification with the One. Asclepignia believed this could not be achieved simply through study, as was thought by Hypatia, but also required the practice of pagan magic: the manipulation of the metaphysical system. A philosopher, according to Asclepignia, must be in contact with the gods and be able to work in conjunction with them.

SOURCES:

Kersey, Ethel M. *Women Philosophers: a Bio-critical Source Book.* NY: Greenwood Press, 1989.

Waithe, Mary Ellen, ed. *A History of Women Philosophers, Vol. 1.* Boston: Martinus Nijhoff Publications, 1987.

Catherine Hundleby, M.A. Philosophy,
University of Guelph, Ontario, Canada

Ascue, Anne (c. 1521–1546).

See Askew, Anne.

Asenath

Egyptian woman of the Bible. Daughter of Potipherah, priest of On or Heliopolis; married Joseph (Gen. 41:45); children: Manasseh and Ephraim.

Ashbridge, Elizabeth (1713–1755)

British autobiographer. Born in 1713 in Middlewich, Cheshire, England; died on May 16, 1755, in Ireland; daughter of Mary and Thomas Sampson; married three times, including Aaron Ashbridge in 1746.

Elizabeth Sampson was raised in a strict, Anglican home in England. While her father worked as a seaman, she was schooled by her mother. In her teens, she ran away to marry and was widowed within five months. Because her father had disowned her, she moved to Ireland where she found lodging with family relatives who were Quakers. Not yet 20, Ashbridge sought free passage to America in exchange for work. Arriving in 1732, she settled in Pennsylvania where she married a schoolteacher named Sullivan, with whom she enjoyed the theater and dancing. Elizabeth explored theology, including Catholicism and atheism, and finally settled on the Quaker Society of Friends. Fiercely opposed to her joining the Quakers, Sullivan responded by joining the army and was killed. Elizabeth remarried in 1746, to Aaron Ashbridge. Seven years later, called to preach, she returned to Ireland and died there in 1755.

Included in the Quaker doctrine is a desire to preserve all writing by members of the Society of Friends. Therefore, a bounty of autobiographies and biographies by Quaker women provide an otherwise scarce female perspective on those eras. Aaron Ashbridge transcribed Elizabeth's journals and notes; in 1774, almost 20 years after her death, he published *Some Account of the Fore Part of the Life of Elizabeth Ashbridge.*

Crista Martin,
Boston, Massachusetts

Ashby, Margery Corbett (1882–1981).

See Corbett-Ashby, Margery.

Ashcroft, Peggy (1907–1991)

One of the finest English actresses of her day, who won every major award for Best Supporting Actress for her work in the film A Passage to India. *Born Edith Margaret Emily Ashcroft in the London suburb of Croydon, Surrey, England, on December 22, 1907; died in England on June 14, 1991; daughter of William Worsley Ashcroft and Violetta Maud (Bernheim, who was of German descent) Ashcroft; attended Woodford School, Croydon, and the Central School of Dramatic Art under the tutelage of Elsie Fogerty; married Rupert Charles Hart-Davis (a publisher; divorced); married Theodore Komisarjevsky (Russian director and architect; divorced); married Jeremy Nicholas Hutchinson (a lawyer), in 1940 (divorced); children: (third marriage) son Nicholas (who became a director) and daughter Eliza.*

The first thing one noticed . . . (and one always noticed) about Peggy Ashcroft was her quietness. She seemed stiller than the moon itself.

—**Harold Hobson**

Awards: Ellen Terry Award for her performance as Evelyn Holt in Edward My Son *(1947); Sketch Award for Outstanding Achievement for her role as Catherine Sloper in* The Heiress *(1949); Commander of the British Empire, 1951; King's Gold Medal of Norway for her Oslo performance in the title role in* Hedda Gabler; *Evening Standard Drama Award and the Plays and Players Award for the role of Miss Madrigal in* The Chalk Garden *(1956); Dame Commander of the British Empire (1956); Plays and Players Award for her Rosalind in* As You Like It *(1957); Evening Standard Drama Award for Queen Margaret in* The Wars of the Roses *(1964); Plays and Players London Theater Critics Award for her performances in* A Delicate Balance *and* Landscape *(1969) and again for* The Lovers of Viorne *and her performance as Queen Katherine in* Henry VIII *(1971); Society of West End Theater Awards for Lidya in* Old World *(1976); Evening Standard Drama Award for 50 years in the theater, and Commander of St. Olav of Norway (both 1976); British Academy of Film and Television Arts Award for Frau Messner in* Caught on a Train *and for Jean Wilsher in* Cream in my Coffee *(both 1980); XXeme Festival Internationale de Télévision de Monte Carlo, and British Press Guild Award for the same role (1981, the latter also for her performance in* Cream in my Coffee*); British Theater Association Special Award for her career in the theater (1983); Royal Television Society Award, Broadcasting Press Guild Theater Award, and British Academy of Film and Theater Arts Award, all for Barbie in* The Jewel in the Crown *(1984); Academy of Motion Picture Arts and Sciences Award, Golden Globe Award, New York Film Critics' Circle Award, Los Angeles Film Critics' Circle Award, and National Board of Review Award, all for Best Supporting Actress in the role of Mrs. Moore in* A Passage to India *(1984); British Academy of Film and Television Arts Award and Hollywood South Award for the same role (1985); also Honorary Doctorates in Literature from Oxford University (1961), Leicester University (1964), London University (1965), Cambridge University (1972), Warwick University (1974), and from the Open University, Bristol University, and Reading University (all 1986); Special Laurence Olivier Award for Lifetime Achievement in the Theater, April 1991.*

Stage (unless otherwise noted, all stage appearances were in London): Made stage debut at Birmingham Repertory Theater as Margaret in James M. Barrie's Dear Brutus; *first appeared on the London stage as Bessie in* One Day More *(May 1927); Mary Dunn in* The Return *(May 1927); Eve in* When Adam Delved *(July 1927); Betty in* The Way of the World *(November 1927); Anastasia Vulliamy in* The Fascinating Foundling, *and Mary Bruin in* The Land of Heart's Desire *(both January 1928); toured as Hester in* The Silver Cord, *which starred the celebrated* **Lilian Braithwaite** *(spring 1928); Edith Strange in* Earthbound *and Kristina in* Easter *(both 1928); Eulalia in* A Hundred Years Old, *Lucy Deren in* Requital, *Sally Humphries in* Bees and Honey *(both 1929); as Desde-*

Peggy Ashcroft

mona in Othello *with* Paul Robeson *in the title role, and as Judy Battle in* The Breadwinner *(both 1930); as Angela in* Charles the 3rd, *Anne in* A Knight Passed By, *Fanny in* Sea Fever, *Marcella in* Take Two from One *(all 1931); Stella in* Le Cocu Magnifique, *Salome Westway in* The Secret Woman *and, at the Old Vic*

and Sadler's Wells theaters played Cleopatra in Shaw's Caesar and Cleopatra, *Imogene in Shakespeare's* Cymbeline, *and Rosalind in* As You Like It *(all Sept.–Oct., 1932); in the title role in* Fraulein Elsa *(1932); in addition, appeared at the Oxford University Dramatic Society as Pervaneh in* Hassan *(February*

1931) and again as Juliet in Romeo and Juliet *(February 1932); returning to the Old Vic, appeared as Portia in* The Merchant of Venice, *as Kate Hardcastle in* She Stoops to Conquer, *as Perdita in* The Winter's Tale, *in the title role in Drinkwater's* Mary Stuart, *as Juliet in* Romeo and Juliet, *Lady Teazle in* The School for Scandal, *and as Miranda in* The Tempest *(Dec. 1932–May 1933); as Inken Peters in* Before Sunset, *1933; as Vasantesena in* The Golden Toy *and as Lucia Maubel in* The Life I Gave Him *(both 1934); Therese Paradis in* Mesmer, *in Glasgow (1935); as Juliet in* Romeo and Juliet *(1936); as Nina in Chekhov's* The Seagull *(1936); New York debut (January 8, 1937) as Lise in Maxwell Anderson's* High Tor; *returning to London, joined John Gielgud in a season of classics at the Queen's Theater playing Portia and Lady Teazle, and the Queen in* Richard II, *Irina in Chekhov's* The Three Sisters, *Yelaina Talborg in* The White Guard, *and Viola in* Twelfth Night *(1938); as Dinah Silvester in* Cousin Muriel *and as the replacement for* **Jessica Tandy** *as Miranda in* The Tempest *(both 1940); as Catherine Lisle in* The Dark River *(1943); toured as Ophelia in* Hamlet *opposite John Gielgud (1944); appeared as Titania in* A Midsummer Night's Dream *and in the title role in* The Duchess of Malfi *(1944–45); as Evelyn Holt in* Edward, My Son *(1947), which she recreated in New York (1948); as Catherine Sloper in* The Heiress; *at the Shakespeare Memorial Theater, Stratford-on-Avon, as Beatrice in* Much Ado About Nothing *and Cordelia in* King Lear *(1950); as Viola in* Twelfth Night *for the reopening of the Old Vic in London (1950); in the title role in Sophocles'* Electra *(1951); as Mistress Page in* The Merry Wives of Windsor *(1951); as Hester Collyer in Terence Rattigan's* The Deep Blue Sea *(1952); again at Stratford-on-Avon as Portia in* The Merchant of Venice *and Cleopatra in* Antony and Cleopatra *(1953); in the title role in* Hedda Gabler *(1954); as Beatrice in* Much Ado About Nothing *(1955); as Miss Madrigal in Enid Bagnold's* The Chalk Garden *(1956); as Shen Te in Berthold Brecht's* The Good Woman of Setzuan *(1956); again at Stratford, as Rosalind in* As You Like It, *and Imogen in* Cymbeline *(1957); at the Edinburgh Festival, Scotland, in a solo performance titled* Portraits of Women *(1958); as Julia Raik in* Shadow of Heroes *(1959); as Rebecca West in Ibsen's* Rosmersholm *(1959–60); at Stratford again as Katherina in* The Taming of the Shrew *and as Paulina in* The Winter's Tale *(May 1960); recreated the title role in* The Duchess of Malfi *for the same company (1960) and in the anthology* The Hollow Crown *(1961); Stratford again as Emilia in* Othello *(1961); as Madame Ranevska in* The Cherry Orchard *(1961); appeared in*

an anthology The Vagueries of Love *(1961–62); at Stratford, played* ***Margaret of Anjou*** *in the trilogy* The Wars of the Roses *(1963), reprised in London (1963–64); as Madame Arkadina in* The Seagull *(1964), followed by a second stint in* The Wars of the Roses *at Stratford (1964); as the Mother in* Days in the Trees *(1966); as Mrs. Alving in Ibsen's* Ghosts *(1967); in* The Hollow Crown *(1968); as Agnes in* A Delicate Balance *and Beth in* Landscape *(both 1969); at Stratford, as* ***Catherine of Aragon*** *in* Henry VIII; *as Volumnia in* The Plebians Rehearse the Uprising *and again as Catherine of Aragon in* Henry VIII, *the last two in London (1971); as Claire Lannes in* The Lovers of Viorne *(1971); as the wife in* All Over *(1972); as Lady Boothroyd in* Lloyd George Knew My Father *(1973); as Beth again in* Landscape *and as Flora in* A Slight Ache *(both 1973); with the National Theater at the Old Vic as Ella Rentheim in* John Gabriel Borkman, *as Winnie in* Happy Days, *and as* ***Lilian Baylis*** *in the National Theater's farewell to the Old Vic titled* Tribute to the Lady *(all 1975–76); as Lidya in* The Old World *(1976); as Fanny Farrelly in Lillian Hellman's* Watch on the Rhine *(1980), as Jean Wilsher in* Cream in my Coffee *(1980), in* Recital, Four Centuries of Poetry and Musical Reflections from Shakespeare to Neruda and from Bach to Villa *(at a number of theaters and at the Greenwich Festival, 1981); as the Countess of Roussillon in* All's Well that Ends Well *at Stratford but transferred to London (1982); as Lilian Baylis in* Save the Wells *at the Royal Opera House (1986) and in* The Hollow Crown *(1986, her last appearance before a live audience).*

Filmography: The Wandering Jew *(1933);* The Thirty-nine Steps *(1939);* Rhodes of Africa *(1936);* Channel Incident *(1940);* Quiet Wedding *(1941);* New Lot *(1942);* The Nun's Story *(1958);* Secret Ceremony *(1968);* Three into Two Won't Go *(1969);* Sunday, Bloody Sunday *(1971);* Der Füssganger *(The Pedestrian, 1975);* Joseph Andrews *(1976);* Hullabaloo over George and Bonnie's Pictures *(1978);* When the Wind Blows *(voice over, 1987). Her final appearances were on television except for the climax of her career, her performance as Mrs. Moore in the film* A Passage to India *(1984).*

One of the finest English-speaking actresses of the 20th century, Dame Peggy Ashcroft was born Edith Margaret Emily Ashcroft on December 22, 1907, into a solid middle-class family in the London suburb of Croydon. Her father, a real estate agent, was killed in the First World War. Her mother, the former Violetta Maud Bernheim, who was of mixed Danish and German-Jewish origin and who died in 1925, had been an amateur actress. Though she allowed her daughter to enroll in the Central School of Speech Training and Dramatic Art where Ashcroft studied under the School's founder and director, 🕭▶ **Elsie Fogerty**, Violetta made it clear that she did not want her daughter to pursue a career on the stage.

At Miss Fogerty's, the young Peggy Ashcroft, as she chose to be known, was a fellow student of Laurence Olivier and *****Athene Seyler**, and became a close friend of *****Diana Wynyard**. While still at school, Ashcroft made her debut with the Birmingham Repertory Company in the role of the Dream Child in *Dear Brutus* by James M. Barrie, with the not-yet-famous Ralph Richardson playing her father. For the next two years she performed at a number of London's smaller, out-of-the-way theaters but shortly made her debut on a West End stage in the role of Sally Humphries in *Bees and Honey* at the Strand Theater in May 1929.

Unlike many actresses who spend years achieving recognition, Ashcroft was already being described as a presence on the London stage when she suddenly dazzled the critics in the role of Naomi in *Jew Süss* at the age of 22 (September 1929). At that time, the African-American actor Paul Robeson had been engaged to play Shakespeare's Moor, Othello, the first black actor to do so, with the inducement that he could personally select his Desdemona. Robeson chose Ashcroft, and the richness of her beautiful voice, as well as the warmth that she brought to the part, demonstrated her ability to tackle classical as well as modern roles. The spectacle of a black actor embracing a white actress, hitherto unknown on the London stage, attracted extraordinary attention and resulted in enormous publicity for Ashcroft. Despite the presence of Ralph Richardson as Roderigo and *****Sybil Thorndike** as Emilia, this particular Othello was not a critical success; indeed, John Gielgud called it a great failure. Ashcroft was widely regarded as having given the production whatever value it had, with Gielgud noting that "in the handkerchief scene she acted so lightly and so touchingly that her performance saved the evening." From that time on, Peggy Ashcroft was a star in her native land. The chance to appear on the London stage in a major Shakespearian production proved to be more than a great step forward in her career, however, for Ashcroft later admitted freely that she had been attracted to Robeson and that, though both were married, they had had a brief affair.

Achieving stardom at such an early age led Ashcroft to be typecast; she was engaged to play

🕭▶ **Fogerty, Elsie** (1865–1945)
English drama teacher. Born in 1865; died in 1945.

Elsie Fogerty founded and was principal of the Central School of Speech Training at the Royal Albert Hall. Having established her school in 1898, she received London University recognition for diploma in dramatic art in 1923. She was also honored with a CBE (Commander of the British Empire) in 1934.

one ingenue after another for many years, until well into her 30s, and almost always as a troubled young maiden. This tendency was mitigated by opportunities to appear in a variety of Shakespearian roles, and, as early as 1932 and 1933, she was performing regularly at The Old Vic Company, which had staged all of the Bard's plays in repertory in 1914–18 and would do so again in 1953–58. In 1932, she played Juliet in *Romeo and Juliet* with *****Edith Evans** as the nurse, and with John Gielgud and Laurence Olivier alternating in the roles of Romeo and Mercutio. This was a stunning performance on Ashcroft's part for she attuned her interpretation to whichever actor was playing Romeo on a given evening. Ever after, she was to be remembered as the finest Juliet of her generation. This was the first time that Ashcroft was directed by Gielgud with whom she would form a most rewarding partnership. She was his co-star at his Queen's Theater Season in 1937–38, as Portia in *The Merchant of Venice*, as Irina in *The Three Sisters*, as Lady Teazle in *The School for Scandal*, and as the queen in *Richard II*. Later, for the Oxford Dramatic Society, she would play Cordelia to his King Lear, Ophelia to his Hamlet, Emilia to his 1961 Othello, and Beatrice to his Benedict. Years later, he would direct her in two of her greatest successes *The Heiress* and *The Chalk Garden*. Eventually, Ashcroft became best known for her ability to play rejected, lonely, and oppressed women with unsentimental sympathy and psychological truth.

During these years, Ashcroft also became associated with Theodore Komisarjevsky, the distinguished Russian director, stage designer and architect, who in his native land had been a close associate of Constantine Stanislavsky, founder of the Moscow Art Theater and originator of the "Stanislavsky Method" of acting designed to enable actors to meet the requirements of the realistic plays being written since the 1870s. Arriving in England from France in 1919, imbued with Stanislavsky's techniques and innovations, Komisarjevsky's production of Anton Chekhov's *The Seagull* (1936) revolutionized the presentation of modern drama on the London stage and served to extend the appreciation of Chekhov's work in the English-speaking theater by seeing to it that his plays were performed "in the Russian manner," i.e., as the author had intended. Through her association with the sensitive, moody and oft-times difficult Komisarjevsky, who briefly became her second husband, Ashcroft emerged as one of the great interpreters of Chekhov on the English stage.

By the time she was 40, Ashcroft had played in so many classical roles that it came almost as a surprise to see her triumph in two modern plays, one right after the other. The first was in Robert Morley's *Edward, My Son* (1947), in which she played a simple housewife in the first act, the wealthy wife of a newspaper tycoon in the second, and a disillusioned, bitter alcoholic woman in the third. The second role was as Catherine Sloper in *The Heiress,* the stage adaptation of Henry James' novella *Washington Square* (1949), in which she turned what might have been a routine melodrama into tragedy. The postwar years were troubled ones for the theater in England, but there was never a dearth of fine acting. In fact, the period from 1945 to 1975 was a fruitful era that might almost be called a latter-day "golden age" in the British theater despite the economic problems that existed and the inroads on the theater made by the advent of television.

Ashcroft's performances, along with those of Michael Redgrave and other fine actors, led to the founding of the Shakespeare Memorial Theater at Stratford-Upon-Avon, a national theater that under the direction of Anthony Quayle replaced the Old Vic as the foremost venue for classical drama in Britain, and, while bringing together Ashcroft, Gielgud, Olivier, and Wynyard in a regular series of productions (1949–56), also nurtured the careers of an entire new generation of distinguished actors including Paul Scofield, Richard Burton, Anthony Hopkins, and Albert Finney.

Never much of a traveler, Ashcroft preferred performing on the London stage, enabling her to spend her leisure time at her home in suburban Hampstead. She had made her New York debut as Lise in Maxwell Anderson's *High Tor* (1937) but only performed there once again as Evelyn Holt in *Edward, My Son* (1948). Unlike many British actresses, she evinced no great interest in either New York or Hollywood. Nevertheless, in 1954, she took her production of *Antony and Cleopatra* to the Continent, spending most of the year on tour, playing in The Hague, Amsterdam, Antwerp, Brussels, and Paris with Gielgud as her partner. Returning to London in September, she opened in the difficult title role in the pioneering modern drama *Hedda Gabler,* by Henrik Ibsen, enjoying such a triumph that she took the production to Oslo, Norway, where the drama had originated in 1890. There she performed before King Haakon, who was so impressed with her command of this classic Norwegian role that he presented her with the King's Gold Medal. Due at least in part to this triumph, Ashcroft's career was crowned in 1956 when, at age 48, she was created a Dame Commander of the British Empire (CBE) during the annual Birthday Honors presented by the Queen *Elizabeth II. By the 1960s, Ashcroft was unquestionably the most celebrated classical actress on the English stage.

As she moved into her 50s, Ashcroft appeared in one classic and modern role after another, continually dazzling audiences and critics with her versatility in such parts as Katherina in Shakespeare's *The Taming of the Shrew* and Paulina in his *The Winter's Tale* (both 1960); as Emilia in *Othello,* and as Madame Ranevska in Chekhov's *The Cherry Orchard* (1961, which she repeated on television the following year). In 1962, she was prevailed upon to make a second foreign tour at the Paris Theater Festival. That autumn, her career reached yet another peak when the newly erected playhouse in her hometown of Croydon was renamed the Peggy Ashcroft Theater.

In Britain, Ashcroft toured somewhat more frequently and was a regular performer at the Shakespeare Festival at Stratford-Upon-Avon. In July 1963, the Royal Shakespeare Company at Stratford undertook a new theatrical conception when it took Shakespeare's *Henry VI,* parts one, two and three, together with his *Richard III,* all four of which were combined, pruned, and pared into a trilogy entitled *The War of the Roses* held together by Dame Peggy Ashcroft playing the role of the English queen, *Margaret of Anjou,* in, respectively, youth, maturity, and old age. This *tour de force* earned her high praise and was repeated in London and later preserved on videotape when it was performed on television in 1965. According to Gielgud, Ashcroft helped Peter Hall enormously during his years as director at Stratford and gave some of her best performances for his theater.

Apart from acting, Ashcroft also served her profession in various administrative capacities.

She was elected to the Council of the English Stage Company in January 1957, where she served on the artistic committee; was a member of the Arts Council 1962–65, and served as president of the Apollo Society in 1964, which she had founded in 1943. In 1968, her career entered a new phase when she was named director of the Royal Shakespeare Company, a position she held with distinction for the year. She also sat on the Council of Equity.

Ashcroft's career drew to a close on a triumphal note, when, in 1984, she appeared as Mrs. Moore in the motion picture of E.M. Forster's novel *A Passage to India.* Far from having declined into lesser parts, Dame Peggy endowed this pivotal role with such wisdom and sweetness that her scenes fairly dominated the film. Ashcroft received every acting award granted in 1984 and 1985 for this performance, including the Academy Award for Best Supporting Actress, though she was unfortunately too ill to receive it in person. After 1982, Ashcroft ceased to appear on the stage except for two brief appearances in *Save the Wells* and *The Hollow Crown* both in London for The Royal Shakespeare Company in 1986, but she did make an occasional television appearance and these were the last roles that she attempted.

Essentially a stage actress, Ashcroft made few films in her career, but since her death these have become monuments to her varied talents. She first acted on radio in *Danger* (1930) and performed regularly over 100 times thereafter until 1986, exclusively for the BBC. Though she early debuted on British television, appearing in Shakespeare's *The Tempest* and *Twelfth Night,* in 1939, she was sparing in her television work, performing for the medium a total of only 19 times thereafter and not again until 1958, when she appeared in the stark drama of World War II "Shadow of Heroes." Her later television appearances included roles in *The Cherry Orchard* (1962), *The Wars of The Roses* (1964), *Rosmersholm* (1965), *Days in the Trees* and *Dear Liar* (both 1966), *From Chekhov with Love* (1968), *The Last Journey* (1971), as Dowager Queen Mary in *Edward and Mrs. Simpson* (1978); *Caught on a Train* and *Cream in my Coffee* (both 1980), in Ibsen's rarely performed *Little Eyolf* (1982), *The Jewel in the Crown* (1984), and, after her triumph in *A Passage to India,* her last three roles of any kind: with Sir John Gielgud and Sir Ralph Richardson in readings from Shakespeare in the fifth program in the BBC television series *Six Centuries of Verse* (1984); as Agatha Christie in *Murder by the Book* (1986); and finally, at 79, as Mrs. Dubber in *A Perfect Spy,* a television

adaptation of the novel by John LeCarré (1987). Ashcroft also made 20 phonograph recordings, most of them on the Argo and Caedmon labels.

As an actress, Peggy Ashcroft was most noted for her extraordinary versatility, her ability to excel in both classical and modern drama, and her willingness to undertake roles that many would have considered unsuitable, if not beyond her range. Shakespeare, Sophocles, Webster, Congreve, Golden, and Sheridan, were, among the classics, all grist for her dramatic mill; Ibsen, Chekhov, Shaw, Barrie, Wilde, Maugham, Schnitzler, Pirandello, Berthold Brecht, Maxwell Anderson, *Lillian Hellman, Samuel Beckett, Harold Pinter, *Enid Bagnold, and Terence Rattigan served her among the moderns. Indeed, her performances in Beckett's *Happy Days,* Bagnold's *The Chalk Garden,* and Rattigan's *The Deep Blue Sea* were considered among her very finest, earning her both great critical and personal success. As a result of her continuous experimentation, she grew steadily in stature, moving from triumph to triumph and holding her own against co-stars who included the greatest actors of the day—Laurence Olivier, John Gielgud, Ralph Richardson, Anthony Quayle, and Michael Redgrave. Beautiful, delicate, and graceful were the adjectives most used to describe her acting in her youth. In later years, eloquent, intense, imaginative, and memorable, were the terms brought into service; and critics and playwrights referred to her integrity, her inner serenity, and her moral gravity. To many, her Juliet was as definitive a performance in the role as one was ever likely to see, while her unique and original interpretations of other famous roles brought new life to them. She played Hedda Gabler for the humor she sensed in the part; she went from youth to maddened old age as Margaret of Anjou in *The War of the Roses,* and the contrast between the vibrant girl so full of life in the earlier scenes of *The Three Sisters* and the sorrowful young woman of the last act was considered a heartbreaking masterpiece of interpretation. Although she gave luster to parts written by virtually ever major British playwright, both classical and modern, she had a remarkable affinity for the characters created by Ibsen and Chekhov and must be considered to have been one of the greatest interpreters of continental playwrights on the English-speaking stage. She also proved herself adept at interpreting American roles, and Edward Albee considered her his favorite actress.

In her early years on the stage, she was considered by some to be "too genteel, too cool, too English bourgeois." Although she was adept at bringing out the humor in a role, comedy was not her forte, and she rarely undertook comedy per se, even though she had excelled in the role of Cecily in *The Importance of Being Earnest*. Her performance in the title role in Sophocles' *Electra* received mixed reviews as did her Rebecca in Ibsen's *Rosmersholm* (1959), and her interpretation of the title role in John Webster's *The Duchess of Malfi* was considered by some to be inadequate. In both cases, however, even the critics who carped found virtues in what she brought to these roles.

Ashcroft's physical strengths lay in her voice and for many years her youthfulness, although as she neared 60 she rapidly lost all traces of youth, aging into a quintessential elderly English lady. Her moral strengths lay in the simplicity of her acting, the integrity that she brought to her interpretations, and her unwillingness to subordinate either the play or the other members of a cast to her own benefit. A strong, willful person, unafraid to speak her views, Ashcroft was nevertheless enormously popular within her profession, never domineering, always professional, and ever ready to help younger performers and put them at their ease. Gielgud called her "the most perfect partner" and said that her influence on a company was extraordinary. Pretty as a girl but by no means a beautiful woman, Ashcroft nevertheless had a wonderful sweetness of expression and a marvelously expressive face.

In her private life, she enjoyed less success. Married three times, first to the publisher Rupert Charles Hart-Davis, then to the brilliant Russian director and architect Theodore Komisarjevsky and finally, in 1940, to a lawyer, Jeremy Nicholas Hutchinson, all of her marriages ended in divorce. By her last husband, however, she had two children, a son Nicholas, who became a director and a daughter Eliza. Offstage, she was a private, quiet, and unassuming person who devoted herself to rearing her children and gave few interviews. She was an ardent cricket fan but, more important, an active supporter of popular causes, especially those involving human rights. She protested apartheid in South Africa and the suppression of dissident writers in both the USSR and Czechoslovakia. Having become a dedicated socialist ever since reading Shaw's lengthy prefaces to his plays, she took part in political demonstrations, circulated petitions, and did what she could to raise money to support her preferred cause, Amnesty International, and the magazine *Index of Censorship*.

Dame Peggy Ashcroft never formally retired and in 1985 spoke only of resting after her year filming in India, but she did little thereafter. She suffered a stroke on May 23, 1991, and died three weeks later on June 14. She was 83 and had been an actress for just under 70 years. Though she was on a par with Dame Edith Evans and Dame *Flora Robson, a more accomplished actress than *Vivien Leigh, and a more versatile one than *Judith Anderson, she did not achieve quite the same fame or popular acclaim in the United States. Yet she will be remembered as one of the great actresses of the English-speaking theater in the 20th century.

SOURCES:

Beauman, Sally. *The Royal Shakespeare Theater: A History of Ten Decades*. Oxford University Press, 1982.

Elsom, John. *The Post-war British Theater*. London: Routledge & Kegan Paul, 1976.

Findlater, Richard. *The Player Queens*. NY: Taplinger, 1976.

Tanitch, Robert. *Ashcroft*. London: Hutchinson, 1987.

SUGGESTED READING:

Hayman, Reginald. *John Gielgud*. NY: Random House, 1971.

Rowell, George. *The Old Vic Theater: A History*. Cambridge University Press, 1993.

R.H. Hewsen, Professor of History, Rowan University, Glassboro, New Jersey

Asherson, Renée (1915—)

English actress. Born Renée Ascherson in London, England, in 1915; daughter of Charles Stephen Ascherman and Dorothy Lilian (Wiseman); educated in Maltman's Green, Gerrard's Cross, Switzerland, and Anjou, France; studied for the stage at the Webber-Douglas Dramatic School; married Robert Donat (an actor).

Renée Asherson made her stage debut at age 15, playing a walk-on in John Gielgud's production of *Romeo and Juliet*. Mostly known for her theatrical and television career, she played Katherine in Laurence Olivier's film of *Henry V* in 1944. Her other films include *The Way Ahead* (1944), *The Way to the Stars* (1944), *Caesar and Cleopatra* (1945), *Once a Jolly Swagman* (also titled *Maniacs on Wheels*, 1948), *The Cure for Love* (1949), *The Small Back Room* (1949), *Pool of London* (1950), *Malta Story* (1953), *The Day the Earth Caught Fire* (1962), *Rasputin, the Mad Monk* (1966), *Theatre of Blood* (1973), and *A Man Called Intrepid* (1979).

Ashford and Simpson.

See Simpson, Valerie (b. 1948).

Ashford, Daisy (1881–1972)

British children's author. Born Margaret Mary Julia Ashford on April 7, 1881, in Petersham, Surrey, Eng-

land; died in Hellesdon, Norwich, England, on January 15, 1972; daughter of William Henry Roxburghe and Emma Georgina (Walker) Ashford; married James Devlin, in 1920.

Author of Where Love Lies Deepest (1893); The Hangman's Daughter (1894); The Young Visiters (1919).

By the time she was ten, Daisy Ashford had written her greatest work, The Young Visiters. When it appeared nearly two decades later and achieved enormous success, Ashford had no interest in following it up nor in revealing her identity as its author.

Emma Walker was the mother of five when she and William Ashford, a civil servant in the War Office, married. William had also been married before. Together they had three more children, including Margaret Mary Julia Ashford, whom the family sometimes called Daisy. The eight children were educated at home by a governess or private tutor, and Ashford started making up stories when she was just four. Not yet able to write, she dictated to her father. The Life of Father McSwinney was her first known story (it was published in 1983, almost 100 years later, as part of a children's collection).

In 1889, the Ashfords moved to Lewes in Sussex, where Margaret continued to tell stories and penned—on her own—The Young Visiters at age eight. Though this novel was not published, two other books were, under the name Daisy Ashford. These works were modestly successful, as readers were charmed by the youthful narrator and the misspellings without realizing the author's age.

When Margaret Ashford was 17, she spent a year at the convent school Hayward's Heath, and then five more years at home, before she moved to London with her sister. As a secretary for the British Legation at Berne during World War I, Ashford spent time in Switzerland. When her mother Emma died, Margaret's early masterpiece was rediscovered among her papers. The Young Visiters was published in 1919, with an introduction by J.M. Barrie (author of Peter Pan). While Ashford maintained her anonymity, the book had 18 reprints in its first year, buoyed largely by the rumor that Barrie was the actual author. The following year, Margaret married James Devlin, with whom she had four children and ran a farm and a hotel near Norwich. She lived a quiet country life as her novel was made into a play, a musical, and a movie. James Devlin died in 1956. Ashford died 16 years later, in 1972, at age 90.

Not until her death was her identity as the author of The Young Visiters revealed.

Crista Martin,
Boston, Massachusetts

Ashford, Evelyn (1957—)

American track-and-field athlete who won four gold medals while competing in three Olympic Games. Born on April 15, 1957, in Shreveport, Louisiana; attended University of California at Los Angeles (UCLA); married Ray Washington; children: daughter Rana (Raina).

Competed in Olympics (1976); won Olympic gold medal in 100-meters and 4x100-meter relay (1984); won Olympic gold medal in 4x100-meter relay (1988); won Olympic gold medal in 4x100-meter relay (1992); recipient Flo Hyman award, Women's Sports Foundation, 1989.

At the 1976 Olympics in Montreal, Canada, a 19-year-old unknown sprinter named Evelyn Ashford surprised the crowd by placing 5th in the 100-meter race. After her impressive performance, she returned home to California to begin four years of intensive training for the 1980 Moscow Olympics. Three years later, she was ready. At the 1979 Montreal World Cup Meet, she turned in impressive wins over East Germany's *Marlies Göhr and *Marita Koch, two of the world's best women sprinters. In doing so, Ashford replaced Göhr as the favorite for the 100-meter Olympic gold medal in 1980. As Ashford trained for what appeared to be her best chance, the Soviet Union invaded Afghanistan, and President Jimmy Carter decided that the United States would boycott the Moscow Olympiad in protest. Ashford's dream, along with those of hundreds of other American athletes, was put on hold.

Evelyn Ashford was born on April 15, 1957, in Shreveport, Louisiana. As the daughter of an air-force sergeant, she and her brother and three sisters grew up moving from one military base to another. In high school, Ashford joined the boy's track team, since a girls' team was nonexistent. By her senior year, she had gained regional and statewide recognition.

In 1975, the University of California at Los Angeles (UCLA) offered her a track scholarship under the tutelage of **Pat Connolly**, who had recently been hired as the women's track coach. In Ashford's first 100-meter time trial, she ran so fast that Connolly thought she had misread the stopwatch. For the next ten years, Connolly would train Ashford. Some say she saw in Ash-

Evelyn Ashford, crossing the finish line of the women's 100-meter dash in the Olympic trials.

medal, so I decided to go ahead and try for it again." For a second time, she began to gain recognition and topple records. She won the World Cup sprints in 1981, and, in 1983, again beat Göhr, establishing a world-record time of 10.79. That same year, at the World Championship in Helsinki, Finland, Ashford suffered a setback when she pulled a hamstring halfway through the race and lost to Göhr. Then, at the U.S. Trials, though she barely won the 100-meter final due to a pulled right leg muscle, she recovered in the 200.

It didn't matter to Ashford that her deferred Olympic dream would not be played out on foreign soil. She was just as pleased to perform amid friends and family in her home state of California. In pay-back fashion, the Soviet Union and some of its allies boycotted the 1984 California games. Ashford remained confident, even against her nemesis. When she lost to Göhr in Helsinki, she had made a prediction about the 1984 Olympic gold: "It's going to me or Göhr, and it's going to be me."

It was Ashford. The 27-year-old not only beat out Göhr in the 100-meter, but she also set a new Olympic record of 10.97 seconds, becoming the first woman to run under 11 seconds in the history of the games. A second gold was won anchoring the 4x100-meter relay with teammates *Alice Brown, *Jeanette Bolden, and *Chandra Cheeseborough. Her dream realized, Ashford enjoyed the economic benefits that come with gold medals, including lucrative endorsements and an opportunity to become a reporter for "World Class Woman," a cable television program about women athletes. Yet another deferred dream, the birth of daughter Raina, was realized in May 1985.

The year following Raina's birth, after losing the 40 pounds she had gained during pregnancy, Ashford ranked first in the world in the 100-meters for the fourth time and ran a 10.88, the best 100-meter time in the world for 1986. In February of that year, at the Vitalis Olympic Invitations, she won the 55-meter dash in 6.6 seconds. These wins added interesting statistics to the controversial issue of childbirth and athletics. "Motherhood made me a better runner," she said. "My endurance was better. I could run a mile, two miles, or four miles and have fantastic times. I could lift the same weight I lifted before I got pregnant. But it did take a while to get the sprinting speed back."

The 1988 Seoul Olympics brought Ashford another gold medal in the 400-meter relay and a

ford the Olympic gold that had so often eluded her during her own career in the '50s. "She was like my mother for a few years," Ashford told a reporter. "She took my parents' place in my mind and maybe in hers, but after 1980 I kind of woke up. We were still friends but not mother-daughter. I grew up. It was hard for both of us."

In 1979, Ashford lost interest in her studies, dropped out of UCLA, and went to work in a shoe store, making it more difficult to put in the long hours of needed practice. Though Connolly agreed to continue training her, they began to have philosophical differences regarding coaching style. Ashford finally decided to let her husband Ray Washington, coach of men's basketball at Mount San Jacinto Junior College, take over her training, and Connolly bowed out gracefully.

Evelyn Ashford was so devastated by Carter's boycott of the Soviet Olympics that she seriously considered giving up her track career. But while taking a cross-country car trip with her husband, she contemplated the future, and returned home intent on studying fashion design and training for the 1984 Olympics in Los Angeles. "I still had the burning desire to get a gold silver in the 100-meter dash, putting her in the same league as *Wilma Rudolph and *Wyomia Tyus as a career triple gold-medal winner. Another victory in the 100-meter relay at the 1992 Games in Barcelona, Spain, capped Ashford's brilliant career with a fourth gold medal.

SOURCES:

Davis, Michael D. *Black American Women in Olympic Track and Field*. Jefferson, NC: McFarland, 1992.

Hoobing, Robert. *The 1984 Olympics*. U.S. Postal Service, 1985.

The Boston Globe. Sports section, August 9, 1992.

Barbara Morgan,
Melrose, Massachusetts

Ashley, Edwina (1901–1960).

See Mountbatten, Edwina.

Ashley, Laura (1925–1985)

Welsh textile designer who built with her husband an international fashion and home-decoration business. Born Laura Mountney in Wales, on September 7, 1925; died in Wales, on September 17, 1985; eldest of four children of Stan (a civil service clerk) and Bessie (Davies) Mountney; married Bernard Albert Ashley, in February 1949; children: Laura Jane (b. 1953); David (b. 1954); Nick (b. 1956); Emma Mary Ashley (b. 1965).

The 1970s ushered in the Laura Ashley decade in England. When Ashley's newest London shop opened on Fulham Street, in May 1970, women from 14 to 40 queued up for blocks to sample the high, prim necklines, muted Victorian prints, and long concealing skirts. Romance and nostalgia had renewed the desire to dress up, silencing the psychedelic excesses of the '60s. For Ashley, who strove to create "a kind of scrubbed simple beauty," it was a happy coincidence that just as the company approached a major expansion, the marketplace was in a retrospective mood.

The wholesome (some said puritanical) Laura Ashley image was part and parcel of the woman herself, the reflection of a philosophy of life forged in childhood. Ashley formed an early bond with her Aunt Elsie, who introduced her to books, gardening, and proper English tea. Most of all, Elsie provided a sanctuary from Laura's three younger siblings and the harried atmosphere of her South London house. Holiday visits to her maternal grandmother established Ashley's deep religious roots and abiding love of Wales. "It was here, away from the brash newness of Thirties London suburbia," wrote her biographer **Anne Sebba**, "that she was able to

transport herself to the world of late Victorian security. It was a world where neither moral value nor furniture had changed much in the previous fifty years."

After secretarial school, Ashley joined the newly formed Girls' Training Corps, and, at 17, took her first job as a shorthand-typist at the Ministry of Health. In 1944, she joined the Women's Royal Naval Service (WRENS), and spent two years in Paris and Brussels. At an Air Cadets' dance, she met her future husband and business partner Bernard Ashley and fell in love on the spot. "Laura never talked a lot," said Bernard, "often she said nothing. But from the moment I first spoke to her she took me over and away from the hold my mother had on me." Separated by wartime service, the couple wed in February 1949.

Like many women of her time, Ashley entered marriage with a firm concept of what a wife should be. Reinforced by Bernard's romantic notions, that model stuck for 40 years, even when it became impractical, if not impossible, to maintain. Her world revolved around her husband. Outside work was accomplished after he left in the morning and before he came home in the evening. Writes Sebba: "This was not only so that the domestic chores could be achieved, apparently without effort, and the evening meal prepared by the time Bernard returned, but so that he need never be aware that his wife was involved in work at all; something which always antagonized him." Settling into their 99-step walk-up on St. George's Square, Ashley took a secretarial position close to home in the handicrafts department at the headquarters of the National Federation of Women's Institutes and looked forward to her first pregnancy. She would later tell her daughter, "Falling in love is for having children."

The couples' business venture began with Ashley's quest to find fabrics with small prints, stripes, or flowers in one color, suitable for a patchwork quilt. Finding none, she set out to print her own, pouring over library books to learn how to construct a silk screen. Then, Bernard became intrigued with the project. He spent evenings pouring over books on printing methods, and within a month had constructed a textile printing-screen stencil. Less than six months after the birth of the couple's first child, the fledgling Ashley Mountney Company was born, providing single-design table mats and scarves to various London buyers. Bernard moved on to printing linen tea towels with Victorian themes, followed by aprons and oven gloves. The B.D.—basic dress—which brought them into the fashion industry was an outgrowth of Laura's design for a gardening smock, composed of an identical back and front sewn together with three large patch pockets in the front. The most simple design often met with the greatest success.

The business grew along with the family: two more children followed and a fourth arrived in 1965. The early years were a struggle emotionally and financially, with several relocations. Profits were turned back into the business to se-

cure larger quarters, additional workers, and better equipment. Once the children were born, Ashley felt her first duty was to them. Often she put them to bed for the night at 4:30 in the afternoon, so she could tend to business without feeling guilty of neglect. By the mid-'60s, the couple had established a profitable factory and shop, Gwalia House, in the farming community of Machynlleth, Wales, where Laura began experimenting with new prints and clothing design. The end of the decade brought another move to larger quarters in an old railway station in Carno, Wales. This facility housed the company

Laura Ashley, with her husband Bernard Ashley.

for many years, providing work for local citizens and ultimately turning mid-Wales into a highly desirable area for industrial development.

From the beginning, Laura handled the design aspects of the business while Bernard made deals and took care of operations; she was careful not to encroach on what she considered his territory. Their temperaments were at opposite extremes: he was given to outbursts, she to stony silences. As employers, they were at once benevolent and authoritarian. Preferring to be called L.A. (Bernard was B.A.), Laura could be unyielding if a staff member "fell short of her high standards or overstepped the boundaries of power." However, both she and her husband took pains to know each employee personally, often providing help if there was a problem or crisis. Once, when a shop manager had nowhere to live, they purchased a house for her and paid for extensive repairs and furnishings.

In 1968, Ashley Shops Ltd. was formed as a subsidiary company expressly for retailing, and the first "Laura Ashley" shop opened in London's Kensington district. By 1975, the company had a turnover of £5 million, owned 40 shops and three factories, and employed 1,000 people worldwide. Toward the end of the 1980s, after a fitful beginning in San Francisco, California, there were 13 Laura Ashley stores in the United States, as well as a number of licensing agreements with major U.S. companies to produce "Laura Ashley" designs on sheets, wallpaper, and other home furnishings.

In America, Laura Ashley was heralded as a brilliant entrepreneur; the female head of a multimillion-dollar international company and, most probably, an ardent feminist. But in the flesh, interviewers heard a conflicting viewpoint. "I see women's role in life in the light of sweetness. Men should be the hunters. Women are keepers of the hunters: it's a straightforward, set philosophy of mine." With the possibility of alienating American feminists, Ashley altered her view somewhat, allowing the keepers a little latitude. She remarked: "A woman sees the home as her base and she dresses to complement that environment almost as part of the decoration. Of course that doesn't mean that she doesn't leave her home to work, it just means that the home is where she visualizes herself." Thriving on interviews, Ashley lost all remnants of shyness; she relished opportunities to contradict her preconceived business persona, which, in turn, delighted the press. Buoyed by the efforts of an aristocratic new director of publicity for the U.S. company, and photographs of Lady *Diana Spencer (future princess of Wales), wearing a "Laura Ashley" flounced skirt, the company quickly won over the American market, which flourished under the directorship of Ashley's eldest son David.

The business ultimately brought fame, wealth, and a dramatic upgrade in lifestyle, which included several houses on the Continent, glamorous vacations, a private plane—piloted by Bernard—and a boat. (Ashley overcame an intense fear of the water to share her husband's love of boating.) Despite these luxuries, she missed contact with her children and disliked the rootless feeling of life on the move. When not busy with company work, Ashley tended her gardens, decorated her houses, and entertained. As she grew older, she involved herself more with the home-furnishings market (expanded to include every room in the house), for which she engaged in meticulous historical research. In 1982, the first *Laura Ashley Book of Home Decorating* was published and quickly sold out its first printing.

Just weeks after handing over the role of company design director to her son Nick, Ashley was celebrating her 60th birthday and the birth of a new granddaughter when she suffered a headlong fall down a flight of stairs and sustained severe injuries. Never again to regain consciousness, she survived on life-support for ten days until her death on September 17, 1985. She was buried in the Welsh countryside she so loved.

The business, worth approximately £200 million at the time of her death, continues to flourish. Biographer Sebba, looking beyond the enterprise, finds Ashley deserving a permanent place in British social history on two counts: "In the Seventies, countering a strong tide, she made it possible for women to look and feel like women without hindering any of their manifold desires for career and job satisfaction. In their homes, and home was the centre of Laura Ashley's world, she rescued a corner of the past that had belonged to ordinary people and restored it to the descendants of those same people with enhanced value."

SOURCES:

Sebba, Anne. *Laura Ashley: A Life by Design.* London: Weidenfeld and Nicolson, 1990.

Barbara Morgan,
Melrose, Massachusetts

Ashrawi, Hanan (1946—)

Palestinian political leader. Name variations: Hanan Mikhail-Ashrawi. Born Hanan Mikhail in Ramallah, about six miles north of Jerusalem (which became the Israeli-occupied West Bank) in 1946; youngest of five daughters of Daoud (a doctor) and Wad'ia Mikhail; attended the American University in Beirut, Lebanon, M.A. in literature (1960s); married Emile Ashrawi (a photographer, filmmaker, and artist); children: two daughters, Amal and Zeina.

Active in the General Union of Palestinian Students (GUPS); only woman from Lebanon on the GUPS delegation at an international conference in Amman, Jordan (1969); joined the teaching staff of Bir Zeit University in the West Bank (1973); received a doctorate in English literature at University of Virginia (1981); rejoined the faculty at Bir Zeit as a professor of English, and became dean of the Faculty of Arts; quit her Palestinian Cabinet post as minister of Higher Education in protest over lack of accountability in the Palastinian government (1998).

Hanan Ashrawi

With her frequent appearances on American television news shows, some believe that Hanan Ashrawi has done more "to change the image of

the Palestinians living under Israeli occupation, than any war, uprising, or terrorist attack," writes **Barbara Victor**. Ashrawi's conciliatory manner has served well in breaching the wall between Palestinians and Israelis in the peace talks. "We wish to address the Israeli people, with whom we have a prolonged exchange of pain," she said. "Let us share hope instead."

Hanan Ashrawi was born in 1946 into a Christian-Muslim household in Ramallah, then a town under British mandate (which became the Israeli-occupied West Bank). Her father, who had been a physician in the Palestinian army, was a prominent politician who defied traditional Muslim precepts by viewing his five daughters as a gift not a curse; he encouraged them to fight for their beliefs.

Though Ashrawi met Yasir Arafat, leader of the Palestinian Liberation Organization (PLO) at a 1969 international conference in Amman, Jordan, her radicalization and open support of the PLO did not come about until Israel's 1982 invasion of Lebanon and the massacre of Palestinians in Beirut during raids on Sabra and Chatila refugee camps. "I said to myself, 'This has got to stop,'" remarked Ashrawi. "Palestinians must not be an easy prey to everybody." Since then, she has sought self-determination for her people, espousing pragmatic approaches with calm and projecting an apparent willingness to reason, while continuing to appear on Western evening news shows. She is known in some circles as the "Nightline Palestinian."

In her book *This Side of Peace*, Ashrawi offers a personal account of the negotiations leading up to the signing of the accord by Israel's Yitzak Rabin and PLO leader Arafat on the White House lawn—an accord that she did not agree with and which brought on her resignation from the PLO. Though she says she is committed to peace, Ashrawi is determined to hang tough on the Arab claim to Jerusalem. She heads the Commission for Citizens' Rights, which serves as defender and monitor of the nascent government. "The challenges of building a nation are probably more difficult than facing an 'external enemy,'" she has said. "I don't think we'll fail, but it will cost."

SOURCES:

Ashrawi, Hanan. *This Side of Peace: A Personal Account.* NY: Simon & Schuster, 1995.
Current Biography. NY: H.W. Wilson, 1992.

SUGGESTED READING:

Victor, Barbara. *A Voice of Reason: Hanan Ashrawi and Peace in the Middle East.* Harcourt, Brace, 1994.

Ashton, Helen (1891–1958)

British novelist. Born Helen Rosaline Ashton on October 18, 1891, in London, England; died in 1958; daughter of Arthur J. (king's counsel) and Emma (Burnie) Ashton; sister of Leigh Ashton (director of the Victoria and Albert Museum); educated at London University; earned a medical degree from London University, but largely applied her medical knowledge to her writing, which included 26 novels; married Arthur Edward North Jordon (a lawyer), in 1927.

Selected works: Pierrot in Town *(1913);* Almain *(1914);* A Lot of Talk *(1927);* Doctor Serocold *(1930);* Mackerel Sky *(1931); (with Katherine Davies)* I Had a Sister *(1937);* William and Dorothy *(1938);* Yeoman's Hospital *(1944);* Parson Austen's Daughter *(1949).*

Helen Ashton grew up in London, Stockton, and Wiltshire. Her father Arthur Ashton held the posts of king's counsel and recorder of Manchester before attaining the bench as judge of appeal on the Isle of Man. Helen had a privileged though relatively normal childhood, with aspirations in medicine that first led her to work as a volunteer nurse during World War I. Following her service, she completed an M.B. and a B.Ch. (equivalent of an American M.D.) at London University and took the role of house physician at the Great Ormond Street Children's Hospital in London.

Though Ashton's marriage in 1927 to barrister Arthur Jordan ended thoughts of a medical career, it did not impede her writing. After seeing her first novel *Pierrot in Town* published by age 22, she continued to write novels and fictionalized biographies, which would total 26 books by the end of her career. Applying her medical background to books such as *Doctor Serocold* (1930), Ashton received greater public reception than she did with an imagined account of *Jane Austen*'s life in *Parson Austen's Daughter* (1949). Ashton and Jordan moved to Gloucestershire but enjoyed spending holidays in Ireland, where they went trout fishing. Ashton died in 1958. She was 66 years old.

Crista Martin,
Boston, Massachusetts

Ashton, Winifred (1888–1965).

See Dane, Clemence.

Ashton-Warner, Sylvia (1908–1984)

New Zealand writer and teacher who achieved international fame as an innovator of child-based educational methods, vivifying her experiences teaching Maori children, and promulgating an educational scheme based on "organic" integration of the inner and outer self. Name variations: Sylvia Henderson, Sylvia. Born Sylvia Constance Warner on December 17, 1908, in Stratford, New Zealand; died on April 28, 1984, in Tauranga, New Zealand, of abdominal cancer; one of nine children of Margaret (Maxwell) Warner (a teacher) and Francis Ashton Warner (a house-husband); attended Wairarapa College in Masterton, 1926–1927; Auckland Teacher's Training College, 1928–1931; married Keith Dawson Henderson (a teacher), on August 23, 1931; children: Jasmine, Elliot, Ashton.

Awards: New Zealand State Literary Funds' Scholarship in Letters (1958); Delta Kappa Gamma Society International Educator's Award (1980); New Zealand Book Award (1980) for I Passed This Way; *Member of the Order of the British Empire (1982).*

With husband, taught in several country schools in New Zealand with largely Maori populations (1931–55); described her experiences in autobiographical novels and educational treatises, which profoundly influence child-based educational methods throughout the world (beginning in the mid-1950s); taught in alternative elementary school, Aspen Colorado (1970–71); was professor of education, Simon Fraser University, Vancouver, British Columbia (1971–73).

Selected writings: Spinster *(1958);* Incense to Idols *(1960);* Teacher *(1963);* Bell Call *(1964);* Greenstone *(1966);* Myself *(1967);* Three *(1970);* Spearpoint: Teacher in America *(1972);* O Children of the World *(1974);* I Passed This Way *(1979);* Stories from the River *(1986).*

Horoera School for Maoris was accessible by horse over eight roadless miles along a beach at low tide. Here in New Zealand during the late 1930s—using State-mandated traditional readers promoting British culture—Sylvia Ashton-Warner failed, by her own estimation and that of the school inspectors, to teach non-western Maori children to read. Desperate, intellectually lonely, she sank into a profound depression from which she surfaced through exploration of her "undermind," which she identified as the wellspring of her creativity and the source of creativity in others, especially children.

Later in 1941, in another outlying Maori school, Pipiriki, located 50 miles upriver from the coastal town of Wanganui, the story was different; with élan, she taught Maori children by listening intently, encouraging them to excavate their inner lives, to transform their most relevant feelings and sensibilities into manageable words, culminating in English literacy. In this isolated corner of New Zealand, Sylvia Ashton-Warner

had invented a theory and style of teaching that would have global repercussions, transforming the manner in which children throughout the world would be educated in the last half of the 20th century. Many thought she had discovered a way to prevent future war.

In her autobiography, *I Passed This Way* (1979), Sylvia Ashton-Warner summarizes the teaching principles of "organic teaching," a mode that begins with gathering a "key vocabulary":

> Touch the true voice of feeling and it will create its own vocabulary and style, its own power and peace.
> Supply the conditions where life comes in the door: let it.
> Supply the conditions where the native, inborn imagery of our child can surface under its own power to be captioned or named, harnessed, put to work and to make its contribution to society.
> Supply the conditions where the impulse to kill can surface to be isolated and defused.

Born on December 17, 1908, in Stratford, New Zealand, Sylvia Constance Warner was a middle child of nine in an impoverished family. Her mother, New Zealand-born Margaret (Maxwell) Warner, was an elementary school teacher and the family breadwinner; her father, Francis Ashton Warner, was housebound, an invalid suffering from rheumatoid arthritis. As a young man, he had immigrated to New Zealand from Great Britain, toting a wooden box of family heirlooms, some dating from the 15th century, including a coat-of-arms. After marriage and before Sylvia was born, he managed to work as a clerk for four or five years; thereafter, he was an invalid at home, bedridden or on crutches, and sometimes hospitalized for his painful, crippling rheumatoid arthritis. As a two-year-old, Sylvia was left to his sole care while her mother worked. She was influenced by his humor and storytelling, his bed remembered as an oasis; he is commemorated in her novel *Greenstone* (1966).

Margaret Warner, Sylvia's mother, supported her family by school teaching, at first changing positions frequently for diversity's sake, later losing job after job, perhaps because of frequent pregnancies, perhaps because of bad inspector reports; by reputation, she was fiercely proud. For one year in 1919, unable to find a teaching position, she reluctantly accepted charitable aide, which required her to take work as a housekeeper and give her younger children to foster care. During the same period, she adopted the hyphenated Ashton-Warner form of her name.

No matter how destitute the Ashton-Warner family, there was always a piano in the house, although it was never owned and was sometimes repossessed, there not being enough money for rent or grocery bills or payments on the piano. A child was always practicing, for Sylvia's mother exempted anyone from chores who was at the keyboard. Chores were strenuous; the Ashton-Warners lived in rural circumstances, sawing and chopping wood for heat and cooking, sometimes preparing food on an open fire in front of their house, not possessing an indoor bathroom until Sylvia Ashton-Warner was 14 years old.

Sylvia attended eleven primary and three secondary schools. Her mother was her first teacher and, according to Sylvia's biographer **Lynley Hood**, strict, brutal, and old-fashioned; she tied Sylvia's left hand behind to force right-handedness, an accepted practice at the time. Sylvia achieved dazzling ambidexterity, simultaneously drawing rabbits with one hand and mice with the other, or, on the blackboard, starting a sentence simultaneously at the far right and far left and completing it in the middle.

Sometimes Sylvia was not promoted in grade sequence, only to catch up with a month or two of intense application. In her autobiography, she explains that her elementary education occurred to a considerable extent in fantasy games with her sisters, prowling the out-of-doors, the forests and swamps. In order to reach the Masterton district high school, she rode a horse first seven miles, then, after a family move, eleven miles, often doing her untidy homework in the saddle.

Sylvia Ashton-Warner emphatically did not want to be a teacher; instead, she dreamed of a career as a concert pianist or commercial artist. Despite her native talent as an artist and musician, she lacked training and opportunity to realize her ambitions. Moreover, teaching and nursing were accepted career paths for women in 1925. Between 1926 and 1927, she was a teaching apprentice at Wellington South School, living away from home, boarding at the Y.W.C.A. In 1928, aged 19, she entered Auckland Teachers' Training College where she was certified as a teacher in 1931 during the Great

Depression. Though there was no work available for new teachers, which accounted for a defeated return to her mother's home, Sylvia Ashton-Warner was eventually placed at the Eastern Hutt School in Wellington where she taught until August 23, 1931, when she married a Training College companion, Keith Dawson Henderson.

The Hendersons settled in a provincial school district, Manuka in Whaeorino, where Keith Henderson continued to teach older elementary school students. Sylvia did not hold a teaching job during this period. In the late 1930s in New Zealand, wives were not allowed to teach in the same schools as their husbands, although exceptions were made for what were considered less desirable assignments in Maori schools. Neither Manuka, nor Mangahume, Keith's next assignment, were Maori. Sylvia had three children: Jasmine in 1935, Elliot in 1937, and Ashton in 1939. According to her biographer, she displayed little interest in domestic duties; her husband cooked, washed clothing, and cared for the children, while she devoted herself to writing and painting.

In 1939, Ashton-Warner persuaded her husband to apply for an assignment to a Maori school so that she could return to teaching. They were appointed to Horoera School in East Cape near Te Araroa, several days travel into the remote reaches of New Zealand. Sylvia immersed herself in Maori culture and language, becoming fluent. She came to realize that one reason Maori children were unable to learn to read was that they simply did not respond to orthodox readers, to English words like *train* and *can,* for the simple reason that they had never seen trains and cans. She was critical of Western cultural ruthlessness: "The main idea in Maori schools was to promote the English culture and it was not so long ago that Maori children were strapped for speaking Maori in school." Tentatively, she added a few Maori words like *kai* (food) and *hoiko* (horse), noting greater success. But she was afraid of the inspectors. She became despondent and eventually was unable to leave her bed. She remained so for months until she received psychotherapy, living in Wellington for months away from husband and children.

With the help of a Freudian therapist, Ashton-Warner believed that she reassembled a self, learning to identify what she called "fear" (selfishness) with survival of the individual and "sex" (selflessness) with survival of the species. She emerged determined to balance her self-defined career as an artist with her activities as a nurturing teacher.

Aged 32, she returned to teaching at Pipiriki School for Maoris; she also established a room of her own, a cottage in the woods to which she retreated to play the piano, to paint and sculpt and write; in every new residence of her married life thereafter, a cottage, cave, or room was designated for creative retreat at the end of each day of teaching and on weekends. The classroom was also a place for creativity; she painted murals on its walls, played sonatas on the piano while her children molded clay, controlled children with music, encouraged dance, and practiced the theory that children will learn best if their first words and stories are their own, a key vocabulary emanating from words of fear, crucial family words like *mommy,* and words of sex, like *kiss.* In *Teacher* (1963), she writes:

> Back to these first words. To these first books. They must be made out of the stuff of the child itself. I reach a hand into the mind of the child, bring out a handful of stuff I find there, and use that as our first working material. Whether it is good or bad stuff, violent or placid stuff, coloured or dun. To effect an unbroken beginning. And in this dynamic material, with the familiarity and security of it, the Maori finds that words have intense meaning to him, from which cannot help but arise a love of reading.

Organic reading assumes that all "art is communication. We never really make things for ourselves alone. The books are to be read to another."

*R*elease the native imagery of our child and use it for working material.

—Sylvia Ashton-Warner

Sylvia established her style of teaching during the years of the second World War; as a writer, she assumed her maiden name, Ashton-Warner, as her *nom de plume.* She theorized that, by releasing suppression, aggression might be channeled into permissible, expressive art and words: "I have always been more afraid of the weapon unspoken than of the one on a blackboard." Herbert Read, the influential British author of *Education Through Art,* recognized that she had, indeed, "discovered a method of teaching that can make the human being naturally and spontaneously peaceable." Worldwide desire to reeducate human beings in order to avoid nuclear extermination crescendoed during the Cold War period, coinciding with the publication of Ashton-Warner's novels and educational treatises about her discoveries teaching Maoris.

She had perceived that "inescapably war and peace wait in the infant room; wait and vie" and that enabling children to be creative in order to vent their violence was more than a teaching matter: "It's an international matter."

Sylvia Ashton-Warner was also representative of a wave of women seeking to expand their opportunities in the 1930s and '40s. *Dora Russell,* the British feminist and educator, describes her as:

> a dynamic personality, much self-absorbed, in whom stirred many of the inter-war discontents—the lack of opportunity for those who had striven to make something of themselves; the rising of rebellion of women against their traditional status; disillusion indeed with almost everything that derived from authority and tradition.

In her cottage retreat, Ashton-Warner explored her artistic gifts and sometimes entertained her friends, particularly **Joy Alley,** the district nurse, whom she disguised as her lover Dr. Saul Mada in her journal of these years, *Myself* (1967). She established an intimate friendship by letter with **Barbara Dest,** the New Zealand writer. By 1948, Ashton-Warner was beginning to publish short stories in the New Zealand *Listener.* She was also writing a journal, the raw material of *Teacher,* and a novel that remained unpublished except for parts that appeared in serial form in the New Zealand *Monthly Review* between 1959 and '60.

In 1955, aged 46, Sylvia Ashton-Warner retired from teaching. She had written and illustrated books for school children to read; she was frustrated by lack of official recognition of her transitional readers designed as a bridge between the "key vocabulary" and mainstream *Janet and John* (the New Zealand equivalent to the American "Dick and Jane"). Indeed, it appears that the district office claimed her manuscripts were accidently destroyed when they were in their possession.

Focusing on issues of educational theory and racial understanding, her first novel, *Spinster* (1958), was published in England and the United States to critical acclaim, named by *The New York Times* as one of the ten best books of the year. In *Spinster,* she fictionalized her experiences teaching Maoris. Reviewers thought it "a first novel of singular literary quality and impact," receiving it with "an exhilarating sense of personal discovery." In 1962, she presented her teaching scheme in *Teacher,* writing in her introduction that she believed her contribution "universal": "For black, for white, for yellow and brown . . . it is universal. With tragic and desperate application to the racial minorities learning another culture." Educators around the world, and particularly in North America, were captivated. **Jeannette Veatch**, a university professor from the United States, journeyed to New Zealand to meet her as did Sir Herbert Read and many others. She received more attention from abroad than she did from educators and literati in New Zealand, a source of bitterness for her, accounting for her refusal to allow her name to be listed in *Who's Who* in New Zealand.

In 1971, two years after her husband's death, Ashton-Warner accepted a position teaching American children in an alternative elementary school in Aspen, Colorado. In this period characterized by the civil rights movement and opposition to the Vietnam War, parents were seeking to remake the world by establishing experimental schools for their children. In *Spearpoint* (1972), Ashton-Warner described her disillusionment with ideals of equality and freedom-as-license; "organic" teaching did not work well in chaos. She concluded that American children had been dehumanized by television:

> As our child sits hour after hour before the man-made screen, as the radio intrudes on the background of his mind or as the rabble-rousing beat of the latest hit booms through the trembling house, it is not the channel outward [that] is blocked to his imagery; it is that his defenseless mind, the frail, unique human marvel of his living feeling, is bombarded into sedation by overstimulation or even into extinction . . . . Our child no longer feels with love or with hatred; he does not feel at all.

She left Aspen, but before returning to New Zealand she trained teachers for two years at Simon Fraser University in Vancouver, British Columbia.

Sylvia Ashton-Warner died of abdominal cancer on April 28, 1984, in her self-designed home in Tauranga, New Zealand. Appropriately, she died in her "Selah," the name she gave all of her rooms, cottages, and caves of self-determined, creative retreat. *Selah* in Hebrew means "to pause or rest."

SOURCES:
Ashton-Warner, Sylvia. *I Passed This Way.* NY: Knopf, 1979.
———. *Spearpoint: Teacher in America.* NY: Knopf, 1972.
———. *Teacher.* London: Virago, 1980.
Hood, Lynley. *Sylvia!: The Biography of Sylvia Ashton-Warner.* NY: Viking, 1988.
Russell, Dora. Introduction to *Teacher* by Sylvia Ashton-Warner. London: Virago, 1980.

SUGGESTED READING:
Cliett, William. "Sylvia Ashton-Warner's Message for American Teachers," in *Childhood Education.* Vol. 61, 1985, p. 207.
Veatch, Jeannette. "Individualised Reading: a Personal Memoir," in *Language Arts.* October 1986.
Wasserman, Selma. "Aspen Mornings with Sylvia Ashton-Warner," in *Childhood Education.* Vol. 48, 1972, p. 348.

COLLECTIONS:
Private papers and manuscripts held in the Sylvia Ashton-Warner Archives, Mugar Memorial Library, Boston University.

RELATED MEDIA:
British film *Two Loves* (1961), based on *Spinster,* directed by Charles Walters, with **Shirley MacLaine**, Laurence Harvey, Jack Hawkins.
New Zealand film *Sylvia* (1985), based on *Teacher* and *I Passed This Way,* directed by Michael Firth.

Jill Benton, Professor of English and World Literature, Pitzer College, Claremont, California

Ashwell, Lena (1872–1957)

English actress. Born in 1872; died in 1957; daughter of C. Ashwell B. Pocock, R.N.; educated in Toronto, Canada; studied singing at Lausanne Conservatoire and Royal Academy of Music; married Arthur Playfair (an actor), in 1896 (divorced 1908); married a Dr. Simson, in 1908.

At the turn of the century, Lena Ashwell was one of London's leading actresses. In 1895, she portrayed Elaine in Sir Henry Irving's production of *King Arthur* at the Lyceum and would again act for him in 1903 in *Dante.* Ashwell scored her first major triumph in *Mrs. Dane's Defence,* directed by Sir Charles Wyndham in 1900. In 1907, she starred under her own management at the Kingsway Theatre. From 1914 to 1918, during World War I, she provided concerts and plays for troops at the front. For the next ten years, she ran the Lena Ashwell Players, which toured the suburbs. Ashwell also founded the Century Theatre after 1924 to provide quality plays at quality prices and to give opportunities for beginning actors. She was awarded the Order of the British Empire (OBE) in 1917.

Askew, Anne (c. 1521–1546)

English Protestant martyr whose adherence to Sacramentarian doctrines led to her execution and subsequent renown as one of the heroines of the English Reformation. Name variations: Askewe, Ascue, Ayscoughe; (married name) Kime, Kyme, Keme. Pronunciation: ASS-que. Born Anne Askew at Stallingborough, near Grimsby in Yorkshire, England, around 1521; burned at the stake in London on July 16,

1546; daughter of Sir William Askew (a knight); mother unknown; married Thomas Kyme (separated); children: two. Following separation from husband, moved to London and presented for heresy (1545).

One July day in the closing years of Henry VIII's reign, a crowd gathered at London's Smithfield Market anticipating the terrible drama about to unfold. Four convicted heretics were brought in and tied to stakes placed at the center of the marketplace. At the last moment, the sole woman among them was presented with papers from the lord chancellor of England promising the king's pardon if she recanted her heretical opinions. The young woman refused even to look upon the papers, declaring that she had not come this day to deny her Lord and Master. Emulating her steadfast example, her three fellows also refused to regard the proffered pardons. Seeing that any further effort to secure a last-minute recantation was futile, the lord mayor of London cried out, "*Fiat Justicia!*" ("Let justice be done!") Lighted torches touched the faggots placed under each stake, and, as the flames leaped up, the surrounding crowd witnessed the untimely end of Anne Askew, one of England's most famous religious martyrs.

I confess there is something in the story of this noble woman which nerves me greatly. Was ever courage greater than hers? Was ever steadfastness more glorious? Did ever hero, plunging into the thick of the battle, . . . surpass the heroism of Anne Askew?

—Anonymous

Despite the great fame she earned by her heroic death, little for certain is known about Anne Askew's earlier life. She is stated to have been born at Stallingborough, near Grimsby in Yorkshire, about the year 1521. She was raised, however, at Kelsey, in Lincolnshire, the second daughter of Sir William Askew, who descended from an old and established Lincolnshire family, and an unknown mother. The first decades of the 16th century saw aristocratic families like the Askews increasingly attuned to the new humanistic learning being imported from Italy and France. This "New Learning" was frequently bestowed on daughters and sons alike, and in keeping with this intellectual fashion, Anne was educated to a high standard. We know that she assiduously studied the Bible, which in her youth became widely available for the first time in a complete English translation. During her stays in the city of

❧▶

Anne of Cleves.
See
*Six Wives of
Henry VIII.*

Lincoln, she often read the public Bible chained in the cathedral and even entered into discussions there with clergy about the proper interpretation of the Scriptures. Anne later recalled, how accurately we cannot tell, that she invariably prevailed in these theological disputations. She nevertheless did earn a reputation for her intellectual abilities; John Foxe, the Protestant martyrologist described her as "studious, well-educated, thoughtful, and quick-minded."

While probably still young, Anne married Thomas Kyme, also of Kelsey. Sir William Askew had originally intended the marriage for Anne's elder sister, who died inopportunely after the conclusion of the marriage contract and the payment of her dowry but before the solemnization of the union. So as to prevent the forfeiture of his dowry money, Sir William substituted Anne, against her wishes, for her deceased sister. It was a pragmatic arrangement entirely typical of aristocratic marriages at the time, made more palatable by a social consensus that expected marital affection and love to grow only after marriage, not before. Askew had two children with Kyme, thus fulfilling the major dynastic objective of aristocratic marriage, yet she and her new husband did not develop a happy relationship. Anne refused publicly to explain the reasons for their marital discord, but its undeniable seriousness is emblematized perhaps in Askew's unconventional retention of her maiden name. It may well be that Anne's radical religious opinions and her continuing disagreements with the local priests to some extent caused the marital breakdown and led Kyme eventually to cast her out of his house. Whatever the basis for her leaving, Askew welcomed the separation: by early 1545, she had taken up lodgings in London near the Temple, the center of the capital's legal establishment, and was supposedly seeking a divorce.

It was in these circumstances that, in March, Askew was arrested for heresy and examined under the terms of the Six Articles, which Parliament had passed in 1539 to combat the spread of advanced Protestant beliefs. Although Henry VIII had rejected the authority of the pope and the Roman church more than ten years before, in the process creating the Protestant Church of England, the king nonetheless remained doctrinally orthodox in most religious matters. In the aftermath of Henry's disastrous marriage to ◀❧ **Anne of Cleves** and with Thomas Cromwell's fall, moreover, the conservative faction at court led by Stephen Gardiner and Thomas, duke of Norfolk, gained the upper hand and sought to enforce stricter limits on religious diversity. The legislative centerpiece to this religious reaction was the Act of Six Articles, which attached severe penalties to the denial of certain traditional religious beliefs.

The direction of questioning during her examination implies that Askew had run afoul of the first of the Six Articles, the one having to do with the proper interpretation of the Eucharist (or Holy Communion). The orthodox position enjoined by the Six Articles and shared with the Roman Catholics held that the substance of the bread and wine used in Holy Communion was really transformed into the body and blood of Christ once a priest uttered the words, "*Hoc est corpus meum*" ("This is my body"), over the Host in emulation of Jesus at the Last Supper. Radical Protestants argued, on the other hand, that Jesus spoke these words not literally but figuratively, and that the bread and wine taken in Communion remained bread and wine in substance and thus had a merely symbolic function. This so-called "Sacramentarian heresy" was condemned by the Act of Six Articles, and it provided that those who denied transubstantiation or otherwise despised the sacrament of the Eucharist "shall, together with their supporters, be guilty of heresy and burned."

Askew therefore stood in mortal danger as she underwent her examination for heresy, yet her answers reveal a remarkable self-assurance and *sang froid* as she parried with her accusers. To Christopher Dare's question whether she believed the consecrated bread to be the very body of Christ, Askew avoided a direct answer by countering with another question: "Wherefore was St. Stephen stoned?," she asked. When Dare confessed that he did not know, Askew responded that neither would she answer his vain question. Askew did admit that she would rather read five lines of the Bible than hear five masses, for the Scriptures edified her while the masses did not, but while this statement obliquely attacked the saving power of Holy Communion, it did not amount to heresy. Having frustrated their desire that she incriminate herself, Askew was taken before the lord mayor of London who continued the interrogation but was even less successful in revealing the extent of her conformity to the religious tenets demanded by the Six Articles. In the end, he remanded her to prison to await further proceedings.

Throughout her examinations for heresy, Askew was protected not only by her considerable wit and circumspection, but perhaps more important by the fact that she was a gentlewoman who possessed influential friends and kin. Although she was isolated from her friends for 11 days while languishing in prison, her cousin Brittayne finally succeeded in visiting her, and he shortly thereafter applied to the lord mayor to have her released on bail. The lord mayor refused to release her without the approval of an ecclesiastical authority, at which point Brittayne enlisted the aid of Bishop Bonner, who seems genuinely to have attempted to help Askew. After interviewing her at length, on the 20th of March the bishop presented her with a confession of faith that he had specially drafted in order to remove any doubt about the orthodoxy of her faith. But rather than simply sign the document, Askew appended a declaration that she believed "all manner of things contained in the faith of the Catholic Church, and not otherwise." This last-ditch effort to reintroduce ambiguity about the doctrines to which she was subscribing greatly offended Bonner, who stormed out of the room, furious that his sincere attempts to help Askew had been met, as he saw it, with such brazen contempt and insubordination.

Once again, however, Askew's friends interceded on her behalf and persuaded Bonner to resubmit the confession of faith for her to sign. This she finally did and consequently was released on bond pending trial. Askew was arraigned on June 13, along with two others also accused of being sacramentarian heretics, but as no witnesses appeared to testify against her (the matter having already been settled by the signed confession of faith), Askew was acquitted and set free.

She remained at liberty until the following spring, when renewed accusations of heresy led to a summons issued on May 24, 1546, requiring that both Askew and her estranged husband appear before the Privy Council within ten days. In the intervening months since Askew's acquittal, England's deteriorating diplomatic position in Europe had led Henry VIII to pursue an increasingly conservative religious policy, with the result that accused heretics could now expect more aggressive prosecution and harsher treatment if convicted. One reason for this shift was the opening of the Council of Trent, which even at its inception posed the ominous threat of a politically united Catholic front capable of crushing the scattered Protestant states. In order to forestall this possibility, Henry sought to detach Charles V, the Holy Roman Emperor, from the alliance with France that acted as the diplomatic mainstay of the Council's authority. In an effort to shake off his reputation as a schismatic and woo Charles to his side, Henry both reinstituted a number of traditional Catholic rites and cracked down on those who advocated radical Protestant doctrines.

It was in these more stringent diplomatic and religious circumstances that Anne Askew and Thomas Kyme appeared before the Privy Council on June 19—nearly four weeks after the summons. One account, supplied years later by Askew's nephew, attributes the delay in her appearance to the fact that she was in hiding and was captured only when one of her letters was intercepted. In any case, her second examination began with inquiry being made into her separation from Kyme and her refusal to acknowledge him as her husband. Askew insisted that she would explain her marital situation only to the king personally, whereupon the Privy Councillors evidently decided that Kyme was of no interest to them, and he was allowed to return home. After further discussion with Askew, however, the Privy Council found that "she showed herself to be of a naughty opinion," and they remanded her to Newgate Prison.

The following day, Askew and the Council debated for five hours, and her statements during this examination (at least as reported by her) reveal an even more assertive and opinionated woman than one interrogated before the lord mayor and Bishop Bonner a year earlier. At one point, when Bishop Gardiner complained that she spoke in parables and admonished her to make direct answer to the questions put to her, she replied that this was best for him, "for if I show the open truth ye will not accept it." Askew's examination continued for several successive days during which the Privy Councillors urged her to "confess the Sacrament to be flesh, blood, and bone." Yet all efforts to secure from her a voluntary recantation failed, and Gardiner began to warn darkly that she was in danger of going to the stake. On June 20, Askew fell seriously ill and seems to have expected to die at any moment of her sickness. Although repeatedly implored to renounce her erroneous opinions and sign a "bill of the Sacrament," Askew remained defiant. Accordingly, she was arraigned at Guildhall on the 28th along with three others: Dr. Nicholas Shaxton, former bishop of Salisbury, John Hadlam, a tailor, and Nicholas White, an attorney. All four admitted to their heresies, were summarily convicted, and condemned to be burned.

Efforts the next day by the bishops Bonner and Heath to exhort the condemned Sacramentarians succeeded in inducing Shaxton and White to abjure their heresies. But Askew was adamant. Bonner even brought in the newly rec-

Parr, Catherine.
See Six Wives of Henry VIII.

tified Shaxton to urge Askew to save herself. As she recounted, "Then came there to me Nicholas Shaxton and counselled me to recant as he had done. I said to him that it had been good for him never to have been born; with many other like words." Instead, she drafted her own confession of faith from her cell in Newgate, a shortened version of which she sent to Thomas Wriothesley, the lord chancellor, asking that he in turn forward it to the king. In it, Askew made plain her uncompromising Sacramentarian views.

Although she already stood condemned, Askew had to undergo yet another ordeal before her final suffering. On the afternoon of the 29th, Sir Richard Rich sent her to the Tower of London for a further round of interrogation, this time with the application of torture. The judicial torture of a condemned criminal was a highly unusual occurrence, and it has been alleged that the king himself authorized Askew's racking in order to ascertain whether she had infected certain ladies at court with heretical doctrines. Certainly the interrogation administered by Rich and Wriothesley in the Tower focused on the identity of her patrons. In fact, Askew's suspected relations with several highly placed aristocratic ladies like the duchess of Suffolk, the countesses of Sussex and Hertford, Lady Denny, Lady Fitzwilliam, and perhaps even the queen, Catherine Parr, may have been the motivating factor behind her rearrest for heresy in 1546. Henry, given the exigencies of his diplomatic policy, could not tolerate a notorious heretic such as Anne Askew gaining influence over the most powerful ladies of the realm. The conservatives at Court, for their part, saw Askew as a promising source of incriminating evidence that might be used to strengthen their hand against the advanced Protestant faction.

Despite a severe racking, however, during which Wriothesley and Rich personally lent a hand, Askew refused to divulge the names of any of her presumed confederates. She acknowledged only that, among the numerous gifts made to her by anonymous members of the public, small sums of money were said to have been conveyed to her by minions of Ladies Denny and Hertford, though she did not know even that to be a fact.

Now seriously injured from her torture and unable to walk, Askew returned to prison. Then on July 16, she was carried in a chair to Smithfield and chained to a stake along with the tailor Hadlam, John Lascelles, a gentleman of the court, and a priest named John Helmsley. None other than Dr. Shaxton, her former compatriot, delivered the sermon from a pulpit erected on the spot. Presiding over the ceremony were the lord chancellor, the dukes of Norfolk and Bedford, the lord mayor, and other notables seated on a dais. As Shaxton preached, Askew, ever contentious, offered a running commentary on his sermon, praising him where she agreed with his words, but other times saying, "There he misseth and speaketh without the book." Unrepentant to the end, pious, and steadfast in her faith, Anne Askew died a religious martyr.

SOURCES:

"Above Rubies;" or, Memorials of Christian Gentlewomen. Nashville, TN: Publishing House of the M.E. Church, South, n.d.

Dickens, A.G., and Dorothy Carr, eds. *The Reformation in England to the Accession of Elizabeth I.* London: Edward Arnold, 1967.

Foxe, John. *Foxe's Book of English Martyrs.* Waco, TX: Word Books, 1981.

Gairdner, James. *Lollardy and the Reformation in England,* Vol. II. London, 1908 (reprinted, NY: Burt Franklin, n.d.).

Hughes, Philip. *The Reformation in England,* Vol. II: *Religio Depopulata.* London: Hollis & Carter, 1953.

Wriothesley, Charles. *A Chronicle of England During the Reigns of the Tudors.* Camden Society, new series, Vol. 11. London: Camden Society, 1875.

SUGGESTED READING:

Bale, John. *The First Examinacyon of Anne Askewe.* Marburg, 1546.

———. *The Lattre Examinacyon of Anne Askewe.* Marburg, 1547.

Dickens, A.G. *The English Reformation.* NY: Schocken, 1964.

Wabuda, Susan Ruth. "Anne Askew (c.1520–1546): A Study of Women and Religious Dissent in England." Unpublished M.A. thesis, Wesleyan University, 1980.

Geoffrey Clark, Assistant Professor of History, Emory University, Atlanta, Georgia

Asp, Anna (1946—)

Swedish production designer. Born in 1946 in Sweden; attended Stockholm's Academy of Fine Arts and Dramatic Institute.

The art director (also known as a production designer) is responsible for every facet of a film's decor, including the acquisition of props and the construction of sets. The work dominates the visual results and sets the mood. A good art director must have a strong grasp of costume design, costs, lighting, cinematography. In essence, she translates the words on the printed page into the visual medium known as the motion picture.

Anna Asp's production designs have graced the sets of Scandinavia's major directors: Ingmar Bergman, Andrei Tarkovsky, and Bille August.

Her films include *Giliap* (1973); *Ansikte mot ansikte* (*Face to Face*, 1976); *Hostsonaten* (*Autumn Sonata*, 1978); *Min Alskade* (1979); *Fanny and Alexander* (1982); *After the Rehearsal* (1984); *Offret-Sacrificatio* (*The Sacrifice*, 1986); *Pelle Erobreren* (*Pelle the Conqueror*, 1987); *Katinka* (1988). In 1982, she won an Academy Award for art direction on *Fanny and Alexander.*

Aspasia Manos (1896–1972).

See Manos, Aspasia.

Aspasia of Miletus

(c. 464 BCE–c. 420 BCE)

One of the most famous women of the ancient Greek world, known for her philosophical and rhetorical education, political influence, and charm. Pronunciation: As-PAS-ia. Flourished around 430 BCE; dates of birth and death unknown. Born in Miletus (in modern Turkey) around 464 BCE; died, probably, in Athens around 420 BCE; daughter of Axiochus; mother unknown; most likely attended schools of the Sophists in Miletus and Athens; attended and engaged in philosophical disputations with Socrates; mistress of Pericles, c. 442 (died 429); mistress of Lysicles, 429 (died 428); children: (with Pericles) a son, Pericles (original name unknown); (with Lysicles) a son, Poristes (name uncertain).

In Aristophanes' comedy, *The Acharnians*, Dicaeopolis charges that the Peloponnesian War (431–404 BCE) was caused when some drunken Athenian, "going to Megara, stole a prostitute named Simaetha. Afterwards, the Megarians, raging mad, stole two of Aspasia's prostitutes in return. Whence the origin of the war upon all the Greeks: from the theft of three little wenches."

The charge is intended to be funny because it parodies the famous rape of Helen as the cause for the Trojan War. Also humorous to an Athenian audience was the lampooning of the most prominent woman in Athens and associating her with the lowest kind of prostitute. When seen for what it is, the quote il-

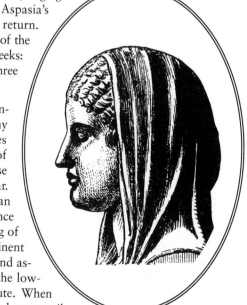

Aspasia of Miletus

lustrates many of the problems inherent in nearly all the sources we have for the life of Aspasia of Miletus.

Aspasia was born at Miletus (in modern Turkey) sometime during the second quarter of the fourth century BCE. Her mother's name is not known; her father was said to be Axiochus, but he is otherwise unknown. Her family probably belonged to a respectable social class; at least she seems to have been free born. She may have attended or had contact with the schools of the Sophists (philosophers who taught for a fee) in her native Miletus before she came to Athens in the mid-440s. We know nothing else about how she spent her early years in Miletus, why she went to Athens, or whether she went alone. There is an interesting, but unlikely, possibility that she traveled together with her famous fellow Milesian Hippodamus, who also arrived in Athens in the middle of the fifth century and became friends with Pericles, the most important man in Athens between 450 and 429.

Aspasia intrigued, fascinated, and scandalized her contemporaries in Athens. Respectable Athenian women rarely left the house except for religious occasions and public ceremonies. Nor did they mingle much with men inside the house. They oversaw slaves, cooked, spun wool, made clothes, and raised their children in separate women's quarters, which, in some houses, had no physical connection to the men's rooms. A wife did not accompany her husband to drinking parties given by his friends, nor did she customarily attend her husband's own. A respectable Athenian woman may have been able to read and write—and a well-to-do woman would certainly be read to—but she was not expected to engage in serious literary or philosophical study or to be able to debate political and philosophical topics with men. In Pericles' own words, Athenian women earned praise by keeping out of sight and not being talked about by men.

But Aspasia was different. Her own thinking may have been more like that of her fellow Sophist, Gorgias of Leontini: Women should have a good reputation outside their own house but not be seen outside it. Despite her own public appearances, when she gave advice, it seems, she suggested a fairly traditional role for women. It would have been hard for Aspasia herself, however, to have conformed to the traditional, praiseworthy role of a Greek married women, for Aspasia was an outsider. As an alien woman, she would have found it difficult to survive alone in male-dominated, ethnocentric Athens. She came to the notice of Pericles—the most powerful man in an ostensibly democratic Athens—shortly after her arrival, and then became his mistress, thus ensuring that she could live in the city. Pericles had divorced his unnamed wife sometime before, but he could not actually marry Aspasia because she was not an Athenian: an official marriage was recognized only between a man and a woman whose parents had been Athenian. Thus, Aspasia, who lived openly with Pericles, was considered a woman of easy virtue. She is referred to as the noblest sort of prostitute, a *hetaira*, or companion, who was expected to be literate, cultured, conversant with contemporary affairs, affable, musically talented, as well as a sexual partner. A *hetaira* was to be intellectually, and sexually, what a wife was not. Aspasia is also called a concubine, connoting a class that was not as cultured, and was expected to provide long-term companionship. She is said to have run a brothel of the lowest sort of prostitutes and to have imported many of the best sort to Athens.

It is hard to evaluate the accuracy of these labels and charges. The sources are clear that Pericles kissed her twice a day, once upon leaving the house in the morning, and once when returning in the afternoon. This was more than the average Greek man would do with his wife. She is also said to have been Socrates' teacher in the art of erotics. Aspasia appeared in public—unlike respectable Athenian women—and she accompanied Pericles to *symposia*. She was visited by Socrates and other philosophers and was included in their disputations. To a Greek male—and the authors of all our sources were men, most of them Greek—such behavior was clear proof that she was a prostitute. Even if she was not a prostitute, her actions and public appearances insured that Athenian rumor mills labeled her as one.

Aspasia's relationship with Pericles was an unusual one for a woman to have with an Athenian man: open, erotic, intellectual, and mutually respectful. The biographer Plutarch (45–125 CE), who provides much information about Aspasia, though he lived much later and did not fully understand all his sources, says Pericles respected Aspasia for her wisdom and political sense. It may be, as Wolfram Martini argues, that Greek values were changing in the time of Aspasia, and that emotional relationships between man and wife were more valued than they had been before. Nevertheless, when Aspasia is mentioned in sources roughly contemporary with her, she is often treated with irony, praised only to be damned in the end.

Aspasia is said to have been part of Socrates' circle. Socrates supposedly listened to her advice on matchmaking and on the qualities of a good wife. She is said to have taught him rhetoric and to have been the author of public funeral speeches, including the famous one delivered by Pericles in 431 BCE. It is difficult to know what to make of these assertions. Aspasia may well have known the Sophists' theories of rhetoric, but when Plato makes Socrates say in the *Menexenus* that he learned rhetoric from Aspasia, Plato is being ironic. Socrates claims that anyone can give a funeral oration over Athenians in Athens, even a woman. The irony is two fold, however: it is against Aspasia and also against Pericles. Neither Plato nor Socrates favored Pericles' politics; neither favored Pericles' democracy (which put Socrates to death); and neither thought highly of rhetoric. Aspasia was probably learned in rhetoric, but it is difficult to believe that the misogynistic Athenian men would have thought they could learn about rhetoric—public discourse—from a woman.

Aspasia owed part of her prominence in Athens to the fact that she was Pericles' mistress. This gave her visibility and some degree of status. Nevertheless, her relationship with him did not confer the honor and respect accorded to Athenian married women. Still, to later generations, who did not know the specific rules governing legitimate marriage at Athens, it could seem that Aspasia and Pericles were married. They did have a son, who must have been born between 445–440, yet due to Aspasia's status as a foreigner, the boy was not automatically allowed to become an Athenian citizen. He failed to qualify under Pericles' own citizenship law of 451–450, which specified that both parents had to be Athenian citizens.

Because of her association with Pericles, Aspasia was the subject of much abuse, aimed at harming Pericles as well. The opening quote from Aristophanes represents the type of attacks that could be made. In 431–430, she was prosecuted in court on a charge of sacrilege, which was a common accusation against the Sophists (and against Socrates). The sources treat the charge as an attack against Pericles, but suggest that Aspasia was known for her philosophic views. As a woman, she could not defend herself in court, so Pericles defended her—"with copious tears"—and secured her acquittal. Some sources charged that Pericles started the great Peloponnesian War by having a decree passed against the Megarians just to satisfy Aspasia (a slightly different version of what the comedic quote alleges), or to draw attention away from the political attacks that were being launched against him and his friends.

In 429, a plague devastated Athens. It took the lives of Pericles' two legitimate sons. At this time, the Athenian Assembly took pity on Pericles and, in an unprecedented move, voted to circumvent Pericles' own citizenship laws and allow his and Aspasia's son to be enrolled as a citizen. The son's name was changed to Pericles. Aspasia thus enjoyed the honor of having a son who was an Athenian citizen—an honor not shared by any other foreign woman at the time. Later, her son Pericles became a general. Unfortunately, he was one of the ten generals defeated in a naval battle at Arginusae in 406, and the Athenian Assembly tried him along with the other generals and condemned them all to death.

Approximately six months after Pericles saw his and Aspasia's son become a citizen, Pericles, too, died from the plague. Aspasia then lived with a popular leader (sometimes called a sheep-dealer) named Lysicles. One source claims that Lysicles' relationship with Aspasia was the reason he became the first man in Athens after Pericles' death. They had a son, whose name is given as Poristes, but that may also be a joke name, meaning "Moneymaker," a reference to the activities of Lysicles. Unfortunately, Lysicles died the next year and in 428 Aspasia was on her own again, this time with two young sons.

After 428 we do not know what happened to Aspasia. She may have been alive when Aristophanes mentioned her in the *Acharnians* (produced in 425), but we cannot say for sure. We do not know whether she saw her son Pericles become a general and be condemned. It is worth noting that her friend Socrates happened to be a president of the Assembly when the case against the generals was brought before it. He strenuously opposed the plan to try all the generals together and then put them all to death—an illegal process—but he could not save his friend's son. Aspasia died and was buried in Attica, in the region of Athens, and her grave site was famous in antiquity.

Aspasia has fascinated writers, artists, and philosophers from her own time to the present day. Perhaps the fragmentary and suggestive statements we have about her have made her all the more intriguing. As a result, she is one of the best known, and least typical, women of ancient Greece.

SOURCES (ORIGINAL):

Plato. *Menexenus.* Translated by R.G. Bury with accompanying Greek text, in *Plato.* Vol. VII. Cambridge,

Mass. & London: Harvard University Press & Heinemann, 1929.

Plutarch. *Life of Pericles.* Translated by B. Perrin with accompanying Greek text, in *Plutarch's Lives.* Vol. III. Cambridge, Mass. & London: Harvard University Press & Heinemann, 1916.

SOURCES (SECONDARY):

Coventry, Lucinda. "Philosophy and Rhetoric in the Menexenus," in *Journal of Hellenic Studies.* Vol. 109, 1989, pp. 1–15.

Halperin, David M. "Why is Diotima a Woman," in *One Hundred Years of Homosexuality.* London: Routledge, 1990, pp. 113–151.

Henry, Madeleine M. *Prisoner of History: Aspasia of Miletus and Her Biographical Tradition.* Oxford: Oxford University Press, 1995.

Martini, Wolfram. "Aspasia as Heroine and Lover: Images of Women in the High Classical Period," in *Apollo.* Vol. 140, July 1994, pp. 12–17.

SUGGESTED READING:

Pomeroy, Sarah B. *Goddesses, Whores, Wives, and Slaves.* NY: Shocken, 1975.

Women in the Classical World: Image and Text. Edited by Elaine Fantham, Helene Peet Foley, Natalie Boymel Kampen, Sarah B. Pomeroy, and H. Alan Shapiro. Oxford: Oxford University Press, 1994.

Robert W. Cape, Jr., Assistant Professor of Classics and Director of Gender Studies, Austin College, Sherman, Texas

Aspasia the Younger (fl. 415–370 BCE)

Greek concubine. Name variations: real name, according to Plutarch, was Milto; Aspasia the Wise. Flourished around 415–370 BCE; daughter of Hermotimus.

The fame of *Aspasia of Miletus was so widespread that her name became proverbial for the refined *hetaira.* The son of the Persian king and aspirant to the throne Cyrus the Younger (c. 423–401 BCE) named his favorite concubine Aspasia. Her original name may have been Milto, and her father's name is given as Hermotimus. She was born free and the sources say she was well educated. We do not know anything about her before she came to the court of Cyrus.

She is called Aspasia the Younger, but ancient tradition held that Cyrus called her "the Wise," for the following incident. Several girls were brought in to Cyrus at a party and they were assigned couches. As Cyrus flirted with the girls, they reciprocated—all, that is, except Aspasia. She refused to play Cyrus' game and when he came closer she is reported to have said, "whosoever lays his hands on me will surely regret it." All the others feared for the girl's life after making such a remark to the prince, but Cyrus was impressed and said she was the only one in the whole lot with a free spirit. He then made her his concubine, called her Aspasia in honor of Aspasia of Miletus, and she became his favorite.

Cyrus was murdered by his brother, Artaxerxes (c. 451–360 BCE), who became the king of Persia, in 401 and Aspasia the Younger, as spoils of war, became part of Artaxerxes' harem. She soon became his favorite as well. She seems to have had some degree of influence over Artaxerxes at the royal court, but we cannot tell how much or in what situations.

When Artaxerxes grew old, he perceived that two of his sons were organizing factions to support their claims to the throne. He decided to make his eldest son, Dareius, heir-apparent. According to Persian custom (as relayed by Plutarch), when an heir to the throne is named he is allowed to make one request of the king. Dareius asked to have Aspasia. Shocked, and somewhat angered, Artaxerxes decided to let Aspasia choose whether she wanted to go with Dareius or stay with him. She chose Dareius, which also angered the king. Nevertheless, Aspasia stayed with Dareius until Artaxerxes connived a devious plan to take her away by making her the priestess of the goddess Artemis, called "Anaitis," who was required to remain chaste for the rest of her life. That way Artaxerxes could still honor Aspasia and at the same time legitimately separate her from his son. But it seems that Aspasia did not feel honored, and she longed to return to Dareius.

Dareius was incensed at losing Aspasia and entered a conspiracy to murder his father, but it failed and he was discovered. Dareius was tried, found guilty, and executed. Nothing more is heard of Aspasia. She was probably around 60 years old and could have died shortly after Dareius. As with many women from ancient Greece, Aspasia the Wise slips silently from the historical record.

SOURCES:

Plutarch. *Life of Artaxerxes.* Translated J.W. Cohoon with accompanying Greek text, in *Plutarch's Lives.* Vol. XI. Cambridge, MA: Harvard University Press, 1926.

Robert W. Cape, Jr., Assistant Professor of Classics and Director of Gender Studies, Austin College, Sherman, Texas

Asquith, Cynthia (1887–1960)

British author best known for her diary of the First World War years, which was published posthumously. Born Cynthia Mary Evelyn Charteris in Wiltshire, England, in 1887; died in 1960; daughter and one of seven children of Hugo (Lord Elcho, 11th earl of Wemyss) and Mary (Wyndham) Charteris; married Herbert Asquith (second son of Prime Minister Herbert Henry Asquith and first wife Helen Melland), in 1910; children: John (b. 1911); Michael (b. 1914); Simon (b. 1919).

Like many aristocratic, well-educated British women of her era, Lady Cynthia Asquith found an outlet in writing. After World War I put an end to her husband's career as a lawyer, her talent supplemented the family income. Asquith authored autobiographies, biographies, novels, children's stories, a play, and diaries of the war years (1915–18), which she undertook to appease a friend who had presented her with her first handsomely bound blank volume. Kept under lock and key until the end of her life, these works were passed on to her children, who published them posthumously in 1968.

The third of seven children born to Lord Elcho, later the 11th earl of Wemyss, Asquith grew up in the large family home—Stanway House—near Cheltenham in Gloucestershire. In the tradition of the day, she was educated at home by tutors, a process she called "a most haphazard, happy-go-lucky affaire." After a girlhood spent alternately amid the social whirl of her parents and of her own famous and near famous young contemporaries, in 1910 she married Herbert ("Beb") Asquith, the poet son of Prime Minister Herbert Henry Asquith, who was beginning a career as an attorney. In 1914, Beb enlisted in the Royal Field Artillery, leaving Asquith and her two young sons (a third son was born in 1919) to take up the practice of "cuckooning" (a term she came up with for flitting from home to home of her friends while her own town house, which she was not wealthy enough to maintain, was leased out).

During the war, with Beb away for long periods recovering from wounds and shell shock, Asquith did some volunteer hospital work while maintaining a social life that included a number of male admirers. D.H. Lawrence, whose letters to her are considered some of his finest, called Asquith a "Pre-Raphaelite 'dreaming woman,'" and supposedly patterned his character of Lady Chatterley after her. After the war, Asquith became secretary to playwright James M. Barrie, author of *Peter Pan*, a position she held for 20 years. (She later wrote his biography, *Portrait of J.M. Barrie*.)

Asquith has been praised for her easy, informal style and is regarded as a valuable chronicler of the "lost, gracious world" which would perish in the First World War. Much in the style of *Margot Asquith (Beb's stepmother; second wife of Herbert Asquith), Cynthia's reminiscences provide colorful portraits of the well-known personalities that wandered through her life: Arthur Balfour, Charles Whibley, H.G. Wells, and *Clementine Churchill. An entire chapter in her

Cynthia Asquith

first autobiography, *Haply I May Remember*, is devoted to the string of popular painters who were eager to translate her beauty to the canvas: Edward Burne-Jones, Augustus John, Charles Furse, John Sargent, and Ambrose McEvoy.

Asquith withstood a nagging concern over her eldest son John, who, though precociously talented musically, was probably suffering from autism, an undiagnosed condition at that time. Her diaries reveal her slow realization that he would never get well and her anguished search for proper care for him. His death in 1937 was followed by the death of her brothers in World War II.

Cynthia Asquith died in 1960, shortly after finishing work on her last biography *Married to Tolstoy*, an account of the intense, tempestuous 48-year union between Leo and *Sonya Tolstoy, based on four obscure diaries.

SOURCES:
Asquith, Cynthia. *Haply I May Remember*. NY: Scribner, 1950.

————. *Remember and be Glad.* NY: Scribner, 1952.

Asquith, Lady Cynthia. *Diaries 1915–1918.* NY: Alfred A. Knopf, 1969.

Blodgett, Harriet, ed. *The Englishwoman's Diary.* London: Fourth Estate, 1992.

This England. Summer 1988, p. 75.

SUGGESTED READING:

Asquith, Cynthia. *Her Majesty, The Queen.* NY: E.P. Dutton, 1937.

————. *Portrait of Barrie.* Westport, CT: Greenwood Press, 1971.

Beauman, Nicola. *Cynthia Asquith.* London: Hamish Hamilton, 1988.

Barbara Morgan, Melrose, Massachusetts

Asquith, Lady (1887–1969).

See Bonham-Carter, Violet.

Asquith, Margot Tennant
(1864–1945)

British writer and political personality. Born Margaret Emma Alice Tennant in Peebleshire, Scotland, in 1864; died on July 28, 1945, in London, England; sixth daughter and one of 12 children of Sir Charles (an industrialist) and Emma (Winsloe) Tennant; married Herbert Henry Asquith, on May 10, 1894; children: (five) only two, Anthony (1902—) and Elizabeth Bibesco (1897–1943), survived infancy; (five stepchildren) Raymond (1878–1916); Herbert (1881–1947); Arthur (1883–1939); Cyril (1890–1954); Violet Bonham-Carter (1887–1969) also known as Lady Asquith of Yarnbury.

Margot Tennant Asquith, daughter of wealthy industrialist Charles Tennant, grew up in a castle on the Scottish moors, 30 miles from Edinburgh. Calling herself "a child of the heather and quite untamable," Asquith received a haphazard education. She had governesses until the age of 15, then spent a few months at a London finishing school and later studied in Dresden, Germany. In her privileged and self-proclaimed "glorious" youth, the only unhappy memories were violent quarrels with her 12 siblings.

Asquith was a fashionable debutante and fearless hunter; her life before her marriage at age 30 revolved around affairs of the heart and an endless social whirl of entertainment. To the wealthy and bored Victorian elite, of which she was a part, Asquith brought an enthusiasm for life and an element of the unexpected. More interesting looking than beautiful, with a slight frame and what was once described as a "hawky" nose, her keen intellect and magnetic personality attracted a vast circle of smart and influential friends, including Benjamin Jowett, vice-chancellor of Oxford, and prime minister William Gladstone, as well as writers John Addington, John Symonds, and ***Virginia Woolf**. Asquith was a member of The Souls, a group of aesthetes who, in addition to intellectual and literary pursuits, advocated greater freedom for women, particularly in self-expression and dress.

Her marriage in 1894 to the Liberal home secretary, Herbert Henry Asquith, caused quite a stir in London society. A widower with five children, whose first wife **Helen Melland** had died in 1891, Herbert was not fashionable or wealthy, "played no games and cared for no sport." A man of unerring instincts and profound modesty, he went on to a distinguished political career, becoming chancellor of the exchequer in 1906 and prime minister in 1908. Forced to resign in 1916 because of dissatisfaction with the nation's war record, Herbert remained Liberal leader until 1926. Asquith blossomed as a brilliant and witty political hostess,

Margot Asquith

but it was more the people—she had a self-professed weakness for great men—than ideas or issues that caught her attention. Although inclusion in the "Margot set" became a mark of distinction, her flamboyant behavior and caustic tongue often caused hostility.

Her newly acquired stepchildren, including *Violet Bonham-Carter, ranged in age from four to fifteen, and kept Asquith in a state somewhere between total frustration and complete awe. "Skeletons with brains," she called them and complained that they lacked temperament and overvalued intelligence. "They rarely looked at you, and never got up when anyone came into the room." They also slept well, which Asquith, a light sleeper herself, likened to something close to sin. The children were equally ambivalent about their new mother. One of them said later, "She filled us with admiration, amazement, amusement, affection, sometimes even with a vague sense of uneasiness as to what she might, or might not, do next." Asquith also had five children of her own, but only two, Anthony and Elizabeth, survived infancy. Anguish over the losses stayed with her throughout life.

Despite her limited formal education, Asquith was an avid reader and a prolific writer, keeping diaries from an early age, and actively corresponding by letter. The first of her two-volume autobiography, published in 1920 when she was 56 years old, was greeted with considerable embarrassment from her family and friends, and shock and condemnation from the critics. Despite its lively account of English history from the waning days of Victoria to the beginning of the Edwardian age, its instant popularity was due mainly to its indiscretions and revelations about English politics and society. *The Times* attacked it as a "scandal which cannot be justified or excused." A critique in the *Spectator* was indicative of general reaction. "The publication could only be justified had the book been by a dead woman about dead men and women." Subsequently, Asquith authored several less controversial books: one on travel, *Places and Persons* (1925), essays entitled *Lay Sermons* (1927), a biographical novel, *Octavia* (1928), and two additional books of reminiscence.

Later in life, when the flap over her autobiography had died down and her husband was no longer in political office, the Asquith house in Sutton Courtenay in the Thames valley was still the weekend destination of a host of incongruous people. After dinner conversations were seemingly endless and sometimes resembled shouting matches. Desmond MacCarthy likened one Sunday afternoon luncheon to a wild game of pool. "One is trying to send a remark into the top corner pocket . . . where at the same moment another player is attempting a close-up shot at his own end: while anecdotes and comments whizz backwards and forwards, cannoning and clashing as they cross the table."

Often communicating with guests by scribbled notes delivered from her bedroom by a footman, Asquith engaged them in killer games of bridge and less strenuous golf outings. There was always time reserved for joyous romps with her grandchildren, when she would regale them with terrifying ghost stories.

Asquith's grandson, Mark Bonham Carter, in his introduction to an edited edition of her autobiography, finds it difficult to fully capture his grandmother's personality, and admits that even her own book fails to bring out her intensely human qualities and endearing virtues: "a simple but deep religious faith; complete physical and social courage; a surprising clear-sightedness about herself and others; generosity/zest and vitality to an unusual degree; candor and honesty to a supreme degree; and a warmth of heart which included all those close to her or connected with her and the young in particular."

Margot Asquith spent the last years of her life in London's Savoy Hotel, saddened by war and the death of her daughter ❧▶ Elizabeth Bibesco in 1943. Asquith continued to attract new friends up to her death in 1945, at the age of 81.

SOURCES:

Carter, Mark Bonham, ed. *The Autobiography of Margot Asquith*. Cambridge, MA: The Riverside Press, 1962.

Barbara Morgan,
Melrose, Massachusetts

❧▶ Bibesco, Elizabeth (1897–1943)

*English writer. Name variations: Princess Bibesco. Born Elizabeth Asquith in 1897; died in 1943; daughter of Herbert Henry Asquith (1852–1928, later earl of Oxford and Asquith) and *Margot (Tennant) Asquith; stepsister of *Violet Bonham-Carter (1887–1969); married Prince Antoine Bibesco, in 1919.*

Elizabeth Bibesco wrote *I Have Only Myself to Blame* (1921), *Balloons* (1923), *There is No Return* (1927), *Portrait of Caroline* (1931).

Asquith of Yarnbury, Baroness
(1887–1969).

See Bonham-Carter, Violet.

Assandra, Caterina (fl. 1580–1609)

Italian composer. Name variations: Catterina Alessandra. Born in Pavia between 1580 and 1609; sometimes confused with another composer of this name who appeared in 1772; studied with Benedetto Re.

Although Caterina Assandra's reputation spread beyond the borders of Italy as a composer, she is sometimes confused with another 18th-century composer of the same name. To compound the matter, the date of her birth is approximate, the date of her death unknown. We know, however, that she became a nun in the cloister of Sant' Agata in Lomello near Pavia. During the first half of the 17th century, she composed many works, including *Siren colestis* and *Promptuarium musicum*. Like a number of Northern Italian composers of the period, she published motets for a few voices and organ continuo in the new concertato style.

John Haag,
Athens, Georgia

Assing, Ludmilla (1821–1880).
See Ney, Elisabeth for sidebar.

Assisi, Clara d' (c. 1194–1253).
See Clare of Assisi.

Astafieva, Serafima (1876–1934)

*Russian dancer and teacher. Name variations: Serafina or Serafine. Born in Russia in 1876; died in 1934; graduated from the St. Petersburg Imperial School of Ballet in 1895; married Joseph Kchessinksy-Nechui (older brother of ballerina *Matilda Kshesinskaia), in 1896 (divorced 1905).*

The career of Serafima Astafieva began in the corps de ballet of the Maryinsky Theater. Following her divorce in 1905, she resigned from the theater, and, from 1909–11, was a member of Diaghilev's Ballets Russes. She then opened a ballet school in London where *Alicia Markova and Anton Dolin, among others, trained. Another pupil of Astafieva's was *Margot Fonteyn.

Astaire, Adele (1898–1981)

American dancer and actress. Born Adele Austerlitz in Omaha, Nebraska, on September 10, 1898; died in 1981; daughter of Ann (Geilus) and Frederick E. Austerlitz (a traveling salesman); older sister of Fred Astaire; married Lord Charles Cavendish, in 1932 (died 1944); married Kingman Douglass (a Wall Street investment broker); children: (first marriage) three (all died shortly after their birth).

One half of the most famous brother-and-sister act in the history of Broadway, Adele Astaire was two years older than her brother Fred. When she was three, her mother enrolled her in dancing school in Omaha, while her brother tagged along. Determined that her children be theatrical stars, Ann Austerlitz took them to New York when Adele was eight to study at the Ned Wayburn School of Dance (Wayburn is said to be the originator of modern tap dancing) and at the Metropolitan Ballet School. Between 1906 and 1916, the brother-and-sister dance team toured the United States on the Orpheum and Keith vaudeville circuits. Between stops, they attended school in Weehawken, New Jersey, and their mother served as tutor, agent, and promoter.

Their Broadway debut came in 1917 in Sigmund Romberg's *Over the Top*, with which they subsequently toured. But it was not until the following year that they had their first major success in *The Passing Show of 1918*, which starred Frank Fay, Charles Ruggles, and *Nita Naldi. From that time on, the Astaires' billing could be found on the marquee. In 1919, Adele appeared as Molly in Fritz Kreisler's *Apple Blossoms*, and, in 1921, as Aline Moray in *Love Letter*. Since the Astaires had not had a speaking part to this point, critics took a cue from their stage name and determined they were French.

Their duets were comedic rather than romantic, "and of that act," wrote Sheridan Morley, "Adele was very much the star." In 1922, they danced their way through two shows: *The Bunch and Judy* and Alex Aaron's *For Goodness Sake*, which had been written especially for them. When they opened the latter in London retitled *Stop Flirting*, they became instant luminaries of the British stage. Gushed the London *Times:* "Columbus may have danced with joy at discovering America, but how he would have cavorted had he also discovered Fred and Adele Astaire!" In 1924, they performed in George Gershwin's hit *Lady Be Good*, dancing to the tunes of "Fascinating Rhythm," "So Am I," and "Oh, Lady, Be Good." Once again, they reprised their roles in London in 1926. Gershwin's *Funny Face* followed on Broadway in 1927 (London 1928), during which the Astaires performed their celebrated "run-around" dance. Their first flop came with Ziegfeld's *Smiles* (also starring *Marilyn Miller) in 1930.

Adele Astaire, with brother Fred.

During one of their London forays, Adele had met England's Lord Charles Cavendish, second son of the duke of Devonshire. Resolved not to marry until after a hit, she waited until their 1931 success, *The Band Wagon*, before marrying Cavendish in 1932. It was the dance duo's final season together. Despite frequent entreaties to team up with her brother once more, Adele went into a determined retirement. Fred was equally determined: he never set foot on another stage without her; the rest of his career was played out on the soundstages of Hollywood.

Following the death of her husband in 1944 and the infant deaths of all three of her children, Adele Astaire returned to America and remarried. She lived the rest of her life in Manhattan, where she continued to avoid show business and the prying eyes of the press. Brother and sister can be seen on celluloid in only one film: *Mary Pickford's *Fanchon the Cricket* (1915).

SOURCES:

Lamparski, Richard. *Whatever Became of . . . ? 1st and 2nd Series.* NY: Crown, 1967.

Morley, Sheridan. *The Great Stage Stars.* London: Angus & Robertson, 1986.

Astakhova, Polina (1936—)

Ukrainian gymnast. Born on October 30, 1936; grew up in the Ukraine.

Won Olympic gold medal on uneven bars (1960, 1964), silver medals on floor exercise (1960, 1964), bronze medals in the all-around (1960, 1964), and team gold (1956, 1960, 1964), all while representing the Soviet Union.

Though she had to compete in the imposing shadows of *Larissa Latynina and *Vera Caslavska in three Olympic Games, the talented gymnast Polina Astakhova took five gold, two silver, and three bronze medals. In Melbourne in 1956, Astakhova received an all-around bronze for the portable apparatus and a team all-around gold. In Rome in 1960, she took a bronze in the all-around, a silver in the floor exercises, a gold in team all-around, and a gold on the uneven parallel bars. In Tokyo in 1964, she won a bronze in the all-around, a silver in the floor exercises, a gold in the team all-around, and a gold in the uneven parallel bars.

Astell, Mary (1666–1731)

English writer of feminist, political, and religious works that addressed some of the most controversial issues of her time, including the education of women, the institution of marriage, and the role of God in everyday life. Name variations: Madonella. Pronunciation: as-TELL. Born Mary Astell on November 12, 1666, in Newcastle-upon-Tyne, England; died in London on May 9, 1731, from breast cancer; daughter of Peter (a coal merchant) and Mary (Errington) Astell; no formal education, but was tutored for a few years by her father's older brother Ralph; never married; no children.

Probably had a conventional middle-class upbringing for girls of that period, though the death of her father when she was 12 left the financial stability of the family threatened; moved to London to live on her own (mid-1680s); came to attention of archbishop of Canterbury (1689); published first work (1694); active as a writer until 1709, when she helped to establish a school for girls and became headmistress; some of her works reissued (1722 and 1730).

Selected publications: A Serious Proposal to the Ladies, For the Advancement of Their True and Greatest Interest *(1694);* Letters Concerning the Love of God *(1695);* A Serious Proposal To The Ladies, Part II, Wherein a Method is Offer'd for the Improvement of Their Minds *(1697);* Some Reflections upon Marriage *(1700);* Moderation Truly Stated *(1704);* A Fair Way with Dissenters and Their Patrons *(1704);* An Impartial Enquiry into the Late Causes of Rebellion and Civil War *(1704);* The Christian Religion as Profess'd by a Daughter of the Church *(1705);* Bart'lemy Fair: or, An Inquiry after Wit *(1709).*

Why educate women? This question, simple as it sounds, provoked many different answers in England throughout the 17th and 18th centuries. Mary Astell's response was unique: rather than force women to be slaves to morally corrupt men, educate women so that they can serve and love God. To her, the idea seemed absolutely reasonable, and her confidence in her vision never wavered. With one eye looking forward and the other looking back to a time when devotion to divine rule, whether by God or King, had been more fashionable, Mary Astell wrote a small but influential body of works that represent a curious mixture of conservative religious and political thought and feminist social policy. That her voice entered into significant debates taking place in England in the late 17th and early 18th centuries is a remarkable testament to her fortitude, good fortune, and faith. By the end of the 18th century, when the British feminist movement was ushered in by *Mary Wollstonecraft and others, much of what they championed, although they did not acknowledge it *per se*, was built upon a foundation that Astell had helped create. More than anything, her contribution was that she regarded the development of women's minds as a serious moral and political issue.

The family of Astell would qualify as middle-class gentry. At the time of her birth, Newcastle-upon-Tyne was one of England's most important regional cities, at the center of the growing coal industry. The area presented many opportunities for its citizens to prosper, especially boys and grown men, who could take advantage of its schools, apprentice positions, and thriving markets. Peter Astell, like his father before him, was involved in the business of selling, weighing, delivering, and collecting revenues for Newcastle coal; both were members of the guild of the Hostmen, which controlled the coal market. Mary Astell's mother, also named Mary, was born into a moderately wealthy Catholic family from Newcastle, but her children were raised as devout Anglicans, which was by then the state religion of England. When Peter died in 1678, he left an estate worth over £500, which was enough to indicate his success in business, but his survivors, including his wife, two children, and an older unmarried sister, required some charity from the guild. The aunt must have had a significant role in Mary Astell's childhood; Astell's modern biographer, **Ruth Perry**, reports that the aunt died in 1684, and the mother died in 1695.

In addition to her father, two other male figures were of great importance in Astell's youth. One was her uncle Ralph, who served as her tutor. Her writings demonstrate that although he died when Mary was just 13 years old, he left his intellectual stamp on her. A graduate of Oxford University and a published poet, Ralph Astell had been influenced by the school of philosophy known as Cambridge Platonism and instructed his niece in its principal tenet, which was the use of one's reason to establish a relationship with God. Clearly Ralph Astell also taught his young charge literature, especially English poetry, for Abraham Cowley, who was one of his favorite poets, became the poet imitated by his niece in her adolescent writings. Ralph and Peter Astell had both been supporters of the royalist cause during the English Civil War, and Ralph's one extant publication is a 16-page poem that celebrates the restoration of the monarchy. Ralph Astell was trained to be an Anglican curate, but he seems to have been dismissed from his post because of a drinking problem. Another significant male figure in Astell's life, if only as a point of comparison, was her brother Peter, two years her junior. As a male, he could go to school and was eligible for an apprenticeship to a lawyer, and in this profession he was successful enough to pay off all the family debts before 1695. For Mary Astell, however, there was no school in Newcastle that admitted females, nor was there a respectable profession open to her that offered her economic independence; the destiny of most girls was confined to marriage. The writings of Mary Astell suggest that she yearned for the freedom and opportunities her brother had at his disposal.

Indeed, the poems of Astell's teenage years make clear her ambition, her creative energy, and her search for faith and identity. If she had not struggled as she did to create herself, no one could have invented her. As a writer, her voice was clear and unmistakable. Often angry and sarcastic, sometimes reflective, but always direct, her prose is different from that of every other woman writer of her time. She seems to have discovered her voice early. We can find it in her poetry, in which she somewhat defiantly represents her own struggles, especially those caused by her intellect and her femaleness. In "Solitude," a poem written in 1684, a few months before her 18th birthday, her opening stanza demonstrates that she does not hesitate to place herself in opposition to the social mores of the time.

> Now I with gen'rous Cowley see,
> This trifling World and I shall ne're agree.
> Nature in business me no share affords,
> And I no business find in empty words:
> I dare not all the morning spend
> To dress my body, and not lend
> A minuit to my Soul, nor can think fit,
> To sell the Jewel for the Cabinet.

Many of Astell's poems also show the importance of God and faith in her life. She clearly believed that if she loved God, God would not love her the less because she was a female. "No, to its native place my Soul aspires,/ And something more than Earth desires/ Heav'n only can its vast Ambition fill,/ And Heav'n alone must exercise my mind and quill."

While her poetry is not outstanding in a technical sense, it is well to remember how young she was when she wrote it, and applaud its sheer competency in terms of form and content. More than anything perhaps, Astell's poetry demonstrates her struggle at this stage of life to find a balance between her ambitions and her lack of opportunity, her need for companionship, and her disdain for both men and women who felt more comfortable in a social arena. Her poem "In Emulation of Mr. Cowley's Poem Call'd the Motto," written when she was 21, contains her best answer, described in the last three stanzas, to the problems created by her sense of self:

> Nature permits not me the common way,
> By serving Court, or State, to gain
> That so much valu'd trifle, Fame;
> Nor do I covet in Wit's Realm to sway:
> But O ye bright illustrious few,
> What shall I do to be like some of you?
> Whom this misjudging World [does] underprize,
> Yet are most dear in Heav'ns all-righteous eyes!
>
> How shall I be a Peter or a Paul?
> That to the Turk and Infidel,
> I might the joyfull tydings tell,
> And spare no labour to convert them all:
> But ah my sex denies me this,
> And Mary's Priviledge I cannot wish;

Yet hard I hear my dearest Saviour say,
They are more blessed who his Word obey.

Up then my sluggard Soul, Labour and Pray,
For if with Love enflam'd thou be,
Thy Jesus will be born in thee,
And by thy ardent Prayers thou canist[?] make way,
For their Conversion whom thou mayst not teach,
Yet by a good Example always Preach:
And tho' I want a Persecuting Fire,
I'll be at lest a Martyr in desire.

Makin, Bathsua.
See Aphra Behn
for sidebar.

When she was about 20, Astell moved to London to live, a bold and unusual act for a young woman of her social class. She settled in the Chelsea area, then a semi-rural western suburb of London known for its tolerance of respectable single women on their own. Her first years in London must have been difficult, both emotionally and economically. Throughout the late 17th and 18th centuries, it was a common practice for authors to dedicate their works to prominent men and women in the hope that the honored figure would become their patron, or at least give them money, and when Astell presented a manuscript collection of her poems to William Sancroft, archbishop of Canterbury, she thanked him in the dedication for receiving the work of "a poor unknown, who hath no place to fly unto, and none that careth for her soul, when even my kinsfolk had failed, and my familiar friends had forgotten me." The fact that her work was not dedicated to an aristocratic or rich woman highly regarded in the London social scene suggests both that she clung steadfastly to the sentiments expressed in her poetry, and that since her arrival in London she had not yet been able to form the network of friendships with influential women she would have later in life. Astell must have hoped that Sancroft, as the leader of England's state religion, could offer her the recognition and protection of the Church that she devoutly believed in. Also there was the notion, always in Astell's mind, that her relationship with God was the most important one in her life, leading naturally to the conclusion that ideas such as the thoughts expressed in her poetry, given to her by God, should in turn be given to the chief representative of his church. Perry believes that Sancroft did respond positively to Astell, perhaps by arranging an introduction to Richard Wilkin, the publisher of religious books who brought all of her works into print.

Astell's first published work, in 1694, entitled *A Serious Proposal To The Ladies,* presents the same enthusiastic devotion to God expressed in her poetry, albeit in a way that is less self-con-scious than socially conscious. One logical and yet radical decision was to address it specifically "to the Ladies." Readers might have been shocked, since authors of other 17th-century works advocating the education of women (and there were several) addressed their proposals to male readers. Indeed, **Bathsua Makin**, in *An Essay to Revive the Antient Education of Gentlewomen* (1673), not only directed her remarks to her male readers but adopted a male persona for herself. "I am a Man my self, that would not suggest a thing prejudicial to our Sex." Female authors often used such a strategy in order to reassure their male audience that what they were proposing would not threaten the male prerogative, demonstrating their presumption that the majority of their readers would be men. Mary Astell, however, did not believe at all in playing to the male audience. In fact, she did nothing to hide the fact that a female was author of the work, announcing on the title page that it was written by a "Lover of her Sex." It might be said that through her use of the pronouns "we" and "us" she tried to appeal to the women directly by means of her femaleness, as well as to persuade or counsel them that they would be better Christians if they followed her lead: "Let us learn to pride our selves in something more excellent than the invention of a Fashion, and not entertain such a degrading thought of our own worth, as to imagine that our Souls were given us only for the service of our Bodies, and that the best we can make of these, is to attract the Eyes of Men." Although Astell published the work anonymously, her authorship was well known to London readers.

Astell's book was stylistically uncommon, also, in the informality of its language and its direct and insistent tone. In urging her female readers to read the entire book and to consider the seriousness of her proposal, she maintained, "This is a Matter infinitely more worthy your Debates, than what Colours are most agreeable, or what's the Dress become you best. Your *Glass* [mirror] will not do you half so much service as a serious reflection on your own Minds, which will discover Irregularities more worthy your Correction, and keep you from being either too much elated or depress'd by the Representations of the other."

The proposal she strongly advocated was the establishment of a female "*Monastery,* or if you will . . . we will call it a *Religious Retirement,*" which would allow women "to attend the great business they came into the world about, the service of GOD and improvement of their own Minds, [where they] may find a convenient and blissful recess from the noise and hurry of the world." The suggestion aroused controversy partly because use of the word *monastery* invoked both an institution and an idea embraced by the Catholic Church, the "enemy" church to the Church of England. Astell offered a vague program of study in her book, which should have reassured the English Anglicans that such female academies would not be seedbeds of Catholic thought; it did not, however. The simple lifestyle the women would lead also worried the readership. In their minds, Astell's description paints the picture of nun-like women who dress simply, wear no make-up or perfume, eat no meat, and pass their time in study, prayer, listening to music, and teaching.

Astell believed that a female monastery could benefit English society as a whole as well as offer a respectable and useful refuge for those young women, particularly the daughters of the more wealthy families, who might not want to marry or might simply want the opportunity to develop their minds before marriage.

> [H]ere Heiresses and Persons of Fortune may be kept secure from the rude attempts of designing Men; And she who has more Money than Discretion need not curse her Stars for being expos'd a prey to bold importunate and rapacious Vultures. She will not here be inveigled and impos'd on, will neither be bought nor sold, nor be forc'd to marry for her own quiet, when she has no inclination to it, but what the being tir'd out with a restless importunity occasions. Or if she be dispos'd to marry, here she may remain in safety till a convenient Match be offer'd by her Friends, and be freed from the danger of a dishonourable one.

In an age when the daughters of the rich were often victimized by marriages arranged by their parents for economic or political reasons, Astell's alternative would have given women a choice about their futures. The proposal must have been colored by Astell's own history, since such an option when she was a young woman in Newcastle would surely have led to a far different life.

Mary Astell's next book took the form of a correspondence, exchanged with the Reverend John Norris, who was author of a number of important books of philosophy and one of England's most important Cambridge Platonists, whose writings showed the influence of the contemporary French philosopher Nicolas Malebranche. Simply stated, Norris believed that only God could create the pleasures that human beings can experience, that truth is created by God, that human beings should love God, and that God should be the object of all knowledge. The central importance of God in his philosophy made Norris an attractive thinker to Astell, as she too believed that human beings should direct all their energies, intellectual and otherwise, toward God. Astell seems to have initiated the correspondence with Norris, but he arranged for the publication of their letters, partly because he was so surprised that a woman could engage him in such a lengthy and intellectually challenging exchange. His attitude is explained in the preface:

> The Letters hereialid open to thy View are a late Correspondence between my self and a Gentlewoman, and to add to thy Wonder, a young Gentlewoman. Her Name I have not the Liberty to publish. For her Person, as her Modesty will not suffer me to say much of her, so the present Productions of her Pen make it utterly needless to say any thing, unless it be by way of Prevention to obviate a Diffidence in some who from the surprizing Excellency of these Writings may be tempted to question whether my Correspondent be really a Woman or no.

There are 13 letters in all, with the last two serving as a review of the correspondence. All were written between September 1693 and September 1694, which makes the work contemporaneous with Astell's *A Serious Proposal to the Ladies,* but the boldness of *A Serious Proposal* is not evident in this correspondence. In the first letter, we see a more reflective and less accusatory author, although the assertion of her female self is still very pronounced:

> Though some morose Gentlemen wou'd perhaps remit me to the Distaff or the Kitchin, or at least to the Glass and the needle, the proper Employments as they fancy of a Woman's Life; yet expecting better things from the more Equitable and Ingenious Mr. Norris, who is not so narrow-Soul'd as to confine Learning to his own Sex, or to envy it in ours, I presume to beg his Attention a little to the Impertinencies of a Woman's Pen.

While Astell clearly regards Norris as the teacher in their relationship, this did not prevent her from offering a slight corrective to his belief that God creates all the pleasures human beings can feel. She even extends Norris' argument a bit further, saying that God must also be the creator of pain, and that humans should thank God for pain and learn the lesson that must be the reason for it. The volume presents an honest and rigorous intellectual exchange in which the correspondents agree far more than they amend or disagree.

In 1697, Astell offered a second part to her earlier *A Serious Proposal.* Titled *A Serious Proposal to the Ladies, Part II: Wherein a Method is Offer'd for the Improvement of their Minds,* it reveals the author's frustration that her earlier proposal had not yet been put into practice.

> It is not enough to wish and to would it, or t'afford a faint Encomium upon what you pretend is beyond your Power; Imitation is the heartiest Praise you can give, and is a Debt whose Justice requires to be paid to every worthy Action. What Sentiments were fit to be rais'd in you to day ought to remain to morrow, and the best Commendation you can bestow on a Book is immediately to put it in Practice. . . . If you *approve,* Why don't you follow? And if you *Wish,* Why shou'd you not *Endeavour?*

This work, much longer than its predecessor, is divided into four sections. In them, she discusses the relationship between ignorance and vice and knowledge and purity; how women might cleanse themselves of some of their bad qualities; how a (female) mind should be developed and put to use; and how a woman should govern her will and her passions. The prose is as lively as the earlier part, although it loses some of its rhetorical flair as Astell works to explain the principles and theories of her proposal in greater detail.

What is most clearly expressed in this part is the essentially religious (as opposed to purely feminist) vision that guided Astell's thinking and being. It was her hope that her proposals would promote a lifestyle for women that would give them a chance for equality before and with God more than it did equality with men in a political or social sense.

> For it is to little purpose to Think well and speak well, unless we *Live well,* this is our Great Affair and truest Excellency, the other are no further to be regarded than as they may assist us in this. She who does not draw this Inference from her Studies has Thought in vain, her notions are Erroneous and Mistaken. And all her Eloquence is but an empty noise, who employs it in any other design than in gaining Proselytes to Heaven.

A Serious Proposal touched a chord in late 17th-century English society and became Astell's most popular work, published in five editions by 1701. The work that followed it, *Some Reflections upon Marriage* (1700), was similarly controversial. Prompted by the social debate then raging about the life history of the recently deceased *Hortense Mancini, duchess of Mazarin, Astell and other London literary figures used the unorthodox marriage of the French noblewoman as a point of departure for discussions of legal and moral authority within the institution of marriage. At the center of the controversy was the fact that the duchess, as a young woman, had abandoned her husband, the duke of Mazarin, because of his religious fanaticism, sexual perver-

sions, jealousy, and a tendency to spend her considerable family fortune. When she was ordered by a French court to return to her husband and submit to his authority, she escaped to England. Charles II, king of England, who knew the duchess from the days of his own exile in Paris, awarded her a large pension, which allowed her to lead a fast-paced, eccentric, and debauched life that rivaled the conduct of some of the most famous male courtiers of the time.

While Astell's conservative outlook could not allow her to agree with those who said the duchess had a right to leave her marriage, she wrote in sympathy of the duchess' plight.

> To be yok'd for Life to a disagreeable Person and Temper; to have Folly and Ignorance tyrannize over Wit and Sense; to be contradicted in every thing one does or says, and bore down not by Reason but Authority; to be denied one's most innocent desires, for no other cause but the Will and Pleasure of an absolute Lord and Master, whose Follies a Woman with all her Prudence cannot hide, and whose Commands she cannot but despise at the same time she obeys them; is a misery none can have a just Idea of, but those who have felt it. . . . But Madam *Mazarin* is dead, may her Faults die with her; may there be no more occasion given for the like Adventures, or if there is, may the Ladies be more Wise than Good than to take it!

Astell saw the problem as one relating to the moral weakness of human beings rather than the institution of marriage itself. For Astell, the ideal of marriage was created by God, and therefore beyond reproach or human correction; but marriage as it existed in her society was not a representation of God's vision so much as a manifestation of how frail human beings could misuse and abuse the power and the practices of the institution.

Although women were not blameless, Astell found the greatest fault with men because they were the ones who gave a higher priority to financial concerns than to the potential for friendship between spouses:

> But if Marriage be such a blessed State, how comes it, may you say, that there are so few happy Marriages? Now in answer to this, it is not to be wonder'd that so few succeed, we should rather be surpriz'd to find so many do, considering how imprudently Men engage, the Motives they act by, and the very strange Conduct they observe throughout. For pray, what do Men propose to themselves in Marriage? What Qualifications do they look after in a Spouse? What will she bring is the first enquiry? How many Acres? Or how much ready Coin?

In Astell's mind, friendship should be the "chief inducement" to the choice of spouse because "we can never grow weary of our Friends; the longer we have had them the more they are endear'd to us." For her time period, Astell's view was idealistic and somewhat unrealistic, especially in regard to upper-middle-class and aristocratic marriages. But friendship between spouses gained in social value throughout the century as many who entered into the institution began to write about it.

For Astell, her views of governance and obedience within marriage mirrored her views on how society at large should be governed and who should rule. As a monarchist, Astell greatly distrusted the Whig political party and others who were advancing an argument and legislative program in Parliament that would strip away the power of the monarch in favor of power held by the Parliament. In the preface to the third edition of *Some Reflections*, published in 1706, she expresses her belief that many members of Parliament were corruptible men who embraced society's generally low opinion of women. In her mind, such men were not fit husbands nor fit rulers.

> For if arbitrary power is evil in it self, and an improper method of governing rational and free agents, it ought not to be practis'd any where; nor is it less, but rather more mischievous in families than in kingdoms, by how much 10,000 tyrants are worse than one. What though a husband can't deprive a wife of life without being responsible to the law, he may, however, do what is much more grievous to a generous mind, render life miserable, for which she has no redress. . . . If all men are born free, how is it that all women are born slaves? As they must be, if the being subjected to the inconstant, uncertain, unknown, arbitrary will of men, be the perfect condition of slavery?

For Astell, the only hope for the institution of marriage and the society at large was for those involved to correct the flawed practices that had been established by frail, fearful, and mistaken human beings who had fallen away from leading lifestyles inspired and directed by God.

In England at the start of the 18th century, political battles were waged with more ferocity than domestic ones, and religious battles often turned political. One of the most troubling and divisive issues of the time was whether non-Anglicans could go to an Anglican service once a year, declare "occasional conformity" with the state religion, and thus be qualified for government service and eligible for local and national elective offices. Tories were strongly against "oc-casional conformity," which they thought threatened the primacy of the Church of England and the power of the monarch as head of the Anglican religion.

In 1704, the Parliament had before it three bills that would prevent occasional conformity, and before each vote, first in the House of Commons and then in the House of Lords, many pamphlets were published advocating the Whig or the Tory position. The Tory party was strong in the House of Commons, which would vote for the bills, but the Whig party controlled the House of Lords, where the vote was against them. That year, Astell entered into the public debate, writing three pamphlets: *Moderation Truly Stated, A Fair Way with Dissenters and Their Patrons,* and *An Impartial Enquiry into the Causes of Rebellion and Civil War.* According to Ruth Perry, "Her strongly held opinions were convincing when delivered with the conversational informality possible in the pamphlet. Her sense of historical parallels, her moralizing, and her penchant for philosophical formulation worked well together and gave animation and variety to her reflections." All three pamphlets were regarded well enough for opposing writers to attack in response.

Many Anglicans, Astell included, considered those who pledged occasional conformity to be hypocrites, although Astell described them as "moderates." In *Moderation Truly Stated,* she wrote: "To be *Moderate* in Religion is the same thing as to be Lukewarm, which God so much abhors, that he has threatened to spew such out of his Mouth." Suspicious of those who could be false in matters pertaining to God and religion, she had a dreadful fear of the havoc they could wreak in government. In *An Impartial Enquiry into the Causes of Rebellion and Civil War,* she wrote in her usual blunt style:

> Few govern themselves by Reason, and they who transgress its Laws, will always find somewhat or other to be uneasie at, and consequently will ever desire, and as far as they can endeavour, to change their Circumstances. But since there are more Fools in the World than Wise Men, and . . . Riches and Power are what Men covet, supposing these can procure them all they wish; Hopes to gain more, or at least to secure what one has, will always be a handle by which Human Nature may be mov'd, and carry'd about as the cunning Manager pleases. And therefore of *Necessity* in all Civil Wars and Commotions, there must be some Knaves at the head of a great many Fools.

In the next year, after the Tories had lost the battle over occasional conformity and were badly split within their own ranks, Mary Astell published *The Christian Religion, As Profess'd by a Daughter of the Church of England,* a long work that asserts her own confidence in her faith, her church, and herself in bold terms: "I am a Christian then, and a member of the Church of *England,* not because I was Born in *England,* and Educated by Conforming Parents, but because I have, according to the best of my Understanding, and with some application and industry, examin'd the Doctrine and Precepts of Christianity, the Reasons and Authority on which it is built." Excluding the long table of contents and the index, this document is 418 pages long. The prose is direct and easy to understand, and the five sections return to many of the themes, like friendship and the development of reason, addressed in her earlier works.

By this time, English readers had good reason to know who Mary Astell was. Popular authors like Daniel Defoe, Richard Steele, and Joseph Addison attacked and satirized her in some of their works, and her own publisher made sure to keep all of her books in print and available to the public. The printer Richard Wilkin published a second edition of her *Letters Concerning God* in 1705, after a second edition of *Some Reflections Upon Marriage* had appeared in 1703, and a fourth edition of *A Serious Proposal in Two Parts* in 1704.

Astell published only one more original work in her lifetime, *Bart'lemy Fair: or, An Inquiry After Wit* (1709). It was written in response to an anonymously published work, *A Letter Concerning Enthusiasm,* which compared the religiously faithful French Huguenots—and, by implication, others who were also fervently loyal to their faith—with people who experience bouts of insanity. Thus, the *Letter* calls religious faith into question by likening it to a mere explosion of emotions, in contrast to Astell's belief that reason should be at the center of one's faith. Although Astell did not know it, the author of *A Letter* was Anthony Ashley Cooper, the third earl of Shaftesbury, one of England's most influential noble-philosophers. His later work of 1711, *Characteristics of Men, Manners, Opinions, Times,* advanced an essentially optimistic view that man's innate goodness, or at least the goodness of the upper-class males, would lead society to greater glory. This, too, would have been rejected by Astell, who was especially suspicious of rich and powerful men.

Soon after the appearance of *Bart'lemy Fair,* Astell's writing came to an end, after she became immersed in the work of establishing a charity school for the daughters of pensioners (retired servicemen, generally) of the Royal Hospital in Chelsea, where she was headmistress for the next several years. Helping Astell, particularly with financial support, were a number of her upper-class female friends. Little is known about her life after Astell retired from the school. Judging from the letters she wrote, she suffered from bouts of sickness, read as much as she could, attended church faithfully, and socialized. She died in 1731 from spreading breast cancer.

It is ironic that Mary Astell is remembered and honored more by feminist scholars today than by the women of her own era. As Perry says, "She was forgotten almost immediately, with a rapidity which is surprising, even granted her own frequent observation that history tended to record the exploits of men and to ignore those of women." Perhaps this was so because she uttered the truth as she saw it so plainly and so simply. Moreover, the challenges in her writings were to the women of her time rather than the men. Although she wanted to "rescue my Sex," the majority of them were not yet ready to listen to her.

SOURCES:

Astell, Mary. *The Christian Religion, As Profess'd by a Daughter of the Church of England.* London, 1705.
———. *The First English Feminist: Reflections upon Marriage and other Writings by Mary Astell.* Ed. with an intro. by Bridget Hill. NY: St. Martin's Press, 1986.
———. *Letters Concerning the Love of God.* London, 1695.
———. *A Serious Proposal to the Ladies.* 4th Edition. 1701. Reprint. NY: Source Book Press, 1970.
Makin, Bathsua. *An Essay to Revive the Antient Education of Gentlewomen. London,* 1673 (reprint, Los Angeles: The Augustan Reprint Society, 1980).
Perry, Ruth. *The Celebrated Mary Astell: An Early English Feminist.* Chicago: University of Chicago Press, 1986.

SUGGESTED READING:

Browne, Alice. *The Eighteenth Century Feminist Mind.* Detroit, MI: Wayne State University Press, 1987.
Rogers, Katharine M. *Feminism in Eighteenth-Century England.* Urbana, IL: University of Illinois Press, 1982.
Smith, Hilda L. *Reason's Disciples: Seventeenth-Century English Feminists.* Urbana, IL: University of Illinois Press, 1982.
Smith, Horence M. *Mary Astell.* 1916 (reprint, NY: AMS Press, 1966).
Uphaus, Robert W., and Gretchen M. Foster. *The "Other" Eighteenth Century: English Women of Letters 1660–1800.* East Lansing, MI: Colleagues Press, 1991.
Williamson, Marilyn L. *Raising Their Voices: British Women Writers, 1650–1750.* Detroit, MI: Wayne State University Press, 1990.

Linda E. Merians, Associate Professor of English, La Salle University, Philadelphia, Pennsylvania

Astin (fl. 5th c. BCE).

See Vashti.

Astley, Thea (1925—)

Australian novelist. Born Beatrice May Astley, August 25, 1925, in Brisbane, Queensland; daughter of Cecil and Eileen (Lindsay) Astley; educated at Teachers Training College; married Edmund John (Jack) Gregson, on August 27, 1948, in Sydney; children: one son, Edmond.

Selected works: Girl With a Monkey (1958); A Descant for Gossips (1960); A Boatload of Home Folk (1968); Hunting the Wild Pineapple (1979); Beachmasters (1985); Reaching Tin River (1990); Vanishing Points (1992); Coda (1994).

In the bush country of Australia, Thea Astley was raised in a Catholic household and a convent school. Traveling with her father Cecil Astley, a journalist with the newspaper *The Queenslander,* Thea became acquainted with the ruggedness of rural Australia and its amalgam of people, imagery she would later use in her writing. After attending Teachers Training College, Astley began her career in the same rural areas she had traveled as a child. For five years, she boarded at a room in the town pub or with a local family while she taught at the town school. Each year saw her in a new place, but Astley felt the lack of privacy such small places engendered. In 1948, she moved to Sydney and took a teaching position at a local high school. In the same year, she married Jack Gregson, with whom she subsequently had a son, Edmond.

Astley's work is satiric, starting with her first publications, *Girl With a Monkey* (1958) and *A Descant for Gossips* (1960). In 1968, she was invited to a post as senior tutor at Macquarie University in Sydney. There, she taught English and Australian literature and continued working on short stories, novellas, and novels, which emphasized the social intricacies, hindrances, and prejudices of small-town life. In 1980, Astley retired from her post as senior tutor and moved, with Gregson, to Nowra, Queensland, a rural town 100 miles south of Sydney. They then moved further north in Queensland.

SOURCES:

Gilbert, Pam. *Coming Out From Under.* London: Pandora, 1988.

Crista Martin,
Boston, Massachusetts

Aston, Luise (1814–1871)

German author and feminist pioneer. Name variations: Louisa. Born Luise Hoche on November 26, 1814, in Gröningen near Halberstadt into a conservative Lutheran family; died in obscurity on December 21, 1871, in Wangen-Allgäu, in southern Germany; daughter of Johann Gottried Hoche (a Lutheran minister and church official); twice married Samuel Aston (an English industrialist); married Eduard Meier (a physician from Bremen), in 1850.

Became a well-known and controversial spokeswoman for women's rights in her verse and novels (early 1840s); brief moment of fame during ill-fated revolution (1848), when her writings were much discussed; fleetingly served as editor of a radical journal; like other German revolutionaries, was unable to reach a broadly based audience and quickly faded from the spotlight after the suppression of the revolution (1849).

Born in 1814 into a traditional, conservative family, Luise Hoche Aston grew up in a period of harsh political and intellectual repression. To combat this atmosphere, much of her generation was attracted to radical ideas, including liberalism, nationalism, and—for women—the idea of female equality. A prolific, but often undisciplined writer, Aston produced a number of books of verse and novels written in the highly emotional style of pre-1848 German Romanticism. In her private life, too, Luise was a romantic, often allowing her heart to dominate her intellect. She quickly decided to marry an English industrialist, Samuel Aston, whom she met in Magdeburg; the marriage, however, was a failure. Some time later, she and Samuel were reconciled and married a second time; and, again, the union resulted in failure. Aston was somewhat more successful in her writings, in which conflicting human emotions could be tamed by the writer's wishes, and unsatisfactory endings were set aside for perfect ones. Her 1846 cycle of poems, *Wilde Rosen* (*Wild Roses*), made Aston famous for their exuberantly emotional eroticism.

After divorcing her husband a second time in 1846, Aston decided a move to Berlin would advance her career as a writer and advocate of women's rights. Her radical views and unconventional (to conservatives) behavior quickly brought her to the attention of the authorities of the highly efficient Prussian police state. Threatened with prison, she left Berlin but returned when that city erupted into revolutionary violence in the spring of 1848. Indeed, the year 1848 was the high point of Aston's life. For part of the year, she participated as a nurse in the military campaign against Denmark in the disputed provinces of Schleswig-Holstein. Upon her return to Berlin, Aston became a leading member of the revolutionary faction led by a fascinating demagogue and rabble rouser Friedrich Wilhelm Held. For a brief time in 1848, she edited a journal, *Der Freischärler für Kunst und Soziales Leben* and wrote most of the articles.

By the closing weeks of 1848, Held had been abandoned by his disillusioned disciples and the revolution collapsed. Luise Aston was expelled from Berlin by the police, her revolutionary dream of a united and democratic Germany having gone up in smoke. In 1850, she again married, this time to a physician from Bremen, Eduard Meier. Although she continued to write, and published a poetry cycle in 1850, her reputation both as a writer and political activist declined drastically in Otto von Bismarck's conservative regime. Largely forgotten by her contemporaries, and virtually unknown to the new generation of Socialists and feminists, Aston died in Wangen-Allgäu on December 21, 1871, the year of Bismarck's triumphant unification of Germany into a conservative and Prussian-dominated *Reich*.

SOURCES:

Aston, Luise. *Wilde Rosen: 12 Gedichte.* Berlin: Moeser & Kühn, 1846.

——. *Meine Emancipation, Verweisung und Rechtfertigung.* Brussels: Vogler, 1846.

——. *Aus dem Leben einer Frau.* Hamburg: Hoffmann & Campe, 1847.

——. *Lydia.* Magdeburg: Baensch, 1848.

——. *Revolution und Contrerevolution: Roman.* 2 vols. Mannheim: Grohe, 1849.

——. *Freischärler-Reminiscenzen: 12 Gedichte.* Leipzig: Weller, 1850.

Robertson, Priscilla. *Revolutions of 1848: A Social History.* NY: Harper Torchbooks, 1960.

Schulte, J.F. *Johanna Kinkel: Nach ihren Briefen und Erinnerungsblättern. Zum 50. Todestage Johanna Kinkels.* Münster: H. Schöningh, 1908.

John Haag, Associate Professor of History, University of Georgia, Athens, Georgia

Astor, Augusta (fl. 1820s–1890s)

American philanthropist. Name variations: Mrs. John Jacob III. Born Charlotte Augusta Gibbes; married John Jacob Astor III (1822–1890); children: William Waldorf Astor (1848–1919, who married Mary Dahlgren Paul).

Known as Mrs. John Jacob Astor III, Augusta Astor was small, blonde, and frail. In her early years of what was said to be a happy marriage, she and her husband lived simple, economical lives. During the Civil War, though her family originally came from the South, Augusta encouraged the recruiting of a regiment of black troops for the North. Described by contemporaries as a woman of good character, she gave balls, held a literary circle, and gave $225,000 for the Astor Pavilion, the first building of the Memorial Hospital for the treatment of cancer. She also supported the Children's Aid Society and helped pay transportation costs for 1,500 New York slum youths who were resettled in foster homes in the midwest.

Astor, Brooke (b. 1902)

American foundation executive and civic worker. Name variations: Mrs. Vincent Astor. Born Brooke Russell in Portsmouth, New Hampshire, in April 1902; daughter of John Henry (a marine commandant) and Mabel (Howard) Russell; Columbia University, LL.D., 1971; married J. Dryden Kuser, in 1918 (divorced, c. 1929); married Charles "Buddie" Marshall (a stockbroker who died in 1952); married Vincent Astor (died 1959), in October 1953; children: (first marriage) Anthony (who took the name of Marshall).

Known as the Fairy Godmother of New York City, Brooke Astor gave away every penny in the family foundation that had been funded by John Jacob Astor's fur trade and real estate fortune. Over a span of 38 years, she handed out $193,317,406 to charitable causes around the city—Carnegie Hall, The Bronx Zoo, the South Street Seaport, industrial projects in the Bronx, rebuilding Bedford-Stuyvesant in Brooklyn—then closed the foundation in March of 1998. She was then age 96. Astor received hundreds of awards, including the Governor's Arts Award (May 1985); two awards from President Ronald Reagan: the Presidential Citizen's Medal and The National Medal of Arts Award (both 1988); and the Presidential Medal of Freedom from President Bill Clinton (1998). She wrote two autobiographies, *Patchwork Child* (1962) and *Footprints* (1980), and was a consulting and feature editor for the magazine *House and Garden*.

Astor, Caroline Schermerhorn (1830–1908)

American arbiter of New York Society. Born Caroline Webster Schermerhorn in New York, New York, on September 22, 1830; died in her Fifth Avenue mansion in New York City on October 30, 1908; daughter of a wealthy Dutch merchant; married William Backhouse Astor, Jr. (1830–1892, grandson of John Jacob and *Sarah Todd Astor), in 1853; children: Emily Astor Van Alen (who married James J. Van Alen and died in childbirth); Helen Astor Roosevelt (who married James Roosevelt); Charlotte Augusta Astor Drayton (who married James Coleman Drayton); Caroline Astor Wilson (who married Orme Wilson); and John Jacob Astor IV (who married Ava Lowle Willing and Madeleine Talmadge Force).

Born in 1830, the daughter of a wealthy merchant of the Dutch aristocracy, Caroline Schermerhorn was the Grande Dame of American society from the 1860s to the turn of the century. Following her marriage to William Backhouse Astor, Jr., she felt it her duty to make sure that those who belonged to the powerful elite were separated from those who did not. It was Caroline Astor who, though she did not coin the term, helped compose the list of the famous "four hundred," the cream of New York Society. She wintered in New York, spent spring in Europe, and summered in Newport, Rhode Island. Determined to be the one-and-only Mrs. Astor, she held lavish parties to undermine the prominence of her sister-in-law, *Augusta Astor (Mrs. John Jacob Astor III).

Astor, Gertrude (1887–1977)

American actress. Born in Lakewood, Ohio, on November 9, 1887; died on her 90th birthday, on November 9, 1977.

Though she was usually cast as a vamp or the other woman, Gertrude Astor is also remembered for her brilliant comedic timing opposite Harry Langdon in *The Strong Man*, a 1926 silent film. Astor began her career as a stage actress at age 13, before joining Universal 14 years later, where she became one of the most popular leading ladies in that studio's silents. She worked with many directors, including George Cukor, Allan Dwan, and Henry Hathaway. Also a favorite of John Ford, Astor appeared in many of his films. At a studio luncheon in her honor in 1975, she reminisced about her years making over 300 movies. Her favorite, she noted, was *Uncle Tom's Cabin* (1927), though she paid heavily for getting the part. "The director [Harry Pollard] didn't want me, and he didn't like me," she cracked, "so he made me kneel for three weeks by the side of the girl's bed crying."

Her other films include *The Devil's Pay Day* (1917), *Beyond the Rocks* (1922), *The Impossible Mrs. Bellew* (1922), *Flaming Youth* (1923), *Alice Adams* (1923), *The Torrent* (1924), *Stage Struck* (1925), *Ship of Souls* (1925), *The Boy Friend* (1926), *The Old Soak* (1926), *The Country Beyond* (1926), *Kiki* (1926), *The Taxi Dancer* (1927), *The Cat and the Canary* (1927), *Rose-Marie* (1928), *Untamed* (1929), *Come Clean* (a short, in which she played the wife of Oliver Hardy, 1931), *Western Unlimited* (1932), *Empty Saddles* (1936), *Hold Back the Dawn* (1941), *Father Makes Good* (1950), *Around the World in 80 Days* (1956), *All in a Night's Work* (1961), and *The Man Who Shot Liberty Valance* (1962).

SOURCES:
Ragan, David. *Who's Who in Hollywood: 1900–1976.* New Rochelle, NY: Arlington House, 1976.

Astor, Mrs. John Jacob (1761–1832).

See Astor, Sarah Todd.

Astor, Mrs. John Jacob III (fl. 1820s–1890s).

See Astor, Augusta.

Astor, Lady (1879–1964).

See Astor, Nancy Witcher.

Astor, Madeleine Talmadge (c. 1893–1940)

American socialite. Name variations: Madeleine Force Astor; Madeline. Born around 1893; died in 1940; married John Jacob Astor IV, in 1911 (he died on April 15, 1912, on the Titanic*); married twice more; children: John Jacob Astor V (b. August 14, 1912). John Jacob Astor's first wife was* Ava Willing Astor*, the mother of Vincent Astor (b. 1891).*

Madeleine Astor had been married to John Jacob Astor IV for only a few months when she boarded the *Titanic* at Cherbourg. The couple's entourage included a manservant, a maid, a nurse, and an Airedale named Kitty. When news of the iceberg first reached the Astors, Madeleine has been quoted as saying, "I rang for ice, but this is ridiculous." John Jacob Astor went down with the ship, but Madeleine and the dog Kitty survived the sinking, and Madeleine went on to marry twice more.

Astor, Mary (1906–1987)

Urbane American actress, best known for her courtroom battle for child custody and her role as Brigid O'Shaughnessy in The Maltese Falcon. *Born Lucile Vasconcellos Langhanke in Quincy, Illinois, on May 3, 1906; died of complications from emphysema on September 25, 1987, in Los Angeles, California;*

Caroline
Schermerhorn
Astor

daughter of Otto Ludwig Langhanke and Helen (Vasconcells); married Kenneth Hawks (producer; brother of Howard Hawks), February 24, 1928 (died in a plane crash on January 2, 1930, while on a film assignment); married Franklyn Thorpe (a gynecologist), on June 29, 1931 (divorced 1935); married Manuel del Campo, in 1937 (divorced 1941); married Thomas Gordon Wheelock (a stockbroker), on December 24, 1945 (separated 1951, divorced 1955); children: (second marriage) Marylyn Hauoli (b. June 15, 1932); (third marriage) Anthony Paul (b. June 5, 1939).

Filmography—silents: Sentimental Tommy *(her role was lost in the cutting room);* The Beggar Maid *(2-reel art film, 1921);* The Young Painter *(2-reel art film, 1921);* The Man Who Played God *(UA, 1922);* John Smith *(Selznick, 1922);* Bought and Paid For *(1922, directed by William C. DeMille);* The Bright Shawl *(1923);* Second Fiddle *(1923);* Success *(MGM, 1923);* The Marriage Maker *(Paramount, 1923);* Puritan Passions *(1923);* The Rapids *(1923);* Woman-Proof *(Par., 1923);* The Fighting Coward *(Par., 1924);* Beau Brummel *(WB, 1924);* The Fighting American *(Universal, 1924);* Unguarded Women *(Par., 1924);* The Price of a Party *(1924);* Inez from Hollywood *(First National, 1924);* Enticement *(1924);* Oh Doctor! *(Universal, 1925);* Don Q, Son of Zorro *(UA, 1925);* The Pace that Thrills *(FN, 1925);* Playing with Souls *(FN, 1925);* The Scarlet Saint *(FN, 1925);* Don Juan *(1926);* High Steppers *(FN, 1926);* The Wise Guy *(FN, 1926);* Forever After *(1926);* The Rough Riders *(Par., 1926);* The Sea Tiger *(FN, 1927);* Sunset Derby *(FN, 1927);* Rose of the Golden West *(FN, 1927);* Two Arabian Nights *(UA, directed by Howard Hughes, 1927);* No Place to Go *(FN, 1927);* Sailors' Wives *(1927);* Three-Ring Marriage *(FN, 1928);* Dressed to Kill *(Fox, 1928);* Once There Was a Princess *(1928);* Heart to Heart *(1928);* Romance of the Underworld *(Fox, 1928);* Dry Martini *(Fox, 1928);* New Year's Eve *(Fox, 1929);* The Woman from Hell *(Fox, 1929).*

Sound: Ladies Love Brutes *(Par., 1929);* The Runaway Bride *(RKO, 1929);* Holiday *(with Ann Harding, RKO, 1930);* The Lash *(FN, 1931);* Smart Woman *(RKO, 1931);* The Sin Ship *(RKO, 1931);* Other Men's Women *(WB, 1931);* White Shoulders *(RKO, 1931);* The Royal Bed *(RKO, 1931);* The Lost Squadron *(RKO, 1932);* Men of Chance *(RKO, 1932);* A Successful Calamity *(WB, 1932);* Those We Love *(World Wide, 1932);* The Dark Tower *(screenplay by George S. Kaufman, 1932);* Red Dust *(MGM, 1932);* The Little Giant *(FN, 1933);* Jennie Gerhardt *(Par., 1933);* Convention City *(FN, 1933);* The Kennel Murder Case *(WB, 1933);* The World Changes *(FN, 1933);* Easy to Love *(WB, 1934);* Upperworld *(WB, 1934);* Return of the Terror *(FN-WB, 1934);* The Man with Two Faces *(FN, 1934);* The Case of the Howling Dog *(WB, 1934);* I Am a Thief *(WB, 1935);* Red Hot Tires *(WB, 1935);* Straight from the Heart *(Universal, 1935);* Dinky *(WB, 1935);* Page Miss Glory *(WB, 1935);* Man of Iron *(WB, 1935);* The Murder of Dr. Harrigan *(FN, 1936);* And So They Were Married *(Columbia, 1936);* Trapped by Television *(Columbia, 1936);* Dodsworth *(UA, 1936);* Lady from Nowhere *(Columbia, 1936);* Prisoner of Zenda *(UA, 1937);* The Hurricane *(UA, 1937);* Paradise for Three *(MGM, 1938);* No Time to Marry *(Columbia, 1938);* There's Always a Woman *(Columbia, 1938);* Woman Against Woman *(MGM, 1938);* Listen, Darling *(MGM, 1938);* Midnight *(Par., 1939, with Claudette Colbert);* Brigham Young—Frontiersman *(Fox, 1940);* The Great Lie *(WB, 1941);* The Maltese Falcon *(WB, 1941);* Across the Pacific *(WB, 1942);* The Palm Beach Story *(Par., 1942);* Thousands Cheer *(MGM, 1943);* Young Ideas *(MGM, 1943);* Blonde Fever *(MGM, 1944);* Meet Me in St. Louis *(MGM, 1944);* Claudia and David *(Fox, 1946);* Fiesta *(MGM, 1947);* Cynthia *(MGM, 1947);* Desert Fury *(Par., 1947);* Cass Timberlane *(MGM, 1947);* Act of Violence *(MGM, 1949);* Little Women *(MGM, 1949);* Any Number Can Play *(MGM, 1949);* A Kiss before Dying *(UA, 1956);* The Power and the Prize *(MGM, 1956);* The Devil's Hairpin *(Par., 1957);* This Happy Feeling *(Universal, 1958);* Stranger in My Arms *(Universal, 1959);* Return to Peyton Place *(Fox, 1961);* Youngblood Hawke *(WB, 1964);* Hush Hush, Sweet Charlotte *(Fox, 1965).*

"I became a valuable piece of property to my parents, closely guarded, closely watched," wrote Mary Astor in the highly successful autobiography *My Story.* "The nun cloistered in a convent is trained in character, . . . the closely guarded young girl of European countries is trained for womanhood and marriage. For me there was no goal—except tomorrow's movie job."

Born Lucile Vasconcellos Langhanke in Quincy, Illinois, in 1906, Mary Astor was the daughter of a jealous mother, whose quarrels with her husband were inevitably "about the baby," and a frustrated, ambitious father, whose idea of success was always out of reach. Hers was a solitary childhood; the household was tense and took its cue from Otto Langhanke's moods and grandiose schemes. She was their only child.

When Astor was seven, the family moved from their tiny flat over a saloon in Quincy to a large Victorian farmhouse, where Otto taught German and worked at another of his "Great Ideas," creating a magnificent "Edelweiss Poultry Farm." The next four years were

Mary Astor

blessed, wrote Astor, but with the onset of the First World War, her father's pro-German sympathies cost him his job; his textbook on the study of German could not find a publisher; and his daughter's echoing of his view ("The Germans'll win, the Germans'll win")—along with her perfectly brushed curls—cost Astor her grade-school popularity. As a child, she was usually the cause of her father's irritation. His harangue would start at the dinner table, wrote Astor, "and Mother and I would eat as unobtrusively as possible, our eyes on our plates, and at the close of the meal, after Daddy had stormed out, we would wordlessly do the dishes."

When the poultry business failed, Otto's daughter became the next enterprise. He decided she was to be a great musician. A piano was purchased, a teacher hired. The lessons went well enough, but the practice was an ordeal for Astor. "My nerves jangled at the loud, sharp 'No!' from another room if I missed the lift of a phrase," she wrote. "I sat on edge, waiting for the caustic . . . '*Can't* you get some life into it?'" At the end of the war in 1916, the family moved back to town, where the piano practice continued. Fortunately, her father became aware that the regimen was wearing her down. She recalls him asking gently, "Don't you want to *be* somebody?":

> "Daddy," I said, "I *am* somebody, I am myself."
> "Well, what do you want to do then? . . ."
> "I just want to grow up, and go to high school and maybe Gem City Business College. I want to work a little, and then get married and have children."
> The heavens and earth opened in wrath; fire and brimstone rained down on my head. I was lectured as I had never been lectured before; I was shaken with a violence and fury that I had never seen in my father in even his worst moods. . . . It was the end of any possible understanding between my father and me.

It was also the end of her saying "no" to his demands for a long, long time.

On a whim, along with a friend, Astor entered a film-fan magazine competition with Brewster Publications, publisher of *Shadowland* and *Motion Picture Magazine*. At year's end, four finalists would be selected from the monthly winners for screen tests; one would get a studio contract. When Astor was a monthly finalist, among a list of eight, Otto Langhanke pulled her out of school and moved the family to Chicago. He had another Great Idea. She would become an actress; after all, motion pictures were the new gold rush.

Unable to get a job teaching without taking a city qualifying exam, Otto turned to making advertising cards for store windows. Astor's mother took a volunteer position teaching English literature and drama at the Kenwood-Loring School for Girls, an exclusive private school, on condition that her daughter receive free attendance. Astor loved the school and loved learning. In later life, she would sometimes read up to ten books a week: psychology, biography, history, poetry. On Saturdays, Astor also trained at a drama school with a friend of her mother's, **Bertha Iles.**

Upon Astor's graduation from Kenwood-Loring in 1919, the family set out for New York with $300 and their newly trained investment. They leased an apartment on West 110th street. Otto Langhanke began to pound the pavement with rapid results. After New York photographer Charles Albin took one look at the young girl and saw a "Madonna quality," he asked her to sit for some portrait shots. In turn, he introduced her to *Lillian Gish, who also took an interest and directed an Astor screen test at D.W. Griffith's studio at Mamaroneck.

"The test was long and difficult," wrote Astor. "Lillian sat in a camp chair beside the camera, suggesting shots, suggesting angles and lighting and movements. She had me recite a few lines of poetry. It took hours, but they were exciting, rapturous hours." But after the test the Langhanke's heard nothing. They began to live on coffee, cereal, and bread. A few years later, Gish explained the silence to Astor: "Mr. Griffith is peculiar. . . . He likes to make his own discoveries, and I think I pushed too hard." It would take 30 more years, however, for Gish to fully fess up: after taking one look at Otto Langhanke, Griffith had told Gish, "The man is a walking cash register; . . . he'll always be an interfering nuisance." Wrote Astor:

> Of course, D.W. was right. In about ten years the Motion Picture Producers Association would tell Daddy the same thing, and they would state it flatly: I would simply not get any more work if he continued to represent me. He was just too much trouble; every item of a contract became an argument. They could not tolerate his arrogance.

With the help of the Albin photos, Lucile Langhanke was given a six-month contract with Famous Players-Lasky and a new name: Mary Astor. But at the end of the term, she had only a shelved one-reeler and a feature picture to her credit; her part could be found on the cutting-room floor. She was soon signed, however, with artist Léjaron Hiller, who was experimenting with diffusion photography in a series of two-reelers. She found her name atop the marquee of the Rivoli Theatre: Mary Astor in *The Beggar Maid;* the critics called it "a little gem." Astor was now practicing the piano six hours a day, taking vocal lessons at Carnegie Hall, and attending dance class at the Denishawn school under the tutelage of *Ruth St. Denis and Ted Shawn. She found the dance an "exhilarating outlet for all my built-up aggressions."

After six more two-reelers, she made her first feature, a small part in *John Smith* for Louis J. Selznick. Her most important film of that period was the lead opposite Richard Barthelmess in *The Bright Shawl*. In April 1923, she signed a much better contract with Famous Players (one year, $500 a week) and was sent to the West Coast. Astor arrived in Hollywood with her mother (her father stayed behind to look after work on their new apartment) two weeks before her 17th birthday.

When John Barrymore asked Warner Bros. to test her to play opposite him in *Beau Brummel,* Otto Langhanke closed the apartment in New York and joined his family in Hollywood. The intelligent 17-year-old fell head over heels for the 40-year-old Barrymore (during the test, he had whispered in her ear: "You are so goddamned beautiful, you make me feel faint"). "So on afternoons when we were not working on the picture," wrote Astor:

> Mother and Daddy sat in the dining room, reading and whispering, while in the living room Jack talked to me. He talked about fundamentals of breathing and of diction, and gave me exercises in both. He explained to me about "authority" and "vitality." . . . He finally told Mother and Daddy that he must work alone with me. . . . They hesitated. He knew what they were thinking, and he beat them to the point. "Don't be ridiculous!" he said. "This is a *kid!*" Every Sunday for the rest of the summer he sent his car for Mother and me, and we rode to his suite at the Beverly Hills Hotel. There Mother sat on the veranda and sewed.

Beau Brummel would bring her success and stardom throughout the 1920s, '30s and '40s, but the early scripts were unexciting and her teenage attention was focused on Barrymore. The affair was important to both; he talked of marriage, she shied away. After the filming, they remet in New York while he was doing *Hamlet,* then Barrymore went on tour for 17 months. During that time, Astor was hard at work, shooting silent after silent. In early 1925, her parents bought an ornate home on Temple Hill Drive. They also acquired a maid, a gardener, a Pierce-Arrow limousine, and a chauffeur. But all her thoughts were centered on John Barrymore. She started a diary, filled it with coded words and symbols, and diligently noted cables "from J.B."

When they met again in New York, Barrymore had been signed to do *Richard III* in London the following season and wanted her to play *Anne of Warwick. When they approached her father over dinner, he quickly put the kibosh on it, saying "We couldn't afford it." There was a large difference in take-home pay between movies and the theater. Astor said nothing. "I think now that this was the critical moment,"

she later wrote, "I think Jack sat there waiting for me to assert myself."

Though they started filming *Don Juan* together (a movie that heralded the beginning of sound with the first Vitaphone recording of background music), Astor began to hear rumors of his interest in *Dolores Costello, his leading lady in the just finished adaptation of *Moby Dick* (renamed *The Sea Beast*). It didn't help that Dolores' sister **Helene Costello** had a part in *Don Juan*. The day Dolores visited the set, something inside of Astor clicked. That night, when her father shook her for not practicing her singing, she raged: "You keep your hands off me! . . . I'm nineteen years old, and I won't take any more of this shoving around and being slapped."

Shortly after, she met Kenneth Hawks, a producer and brother of director Howard Hawkes, and they were married. She also made new friends, *Bessie Love and **Marian Spitzer,** a journalist for the *New York Globe*. Since her husband was determined to be the breadwinner, her earnings continued to go to her parents in the mansion on Temple Hill Drive. Her father was using the money to improve the property, he said, property that was now split three ways between her mother, her father, and herself. It was a good marriage, but Hawkes wasn't entirely interested in the physical part of the relationship, and she had an affair. This too went into the diary. In 1930, while filming a parachute drop with two Ford tri-motor planes flying close together, Hawkes was killed, along with nine others.

The disaster left Astor husbandless and broke. In the preceding ten years, she had earned close to half a million dollars but had only $3,000 in her bank account. When a friend of hers suggested to her father that he sell Temple Hill and live in a place less grand, he laughed. While her parents lived in a house with two cars and three servants, Astor rented a small apartment in Hollywood. She rushed into another marriage with physician Franklyn Thorpe, the high point of which was the birth of her daughter.

Otto Langhanke continued to protest that they needed her money for maintenance on the Temple Hill house. Astor finally went to him, offered him her third, and said they would receive no more money. Her parents then sued her for maintenance. The newspaper colony had a field day. Under one photo of her father, posing over the bridge he had added to the estate's swimming pool, ran the headline: "Down to their last swimming pool." After she agreed to $100 a month continued support, the case was dismissed.

During her marriage to Thorpe, Astor journeyed to New York on holiday and became an exhilarated addition to the New York literati: *Edna Ferber, Bennett Cerf, Moss Hart, and Oscar Levant. She also became a close friend of George S. Kaufman, who accompanied her everywhere. Returning home, she filmed *Red Dust* with Clark Gable and *Jean Harlow. (The movie was later remade as *Mogambo* with *Grace Kelly playing the part Astor originated.) Astor continued to see Kaufman while he was working on a play in Palm Springs. Aware that her marriage to Thorpe was a sham, she asked for a divorce, but her husband threatened the use of her diary in divorce court.

> For a long time after the trial I was shy of people. I was afraid of what the notoriety might do to my work. . . . Wearing glasses and wrapped in scarves, I went one night to see [*Dodsworth*]. . . . My first line was spoken off screen, but the moment they heard it the audience burst into spontaneous applause. . . . I was told that it happened at every performance at that theatre.
>
> —Mary Astor

Knowing the consequences of such disclosure would not only touch her life but the lives of her daughter Marylyn and many others, Astor was frightened and agreed to an uncontested divorce and her husband's legal custody of the child. When friends convinced her to assert herself and connected her with a lawyer who vowed that the diary would never be admissible in court, Astor sued for custody of her daughter. Before long, she was called into a meeting with a room full of major Hollywood producers (Thalberg, Goldwyn, Warner, Cohn, and others), asking her to back down. The trial would create a scandal, they said, and give the industry a bad name; she would "probably lose the case and the child too." Astor was puzzled until she later learned that someone mentioned in the diary was distributing a forgery, a more salacious version that contained a "box score" of name after Hollywood name; he hoped the falsified account would incite her producers to pressure Astor into a dismissal of the suit. Portions of the phoney diary were leaked to the press, quoted, and requoted. "I could not sue the fourth estate," wrote Astor, "because, of course, each paper was 'simply quoting' material from another paper. I could only cry futilely, 'There *wasn't* any "box score" and I never called the damned thing "Dear Diary."'"

A few pages of the authentic diary landed in the pages of the *Los Angeles Examiner.* "This was mostly the account, romantic and sentimental, certainly not pornographic, of my friendship with George Kaufman," wrote Astor. "The entire association as revealed by those papers should have been interpreted as nothing more than a close friendship. But when people thought of 'the diary' they thought not of these rather mild pages, but of the lurid lines quoted from the forgery."

Considered the Hollywood trial of the 1930s, Astor's custody battle lasted for 30 days. Outside the courtroom, vendors hawked their wares; inside, the room was packed. Her lawyer proved as good as his word. He called for the diary to be admitted, fairly sure that they only had these Kaufman fragments, and he was right. A portion of a document cannot be used as evidence in court; rather, it must be whole. The judge ordered joint custody, and the diary, impounded and sealed, would be destroyed by court order in 1952 (or at least that's what Astor thought; historian Robert Parish claims it reposes in the managing editor's confidential file at the *New York Daily News*).

Surprisingly, the notoriety helped rather than hurt Astor's career. In the eyes of moviegoers, she was a woman who put her reputation on the line to fight for her child. Her next part of Edith Cortwright, the sympathetic widow in *Dodsworth,* also helped her public image. Two years later, she married once more and had a son Anthony Paul. But her new husband joined the Canadian Air Force and flew off to war.

In 1940, *Bette Davis asked Astor to join the cast of *The Great Lie.* Astor was to play a self-centered, world-famous pianist, and all those piano lessons were about to pay off. She remarked, "It was the greatest challenge I had so far met in my career." Mid-filming, Davis appeared in her dressing room complaining of the story and claiming that the most interesting conflict in the movie was between their characters. Davis asked Astor if she'd be interested in working with her in building up the characters. They wrote dialogue together, went over their scenes, and became "as simpatico as a pair of dancers." The following year, Astor won an Oscar for Best Supporting Actress for the film. Though some asserted that she stole the picture from Davis, Astor adamantly denied it: "She handed it to me on a silver platter."

In 1941, Astor learned to fly and began to take on radio assignments: "Lux" and "Screen Guild." She had her own show for a year, "Hollywood Showcase," and a show for Roma Wines. Then, in a part originally intended for *Geraldine Fitzgerald, she portrayed Brigid O'Shaughnessy, the perpetual liar, in Dashiell Hammett's *Maltese Falcon*. "With her breathless, orgasmic voice," writes **Marjorie Rosen** in *Popcorn Venus*, Astor's performance was a "masterpiece of deception." In fact, as Jay Nash and Stanley Ross report, Astor "purposely hyperventilated to capture a breath-catching look, and she is so convincing that Bogart can only blurt admiration for her lies, . . . 'You're good, you're real good.'" The film was John Huston's first directing chore, but his casting was perfection: Humphrey Bogart, Peter Lorre, *Gladys George, and Sydney Greenstreet. *The Maltese Falcon* set became so notorious for hijinks and salty talk that the studio placed it off limits to the press. Astor would also star with Bogart in *Across the Pacific* in 1942.

In 1944, her father Otto died. Astor became reclusive and began to drink more; she also halfheartedly converted to Catholicism. In 1942, she had signed a six-year contract with MGM. Despite Metro's promise of a buildup, the studio was putting the 38-year-old Astor in a series of mother roles in undistinguished films. "My femme fatale image of the Diary days went down the Culver City drain," she wrote. She was *Kathryn Grayson's mother in *Thousands Cheer*, *Elizabeth Taylor's mother in *Cynthia*, *Judy Garland and *Margaret O'Brien's mother in *Meet Me in St. Louis,* and strong-willed *Lizbeth Scott's mother in *Desert Fury*.

In frustration, Astor took six months off to do **Clare Kummer**'s *Many Happy Returns* in New York with Henry Hull. Though the play was panned, she walked away with excellent reviews. She married for a fourth time in 1945, to the stockbroker Thomas Gordon Wheelock, and they drank together. A few months later, she was diagnosed with cirrhosis of the liver. Astor began to develop what were considered psychosomatic symptoms, breathing problems, aches and pains. A little dance she was supposed to perform with her "daughters" (*June Allyson, Elizabeth Taylor, *Janet Leigh, and Margaret O'Brien) while shooting *Little Women* was too much for her. The director allowed her to stand by and watch.

Tired of working and tired of supporting people, Astor wanted out of her contract with Metro. Her nerves were taut; she was jumpy, hated noise, and was relying heavily on the sedative Seconal. Though she couldn't sleep, she spent most of 1949 in bed, taking more pills, consuming more Vodka. After an overdose (and pumped stomach) that newspapers dubbed an attempted suicide, Astor was taken to a sanitarium. While there, someone handed her Thomas Merton's *The Seven Story Mountain,* and she began to find her way back.

But 1951 brought more disintegration. Astor fought the decline by becoming more and more involved with the Catholic Church. With no film work, debts began to pile up. She dealt with a broken fibula, another divorce. The actress *Louise Fazenda sent over a loan, and others helped. When Astor entered the Motion Picture Relief Hospital with bronchial pneumonia, a serious embedding of large fibroids in the uterus was discovered that may have caused the "psychosomatic" aches and pains. An operation found them benign.

Astor was now 46, inactive in Hollywood, and had not been seen socially for three years. "I did not yet know that I had a real recognized disease, the disease of alcoholism, which is now known to be as insidious and fatal as cancer or

Mary Astor portrayed Brigid O'Shaughnessy in The Maltese Falcon *opposite Humphrey Bogart.*

tuberculosis, and no more shameful, and just as 'arrestable.'" Then she was offered the job of replacing *Shirley Booth on Broadway in *Time of the Cuckoo*. Astor followed with one theater job after another for four years, but she was still in debt, still sickly, still drinking. Her sobriety was reserved for television and the stage.

Nothing pleased her more than a good feud.

—Noel Annan

In 1955, she returned to Los Angeles. It took a few more years before she realized she could not tolerate even one drink. Her life did an about-face. After a heart condition effectively ended her career in 1965, Astor spent her last years at the Motion Picture Country Home. Her second book, the autobiographical *A Life on Film*, was published by Delacorte in 1967; she also wrote several novels, including *The Incredible Charlie Carewe* and *A Place Called Saturday*. At age 81, Mary Astor died of complications from emphysema on September 25, 1987.

SOURCES:

Astor, Mary. *My Story*. NY: Doubleday, 1959.

Katz, Ephraim. *The Film Encyclopedia*. NY: Harper, 1994.

Nash, Jay Robert, and Stanley Ralph Ross. *The Motion Picture Guide*. Chicago, IL: Cinebooks, 1986.

Parish, James Robert, and Ronald L. Bowers. *The MGM Stock Company*. New Rochelle, NY: Arlington House, 1973.

Thomson, David. *A Biographical Dictionary of Film*. 3rd ed. NY: Knopf, 1994.

Astor, Minnie (1906–1978).

See Cushing Sisters.

Astor, Nancy Witcher (1879–1964)

First woman member of the House of Commons, who was known for her iconoclastic wit and the many controversies into which she entered. Name variations: Lady Astor, Nancy Viscountess Astor. Born Nancy Witcher Langhorne on May 19, 1879, at Danville, Virginia; died on May 2, 1964, at Grimsthorpe, Lincolnshire; fifth child of Chiswell Dabney Langhorne (a railroad developer) and Nancy Witcher Keene; sister of Irene Gibson (the Gibson girl); married Robert Gould Shaw, in October 1897 (divorced, February 1903); married Waldorf Astor, on May 3, 1906; children: (first marriage) Robert (Bobbie) Shaw; (second marriage) William (Bill) Waldorf, Nancy Phyllis Louise (Wissie), Francis David Langhorne, Michael Langhorne, John Jacob (Jakie); aunt of actress Joyce Grenfell.

Throughout her life, American-born Nancy Astor was surrounded by controversy. The first woman member of the British House of Commons, she gained an international reputation for crusading zeal and biting wit. To poet *Anne Morrow Lindbergh, she was "screamingly funny." To her close friend playwright George Bernard Shaw, she was "a reckless unladylike Lady." But to critics she was "the Pollyanna of the political world," "the most honest of hypocrites." One said, "For her a declaration of good will is equivalent to a realization of justice."

Lady Astor was born Nancy Witcher Langhorne on May 19, 1879, in Danville, Virginia. Her father was Chiswell (Chillie) Dabney Langhorne, an impoverished auctioneer and Civil War veteran, who later made a fortune as a railroad contractor. Her mother, Nancy Witcher Keene, had worked in a hospital during the Civil War. Said Nancy of her parents, "Very early in life I sensed that she had the stronger character. But Father had the power. He held the purse strings." Her sister ❧➤ Irene Gibson was a famous beauty, immortalized as the Gibson girl by the then little-known artist Charles Dana Gibson. Though Chillie first referred to Gibson as "this damn charcoal artist," Charles and Irene were married in 1895. Nancy's younger sister **Nora Langhorne Phipps** had two children, Tommy and Joyce. The shy, overweight Joyce grew up to be the talented comedienne *Joyce Grenfell.

First raised in a wooden frame house, at six Nancy moved with her family to an impoverished part of Richmond. Around 1892, however, her father—whose income had radically improved—bought an estate named Mirador, located in Greenwood, Virginia, 17 miles west of Charlottesville. A typical Southern belle, Nancy rode to the hounds in daytime and attended fancy-dress balls at night. When she was 17, she was sent to Miss Brown's Academy for Young Ladies, a finishing school in New York. Finding herself snubbed by the daughters of the city's elite, she retaliated by wearing garish clothes. Already possessing a caustic temperament, the highly attractive Nancy told her classmates that her father was a drunk and her mother took in washing.

In October 1897, after turning down 16 proposals, Nancy Langhorne married New Englander Robert Gould Shaw, scion of a socially prominent family. Shaw was mentally ill and an alcoholic. Though she gave him one son, "Bobbie," the marriage was doomed from the start. Nancy fled Shaw the second night of her honeymoon and possibly several times thereafter. The couple separated permanently in 1901 and divorced in 1903, when Shaw had already committed bigamy. A year later, Nancy started visiting England for the social and hunting seasons. She first fell in love with Lord John Baring Revelstoke of the prominent banking family. In the end, she found Revelstoke too worldly and snobbish; he in turn wondered if she was up to entertaining royalty.

In 1906, on a second trip to England, she married the handsome and dignified Waldorf (later second viscount) Astor. Born in New York, Waldorf was educated at Eton and New College, Oxford. Like his American-born father William Waldorf Astor, he was a naturalized British subject. One of the richest families in the world, the Astors possessed political influence as well. They owned the *Pall Mall Gazette* and later the *Observer;* young Waldorf sat in Parliament as a Conservative representing the working-class Sutton division of Plymouth. The couple would have four sons and one daughter.

Almost immediately, Lady Astor turned their magnificent country house "Cliveden," near Taplow on the Thames, into a showplace where entertainment was conducted on a grand scale. Here British royalty mixed with prominent political and literary figures. Dinners for 50 to 60 were frequent; major balls would have 600 guests. Commented the leading civil servant Thomas (Tom) Jones of Lady Astor's role at Cliveden: "She was and remained the center of attraction; no visitor could compete with her beauty, athletic figure, immense vitality, and her darting tongue." At that time she was an avid reader, a lover of words. Cliveden visitors included Rudyard Kipling, Hilaire Belloc, and Henry James, who was escorted there by *Edith Wharton in the summer of 1912. "Though but a reclaimed barbarian," wrote Wharton, Nancy was "full of possibilities and fine material, with all her bounty, spontaneity and charm, too."

In her prime, Lady Astor was a short, trim woman, though her alertness made her appear taller. Her eyes were blue, her complexion fair, her nose and chin strong and finely shaped. Her personality was far from simple. Writes her biographer Christopher Sykes:

> There was never a person of more contradiction than Nancy. It is almost true to say that she had in greater or lesser degree the opposite of all her qualities. She could be fanatic, she could be extraordinarily broad-minded; she could be cruel, she could bring comfort as no one else was able to; she could be foolish, she could be remarkably intelligent; she could be tyrannical, she could be humbly self-critical.

❦▶ Gibson, Irene Langhorne (1873–1956)

The original "Gibson girl." Born in Danville, Virginia, in 1873; died in 1956; third child of Chiswell Dabney Langhorne (a railroad developer) and Nancy Witcher Keene; sister of *Nancy Astor; married Charles Dana Gibson, in 1895; children: daughter Babs.

Irene was the beauty of the Langhorne family. She opened the ball of the Philadelphia Academy, was queen of the Mardi Gras, and led the grand march at the Patriarch's Ball in New York (1894). After refusing 60 proposals of marriage (it is not known who kept track), she agreed to marry the Yankee artist Charles Dana Gibson (1867–1944), one of the top illustrators of his day. For 20 years, Charles drew the "Gibson girl," modeled after her. Immensely popular, the patrician Gibson girl was competent and assured, fashionably dressed, and moved through an undemanding world. Embodying the American dream of the Gilded Age, women modeled their clothes and hair after Irene Gibson. Her likeness was everywhere: printed on pillow covers, chinaware, and silver spoons.

In 1914, when Lady Astor suffered from an internal abscess and was close to becoming an invalid, she converted from her nominal Anglicanism to Christian Science. Henceforth, she seldom became ill. Indeed, she was so enthusiastic about her new faith that she was able to convert her close friend, the prominent civil servant Philip Kerr, later 11th Marquis of Lothian.

During World War I, the Astors turned Cliveden into a hospital. In total, 1,400 troops were tended. Feeling the impact of the conflict severely, Lady Astor later wrote: "After two years in that first war, we did not look at the casualty lists any more. There was nothing to look for. All our friends had gone." Throughout this time, Waldorf Astor was holding high positions: in 1917, parliamentary secretary to Prime Minister David Lloyd George; in 1918, parliamentary secretary to the Ministry of Food and Local Government Board and in 1919 to the Ministry of Health. In 1918, on the death of his father, Waldorf succeeded to his viscounty. Much against his will, he was elevated to the House of Lords.

In the resulting by-election, Lady Astor agreed to stand for Parliament in his place, running as a Conservative supporter of the Lloyd George coalition. "I am a Virginian," she said, "so naturally I am a politician." The campaign did not lack color. Refusing to look dowdy in order to please voters, she campaigned in highly fashionable garb. She claimed that her Labour

Party opponent represented the "shirking class-es," she the "working classes." When someone commented that she should be home looking after her children, she replied, "This is true, but I feel that someone ought be looking after the more unfortunate children."

While campaigning, she had "unlimited ef-frontery," said Oswald Mosley (soon to be hus-band of *Diana Mitford):

> She was less shy than any woman—or any man—one has ever known. She'd address the audience and then she'd go across to some old woman scowling in a neighbour-ing doorway, who simply hated her, take both her hands and kiss her on the cheek or something of that sort. She was absolutely unabashed by any situation. Great effron-tery but also, of course, enormous charm. People were usually overcome by it. She was much better when she was interrupted. She must have prayed for hecklers....

On December 1, 1919, Lady Astor became the first woman to sit in the British Parliament, remaining in the Commons for 26 years. To mark her entrance, she was introduced by Lloyd George and former prime minister Arthur Bal-four. Yet some members sought to make her un-comfortable. Wrote **Mary Stocks:**

> From the first moment of her appearance in that exclusive club a terrifying responsibility rested upon her. She carried the repute of fu-ture women MPs in her elegant gloved hands. . . . Everybody waited to see what she would say or do; and those who resented fe-male incursion into that sacred male pre-serve devoutly prayed that she might say or do the wrong thing.

Lady Astor said many things, and what she said was often out of order; during sessions, she would audibly comment or interrupt any speech with which she disagreed. She tried to limit one Conservative speech by pulling the speaker down by the coat-tails. "People who live in two houses do not realise what it is like to live in two rooms. That's what is wrong with the Conserva-tives." By such antics, Lady Astor immediately made her mark. Rather than claiming herself equal to her male colleagues, she maintained that women were the superior sex. "I married beneath me," she used to say. "All women do."

From the time she entered Parliament, she spoke for the prohibition of alcoholic beverages. Noting the enormous fortunes made from brew-ing, she claimed that the Peerage might be called the Beerage. When in 1930 the British lost a major cricket competition, she said, "The reason England lost the Ashes was that the Australians did not drink." In 1923, she introduced a bill raising the drinking age to 18. Once it passed the Commons, her husband conducted the bill through the House of Lords, and it became law.

In Parliament, Lady Astor continually pressed issues concerning women and children. Women were particularly appreciative of her causes, which included votes for females at 21, equal rights in the civil service, better conditions in women's prisons, the preservation of the women's police forces, milk for the needy, allowances for widows, birth control, the suppression of prostitution, and the elimination of venereal disease. She was equally active on behalf of children, fighting child labor in unregulated trades and calling for the protection of the young from indecent assault, the raising of the school age, and the introduction of juvenile courts. She was a staunch defender of the famous nursery school program of *Margaret McMillan. Extremely constituent-minded and representing a naval district, Astor often spoke for British mariners. For instance, she demanded improved conditions for naval wives and children and better educational facilities for enlisted men.

Her bumptiousness and self-assurance made her the right woman for parliamentary trailblazing, wrote Harold Nicolson:

> Her courage . . . was such that no subsequent woman Member ever felt inferiority when faced with that predominantly male assembly. It was Lady Astor who, from the very day of her introduction, taught her contemporaries that the expansion of woman's liberty could be achieved, not by mute acquiescence, but by voluble pugnacity. She taught her sex to fight.

In 1922, Lady Astor visited the United States, where she met a host of dignitaries, including President Warren G. Harding. Outspoken as usual, she attacked the wearing of short skirts, stressed that the United States had been founded by Protestants, called the proposed bonus for veterans "a dangerous thing," and claimed that America should have joined the League of Nations. Her speeches were published under the title *My Two Countries* (1923).

Another visit was even more provocative. In 1931, the Astors visited the Soviet Union with playwright George Bernard Shaw. When Lady Astor asked Joseph Stalin how long he was going to keep on killing people, the Russian dictator said, "As long as necessary." (Her very next question focused on Soviet nurseries.) Though Shaw returned to Britain fervently enthusiastic over the Soviet system, Lady Astor strongly assailed it.

During the 1930s, Lady Astor condemned the Nazi system early on, while calling for accommodation with Germany. In May 1933, she denounced Nazism as tyranny. That June, she protested to the German embassy about illiberal treatment of professional women. When in 1936 she met German diplomat Joachim von Ribbentrop, she told him Adolf Hitler's performances were absurd and mocked the *führer*'s appearance. In 1938, she intervened on behalf of the uncle of American jurist Felix Frankfurter, detained by the Nazis in Austria.

Yet Lady Astor was equally outspoken in defense of appeasement. In May 1937, she called for an Anglo-German pact, saying that one must either live with people one did not wholly approve or face a new world war. In June, while in New York, she said that hatred of Nazism should not breed hostility towards Germany itself. She also warned Jews not to allow their anti-Nazism to result in support of communism. When criticized for the latter remark, she simply claimed that she had been making "a plea for an atmosphere of constructive goodwill." A strong admirer of Prime Minister Neville Chamberlain, whom she saw as Britain's greatest leader since Lloyd George, she strongly endorsed the Munich agreement. When Winston Churchill called the pact "a total and unmitigated defeat," she heckled "Nonsense!" Yet once Hitler seized Prague, she urged Chamberlain to protest.

In the immediate years before World War II, the Astor country house Cliveden became the subject of much controversy, so much so that the press even spoke of a "Cliveden set." It was claimed that the Astor mansion was headquarters to a shadow foreign office where schemes were hatched to assure Hitler's dominance in Europe. The myth was first given currency by Claud Cockburn, a former New York correspondent of *The Times* (London) and publisher of a mimeographed bulletin entitled *The Week*. In the issue of November 17, 1937, Cockburn told of a plan, laid at the Astor house, by which Lord Halifax, lord president of the Council and a prominent appeaser, would bargain with Hitler. In exchange for an Anglo-German truce, Britain would not interfere with Germany's eastern expansion. The story was wrong in every particular. For example, Halifax was not present while foreign secretary Anthony Eden, a foe of appeasement, was. Indeed, writes biographer Sykes, "When it comes to evidence of Appeasement policy and action, the Astors never seem to be there." Yet the damage was done. The term "Cliveden set" was picked up by a host of other journals, ranging from the Communist *Daily*

Opposite page

Nancy

Witcher

Astor

Worker to the liberal *Manchester Guardian.* Even the British fascist organ *Action* accused Cliveden of representing "the powers of money and the press." David Low of the (London) *Evening Standard* drew savage cartoons while Labourite Sir Stafford Cripps called Lady Astor "the honorable member for Berlin."

When war broke out in September 1939, Lady Astor's sons went into service almost immediately. Cliveden became part nursery for evacuated children, part hospital for Canadian troops. When Waldorf served as lord mayor of Plymouth for five years, Nancy was most effective as co-mayor, often substituting for him in times of ill-health. During the bombing raids, she was continually in the Plymouth shelters, nursing babies and raising morale by performing cartwheels. After a major blast on March 21, 1941, which began a sustained blitzkrieg on the city, she said, "There goes thirty years of our lives, but we'll build it again." At the same time, she was saying, "Hate is a deadly poison. Kill the Germans, don't hate them." She wrote a friend, "Only I and the P.M. [Prime Minister] enjoy the war, but only I say so."

In Commons, she fought to curb the import on champagne, wanted supplies rationed to brewers, and demanded the evacuation of children from urban areas. Ever mindful of women's concerns, she pushed allowances to soldier's wives, equal compensation for women injured in air raids, admission of women to the foreign service, and—a favorite cause—the enlargement of the women's police force. In part due to her efforts, a national fire-fighting service was established.

In 1940, during the debate over the abortive Norwegian campaign, she supported the summoning of Winston Churchill as prime minister. (Her personal choice had been the 77-year-old Lloyd George.) Personal relations with Churchill, however, had seldom been good, and there had been one quite famous exchange:

> **Astor:** Winston, if I were married to you, I'd put poison in my coffee.
> **Churchill:** Nancy, if you were my wife, I'd drink it.

Certain stands were almost designed to court unpopularity. In 1942, Lady Astor warned of Roman Catholic influence over the foreign service and overseas propaganda agencies. In the same year, she said of the Soviet Union, "I am grateful to the Russians, but they are not fighting for us. They are fighting for themselves." Opposing the internment of British fascist leader Sir Oswald Mosley without trial, she comment-ed, "It's not the British way to keep people in prison if they are uncondemned."

By 1945, Lady Astor had lost her influence in Parliament; she seemed unable to focus on an issue. Commented information minister Brenden Bracken in the midst of a debate, "Would the noble lady tell the House exactly what she means?" She lacked the support of the local Conservative Association and, as the Labour Party won the elections by a wide margin, she would undoubtedly have been defeated. When, however, her husband persuaded her not to seek reelection, she never forgave him. For the first time in their marriage, and until Waldorf's death in 1952, their relationship was shaky. Moreover, she never recovered from the blow of being out of office.

During her trips to America, she was more provocative than ever. In 1946, in the midst of a debate concerning a loan to Great Britain, she said at a press conference in Washington, "You should get down on your knees and thank God for Britain." When asked her reaction to the city of Savannah, Georgia, to which she had been unexpectedly diverted because of weather, she replied: "The city is beautiful, as everybody knows it is. It's one of the most beautiful cities of America. But the way y'keep it. It's revoltin'. Never seen anything so revoltin' in m'life."

In 1947, during another visit to the United States, she experienced more criticism by calling the Zionist movement "purely political." Six years later, when she returned to the States, she met Senator Joseph R. McCarthy, then approaching the height of his Communist witchhunt. She told the Wisconsin Republican that she wished the glass of whiskey in his hand were poison, a comment that caused one editor to demand her arrest.

On May 2, 1964, Lady Astor died of a stroke at her daughter's house, Grimsthorpe, Lincolnshire. When she saw all her children assembled around her for the last time, she asked, "Am I dying or is this my birthday?" Her son Jakie replied, "A bit of both."

SOURCES:
Annan, Noel. *New York Review of Books.* February 8, 1973.
Astor, Michael. *Tribal Feeling.* John Murray, 1964.
Astor, Nancy W. *My Two Countries.* NY: Doubleday, 1923.
Collis, Maurice. *Nancy Astor: An Informal Biography.* NY: Dutton, 1960.
Grigg, John. *Nancy Astor: A Lady Unashamed.* Boston, MA: Little, Brown, 1980.
Langhorne, Elizabeth. *Nancy Astor and Her Friends.* Praeger, 1974.

Sykes, Christopher. *Nancy: The Life of Nancy Astor*. NY: Harper and Row, 1972.

SUGGESTED READING:

Jones, Thomas. *A Dairy with Letters, 1931-1950*. Oxford University Press, 1954.

Lindbergh, Anne Morrow. *The Flower and the Nettle: Diaries and Letters, 1936–1939*. NY: Harcourt Brace Jovanovich, 1976.

Justus D. Doenecke, Professor of History, New College of the University of South Florida, Sarasota, Florida

Astor, Sarah Todd (1761–1832)

German-born American fur trader who worked with, and consulted for, her husband John Jacob Astor in their successful business and philanthropic ventures. Born Sarah Todd in New York, New York, in 1761; died in 1832; only daughter and youngest child of Adam and Sarah (Cox) Todd; married John Jacob Astor, on September 19, 1785; children: eight, five of whom lived to adulthood, including William Backhouse Astor (1792–1875, who married Margaret Rebecca Armstrong) and **Magdalen Astor** *(who married Danish major-general Adrien Benjamin de Bentzon, grandfather of* ***Marie Thérèse Blanc***).

As was often the case in the early merchant families of New York, the marriage of Sarah Todd and John Jacob Astor may have hinged on the bride's dowry and family connections. Although John Jacob later told his grandchildren that he married Sarah "because she was so pretty," one has to wonder about the appeal of the $300 she brought to the union. Perhaps, however, he also saw in her the ambition and propensity for hard work that were to make her an invaluable helpmate.

John Jacob Astor met his future bride when he rented a room in the Manhattan boarding house Sarah ran with her widowed mother. He had come to New York by way of London where, after leaving his home in Germany to escape his stepmother and his father's butcher business, he worked for an older brother making and selling musical instruments until he had saved enough to book passage to America. On the crossing, a fellow passenger told him there was money to be made in furs, so, after landing in Baltimore, he made his way to New York and a job working for a furrier at two dollars a week.

From the beginning of their marriage in September 1785, Sarah and John Jacob Astor worked as a team. Her dowry allowed them to open their own business, where they sold pianos and flutes sent by his brother in England, and with the profits they bought furs. As they undertook the dirty, smelly task of processing the pelts,

Sarah's knowledge of fur quality soon grew and even surpassed that of her husband's. While he was away on buying expeditions, she not only took full charge of managing the business, but also cared for their eight children, all born between 1788 and 1802 in their flat above the store. Three of the children died in childhood.

By 1801, the success of the business made it possible to buy a handsome house near the corner of Broadway and Vesey Streets, which would later become the location of the famous Astor House. At Sarah's suggestion, they also began to invest some of their profits in New York City real estate, which would later comprise the bulk of the Astor fortune. John Jacob increasingly utilized Sarah's ability to evaluate furs, which he then transported to China in exchange for even more valuable commodities like silks, tea, and spices. As their income increased, she proposed that he pay her for her consulting services. They agreed on a rate of $500 an hour, which she used for various religious contributions.

Although John Jacob did not realize his dream of a fur monopoly, the real-estate earnings more than compensated. When Sarah Astor died in 1832, the Astor fortune was estimated as the greatest in the country. Upon his death in 1848, John Jacob Astor was worth somewhere between $20 and $30 million, an enormous sum for that time.

SOURCES:

Bird, Caroline. *Enterprising Women*. NY: W.W. Norton, 1976.

Johnson, Allen, ed. *Dictionary of American Biography*, Vol. I. NY: Scribner, 1957.

SUGGESTED READING:

Kavaler, Lucy. *The Astors: A Family Chronicle of Pomp and Power*. NY: Dodd, Mead, 1966.

Barbara Morgan, Melrose, Massachusetts

Astor, Mrs. Vincent (b. 1902).

See Astor, Brooke.

Astor, Mrs. William Backhouse, Jr. (1830–1908).

See Astor, Caroline Schermerhorn.

Astorga, Nora (1949–1988)

Nicaraguan diplomat and revolutionary. Born Nora Astorga Gadea in 1949; died of cancer in Managua on February 14, 1988; studied law and became an attorney; married Jorge Jenkins; children: five, including one adopted son.

Assisted in the assassination of General Reynaldo Perez Vega, notorious security chief for the Somozas and a sadistic torturer; founding member of the Associ-

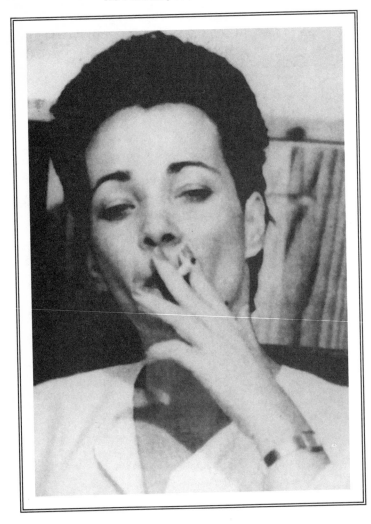

ation of Women Confronting the National Problem (AMPRONAC), the Sandinista organization of women supporters of the Sandinista National Liberation Front (FSLN); served as deputy minister of foreign affairs.

Born Nora Astorga Gadea into an affluent family of the Nicaraguan oligarchy in 1949, Nora had a contented, secure childhood. Her father, a wealthy lumber exporter and rancher, came from a family that had prospered for decades under the long-established Somoza regime. Nora's grandfather served the Somozas as minister of defense. Like many members of her nation's economic and political elite, she studied in the United States, at Catholic University in Washington, D.C. When she began studying for a law degree at Managua's Universidad Centroamericana, Nora became increasingly convinced that the brutal rule of the Somoza family and its political dynasty must be terminated.

The Somoza clan had ruled Nicaragua since 1937, when Anastasio Somoza (1895–1956) became president until 1947, and again from 1951

until his assassination in 1956. Speaking excellent English, Somoza began working for the U.S. Marines who occupied Nicaragua from 1912 until 1933 to protect American corporate and strategic interests in an impoverished "banana republic." A nationalist movement that attempted to free Nicaragua was led by one of the most effective guerrilla leaders of modern history, Agusto César Sandino (1895–1934). From 1927 through 1933, Sandino was at the head of a successful national insurrection. Lured to the capital city of Managua for a peace conference, Sandino was seized and shot in February 1934. Despite his murder and the demise of his movement, the Sandino myth grew with each passing year as Nicaraguan intellectuals, many of them from oligarchic families, thrilled to novels, plays and songs celebrating their martyred leader.

While growing up, Nora Astorga idealized and romanticized the legend of the Sandinista forces. She also read about courageous women: Sandino's wife ❧➤ **Blanca Araúz**, a trained telegrapher who ran the rebel forces communications units; **Teresa Villatoro**, a Salvadorean who led one of the guerrilla columns (and was incidentally also Sandino's mistress); and **Maria Altamirano**, who was placed in charge of one of the rebel base camps.

By the time she graduated from law school, Astorga was a confirmed social radical. At age 22, she married Jorge Jenkins, a student radical, with whom she had two children. The couple studied together for a year in Italy, he studying architecture and she banking law. The marriage ended after five years. As a law student, Astorga joined a revolutionary cell, passing messages and buying illegal supplies. Whereas student radicalism has been shown to often fizzle once students move into adult roles, this was not the case with Nora Astorga, though she benefitted from her status in the ruling class. By this time, the Somoza dynasty's corruption had reached monumental proportions; even a normally indulgent U.S. State Department began to characterize the Nicaraguan regime as a "kleptocracy," which relentlessly plundered the poor nation. The largest country in Central America, Nicaragua was endowed with sufficient natural resources to support all of its citizens in a decent manner, but not when the Somozas amassed a private fortune of at least $500 million. The regime was tolerated because of the emergence of an assertive revolutionary state in Cuba in 1959 under young and charismatic leaders Fidel Castro and Ernesto "Che" Guevara.

When a massive earthquake in Nicaragua devastated the capital city of Managua on December 23, 1972, leaving many thousands dead and even more homeless, the Somoza government's response was inept and corrupt. The old regime finally went too far, as international aid earmarked for earthquake victims was pocketed by the dynasty and its hangers-on. From this point on, the political opposition grew rapidly, and soon a full-scale guerrilla organization, the Sandinista National Liberation Front (FSLN) was born. Nora Astorga quickly joined the rebel group.

A successful lawyer for a leading construction company, she had an ideal cover for her work as a clandestine member of the FSLN. At the center of Nicaragua's oligarchic system, she was able to gather political and economic intelligence and pass it on to her friends in the revolutionary movement. As the government began to fail, her work grew increasingly dangerous. On March 8, 1978—International Women's Day (surely not a coincidence)—Astorga played a central role in an important assassination. The Sandinistas wanted to kidnap the notorious security chief and sadistic torturer General Reynaldo Perez Vega. Astorga lured Vega to her bedroom, where he was strangled when he resisted. His death would remain a celebrated but also controversial part of Nora Astorga's revolutionary career for the rest of her life. In later years, she remarked, "It was not murder but political justice." Assisted by the underground, Astorga escaped to a rebel training camp to become commander of a military squad. After the triumph of the revolution, she received the title of *Comandante Guerrillero*, of which she was extremely proud. For Sandinista loyalists, she had become an instant heroine. The other side labeled her an immoral, scheming Marxist femme fatale who unfairly lured a soldier to his doom.

In January 1978, Somoza henchmen murdered the regime's most outspoken critic, Pedro Joaquin Chamorro, who published the newspaper *La Prensa*. In August 1978, Sandinista partisans captured the National Palace. Taking hostages, they forced the regime to pay a large cash ransom and provide safe conduct for them out of the country. A national uprising erupted, and the corrupt Somoza system rapidly collapsed. In July 1979, Anastasio Somoza, Jr. fled to the United States. Power was transferred to a five-member *junta* of National Reconstruction, which pledged political democracy and economic justice. The *junta* included Sandinista leaders but also *Violetta Barrios de Chamorro, the widow of the slain editor of *La Prensa*. In 1980, Nora Astorga was appointed chief special prosecutor for the trials of some 7,500 members of Somoza's National Guard, many of whom drew long prison terms.

❧▶ Araúz, Blanca
Nicaraguan rebel. Name variations: Arauz.

A trained telegrapher, Blanca Araúz ran the rebel forces communications units for her husband Agusto César Sandino (1895–1934), one of the most effective guerrilla leaders in modern history; he was assassinated in 1934.

Although the response of the U.S. government to the new situation in Managua was initially cautious because of the nationalistic and leftist components of Sandinista policy, it still appeared that the two nations could move to create a more stable and just political and social order in Central America. This situation changed significantly in 1981, however, when the staunchly conservative Reagan administration decided that the Sandinista government represented a direct threat to American security interests in the region. Of the new situation in Central America, some Washington strategists took a hard-line Cold War view, postulating that Managua was another Cuba and would destabilize a region long subservient to American economic and strategic interests. American-funded contra mercenaries and massive CIA involvement throughout the 1980s were a sad chapter in the region's history.

Nora Astorga regarded her work as a founding member of the Association of Women Confronting the National Problem (AMPRONAC), the Sandinista organization of women supporters of the FSLN, as the most important part of her work for the national rebirth of the Nicaraguan people. In July 1979, AMPRONAC had no more than 8,000 members and supporters (a small number in a national population of 2,400,000); yet women played an important role in the revolution and comprised 30% of the total number of FSLN combat forces in the summer of 1979 when the guerrillas marched into Managua in triumph. Despite that fact, few women were assigned important roles in the new government. Nora Astorga was joined by **Lea Guido** who served as minister of health, **Daisy Zamora** who became deputy minister of culture, and **Dora Maria Tellez** who advanced to the position of vice president of the Council of State. (Daisy Zamora would honor the memory of her friend "Norita" after her 1988 death with a deeply felt poem.) These were tangible signs of progress, but even the creation of a new organization—the Luisa Amanda Espinosa Association of Nicaraguan Women (AMNLAE) in September 1979—failed to fully mobilize many of the poor, malnourished, and illiterate rural women who constituted the bulk of women in a nation where traditional *machismo* and male dominance still reigned.

Nora Astorga served as deputy minister of foreign affairs, and was an intelligent but glamorous speaker for the beleaguered Sandinista revolution. Conversing in idiomatic American English (as well as Italian), she wore high heels and was smartly dressed. As one of the few women diplomats of such high rank, she presented the Sandinista point of view cogently and persuasively, especially in 1983 and 1984 when the Contadora group of Latin American nations sought a peaceful settlement to Central America's bloody politics. Many observers believed that she would be an effective ambassador to Washington, but the Reagan administration rejected her on "moral grounds," arguing that she had been involved in a murder and had had several children out of wedlock. It seems possible that the real reason for her rejection was her potential as a very effective speaker for the Sandinista cause. But she remained *persona non grata* to the CIA because of her involvement in the death of General Perez Vega, one of the agency's key men in Central America.

In 1986, Astorga was appointed chief Nicaraguan delegate to the United Nations. That same year, she discovered that she had breast cancer, a disease she would fight with valor. Back at work seven weeks after surgery, she impressed her fellow delegates with her diligence. Her approach to diplomacy was unique. Astorga often sent red roses with personally signed diplomatic notes. Aware of American antagonism towards her country, she argued: "Revolutions are not exportable like Coca-Cola or paperbacks or something like that. You don't produce it internally and send it away. Revolutions are made in a country when the conditions in that particular country are for a process of change."

Nora Astorga was a passionate speaker for the rights of small nations. In many ways, she was a typical Latin American revolutionary from the ruling elite. While serving at the UN, she lived in a large house in the exclusive suburb of Scarsdale with her mother and five children, including an adopted son, the child of a revolutionary comrade who had died fighting Somoza. Despite the growing tensions between Washington and Managua, she felt at home in the United States and had many American friends who sympathized with the Sandinista revolution. In ill health, she continued to speak before warmly appreciative American audiences, including feminist groups. Nora Astorga died of cancer in Managua on February 14, 1988. Two years later, the Sandinistas voluntarily relinquished power and free elections were held, a fitting tribute to Astorga and those like her who struggled to free Nicaragua from tyranny.

SOURCES:

Canine, Craig. "What Becomes a Legend Most?," in *Newsweek*. Vol. 103, no. 14, April 2, 1984, p. 49.

Cox, Jack. *Requiem in the Tropics: Inside Central America*. NY: UCA Books, 1987.

Garvin, Glenn. *Everybody Had His Own Gringo: The CIA & the Contras*. Washington, DC: Brassey's (United States), 1992.

Meyer, Harvey K. *Historical Dictionary of Nicaragua*. Metuchen, NJ: Scarecrow Press, 1972.

Molyneux, Maxine D. "Women's Role in the Nicaraguan Revolutionary Process: The Early Years," in *Promissory Notes: Women in the Transition to Socialism*. Edited by Sonia Kruks, Rayna Rapp, and Marilyn B. Young. NY: Monthly Review Press, 1989, pp. 127–147.

"Nora and the Dog," in *Time*. Vol. 123, no. 14, April 2, 1984, p. 24.

Randall, Margaret. *Sandino's Daughters: Testimonies of Nicaraguan Women in Struggle*. London: Zed Press, 1981.

———. *Sandino's Daughters Revisited: Feminism in Nicaragua*. New Brunswick, NJ: Rutgers University Press, 1994.

———. "When art meets politics: three worlds, three stories," in *Women's Review of Books*. Vol. 7, Nos. 10–11, July 1990, pp. 21–22.

Rohter, Larry. "Managua Journal: Ghosts in Nicaragua? No, Somozas in the Flesh," in *The New York Times*. July 28, 1995, p. A2.

Saxon, Wolfgang. "Nora Astorga, a Sandinista Hero And Delegate to U.N., Dies at 39," in *The New York Times Biographical Service*. February 1988, p. 199.

Sciolino, Elaine. "Nicaragua's U.N. Voice," in *The New York Times Magazine*. September 28, 1986, pp. 28ff.

"Señorita Nora Astorga," in *The Times* [London]. February 16, 1988, p. 16.

Walker, Thomas W., ed. *Nicaragua in Revolution*. NY: Praeger Publishers, 1982.

John Haag, Associate Professor of History, University of Georgia, Athens, Georgia

Astrid.

Variant of Estrith.

Astrid Bernadotte or Astrid of Belgium (1905–1935)

See Astrid of Sweden.

Astrid of Sweden (1905–1935)

Queen of the Belgians. Name variations: Astrid Bernadotte; Astrid of Belgium. Born Astrid Sofia Lovisa Thyra Bernadotte, princess of Sweden, on November 17, 1905, in Sweden; died in an automobile accident on August 29, 1935, near Küssnacht, Switzerland; buried in Laeken, Brussels, Belgium; daughter of Charles of Sweden and Ingeborg of Den-

*mark (1878–1958); married Leopold III (b. 1901), king of the Belgians, on November 4, 1926; children: Baudoin (1930–1993), king of the Belgians; Albert II (b. 1934), king of the Belgians; *Josephine-Charlotte of Belgium (b. 1927).*

Astrid of Sweden was already a princess when she married Prince Leopold III of Belgium in 1926. Since her mother *Ingeborg of Denmark was a sister of the king of Sweden, she had led a royal life. Among the people of Belgium, however, Astrid was known as the kind who did her own shopping, willingly stopped to talk with people on the streets, and did not put on airs. She had three children with Leopold. In 1934, she assumed the title of queen when her husband ascended the throne, but their royal glow was short-lived. On August 29, 1935, while driving in Switzerland with Leopold at the wheel, the king and queen were in an accident, which Astrid did not survive. Leopold, though badly injured, lived. Six years later, when he remarried, the people of Belgium were unwelcoming to their new queen, *Liliane Baels, who was unable to win the hearts of those still devoted to Queen Astrid. During the German occupation of Belgium in the 1940s, Leopold temporarily lost his throne. Though he resumed it in 1950, public support waned, in part due to Leopold's less charming second wife. He abdicated in 1951.

SOURCES:

Arango, E. Ramón. *Leopold III & the Belgian Royal Question*. Baltimore, Maryland: Johns Hopkins Press, 1961.

Crista Martin,
Boston, Massachusetts

Astrid of the Obotrites (c. 979–?)

*Queen of Sweden. Born around 979; married Olof or Olaf Sköttkonung or Skötkonung, king of Sweden (r. 994–1022); children: *Ingigerd Olafsdottir (c. 1001–1050); Anund Jakob, king of Sweden (r. 1022–1050). Olaf also had children with *Edla.*

Astrith.

Variant of Estrith.

Astronauts: Women in Space

Bondar, Roberta (1945—). First Canadian woman astronaut. Pronunciation: BONN-dar. Born Roberta Lynn Bondar on December 4, 1945, at Sault Ste. Marie, Ontario, Canada; daughter of Edward Bondar and Mildred Bondar; attended University of Guelph, B.S., 1968, University of Western Ontario, M.S., 1971, Uni-

Astrid of Sweden

versity of Toronto, Ph.D., 1974, McMaster University, M.D., 1977. Selected Canadian astronaut (1983); flew on one Spacelab mission before resigning from astronaut corps (1992); published with sister, Dr. Roberta Bondar, On the Shuttle: Eight Days in Space (1993).

Cobb, Jerrie (1931—). First American woman to pass NASA astronaut tests and qualify for spaceflight. Born Geraldyn Menor Cobb on March 5, 1931, at Norman, Oklahoma; daughter of William Harvey Cobb (an Air Force officer) and Helena Butler Stone Cobb (a teacher). Licensed pilot since 1947, setting world records (1956–60); first American woman to pass NASA astronaut tests (February 1960); became a NASA consultant (1960–62); published, with Jane Rieker, Woman Into Space: The Jerrie Cobb Story (1963); established airlift service to Amazonia, the Jerrie Cobb Foundation (1964—); nominated for Nobel Peace Prize (1981).

Collins, Eileen Marie (1956—). American astronaut who was the first female pilot of the space shuttle. Born Eileen Marie Collins on November 19, 1956, at Elmira, New York; daughter of James E. Collins and

Rose Marie Collins; attended Corning Community College, A.S., 1976, Syracuse University, B.A., 1978, Stanford University, M.S., 1986, Webster University, M.A., 1989; married James Patrick Youngs. Joined the Air Force (1978); as second female Air Force test pilot, graduated from Air Force Institute of Technology and Air Force Test Pilot School (1985–90); selected by NASA (1990); pilot on one mission (1995); appointed space shuttle commander of the Columbia, the first woman to lead the crew of four (1998).

Jemison, Mae (1956—). American astronaut who was the first African-American woman to fly in space. Born Mae Carol Jemison on October 17, 1956, at Decatur, Alabama; daughter of Charlie Jemison (a contractor) and Dorothy Jemison (a teacher); attended Stanford University, B.S. and B.A., 1977, Cornell University, M.D., 1981; divorced. Peace Corps medical officer (1983–85); selected by NASA (1987); flew on one mission (1992), before resigning; wrote afterward in **Doris L. Rich**'s biography of **Bessie Coleman**, Queen Bess (1993).

McAuliffe, Christa (1948–1986). First private American citizen selected to fly in space and first civilian to die on the space shuttle. Born Sharon Christa Corrigan on September 2, 1958, in Boston, Massachusetts; died on space shuttle, January 28, 1986; daughter of Edward C. Corrigan (an accountant) and Grace Corrigan (a teacher); attended Framingham State College, B.A., 1970, Bowie State College, M.Ed., 1978; married Steve James McAuliffe, on August 23, 1970; children: Scott (b. 1976) and Caroline (b. 1979). Taught in several Maryland and New Hampshire schools and developed a women's history course (1970–85); won NASA's Teacher-in-Space competition (1985); killed on space shuttle Challenger, January 28, 1986.

Ochoa, Ellen (1958—). American astronaut who was the first female Hispanic astronaut. Pronunciation: O-cho-AH. Born Ellen Lauri Ochoa on May 10, 1958, at Los Angeles, California; daughter of Joseph L. Ochoa and Rosanne Ochoa; attended San Diego State University, B.S., 1980, Stanford University, M.S., 1980, Ph.D., 1985; married Coe Fulmer Miles. Optical researcher (1985–90); won Hispanic Engineering National Achievement Award (1989); selected by NASA (1990); flew on one mission (1993) and awaiting future assignments.

Resnik, Judith (1949–1986). American astronaut who was the first Jewish astronaut to fly in space and first woman astronaut killed in flight. Pronunciation: REZ-nick. Born Judith Arlene Resnik on April 5, 1949, at Akron, Ohio; killed in space on January 28, 1986; daughter of Dr. Marvin Resnik (an optometrist) and Sarah Polensky Resnik (a secretary); married Michael D. Oldak, on July 14, 1970 (divorced 1976); attended Carnegie-Mellon University, B.S., 1970, University of Maryland, Ph.D., 1977. Selected for first group of women astronauts (1978) and completed one mission as second American woman in space (1984); killed on Challenger space mission (1986).

Ride, Sally (1951—). First American woman to fly in space. Born Sally Kristen Ride on May 26, 1951, at Los Angeles, California; daughter of Dr. Dale (an educator) and Joyce (Anderson) Ride (a counselor); attended Swarthmore College, 1968–1970, Stanford University, B.S. and B.A., 1973, M.S., 1975, Ph.D., 1978; married Dr. Steven Hawley, on July 26, 1982 (divorced 1987). Selected for first group of women astronauts in 1978 and first American woman in space, June 18, 1983; after second flight in 1984, served on the Rogers Commission to investigate the Challenger disaster and was a special assistant to the NASA administrator; resigned from NASA (1987); currently director of the Space Science Institute at the University of California at San Diego; inducted into Women's Hall of Fame, Seneca Falls, New York, 1988; published To Space and Back (1986), Voyager: An Adventure to the Edge of the Solar System (1992), and The Third Planet: Exploring the Earth From Space (1994).

Savitskaya, Svetlana (1948—). Soviet astronaut who was the second woman in space and first woman to walk in space. Pronunciation: SVET-lawn-AH Sah-VIT-sky-AH. Born Svetlana Savitskaya on August 8, 1948, in Moscow, Soviet Union; daughter of Yevgeny Yakovlevich (a pilot) and Lidiya Pavlovna Savitsky; graduated from Moscow Aviation Institute, 1972; married Viktor Stanislavovich Khatkovsky; son Konstantin (1986). World champion flyer (1970); set world flying records (1974–81); chosen as cosmonaut (1980) and flew on two missions (1982, 1984), becoming the first woman to walk in space; published Yesterday and Always (1988); elected to Congress of People's Deputies (1989); active cosmonaut awaiting assignment as spacecraft commander.

Sullivan, Kathryn (1951—). First American woman to walk in space and first female payload commander. Born Kathryn Dwyer Sullivan on October 3, 1951, at Paterson, New Jersey; daughter of Donald P. Sullivan (an aerospace design engineer) and Barbara K. Sullivan; University of California at Santa Cruz, B.S., 1973, Dalhousie University, Ph.D., 1978. Selected for first group of women astronauts (1978) and flew on three missions (1984); was the first American woman to walk in space (1990, 1992), and the first female payload commander; wrote foreword in Your

Future in Space: The U.S. Space Camp Training Program (1986); chief scientist of the National Oceanographic and Atmospheric Administration (1992–96); appointed to head the nonprofit Center of Science and Industry in Columbus, Ohio (1996).

Thornton, Kathryn (1952—). American astronaut who was the first woman to fly on a classified Department of Defense mission and holder of spacewalking record for female astronauts. Born Kathryn Ryan Cordell on August 17, 1952, at Montgomery, Alabama; daughter of William Carten Thornton and Elsie Elizabeth Ryan Cordell (restaurant owners); attended Auburn University, B.S., 1974, University of Virginia, M.S., 1977, Ph.D., 1979; married Stephen Thomas Thornton; children, stepson Kenneth (b. 1963), stepson Michael (b. 1965), Carol Elizabeth (b. 1982), Laura Lee (b. 1985), Susan Annette (b. 1990). Selected by NASA (1984); flew on three missions (1989); became the first female astronaut to fly on a classified Department of Defense mission (1992), achieving the female spacewalking record; helped repair the Hubble telescope (1993); went on fourth mission as payload commander of the second United States Microgravity Laboratory (1995).

On July 20, 1969, the world was enthralled when two American astronauts landed on the moon, and Neil Armstrong declared: "That's one small step for a man . . . one giant leap for mankind." By the end of the 20th century, women had yet to set foot on the moon, and the pronoun *he* permeated space history. Nevertheless, pioneering female astronauts have overcome political, societal, and bureaucratic obstacles and have secured opportunities for future female space explorers. A diverse group of women not only serve admirably as space travelers but also as astronautic engineers, scientists, and administrators.

Jerrie Cobb

The inclusion of women in space exploration has been a frustrating endeavor. In the late 1950s, the Air Force first tested women at Wright-Patterson Air Force Base in Dayton, Ohio, to determine if they were physiologically suitable for space flight. Then, in 1960, Geraldyn "Jerrie" Menor Cobb became the first American woman to undergo and successfully complete NASA's grueling astronaut tests. A pilot since age 12, Cobb played semi-pro softball with the Sooner Queens for three years, accumulating enough money to buy a war-surplus airplane to patrol oil pipelines and teach flying lessons. Cobb also ferried aircraft to South America, Europe, and India.

Setting speed and altitude records, Cobb was hired as a test pilot by the Aero Design and Engineering Company in April 1959. Most test pilots were men with military training; only a few women were skilled enough to test the strength and endurance of new airplanes. After securing several world records, Cobb won the Woman of the Year in Aviation Award in 1959. Later that year, at the Miami Air Force Association conference, Cobb talked to Dr. W. Randolph Lovelace, chair of NASA's Life Sciences Committee for Project Mercury. Lovelace wanted to study the effects of spaceflight on women and asked Cobb to be his test subject.

Cobb accepted Lovelace's invitation. Though she realized that in 1958 President Dwight Eisenhower had directed that NASA consider only male military test pilots for astronauts, she hoped that her talent would outweigh such restrictions. Following her arrival at the Lovelace Foundation in Albuquerque, New Mexico, in February 1960, Cobb passed the same rigorous tests, physical and psychological, as the male Mercury astronauts, everything from swallowing lengthy hose for gastric analysis to withstanding exposure to extreme temperatures. Cobb rated higher than many male candidates, especially in adjustment tests, and revealed that in some ways women were more capable than men to meet space travel's physical demands.

As a result of Cobb's success, Lovelace predicted that women would have a major role in future spaceflight. He suggested that Cobb undergo further tests at the Lewis Research Center in Cleveland, Ohio, where her ability to react and to control a space capsule would be analyzed. Cobb successfully completed those tests; she also passed Navy pilot tests at the Pensacola Aerospace Medical Research Laboratory, and floated in a darkened underground isolation water tank in Oklahoma City for nine hours and forty minutes, three hours longer than any male astronaut. Lovelace publicized Cobb's successes and announced that she was ready to go into space. In the ensuing publicity frenzy, Cobb was labeled a "lady astronaut" and featured on television and in major magazines. One NASA official responded, "Talk of an American spacewoman makes me sick to my stomach."

Encouraged by Cobb, famed pilot *Jacqueline Cochran, who had organized World War II women pilots, enlisted Cobb and Lovelace to help her select women for astronaut testing. Cochran financed the tests. The stipulations required that each applicant must have a commercial pilot's license with 1,500 hours of flying time. Thirty-one women applicants qualified. In 1961, 12 American women passed the Mercury tests and were designated as Fellow Lady Astronaut Trainees (FLATs). These women, who were firmly committed to the space program and often better trained than their male counterparts, pursued spaceflight training in the "Women in Space Soonest" (WISS) program.

When NASA administrator James Webb chose Cobb to be a NASA consultant and write a report on the potential of women in the space program, she was emphatic that qualified women should become astronauts. Having initially believed that no women could pass the tests, NASA delayed responding to her report, finally explaining that women might be included in future space flight but that the WISS program was canceled and women would not train for Project Mercury. Cobb and the FLATs were rejected as astronauts because they lacked sufficient experience as jet test pilots, a career limited primarily to military men.

*J*ohnny Carson made what he considered to be a joke, that the shuttle launch was being postponed until Sally Ride could find the purse to match her shoes. There are a lot of people waiting for her to fail.

—Joyce Ride, on the eve of her daughter's historic mission
as the first American woman in space

Devastated, Cobb refused to give up. Joined by the FLATS, especially **Jane Hart**, the wife of a Michigan senator, Cobb lobbied Congress. On July 17, 1962, she addressed the House Committee on Science and Astronautics, arguing that women had proven that they were as physically and mentally suitable to be astronauts as men. Women weighed less, needed less oxygen and food, and were less likely to suffer heart attacks than men, she noted, as she urged Congress to let America be the first country to send a woman into space. Commenting that female research animals had already been sent to space, Cobb complained, "Millions for chimps, but not one cent for women." An outspoken woman, Hart told Congress, "It is inconceivable to me that the world of outer space should be restricted to men only, like some sort of stag club." She stressed, "I am not arguing that women be admitted to space merely so that they won't feel discriminated against. I am arguing that they are admitted because they have a very real contribution to make."

Then Cobb and Hart had to sit back and listen to leader after NASA leader denounce women

space explorers, recommending their exclusion. Despite her earlier support, Cochran testified that though she thought a corps of female space specialists like the World War II WASPs should be established, it might be too costly. Also, she questioned whether female astronauts would abandon the space program for marriage and pregnancy. Cochran had written Cobb that the time for female astronauts would come and warning that "pushing too hard just now could possibly retard rather than speed that date." An annoyed John Glenn, the first American to orbit the Earth, dismissed the FLATS in his testimony, declaring that the tests were inconsequential. Despite their success in outfitting male astronauts, NASA officials explained that it would be too complicated to design spacesuits to fit female astronauts and accommodate their biological needs. Administrators also argued that hundreds of women would have to be more rigorously tested to determine if women were capable of sustaining spaceflight. In response, the press rallied in support of the FLATS, dubbing them astronauttes, astronettes, and astronautrixes.

Although the military requirement was dropped when the second group of Project Gemini astronauts were selected in 1962, Congress and President John F. Kennedy refused to train women astronauts, believing that they would impede the goal of landing a man on the moon by 1970. Other reasons for not having an official training program for women included fear of public backlash against the space program if a woman was killed in space and possible public-relations problems with the logistics of overnight cohabitation in capsules or the assignment of all-female crews (which some feminists labeled male NASA officials' "worst nightmare").

On June 15, 1963, cosmonaut *Valentina V. Tereshkova became the first woman in space. (She had been selected along with **Zhanna Dmitriyevna Yorkina**, though Yorkina never flew.) After Tereshkova's flight, American journalist *Clare Boothe Luce penned an angry editorial for *Life* magazine, criticizing NASA's refusal to train women astronauts. In 1964, NASA invited female geologists and geophysicists to apply for scientific lunar missions; none were accepted. Then, the feminist movement of the late 1960s began to pry open the doors.

In 1972, Congress passed an amendment of the Civil Rights Act of 1964, stipulating that federal agencies could not discriminate on the basis of gender, and NASA officials began to come around. Besides, some reasoned, women would have a "civilizing influence" on male astronauts and be necessary for domestic chores such as housekeeping and cooking in addition to providing a means for the men's sexual release on future space stations and lengthy missions.

Beginning the following year, Air Force nurses and civilian women participated in NASA-sponsored physiological tests, simulating weightlessness to determine the role women could play in space. Volunteers, such as future astronaut **Marsha Ivins**, underwent tests during the mid-1970s to aid NASA in establishing criteria to select the first women astronauts. At the same time, NASA's transition to the space shuttle resulted in more frequent flights that required larger crews consisting of specialists in science and engineering. The attitudes of NASA officials changed slowly, but women interested in aerospace careers now had hope for future advancement.

After a rigorous selection process, involving interviews and physical examinations, NASA named the first female astronaut candidates in January 1978: **Sally Ride, Judith Resnik, Kathryn Sullivan, *Shannon Lucid, Anna Fisher,** and ❧▸ **Rhea Seddon.** Of 8,079 applications, 1,142 had been submitted by women. Nineteen women were named finalists, and the chosen six, selected on the basis of their achievements and potential for the future, were designated as mission specialists. Though they relinquished their careers and original research for the chance to fly in space, all agreed that it was an opportunity that they could not refuse. Said Seddon, "I feel the burden to succeed especially because of other women who want to go into the space program. They will be looking to us to do well so that NASA will accept more women in the future." At about the same time, physicist **Ann F. Whitaker** was designated one of six American finalists for Spacelab I, a cooperative mission with Europe. She was the only woman chosen.

Sally Ride

Sally Kristen Ride became the first American woman in space 23 years after Cobb passed NASA's astronaut tests. Publicity about Ride's accomplishment rivaled that of the Apollo moon landing, creating renewed enthusiasm for the space program. Ride's childhood experiences bolstered her scientific interests. She had excelled scholastically, attending Beverly Hills' Westlake School for Girls. Dedicated to her studies, she credited her science teacher, Dr. **Elizabeth Mommaerts**, for encouraging her to explore the mysteries of the universe. A nationally ranked junior tennis player, Ride acquired character traits such as discipline, commitment, and

composure that she believed prepared her to become an astronaut. Her parents were also supportive. Said Ride: "Anytime I wanted to pursue something that they weren't familiar with, that was not part of their lifestyle, they let me go ahead and do it. . . . Tennis was an example; so was going into science. I think they were kind of glad when I went into the astronaut program, because that was something they could understand. Astrophysics they had trouble with."

In college, Ride's favorite classes were astronomy and physics. Having watched the moon landing, she dreamed of a dual career as a tennis professional and a space researcher. She did not consider becoming an astronaut because women were excluded from that role. A versatile scholar, Ride also majored in English and edited *Sportswoman* magazine. She focused her graduate work in astrophysics, specializing in x-ray astronomy at the Stanford Plasma Physics Laboratory, and applied to NASA. Believing that her research could benefit the planned space station, NASA included Ride among its six female astronaut-candidates in 1978. "I don't know why they chose me," said Ride, "but I hope it had nothing to do with the fact that I'm a woman. I hope they chose me because I am a scientist." She disliked publicity that focused on her gender, especially reporters' questions about whether she would wear a brassiere and if she feared space flight would damage her reproductive organs.

❧▸ **Seddon, Rhea** (1947—)

American astronaut. Born Margaret Rhea Seddon in Murfreesboro, Tennessee, on November 8, 1947; served a surgical internship and three years of general surgery residency in Memphis, Tennessee; did clinical research into the effects of radiation therapy on nutrition in cancer patients.

In August 1979, out of the original group of six women astronaut trainees, Rhea Seddon was the first woman to achieve the full rank of astronaut and the first to be selected for the space-shuttle program. Before her initial space mission, she worked on orbiter and payload software, functioned as launch and landing rescue helicopter physician, and as technical assistant to the director of Flight Crew Operations. On April 12, 1985, she boarded the *Discovery* shuttle for a 168-hour mission, which, among other things, made an unscheduled attempt to repair a malfunctioning satellite. Her next flight, on June 5, 1991, was on the Spacelab Life Sciences (SLS-1) mission on board the *Columbia*; it was a nine-day mission that explored microgravitational pull on humans and animals.

Sally Ride

June 24 at Edwards Air Force Base, Ride became an instant national hero.

In October 1984, Ride was the initial American woman assigned to a second shuttle mission. Flight 41-G was the first launch with two female astronauts, Ride and Kathryn Sullivan. Though Ride was named to fly on STS 61-M in June 1985, she discontinued her training after the January 1986 *Challenger* explosion. Selected as the only active astronaut on the Rogers Commission to investigate the accident, Ride advised that some astronauts should serve in NASA management positions. She became a special assistant to the agency administrator in Washington, D.C., evaluating NASA objectives.

In 1987, Ride led a team study of NASA and wrote "Leadership and America's Future in Space: A Report to the Administrator." The Ride Report outlined four paths for future space exploration. In particular, she promoted "Mission to Planet Earth," a space-based study of Earth. She also suggested initiating exploration of the solar system without a crew, building outposts on the moon, and sending staffed missions to Mars to recapture American space leadership and increase public interest. Later that year, Ride resigned from NASA's astronaut corps and joined Stanford's Center for International Security and Arms Control. She then became director of the California Space Studies Institute.

Svetlana Savitskaya

The first woman to walk in space, Russia's Svetlana Savitskaya decided to become a pilot at an early age. She set world parachuting records as a teenager and won the world flying aerobatics championship in 1970. Obtaining a degree in aeronautical engineering and completing test pilot school, she achieved world records for speed and altitude in supersonic aircraft. Savitskaya qualified as a cosmonaut in 1980. On August 19, 1982, she became the second woman in space. Despite her technical accomplishments, as Savitskaya prepared to board the Soviet space station, astronaut Valentin Lebedev welcomed her with, "We have an apron all ready for you, Svetlana."

Savitskaya became the first woman to walk in space on July 25, 1983, an action that many critics demeaned by labeling it a propaganda stunt to diminish the impact of American astronaut Kathryn Sullivan's planned spacewalk. Donning a spacesuit modified for her smaller frame, Savitskaya found it difficult to maneuver on her spacewalk, during which she tested space tools and removed an experiment from the sta-

Moving to Houston, Texas, Ride mastered simulators and computer systems, preparing for every conceivable situation that might occur on a shuttle flight from launch to landing. She helped Canadian scientists develop the Remote Manipulator System (RMS), a robotic arm to move items in the shuttle's cargo bay. She rode in a T-38 chase plane for the first shuttle mission, STS-1, in April 1981, photographing the shuttle and relaying weather information to the crew. As the first female capsule communicator in Houston's Mission Control, she communicated with astronauts on the second and third shuttle flights and asked them good-naturedly, "When do I get my turn?"

In April 1982, Commander Bob Crippen announced that Ride would be the first American woman in space. "I wanted a competent engineer who was cool under stress," he explained. On June 18, 1983, half a million spectators watched Ride's launch at Cape Canaveral. As a mission specialist, she monitored experiments and demonstrated the remote arm, retrieving a satellite to return to Earth for repair. Landing on

tion hull to return to scientists on Earth. When asked about her historic walk, Savitskaya remarked, "A hundred years from now, no one will remember it, and if they do, it will sound strange that it was once questioned whether a woman should go into space."

Although the Soviets planned for an all-woman crew commanded by Savitskaya, the mission was canceled due to mechanical difficulties and because of her pregnancy. She was honored twice in the 1980s as a Hero of the Soviet Union and received the Order of Lenin and numerous sports medals, including the Gold Space Medal.

Kathryn D. Sullivan

Kathryn D. Sullivan, the first American woman to walk in space, became intrigued by science experiments in the second grade and watched the Apollo landing, calling it an "unforgettable experience." She regretted that "'astronaut' in those days was not a career option that school guidance counselors or parents urged on young students—and certainly not one for young women." In graduate school, Sullivan focused on marine geology and participated in oceanographic expeditions to evaluate the sea floor east of Newfoundland's Grand Banks. While finishing her dissertation, she became aware of NASA's changed attitudes toward female astronauts. Recognizing parallels between marine geologists and astronauts (both explored in uncharted territory), she applied to NASA because "no self-respecting geologist could pass up the chance to see our beautiful planet from such an incredible perspective with her own eyes."

NASA recognized Sullivan's skills, including her ability to communicate and coexist with others in small spaces as evidenced on marine research ships. An expert with remote sensing equipment, she was the co-investigator for the Shuttle Imaging Radar-B (SIR-B) experiment. This mission, which included Sally Ride, was launched on October 5, 1984, the first shuttle flight with two women aboard. On October 11, Sullivan became the first American woman to spacewalk when she tested refueling satellites in orbit and deployed the Earth Radiation Budget Satellite. Male astronauts had completed almost 40 spacewalks before Sullivan made her pioneering stroll.

In 1985, Sullivan became an adjunct geology professor at Rice University, and President Ronald Reagan named her to the National Commission on Space, where she prepared the report "Pioneering the Space Frontier," outlining space goals into the 21st century. She helped deploy the

Kathryn D. Sullivan

Hubble telescope in April 1990 and studied protein crystal growth and polymer membrane processing. Sullivan was the first female payload commander in the spring of 1992, focusing on how atmospheric composition influences the Earth's climate and environment. In 1994, she was appointed chief scientist to the National Oceanic and Atmospheric Administration, and, in 1996, was appointed head of the Center of Science and Industry Museum in Columbus, Ohio.

Judith Resnik

Judith Arlene Resnik, the first Jewish astronaut, dedicated her life to scientific achievement. The granddaughter of Russian immigrants who valued hard work, Resnik excelled in high school. Taking advanced courses in mathematics and science, the ambitious Resnik graduated as class valedictorian, earning a perfect score on the SAT. In college, she enjoyed applying science to practical problems, majoring in electrical engineering. Graduating with honors, she married her college

Judith Resnik

might interfere with her career. She resented personal questions. In April 1981, she was a technical commentator for NBC at the shuttle's maiden launch. When Tom Brokaw asked how she responded when men said that she was too cute to be an astronaut, Resnik sternly quipped, "I just tell them I'm an engineer."

In 1984, Resnik flew on the shuttle *Discovery*. The flight was delayed by computer problems, finally launching on August 30. She deployed satellites, tested the shuttle's solar sail, and monitored crystal growth experiments. Resnik also manipulated the remote arm to remove dangerous ice built up on the shuttle. The crew filmed themselves and were featured in the IMAX movie, *The Dream is Alive*.

Christa McAuliffe

After her return to Earth, Resnik traveled to Washington, D.C., to describe her adventures in space to NASA's Teacher-in-Space contest finalists, including Christa McAuliffe, the first private civilian selected to travel in space. McAuliffe had watched Alan Shepard's flight as a teenager, saved magazine articles about the Mercury 7 astronauts, heard Neil Armstrong's historic words while driving through a rainstorm in Pennsylvania, and longed to go into space. "I remember the excitement in my home when the first satellites were launched," she recalled. In college, she majored in history and dreamed of improving society. History professor **Carolla Haglund** inspired McAuliffe to study the frontier, including space.

After her marriage in 1970, McAuliffe taught junior high history, civics, and English in several schools in the Washington, D.C. area. Teaching disadvantaged children, she introduced them to significant historical sites in their community. When her husband was appointed assistant state attorney general, McAuliffe moved to New Hampshire and accepted a teaching position at Concord High School. She developed a course, "The American Woman," in which students learned how women, including Sally Ride, had influenced history.

When Reagan announced the NASA Teacher-in-Space project in 1984, primarily to counter public support for political rival Walter Mondale, McAuliffe decided to apply as an example to her students. If selected, McAuliffe planned to keep a journal, describing her selection and training, the shuttle flight, and postflight reflections. She compared her voyage into space to a pioneer woman heading west in a Conestoga wagon. "My perceptions as a non-as-

sweetheart and moved to New Jersey where she worked in the missile and surface radar division of RCA. When her husband enrolled in Georgetown's law school, Resnik began studies at the University of Maryland and worked as a biomedical engineer at the National Institute of Health.

Shortly before finishing her doctorate, Resnik saw NASA's announcement for shuttle astronauts on a bulletin board at work, and she applied. She embarked on a fitness and dietary program, earned a pilot's license, and read astronaut Michael Collins' book, *Carrying the Fire*, which discussed how NASA applicants were reviewed. She then located Collins' office at the National Air and Space Museum where he was administrator and boldly introduced herself: "My name's Judy Resnik, and I want to be an astronaut."

After her selection, Resnik devoted her life to mission training. *Time* magazine described her as: "The most doggedly determined astronaut, male or female, ever to suit up." Resnik disliked publicity, worrying that negative press tronaut would help complete and humanize the technology of the Space Age," she declared. "Future historians would use my eyewitness accounts to help in their studies of the impact of the Space Age on the general population."

Committed to educating future space travelers and researchers, McAuliffe noted, "I really hope the students get exited about the Space Age because they see me as an a ordinary person up there in space." She elaborated, "Not everybody has had an astronaut in his or her life, but almost everyone has had a teacher." She wanted her mission to demonstrate that "space is for everyone" and emphasized that thousands of earthbound employees worked for NASA as engineers, scientists, and administrators. **Barbara Morgan**, an Idaho teacher who was selected as McAuliffe's alternate, mused, "I hope that when people see Christa in space, they won't want to become astronauts; they'll want to become teachers."

Chosen from 10,463 applicants, McAuliffe was unanimously selected as the Teacher-in-Space on July 19, 1985. NASA believed that she was the most qualified person to explain her experiences and convince children and parents that space was a valuable frontier to explore. McAuliffe enthusiastically prepared for her flight, outlining two lessons, "The Ultimate Field Trip," a tour of the shuttle, and "Where We've Been, Where We're Going, Why?," a discussion about the history and future of space flight. She also planned to demonstrate the scientific and commercial benefits of space, showing how microgravity aided production of crystals and other vital substances.

Assigned to the same crew as Judy Resnik, McAuliffe cherished a friendship with her as they trained together during the fall and winter of 1985. After delays due to bad weather, pressured NASA officials ignored engineers' warnings and decided to launch the shuttle in freezing temperatures on January 28, 1986. Despite wintry winds, family and friends of McAuliffe and Resnik joined teachers waiting in the bleachers to watch the launch. Seventy-three seconds after liftoff, the *Challenger* exploded, and the entire crew perished in a fireball. It was the worst disaster in spaceflight history; their bodies would not be recovered from the Atlantic Ocean until April.

While the nation mourned, President Reagan paid tribute to the dead at a national service at the Johnson Space Center. Bronze replicas of the crew adorn the *Challenger* Monument in Arlington National Cemetery by the common grave of unidentified astronauts. Christa McAuliffe was buried in Concord's Blossom Hill Cemetery; her gravestone reads, "She tried to

Christa McAuliffe

protect our spaceship Earth. She taught her children to do the same." Scholarships and memorials throughout the world, and two craters on the moon, bear McAuliffe's and Resnik's names.

Kathryn Thornton

The *Challenger* disaster did not deter women from pursuing spaceflight. Although they acknowledged the dangers involved, female astronauts concurred that the risks of space were negligible compared to everyday earthly hazards. Remarking that driving on Houston roads posed more threats than being launched in the shuttle, Kathryn Thornton, the first woman on a secret Department of Defense flight, holds the record for spacewalking by a female astronaut. Growing up in Alabama, she played "moon landing" with her siblings but admitted, "I didn't know when I was a child that I wanted to be an astronaut because there weren't any women astronauts." A physicist, Thornton has worked at the Max Planck Institute for Nuclear Physics in Heidelberg, West Germany,

Mae
Jemison

Space Telescope. In December 1993, Thornton was the only woman on the Hubble servicing crew. Perched in deep space on the end of the shuttle's robotic mechanical arm, she skillfully completed her tasks and established new space-walk records. Thornton and her colleagues salvaged an expensive and crucial piece of hardware, boosting public support for NASA and continued space exploration.

During her post-flight media tour, Thornton advocated scientific education for youngsters. Concerned about her children, she admitted, "Leaving home each time is the hardest thing of all." While in space, she talked daily to her daughters by videophone. Balancing her career and family, Thornton noted, "Women can't have it all—we can have a little bit all of the time, or all of it a little bit of the time, but we never have it all, all of the time."

Roberta Bondar

Roberta Bondar, the first Canadian female astronaut, enjoyed listening to science fiction radio stories as a child with her sister Barbara. Pretending they were astronauts, the girls built a spaceship from wood, cardboard, and wire and wore space helmets ordered from a bubble gum company. Educated as a neurologist, Bondar served as director of the Multiple Sclerosis Clinic at McMaster University, researched aspects of aerospace medicine, and won an award for the best paper published in *Canadian Aeronautics and Space*.

Bondar was one of six Canadian astronauts selected in December 1983. The Canadian astronaut program was established to provide a payload specialist for the space station, and 4,300 applicants responded to newspaper advertisements. Bondar began training with the Canadian Space Agency in February 1984 and was named chair of Canada's life sciences subcommittee for the space station. While training for her mission, Bondar was a civil aviation medical examiner and served on the science staff at Sunnybrook Hospital, where she researched the blood flow in the brains of stroke patients; she also tested subjects in microgravity aboard a special NASA plane that simulated zero gravity.

As a payload specialist on the Internal Microgravity Laboratory (IML-1) Spacelab mission in December 1990, Bondar studied microgravity's effects on material processing and living organisms. She was the mission's principal investigator for 55 experiments, including studies of taste in space and cerebral blood flow velocity during weightlessness. Monitoring her blood pressure,

and at the Army Foreign Science and Technology Center in Charlottesville, Virginia. She applied to NASA, believing that becoming an astronaut would be the best way to utilize her scientific training and technical ability. She was selected in May 1984 from almost 5,000 applicants.

Thornton's first mission in November 1989 transported a classified military payload. She deployed a spy satellite and supervised experiments for the Star Wars missile defense system. After a brief maternity leave, she entered training for her second flight. In May 1992, Thornton returned to space to repair a telecommunications satellite and to test space-station construction techniques. During her first spacewalk, she experimented with rescue procedures to capture untethered astronauts drifting in space. Her spacewalk of seven hours and forty-five minutes exceeded the combined total of the two previous woman spacewalkers, Sullivan and Savitskaya.

Returning to Earth, Thornton prepared for an even greater challenge, repair of the Hubble she reported how her body adjusted during reentry through the atmosphere and return to Earth.

With the help of her sister, Bondar wrote a book about her experiences in space. In 1984, she resigned from the astronaut corps and returned to the University of Ottawa to teach.

Mae Jemison

Mae Jemison, the first female African-American astronaut, followed her dreams despite discouragement from teachers and friends. Growing up in Chicago, she admired Lt. Uhura, a fictional black astronaut on "Star Trek," read space books, and watched the lunar landing. "I always assumed I would go into space ever since I was a little girl," she recalled. In college and medical school, she encountered subtle racism as engineering professors ignored her or treated her condescendingly. "I felt," she said, "totally invisible." Jemison coped by developing "internal motivation": "Basically, you have to understand and believe in yourself and do what it is you know you are capable of despite what anyone else may tell you."

After assisting refugees in Thailand when she was a medical student, Jemison joined the Peace Corps in 1983, serving in Sierra Leone and Liberia as the area medical officer and researching vaccines for hepatitis and rabies. Two years later, she returned to the United States as a general practitioner for CIGNA Health Plans of California. Inspired by the women and minorities in NASA's class of 1978, Jemison consulted black astronaut Ron McNair about fulfilling her desire to travel in space. She was one of 15 candidates chosen from 2,000 applicants in June 1987.

Her mission, originally scheduled for August 1988, was postponed until September 1992 because of the *Challenger* tragedy. Flying aboard the shuttle *Endeavor* on the first cooperative mission with Japan, Jemison focused on scientific experiments, observing the behavior of fish, frogs, and hornets in microgravity. She conducted tests to determine how to force body fluids that move upward into the chest when astronauts are in microgravity back into their legs for a safe return to Earth. Jemison demonstrated how the Autogenic Feedback Training Vestibular Symptomatology Suit measured vital signs and how the wearer could use biofeedback to soothe space sickness.

After Jemison's mission, Chicago hosted a six-day celebration. She talked to children, advising them to follow their hearts and avoid people with "limited imagination." She especially encouraged blacks to seek careers with the space program, saying, "This is one time when we can

Ellen Ochoa

get in on the ground floor." Six months after her flight, Jemison left NASA to teach a class on space-age technology and developing countries at Dartmouth College. She has since established the Jemison Group in Houston to improve health care in West Africa. Jemison fulfilled a childhood ambition in 1993 when she played Lt. Palmer on "Star Trek: The Next Generation."

Ellen Ochoa

Ellen Ochoa, the first Hispanic female astronaut, graduated as valedictorian when she earned a degree in physics at San Diego State University. A gifted flutist, Ochoa originally had majored in music and won symphony awards. At Stanford University, she was one of the few women enrolled in electrical engineering. "Other than feeling a little self-conscious at times, I never really felt that I was treated different in any way," Ochoa recalled. Supported by fellowships from IBM, she wrote a dissertation about using photorefractive crystals in optical systems to detect defects in images.

Eileen M. Collins

Eileen M. Collins

Air Force Lieutenant Colonel Eileen Collins, the first female shuttle pilot, grew up in Elmira, New York, an aviation-oriented town. Working odd jobs as a teenager to save money for flight lessons, Collins also had dreams of flying in space. After completing her academic education, including two years of Air Force ROTC at Syracuse University, she was commissioned as a second lieutenant in 1978, and was in the first group of women that the Air Force trained to fly. When a female student failed a proficiency check ride, news of her blunders quickly spread, and Collins recalled, "All of a sudden, I realized there is a lot of pressure on me. I can't afford to fail because I will be hurting chances for young women who want to come here some day."

Collins mastered military flying and received medals for combat service in Grenada in October 1983. For two years, she honed her flying skills at Travis Air Force Base in California, then enrolled at the Air Force Institute of Technology in 1985. At the same time, Collins was an assistant professor of mathematics at the United States Air Force Academy and a T-41 instructor pilot with the 557th Flying Training Squadron. In 1989, she was accepted at the exclusive Air Force Test Pilots School at Edwards Air Force Base, graduating in 1990 as the Air Force's second female test plot (Major **Jackie Parker** was the first). With over 3,500 flying hours in 30 types of aircraft, Collins had the piloting skills that NASA desired. She was chosen as a future shuttle pilot in January 1990. Before her selection, women astronauts were utilized primarily for research and repair assignments.

Dedicating herself to pilot training, Collins became the first woman to pilot the space shuttle on February 3, 1995, when she was second in command of a crew of six that made an historical rendezvous with the Russian space station Mir. Collins invited the surviving FLATS to Cape Canaveral to watch her launch, carrying memorabilia for them, including ***Amelia Earhart**'s scarf, aboard the shuttle. "The space program is critical to the future of all mankind," notes Collins, "as some of our biggest problems on Earth can be solved in space." On March 5, 1998, **Hillary Rodham Clinton** announced Collins' appointment as the first female space shuttle commander. She would lead a crew of four on the *Columbia*.

Ochoa excelled as a researcher with the Imaging Technology Branch of Sandia National Laboratories in Livermore, California; she developed optical methods to improve object recognition and designed optical filters for noise removal, receiving two patents. In 1988, she transferred to NASA's Ames Research Center at Moffett Field, California, leading a research group in optical processing, especially recognition systems for space. Within six months, she was chosen as chief of the Intelligent Systems Technology Branch, directing a group of engineers and scientists to develop high performance computational systems for aerospace missions.

Ochoa penned professional papers for journals and won the Hispanic Engineering National Achievement Award as the most promising government engineer in 1989. In January 1990, NASA chose Ochoa as the first female Hispanic astronaut; she was one of 23 candidates selected from 2,000 applicants. Ochoa flew on her first mission in April 1993, retrieving a solar observation satellite and studying the Earth's atmosphere.

Although a small minority, NASA's growing troupe of female astronauts are thriving in a male-dominated agency. Worldwide, female astronauts still continue to be designated as pioneers: **Susan Jane Helms** was the first woman astronaut to graduate from a military service academy, Shannon Lucid was the first woman to fly on three flights and the first to stay on Mir for over six months, **Anna Fisher** was the first mother in space, **Jan Davis** was the first female astronaut to travel in space with her spouse, **Helen Patricia Sharman** was the first British astronaut in space, and **Chiaki Naito-Mukai** was the first female Japanese astronaut. In June 1991, **Tamara Jernigan**, Rhea Seddon and **Millie Hughes-Fulford** were the first three women to fly together on a mission. **Bonnie Dunbar** and **Ellen Baker** were on the first shuttle mission to dock with the Soviet space station Mir in June 1995. Dunbar, who speaks Russian fluently and was backup to Norman Thagard, trained in Russia for one year prior to the mission. Baker is a physician who conducted medical tests on the Mir crew to understand how living in space for long periods of time affects the human body.

Since the early 1960s, women worldwide have played prominent roles in aerospace science, engineering, and administration, designing miniature electronic circuits, inventing the first satellite-tracking technology, analyzing aerodynamic performance, devising nutritious meals for astronauts, and developing adequate life support systems, clothing, and medical care for space explorers. Dr. *Irmgard Flügge-Lotz was called the female Wernher von Braun for her work on satellite, rocket, and missile controls. Women also molded space policy. Dr. **Carolyn L. Huntoon**, a physiologist and director of the Johnson Space Center in Houston, was the only female panelist on the committee that selected the first six American women astronauts.

Having won a variety of aerospace, professional, and international awards, women have secured their place in space. As their legacy, female astronauts and aerospace engineers, scientists, and administrators have invested their myriad talents and achievements to weave an intricate tapestry to nurture future space travelers and residents. As astronaut **Mary Cleave** reflected, "The early astronauts were the explorers. We are the homesteaders."

SOURCES:

Bernstein, Joanne, and Rose Blue, with Alan Jay Gerber. *Judith Resnik: Challenger Astronaut.* NY: Lodestar Books, 1990.

Corrigan, Grace George. *A Journal for Christa: Christa McAuliffe, Teacher in Space.* Lincoln: University of Nebraska Press, 1993.

Hawthorne, Douglas B. *Men and Women of Space.* San Diego, CA: Univelt, 1992.

Hohler, Robert T. *"I Touch the Future . . .": The Story of Christa McAuliffe.* NY: Random House, 1986.

Hurwitz, Jane, and Sue Hurwitz. *Sally Ride: Shooting for the Stars.* NY: Fawcett Columbine, 1989.

Lasagna, Louis. "Why Not 'Astronauttes' Also?," in *The New York Times Magazine.* October 21, 1962, pp. 52–53.

Phelps, J. Alfred. *They Had a Dream: The Story of African-American Astronauts.* Novato, CA: Presidio, 1994.

SUGGESTED READING:

Briggs, Carole S. *Women in Space: Reaching the Last Frontier.* Minneapolis: Lerner Publications, 1993.

Flowers, Sandra H. *Women in Aviation and Space.* Washington, DC: Department of Transportation, Federal Aviation Administration, 1990.

Fox, Mary Virginia. *Women Astronauts Aboard the Shuttle.* Rev. ed. NY: Messner, 1987.

Hoyt, Mary Finch. *American Women of the Space Age.* NY: Atheneum, 1966.

Sharman, Helen, and Christopher Priest. *Seize the Moment: The Autobiography of Helen Sharman.* London: Victor Gollancz, 1993.

Vaughan, Diane. *The Challenger Launch Decision.* Chicago, IL: University of Chicago Press, 1996.

COLLECTIONS:

Astronaut biographical information is available from the public relations office and history office at Johnson Space Center, Houston, Texas, and additional archival materials are at the NASA History Office and the Smithsonian Institute's National Air and Space Museum Library, Washington, D.C.

Elizabeth D. Schafer, Ph.D., Freelance Writer in History of Technology and Science, Loachapoka, Alabama

Athaliah (r. 842–836 BCE)

Biblical woman who seized control of Judah (842 BCE), which she ruled until her murder by Judaeans opposed to her foreignness and religious toleration.

Name variations: Athalia. Flourished between 860 and 836 BCE; assassinated in 836 BCE; daughter of Ahab and Jezebel of Israel; married Jehoram (or Joram), king of Judah; children: son Ahaziah (or Azariah).

Athaliah, meaning "the Lord is exalted," was the daughter of Ahab and *Jezebel of Israel. Her marriage to Jehoram, the crown prince of Judah, sealed a political alliance between Israel and Judah. However, not all within Judah were pleased by the alliance, especially as Israel—religiously much more tolerant than Judah—permitted the worship of many deities. As a result, with the coming of Athaliah to Jerusalem came also the worship of various ba'als, especially Melqart, a development that was anathema to all religiously conservative Judaeans. Even so, religious toleration was itself tolerated for the sake of the Israeli-Judaean alliance, for as long as Athaliah's husband and son reigned.

Jehoram died in 843 BCE and his son by Athaliah, Ahaziah, came to the throne without apparent opposition. Nevertheless, factional opposition quickly coalesced when Ahaziah refused to abandon his father's political and religious policies. After about a year, Jehu, a critic of those policies, successfully hatched an assassination plot. When Ahaziah was murdered, his son and heir, Joash, was but an infant, and the opposition obviously thought the moment opportune to seize the initiative. Jehu and those supporting him, however, did not reckon with Athaliah, who, amid the bloody removal of potential royal rivals, seized power. Such bloody transitions of power were certainly not unknown to Jerusalem, but at least three things conspired to make Athaliah extremely unpopular thereafter with significant numbers of her subjects: first, she was of foreign origin, for although she had been married to a scion of the House of David, none of David's blood ran through her veins; second, during her palace revolution, Athaliah had caused the death of some who *were* of David's house; and third, Athaliah openly worshipped Melqart and other pagan deities.

Not murdered in Athaliah's coup was her grandson, Joash, and, indeed, it is extremely unlikely that Athaliah ever desired his death. In fact, the opposite was almost certainly the case; that is, Athaliah likely acted as decisively as she did in order to secure her line's future through Joash. Nevertheless, the hostile extant sources accuse Athaliah of acting out of purely selfish motives, and desirous of Joash' extermination. This unfair characterization almost certainly had its origins in the actions of ◄ Jehosheba, who was the sister of the late Jehoram, and thus the one-time sister-in-law of Athaliah. This Jehosheba was married to Jehoiada, who at the time was the High Priest of Yahweh's Temple. As such, it is quite likely that Jehosheba and her husband had much to resent in the religious policy that permitted the worship of ba'als in Jerusalem.

When Athaliah's palace bloodbath was underway, Jehosheba spirited Joash away, supposedly to save him from the evil designs of his grandmother. Joash remained in seclusion for a little more than

Jehosheba (fl. 9th c.)

Biblical woman. Name variations: Josaba. Flourished in the 9th century; sister of Jehoram of Judah; sister-in-law of Athaliah; married Jehoiada (a high priest).

Jehosheba, with the help of her high priest husband Jehoiada, safeguarded the life of her nephew Joash when the entire royal family was slain by *Athaliah. When Joash was six, Jehosheba and Jehoiada organized a revolution in his favor, causing Athaliah and her followers to be put to death.

six years (842–836 BCE), during which time Athaliah ruled with enough strength to later be credited with having been one of the most powerful royal women of the ancient Near East. Why Athaliah permitted her grandson to be held captive against her interests cannot be said for certain; perhaps, knowing that Joash was in the safekeeping of close relatives, she allowed this situation to continue in the hopes that it would bind the faction of the Temple in the short run to her rule, and in the long run to the rule of her dynasty. If so, then Athaliah miscalculated, for a little over six years into her reign (836) Joash was produced in the Temple as the rightful king of Judah. When Athaliah hurried to the Temple to try to put an end to this mutiny, she was murdered at the sanctuary's Horse Gate. Joash thereafter ruled, initially under a regency. Ironically, Joash would later betray those who engineered his grandmother's downfall by acknowledging more gods than Yahweh.

SUGGESTED READING:
The Bible: 2 *Chronicles* 20.

RELATED MEDIA:
The story of Athaliah forms the subject of one of Racine's best tragedies; it has also been musically adapted by Handel and Mendelssohn.

William S. Greenwalt, Associate Professor of Classical History, Santa Clara University, Santa Clara, California

Athanasia (d. about 860).
See Anastasia.

Athenais, empress (c. 400–460).
See Eudocia.

Atherton, Gertrude (1857–1948)
American author of novels and short stories. Born Gertrude Franklin Horn on October 30, 1857, in San Francisco, California; died in San Francisco on June 14, 1948; daughter of Thomas L. (a businessman) and Gertrude (Franklin) Horn (a homemaker); attended Clark Institute, St. Mary's Hall, and Sayre Institute; married George Henry Bowen Atherton, on February 15, 1876 (died 1887); children: George (d. 1882), Muriel.

Published first novel, What Dreams May Come *(1888). Wrote over 50 books, including* Los Cerritos *(1889);* The Doomswoman *(1892);* Before the Gringo Came *(1894, revised under the title* The Splendid Idle Forties, *1902);* Patience Spearhawk and Her Times *(1897);* The Californians *(1898, revised 1935);* Senator North *(1900);* The Conqueror: Being the True and Romantic Story of Alexander Hamilton *(1902);* The Living Present *(1917);* The White Morning *(1918);* Black Oxen *(1923);* The Immortal Marriage *(1927);* The Jealous Gods *(1928);* Dido, Queen of Hearts

(1929); The Sophisticates *(1931) and* The Horn of Life *(1942). Also published stories and articles in* Cosmopolitan, Lippincott's, North American Review, Harper's, Godey's, Yale Review, San Francisco Examiner, New York Times. *Elected to National Institute of Arts and Letters (1938); chosen first recipient of California's Most Distinguished Woman award (1940).*

Gertrude Atherton's maternal grandfather, Stephen Franklin, migrated to California from New Orleans in 1849 in hopes of sharing in the wealth of the gold rush. The rough life in San Francisco seemed incompatible with Franklin's strict Presbyterian notions of propriety, but after two years he determined that the area had become sufficiently civilized to send for his wife Eliza and 15-year-old daughter, Gertrude Franklin. The attractive young woman quickly became a belle in a society where men greatly outnumbered women. She apparently had no desire to marry while an exciting social life was available. Nonetheless, at age 19, Gertrude Franklin submitted to her parents' urging to marry Thomas Horn, a rich tobacco merchant. Nine months later, their daughter Gertrude was born.

Her parents' marriage was rocky from the outset, exacerbated by what was seen as her mother's immaturity and frivolity and her father's drinking and business failures. They divorced when Gertrude was only three years old. With no skills and no inclination to earn her own living, the senior Gertrude took her small daughter to her parents' ranch several miles outside San Jose, where young Gertrude often stayed with her grandparents while her mother resumed her social life in San Francisco.

The child flaunted the rules of appropriate behavior, became destructive, and essentially ungovernable. When she was seven years old, her mother married John F. Uhlhorn. The second marriage provided two half sisters and a despised stepfather who managed to drink and gamble away his own and his wife's money. Meanwhile, Gertrude moved into adolescence. She attended three different girls' academies in four years, and although she seemed quite intelligent she never applied herself to her studies. She was finally packed off to the Sayre Institute in Lexington, Kentucky, where her grandfather hoped Gertrude would conform to the supervision of a stern Presbyterian great aunt. Instead, she was sent back to California after a year, lest her outrageous behavior corrupt her cousins.

During those chaotic years, Atherton developed a passion for reading. She began with romances, standards such as *Little Women* and

Gertrude Atherton

Jane Eyre, and fairy tales. When she was 14, her grandfather decided that she should read aloud to him for two hours each night. Thus he would help her to become an "intellectual woman." For the first time, Gertrude, who knew her conduct had always displeased her grandfather, attempted to win his approval through exercise of her intelligence. Together they read history and literary classics. The world of books became the happiest and most stable part of her life.

The Uhlhorn marriage ended in divorce. When Gertrude returned from Kentucky she found her mother with a new suitor. He was George Atherton—spoiled, handsome, aristocratic and 14 years younger than her mother. George's attentions turned from the mother to the daughter, and Gertrude responded. On February 15, 1876, the two eloped.

Both families were dismayed at the match. Gertrude remained estranged from her mother and her grandfather for three years until after the birth of her daughter Muriel. The senior

Athertons had hoped George would marry someone more socially connected and less independent in spirit. As George had few business talents and fewer intellectual interests, the marriage had little chance of success. When, in 1882, their six-year-old son Georgie died of diphtheria, Gertrude turned her energies to work on a novel. In three months, she had completed the manuscript for *The Randolphs of Redwoods*. She had been inspired by a newspaper article about the declining fortunes of a prominent family and, as she would often do, Gertrude used a news item as a springboard for her fiction. The story was serialized in the San Francisco journal *The Argonaut* under the pseudonym "Asmodeus" (a Hebrew demon who destroyed domestic happiness). It caused a sensation for its unconventional portrayal of alcoholism and sensuality. It also caused a furor in the Atherton family. Her mother-in-law believed that publication by a woman was unseemly, while George was jealous of the time devoted to writing and of Gertrude's ability to make money and her refusal to share it with him.

Two years later, she completed a manuscript for the novel *What Dreams May Come*, sent it off to publishers, and moved from the Atherton family compound to her own flat in San Francisco. By this time, her marriage was a fiction maintained for appearances. Atherton admitted in her autobiography that she often wished George were dead so she could strike out on her own. In fact, George died at sea in 1887 en route to Chile. His shipmates embalmed him in a barrel of rum, and in that container his remains were returned to San Francisco.

Atherton moved to New York later that year to earn her living as a writer. Her daughter Muriel remained behind where she was raised almost completely by her two grandmothers. Atherton frequently boasted that she was devoid of maternal qualities. In New York, she found a publisher for *What Dreams May Come*. She worked at her writing for six or seven hours a day, producing a column called "Letter from New York" for a San Francisco paper and completing another novel, *Hermia Suydam*. This story featured a heroine who resembled the author in looks, literary aspirations, and disgust with marriage. Hermia, however, shocked her contemporaries with an extramarital affair, something the self-contained Atherton would never do. *Hermia Suydam* engendered a storm of criticism from the guardians of Victorian morality. Although the notoriety did not entirely displease her, Gertrude had no real ties in New York, so she set off for Europe.

The peripatetic pattern would continue through much of Atherton's life. She would travel from coast to coast in the United States, back and forth to Europe, to Cuba, to the West Indies, to Egypt. She would reside in Munich for a five-year period and finally settle in San Francisco during her last decade. Much of her travel involved gathering background for her books, but, ironically, Atherton often retired to an entirely different locale from the setting of the book she was writing. Thus in 1889 she wrote a historical novel about California, *Los Cerritos*, at a Sacred Heart convent in France.

Her early novels did well in England where the reading public seemed captivated by stories of the United States, especially of the West. Typically, Atherton wrote of loveless marriages, of young girls instructed by wise, bookish older men, of disillusionment. During an early stay in London, she met Henry James whom she admired, but who was appalled by Atherton's brashness and self-promotion.

If Atherton and her work did not win favor from Henry James, she did make a favorable impression on fellow California writer and critic Ambrose Bierce. Bierce praised her 1892 novel *The Doomswoman*, but also pointed out the uneven quality that was bound to occur when one wrote as hurriedly and with as little revision as did Atherton. Her association with Bierce was one of the longest relationships of Atherton's life, but it was a relationship that flourished only when the two were miles apart and communicated through tart yet intimate letters.

Patience Spearhawk and Her Times, first published in London in 1897, may have been inspired by several actual murder trials where the victim was poisoned. Again, the heroine resembles Atherton, while her handsome but weak husband, whom she is accused of murdering, resembles George Atherton. Patience Spearhawk is obstinate and self-assertive; she delights in shocking people. Aside from the authenticity of the characters, Atherton drew her settings from life. She attended a murder trial to appreciate the courtroom atmosphere, and she even visited a prison and sat in the electric chair at Sing Sing.

But if Gertrude Atherton wrote of women who defied convention, she also came to admire men who exercised power. Two of her more highly regarded books, *Senator North* (1900) and *The Conqueror: Being the True and Romantic Story of Alexander Hamilton* (1902), featured male heroes who exemplified the jingoistic spirit that was prevalent after the Spanish-American War of 1898. She gathered material for *Senator North* in the chambers of Congress and at receptions in Washington D.C. She cultivated Senator Eugene Hale of Maine whom she used as a model for North, a mature and sexually attractive hero whose integrity and power win a strong and independent woman.

Some commentators have argued that if any one of Atherton's books has enduring value, it is her fictional biography of Alexander Hamilton, *The Conqueror*. As usual, Atherton traveled to the place where the story was set to gather material. In this case, she visited Hamilton's birthplace, the island of Nivis in the West Indies, as well as St. Kitts and St. Croix where Hamilton had lived as a child. Atherton read dozens of books dealing with Hamilton, and carried with her a copy of his portrait as an inspiration. Using techniques of both biography and novel, she was able to combine an uncritical romantic picture of Hamilton with careful attention to context and surrounding details. The book did well from the beginning, and eventually sold over a million copies. With the success of *The Conqueror,* Atherton came to believe that the value of her work had been vindicated.

The author returned to California in 1906, in time to experience the Great Earthquake on August 18. She took pride in calmly withstanding the shock by standing in a doorway, but all of her own records of the first 50 years of her life were lost in the earthquake and subsequent fire. In a piece for *Harper's Weekly,* Atherton compared the damage to the city to the ruins in the ancient world. Later, she would describe the "fresh, handsome, and bustling" San Francisco that was rebuilt on the wreckage. In the aftermath of the earthquake, she also developed her association with James D. Phelan, a banker, developer, and former mayor of San Francisco. A supportive, platonic friend and benefactor, Phelan kept a suite for Gertrude at his home Villa Montalvo from 1920 until his death in 1930.

During the first decade of the 20th century, the organized women's movement reached its peak in both the United States and England. Atherton had the makings of a feminist: her entire adult life had demonstrated independence and self sufficiency, and she had written of the limitations of conventional marriage and domesticity. Yet she did not have time or patience with women's groups. In 1910, however, she became involved in the campaign for the vote. Her major effort was to write a play, *Julia France and Her Times,* set in the British suffrage movement. Neither the play, which had only one performance

in Toronto, nor the novel, published in 1912, was a success. "I have no love for it myself," Atherton wrote.

During World War I, she visited France and turned her attention to the activities of French women in support of the war effort. The experience with nursing or with munitions work, she believed, was giving women confidence in their own abilities. After the war, however, they might be repulsed by the men who had caused and prolonged the slaughter and refuse to bear children who would be blown to pieces. Two of her works during the war, *The Living Present* (1917) and *The White Morning* (1918), describe future societies run by women.

In her own contribution to the war effort, Atherton helped found a relief organization, *Le Bien-Etre du Blesse* (The Well-Being of the Wounded), to provide nutritious food to supplement the diets of hospitalized soldiers. In addition, she edited a highly patriotic journal, *American Woman's Magazine,* that condemned pacifists and slackers.

There is a good deal of fun to be got out of the Battle with Life, which begins with birth and ends only with death. Many go under, but millions do not. They fight to the end, and if they never quite got the best of Life, at least Life did not get the best of them.

—Gertrude Atherton

After the war, Atherton returned to California. She worked briefly doing screenwriting as one of Samuel Goldwyn's "Eminent Authors," but quickly became disenchanted with Hollywood. She seemed to feel that both her health and her reputation were in a stagnant state when she learned about the Steinbach Treatment, a rejuvenation procedure developed by an Austrian doctor. She began treatments in 1922 and claimed an almost miraculous rebirth of her physical and mental capacities. During the next year, she published *Black Oxen,* in which the heroine is "reactivated," her restored beauty and creativity making her the object of desire for younger men. The controversial *Black Oxen* was the bestseller of 1923 and was made into a film the following year.

During the 1920s, Atherton published three novels dealing with the ancient world. *The Immortal Marriage* (1927) was the story of Pericles and *Aspasia of Miletus. She went to Greece, visited museums with collections of Greek antiquities, and consulted documents. Although not such a commercial success as *Black Oxen*, *The Immortal Marriage* was praised in both popular and scholarly circles. *The Jealous Gods* (1928) and *Dido, Queen of Hearts* (1929) had less public appeal.

The last part of Gertrude Atherton's life, the period after 1930, was spent mostly in California. Much of her fiction had been set in California and provided a sort of chronicle of that state's history, including *Rezanov* (1906) about a Russian explorer; *The Splendid Idle Forties* (1902), a collection about the Mexican period; *Los Cerritos* (1890), set in the 1880s; *Ancestors* (1907), set at the time of the earthquake; *The Sisters-in-Law* (1921); and *The House of Lee* (1940), dealing with the post-World War I era. In 1932, she produced her autobiography, *Adventures of a Novelist*, in which the author became one of her California heroines.

In her later years, Atherton received a number of important honors. The French government recognized her wartime service with the Legion of Honor in 1925. Mills College awarded her an honorary Doctor of Literature degree in 1935, and the University of California at Berkeley followed with an honorary Doctor of Laws in 1937. She was elected to the National Institute of Arts and Letters and, in 1940, she was the first person named to California's Most Distinguished Women. Gertrude Atherton died of a stroke at the age of 91. She had been writing every day until a month before her death.

SOURCES:

Atherton, Gertrude. *Adventures of a Novelist*. NY: Liveright, 1932.

Leider, Emily Wortis. *California's Daughter: Gertrude Atherton and Her Times*. Stanford, CA: Stanford, 1991.

McClure, Charlotte S. *Gertrude Atherton*. Boston: Twayne, 1979.

Wilkins, Thurman. "Gertrude Atherton." *Notable American Women, 1607–1950*. Cambridge, MA: Belknap, 1971, pp. 64–65.

COLLECTIONS:

Collections of Gertrude Atherton's papers and manuscripts are located in the Library of Congress and at the Bancroft Library, University of California at Berkeley.

Mary Welek Atwell, Associate Professor of Criminal Justice,
Radford University, Radford, Virginia

Atia the Elder (c. 80 BCE–?).

See Octavia for sidebar.

Atkins, Anna (1797–1871)

English botanist and photographer who specialized in scientific illustration and was the first to produce a photographically illustrated book. Born Anna Children in 1797 in Tonbridge, England; died in 1871 in Halstead Place, England; daughter of John George Children (a zoologist and fellow and secretary of the Royal Society); married John Pelly Atkins (a railway promoter and owner of Jamaican coffee plantations), in 1825.

Anna Atkins, the first person to publish a book illustrated with photographs, worked closely with her father, zoologist John George Children, a respected scientist and longtime associate of the British Museum. She began her career in 1823 by producing drawings for his translation of Jean-Baptiste-Pierre-Antoine de Monet de Lamarck's, *Genera of Shells*.

It was after his retirement in 1840, however, that Children spent time with his daughter and her husband at their home in Kent, where he began to experiment with the mechanics of cyanotype or blueprinting that he had picked up from both the work of William Henry Fox Talbot on photogenic drawing, and his acquaintance with Sir John Herschel, the astronomer and scientist who had done pioneering work on the process as early as 1819. Atkins, in turn, refined the process and, in 1843, produced a study of algae titled *British Algae: Cyanotype Impressions*, containing her own original cyanotypes. In the introduction, she explained that she had used the new process because many of her specimens were so small that it was difficult to make accurate drawings of them.

Following her father's death in 1852, Atkins, possibly in collaboration with her friend **Anne Dixon**, produced *Cyanotypes of British and Foreign Flowering Plants and Ferns* (1864), thus establishing herself in both the scientific and photographic communities and insuring a place in those fields for a generation of women to follow.

SOURCES:

Rosenblum, Naomi. *A History of Women Photographers*.

Williams, Val. *The Other Observers: Women Photographers in Britain 1900 to the Present*. London, England: Virago Press, 1986.

Barbara Morgan,
Melrose, Massachusetts

Atkins, Vera.

See Noor, Inayat Khan for sidebar.

Atkinson, Eleanor (1863–1942)

American author of 11 books, primarily for children, including Johnny Appleseed. *Name variations: (pseudonym) Nora Marks. Born Eleanor Stackhouse, Janu-*

ary 7, 1863, in Renselaer, Indiana; died on November 4, 1942, in Orangeburg, New York; daughter of Isaac M. and Margaret (Smith) Stackhouse; educated at Indianapolis Normal Training School; married Francis Blake Atkinson (journalist), in 1891; children: two daughters (who write under the pseudonyms Dorothy and Eleanor Blake).

Selected works: Greyfriars Bobby (1912); Johnny Appleseed (1915).

Following graduation from Indianapolis Normal Training School, Eleanor Atkinson began her career as a teacher, first in Indianapolis, then in Chicago. She left teaching to write for the Chicago Tribune, where she used the pseudonym Nora Marks. She was introduced to Francis Blake Atkinson, the news editor for the Chicago Evening Post, whom she married in 1891. Together, the Atkinsons applied their knowledge of periodicals and children to produce The Little Chronicle, a weekly paper for grammar and high-school students. Once the paper was established, they sold it and took their talents to F.E. Compton Company, where they edited and wrote a student encyclopedia. Meanwhile, Eleanor wrote novels for children, the most famous of which is Johnny Appleseed. The book was published in 1915, three years before Atkinson retired from writing.

The Atkinsons had two daughters who became authors and assumed the pseudonyms Dorothy Blake and Eleanor Blake. Following her husband's death, Atkinson moved from Chicago to Long Island, where she lived with her daughter "Eleanor." Atkinson died on November 4, 1942, in Orangeburg, New York.

SOURCES:

The New York Times. November 11, 1942, p. 25.

Crista Martin,
Boston, Massachusetts

Atossa (c. 545–c. 470s BCE)

Persian queen whose support for the accession of her son Xerxes secured for him the Persian throne after the death of Darius. Born around 545 BCE; probably died in the 470s BCE; daughter of Cyrus, II the Great (c. 590–529 BCE), the first Persian king, and possibly ✤➤ *Cassandane; married Cambyses II (died 522 BCE); married Smerdis, in 522 BCE; married Darius I the Great, in 521 BCE; children: (third marriage) Xerxes I, king of Persia (c. 518–465 BCE).*

Subsequent to her father's death, she was married to her (probably) half-brother, Cambyses, to the pseudo-Smerdis, and finally to Darius, all of whom attempted to consolidate their control of the Persian

Empire by marrying Atossa. A figure much respected within the royal harem, Atossa's greatest influence seems to have been felt when her support for the accession of her son Xerxes secured for him the Persian throne after the death of Darius (486).

Born around 545 BCE, Atossa was the daughter of Cyrus, whose successful overthrow of Median hegemony (dominance) and subsequent conquests in Anatolia, throughout the Near East including Iran, and even into central Russia founded the Persian Empire. Upon the death of her father in 529 BCE, Atossa's brother, Cambyses, came to the throne. Since polygamy was practiced at the Persian court, we do not know whether or not Atossa and Cambyses were full siblings, but the likelihood is that they were not, for Cambyses married Atossa to consolidate his claim to his father's power, and such a consolidation implies that Atossa was associated with some faction of interest distinguishable from that of Cambyses. As such, they probably had different mothers.

Although Cambyses continued the imperialism of his father by conquering Egypt, his reign was disrupted by a rebellion led by a Persian pretender who whipped up support by pretending to be Cambyses' dead brother, Smerdis (hence this pretender is known as the pseudo-Smerdis). When Cambyses died from a gangrenous wound received in an equestrian accident, the pseudo-Smerdis married Atossa in an effort to secure the throne. However, this usurpation was brief, since a counter-revolution led by the Persian noble Darius I ousted the pseudo-Smerdis within a year. In turn, Darius also married Atossa to legitimate his seizure of royal authority. The daughter of Persia's royal founder, the sister of his successor, and the wife of three kings, Atossa's status at the Persian court was very high, if not unchallenged, in Darius' harem.

Darius' reign (521–486 BCE) was a long and successful one, during which—after his conquest of modern Pakistan in the east and parts of Macedonia, Greece, Bulgaria and Rumania in

✤➤ **Cassandane** (fl. 500s BCE)

*Queen of Persia. Married Cyrus II the Great (c. 590–529 BCE), first Persian king; children: possibly *Atossa (c. 545–470s BCE); possibly Cambyses II (d. 522 BCE), king of Persia; and possibly Smerdis.*

the west—the Persian Empire reached its zenith. Although Darius was an extremely successful conqueror, able administrator, and an efficient consolidator of Persian power over an immense area, he is ironically known today as much for his one minor setback—the defeat of his army (he was not present) by the Athenians at the Battle of Marathon in 490—than for his many accomplishments. After Marathon, Darius swore that he would be avenged upon the Athenians, yet, as luck would have it, before he could mobilize the large army he felt would be necessary to eradicate the one blot on his reign's military record, he died. Because he had many wives (so far as we know, all married in order to tie their families more closely to his rule) and many children by these wives, when Darius died, a scramble to succeed him began between a number of half brothers, each relying upon their mothers' constituencies for support. At this moment, Atossa seems to have exerted the greatest influence of her life, for she incapacitated the efforts of her rivals and saw to it that Xerxes, her son by Darius, inherited his father's position. As such, Atossa was especially important during the first few years of Xerxes' reign, as he found it necessary to ferret out all possible challenges to his succession.

Although Xerxes is best known for his own unsuccessful invasion of Greece in 480—undertaken both to carry on the legacy of Darius and to unify the various factions of the Persian state against a common enemy—his reign was not one of unmitigated hostility to all Greeks or the products of Greek culture. In fact, many Greeks along the Anatolian coast of the Aegean Sea were Persian subjects, and their presence within the empire facilitated cultural exchange between the Persians and the Greeks. Although many Greek artists, architects, and intellectuals plied their trades under Xerxes' authority, one of the most striking examples of this accommodation was Atossa's trusting of her own health to the Greek physician Democedes, who seems to have treated her with some success against a cancer. In the 5th century, Greek medical "science" was as advanced as any, so the employment of Democedes implies that Atossa was well-informed as to the respective talents of the various peoples then under Persian sway. However, this is hardly surprising of the woman whom the Old Testament knew as "*Vashti," and whom that work credited as being one of history's most influential queens. The Biblical Vashti is possibly a composite of Atossa, Xerxes' wife Amestris, and others (see *Vashti*). Atossa probably died in the 470s BCE.

SUGGESTED READING:

Olmstead, A.T., *History of the Persian Empire*. University of Chicago Press, 1948.

William S. Greenwalt, Associate Professor of Classical History, Santa Clara University, Santa Clara, California

Attwell, Mabel Lucie (1879–1964)

English artist, illustrator, and author of children's stories and verse. Born on June 4, 1879, in Mile End, London; died on November 5, 1964, in Fowey in Cornwall; ninth of ten children; attended Heatherley's and St. Martin's School of Art; married Harold Earnshaw (an illustrator), in 1908; children: Peggy (b. 1909), Peter (b. 1911), and Brian (1914–1936).

At the height of her enormous popularity, British illustrator Mabel Lucie Attwell's trademark wide-eyed, chubby-kneed toddlers gained worldwide recognition. Fueled by the public's fascination with her colorful book illustrations, a huge industry of china, textiles, toys, dolls, and postcards was born. The round-faced tots, invariably two or three years old, even adorned the trenches of young British soldiers during World War I.

Attwell's childhood was not the ideal she often depicted in her illustrations. Born in Mile End, London, one of 10 children, she received a strict Victorian upbringing. Often overwhelmed by the size and exuberance of her family, she developed into a shy young girl, who neglected her schoolwork in favor of doodling on book covers and daydreaming. Her talent went virtually unnoticed until, at age 15, she amazed the family by receiving two guineas in payment from a publisher for a painting she submitted. After leaving school, she worked up the courage to take her portfolio to a London publisher, who surprised her with payment for some of the work. From then on, Attwell made a living from her drawing and saved enough to pay for formal art instruction. By 1905, she was illustrating books by **May Baldwin, *Mrs. Molesworth, Mabel Quiller-Couch**, and others, usually providing between four and eight color plates for each volume.

While studying at St. Martin's School of Art, Attwell met and fell in love with fellow student Harold ("Pat") Earnshaw, a gifted artist specializing in pen and watercolor illustrations. The couple married in 1908 and settled in Dulwich, South London, where their three children were born. Daughter Peggy, born in 1909, became Attwell's inspiration for her archetypal toddler. A son Peter was born in 1911, and Brian followed in 1914. Marriage and children provided an environment in which Attwell blossomed both emotionally and professionally.

Some of her best-remembered illustrations were produced during this time for Cassell & Co. and Raphael Tuck & Son. For Cassell, she illustrated *Grimm's Fairy Tales and Stories* and *Legends* (both in 1910). For Raphael Tuck, *Old Rhymes* (1909), *Mother Goose* (1910), *Alice in Wonderland* (1911), *Grimm's Fairy Stories* (1912), *Our Playtime Picture Book* (1913), *Hans Andersen's Fairy Tales* (1914), *The Water Babies* (1915), *Children's Stories from French Fairy Tales* (1917), and *Baby's Book* (1922). Individual stories from these books were reissued separately in the 1920s and 1930s, especially those by Andersen and Grimm.

Attwell illustrated two gift books for Hodder & Stoughton, *Peeping Pansy* (1918) by *Marie of Rumania, who also hosted Attwell's four-week stay at the Royal Palace at Bucharest, and *Peter Pan and Wendy* (1921) by J.M. Barrie, who was a great admirer of her work. In 1922, *The Lucie Attwell Annual* was launched and survived for half a century, undergoing occasional title changes.

In 1932, shortly after Attwell and her family moved to a new country home at West Dean in Sussex, her husband was taken seriously ill; he would die four years later. In 1934, her youngest son died unexpectedly of pneumonia. Despite these losses, Attwell continued her work, and in 1937 was honored with Royal patronage when she was asked to design a special Christmas card for Princess *Margaret Rose. Attwell china was also ordered for the nursery of Princesses *Elizabeth (II) and Margaret. Years later, Prince Charles would request her china in a nursery for his children.

Attwell spent the last 20 years of her life at Fowey in Cornwall, where she died on November 5, 1964. Her world of children is still admired by people of all ages throughout the world. She has been likened to the character of Peter Pan, who never grew up. Wrote **Mary Anne Field**: "Hers was a world peopled by children whose innocence, laughter and love dispel the reality. She saw the child in the adult and then drew the adult as a child."

SOURCES:

Dalby, Richard. *The Golden Age of Children's Illustration.* NY: Gallery Books, 1991.

Field, Mary Anne. "The Cherubic Children of Mabel Lucie Attwell," in *This England.* Autumn 1989.

SUGGESTED READING:

Beetles, Chris. *Mabel Lucie Attwell.* London: Pavilion Books.

Barbara Morgan,
Melrose, Massachusetts

From a drawing by Mabel Lucie Attwell.

Atwater, Helen (1876–1947)

American home economist who became the first female full-time editor of the Journal of Home Economics *(1923). Born in Somerville, Massachusetts, on May 29, 1876; died in Washington, D.C., on June 26, 1947; graduated from Smith College, Northampton, Massachusetts, in 1897.*

Helen Atwater's first job after graduating from Smith College was as an assistant to her father, a food chemistry specialist. Following his death, she joined the staff of the Office of Home Economics in the U.S. Department of Agriculture. As a frequent contributor to the *Journal of Home Economics,* a publication of the American Home Economics Association, she went to work for them in 1923, becoming their first woman editor that year, and stayed until her retirement in 1941.

In 1930, she participated in the White House Conference on Child Health and Protection, and, in 1942, served as chair of the Committee on Hygiene in Housing of the American Public Health Association. In 1948, a year after her death, the American Home Economics Association honored her by establishing the Helen Atwater International Fellowship Award.

Barbara Morgan,
Melrose, Massachusetts

Atwell, Winifred (1914–1983)

Trinidad-born British pianist and entertainer who dominated the pop charts in the 1950s with a string of hits. Born in Tunapuna, Trinidad, in 1914; died in Sydney, Australia, on February 27, 1983.

Winifred Atwell, born in 1914 in Tunapuna, Trinidad, was trained as a classical pianist. Soon after arriving in London in 1946, she turned to the popular idiom, playing medleys in a vigorous ragtime style, which she played on a "honky-tonk" piano. Her 1952 Decca recording of George Botsford's "Black and White Rag" was immensely popular as it helped to relieve some of the gloom of a Britain still suffering from postwar austerity and economic anemia. For Queen *Elizabeth II's coronation in 1953, Atwell recorded "Flirtation Waltz," "Britannia Rag" and, especially for the royal occasion, a "Coronation Rag."

An even greater commercial success followed when Atwell hit upon the concept of recording a song medley that, in effect, was a sing-along of the type commonly found in pubs throughout the British Isles. Although scorned by highbrows, the Philips album "Let's Have a Party" hit the top of the charts. Armed with a winning formula, Atwell released "Let's Have Another Party" in 1954. Not surprisingly, the two hit albums quickly resulted in a flood of imitations, few if any of them as exuberant or commercially successful as were Atwell's.

In 1955, she returned to the Decca label and delighted its board of directors by turning in a string of hits that made it into the Top 20 category. Best known of her smash successes from these years was the 1956 "Poor People of Paris," which became very popular in the United States as performed by Les Baxter. The advent of rock 'n' roll in the late 1950s spelled the end of Atwell's domination of the charts, although she tried to join the new phenomenon in 1957 with her "Let's Rock 'n' Roll." Winifred Atwell died in Sydney, Australia, on February 27, 1983, fondly remembered by her now-aging, but still loyal, fans.

John Haag, Associate Professor of History,
University of Georgia, Athens, Georgia

Aubert, Constance (1803–?)

French journalist and novelist who wrote for and edited several French fashion journals, and collaborated with her mother on novels. Born in 1803 in France; daughter of Laure d'Abrantès (1784–1838, a novelist and biographer) and General Junot.

Constance Aubert's mother, *Laure d'Abrantès, who had grown up a family friend of the Bonapartes, turned to writing only when her alcoholic husband killed himself and she was left to support herself and her daughter. In her adulthood, Constance Aubert collaborated with her mother on several novels, but she is best known for her journalism. She worked as a fashion columnist for *Le Temps,* as a contributor for *Journal des Dames* (*Ladies Journal*), and as an editor for several fashion and style publications, including *Les Abeilles parisiennes* (*The Bees of Paris*). Neither Aubert nor her mother achieved enough success to prevent d'Abrantès' 1838 death in conditions of extreme poverty. It was not until 1859 that Aubert published her book *Manuel d'économie élégante* (*Handbook of Economy and Style*).

Aubert was one of many French intellectual women who turned to journalism when their gender barred them from other outlets. The resulting feminist perspective is apparent in Aubert's contributions to *Journal des Femmes* (*The Women's Journal*), which was initially established and run only by women, in part a reaction to the less feminist *Journal des Dames.*

Crista Martin,
Boston, Massachusetts

Aubespine, Madeleine de l' (1546–1596)

French poet. Name variations: Madame de Laubespine; Dame de Villeroy. Born in 1546 in France; died in 1596 in France; daughter of Jean de Brabant; married Nicolas de Neufville.

Madeleine de l'Aubespine was born into the French aristocracy and became lady-in-waiting to the French queen, *Catherine de Medici. After her marriage to the king's secretary, Nicolas de Neufville, the well-educated Madeleine turned to writing poetry to entertain herself and her friends. She also provided an impetus for other French poets by creating one of the earliest salons, opening her home for writers and poets to share their works. Madeleine's own works, mostly sonnets, earned her the admiration and respect of many of Europe's finest poets, including Pierre de Ronsard. She died at about age 50.

Laura York,
Anza, California

Aubigny, Agatha d'.

See Adelicia of Louvain (1102/3–1151) for sidebar.

Aubin, Penelope (c. 1685–1731)

British author and translator. Born around 1685 in London, England; died in England around 1731; married a government employee, name unknown.

Selected works: The Strange Adventures of the Count de Vinevil *(1721);* The Life of Madame de Beaumont *(1721);* The Life of Charlotta DuPont *(1723);* The Life and Adventures of the Lady Lucy *(1726).*

In the late 17th and early 18th century, fictional novels by women made their debut in England. At a time when it was considered disreputable for women to write, let alone receive payment for their work, Penelope Aubin experienced relative success and would become known as a respected foremother of the fictional novel.

Little, however, is known about the author. The only published account of her life, by Abbé Prévost, appeared during the pinnacle of her success. She was the daughter of a poor French officer, who immigrated to England around the time of her birth, and his English, likely Protestant, wife. Aubin's lineage drew her back and forth between British allegiance and an attraction to things French, a dichotomy apparent in several of her works. She was married to a financially secure man who held a government post, though his name is unknown, and she was a devout Roman Catholic.

These latter factors allowed Aubin, in good conscience, to continue writing. She reportedly required no fee for her work, and her novels bore a strict moral message. In the preface to *The Life of Charlotta DuPont* (1723), she wrote, "My design in writing is to employ my leisure hours to some advantage to myself and others . . . . I do not write for bread, nor am I vain or fond of applause; but I am very ambitious to gain the esteem of those who honour virtue." In fact, however, it is believed her publication career did begin for money. Unlike her peers, who wrote romantic and whimsical novels that Aubin thought blended together in their sameness, she hoped to encourage heroism and intelligence in her readers. In 1707, three anonymously published poetic pamphlets by Aubin re-

ceived broad distribution. She was then silent for 13 years, during which time she married. Aubin reemerged more well-to-do in 1721, and over the next eight years published six novels, four translations (from French and Asian works), a drama, and a moral treatise. In these later years, despite her professions of monetary disinterest, Aubin noted with pride that her many books were widely enjoyed and sold well. She was also a public speaker of popular demand for a short period. In 1729, she established an oratory in London, at which patrons paid a small sum to hear her lecture. Aubin claimed a friendship with author **Elizabeth Singer Rowe**, though it is unconfirmed if the two knew each other. There is some suspicion that Aubin invoked her peer's name to improve sales of her books, particularly *Charlotta DuPont*, which is dedicated to Rowe.

SOURCES:

Batlestein, Martin C., ed. *British Novelists, 1660–1800.* Detroit: Gale Research Company, 1985.

Blain, Virginia, Pat Clements, and Isobel Grundy, eds. *The Feminist Companion to Literature in English.* New Haven: Yale University Press, 1990.

Goreau, Angeline. *The Whole Duty of a Woman: Female Writers in Seventeenth Century England.* Garden City, NY: Dial Press, 1985.

MacCarthy, B.G. *The Female Pen: Women Writers and Novelists 1621–1818.* NY: New York University Press, 1994.

Williamson, Marilyn L. *Raising Their Voices: British Women Writers, 1650–1750.* Detroit: Wayne State University Press, 1990.

Crista Martin,
Boston, Massachusetts

Aubrac, Lucie (1912—)

French Resistance leader during World War II who helped found the powerful Libération Sud and was responsible for numerous escapes. Name variations: Lucie Bernard, Lucie Samuel. Born Lucie Bernard in the Mâcon area of Burgundy, France, on June 29, 1912; daughter of winegrowers; attended the Sorbonne, 1931–38; married Raymond Samuel, on December 14, 1939; children: Jean-Pierre (b. May 3, 1941), Catherine (b. February 19, 1944), Elisabeth (b. 1946).

Selected writings: La Résistance (*Naissance et Organisation, Paris, 1945);* "Présence des femmes dans toutes les activités de la Résistance," *in* Femmes dans la Résistance (*Monaco: Editions du Rocher, 1977);* Ils partiront dans l'ivresse (*Paris, 1984;* Outwitting the Gestapo, *translated by Konrad Bieber, with the assistance of Betsy Wing, University of Nebraska Press, 1993).*

During World War II, the French Resistance turned civilians—people who worried about bills, taxes, coughs, and impetigo—into counter-

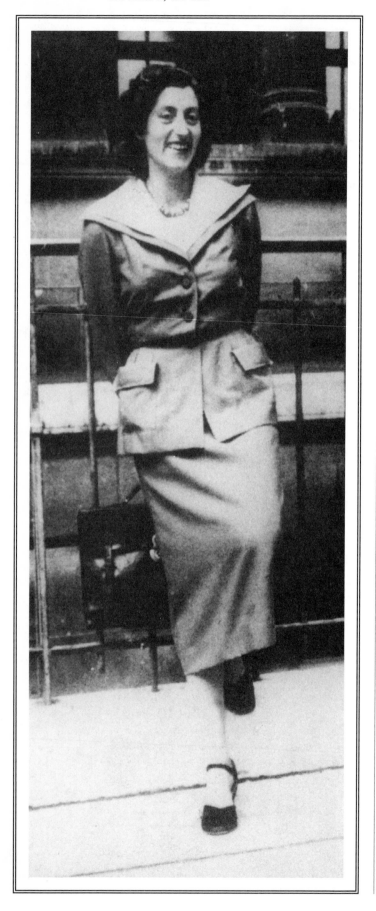

feiters, forgers, thieves, saboteurs, and killers. An estimated 222,000 belonged to resistance movements, while many townspeople, though uninvolved, were sympathetic. Without the aid of televisions, transistor radios, tape recorders, and untapped telephone lines, the dissemination of information was difficult. The Resistance relied on a network of underground, hand-delivered newspapers. During the war, French women shared the same risks and responsibilities as men. As liaison agents, they used shopping bags, bike baskets, and baby carriages to smuggle everything from messages to guns; they procured forged papers and provisions and became false fiancées accompanying male agents into prisons. They also spent their moonlighting hours assisting in derailments, while working amid double agents. One of the most active members of the Resistance was Lucie Aubrac. From 1940 to 1944, she participated in raids, arranged contacts, delivered patriots from the Gestapo, and organized their escape from France. Aubrac specialized in organizing prison escapes, three of which included her *résistant* husband. "A long list of men and women," writes **Maria Wilhelm**, "owe their lives to her."

The daughter of Catholic winemakers, Lucie Aubrac was a pacifist in her youth; her father, an infantryman, had been critically wounded in World War I. Graduating from the Sorbonne with an *agrégée d'histoire* (one of France's highest academic degrees), she first taught history at Strasbourg lycée for girls. When she met her husband Raymond Samuels in 1938, he was fulfilling his military service as a second lieutenant in the Engineer Corps, building roads and bridges. He had spent the preceding years in America, at Massachusetts Institute of Technology (MIT) in Boston, and had been offered a job as an assistant to a professor at MIT. Lucie also had been granted a fellowship in the United States to work on her dissertation. But when Hitler marched into Poland in September 1939, even though Raymond was Jewish, both decided to stay in France. They were married that December.

On May 10, 1940, the Germans attacked through Belgium, outflanking the Maginot Line. Within days, the French forces were in a state of collapse. Paris was declared an open city and surrendered without resistance on June 14, 1940. To shore up the government and public morale, 84-year-old Marshal Pétain was named premier. Convinced that a continuation of the war would result in the physical ruin of France, Pétain essentially requested an armistice. The following day, in direct contradiction, General Charles de Gaulle broadcast from London his first appeal calling for the French to defend their national honor and resist the German forces.

The armistice granted by the Germans left them in occupation of roughly the northern three-fifths of France, including Paris. As the Germans consolidated their hold on northern France, Pétain's government moved to the spa resort of Vichy in the unoccupied zone. Meanwhile, Pierre Laval and a group of political leaders at Vichy restructured the government in an authoritarian manner that enhanced Pétain's powers and aligned France more closely with the victorious Axis powers. A law of October 1940 barred Jews from public office, teaching, and military command. Pétain's humane reputation with respect to soldiers under his command had obvious limits as Vichy's police helped round up *résistants* and thousands of French Jews for deportation to the German extermination camps. By 1944, his government would be acting as a virtual proxy for the Germans.

"The defeat and the Occupation gave birth in France to a new national feeling," wrote Aubrac, "stimulated among all classes of society by the presence of German soldiers on French soil. . . . The commandeering of foodstuffs and industrial commodities, the billeting of German soldiers, the curfew, and patrolling of French streets by German soldiers" all served to produce a conditioned reflex.

> A little like children in the presence of a boorish teacher, the French tended from the outset to make fun of the Germans. Travellers in the *Métro* would deliberately direct Germans to stations miles out of their way; bus conductors would skip stops where Germans wanted to get off; while shop assistants loved to sell Germans all the duddest and most unsalable articles, after a glowing display of flattery. . . . The servility of the French press in Paris was so blatant that the critical sense of the French people reacted immediately. The corrupt and notorious pro-German agents and the newly-acquired German stooges filled people with the same degree of disgust. A kind of instinctive national solidarity found expression in innumerable cases where escaped war prisoners needed help.

One such prisoner was her captured French army husband who, by August of 1940, was sitting out his days in the Uhlans barracks at Sarrebourg, where the members of his regiment were confined as prisoners of war. While visiting, Aubrac managed to slip him some fever-inducing pills. Since the Germans were then still observing the tenets of the Geneva Convention, they transferred the feverish Raymond to a hospital run by the Red Cross. That night, he went over the wall. After his escape, the couple relocated to the capital of the resistance, Lyon, in September 1940, in the unoccupied zone of France. There, they helped start a publication and a movement, *Libération Sud* ("Liberation South").

The sellout of the French press to Vichy became the impetus for the underground counterpress, and each insurgent newspaper spawned its own secret army. Four of the most important resistance groups in France during World War II, writes historian Alexander Werth, were *Combat* (edited by Albert Camus, with frequent contributions by Jean-Paul Sartre); *Libération Sud, Franc-Tireur,* and *Témoignage Chrétien,* all of which would continue to publish after the war. (Another famous woman of the Resistance, ❧▶ **Bertie Albrecht**, was a member of *Combat*.)

The aim of *Libération Sud* was to incite popular revolt and a general strike, and to alert the French to the treacherous machinations of Pétain's Vichy government. The movement's leader was Emmanuel d'Astier de la Vigerie, a former naval officer, "and a remarkable writer," according to Werth. Members wanted to assemble Communists, Socialists, and trade unionists (both Socialist-Communist and Catholic) into a powerful resistance movement; they wanted to mobilize the masses, especially in the industrial centers.

A large portion of the university element of *Libération Sud* was made up of students from the University of Strasbourg, who had been evacuated to Clermont-Ferrand at the beginning of the war. Like the Aubracs, intellectuals had fled to the Vichy zone in 1940. "Among these groups were easily found people who could reinforce this or that strike movement," wrote Aubrac, "or organize attacks on trains, carrying new French war material *nach Berlin*."

In the autumn of 1941, Lucie was teaching history and geography in a Lyon girls' school on the place Edgar-Quinet. Raymond was an engineer, working for the Chemin Company; he was directing repair work on landing strips at an airport. They lived in a small house on the avenue Esquirol, with Maria their maid, and their small son Jean-Pierre, whose Resistance name was Boubou.

The Resistance worked under the theory of *cloisonnement* (containment): know as little as possible. This way, captured agents could divulge very little under torture. Even within the Resistance, they only knew each other by assumed names. To all his Resistance contacts,

❧▶
See sidebar
on the
following page

Opposite page

Lucie

Aubrac

Albrecht, Bertie (?–1943)

French partisan. Born of Swiss parents in Marseille; died at Fresnes prison on May 29, 1943.

Before the start of World War II, Bertie Albrecht worked on the personnel staff in several industrial plants in Paris. When Marshal Pétain called for armistice, she was employed in a factory in Vierzon, a perfect village for Resistance work; the town sat on the demarcation line between occupied and Vichy France. In December 1940, she sought out Henri Frenay in Vichy, whose group would eventually be known as Combat. Albrecht typed and distributed their underground newspaper, a roneotyped newsletter called "Petites Ailes."

Moving to Lyon, she took a cover job, that of regional director for unemployed women at the Ministry of Labor. At first she was able to set up new resistance cells with women in the neighborhood, but suspicions were aroused. When the French police knocked at her door, she delayed admitting them until she had destroyed incriminating documents. Reminded that burning papers was against the law, Albrecht replied, "Sirs, you do your job, I do mine, and I prefer mine to yours." Interned at Vals, she demanded a trial, but those at Vichy ignored her. She then attempted a 13-day hunger strike. When prison doctors refused to force-feed her, she was transferred to St. Joseph, and her case came to trial in October 1942. Though she was sentenced to six months and fined 60,000 francs, the Vichy government ordered her transferred to a concentration camp.

To buy time, Albrecht feigned insanity and outmaneuvered a legion of psychiatrists who examined her. She was then taken to an asylum at Bron, and, on December 29, fellow Combat regulars helped her escape. But her face was now well-known, and she was encouraged to leave the country. Refusing, Albrecht plunged into underground work, even replacing Frenay when he was away. When the Gestapo caught up with her again, she was taken to Mâcon prison, then to Fresnes. For years, her death was shrouded in mystery. It was later learned that, fearing what she might say under torture, Bertie Albrecht hung herself in the cell she was occupying at Fresnes prison on May 29, 1943.

Raymond Samuels was a man named Balmont or Ermelin, and later Aubrac. For the Germans and the French police, his identity papers carried the name Vallet with an address on Croix-Rousse hill where he kept a small apartment in case of arrest. He did not want the Gestapo coming to their home.

Lucie was known as Catherine to fellow resistance leaders. She used an old identity card with her maiden name and the address of her old student residence in Paris; thus, if caught, she was Lucie Bernard. So that she might get a quick leave of absence or day off from teaching with-

out inciting suspicion, a sympathetic doctor faked her medical records, giving her a history of cured TB and anemia. For the next few years, her anemia was put to good use. She describes one such incident in her memoir, *Outwitting the Gestapo*. When *Libération Sud* learned that four *résistants*, who had been wounded or beaten and tortured, were being held as prisoners in Saint-Etienne Hospital, Lucie Aubrac took the train from Lyon to Saint-Etienne.

> I walk into the hospital as if perfectly at home, with my canvas bag slung over my arm, and I get to the toilets without being stopped. I slip on the white gown and put the stethoscope around my neck, then with total self-confidence I walk toward one of the general medical wards. A nurse greets me and shows no sign of surprise. Everything is going fine. Ten beds to this ward. I go up to one of them, where an old woman lies dozing. At the foot of the bed I pick up the medical chart, note the temperature curve, the date of admission, the diagnosis, the frequency and the name of the medications. For this first morning, I limit myself to one walk up and down the corridors.

On the second and third day, she commuted from Lyon (one hour by train, then a trolley) to the hospital. The staff grew accustomed to her presence. On the fourth day, she located the section on the second floor where the prisoners were being held. She watched as a doctor entered the prison section of the hospital; she waited until he came out an hour later, followed by two interns and a male nurse.

> As they are leaving, the nurse stops to light a cigarette. I walk up to him and say: "Can I have a light?" We both stop walking while I slowly take out a cigarette from my purse and light it just as slowly. By now the three others are way ahead of us.
> "Are they in such bad shape?"
> "Oh," he answers, "two of them have to be operated on, but we drag the process out as long as we can because afterward, the Gestapo will take them back. It's wretched."
> He hurries off to rejoin the group. I turn on my heels as if I have something urgent to attend to. As I pass by two policemen who saw me talking to the nurse, I mumble: "They forgot to take number three's blood pressure again." And without further explanation I enter the room.

Finding the prisoners, she leaned in with her stethoscope, and apprised them each of escape plans, while also noting the patient's name and health status from each chart. These were the names the Gestapo were using, and these were the names the Resistance employed when they drove up a day later in three black Citroëns, the kind used by the Gestapo, with three faked license plates and German windshield stickers. They demanded the prisoners and walked off with them.

By 1942, individual resistance movements inside France were becoming more than an irritant to Nazi Germany. Outside France, however, London-based de Gaulle was having difficulty convincing the Allies to recognize his authority. Though he headed all French forces outside his country, he needed to show that a united France was behind him. His lieutenant Jean Moulin, under the code names Rex and Max, was dispatched to France to create the *Conseil National de la Résistance* (CNR, National Council of Resistance). It was not an easy task: de Gaulle wanted to be commander in chief of resistance forces inside France, but resistance leaders were suspicious of him, speculating that he might be a puppet of the British.

"The CNR," Aubrac told Werth, "was created towards the *end* of the Resistance, just in order to give the world the idea that de Gaulle had 'the whole of France behind him.'. . . For a long time the Resistance didn't know much about him. In Normandy, before he arrived, they used to ask: 'What's he like—big or small, thin or fat?'" Tensions also arose over a prolonged debate as to whether or not the French Communist groups would join. They subsequently did.

Amazingly, for the most part Moulin brought off the unification. A former prefect in Chartes, he had been arrested and tortured by the Germans, fled to London in September 1941, then returned to France in January 1942. (*Laure Diebold** would be appointed Moulin's secretary on September 1). By March 1943, Moulin had unified the three principal movements in the South under the banner MUR (*Mouvements Unis de la Résistance),* which included *Libération Sud.* It was a shadow army with four subgroups: *Armée Secrète, Groupes Francs* (of which Lucie Aubrac was a member), *Maquis,* and *Parachutages.* General Délestraint was made head of the unified Secret Army, about 80,000 strong, with a member of Combat and Raymond Aubrac as his deputies.

The activities, the risk, and the size of the units escalated. Until February 16, 1943, the Resistance had been comprised mostly of political idealists. Many of the French had remained nonpartisan. Then, the Germans, facing a shortage of manpower for their factories, instituted STO (*Service du Travail Obligatoire).* All French men born between January 1920 and December 31,

1922, were conscripted, hauled out of French factories, rounded up in the street, transported, and forced to work in German industry. This spurred the Resistance and many more joined its ranks. Many of the French workers, as well as Jews, aided by the Resistance movements, began to "get lost" in the countryside. They were also aided by MUR with its "forged papers service." For over two years, MUR was involved "in some of the most fantastic activities connected with the Resistance," writes Werth. "All this work was a good deal more complicated and more dangerous than the mere production of clandestine newspapers." The MUR not only forged documents, ration cards, and identity cards, but they unnerved the Germans, and the entire system, by spreading rumors that *genuine* labor and identity cards were forgeries.

From March to May of 1943, Raymond Aubrac was once again in jail. He and other leaders had been arrested on March 15, but the French police didn't know who they had; as far as they were concerned, he was a man named François Vallet involved in black-market activities. While the MUR considered escape plans, Lucie—suspecting the French prosecutor who would not sign for bail was a coward—went to his house and threatened him with the vengeance of the entire underground community. Then she walked home terrified. Raymond was released on May 14, 1943, and jumped bail. The other leaders also escaped.

On June 21, 1943, in a Lyon suburb, Moulin and seven other resistance leaders, including Raymond, gathered at a partisan doctor's clinic at Caluire for a clandestine meeting. A month earlier, Moulin had offered Raymond command of the Secret Army in the Northern Zone (occupied France, from the Pyrenees to the Belgian border). Seconds after Moulin's arrival, sirens wailed, and they were arrested by the Gestapo headed by Klaus Barbie. Délestraint had been arrested earlier.

The Resistance had no idea where Moulin and the others were taken, nor whether the Gestapo knew the importance of their prisoners. Lucie suspected they were being held at the Gestapo's Montluc prison. Aware of the danger, she wrapped clean clothes in a sheet of newspaper containing a crossword puzzle, went to Montluc, handed them to a guard in the prison guard house, and requested they be given to Claude Ermelin, a name Raymond was then using. She concluded that if the guard accepted the package, Raymond was being held there, and that was the name by which they knew him. The guard took the package and was gone for some time. When he returned, he handed her some dirty socks rewrapped in the newspaper. In squares of the crossword puzzle, faintly written, were seven letters: MAXWELL. It was then she knew: Raymond Aubrac was in Montluc and Jean Moulin, under the codename Max, was still alive.

Still unsure of how much the Germans knew, she went to Gestapo headquarters. There, she asked to speak to the head of German police services, and was ushered in front of Klaus Barbie. Aubrac was amazed that this young, plain-looking man, shorter than she, who had all Lyon shaking, was the Butcher of Lyon. She told Barbie that she hadn't seen her fiancé since yesterday, that he'd recently had a bad bout with tuberculosis and was going for a check up (the Germans hated infectious diseases), and that the French police told her the Germans had arrested him, along with others, at the doctor's in Caluire. She begged Barbie for his quick release: "his health," she said, "is so frail." When he asked for the man's name, she replied Claude Ermelin. Smiling, Barbie threw a file on the table. "His name is not Ermelin but Vallet," said Barbie, who went on to describe Raymond's arrest as a Gaullist and his identity as a terrorist. Barbie said he would not be released; instead, he would be executed. But, by the time Lucie departed, she had convinced Barbie, with the help of sincere tears, that she had met Vallet on the Cote d'Azur and had fallen in love. Now, Lucie told him, she was pregnant (which was true), and they had planned to marry soon.

Next, Aubrac sent her son Boubou away to a children's home in the mountains. Then, she sat down with other members of the Resistance. To prepare for the rescue, D'Astier gave her 350,000 francs to pay Resistance workers who had little on which to live. They could attack the prison van on its daily trip between Montluc and the health-science school where the prisoners were interrogated in the basement. The question was: how to get Raymond into that van?

Aubrac engineered an appointment with a German colonel who might help. She reiterated her story, telling him she only wanted to see her fiancé once before he died. A well-placed case of cognac cinched the deal: Raymond would be brought out of the prison to the German colonel's office where he was to be briefly reunited with Lucie; the Resistance could then hijack the German pickup truck on its return trip. In case the escape should fail, Aubrac sought out a doctor who inoculated ten wrapped sourball candies with a form of typhus virus; they would stand a better chance of springing him from a hospital than a prison.

On the day of her meeting with Raymond, Lucie managed to give him the hard candies, but the timing of the Resistance was off, and they failed to stop the prison truck. And, though she checked, no prisoner entered a hospital with typhoid. (The doctor later realized that the candies were useless due to the presence of an antiseptic agent used to keep the sugars from breaking down.)

In the failed attempt, they had seen something that would necessitate a new plan: the German guards in the back of the truck had their submachine guns trained on the cargo. If the guards heard gunfire, they would kill the prisoners. The driver and the front-seat guard had to be killed silently. The Resistance group needed a silencer (which they knew of only from gangster movies). Aubrac was soon on a train on her way to the border, where Swiss customs officials gave her two boxes, each containing a silencer.

Once again, Aubrac had to maneuver the Germans into transporting Raymond between Montluc and the health and science building. Planning to invoke the French law of *marriage in extremis* from the Napoleonic code, she made another appointment; this time with a German Gestapo lieutenant. He was sympathetic to the frightened, unmarried pregnant woman who cried for her family and her good name. He told her that the man they were executing was not who she thought he was, that he was a terrorist, a man named Vallet. As if to underscore the seriousness, he told her an envoy of General de Gaulle was also involved in the matter and died more than a month ago. Lucie begged to meet Vallet face-to-face to convince him to accept the marriage and sign a contract. She told the lieutenant that hers was a family with land holdings, and she didn't want her inheritance going to his family. Reluctantly, the German lieutenant agreed. She left with an important piece of information: Jean Moulin was dead.

Meanwhile, their group leader had been captured and, while breaking away, had been wounded. Since he was seriously ill, the group wanted to postpone the escape. Aubrac, who knew they had few chances left, took command, and convinced them to proceed. At this point, she was six months pregnant.

On October 21, 1943, at Gestapo headquarters, Lucie Aubrac met her husband once again; he signed the marriage contract and managed a quick wink. Emerging from the Gestapo building, she walked to town hall to file the contract, had a cup of hot chocolate in the Marquise de Sévigné tearoom, went to her husband's hideout to grab a pistol and change clothes, then climbed into the back seat of a Citroën behind the driver and the sharpshooter, who had a submachine gun on his lap, capped by a silencer. When the gate of the health-and-science building opened and the German pickup truck came out, the Citroën pulled alongside the German driver. The submachine gun was soundless and the German truck, its driver dead, slowed to a curb. Guns raised, the guards jumped out to see if the vehicle was malfunctioning. Three cars filled with partisans moved in, killing the German guards, and Raymond, with the other prisoners, was freed.

While Barbie's girlfriend looked on, Raymond Aubrac had been badly beaten during four months of interrogations under Klaus Barbie. Jean Moulin had also been savagely tortured and killed because he would not talk. "His head all bloody," wrote Moulin's sister, "his insides burst open, he reached the limit of human suffering, without once betraying a single secret, he who knew them all."

On November 3, while Raymond convalesced in hiding, the Aubracs learned that Lucie's identity had been uncovered and the Gestapo had come to their home, looking for her. The news was worse the following day. The Gestapo had discovered where she had placed her son. Men of the Resistance hurried to his school in the mountains. While his parents waited in terror for news, the Resistance beat the Gestapo. The Aubracs now knew they must take their son and leave the country.

"Everyone knows what would happen to me if I were caught," she wrote. "Many people fear the repercussions of my possible arrest. I know far too many things, dating from the fall of 1940 when Libération was established. I know too many people at every level. Many who are well known, some of them sought by the Germans; many heads of sections in the various services; many of the liaison people in the provinces. In other words, I have become very dangerous."

But getting resistance wives out of the country along with resistance leader husbands was difficult; space was at a premium. The underground convinced the British of Lucie's importance by making her a representative of the United Resistance Movement with a seat at the conservative assembly of the French Committee of National Liberation in Algiers in 1944. Thus,

Aubrac became the first French woman parliamentarian. That year, de Gaulle finally awarded French women the right to vote and run for office. The law was first exercised in 1946.

On Tuesday, February 8, 1944, using the light of the moon, a plane left a French meadow for London, carrying the Aubracs. Four days later, on February 12, she had her first daughter in a London hospital. News of the escape and birth was radioed into France over the BBC: "Boubou has a little sister, Catherine, born on the twelfth." Their daughter Elisabeth was born in 1946.

After the war, d'Astier became a member of de Gaulle's Cabinet during the Liberation, then a member of Parliament; he finally returned to journalism before he died. Raymond, whose parents were killed at Auschwitz, returned to France with the landing forces in Provence in August 1944. He was appointed commissaire régional de la République by de Gaulle and resumed his work as engineer with the Ministry of Reconstruction, responsible for mine clearance.

Lucie helped establish the new Public Administration in Normandy and was a member of the Consultative Assembly in Paris, as well as the Second World War Historical Committee. She resumed teaching in Paris, in Rabat (Morocco), and Rome, then retired in 1966 but remained active in movements concerning racism and in remembrance of the Resistance. In her memoirs, first published in France in 1984, as *Ils partiront dans l'ivresse* (*Outwitting the Gestapo*), she chronicles nine months, while she was pregnant with her second child, of her nearly 60 months of life during the French Resistance.

In 1983, Klaus Barbie, the Butcher of Lyon, went on trial in Lyon. Since French law does not permit sentencing for repressing the Resistance, he was held for war crimes and crimes against humanity. Barbie's defense was to attack the Resistance, tarnish the heroes, sow doubt. He insinuated that Moulin committed suicide, while revisionists denied the existence of death camps. In effect, Barbie put the Resistance on trial. In 1987, he was sentenced to life in prison. Earlier that year, the Aubracs won a libel suit against Barbie's lawyer for slander.

SOURCES:

Aubrac, Lucie. *La Résistance (Naissance et Organisation)*. Paris, 1945.

———. *Outwitting the Gestapo*. Trans by Konrad Bieber, with the assistance of Betsy Wing. University of Nebraska Press, 1993 (first published in France in 1984 as *Ils partiront dans l'ivresse*.)

Werth, Alexander. *France: 1940–1955*. NY: Henry Holt, 1956.

Aubrey of Buonalbergo (fl. 1000s)

Duchess of Apulia. Flourished in the 1000s; first wife of Robert Guiscard (d. 1085), a Frankish noble, duke of Apulia and Calabria, count of Sicily (r. 1057–1085); children: Bohemund I of Antioch (r. 1098–1111, who married *Constance of France).

Aubry, Cécile (1929—)

French actress. Born Anne-Marie-José Bénard in Paris, France, on August 3, 1929; married a Moroccan prince (later divorced).

Following her meteoric rise in 1949, the petite Cécile Aubry made few films. She was discovered by Henri-Georges Clouzot and cast in his highly popular film *Manon*, based on a modernization of Abbé Prévost's 18th-century novel *Manon Lescaut*. Aubry played the title character who is condemned by local villagers for her affair with a Resistance fighter played by Michel Auclair. (The movie was later remade as *Manon 70* with **Catherine Deneuve**.) Cécile Aubry's other films include *The Black Rose* (United States, 1950), *Barbe-Bleu* (Bluebeard, 1951), *Bonjour la Chance* (1954), and *The Reluctant Thief* (Italian, 1955). After her marriage, she went on to write and illustrate children's books and produce for children's television.

Auclert, Hubertine (1848–1914)

Founder of the women's suffrage movement in France who struggled for 30 years to win the vote through her suffrage league, her militant newspaper, and dramatic tactics including a tax boycott and violent demonstrations. Name variations: "Liberta," Jeanne Voitout. Pronunciation: o-CLAIR. Born Marie-Anne-Hubertine Auclert on April 10, 1848, in the village of Tilly, in the department of Allier, France; died in her apartment in Paris, France, on April 8, 1914; fifth of seven children of Jean-Baptiste (a well-to-do peasant landowner) and Marie (Chanudet) Auclert (daughter of neighboring landowners); residential pupil at the Catholic Convent of the Dames de l'enfant Jésus in Montmirail (Allier, France) from age nine (1857) through sixteen (1864); married Antonin Lévrier (a judge in the French colonial service) in Algiers, in July 1888 (died, February 1892); no children.

Father died (1861); rejected in effort to join Sisters of Charity of St. Vincent de Paul at end of her studies (1864); sent back to convent as a pensioner by her oldest brother on the death of their mother (1866); inherited independent fortune at age 21 (1869); claimed inheritance and moved to Paris (1873), joining

Opposite page

Hubertine Auclert

pioneering feminist league of Léon Richer and Maria Deraismes; founded her own feminist society, Women's Rights (1876); split from Richer and Deraismes during feminist congress of 1878, to seek women's suffrage; participated in socialist congress of 1879 to seek feminist-socialist alliance; organized voter registration campaign and feminist tax boycott in Paris (1880–81); founded feminist society, Women's Suffrage, and suffragist newspaper, La Citoyenne (The Citizeness) (1881); lead numerous petition campaigns and demonstrations (1881–85); ran as illegal candidate for French parliament (1885); left Paris to marry her longtime feminist collaborator (1888–92); returned to Parisian feminism as newspaper columnist (1893); resumed suffragist petition campaigns (1898); took active role in feminist congress and revived Women's Suffrage (1900); led militant demonstration to burn French Civil Code (1904); led violent election-day demonstrations and convicted of misdemeanor (1908); ran as illegal candidate for French parliament (1910); remained leading voice of militant suffragism as moderate suffragist movement grew in France (1910–14).*

Publications—many pamphlets and newspaper columns plus: Les Femmes arabes en Algérie (Arab Women in Algeria; Paris, 1900); Le Vote des femmes (The Vote for Women; Paris, 1908); Les Femmes au gouvernail (Women at the Helm; Paris, 1923).

Women's suffrage received enormous publicity during the Parisian municipal elections of May 1908. Although French women had no legal right to vote or to run for office, **Jeanne Laloë**, a young reporter for *Le Matin*, announced her candidacy for the Municipal Council and began to write newspaper stories about her campaign. French suffragists, who had worked for political rights for 30 years, worried that this unprepared campaign was merely a newspaper's publicity gimmick. Militant suffragists, led by the founder of the movement, Hubertine Auclert, decided to make a more forceful demonstration. On polling day, the 60-year-old Auclert, wearing widow's black, led a suffragist parade through Paris. Later, on that same Sunday afternoon, Auclert marched into a poll, brushed aside electoral officials, and walked to a table where men were depositing their paper ballots in a wooden box. Before the eyes of stunned officials, she seized the ballot box, smashed it to the floor, and stamped on the spilled ballots. After a brief speech denouncing "unisexual suffrage," Auclert was arrested. At her subsequent trial, she proudly accepted the comparison to the "violent suffragettes" of Britain and vowed to continue the struggle to win the vote.

Hubertine Auclert was born in the department of Allier in central France in 1848. Her father, Jean-Baptiste, was a prosperous landowner who served as mayor of the village of Tilly, a republican in an age of monarchy. Auclert received eight years of formal education (1855–64) as a residential pupil at the convent of the Dames de l'enfant Jésus in Allier, and she developed her youthful personality in ascetic piety. At age 16, she felt called to a religious life, and she sought in 1864 to join the Sisters of Charity of St. Vincent de Paul. They apparently found her egalitarian Christianity too radical and rejected her.

Auclert lived with her widowed mother in 1864–66, and their conversations during these years awakened the young woman to the subjection of women. When Madame Auclert died in 1866, Hubertine learned that lesson in a more painful manner. Her older brother Théophile assumed control of the family properties and returned his sister to the now-hated convent as a "paying resident." After Hubertine Auclert received her share of the family estate, however, neither her brother, nor the convent, nor the provinces could keep her. Her inheritance did not bring great riches, but it brought freedom: it provided Auclert with sufficient income that she need never take a job or a husband.

Auclert's feminist awakening was completed in 1872 when she read the press accounts of a great meeting held in Paris by the women's right league of *Maria Deraismes** and Léon Richer. She was especially moved by Victor Hugo's famous message to that meeting:

> It is sad to say, that there are still slaves in today's civilization. The law uses euphemisms. Those whom I call slaves, it calls minors; these minors according to the law and slaves according to reality, are women. . . . Women cannot own, they are outside the legal system, they do not vote, they do not count, they do not exist. There are citizens, THERE ARE NOT CITIZENESSES. This is a violent fact; it must cease.

After reading accounts of that speech, Hubertine Auclert resolved to go to Paris and to devote herself to the cause of women's rights.

Auclert joined Léon Richer's group, *L'Avenir des femmes* (Women's Future), in 1873. The league called for numerous reforms in French civil and criminal law to improve the position of women: the right of women to file paternity suits against their seducers, the equal sharing of paternal authority and rights within the family, the abolition of a husband's control over the property and earning of his wife, the end of the legal

double standard concerning adultery, the acceptance of a woman's testimony in civil and public law, and the legalization of divorce.

Auclert worked for these reforms as a public speaker, a journalist, and a supporter of Richer's league for three years (1873–76). As she learned her way in Parisian politics, however, she became convinced that Richer and the other leaders of French feminism were making a major mistake in their program. In order to win the many objectives of Richer's program, Auclert concluded, they must demand the complete political rights of women. When women had the vote, the Chamber of Deputies would pay attention to them. Richer refused to add political rights to his program, so the 28-year-old Auclert left *L'Avenir des femmes* to launch her own association.

Hubertine Auclert founded a society named Le Droit des femmes (Women's Right) in 1876. Through this association, soon renamed *Le Suffrage des femmes* (Women's Suffrage), Auclert founded the women's suffrage movement in France. The group initially attracted only 20 members and rose to a maximum of 150, but they were enough to put the issue before the French public. Auclert hoped to present the case for political rights at the women's rights congress of 1878 (*Congrès international du droit des femmes*), which Richer and Deraismes organized. Instead, she learned that the moderate mainstream of French feminism strongly opposed calling for the vote: Deraismes and Richer refused to allow her to speak of women's suffrage at the congress.

Auclert responded by publishing her proposed speech as a pamphlet, "The Political Rights of Women—A Question That is Not Treated at the International Congress of Women." Her attack was blistering:

> I know that the partisans of the emancipation of women find the claim of political rights premature. I have nothing to reply to them, except that woman is a despoiled creature who demands justice, not a beggar who pleads for charity from man. . . . What can the oppressors think, if those who desire to liberate women are anxious about not offending their oppressors and timidly ask for a little more education, a bit more bread, slightly less humiliation in marriage.

With these words, Auclert left behind the moderate feminist movement and began a search for new allies.

During the winter of 1878–79, Hubertine Auclert began attending Parisian socialist meetings in hopes of finding allies on the far left of French politics. This led to her being chosen as a delegate to the annual congress of French socialists held at Marseilles in October 1879. Auclert addressed that congress as "the slave delegate of nine million slaves," and proposed to French workers an "alliance against our common oppressors." She defiantly challenged French socialists to add women's suffrage to their program:

> If you, proletarians, wish to protect privileges, the privileges of sex, I ask you what authority you have to protest against the privileges of class? . . . In the future society, pretended socialists [say], women will have their rights. In this they imitate the priests who promise to the disinherited of the earth the joys of heaven. Neither the disinherited of wealth nor the disinherited of rights, neither the poor nor women can always content themselves with holy promises. Women of France, I tell you from the height of this podium: those who deny our equality in the present will deny it in the future.

Auclert's speech won a socialist resolution in favor of women's suffrage, the first won from any political party in France. During the early 1880s, however, French socialists discouraged Auclert by giving women's rights only lip service, and her enthusiasm for the party waned by 1885.

Auclert launched her most energetic campaigns for women's suffrage in the early 1880s. Her small association, renamed *Suffrage des femmes* (Women's Suffrage) and a newspaper that she founded, financed, and edited, *La Citoyenne* (The Citizeness) sponsored numerous efforts to publicize their claims. In February 1880, she led a delegation of suffragists in an attempt to register to vote at the town hall. Denied registration, Auclert protested by announcing that she would no longer pay her taxes: "I have no rights, therefore, I have no taxes; I do not vote, I do not pay." After several months of controversy, Auclert backed down when the government came to seize her furniture—but she launched a new series of court cases to appeal these procedures. Her other demonstrations of the 1880s included the interruption of marriage ceremonies at town hall (to warn brides of their legal subjection to their husbands), polls of parliament, regular petitions on behalf of all forms of women's rights (22 petitions between 1880 and 1887), contacts with the American suffrage movement, parades in Paris (reaching 200 marchers in 1885), and even illegal candidacies for office. Perhaps Auclert's most lasting accomplishment during these struggles was to give the women's movement the word "feminist" in 1882: she was apparently the first advocate of women's rights (in any country) to adopt this label.

By the late 1880s, Auclert was frustrated and disillusioned. After 15 years of labor, she had not even persuaded the moderate majority of the feminist movement to support women's suffrage. Her organization never attracted many members, nor her newspaper many subscribers. The Parisian press ridiculed her.

And Auclert was deeply lonely. The love of her life, a strong supporter of her feminism named Antonin Lévrier, was a judge. When the Ministry of Justice transferred Lévrier out of Paris, he proposed marriage but Auclert chose to stay in Paris to work for feminism. When Lévrier was posted overseas in 1885, he again proposed marriage and Auclert again declined. When his career moved Lévrier back to Algeria and his health declined, Auclert reconsidered. Deeply frustrated in Paris, Auclert married Lévrier in Algiers in July 1888. For the period 1888–92, her contact with French feminism was limited to writing letters and articles. One series of those articles formed the basis of her subsequent book, *Les Femmes arabes en Algérie* (*Arab Women in Algeria*, Paris, 1900), outraged at the life of women in the most important French colony.

Though Hubertine Auclert returned to Paris after Lévrier's death in 1892, she only gradually returned to the women's rights movement. She felt like an outcast when she tried to participate in the feminist congress of 1896, but she had recovered her vigor and dedication by the time of the next congress in 1900. Auclert launched a vigorous second feminist career in that year and reestablished her organization, *Suffrage des femmes*. She did not found another newspaper, but she became a regular columnist (under the rubric "Le Féminisme") for an important Parisian daily paper, *Le Radical*.

During the first decade of the 20th century, Auclert worked with the same energy that she had shown in her 30s. French feminism was then beginning the transition from small, pioneering societies to large, active organizations with tens of thousands of members. Although she never became an insider in these large, moderate organizations, Auclert and her society revived the issue of women's suffrage and contributed significantly to the acceptance of this issue by the French women's rights movement. She revived the tactics of her suffrage campaigns of the 1880s, such as petitions to the Chamber of Deputies, but during the years 1904–08 Hubertine Auclert also introduced more militant suffragist tactics to France.

Auclert's most famous demonstration, during the Parisian municipal elections of 1908, earned her the appellation "the French suffragette." Her seizure and destruction of a ballot box was, with *Madeleine Pelletier's breaking of a polling place window a week later, the greatest violence used by French suffragists before World War I. Auclert was not by nature a violent person, and she tried to explain her militancy in court:

> It is regrettable that I committed this act which brings me before you; regrettable because I am strongly opposed to violence. But I acted this way because I have been pushed to the limit—as all of my suffragette comrades have been—by the egoism of men.
>
> Please consider that for many years I have tried in vain to claim the political rights of women, in a lawful manner. . . . I am very respectful of legality, I am not a violent person. But I believe that there are moments in life when violence is excusable.
>
> Driven to desperation by seeing my legal efforts lead to nothing, I bore in mind that when men were excluded from politics, as women are today, they built barricades.... They cannot be surprised that women, in their turn, revolt.

When Hubertine Auclert made that speech in court, she was 60 years old and near the end of her career. She lived long enough to witness the acceptance of suffragism by French moderate feminists at a congress in 1908, and to watch as they founded a new league committed to moderation, the *L'Union française pour le suffrage des femmes* (French Union for Women's Suffrage), rather than join her organization. She tried to lead the new suffrage movement to more vehement tactics by participating in a series of women's candidacies in the parliamentary elections of 1910, and lived long enough to see a suffrage movement with more than 10,000 members plan marches in the streets in 1914.

I leave to men the privilege of paying the taxes that they adopt and portion out according to their pleasure. . . . I have no rights, therefore, I have no taxes; I do not vote, I do not pay.

—Hubertine Auclert

SOURCES:

Hause, Steven C. *Hubertine Auclert: The French Suffragette.* New Haven, CT: Yale University Press, 1987.

SUGGESTED READING:

Bidelman, Patrick K. *Pariahs Stand Up! The Founding of the Liberal Feminist Movement in France, 1858–1889.* Westport, CT: Greenwood, 1982.

Hause, Steven C., and Anne R. Kenney. "The Limits of Suffragist Behavior: Legalism and Militancy in France, 1876–1922," in *American Historical Review.* Vol. 86, 1981, p. 781.

Hause, Steven C., with Anne R. Kenney. *Women's Suffrage and Social Politics in the French Third Republic.* Princeton, NJ: Princeton University Press, 1984.

Klejman, Laurence, and Florence Rochefort. *L'Egalité en marche: Le Féminisme sous la Troisième République.* Paris: Fondation nationale des sciences politiques, 1989.

Moses, Claire G. *French Feminism in the 19th Century.* Albany, NY: SUNY Press, 1984.

Sowerwine, Charles. *Sisters or Citizens? Women and Socialism in France since 1876.* Cambridge, England: Cambridge University Press, 1982.

Taïeb, Edith, ed. *Hubertine Auclert: La Citoyenne: Articles, 1848–1914.* Paris: Syros, 1982.

COLLECTIONS:

Papers located in the Bouglé Collection at the Bibliothèque historique de la ville de Paris; important dossiers located in the Bibliothèque Marguerite Durand (Paris) and in the Archives du Préfecture de Police (Paris).

Steven C. Hause, Professor of History and Fellow in International Studies, University of Missouri-St. Louis, and author of *Hubertine Auclert: The French Suffragette*

Audley, Alice (d. 1374)

Baroness Neville of Raby. Name variations: Alice Neville. Died in 1374; married Ralph Neville, 2nd baron Neville of Raby; children: John Neville, 3rd baron Neville of Raby; *Margaret Neville (d. 1372).

Audley, Margaret (fl. 1340s)

Countess of Stafford. Flourished in 1340; daughter of Hugh Audley, earl of Gloucester, and *Margaret de Clare (c. 1293–1342); married Ralph Stafford, 1st earl of Stafford; children: Ralph (d. 1348), 1st earl of Stafford; Hugh (c. 1344–1386), 2nd earl of Stafford; Beatrice Stafford (who married Thomas Roos, 5th baron Ros).

Audley, Margaret (d. 1564)

Duchess of Norfolk. Name variations: Margaret Howard. Died on January 9, 1564; daughter of Thomas Audley and Elizabeth Grey; married Henry Dudley; married Thomas Howard, 3rd duke of Norfolk, after 1557; children: Thomas Howard (1561–1626), earl of Suffolk; William Howard (1563–1640).

When her sister **Mary Audley** died unmarried, Margaret Audley inherited her father's property.

Audley, Maxine (1923–1992)

English actress. Born in London, England, on April 29, 1923; died in 1992; daughter of Henry Julius Hecht and Katharine (Arkandy) Hecht; educated at Westonbirt School; trained for the stage at the Tamara Daykharhanova School in New York and at the London Mask Theatre School; married Leonard Cassini (divorced); married Andrew Broughton (divorced); married Frederick Granville (divorced).

Maxine Audley make her first stage appearance as a walk-on in *Midsummer Night's Dream* at the Open Air Theatre in July 1940. Following years of stage work, she also appeared in such films as *Anna Karenina* (1947), *The Sleeping Tiger* (1954), *The Barretts of Wimpole Street* (1957), *The Prince and the Showgirl* (1957), *King in New York* (1957), *The Dunkirk Story* (1958), *The Vikings* (1958), *Our Man in Havana* (1959), *The Trials of Oscar Wilde* (1960), *The Agony and the Ecstasy* (1965), *House of Cards* (1969), and *The Looking-Glass War (1970).* Her British television credits include Queen *Elizabeth I in *Kenilworth*, Celia in *The Cocktail Party*, Tanis in *Portrait in Black*, Mrs. Wilton in *John Gabriel Borkman.* Audley also appeared in the television serials "The Voodoo Factor" and "Danger Man," and played Mrs. Marlow on "Prime Suspect."

Audofleda (c. 470–?).

See Amalasuntha for sidebar.

Audouard, Olympe (1830–1890)

French novelist, travel writer, and journalist. Pronunciation: OH-dö-är. Born in 1830; died in 1890; married and divorced.

The French writer Olympe Audouard married a notary in Marseilles. Though she soon separated from him, she was unable to obtain a divorce until 1885. Supported by her writing, Audouard traveled in Egypt, Turkey, and Russia. From 1860, she founded various journals in Paris (including the literary review *Le Papillon*), and made a successful lecture tour through America in 1868–69. After her return to France, she became interested in the occult and was an ardent advocate of women's rights, possibly fueled by her marriage as well as an experience in Paris where she was thwarted in starting a political journal because of her gender. Her novels and books of travel include *How Men Love* (1861), *The Mysteries of the Seraglio and of the Turkish Harems* (1863), *War on Man* (1866), *Across America* (1869–71), and *Parisian Silhouettes* (1883).

Audoux, Marguerite (1863–1937)

French novelist. Born in 1863 in France, orphaned; died in 1937. Worked as a servant and wrote in her spare time, including the autobiographical Marie-Claire *(1910).*

After her mother died while giving birth and her father abandoned her as an infant, Marguerite Audoux was banished to an orphanage, where she grew up before being hired as a farm servant in Sologne. Several long years later, Audoux moved to Paris and took work as a seamstress. The author Charles-Louis Philippe befriended Audoux and introduced her to the literary circles of Paris. In her spare hours away from her needle and thread, Audoux wrote *Marie-Claire,* a largely autobiographical and acutely realistic depiction of working-class life in France. The novel, published in 1910, received critical acclaim and international circulation for its subtle exposure of the indentured nature of working-class life. Audoux continued to write following her debut, but no other novel was so well received or so respected as her first.

Crista Martin,
Boston, Massachusetts

Audovera (d. 580).

See Fredegund for sidebar.

Audran, Stéphane (1932—)

French actress. Born Colette Suzanne Jeannine Dacheville in Versailles, France, on November 2, 1932; married Jean-Louis Trintignant (divorced); married Claude Chabrol (a director), in 1964 (divorced in late 1980s).

Filmography: La Bonne Tisane *(Kill or Cure, 1958);* Les Cousins *(The Cousins, 1959);* Les Bonnes Femmes *(with* **Bernadette Lafont***, 1960);* Les Godelureaux *(1961);* L'Oeil du Matin *(The Third Lover, 1962);* Le Signe de Lion *(The Sign of Leo, 1962);* Landru *(Bluebeard, 1963);* Le Tigre aime la Chair fraiche *(The Tiger Likes Fresh Blood, 1964);* Paris Vu Par *(Six in Paris, 1965);* La Ligne de Démarcation *(directed by Eric Rohmer, 1966);* Le Scandale *(The Champagne Murders, 1967);* Les Biches *(1968);* La Femme Infidèle *(1969);* La Rupture *(The Break Up, 1970);* Le Boucher *(1970);* La Dame dans l'Auto avec des Lunettes et us Fusil *(The Lady in the Car with Glasses and a Gun, 1970);* La Peau de Torpedo *(directed by Jean Delannoy, 1970);* Sans Mobile Apparent *(Without Apparent Motive, 1971);* Juste Avant la Nuit *(Just Before Nightfall, 1971);* The Discreet Charm of the Bourgeoisie *(1972);* Les Noces rouges *(Wedding in Blood, 1972);* Folies Bourgeoises *(1976);* Blood Relatives *(1978);* And Then There Were None *(1974);* The Black Bird *(1975);* Silver Bears *(1977);* Eagle's Wing *(1978);* Violette Nozière *(Violette, 1978);* Le Gagnant *(1979);* La Soleil en Face *(1979);* The Big Red One *(1980);* Coup de Torchon *(Clean Slate, 1981);* Brideshead Revisited *(1981);* Le Beau Monde *(1981);* Boulevard de Assassins *(1982);* Les Affinites Electives *(1982);* Le Paradis pour Tous *(1982);* Thieves After Dark *(1983);* Le Sang des Autres *(1984);* Mistral's Daughter *(1984);* The Sun Also Rises *(1984);* Night Magic *(1985);* La Cage aux Folles III *(1985);* Le Gitane *(1985);* Suivez Mon Regard *(1986);* Les Saisons du Plaisir *(1987);* Poor Little Rich Girl: The Barbara Hutton Story *(1987);* Babette's Feast *(1987);* Sons *(1989);* Jours tranquiles à Clichy *(Quiet Days in Clichy, 1990);* Le Messe en si mineur *(1990); and* Betty *(1993).*

An enormously popular star in France, Stéphane Audran is known for her ability to play the vapid sophisticate or elegant mannequin, while hinting at far more intensity below the surface. After a series of small parts, she first starred in *L'Oeil du Matin* (*The Third Lover*, 1962); she has since appeared in nearly 50 films, 21 of them directed by her ex-husband Claude Chabrol. In *Paris Vu Par* (*Six in Paris*, 1965), "she was the quarrelsome mother," writes David Thomson, "whose son puts cotton wool in his ears so that he never hears her cry for help in an emergency." Thomson regarded the part as a "sardonic, marital joke" on the part of Chabrol. In her next two husband-directed movies, Audran portrayed traditional "fashion plates." It was Chabrol's *Les Biches* in 1968, however, that "properly discovered her as an actress," continues Thomson. "In one sense, her acutely made-up beauty needed very little heightening to suggest lesbianism, but the eventual sexual reversal of the film allowed her a new poignancy that was an advance for both actress and director." For her performance, she walked off with the Berlin Festival's Best Actress prize. Audran also received Britain's Academy Award for *Juste Avant la Nuit* (*Just Before Nightfall*, 1971) and Luis Buñuel's witty *The Discreet Charm of the Bourgeoisie* (1972), which also starred *Delphine Seyrig.

In the late 1970s, Audran began to take roles as a supporting actress; she won a César award for her performance as the dowdy middle-aged woman contrasted with **Isabelle Huppert** in *Violette Nozière* (*Violette*, 1978). In 1987, Audran was again lauded for her performance in the title role of *Babette's Feast*, based on a short story by *Isak Dinesen. An instant classic, the film concerns Babette Hersant who—fleeing from government reprisals against the Paris Commune, which had already claimed her

husband and son—arrives in a remote village in northern Norway (though the movie was shot in Jutland). In exchange for asylum, she takes a job as unpaid housekeeper for two aging sisters (played by **Birgitte Federspiel** and **Bodil Kjer**), daughters of a strict Lutheran minister who had imposed a rigid asceticism on the community before his death. For 14 years, she cares for them, cooking their frugal fare. Then Babette wins the lottery and offers to cook them a dinner to celebrate the centenary of their departed father. She methodically spends every penny of her winnings and prepares a sumptuous feast of quail, turtle soup, baba au rhum, and blinis with crème fraîche and caviar for all of the villagers who later learn that she was once head chef at the Café Anglais in Paris. "With her marvelous screen presence and mature beauty, Stéphane Audran is an ideal Babette," wrote James Reid Paris. In this parable about the healing power of art, Audran said she felt as though she was "transcending the ingredients and performing a sacred act." The film "speaks of the communication among the people. It is a miracle; it involves the union of the spirit and matter. A metaphysical tale."

SOURCES:

Paris, James Reid. *Classic Foreign Films: From 1960 to Today.* NY: Citadel Press, 1993.

Thomson, David. *A Biographical Dictionary of Film.* 3rd ed. NY: Knopf, 1994.

Audry, Jacqueline (1908–1977)

French film director. Born Jacqueline Audry in Orange, France, on September 25, 1908; died in 1977; sister of **Colette Audry** *(1906–1990, a novelist, playwright, literary critic, and screenwriter of* The Battle of the Rails *[Bataille du Rail]); married Pierre Laroche (1902–1962, a scriptwriter).*

Filmography: Les Chevaux du Vercors *(short, 1943);* Les Malheurs de Sophie *(1944);* Gigi *(1948);* Sombre dimanche *(1948);* Minne ou l'ingenue libertine *(Minne, 1950);* Olivia *(Pit of Loneliness, 1951);* La Caraque blonde *(1952);* Huis Clos *(No Exit, 1954);* Mitsou *(1956);* La Garçonne *(1956);* L'Ecole des cocottes *(1957),* C'est la faute d'Adam *(1957);* Le Secret du chevalier d'Eon *(1959);* Les Petits Matins *(1961);* Cadavres en vacances *(1961);* Cours de bonheur conjugal *(1964);* Fruits amers *(1966);* Le Lys de mer *(1969);* Un grand Amour de Balzac *(1972).*

Jacqueline Audry began her motion-picture career in the area of continuity in 1933. For the next ten years, she served as assistant director to such luminaries as G.W. Pabst, Jean Delannoy, and Marcel Ophüls. In 1943, Audry directed her first film, a short entitled *Les Chevaux du Vercors*. Two years later, she shot her first full-length feature *Les Malheurs de Sophie* and subsequently directed a number of films that were popular in France, many of which were written by her husband Pierre Laroche.

Audry brought two of *Colette's stories to the screen. In 1950, she cast **Danièle Delorme** as Gigi, **Yvonne de Bray** as Gigi's grandmother, and **Gaby Morlay** as the great aunt, to make *Gigi*. (Vincente Minnelli directed the 1958 musical version, which starred **Leslie Caron**.) In 1957, Audry directed Colette's love story *Mitsou*, again with Delorme in the title role. Wrote *Pauline Kael, the movie "achieves some of the story's absurdly touching quality."

Though in her earlier films Audry often chose to make what would be considered in any country "studio pictures," she ultimately set herself apart as the only French filmmaker to exclusively explore women characters. In particular, her film *Olivia*, made in 1951, is considered a milestone because of its exploration of lesbian themes, certainly a subject considered taboo in the 1950s. Released in America as *Pit of Loneliness*, it was adapted from the English novel *Olivia*, which was published anonymously; the script was written by Colette. In the story, which starred *Edwige Feuillère and *Simone Simon, two women run a finishing school. The elegant and provocative Feuillère is looked up to by the girls, and she in turn takes a more than passing interest in the English student Olivia. The film, claims Kael, does not measure up to an earlier study of lesbianism at school, *Mädchen in Uniform*. "Audry was more adept at light comedy, than at this sort of subtle sensuousness. Feuillère has superb presence but the movie is so determinedly 'delicate' that it seems to move at a snail's pace." Audry also directed Jean-Paul Sartre's *Huis clos* (*No Exit*) in 1954.

SOURCES:

Kael, Pauline. *5001 Nights at the Movies*. NY: Holt, 1985.

Kuhn, Annette, ed. with Susannah Radstone. *The Women's Companion to International Film*. Berkeley and Los Angeles: University of California Press, 1994.

Manvell, Roger, ed. *The International Encyclopedia of Film*. NY: Crown Publishers, 1972.

Auer, Judith (1905–1944)

Swiss-born German political activist who fought courageously against the Nazi regime despite constant threats to her life. Born Judith Vallentin in Zurich, Switzerland, on September 19, 1905; died on the guillotine at Berlin's Plötzensee Penitentiary on October 27, 1944; married Erich Auer, in 1926; children: one daughter (b. 1929).

Active in youth activities in Berlin, joining the German Communist Party (KPD; 1927); centered her work in the Communist-dominated working-class district of Wedding, known as "Red Wedding" during the period of the Weimar Republic; active in underground resistance activities, including the preparation and distribution of pamphlets and flyers warning the populace of Hitler's plans for war (1930s); member of the Saefkow-Jacob-Bästlein resistance group (1940–44); arrested and sentenced to death for high treason (1944).

The oldest of four children, Judith Vallentin Auer was born the daughter of a writer in Zurich, Switzerland, on September 19, 1905, into comfortable circumstances. Tragedy entered her young life in 1918 when both her parents died within weeks of each other. Jewish friends of her family made it possible for her to continue her education, which took Auer to music schools in Leipzig and Berlin. She also began to study Marxism and revolutionary social theories in 1924 after meeting Ernst Putz, a German Communist organizer, at a student work-and-study camp in the Rhön district. Auer developed a strong social conscience, asking fundamental questions about the social injustices that were never far from her eyes in the great cities of Germany. Believing that Communism was the answer to these evils, she joined the Communist youth movement in Leipzig.

In 1925, she moved from Leipzig back to Berlin, becoming active in Communist youth work in the overwhelmingly working-class section of Wedding. At this time, her financial support ceased, and she was forced to end her studies and support herself by working as a typist. She became more closely linked with the world of German Communism in 1926 when she married Erich Auer, an up-and-coming functionary in the Communist youth movement, and the next year she joined the KPD (German Communist Party).

The Auers spent 1928–29 in Moscow. Although economic conditions were poor and the Stalinist grip on the Soviet Communist Party was rapidly tightening, the couple had positive impressions of a society rapidly industrializing and apparently creating the political, economic and cultural foundations of a genuine Socialist society. By the time they returned to Berlin in 1929, German democracy was entering its final crisis. For convinced Marxists like Judith Auer, the time for revolutionary upheaval had arrived.

Opposite page
Stephane Audran in Babette's Feast, based on a short story by Isak Dinesen.

These ideas, however, proved to be illusions, for Adolf Hitler and his National Socialist movement were infinitely more cynical and adroit than the political Left, seizing power in Germany in 1933, aided by Communists who refused to make democracy work and conservatives who believed they could manipulate Hitler to do their bidding. The Nazis crushed most opposition to their rule in a few brief months, but underground cells of Communists and Social Democrats continued to prepare for the day when the regime could be toppled.

During the following years, Auer remained active, preparing pamphlets and studying party literature. Starting in 1937 she worked as a buyer for the Oberspree Cable Works, a job that provided her not only with an income but also a cover for her illegal party work. Despite her daughter's birth in 1929, Auer continued her anti-Nazi underground work. Among her close friends and colleagues was **Aenne Saefkow**, wife of Anton Saefkow, one of the leading Communist functionaries of the illegal party.

The outbreak of World War II made Communist underground work in Germany more difficult as the Gestapo and its large network of spies and informers tightened their grip. Auer carried out a large number of missions for the Communist central command. She was treasurer of the underground organization created in Berlin-Brandenburg by Anton Saefkow, Franz Jacob, and Bernhard Bästlein. She delivered food and food ration cards to fugitive party members who dared not show their faces in public. She also acted as a courier for endangered members of Communist cells, including the Theodor Neubauer group in Thuringia and other organizations operating in Dresden, Leipzig, Hanover, and Liegnitz. She offered her home in the suburb of Bohnsdorf as a refuge to Franz Jacob, who was in hiding from the Hamburg Gestapo.

Judith Auer's luck ran out in July 1944 when she was arrested. At her trial before the notorious *Volksgerichtshof* (People's Court), she was sentenced to death along with two other Communists, Bruno Hämmerling and Franz Schmidt. Her execution took place at Berlin's Plötzensee prison where, between 1933 and 1945, 1,574 men and women were executed for political offenses by the Nazi regime. On October 27, 1944, she wrote a last letter to her young daughter from her cell at Plötzensee, giving practical advice on how to stop sucking her thumb, on deriving inspiration from the life and music of Beethoven, and on the necessity of "above all else always being inspired by love; the mistakes one makes out of love are never sins, because they can always be rectified." Auer was executed on that same day. Six months later, Berlin was a city in ruins, Adolf Hitler was dead in his bunker, and the Nazi regime Judith Auer had given her life to overthrow had been toppled by the Soviet Army.

One aspect of German unification in 1990 was a conservative nationalist spirit that called for the elimination of all public reminders of the Communist resistance to Nazism. As a result, the Judith-Auer-Strasse in the city of Magdeburg has been renamed.

SOURCES:

Ehrenbuch der Opfer von Berlin-Plötzensee. Berlin: verlag das europäische buch, 1974.

Kraushaar, Luise. *Deutsche Widerstandskämpfer 1933–1945: Biographien und Briefe.* 2 vols. Berlin: Dietz Verlag, 1970.

Merson, Allan. *Communist Resistance in Nazi Germany.* London: Lawrence and Wishart, 1985.

Nitzsche, Gerhard. *Die Saefkow-Jacob-Bästlein-Gruppe: Dokumente und Materialien des illegalen antifaschistischen Kampfes (1942 bis 1945).* Berlin: Dietz Verlag, 1957.

Steinbach, Peter, and Johannes Tuchel, ed. *Lexikon des Widerstandes 1933–1945.* Munich: Verlag C.H. Beck, 1994.

Zorn, Monika. *Hitlers zweimal getöte Opfer: Westdeutsche Endlösung des Antifaschismus auf dem Gebiet der DDR.* Freiburg im Breisgau: Ahriman-Verlag, 1994.

John Haag, Associate Professor of History, University of Georgia, Athens, Georgia

Auerbach, Beatrice Fox

(1887–1968)

American business executive who for many years was the only female department-store president in the country. Name variations: Beatrice Fox. Born in Hartford, Connecticut, on July 7, 1887; died on November 29, 1968; eldest daughter of Moses and Theresa Stern Fox; married George Auerbach.

Came into the family business, G. Fox & Co., when her husband died (1927); became company president (1938); introduced the five-day work week, excellent retirement and medical plans, and a subsidized lunchroom; was one of the first to hire African-Americans in jobs that were not dead-end positions; initiated a statewide toll-free telephone service, a free delivery service, and fully automated billing; by 1959, G. Fox & Co. was the largest privately owned department store in the United States.

On July 7, 1887, Beatrice Fox, eldest daughter of Moses and Theresa Stern Fox, was born in Hartford, Connecticut, into an affluent Jewish family. Beatrice's paternal grandfather had emigrated from Germany in the 1840s, opening up a one-room fancy goods shop that was transformed by his son Moses into G. Fox & Co., a profitable retail enterprise. Beatrice attended public and private schools in Hartford, as well as a finishing school in New York City. During these years, she often traveled to Europe with her parents, and it was on one of these trips that she met her future husband, George Auerbach.

After the marriage, the Auerbachs moved to Salt Lake City, but they returned to Hartford in 1917 when the family store burned to the ground. Determined to rebuild the business, Moses Fox hired his son-in-law to assist him in the task. The new and remodeled store was a great success, and George served as its secretary-treasurer while Beatrice concentrated on being a wife and mother. Upon her husband's death in 1927, Beatrice took on what she saw as a temporary job to assist her father. Years later, she recalled that she "just came down" to the store, believing she would return to domesticity within a few months. As it turned out, she said, "I found myself fascinated and I stayed."

Increasingly, Auerbach took on her father's managerial responsibilities as he grew older and his health began to fail. She learned an immense amount about business from 1927 to 1938. After her father's death in 1938, she inherited the major share of stock in the firm and was named its president. Not only did she keep the family business intact during the worst years of economic depression in the early 1930s, but she was also responsible for a number of important innovations. Concerned about her employees' morale, she introduced a five-day work week, keeping the store closed on Sundays and Mondays, except during the Christmas shopping season. Auerbach offered her employees excellent retirement and medical plans as well as a subsidized lunchroom. The **Theresa Stern Fox** Fund was put in place to provide employees with interest-free loans for family emergencies. Decades ahead of her time, Auerbach made it company policy to hire African-Americans for jobs that provided opportunities for advancement and were not just menial or dead-end. Genuinely concerned about her 3,500 employees, she often commented, "Our entire approach has been a community one."

Always an innovative manager and marketer, Auerbach increased the sales volume of G. Fox & Co. tenfold during her 27 years as head, to $60 million in 1965, the year of her retirement. To accomplish such impressive growth, she initiated a statewide toll-free telephone service, a free-delivery service, and fully automated billing. Customer satisfaction was paramount in store design, and certain appliances were only sold at sales counters where repairers were on hand to provide service. These and other innovations kept customers satisfied and loyal, so that by 1959 an $8 million addition was built to increase floor space. By this year, G. Fox & Co. was the largest privately owned department store in the United States and could boast of the largest business volume of any enterprise between New York and Boston. In 1965, Beatrice Fox Auerbach retired as the firm's president, at the same time overseeing a deal that exchanged her family's privately held G. Fox & Co. stock for $40 million worth of publicly held stock in the May Company chain of department stores. She had been for many years the only female president of a major department store in the United States.

An active community leader throughout her business career, Auerbach expanded this role in her active retirement years, remarking: "One thing you can be certain of is that I won't be spending it on yachts and horses, but for the benefit of people." As early as 1941, she had established the Beatrice Fox Auerbach Foundation to fund various educational and civic projects. She also provided funds for a program in retailing and related subjects at the Connecticut College for Women in order to provide professional education for women. An important beneficiary of her foundation work was the Service Bureau for Women's Organizations, founded in 1945 to train women's groups in community-organization strategies.

Auerbach served as a director of the May Company until her death. Her two sons-in-law served as president and board chair of the main Hartford store, still called G. Fox & Co. though it was now a subsidiary of the May Company. With superb business acumen, Auerbach upgraded the appeal of G. Fox & Co. from a middle-class to an upper-middle-class consumer, a feat few retail executives of the period accomplished. She died on November 29, 1968, mourned by her family, generations of employees and customers, and the citizenry of Hartford, Connecticut.

SOURCES:

Ingham, John N., and Lynne B. Feldman. *Contemporary American Business Leaders: A Biographical Dictionary.* NY: Greenwood Press, 1990.

Neu, Irene D. "The Jewish Businesswoman in America," *American Jewish Historical Quarterly.* Vol. 66, no. 1, September 1976, pp. 137–154.

John Haag, Associate Professor of History, University of Georgia, Athens, Georgia

Auerbach, Charlotte (1899–1994)

German-born Scottish geneticist whose studies on the effects of radiation on mutation of genes are universally recognized. Name variations: Lotte Auerbach. Born on March 17, 1899, in Krefeld, Germany; died on March 17, 1994, in Scotland; achieved doctorate in genetics from the University of Edinburgh in 1935; never married; children: adopted a German girl and her baby boy.

Left Nazi Germany to escape persecution (1933); completed doctorate in genetics from University of Edinburgh (1935); became a laboratory technician despite her qualifications, slowly working her way up the career ladder; appointed lecturer (1947) and reader (1958); researched the mutagenic action of chemicals, which resulted in many publications, including several books for general audiences, like Genetics in the Atomic Age *(1956) and* The Science of Genetics *(1962); awarded the D.Sc. from Edinburgh (1947); elected to a Royal Society of Edinburgh fellowship (1949); became a fellow of the Royal Society of London (1957); a foreign associate member of the Royal Danish Academy of Science (1968); foreign associate member of the United States National Academy of Sciences (1970); received honorary degrees from Leiden, Dublin, and Cambridge Universities; received the Darwin Medal of London's Royal Society (1976).*

Charlotte Auerbach was born into an affluent and respected Jewish academic family on March 17, 1899, in Krefeld, Germany. Her father was a physical chemist and her grandfather a distinguished anatomist who had discovered "Auerbach's plexus" in the human intestine. Auerbach studied physics, chemistry and biology at the Universities of Berlin, Würzburg and Freiburg. A brilliant student, she was also opinionated, and a disagreement with her doctoral advisor at the University of Berlin resulted in her dropping out of the program without having been granted her degree. A number of seemingly condemning factors—including the fact that her family no longer had money and that she was a Jewish woman—forced her to conclude that even with a Ph.D. she stood little chance of achieving academic success. So she took a job as a secondary-school teacher in Berlin, continuing to read avidly in the sciences, particularly in the field of genetics and biology.

When the Nazis seized power in 1933, she immigrated to Scotland. With the help of friends, she survived on extremely meager resources, taking advantage of her newfound freedom to finally earn a Ph.D. In 1935, she was awarded a doc-

toral degree in genetics from the University of Edinburgh. Lotte, as she was known to her close friends, continued to live in Edinburgh with her mother, who had also been able to flee Nazi Germany. Despite her obvious intellectual gifts, Auerbach was only able to find a low-paying, vaguely defined job at the University of Edinburgh's Institute of Animal Genetics that included such chores as washing of laboratory glassware. She became a British citizen in 1939.

Throughout the war years, Auerbach kept working at her menial job, but the course of her career had been set a few years earlier when she met the American Nobel Prize-winning geneticist Hermann J. Muller in Edinburgh. Muller, who had discovered the mutational genetic impact of ionizing radiation, advised her to study the nature and causes of these complex mutational changes. He became her lifelong mentor, persuading Auerbach to thoroughly investigate the mutagenic action of chemicals. In a fruitful collaborative partnership with the pharmacologist J.M. Robson, Auerbach was able to demonstrate in unambiguous terms the highly mutagenic nature of mustard gas. This research, deemed sensitive in wartime by British authorities, did not appear in print until 1946. Although she was no longer young after the war, much of Auerbach's most important research was accomplished during this period. Painstaking and innovative, she compared the mutagenic effects of alkylating agents and ionizing radiation in the fruitfly. It was not until 1947 that she finally received an academic appointment as a lecturer. She was 58 when she became a reader and 67 when she received a chaired professorship as an internationally recognized researcher. As the importance of her work became more widely known, her international stature grew.

Known as an impassioned communicator to generations of Edinburgh science students, evidently Auerbach was more proficient at lecturing than carrying out demonstrations. One group of her students watched mice—brought in to demonstrate the genetics of mouse coat colors—get the better of her and escape. Convinced that students needed to be inspired at an early stage in their learning experience, she wrote a series of popular accounts in the 1950s, which include *Genetics in the Atomic Age* (first published in 1956, revised edition 1965) and *The Science of Genetics* (first published in 1962, revised edition 1969). Advancing years did little to stifle her enthusiasm or the quality of her work, and she continued throughout the 1960s at the MRC Mutagenesis Research Unit in Edinburgh. With a dedicated staff and enthusiastic students, Auerbach and her team unraveled the myriad mysteries found in the process of cellular mutation.

She received many honors and awards. In 1947, Auerbach was awarded the D.Sc. from Edinburgh and elected to a Royal Society of Edinburgh fellowship in 1949. She became a fellow of the Royal Society of London in 1957, a foreign associate member of the Royal Danish Academy of Science in 1968, and a foreign associate member of the United States Academy of Science in 1970. She received honorary degrees from Leiden, Dublin and Cambridge Universities. In 1976, she was given the Darwin Medal of London's Royal Society.

Auerbach loved Scotland and some of her happiest times were spent walking with friends in the West Highlands, admiring the scenery. She never married, but she acquired an adopted family just before the death of her mother in 1955 when she befriended a German girl and her baby boy, assisting in the child's upbringing. The boy eventually married and had children of whom Lotte was immensely proud. To these children, she was simply "Gran." Charlotte Auerbach died on March 17, 1994.

SOURCES:
"Professor Charlotte Auerbach," in *The Times* [London]. April 9, 1994, p. 21.
The Year Book of the Royal Society of London 1977. London: The Royal Society, 1977.

John Haag, Associate Professor of History, University of Georgia, Athens, Georgia

Augspurg, Anita (1857–1943).

See joint entry under Heymann, Lida.

Augusta, Mlle (1806–1901)

French dancer. Name variations: Comtesse de Saint-James. Born Caroline Augusta Josephine Thérèsa Fuchs in 1806; died in 1901.

Mlle Augusta's greatest success was her U.S. debut in *Les Naïades* in 1836. Ten years later, in February 1846, she was the first to dance *Giselle* in New York, a month after **Mary Anne Lee** had danced the ballet in Boston. Augusta was also known for her versions of *La Sylphide* and *La Muette de Portici.*

Augusta Guelph (1737–1813)

Duchess of Brunswick-Wolfenbuttel. Name variations: Princess royal. Born on July 31, 1737, at St. James's Palace, London, England; died on March 23, 1813, in London; buried at St. George's Chapel, Windsor; daughter of Frederick Guelph, prince of Wales, and **Augusta of Saxe-Gotha (1719–1772)*; sister of George III, king of England; married Charles Bevern, duke of Brunswick-Wolfenbuttel, on January 17, 1764; children: seven, including **Augusta of Brunswick-Wolfenbuttel* (1764–1788, who married Frederick I, king of Wurttemberg); **Caroline of Brunswick* (1768–1821, who married George IV, king of England); Amelia Caroline Dorothea (1772–1773).

Augusta Guelph (1768–1840)

English princess. Name variations: Princess Augusta, Augusta Sophia. Born August Sophia on November 8, 1768, at Buckingham House, London, England; died on September 22, 1840, in London; buried at St. George's Chapel, Windsor; daughter of George III, king of England, and *Charlotte of Mecklenburg-Strelitz.

Augusta Guelph (1822–1916)

Duchess of Mecklenburg-Strelitz. Born Augusta Caroline Charlotte Elizabeth Mary Sophia Louise Guelph on July 19, 1822; died on December 4, 1916, in Neustrelitz, Mecklenburg, Germany; daughter of Adolphus Guelph, 1st duke of Cambridge, and *Augusta of Hesse-Cassel (daughter of Landgrave Frederick III); married Frederick, grand duke of Mecklenburg-Strelitz, on June 28, 1843; children: two, including Adolphus Frederick V, grand duke of Mecklenburg-Strelitz.

Augusta Maria of Baden-Baden (1704–1726)

Duchess of Orleans. Name variations: Augusta-Marie of Baden; Augusta Maria von Baden-Baden. Born on November 10, 1704; died on August 8, 1726, shortly after giving birth to a daughter; daughter of Louis William (b. 1655), margrave of Baden-Baden; married Philippe Louis also known as Louis Philip or Philippe (1703–1752), 3rd duke of Orleans (r. 1723–1752), on July 13, 1724; children: Louis-Philippe (1725–1785), 4th duke of Orleans (1752–1785); Louise Magdalen (1726–1726, lived seven days).

Augusta Maria of Holstein-Gottorp (1649–1728)

Margravine of Baden-Durlach. Name variations: Augusta Marie. Born in 1649; died in 1728; daughter of *Marie Elizabeth of Saxony (1610–1684) and Freder-

ick III, duke of Holstein-Gottorp; married Frederick VII, margrave of Baden-Durlach, on May 15, 1670; children: *Albertina of Baden-Durlach (1682–1755); Charles III William, margrave of Baden-Durlach (b. 1679).

Augusta of Bavaria (1788–1851).

See Amalie Auguste.

Augusta of Brunswick-Wolfenbuttel (1764–1788)

Queen of Wurttemberg. Name variations: Augusta Caroline of Brunswick. Born Augusta Caroline Fredericka Louise Bevern on December 3, 1764; died age 24 on September 27, 1788; daughter of *Augusta Guelph (1737–1813) and Charles II Bevern, duke of Brunswick-Wolfenbuttel; married Frederick II (1754–1816), duke of Wurttemberg (r. 1797–1802), elector of Wurttemberg (r. 1802–1806), also known as Frederick I, king of Wurttemberg (r. 1806–1816), on October 11, 1780; children: William I, king of Wurttemberg (r. 1816–1864); *Catherine of Wurttemberg (1783–1835); Sophia Dorothea (1783–1784); Paul Charles Frederick (1785–1852), duke of Wurttemberg (b. 1785).

Augusta of Hesse-Cassel (1797–1889)

Duchess of Cambridge. Born on July 25, 1797, at Cassell, Germany; died on April 6, 1889, at St. James's Palace, London, England; buried at St. George's Chapel, Windsor; daughter of Frederick III, landgrave of Hesse-Cassel, and *Caroline of Nassau-Usingen (1762–1823); married Adolphus Guelph, 1st duke of Cambridge, on May 7, 1818; children: George Guelph, 2nd duke of Cambridge; *Augusta Guelph (1822–1916); *Mary Adelaide (1833–1897).

Augusta of Reuss-Ebersdorf (1757–1831)

German duchess. Born on January 9, 1757; died on November 16, 1831; daughter of Henry XXIV, count of Reuss-Ebersdorf, and Caroline Ernestine, countess Erbach-Schonberg (b. 1727); grandmother of Queen *Victoria; married Francis Frederick (1750–1806), duke of Saxe-Coburg-Saalfeld; children: Sophie (b. 1778); *Antoinette Saxe-Coburg (1779–1824); *Anna Juliana of Saxe-Coburg-Saalfeld (1781–1860); Ernest I, duke of Saxe-Coburg and Gotha (b. 1784); Ferdinand Saxe-Coburg (b. 1785); *Victoria of Coburg (1786–1861, mother of Queen Victoria); Marianne (b. 1788); Leopold I, king of Belgium (b. 1790); Maximilian (b. 1792).

Augusta of Saxe-Gotha (1719–1772).

See Caroline Matilda for sidebar.

Augusta of Saxe-Weimar (1811–1890)

Empress of Germany and queen of Prussia. Name variations: Marie Louise Augusta of Saxe-Weimar. Born Marie Luise Katharina Augusta, princess of Grand Duchy of Weimar, on September 30, 1811, in Saxe-Weimar, Germany; died in Berlin on January 7, 1890; second daughter of Karl Friedrich also known as Charles Frederick, grand duke of Saxe-Weimar, and *Marie Pavlovna (1786–1859); educated at home; married William I (1797–1888), the future Kaiser Wilhelm I, emperor of Germany (r. 1871–1888), on June 11, 1829; children: Frederick Wilhelm III also known as Frederick III (b. 1831), king of Prussia and emperor of Germany (r. 1888); Louise of Baden (1838–1923).

Because her father Charles Frederick, grand duke of Saxe-Weimar, insisted on a well-educated and cultured court, Princess Augusta of Saxe-Weimar was raised as a scholar. Her royal blood would lead to her match, in 1829, with Prince Wilhelm of Prussia (the future kaiser Wilhelm I). The prince had long loved his cousin, **Elisa Radziwill**, but it was considered inappropriate for the two to marry since Elisa was not of royal lineage. Still deeply in love with Elisa, Wilhelm had nevertheless renounced her and continued to live as a bachelor until he was 32 years old.

Princess Augusta was 18 when she married Wilhelm, and the two could not have been more different. She was a learned liberal, he a relatively uneducated conservative, 16 years her senior. From the first, they were ill-matched, as Augusta freely announced her opinions, often in direct contrast with her husband. A beautiful but vain woman, Augusta did not accept her aging gracefully. She indulged in glittery, expensive garments and jewelry, and used heavy makeup. She was also known for her impassioned displays, her passionate friendships, her explosions of anger, and her fiercely held opinions. Wilhelm and Augusta fought frequently and led separate lives, sequestered on different floors in their home in Berlin, Germany.

In 1858, when Wilhelm was named king of Prussia, succeeding his brother, Augusta was 47 years old. During the regency, the couple had done away with any pretense of a unified marriage. Augusta had often spent time away from Berlin, either with her brother in Weimar or with her daughter *Louise of Baden. Augusta's opinions had been unwelcome in Berlin, and she turned her attentions from politics to Catholicism. (Though she never converted, she no longer practiced Lutheranism, the predominant religion of the regency.) Augusta returned to Berlin for the crowning, and fully immersed herself in the pomp and ceremony she so enjoyed. In 1871, as Wilhelm was named emperor of Germany, she stood by his side, and again in 1879 she thrilled at an elaborate golden anniversary party, despite the obvious irony. By this time, both Wilhelm and Augusta were in declining health. Under her layers of make-up and finery, Augusta was pale and aging. Confined to a wheelchair in her later years, she had become an object of quiet ridicule in Germany, no longer beautiful enough for the public to endure the spectacle she tended to create.

In March of 1888, 91-year-old Wilhelm developed a cold. Days later, in the hours before his death on March 9, he asked for the picture of Elisa Radziwill, which he had kept on his desk. Wilhelm and Augusta's son, Wilhelm II, was named king of Prussia and emperor of Germany.

Augusta caught the flu at the beginning of 1890, and her weakened body succumbed on January 7. Having never loved her husband nor been loved by him, she had thrown herself fully into the only comfort her titles offered—beribboned and bejeweled celebrity. Augusta lay in state for three days before she was buried on January 11, 1890.

SOURCES:

Aronson, Theo. *The Kaisers.* Indianapolis: Bobbs-Merrill, 1971.

Crista Martin,
Boston, Massachusetts

Augusta of Schleswig-Holstein
(1858–1921)

Empress of Germany. Name variations: Augusta Victoria; (Ger.) Auguste Viktoria. Born Augusta Victoria Fredericka Louise Feodore Jenny on October 22, 1858, in Dolzig, Germany; died on April 11, 1921, at Doorn, Netherlands; eldest daughter of Frederick, duke of Schleswig-Holstein-Sonderburg-Augustenberg, and *Adelaide of Hohenlohe-Langenburg (1835–1900); married William II (1859–1941), also known as Wilhelm II, kaiser of Germany (r.

1888–1918), on February 27, 1881; children: Frederick William (1885–1951, crown prince of Prussia, who married *Cecilia of Mecklenburg-Schwerin); Eitel-Frederick (1883–1942, who married *Sophie Charlotte of Oldenburg); Augustus William (1887–1949, who married *Alexandra Victoria of Schleswig-Holstein); Adalbert (who married *Adelaide of Saxe-Meiningen); Oscar; Joachim (who married *Marie of Anhalt); *Victoria Louise (1892–1980, who married Ernest Augustus of Cumberland). Following the death of Augusta in 1921, Wilhelm II married *Hermine of Reuss on November 5, 1922.

Augusta of Tuscany (1825–1864)

Austrian archduchess. Name variations: Auguste Ferdinand; Augusta of Austria. Born on January 4, 1825, in Florence, Italy; died on April 26, 1864, in Munich; daughter of *Maria Anna of Saxony (1799–1832) and Leopold II, grand duke of Saxony; married Luitpold (1821–1912), regent of Bavaria from 1886 to 1912; children: Ludwig III, king of Bavaria (r. 1913–1918); Therese (1850–1925); Leopold (1846–1930); Arnulf (1852–1907).

Augusta of Wurttemberg
(1826–1898)

Princess of Saxe-Weimar. Born Augusta Wilhelmina Henrietta on October 4, 1826; died on December 3, 1898; daughter of *Pauline of Wurttemberg (1800–1873) and William I (1781–1864), king of Wurttemberg (r. 1816–1864); married Hermann Henry, prince of Saxe-Weimar, on June 17, 1851; children: *Pauline of Saxe-Weimar (1852–1904); William Charles (b. 1853); Bernard William (b. 1855), count of Crayenberg; Alexander William (b. 1857); Ernest Charles (b. 1859); Olga Marie (1869–1924, who married Leopold Wolfgang, prince of Ysemburg-Birste).

Augusta Victoria (1890–1966)

Countess Douglas. Name variations: Auguste Victoria Hohenzollern. Born on August 19, 1890, in Potsdam, Germany; died on August 29, 1966, in Münchhof, Kr. Stockach, Baden, Germany; daughter of William (1864–1927), prince of Hohenzollern, and *Marie Therese of Bourbon; married Manuel II (1889–1932), king of Portugal (r. 1908–1910, deposed in 1910), on September 4, 1913; married Carl Robert, count Douglas, on April 23, 1939; childen: (second marriage) possibly **Dagmar Rosita Douglas** who married John George Spencer-Churchill, 11th duke of Marlborough.

Augustat, Elise (1889–1940)

German Reichstag deputy. Born Elise Queck on July 29, 1889, in Waldkeim, Germany; died on March 13, 1940, as a result of injuries sustained while imprisoned at Ravensbrück.

Born on July 29, 1889, into a poor family in the small East Prussian town of Waldkeim, Elise Augustat was a housewife and worker who first was elected to the German Reichstag in September 1930 on the Communist ticket. Augustat represented Hamburg, a stronghold of militant Communism and a scene of an abortive uprising in 1923. Like all German parliamentary delegates of the period, she did not question the directives of her party leadership, voting the strict party line on each issue. Well known to the local Nazis, Augustat was arrested on charges of high treason soon after the Hitler regime came to power in early 1933. She was eventually released but kept under surveillance during the following years, living in the village of Lägerdorf in Germany's northernmost province of Schleswig-Holstein.

When World War II began in September 1939, Augustat was again arrested. This time, she was not confined in a Hamburg prison but sent to the notorious women's concentration camp Ravensbrück. Here, the body of the 50-year-old woman, already weakened by her earlier ordeals, could not withstand the privations and indignities that were routine at every German concentration camp. Mortally ill in December 1939, she was granted a "leave of absence" from Ravensbrück. She returned to Lägerdorf, where she died on March 13, 1940.

SOURCES:

Feig, Konnilyn G. *Hitler's Death Camps: The Sanity of Madness.* NY: Holmes & Meier, 1981.

Schumacher, Martin, ed. *M.d.R. Die Reichstagsabgeordneten der Weimarer Republik in der Zeit des Nationalsozialismus.* Düsseldorf: Droste Verlag, 1991.

John Haag, Associate Professor of History, University of Georgia, Athens, Georgia

Augustesen, Susanne (1956—)

Danish soccer player. Born in Denmark in 1956.

In 1971, Denmark's women footballers defeated Mexico 3–0 to win the world championship for the second successive year. To the delight of the Danes, all three goals were scored by Susanne Augustesen, a 15-year-old schoolgirl. Thirty-one-year-old **Helene Hansen**, the oldest member of the team, also dominated the game.

Aulnoy, Marie Catherine, Countess d' (c. 1650–1705)

*Popular French author of the 17th century. Name variations: Aunoy or Anois; wrote under pseudonyms of Dunnois and Madame D. Born Marie Catherine Jumel de Barneville about 1650 at Barneville near Bourgachard (Eure); died in Paris, France, on January 14, 1705; her mother became the marquise de Gudaigne at the time of her second marriage; niece of **Marie Bruneau des Loges** (friend of Malherbe and Balzac, called the "tenth Muse"); married François de la Motte (a gentleman in the service of César, duc de Vendôme, who became Baron d'Aulnoy in 1654), on March 8, 1666; children: five, not all with her husband.*

Selected writings: Histoire d'Hypolite comte du Duglas (Hippolyte, Count of Douglas, *1690); Mémoires de la cour d'Espagne (*Memoirs of the Court of Spain, *1690); Relation du voyage en Espagne (*Account of Travels in Spain, *1691); Histoire de Jean de Bourbon (1692); Mémoires sur la cour de France (1692); Nouvelles espagnolles (*Spanish Stories, *1692); Mémoires de la cour d'Angleterre (1695); Contes nouvelles ou les Fées à la mode (fairy tales, 3 vols., 1698); Le Comte de Warwick (*The Earl of Warwick, *1703).*

In accounts of the life of Marie Catherine d'Aulnoy, one of the most popular authors of the 17th century, it is often difficult to separate fact from fiction. The same can be said of her historical novels, noted for their "imaginative interpretation of historical fact."

Born into minor nobility, she married Baron d'Aulnoy in 1666, and had several children. Sometime after the birth of her fourth child in 1669, Aulnoy became embroiled in a plot with her mother—who by a second marriage had become marquise de Gudaigne—to have her husband Baron d'Aulnoy committed for high treason. When the conspiracy was exposed, Aulnoy and her mother retreated to England, then on to Spain, but they were eventually allowed to return to France as reward for secret services rendered to the government.

Amid such events, Aulnoy still had time for writing, and she was quite prolific. She was especially noted for her *Contes nouvelles ou fées à la mode,* 24 fairy tales from the original stories found in the *Pentamerone* (1637) by Giovanni Battista Basile. The collection included *L'Oiseau blue* (The Blue Bird), *La Chatte Blanche* (The White Cat), and, her best known, *La Belle aux cheveux d'or* (Goldilocks),

Many of Aulnoy's 27 volumes of novels, memoirs and travel books contain autobiographical accounts of her jaunts in Europe while she was, so to speak, on the lam. She won instant success with her first novel in 1690, *Histoire d'Hypolite comte du Duglas* (*Hippolyte, Count of Douglas*), an adventure-romance set in England. Her *Mémoires de la cour d'Espagne* (*Memoires of the Court of Spain*), unlike other of her memoires that might be better classified as romantic novels, was based on authentic documents. By far her best known travel book was *Relation du voyage en Espagne* (*Accounts of Travels in Spain*), written in letter form, spanning the months between February 20, 1679, and September 28, 1680.

Aulnoy wrote two religious works and a collection of Spanish adventure stories. Her final effort, in 1703, *Le Comte de Warwick* (*The Earl of Warwick*), was the only one of her books in which her name in full appeared on the title page. Aulnoy was honored in 1698 with membership to the female Academy of the Ricovrati in Padua, where she assumed the title of Clio, Muse of History. She died in Paris in 1705.

Barbara Morgan,
Melrose, Massachusetts

Aung San Suu Kyi (1945—)

Burmese human-rights activist, scholar, writer, and recipient of the Nobel Peace Prize. Born Suu Kyi in Rangoon, the capital of Burma (formally Yangon and Myanmar, respectively, since 1989), on June 19, 1945; the youngest of three children of Aung San (leader of the Burmese nationalist movement in the 1940s, which culminated in 1948 in the nation's attaining its independence from 50 years of British rule and three years of Japanese occupation) and Khin Kyi (Burma's ambassador to India and the first woman to head a Burmese diplomatic mission); attended Lady Sri Ram College and Delhi University; B.A. degree from St. Hugh's College at Oxford University (1967); attended University of Kyoto in Japan (1985); attended School of Oriental and African Studies at London University (1987); married Michael Aris (a scholar of Tibetan civilization), in 1972; children: two sons, Alexander and Kim.

Her name, Aung San Suu Kyi, means "A Bright Collection of Strange Victories," ironic in light of the circumstances surrounding her receipt of the 1991 Nobel Peace Prize in recognition of her nonviolent quest for democracy in her ravaged nation. The Nobel Committee called her struggle, "one of the most extraordinary examples of civil courage in Asia in recent decades." Suu Kyi, however, did not attend the awards ceremony in Oslo. She remained under house arrest at her family home in Rangoon—placed there in July 1989 for violating the government ban on political activity. Freedom for the 46-year-old wife, mother, and scholar would not come for another four years.

Aung San Suu Kyi was born Suu Kyi in 1945, the youngest daughter of **Aung San**—respectfully called *Bogyoke* (a term expressing admiration for his leadership role in the Burmese nationalist movement, which, in 1948, won the country's independence from British rule). Unfortunately, Suu Kyi never got to know her father; he was assassinated by a political rival in July 1947, less than six months before Burma became formally independent. Without a leader of stature to succeed Aung San, in 1962 the country fell victim to a military coup led by General Ne Win, described by detractors as "inept and xenophobic."

Suu Kyi came late to the role of political activist and liberator of her country. Indeed, the first 30 years of her life were spent in relatively comfortable, apolitical environments outside her homeland. She left the country at 15 when her mother became Burma's ambassador to India. In New Delhi, she enjoyed an fashionable home and a privileged education, including piano and horseback-riding lessons. She graduated from Oxford University in 1967. After working in England as a teacher and in New York City at the United Nations, she married Michael Aris, a scholar of Tibetan civilization she had met at Oxford. The couple had two sons, Alexander and Kim.

As a housewife and mother, Suu Kyi continued her scholarly pursuits but became increasingly consumed with learning more about the father she never knew. She undertook research for a biographical essay about him, and even added his name to her own, becoming Aung San Suu Kyi. Reading about her father rekindled her own patriotism, though she had always entertained the idea of returning to Burma to serve her people. Before her marriage to Aris, she had elicited his promise that she be allowed to return to her country if she felt the need.

In March 1988, Aung San Suu Kyi returned to Rangoon to care for her dying mother. Just beyond the family estate on Inya Lake, the capital was in turmoil, with student uprisings against the government and armed soldiers in the street. As the student death toll increased, it ignited a rage in the Burmese people, who had for decades watched their once resource-rich land deteriorate into one of the least productive areas in the world. When Ne Win appointed his crony General Sein Lwin as leader of the ruling Burma Socialist Program Party, the population erupted in protest, taking to the streets where they were met with indiscriminate army gunfire. As Suu Kyi listened to reports of the deaths of as many as 3,000 citizens, she could no longer remain a bystander. "As my father's daughter, I felt I had a duty to get involved," she said.

At her first major public appearance in front of a crowd of 500,000, she spoke of basic human rights, including freedom to choose one's government. She attempted to reconcile civil and military authorities by urging the leaders to resume their proper role as protectors of the people. Many observers were struck by her resemblance to her father, in both appearance and mannerisms. As her following grew, civil unrest continued, even after Sein Lwin was replaced with the more conciliatory Maung Maung, who took immediate steps to remove the soldiers from the streets. The government reasserted control over the country with the establishment of the State Law & Order Restorational Council as the supreme political authority in the land. It

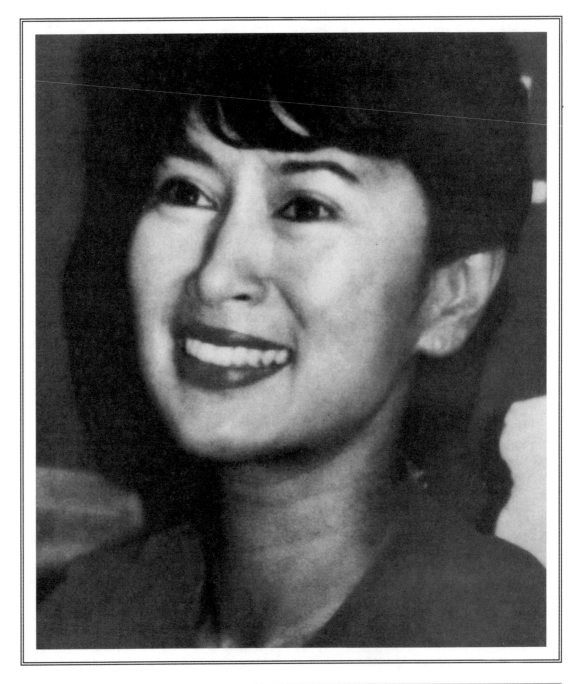

Aung San
Suu Kyi

banned political demonstrations of over four persons and reaffirmed the right to arrest and sentence citizens without trial.

On September 24, 1988, Aung San Suu Kyi founded the National League of Democracy and became its secretary-general. In defiance of the ban on political gatherings, she continued her efforts for "Burma's second struggle for independence," touring towns and villages to elicit support. By the end of 1988, the government began arresting her supporters and undertook a hate campaign against her, accusing her of being a Communist and of engaging in "abnormal sexual practices." On April 5, 1989, at a political gathering, she found herself facing soldiers with guns drawn, who had been sent to kill her. Asking her supporters to move aside, she calmly walked toward the pointed guns. Spared only at the last minute by a countercommand not to shoot, she made light of her courage: "It seemed so much simpler to provide them with a single target than to bring everyone else in."

In June 1989, Suu Kyi publicly speculated that Ne Win had remained in control of the government even after his "retirement" in 1988; she also exhorted members of the army to reexamine their loyalties. In July, she called the government "fascist" in its declaration of martial law. She further commented, "To achieve democracy, the struggle against fascism must be continued with courage." A month later—11 months after she had joined the prodemocracy movement—she disappeared.

In Suu Kyi's early days under house arrest, she was allowed contact with her husband and sons, but family visits and written correspondence were later denied. Although her party won an overwhelming victory in May 1990, the military refused to release her or transfer power as they had promised. Even worldwide condemnation of Suu Kyi's detention did not move the government powers. In addition to the Nobel Peace Prize, in 1990 Suu Kyi was awarded the Thorolf Rafto Memorial Prize for Human Rights and the Sakharov Prize for Freedom of Thought. In June 1990, a birthday card for her was signed by more than 1,000 worldwide. As her imprisonment wore on, the young people of her country began wearing miniature pins bearing her photograph. In July 1995, Suu Kyi was finally freed from her six-year detention; her battle was far from over.

SOURCES:

Graham, Judith, ed. *Current Biography 1992.* NY: H.W. Wilson, 1992.

Nelan, Bruce W. "Heroine in Chains," in *Time.* October 28, 1991, p. 73.

"The Wages of Courage," in *People.* November 28, 1991, p. 129.

Win, Aye Aye. "Burmese dissident freed by military," in *The* [New London] *Day.* July 11, 1995.

SUGGESTED READING:

Aung San Suu Kyi. *Freedom From Fear & Other Writings.* NY: Viking Penguin, 1991.

———, with Alan Clements. *The Voice of Hope.* Seven Stories Press, 1997.

Barbara Morgan,
Melrose, Massachusetts

Aunoy, Marie (c. 1650–1705).

See Aulnoy, Marie Catherine, Countess d.

Aura Pokou (c. 1700–c. 1760).

See Pokou.

Aurelia (c. 120 BCE–54 BCE)

Roman noblewoman and mother of Julius Caesar.
Born around 120 BCE; died in 54 BCE in Rome; daughter of Aurelius Cotta; married Gaius Julius Caesar Maior (a judge); children: Roman emperor (Gaius) Julius Caesar Minor (c. 100–44 BCE); *Julia Minor (c. 100 BCE–51 BCE); Julia Maior.

Little is known of Julius Caesar's mother, outside of her dedication to the proper upbringing of her son who would become general and ruler of the Roman Empire. Of patrician lineage, she married Gaius Julius Caesar, a judge, and gave birth to two daughters and Julius Caesar (c. 100–44 BCE). Though the circumstances of Caesar's birth are unconfirmed and often debated, Aurelia is said to have had difficulty; he was delivered through a surgical opening in her stomach—thus, the medical term *caesarian section*.

Aurelia was known to have had some education, because she spoke a learned Latin. As was the custom of the time, she oversaw the education of her son until he was seven-years-old, after which young Caesar was turned over to his father and uncles. Aurelia remained in charge of her daughters, one of whom, *Julia Minor (c. 100–51 BCE), would be the grandmother of Rome's first emperor, Augustus. Aurelia died in 54 BCE, ten years before her son's assassination at the hands of his political enemies.

SOURCES:

Fry, P.S. *Great Caesar.* London: Collins, 1974.

Kahn, Arthur D. *The Education of Julius Caesar.* NY: Schocken Books, 1986.

Thaddeus, Victor. *Julius Caesar and the Grandeur That Was Rome.* NY: Brentano, 1927.

Crista Martin,
Boston, Massachusetts

Aurelia Fadilla (d. before 138).

See Faustina II for sidebar.

Auriol, Jacqueline (1917—)

French aviator. Born Jacqueline Douet on November 5, 1917, at Challans, France; daughter of Pierre Douet (a shipbuilder and importer of Scandinavian wood); attended school in Nantes; studied art at L'École du Louvre, Paris; married Paul Auriol (son of Vincent Auriol, French diplomat and first president of the Fourth Republic [1947–1954]), in 1938; children: two sons, Jean-Claude and Jean-Paul.

The distinguished French aviator Jacqueline Auriol won the title of "fastest woman in the world" in 1951, then broke her own speed record on December 21, 1952, flying a Mistral jet fighter an average speed of 534.375 miles an hour over a measured 62.1 mile course. Though Auriol's accomplishments were remarkable by any standards, they were made even more so by the fact that she had only been flying for eight

Jacqueline Auriol

years and, in 1949, had been severely injured when a seaplane in which she was a passenger crashed into the Seine. Suffering a fractured skull and broken bones in her face, Auriol was sustained through her long and torturous recovery by her determination to fly again. While undergoing the over 20 operations necessary to rebuild her face, she obtained military and commercial pilot licenses and also learned to fly a helicopter. Lawrence Bell, president of the Bell Aircraft Corporation in Buffalo, New York, where Auriol took helicopter lessons in 1951, called her "the most extraordinary woman in the world. She has met fear head-on and conquered it. She has a complete passion for flying."

The daughter of a wealthy shipbuilder, Auriol was raised and educated in Nantes, France, then studied art in Paris. Through her interest in skiing, she met and fell in love with Paul Auriol, whose father was Vincent Auriol, a prominent leader of the French Socialist Party who had served several years in the government. Since both sets of parents disapproved of the match, Auriol was whisked off to Sweden on one of her father's cargo ships, while Paul toured Italy with his mother. In February 1938, two years after their first meeting, they were finally married in a small mountain chapel. During World War II, while Paul served in the French Resistance, Auriol remained in France, living under an assumed name with the first of the couple's two sons. After the war and Vincent Auriol's election as president of the Republic, Paul became his father's press secretary, and he and Auriol took up residence at the Palace Élysee in Paris. Emerging from her wartime retirement, Auriol became her father-in-law's social emissary. A beautiful, witty, and fashionable woman, she organized and attended a variety of balls, receptions, and charity events, and became a well-known figure in social circles.

Auriol became fascinated with flying through her acquaintance with French pilot Raymond Guillaume, whom she met at a dinner party. Accepting an invitation to fly with him, she came away from the experience a changed woman. "I discovered a world," she said, "where, no matter what your name, the only things that count are merit, skill and courage." Auriol attended flying school at Villacoublay and received her pilot's license in 1948, then soloed an additional ten hours to receive a second degree license. She went on to learn stunt flying from Guillaume, although he insisted that she obtain written permission from her father-in-law before he began instruction. In July 1949, she demonstrated her new skills in an air show outside Paris, where she was the only woman among 20 famous French flyers. Just three days later, she was injured in the seaplane accident.

After a year in French hospitals, where she endured 14 operations, Auriol was still severely disfigured. An examination was arranged by the noted American plastic surgeon Dr. John Converse, who agreed to perform further surgery but only at his own hospital in the United States. Auriol made the trip to New York's Manhattan Eye, Ear and Throat Hospital, where she underwent eight additional operations over a six-month period. While in the United States, she was introduced to Lawrence Bell, of Bell Aircraft, who arranged for her to take helicopter lessons at his plant. After 23 hours of instruction, combined with classwork, Auriol qualified for a helicopter pilot's license on January 23, 1951.

Returning to France with a new face, Auriol was further traumatized when old friends failed to recognized her. Moving away from the social whirl she had once enjoyed, she drove daily to Villacoublay to watch construction of the Havilland Vampire jet, a fighter plane in which she would attempt a new woman's flying record. Her first solo flight in this plane was an emotional one. "That day I experienced a sense of completeness," she later recalled, "an extraordinary sense of power, . . . a sense of being in complete possession of myself." On May 12, 1951, after three weeks of intense preparation for her speed test, Auriol took off from Istres and flew her Vampire jet 509.245 miles an hour in a 62.1 mile closed circuit flight between Istres and Avignon, officially breaking the women's speed record for the same distance set by *Jacqueline Cochran of the United States on December 10, 1947. For her achievement, Auriol was awarded the Cross of Chevalier of the French Legion of Honor, and the Harmon International Trophy for an "aviatrix," which was presented to her at the White House by President Harry Truman. Auriol's return to the United States included a visit to the Manhattan Eye, Ear and Throat Hospital to thank trustees and doctors for restoring her face.

In 1952, Auriol received a second Harmon Trophy for beating her own speed record and went on to become one of France's top test pilots, the only woman in her country engaged in that hazardous profession. Her work included tests in more than 50 types of planes, ranging from American Constellations to tiny sports planes. In August 1953, she flew faster than the speed of sound in the new French jet interceptor, the Mystère IV. She made headlines again in Sep-

tember 1971 as the Concorde's first pilot and subsequently flew tours in Latin America, Africa, and the Orient to help sell the plane. Her private life remained within a circle of family and a few close friends. In a 1952 interview for *Collier's* magazine, Auriol claimed that flying taught her the truth about what really mattered. "Now I know that only life and death are important. When I am in the air, close to both, things finally take on their proper perspective. Nonsense becomes nonsense. The big things stand out, become alive."

SOURCES:

Candee, Marjorie Dent, ed. *Current Biography 1953.* NY: H.W. Wilson, 1953.

Cowles, Fleur. *Friends & Memories.* NY: Reynal in association with William Morrow, 1978.

SUGGESTED READING:

Auriol, Jacqueline. *I Live To Fly.* Translated from the French by Pamela Swinglehurst. London: M. Joseph, 1970.

Barbara Morgan,
Melrose, Massachusetts

Aurora of San Donato (1873–1904)

Princess of Yugoslavia. Name variations. Aurora Demidoff. Born on November 15, 1873; died on June 28, 1904; daughter of Paul Demidoff, prince of San Donato; married Arsen or Arsene Karadjordjevic (b. 1859), prince of Yugoslavia, on May 1, 1892 (divorced 1896); children: Paul, prince and regent of Yugoslavia.

Aury, Dominique (1907–1998)

French editor and writer. Name variations: (pseudonym) Pauline Réage or Reage. Born at Rochefort-sur-Mer, France, in 1907; died on April 26, 1998, in France.

Dominique Aury

French editor Dominique Aury was not publicly unveiled as author of *The Story of O,* the sado-masochistic "classy porn classic," until 1994, when she was 86, even though the book was awarded the Deux-Magots, one of France's premiere literary awards in 1955. In one of the best-kept secrets in postwar publishing history, the pseudonym of this underground

bestseller went unclaimed for 40 years, until Aury was pinpointed in an article in *The New Yorker* by British journalist John De St. Jorre; he also discusses authorship in his book *The Good Ship Venus,* which deals with novels published by Paris' Olympia Press.

Aury admitted to St. Jorre that she had written *O* as a love letter to Jean Paulhan, a prominent French critic, when he intimated that she was incapable of writing an erotic book. St. Jorre identified *O*'s English translator, known as Sabine d'Estree, as Dick Seaver, a former copublisher of Grove Press, who brought out the book in the United States in 1965. "The French, they are a funny race," wrote Herb Lottman in *Publishers Weekly*. "Everybody has always 'known' that Aury wrote *O*. Even I knew it, for years. I'm sure that I even saw references to it in print, but never in an authorized form." A well-known translator, Dominique Aury worked for Gallimard in Paris, starting in 1950, and continued to do so well into her 80s.

SOURCES:
O'Brien, Maureen. *Publishers Weekly.* August 1, 1994, p. 13.

Aus der Ohe, Adele (1864–1937)

German pianist who played Tchaikovsky's First Piano Concerto at Carnegie Hall with the composer himself conducting. Born in Hannover, Germany, on December 11, 1864; died in Berlin on December 7, 1937; a pupil of Franz Liszt.

As a child, Adele Aus der Ohe studied with Theodor Kullak (1818–1882). Starting at age 12, Aus der Ohe studied for seven years with Franz Liszt, and, in 1886, made her American debut in New York, performing Liszt's First Piano Concerto. American audiences idolized her, and she made 17 annual tours of the United States. The Boston Symphony Orchestra was particularly partial to her talents, and she played with this group on 51 occasions between 1887 and 1906. One of the highlights of Aus der Ohe's career was her performance of the Tchaikovsky First Piano Concerto at the Carnegie Hall inaugural concerts in 1891, with the composer Peter Ilyitch Tchaikovsky conducting. Tchaikovsky loved her performance; Aus der Ohe, however, refused to accept any applause for herself. Two years later, in October 1893, she appeared again as soloist in the same concerto with the composer conducting in St. Petersburg, Russia, a few days before his sudden death. A crippling illness forced Aus der Ohe to abandon her brilliant career in midstream. The

German inflation of the early 1920s destroyed her life's savings, and in her final years she was only able to maintain a dignified level of life because of the generosity of an American foundation of music lovers.

SOURCES:
Yoffe, Elkhonon. *Tchaikovsky in America: The Composer's Visit in 1891.* NY: Oxford University Press, 1986.

John Haag, Associate Professor of History,
University of Georgia, Athens, Georgia

Ausländer, Rose (1901–1988)

Austro-Hungarian acclaimed as one of the foremost lyrical poets of postwar Germany. Born Rosalie Scherzer in 1901 in Czernowitz (now Chernovtsy), Ukraine; died in 1988; married Ignaz Ausländer (divorced three years later).

Selected works: Blindar Summer *(Blind Summer, 1965);* Inventar *(Inventory, 1972);* Doppelspiel *(Double Game, 1977);* Mutterland *(Motherland, 1978);* Ein Stück weiter *(A Little Further, 1979); as well as five other volumes of poetry.*

At the dawn of the 20th century, Rosalie Scherzer was born into a German-speaking Jewish family and raised in the Ukraine region. She left Europe in 1921 for the United States. There, she met and married Ignaz Ausländer, but the marriage was short-lived and Rose returned to her hometown of Czernowitz in 1931, as World War II loomed. Though she was never captured, Ausländer spent the war years hiding in the ghetto cellars of Czernowitz. With Germany's defeat, she returned to America but in 1947 her mother died. Ausländer had an emotional breakdown. As yet unpublished, she attempted to write in English but was unsuccessful and felt displaced. In 1964, she returned to Europe where she quietly worked in her native German. The following year, her first volume of poetry was published but received little notice. Not until the 1970s, when Ausländer was in her seventh decade, did her work receive critical acclaim. At the time of her death in 1988, Rose Ausländer was recognized as a preeminent poet of German literature detailing the war and postwar experience of the Jews.

Crista Martin,
Boston, Massachusetts

Aussem, Cilly (1909–1963)

Tennis star of the late 1920s and early 1930s, and only German to hold a Wimbledon title before 1985, who briefly represented hope of a better future for Germans during their severe economic crisis after World War I. Name variations: Cilly, Cäcilie. Born Cäcilie Aussem in

Cologne, Germany, on January 4, 1909; died in Portofino, Italy, in March 1963; married Murai della Corte Brae (an Italian count), in 1935; no children.

Winner of the German mixed-doubles championship in Berlin (1926); winner of the German national singles title (1927); rescued from her faltering game by American champion Bill Tilden and won the French mixed-doubles championships with Tilden and the women's singles title (1930); ranked the world's number two player and won the Wimbledon's women's singles title (1931); at the height of her career, ill health forced her retirement (1935).

During the first decades of the 20th century, Great Britain, Australia, and the United States dominated tennis, although some of the world's top-ranked women players hailed from other countries, including *Suzanne Lenglen from France, ❧▸ Lili de Alvarez from Spain, and *Molla Bjurstedt Mallory from Norway. Before Boris Becker and Steffi Graff established German dominance on the courts in the 1980s and 1990s, German champions were few and far between. Cilly Aussem, born in Cologne on January 4, 1909, was the first and only German international tennis champion of her time. Very well known for a brief period, she was then largely forgotten, partly because the politics of World War II helped obliterate her achievements and partly because her career was cut short by illness. But her accomplishments on the court do not merit such oblivion. In the words of American tennis great *Helen Hull Jacobs, Aussem should be remembered "for the almost unparalleled swiftness of her rise to tennis heights against the sort of odds that are seldom overcome."

When she began playing at age 14, many remarked on Cilly Aussem's good looks. Said Norah Gordon Cleather: "She had a lovely, heart-shaped little face with big amber eyes, and wore her russet-coloured hair parted in the middle, a fashion that enhanced her doll-like appearance." Aussem was pretty, petite, and determined, qualities that eventually transformed her from an above average tennis player to the best in the world. In 1926, Aussem was 17 when she won the mixed-doubles title in Berlin; the following year, she took the national singles title. Suzanne Lenglen, the French tennis champion, dominated the international courts at the time, and, because Germany had never been a tennis powerhouse, few took notice of a German champion in 1927, until she defeated Lili de Alvarez at the Le Tourquet tournaments in France.

Cilly Aussem's game was unimaginative but tenacious. She relied on quick footwork and clever placing to win. Scampering along the baseline, she would flick the ball into unexpected places, catching her opponent off guard. In the French championship semi-finals in 1928, she demonstrated this style when she defeated the English player Phoebe Holcroft-Watson. Driving the ball from corner to corner, Aussem wore Holcroft-Watson down and advanced to the finals. But the finals, played against the American champion *Helen Newington Wills, demonstrated the weakness of Aussem's game. She was a cautious, unaggressive player, with a weak service, often resulting in double faults. Aussem displayed little self-confidence on the courts, and her lack of power, combined with her tentative manner, caused many to assess her as a typical German tennis player of the time— good enough to play the best but never good enough to beat them.

In the summer of 1928, the international championships in the Netherlands proved to be a replay of that year's French championships. This international tournament was the most important before Wimbledon, and Aussem was determined to win it. She advanced to the finals where she faced Kea Bouman, the Dutch player who had won the French championship in 1927. Bouman started slowly, playing the first match conservatively. Few drives went beyond the service line and there was no aggressive net attack. During long rallies, Aussem and Bouman maneuvered for an opening, allowing safety and placement to take precedence over speed and depth. Aussem won the first set, and the second set should have been hers as well, but her unaggressive style proved her undoing and Bouman took the second set 6–4. Always persistent, Aussem fought for the third set, only to see victory slip

❧▸ Alvarez, Lili de

Spanish tennis player. Name variations: Lili d'Alvarez. Born in Rome, Italy.

Born in Rome of Spanish descent, Lili de Alvarez was one of Europe's most popular tennis stars. Fluent in five languages, she was a beautiful, sophisticated woman, who introduced the first culottes to be seen at Wimbledon. "She wore the Lenglen bandeau with a twist, slanted to one side, and brought trousers—voluminous, calf-length slacks—to the game," writes Billie Jean King in *We Have Come a Long Way*. "She was a bold, exciting player who hit the ball on the rise, and aimed for winners." Termed brilliant but erratic, Alvarez played in the finals at Wimbledon in 1926, 1927, 1928.

Cilly Aussem, 1988 West German postage stamp.

fail. He began to analyze the game and realized there was a "why" and a "how" to tennis. Tilden concluded that the mind was as important as the racquet arm in the game. Using this approach, he began to work on his weaknesses—a long, tough process as Tilden did not win a major title until he had reached the age of 27.

Watching Cilly Aussem's cautious, tentative style, Tilden was reminded of himself, and he believed his coaching could transform the German player. In 1930, she could scarcely believe her good fortune when one of the world's greatest proposed to coach her. Tilden began by building Aussem's confidence, teaching her to enjoy the game again. After a few weeks of training, she played *Elizabeth Ryan, who defeated her. Depressed, Aussem told Tilden she had disgraced Germany. Tilden quickly set her straight, declaring that no one cared whether she won or lost a tournament except herself and her mother. Few Germans were even that aware of her playing schedule, and the few who were undoubtedly paid no attention whatsoever to her wins and losses. Buoyed by this pep talk, Aussem went back to intensive training.

Tilden emphasized footwork, timing, and stroke production during endless hours of practice. He strengthened and steadied Aussem's service. Previously only a baseliner, she was extremely limited in her strokes, so Tilden added a creditable volley and smash as well as powerful overheads to her repertoire. He also improved placement of her drives. Most of all, Tilden taught Aussem to enjoy the game and to forget her fear of losing. Under his careful coaching, her natural abilities began to reassert themselves. The transformation was remarkable as Jacobs noted:

> I was on the Riviera this same spring and, although illness forced me into the role of spectator during most of the tournaments so that I had no opportunity to play Cilly, I was astonished at the progress of her game. One could see from match to match the hand of Bill Tilden in her sweeping forehand drive and accurate, cleverly placed backhand. I marked her at once as a player to treat with great respect and to play with infinite attention to strategy, should we ever meet.

Aussem and Tilden won the French hard-court championship mixed doubles that year. For the first time, Aussem could serve, smash, and volley with the best. Then she beat Elizabeth Ryan in the singles at the French championships. When she arrived at Wimbledon in the summer of 1930, her game had never been better. Jacobs, who played Aussem in the quarter-final round, commented:

away. At Wimbledon not long afterwards, she played similarly, and lost to d'Alvarez. In 1929, Aussem lost at Wimbledon to **Joan Ridley**, an English player whose skills were not even in the same category. Watching Aussem's defeat, Helen Hull Jacobs summed up her failures:

> The German girl lacked a very potent quality in her match play temperament. She had arrived at the point where she would either go forward or backward very fast, and the course she was to take depended upon her ability to develop this quality-fearlessness. Cilly played as if she were so afraid of losing that the game itself had little pleasure for her.

Jacobs and many others thought Aussem would quickly fade from the scene. But at this low point in her career, the young German attracted the attention of Bill Tilden, the American star. William Tatem Tilden dominated men's tennis during the 1920s and early 1930s. A large man with a cannonball service, he was Aussem's opposite in every respect. Tilden had great faith in his abilities, which were considerable as he won seven Wimbledon championships before turning professional. His maxim was, "Never give your opponent the shot he likes to play." As a child star, his natural abilities had taken him far when, without warning, his game began to

Bill Tilden had succeeded in teaching her the sharply angled, short drive that leaves the opponent in such a vulnerable position and, as much as I varied my game to make the production of this shot more difficult, she played it with maddening regularity. Cilly's speed of foot and position play were vital factors in the soundness of her game against any attack or defense that I could launch. When finally the length and angles of my shots began to improve, it was too late. The set and match were over at 6–1.

The next day at the semi-finals, Aussem played Ryan. She had beaten Helen Jacobs 6–2 and 6–1 the previous day, so defeating Ryan was a possibility. Aussem lost the first set to Ryan 3–6 and won the second 6–0. In the final set, she crumpled to the ground in a faint, and another Wimbledon championship eluded her.

At this point, however, Cilly Aussem was a star on the international tennis circuit. Her aggressive style of play had gained her many fans, and she was ranked the number two player in the world. Picture postcards of the German with the pretty face were the rage in Europe. Aussem enjoyed the limelight and the spectators who mobbed her, although fans could be somewhat dangerous to the petite player. Once at Wimbledon, enthusiasts literally swept Aussem off her feet and Teddy Tinling, the master of ceremonies of center court, had to rescue her. The 6'6" Tinling snatched the 5' Aussem from her admirers, safely depositing her in her dressing room.

Aussem never possessed great physical stamina, relying instead on an iron will and a fighting spirit to play the game. Exhausted at the end of the 1930 season, she spent the winter resting, but by May 1931 she was ready for the next challenge. Helen Wills, the American star who had won the Wimbledon single's championship every year from 1927–30, withdrew from competition, wishing to spend time with her new husband. Her absence left a vacuum on the international circuit that Aussem was determined to fill. She won the French championship easily, mowing down her opponents, and arrived at Wimbledon determined to do the same.

Reaching the semi-finals, Aussem faced *Simone Mathieu, the French player known for her inexhaustible style. Aussem easily defeated Mathieu 6–0 in the first set and looked to be a sure winner in the second. Mathieu, however, found her form and took the second set 6–2. In the old days, the threat of defeat would have immobilized Aussem, but Tilden's training reasserted itself and Mathieu went down 6–3 in the third set. Aussem had reached the finals at Wimbledon for the first time in her career. This match was unique because two Germans, Cilly Aussem and *Hilde Krahwinkel (Sperling), faced each other in the finals, an unprecedented occurrence that would not happen again for many decades. Sperling and Aussem were opposites in almost every respect. In later years, Tilden said of the tall, ungainly Sperling:

> She is one of the best yet most hopeless looking tennis players I have ever seen. Her game is awkward in the extreme, limited to cramped unorthodox ground strokes without volley or smash to aid her, yet she has been the most consistent winner in women's tennis each year since 1934. She is another proof of that great tennis truth that it is where and when you hit a tennis ball, not how, that wins matches.

The final match was excruciating for both players. Sperling had blistered her feet in the semi-finals, which she played against Helen Jacobs, defeating her 10–8, 0–6, 6–4. Aussem suffered a similar situation in her match against Mathieu, and in consequence neither player was at her best. Sperling was a dogged player whose height and grip worked against her. As a child, she had injured the ligaments in the fourth and fifth fingers of her right hand, causing them to drop at right angles to the palm of her hand. Gripping the racquet was very difficult, a handicap she struggled to overcome. But she was a tenacious player, and the smaller, more nimble Aussem did not underestimate her. Said **Allison Danzig**, while describing the match:

> Today, with the championship at stake, Fräulein Aussem did not trust herself to rush to the net or depend too much on her backhand. She stuck stubbornly to the baseline, sparking from one side of the court to the other and running so fast that she always was in time to return Fräulein Krahwinkel's drives with her high, swift forehand. Fräulein Aussem was so fast, in fact, with her short rushes along the back line that she was able to get her forehand into use on strokes that nine out of ten players would have answered with their backhand. Against such a game Fräulein Krahwinkel could do little.

Cilly Aussem won the championship 6–2 and 7–5, the first German to ever win a Wimbledon title.

Aussem's unexpected victory inspired celebrations throughout a defeatist Germany then suffering from the economic depression and political chaos that had followed World War I. Shortly before her surprising upset, Max Schmeling had also won a boxing bout in Cleveland, and sports fans in their country now went wild. The *Leipziger Neueste Nachrichten* echoed a common sentiment in the headline, "Cilly and Max would not be beaten. Neither will we." For Germans, their victories marked a turning point, an end to ignominious defeat that had plagued the country since 1918. The *Leipziger Neueste Nachrichten* could barely contain its delight:

This third of July is worthy of remembrance in German sport. Two figures, Cilly and Max, appeared as world champions in their games. Higher honors are impossible. We do not desire to overrate the results, but they prove to our great satisfaction that the German folk, although not yet free from the Young Plan and the Versailles Treaty, are not in the slightest thinking of dropping out of world affairs.

The *Vossische Zeitung* of Berlin echoed this theme under the headline, "The Wimbledon Turning Point":

Krahwinkel and Aussem bestowed upon German tennis a new authority in the hour of our deepest humiliation. Both worked themselves up through the world's best and accomplished grandiose feats on unfamiliar grass courts. Their example is an assurance that German women's tennis never will lose touch with international stardom.

Cilly Aussem's victory at Wimbledon represented a resurgence of hope in Weimar Germany. For a moment, the humiliation of defeat, Nazi diatribes against the Jews, and financial woes brought on by the Great Depression were put aside. Aussem proved that Germans could forge ahead with renewed hope and determination. Like the "fragile Fräulein with the will of iron," the German people would one day stand in the winner's circle.

With tennis immortality so close at hand [Aussem] abandoned all adventure and played the final with a steadfast refusal to err.

—Davidson and Jones on Aussem's championship bout at Wimbledon, 1931

Success followed success for Aussem in 1931. She was the "Tennis Queen of Europe," winning the national singles championships of France, Germany, Hungary, and Austria. In the fall of 1931, she traveled to South America where she defeated **Irmgard Rost,** a fellow countrywoman, in Argentina. During this tour, appendicitis struck, however, and Aussem underwent surgery upon her return to Germany. Unfortunately, she returned to competition before she had fully recovered. Still only 22 years old, she was dogged by poor health during every match. In 1932, she was forced to retire from the French championships, falling behind in matches against *Betty

Nuthall. When Aussem played against Helen Hull Jacobs at Wimbledon in 1934, Aussem was a different athlete. Jacobs recounted:

When we met for the second and last time at Wimbledon in 1934, Cilly did not remotely resemble the player of 1931. I don't believe I ever played much better in my life than I did on this day to win 6–0, 6–2, but I faced an opponent on the wane. Cilly seemed to have lapsed into her old, hopeless, match-play psychology, probably induced by numerous setbacks she suffered after her operation. The aggressive power of her fame was gone and with it the will to win.

In 1935, Aussem married an Italian count, Murai Della Corte Brae. Although it was often rumored that Aussem and Bill Tilden were engaged, theirs was a strong friendship rather than a romantic relationship. Not long after her marriage, Aussem contracted a jungle fever, which further eroded her health and affected her eyesight. She ended her tennis career in 1936.

A superstar in the 1930s, Cilly Aussem faded from view. Her health remained frail, and she was only 54 when she died in Italy in 1963. *Der Spiegel,* Germany's foremost publication, devoted a short six lines to her obituary. Aussem was no longer listed in the German *Who's Who,* and her accomplishments were mostly forgotten in the tennis world. Still, there were those who remembered her remarkable ascent to the top ranks of tennis. In May 1988, Aussem was featured on a German postage stamp. The passage of time has brought greater perspective to her accomplishments, and Cilly Aussem has been restored to her rightful place as a champion.

SOURCES:
Cleather, Norah Gordon. *Wimbledon Story.* London: Sporting Handbooks, 1947.

Davidson, Owen, and C.M. Jones. *Great Women Tennis Players.* London: Pelham Books, 1971.

Davy, Charles. "Wimbledon Again," in *Saturday Review* [London]. Vol. 151, no. 3947, June 20, 1931, pp. 896–897.

"'Hoch' Cries Germany as Max and Cilly Win," in *Literary Digest.* Vol 110, no. 3, July 18, 1931, pp. 38–39.

Jacobs, Helen Hull. *Gallery of Champions.* NY: A.S. Barnes, 1970.

Kuhn, Ferdinand Jr. "Shiedds Defaults; Title Goes to Wood. Fräulein Aussem Victor," in *The New York Times.* July 4, 1931, p. 7.

"Lawn Tennis. The Championships. Fräulein Aussem's Victory," in *The Times* [London]. July 4, 1931, p. 6.

"Menzel and Miss Aussem Win Singles Titles in Germany," in *New York Times.* August 10, 1931, p. 22.

"Register-Cilly Aussem," in *Der Spiegel.* Jg. 17, nr. 14, April 3, 1963, p. 96.

Robertson, Max. *The Encyclopedia of Tennis.* London: George Allen & Unwin, 1974.

———. *Wimbledon. Centre Court of the Game. Final Verdict.* 3rd ed. London: BBC Books, 1987.

Wills, Helen. "European Tennis," in *Saturday Evening Post*. Vol. 203, no. 15, October 11, 1930, pp. 11+.

"Wimbledon 1931-ein deutscher Erfolg," in *Essner Volkszeitung*. July 12, 1931.

Karin Loewen Haag,
freelance writer, Athens, Georgia

Austen, Alice (1866–1952)

American photographer. Name variations: Elizabeth Alice Austen. Born Elizabeth Alice Munn in 1866 in New York; died in 1952 in Staten Island, New York; daughter of Edward Stopford Munn and Alice (Austen) Munn; attended Miss Errington's School for Young Ladies.

Alice Austen was quite young when her father deserted the family. Alice's mother returned to her family's mansion, called Clear Comfort, on Staten Island, claiming her maiden name for both herself and her child. After receiving her first camera as a gift from an uncle at the age of 10, Austen was rarely without one. She used her stately house, family, friends, sporting activities, and social events for subject matter, and, by the age of 18, she was a serious photographer with professional standards. Much of her work was done in Manhattan, documenting working people and immigrants of various ethnic backgrounds. She also spent many summers abroad. Of all the thousands of pictures Austen took and developed on glass-plate negatives—many of extraordinary quality—she never tried to sell one, thus retaining her amateur standing.

Austen lost her money in the stock-market crash of 1929, and by 1945 was forced to give up her home. With her family gone, she was reduced to living at the Staten Island Farm Colony—a poorhouse. Fortunately, the Staten Island Historical Society saved 3,500 of her glass plates, some of which they displayed in a retrospective exhibition in 1951.

Around 1950, historian Oliver Jensen interested magazines such as *Pageant, Holiday,* and *Life* in publishing Austen's work, thus providing her with the funds to move into a private nursing home on Staten Island, where she lived until

"Newsgirl and newsboy in front of New York City Hall, 1896" (photograph by Alice Austen).

her death in 1952. A solo exhibition of Austen's work was presented at Neikrug Galleries, New York, in 1978.

SOURCES:
Robertson, Archie. "The Island in the Bay," in *American Heritage.* Vol XVII, no. 5. August 1966, p. 24.
Rosenblum, Naomi. *A History of Women Photographers.* NY: Abbeville Press, 1994.

Austen, Elizabeth Alice (1866–1952).

See Austen, Alice.

Austen, Jane (1775–1817)

British novelist whose domestic satires of 19th-century British gentry with their witty and astute depictions of human nature are literary classics, which continue in print and in film, enthralling modern readers. Name variations: Jennie. Pronunciation: AW-sten. Born Jane Austen on December 16, 1775, in the village of Steventon, England; died on July 18, 1817, in Winchester, England, probably of Addison's disease; daughter of George Austen (a cleric) and Cassandra (Leigh) Austen; attended boarding school for girls in Oxford, then Southampton, run by Ann Cooper Cawley, 1783, and the Abbey School in Reading, 1784–1786; never married; no children.

Lived with her family in Steventon (1775–1801), Bath (1801–06), Southampton (1801–09), Chawton (1809–1817); shortly before her death moved to Winchester for medical care; published her first novel (1811).

Selected writings: Sense and Sensibility *(1811);* Pride and Prejudice *(1813);* Mansfield Park *(1814);* Emma *(1815);* Northanger Abbey *and* Persuasion *(1818);* Lady Susan and the Watsons *(1882);* Love & Freindship [sic] and other Early Works *(1922);* Fragment of a Novel Written by Jane Austen January-March 1817 *(Sanditon, 1925);* Plan of a Novel according to Hints from Various Quarters *(1926);* Volume the First *(juvenilia, 1933);* Volume the Third *(juvenilia, 1951);* Volume the Second *(juvenilia, 1963).*

On Thursday morning, July 24, 1817, Jane Austen was buried in the center of the north aisle of her beloved Winchester Cathedral in a private ceremony held early to avoid disrupting the 10 o'clock services. As custom dictated, only men were in attendance—three brothers and a nephew. Jane's sister and lifelong companion **Cassandra** remained behind in the lodging they had shared. Earlier she had watched the mournful procession from an upper-story window, "I watched . . . the length of the street; and when it turned from my sight . . . I had lost her for ever." Jane Austen was 41.

The words that the Austen family caused to be inscribed on the tomb's black marble slab paid tribute to the "benevolence of her heart" and "the sweetness of her temper." Ignored were her authorship and her caustic wit. The novels were published anonymously during Jane's lifetime—the frontispieces bore the coy attribution "By a Lady." And yet, the steady growth of Jane Austen's fame, the continued reissue of her novels to this day, and the durable appeal of her understated humor and her light satire of the 19th-century English gentry attest to the wisdom in Edmund Wilson's remark that only Shakespeare's and Jane Austen's reputations prove impervious to changes in taste and literary fashion.

Jane Austen was born on December 16, 1775, in the village of Steventon, Hampshire. The seventh of eight children, the younger of two daughters, she grew up among the parsons and squires, naval and army officers, Oxford and Cambridge fellows whom she would later satirize with gentle humor in her novels. Her father, George Austen, a conventional 18th-century cleric-scholar, had attended St. Johns, Oxford, where he later became a fellow. In 1764, he married **Cassandra Leigh**, the youngest daughter of Rev. Thomas Leigh, Fellow of All Souls College, Oxford. His bride boasted aristocratic relatives in the Leighs of Stoneleigh Abbey, Warwickshire; she was also the niece of Theophilus Leigh, master of Balliol for more than a half-century. By the time of their marriage George Austen was himself comfortably situated, thanks to the generosity of two kinsmen. He was given the living of Steventon (the revenue from the church) by Thomas Knight, a wealthy landowner whose son would later adopt George Austen's third son, Edward, as his heir; his uncle, Francis Austen, a wealthy solicitor who had provided for George Austen after he was orphaned at age nine, had given him the living of Deane. These revenues combined with the monies from farming some of his land and tutoring private pupils resulted in a respectable annual income of £600.

The Steventon rectory would be Jane's home for the next 25 years. During her childhood, the seven-bedroom parsonage was home for the seven children—the second son, George, suffered from some sort of handicap and lived elsewhere—and her father's private pupils. Of necessity, Jane shared a bedroom with her sister Cassandra, a practice they continued for most of their lives. And room was always found for visiting relatives—among them the family of Mrs.

Austen's sister, the Coopers, and George Austen's sister, **Philadelphia Hancock,** and her daughter **Eliza.** Eliza had grown up in French society and married a French noble in 1781 when Jane was six. In 1794 during the French Revolution, he was guillotined; Eliza would later (in 1797) marry Jane's brother Henry. She must have fascinated a young Jane growing up in a small English village.

Jane Austen's formal education was brief, desultory, and, at one point, almost fatal. In

1783, Jane, her sister Cassandra, and their cousin, another **Jane (Cooper)**, were sent to a girls' boarding school in Oxford run by Mrs. Cawley, a family connection. Although Jane was rather young to be sent away to school—she was only seven—her emotional ties to Cassandra were so strong that Mrs. Austen decided not to separate them. She once remarked that if Cassandra were going to have her head cut off, Jane would insist on sharing her fate. Shortly after the girls were enrolled, the school was moved to Southampton; there all three girls came down with "putrid fever" (probably either diphtheria or typhoid). For some reason, Cawley neglected to inform the girls' parents; however, after an already homesick Jane Cooper managed to get a letter to her mother, Mrs. Austen's sister, the two women descended on the school and removed their daughters. Jane Austen was very ill and almost died; her aunt, Mrs. Cooper, caught the infection from her daughter and died of it.

Next—1785—Jane and Cassandra were sent to a girls' boarding school in Reading called the Abbey because it was built on the ruins of a medieval monastery. While less dangerous to the girls' health, it was educationally ineffectual. **Mrs. Latournelle**, who ran the school, was memorable mostly for her cork leg. Supervision was lax and lessons were casual. The girls spent much of their time gossiping in the gardens. In 1787, George Austen decided to bring his daughters home. By then, his son James was at Oxford and Frank was at the Naval Academy in Portsmouth; Edward, already adopted by the Knights, was on the Grand Tour. Only two boys, Henry and Charles, continued to live at home. (Henry would soon join James at Oxford; in about four years Charles would leave for the Naval Academy.) Jane and Cassandra continued to share a bedroom but were now given an adjacent room as a combination sitting and dressing room. Here Jane wrote her first short pieces of fiction.

Though what passed for Jane's formal education was over by the time she was 11 years old, her intellectual horizon was considerably broader than that of most women of her social class. The usual emphasis was on acquiring the traditional female accomplishments of drawing, music, and needlework—with perhaps smatterings of foreign languages. Jane knew French along with some Italian. She enjoyed the piano and played it throughout her life, but shared neither Cassandra's passion for, nor ability in, drawing and watercolor. (The only authenticated portrait we have of Jane is a sketch by Cassandra.) But her education, which was completed at home, went beyond the norm. Following her brothers' reading suggestions, she read widely in history and in both classical and contemporary literature in her father's library, which contained 500 volumes in 1801. Perhaps more important for her subsequent development as a novelist, the Austens also subscribed to local circulating libraries, from which they frequently obtained the most recent novels. They obviously did not share the contemporary notion that novels would exert undesirable influences on the imaginations of susceptible young ladies. According to Jane, the Austens were "great novel readers, and not ashamed of being so." Indeed, the Austens often read aloud to each other; George Austen was supposed to have had an especially pleasing voice. They also staged their own amateur theatricals in a barn during the summer, moving into the dining room during the winter months.

The Austens were of consequence in local society, not only because George Austen was the parson, but also because he was regarded as the social representative of his kinsman Thomas Knight, who, though the chief landowner of the district, lived elsewhere. After Jane's coming out when she turned 16, she attended the usual social events—dinners, dances, musical evenings. During the winter, formal dances were held once each month at the Basingstoke Assembly Rooms; informal dances were often held at friends' homes with the music provided by one of their number playing the piano. She often visited friends and relatives in London, Bath, and Southampton, where she attended plays and dinners. As her brothers married and had children, she enjoyed the company of a growing number of nieces and nephews during her visits.

That neither Jane nor Cassandra married was in part the result of circumstance. Thomas Craven Fowle, to whom Cassandra was engaged in 1795, died of yellow fever in 1797 while serving as a military chaplain in the West Indies. He left his bereaved fiancée a legacy of £1,000. Jane had several suitors, including a flirtation in 1796 with Tom Lefroy, a future chief justice of Ireland, who recalled in his old age his "boyish love" for Jane. Their flirtation ended when his aunt and Jane's good friend, Mrs. **Anna Lefroy**, recognized that her impoverished nephew was in no financial position to marry and cut his visit short in order to prevent any more "mischief" between the two.

It was during Jane's late teenage years that the fiction writing in which she had been indulging in her sitting room began to show signs of her later remarkable talent. By 1793 or 1794, the short stories and comedies that she wrote for the family's amusement had evolved into a short epistolary novel called *Lady Susan.* Early versions of her later novels followed—*Eleanor and Marianne* (later *Sense and Sensibility*) and *First Impressions* (later *Pride and Prejudice*). We may assume that George Austen was not unaware of his daughter's talent; in November 1797, he offered *First Impressions* to the publisher Cadell, who rejected the manuscript without having read it. By then Jane was at work on *Susan* (*Northanger Abbey*), which she completed no later than 1799.

In 1800, Jane returned from a stay with friends in Ibthrop to learn from her mother that George Austen, who was almost 70 years old, had decided to retire to Bath and turn over the Steventon rectory to his eldest son, James. That Jane responded to the news by fainting suggests that neither she nor Cassandra, the only children still living at home, had been told that their father was contemplating uprooting them from the only world either of the young women had ever known. Naturally, as dependent daughters, they had no choice in the matter. Jane's initial dislike of Bath only increased following the family's relocation. Even so, she cannot be said to have led a solitary life. She took part in Bath society and continued her occasional visits to relatives and friends. During a family seaside holiday in either 1801 or 1802, Jane met a somewhat mysterious suitor, who, according to stories passed down in the family, fell in love with Jane and promised to visit the family in Bath. The attraction seems to have been mutual, and even Cassandra appears to have approved. But instead of the stranger's visit, Jane soon received word of his death. Around that same time, on an evening in 1802, Jane received and accepted a marriage proposal from Harry Biggs Withers, whose sisters were friends of Jane and Cassandra. Biggs Withers was his family's heir and was about to become a cleric. Although at 21 he was six years younger than Jane, she accepted his proposal. The next morning, however, she announced that she had changed her mind. The two Austen sisters prevailed upon their brother James to escort them back to Bath immediately, thus escaping a socially embarrassing situation.

The abortive sale of *Susan* (later *Northanger Abbey*) in 1803 to the publisher Richard Crosby for the sum of £10—he advertised the novel but then did not publish it—and Jane's inability to complete *The Watsons,* which she began in 1804 and abandoned in 1805, marked the end of Jane

Austen's early productive phase and the onset of an extended period of literary inactivity. She was entering a difficult time in her life. Condemned to live in a town she increasingly disliked, surely disillusioned at being deprived of the satisfaction of her novel's publication, she was soon rocked by tragedy among her friends and family. In December 1804, she learned that her dear friend, Anna Lefroy, had died as the result of a fall from a horse. A month later, in January 1805, her father died. The emotional blow of George Austen's death was compounded by the severe financial hardship that it brought in its wake. Deprived of his income, Mrs. Austen and her daughters had only the £210 deriving from Mrs. Austen's annuity and the interest on Cassandra's legacy from Tom Fowle to support them. Severely straitened circumstances were avoided only because Jane's brothers agreed to contribute specific yearly amounts and thus raise Mrs. Austen's annual income to roughly £450. In April, **Martha Lloyd,** an old friend of the family and their brother James' sister-in-law, moved in with them. She brought her own small income. Even so, in 1806, the women moved to Southampton in order to share first lodgings and then a house with Jane's brother Frank and his new bride. Although Jane considered the move from Bath a "happy escape," as she later wrote Cassandra, they still lacked a permanent home. That source of insecurity ended only in 1809, when Jane's brother Edward offered them a six-bedroom "cottage," in the village of Chawton in Hampshire, which was only about a mile from Edward's Hampshire estate and near Steventon, where brother James now served as the local rector.

She sat musing on the difference of woman's destiny.

—From Jane Austen's *Emma*

Jane Austen had written nothing since putting aside *The Watsons* in 1805, but now, with the return to familiar surroundings and the small country society of family and friends, she picked up her pen again. In the general sitting room, where, according to her nephew, a creaking door warned her of imminent intrusion, she began revising manuscripts that she had laid aside a decade before. Of *Eleanor and Marianne* she made *Sense and Sensibility*; *First Impressions* became *Pride and Prejudice. Sense and Sensibility,* which she published anonymously at her own expense in November 1811, was an immediate success. After completing the revision of *Pride and Prejudice,* Jane began working on

From the movie Emma, *starring Gwyneth Paltrow (Miramax, 1996).*

Mansfield Park in 1812. *Pride and Prejudice* appeared in January 1813, and second printings of both *Sense and Sensibility* and *Pride and Prejudice* were issued later in that same year. She received, however, no additional income from the second edition of *Pride and Prejudice*—she had sold it outright for £110. *Mansfield Park,* which appeared in 1814, sold out in six months. By then Jane was already at work on *Emma,* which came out in December 1815.

Despite the success of her novels (only the second edition of *Mansfield Park* in 1816 showed disappointing sales), Jane Austen receive little money and less fame as a result of her fiction. She made £150 from *Sense and Sensibility* in 1811; from her later novels, she realized a total of £700. As for her anonymity, the customs of the time, to which Jane Austen firmly adhered, prescribed that ladies of good breeding shun the limelight. It was not until 1813 that word of her authorship spread beyond the family circle, and even then only a few knew to whom the attribution "By a Lady" actually referred. One, interestingly enough, was an ardent fan: the prince re-

gent, later George IV, kept a set of her novels at each of his houses. At his request—in regal terms, he granted her permission—*Emma* was dedicated to him. The larger reading public would only come to know the author's name after her death, when her brother Henry, who supervised the posthumous publication of *Northanger Abbey* and *Persuasion,* appended a biographical note identifying Jane Austen as the author of these and previous novels.

By 1816, Jane was seriously ill. Even so, in August she managed to finish *Persuasion,* which she had begun a year earlier. In that same year, through the emissary of her brother Henry, she bought back the rights to *Susan* and revised it under a new title, *Northanger Abbey.* In January 1817, she began *Sanditon* but abandoned it in March; she grew increasingly weak as her health declined. Diagnosed as suffering from "bile," she probably had Addison's disease, which, at that time, was fatal. In May 1817, at the suggestion of her doctor, she moved to Winchester to be near a surgeon named Lyford who enjoyed considerable reputation. There, in lodgings in College Street,

nursed by her sister Cassandra and attended by her brothers, James and Henry, she died on July 18, 1817, at age 41. Six days later, she was interred in her beloved Winchester Cathedral.

SOURCES:

Austen, Jane. *Jane Austen's Letters to her sister Cassandra and Others.* Collected and edited by R.W. Chapman. London: Oxford University Press, 1952.

Austen-Leigh, James Edward. *Memoir of Jane Austen.* Introduction, Notes, & Index by R.W. Chapman. 1870 (available in many editions).

Cecil, David. *A Portrait of Jane Austen.* NY: Hill and Wang, 1978.

Halperin, John. *The Life of Jane Austen.* Baltimore, MD: Johns Hopkins University Press, 1984.

Laski, Marghanita. *Jane Austen and her World.* NY: The Viking Press, 1969.

SUGGESTED READING:

Austen, Jane. *My Dear Cassandra: The Letters of Jane Austen.* Edited by Penelope Hughes-Hallett. NY: Clarkson Potter, 1991.

Nokes, David. *Jane Austen: A Life.* NY: Farrar, Straus, 1997.

Tomalin, Claire. *Jane Austen: A Life.* NY: Knopf, 1997.

Tucker, George Holbert. *Jane Austen, the Woman. Some Biographical Insights.* NY: St. Martin's Press, c. 1994.

RELATED MEDIA—A SELECTION:

"Emma" (sound recording; 205 min), performed by **Anna Massey**, abridged by **Ursula Wood**, Norton, distributed by Audio-Forum, 1979.

Clueless, starring **Alicia Silverstone**, a movie freely adapted from *Emma*, 1995.

Emma, starring **Gwyneth Paltrow**, by writer-director Douglas McGrath, 1996.

"Mansfield Park" (VHS; 261 min), BBC Video, 1987.

"Persuasion" (sound recording; 260 min), performed by Alison Fiske, abridged by Donald Bancroft, Norton, distributed by Audio-Forum, 1979.

Persuasion, movie starring Amanda Root and Susan Fleetwood, directed by Roger Michell, 1995.

Pride and Prejudice, starring Greer Garson and Laurence Olivier, screenplay by Aldous Huxley, directed by Robert Z. Leonard, Loew's, 1940.

"Pride and Prejudice" (sound recording; 57 min), read by Claire Bloom, 1958.

"Pride and Prejudice, or, First Impressions" (VHS; 226 min), BBC production, starring Elizabeth Garvie and David Rintoul, directed by Cyril Coke, 1985.

"Pride and Prejudice" (6 hour) BBC production, starring **Jennifer Ehle**; adapted by Andrew Davies and directed by Simon Langton, 1996.

"Sense and Sensibility" (VHS; close captioned; 174 min), starring Irene Richard and Tracey Childs, BBC Video, CBS/Fox Video, 1987.

From the movie Sense and Sensibility, *starring Emma Thompson and Kate Winslet (Columbia Pictures, 1995).*

"Sense and Sensibility" (sound recording; 56 min); read by Claire Bloom, 1979.

Sense and Sensibility, movie starring and adapted by **Emma Thompson**, Alan Rickman, and Kate Winslet, directed by Ang Lee, produced by Columbia Pictures, 1995.

COLLECTIONS:

Early editions, miscellaneous and collateral materials including translations, critical studies, works by Jane Austen's contemporaries, background literature about her life and times, and audiovisual representations located in the Henry and Alberta Hirshheimer Burke Collection, Goucher College, Baltimore, Maryland.

Letters and manuscripts, Pierpoint Morgan Library, New York.

> **Carole Shelton**, Adjunct Professor of History, Middle
> Tennessee State University, Murfreesboro, Tennessee

Austin, Lovie (1887–1972).

See Armstrong, Lil Hardin for sidebar.

Austin, Mary Hunter (1868–1934)

American author, primarily of naturalist fiction about the Southwest, who celebrated the environment, preserved Native American and Spanish Colonial culture, and mingled with the cultural icons of her times. Name variations: refers to herself as both I-Mary and Mary-by-Herself; (pseudonym) Gordon Stairs. Pronunciation: Os-ten. Born Mary Hunter on September 9, 1868, in Carlinville, Illinois; died in Santa Fe, New Mexico, on August 13, 1934; daughter of Captain George (a lawyer) and Susannah Savilla Graham Hunter (a nurse); attended State Normal School at Bloomington and graduated from Blackburn College of Carlinville, 1888; married Stafford Wallace Austin (a vineyardist, irrigation manager, schoolteacher), on May 18, 1891 (divorced, August 21, 1914); children: Ruth (1892–1918).

Moved to California (1888); taught school (1897–99); published first book (1903); separated from husband and child and moved to the artists colony of Carmel (1906); lived through and reported the San Francisco Earthquake and Fire (1906); traveled in Europe (1908–10); commuted between New York City and Carmel (1911–24); publicist for the Panama-Pacific Exposition (1915); served as advisor and lecturer for Herbert Hoover's U.S. Food Administration (1917); named associate in Native American Literature at the School of American Research (1918); lectured for Fabian Society in England (1921); built house in Santa Fe (1925); organized the Spanish Colonial Arts Society of Santa Fe (1927); served as delegate to Seven States Conference (1927); led discussions at Mexican Ministry of Education seminars (1930); pub-

lished autobiography (1932); bequeathed most of her estate to the Indian Arts Fund (1933).

Fiction: The Land of Little Rain (1903); Isidro (1905); Lost Borders (1909); (as Gordon Stairs) Outland (1910); Woman of Genius (1912); The Ford (1917); The Man Jesus (1925); Starry Adventure (1931); One Smoke Stories (1934). Nonfiction: The Flock (1906); California, Land of the Sun (1914); The American Rhythm: Studies and Re-expressions of American Songs (1923); Everyman's Genius (1925); (with photographer Ansel Adams) Taos Pueblo (1930); Earth Horizon: An Autobiography (1932); Earth Horizon: An Autobiography (1934). Plays: The Arrow Maker (1911); Fire (1912); The Man Who Didn't Believe in Christmas (1916). Articles and essays on contemporary events, Native American Folk Culture, and Regionalism in American Fiction in numerous periodicals and published literature collections.

At the stroke of midnight on September 9, 1868, Susannah Hunter gave birth to the daughter she did not want. Struggling to keep herself, her husband, and their son financially afloat in the years after a debilitated Captain Hunter returned from the Civil War, she did not welcome another mouth to feed. Mary Hunter Austin bore the brunt of her mother's anger; Mary's younger siblings, born in more prosperous times, felt the acceptance for which she always longed. As a child, Mary could not understand why her mother pulled away from her but cuddled her siblings; she knew that her knack for saying the very thing the adults were skirting disturbed her mother, but she felt unable to curb this tendency. Mary also found it difficult to distinguish between events she experienced and events she heard about. She believed she had experienced things if she could see them in her mind, but Susannah labeled her stories "lies."

Oddly enough, it was Susannah who introduced Mary to an internal source of assurance and comfort. As her brother Jim practiced his alphabet at the table one afternoon, four-year-old Mary mimicked him. When he came to the letter "I," Mary questioned Susannah, "Eye?" Her mother answered, "No, I, myself, I want a drink, I Mary." That day, Mary became aware of I-Mary within herself. From that time on, the physical Mary-by-herself associated I-Mary with the print in Jim's book and attempted to summon the invulnerable I-Mary from that source whenever possible. Precocious with the written word, Mary began school in the third grade, but she suffered socially until she learned to weave tales to entertain the other children.

Mary
Hunter
Austin

Austin identified with her father and spent time in the family orchard with him. George Hunter encouraged his daughter to read and to explore the natural world. Under a walnut tree in the orchard, she discovered a Presence that would give her strength throughout her life: at the age of five, she recounted in *Earth Horizon,* "Earth and sky and tree and wind-blown grass and the child in the midst of them came alive together with a pulsing light of consciousness." Austin became aware of an extraordinary reality in this mystical experience, which she called "the Practice of the Presence of God."

Mary suffered the loss of her two strongest supporters in 1878 when her father and her younger sister Jennie, whom she named "the only one who ever unselfishly loved me," died. She moved with her family into a small cottage in Carlinville away from the orchard and meadows. Her mother worked as a nurse and participated actively in the Methodist church and the Woman's Christian Temperance Union (WCTU). The WCTU campaigned against alcohol use and provided women an opportunity to learn skills such as public speaking while maintaining their role as arbiters of morality. Austin often accompanied her mother to the meetings and formulated her ideas about marriage, the role of women, and concern for the right of women to control their own bodies. As an adult, Austin still felt a vast distance between herself and her mother, but learned to appreciate Susannah's efforts, along with those of the Carlinville women, on behalf of women on the American frontier.

At age 16, Austin entered Blackburn College but an illness forced her to withdraw. The following year, her mother sent her to the State Teachers' College. Though Mary did not desire it, teaching presented the only socially acceptable vocation for Gilded Age women in the Midwest, but the curriculum drove Austin to a nervous breakdown. When the local doctor, reflecting the views of the day, declared that, as a woman, she had overtaxed her brain and she should not aspire to work beyond her capacity, Mary responded by regaining her health and convincing her mother to let her return to Blackburn. She studied science, became the editor of the school newspaper, and was elected class poet.

After graduation in 1888, Austin and her mother went West to meet her brother Jim on the land claims he had made under the Homestead Act of 1862 and the Timber Culture Act of 1873. Both acts encouraged settlement of the American West. Austin disagreed with the move and nearly suffered another breakdown on the trip to Tejon in the southern Joaquin Valley in California. She wrote about the experience, which she recorded in her notebook, in "One Hundred Miles on Horseback." The entire family, Mary in particular, suffered from slight malnutrition once there. The dry land had few edible native plants, and Susannah disliked the expensive town-bought canned fruits, vegetables, and milk. Austin recovered her strength by roaming. Wanting to better understand her surroundings, she obtained government documents about the area, including agricultural reports, geological and botanical surveys from General Edward Fitzgerald Beale, the owner of the Tejon Ranch. She also spent days on her horse, accompanying the sheepherders, Indians, and Spanish-speaking *vaqueros* (cowboys), learning the work of the ranch and taking notes. While her friendships with these men fulfilled her spiritually and mentally. Single Anglo-American women did not freely associate with men in general, and with nonwhites in particular. However, these men provided inspiration and material for Austin's later work, particularly *The Flock, One Smoke Stories, Isidro,* and *The Ford.*

General Beale helped the Hunters financially by arranging for them to run an inn along the stage route. The family relinquished their timber claim but kept working to obtain title to the other claims. Previously oblivious to her family's difficulties, Austin suddenly realized their financial insecurity and understood that she could not continue to depend upon Susannah and Jim for her welfare.

In 1889, Austin took a provisional teaching position in Mountain View near Bakersfield, but she failed the required teaching credentials examination that December. She tutored privately before failing the exam once again in May. While boarding with a family in Mountain View, Austin became aware of local farmers' problems in obtaining water rights, observations that would later inform her novel *The Ford.* Simultaneously, relations with her family further deteriorated, and Mary decided that marriage could provide her both economic means and a way to build her own life. By chance, a neighbor named Stafford Wallace Austin began to court her. Cultured and intelligent, Wallace fancied himself a gentleman farmer. While Mary did not feel love for him, they shared some interests, and Wallace did not balk when Mary frankly informed him of her career intentions. They married on May 18, 1891.

Marriage disappointed both of them: he did not encourage her work, while she did not keep a clean house or take much interest in his vineyard. They had little money. When Wallace failed at grape-growing and refused to take a teaching job, Mary insisted he seek other work. In 1892, they moved to Bakersfield where Wallace found an irrigation construction job; Austin continued to write and discovered she was pregnant. Then Wallace moved to San Francisco to work with his brother. Left behind to pack up, she took the opportunity to write two short stories as I-Mary based on her experiences around Tejon. In San Francisco, Austin sought advice from poet *Ina Coolbrith on submitting manuscripts; afterwards, she presented the tales to *Overland Monthly,* which accepted them both. Two months later, the couple moved to the Owens Valley so Wallace could manage an irrigation project at Lone Pine.

The townspeople of "The Little Town of the Grape Vines" were primarily of Mexican origin, and she felt a rapport with them. When Wallace lost his job, Mary worked at a boardinghouse while he took odd jobs and rejected a position as a school principal. Her husband's refusal to take on work that he disliked greatly frustrated her.

Mary stayed with her mother to have her child, Ruth; the labor lasted 48 hours and left her ill. While there, the local court served Mary with a legal notice for debts incurred by Wallace before and during their marriage. Austin arranged to sell their Mountain View property and pay their debts in installments. When Wallace took a teaching job in the Owens Valley, Austin hoped for a new start. Instead, they grew further apart.

Mary continued to seek spiritual strength and healing through the natural world. She became friends with the Paiute Indians, who inspired *The Basket Woman,* and renewed friendships with the *señoras,* miners, and sheepherders in town. She worried about her frail child and only later accepted the mental handicaps of her daughter and determined that Ruth had inherited them from the Austin family. Mary had trouble writing with the distractions provided by Ruth, the disapproval of neighbors, and lack of support from her husband, but the Austins needed money and Mary needed to write.

Hoping to sort out her situation, in 1895 she took a teaching job in Bishop, away from her husband. But Mary had to leave Ruth in her room unattended while she taught, thereby drawing criticism and unsolicited aid from her neighbors. Austin covered her embarrassment about the situation with aloofness. Though Wallace disapproved, she eventually placed Ruth with a child-less farm couple nearby. After her mother's death in 1896, Mary tempered her grief with the realization of her new found freedom. At about this time, she learned the principles of Paiute prayer from a medicine man, Tinnemaha, learning to detach herself and concentrate upon writing. When Austin arranged to teach in Bishop for another year, she became friends with the female physician, Dr. **Helen MacKnight** (Doyle), who cared for Ruth.

In 1897, in hopes of reviving her marriage, Austin agreed to take a position teaching at Lone Pine under Wallace as the school superintendent. Finally, their combined salaries allowed them to pay off most of their debt, but Mary suffered from nervous tension. Seeking treatment in Los Angeles, she established contact with magazine editor Charles Lummis and his wife **Eve.** By the time she returned home, Wallace had taken a job as a land registrar in Independence and expected her to fulfill his superintendent duties as well as teach. The following summer, Austin again went to the hospital, this time in Oakland. While there, she met philosopher William James and discussed Paiute prayer methods with him. Reinspired, Austin turned her attention to studying the Paiute lifestyle; she became convinced that all rhythmic movement held creative force and tried to capture this in her writing. In 1899, she decided to move to Los Angeles, taking Ruth with her while Wallace remained in Independence.

Mary's friendship with the Lummis family bloomed and provided her with opportunities to meet others who would later open doors for her, including anthropologist Frederick Webb Hodge, feminist *Charlotte Perkins Gilman, naturalist John Muir, and author George Sterling. Then Wallace Austin insisted his wife return to Independence. The couple attempted to share their lives by organizing a little theater and taking hiking trips together. In addition to her first book, Austin began working on *Isidro* and published a stream of poems in a children's magazine. She began writing about her surroundings, revealing her intimate connection with the earth in a rhythmic style. In her new house, Austin could look out her sunroom window as she wrote; she felt "two tall, invisible presences" stand over her there. When Houghton Mifflin published *The Land of Little Rain* in 1903, she explained her life in a short biography requested by the publisher: "All of Mary Austin's work is like her life, out of doors, nights under the pines, long days watching by waterholes to see the wild things drink, breaking trail up new slopes, heat, cloud bursts, snow; wild beasts and mountain bloom, all equally delightful because understood."

Austin took a trip along the California coast and returned home determined to make changes. She placed Ruth in a Santa Clara sanatorium in 1904, making the arrangement permanent in 1905, and never saw her daughter again. Her love for the land caused her to participate in the controversy over Los Angeles' bid to claim Owen's Valley water rights for use by the city over 200 miles away. Owen's Valley eventually lost control of its water and thereby its chance to grow. Unable to stand by and watch the valley wilt, she left Wallace and moved to Carmel. Austin would later use the experience as additional material for *The Ford*.

Carmel life allowed Mary to spend time with George Sterling and his Bohemian Club crowd: photographer Arnold Genthe, writer Jack London, poet **Nora May French**, and others. Austin purchased some property and began working in her "wick-i-up" among the branches of a huge oak. In 1906, while meeting with her publisher's representative in San Francisco, she had a premonition of disaster. The next morning, the city shook awake with the massive earthquake and resultant fire. Austin published her account of the catastrophe.

In her new setting, Austin's personality changed. She lost touch with her surroundings and the Presence. She developed a reputation, fortified by her unconventional apparel, as an egotist with a priestess complex. During this period, she wrote *Lost Borders* in which her description of the desert has been used to describe Austin herself by several authors: "If the desert were a woman, I know well what like she would be . . . and you could not move her, no, not if you had all the earth to give, so much as one tawny hairsbreadth beyond her own desires." She began collaborating with other writers and thrived on the intellectual ferment.

In 1907, Austin was told she had terminal breast cancer. Relying upon I-Mary, she chose to avoid surgery, accept her fate, and go to Italy "to die quietly." Fortuitously, some friends invited her to Florence. En route by steamer, Austin was invited by a Vatican representative to study Christian prayer in Rome, an attempt to ease her suffering. Her subsequent cure reaffirmed her belief in the Friend of Man and I-Mary. While she was abroad, Austin studied the life of Jesus Christ and the artistic depictions of him, and met a number of influential people including the dancer *Isadora Duncan, writer H.G. Wells, suffragist *Anne Martin, poet William Butler Yeats, author Henry James, and novelist Joseph Conrad. Her experience brought her greater confi-

dence. She wrote *Outland,* based upon notes developed with George Sterling and published under a pseudonym, Gordon Stairs, in 1910. Austin marched in suffragist parades in London before sailing for New York City to produce her play, *The Arrow Maker.*

While in New York, she developed an ardent friendship with journalist Lincoln Steffens, and became associated with other women in the suffrage and labor movements, including advocate *Margaret Sanger, journalist *Ida Tarbell, and labor leader *Elizabeth Gurley Flynn. When the relationship with Steffens soured, Austin poured her heartache into the autobiographical *A Woman of Genius.* Her career going smoothly, she attributed her lack of emotional fulfillment to her success, her genius.

Longing for the West, Austin returned to Carmel in December 1912 and began a new friendship with Dr. Daniel Trembly MacDougal, a botanical research scientist for the Carnegie Institution. Her eccentricity became local legend: dressed in robes, her hair flowing below her waist, she would wander the woods, waving her arms as she talked.

Despite continued publication, her sales were disappointing, and Austin was plagued financially. Since New York held the key to connections essential for her career, she returned to the city and took a studio at the National Arts Club. Soon she found herself in another intellectual circle, an evening salon hosted by the rich young widow, *Mabel Dodge Luhan. Luhan, who shared Austin's inclination towards mysticism, became one of her closest friends.

When funds allowed, she retreated to Carmel or the Southwest for renewal. While in Carmel in 1914, Wallace formally charged her with willful desertion and abandonment without cause. Their divorce became final in August. Mary returned to New York and finished her unorthodox manuscript of *The Man Jesus;* the book was not well received. In 1916, she became involved in the Mexican Revolution, speaking out on behalf of the revolutionaries. In early 1917, as part of the war effort, Austin was consulted by her old friend Herbert Hoover, then heading the U.S. Food Administration, on ways to educate women in the preservation of foodstuffs. The same year, she began a long-standing quarrel with her brother George over the welfare of their niece, Mary. She resolved to establish a relationship with her niece just as she learned that her own daughter had died.

After traveling to Santa Clara and arranging for cremation of Ruth's remains, Austin went to

Santa Fe, New Mexico, to do research at the School of American Research. She immediately became involved in community affairs—holding teas at the new Museum of New Mexico, organizing a community theater, and giving a series of lectures about writing. Her post as an associate in Native American Literature did not include remuneration; finances continued to plague her, yet she insisted on trying to adopt her niece who resisted her efforts. Austin escaped to Mabel Luhan's home in Taos where she finished *26 Jayne Street.*

Returning to New York, she joined a new circle of bohemian friends, including authors *Willa Cather and Sinclair Lewis. To shore up her reputation, in 1921, Austin journeyed to England to renew contacts and lecture at the Fabian Society on "The American Rhythm." She believed that the "new" American free verse had roots in the ancient American Indian rhythmic measures. When she returned to New York that winter, magazine editors sought articles from her, and the National Arts Club honored her with a testimonial dinner in January. Austin scraped together enough funds to travel to Carmel that summer and for a 2,500-mile-long automobile trip through the Southwest for research the following year. Her trips allowed her to visit MacDougal, but she resented having to do what she termed "hack work" (primarily articles) to survive financially. She gave a speech to the National Popular Government League in opposition to the Bursum bill, which sought to deprive the Pueblo Indians of their land and water rights, and organized speaking engagements for a delegation of New Mexican Indians in 1923. About this time, Austin developed high blood pressure, which limited her activities until she finally had a complete breakdown at the Luhans' home in Taos.

Determined to leave New York and recapture her connection with the Presence, she purchased property in Santa Fe before returning East. Illness and a frenetic workload continued to bedevil her; as Augusta Fink, author of *I-Mary,* points out, at the very time she was writing about them in *Everyman's Genius,* her techniques for tapping into the "deep-self" began to fail her. Selling her Carmel property to finance her move to Santa Fe in March 1925, she built her house, Casa Querida (The Beloved House), near Frank and **Alta Applegate**, Indian and Spanish Colonial art aficionados. Austin resumed her writing and reentered community affairs. She supported the new Indian Arts Fund by purchasing a lot north of her home and deeding it to the fund as a museum site. She orga-

nized a group of writers, the Genius Club, and collaborated with the Applegates to form the Spanish Colonial Arts Society in 1927.

Despite outward appearances, Austin continued to fight illness and found it difficult to concentrate for long periods of time. Short articles brought quick money. While researching for a series of articles, Mary established a relationship with San Francisco philanthropist Albert Bender. When Bender brought photographer Ansel Adams to Santa Fe to collaborate with her, the result was *Taos Pueblo.* Shortly thereafter, New Mexico's governor appointed Mary as a delegate to the 1927 Seven States Conference on water resources; at the conference, she fought for Arizona in its quarrel with California for control of the water in the Colorado River. She followed this experience with an article against the building of Boulder Dam (later named Hoover Dam) on the Colorado in *The Nation.*

> [My books] originate in an inherent sensitivity to the spirit of existence which has been set in motion by the activities of my horison [*sic*], the zone in which sky and earth meet and commingle.
>
> —Mary Austin, *Earth Horizon*

In January 1928, Austin undertook a lecture tour in the Northeast. The woman wearing a blue velvet gown with oxfords and a Spanish comb in her hair commanded the attention of her audiences. A burst of energy and renewed awareness of I-Mary, propelled Austin. She began *Starry Adventure* and published a series of articles entitled "Experiences Facing Death." In 1929, she took time out from her work to lecture on primitive drama and produce a Spanish play at Yale University. While away, she received news of the sale of El Sanctuario, the chapel at Chimayo, a priceless treasure of Spanish colonial art. Austin used her contacts to locate an anonymous donor to purchase the property for safekeeping. Despite her revived career, money problems persisted, and she probably agreed to write her autobiography, *Earth Horizon,* to reduce debt. Writing about her life bored and depressed her, but dogged by continuing illness, she hastened to complete her work in hopes of acquiring enough cash for treatment.

The next two years proved productive. In 1930, she traveled to Mexico to conduct discussions on Indian art and culture for the Ministry of Education and found her own sense of the American Rhythm expressed in the murals of

Diego Rivera. In Santa Fe, Austin continued her work with Spanish Colonial arts and helped establish a bilingual program for Spanish-speaking children and a native arts and crafts curriculum for Indians. Her activities extended to fighting federal legislation harmful to the Pueblo Indians and raising funds for the Arts Society.

As she arrived in New York in October 1932 for the release of her autobiography, she learned that H.G. Wells considered her characterization of him in *Earth Horizon* libelous. She quickly made revisions, but the strain resulted in a heart attack. The financial uncertainties of the Great Depression made earning a livelihood as a writer more difficult, and Mary continued to work. Despite a second heart attack, she undertook a lecture trip to Los Angeles. While the trip was successful, she suffered another attack upon her return to Santa Fe. Austin continued to work on her manuscripts the following spring but suffered spells of severe illness. She recovered sufficiently to appear at the Santa Fe Poet's Roundup on August 9, where she read several poems from *The Children Sing in the Far West*. She submitted a Spanish colonial arts book manuscript to her publisher the next day and suffered a final heart attack on the 12th. She died in her sleep the following day. Her ashes rest amid boulders near the summit of Mount Picacho to the east of Casa Querida; her final resting place overlooks the valley of Santa Fe, the mix of its cultures, and the blending of earth and sky in a harmony that Mary Hunter Austin sought in her writings and in her life.

SOURCES:

Austin, Mary. *Earth Horizon: An Autobiography.* NY: Literary Guild, 1932.

Doyle, Helen MacKnight. *Mary Austin: Woman of Genius.* NY: Gotham House, 1939.

Fink, Augusta. *I-Mary: A Biography of Mary Austin.* Tucson: University of Arizona Press, 1983.

Pearce, T. M. *Mary Hunter Austin.* Twayne's United States Authors Series. New Haven: College & University Press, Twayne, 1965.

SUGGESTED READING:

O'Grady, John P. *Pilgrims to the Wild: Everett Ruers, Henry David Thoreau, John Muir, Clarence King, Mary Austin.* Salt Lake City, UT: University of Utah Press, 1993.

Pearce, T.M., ed. *Literary America, 1903–1934: The Mary Austin Letters.* Contributions in Women's Studies, No. 5. Westport, CT: Greenwood Press, 1979.

A comprehensive list of her works appears in the University of California Library *Research Digest*, Monograph *2 (Berkeley, 1934).

COLLECTIONS:

The largest are the "Mary Austin Collection," Henry E. Huntington Library, San Marino, California, and the "Special Collection, Mary Austin," Coronado Room, University of New Mexico Library. Small collections exist at the Bancroft Library at University of California, Berkeley; the Mills College Library, Oakland, California; University of California, Los Angeles; the University of Arizona; Blackburn College; and the Southwest Museum of Los Angeles. Her house in Independence, California, is a California Historical Landmark.

Laura Anne Wimberley, Department of History, Texas A&M University, College Station, Texas

Austin, Sarah (1793–1867).

See Duff-Gordon, Lucie for sidebar.

Austin, Tracy (1962—)

American tennis player. Born in 1962; grew up in Rolling Hills, California. Won 25 U.S. national junior titles; won two U.S. Open championships (1979, 1981); the Italian Open (1979); with her brother John, mixed doubles at Wimbledon (1980); married Scott Holt (a mortgage broker); children: Dylan Matthew Holt (b. 1996).

In 1977, at 4'11" with braces and ponytail, weighing 89 pounds, 14-year-old Tracy Austin was the youngest player in 70 years to ever compete at Forest Hills; that same year, she also unsuccessfully faced *Chris Evert on Centre Court at Wimbledon. In 1979, 16-year-old Austin was the youngest player to win the women's singles title in the history of the U.S. Open, beating a 24-year-old Evert. For three months in 1980, Austin was ranked number one in the world, having beaten all the top players. The following year, she employed her relentless baseline game to defeat *Martina Navratilova and once again take the U.S. Open title.

But chronic sciatic-nerve problems effectively ended Austin's career by 1982, though she returned to play mixed doubles in 1984. Austin told *Billie Jean King: "The press kept harping on how little I was in my pinafores and my pigtails. They said my mom tried to make me look like a little girl. But I *was* a little girl. I didn't mature quickly, physically or emotionally. Some of these girls at fourteen wear makeup, are five feet eight, and have developed physically. That didn't happen to me." Austin felt that her early wins were a disservice to subsequent young players, putting incredible pressure on them to follow her lead. "I *never* expected to win the U.S. Open at sixteen. . . . There wasn't any pressure, it just happened." Tracy Austin was the youngest player ever inducted into the International Tennis Hall of Fame.

SOURCES:
King, Billie Jean. *We Have Come a Long Way*. McGraw-Hill, 1988.

Austrebertha (635–704)

Medieval abbess. Born in 635; died in 704; daughter of Count Badefroi of the Palatine and Frametilda.

Much admired as a holy woman, Austrebertha was the child of Count Badefroi of the Palatine and **Frametilda**, who was canonized. Badefroi and Frametilda tried to arrange a marriage for their daughter to a local noble when she was 16, but Austrebertha refused to go along with her parents' wishes; she preferred to live as a servant of God. To escape the wedding, the young woman secretly took the vows of a nun from a local bishop. During her long life as a holy woman, Austrebertha served as abbess at two establishments, in Port and later in Pavilly. Her noble birth and extreme dedication to serving God influenced the lives of many young noblewomen, who took Austrebertha as their model in freeing themselves from matrimonial ties. The abbess' charitable works and leadership abilities gained her the admiration of believers across Western Europe.

Laura York,
Anza, California

Austria, archduchess of.

See Visconti, Virida (1350–1414).
See Eleanor Stewart (d. 1496).
See Joanna of Austria (1546–1578).
See Elizabeth of Habsburg (1554–1592).
See Gonzaga, Anna Caterina (1566–1621).
See Isabella Clara Eugenia (1566–1633).
See Maria Antonia of Austria (1683–1754).
See Alexandra Pavlovna (1783–1801).
See Maria of Wurttemberg (1797–1855).
See Sophie of Bavaria (1805–1872).
See Maria Annunziata (1843–1871).
See Augusta of Tuscany (1825–1864).
See Marie Annunziata of Naples (d. 1877).
See Elizabeth (1831–1903).
See Maria Theresa of Portugal (1855–1944).
See Marie Valerie (1868–1924).
See Maria Cristina of Sicily (1877–1947).
See Elizabeth von Habsburg (1883–1963).
See Ileana (1909–1991).

Austria, duchess of.

See Margaret of Babenberg (fl. 1252).
See Cunigunde of Hungary (d. 1285).
See Agnes of Bohemia (1269–1297).
See Johanna of Pfirt (1300–1351).

See Elizabeth of Bohemia (1358–1373).
See Beatrice of Brandenburg (1360–1414).
See Johanna of Bavaria (c. 1373–1410).
See Catherine of Burgundy (1378–1425).
See Cimburca of Masovia (c. 1396–1429).
See Elizabeth of Luxemburg (1409–1442).
See Mary of Bavaria (1551–1608).

Austria, empress of.

See Maria Theresa of Austria (1717–1780).
See Maria Josepha of Bavaria (1739–1767).
See Maria Louisa of Spain (1745–1792).
See Maria Teresa of Naples (1772–1807).
See Maria Ludovica of Modena (1787–1816).
See Maria Anna of Savoy (1803–1884).
See Elizabeth of Bavaria (1837–1898).

Austrian Tyrol, archduchess of.

See Medici, Claudia de (1604–1648).

Auvergne, duchess of (1606–1627).

See Montpensier, Anne Marie Louise d'Orléans, duchesse de for sidebar on Marie de Bourbon.

Auzello, Blanche (d. 1969).

See Rubenstein, Blanche.

Auzou, Pauline Desmarquets (1775–1835)

French painter. Name variations: Mme Auzou; Pauline Desmarquêts Auzou. Born in Paris in 1775; died in 1835; studied under Regnault.

Influenced by *Marguérite Gérard, Pauline Auzou began painting interior scenes in the 1790s, portraying young women reading or playing musical instruments. She won a *médaille de première classe* with this theme in 1808. Her most popular works were French historical paintings and portraits, including *Diana of France and Montmorency*. Several of her pictures have been engraved.

Ava of Melk (d. 1127)

German religious writer. Name variations: Frau Ava. Birth date unknown; died in 1127 in Melk, Austria; married; two children.

Few facts are available on Ava of Melk, but she is the earliest female writer known to have written in German. Her high level of literacy suggests that she was born into the nobility, as does the fact that she retired to a convent but was not a nun, an option reserved for those women who could bring money or property to the convent for their support. As for her life prior to the convent, she records in one of her books that she had been married and had borne two children, retiring to the convent at Melk after her husband died. Her works, all composed at Melk, were poems and prose in German with themes from the New Testament, as well as translations of saints' lives.

Laura York,
Anza, California

Avedon, Barbara Hammer

(1930–1994)

American television writer who, with Barbara Corday, created "Cagney and Lacey." Name variations: Barbara Hammer (ceased using her married name in the 1990s). Born Barbara Hammer in New York City in 1930; died in Palm Springs, California, on August 31, 1994; married and divorced; children: one son, Josh.

Television credits, 1969–1983: (co-written with Barbara Corday) episodes of "The Doctors," "Medical Center," "Maude," "Sons and Daughters," "Fish," "Trapper John, M.D.," "Grandpa Goes To Washington," "Harper Valley PTA," "Turnabout; (co-creator of the series) "Cagney and Lacey"; television movie: "This Girl For Hire" (1983).

Barbara Hammer Avedon

Though Barbara Avedon is most known for her work in television, her final piece of writing appeared in a periodical called *The Desert Woman*. The last line reads, "Each star in the ink black sky reminds us that if we do right, our light will shine long after we are gone." It is a fitting tribute to the co-creator of "Cagney and Lacey," the first television series to give the viewing public a crime show in which the two central characters were female.

A longtime political activist, Avedon met **Barbara Corday** in 1968 when Corday joined the grassroots antiwar organization begun by Avedon and actress *Donna Reed. Called Another Mother For Peace, the group made famous the slogan, "War is not healthy for children and other living things." Soon after, Avedon and Corday became writing partners. For the next few years, the team wrote for many successful episodic television shows. In 1974, they created and wrote the original pilot script for the series "Cagney and Lacey." It took the partners (plus Corday's then-husband Barney Rosenzweig) another eight years to convince a network (CBS) to back it.

The series, which starred **Tyne Daly** and **Sharon Gless**, looked at the lives and careers of two New York City women detectives. As **Gloria Emerson** of *Vogue* noted, "Daly plays a woman (Mary Beth Lacey) of principles, who runs out of hand lotion from time to time, wishes she could see more of her husband, Harvey, and have time for her kids." Gless' character, Christine Cagney, was Lacey's opposite. Single, pretty and datable, Cagney was in Emerson's words, "sweeter, more accommodating." Fortunately for the audience, the producers allowed the character room to grow. In the 1984–85 season, John Leonard of *New York Magazine* said, "The series is really about friendship and increasingly about adult sexuality, especially Cagney's . . . the sexuality on *Cagney and Lacey* is complicated by intelligence and doubt. . . . On Monday nights, I am watching grown-ups."

Ironically, though the series, which ran from March 1982 to August 1988, was never a ratings grabber, it nonetheless changed forever the way women are portrayed on television and will likely continue to be seen in syndication, as Avedon said, "long after we are gone."

SOURCES:

Emerson, Gloria. "The Rewards of Tough Police," in *Vogue*. May 1983.

Hammer, Barbara. "A Desert Woman's Reflection," in *The Desert Woman*. Vol. 1, Issue 1, November 1994, pp. 12–13.

Leonard, John. *New York Magazine* November 26, 1984.

Thuna, Leonora. *The Journal of the Writers Guild of America*. October 1994.

Uhnak, Dorothy. "I'd Walk Through A Dark Alley with Cagney or Lacey Behind Me: A Female Cop's Testimonial," in *TV Guide*. February 2, 1985.

Deborah Jones, freelance writer,
Studio City, California

Avelina de Forz (1259–1274).

See Isabella de Redvers for sidebar.

Avellaneda, La (1814–1873).

See Gómez de Avellaneda, Gertrudis.

Averina, Tatiana (1951—)

Russian speedskater. Name variations: Tatyana. Born in the USSR in 1951; grew up and trained in the central Russian city of Gorky.

Won the Olympic gold medal in 1,000 and 3,000 meters and a bronze in the 500 and 1,500 meters (1976); won world championship (1978).

The Soviet speedskater Tatiana Averina held the world records in the 500, 1,000, and 1,500 meters when she entered the 1976 Olympics at Innsbruck, Austria. The 25-year-old college student won the gold in the 1,000 meters with an Olympic record of 1:28.43. *Leah Poulos Mueller came in 14/100ths of a second behind her. Averina took a second gold in the 3,000 meters with an Olympic record of 4:45.19, ahead of East Germany's *Andrea Mitscherlich Schöne. Though *Sheila Young took the 500 meter, third-place finisher Averina also broke the Olympic record in that event. Galina Stepanskaya, a last-minute addition to the Soviet skating team, took the 1,500, while Averina came in third.

Avice or Avisa of Gloucester
(c. 1167–1217).

See Isabella of Angoulême for sidebar.

Avoie (c. 915–965).
See Hedwig.

Awashonks (fl. mid-late 17th c.)

Sunksquaw of the Sakonnet tribe. Name variations: The Queen. Born Awashonks in the middle to late 1600s in the vicinity of present-day Little Compton, Rhode Island; death date unknown; married Tolony.

Though *sunksquaw* is the title given the hereditary female head of state of the Wampanoag Confederacy tribes, Awashonks was one of the numerous women warriors misidentified as a queen by early British colonists. Along with *Wetamoo and *Magnus, Awashonks participated as a tribal chieftain during Metacom's (King Philip's) War (1675–76). Unlike her counterparts, when she was forced to surrender, Awashonks convinced her warriors to fight with the British, in order to save her people from being sold into slavery in the West Indies.

SOURCES:
Allen, Paula Gunn. *The Sacred Hoop: Recovering the Feminine in American Indian Traditions.* Boston, MA: Beacon, 1986.

Deborah Jones, freelance writer, Studio City, California

Awolowo, Hannah (1915—)

Nigerian businesswoman and philanthropist whose early ventures in trade grew into a business empire that generated the fortune that allowed her husband to devote himself to politics as a nationalist leader. Name variations: Chief (Mrs) H.I.D. Awolowo, Mama H.I.D. Born Hannah Idowu Dideolu Adelana on November 25, 1915, at Ikenne Remo, Nigeria; daughter of Chief Moses Odugbemi Adelana (a prince) and Elizabeth Oyesile-Adelana (a businesswoman and member of Nigerian royalty); attended Saint Saviour's Anglican School, Saint Peter's School, and Methodist Girls' High School in Lagos; married Obafemi Awolowo (a journalist), on December 26, 1937; children: Segun, Olusegun, Omotola, Oluwole, and Ayo.

Entered business after the departure of her husband to study in England (1944); founded Dideolu Stores Ltd., Ligu Distribution Services Ltd. (after 1946); backed the founding of The Nigerian Tribune, later expanded to include the African Newspapers of Nigeria Ltd., and African Press Ltd. (1949); husband became prime minister of the western region of Nigeria (1951); Chief Obafemi lost bid for national leadership (1959); Obafemi, arrested for treason, began 10-year imprisonment (1962); Obafemi released after government coup (1966); Awolowo campaigned for her husband in two unsuccessful bids for the national presidency (1979 and 1983); continued her philanthropic activities after her husband's death (1987); awarded the 1,000-year-old chieftaincy title of Yeye-Oba for life (1980).

Hannah Idowu Dideolu Adelana was born into a polygamous household, the daughter of the second of her father's three wives, and the only one of the seven children borne by her mother to survive long after birth. She grew up in a lively and happy home, filled with nine half-brothers and half-sisters. Hannah's father was Chief Moses Odugbemi Adelana, a prince with connections to Nigerian royalty; her mother, **Elizabeth Oyesile-Adelana**, was related to the Onijagba royal family, and came from a long line of businesswomen who had grown wealthy through trade.

Members of the large Adelana household were also Christian, and Hannah began her elementary education at age six at the Saint Saviour's Anglican School. In 1928, when she was 13, she went to Saint Peter's School in Lagos, then on to Methodist Girls' High School. In Lagos, she and a half-sister shared a rented room where they were visited regularly by her mother. Hannah learned to prefer school to vacations, because when she returned home, her younger brothers and sisters would be excused from the heavy domestic chores that were turned over to her. But during these times, she also traveled with her mother on her business trips in the textile trade and learned a great deal about the fundamentals of business. Although classmates of hers may have had easier lives, she never regretted the parental discipline, which she later felt had prepared her for the rigors of her adult life.

At age 19, Hannah finished college and returned to teach at Saint Savior's Anglican School. Although she was comfortable economically, business had become as natural to her as breathing, and soon she was making additional money as a seamstress and through the import of hats and other items. While still a teacher, Hannah met Obafemi Awolowo through mutual friends. Soon she began to receive long handwritten letters from Awolowo, who was a journalist with a passionate interest in politics, and the two were married on December 26, 1937, after a three-year courtship. Their first child was a son, Segun, born in 1939, followed by Olusegun, Omotola, Oluwole, and Ayo over the next several years.

[Hannah Awolowo] is a resourceful business woman, and . . . a worthy upholder of the traditions of her mother and grandmother both of whom are successful women traders. With my wife on my side, it has been possible for us to weather all financial storms.

—Chief Obafemi Awolowo

Shortly after their marriage, Obafemi decided that he did not want his wife to work and forbade her to engage in trading. In 1944, when he departed for two years to study law in London, he gave Hannah, then pregnant with their fifth child, £20 (a considerable sum at the time) to provide for the family. Until this time Hannah Awolowo had respected her husband's wishes, but now she withdrew the entire amount from the bank and bought foodstuffs, which she resold at profit. Reinvesting, she watched her earnings grow and made enough money to return her husband's £20 pounds, which reached London at a time when Obafemi was destitute. After that, he never again forbade his wife's business ventures.

When Obafemi returned from his studies in 1946, his perspective had changed. In London, he had become enmeshed in politics, and he was now gripped by the idea of independence for Nigeria. "The entire continent of Africa must be free," he told his wife, "and the dignity of the black man re-stored to him." When he expressed his desire to enter politics, she agreed to a plan that gave him her full moral and economic support.

Hannah opened a small shop at the rear of their home where she sold European textiles. The business was doing well when Obafemi was elected to the West Region House and appointed Leader of Government Business. Expanding the business to a shop on the market square, she also became a distributor for beer and tobacco products, establishing a sales network that expanded eventually throughout Nigeria. This enterprise was a source of some conflict, as Obafemi never smoked or drank and was opposed to the profits made in this way, but eventually he submitted to the arguments of Hannah and their children that these products were legal and enjoyed by millions of Nigerians. Under her control, the distributorships grew into Didelou Stores Ltd. and Ligu Distribution Services Ltd.

In 1949, Obafemi founded *The Nigerian Tribune*, a national daily, with money earned by his wife. Under her guidance, this venture grew into a network of newspapers, journals, and magazines, and she became chair of African Newspapers of Nigeria Ltd. and African Press Ltd. While she advanced their corporate empire, Obafemi became a national political figure and a writer of books, including *Path to Nigerian Freedom*, *The People's Republic*, and *Thoughts on Nigerian Constitution*.

In 1951, Obafemi was president of the Action Group Party (AG), which won the elections in the western region of Nigeria, where he headed the new government and became prime minister under a new constitution in 1954. As a regional leader, Obafemi sponsored many innovative programs that were new to Africa, introducing free primary education for all school-age children in 1954 and establishing the first television station in the whole of black Africa in 1959. In 1960, he opened a first-class sports facility, the Liberty Stadium, in Ibadan.

By 1959, Obafemi had built the AG party into a national political power through which he hoped to gain control of the national government, but he failed to win in the elections. A new government was formed under Nnamdi Azikiwe and his party, the National Council of Nigeria and the Cameroons (NCNC). The political loss set up a chain of events that were to have a disastrous impact on the Awolowo family. Since Nigerian party loyalty usually followed tribal origins, most members of AG were Yorubas, like the Awolowos, while most members of the

NCNC were Ibos. Under their new parliamentary form of government operating after Nigerian independence, Obafemi Awolowo was the leader of the loyal opposition; but the traditions of parliamentary rule were not yet strong enough to overcome tribal hostility, and Azikiwe and the NCNC set out to obliterate the opposition party.

In 1962, the Awolowos were experiencing unbounded success. Obafemi was poised for national office, Hannah's business ventures were thriving, their eldest son had become a lawyer, and their four other children were in the process of completing their educations. Then a series of swift moves by the Azikiwe administration placed Obafemi under house arrest. Thousands demonstrated in vain against his incarceration, but the police began to appear at the house, all hours, day and night, to question the couple and search the house for incriminating documents. A fruitless search only angered the police and caused them to leave the house in a shambles.

On November 2, 1962, Obafemi was arrested with 18 other members of his party and charged with treason; if convicted, he faced a death sentence. When the case went to trial, Hannah sat stoically in the courtroom day after day. Thrice daily, she visited the jail to take her husband home-cooked meals. Segun, a 23-year-old attorney, became her main support, accompanying her to prison, taking over his father's duties, and managing details of his mother's business, until one morning when he was killed in a car accident on his way to visit his father in prison. When Hannah returned home from viewing her son's body in the morgue, the police had again searched the house and left the possessions of the family strewn over the floor.

The nightmare continued. After a long trial, Obafemi was sentenced to ten years in Calabar prison, where regular visits were prohibited. For four years, Hannah saw him as often as she was allowed, tended her businesses, and looked after her family, until a coup felled the government in 1966. Obafemi was released by its leader, Colonel Gowon.

Known as an honest man who never took a bribe, Obafemi had introduced many innovative programs to Nigeria. His main fault seemed to be that his success as an able and honest administrator gave him more political stature than the opposition could tolerate. Obafemi later remarked on how ironic it was that he, who had given so much of his life to gain independence for Nigeria, had spent the first years of his country's newly won freedom in jail.

After the release of Obafemi, the Awolowo family remained out of public view for many years. In 1979, when her husband decided to run for the presidency, Hannah consented reluctantly to the plan. She toured the country with him for the Unity Party of Nigeria (UPN), but Obafemi lost, then ran and lost again in 1983. On May 9, 1987, Chief Awolowo died in his sleep. His passing was marked by the closing of markets for two days, and more than a million Nigerians attended his funeral.

Obafemi Awolowo would have given most of the credit for his remarkable career to the woman he called "a jewel of inestimable value." He often named the three factors in his life to which he owed his success as "the grace of God, a spartan self-discipline, and a good wife." For most of their marriage, Hannah Awolowo was the family's sole breadwinner, and while funding her husband's political career, she gave his aspirations her full support, allowing him to chart an independent political course, and making him beholden to no one.

After her husband's death, Hannah Awolowo made large donations to the Methodist Girls' High School, the Ikenne Community Hospital, and the Awolowo Memorial Museum. In memory of her husband, she sponsored the building of the Obafemi Awolowo Memorial Anglican Church, and she became widely known for her many philanthropic contributions throughout the country. **Tola Adeniyi** documented Hannah Awolowo's remarkable life in her book, *The Jewel: The Biography of Chief (Mrs) H.I.D. Awolowo.*

In 1980, Hannah's contributions to the people of Nigeria were recognized when she was awarded the title of Yeye-Oba for life. Among her people, few women ever achieved the rank of "chief," and fewer still have been raised to this high rank of chieftaincy, recognized for a thousand years.

SOURCES:

Adeniyi, Tola. *The Jewel: The Biography of Chief (Mrs) H.I.D. Awolowo.* Ibandan, Nigeria: Gemini Press, 1993.

Akinola, Anthony. "Politics without Awo," in *West Africa.* No. 3642, June 1, 1987, pp. 1040–1041.

"Awo's Last Journey," in *West Africa.* No. 3643, June 8, 1987, pp. 1088–1089.

"Awolowo's Burial," in *West Africa.* No. 3641, May 25, 1987, pp. 996–997.

"Chief Awolowo's Legacy," in *West Africa.* No. 3640, May 18, 1987, p. 947.

"A Flood of Tributes," in *West Africa*. No. 3640, May 18, 1987, pp. 952 and 980.

Leith-Ross, Sylvia. *African Women. A Study of the Ibo of Nigeria*. NY: Frederick A. Praeger, 1965.

Mba, Nina Emma. *Nigerian Women Mobilized. Women's Political Activity in Southern Nigeria, 1900–1965*. Berkeley, CA: Institute of International Studies, 1982.

Obe, Ad'Obe. "Succeeding Oduduwa," in *West Africa*. No. 3640, May 18, 1987, pp. 950–952.

Okutubo, Taiwo. "Awo Comes Home," in *West Africa*. No. 3644, June 15, 1987, p. 1140.

Williams, David. "A Personal Memoir," in *West Africa*. No. 3640, May 18, 1987, p. 948.

Karin Loewen Haag, freelance writer, Athens, Georgia

Awura Pokou (c. 1700–c. 1760).

See Pokou.

Axelrod, Luibo (1868–1946).

See Akselrod, Luibo.

Axiothea of Phlius.

See joint entry under Lasthenia of Mantinea.

Axioti, Melpo (c. 1906–c. 1973)

Greek novelist and poet. Name variations: Melpo Axiote. Born around 1906 in Athens, Greece; died around 1973.

Selected novels: Difficult Nights *(1938);* Would You Like to Dance, Maria? *(1940);* Twentieth Century *(?);* Cadmo *(1972). Poetry:* Coincidence *(1939);* Contraband *(1959). Non-Fiction:* Chronicles *(1945).*

Harriet Hubbard Ayer

Melpo Axioti, a Greek author who wrote extensively in both prose and verse, was born around 1906 in Athens, Greece. When she was a young girl, her mother abandoned the family, and Axioti was raised by her father. From 1918–22, she attended school at a Roman Catholic convent on the island of Tinos. While there, Axioti acquired a strong command of French language and literature. By 1930, she returned to Athens. In 1938, she published her first novel, *Difficult Nights,* which generated mixed reviews. Shortly after, Axioti completed a collection of poems, *Coincidence*

(1939), and another novel, *Would You Like to Dance, Maria?* (1940). In 1940, she became a member of the Communist Party along with other prominent female writers in Greece. Indeed, her political affiliation is frequently reflected in her work. Sent into exile in 1947, Axioti fled to France and subsequently to East Germany, where, at the Classics Institute of Humboldt University, she taught Modern Greek. She returned to her homeland in 1964. In later years, she continued to publish poetry and fiction. Melpo Axioti died in 1973, and her funeral roused demonstrations in the streets of Athens.

M.C. English, Boston University, Boston, Massachusetts

Axis Sally (1900–1988).

See Gillars, Mildred E.

Axmatova, Anna (1889–1966).

See Akhmatova, Anna.

Ayala, Josefa de (1630–1684).

See de Ayala, Josefa.

Ayer, Harriet Hubbard (1849–1903)

American cosmetics entrepreneur and journalist. Born Harriet Hubbard in Chicago, Illinois, in 1849; died in 1903; graduated from the Convent of the Sacred Heart, Chicago, Illinois; married Herbert C. Ayer (divorced); children: two daughters.

Harriet Hubbard Ayer's great beauty, facility with words, and business savvy came together out of necessity and turned her into one of the first cosmetic notables of the 19th century. After her marriage to wealthy Chicago businessman Herbert C. Ayer ended, and he subsequently lost his fortune, Ayer was left to support herself and her two small daughters. After close to 20 years as a wealthy society matron, she went to work as a saleswoman in a fashionable New York furniture store. Turning her "fall from grace" into an advantage, she soon had a cadre of special customers and was making business trips to Europe to find special pieces of furniture for them, often calling on the very people she had once known in her more leisurely past life.

On one such junket abroad, Ayer visited M. Mirault, a chemist in Paris, who had, in better days, made the special violet Parma perfume that had become Ayer's trademark. On an impulse, Ayer purchased from him the formula for a cream his grandfather had supposedly made for *Mme Récamier, the famous beauty who had plotted against Napoleon (and had used the potion for 40 years with, some say, stunning results). In 1886, with hopes of manufacturing the cream herself, Ayer obtained $50,000 backing from a rich Chicago customer, James Seymour, who insisted that she put her own name on the product.

Ayer continued to sell furniture by day, while at night she perfected her formula. It was her promotions, however, that pushed the concoction over the top and set a new standard for cosmetic publicity. She crafted imaginative pamphlets about Récamier's beauty secrets and how she had discovered them. Since medical ointments were the most socially accepted of the day, Ayer first claimed that the cream was a remedy for sunburn. She used the endorsements of society friends and a testimonial by actress and beauty *Lillie Langtry—who must have relished the idea of the elixir, having reportedly been known to "rub her face with minced raw meat." Ayer went so far as to put the Hubbard coat of arms, as well as her name, on the jars, a personal approach so revolutionary and shocking that an ardent suitor who had proposed marriage suddenly broke off the relationship.

Due to a bizarre turn of events, Ayer's success lasted only a few years. She was reportedly sued by her original backer James Seymour because, as one story goes, she refused his advances. (To further complicate matters, her daughter Hattie had married Seymour's son Lewis.) Seymour, in another strange twist, supposedly convinced Hattie to commit her mother to an insane asylum. Hattie complied. When Ayer was released, she took up the cause of treatment of the insane and helped organize legal help for similar victims. The cosmetic business was all but forgotten.

In 1896, Ayer resurfaced on the staff of the New York *World*, writing a beauty column for the new woman's page in the Sunday edition. She soon became as well known for her "working-woman's costume," with a skirt cut off a full four inches from the floor, as she did for her health and beauty advice. In 1899, she published a bestseller, *Harriet Hubbard Ayer's Book: A Complete and Authentic Treatise on the Laws of Health and Beauty*. She continued to experiment with creams and deodorants, and even a formula for straightening hair (which would eventually make a fortune for *Madame C.J. Walker).

Following Ayer's death in 1903, the right to her cosmetic products and the use of her name were sold by her heirs. Forty years later, the cosmetic industry was the 20th largest in the United States, with an estimated half billion dollars spent on improving the appearance of the female population. The floodgates opened to scores of profiteers, mostly men. Women, too, like *Helena Rubenstein and *Elizabeth Arden followed in Ayer's footsteps and became some of the biggest female money makers of the 20th century.

SOURCES:
Bird, Caroline. *Enterprising Women*. NY: W.W. Norton, 1976.

Barbara Morgan,
Melrose, Massachusetts

Ayesha (c. 613–678).
See A'ishah bint Abi Bakr.

Ayling, Jean (1894–1976).
See Wrinch, Dorothy.

Aylward, Gladys (1902–1970)

English missionary in China and Taiwan who worked to end the traditional Chinese practice of binding women's feet, led a large group of orphans out of occupied China, and set up orphanages in Hong Kong and Taiwan. Name variations: Ai-weh-deh, Ai Weh Teh, Hsiao Fu-jeh. Pronunciation: AIL-wood. Born Gladys May Aylward on February 24, 1902, in Edmonton, north of London, England; died of influenza on January 2, 1970, in Taipei, Taiwan; daughter of a postman and a postal worker; left school at 14; at 28, studied for three months at the China Inland Mission in London; never married; children: adopted five officially, many unofficially.

Left school to work as a shop assistant; later went into domestic service; became an evangelical Christian at age 18 (1920); began training at the China Inland Mission but was not recommended for further training (1928); went back into domestic service in London; finally departed for China (1930); settled in Yangcheng in Shensi (or Shansi) province; helped set up an inn and appointed Inspector of Feet; adopted Chinese nationality (1936); led about 100 orphans out of war-torn China to safety in Sian (1940); worked in Tsingsui, near Lanchow in northwest China (1944); moved to Chengtu, Szechwan, where she continued her missionary work and was appointed Biblewoman at the Chinese Seminary (1945); returned to England (1949); went to Hong Kong and then Taiwan, settling in Taipei where she set up an orphanage (1957).

In late April 1940, an oxcart stopped outside the Scandinavian-American Mission in Hsing-P'ing (Xingping), northwest China, to deliver the fragile body of a 38-year-old Western woman who was delirious and on the verge of death. Across her back, she bore the scar of a recent bullet wound. Sent to the hospital in Sian

(Xi'an), she was diagnosed with typhoid fever and internal injuries, but a month passed before she was identified. She was Gladys Aylward, also called Ai-weh-deh (the Virtuous One), a Christian evangelist who had brought many children to safety from behind the Japanese lines. Remarkably, Aylward survived, believing that God had more work for her to do.

Gladys May Aylward was born in north London on February 24, 1902, and grew up a high-spirited, happy child. "She remembered her father coming home," wrote her biographer Alan Burgess, "clumping up the road in his heavy postman's boots." Her mother would be in the kitchen preparing tea, while Gladys and her sister Violet would be "screaming around the house or running wild with the other children in the street." During World War I, when the Zeppelins came over to bomb London, wrote Burgess:

Gladys Aylward

> she remembered how she'd first discovered the antidote to being "frightened." She would bring all the children in the street into

the front parlor and sit them down against the inside wall. Then she would sit at the tiny old foot-operated organ, pedal furiously and scream out a hymn at a decibel scale calculated to reach almost as high as those ominous silver cocoons droning through the sky.

Aylward tried hard as a student, but she did not fare well at school. At age 14, she quit to work in a penny bazaar and then a grocer's shop. At the cessation of war, she went into domestic service as a parlormaid in London's West End. Aylward loved being in the heart of the big city, and in particular going to the theater. Like many young girls, she dreamed of becoming an actress.

Though she had been brought up a Christian, Aylward's only religious experience was going to Sunday school. She was 18 on the evening she allowed herself, somewhat against her will, to be led by a group of young evangelicals into a church meeting. When it was over, writes **Phyllis Thompson**:

> She was hurrying to get away . . . when someone at the door grasped her hand, enquired her name, and then said, "Miss Aylward, I believe God is wanting you." Gladys was alarmed. "No fear!" she said quickly, "I don't want any of that!"

But the encounter must have made a strong impression. Aylward went back to see the cleric of the church and decided to join the movement. "Her friends," wrote Burgess, "seeing which way her inclinations were turning, declared quite bluntly that she was 'barmy.' 'Don't be silly, Glad,' they protested. . . . '[L]et's go phone those nice chaps we met in the park.'"

Sometime after, in her late 20s, Aylward read a newspaper commentary about China and the millions of people who had never heard of the Gospel. The article was to change her life. She sought training at the China Inland Mission (C.I.M.) in London, but she soon found the study of theology and languages difficult. After three months in the program, the chair of the C.I.M. committee reported: "It is with great regret that I have to recommend to you that we do not accept Miss Aylward. She has a call to serve God—she is sincere and courageous—but we cannot take the responsibility of sending a woman of 26, with such limited Christian experience and education, to China." She was also too old, he felt, to learn the Chinese language.

Aylward knew her weaknesses and appreciated the mission's concern that she would find it hard to learn a Chinese dialect. She remained convinced, however, that God meant her to serve in China. Sent by the C.I.M. to Bristol to work as housekeeper for a retired missionary couple who had just returned from China, she learned a great deal through stories of their experiences and their deep faith in God.

Aylward next went to work as a Rescue Sister of "fallen women" near the docks of Swansea in South Wales. There, the five-foot, 110-pound Aylward wandered the streets, talking to the homeless, penniless women and girls, and led them back to the hostel run by the mission for down-and-outs. The younger prostitutes thanked her; the older ones began treating her with "tolerant amusement."

"Although these experiences had strengthened Gladys' spirit," wrote Burgess, "they had added nothing to her bank balance. It became more and more obvious that if she was ever going to get to China . . . she would have to pay her own fare." The only way she knew to make money was as a housemaid, so she returned to London, bent on saving up enough to travel to the East by herself. But the first day at her new post in Belgrave Square, she began to despair of ever reaching China. Sitting alone on her bed in her new quarters, she placed the few coins she had on her Bible and cried out, "Oh God, here's my Bible! Here's my money! Here's me! Use me!" At that moment her door was opened by a housemaid calling Aylward downstairs; their mistress wished to reimburse her for her travel fare. Those three shillings became a sign from God, the beginning of her fund toward a ticket to China. "In spirit," wrote Burgess, "she was half way there."

Aylward worked evenings and weekends to earn money. The people at the railway ticket office tried to explain to her that the cheapest way to China was by water and would cost £90. Yes, they agreed, there was an even cheaper way—overland through Holland, Germany, Poland, and Russia, then through Siberia on the Trans-Siberian Railroad, until she made a junction connection with the Manchurian railway, which would take her to a steamer that would take her to Tientsin—but that route was impossible because there was an undeclared war on between Russia and China. Realizing that their unlikely traveler was not to be deterred from making the long, dangerous journey, they allowed her to pay little by little on her ticket toward the full amount.

As yet, Aylward had no specific destination in China. She learned of a 73-year-old missionary named **Jeannie Lawson**, who, upon returning to England, was immediately miserable and went back to China. Lawson was seeking a young person to help her continue her work. Aylward wrote to her, and the two agreed to meet at Tientsin (Tianjin). On October 18, 1930, Aylward finally set out from Liverpool Street Station on her arduous overland journey with two £1 traveler's checks and ninepence sewn into her corset. She carried two suitcases. One held her clothes; the other contained corned beef, fish, beans, crackers, soda biscuits, rye crisp, tea, coffee, hard-boiled eggs, a sauce pan, a kettle, and an alcohol stove.

Ten days later, she crossed into Siberia. As the train progressed, soldiers got on and civilians got off at each stop. At the town of Chita, a railway official tried to persuade her to disembark, but Aylward could not understand what he was saying and insisted on staying aboard. Hours later, the train halted, the lights went out, and the soldiers got off. Aylward was now alone, and at the front line of the war about which she had been warned. With no choice other than to make the long walk back down the tracks to Chita, she carried her baggage through the freezing snow, trusting in God to protect her.

From Chita, Aylward managed to find her way to Vladivostok, where she was to make another connection. Though she had paid her fare from London to Tientsin, it soon became apparent that her ticket was useless. She was also nearly penniless, and officials, desperate for skilled factory workers, wanted to keep her in Russia. While in her hotel, she was approached by an English-speaking woman who warned her that if she did not get out of the country immediately she might be sent to a remote part of Russia and never be heard from again. Scrutinizing Aylward's passport, the stranger pointed out that an official had changed Aylward's profession from missionary to machinist. The woman arranged for Aylward's escape and travel by the first ship out. Its destination: Japan.

In Kobe, Japan, Aylward was able to stay at the Mission Hall before turning in her unused vouchers for a steamer to Tientsin. There, she was told that Mrs. Lawson was in a mission at Tsechow in Shensi (Shaanxi) province, north of the Yellow River in northwest China, many weeks away by train, bus, and mule. A Mr. Lu offered to escort her. When they arrived at the mission, they were told that Lawson was in Yangcheng (Yangzheng), a walled town two days away, along an ancient mule trail between Honan and Hopeh. The country, she was warned, was unpenetrated by Christianity. Wild and mountainous, the area was filled with bandits, immense stretches of lonely roads, and primitive people who thought all foreigners were devils.

Aylward finally found Lawson living in a house on the main road outside the city gate, amid private houses and inns. Though the house was a wreck, it was large and had a courtyard, and Lawson wanted to turn it into an inn for muleteers. Her plan was to read Bible stories at night to the guests, who would then spread news of the inn as they traveled the country. The Inn of Eight Happinesses was soon opened and quickly boycotted. When the local inhabitants weren't throwing clods of earth at Aylward or calling her a foreign devil, they were dragging her to witness judicial beheadings. It became Aylward's job to stand in the road when a mule-train appeared, announcing, "*Muyo beatch, muyo goodso, how, how, how, lai, lai, lai.*" ("We have no bugs, we have no fleas, good, good, good, come, come, come."), then grab the head of the lead mule to pull it into the inn.

Aylward also accompanied Lawson on her visits to neighboring villages to preach and tell stories. ("The story I'm going to tell you tonight, concerns a man called Jesus Christ whose honorable ancestor was the Great God who lived in the clouds high above.") Gradually, she picked up the local dialect. A year later, the 74-year-old Lawson fell off a balustrade and was severely injured. Before she died, she told Aylward: "God called you to my side, Gladys; He wants you to carry on His work here. He will provide. He will bless and protect you."

By this time, a government decree had been passed in China, prohibiting the tradition of binding the feet of girls at birth. In the view of the ancients, binding stunted the foot's natural growth, keeping it small but attractive. The local mandarin, a powerful figure responsible for the administration of Yangcheng, needed a woman with "big feet," who had not been crippled by the custom, to travel throughout the province and verify that the cruel tradition was no longer being observed. Thus, Gladys Aylward, who wore a size three, became Inspector of Feet, traveling the province on a mule accompanied by two soldiers. For this job, she received one daily measure of millet and money for vegetables, recompense that was sorely needed at the mission at Yangcheng. After capitalizing on the opportunity at every village to tell her stories, Aylward would then state her case to the women plainly:

> If God intended little girls to have horrible stubby little feet, he'd have made them like that in the first place, wouldn't he? Feet are to walk with, not to shuffle up and down

with, aren't they? I don't care if the husbands say you should do it or not. They should try it sometimes, and see if they like hobbling about on little club feet. Any man who tells you to do it goes to prison at once; that's the law now.

Generally, as girls were unbound, wiggling their toes with delight, the women of the town would cheer. Gladys Aylward had gained "much face."

Aylward's years at the inn were happy. "This is indeed my country and these are my people," she wrote her family. "I live now completely as a Chinese woman. I wear their clothes, eat their food, speak their language—even their dialect—and I am thinking like they do." Aylward's religion was never a complex, theoretical spirituality but a simple belief in God's power for good, which relied on humility, love, and faith. She didn't try to inflict Christian morality. Always penniless and living among the people she helped, she was driven by a compassion for human suffering.

In 1936, Aylward became a naturalized Chinese citizen. By that time, China and Japan had been pursuing an undeclared war for several years. In July 1937, the full-scale, official Sino-Japanese war was underway. The following year, when the Japanese bombing reached Yangcheng, one raid destroyed the town as well as the inn. Aylward was rescued from beneath the rubble. Amid the chaos, she improvised a hospital and established small Christian communities in the region, sometimes visiting villages under Japanese occupation and reporting any observations on her travels that might prove useful to the Chinese Nationalists. She had been asked to work in this capacity by a young Chinese colonel, a member of Chiang Kai-shek's intelligence service, who had set up headquarters in her city. Yangcheng was considered an important military objective and changed hands several times, often forcing the townspeople into caves in the hills. Aylward began to report regularly to the colonel and in the process fell in love. Wrote Burgess:

> They talked at odd moments in between battles and births and baptisms. They exchanged scraps of news, had a meal together, talked of the future they would build in the new China. His concern, his gentleness, his tenderness toward her never wavered. They discussed marriage; he was eager that they should marry at once, live together as man and wife as best they could, war or no war. It was Gladys who said, "No." The war had to be won first. . . . She wrote to her family in faraway England and told them that she was going to marry a Chinese, and hoped that they would understand.

She would later learn that she had waited too long; she and her Chinese colonel would go their separate ways.

The war left many children orphaned, and most of those in Yangcheng were brought to Aylward, who lived in the bombed out inn. Eventually, she found herself in charge of more than 200 unruly children, including five of her own that she had officially adopted. She taught them lessons, read them stories from the Bible, and begged food from everyone, including the Japanese, to keep them fed. Aware that Madame Chiang Kai-shek (*Song Meiling) had started a fund for government-run orphanages, Aylward wrote for help and was told that the children would be looked after if she could get them to Sian, in Free China, and that money would be sent for the work of the Mission in Yangcheng. Aylward directed one of her converts, Tsin Pen-kuang, to set off with about 100 orphans toward the Yellow River (Huang He), which they would cross, then take the railway to Sian. Five weeks later, she heard that they had arrived safely and that Tsin Pen-kuang was returning to escort the rest of the children out. But along the way, he and the funds were captured by the Japanese; it was presumed that Tsin Pen-kuang had been shot.

As the situation grew worse and the Chinese army was preparing to retreat, Aylward organized another large group of orphans and had them taken to safety nearby. Believing that "Christians never retreat," she returned to Yangcheng and intended to stay, until she learned that the impending Japanese army had put a price on her head because of her intelligence work for the Chinese Nationalists. Praying for guidance, she opened her Bible, and her eyes fell on the words, "Flee ye; flee ye into the mountains." The Japanese arrived that very night. Amid a hail of bullets, Aylward barely escaped the city to join the children; one bullet grazed her shoulder blades.

Though she had no money, Aylward decided to take the second group of orphans to Sian. The Japanese occupation was now so extensive that the only route open was a dangerous one, over the mountains and down to the 3,000-mile-long Yellow River. Taking just a little grain for food, she set off with approximately 100 children, most of them aged four to sixteen.

Following mule tracks over the mountains, the band slept in whatever shelter they could find with only each other for warmth; many of the smaller children had to be carried by the older ones. Aylward always carried at least one child while others clung to her. As they all grew more and more tired, she sang hymns to keep up their spirits. On the 12th day, they came in sight of the Yellow River, which was swift, deep, and about a mile across. When they reached the town of Yuan Chu on its banks, they found it deserted except for a few soldiers. There was no food to be had, and, worse, the ferry to cross the river was nowhere in sight. At any moment, the Japanese were expected to arrive.

Unable to decide what to do, Aylward waited on the banks of the river for three days, despairing of a boat. Then a young girl asked Aylward if she believed the story of Moses taking the children of Israel across the Red Sea. When Aylward said that she did, the girl asked, "Then why don't we go across?" Aylward replied, because "I'm not Moses." The child responded, "Of course you're not Moses, but God is God! He can open the river for us." The words renewed Aylward's faith, and she knelt down to pray. Their encampment was soon interrupted with the arrival of a Chinese officer. When Aylward explained that they were harmless refugees, the officer signaled to the Chinese across the river, and boats were sent to carry them to safety.

Life is pitiful, death so familiar, suffering and pain so common, yet I would not be anywhere else.

—Gladys Aylward, during the Japanese occupation of China

After a few days of rest in the town of Mien Chu, Aylward and the children continued their journey by foot and by rail, then crossed another mountain range until they finally reached Sian in late April 1940. They had traveled for 27 days, only to find that the city was full and closed to more refugees. They journeyed another day, to an orphanage in the nearby town of Fufeng. Only a few hours after Aylward deposited the children, she collapsed from exhaustion. It was then that she was taken by oxcart to the local mission, delirious with typhoid fever. Over the following months, she recovered slowly in a hospital in Sian under the care of two English missionaries.

The following years were restless ones for Aylward. She first worked among the refugees in Sian, and, in 1944, as conditions of war subsided, she moved to a remote village called Tsingsui, some distance from Lanchow (Lanzhou), in northwestern China. She then felt called to work in Szechwan (Sichuan), in the hot and humid south of China, where she stayed for four years. In the city of Chengtu (Chengdu), she prayed and preached with the missionaries of the C.I.M., was appointed Biblewoman at the Chinese Theological Seminary, and worked with lepers. She also adopted a young Chinese Christian named Gordon, whom she nursed back to health after an accident left him without the use of his hands for some time.

By 1948, the Communists' hold on China caused many to flee the country, including missionaries, who were prime targets. Aylward remained unconcerned about her safety, while friends feared for her life; she was finally per-suaded to visit her family whom she had not seen for 17 years. Donations paid for the fare.

Arriving in England in the spring of 1949, Aylward soon found fame when Alan Burgess, a producer from the BBC, dramatized her story in a program called "Gladys Aylward: One of the Undefeated." A booklet and later a book called *The Small Woman* were written with her cooperation, and, though not a professional speaker, she gave many talks, chatting naturally about the extraordinary events of her life. Her audiences found her captivating. Although

From the movie The Inn of the Sixth Happiness, *starring Ingrid Bergman, loosely based on the life of Gladys Aylward.*

she did not enjoy the talks, she found it an effective way to raise money for more Chinese mission work.

But Aylward missed China. Though she made many friends in London's Chinese community, she did not feel at home in England. She was disturbed by stories of the horrors of life in China under Communist rule but was persuaded that a return there would be too dangerous. In 1957, after the death of her mother, she finally felt free to leave England again. She stayed for a short while in Hong Kong, working among the refugees from Communism, and went later that same year to the island of Formosa, known today as Taiwan, which was the home of Free China. Over the following years, she ran mission halls and orphanages and traveled the world on speaking and preaching tours, raising money for her work. She settled in the city of Taipei and adopted many children.

Two distressing events marked Aylward's later life. One was the film *The Inn of the Sixth Happiness*, starring *Ingrid Bergman, based on the book about her life. Although she had signed an agreement with 20th Century-Fox, she felt her work was cheapened by the story, which distorted events and was changed to include a love scene. In addition, the husband of one of her adopted daughters, who was the superintendent of the Aylward Orphanage in Taipei, caused a scandal when he abused Aylward's trust by embezzling funds. Otherwise, Aylward was happy in the work of her last years in Taipei, which were spent peacefully among the people she loved. At age 67, she caught influenza and died on January 2, 1970. The fame of her work led to memorial services around the world. Today her accomplishments continue through a children's home in Taipei, the Hope Mission in Hong Kong, and the Gladys Aylward Charitable Trust, based in England.

SOURCES:

Burgess, Alan. *The Small Woman*. London: Evans Brothers, 1957 (reprinted by Pan Books, London).

Gladys Aylward: One of the Undefeated. London: Edinburgh House Press, 1950.

Hunter, C. *Gladys Aylward*. Eastbourne, England: Coverdale, 1970.

Thompson, Phyllis. *A London Sparrow: The Story of Gladys Aylward*. London: Word Books, 1971 (reprinted by Pan Books, London).

RELATED MEDIA:

The Inn of the Sixth Happiness, a film romanticizing the journey of Aylward and the orphans from China to Sian, starring Ingrid Bergman as Aylward and Athene Seyler as Mrs. Lawson, 20th Century-Fox Films, 1958.

Francesca Baines, freelance writer,
London, England

Ayres, Agnes (1896–1940)

American actress. Born Agnes Hinkle on September 4, 1896, in Carbondale, Illinois; died on December 25, 1940.

Filmography: Forbidden Fruit *(1919)*, The Affairs of Anatol *(1921)*, The Sheik *(1921)*, Clarence *(1922)*, Racing Hearts *(1923)*, Tess of the Storm Country *(1923)*, The Ten Commandments *(1923)*, When a Girl Loves *(1924)*, Morals for Men *(1925)*, Her Market Value *(1926)*, Son of the Sheik *(1926)*, The Awful Truth *(1926)*, Into the Night *(1928)*, Eve's Love Letters *(1929)*, The Donovan Affair *(1929)*, Souls at Sea *(1937)*.

American leading lady of the silent screen, Agnes Ayres began working in Essanay shorts around 1915. She was at the height of her career when she played opposite Rudolph Valentino in *The Sheik* (1921) and also starred opposite Wallace Reid. Retiring with the advent of sound, Ayres returned to the screen only once, for a bit in the 1937 movie, *Souls at Sea*. She died three years later, age 44, of a cerebral hemorrhage.

Ayres, Anne (1816–1896).

See Cannon, Harriet for sidebar.

Ayres, Ruby Mildred (1883–1955)

English novelist of 150 books, with sales totaling more than eight million copies. Born in 1883 in Watford, Hertshire, England; died on November 14, 1955, in Weybridge, England; married Reginald William Pocock (insurance broker), in 1909.

Selected works: Castles in Spain *(1912)*; Dark Gentleman *(1953)*.

Ruby Ayres' father was an architect in the county of Hertshire, where she was raised. In 1909, with her marriage to London insurance broker Reginald Pocock, Ayres moved to Harrow and seems to have hardly risen from her desk. In the 41 years between her first novel, *Castles in Spain*, and her last, *Dark Gentleman*, Ayres produced 150 books—in excess of three a year. She claimed to begin each new book by first setting "the price. Then I fix the title. Then I write the book."

The novels, romances that bring together a wealthy heroine and an even richer gentleman despite minor difficulties, sold more than eight million copies. A number of her stories were serialized in British newspapers or made into movies. Ayres also authored one play, *Silver*

Wedding, which was produced in 1932. In the 1940s, after over 30 years of marriage, Ayres husband was killed in a train accident. Ayres then moved to Weybridge, where she lived with her sister until she died in 1955. At the time of her death, Ayres had enjoyed two years of retirement from her resolute writing pace.

Crista Martin,
Boston, Massachusetts

Ayrton, Hertha Marks (1854–1923)

British physicist, noted for work on the motion of waves and formation of sand ripples, and the behavior of the electric arc. Name variations: adopted the name Hertha while at Girton College. Born Phoebe Sarah Marks in Portsmouth, England, in 1854; died in 1923; third of five children of Alice and Levi Marks (a clockmaker and jeweler); attended boarding school, London; Girton College, Cambridge (1876–1880); Finsbury Technical College (1884–1885); married William Edward Ayrton, in 1885; one daughter, Barbara Bodichon (Barbie) Ayrton, 1892.

Hertha Marks Ayrton was a nonconformist from youth, a fact that may well have contributed to her interest in scientific research and invention, fields not widely open to women during the second half of the 19th century. Faced with a male-dominated scientific community all her life, she maintained an ongoing interest in women's suffrage and believed sexism had no place in the laboratory. "The idea of 'women and science' is entirely irrelevant," she once said. "Either a woman is a good scientist, or she is not; in any case she should be given opportunities, and her work should be studied from the scientific, not the sex, point of view."

Ayrton's father, a Polish-Jewish refugee, struggled as a clockmaker to provide for his young family. When he died in 1861, her mother kept food on the table with money from her needlework. Though money was scarce, Ayrton was able to attend boarding school in London because she had an aunt who ran one. In 1876, after failing scholarship exams for Girton College (examinations would consistently prove difficult for her), she was finally able to enter with some financial help from friends. An eccentric philanthropist, *Barbara Bodichon, who was interested in women's causes, also became a benefactor. While in college, through her association with a "freethinking" cousin, Ayrton became a religious skeptic, although later in life she would express pride in her Jewish heritage. She also changed her name to Hertha, an expression of

new-found independence. Placing a disappointing 15th in her class on the Cambridge University baccalaureate honors examinations, Ayrton left Girton to teach mathematics.

In 1884, bolstered by her success in obtaining a patent for an instrument for dividing lines into any number of equal parts (a boon to architects, engineers, and artists), Ayrton entered Finsbury Technical College, again with the help of Bodichon. There, she met her husband William Edward Ayrton, a professor of physics and a widower, whose first wife, **Matilda Chaplin Ayrton** (1846–1883), had been a pioneering woman physician. The couple married in 1885, and, with the exception of a series of lectures on electricity delivered in 1888, much of Ayrton's early married life was occupied by domestic duties and caring for her baby daughter Barbara, born in 1892.

In 1893, Ayrton began experiments with electricity, presenting papers on her work while making plans to publish a book. In 1898, she became the first woman member of the Institution of Electrical Engineers. However, in 1901, her paper, "The Mechanism of the Electric Arc," had to be read to the Royal Society by an associate of her husband because the society would not allow women to present their work. In that year, she also began investigating ripple marks in sand and finished her book *The Electric Arc*. Published in 1902, it became the accepted textbook on the subject and cemented her reputation. During the summer of 1903, she met and befriended fellow scientist *Marie Curie, who was visiting England.

The Royal Society relented in 1904, and Ayrton became the first woman to present a paper, "The Origin and Growth of Ripple Marks." Although she was not allowed to become a fellow of the Society, in 1906 they awarded her their Hughes Medal for original research.

From 1905 to 1910, Ayrton worked for the War Office and Admiralty on electric searchlights (a project inherited from her husband for which she produced several reports that were ultimately credited to him), and on what would be her last scientific triumph, the invention of the Ayrton fan, which she described as a device that would make it possible "for our men to drive off poisonous gases and bring in fresh air from behind by simply giving impulses to the air with hand fans." After World War I, she researched various industrial applications for the fan.

Until her death in 1923, Ayrton continued her work as a scientist and suffragist. In her later years, she became more militant in her defense of equality for women.

SOURCES:

Macksey, Joan, and Kenneth Macksey. *The Book of Women's Achievements*. NY: Stein and Day, 1976.

Ogilvie, Marilyn Bailey. *Women in Science: Antiquity through the Nineteenth Century*. Cambridge, MA: MIT Press, 1993.

Uglow, Jennifer S., comp. and ed. *The International Dictionary of Women's Biography*. NY: Continuum, 1985.

Barbara Morgan,
Melrose, Massachusetts

Ayscough, Anne (c. 1521–1546).

See Askew, Anne.

Ayscough, Florence (1875/78–1942)

American poet and translator. Born Florence Wheelock between 1875 and 1878 in Shanghai, China; died on April 26, 1942, in Chicago, Illinois; daughter of Thomas Reed and Edith Haswell (Clarke) Wheelock; educated at Mrs. Quincy Shaw's School in Brookline, Massachusetts; married Francis Ayscough, around 1895 in Shanghai (died 1933); married Harley Farnsworth MacNair, in 1935.

Taught Chinese art and literature at the college level and wrote eight books encompassing Chinese history, literary criticism and translation. Selected works: Chinese Women Yesterday and Today (1939).

Florence Wheelock was born and raised in Shanghai, China, daughter of an American mother and a Canadian businessman. After studying with private tutors, she made her first trip to America at age nine to begin her formal schooling in Brookline, Massachusetts, where she was enrolled as a boarder at Mrs. Quincy Shaw's School. There, she met *Amy Lowell, who became her lifelong friend and later collaborator.

After her schooling was complete, Florence returned to Shanghai, where she met and married British importer Francis Ayscough. She also became enamored of the Chinese language and culture and set out to learn its intricacies. On a visit to America, she brought several Chinese word pictures that she translated into English; then her friend Lowell turned the words into rhymed poetry.

Ayscough, who traveled as a lecturer on Chinese art, literature, and society, made her home in Shanghai until her husband died in 1933. She then met Harley MacNair, a professor, whom she married in 1935. The couple moved to Chicago, Illinois, where Ayscough accepted a permanent lecturing post at the University of Chicago. She continued her work trans-lating Chinese literature and documenting China's history and culture. Ayscough named her homes in traditional Chinese fashion: Wild Goose Happiness House and House of the Wu-tung Trees. In 1941, she entered the Chicago Osteopathic Hospital, where she died, after a long illness, in late April of 1942. Harley MacNair compiled and edited the letters of his wife and Lowell, and, in 1945, he published *Florence Ayscough and Amy Lowell: Correspondence of a Friendship*. The following year, he published *The Incomparable Lady*, a biography of his wife.

Crista Martin,
Boston, Massachusetts

Ayverdi, Samiha (1906—)

Turkish novelist and author of political and spiritual essays. Born in 1906 in Istanbul, Turkey.

Selected works: So This Is Love *(1939);* A Night in the Temple *(1940);* The Fire Tree *(1941);* Living Dead *(1942);* The Chaplain *(1948).*

Though she was raised in a traditional old Turkish family and attended public school, when Samiha Ayverdi was 15 she left formal education to pursue self-directed scholarship. Ayverdi has written essays on politics and religion, including explications of the Islamic Jihad, which condone war as a basis for advancing the Muslim religion. Her publishing career flourished in the 1930s and 1940s with several novels.

Crista Martin,
Boston, Massachusetts

Azubah

Biblical woman. Wife of Caleb (1 Chr. 2:18, 19).

Azubah (fl. 860 BCE)

Biblical woman. In 1 Kings 22:42; daughter of Shilhi; children: Jehoshaphat, king of Judah (r. 873–849 BCE).

Azurduy de Padilla, Juana (1781–1862)

Heroine in the Argentine struggle for independence, whose military exploits have long been celebrated throughout Latin America. Name variations: Juana Azurduy. Born in Chuquisaca (now Sucre, Bolivia) in 1781; died in 1862; married Manuel Asencio Padilla, in 1805 (died 1816); children: one daughter.

Juana Azurduy de Padilla was born in Chuquisaca (now Sucre, Bolivia) and was educated in a convent before becoming a nun. After a few years, she left the cloister to marry a soldier, Manuel Asencio Padilla, in 1805. When the independence struggle against Spain in the Viceroyalty of La Plata began in 1810, Azurduy fought side by side with her husband. With his death in battle in 1816 at Viloma, she withdrew with rebel forces to Salta, where General Manuel Belgrano won a significant victory. Much admired for her courage and élan by the local commander, Caudillo Güemes, she received an officer's appointment in 1816 from the national executive of the provisional rebel government, Supreme Director Juan Martín Pueyrredón. Appointed a full lieutenant colonel, Azurduy had the right to wear a uniform and enjoy all the privileges of that rank. To dramatize the importance of her heroic reputation, General Belgrano, a hero of battles in Paraguay and Upper Peru, bestowed the sword of an officer upon her. After Argentina achieved its independence from Spain in 1825, Juana Azurduy retired from the military, returned to her home city of Chuquisaca, and lived quietly with her daughter.

SOURCES:

Kirkpatrick, Frederick Alexander. *A History of the Argentine Republic.* Cambridge, U.K.: The University Press, 1931.

Wright, Ione S., and Lisa M. Nekhom. *Historical Dictionary of Argentina.* Metuchen, NJ: Scarecrow Press, 1978.

John Haag, Associate Professor of History, University of Georgia, Athens, Georgia

Azza al-Maila (?–c. 707)

Arabian composer and songstress. Name variations: (nickname) Maila. Date of birth unknown; died around 707. Was taught music of the older days by Ra'iqa and learned Persian airs from Nashit and Sa'ib Kathir; composed many songs in the Persian idiom.

Azza al-Maila was a Christian freed woman of Medina and one of the most important professional musicians of her era. Her protector and patron was Abdalla ibn Ja'far. His protection was necessary because music was a pleasure forbidden to Muslims, and some accused al-Maila of leading the populace into moral degeneration. This derogatory attitude toward performers is reflected in al-Maila's nickname *Maila,* which some said was given for her eye-catching gait; others said, however, that the name came from *milaye,* which means cloak. Al-Maila was accused of wearing a cloak so as to disguise herself as a man and indulge in drink. Despite her detractors, she was an immensely popular musician and people gathered at her home weekly to hear her concerts. The first singer from Hejaz to sing in rhythmic cadences, al-Maila accompanied herself on the *mizhar* (skin-bellied lute), the *mi'zafa* (psaltery), and the *oud* (wooden-bellied lute). In addition to Persian airs handed down through the centuries, she also composed many songs. Azza al-Maila was the forerunner of other Arab musicians who enjoyed great popularity throughout the Muslim world.

John Haag, Associate Professor of History, University of Georgia, Athens, Georgia